'HE AMERICAN WORKFORCE

FEB '94 $$$6150

1990 U.S. Civilian Labor Force

2005 U.S. Civilian Labor Force

Workforce 2000:
Projected Demographic Trends

1. The population and the workforce will grow more slowly than at any time since the 1930's.
2. The average age of the population and the workforce will rise, and the pool of young workers entering the labor market will shrink.
3. More women will enter the workforce.
4. Non-whites will be a larger share of new entrants into the labor force.
5. Immigrants will represent the largest share of the increase in the population and the workforce since the first World War.

D1368522

MODERN MANAGEMENT

MODERN MANAGEMENT

Diversity, Quality, Ethics, and the Global Environment

SAMUEL C. CERTO
Dean and Professor of Management
Roy E. Crummer
Graduate School of Business
ROLLINS COLLEGE

Allyn and Bacon
Boston London Toronto Sydney Tokyo Singapore

Editor in Chief, Business and Economics: Richard Wohl
Senior Series Editor: Suzy Spivey
Senior Development Editor: Judith S. Fifer
Development Editor: Carol Alper
Production Administrator: Marjorie Payne
Editorial-Production Service: York Production Services
Text Designer: Lesiak/Crampton Design, Inc.
Cover Administrator: Linda Dickinson
Cover Designer: Design Ad Cetera
Composition Buyer: Linda Cox
Manufacturing Buyer: Megan Cochran

Copyright © 1994 by Allyn and Bacon
A Division of Simon & Schuster, Inc.
160 Gould Street, Needham Heights, MA 02194

Previous editions were published as
Modern Management: Quality, Ethics, and the Global Environment
Copyright © 1992
Principles of Modern Management: Functions and Systems
Copyright © 1989 by Allyn and Bacon

Copyright © 1986, 1983, 1980 by Wm. C. Brown Publishers

All rights reserved. No part of the material protected by this copyright notice may be reproduced or utilized in any form or by any means, electronic or mechanical, including photocopying, recording, or by any information storage and retrieval system, without the written permission of the copyright owner.

Library of Congress Cataloging-in-Publication Data

Certo, Samuel C.
Modern management : diversity, quality, ethics, and the global environment / Samuel C. Certo. — 6th ed.
p. cm
Includes bibliographical references and index.
ISBN 0-205-15336-4
1. Management. 2. Industrial management. 3. Social responsibility of business. I. Title
HD31.C4125 1994
658—dc20 93-27073
CIP

Printed in the United States of America
10 9 8 7 6 5 4 3 2 1 99 98 97 96 95 94

The credits and acknowledgments for figures, tables, boxes, and cases are found on pages 681–684. These pages should be considered extensions of the copyright page.

Photo Credits
Photo credits are found on page 684, which should be considered an extension of the copyright page.

To Mimi, Trevis, Matthew, Sarah, and Brian—
My reason for being

ABOUT THE AUTHOR

Dr. Samuel C. Certo is presently Dean and Professor of Management at the Roy E. Crummer Graduate School of Business at Rollins College. He has been a professor of management for eighteen years and has received prestigious awards including the Award for Innovative Teaching from the Southern Business Association, the Instructional Innovation Award granted by the Decision Sciences Institute, and the Charles A. Welsh Memorial Award for outstanding teaching at the Crummer School. Dr. Certo's numerous publications include articles in such journals as *Academy of Management Review, The Journal of Experiential Learning and Simulation,* and *Training.* He has also written several successful textbooks including *Modern Management: Diversity, Quality, Ethics, and the Global Environment; Strategic Management: Concepts and Applications;* and *Supervision: Quality and Diversity Through Leadership.* A past chairman of the Management Education and Development Division of the Academy of Management, he has been honored by that group's Excellence of Leadership Award. Dr. Certo has also served as president of the Association for Business Simulation and Experiential Learning, as associate editor for *Simulation & Games,* and as a review board member of the *Academy of Management Review.* His consulting experience has been extensive with notable experience on boards of directors.

NOTE TO STUDENTS FROM THE AUTHOR

YOUR CAREER GUIDEBOOK FOR THE FUTURE

Management success is what happens when preparation meets opportunity. Take advantage of this text and this course as a vehicle for preparing for management opportunities that you inevitably will have. Keep this text in your professional library as a *reference book,* which can be used to enhance your preparedness for opportunities throughout various stages of your future management career.

CONTENTS

Preface *xxiii*
Acknowledgments *xxx*

PART 1 **INTRODUCTION TO MANAGEMENT** *1*

CHAPTER 1 **MANAGEMENT AND MANAGEMENT CAREERS** *2*

INTRODUCTORY CASE: Robert Stempel Faces Serious Problems at General Motors *3*

The Importance of Management *4*

The Management Task *6*
- *The Role of Management* *6*
- *Defining Management* *6*
- *The Universality of Management* *12*

Management Careers *13*
- *A Definition of Career* *13*
- *Promoting Your Own Career* *14*
- *Special Career Issues* *16*

Management Highlights: A Special Feature for the Remaining Chapters *18*
- *Global Highlights* *19*
- *Ethics Highlights* *19*
- *Diversity Highlights* *19*
- *Quality Highlights* *19*

CASE STUDY: Dorothy Terrell: The Road to President, Sun Express *23*

CNN **VIDEO CASE:**
On a Management Career Path with Style: Josie Natori, House of Natori *24*

CNN **VIDEO EXERCISE:**
Your Interview with Josie Natori *25*

CHAPTER 2 **THE HISTORY OF MANAGEMENT** *26*

INTRODUCTORY CASE: "Mickey's Kitchen" at The Disney Store *27*

The Classical Approach *28*
- *Lower-level Management Analysis* *28*

GLOBAL HIGHLIGHT:
Delta Faucet Company *30*

DIVERSITY HIGHLIGHT:
Northern Island Federal Credit Union *32*

- *Comprehensive Analysis of Management* *33*
- *Limitations of the Classical Approach* *35*

The Behavioral Approach 35
The Relay Assembly Test Room Experiments 35
The Bank Wiring Observation Room Experiment 36
The Management Science Approach 37
The Beginning of the Management Science Approach 37
QUALITY HIGHLIGHT: Baldrige Award 38
Management Science Today 38
Characteristics of Management Science Applications 39
The Contingency Approach 39
ETHICS HIGHLIGHT: Charles Schwab 40
The System Approach 40
Types of Systems 40
Systems and "Wholeness" 40
The Management System 41
Information for Management System Analysis 42
CASE STUDY: Scientific Management at the Watertown Arsenal 46
VIDEO CASE: A Born Entrepreneur: Fred DeLuca, Subway Sandwiches 47
VIDEO EXERCISE: Planning Major Changes at Subway Sandwiches 48

CHAPTER 3 **CORPORATE SOCIAL RESPONSIBILITY AND BUSINESS ETHICS** 50
INTRODUCTORY CASE: Larami Corporation "Super Soaks" Society? 51
Fundamentals of Social Responsibility 52
The Davis Model of Corporate Social Responsibility 52
QUALITY HIGHLIGHT: Xerox Corporation 53
Areas of Corporate Social Responsibility 54
Varying Opinions on Social Responsibility 54
ETHICS HIGHLIGHT: IBM 54
GLOBAL HIGHLIGHT: DuPont 60
Social Responsiveness 61
Social Responsiveness and Decision Making 61
Approaches to Meeting Social Responsibilities 62
DIVERSITY HIGHLIGHT: Opryland 64
Social Responsibility Activities and Management Functions 65
Planning Social Responsibility Activities 66
Organizing Social Responsibility Activities 68
Influencing Individuals Performing Social Responsibility Activities 69
Controlling Social Responsibility Activities 69
How Society Can Help Business Meet Social Obligations 71
Business Ethics 72
A Definition of Ethics 73
Why Ethics Is a Vital Part of Management Practices 73

A Code of Ethics 74
Creating an Ethical Workplace 75
CASE STUDY: Procter & Gamble: A Socially Responsible Company 81
VIDEO CASE: Promoting Cosmetics with a Conscience: Anita Roddick, Body Shop International 82
VIDEO EXERCISE: Making Ethical Decisions for the Body Shop 83

PART I INTEGRATIVE CASE: Juane Blanes Wins Hearts as Well as Quality 84

PART 2 PLANNING 87

CHAPTER 4 ORGANIZATIONAL OBJECTIVES 88
INTRODUCTORY CASE: Entrepreneur Suffers Growing Pains at Arkansas Freightways 89
General Nature of Organizational Objectives 90
Definition of Organizational Objectives 90
GLOBAL HIGHLIGHT: Asea Brown Boveri 91
Importance of Organizational Objectives 92
Types of Objectives in Organizations 93
Organizational Objectives 93
Individual Objectives 93
Areas for Organizational Objectives 94
ETHICS HIGHLIGHT: IBM France 95
Working with Organizational Objectives 95
Establishing Organizational Objectives 96
QUALITY HIGHLIGHT: American Management Association 96
DIVERSITY HIGHLIGHT: The Department of Transportation 97
Guidelines for Establishing Quality Objectives 100
Guidelines for Making Objectives Operational 100
Attainment of Objectives 102
How to Use Objectives 102
Management by Objectives (MBO) 103
Factors Necessary for a Successful MBO Program 104
MBO Programs 104
Advantages and Disadvantages 104
CASE STUDY: Planning for Survival At Brant Manufacturing 109
VIDEO CASE: The Essence of Essence Communications: Edward Lewis, Essence Magazine 110
VIDEO EXERCISE: Setting Organizational Goals, Means, and Measures for Essence 111

CHAPTER 5 FUNDAMENTALS OF PLANNING 112
INTRODUCTORY CASE: Poor Planning at Weyerhaeuser Kills a Good Product 113
General Characteristics of Planning 114
Defining Planning 114
Purposes of Planning 114

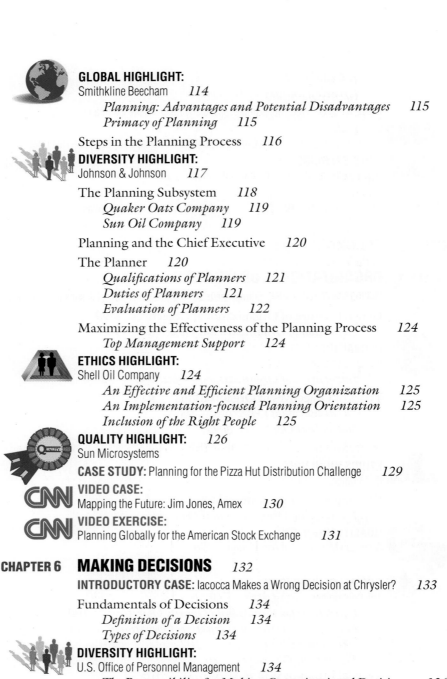

GLOBAL HIGHLIGHT:
Smithkline Beecham *114*
Planning: Advantages and Potential Disadvantages 115
Primacy of Planning 115

Steps in the Planning Process *116*

DIVERSITY HIGHLIGHT:
Johnson & Johnson *117*

The Planning Subsystem *118*
Quaker Oats Company 119
Sun Oil Company 119

Planning and the Chief Executive *120*

The Planner *120*
Qualifications of Planners 121
Duties of Planners 121
Evaluation of Planners 122

Maximizing the Effectiveness of the Planning Process *124*
Top Management Support 124

ETHICS HIGHLIGHT:
Shell Oil Company *124*
An Effective and Efficient Planning Organization 125
An Implementation-focused Planning Orientation 125
Inclusion of the Right People 125

QUALITY HIGHLIGHT: *126*
Sun Microsystems

CASE STUDY: Planning for the Pizza Hut Distribution Challenge *129*

VIDEO CASE:
Mapping the Future: Jim Jones, Amex *130*

VIDEO EXERCISE:
Planning Globally for the American Stock Exchange *131*

CHAPTER 6 **MAKING DECISIONS** *132*

INTRODUCTORY CASE: Iacocca Makes a Wrong Decision at Chrysler? *133*

Fundamentals of Decisions *134*
Definition of a Decision 134
Types of Decisions 134

DIVERSITY HIGHLIGHT:
U.S. Office of Personnel Management *134*
The Responsibility for Making Organizational Decisions 136

Elements of the Decision Situation *138*
State of Nature 138
The Decision Makers 139

GLOBAL HIGHLIGHT:
United Technologies *139*
Goals to Be Served 139
Relevant Alternatives 139
Ordering of Alternatives 140
Choice of Alternatives 140

The Decision-Making Process *140*
Identifying an Existing Problem 141
Listing Alternative Problem Solutions 141

ETHICS HIGHLIGHT:
Pharmacy Industry *142*
Selecting the Most Beneficial Alternative 142

Implementing the Chosen Alternative 142
Gathering Problem-Related Feedback 142

Decision-Making Conditions 143
Complete Certainty Condition 143
Complete Uncertainty Condition 144
Risk Condition 144

QUALITY HIGHLIGHT:
PepsiCo 144

Decision-Making Tools 145
Probability Theory 145
Decision Trees 146

CASE STUDY: GM: Which Way Is Up? 151

VIDEO CASE:
Making Decisions that Count: John Georges, International Paper 152

VIDEO EXERCISE:
Team Decision Making at International Paper 153

CHAPTER 7 STRATEGIC PLANNING 154

INTRODUCTORY CASE: Sea World Plots a New Competitive Course 155

Strategic Planning 156
Fundamentals of Strategic Planning 156
Strategy Management 156

ETHICS HIGHLIGHT:
Quaker Oats 159

GLOBAL HIGHLIGHT:
The Limited, Inc. 161

QUALITY HIGHLIGHT:
Lutheran General Health Care System 164

DIVERSITY HIGHLIGHT:
Methodist Hospital 172

Tactical Planning 174

Comparing and Coordinating Strategic and Tactical Planning 174

Planning and Levels of Management 175

CASE STUDY: EPI Products 179

VIDEO CASE:
Spicing up Sales: Charles McCormick, McCormick and Company 180

VIDEO EXERCISE:
Strategic Planning at McCormick Spice 181

CHAPTER 8 PLANS AND PLANNING TOOLS 182

INTRODUCTORY CASE: Fiat Plans Car Production 183

Plans 184
Plans: A Definition 184

ETHICS HIGHLIGHT:
Toyota Motor Corporation 184

Dimensions of Plans 184
Types of Plans 186

DIVERSITY HIGHLIGHT:
Security Pacific Bank *188*
Why Plans Fail 189
Planning Areas: Input Planning 189

GLOBAL HIGHLIGHT:
Mexico *189*

QUALITY HIGHLIGHT:
Toyota Motor Corporation *191*

Planning Tools *192*
Forecasting 192
Scheduling 198

CASE STUDY: Carol Kirby of Baskin-Robbins: Planning a New Image *205*

VIDEO CASE:
A Lucky Star: James Kinnear, Texaco *206*

VIDEO EXERCISE:
Creating a PERT Network for James Kinnear *207*

PART II INTEGRATIVE CASE: Planning for World-Class Performance at Bristol-Meyers Squibb, Mayaguez *208*

PART 3 ORGANIZING *211*

CHAPTER 9 FUNDAMENTALS OF ORGANIZING *212*

INTRODUCTORY CASE: MCI Communications Organizes to Be More Competitive *213*

A Definition of Organizing *214*
The Importance of Organizing 214
The Organizing Process 215
The Organizing Subsystem 216

Classical Organizing Theory *217*
Structure 218

DIVERSITY HIGHLIGHT:
The Banking Industry *219*

GLOBAL HIGHLIGHT:
Crown Cork & Seal Company *221*

ETHICS HIGHLIGHT:
Gerber Products Company Division of Labor *222*

QUALITY HIGHLIGHT:
Mercedes Benz *225*
Span of Management 226
Scalar Relationships 228

CASE STUDY: Organizing the Sedona Fire Dept. *233*

VIDEO CASE:
Organizing a Family Business: Stanley and Edwin Shulman, Alixandre Furs *234*

VIDEO EXERCISE:
Creating an Organizational Structure at Alixandre Furs *235*

CHAPTER 10 **RESPONSIBILITY, AUTHORITY, AND DELEGATION** *236*

INTRODUCTORY CASE: "Famous" Amos: The Organizing Challenge *237*

Responsibility *238*

Dividing Job Activities *238*

QUALITY HIGHLIGHT:
Motorola *240*

Clarifying Job Activities of Managers *240*

Authority *242*

Types of Authority *243*

ETHICS HIGHLIGHT:
General Electric *246*

Accountability *247*

DIVERSITY HIGHLIGHT:
Procter & Gamble *248*

Delegation *249*

Steps in the Delegation Process *249*

Obstacles to the Delegation Process *249*

Eliminating Obstacles to the Delegation Process *251*

Centralization and Decentralization *251*

GLOBAL HIGHLIGHT:
Levi Strauss & Company *253*

CASE STUDY: Empowerment at Iomega *259*

VIDEO CASE:
Working Patterns: John Lehmann, Butterick Company *260*

VIDEO EXERCISE:
Delegating Responsibility at Butterick *261*

CHAPTER 11 **MANAGING HUMAN RESOURCES** *262*

INTRODUCTORY CASE: Getting the Right People for Universal Studios *263*

Defining Appropriate Human Resources *264*

Steps in Providing Appropriate Human Resources *264*

Recruitment *264*

Selection *272*

GLOBAL HIGHLIGHT:
Compaq Computer Company Training *273*

QUALITY HIGHLIGHT:
Aetna Life & Casualty Co. *277*

Performance Appraisal *280*

DIVERSITY HIGHLIGHT:
US West *280*

ETHICS HIGHLIGHT:
Mobil Chemical Company *282*

CASE STUDY: Managing Diversity at Levi Strauss *287*

VIDEO CASE:
The American Workforce: Retraining to Stay Competitive *288*

VIDEO EXERCISE:
Keeping Frigidaire Cool through Job Analysis *289*

CHAPTER 12 **ORGANIZATIONAL CHANGE AND STRESS** *290*

INTRODUCTORY CASE: PepsiCo Reorganizes Pizza Hut and Taco Bell *291*

Fundamentals of Changing an Organization *292*

Defining "Changing an Organization" *292*

Change versus Stability *293*

GLOBAL HIGHLIGHT: Banco Español de Credito *293*

Factors to Consider When Changing an Organization *294*

The Change Agent *295*

QUALITY HIGHLIGHT: Hutchinson Technology *295*

Determining What Should Be Changed *296*

ETHICS HIGHLIGHT: *296* Sonoco

The Kind of Change to Make *297*

DIVERSITY HIGHLIGHT: *300* McDonald's Corporation

Individuals Affected by the Change *293*

Evaluation of Change *305*

Change and Stress *306*

Defining Stress *306*

The Importance of Studying Stress *307*

Managing Stress in Organizations *307*

CASE STUDY: Managing Change in Transition: Kathleen A. Cote of ComputerVision *313*

VIDEO CASE: Spirit under Stress: Susie Tompkins, Esprit de Corps *314*

VIDEO EXERCISE: Effecting Change at Esprit de Corps *315*

PART III INTEGRATIVE CASE: USAir Begins with You, but Where Does It End? *316*

PART 4 **INFLUENCING** *319*

CHAPTER 13 **FUNDAMENTALS OF INFLUENCING AND COMMUNICATION** *320*

INTRODUCTORY CASE: Eaton Managers Concentrate on Influencing People *332*

Fundamentals of Influencing *322*

Defining Influencing *322*

The Influencing Subsystem *322*

Communication *325*

Interpersonal Communication *325*

GLOBAL HIGHLIGHT: Compression Labs *325*

Interpersonal Communication in Organizations *325*

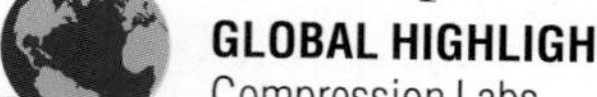

DIVERSITY HIGHLIGHT: Bull Worldwide Information Services *329*

ETHICS HIGHLIGHT: Dow Corning *333*

QUALITY HIGHLIGHT: Holiday Inn *335*

CASE STUDY: The Wal-Mart Influence *343*

VIDEO CASE:
PG&E's Master Communicator: Richard Clarke, Pacific Gas & Electric *344*

VIDEO EXERCISE:
Mastering Communication at PG&E *345*

CHAPTER 14 LEADERSHIP *346*

INTRODUCTORY CASE: Liz Claiborne: The Wizard of Working Women's Fashions *347*

Defining Leadership *348*

Leader versus Manager *348*

The Trait Approach to Leadership *349*

The Situational Approach to Leadership: A Focus on Leader Behavior *350*

GLOBAL HIGHLIGHT:
China *350*

Leadership Situations and Decisions *350*

ETHICS HIGHLIGHT:
NBC News *356*

Leadership Behaviors *357*

QUALITY HIGHLIGHT:
Potlatch Corporation *361*

Recent Emphasis on Leadership *365*
Transformational Leadership *366*
Substitutes for Leadership *366*
Women as Leaders *367*
Ways Women Lead *367*

DIVERSITY HIGHLIGHT:
Corning *367*

CASE STUDY: Al Scott's Vision of Quality for Wilson Sporting Goods *371*

VIDEO CASE:
When Inexperience Paid Off: Richard Branson, The Virgin Group *372*

VIDEO EXERCISE:
Planning an Executive Retreat for Virgin Atlantic Airways *373*

CHAPTER 15 MOTIVATION *374*

INTRODUCTORY CASE: American Greetings Motivates Through Lateral Moves *375*

The Motivation Process *376*
Defining Motivation *376*
Process Theories of Motivation *376*
Content Theories of Motivation: Human Needs *379*

GLOBAL HIGHLIGHT:
Maslow's Hierarchy and Japanese, Chinese, and U.S. Workers *381*

Motivating Organization Members *383*
The Importance of Motivating Organization Members *383*
Strategies for Motivating Organization Members *384*

DIVERSITY HIGHLIGHT:
Greyhound *387*

QUALITY HIGHLIGHT:
Apple Computer *389*

ETHICS HIGHLIGHT:
Government *391*

CASE STUDY: Motivation at America West Airlines *397*

CNN Video Case:
Motivation through Intrapreneurship *398*

CNN Video Exercise:
Analyzing Motivation at Federal Express *399*

CHAPTER 16 GROUPS AND CORPORATE CULTURE *400*

INTRODUCTORY CASE: Groups Are Important to Progress at Rolls-Royce *401*

Defining Groups *402*

Kinds of Groups in Organizations *402*

Formal Groups 402

DIVERSITY HIGHLIGHT:
The Equitable *403*

ETHICS HIGHLIGHT:
Calvary Hospital *405*

QUALITY HIGHLIGHT:
Standard Steel *408*

Informal Groups 410

Managing Work Groups *412*

Determining Group Existence 412

Understanding the Evolution of Informal Groups 412

Maximizing Work Group Effectiveness 414

GLOBAL HIGHLIGHT:
Mazda *415*

Corporate Culture *418*

CASE STUDY: Rewards in a Self-Managed Work Team at Boeing *425*

VIDEO CASE:
Building a Corporate Culture: Kay Unger, Gillian Group *426*

VIDEO EXERCISE:
Making Decisions by Committee at the Gillian Group *427*

PART IV INTEGRATIVE CASE: The Navajo Arts and Crafts Enterprise: Bringing Together Culture and Business *428*

PART 5 CONTROLLING *431*

CHAPTER 17 PRINCIPLES OF CONTROLLING *432*

INTRODUCTORY CASE: A Lack of Control at USA Today *433*

Fundamentals of Controlling *434*

Defining Control 434

Defining Controlling 434

GLOBAL HIGHLIGHT:
Euro Disneyland *437*

QUALITY HIGHLIGHT:
Modern of Marshfield Inc. *440*

Types of Control 440

ETHICS HIGHLIGHT:
Propane Appliances *441*

DIVERSITY HIGHLIGHT:
Cosmetics Industry *443*

The Controller and Control *443*
The Job of the Controller *443*
How Much Is Needed? *444*

Power and Control *446*
A Definition of Power *446*
Total Power of a Manager *446*
Steps for Increasing Total Power *446*

Performing the Control Function *447*
Potential Barriers to Successful Controlling *448*
Making Controlling Successful *449*

CASE STUDY: Measuring Performance at Texaco *453*

VIDEO CASE:
In the Driver's Seat: Frank Olson, Hertz Corporation *454*

VIDEO EXERCISE:
Controlling Costs at Hertz *455*

CHAPTER 18 **PRODUCTION MANAGEMENT AND CONTROL** *456*

INTRODUCTORY CASE: BRIDGESTONE (USA): Eliminating the Fire and Building Bridges of Quality *457*

Production *458*
Defining Production *458*
Productivity *458*
Quality and Productivity *459*

QUALITY HIGHLIGHT:
Adidas USA *462*
Automation *463*

GLOBAL HIGHLIGHT: *463*
GMFanuc
Strategies, Systems, and Processes *464*

Operations Management *465*
Defining Operations Management *465*
Operations Management Considerations *466*

ETHICS HIGHLIGHT:
Firestone *467*

DIVERSITY HIGHLIGHT:
Americans with Disabilities Act *471*

Operations Control *472*
Just-in-Time Inventory Control *472*
Maintenance Control *472*
Cost Control *473*
Budgets *474*
Ratio Analysis *475*
Materials Control *476*

Selected Operations Control Tools *477*
Using Control Tools to Control Organizations *477*
Inspection *478*

Management by Exception 478
Management by Objectives 478
Breakeven Analysis 479
Other Broad Operations Control Tools 481

CASE STUDY: Caterpillar's Factory, a Star 487

VIDEO CASE:
Profits and People: Robert Rich, Rich Products 488

VIDEO EXERCISE:
Computing a Breakeven Analysis for Rich Products 489

CHAPTER 19 INFORMATION 490

INTRODUCTORY CASE: Sam Walton Taught Others at Wal-Mart to Use Information 491

Essentials of Information 492
Factors Influencing the Value of Information 492
Evaluating Information 494
Computer Assistance in Using Information 496

ETHICS HIGHLIGHT:
Burroughs Wellcome 497

The Management Information System (MIS) 500

GLOBAL HIGHLIGHT:
Pohang Iron & Steel Company 500
Describing the MIS 501

DIVERSITY HIGHLIGHT:
Target 502

QUALITY HIGHLIGHT:
Nashua 502
Establishing an MIS 505

The Management Decision Support System (MDSS) 509

CASE STUDY: Information Mainframes Are Not Dead at 3Com 515

Video Case:
The Shape of the World: Caleb Dean Hammond III, Hammond Inc. 516

Video Exercise:
Improving the MIS at Hammond Inc. 517

PART V INTEGRATIVE CASE: Buy Me a Light—a Mag Light 518

PART 6 TOPICS FOR SPECIAL EMPHASIS 521

CHAPTER 20 INTERNATIONAL MANAGEMENT 522

INTRODUCTORY CASE: Estée Lauder's Moscow Perfumery Plans for Expansion 523

Fundamentals of International Management 524

The Multinational Corporation 526
Defining the Multinational Corporation 526

ETHICS HIGHLIGHT:
U.S. Companies Send Hazardous Waste to Mexico 527
Complexities of Managing the Multinational Corporation 528

GLOBAL HIGHLIGHT:
U.S. Companies in China 528
Risk and the Multinational Corporation 528

Management Functions and Multinational Corporations 530
Planning for Multinational Corporations 530
Organizing Multinational Corporations 531

DIVERSITY HIGHLIGHT:
European Organization Structures 531

Influencing People in Multinational Corporations 533

Controlling Multinational Corporations 535

Comparative Management: An Emphasis on Japanese Management 536
Defining Comparative Management 536

QUALITY HIGHLIGHT:
The Deming Prize 536
Insights from Japanese Motivation Strategies 537
Insights from Japanese Management Practices: Theory Z 537

CASE STUDY: The Jolly Green Giant's *Maquiladora* 543

CNN VIDEO CASE:
International Joint Venturing: Sharing Risks and Benefits 544

CNN VIDEO EXERCISE:
Risks and Rewards of International Joint Ventures 545

CHAPTER 21 QUALITY: BUILDING COMPETITIVE ORGANIZATIONS 546

INTRODUCTORY CASE: Iomega Corporation: Success Built on Continuous Improvement 547

Fundamentals of Quality 548
Defining Total Quality Management 548

QUALITY HIGHLIGHT:
Ford Motor Company 548
The Importance of Quality 550
The Quality Awards 551
Achieving Quality 552

ETHICS HIGHLIGHT:
American Marketing Association 554

Quality through Strategic Planning 556
Environmental Analysis and Quality 556
Establishing Organizational Direction and Quality 557
Strategy Formulation and Quality 558
Strategy Implementation and Quality 559
Strategic Control and Quality 560

GLOBAL HIGHLIGHT:
U.S. Lagging on ISO 9000 560

The Quality Improvement Process 562
The Incremental Improvement Process 562
Reengineering Improvements 564

DIVERSITY HIGHLIGHT:
Digital Equipment Corporation 565

CASE STUDY: JAS's Trackmaster: The Result of Total Quality Management 569

CNN VIDEO CASE:
Quality in the Auto Industry: GM's Saturn Keeps Orbiting 570

CNN VIDEO EXERCISE:
Will Success Spoil Saturn? 571

CHAPTER 22 **DIVERSITY AND MANAGEMENT** *572*

INTRODUCTORY CASE: Ortho Pharmaceutical: Showcase for Cultural Diversity *573*

Defining Diversity *574*
Social Implications of Diversity *574*

QUALITY HIGHLIGHT:
Frito Lay *575*

Advantages of Diversity in Organizations *575*
Keeping and Gaining Market Share *575*
Cost Savings *576*
Increased Productivity and Innovation *576*
Better Quality of Management *576*

DIVERSITY HIGHLIGHT:
General Electric *577*

Challenges Managers Face in Working with Diverse Populations *578*
Changing Demographics *578*

GLOBAL HIGHLIGHT:
AT&T *578*

Ethnocentrism, Prejudices, Stereotypes, and Discrimination *580*

Strategies for Promoting Diversity in Organizations *583*
Workforce 2000 *583*
Equal Employment and Affirmative Action *584*

ETHICS HIGHLIGHTS: *587*
Procter & Gamble

Pluralism *587*

The Role of the Manager *588*
Planning *589*
Organizing *589*
Influencing *589*
Controlling *590*

Management Development and Diversity Training *590*

CASE STUDY: Rebuilding LA *595*

CNN VIDEO CASE:
The Glass Ceiling: Shattered or Still in Place? *596*

CNN VIDEO EXERCISE:
Taking a SWOT at the Steelcase Ceiling *597*

PART VI INTEGRATIVE CASE: Global Quality at Federal Express *598*

QUALITY MODULES

QUALITY MODULE 1 **THE MALCOLM BALDRIGE NATIONAL QUALITY AWARD: A BLUEPRINT FOR EXCELLENCE** *601*

Malcolm Baldrige National Quality Award Criteria (1992) *601*

Description of the Award Criteria *602*

The Bottom Line: Continuous Improvement Is What Counts *607*

QUALITY MODULE 2 **SELECTED BALDRIGE AWARD WINNERS FROM THE MANUFACTURING COMPANIES AWARD CATEGORY** *608*

Texas Instruments: A 1992 Winner *608*
The Five Quality Thrusts *609*
Making the Most of the Baldrige Process *610*
Get on the Field and Play! *611*

Xerox Corporation: A 1989 Winner 612
Benchmarking Process Reveals Areas Needing Improvement 612
A Strategy to Regain That Critical Competitive Edge 612
Increased Effectiveness Leads to Baldrige Application—and Xerox Wins 617
The "Race for Quality" Has No Finish Line 618
The Success Is Shared Far and Wide 618
Quality Has Many Rewards—Happy Customers Is Number One 619
The "Race without a Finish Line" Keeps on Going 619

Motorola, Inc.: A 1988 Winner 620
Identifying System Weaknesses Breaks Down Barriers 620
The Six Sigma Solution Sets Tight Performance Parameters 621
It Starts with Comprehensive Employee Training 621
Reviews Keep the System Going Strong 622
Quality Teams Conduct the Systems Reviews 622
Review Team Members Selected on a Rotating Basis 623
Corporate Championship Creates Quality Champs 624

QUALITY MODULE 3 SELECTED BALDRIGE WINNERS FROM THE SERVICES COMPANIES AWARD CATEGORY 625

AT&T Universal Card Services: A 1992 Winner 625
Delighting External Customers 625
Gauging External Customer Satisfaction 626
Delighting Internal Customers 626
The Baldrige Connection 628
The Ten Most Wanted 629
Some Advice from a Baldrige Winner 608

The Ritz-Carlton® Hotel Company: A 1992 Winner 630
Employee Training Is Extensive 631
Three Keys of the Baldrige Success 631
Big Benefits of the Baldrige Process 633
Advice to Other Companies 634

Federal Express Corporation: A 1990 Winner 635
A Ten-Step Process for Improvement 635
A Dozen Service Quality Indicators Help Keep Efforts on Track 637
Employee Satisfaction Ranks up There with Customer Satisfaction 638
Not Awards, but Improvement Is the Prime Objective 638

Solectron Corporation: A 1991 Winner 639
Culture Based on Continuous Improvement and Customer Satisfaction 639
Fluctuating Defect Rates Led to Balrdige Criteria 639
The Customer Drives Solectron's Quality Efforts 640
Institute a Formal Quality Training Program 642
Create an Environment that Encourages a Quality Attitude 644
The Quality Journey Knows No End 645

QUALITY MODULE 4 SELECTED WINNERS FROM THE BALDRIGE SMALL BUSINESSES AWARD CATEGORY 646

Granite Rock: A 1992 Winner 646
Nine Objectives for Total Quality 646
Four Steps to Success 647
Connecting with Customers 648
Believers in the Baldrige 650

Globe Metallurgical Inc.: A 1988 Winner 652
Simply "Telling It Like It Is" Brings Baldrige Surprise 652
The Development of a First-Rate Quality Process 653
Prizes Accrue as Quality Improvements Continue 658

GLOSSARY *659*

ENDNOTES *669*

CREDITS *681*

INDEXES *687*

PREFACE

As with the previous five editions, the purpose of this book is to prepare students to be managers. Management concepts contained in this new edition reflect traditionally accepted management theory and represent practical tools that managers commonly use to meet organizational challenges. Judgments regarding which management concepts to include were influenced by information from accrediting agencies like the American Assembly of Collegiate Schools of Business (AACSB), organizations established by professional managers like the American Management Association (AMA), and organizations established by management scholars like the Academy of Management.

In addition to presenting traditional wisdom about the management process, this edition continues the distinctive thrust of previous editions of highlighting important current issues facing modern managers. To illustrate the "current issues" component, this edition gives special attention to: **diversity, quality, ethics** and the **global environment.** This edition not only provides individual chapters on each of these current issues, but integrates the topics throughout the text. Overall, this book is carefully crafted to present traditional management concepts, important current management issues, and insights regarding how students should handle both to ensure organizational success.

The Modern Management Learning Package, this book and its ancillaries, has maintained its popularity and position as a market leader since it was first published nearly two decades ago. Over the years, this package has been used in colleges and universities as well as in professional management training programs, has been translated into foreign languages for distribution throughout the world, and has been used by nearly 500,000 students. Many credit the continuing popularity of the Modern Management Learning Package to my strong and continuing convictions that important management concepts must be clearly and concisely presented to students but modified to reflect our modern society, that learning materials must reflect an empathy for and enhancement of the student learning process, and that instructional support materials must facilitate the design and conduct of principles of management courses of only the highest quality. Starting with the text, the following sections describe each major component of this newest Modern Management Learning Package and illustrate how these convictions are even more pronounced in this sixth edition.

TEXT: THEORY OVERVIEW

Over all, management theory in this text is divided into six main sections: "Introduction to Management," "Planning," "Organizing," "Influencing," "Controlling," and "Topics for Special Emphasis." Naturally, updates of theories and examples have been extensively made throughout each section. More specifically, Section 1, "Introduction to Management," lays the groundwork necessary for studying management. Chapter 1, "Management and Management Careers" not only exposes students to what management is, but also gives them an understanding of special career issues such as the progress of women in management, dual career couples, and the multicultural workforce. This chapter also highlights Peters and Waterman's *In Search of Excellence,* which provides practical insights on how to manage a successful organization. Chapter 2, "The History of Management," presents several fundamental but different ways in which managers can perceive their jobs. The last chapter in this section, Chapter 3, "Corporate Social Responsibility and Business Ethics," discusses the responsibilities that managers have to society and how business ethics apply to modern management. This chapter is presented early in the text to enable students to reflect on societal implications of management action throughout their text and course.

Section 2, "Planning," elaborates on planning activities as a primary management function. This section begins with Chapter 4, "Organizational Objectives" in order to emphasize the setting of organizational objectives as the beginning of the planning process. Chapter 5, "Fundamentals of Planning," presents the basics of planning. Chapter 6, "Making Decisions," discusses the decision-making process as a component of the planning process. Chapter 7, "Strategic Planning" highlights Porter's model for industry analysis, the BCG Growth-Share Matrix, the GE Portfolio Matrix, strategy implementation, and strategic control. Chapter 8, "Plans and Planning Tools," discusses various managerial planning tools available to help formulate plans.

Section 3, "Organizing," discusses organizing activities as a major management function. Chapter 9 presents the fundamentals of organizing, and Chapter 10 elaborates on how to organize various worker activities appropriately. Chapter 11, "Managing Human Resources," discusses hiring people who will make a desirable contribution to organizational objectives. Chapter 12 is "Organizational Change and Stress." Coverage focuses on how managers change organizations and the stress-related issues that can accompany such action. The discussion highlights the definition of stress and the importance of studying and managing stress.

Section 4, "Influencing," discusses how managers should deal with people. The four chapters in this section (Chapters 13–16) respectively discuss the fundamentals of influencing and communication, leadership, motivation, and groups and corporate culture. The leadership chapter highlights more traditional concepts such as the Vroom-Yetton-Jago leadership model, the Michigan studies, and the Path-Goal Theory of Leadership, as well as more recently developing topics such as transformational leadership, and leadership and trust. For this edition, newly added leadership content focuses on substitutes for leadership and women as leaders. Practical emphasis added to the motivation chapter for this edition focuses on how American Greetings Corporation motivates employees through lateral moves, how Greyhound Financial Corporation enhances organizational diversity through job rotation, and how Maslow's hierarchy of needs relates to Japanese, Chinese, and U.S. workers. The last chapter in this section emphasizes groups as a key to organizational success.

Section 5, "Controlling," analyzes the performance of control activities as another basic management function. Chapter 17, "Principles of Controlling," presents the basics of controlling. Chapter 18, "Production Management and Control," has been significantly revised. New topics include quality and production, automation, and production strategies, systems, and processes available to managers. Added focus on operations control emphasizes cost, materials, and inventory control as well as aggregate planning and master scheduling. New discussion also focuses on inspection as an operations control tool. Chapter 19, "Information," defines *information* and elaborates on its role in the controlling process. The relationship between quality and productivity is featured with special emphasis on the work of W. Edwards Deming.

The last section of this text is "Topics for Special Emphasis." Chapter 20, "International Management," discusses the basics of international and multinational organizations. Planning for multinational corporations, organizing multinational corporations, and influencing people in multinational corporations are all major topics. Special discussion focuses on learning from Japanese management techniques. Chapter 21 is "Quality: Building Competitive Organizations." This chapter focuses on building quality throughout all phases of organizational activity. Discussions focus on defining quality, achieving quality through strategic planning, and management skills necessary to build quality throughout an organization. The ideas of Philip B. Crosby, W. Edwards Deming, and Joseph M. Juran, internationally known quality experts, are highlighted. Significant revision of this chapter focuses on Total Quality Management (TQM), awards given for quality in organizations, and incremental improvements as well as reengineering as means to improve quality in organizations. Chapter 22, "Diversity Issues for Managers," is a new chapter in this edition. This chapter defines diversity, explains organizational advantages to promoting diversity in organizations, and outlines how managers can promote diversity in organizations. The chapter also discusses the challenges and dilemmas that a manager faces in attempting to build a diverse workforce.

Four special Quality Modules featuring winners of the Malcolm Baldrige National Quality Award have been added to this edition to enrich the text's quality theme and take a closer look at how real companies are incorporating TQM. Quality Module 1 looks into the purpose for establishing the Malcolm Baldrige National Quality Award and then discusses the criteria a company must meet to apply and then win. Quality Modules 2, 3, and 4 look at profiles of selected Baldrige winners in the manufacturing companies award category, the services companies award category, and the small businesses award category. Included are the total quality management stories of Texas Instruments, The Ritz-Carlton® Hotel Company, and the small business, Granite Rock—all 1992 winners of the Baldrige award—as well as profiles of some of the winners from past years. These Baldrige success stories will provide instructional and inspirational reading for students and faculty alike.

TEXT: STUDENT LEARNING AIDS

Several features of this text were designed to make the study of management more efficient, effective, and enjoyable. A list of these features and an explanation of each follow.

LEARNING OBJECTIVES The opening pages of each chapter contain a set of learning objectives that are intended as guidelines on how to study the chapter.

CHAPTER OUTLINES The opening pages of each chapter also contain a chapter outline that previews the textual material and helps the reader keep the information in perspective while it is being read.

INTRODUCTORY CASES WITH "BACK TO THE CASE" SECTIONS The opening of each chapter contains a case study that introduces readers to management problems related to chapter content. Detailed "Back to the Case" sections appear throughout each chapter, applying specific areas of management theory discussed in the chapter to the introductory case. All of these cases involve real companies such as Rolls-Royce, Liz Claiborne, and USA Today, and highlight contemporary issues. Over half of the introductory cases are new to this edition.

CASE STUDIES The concluding pages of each chapter contain a real-life case that further applies chapter content to related management situations. All end-of-chapter cases are based on real companies and are new or substantially revised and updated. The cases cover a wide range of subjects, including recent accounts about business and government, and featuring accounts of managing cultural diversity. Among the companies focused on are General Motors, Pizza Hut, and Wilson Sporting Goods.

CNN VIDEO CASES A very innovative and exciting feature is the CNN Video Case that follows each chapter. The case is comprised of textual material profiling management action in a real company as well as a specially edited CNN "Pinnacle" interview, "Inside Business" program, or other CNN news special that is provided to the instructor for classroom viewing. The written and video materials were carefully designed to illustrate chapter material. Over all, the CNN Video Case makes management concepts "come alive" in the classroom. The textual material for each CNN Video Case concludes with discussion questions.

CNN VIDEO EXERCISES An exciting new feature of the sixth edition is the CNN Video Exercise, specially designed to complement the CNN Video Case. This hands-on, experiential exercise is based on the scenario presented in the CNN Video Case and offers the opportunity for students to practice what they have learned by making management decisions in an exercise format.

INTEGRATIVE CASES Each of the six major parts of the text ends with a case relating to that section as a whole. These cases provide students with the opportunity to review and apply material from entire sections of the text. All integrative cases are based on real, undisguised situations.

MARGIN NOTES Each chapter contains margin notes that can be helpful in the initial reading and for review. Margin notes highlight the key terms in each chapter and also provide brief definitions for the student's review.

MANAGEMENT HIGHLIGHTS Management Highlights are another exciting feature of this text. Management Highlights are extended examples emphasizing how modern managers face contemporary issues in real companies. Chapters have four highlights that illustrate the following timely and important management issues: diversity, quality, ethics, and the global environment. Companies featured in Management Highlights include Motorola, General Electric, and Levi Strauss.

ACTION SUMMARIES Each chapter ends with an action-oriented chapter summary. In this summary, students respond to several objective questions that are clearly linked to the learning objectives stated at the beginning of the chapter. Students can check their answers with the answer key at the end of the chapter. This key also lists the pages in the chapter that can be referred to for a fuller explanation of the answers.

INTRODUCTORY CASE WRAP-UP Each chapter ends with several questions about its introductory case. These questions provide the opportunity to apply chapter concepts directly to the case.

ISSUES FOR REVIEW AND DISCUSSION The concluding pages of each chapter contain a set of discussion questions that test the understanding of chapter material and can serve as vehicles for study and for class discussion.

GLOSSARY Major management terms and their definitions are gathered at the end of the text. The terms appear in boldface type with references to the text pages on which the discussion of each term appears.

ILLUSTRATIONS Figures, tables, and photographs depicting various management situations are used throughout the text to help bridge the gap between management theory and authentic situations.

SUPPLEMENTARY MATERIALS

A number of supplementary materials have been developed to complement the use of *Modern Management,* Sixth Edition. Although the text itself was designed to offer a desirable amount of material for a high-quality course in principles of management, special supplements are available to further enrich the learning situation in which the text is used.

EXPERIENCING MODERN MANAGEMENT: A WORKBOOK, Sixth Edition

This is a combination study guide and source book of more than sixty-seven experiential exercises and is to be used in conjunction with the text. The sixth edition of this workbook, by Professor Lee Graf of Illinois State University and author Samuel C. Certo, contains a number of new and modified exercises that correspond to the revised text. Diversity, quality improvement, ethics, and international management are the dominant issues in these new exercises. Workbook elements that correspond to each text chapter include the following:

AN EXTENDED CHAPTER SUMMARY Extended summaries are helpful for a quick review of text material. Summaries are keyed to chapter learning objectives in the text in order to facilitate student learning.

LEARNING ASSESSMENT ACTIVITIES For each chapter of the text, the workbook contains a series of twenty-five objective questions that test the understanding of chapter content. Correct answers and the text page numbers on which answers are explained are furnished for all questions.

EXPERIENTIAL EXERCISES, ACTIVITIES, PROJECTS, CASES A number of varied in-class and out-of-class learning activities that further illustrate the content of each text chapter are provided. Exercises are provided for use in large classes, small classes, and for assignment to individuals. Figure 1 at the beginning of the activity manual/study guide outlines how each exercise can be best used. In addition, a suggested sequence for using the text and the workbook jointly is shown on the next page. Finally, the workbook table of contents identifies the topic and explains the fundamental objective of each of the exercises.

Computer Simulations in Management (CSM)

This software contains six computer-assisted experiential exercises designed to help students understand how software application programs can be used in practical management situations. The exercises focus on major sections in the text; topics addressed in these exercises include using decision trees, assessing management style, and computer-assisted scheduling.

Total Quality Management Paperbacks

Allyn and Bacon offers three paperbacks on total quality management: *Profiles in Quality: Blueprints for Action from 50 Leading Companies, Profiles of Malcolm Baldrige Award Winners,* and *Profiles of ISO 9000.* Quality Improvement Programs from companies such as Federal Express, General Electric, Boeing, AT&T, Amana, and Hewlett Packard are featured.

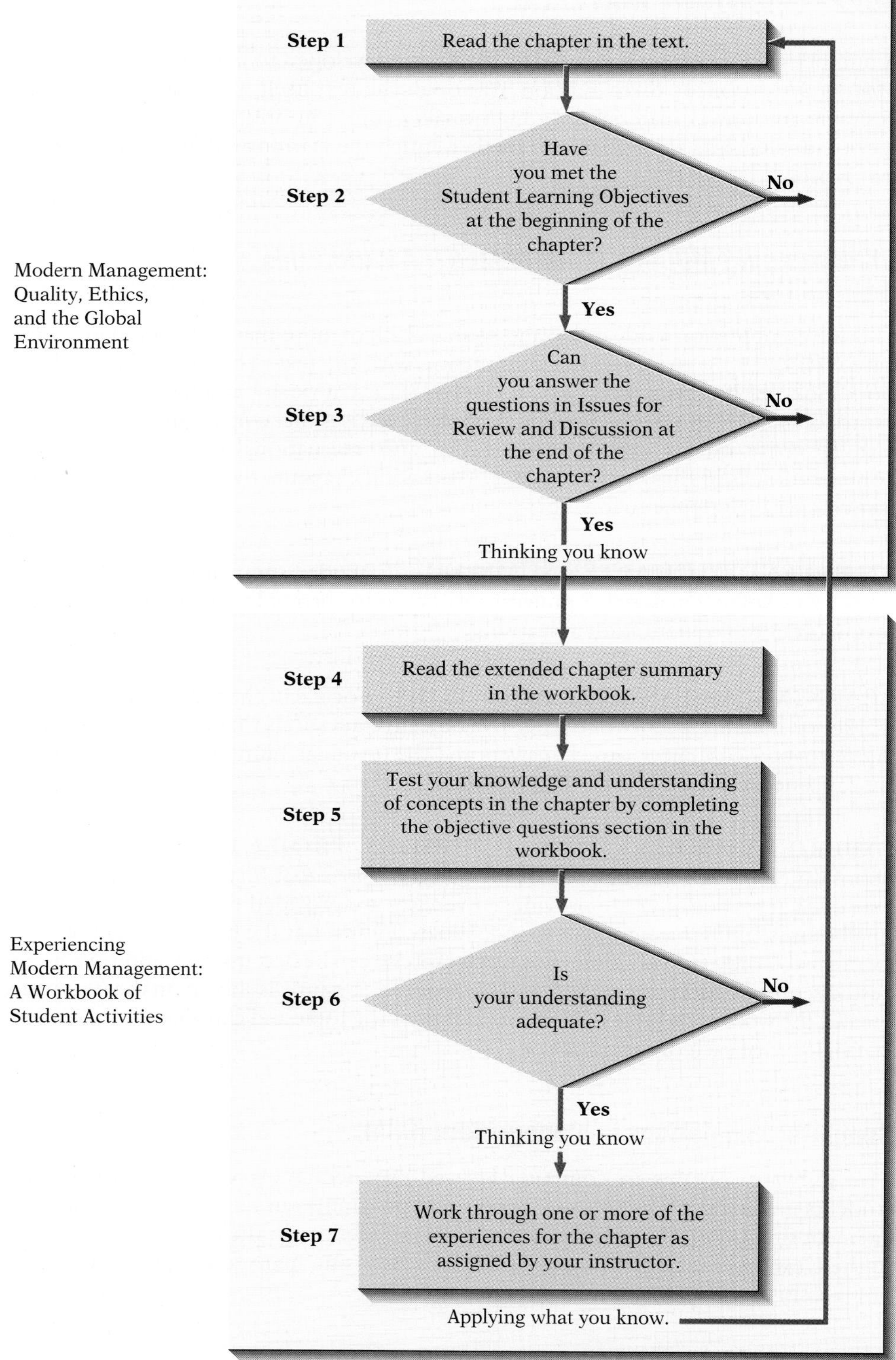

Figure 1
Suggested sequence for using the text and student workbook jointly.

OTHER INSTRUCTIONAL AIDS

In addition to the supplements just described, several other ingredients of the *Modern Management* learning package also have been designed to enhance the learning environment in which this text is used. Detailed descriptions of these items are located in the Instructor's Annotated Edition. These include

Instructor's Annotated Edition
Instructor's Resource Manual
Test Bank
Allyn and Bacon Test Manager,
a computerized test bank
Acetate transparencies
CNN Videos
Video User's Guide
Videodisc: Experiencing Management: What Managers Do
Business Line Fax Service
Mosaic Workplace Video Series
(also available on videodisc)

ACKNOWLEDGMENTS

I continue to receive much positive feedback regarding the *Modern Management* learning package. Compliments from colleagues, students, and practicing managers regarding the quality of this text and its ancillaries are gratifying indeed! Much of this positive feedback, however, actually relates to valuable contributions to this project made by respected colleagues. I am pleased to recognize the contributions of these individuals and extend to them my warmest personal regards for not only their professional insights, but their personal support and encouragement during the development of this project.

Professor Lee A. Graf, Illinois State University, has truly been a driving force in clarifying how this text and its accompanying workbook should be improved to better meet the needs of the management students of today. Lee Graf is a close personal friend and highly esteemed colleague whom I deeply respect for his competence, pedagogic insight, and high professional standards. Dr. Graf has not only made a significant contribution to this edition, but to all previous editions.

Other colleagues have also made important contributions to this text and its ancillaries. I would like to thank these individuals for their dedication and professionalism in making this project all that it can be. These professionals and the contribution that each has made are listed below:

Robert E. Kemper at Northern Arizona University for assistance in the revision of Chapter 18, "Production Management and Control"

Toni Carol King at Binghamton University for assistance in writing Chapter 22, "Diversity and Management," new to the sixth edition

Maurice Manner at Marymount College for assistance in the revision of Chapter 20, "International Management"

Richard Ratliff, Shari Tarnutzer, and their colleagues at Utah State University for assistance in the revision of Chapter 21, "Quality: Building Competitive Organizations"

Larry Waldorf at Boise State University for assistance in the revision of Chapter 14, "Leadership"

Dean Danielson of San Joaquin Delta College for preparing the transparency package

David J. Hoag of St. Louis Community College for revising the Instructor's Resource Manual and preparing annotations for the Instructor's Annotated Edition

Mary Oates Johnson for preparing the CNN Video User's Manual

Robert E. Kemper for revising the Test Bank

Betty Pritchett of Kennesaw State College for preparing the Pedagogical Notes to the Instructor

Shari Tarnutzer of Utah State University for preparing annotations for the Instructor's Annotated Edition

Mary S. Thibodeaux of University of North Texas for preparing annotations for the Instructor's Annotated Edition

The case studies and integrative cases were specially written for this text by the following team of case writers:

Stephen Beckstead, Utah State University

Robert E. Kemper, Northern Arizona University

Sylvia Keyes, Bridgewater State University

Cheryl Macon, Butler County Community College

Tony Ortega, California State University at Bakersfield

Peter B. Peterson, The Johns Hopkins University

Mildred Pryor, Center for Excellence, East Texas State University

Mary S. Thibodeaux, University of North Texas

Leslie A. Toombs, University of Texas at Tyler

In addition, Leslie Brunetta, Mary Oates Johnson, Meredith Rutter, Robin Deschert Schachat, and Mary Walsh researched and made contributions to many of the case studies, CNN video cases, CNN video exercises, and integrative cases.

Every author appreciates the valuable contribution reviewers make to the development of a text project. Reviewers offer that "different viewpoint" that requires an author to constructively question his or her work. I again had an excellent team of reviewers. Thoughtful comments, concern for student learning, and insights regarding instructional implications of the written word characterized the high-quality feedback I received. I am pleased to be able to recognize members of my review team for their valuable contributions to the development of this text:

Chandler Atkins, Adirondack Community College

Ronald Courchene, Allegheny Community College

Jim Day, Shawnee State University

Carl Gates, Sauk Valley Community College

John Heinsius, Modesto Junior College

John Herrmann, California State University at Long Beach

Eileen Bartels Hewitt, University of Scranton

Susan Jackson, New York University

Colleen Jones, Suffolk University

Cheryl Macon, Butler County Community College

Maurice Manner, Marymount College

Malcolm B. McGregor, Ozark Technical Community College

Thomas Meier, West Virginia University

Stephen Mosher, University of North Dakota

Tony Ortega, California State University at Bakersfield

Shari Tarnutzer, Utah State University

Stephen Walter, Davenport College

Another source of valuable feedback that I have used for developing and implementing the *Modern Management* learning package has been the helpful comments from colleagues. These individuals have, over the years, provided reviewer comments or have responded to an opinion survey. Surveys are conducted to expand the breadth of relevant feedback about the instructional value of various components of the text as well as the *Modern Management* learning package as a whole. I would like to personally thank my colleagues who have spent the time and effort to provide data that was critical in defining the character and scope of this text and its ancillaries.

Christopher Aglo-Ostoghile, *Prairie View Agriculture and Technology College*
Milton C. Alderfer, *Miami Dade Community College North*
Billie Allen, *University of Southern Mississippi*
Arturo Alonzo Jr., *St. Philip's College*
David Anstett, *College of St. Scholastica*
Robert J. Ash, *Rancho Santiago College*
Donald L. Ashbaugh, *University of Northern Iowa*
Jack Ashmore, *Bee County College*
Donald Baack, *Pittsburg State College*
Lorraine Bassette, *Prince George's Community College*
David Baxter, *San Diego Mesa College*
Charles Beavin, *Miami-Dade Community College*
Lee A. Belovarac, *Mercyhurst College*
Jack Blanton, *University of Kentucky*
Pam Braden, *Parkersburg Community College*
Don B. Bradley, *University of Central Arkansas*
Terry H. Brattin, *Texas State Technical University–Harlingen*
William Brichner, *San Jose State University*
Duane Brickner, *Southern Mountain Community College*
John W. Brown, Jr., *SUNY Brockport*
W. Brown, *Berry College*
Robert Bruns, *Central College*
Shirley Bryan, *Pennsylvania State University–Berks*
F. M. Buchanan, *Salisbury State College*
Alison Buck, *Phillips University*
Robert S. Bulls, *J. Sargeant Reynolds Community College*
Ellen Burns, *Phillips University*
Thomas Burns, *Keystone Jr. College*
David T. Bussard, *Susquehanna University*
Dennis G. Butler, *Orange Coast College*
Austin Byron, *Northern Arizona University*
Edward Cahaly, *Stonehill College*
Robert E. Callahan, *Seattle University*
Elizabeth A. Cameron, *Alma College*
Perry Camingore, *Brazosport College*
Joseph E. Cantrell, *DeAnza College*
Valeriano Cantu, *Angelo State University*
Justin Carey, *St. John's University*
Mario Carrillo, *Colorado School of Mines*
Thomas Case, *Georgia Southern University*
Tommy Cates, *University of Tennessee at Martin*
C. Dale Caudill, *Morehead State University*
Herschel Chait, *Indiana State University*
Pamela Chandler, *University of Mary Hardin–Baylor*
John F. Chisholm, *Allegheny Community College*
Daniel W. Churchill, *Mount Ida College*
Robert A. Cisek, *Mercyhurst College*
Joseph Clairmont, *Bay De Noc Community College*
William Clark, *Leeward Community College*
Debra M. Clingerman, *California University of Pennsylvania*
Larry A. Coleman, *Indiana State University*
Terry Comingor, *Brazosport College*
John Coppola, *Cosumnes River College*
Pati Crabb, *Bellarmine University*
D. Dexter Dalton, *St. Louis Community College at Meramec*
D. James Day, *Shawnee State University*
John R. Deegan, *Texas Wesleyan College*
Linda Dell'Osso, *California State Polytechnic University–Pomona*
Sezai Demiral, *Edinboro University of Pennsylvania*
Richard L. Dickinson, *California State University–Sacramento*
Dale L. Dickson, *Mesa College*
Daniel J. Duffy, *Loyola College–Evergreen*
Robert Dunn, *Alexander City State College*
John Eberle, *Embry-Riddle Aeronautical University*
Sidney W. Eckert, *Appalachian State University*
Jeb Egbert, *Ambassador College*
Randi Sue Ellis, *North Harris County Community College*
Chuck England, *Bridgewater State College*
Mary Sue Ewald, *Missouri Baptist College*
Vincent E. Faherty, *University of Northern Iowa*
Jeffrey W. Fahrenwal, *Central College*
Deborah Fajcak, *Harding Business College*
Jay Felton, *North Harris County Community College*
Judy Field, *Willmar Community College*

Stephen Field, *University of West Florida*
Richard Forsyth, *University of Wisconsin–Green Bay*
Paula S. Funkhouser, *Truckee Meadows Community College*
Dick Gardner, *West Virginia University*
Gerald Garrity, *Anna Maria College*
Carl Gates, *Sauk Valley College*
Pat Gaudette, *Pine Manor College*
Beth Gershon, *University of La Verne*
Faith Gilroy, *Loyola College–Evergreen*
Carolyn Goad, *Oakland City Community College*
R. Goddard, *Appalachian State University*
Robert Goldberg, *Northeastern University*
David Goldenberg, *Bellarmine University*
Sonia Goltz, *University of Notre Dame*
Thomas Goodwin, *Johnson and Wales College*
Jack N. Grose, *Mars Hill College*
Raymond M. Guydosh, *SUNY Plattsburgh*
Luther Guynes, *Los Angeles City College*
James L. Hall, *University of Santa Clara*
Ed Hammer, *University of Tennessee–Chattanooga*
Kathleen Harcharik, *California State Polytechnic University–Pomona*
James Harvey, *University of West Florida*
Dorothy B. Heide, *California State University–Fullerton*
Wayne Hemberger, *Edinboro University of Pennsylvania*
John W. Henry, *Georgia Southern University*
Bill Herlehy, *Embry-Riddle Aeronautical University*
Irving L. Herman, *California State University–Sacramento*
J. C. Hill, *Appalachian State University*
Marvin Hill, *Northern Illinois University*
Robert T. Holland, *Woodbury University*
William Houlihan, *Detroit College of Business*
Fred House, *Northern Arizona University*
Edmund Hunter, *Delaware County Community College*
Warren Imada, *Leeward Community College*
William Jacobs, *Lake City Community College*
Ernest Jaski, *Richard J. Daley College*
David J. Jobson, *Keystone Jr. College*
Alan E. Johnson, *Embry-Riddle Aeronautical University*
Edwin Johnson, *Parkersburg Community College*
Karen R. Johnson, *University of New Hampshire*
Paul W. Joice, Sr., *Walla Walla College*
Bette-Jean Jones, *Embry-Riddle Aeronautical University*
Charlie Jones, *East Central Oklahoma University*
Frazier C. Jones, *Montreat-Anderson College*
Marvin Karlins, *University of South Florida*
Frank Kattwinkel, *St. Leo College*
Fred Jeffrey Keil, *J. Sargeant Reynolds Community College*
Robert E. Kemper, *Northern Arizona University*
George Kevorkian, *Northern Virginia Community College*
Sylvia Keyes, *Bridgewater State College*
Scott King, *Sinclair Community College*
Jerome M. Kinskey, *Sinclair Community College*
Barney J. Klecker, *Normandale Community College*
John P. Kohl, *San Jose State University*
Bob Kovacev, *California State University–Fullerton*
Dennis Lee Kovach, *Community College of Allegheny North*
Arthur LaCapria, Jr., *El Paso Community College*
William Lacewell, *Westark Community College*
Patricia Laidler, *Massasoit Community College*
Philip M. Lee, *Campbellsville College*
Jery Lemmons, *State Technical Institute–Memphis*
Charles LePore, *Embry-Riddle Aeronautical University*
Robert Lerosen, *Northern Virginia Community College*
Ardyce S. Lightner, *D'Youville College*
Malcom H. Livick, *Blue Ridge Community College*
Mary Alice Lo Cicero, *Oakland Community College*
Chris Lockwood, *Northern Arizona University*
John F. Logan, *Thiel College*
David J. Lonergan, *Greater Hartford Community College*
David H. Lydick, *St. Leo College*
Robert J. Lyons, *Sweet Briar College*
Willard Machen, *Amarillo College*
Anita Marcellis, *College of St. Elizabeth*
Daniel W. McAllister, *University of Nevada, Las Vegas*
John D. McCurdy, *Embry-Riddle Aeronautical University*
Barbara McDonnell, *College of Notre Dame of Maryland*
Robert L. McElwee, *University of Akron*
James L. McGuigan, *Community College of Allegheny County*

James M. McHugh, *St. Louis Community College–Forest Park*
Pat McLaughlin, *Merrimac College*
Edward Meier, *Concordia College*
Peggy C. Mifflin, *Indiana State University*
E. S. Mills, *Kendall College*
Robert A. Moore, *Southern Utah State*
James Moreau, *Rock Valley College*
Bill Morris, *Devry Institute of Technology*
J. B. Mosca, *Monmouth College*
Alexander Mosley, *Miami-Dade Community College*
Bonnie S. Moyers, *Blue Ridge Community College*
Eugene Murkison, *Georgia Southern University*
John E. Murray, *Massasoit Community College*
M. James Nead, *Vincennes University*
Thomas Nist, *La Roche College*
Janet M. Noble, *University of Maryland*
James Nordin, *Coffeyville Community College*
Christopher E. Nussbaumer, *Austin Peay State University*
Erna O'Connor, *Kishwaukee College*
Diana Page, *University of West Florida*
Karl Pape, *Embry-Riddle Aeronautical University*
Michael H. Parson, *Hagerstown Junior College*
John Paxton, *Southwest Missouri State University*
Joseph O. Pecenka, *Northern Illinois University*
Dennis Pennington, *Spartanburg Methodist College*
Shri Penugonda, *Wilkes College*
Joseph Platts, *Miami-Dade Community College*
Shane Premeaux, *McNeese State University*
Rebecca Pyrne, *Wilmington College*
William Racker, *Anoka-Ramsey Community College*
Kenneth J. Radig, *Medaille College*
Harry Ramsden, *University of La Verne–NAS No. Island*
Richard Raspen, *Wilkes College*
Mary C. Raven, *Mount Mary College*
William R. Rawlinson, *Solano Community College*
Morris Dale Reed, *East Central University*
Harriet Rice, *Los Angeles City College*
Charles A. Rickman, *University of Arts and Sciences*
Robert Roller, *Oral Roberts University*
Peggy Romanelli, *Oral Roberts University*
Stanford H. Rosenberg, *La Roche College*
Greg Runyon, *Trevecca Nazarene College*
Mary Beth Ruthem, *Jefferson Tech College*
Robb Ruyle, *Mesa College*
R. Richard Sabo, *California State Polytechnic University*
Madan Saluja, *Lake Superior State College*
Richard D. Sambuco, *West Virginia Northern Community College*
Cheryl Savage, *California State Polytechnic University–Pomona*
Clemmie Saxon, *Howard University*
Dietrich L. Schaupp, *West Virginia University*
Suzanne Seedorf, *Northeast Iowa Technical Institute*
Charles R. Schatzer, *Solano Community College*
David Shepard, *Virginia Western Community College*
Frederick Sheppard, *Bridgewater State College*
Steven Shiring, *Butler County Community College*
Charles B. Shrader, *Iowa State University*
Sara Shryock, *Black Hills State College*
Jack Skaggs, *Oklahoma Christian College*
Mary S. Thibodeaux, *University of North Texas*
Leslie Toombs, *University of Texas at Tyler*
G. A. Vargas, *California State University, Fullerton*
Ronald Vickroy, *University of Pittsburgh at Johnstown*

I would also like to acknowledge the personal interest and encouragement for this project shown by my colleagues in the Crummer Graduate School of Business at Rollins College. The faculty has been very supportive of this project. In addition, my management colleagues, James M. Higgins, Theodore T. Herbert, and Max R. Richards, have all helped me to validate my professional judgments and crystalize my book concept. I am fortunate indeed to work with a faculty that possess such expertise and high professional standards.

The support that Allyn and Bacon has given throughout this project has been invaluable. As editors, Rich Wohl and Suzy Spivey have shown amazing insight and book savvy in helping me to develop this revision. Professionals such as Judy Fifer, Carol Alper, and Marjorie Payne, played critical roles in both the planning and evolution of this project. Mary Jo Gregory has ushered my manuscript through the production process smoothly and efficiently. Bill Barke, the president of Allyn and Bacon, provided me many important insights about the more general world of publishing that have helped me to improve this text. I thank the entire Allyn and Bacon family for its patience in listening to my ideas and appropriately improving, discarding, or accepting them. The healthy exchange of ideas between author and publisher that characterized this revision process is a primary reason that the text you see is of such high quality.

From a more personal viewpoint, my family was always there to help me handle the difficult challenges that inevitably accompany the task of publishing a comprehensive text of this magnitude. My wife, Mimi, is simply the best! My children, Trevis, Matthew, Sarah, and Brian have no idea that the care they show is so inspirational to me. The strength shown by my father, Sam, and my mother, Annette, in handling personal challenges throughout their lives will always "show me the way."

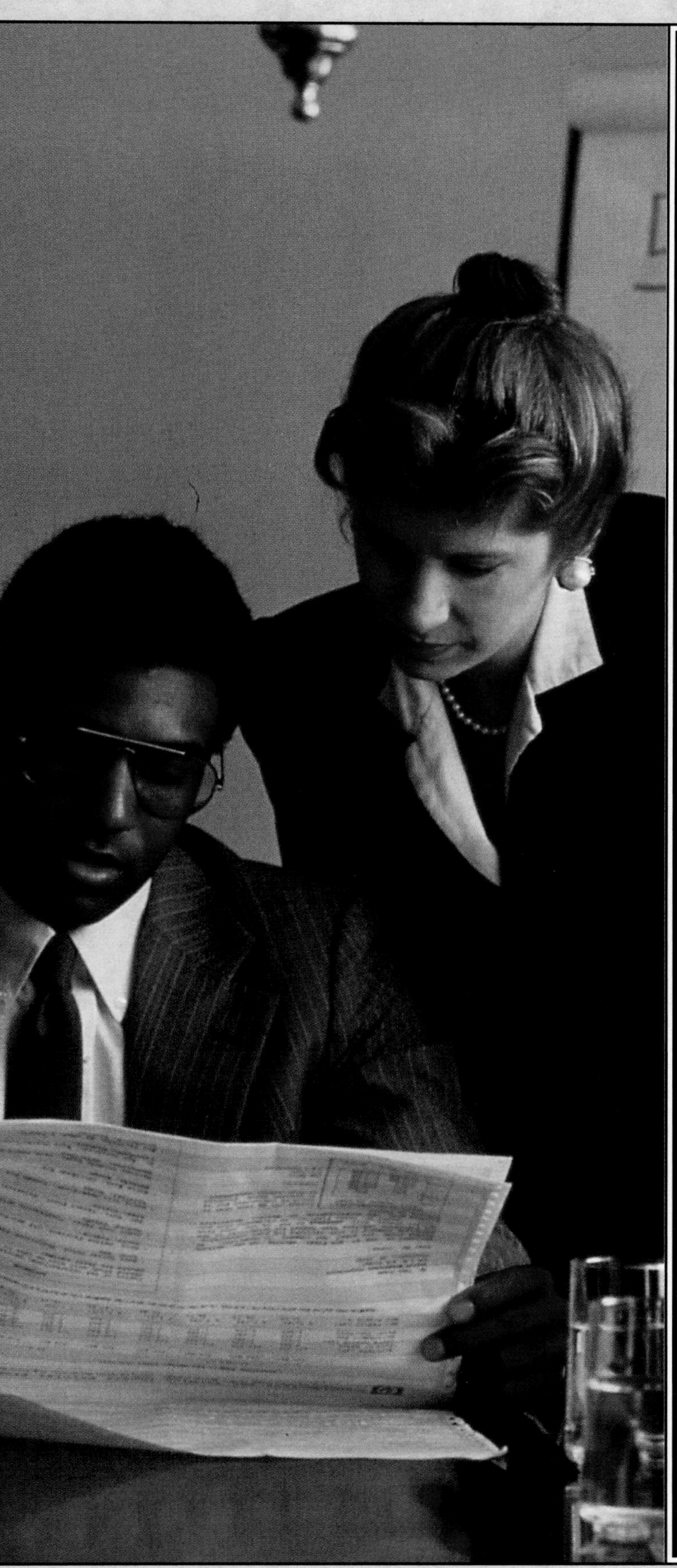

INTRODUCTION TO MANAGEMENT

The purpose of this section is to introduce the field of management. In general terms, the introduction is accomplished through extended discussion on how management is defined, on various approaches to management that have evolved over the years, and on social responsibility and ethics.

PART 1

In more specific terms, this section offers a thorough explanation of the steps of the management process, of managerial effectiveness and efficiency, of the skills needed by managers, and of what can be expected from a management career. The explanation of different ways to perform the manager's job emphasizes the classical, behavioral, management science, contingency, and systems approaches. Last, this section discusses fundamentals of social responsibility, social responsiveness, social responsibility and management functions, and ethics.

As you study chapters in this section, keep in mind that this material is extremely important. An understanding of these foundation concepts will significantly influence your ability to understand the material in the remaining sections of the text.

CHAPTER

1

MANAGEMENT AND MANAGEMENT CAREERS

STUDENT LEARNING OBJECTIVES

From studying this chapter, I will attempt to acquire:

1. An understanding of the importance of management to society and individuals.
2. An understanding of the role of management.
3. An ability to define management in several different ways.
4. An ability to list and define the basic functions of management.
5. Working definitions of managerial effectiveness and managerial efficiency.
6. An understanding of basic management skills and their relative importance to managers.
7. An understanding of the universality of management.
8. Insights concerning what careers are and how they evolve.

CHAPTER OUTLINE

INTRODUCTORY CASE
Robert Stempel Faces Serious Problems at General Motors

THE IMPORTANCE OF MANAGEMENT

THE MANAGEMENT TASK

The Role of Management
Defining Management

THE UNIVERSALITY OF MANAGEMENT

MANAGEMENT CAREERS

A Definition of Career
Promoting Your Own Career
Special Career Issues

MANAGEMENT HIGHLIGHTS: A SPECIAL FEATURE FOR THE REMAINING CHAPTERS

Global Highlights
Ethics Highlights
Diversity Highlights
Quality Highlights

CASE STUDY
Dorothy Terrell: The Road to President, SunExpress

VIDEO CASE
On a Management Career Path with Style: Josie Cruz Natori, House of Natori

VIDEO EXERCISE
Your Interview with Josie Natori

INTRODUCTORY CASE

Robert Stempel Faces Serious Problems at General Motors

To fully fathom the depth and pervasiveness of the ailments that forced General Motors to order the greatest reorganization in its modern history, consider the Cadillac Seville STS. GM is billing the redesigned $38,000 luxury sedan as its flagship, the embodiment of its engineering superiority, its answer to Mercedes and Lexus. The car is vastly superior to the model it replaces and has won several awards from enthusiast publications.

Bob Stempel has an opportunity that was denied all of his predecessors: the crisis required to bring about revolutionary change.

And yet its introduction was delayed for a year because of design problems. A new multivalve V-8 engine planned for the car won't be ready for another year. Production ran behind schedule owing to difficulties with the paint system, among other things. The plant in Hamtramck, Michigan, where the Seville is built, has operated at little more than 50 percent of capacity since it opened in 1985, rendering it perpetually uneconomic.

Such are the wonders and the woes of the world's biggest manufacturing company. GM is capable of achievements bordering on brilliance. Today it builds the best cars and trucks in its history. This model year it is introducing 16 new vehicles—the most ever. J.D. Power & Associates ranks Cadillac and Buick among the industry's ten top makes for customer satisfaction. GM is a world leader in several critical technologies, including antilock brakes and electric cars.

But the company is foundering. Even with the massive cutbacks announced by Chairman Robert Stempel in mid-December, it lags behind its major competitors in almost every measure of efficiency. By some key standards—how many worker-hours it takes to assemble a car, for instance—GM is an astounding 40 percent less productive than Ford. Last year GM lost, on average, $1,500 on every one of the more than 3.5 million cars and trucks it made in North America. . . .

Great men demand great times. Bob Stempel has an opportunity that was denied all of his predecessors: the crisis required to bring about revolutionary change. Stempel said in December that he is making fundamental alterations in the way GM does business. If he fails, it would be a tragedy for Detroit, for the Midwest, for the U.S. economy, and for a million or more GM workers and retirees—not to mention all those potential customers for the high-quality, made-in-America automobiles. But if he and the rest of GM management are successful, even his competitors will have reason to cheer the renewed vitality of an American corporate institution.

In order to cope with the many problems facing General Motors, Chairman Robert Stempel is making fundamental changes in the way that GM does business.

This case is excerpted from Alex Taylor III, "Can GM Remodel Itself?," *Fortune*. (January 13, 1992), 26–34. © 1992 Time Inc. All rights reserved.

WHAT'S AHEAD As discussed in the introductory case, General Motors is suffering from a number of serious organizational problems. The case concludes by implying that the problems facing Chairman Robert Stempel are formidable. Information in this chapter is designed to describe what management is and how it relates to an individual like Stempel facing the challenge of solving complex organizational problems. In this chapter, management is described through (1) a discussion of its importance both to society and to individuals, (2) a description of the management task, (3) a definition of management, (4) a discussion of its universality, and (5) insights about management careers.

THE IMPORTANCE OF MANAGEMENT

Managers influence all phases of our modern organizations. Plant managers run manufacturing operations that produce our clothes, food, and automobiles. Sales managers maintain a sales force that markets goods. Personnel managers provide organizations with a competent and productive work force. The "jobs available" section in the classified advertisements of any major newspaper describes many different types of management activities and confirms the importance of management (see Figure 1.1).

Our society simply could not exist as we know it today or improve its present status without a steady stream of managers to guide its organizations.[1] Peter Drucker makes this point in stating that effective management is probably the main resource of developed countries and the most needed resource of developing ones.[2] In short, countries desperately need good managers.

In addition to being important to our society as a whole, management is vital to many individuals simply because they earn their livings by being managers. Government statistics show that management positions have increased from approximately 10 percent to approximately 18 percent of the work force since 1950.[3] Managers typically come from varying backgrounds and have diverse educational specialties. Many individuals who originally trained to be accountants, teachers, financiers, or even writers eventually make their livelihoods as managers. In the short term, the demand for managers may vary somewhat from year to year. In the long term, managerial positions can yield high salaries, status, interesting work, personal growth, and intense feelings of accomplishment.

In fact, there is some concern that certain managers are paid too much when you consider how well or how poorly their organizations are doing.[4] To illustrate how substantial management salaries can be, consider the results of a 1990 poll by *Forbes* magazine ranking the highest total compensation amounts paid by organizations to managers.* Figure 1.2 lists the top ten compensation packages paid to managers during 1991, the companies that paid them, and the managers who received them.[5]

BACK TO THE CASE The information just presented furnishes an individual such as Stempel with insights concerning the significance of his role as manager. His role as a manager is important not only to society as a whole but also to himself as an individual. In general, as a manager he makes some contribution to creating the standard of living that we all enjoy and thereby earns corresponding rewards. Even given the present status of General Motors, the societal contributions that it can make are significant and far reaching. If Stempel is able to solve the organizational problems that confront him at GM, the positive impact that the company could have on society will be even greater.

*The *Forbes* poll defined *total compensation* as the total amount paid to a manager through salary, bonus, and other sources like benefits, and value of company stock owned.

SR. MANAGEMENT DEVELOPMENT SPECIALIST

We are a major metropolitan service employer of over 5,000 employees seeking a person to join our management development staff. Prospective candidates will be degreed with 5 to 8 years experience in the design, implementation, and evaluation of developmental programs for first-line and mid-level management personnel. Additionally, candidates must demonstrate exceptional oral and written communications ability and be skilled in performance analysis, programmed instruction, and the design and implementation of reinforcement systems.

If you meet these qualifications, please send your résumé, including salary history and requirements to:

Box RS-653

An Equal Opportunity Employer

BRANCH MGR–$30,500. Perceptive pro with track record in administration and lending has high visibility with respected firm.

Box PH-165

AVIATION FBO MANAGER NEEDED

Southeast Florida operation catering to corporate aviation. No maintenance or aircraft sales–just fuel and the best service. Must be experienced. Salary plus benefits commensurate with qualifications. Submit complete résumé to:

Box LJO-688

DIVISION CREDIT MANAGER

Major mfg. corporation seeks an experienced credit manager to handle the credit and collection function of its Midwest division (Chicago area). Interpersonal skills are important, as is the ability to communicate effectively with senior management. Send résumé with current compensation to:

Box NM–43

ACCOUNTING MANAGER

Growth opportunity. Michigan Ave. location. Acctg. degree, capable of supervision. Responsibilities include G/L, financial statements, inventory control, knowledge of systems design for computer applications. Send résumé, incl. salary history to:

Box RJM-999

An Equal Opportunity Employer

PERSONNEL MANAGER

Publicly owned, national manufacturer with 12 plants, 700 employees, seeks first corporate personnel director. We want someone to administer programs in:

- Position and rate evaluation
- Employee safety engineering
- Employee training
- Employee communications
- Employee benefits
- Federal compliance

Qualifications: minimum of 3–5 years personnel experience in mfg. company, ability to tactfully deal with employees at all levels from all walks of life, free to travel. Position reports to Vice President, Operations. Full range of company benefits, salary $32,000– 40,000. Reply in complete confidence to:

Box JK-236

FINANCIAL MANAGER

CPA/MBA (U of C) with record of success in management positions. Employed, now seeking greater opportunity. High degree of professionalism, exp. in dealing w/financial inst., strong communication & analytical skills, stability under stress, high energy level, results oriented. Age 34, 11 yrs exper. incl. major public acctng, currently 5 years as Financial VP of field leader. Impressive references. **Box LML-666**

MARKET MANAGER

Major lighting manufacturer seeks market manager for decorative outdoor lighting. Position entails establishing and implementing marketing, sales, and new product development programs including coordination of technical publications and related R & D projects. Must locate at Denver headquarters. Send resume to **Box WM-214**

No agencies please

GENERAL MANAGER

Small industrial service company, privately owned, located in Springfield, Missouri, needs aggressive, skilled person to make company grow in profits and sales. Minimum B. S. in Business, experienced in all facets of small business operations. Must understand profit. Excellent opportunity and rewards. Salary and fringes commensurate with experience and performance. **Box LEM-116**

FOUNDRY SALES MANAGER

Aggressive gray iron foundry located in the Midwest, specializing in 13,000 tons of complex castings yearly with a weight range of 2 to 400 pounds, is seeking experienced dynamic sales manager with sound sales background in our industry. Salary commensurate with experience; excellent benefit package. **Box MO-948**

FIGURE 1.1 The variety of management positions available

Pay Rank	CEO, Company	Compensation* 1991 Sal + Bonus	Value of 1991 Stock Grants	Total
1	**Robert C. Goizueta,** Coca-Cola	2,962	55,971	58,933
2	**Hamish Maxwell,** Philip Morris	1,741	28,201	29,942
3	**Stanley C. Gault,** Goodyear Tire and Rubber	735	21,801	22,536
4	**Lawrence A. Bossidy,** Allied-Signal	809	21,393	22,202
5	**William A. Schreyer,** Merrill Lynch	5,850	9,908	15,758
6	**Stephen M. Wolf,** UAL	575	13,605	14,180
7	**Noland D. Archibald,** Black and Decker	1,336	12,194	13,529
8	**Robert E. Allen,** American Telephone & Telegraph	2,061	10,716	12,777
9	**Richard J. Mahoney,** Monsanto	1,530	9,078	10,608
10	**John F. Welch, Jr.,** General Electric	3,207	7,047	10,254

* All dollar amounts in thousands

FIGURE 1.2 The ten highest total compensation amounts recently paid to managers

THE MANAGEMENT TASK

Besides understanding the significance of being a manager and its related potential benefits, prospective managers should know what the management task entails. The sections that follow introduce the basics of the management task through discussions of the role and definition of management.

The Role of Management

Essentially, the role of managers is to guide organizations toward goal accomplishment. All organizations exist for some purpose or goal, and managers have the responsibility of combining and using organizational resources to ensure that the organizations achieve their purposes. Management moves organizations toward purposes or goals by assigning activities that organization members perform. If the activities are designed effectively, the production of each individual worker represents a contribution to the attainment of organizational goals. Management strives to encourage individual activity that will lead to reaching organizational goals and to discourage individual activity that will hinder organizational goal accomplishment. "There is no idea more important to managing than goals. Management has no meaning apart from its goals."[6] Management must keep organizational goals in mind at all times.

Defining Management

Students of management should be aware that the term *management* can be and often is used in several different ways.[7] For instance, it can refer simply to the process that managers follow to accomplish organizational goals. It can also be used to refer to a body of knowledge. In this context, it is a cumulative body of information that furnishes insights on how to manage. Management also can be the term used to pinpoint the individuals who guide and direct organizations or to designate a career devoted to the task of guiding and directing organizations. An understanding of the various uses and related definitions of the term should help students and practitioners eliminate miscommunication during management-related discussions.

Management is the process of reaching organizational goals by working with and through people and other organizational resources.

As used most commonly in this text, **management** is the process of reaching organizational goals by working with and through people and other organizational resources. A comparison of this definition with the definitions offered by several contemporary management thinkers shows that there is some agreement that management has the following three main characteristics: (1) It is a process or series of continuing and related activities; (2) It involves and concentrates on reaching organizational

TABLE 1.1 Contemporary definitions of management

Management—
1. Is the process by which a cooperative group directs actions of others toward common goals (Massie and Douglas).
2. Is the process of working with and through others to effectively achieve organizational objectives by efficiently using limited resources in a changing environment (Kreitner).
3. Is the coordination of all resources through the processes of planning, organizing, directing, and controlling in order to attain stated objectives (Sisk).
4. Is establishing an effective environment for people operating in formal organizational groups (Koontz and O'Donnell).
5. Entails activities undertaken by one or more persons in order to coordinate the activities of others in the pursuit of ends that cannot be achieved by any one person (Donnelly, Gibson, and Ivancevich).

goals; and (3) It reaches these goals by working with and through people and other organizational resources (see Table 1.1). A discussion of each of these characteristics follows.

The Management Process: Management Functions

The four basic **management functions**— activities that make up the management process — are as follows:

Management functions are activities that make up the management process.

1. *Planning.* Planning involves choosing tasks that must be performed to attain organizational goals, outlining how the tasks must be performed, and indicating when the tasks should be performed. Planning activity focuses on attaining goals. Managers, through their plans, outline exactly what organizations must do to be successful. They are concerned with organizational success in the near future (short term) as well as in the more distant future (long term).
2. *Organizing.* Organizing can be thought of as assigning the tasks developed during planning to various individuals or groups within the organization. Organizing creates a mechanism to put plans into action. People within the organization are given work assignments that contribute to goal attainment. Tasks are organized so that the output of individuals contributes to the success of departments, which contributes to the success of divisions, which in turn contributes to the overall success of organizations.
3. *Influencing.* Influencing is another of the basic functions within the management process. This function — also commonly referred to as motivating, leading, directing, and actuating — is concerned primarily with people within organizations.* Influencing can be defined as the process of guiding the activities of organization members in appropriate directions. An appropriate direction is any direction that helps the organization move toward goal attainment. The ultimate purpose of influencing is to increase productivity. Human oriented work situations usually generate higher levels of production over the long term than do work situations that people find distasteful.

*In early management literature, the term *motivating* was more commonly used to signify this people-oriented management function. The term *influencing* is used consistently in this text because it is broader and allows more flexibility in discussions of people-oriented issues. Later in the text, motivating is discussed as a major part of influencing.

FIGURE 1.3 Interrelations of the four functions of management to attain organizational goals

4. *Controlling.* Controlling is the management function for which managers (a) gather information that measures recent performance within the organization; (b) compare present performance to preestablished performance standards; and (c) from this comparison, determine if the organization should be modified to meet preestablished standards. Controlling is an ongoing process. Managers continually gather information, make their comparisons, and then try to find new ways of improving production through organizational modification.

Management Process and Goal Attainment

Although the four functions of management have been discussed individually, planning, organizing, influencing, and controlling are integrally related and cannot be separated. Figure 1.3 illustrates this interrelationship and also that managers use these activities solely for the purpose of reaching organizational goals. Basically, these functions are interrelated because the performance of one depends on the performance of the others. To illustrate, organizing is based on well-thought-out plans developed during the planning process, and influencing systems must be tailored to reflect both these plans and the organizational design used to implement them. The fourth function, controlling, proposes possible modifications to existing plans, organizational structure, or the motivation system to develop a more successful effort.

To be effective, a manager must understand how the four management functions must be practiced, not simply how they are defined and related. Thomas J. Peters and Robert H. Waterman, Jr., studied numerous organizations — including Frito-Lay and Maytag — for several years to determine what management characteristics best described excellently run companies. Table 1.2 contains the list and descriptions of characteristics finally developed by Peters and Waterman and published in their book *In Search of Excellence.* This list implies that planning, organizing, influencing, and controlling should be characterized by a bias for action; a closeness to the customer; autonomy and entrepreneurship; productivity through people; a hands-on, value-driven orientation; "sticking to the knitting"; a simple form with a lean staff; and simultaneous loose-tight properties.

The information in this section has been only a brief introduction to the four management functions. Later sections are devoted to developing these functions in much more detail.

Organizational resources are assets available for activation during normal operations, including human resources, monetary resources, raw materials resources, and capital resources.

Management and Organizational Resources

Management must always be aware of the status and use of **organizational resources.** These resources, composed of all assets available for activation during the production process, are of four basic types: (1) human, (2) monetary, (3) raw materials, and (4) capital. As Figure 1.4 depicts, organizational resources are combined, used, and transformed into finished products during the production process.

TABLE 1.2 Characteristics of excellently run companies

1. *A bias for action,* for getting on with it. Even though these companies may be analytical in their approach to decision making, they are not paralyzed by that fact (as so many others seem to be). In many of these companies, the standard operating procedure is "Do it, fix it, try it." Moreover, the companies are experimenters supreme. Instead of allowing 250 engineers and marketers to work on a new product in isolation for fifteen months, they form bands of 5 to 25 and test ideas out on a customer, often with inexpensive prototypes, within a matter of weeks. What is striking is the host of practical devices the excellent companies employ to maintain corporate fleetness of foot and counter the stultification that almost inevitably comes with size.
2. *Close to the customer.* These companies learn from the people they serve. They provide unparalleled quality, service, and reliability — things that work and last. They succeed in differentiating — *à la* Frito-Lay (potato chips), Maytag (washers), or Tupperware — the most commodity-like products. IBM's marketing vice president, Francis G. (Buck) Rodgers, says, "It's a shame that, in so many companies, whenever you get good service, it's an exception." Not so at the excellent companies. Everyone gets into the act. Many of the innovative companies got their best product ideas from customers. That comes from listening — intently and regularly.
3. *Autonomy and entrepreneurship.* The innovative companies foster many leaders and many innovators throughout the organization. They are a hive of what we've come to call champions; 3M has been described as "so intent on innovation that its essential atmosphere seems not like that of a large corporation but rather a loose network of laboratories and cubbyholes populated by feverish inventors and dauntless entrepreneurs who let their imaginations fly in all directions." They don't try to hold everyone on so short a rein that creativity is stifled. They encourage practical risk taking, and support good tries. They follow Fletcher Byrom's ninth commandment: "Make sure you generate a reasonable number of mistakes."
4. *Productivity through people.* The excellent companies treat the rank and file as the source of quality and productivity gain. They do not foster we/they labor attitudes or regard capital investment as the fundamental source of efficiency improvement. As Thomas J. Watson, Jr., said of his company, "IBM's philosophy is largely contained in three simple beliefs. I want to begin with what I think is the most important: *our respect for the individual.* This is a simple concept, but in IBM it occupies a major portion of management time." Texas Instrument's chairman Mark Shepherd talks about it in terms of every worker's being "seen as a source of ideas, not just acting as a pair of hands"; each of his more than 9,000 People Involvement Program, or PIP, teams (Texas Instrument's quality circles) does contribute to the company's sparkling productivity record.
5. *Hands-on, value driven.* Thomas Watson, Jr., said that "the basic philosophy of an organization has far more to do with its achievements than do technological or economic resources, organizational structure, innovation, and timing." Watson and Hewlett-Packard's William Hewlett are legendary for walking the plant floors. McDonald's Ray Kroc regularly visited stores and assessed them on the factors the company holds dear, Q.S.C. & V. (Quality, Service, Cleanliness, and Value.)
6. *"Stick to the knitting."* Robert W. Johnson, former Johnson & Johnson chairman, put it this way: "Never acquire a business you don't know how to run." Or as Edward G. Harness, past chief executive at Procter & Gamble, said, "This company has never left its base. We seek to be anything but a conglomerate." While there were a few exceptions, the odds for excellent performance seem strongly to favor those companies that stay reasonably close to businesses they know.
7. *Simple form, lean staff.* As big as most of the companies we have looked at are, none was formally run with a matrix organization structure, and some which had tried that form had abandoned it. The underlying structural forms and systems in the excellent companies are elegantly simple. Top-level staffs are lean; it is not uncommon to find a corporate staff of fewer than 100 people running multi-billion-dollar enterprises.
8. *Simultaneous loose-tight properties.* The excellent companies are both centralized and decentralized. For the most part, as we have said, they have pushed autonomy down to the shop floor on product development teams. On the other hand, they are fanatic centralists around the few core values they hold dear. 3M is marked by barely organized chaos surrounding its product champions. Yet one analyst argues, "The brainwashed members of an extremist political sect are no more conformist in their central beliefs." At Digital, the chaos is so rampant that one executive noted, "Damn few people know who they work for." Yet Digital's fetish for reliability is more rigidly adhered to than any outsider could imagine.

Human resources are the people who work for an organization. The skills they possess and their knowledge of the work system are invaluable to managers. Monetary resources are amounts of money that managers use to purchase goods and services for the organization. Raw materials are ingredients acquired to be used directly in the manufacturing of products. For example, rubber is a raw material that a company such as Goodyear would purchase with its monetary resources and use directly in the manufacturing of tires. Capital resources are the machines an organization uses during the

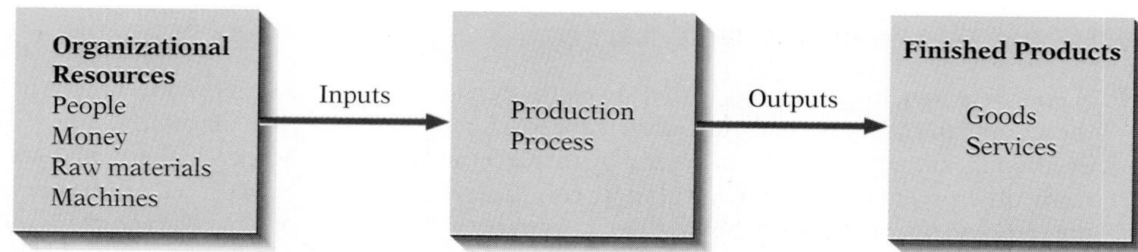

FIGURE 1.4 Transformation of organizational resources into finished products through the production process

manufacturing process. Modern machines, or equipment, can be a major factor in maintaining desired production levels. Worn-out or antiquated machinery can make it impossible for an organization to keep pace with competitors.

Managerial effectiveness is the degree to which management attains organizational objectives. It is measured by how close organizations come to achieving their goals.

Managerial Effectiveness. As managers use their resources, they must strive to be both effective and efficient. **Managerial effectiveness** is defined in terms of resource utilization in relation to organizational goal attainment. If organizations are using their resources to attain their goals, the managers are effective. In reality, there are degrees of managerial effectiveness. The closer that organizations come to achieving their goals, the more effective the managers are said to be. Managerial effectiveness can be depicted as being on a continuum ranging from ineffective to effective.

Managerial efficiency is the degree to which organizational resources contribute to productivity. It is measured by the proportion of organizational resources used during the production process.

Managerial Efficiency. **Managerial efficiency** is defined in terms of the proportion of total organizational resources that contribute to productivity during the manufacturing process. The higher this proportion, the more efficient the manager. The more resources wasted or unused during the production process, the more inefficient the manager. In this situation, *organizational resources* refers not only to raw materials that are used in manufacturing goods or services, but also to related human effort.[8] As with management effectiveness, management efficiency is best described as being on a continuum ranging from inefficient to efficient. *Inefficient* means that a very small proportion of total resources contributes to productivity during the manufacturing process; *efficient* means that a very large proportion contributes.

As Figure 1.5 shows, the concepts of managerial effectiveness and efficiency are obviously related. A manager could be relatively ineffective, the organization making very little progress toward goal attainment, primarily because of major inefficiencies or

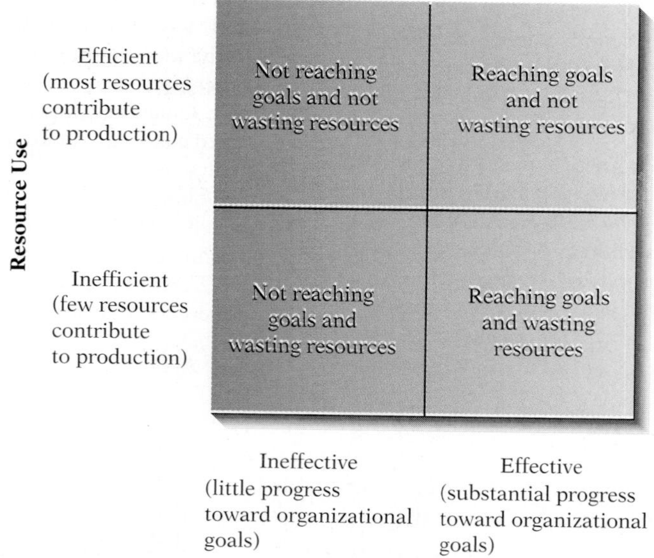

FIGURE 1.5 Various combinations of managerial effectiveness and managerial efficiency

poor utilization of resources during the production process. In contrast, a manager could be somewhat effective despite being inefficient. Demand for the finished goods may be so high that the manager can get an extremely high price per unit sold and thus absorb inefficiency costs.

For example, some oil companies in Saudi Arabia could probably absorb many managerial inefficiencies when oil sells at a high price. Management in this situation has a chance to be somewhat effective despite its inefficiency. Thus, a manager can be effective without being efficient and vice versa. To maximize organizational success, however, both effectiveness and efficiency are needed.

BACK TO THE CASE

The preceding material contains more specific information on what management is and what managers do. According to this information, a manager such as Stempel must have a clear understanding of General Motors' objectives and guide the organization toward reaching these objectives. This guidance, of course, will involve the manager's working directly with other top managers at General Motors' headquarters as well as perhaps various managers at GM facilities throughout the country.

Stempel must be heavily involved in planning, organizing, influencing, and controlling. In other words, he will have to outline how certain activities must be performed to reach objectives, assign these activities to appropriate GM personnel, encourage the personnel to perform their jobs, and make any changes necessary to ensure reaching GM's objectives. As he performs these four functions at General Motors, Stempel must remember that the activities themselves are interrelated and must blend together appropriately.

The wise use of General Motors' resources by Stempel is critical. He must strive to be both effective and efficient—to reach General Motors' objectives without wasting company resources.

Management Skills. No discussion of organizational resources would be complete without the mention of management skills, perhaps the primary determinant of how effective and efficient managers will be.

According to a classic article by Robert L. Katz, managerial success depends primarily on performance rather than personality traits.[9] Katz also states that a manager's ability to perform is a result of the managerial skills possessed. A manager with the necessary management skills will probably perform well and be relatively successful. One without the necessary skills will probably perform poorly and be relatively unsuccessful.

Katz indicates that three types of skills are important for successful management performance: technical skills, human skills, and conceptual skills. **Technical skills** involve using specialized knowledge and expertise in executing work-related techniques and procedures. Examples of these skills are engineering, computer programming, and accounting. Technical skills are mostly related to working with "things"— processes or physical objects. **Human skills** are skills that build cooperation within the team being led. They involve working with attitudes, communication, individuals and groups, and individual interests — in short, working with people. **Conceptual skills** involve the ability to see the organization as a whole. A manager with conceptual skills is able to understand how various functions of the organization complement one another, how the organization relates to its environment, and how changes in one part of the organization affect the rest of the organization.

Technical Skills are the ability to apply specialized knowledge and expertise to work-related techniques and procedures.

Human skills are skills involving the ability to build cooperation within the team being led.

Conceptual skills are skills that involve the ability to see the organization as a whole.

As one moves from lower-level management to upper-level management, conceptual skills become more important and technical skills less important (see Figure 1.6). The supportive rationale is that as managers advance in an organization, they become less involved with the actual production activity or technical areas and more involved with guiding the organization as a whole. Human skills, however, are extremely important to managers at top, middle,[10] and lower (or supervisory) levels.[11] The common denominator of all management levels is people.

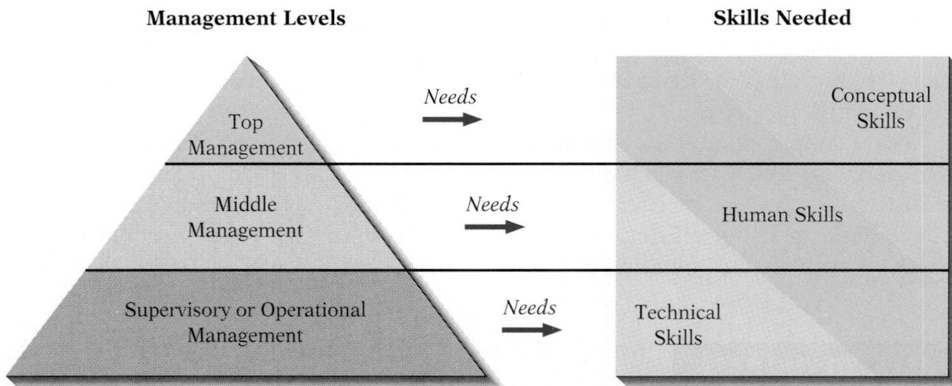

FIGURE 1.6 As a manager moves from the supervisory to the top management level, conceptual skills become more important than technical skills, but human skills remain equally important

THE UNIVERSALITY OF MANAGEMENT

Universality of management principles means that the principles of management are applicable to all types of organizations and organizational levels.

Management principles are **universal;** that is, they apply to all types of organizations (businesses, churches, sororities, athletic teams, hospitals, and so on) and organizational levels. Naturally, managers' jobs are somewhat different in each of these organizations because each organization requires the use of specialized knowledge, exists in unique working and political environments, and uses different technology. However, job similarities also exist because of the common basic management activities necessary in all organizations: planning, organizing, influencing, and controlling.

Henri Fayol, one of the earliest management writers, stated that all managers should possess certain characteristics, such as positive physical qualities, mental qualities, and special knowledge related to the specific operation.[12] B. C. Forbes, also describing managerial characteristics, has emphasized the importance of certain more personal qualities in successful managers. He has inferred that enthusiasm, earnestness of purpose, confidence, and faith in their worthwhileness are primary characteristics of successful managers. Forbes has described Henry Ford as follows:

> At the base and birth of every great business organization was an enthusiast, a man consumed with earnestness of purpose, with confidence in his powers, with faith in the worthwhileness of his endeavors. The original Henry Ford was the quintessence of enthusiasm. In the days of his difficulties, disappointments, and discouragements, when he was wrestling with his balky motor engine — and wrestling likewise with poverty — only his inexhaustible enthusiasm saved him from defeat.[13]

Fayol and Forbes can describe these desirable characteristics of successful managers only because of the universality concept: the basic ingredients of the successful management situation are applicable to organizations of all types.

BACK TO THE CASE

Stempel will be successful as the chairman of General Motors only if he possesses technical skills, human skills, and conceptual skills. In order to be successful, a relatively low-level manager at General Motors would generally need, probably in order of importance, human skills, then technical skills, and, finally, conceptual skills. As a top manager at the company, Stempel would normally need, probably in order of importance again, human skills, conceptual skills, and then technical skills. In general, as lower-level managers at General Motors take over middle- and upper-level management positions, the ranking of skills importance changes by adding more importance to conceptual skills and less importance to technical skills.

Managers such as Stempel usually find that, as they gain experience in managing, their cumulative management experience is valuable in whatever management positions they may hold either at General Motors, in some other automobile manufacturing company, or even in some other business altogether. Stempel will likely discover that as his enthusiasm, earnestness, confidence, and faith in his own worthwhileness become more pronounced personal qualitities, he will tend to become a more successful manager.

MANAGEMENT CAREERS

Thus far, this chapter has focused on outlining the importance of management to our society, presenting a definition of management and the management process, and explaining the universality of management. Individuals commonly study such topics because they are interested in pursuing a management career. This section presents information that will help students preview what might characterize their own management careers and describes some of the issues they might face in attempting to manage the careers of others within an organization. The specific focus is on career definition, career and life stages and performance, and career promotion.

A Definition of Career

A **career** is an individual's perceived sequence of attitudes and behaviors associated with the performance of work-related experiences and activities over the span of the person's working life.[14] This definition implies that a career is cumulative in nature. As individuals accumulate successful experiences in one position, they generally develop abilities and attitudes that qualify them to hold more advanced positions. In general, management positions at one level tend to be stepping-stones to management positions at the next higher level.

A **career** is an individual's perceived sequence of attitudes and behaviors associated with the performance of work-related experiences and activities over the span of the person's working life.

Career Stages, Life Stages, and Performance

Careers are generally viewed as evolving through a series of stages.[15] The evolutionary stages — exploration, establishment, maintenance, and decline — appear in Figure 1.7. This figure highlights the performance levels and age ranges commonly associated with each stage. The levels and ranges indicate what is likely at each stage, not what is inevitable.

Exploration Stage

The first stage in career evolution is the **exploration stage,** which occurs at the beginning of a career and is characterized by self-analysis and the exploration of different types of available jobs. Individuals at this stage are generally about fifteen to twenty-five years old and involved in some type of formal training, such as college or vocational education. They often pursue part-time employment to gain a richer understanding of what it might be like to have a career in a particular organization or industry. Typical jobs held during this stage might include cooking at Burger King, stocking at a Federated Department Store, or being an office assistant at a Nationwide Insurance office.

The **exploration stage** is the first stage in career evolution, which occurs at the beginning of a career and is characterized by self-analysis and the exploration of different types of available jobs.

Establishment Stage

The second stage in career evolution is the **establishment stage,** during which individuals who are about twenty-five to forty-five years old typically start to become more productive, or higher performers (as Figure 1.7 indicates by the upturn in the dotted line). Employment sought during this stage is guided by what was learned during the exploration stage. In addition, the jobs sought are usually full-time. Individuals at this stage commonly move to different jobs within the same company, to different companies, or even to different industries.

The **establishment stage** is the second stage in career evolution, during which individuals of about twenty-five to forty-five years of age typically start to become more productive or higher performers.

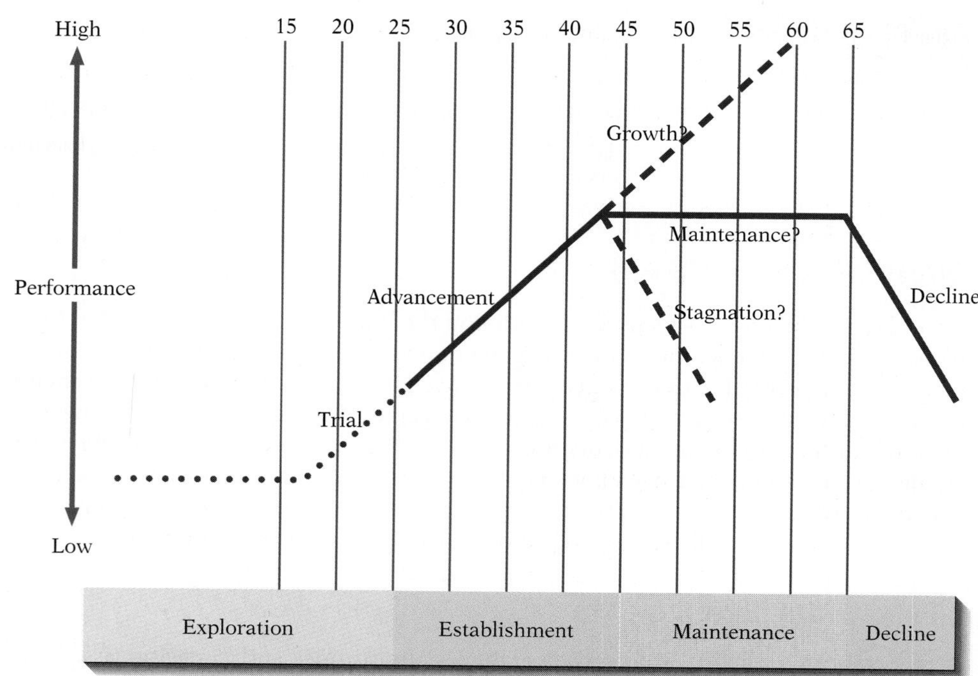

FIGURE 1.7 The relationships among career stages, life stages, and performance

Maintenance Stage

The **maintenance stage** is the third stage in career evolution, during which individuals of about forty-five to sixty-five years of age become more productive, stabilize, or become less productive.

Career plateauing is defined as a period of little or no apparent progress in the growth of a career.

The third stage in career evolution is the **maintenance stage.** In this stage, individuals who are about forty-five to sixty-five years old show either increased performance (career growth), stabilized performance (career maintenance), or decreased performance (career stagnation).

From a managerial viewpoint, it is better to have growth than maintenance or stagnation. Some companies, such as IBM, Monsanto, and Brooklyn Union Gas, attempt to eliminate career plateauing.[16] **Career plateauing** is defined as a period of little or no apparent progress in the growth of a career. Table 1.3 on page 15 shows how Coca-Cola USA has tried to avoid career maintenance and stagnation by ensuring that employees know where to go for career development guidance, know what jobs are open within the company, and know what avenues are available for self-development.[17]

Decline Stage

The **decline stage** is the fourth and last stage in career evolution, which occurs near retirement and during which individuals about sixty-five years of age or older show declining productivity.

The last stage in career evolution is the **decline stage,** which involves people of about sixty-five years and older whose productivity may be declining. These individuals are either close to retirement, semiretired, or retired. People at this stage may find it difficult to maintain prior performance levels, perhaps because they begin to lose interest in their careers or fail to keep their job skills up-to-date. As people live longer and stay healthier, many of them become part-time workers in businesses such as Publix supermarkets and McDonald's and in volunteer groups such as the March of Dimes and the American Heart Association. Some retired executives put their career experience to good use by working with the government-sponsored organization SCORE — Service Corps of Retired Executives. This program offers experienced management advice and consultation to small businesses trying to gain footholds in their markets.

Promoting Your Own Career

Practicing managers[18] and management scholars generally agree that careful formulation and implementation of appropriate tactics can enhance the success of management careers.[19] Planning your career path, the sequence of jobs that you will do along the course of your working life, is your first step in promoting your career. For some peo-

TABLE 1.3 Aspects of Coca-Cola USA that help enhance career growth of employees

- *Newsmakers* is a monthly publication listing moves within Coca-Cola USA. This gives people information on the kinds and number of internal career moves taking place.
- Job posting and the Exempt Job Opening Listing indicate specific open positions of the lower and mid-level management levels.
- Career opportunities booklets provide a broad overview of each department, as well as specific qualifications for typical positions.
- The thirty-page *Career Planning Workbook*, designed specifically for Coca-Cola USA, gives individuals an opportunity to assess their strengths, values, and alternative career directions and provides a structured means of developing a career plan. A work sheet captures all the critical information in one place.
- Career planning can also be explored through a two-day "Career Strategies Workshop." Participants examine themselves, possible career options, and strategies for attaining their goals. A special feature of the program is the opportunity to meet key human resource people representing each functional area in Coca-Cola USA as well as the larger structure of the Coca-Cola Company.
- The company helps employees develop their skills through an extensive in-house training program. The *Employee Training Catalog*, distributed annually with quarterly updates, lists courses offered by Coca-Cola USA by performance factor, such as organizing and planning. Therefore, if a particular skill area is identified during a performance evaluation or a career discussion, the appropriate course can easily be selected.
- A 100 percent reimbursement tuition aid program offers employees the opportunity to return to school to enhance their formal educations.
- On- and off-the-job developmental activities are considered primary opportunities for growth. Employees may ask for feedback from their managers, act as instructors or trainers, take on new projects, participate on a task force or project team, or join professional organizations. All of these activities allow the development of new professional skills and contribute to professional growth.

ple this means planning to ascend the hierarchy of a particular organization. For others it will mean planning a career path within a particular profession or series of professions. For everyone, however, career planning should be an ongoing process, beginning with the career's early phases and continuing throughout the career.

In promoting your own career, you must be proactive and see yourself as a business that your are responsible for developing.[20] Your plan should not be seen as limiting your options. Consider both your strengths and your liabilities and assess what you need from a career. Then explore all the avenues of opportunity open to you both inside and outside the organization. Set your career goals, continually revise and update these goals as your career progresses, and take the steps necessary to accomplish these goals.

Another important tactic in promoting your own career is to work for managers who carry out realistic and constructive roles in the career development of their employees.[21] (The cartoon on this page lightheartedly depicts a manager who is not inter-

"As this is your proposal, Cosgrove, its failure could mean the end of your career. I think, however, that is an acceptable risk."

From Warren Keith Schilit, "What's the Logic of Strategic Planning?" *Management Review* (November 1988), 42. © Leo Cullum, 1991.

ested in the careers of his employees.) Table 1.4 outlines what career development responsibility, information, planning, and follow-through might include. This table also contains an example of a complementary career development role for a professional employee. Table 1.5 lists several additional tactics for enhancing career success.

To enhance their career success, individuals must be *proactive* rather than *reactive*.[22] That is, they must take specific actions to demonstrate their abilities and accomplishments. They must also have clear ideas of the next positions they are seeking, the skills they must acquire to function appropriately in those positions, and plans for how they will acquire those skills. Finally, they need to think about the ultimate positions they will want and the sequence of positions they must hold in order to gain the skills and attitudes necessary to qualify for those positions.

Women, in their roles as managers, guide organizations toward goal accomplishment.

Special Career Issues

Women in Management

Women in their roles as managers must meet the same challenges in their work environments as men do. However, because women have only recently begun to join the ranks of management in large numbers, they often lack the social network systems and mentor relationships that are so important in the development of a management career. Traditionally, women were also expected to manage families and households while simultaneously handling the pressures and competition of the work force. Some women also encounter sexual harassment in the workplace.

However, Tom Peters, author of the aforementioned classic management book *In Search of Excellence,* believes that women may have an enormous advantage over men in future management situations.[23] He predicts that, in the late nineties, networks of relationships will replace rigid organizational structures and star workers will be replaced by teams made up of workers at all levels who are empowered to make decisions. Detailed rules and procedures will be replaced by a flexible system that calls for judgments based on a system of key values and for a constant search for new ways to get the job done. Strengths that are often attributed to women — placing high priority on interrelationships, listening, and motivating others —will be the dominant virtues in the corporation of the future.

Dual-Career Couples

Because of the growing number of women at work, many organizations need to consider how dual-career couples affect the work force. The traditional scenario in which a woman takes a supporting role in the development of her spouse's career is being replaced with one of equal work and shared responsibilities for both spouses. This re-

TABLE 1.4 Manager and employee roles in enhancing employee career development

Dimension	*Professional Employee*	*Manager*
Responsibility	Assumes responsibility for individual career development	Assumes responsibility for employee development
Information	Obtains career information through self-evaluation and data collection: What do I enjoy doing? Where do I want to go?	Provides information by holding up a mirror of reality: How manager views the employee How others view the employee How "things work around here"
Planning	Develops an individual plan to reach objectives	Helps employee assess plan
Follow-through	Invites management support through high performance on the current job by understanding the scope of the job and taking appropriate initiative	Provides coaching and relevant information on opportunities

TABLE 1.5 Tips for enhancing your management career

- Remember that good performance that pleases your superiors is the basic foundation of success, but recognize that not all good performance is easily measured. Determine the real criteria by which you are evaluated and be rigorously honest in evaluating your own performance against these criteria.
- Manage your career; be active in influencing decisions, because pure effort is not necessarily rewarded.
- Strive for positions that have high visibility and exposure where you can be a hero observed by higher officials. Check to see that the organization has a formal system of keeping track of young people. Remember that high-risk line jobs tend to offer more visibility than staff positions like corporate planning or personnel, but also that visibility can sometimes be achieved by off-the-job community activities.
- Develop relations with a mobile senior executive who can be your sponsor. Become a complementary crucial subordinate with different skills from your superior.
- Learn your job as quickly as possible and train a replacement so that you can be available to move and broaden your background in different functions.
- Nominate yourself for other positions: modesty is not necessarily a virtue. However, change jobs for more power and influence, not primarily for status or pay. The latter could be a substitute for a real opportunity to make things happen.
- Before taking a position, rigorously assess your strengths and weaknesses, what you like and don't like. Don't accept a promotion if it draws on your weaknesses and entails mainly activities that you don't like.
- Leave at your convenience, but on good terms without parting criticism of the organization. Do not stay under an immobile superior who is not promoted in three to five years.
- Don't be trapped by formal, narrow job descriptions. Move outside them and probe the limits of your influence.
- Accept that responsibility will always somewhat exceed authority and that organizational politics are inevitable. Establish alliances and fight necessary battles, minimizing upward ones to very important issues.
- Get out of management if you can't stand being dependent on others and having them dependent on you.
- Recognize that you will face ethical dilemmas no matter how moral you try to be. No evidence exists that unethical managers are more successful than ethical ones, but it may well be that those who move faster are less socially conscious. Therefore, from time to time you must examine your personal values and question how much you will sacrifice for the organization.
- Don't automatically accept all tales of managerial perversity that you hear. Attributing others' success to unethical behavior is often an excuse for one's own personal inadequacies. Most of all, don't commit an act which you know to be wrong in the hope that your supervisor will see it as loyalty and reward you for it. Sometimes the supervisor will, but he or she may also sacrifice you when the organization is criticized.

quires a certain amount of flexibility on the part of the couple as well as on the organizations for which they work. Issues such as whose career takes precedence if a spouse is offered a transfer to another city, or who takes the ultimate responsibility for family concerns, point up the fact that dual-career relationships involve trade-offs and that it is very difficult to "have it all."

Studies of dual-career couples reveal that many people cope with their career difficulties in one of the following ways.[24] The couple might develop a commitment to both spouses' careers so that, when a decision is made, the right for each spouse to pursue a career is taken into consideration. Each member of the relationship is flexible about handling both home- and job-oriented issues. They work out coping mechanisms such as negotiating child care or scheduling shared activities in advance to better manage their work and their family responsibilities. Dual-career couples often find that they must limit their social lives and their volunteer responsibilities in order to slow the pace of their lives. Finally, many couples find that they must take steps to consciously facilitate their mutual career advancement. Organizations that want to retain an employee may find that they need to assist the employee's spouse in his or her career development as well.

A Multicultural Work Force

The term *multicultural* refers to the mix of many different ethnic groups that will be working in business in the United States in the 1990s. Various minority groups are included in that term, including African Americans, Hispanics, Asians, Africans, Native

Americans, and Caribbean Islanders. The U.S. Department of Labor estimates that almost one-third of new entrants into the labor force in the 1990s will be members of various minority groups.

Minority groups are still underrepresented in management. The Rutgers University Graduate School of Management and the Program to Increase Minorities in Business found in a 1986 survey of 400 Fortune 1,000 corporations that less than 9 percent of all managers were members of a minority. One reason is a shortage of education among minorities in the fields most in demand by businesses: hard sciences, business administration, and engineering. As a result, many minority members end up in staff rather than line positions and are consequently more likely to be laid off in the event of a downturn. Finally, in some instances discrimination may be responsible for minority workers' being passed over for promotions.

As more and more of the new entrants into the labor market are members of various minority groups, it will be even more important for businesses to recruit talented minority workers. Building community visibility may be the first step companies can take to help minority applicants find them. Arranging internships and career fairs as well as providing financial support are concrete steps that a firm can take. Managers can look within the firm for people who can be promoted. Firms may need to conduct their own training and education programs to provide workers the skills they need to join the ranks of management.

Instead of looking for people who fit into the existing corporate culture, managers should consider talent and diversity. Some managers will be uncomfortable dealing with workers from different backgrounds and different cultures; corporations may need to provide support and reeducation for their own managers, to train them to be sensitive to other cultures. For example, much business jargon in the United States is sports-oriented, such as telling someone to "play hardball." Such terms can be confusing to those from other cultures.

Some American businesses are making a concerted effort to attract and promote minorities. A 1986 *Black Enterprise* magazine survey listed twenty-five firms that were rated by African Americans as good places to work. The survey included Xerox, IBM, Hewlett-Packard, Avon, Philip Morris, AT&T, and Equitable. The multicultural work force of the 1990s will need a new, more flexible and open style of management to reflect the new mix of backgrounds and cultures.[25, 26]

MANAGEMENT HIGHLIGHTS: A SPECIAL FEATURE FOR THE REMAINING CHAPTERS

The **law of the situation** indicates that managers continually analyze circumstances within their organizations and apply management concepts to fit them.

The **law of the situation,** based upon the classic work of Mary Parker Follett, indicates that managers must continually analyze unique circumstances within their organizations and especially apply management concepts to fit those circumstances.[27] Managers can understand planning, organizing, influencing, and controlling, but unless they can apply these concepts to deal with specific organizational circumstances, the knowledge is of little value.

Management highlights, a special feature in the remaining chapters, focus on four key areas of management: ethics, quality, diversity, and management in a global environment. The feature provides a wealth of examples that show how chapter concepts can be applied to manage organizations. This feature has been purposefully designed to convey a practical understanding of chapter content by emphasizing the application of management concepts by real managers in real organizations. The management sections, titled "Global Highlight," "Ethics Highlight," "Diversity Hightlight," and "Quality Highlight," offer an assortment of applications involving management positions and companies ranging from top-level to lower-level managers in organizations such as Motorola, Nike, General Electric, and Exxon. Application examples in each chapter emphasize issues related to four important contemporary management themes:

Global Highlights

Modern managers are faced with many challenges involving global business. Some such challenges involve building organizations in developing countries, fighting foreign competition, developing joint ventures with foreign companies, and building a productive work force covering several foreign countries. This management feature illustrates the application of management concepts in meeting international challenges.

Managers continually face the challenges involving four key issues of management: diversity, quality, ethics, and the global environment.

Ethics Highlights

Modern managers face the challenge of developing and maintaining social responsibility and ethical practices that are appropriate for their particular organizations. Some such challenges involve issues like settling such questions as who within an organization should be involved in performing socially responsible activities, determining the role of ethics in an organization, encouraging ethical behavior in organizations, and determining internal funding for socially responsible activities. This management feature illustrates the application of management concepts in meeting a firm's social responsibility and ethical challenges.

Diversity Hightlights

Modern managers constantly face the growing challenge of handling situations involving diversity in organizations. *Diversity* is defined as differences in people regarding issues like age, gender, ethnicity, nationality, and ability. In essence, managers continually face situations involving significant variability in all people that interface with organizations. Examples could be organization members as well as customers who reflect a mix of blacks, Hispanics, Asians, and Native Americans.[28] Such a mix can also involve people who are older, women, and the handicapped. This management feature presents practical insights about how to appropriately build organizational diversity into an organizational resource that understands and responds to diversity in the broader organizational environment, including customer diversity, and thereby enhances organizational success. In addition, more discussion of diversity is presented in Chapter 22—Diversity Issues for Managers.

Quality Highlights

Modern managers, perhaps more than any other generation of managers, face the challenge of developing and maintaining high quality in the goods and services they offer the marketplace. High-quality products are defined as goods or services that customers rate as being excellent. Most management theorists and practicing managers agree that if an organization is to be successful in the national and international business world of today, it must offer high-quality goods and services to its customers.

The maintaining of high-quality products has grown from an issue pertinent to the future success of individual businesses to an issue pertinent to the economic success of the United States as a whole. Congress passed the Malcolm Baldrige National Quality Improvement Act in 1987 to encourage a focus on quality products in business organizations throughout the United States.[29] This law establishes the granting of annual national quality awards, called the "Malcolm Baldrige National Quality Awards," to a company or companies doing exemplary work in the area of quality. The Baldrige award, named after the late U.S. Secretary of Commerce, is the highest level of national recognition that a company in the United States can receive, and it demonstrates the growing cooperation of business and government to improve the quality of U.S. goods and services.

Virtually every activity a manager performs can have some impact on the quality of goods or services that an organization produces. Activities such as developing organizational objectives, training organization members, strategic management, and designing organization structures can all affect the quality of goods offered by a company. This management feature illustrates how various management activities can affect product quality.

Studying all of these management highlights carefully will be valuable to you. They help you to build realistic expectations about what being a manager actually means. As applied to career-building, these cases illustrate that, as managers show the ability to solve various organizational problems, they become more valuable to organizations and are more usually recipients of organizational rewards such as promotion and significant pay increases.

BACK TO THE CASE Like those at any company, managers at General Motors are at various stages of career development. As an example of how the stages of career development might relate to managers at General Motors, let's focus on one particular manager, Martin Plane. Assume that Martin Plane is the head of manufacturing at the General Motors' Saturn plant. He is forty-five years old and is considered a member of the company's middle management.

Plane began his career (exploration stage) in college by considering various areas of study and by holding a number of different types of primarily part-time positions. He delivered pizzas for Domino's Pizza and worked for Scott's, a lawn-care company. He began college at age eighteen and graduated when he was twenty-two.

Plane then moved into the establishment stage of his career. For a few years immediately after graduation, he held full-time trial positions in the automobile manufacturing industry as well as in the restaurant and retailing industries. What he learned during the career exploration stage helped him choose the types of full-time trial positions to pursue. At the age of twenty-six, he accepted a trial position as a supervisor in one General Motors' Detroit factory. Through this position, he discovered that he wanted to remain in the automotive industry in general and at General Motors in particular. From the age twenty-seven to age forty-five, he held a number of supervisory and middle management positions within the company.

Now Plane is moving into an extremely critical part of his career, the maintenance stage. He could probably remain in his present position and maintain his productivity for several more years. However, assume that he wants to advance his career. He must now emphasize a proactive attitude by formulating and implementing tactics aimed at enhancing his career success, such as seeking training to develop critical skills, or moving to a position that is a prerequisite for other, more advanced positions at General Motors.

In the future, as Plane approaches sixty-five (the decline stage), it is probable that his productivity at General Motors will decline somewhat. From a career viewpoint, he may want to go from full-time employment to semiretirement. Perhaps he could work for the same company or another company in the same industry on a part-time advisory basis or even pursue part-time work in another industry. For example, he might be able to teach a small business management course at a nearby college.

ACTION SUMMARY

Reread the learning objectives that follow. Each objective is followed by questions. Answering these questions accurately will help you to retain the most important concepts discussed in this chapter. After answering each question, check your answer with the answer key at the end of this chapter. (*Hint:* If you have doubt regarding the correct response, consult the page whose number follows the answer.)

Circle: ***From studying this chapter, I will attempt to acquire:***

1. An understanding of the importance of management to society and individuals.

T, F **a.** Managers constitute less than 1 percent of the U.S. work force.

T, F **b.** Management is important to society.

2. An understanding of the role of management.

a, b, c, d, e **a.** The role of a manager is: (a) to make workers happy; (b) to satisfy only the manager's needs; (c) to make the most profit; (d) to survive in a highly competitive society; (e) to achieve organizational goals.

T, F **b.** Apart from its goals, management has no meaning.

3. An ability to define *management* in several different ways.

a, b, c, d, e **a.** Management is: (a) a process; (b) reaching organizational goals; (c) utilizing people and other resources; (d) all of the above; (e) a and b.

T, F **b.** Management is the process of working with people and through people.

4. An ability to list and define the basic functions of management.

a, b, c, d, e **a.** Which of the following is not a function of management: (a) influencing; (b) planning; (c) organizing; (d) directing; (e) controlling.

a, b, c, d, e **b.** The process of gathering information and comparing this information to preestablished standards is part of (a) planning; (b) influencing; (c) motivating; (d) controlling; (e) commanding.

5. Working definitions of managerial effectiveness and managerial efficiency.

T, F **a.** If an organization is using its resources to attain its goals, the organization's managers are efficient.

T, F **b.** A manager who is reaching goals but wasting resources is efficient but ineffective.

6. An understanding of basic management skills and their relative importance to managers.

a, b, c, d, e **a.** Conceptual skills require that management view the organization as: (a) a profit center; (b) a decision-making unit; (c) a problem-solving group; (d) a whole; (e) individual contributions.

T, F **b.** Managers require fewer and fewer human skills as they move from lower to higher management levels.

7. An understanding of the universality of management.

T, F **a.** The statement that management principles are universal means that they apply to all types of organizations and organizational levels.

T, F **b.** The universality of management means that management principles are taught the same way in all schools.

8. Insights concerning what management careers are and how they evolve.

T, F **a.** In general, as careers evolve, individuals tend to further develop job skills but show very little or no change in attitude about various job circumstances.

T, F **b.** Individuals tend to show the first significant increase in performance during the establishment career stage.

T, F **c.** Tips for enhancing the success of your career should not be seen as very useful over the long run.

INTRODUCTORY CASE WRAP-UP

"Robert Stempel Faces Serious Problems at General Motors" (p. 3) and its related back-to-the-case sections were written to help you better understand the management concepts contained in this chapter. Answer the following questions about this introductory case to further enrich your understanding of the chapter content:

1. Would you like to have Robert Stempel's job at General Motors? Explain.
2. What do you think you'd like most about being a manager? What would you like least?
3. You have just been appointed a General Motors' vice president who is responsible for three automobile factories. List and describe five activities that you think you'll have to perform as part of this job.

ISSUES FOR REVIEW AND DISCUSSION

1. What is the main point illustrated in the introductory case on General Motors?
2. How important is the management function to society?
3. How important is the management function to individuals?
4. What is the basic role of the manager?
5. How is *management* defined in this text? What main themes are contained in this definition?
6. List and define each of the four functions of management.
7. Outline the relationship between the four management functions.
8. List and describe five of Peters and Waterman's characteristics of excellent companies, and explain how each of these characteristics could affect planning, organizing, influencing, and controlling.
9. List and define the basic organizational resources managers have at their disposal.
10. What is the relationship between organizational resources and production?
11. Draw and explain the continuum of managerial effectiveness.
12. Draw and explain the continuum of managerial efficiency.
13. Are managerial effectiveness and managerial efficiency related concepts? If so, how?
14. According to Katz, what are the three primary types of skills important to management success? Define each of these types of skills.
15. Describe the relative importance of each of these three types of skills to lower-level, middle-level, and upper-level managers.
16. What is meant by "the universality of management"?
17. What is a career?
18. Discuss the significance of the maintenance career stage.
19. What tips for promoting the success of a career are most valuable to you? Explain.
20. What does the law of the situation tell you about the success of your management career?

ACTION SUMMARY ANSWER KEY

1. a. F, p. 4
   b. T, p. 4
2. a. e, p. 6
   b. T, p. 6
3. a. d, p. 6–7
   b. F, p. 7
4. a. d, p. 7–8
   b. d, p. 8
5. a. F, p. 10
   b. F, p. 10–11
6. a. d, p. 11
   b. F, p. 11
7. a. T, p. 12
   b. F, p. 12
8. a. F, p. 13
   b. T, p. 13
   c. F, p. 17

CASE STUDY

Dorothy Terrell: The Road to President, SunExpress

Sylvia Keyes
Bridgewater State College

Dorothy Terrell has been propelled to the top by people, pride, problems, and perseverance. How did this African-American woman become president of SunExpress, a high-tech channel for computer peripherals?

Her employment began in the public sector in the Massachusetts Office for Children. She learned quickly; after three exciting years she was named head of personnel.

Through a contact on a business advisory committee involving training in Boston's inner city, Terrell landed a job at Digital Equipment Corporation (DEC), a major computer firm, as management development manager. At that time, DEC was a place where people moved from job to job as deemed appropriate, so Terrell was able to gain experience in a number of management capacities. The people were terrific and the career lines were primarily dotted, not solid, so Terrell learned to listen and learned the value of specially tailored organization structures. At DEC, Terrell formed a core group of friends, among them three other women, who have maintained their friendship throughout their careers.

However, here her career turned a corner. Her boss and her position at DEC changed, and Terrell was not happy with how the changes were handled. She used this time to reassess her interests and her career; she decided to move on.

She took a position as group personnel manager for a small start-up engineering organization. From that position, Terrell was able to oversee all aspects of the company: manufacturing, engineering, and marketing for a short time.

About two years later, Terrell got a call from a friend who was leaving the DEC Boston plant, where the position of plant manager had opened. The Boston plant was highly diverse: employees came from every segment of Boston and spoke a wide variety of languages. Terrell had wanted the job—not to *go* back to DEC, but to *give* back. Her challenge was to pull this diverse group together, to build a team made up of people who were used to working as individuals. Once again, Terrell found her environment an exciting one. She remained at DEC for three years.

Recognizing that she had only staff and functional experience, Terrell wanted to gain some experience managing technology. So, she returned to the suburbs for a while in the technical area. DEC was starting a plant in Cupertino, California, and Terrell was recommended as a start-up manager. While Terrell told management, "I am not technically competent," they responded that they had enough technical people and needed someone who could make things happen. She and her family moved to California.

There Terrell dealt with the strict California EPA laws that required licenses before DEC's new plant could become operational. She quickly adapted to working with engineers by encouraging them to explain things in lay language. She felt it was vital to work in a close relationship with the people for whom she was responsible and to experience their working conditions firsthand, so she donned a high-tech "bunny suit" (coveralls) and scrubbed her face and worked side-by-side in the clean-room environment. When the job was complete and it was time to move up, she was promoted to group manufacturing manager of the whole Cupertino plant.

By this time, Terrell had become acquainted with Scott McNeally, CEO Sun Microsystems, Inc., who proposed another opportunity for her with the start-up subsidiary SunExpress. Calling DEC to inform them of her decision to become the first president of SunExpress was the most difficult call she had made in her life—DEC had given her sixteen productive years.

As president of SunExpress, Terrell is responsible for the company's entire global operation. When asked what makes her a leader, Terrell responded, "I care about people. I don't take care of people. I try to treat people as adults and when something is happening that's not right, I go after the issue, not the person. I am a good leader because I am a good follower. I don't claim to have all the answers, but I can work with a group to come up with the answers."

DISCUSSION QUESTIONS

1. In what stage of the career cycle was Dorothy Terrell in each of the positions she held?
2. Discuss Terrell's situation with respect to social network systems and mentors.
3. Do you believe that the position of president is easier, the same, or more difficult for this African-American woman than it would be for a Caucasian woman? A Caucasian man?
4. Did Terrell follow a specific career path? Why or why not?

CNN VIDEO CASE

On a Management Career Path with Style

JOSIE CRUZ NATORI
House of Natori

Josie Cruz Natori loves her work. "It is feeding my aesthetic needs, my spiritual needs, and my artistic needs at the same time it is challenging my head." In getting to this stage in her career, Natori took a sharp turn away from two other careers—one potential and another quite established. At nine years of age, pianist Josie Natori soloed with the Manilla Philharmonic. Despite this talent, however, after high school she decided to study economics in college, and after graduating she went to Wall Street. Nine years later she was the first woman vice president at Merrill Lynch; and then she got bored.

Born and raised in the Philippines, Natori sought a new career that would give something back to her home, that would challenge her, and that would feed her need to create something beautiful. Along with the trademark fashions now coming out of the House of Natori, she has managed the creation of the $25 million Natori Company. This includes a factory in Manila, built by her father's construction company, that employs over 600 Filipinos.

Josie Cruz Natori created the House of Natori because she sought a new career that would challenge her and fill her need to create something beautiful.

Josie Natori hired her husband Ken away from a senior position with Shearson Lehman Brothers in 1985 and made him chairman. They work closely together and respect each other's ideas. Recognizing that the business environment is changing all the time, the Natoris are expanding the company into other areas and experiencing growth pains. The first expansion for the company actually occurred before Ken arrived on the scene. That expansion was in 1982, when bedroom accessories such as lingerie bags and bedroom pillows were added to the product line. Today, the company's "total concept" also includes fragrances, and linens and accessories for the bed, the bath, and the table.

Concentrating now on international markets, the company's growing pains continue. Sharing the vision, however, the Natoris stay focused on company goals. Comments Ken Natori, "It might sound corny, but we have a great time together, and we really have a good time with the business. We're in a tough environment, but it's challenging and we're having a good time."

In her various managerial roles across two formal careers, Josie Natori has had many opportunities to plan, organize, influence, and control. With the common denominator of management at all levels being "people," she has a better-than-average understanding of issues in both gender relations and multicultural relations. "I've always felt it was my biggest asset, being a woman *and* being Oriental." Also, given her talents, Natori is as comfortable managing the creative designers for the House of Natori as she is managing financial and other personnel in different arms of the company. "Nothing around here goes without passing my eye. I have the creative concept to start, and I have great people to execute it."

Josie Natori is not tied to any particular line of work. All her life, she knew she wanted to be in business. Management is what she does best, and she can apply the skills of management to whatever she gets involved in and succeed. "Women were very entrepreneurial in the Philippines, and that doesn't mean establishing big business. It could be entrepreneurial selling lemonade in the street. So there was never a question when I applied to a firm in Wall Street. I was very single-minded, a musician."

VIDEO CASE QUESTIONS

1. Show how Josie Natori uses each of the three types of management skills. Which skill does she consider her strongest?
2. Josie Natori has had an unusual career path. At what stage of her career is she now?
3. In the chapter section entitled "The Universality of Management," you read about certain managerial characteristics. From what you have learned about Josie Natori, decide whether those characteristic s describe her. Relate the characteristics to events in her life to support your decisions.
4. What is special about the Natoris' dual-career marriage?

CNN VIDEO EXERCISE

Your Interview with Josie Natori

EXERCISE GOAL: Find examples from your own experience of the four managerial functions.

Imagine that you are applying for a management position at the House of Natori. You have already interviewed with several Natori managers. You are scheduled for a final interview with Josie Natori, and the personnel director has indicated that there are reservations about your application because of your lack of management experience.

Review the discussion of management functions on page 7. Then complete the following diagram by adding brief descriptions of some experiences you have had that meet the definitions, however broadly. For example, you may have planned a school party or a long trip. List as many experiences as you can. Then review the lists and select the one experience that you will discuss in your interview with Josie Natori. Highlight or underline that experience.

Planning

1. ______________________________

____

2. ______________________________

____

3. ______________________________

____

Influencing

1. ______________________________

____

2. ______________________________

____

3. ______________________________

____

Controlling

1. ______________________________

____

2. ______________________________

____

3. ______________________________

____

Organizing

1. ______________________________

____

2. ______________________________

____

3. ______________________________

____

CHAPTER

2

THE HISTORY OF MANAGEMENT

STUDENT LEARNING OBJECTIVES

From studying this chapter, I will attempt to acquire:

1. An understanding of the classical approach to management.
2. An appreciation for the work of Frederick W. Taylor, Frank and Lillian Gilbreth, Henry L. Gantt, and Henri Fayol.
3. An understanding of the behavioral approach to management.
4. An understanding of the studies at the Hawthorne Works of the Western Electric Company.
5. An understanding of the management science approach to management.
6. An understanding of how the management science approach has evolved.
7. An understanding of the system approach to management.
8. An understanding of how triangular management and the contingency approach to management are related.

CHAPTER OUTLINE

INTRODUCTORY CASE
"Mickey's Kitchen" at The Disney Store

THE CLASSICAL APPROACH

Lower-Level Management Analysis

GLOBAL HIGHLIGHT
Delta Faucet Company

DIVERSITY HIGHLIGHT
Northern Island Federal Credit Union

Comprehensive Analysis of Management
Limitations of the Classical Approach

THE BEHAVIORAL APPROACH

The Relay Assembly Test Room Experiments
The Bank Wiring Observation Room Experiment

THE MANAGEMENT SCIENCE APPROACH

The Beginning of the Management Science Approach
Management Science Today

QUALITY HIGHLIGHT
Baldrige Award

Characteristics of Management Science Applications

THE CONTINGENCY APPROACH

ETHICS HIGHLIGHT
Charles Schwab

THE SYSTEM APPROACH

Types of Systems
Systems and "Wholeness"
The Management System
Information for Management System Analysis

CASE STUDY
Scientific Management at the Watertown Arsenal

VIDEO CASE
A Born Entrepreneur: Fred DeLuca, Subway Sandwiches

VIDEO EXERCISE
Planning Major Changes at Subway Sandwiches

INTRODUCTORY CASE

"Mickey's Kitchen" at the Disney Store

You say you want a Mickey Mouse T-shirt and the kids are clamoring for a burger? Well, if you're in or near Montclair, California, The Disney Store has got you covered.

In a shopping mall forty miles east of Los Angeles, The Disney Store, Inc. has opened Mickey's Kitchen. There, you can chow down on French fries shaped like Mickey or Donald or pig out on a Hot Diggity Dog, a meatless Mickey Burger, or the "Soup-a-Dee-Doo-Dah" garden soup.

You can chow down on French fries shaped like Mickey or Donald or pig out on a Hot Diggity Dog.

And, in typical Disney style, the decor is more elaborate than that of the average burger joint. While they munch, diners will be seated in one of four themed areas that are mock sound stages—giant friezes, actually, where a famous Disney cartoon is being "filmed." No actual filming takes place.

The Montclair Mickey's Kitchen was recently joined by a second restaurant at The Disney Store in the Woodfield Mall in Schaumburg, Illinois. While it's likely that there will be more Mickey's Kitchens, "it's premature to announce more" now, said Chuck Champlin, spokesman for Disney's consumer products division headquartered in Burbank, California.

The Montclair Mickey's Kitchen has 190 seats and sells food items ranging from 50¢ to $3.45. The menu, which includes more low-fat items than typical fast-food fare, has been fine-tuned many times, but not substantially altered.

Pinocchio's Pizza includes three varieties of pizza: a cheese pizza or vegetable pizza that sells for $2.75 and barbecue chicken pizza for $2.95.

The PB&J Handwich, a pancake wrapped around a banana half and filled with peanut butter and jelly, has proved popular with children, Champlin said.

For those concerned about fat and calorie content, there is the Goofy Burger, with lean ground beef and fat content of less than 15 percent, which sells for $1.95 for adults and $1.25 for children. The Hot Diggity Dog is a turkey frank that sells for $1.50.

The meatless Mickey Burger consists of a blend of walnuts, mozzarella, bean curd, and vegetables. Rather than being fried, it is browned under a heat lamp.

Champlin said the lower-fat items aren't meant to be a subtle comment on the typically high-fat American diet but to offer diners a variety of choices.

"Our priority is to create fun . . . and the emphasis is to offer really good food with something for everybody."

Capitalizing on the popularity of the Disney characters, the Disney Stores opened restaurants called Mickey's Kitchens that offered such fun fare as Hot Diggity Dogs for kids.

This case is from Vicki Vaughn, "Disney Testing Fast-Food Recipe," *The Orlando Sentinel,* November 4, 1990, D1, D2.

WHAT'S AHEAD There are several different ways to approach management situations and to solve related organizational problems. Managers like the ones managing Disney's new Mickey's Kitchen must understand these approaches if they are to be successful in building successful organizations. This chapter explains five such approaches: (1) the classical approach, (2) the behavioral approach, (3) the management science approach, (4) the contingency approach, and (5) the system approach.

Chapter 1 focused primarily on defining *management*. This chapter presents various approaches to analyzing and reacting to the management situation. Each approach recommends a basically different method of analysis and a different type of action as a result of the analysis.

Over the years, disagreement on exactly how many different approaches to management exist and what each approach entails has been common. In an attempt to organize and condense the various approaches, Donnelly, Gibson, and Ivancevich[1] combined the ideas of Koontz, O'Donnell, and Weihrich[2] with those of Haynes and Massie,[3] and offered these three: (1) the classical approach, (2) the behavioral approach, and (3) the management science approach. They stated that their objective was to simplify the discussion of the field of management without sacrificing significant information.

The following sections build on the work of Donnelly, Gibson, and Ivancevich in presenting the classical approach, the behavioral approach, and the management science approach. The contingency approach is also discussed as a fourth primary approach to analyzing the management task. The fifth approach, the system approach, is presented as a more recent trend in management thinking and is the approach emphasized in this text.

THE CLASSICAL APPROACH

The **classical approach to management** is a management approach that emphasizes organizational efficiency to increase organizational success.

The **classical approach to management** resulted from the first significant, concentrated effort to develop a body of management thought. Management writers who participated in this effort are considered the pioneers of management study. The classical approach recommends that managers continually strive to increase organizational efficiency to increase production. Although the fundamentals of this approach were developed some time ago, modern managers are just as concerned about finding the "one best way" to get the job done as were their predecessors.

For discussion purposes, the classical approach to management breaks into two distinct areas. The first area, lower-level management analysis, consists primarily of the work of Frederick W. Taylor, Frank and Lillian Gilbreth, and Henry L. Gantt. These individuals studied mainly the jobs of workers at lower levels of the organization. The second area, comprehensive analysis of management, concentrates more on the management function as a whole. The primary contributor to this category was Henri Fayol. Figure 2.1 on page 29 illustrates the two areas in the classical approach.

Lower-Level Management Analysis

Scientific management emphasizes the "one best way" to perform a task.

Lower-level management analysis concentrates on the "one best way" to perform a task; that is, it asks how a task situation can be structured to get the highest production from workers. The process of finding this "one best way" has become known as the scientific method of management, or simply, **scientific management.** Although the techniques of scientific managers could conceivably be applied to all management levels, the research, research applications, and illustrations relate mostly to lower-level

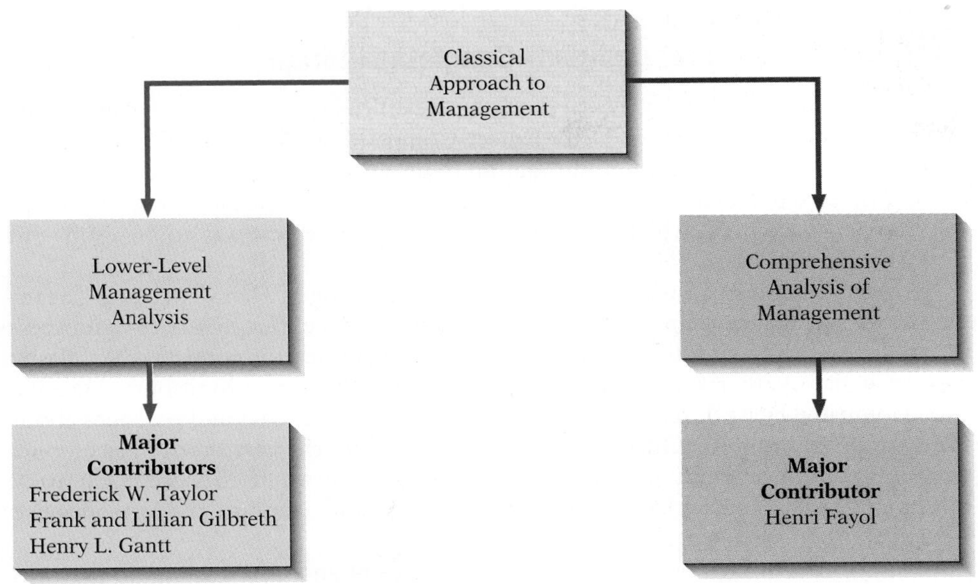

FIGURE 2.1 Division of classical approach to management into two areas and the major contributors to each area

managers. The work of Frederick W. Taylor, Frank and Lillian Gilbreth, and Henry L. Gantt is summarized in the sections that follow.

Frederick W. Taylor (1856–1915)

Because of the significance of his contributions, Frederick W. Taylor is commonly called the father of scientific management. His primary goal was to increase worker efficiency by scientifically designing jobs. His basic premise was that there was one best way to do a job and that that way should be discovered and put into operation.

Perhaps the best illustration of Taylor's scientific method and his management philosophy lies in a description of how he modified the job of employees whose sole responsibility was shoveling materials at the Bethlehem Steel Company.[4] During the modification process, Taylor made the assumption that any worker's job could be reduced to a science. To construct the "science of shoveling," he obtained answers—through observation and experimentation—to the following questions:

1. Will a first-class worker do more work per day with a shovelful of five, ten, fifteen, twenty, thirty, or forty pounds?
2. What kinds of shovels work best with which materials?
3. How quickly can a shovel be pushed into a pile of materials and pulled out properly loaded?
4. How much time is required to swing a shovel backward and throw the load a given horizontal distance at a given height?

As Taylor began formulating answers to these types of questions, he developed insights on how to increase the total amount of materials shoveled per day. He increased worker efficiency by matching shovel size with such factors as the size of the men, the weight of the materials, and the height and distance the materials were to be thrown. After the third year that Taylor's shoveling efficiency plan was in operation, records at Bethlehem Steel indicated that the total number of shovelers needed was reduced from about 600 to 140, the average number of tons shoveled per worker per day rose from sixteen to fifty-nine, the average earnings per worker per day rose from \$1.15 to \$1.88, and the average cost of handling a long ton (2,240 pounds) dropped from \$0.072 to \$0.033—an impressive application of scientific management to the task of shoveling.[5]

Managers at the Delta Faucet Company focus on automation in order to find efficient ways to perform jobs in their Chickasha, Oklahoma manufacturing plant.

GLOBAL HIGHLIGHT
Delta Faucet Company Competes Globally

When it became necessary to compete efficiently in the global manufacturing environment, managers at Delta Faucet Company in Chickasha, Oklahoma, recently focused their attention on automation to help them find the most efficient ways to perform jobs in Delta's manufacturing plant. This effort illustrates the scientific approach to management, which emphasizes finding the one best way to do a job—in this case, through the use of machines.

Experts analyzed the assembling and packaging of one of Delta's products, a faucet aerator. An aerator is a part attached to the end of a faucet that increases water pressure by introducing air into the stream of water. Delta's aerator consists of six plastic parts that fit together for easy assembly. With the help of the Kingsbury Machine Tool Company, Delta developed a special machine that assembles and packages about fifty aerators per minute. Once assembled and packaged, the aerators are placed on a conveyor belt for distribution to another part of the plant where they are made ready for shipment. This enables Delta to assemble, package, and distribute the aerators more efficiently.

One benefit of Delta's search for the most efficient and effective way to perform each of its jobs is that the company will be able to compete more effectively in an international marketplace. In Delta's case, finding the "one best way" to do a job is the key to successful expansion into international markets. ▶

Frank Gilbreth (1868–1924), Lillian Gilbreth (1878–1972)

A **motion study** finds the best way to accomplish a task by analyzing the movements necessary to perform the task.

The Gilbreths were also significant contributors to the scientific method. By definition, therefore, they ascribed to the idea of finding and using the one best way to perform a job. The primary investigative tool in their research was **motion study,** which consisted of reducing each job to the most basic movements possible. Motion analysis is still used today to establish job performance standards. Each movement or motion that is used to do a job is studied in terms of how much time the movement takes and how

TABLE 2.1 Primary variables considered in analyzing motions

Variables of the Worker	*Variables of the Surroundings, Equipment, and Tools*	*Variables of the Motion*
1. Anatomy	1. Appliances	1. Acceleration
2. Brawn	2. Clothes	2. Automaticity
3. Contentment	3. Colors	3. Combination with other motions and sequence
4. Creed	4. Entertainment, music, reading, etc.	4. Cost
5. Earning power	5. Heating, cooling, ventilating	5. Direction
6. Experience	6. Lighting	6. Effectiveness
7. Fatigue	7. Quality of material	7. Foot-pounds of work accomplished
8. Habits	8. Reward and punishment	8. Inertia and momentum overcome
9. Health	9. Size of unit moved	9. Length
10. Mode of living	10. Special fatigue-eliminating devices	10. Necessity
11. Nutrition	11. Surroundings	11. Path
12. Size	12. Tools	12. "Play for position"
13. Skill	13. Union rules	13. Speed
14. Temperament	14. Weight of unit moved	
15. Training		

necessary it actually is in performing the job. Inefficient or unnecessary motions are pinpointed and eliminated in doing the job.[6]

During a motion analysis, the Gilbreths considered the work environment, the motion itself, and behavioral variables concerning the workers. Table 2.1 lists the primary factors in each of these groups. The analysis of each of the variables in a task situation was obviously a long, involved, and tedious process.

Frank Gilbreth's experience as an apprentice bricklayer led him to do motion studies of bricklaying. He found that bricklayers could increase their output significantly by concentrating on performing some motions and eliminating others. Table 2.2 shows a portion of the results of one of Gilbreth's bricklaying motion studies. For each bricklaying activity, Gilbreth indicated whether it should be omitted for the sake of efficiency

TABLE 2.2 Partial results for one of Gilbreth's bricklaying motion studies

Operation No.	The Wrong Way *Motions Per Brick* $\frac{1}{4}\ \frac{1}{2}\ \frac{3}{4}\ \frac{4}{4}$	The Right Way *Motions Per Brick* $\frac{1}{4}\ \frac{1}{2}\ \frac{3}{4}\ \frac{4}{4}$	Pick and Dip Method: The Exterior Four Inches (Laying to the Line)
1	Step for mortar	Omit	On the scaffold the inside edge of mortar box should be plumb with inside edge of stock platform. On floor the inside edge of mortar box should be twenty-one inches from wall. Mortar boxes never over four feet apart.
2	Reach for mortar	$\frac{4}{4}$	Do not bend any more than absolutely necessary to reach mortar with a straight arm.
3	Work up mortar	Omit	Provide mortar of right consistency. Examine sand screen and keep in repair so that no pebbles can get through. Keep tender on scaffold to temper up and keep mortar worked up right.
4	Step for brick	Omit	If tubs are kept four feet apart, no stepping for brick will be necessary on scaffold. On floor keep brick in a pile not nearer than one foot nor more than four feet six inches from wall.
5	Reach for brick	Included in 2	Brick must be reached for at the same time that the mortar is reached for, and picked up at exactly the same time the mortar is picked up. If it is not picked up at the same time, allowance must be made for operation.
6	Pick up right brick	Omit	Train the leader of the tenders to vary the kind of brick used as much as possible to suit the conditions; that is, to bring the best brick when the men are working on the line.
7	Mortar box to wall	$\frac{4}{4}$	Carry stock from the staging to the wall in the straightest possible line and with an even speed, without pause or hitch. It is important to move the stock with an even speed and not by quick jerks.
8	Brick pile to wall	Included in 7	Brick must be carried from pile to wall at exactly same time as the mortar is carried to the wall, without pause or jerk.
9	Deposit mortar on wall	Included in 7	If a pause is made, this space must be filled out. If no pause is made, it is included in No. 7.
10	Spreading mortar	Omit	The mortar must be thrown so as to require no additional spreading and so that the mortar runs up on the end of the previous brick laid, or else the next two spaces must be filled out.
11	Cutting off mortar	Omit	If the mortar is thrown from the trowel properly, no spreading and no cutting is necessary.
12	Disposing of mortar	Omit	If mortar is not cut off, this space is not filled out. If mortar is cut off, keep it on trowel and carry back on trowel to box, or else butter on end of brick. Do not throw it on mortar box.

and why. He reduced the twelve motions per brick listed under "The Wrong Way" to the two motions per brick listed under "The Right Way." Gilbreth's bricklaying motion studies resulted in reducing the number of motions necessary to lay a brick by approximately 70 percent and tripling bricklaying production.

Lillian Gilbreth, in addition to collaborating with her husband, researched and wrote on motion studies after her husband's death. She applied the scientific method to the role of the homemaker and to the handicapped.

Henry L. Gantt (1861–1919)

A third major contributor to the area of scientific management was Henry L. Gantt. He, like Taylor and the Gilbreths, was interested in increasing worker efficiency. Gantt attributed unsatisfactory or ineffective tasks and piece rates (incentive pay for each product piece an individual produces) primarily to the fact that they were set on what had been done in the past or on somebody's *opinion* of what could be done. According to Gantt, *exact scientific knowledge* of what could be done should be substituted for opinion. He considered this the role of scientific management.

Gantt's management philosophy is described by his statement that "the essential differences between the best system of today and those of the past are the manner in which tasks are 'scheduled' and the manner in which their performance is rewarded."[7] Following his own rationale, Gantt tried to improve systems or organizations through task-scheduling innovation and reward innovation.

Scheduling Innovation. The Gantt chart, the primary scheduling device that Gantt developed, is still cited as the scheduling tool that is most commonly and widely used by modern managers.[8] Basically, this chart provides managers with an easily understood summary of what work was scheduled for specific time periods, how much of this work was completed, and by whom it was done. The Gantt chart is covered in much more detail in chapter 7.

DIVERSITY HIGHLIGHT
North Island Federal Credit Union Uses Scheduling to Respond to Needs of Female Employees

Because managers at North Island Credit Union listen to employees' personal and professional concerns, the morale among employees, such as this group celebrating a branch reopening, remains high.

Companies interested in attracting and retaining a quality, diverse work force need to manage workers differently now than they have in the past. One of the differences in managing today is how managers design employee work schedules.

The North Island Federal Credit Union, located in San Diego, California, is developing innovative scheduling techniques that are aimed at meeting the needs of its specific, diverse work force. Because North Island Federal has a high percentage of female employees who also have child-care responsibilities, most worker needs seem to focus on when and how employees are scheduled to work. North Island Federal is also offering work scheduling alternatives, such as extended maternity leave and plans that allow parents time off to care for sick children or elderly parents.

North Island Federal's scheduling techniques focus on having work schedules that are flexible and reflect individual worker needs. Specific scheduling programs at North Island Federal include flex-time, a program enabling workers to choose which hours they work; compressed work weeks, a program enabling workers to work fewer but longer days; worksteading, a program which allows certain employees to work at home; and job sharing, a program in which two or more employees share a job and carry out its responsibilities together. North Island Federal can be sure that such scheduling programs are appropriate by carefully listening to employees' personal as well as professional concerns and by developing a realistic, step-by-step plan that focuses on meeting both sets of concerns. ▶

Reward Innovation. Gantt seemed more aware of the human side of production than either Taylor or the Gilbreths. He wrote that "the taskmaster (manager) of the past was practically a slave driver, whose principal function was to force workmen to do that which they had no desire to do, or interest in doing. The task setter of today under any reputable system of management is not a driver. When he asks the workmen to perform tasks, he makes it to their interest to accomplish them, and is careful not to ask what is impossible or unreasonable."[9]

Whereas Taylor had pioneered a piece-rate system under which workers were paid according to the amount they produced, and advocated the use of wage incentive plans, Gantt developed a system wherein workers could earn a bonus in addition to the piece rate if they went beyond their daily production quota. Gantt believed that worker compensation needed to correspond not only to production through the piece-rate system but also to overproduction through the bonus system.

BACK TO THE CASE

The managers of Mickey's Kitchen, The Disney Store's new restaurants, could use a classical approach to management to stress organizational efficiency — the "one best way" to perform jobs at Mickey's Kitchen — to increase productivity. As a simplified example, Mickey's Kitchen managers might want to check whether the dispenser used to apply mustard and catsup is of the appropriate size to require only one squirt or whether more than one squirt is necessary to adequately cover the new lean ground beef Goofy Burger bun.

The managers also could use motion studies to eliminate unnecessary or wasted motions by their employees. For example, are Hot Diggity Dogs, french fries, and drinks located for easy insertion into customer bags, or must an employee walk unnecessary steps during the sales process? Would certain Mickey's Kitchen employees be more efficient over an entire working day if they sat, rather than stood, while working?

The classical approach to management might also guide Mickey's Kitchen managers in scheduling more efficiently. By ensuring that an appropriate number of people with the required skills are scheduled to work during peak hours and that fewer are scheduled to work during slower hours, managers would maximize the return on their labor costs.

Mickey's Kitchen managers also might want to consider offering their employees some sort of bonus if they reach certain work goals. But managers should make sure that the goals that they set are realistic, since unreasonable or impossible goals tend to make workers resentful and unproductive. For example, managers might ask that certain employees reduce errors in filling orders by 50 percent during the next month. If and when these employees reached the goal, Mickey's Kitchen managers could give them a free lunch as a bonus.

Comprehensive Analysis of Management

Comprehensive analysis of management involves studying the management function as a whole.

Whereas scientific managers approach the study of management primarily in terms of job design, managers who embrace the comprehensive view—the second area of the classical approach—are concerned with the entire range of managerial performance.

Among the well-known contributors to the comprehensive view were Chester Barnard,[10] Alvin Brown,[11] Henry Dennison,[12] Luther Gulick and Lyndall Urwick,[13] J.D. Mooney and A.C. Reiley,[14] and Oliver Sheldon.[15] Perhaps the most notable of all contributors, however, was Henri Fayol. His book *General and Industrial Management* presents a management philosophy that many modern managers still look to for advice and guidance.[16]

Henri Fayol (1841–1925)

Because of his writings on the elements of management and the general principles of management, Henri Fayol is usually regarded as the pioneer of administrative theory. The elements of management he outlined—planning, organizing, command, coordination, and control—are still considered worthwhile divisions under which to study, analyze, and put into action the management process.[17] (Note the similarities between Fayol's elements of management and the management functions outlined in chapter 1—planning, organizing, influencing, controlling.)

The general principles of management suggested by Fayol also still are considered by most managers to be useful in contemporary management practice. These principles follow in the order developed by Fayol and are accompanied by corresponding definitional themes:[18]

1. *Division of work.* Work should be divided among individuals and groups to ensure that effort and attention are focused on special portions of the task. Fayol presented work specialization as the best way to use the human resources of the organization.
2. *Authority.* The concepts of authority and responsibility are closely related. *Authority* was defined by Fayol as the right to give orders and the power to exact obedience. Responsibility involves being accountable and, therefore, is naturally associated with authority. When one assumes authority, one also assumes responsibility.[19]
3. *Discipline.* A successful organization requires the common effort of workers. Penalties, however, should be applied judiciously to encourage this common effort.
4. *Unity of command.* Workers should receive orders from only one manager.
5. *Unity of direction.* The entire organization should be moving toward a common objective, in a common direction.
6. *Subordination of individual interests to the general interests.* The interests of one person should not have priority over the interests of the organization as a whole.
7. *Remuneration.* Many variables, such as cost of living, supply of qualified personnel, general business conditions, and success of the business, should be considered in determining the rate of pay a worker will receive.[20]
8. *Centralization.* Fayol defined *centralization* as lowering the importance of the subordinate role. Decentralization is increasing the same importance. The degree to which centralization or decentralization should be adopted depends on the specific organization in which the manager is working.[21]
9. *Scalar chain.* Managers in hierarchies are actually part of a chainlike authority scale. Each manager, from the first-line supervisor to the president, possesses certain amounts of authority. The president possesses the most authority; the first-line supervisor possesses the least authority. The existence of this chain implies that lower-level managers should always keep upper-level managers informed of their work activities. Existence of and adherence to the scalar chain are necessary if organizations are to be successful.
10. *Order.* For the sake of efficiency and coordination, all materials and people related to a specific kind of work should be assigned to the same general location in the organization.
11. *Equity.* All employees should be treated as equally as possible.
12. *Stability of tenure of personnel.* Retaining productive employees should always be

a high priority of management. Recruitment and selection costs, as well as increased reject rates, are usually associated with hiring new workers.

13. *Initiative.* Management should take steps to encourage worker initiative, which can be defined as new or additional work activity undertaken through self-direction.

14. *Esprit de corps.* Management should encourage harmony and general good feeling among employees.

Fayol's general principles of management cover a broad range of topics, but organizational efficiency, the handling of people, and appropriate management action seem to be the three general themes stressed. With the writings of Fayol, the study of management as a broad comprehensive activity began to receive the attention it deserved.

Limitations of the Classical Approach

Individual contributors to the classical approach were probably encouraged to write about their experiences largely because of the success they enjoyed. Structuring work to be more efficient and defining the manager's role more precisely yielded significant improvement in productivity, which individuals such as Taylor and Fayol were quick to document.

The human variable for the organization, however, may not be adequately emphasized in the classical approach. People today do not seem to be as influenced by bonuses as they were in the nineteenth century. It is generally agreed that critical interpersonal areas, such as conflict, communication, leadership, and motivation, were not emphasized enough in the classical approach.

THE BEHAVIORAL APPROACH

The **behavioral approach to management** emphasizes striving to increase production through an understanding of people. According to proponents of this approach, if managers understand their people and adapt their organizations to them, organizational success usually follows.

The **behavioral approach to management** is a management approach that emphasizes increasing organizational success by focusing on human variables within the organization.

The behavioral approach is usually described as beginning with a series of studies conducted between 1924 and 1932. These studies investigated the behavior and attitudes of workers at the Hawthorne (Chicago) Works of the Western Electric Company.[22] Accounts of these studies are usually divided into phases: the relay assembly test room experiments and the bank wiring observation room experiment.

The Relay Assembly Test Room Experiments

The relay assembly test room experiments originally had a scientific management orientation.[23] The experimenters believed that if productivity were studied long enough under different working conditions (including variations in weather conditions, temperature, rest periods, work hours, and humidity), the working conditions that maximized production would be found. The purpose of the relay assembly test room experiments was to determine the relationship between intensity of lighting and efficiency of workers, as measured by worker output. Two groups of female employees were used as subjects. The light intensity for one group was varied, while the light intensity for the other group was held constant.

The results of the experiments surprised the researchers. No matter what conditions employees were exposed to, production increased. A consistent relationship between productivity and lighting intensity seemed nonexistent. An extensive interviewing campaign was begun to determine why the subjects continued to increase production. The following are the main reasons, as formulated from the interviews:

1. The subjects found working in the test room enjoyable.
2. The new supervisory relationship during the experiment allowed the subjects to work freely, without fear.
3. The subjects realized that they were taking part in an important and interesting study.
4. The subjects seemed to become friendly as a group.

The experimenters concluded that human factors within organizations could significantly influence production. More research was needed to evaluate the potential impact of this human component in organizations.

The Bank Wiring Observation Room Experiment

The purpose of the bank wiring observation room experiment was to analyze the social relationships in a work group.[24] More specifically, the study focused on the effect of group piecework incentives on a group of men who assembled terminal banks for use in telephone exchanges. The group piecework incentive system dictated that the harder a group worked as a whole, the more pay each member of that group received.

The experimenters believed that the study would find that members of the work group would pressure one another to work harder so that each group member would receive more pay. To the surprise of the researchers, the opposite occurred. The work group pressured the faster workers to slow down their work rate. In essence, the men whose work rate would have increased individual salaries were pressured by the group, rather than the men whose work rate would have decreased individual salaries. Evidently, the men were more interested in preserving the work group than in making more money. The researchers concluded that social groups in organizations could effectively exert enough pressure to influence individuals to disregard monetary incentives.[25]

Taken together, the series of studies conducted at the Hawthorne plant gave management thinkers a new direction for research. Obviously, the human variable in the organization needed much more analysis, since it could either increase or decrease production drastically. Managers began to realize that they needed to understand this influence in order to maximize its positive effects and minimize its negative effects. This attempt to understand people is still a major force of today's organizational research.[26] The cartoon humorously illustrates a manager whose lack of understanding of an employee results in employee discontent and perhaps eventually produces a relatively unproductive employee. More current behavioral findings and their implications for management are presented in much greater detail in later sections of this text.

Cathy Copyright © 1990, Cathy Guisewite. Reprinted with permission of Universal Press Syndicate.

BACK TO THE CASE Comprehensive analysis of organizations implies that Mickey's Kitchen managers might be able to improve their restaurant by evaluating the entire range of their managerial performance—especially with regard to organizational efficiency, the handling of people, and appropriate management action. For example, Mickey's Kitchen managers should check with their employees to make sure they are receiving orders from only one source—that one manager hasn't instructed an employee to man the french fry station moments before an assistant manager directs the same employee to prepare Pinocchio's Pizzas. Along the same lines, Mickey's Kitchen managers might want to verify that all of their employees are being treated equally—that fry cooks, for example, don't get longer work breaks than order takers.

The behavioral approach to management suggests that Mickey's Kitchen managers should consider the people working for them and evaluate the impact of their feelings and relationships on the productivity of the new restaurants. Managers at Disney's restaurants could, for example, try to make the work more enjoyable, perhaps by allowing their employees to work at different stations (grill, beverage, french fry, cash register, etc.) each day. Managers might also consider creating opportunities for employees to become better acquainted with each other, perhaps through a Mickey's Kitchen employee picnic. In essence, the behavioral approach to management stresses that Mickey's Kitchen managers should recognize the human variable in their restaurants and strive to maximize its positive effects.

THE MANAGEMENT SCIENCE APPROACH

Churchman, Ackoff, and Arnoff define the management science, or operations research (OR), approach as (1) an application for the scientific method to problems arising in the operation of a system and (2) the solving of these problems by the solving of mathematical equations representing the system.[27] The **management science approach** suggests that managers can best improve their organizations by using the scientific method and mathematical techniques to solve operational problems.

The **management science approach** is a management approach that emphasizes the use of the scientific method and quantitative techniques to increase organizational success.

The Beginning of the Management Science Approach

The management science, or operations research, approach can be traced to World War II. During this era, leading scientists were asked to help solve complex operational problems that existed in the military.[28] The scientists were organized into teams that eventually became known as operations research (OR) groups. One OR group was asked to determine which gunsights would best stop German attacks on the British mainland.

These early OR groups typically included physicists and other "hard" scientists, who used the problem-solving method with which they had the most experience: the scientific method. The **scientific method** dictates that scientists:

The **scientific method** is a method of problem-solving that involves the following sequential steps:

1. Systematically *observe* the system whose behavior must be explained to solve the problem.
2. Use these specific observations to *construct* a generalized framework (a model) that is consistent with the specific observations and from which consequences of changing the system can be predicted.
3. Use the model to *deduce* how the system will behave under conditions that have not been observed but could be observed if the changes were made.
4. Finally, *test* the model by performing an experiment on the actual system to see if the effects of changes predicted using the model actually occur when the changes are made.[29]

1. Observing.
2. Constructing a model.
3. Deducing.
4. Testing the model.

The OR groups were very successful in using the scientific method to solve their operational problems.

Management Science Today

After World War II, the world again became interested in manufacturing and selling products. The success of the OR groups had been so obvious in the military that managers were anxious to try management science techniques in an industrial environment. After all, managers also had complicated operational problems.

By 1955, the management science approach to solving industrial problems had proven very effective. Many people found this approach valuable and saw great promise in refining its techniques and analytical tools. Managers and universities alike anxiously began these refinement attempts.

By 1965, the management science approach was being used in many companies and applied to many diverse management problems, such as production scheduling, plant location, and product packaging.[30]

In the 1980s, surveys of firms using management science techniques indicated that these techniques are used extensively in very large, complex organizations. The benefit of using these techniques in smaller organizations has not yet been fully realized. Finding new and beneficial ways of applying management science techniques to smaller organizations is undoubtedly a worthwhile challenge facing managers in the 1990s and beyond.[31]

QUALITY HIGHLIGHT
Baldrige Award Exemplifies Quality

The application of scientific management to quality standards is the basis for the prestigious Baldrige Award, as explained in the following "Quality Highlight."

Since it was established in 1987, the Malcolm Baldrige National Quality Award has become the sought-after award for quality standard for U.S. businesses. It is to corporate America what the Oscars are to the motion-picture industry or the Grammys are to the music industry.

The award does not just emphasize quality. Guidelines for award application provide a detailed plan for improving quality in all areas of a company's business.

Employees of The Ritz-Carlton Hotel, a recent winner of the Baldrige Award, meet frequently to discuss quality issues and plan the company's total quality effort.

"The guidelines are outstanding," says James Houghton, chairman and chief executive officer of Corning Glass, which has competed for the award. "We have passed out the guidelines for our divisions and just said, 'If you want to know what quality is all about, take a look at this.'" Corning estimates that staffers spent 14,000 hours competing for the award.

Six prizes are offered each year, two each for manufacturing and service companies and two for small businesses with fewer than 500 employees. Some past award winners include Motorola, Globe Metallurgical, IBM Rochester, Federal Express, Wallace Company, the Ritz-Carlton Hotel Company, AT&T Universal Card Services, Texas Instruments Defense Systems & Electronics Group, and Granite Rock Company

The award is administered by the National Institute of Standards and Technology. To apply, a large company must pay a fee of $4,000 and submit responses to over 90 "Areas to Address" on a 75-page questionnaire. A small company pays $1,200 and answers a 50-page questionnaire.

Applications are scored by volunteer examiners, largely from industry. Companies passing the initial screening enter the second phase of the competition, which includes an on-site visit by four to six examiners who verify information in the application.

Finally, application scores and examiners' reports are given to a panel of nine judges who submit their choices to the U.S. Secretary of Commerce.

Because the process is so detailed, just applying for the Baldrige award forces a company to review its entire operation to discover weaknesses in quality. Applicants also receive reports from the examiners highlighting strengths and weaknesses.

Former Xerox Chairman David Kearns says that 90 percent of the value of applying for the award is in that examiners' report.

Adds David Luther, Corning Glass's vice president for quality: "It's the cheapest consulting you can ever get." ▶

Characteristics of Management Science Applications

Four primary characteristics usually are present in situations in which management science techniques are applied.[32] First, the management problems studied are so complicated that managers need help in analyzing a large number of variables. Management science techniques increase the effectiveness of the managers' decision making. Second, a management science application generally uses economic implications as guidelines for making a particular decision. Perhaps this is because management science techniques are best suited for analyzing quantifiable factors, such as sales, expenses, and units of production. Third, the use of mathematical models to investigate the decision situation is typical in management science applications. Models are constructed to represent reality and then used to determine how the real world situation might be improved. The fourth characteristic of a management science application is the use of computers. The great complexity of managerial problems and the sophisticated mathematical analysis required of problem-related information are two factors that make computers very valuable to the management science analyst.

Today, managers are using such management science tools as inventory control models, network models, and probability models as aids in the decision-making process. Later parts of this text will outline some of these models in more detail and illustrate their applications to management decision making. Because management science thought is still evolving, more and more sophisticated analytical techniques can be expected.

THE CONTINGENCY APPROACH

In simple terms, the **contingency approach to management** emphasizes that what managers do in practice depends on, or is contingent upon, a given set of circumstances—a situation.[33] In essence, this approach emphasizes "if-then" relationships. "If" this situational variable exists, "then" this is the action a manager probably would take. As an example, if a manager has a group of inexperienced subordinates, then the contingency approach would recommend that he or she lead in a different fashion than if he or she had an experienced group.

The **contingency approach to management** is a management approach that emphasizes that what managers do in practice depends on a given set of circumstances—a situation.

In general, the contingency approach attempts to outline the conditions or situations in which various management methods have the best chance of success.[34] This approach is based on the premise that, although there is probably no one best way to solve a management problem in all organizations, there probably is one best way to solve any given management problem in any one organization. Perhaps the main challenges of using the contingency approach are (1) perceiving organizational situations as they actually exist, (2) choosing the management tactics best suited to those situations, and (3) competently implementing those tactics.

Although the notion of a contingency approach to management is not new,[35] the use of the term itself is relatively new. In addition, the contingency approach has become a popular discussion topic for contemporary management writers. The general consensus of their writings seems to indicate that if managers are to apply management concepts, principles, and techniques successfully, they must consider the realities of the specific organizational circumstances they face.[36]

ETHICS HIGHLIGHT
Charles Schwab Protects Clients During Disaster

Stockbrokers take care of their clients' financial affairs. These clients entrust records of their financial transactions to their brokers. Charles Schwab, a large discount stock brokerage with a branch in San Francisco, determined that it owed its clients a duty to make contingency plans in case of a physical disaster. The plans were deemed necessary not only for the good of the company but for the benefit of the company's many clients. If a physical disaster hit and the financial records of clients were destroyed, they would undoubtedly suffer both financially and emotionally.

These contingency plans paid off when, in October of 1989, many parts of the San Francisco Bay area lost electrical power following an earthquake. The company's backup battery system went into operation immediately following the earthquake, and prevented the shutdown of the firm's mainframe computer. Thirty minutes later, a diesel generator took over the task of providing electric power to the computer.

Without prior contingency plans to deal with a lack of electrical power to the mainframe computer, the company could have suffered a severe information loss that would have harmed clients and the company for an extended period of time. Not all companies in the Bay area had such contingency plans. Charles Schwab's ethical concern for its clients resulted in necessary protection for its clients and the company. ▶

During the San Francisco earthquake Charles Schwab, a stock brokerage firm, was able to protect its clients' financial records by using a backup battery system and diesel generator to provide electrical power to the firm's mainframe computer.

THE SYSTEM APPROACH

The **system approach to management** is a management approach based on general system theory — the theory that to understand fully the operation of an entity, the entity must be viewed as a system. This requires understanding the interdependence of its parts.

The **system approach to management** is based on general system theory. Ludwig von Bertalanffy, a scientist who worked mainly in the areas of physics and biology, is recognized as the founder of general system theory.[37] The main premise of the theory is that to understand fully the operation of an entity, the entity must be viewed as a system. A **system** is a number of interdependent parts functioning as a whole for some purpose. For example, according to general system theory, to fully understand the operations of the human body, one must understand the workings of its interdependent parts (ears, eyes, brain, etc.). General system theory integrates the knowledge of various specialized fields so that the system as a whole can be better understood.

Types of Systems

A **system** is a number of interdependent parts functioning as a whole for some purpose.

A **closed system** is a system that is not influenced by and does not interact with its environment.

An **open system** is a system that is influenced by and is constantly interacting with its environment.

According to von Bertalanffy, there are two basic types of systems: closed and open. **Closed systems** are not influenced by and do not interact with their environments. They are mostly mechanical and have necessary predetermined motions or activities that must be performed regardless of the environment. A clock is an example of a closed system. Regardless of its environment, a clock's wheels, gears, and so forth must function in a predetermined way if the clock as a whole is to exist and serve its purpose. The second type of system, the **open system,** is constantly interacting with its environment. A plant is an example of an open system. Constant interaction with the environment influences the plant's state of existence and its future. In fact, the environment determines whether or not the plant will live.

Systems and "Wholeness"

The concept "wholeness" is very important in general system analysis. The system must be viewed as a whole and modified only through changes in its parts. A thorough knowledge of how each part functions and of the interrelationships among the parts must be present before modifications of the parts can be made for the overall benefit of the system. L. Thomas Hopkins suggested six guidelines for system wholeness that should be remembered during system analysis.[38]

1. The whole should be the main focus of analysis, with the parts receiving secondary attention.
2. Integration is the key variable in wholeness analysis. It is defined as the interrelatedness of the many parts within the whole.
3. Possible modifications in each part should be weighed in relation to possible effects on every other part.
4. Each part has some role to perform so that the whole can accomplish its purpose.
5. The nature of the part and its function is determined by its position in the whole.
6. All analysis starts with the existence of the whole. The parts and their interrelationships should then evolve to best suit the purpose of the whole.

Since the system approach to management is based on general system theory, analysis of the management situation as a system is stressed. The following sections present the parts of the management system and recommend information that can be used to analyze the system.

The Management System

As with all systems, the **management system** is composed of a number of parts that function on an interdependent basis to achieve a purpose. The main parts of the management system are organizational input, organizational process, and organizational output. As discussed in chapter 1, these parts consist of organizational resources, the production process, and finished goods, respectively. The parts represent a combination that exists to achieve organizational objectives, whatever they may be.

The **management system** is an open system whose major parts are organizational input, organizational process, and organizational output.

The management system is an open system, one that interacts with its environment (see Figure 2.2). Environmental factors with which the management system interacts include the government, suppliers, customers, and competitors. Each of these represents a potential environmental influence that could significantly change the future of a management system.

Environmental impact on management cannot be overemphasized. As an example, the federal government, through its Occupational Safety and Health Act (OSHA) of 1970, encourages management to take costly steps to safeguard workers. Many managers are frustrated because they believe the safeguards are not only too expensive but also unnecessary.

The critical importance of managers' knowing and understanding various compo-

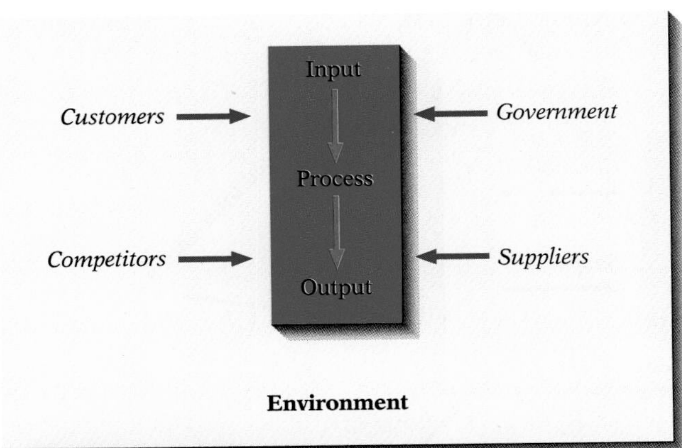

FIGURE 2.2 The open management system

nents of the environments of their organizations is perhaps best illustrated by the constant struggle of supermarket managers to know and understand their customers. Supermarket managers fight for the business of a national population that is growing by less than 1 percent per year. Survival requires that supermarket managers know their customers better than the competition does. Many food retailers are conducting and using market research to uncover customer attitudes about different kinds of foods and stores. Armed with a thorough understanding of their customers, supermarket managers conducting market research hope to win business from competitors who are not benefiting from insights gained through such research.[39]

Information for Management System Analysis

As noted earlier, to better understand a system, general system theory allows for the use of information from many specialized disciplines. This certainly holds true for the management system. Information from any discipline can increase the understanding of management system operations and thereby enhance the success of the system. A broad, sweeping statement such as this, however, presents a problem. Where do managers go to get this information?

The information used to discuss the management system in the remainder of this text comes from three primary sources: (1) the classical approach to management, (2) the behavioral approach to management, and (3) the management science approach to management. The use of these three sources of information to analyze the management system is referred to as **triangular management.** Figure 2.3 presents the triangular management model. The three sources of information in the model are not meant to represent all the information that can be used to analyze the management system. Rather, they are the three bodies of management-related information that probably would be most useful to managers analyzing the management system.

Triangular management is a management approach that emphasizes using information from the classical, behavioral, and management science schools of thought to manage the open management system.

A synthesis of classically based information, behaviorally based information, and management science based information is critical to effectively managing the management system. This information is integrated and presented in this text in the five remaining parts of the book. These parts discuss management systems and planning

FIGURE 2.3 Triangular management model

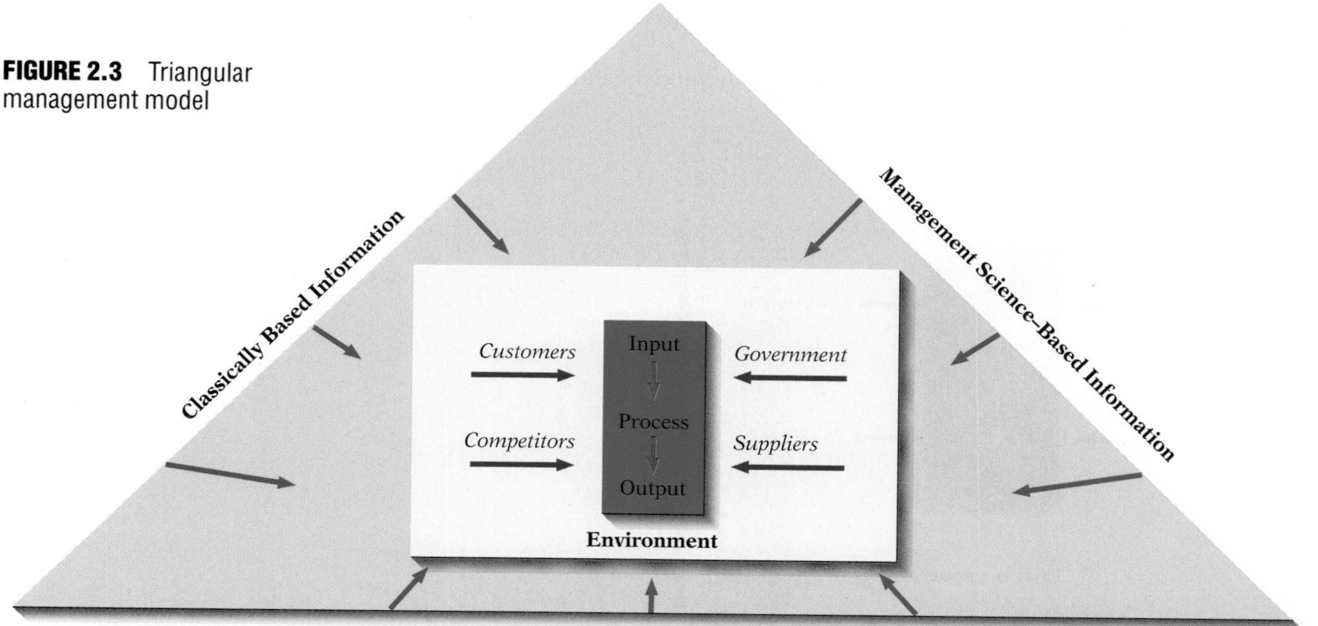

(chapters 4–8), organizing (chapters 9–12), influencing (chapters 13–16), controlling (chapters 17–19), and topics for special emphasis (chapters 20–22).[40] In addition, some information in these parts is presented from a contingency viewpoint to give added emphasis to the practical application of management principles.

BACK TO THE CASE

Mickey's Kitchen managers could use the management science approach to solve any operational problems that arose. According to the scientific method, Mickey's Kitchen managers would first spend some time observing what takes place in their restaurants. Next, they would use these observations to outline exactly how the restaurants operate as a whole. Third, they would apply this understanding of Mickey's Kitchen operations by predicting how various changes might help or hinder the restaurants as a whole. Before implementing possible changes, they would test them on a small scale to see whether they actually affected the restaurants as desired.

If Mickey's Kitchen managers were to follow the contingency approach to management, their actions as managers would depend on the situation. For example, if some customers hadn't been served within a reasonable period because the equipment needed to make PB&J Handwiches had broken down, then a Mickey's Kitchen manager probably would not hold employees responsible. But if the manager knew that Handwich equipment had broken down because of employee mistreatment or neglect, then the management's reaction to the situation would likely be very different.

Mickey's Kitchen managers could also apply the system approach and view their restaurants as a system, a number of interdependent parts that function as a whole to reach restaurant objectives. Naturally, Mickey's Kitchen would be seen as an open system—a system that exists in and is influenced by its environment. Major factors within the environment of Mickey's Kitchen would include customers, suppliers, competitors, and the government. For example, if McDonald's, a competitor, significantly lowered its price for hamburgers to a point well below what Mickey's Kitchen was charging for a hamburger, Mickey's Kitchen management might be forced to consider modifying different parts of their restaurant system in order to meet or beat that price.

ACTION SUMMARY

Reread the learning objectives that follow. Each objective is followed by questions. Answering these questions accurately will help you retain the most important concepts discussed in this chapter. After answering each question, check your answer with the answer key at the end of this chapter. (*Hint:* If you have doubt regarding the correct response, consult the page whose number follows the answer.)

Circle: ***From studying this chapter, I will attempt to acquire:***

1. An understanding of the classical approach to management.

T, F — **a.** The classical management approach established what it considered the "one best way" to manage.

a, b, c, d, e — **b.** The process of finding the one best way to perform a task is called: (a) comprehensive analysis of management; (b) the concept of wholeness; (c) the Hawthorne studies; (d) the management science approach; (e) scientific management.

2. An appreciation for the work of Frederick W. Taylor, Frank and Lillian Gilbreth, Henry L. Gantt, and Henri Fayol.

a, b, c, d, e **a.** Fayol defines fourteen principles of management. Which of the following is *not* one of those principles: (a) scalar chain of authority; (b) esprit de corps; (c) centralizaion; (d) unity of command; (e) directedness of command.

a, b, c, d, e **b.** Which of the following theorists assumed that any worker's job could be reduced to a science: (a) Gilbreth; (b) Gantt; (c) Mayo; (d) Fayol; (e) Taylor.

T, F **c.** Gantt increased worker efficiency by setting standards according to top management's opinion of what maximum performance should be.

3. An understanding of the behavioral approach to management.

T, F **a.** The behavioral approach to management emphasizes striving to increase production through an understanding of the organization itself.

a, b, c, d, e **b.** The behavioral approach began with: (a) the Hawthorne studies; (b) the mental revolution; (c) the Industrial Revolution; (d) motion studies; (e) the Bethlehem Steel studies.

4. An understanding of the studies at the Hawthorne Works of the Western Electric Company.

T, F **a.** The Hawthorne studies showed a direct relationship between lighting and efficiency.

T, F **b.** The Hawthorne experimenters found that people were more concerned with preserving the work group than with maximizing their pay.

5. An understanding of the management science approach to management.

a, b, c, d, e **a.** Which of the following is not one of the philosophies of the management science approach: (a) managers can improve the organization by using scientific methods; (b) mathematical techniques can solve organizational problems; (c) models should be used to represent the system; (d) individual work is better than teamwork; (e) observation of the system must take place.

T, F **b.** In the management science theory, models are used to represent reality and then to determine how the real world situation might be improved.

6. An understanding of how the management science approach has evolved.

a, b, c, d, e **a.** The management science approach emerged after: (a) World War I; (b) the Civil War; (c) the Korean War; (d) World War II; (e) the 1930 depression.

T, F **b.** Although management science was first applied to military problems, it is now applied by companies to diverse management problems.

7. An understanding of the system approach to management.

a, b, c, d, e **a.** An organization that interacts with external forces is: (a) a closed system; (b) a model; (c) an independent entity; (d) an open system; (e) a contingency.

a, b, c, d, e **b.** Which of the following is *not* one of the guidelines proposed by Hopkins in the concept of wholeness: (a) the whole should be the main focus of analysis; (b) all analysis starts with the existence of the whole; (c) the nature of the part is determined by its position in the whole; (d) each part has some role to perform so that the whole can accomplish its purpose; (e) modifications should be made as they occur.

8. An understanding of how triangular management and the contingency approach to management are related.

a, b, c, d, e **a.** The contingency approach emphasizes the viewpoint that what managers do in practice depends over all on: (a) the worker; (b) the situation; (c) the task; (d) the environment; (e) the manager's personality.

a, b, c, d, e **b.** The three sources of information in triangular management are: (a) input, process, and output; (b) management science, classically and behaviorally based; (c) mathematics, psychology, and sociology; (d) managers, directors, and stockholders; (e) executives, administrators, and supervisors.

INTRODUCTORY CASE WRAP-UP

" 'Mickey's Kitchen' at The Disney Store" (p. 27) and its related back-to-the-case sections were written to help you better understand the management concepts contained in this chapter. Answer the following questions about this introductory case to further enrich your understanding of the chapter content:

1. What are three problems that you think the managers of The Disney Store's Mickey's Kitchen will have to solve?
2. What action(s) do you think the managers will have to take to solve these problems?
3. From what you know about fast-food restaurants, how easy would it be to manage Mickey's Kitchen? Why?

ISSUES FOR REVIEW AND DISCUSSION

1. List the five approaches to managing.
2. Define the classical approach to management.
3. Compare and contrast the contributions to the classical approach made by Frederick W. Taylor, Frank and Lillian Gilbreth, and Henry L. Gantt.
4. How does Henri Fayol's contribution to the classical approach differ from those of Taylor, the Gilbreths, and Gantt?
5. What is scientific management?
6. Describe motion study as used by the Gilbreths.
7. Describe Gantt's innovation in the area of worker bonuses.
8. List and define Fayol's general principles of management.
9. What is the primary limitation to the classical approach to management?
10. Define the behavioral approach to management.
11. What is the significance of the studies at the Hawthorne Works of the Western Electric Company?
12. What is the management science approach to management?
13. What are the steps in the scientific method of problem solving?
14. List and explain three characteristics of situations in which management science applications usually are made.
15. Define the contingency approach to management.
16. What is a system?
17. What is the difference between a closed system and an open system?
18. Explain the relationship between system analysis and "wholeness."
19. What are the parts of the management system?
20. What is triangular management?

ACTION SUMMARY ANSWER KEY

1. a. T, p. 28
   b. e, p. 28
2. a. e, pp. 34–35
   b. e, p. 29
   c. F, p. 32
3. a. F, p. 35
   b. a, p. 35
4. a. F, pp. 35–36
   b. T, p. 36
5. a. d, p. 37
   b. T, p. 37
6. a. d, p. 37
   b. T, p. 38
7. a. d, p. 40
   b. e, pp. 40–41
8. a. b, p. 39
   b. b, p. 42

CASE STUDY

Scientific Management at the Watertown Arsenal

Peter B. Petersen
The Johns Hopkins University

An early application of Frederick Taylor's principles of scientific management took place in the U.S. Army prior to World War I. General William Crozier was the Army Chief of Ordnance (weapons and other military supplies) from 1901 to 1918. Crozier was aware of Taylor's work; Taylor's principles of scientific management had been used in private industry since the mid-nineteenth century, and Crozier had observed them being used by companies manufacturing munitions.

Crozier was in charge of the Watertown Arsenal in Boston, Massachusetts, where the Army manufactured and stored weapons. In 1909, Crozier employed consultants to introduce Taylor's scientific management techniques at the arsenal. He and his subordinates identified 24 reasons for inefficiency and poor performance. They included frequent changes in management, lack of a proper supply system, lack of coordination of work done in different shops, lack of sufficient and appropriate tools, loss of time due to breakages and repairs, delays in procuring materials, added transport costs between shops, and failure to take advantage of the machines and tools provided. Crozier employed Carl Barth, a follower of Taylor, to conduct a study at the Watertown Arsenal. The study took two years and was based on Taylor's principles of analyzing existing practices, looking for ways to improve these practices, and standardizing the improvements. In 1911, Barth introduced the new Taylor principles at the arsenal, including making productivity-related premium payments to workers and implementing new methods of working based on the results of time study of jobs.

Initially, the changes in management were favorably received by the workers, who appeared interested and who enjoyed the premium payments they received. Crozier concluded that great economy, as well as substantial benefits to the workers, had been achieved. After two or three months of using the new system, Crozier attempted to extend its use to the foundry also—but the foundry workers saw the new management techniques as a threat to their jobs, and they went out on strike.

Organized labor became involved; they perceived Taylor's principles as a dangerous attempt to introduce restrictions to the freedom of individual workers and eventually to reduce overall wages. Congressional hearings were held, to air testimony by organized labor as well as by Crozier and other proponents of Taylor's management methods. General Crozier testified that employees at the Watertown Arsenal working under the Taylor system had increased their wages by about 25 percent, while the government had realized overall cost savings. The cost of producing a plug for a hydraulic gun carriage, for example, was reduced from 25 cents to 7 cents.

In Crozier's Report of the Chief of Ordnance in 1912, he announced annual savings of $240,000 at the Watertown Arsenal. The cost of production for 12-inch mortar carriages was reduced from $1,536.73 to $988.36, a savings of more than 35 percent. However, despite these clear savings, the Congressional inquiry continued, fueled by the objections of organized labor.

Taylor died in 1915. His methods had gained wide acceptance in American industry. Crozier continued his efforts to introduce principles of scientific management into Army munitions production. In 1914, war broke out in Europe, and demand for American armaments increased. American productivity in arms manufacture became increasingly important. By the time that the United States entered World War I in 1917, Taylor's principles were accepted practice both in private industry and in the Army.

Crozier's attempt to introduce scientific management at the Watertown Arsenal has been criticized for having been conducted too quickly and without communication with the workers whose jobs were affected. Today, he is credited with having created an effective Ordnance Department that helped prepare the United States for participation in World War I, and with having had the persistence and vision to continue his crusade for efficiency in the face of opposition and criticism.

DISCUSSION QUESTIONS

1. What is the basic premise behind Taylor's principles of scientific management? How was that premise applied at the Watertown Arsenal?
2. What two factors were the keys to increased productivity at the Watertown Arsenal?
3. What key variable did General Crozier apparently ignore in his application of Taylor's scientific management principles?
4. Why was the introduction of scientific management at the Watertown Arsenal important?

CNN VIDEO CASE

A Born Entrepreneur

FRED DeLUCA
Subway Sandwiches

A thorough study of management practices cannot account for the rise of every successful entrepreneur; a businessperson like Fred DeLuca of Subway Sandwiches is a "natural." In 1965, at the age of 17, DeLuca approached Peter Buck, a family friend, for advice on financing his college career. He emerged from their discussion a full partner in "Pete's Super Submarine Sandwiches," an idea that would eventually make him a millionaire.

Although DeLuca has never studied management techniques formally, his ability to influence others is uncanny. This skill is particularly important when franchisees come into play. In order to realize their ten-year goal of 32 restaurants, in 1974, DeLuca and Buck began to sell franchises of what they renamed "Subway Sandwiches." Their franchising system is unusual in the fast food industry. The franchise fee itself is extremely low relative to competitors'; it is even lower for existing franchisees seeking to open an additional store. Restaurant start-up costs are also kept intentionally low, often less than ten percent the cost of competing franchises if equipment is leased directly from Subway Sandwiches. If the franchisee purchases equipment, he or she can do so at Subway Sandwiches' cost.

In order to realize his ten-year goal of 32 Subway Sandwich shops, Fred DeLuca began selling franchises. He then expanded that goal to 5,000 shops by 1994.

DeLuca's support does not fade away after the shop has opened, either. Subway Sandwiches headquarters staffs a toll-free information line for its franchisees. Multiple copies of newsletters are available to help the individual owners with an exchange of information and assistance. New franchisees are even regular guests at the DeLuca home. "It's critical to this kind of business to keep the lines of communication open," says DeLuca.

In exchange for low start-up expenses and extensive support structures offered by Subway Sandwiches, the corporate royalty fee that franchises pay to the corporation is higher than usual in the fast food business. Also, new franchises may find themselves in direct competition with established Subway Sandwiches shops nearby; it is a corporate policy not to protect franchise territory. In fact, DeLuca sees Subway Sandwiches' saturation of a market not only as a positive gain to the corporation, but also to individual franchisees because independent sandwich shops often cannot compete successfully in a market dominated by Subway Sandwiches shops.

When Fred DeLuca and Peter Buck went into partnership in 1965, they wanted 32 shops in ten years. They expanded that goal to 5,000 by 1994. At the end of 1990, the total had already topped 5,100. "The most important thing we can do is teach people the concepts of business. . . . A lot of people get into the business with the idea of 'Okay, I'm going to open a store,' but they don't always know all the approaches that are available to them so they can maximize their results in the business. So what you want to do is make sure that you have your skills together if you want to build and sell stores."

In 1989, DeLuca bought a stake in a small chain of chicken restaurants, Cajun Joe's. Franchises are selling briskly, many of them to Subway Sandwiches franchisees: "Cajun Joe's provides them the opportunity to grow," says DeLuca. Teaching business skills and providing opportunity for growth is not only good for the franchisee, however; it has made Fred DeLuca the success he is today.

VIDEO CASE QUESTIONS

1. What management approach did Peter Buck use in setting up his original partnership with Fred DeLuca?
2. Opening a second shop in order to "create an illusion of success" exploited one major input factor in an open system. What is that factor?
3. List three ways in which management science applications might be used to help Subway Sandwiches shops increase in efficiency.
4. How does DeLuca take advantage of Fayol's principle of esprit de corps?

CNN VIDEO EXERCISE

Planning Major Changes at Subway Sandwiches

EXERCISE GOAL: Learn how you could use information from different management approaches to consider a major change in the operation of a fast-food restaurant.

Burger King recently announced plans to offer dinner baskets, free popcorn, and limited table service in order to encourage business during the usually slow dinner hour. Burger King hopes to lure customers from other fast-food chains and from family-style restaurants. Burger King says that, at dinner, people want a more complete meal and a different kind of service. Burger King will offer several basket dinners. Customers will receive free popcorn and select a seat. Their meals will be brought to them.

Imagine that you are an executive at Subway Sandwiches. You have been assigned to analyze the costs and appeal of Burger King's new dinner menu and special dinner service. Should Subway make similar changes?

Make three separate analyses of the studies that you would recommend that Subway should conduct to decide whether a program similar to Burger King's dinner special would succeed at Subway. Using the classical approach, the behavioral approach, and the management science approach to management, list the steps Subway should take to study the issue.

The Classicists	The Behaviorists	The Management Scientists
____________	____________	____________
____________	____________	____________
____________	____________	____________
____________	____________	____________
____________	____________	____________
____________	____________	____________
____________	____________	____________
____________	____________	____________
____________	____________	____________
____________	____________	____________
____________	____________	____________
____________	____________	____________

CHAPTER

3

CORPORATE SOCIAL RESPONSIBILITY AND BUSINESS ETHICS

STUDENT LEARNING OBJECTIVES

From studying this chapter, I will attempt to acquire:

1. An understanding of the term *corporate social responsibility.*
2. An appreciation for the arguments both for and against business assuming social responsibilities.
3. Useful strategies for increasing the social responsiveness of an organization.
4. Insights on the planning, organizing, influencing, and controlling of social responsibility activities.
5. A practical plan for how society can help business meet its social obligations.
6. An understanding of the definition and importance of business ethics.
7. An understanding of how ethics can be incorporated into management practice.

CHAPTER OUTLINE

INTRODUCTORY CASE
Larami Corporation "Super Soaks" Society?

FUNDAMENTALS OF SOCIAL RESPONSIBILITY

The Davis Model of Corporate Social Responsibility

QUALITY HIGHLIGHT
Xerox Corporation

Areas of Corporate Social Responsibility
Varying Opinions on Social Responsibility

ETHICS HIGHLIGHT
IBM

GLOBAL HIGHLIGHT
DuPont

SOCIAL RESPONSIVENESS

Social Responsiveness and Decision Making
Approaches to Meeting Social Responsibilities

DIVERSITY HIGHLIGHT
Opryland

SOCIAL RESPONSIBILITY ACTIVITIES AND MANAGEMENT FUNCTIONS

Planning Social Responsibility Activities
Organizing Social Responsibility Activities
Influencing Individuals Performing Social Responsibility Activities
Controlling Social Responsibility Activities

HOW SOCIETY CAN HELP BUSINESS MEET SOCIAL OBLIGATIONS

BUSINESS ETHICS

A Definition of Ethics
Why Ethics Is a Vital Part of Management Practices
A Code of Ethics
Creating an Ethical Workplace

CASE STUDY
Procter & Gamble: A Socially Responsible Company

VIDEO CASE
Promoting Cosmetics with a Conscience: Anita Roddick, Body Shop International

VIDEO EXERCISE
Making Ethical Decisions for the Body Shop

INTRODUCTORY CASE

Larami Corporation "Super Soaks" Society?

Larami Corp. has produced the summer's hottest toy, Super Soakers, a high-powered plastic toy gun that shoots more water farther than any other toy gun in town. Indeed, it's a toy maker's dream come true. Or nightmare.

In the last few days, stories of Super Soaker-wielding youths squirting people with water, bleach, ammonia, and urine have flooded the offices of lawmakers and police departments around the country. . . . Already one youth in Boston has died, and two others — one in New York, another in New Castle, Pennsylvania — were wounded in shootings triggered by dousings.

Larami has been taking cover . . . expressing sympathy for the family of the 15-year-old Boston youth who was killed.

The controversy has thrust closely held Larami into a dilemma — particularly because the water gun is the company's biggest profit-maker, experts say. Other companies make similar guns, such as Tyco Toys Inc.'s Super Saturator, but Larami's Super Soaker is the top-selling water gun by far.

For the most part, Larami has been taking cover. Earlier this week, it issued a one-page statement, expressing sympathy for the family of the 15-year-old Boston youth who was killed, while noting that the violence and misuse of the water gun is "something we cannot control."

No one in the 50-employee company, other than Al Davis, executive vice president, is authorized to speak to the media or public officials. And Mr. Davis, the Philadelphia-based company said, isn't available for comment.

The mayor of Boston, Raymond Flynn, has urged retailers to stop selling the gun, and Michigan state Sen. Gilbert DiNello has introduced a bill to outlaw the toy. In response, Woolworth's and Bradlee's have pulled the product off the shelves in some of their stores, and the Sharper Image has said it will give to charity the money it receives from the sale of the toy guns in its Boston stores. . . .

The Super Soaker, which comes in three models varying in price from $10 to $30 apiece, is a best-selling toy, according to NPD Group, a Port Washington, N.Y., researcher that supplies industry sales figures to the Toys Manufacturers Association and to toy retailers.

Super Soaker has been taking most of the heat in recent days because it is by far the most popular gun of its kind on the market. Analysts estimate that Larami's water gun represents more than 70% of the water-gun market. The gun's air compression system, which propels water as much as 50 feet away, is patented to keep competitors from copying its technology. But that hasn't stopped others from riding on the wave of this summer's hot toy. For example, Tyco's new Super Saturator, a battery-operated gun, shoots water in spurts, lawnmower-style, as much as 35 feet. The Super Saturator hasn't been linked to any violent incidents. Tyco officials couldn't be reached for comment yesterday.

The mayor of Boston urged retailers to stop selling the Super Soaker, a high-powered toy water gun, after a 15-year-old youth was killed in an incident involving the toy.

From Joseph Pereira, "Toy Maker Faces Dilemmas as Water Gun Spurs Violence," *Wall Street Journal* (June 11, 1992), B1, B9. Reprinted by permission of *Wall Street Journal,* © 1992 Dow Jones & Company, Inc. All Rights Reserved Worldwide.

WHAT'S AHEAD The introductory case describes societal efforts to curb sales of a toy gun being produced by Larami Corporation. Management at Larami must face the difficult challenge of making a profit from its Super Soaker while facing the public criticism that this toy gun is encouraging youth violence resulting in serious injuries and even death. This chapter presents material that managers such as those at Larami can use to help analyze and handle the dilemma of reaching company objectives while protecting or improving the welfare of society. Specifically, the chapter discusses (1) fundamentals of social responsibility, (2) social responsiveness, (3) social responsibility activities and management functions, (4) how society can help business meet social obligations, and (5) ethics.

FUNDAMENTALS OF SOCIAL RESPONSIBILITY

Corporate social responsibility is the managerial obligation to take action that protects and improves both the welfare of society as a whole and the interests of the organization.

The term *social responsibility* means different things to different people.[1] For purposes of this chapter, however, **corporate social responsibility** is the managerial obligation to take action that protects and improves the welfare of society as a whole and organizational interests as well.[2] According to the concept of corporate social responsibility, a manager must strive to achieve both organizational and societal goals.[3]

The amount of attention given to the area of social responsibility by both management and society has increased in recent years and probably will continue to increase in the future.[4] The following sections present the fundamentals of social responsibility of businesses by discussing (1) the Davis model of corporate social responsibility, (2) areas of corporate social responsibility, and (3) varying opinions on social responsibility.

The Davis Model of Corporate Social Responsibility

A generally accepted model of corporate social responsibility was developed by Keith Davis.[5] Stated simply, Davis's model is a list of five propositions that describe why and how business should adhere to the obligation to take action that protects and improves the welfare of society and the organization:

Proposition 1: Social responsibility arises from social power. This proposition is built on the premise that business has a significant amount of influence on, or power over, such critical social issues as minority employment and environmental pollution. In essence, the collective action of all businesses in the country determines to a major degree the proportion of minorities employed and the prevailing condition of the environment in which all citizens must live.

Building on this premise, Davis reasons that since business has this power over society, society can and must hold business responsible for social conditions that result from exercising this power.[6] Davis explains that society's legal system does not expect more of business than it does of each individual citizen exercising personal power.

Proposition 2: Business shall operate as a two-way open system, with open receipt of inputs from society and open disclosure of its operation to the public. According to this proposition, business must be willing to listen to society's representatives in regard to what must be done to sustain or improve societal welfare. In turn, society must be willing to listen to the reports of business on what it is doing to meet its social responsibilities. Davis suggests that ongoing honest and open communications between business and society's representatives must exist if the overall welfare of society is to be maintained or improved.

Proposition 3: The social costs and benefits of an activity, product, or service shall be thoroughly calculated and considered in deciding whether to proceed with it. This proposition stresses that technical feasibility and economic profitability are not the only factors that should influence business decision making. Business also should consider both the long- and short-term societal consequences of all business activities before such activities are undertaken.

Proposition 4: Social costs related to each activity, product, or service shall be passed on to the consumer. This proposition states that business cannot be expected to finance completely activities that may be socially advantageous but economically disadvantageous. The cost of maintaining socially desirable activities within business should be passed on to consumers through higher prices for the goods or services related to the socially desirable activities.

Proposition 5: Business institutions, as citizens, have the responsibility to become involved in certain social problems that are outside their normal areas of operation. This last proposition makes the point that if a business possesses the expertise to solve a social problem with which it may not be directly associated, it should be held responsible for helping society solve that problem. Davis reasons that because business eventually will share increased profit from a generally improved society, business should share in the responsibility of all citizenry to generally improve society.

QUALITY HIGHLIGHT
Xerox Corporation Provides Social Service

The Xerox Corporation developed a program that reflects the Davis model of corporate responsibility. Xerox Corporation has found that following the strategy of maintaining a serious commitment to community improvement helps the company to reach its goal of high quality products. Xerox implements this strategy through its Social Service Leave Program, which provides Xerox employees with a paid leave in order to pursue a community service project. The employees themselves develop the ideas for useful projects to be performed within the community.

The program reflects both Xerox's high regard for the community and its regard for the self-development of its employees. The company recognizes that its respect for employee initiative and social concerns fosters a more effective and positive work force and work environment, which inevitably leads to improved product quality.

According to Marian Whipple, Xerox's Community and Employee Programs manager, employees in good standing at Xerox who have been with the company for at least three years can apply for the leave program. About sixty employees apply each year to a committee that judges the merits of the community projects and awards the leaves. Xerox spends about $300,000 per year on the program, which focuses on such projects as combating homelessness, child abuse, and drug abuse.

Corporate social responsibility programs, such as this operation to distribute groceries to homeless people, can help foster an effective and positive work force and work environment, which leads to improved product quality.

BACK TO THE CASE

Social responsibility is the obligation of a business manager to take action that protects and improves the welfare of society along with the interests of the organization. Management at Larami, as discussed in the introductory case, presently faces the issue of social responsibility that the company may have for curbing youth violence. Following the logic of Davis's social responsibility model, if the sale of the Super Soaker actually does encourage youths to perform violent acts, Larami management will probably have to address this violence issue by somehow modifying the design of the product and the way it is marketed. The real challenge in this situation is to determine whether indeed the sale of the Super Soaker causes these violent acts. Should Larami management hold itself responsible for contributing to the delinquency of minors simply because some young customers use Super Soakers with violent intent? Larami management must carefully weigh the social costs and benefits of providing society with such toys and then proceed with the course of action that will best benefit society as well as Larami.

The information presented thus far in this chapter also implies that Larami management should seriously listen to society's concerns about the Super Soaker. Perhaps the best response to this situation is for Larami management to gather as much information as possible concerning violent acts committed with the

Super Soaker and take steps such as redesigning or refocusing their marketing of the product to minimize its use in any future acts of this nature.

As a result of handling this situation, Larami management could possibly acquire some special expertise in developing products that not only discourage youth violence but also encourage young people to be positive forces in their communities. This expertise could certainly benefit society if Larami management shared it with business people in other fields. For example, Larami management might be able to help the president of a publishing company publish books that discourage youth violence.

Areas of Corporate Social Responsibility

The areas in which business can become involved to protect and improve the welfare of society are numerous and diverse (see Table 3.1 on pages 56 and 57). Perhaps the most publicized of these areas are urban affairs, consumer affairs, and environmental affairs, and employment practices affairs.[7]

Varying Opinions on Social Responsibility

Although numerous businesses are involved in and will continue to be involved in social responsibility activities, much controversy persists about whether such involvement is necessary or appropriate. The following two sections present some arguments for and against businesses performing social responsibility activities.[8]

Arguments FOR Business Performing Social Responsibility Activities

The best-known argument supporting the performance of social responsibility activities by business was alluded to earlier in this chapter. This argument begins with the premise that business as a whole is a subset of society and exerts a significant impact on the way in which society exists. The argument continues that, since business is such an influential member of society, it has the responsibility to help maintain and improve the overall welfare of society. After all, since society asks no more and no less of any of its members, why should business be exempt from such responsibility?

In addition, some make the argument that business should perform social responsibility activities because profitability and growth go hand in hand with responsible treatment of employees, customers, and the community. In essence, this argument implies that performing social responsibility activities is a means of earning greater organizational profit.[9]

However, later empirical studies have not demonstrated any clear relationship between corporate social responsibility and profitability. In fact, several companies that were acknowledged as leaders in social commitment during the 1960s and '70s, including Control Data Corporation, Atlantic Richfield, Dayton-Hudson, Levi Strauss, and Polaroid, experienced serious financial difficulties during the 1980s.[10] (No relationship between corporate social responsibility activities and these financial difficulties was shown, however.)

ETHICS HIGHLIGHT
International Business Machines (IBM) Argues for Philanthropy

There are many good reasons why companies should perform social responsibility activities. IBM, a giant in the computer technology industry, is one company that strongly believes that businesses should indeed pursue such activities.

James Parkel, the Director for Corporate Support and Community Programs at IBM believes that pursuing social responsibility activities is clearly a matter of survival for modern businesses. According to Parkel, people of today are simply not going to accept into their communities companies that are perceived as poor corporate citizens.

One area of social responsibility on which Parkel focuses at IBM is corporate philanthropy, the generous giving to charities to show goodwill toward fellow members of society. Annual corporate charitable gifts at IBM recently reached $5.9 billion or 1.9 percent of pretax profits. Until recently, this money has been donated by IBM with little thought regarding what corporate objectives were and how they might be accomplished. Now, however, donations are being made to try to enhance the attainment of corporate objectives and are becoming known as "strategic philanthropy."

According to the American Association of Fund-Raising for Philanthropy, given current economic conditions, the growth of corporate philanthropy has slowed somewhat over the past few years. As corporate budgets have tightened, even philanthropy is being scrutinized from a profit-generating viewpoint. Overall, education gets the largest share of the corporate philanthropy "pie" by receiving 38 percent of total dollars given by companies. Health care companies such as hospitals rank second. ▶

Many corporations have begun to practice strategic philanthropy—giving which will help to enhance the attainment of corporate objectives. Education receives 38 percent of such corporate giving.

Arguments AGAINST Business Performing Social Responsibility Activities

The best-known argument against business performing social responsibility activities is advanced by Milton Friedman, one of America's most distinguished economists. Friedman argues that to make business managers simultaneously responsible to business owners for reaching profit objectives and to society for enhancing societal welfare represents a conflict of interest that has the potential to cause the demise of business as it is known today.[11] According to Friedman, this demise almost certainly will occur if business continually is forced to perform socially responsible behavior that is in direct conflict with private organizational objectives.[12]

Friedman also argues that to require business managers to pursue socially responsible objectives may in fact be unethical, since it requires managers to spend money that really belongs to other individuals:

> In a free enterprise, private property system, a corporate executive is an employee of the owners of the business. He has direct responsibility to his employers. That responsibility is to conduct the business in accordance with their desires, which generally will be to make as much money as possible while conforming to the basic rules of society, both those embodied in law and those embodied in ethical custom. . . . Insofar as his actions reduce returns to stockholders, he is spending their money. Insofar as his actions raise the price to customers, he is spending the customers' money.[13]

An example that Friedman could use to illustrate his argument is the Control Data Corporation. Former chairman William Norris involved Control Data in many socially responsible programs that cost the company millions of dollars — from building plants in the inner city and employing a minority work force to researching farming on the Alaskan tundra. When Control Data began to incur net losses of millions of dollars in the mid-1980s, critics blamed Norris's "do-gooder" mentality. Eventually, a new chairman was installed to restructure the company and return it to profitability.[14]

Many more arguments for and against business performing social responsibility activities are presented in Table 3.2.

BACK TO THE CASE

Table 3.1 indicates that there are many different areas of social responsibility in which Larami management could become involved. This situation with the Super Soaker, however, can probably best be categorized under the heading of "product line," since society's criticisms focus on how misuse of the product can cause pain, injury, or even death to young people.

Whatever Larami management did to ease this situation with the Super Soaker would probably result in a short-run decrease in Super Soaker sales and perhaps even cost the company additional money as management looked for and invested in better ways to manufacture the product. Although at first glance,

TABLE 3.1 Major social responsibility areas in which business can become involved

Categories of Social Responsibility Items

Product Line
Internal standards for product
- Quality (e.g., does it last?)
- Safety (e.g., can it harm users or children finding it?)
- Disposal (e.g., is it biodegradable?)
- Design (e.g., will its use or even "easy" misuse cause pain, injury, or death?)

Average product life comparisons versus
- Competition
- Substitute products
- Internal standards or state-of-the-art regular built-in obsolescence

Product performance
- Efficacy (e.g., does it do what it is supposed to do?)
- Guarantees/warranties (e.g., are guarantees sufficient, reasonable?)
- Service policy
- Service availability
- Service pricing
- Utility

Packaging
- Environmental impact (degree of disposability; recyclability)
- Comparisons with competition (type and extent of packaging)

Marketing Practices
Sales practices
- Legal standards
- "Undue" pressure (a qualitative judgment)

Credit practices against legal standards

Accuracy of advertising claims—specific government complaints

Nondiscriminatory portrayal of women and minorities in advertising

Consumer complaints about marketing practices
- Clear explanation of credit terms
- Clear explanation of purchase price
- Complaint answering policy
  - —Answered at all
  - —Investigated carefully
  - —Grievances redressed (and cost)
  - —Remedial action to prevent future occurrences

Adequate consumer information on
- Product use (e.g., dosage, duration of use, etc.)
- Product misuse

Fair pricing
- Between countries
- Between states
- Between locations

Packaging

Employee Education, Training, and Support
Policy on leaves of absence for
- Full-time schooling
- Courses given during working hours

Dollars spent on training
- Formal vocational training
- Training for disadvantaged worker
- OJT (very difficult to isolate)
- Tuition (job-related versus non-job-related)
- Special upgrading and career development programs
- Compare versus competition

Special training program results (systematic evaluations)
- Number trained in each program per year
- Cost per trainee (less subsidy)
- Number or percent workers still with company

Plans for future programs

Career training and counseling

Failure rates

Extend personnel understanding
- Jobs
- Skills required later
- Incentive system now available
- Specific actions for promotion
- Provision of day care resources

Corporate Philanthropy
Contribution performance
- By category, for example:
  - —Art
  - —Education
  - —Poverty
  - —Health
  - —Community development
  - —Public service advertising
- Dollars (plus materials and work hours, if available)
  - —As a percent of pretax earnings
  - —Compared to competition

Selection criteria for contributions

Procedures for performance tracking of recipient institutions or groups

Programs for permitting and encouraging employee involvement in social projects
- On company time
- After hours only
- Use of company facilities and equipment
- Reimbursement of operating units for replaceable "lost" time
- Human resource support
  - —Number of people
  - —Work hours

Extent of employee involvement in philanthropy decision making

Environmental Control
Measurable pollution resulting from
- Acquisition of raw materials
- Production processes
- Products
- Transportation of intermediate and finished products

Violations of government (federal, state, and local) standards

Cost estimates to correct current deficiencies

Extent to which various plants exceed current legal standards (e.g., particulate matter discharged)

Resources devoted to pollution control
- Capital expenditures (absolute and percent)
- R & D investments
- Personnel involved full-time, part-time
- Organizational "strength" of personnel involved

Competitive company performance (e.g., capital expenditures)

Effort to monitor new standards as proposed

Programs to keep employees alert to spills and other pollution-related accidents

Procedures for evaluating environmental impact of new packages or products

External Relations

Community Development
Support of minority and community enterprises through
- Purchasing
- Subcontracting

Investment practices
- Ensuring equal opportunity before locating new facilities
- Identifying opportunities to serve community needs through business expansion (e.g., housing rehabilitation or teaching machines)
- Funds in minority banks

Government Relations
Specific input to public policy through research and analysis

Participation and development of business/government programs

Political contributions

Disclosure of Information/ Communications
Extent of public disclosure of performance by activity category

Measure of employee understanding of programs such as:
- Pay and benefits

TABLE 3.1 Continued

- Equal opportunity policies and programs
- Position on major economic or political issues (as appropriate)

Relations/communications with constituencies such as stockholders, fund managers, major customers, and so on

International
Comparisons of policy and performance between countries and versus local standards

Employee Relations, Benefits, and Satisfaction with Work
Comparisons with competition (and/or national averages)
- Salary and wage levels
- Retirement plans
- Turnover and retention by level
- Profit sharing
- Day care and maternity
- Transportation
- Insurance, health programs, and other fringes
- Participation in ownership of business through stock purchases

Comparisons of operating units on promotions, terminations, hires against breakdowns by
- Age
- Sex
- Race
- Education level

Performance review system and procedures for communication with employees whose performance is below average

Promotion policy — equitable and understood

Transfer policy

Termination policy (i.e., how early is "notice" given)

General working environment and conditions
- Physical surroundings
  - — Heat
  - — Ventilation
  - — Space/person
  - — Lighting
  - — Air conditioning
  - — Noise
- Leisure, recreation, cultural opportunities

Fringe benefits as a percent of salary for various salary levels

Evaluation of employee benefit preferences (questions can be posed as choices)

Evaluation of employee understanding of current fringe benefits

Union/industrial relations
- Grievances
- Strikes

Confidentiality and security of personnel data

Minority and Women Employment and Advancement
Current hiring policies in relation to the requirements of all affirmative action programs

Specific program of accountability for performance

Company versus local, industry, and national performance
- Number and percent minority and women employees hired in various job classifications over last five years
- Number and percent of new minority and women employees in last two or three years by job classification
- Minority and women and nonminority turnover
- Indictments for discriminatory hiring practices

Percent minority and women employment in major facilities relative to minority labor force available locally

Number of minority groups and women members in positions of high responsibility

Promotion performance of minority groups and women

Specific hiring and job upgrading goals established for minority groups and women
- Basic personnel strategy
- Nature and cost of special recruiting efforts
- Risks taken in hiring minority groups and women

Programs to ease integration of minority groups and women into company operations (e.g., awareness efforts)

Specialized minority and women career counseling

Special recruiting efforts for minority groups and women

Opportunities for the physically handicapped
- Specific programs
- Numbers employed

Employee Safety and Health
Work environment measures
- OSHA requirements (and extent of compliance)
- Other measures of working conditions

Safety performance
- Accident severity — work hours lost per million worked
- Accident frequency (number of lost time accidents per million hours)
- Disabling injuries
- Fatalities

Services provided (and cost of programs and human resources) for
- Addictive treatment (alcohol, narcotics)
- Mental health

Spending for safety equipment
- Required by law/regulation
- Not required

Special safety programs (including safety instruction)

Comparisons of health and safety performance with competition and industry in general

Developments/innovations in health and safety

Employee health measures (e.g., sick days, examinations)

Food facilities
- Cost/serving to employee, to company
- Nutritional evaluation

TABLE 3.2 Major arguments for and against business performing social responsibility activities

Major Arguments for Social Responsibility

1. It is in the best interest of the business to promote and improve the communities where it does business.
2. Social actions can be profitable.
3. It is the ethical thing to do.
4. It improves the public image of the firm.
5. It increases the viability of the business system. Business exists because it gives society benefits. Society can amend or take away its charter. This is the "iron law of responsibility."
6. It is necessary to avoid government regulation.
7. Sociocultural norms require it.
8. Laws cannot be passed for all circumstances. Thus, business must assume responsibility to maintain an orderly, legal society.
9. It is in the stockholders' best interest. It will improve the price of stock in the long run because the stock market will view the company as less risky and less open to public attack and therefore award it a higher price-earnings ratio.
10. Society should give business a chance to solve social problems that government has failed to solve.
11. Business, by some groups, is considered to be the institution with the financial and human resources to solve social problems.
12. Prevention of problems is better than cures — so let business solve problems before they become too great.

Major Arguments Against Social Responsibility

1. It might be illegal.
2. Business plus government equals a monolith.
3. Social actions cannot be measured.
4. It violates profit maximization.
5. Cost of social responsibility is too great and would increase prices too much.
6. Business lacks social skills to solve societal problems.
7. It would dilute business's primary purposes.
8. It would weaken U.S. balance of payments because price of goods has to go up to pay for social programs.
9. Business already has too much power. Such involvement would make business too powerful.
10. Business lacks accountability to the public. Thus, the public would have no control over its social involvement.
11. Such business involvement lacks broad public support.

such action might seem unbusinesslike, performing such social responsibility activities could significantly improve the public image of Larami and be instrumental in Larami's maintaining long-run company growth.

Conclusions About Business Performing Social Responsibility Activities

The preceding two sections presented several major arguments for and against businesses performing social responsibility activities. Regardless of which argument or combination of arguments particular managers might support, they generally should make a concerted effort to (1) perform all legally required social responsibility activities, (2) consider voluntarily performing social responsibility activities beyond those legally required, and (3) inform all relevant individuals of the extent to which their organization will become involved in performing social responsibility activities.

Performing Required Social Responsibility Activities. Federal legislation requires that businesses perform certain social responsibility activities. In fact, several government agencies have been established and are maintained to develop such business-related legislation and to make sure the laws are followed (see Table 3.3). The Environmental Protection Agency does indeed have the authority to require businesses to adhere to certain socially responsible environmental standards. Examples of specific legislation that require the performance of corporate social responsibility activities are (1) the Equal Pay Act of 1963, (2) the Equal Employment Opportunity Act of 1972, (3) the Highway Safety Act of 1978, and (4) the Clean Air Act Amendments of 1990. The highlight on page 60 discusses DuPont's involvement with a clean air issue.

Voluntarily Performing Social Responsibility Activities. Adherence to legislated social responsibilities represents the minimum standard of social responsibility performance that business managers must achieve. Managers must ask themselves, however, how far beyond the minimum they should attempt to go.

The process of determining how far to go is simple to describe yet difficult and complicated to implement. It entails assessing the positive and negative outcomes of performing social responsibility activities over both the short and long term and then performing only the social responsibility activities that maximize management system success while making some desirable contribution to maintaining or improving the welfare of society.

Recent events at Sara Lee Bakery's New Hampton, Iowa, plant illustrate how company management can voluntarily take action to protect employee health. Many employees at the plant began developing carpal tunnel syndrome, a debilitating wrist disorder caused by repeated hand motions. Instead of simply letting their employees go through physical therapy and watching the morale of the town drop, Sara Lee investigated the problem. Managers took suggestions from factory workers and had their engineers design tools to alleviate forearm problems. The result was a virtual elimination of carpal tunnel syndrome at the plant within a very short time.[15]

Sandra Holmes asked top executives in 560 of the major firms in such areas as commercial banking, life insurance, transportation, and utilities to indicate the possible

TABLE 3.3 Primary functions of several federal agencies involved with social responsibility legislation

Federal Agency	*Primary Agency Activities*
Equal Employment Opportunity Commission	Investigates and conciliates employment discrimination complaints that are based on race, sex, or creed
Office of Federal Contract Compliance Programs	Ensures that employers holding federal contracts grant equal employment opportunity to people regardless of race or sex
Environmental Protection Agency	Formulates and enforces environmental standards in such areas as water, air, and noise pollution
Consumer Product Safety Commission	Strives to reduce consumer inquiries related to product design, labeling, etc., by promoting clarity of these messages
Occupational Safety and Health Administration	Regulates safety and health conditions in non-government workplaces
National Highway Traffic Safety Administration	Attempts to reduce traffic accidents through the regulation of transportation-related manufacturers and products
Mining Enforcement and Safety Administration	Attempts to improve safety conditions for mine workers by enforcing all mine safety and equipment standards

TABLE 3.4 Outcomes of social responsibility involvement expected by executives and the percent who expected them

	Percent Expecting
Positive Outcomes	
Enhanced corporate reputation and goodwill	97.4
Strengthening of the social system in which the corporation functions	89.0
Strengthening of the economic system in which the corporation functions	74.3
Greater job satisfaction among all employees	72.3
Avoidance of government regulation	63.7
Greater job satisfaction among executives	62.8
Increased chances for survival of the firm	60.7
Ability to attract better managerial talent	55.5
Increased long-term profitability	52.9
Strengthening of the pluralistic nature of American society	40.3
Maintaining or gaining customers	38.2
Investor preference for socially responsible firms	36.6
Increased short-term profitability	15.2
Negative Outcomes	
Decreased short-term profitability	59.7
Conflict of economic or financial and social goals	53.9
Increased prices for consumers	41.4
Conflict in criteria for assessing managerial performance	27.2
Disaffection of stockholders	24.1
Decreased productivity	18.8
Decreased long-term profitability	13.1
Increased government regulation	11.0
Weakening of the economic system in which the corporation functions	7.9
Weakening of the social system in which the corporation functions	3.7

negative and positive outcomes their firms could expect to experience from performing social responsibility activities.[16] Table 3.4 lists the outcomes and indicates the percentage of executives questioned who expected to experience them. Although this information furnishes managers with general insights on how involved their organizations should become in social responsibility activities, it does not and cannot furnish them with a clear-cut statement about what to do. Managers can determine the appropriate level of social responsibility involvement for a specific organization only by examining and reacting to specific factors related to that organization.

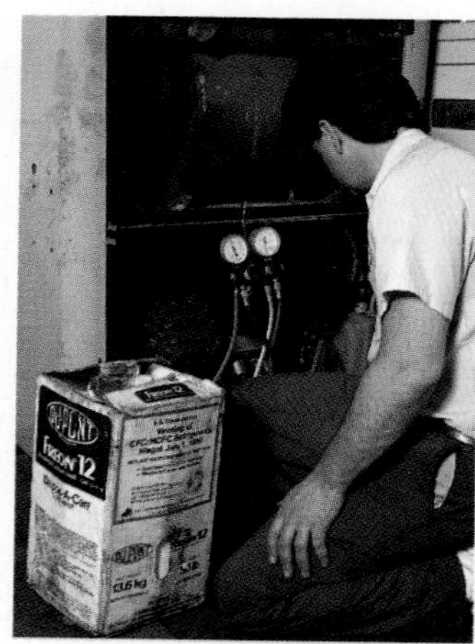

Dupont, in an attempt to ensure that its products would not contribute to further depletion of the ozone layer, has stepped up research efforts to study the environmental effects of gases from its products being released into the atmosphere.

GLOBAL HIGHLIGHT
DuPont Protects the Environment

E.I. DuPont de Nemours and Company, a producer of chemical products, exemplifies a company whose actions affect the environment at both national and international levels. When scientists in the early 1970s began to theorize that certain types of gases—gases related to some of DuPont's products—could be contributing to the breakdown of the ozone layer, DuPont encouraged further research and began looking for alternative products. As more conclusive evidence of ozone depletion caused by these gases became available, the company stepped up research efforts in order to make informed decisions about its products and their impact on the environment. As a company that conducts business in many countries, DuPont wished to assure its customers and concerned citizens throughout thu world that it was sensitive to the ozone issue and that it was acting in a socially responsible manner to ensure that its products would not contribute to further deterioration of the ozone layer.

Critics, however, could argue that DuPont is merely reacting to pressure from stakeholders and/or outside pressures from environmentalists instead of proactively seeking solutions to global environmental problems. ▶

Communicating the Degree of Social Responsibility Involvement. Determining the extent to which a business should perform social responsibility activities beyond legal requirements is a subjective process. Despite this subjectivity, however, managers should have a well-defined position in this vital management area and should inform all organization members of the position. Taking these steps will ensure that managers and organization members behave consistently to support the position and that societal expectations of what a particular organization can achieve in this area are realistic.

BACK TO THE CASE Some social responsibility activities are legislated and therefore must be performed by business. Most of the legislated activities, however, are aimed at larger companies. Even though Larami is a significant company in the toy industry, there probably is no existing legislation that would require Larami management to modify its Super Soaker.

Because Larami management is not required by law to modify its Super Soaker for the benefit of society, whatever modifications management might decide to make would be strictly voluntary. In making this decision, Larami management should assess the positive and negative outcomes of modifying its Super Soaker over both the long and short term and then make whatever modifications, if any, that would maximize the success of Larami as well as offer some desirable contribution to society. Larami management should let all organization members, as well as the public, know how the company feels about this situation with the Super Soaker and why.

SOCIAL RESPONSIVENESS

The previous section discussed social responsibility as a business's obligation to take action that protects and improves the welfare of society along with the business's own interests. This section defines and discusses **social responsiveness** as the degree of effectiveness and efficiency an organization displays in pursuing its social responsibilities.[17] The greater the degree of effectiveness and efficiency, the more socially responsive the organization is said to be. The two sections that follow discuss (1) social responsiveness and decision making and (2) approaches to meeting social responsibilities.

Social responsiveness is the degree of effectiveness and efficiency an organization displays in pusuing its social responsibilities.

Social Responsiveness and Decision Making

The socially responsive organization that is both effective and efficient meets its social responsibilities and does not waste organizational resources in the process. Determining exactly which social responsibilities an organization should pursue and then deciding how to pursue them are perhaps the two most critical decision-making aspects of maintaining a high level of social responsiveness within an organization.

Figure 3.1 is a flowchart that managers can use as a general guideline for making social responsibility decisions that enhance the social responsiveness of their organization. This figure implies that for managers to achieve and maintain a high level of social responsiveness within an organization, they must pursue only the social responsibilities that their organization actually possesses and has a right to undertake. Furthermore, once managers decide to meet a specific social responsibility, they must decide the best way to undertake activities related to meeting this obligation. That is, managers must

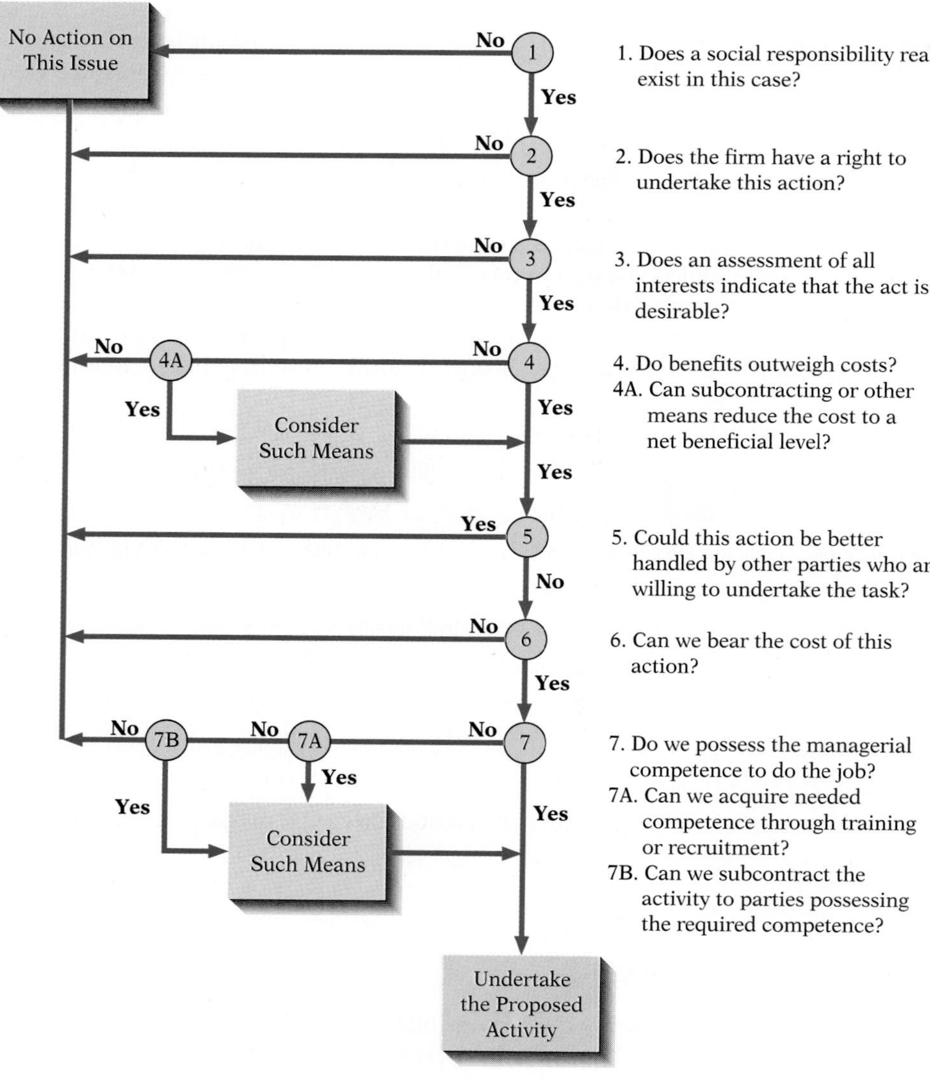

FIGURE 3.1 Flowchart of social responsibility decision making that generally will enhance the social responsiveness of an organization

decide whether their organization should undertake the activities on its own or acquire the help of outsiders with more expertise in the area.

Approaches to Meeting Social Responsibilities

In addition to decision making, various managerial approaches to meeting social obligations are another determinant of an organization's level of social responsiveness. According to Lipson, a desirable and socially responsive approach to meeting social obligations (1) incorporates social goals into the annual planning process; (2) seeks comparative industry norms for social programs; (3) presents reports to organization members, the board of directors, and stockholders on social responsibility progress; (4) experiments with different approaches for measuring social performance; and (5) attempts to measure the cost of social programs as well as the return on social program investments.[18]

S. Prakash Sethi presents three management approaches to meeting social obligations: (1) the social obligation approach, (2) the social responsibility approach, and (3) the social responsiveness approach.[19] Each of these approaches and the types of behavior typical of them on several dimensions are presented in Table 3.5.

TABLE 3.5 Three approaches to social responsibility and the types of behavior associated with each

Dimensions of Behavior	*Approach 1: Social Obligation Prescriptive*	*Approach 2: Social Responsibility Prescriptive*	*Approach 3: Social Responsiveness Anticipatory and Preventive*
Search for legitimacy	Confines legitimacy to legal and economic criteria only; does not violate laws; equates profitable operations with fulfilling social expectations	Accepts the reality of limited relevance of legal and market criteria of legitimacy in actual practice; willing to consider and accept broader extralegal and extramarket criteria for measuring corporate performance and social role	Accepts its role as defined by the social system and therefore subject to change; recognizes importance of profitable operations but includes other criteria
Ethical norms	Considers business value-neutral; managers expected to behave according to their own ethical standards	Defines norms in community-related terms: e.g., good corporate citizen; avoids taking moral stand on issues that may harm its economic interests or go against prevailing social norms (majority views)	Takes definite stand on issues of public concern; advocates institutional ethical norms even though they may be detrimental to its immediate economic interest or prevailing social norms
Social accountability for corporate actions	Construes narrowly as limited to stockholders; jealousy guards its prerogatives against outsiders	Construes narrowly for legal purposes, but broadened to include groups affected by its actions; management more outward looking	Willing to account for its actions to other groups, even those not directly affected by its actions
Operating strategy	Exploitative and defensive adaptation; maximum externalization of costs	Reactive adaptation; where identifiable, internalizes previously external costs; maintains current standards of physical and social environment; compensates victims of pollution and other corporate-related activities even in the absence of clearly established legal grounds; develops industry-wide standards	Proactive adaptation; takes lead in developing and adapting new technology for environmental protectors; evaluates side effects of corporate actions and eliminates them prior to the action's being taken; anticipates future social changes and develops internal structures to cope with them
Response to social pressures	Maintains low public profile, but if attacked, uses PR methods to upgrade its public image; denies any deficiencies; blames public dissatisfaction on ignorance or failure to understand corporate functions; discloses information only where legally required	Accepts responsibility for solving current problems; will admit deficiencies in former practices and attempt to persuade public that its current practices meet social norms; attitude toward critics conciliatory; freer information disclosures than in approach 1	Willingly discusses activities with outside groups; makes information freely available to public; accepts formal and informal inputs from outside groups in decision making; is willing to be publicly evaluated for its various activities
Activities pertaining to government actions	Strongly resists any regulation of its activities except when it needs help to protect its market position; avoids contact; resists any demands for information beyond that legally required	Preserves management discretion in corporate decisions, but cooperates with government in research to improve industry-wide standards; participates in political processes and encourages employees to do likewise	Openly communicates with government; assists in enforcing existing laws and developing evaluations of business practices; objects publicly to government activities that it feels are detrimental to the public's good

Continued

TABLE 3.5 Continued

Dimensions of Behavior	*Approach 1: Social Obligation Prescriptive*	*Approach 2: Social Responsibility Prescriptive*	*Approach 3: Social Responsiveness Anticipatory and Preventive*
Legislative and political activities	Seeks to maintain status quo; actively opposes laws that would internalize any previously externalized costs; seeks to keep lobbying activities secret	Willing to work with outside groups for good environmental laws; concedes need for change in some status quo laws; less secrecy in lobbying than in approach 1	Avoids meddling in politics and does not pursue special-interest laws; assists legislative bodies in developing better laws where relevant; promotes honesty and openness in government and in its own lobbying activities
Philanthropy	Contributes only when direct benefit to it clearly shown; otherwise, views contributions as responsibility of individual employees	Contributes to noncontroversial and established causes; matches employee contributions	Activities of appraoch 2 *plus* support and contributions to new, controversial groups whose needs it sees as unfulfilled and increasingly important

The **social obligation approach** is an approach to meeting social obligations that considers business to have primarily economic purposes and confines social responsibility activity mainly to conformance to existing legislation.

The **social responsibility approach** is an approach to meeting social obligations that considers business as having both societal and economic goals.

The **social responsiveness approach** is an approach to meeting social obligations that considers business to have societal and economic goals as will as the obligation to anticipate upcoming social problems and to work actively toward preventing their appearance.

As the table indicates, each of Sethi's three approaches contains behavior that reflects a somewhat different attitude with regard to business performing social responsibility activities. The **social obligation approach,** for example, considers business as having primarily economic purposes and confines social responsibility activity mainly to conformance to existing legislation. The **social responsibility approach** sees business as having both economic and societal goals. The **social responsiveness approach** considers business as having both societal and economic goals as well as the obligation to anticipate upcoming social problems and to work actively toward preventing their appearance.

Organizations characterized by attitudes and behaviors consistent with the social responsiveness approach generally are more socially responsive than organizations characterized by attitudes and behaviors consistent with either the social responsibility approach or the social obligation approach. Also, organizations characterized by the social responsibility approach generally achieve higher levels of social responsiveness than organizations characterized by the social obligation approach. As one moves from the social obligation approach to the social responsiveness approach, management becomes more proactive. Proactive managers will do what is prudent from a business viewpoint to reduce liabilities whether an action is required by law or not.[20]

DIVERSITY HIGHLIGHT
Social Responsiveness and the Equal Opportunity Act at Opryland

The Equal Opportunity Act was passed in 1972 to eliminate employment discrimination based upon race, sex, or color. The management attitude toward performing Equal Opportunity Act social responsibilities activities at Opryland illustrates the social responsiveness approach.

The inevitability of having a future work force that is characterized by cultural diversity is driving many hotels to aggressively recruit minorities for management-level positions. Such hotels see the careful building of this work force as a means not only of enhancing worker productivity, but also of attracting a more diverse customer, a growing segment of the market.

Because the pool of minority candidates for hotel manager positions is relatively small, many hotels and hotel chains are aggressively recruiting in this area. At the Opryland Hotel, for example, in order to encourage minority participation in the hiring process, its human resource department supports and has developed a wide range of special minority recruitment programs. One such program is called INROADS. By participating in INROADS, the Opryland Hotel gives minority college students the financial means to experience four years of hotel-management training. Upon graduation from such a college program, students would be qualified for entry level management positions in a hotel such as Opryland. Although participating in INROADS will not solve Opryland Hotel minority recruitment challenges in the short run, it does help to increase the supply of minority candidates to fill its management positions in the longer run. ▶

Barbara Lowe, Recruitment Manager at Opryland Hotel, supports a wide range of recruitment programs as a way to attract qualified minority applicants for entry-level management positions.

BACK TO THE CASE Larami management should strive to maintain a relatively high level of social responsiveness in pursuing issues such as the one involving the Super Soaker. To do this, management should make decisions appropriate to the company's social responsibility area and should approach the meeting of those social responsibilities in an appropriate way.

In terms of the Super Soaker situation, Larami management must first decide if the company has social responsibility to fight, through the design and marketing of its products, society's problem of youth violence. Assuming that management decides that Larami has such a responsibility, management must then determine exactly how to accomplish the activities necessary to meet this responsibility. For example, can the people presently employed by Larami develop and implement a modified Super Soaker design or a new marketing campaign that would minimize Super Soaker use in youth violence incidents? Or, should management hire independent consultants to recommend and install such product design and/or marketing modifications? Making appropriate decisions of this nature will help Larami management effectively and efficiently meet social obligations.

In terms of an approach to meeting social responsibilities that probably will increase Larami's social responsiveness, management should try to view its organization as having both societal and economic goals. In addition, Larami management should attempt to anticipate the arrival of social problems, such as the one generated by the Super Soaker situation, and should actively work to prevent their appearance.

SOCIAL RESPONSIBILITY ACTIVITIES AND MANAGEMENT FUNCTIONS

This section discusses social responsibility as a major organizational activity. As such, it should be subjected to the same management techniques used for other major organizational activities, such as production, personnel, finance, and marketing activities. Managers have known for some time that to achieve desirable results in these areas, managers must be effective in planning, organizing, influencing, and controlling. Achieving social responsibility results is not any different. The following sections discuss planning, organizing, influencing, and controlling social responsibility activities.

Planning Social Responsibility Activities

Planning was defined in chapter 1 as the process of determining how the organization will achieve its objectives, or get where it wants to go. Planning social responsibility activities therefore involves determining how the organization will achieve its social responsibility objectives, or get where it wants to go in the area of social responsibility. The following sections discuss how the planning of social responsibility activities is related to the overall planning process of the organization and how the social responsibility policy of the organization can be converted into action.

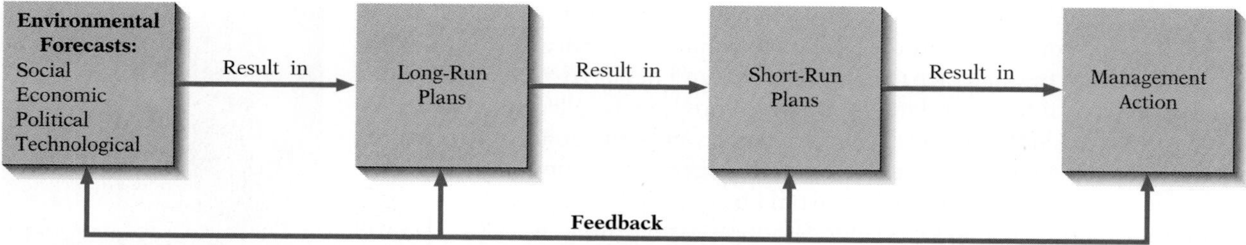

FIGURE 3.2 Integration of social responsibility activities and planning activities

The Overall Planning Process

The model shown in Figure 3.2 depicts how social responsibility activities can be handled as part of the overall planning process of the organization. According to this figure, social trends forecasts should be performed within the organizational environment along with the more typically performed economic, political, and technological trends forecasts. Examples of social trends are prevailing and future societal attitudes toward water pollution, safe working conditions, and the national education system.[21] Each of the forecasts would influence the development of the long-run plans, or plans for the more distant future, and short-run plans, or plans for the relatively near future.

Converting Organizational Policies on Social Responsibility into Action

A *policy* is a management tool that furnishes broad guidelines for channeling management thinking in specific directions. Managers should establish organizational policies in the social responsibility area just as they do in some of the more generally accepted areas, such as hiring, promotion, and absenteeism.

To be effective, social responsibility policies must be converted into appropriate action. According to Figure 3.3, this conversion involves three distinct and generally sequential phases.

Phase 1 consists of top management recognizing that its organization possesses some social obligation. Top management then must formulate and communicate some policy about the acceptance of this obligation to all organization members.

Phase 2 involves staff personnel as well as top management. In this phase, top management gathers information related to meeting the social obligation accepted in phase 1. Staff personnel generally are involved at this point to give advice on technical matters related to meeting the accepted social obligation.

Phase 3 involves division management in addition to organization personnel already involved from the first two phases. During this phase, top management strives to obtain the commitment of organization members to live up to the accepted social obligation and attempts to create realistic expectations about the effects of such a commitment on organizational productivity. Staff specialists encourage the responses within the organization that are necessary to meet the accepted social obligation properly. And division management commits resources and modifies existing procedures so appropriate socially oriented activities can and will be performed within the organization.

BACK TO THE CASE

Larami management should know that pursuing social responsibility objectives could be a major management activity within the company. Therefore, management must plan, organize, influence, and control Larami's social responsibility activities if the company is to be successful in reaching social responsibility objectives.

In terms of planning social responsibility activities, management should determine how Larami can achieve its social responsibility objectives. Management can do this by incorporating social responsibil-

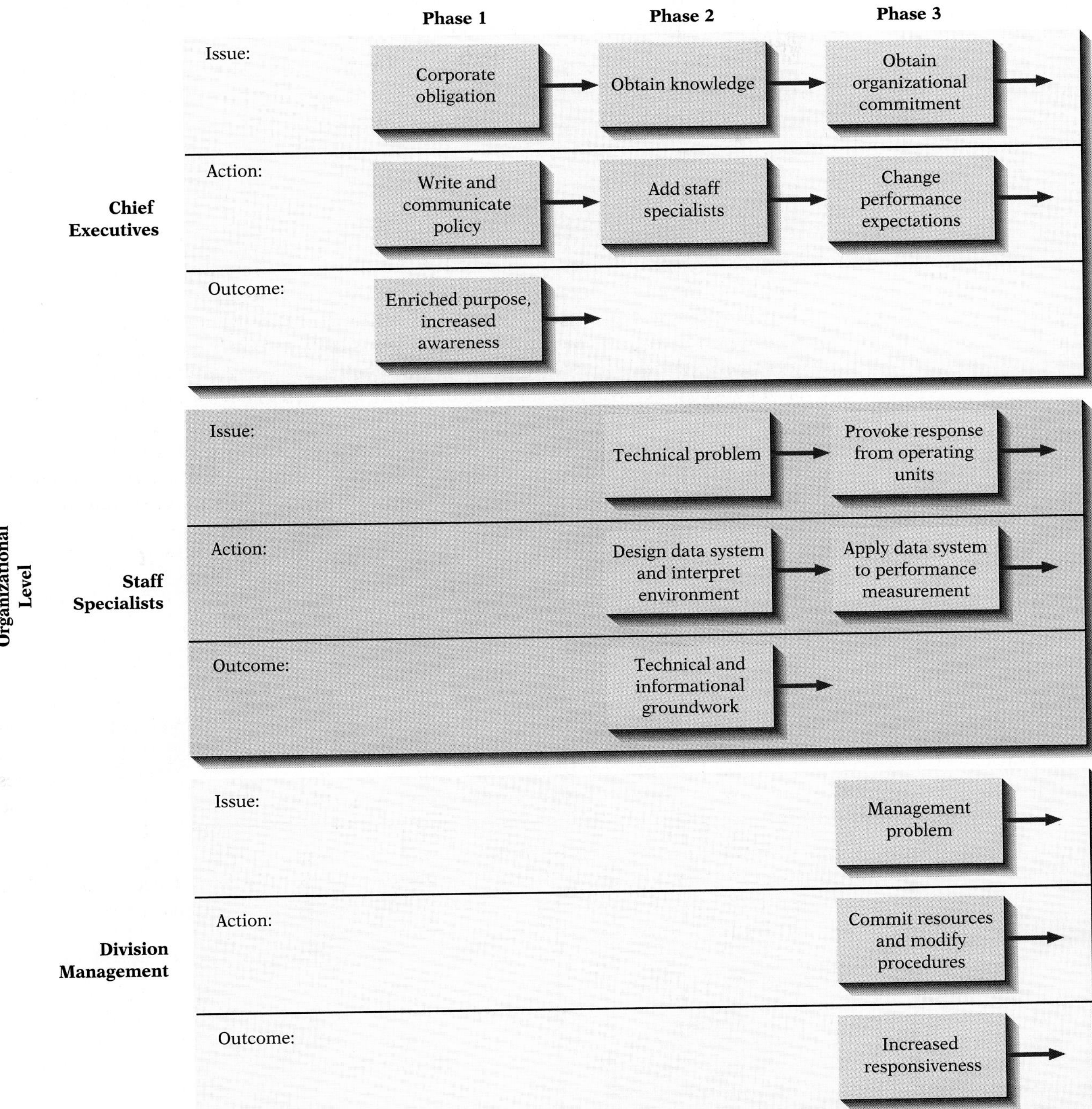

FIGURE 3.3 Conversion of social responsibility policy into action

ity planning into the overall planning process. That is, management can make social trends forecasts along with Larami's economic, political, and technological trends forecasts. In turn, these forecasts would influence the development of plans and, ultimately, the action taken by Larami in the area of social responsibility.

Management also must be able to turn Larami's social responsibility policy into action. For example, management may want to follow the policy of better marketing Larami's toys like the Super Soaker so that young people will be better informed of the dangers of using such toys with undesirable chemicals such as bleach or ammonia. To convert this policy into action, Larami management should first communicate the policy to all organization members. Next, management should obtain additional knowledge of exactly how to market toys such as the Super Soaker in a way that encourages their safe use. Finally, management should make sure all people at Larami are committed to meeting this social responsibility objective and that lower-level managers are allocating funds and establishing appropriate opportunities for organization members to help implement this policy.

Organizing Social Responsibility Activities

Organizing was discussed in chapter 1 as the process of establishing orderly uses for all resources within the organization. These uses, of course, emphasize the attainment of management system objectives and flow naturally from management system plans. Correspondingly, organizing for social responsibility activities entails establishing for all organizational resources logical uses that emphasize the attainment of the organization's social objectives and that are consistent with its social responsibility plans.

Figure 3.4 shows how Standard Oil Company of Indiana decided to organize for the performance of its social responsibility activities. The vice president for law and public affairs holds the primary responsibility in the area of societal affairs within this company and is responsible for overseeing the related activities of numerous individu-

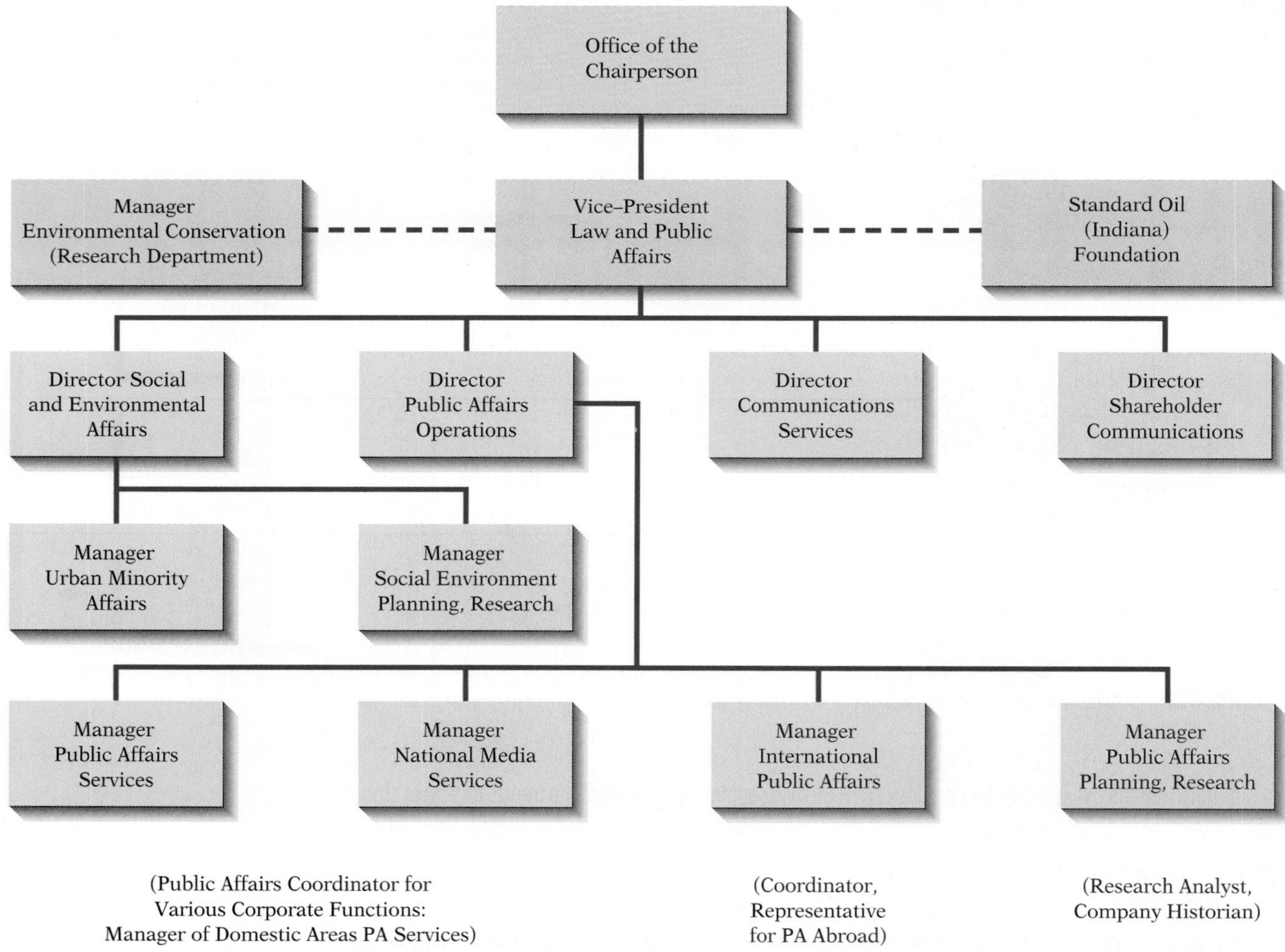

FIGURE 3.4 How Standard Oil Company of Indiana includes social responsibility in its organization chart

als. This chart, of course, is intended only as an illustration of how a company might include its social responsibility area on its organization chart. The specific organizing in this area always should be tailored to the unique needs of each company.

Influencing Individuals Performing Social Responsibility Activities

Influencing was defined in chapter 1 as the management process of guiding the activities of organization members in directions that enhance the attainment of organizational objectives. As applied to the social responsibility area, influencing is simply the process of guiding the activities of organization members in directions that will enhance the attainment of the organization's social responsibility objectives. More specifically, to influence appropriately in this area, managers must lead, communicate, motivate, and work with groups in ways that result in the attainment of existing social responsibility objectives.

Controlling Social Responsibility Activities

Controlling, as discussed in chapter 1, is making things happen as they were planned to happen. To control, managers assess or measure what is occurring in the organization and, if necessary, change these occurrences in some way to make them conform to plans. Controlling in the area of social responsibility entails the same two major tasks. The following sections discuss various areas in which social responsibility measurement takes place and examine the social audit, a tool for determining and reporting progress in the attainment of social responsibility objectives.

Areas of Measurement

To be consistent, measurements to gauge organizational progress in reaching social responsibility objectives could be taken in any of the areas listed in Table 3.1. The specific areas in which individual companies actually take such measurements vary, of course, depending on the specific social responsibility objectives of the companies. All companies, however, probably should take such social responsibility measurements in at least the following four major areas:[22]

1. *The economic function area.* A measurement should be made of whether the organization is performing such activities as producing goods and services that people need, creating jobs for society, paying fair wages, and ensuring worker safety. This measurement gives some indication of the economic contribution the organization is making to society.
2. *The quality-of-life area.* The measurement of quality of life should focus on whether the organization is improving or degrading the general quality of life in society. Producing high-quality goods, dealing fairly with employees and customers, and making an effort to preserve the natural environment are all indicators that the organization is upholding or improving the general quality of life in society. As an example of not upholding the quality of life, some people believe that cigarette companies, because they produce goods that actually can harm the health of society over all, are socially irresponsible.[23]
3. *The social investment area.* The measurement of social investment deals with the degree to which the organization is investing both money and human resources to solve community social problems. Here, the organization could be involved in assisting community organizations involved in education, charities, and the arts.
4. *The problem-solving area.* The measurement of problem solving should focus on the degree to which the organization deals with social problems. Such activities as participating in long-range community planning and conducting studies to pinpoint social problems generally could be considered dealing with social problems.

The Social Audit: A Progress Report

The **social audit** is the process of measuring the social responsibility activities of an organization. It monitors, measures, and appraises social responsibility performance.

A **social audit** is the process of taking measurements of social responsibility to assess organizational performance in the social responsibility area. The basic steps in conducting a social audit are monitoring, measuring, and appraising all aspects of an or-

TABLE 3.6 Portion of sample social audit report

Social Performance Report Part 1—Mainstream Issues

Priority—Consumer Issues

Issue—Discrimination in Credit — Minorities

Potential	New legislation pending in Congress, which should be enacted within two years. Growing public awareness due to increased press coverage. Class actions a possibility.
Progress	New guidelines instituted for small loans (under $5,000), credit cards. Race no longer part of the application, emphasis on employment and credit history. No automatic restrictions.
Problems	No progress in increasing applications from minorities.
Position	Keeping pace with the competition. Better advertising of new policies would help generate new business.

Issue — Complaints and Errors

Potential	Most stated reason for customer choosing another bank is errors. A 3% reduction in closed accounts would be the equivalent of increased profits of $320,000. This could be dramatically increased if complaints were handled more quickly.
Progress	Instituted toll-free line to handle complaints. Feedback has been positive. Cost: $50,000. New manager hired in checking. Instituted a system whereby all checks are double-processed. Errors down 18%. Cost: $80,000.
Problems	No progress in ridding checking and savings account statements of errors.
Position	Perception in the marketplace regarding our service is improved. Substantial reduction in closed accounts (7%).

Priority — Employee Development

Issue—Affirmative Action

Potential	Continued close monitoring by government. Potential liability by class actions now $1 million to $10 million. Program to upgrade underutilized talent in bank (especially women) could significantly increase productivity, as well as decrease recruitment costs. Growing number of qualified minorities in area increase pool of qualified candidates.
Progress	Strong minority program instituted during the year with goals, timetables, and mechanisms for enforcement. The recent record is good: 1988, 18.3% of employees minority; 1989, 19.9%; 1990, 23.7%; 1992 goal is parity.
Problems	Minorities and women still concentrated in the lower ranks:

Percent of Bank Officers Who Are:	1986	1988	1990	1992 Goal
Minority	5.8%	7.1%	9.2%	10.8%
Women	19.7%	22.0%	26.7%	35.0%

To reach 1992 goals, we must concentrate on developing programs to identify and train potential candidates for promotion.

Position	The above effort is largely required. It will offer no competitive advantage or disadvantage, since it is mandated industrywide.

ganization's social responsibility performance. Although companies like General Electric that pioneered concepts of social reporting are still continuing their efforts, few new companies are joining their ranks.[24]

Table 3.6 on page 70 is an example of a social audit that would be prepared by a bank. This table does not illustrate any type of standard format used for writing up the results of a social audit. In fact, probably no two organizations conduct and present the results of a social audit in exactly the same way.[25]

BACK TO THE CASE In addition to planning social responsibility activities at Larami, management also must organize, influence, and control them. To organize social responsibility activities, Larami management must establish orderly use of all resources at Larami to carry out the company's social responsibility plans. Developing an organization chart that shows the social responsibility area at Larami along with corresponding job descriptions, responsibilities, and specifications for the positions on this chart might be an appropriate step for Larami management to take.

To influence social responsibility activities, Larami management must guide the activities of organization members in directions that will enhance the attainment of Larami's social responsibility objectives. Management must lead, communicate, motivate, and work with groups in ways appropriate for meeting those objectives.

To control, Larami management must make sure that social responsibility activities within the company are happening as planned. If they are not, management should make changes to ensure that they will be handled properly in the near future. One tool management can use to check Larami's progress in meeting social responsibilities is the social audit. With the audit, management can check and assess management system performance in such areas as economic functions, quality of life, social investment, and problem solving.

HOW SOCIETY CAN HELP BUSINESS MEET SOCIAL OBLIGATIONS

Although the point has been made that there must be an open and honest involvement of both business and society for business to meet desirable social obligations, the bulk of this chapter has focused on what business should do in the area of social responsibility. This section emphasizes action that society should take to help business accomplish its social responsibility objectives.

Jerry McAfee, chairman of the board and chief executive officer of Gulf Oil Corporation, says that although business has some responsibilities to society, society also has the following responsibilities to business.[26]

1. *Set rules that are clear and consistent.* This is one of the fundamental things that society, through government, ought to do. Although it may come as a surprise to some, I believe that industry actually needs an appropriate measure of regulation. By this I mean that the people of the nation, through their government, should set the bounds within which they want industry to operate.

   But the rules have got to be clear. Society must spell out clearly what it is it wants the corporations to do. The rules can't be vague and imprecise. Making the rules straight and understandable is really what government is all about. One of my colleagues described his confusion when he read a section of a regulation that a federal regulatory representative had cited as the reason for a certain decision that had been made. "You're right," the official responded, "that's what the regulation says, but that's not what it means."

2. *Keep the rules technically feasible.* Business cannot be expected to do the impossible. Yet the plain truth is that many of today's regulations are unworkable. Envi-

ronmental standards have on occasion exceeded those of Mother Nature. For example, the Rio Blanco shale-oil development in Colorado was delayed by the fact that the air-quality standards, as originally proposed, required a higher quality of air than existed in the natural setting.

3. *Make sure the rules are economically feasible.* Society cannot impose a rule that society is not prepared to pay for because, ultimately, it is the people who must pay, either through higher prices or higher taxes, or both. Furthermore, the costs involved include not only those funds constructively spent to solve problems, but also the increasingly substantial expenditures needed just to comply with the red-tape requirements. Although the total cost of government regulation of business is difficult to compute, it is enormous. To cite an example, the Commission on Federal Paperwork estimated the energy industry's annual cost of complying with federal energy-reporting requirements at possibly $335 million per year.

4. *Make the rules prospective, not retroactive.* Nowadays, there is an alarming, distressing trend toward retroactivity, toward trying to force retribution for the past. Certain patterns of taxation and some of the regulations and applications of the law are indications of this trend.

   A case in point is the "Notices of Proposed Disallowance" issued by the Federal Energy Administration (now the Department of Energy) in 1977 against Gulf Oil for alleged overcharges on imported crude oil during the 1973–74 oil embargo. The fact is that during those difficult months we were struggling to supply the nation's energy needs, and increasing imports with the government's support.

   We were doing our level best to follow the existing regulations on pricing imports. The charges against us, as well as many other issues raised by the DOE, were the result of retroactive applications of vague, poorly written and confusing regulations.

   It is counterproductive to make today's rules apply retroactively to yesterday's ball game.

5. *Make the rules goal-setting, not procedure-prescribing.* The proper way for the people of the nation, through their government, to tell their industries how to operate is to set the goals, set the fences, set the criteria, set the atmosphere, but don't tell us how to do it. Tell us what you want made, but don't tell us how to make it. Tell us the destination we're seeking, but don't tell us how to get there. Leave it to the ingenuity of American industry to devise the best, the most economical, the most efficient way to get there, for industry's track record in this regard has been pretty good.

BUSINESS ETHICS

The study of ethics in management can be approached from many different viewpoints. Perhaps the most practical approach is to view ethics as a catalyst causing managers to take socially responsible actions. The movement toward including the study of ethics as a critical part of management education began in the 1970s, grew significantly in the '80s, and is expected to continue growing throughout the '90s. John Shad was the chairman of the Securities and Exchange Commission during the 1980s when Wall Street became involved in a number of insider trading scandals. He recently pledged a $20 million trust fund to the Harvard Business School to create a curriculum in business ethics for MBA students. And television producer Norman Lear gave $1 million to underwrite the Business Enterprise Trust, which will give national awards to companies and "whistle blowers . . . who demonstrate courage, creativity, and social vision in the business world."[27]

The following sections present business ethics as a critical part of management by defining ethics, explaining why ethical considerations are a vital part of management practices, discussing a code of ethics, and giving some suggestions on how to create an ethical workplace.

A Definition of Ethics

Famous humanitarian Dr. Albert Schweitzer defined ethics as "our concern for good behavior. We feel an obligation to consider not only our own personal well-being, but also that of other human beings." This is similar to the precept of the Golden Rule: Do unto others as you would have them do unto you.

In business, **ethics** can be defined as the capacity to reflect on values in the corporate decision-making process, to determine how these values and decisions affect the various stakeholder groups, and to establish how managers can use these observations in day-to-day company management. Ethical managers strive for success within the confines of sound management practices that are characterized by fairness and justice.[28]

Ethics is our concern for good behavior; our obligaton to consider not only our own personal well-being but also that of other human beings.

Business ethics involves the capacity to reflect on values in the corporate decision-making process, to determine how these values and decisions affect the various stakeholder groups, and to establish how managers can use these observations in day-to-day company management.

Why Ethics Is a Vital Part of Management Practices

John F. Akers, former chairman of the board of IBM, recently said that it makes good business sense for managers to be ethical. Without being ethical, he believes, companies cannot be competitive at either the national or international levels. According to Akers,

> Ethics and competitiveness are inseparable. We compete as a society. No society anywhere will compete very long or successfully with people stabbing each other in the back; with people trying to steal from one another; with everything requiring notarized confirmation because you can't trust the other person; with every little squabble ending in litigation; and with government writing reams of regulatory legislation, tying business hand and foot to keep it honest.[29]

While ethical management practices may not necessarily be linked to specific indicators of financial profitability, there is no inevitable conflict between ethical practices and a firm's emphasis on making a profit.[30] As Akers's statement suggests, our system of competition presumes underlying values of truthfulness and fair dealing.

The employment of ethical business practices can enhance overall corporate health in three important areas. The first area is productivity. The employees of a corporation are stakeholders who are affected by management practices. When management employs a consideration of ethics in its actions toward stakeholders, employees can be positively affected. For example, a corporation may decide that business ethics requires a special effort to ensure the health and welfare of employees. Many corporations have established Employee Advisory Programs (EAPs), to help employees with family, work, financial, or legal problems, or with mental illness or chemical dependency. These programs can even be a source of enhanced productivity for a corporation. Control Data Corporation found that its program reduced health costs and sick-leave usage significantly.[31]

A second area in which ethical management practices can enhance corporate health is by positively affecting "outside" stakeholders, such as suppliers and customers. A positive public image can attract customers who view such an image as desirable. For example, Johnson & Johnson, manufacturer of baby products, carefully guards its public image as a company that puts customer health and well-being ahead of corporate profits, as exemplified in its code of ethics in Table 3.7 on page 74. James E. Burke, the chairman of Johnson & Johnson, is one of the directors of Norman Lear's new Business Enterprise Trust, which will support and encourage ethical business management.

The third area in which ethical management practices can enhance corporate

TABLE 3.7 The Johnson & Johnson code of ethics

We believe our first responsibility is to the doctors, nurses, and patients, to mothers and all others who use our products and services.
In meeting their needs everything we do must be of high quality.
We must constantly strive to reduce our costs in order to maintain reasonable prices.
Customers' orders must be serviced promptly and accurately.
Our suppliers and distributors must have an opportunity to make a fair profit.

We are responsible to our employees, the men and women who work with us throughout the world.
Everyone must be considered as an individual.
We must respect their dignity and recognize their merit.
They must have a sense of security in their jobs.
Compensation must be fair and adequate, and working conditions clean, orderly and safe.
Employees must feel free to make suggestions and complaints.
There must be equal opportunity for employment, development, and advancement for those qualified.
We must provide competent management, and their actions must be just and ethical.

We are responsible to the communities in which we live and work and to the world community as well.
We must be good citizens — support good works and charities and bear our fair share of taxes.
We must encourage civic improvements and better health and education.
We must maintain in good order the property we are privileged to use, protecting the environment and natural resources.

Our final responsibility is to our stockholders.
Business must make a sound profit.
We must experiment with new ideas.
Research must be carried on, innovative programs developed and mistakes paid for.
New equipment must be purchased, new facilities provided, and new products launched.
Reserves must be created to provide for adverse times.
When we operate according to these principles, the stockholders should realize a fair return.

health is in minimizing regulation from government agencies. Where companies are believed to be acting unethically, the public is more likely to put pressure on legislators and other government officials to regulate those businesses or to enforce existing regulations. For example, in 1990 hearings were held on the rise in gasoline and home heating oil prices following Iraq's invasion of Kuwait, in part due to the public perception that oil companies were not behaving ethically.

A Code of Ethics

A **code of ethics** is a formal statement that acts as a guide for making decisions and acting within an organization.

A **code of ethics** is a formal statement that acts as a guide for how people within a particular organization should act and make decisions in an ethical fashion. Ninety percent of the Fortune 500 firms, and almost half of all other firms, have ethical codes.[32] Codes of ethics commonly address issues like conflict of interest, competitors, privacy of information, gift giving, and giving and receiving political contributions or business.[33] According to a recent survey, the development and distribution of a code of ethics within an organization is perceived as an effective and efficient means of encouraging ethical practices within organizations.[34] The code of ethics that Johnson & Johnson developed to guide company business practices (Table 3.7) is distributed in its annual report.

Managers cannot assume that merely because they have developed and distributed a code of ethics within a company the organization members have all the guidelines necessary to determine what is ethical and to act accordingly. There is no way that all ethical and unethical conduct within an organization can be written into one code.[35] Codes of ethics must be monitored continually to determine that they are comprehensive and usable guidelines for making ethical business decisions. Managers should view codes of ethics as tools that periodically must be evaluated and refined in order to more efficiently and effectively encourage ethical practices within organizations.

Creating an Ethical Workplace

Managers in most organizations commonly strive to encourage ethical practices, not only to be morally correct but to gain whatever business advantage there may be in having potential consumers and employees regard the company as ethical.[36] Creating, distributing, and continually improving a company's code of ethics is one usual step managers take to establish an ethical workplace.

Another step managers can take to create an ethical workplace is to create a special office or department with the responsibility of ensuring ethical practices within the organization. For example, management at Martin Marietta, a major supplier of missile systems and aircraft components, has established a corporate ethics office. This ethics office is a tangible sign to all employees that management is serious about encouraging ethical practices within the company (see Table 3.8).

Another way to promote ethics in the workplace is to furnish organization members with appropriate training. General Dynamics, McDonnell Douglas, Chemical Bank, and American Can Company are examples of corporations that conduct training programs aimed at encouraging ethical practices within their organizations.[37] Such programs do not attempt to teach managers what is moral or ethical but, rather, give managers criteria they can use to help determine how ethical a certain action might be. Managers can feel confident that a potential action will be considered ethical by the general public if it is consistent with one or more of the following standards:[38]

1. *The golden rule.* Act in a way you would expect others to act toward you.
2. *The utilitarian principle.* Act in a way that results in the greatest good for the greatest number.

TABLE 3.8 Martin Marietta's Corporate Ethics Office

To ensure continuing attention to matters of ethics and standards on the part of all Martin Marietta employees, the Corporation has established the Corporate Ethics Office. The Director of Corporate Ethics is charged with responsibility for monitoring performance under this Code of Ethics and for resolving concerns presented to the Ethics Office.

Martin Marietta calls on every employee to report any violation or apparent violation of the Code. The Corporation strongly encourages employees to work with their supervisors in making such reports and, in addition, provides to employees the right to report violations directly to the Corporate Ethics Office. Prompt reporting of violations is considered to be in the best interest of all.

Employee reports will be handled in absolute confidence. No employee will suffer indignity or retaliation because of a report he or she makes to the Ethics Office. . . .

The Chairman of the Corporate Ethics Committee will be the President of the Corporation. The Committee will consist of five other employees of the Corporation including representatives of the Corporation's operating elements, each of whom will be appointed by the Chairman of the Committee subject to the approval of the Audit and Ethics Committee of the Corporation's Board of Directors.

The Chairman of the Corporate Ethics Committee reports to the Audit and Ethics Committee of the Martin Marietta Corporation Board of Directors.

3. *Kant's categorical imperative.* Act in such a way that the action taken under the circumstances could be a universal law, or rule, of behavior.
4. *The professional ethic.* Take actions that would be viewed as proper by a disinterested panel of professional peers.
5. *The TV test.* Managers should always ask, "Would I feel comfortable explaining to a national TV audience why I took this action?"
6. *The legal test.*[39] Is the proposed action or decision legal? Established laws are generally considered minimum standards for ethics.
7. *The four-way test.*[40] Managers can feel confident that a decision is ethical if they can answer "yes" to the following questions as they relate to the decision: Is the decision truthful? Is it fair to all concerned? Will it build goodwill and better friendships? Will it be beneficial to all concerned?

Finally, managers can take responsibility for creating and sustaining conditions in which people are likely to behave ethically and for minimizing conditions in which people might be tempted to behave unethically.[41] Two practices that commonly inspire unethical behavior in organizations are to give unusually high rewards for good performance and unusually severe punishments for poor performance. By eliminating such factors, managers can reduce much of the pressure that people feel to perform unethically in organizations.[42]

BACK TO THE CASE As indicated earlier, there probably is no legislation that would require Larami's management to modify its Super Soaker situation to more specifically address the youth violence problem. If such legislation were being developed, however, there are certain steps legislators could take to help Larami management meet social responsibilities in this area. For example, laws should be clear, consistent, and technically feasible. This would ensure that Larami management would know what action was expected of them and the company and that the technology existed to help them take this action.

Laws should also be economically feasible, emphasize the future, and allow flexibility. Larami management should be able to follow them without going bankrupt and should not be penalized for what has happened in the past. Larami management also should be given the flexibility to follow these laws to the best advantage of the company. In other words, management should not be told to conform to laws by following specific steps.

Assuming that Larami management is ethical, it would be inclined to consider the well-being of other people. As a result, Larami management would be likely to consider seriously any reasonable action to aid society in its efforts to curb youth violence. If Larami management significantly reduced or limited the overall appeal of its products to youth customers as a result of becoming involved curbing youth violence, however, management could probably be accused of being unethical by company employees, stockholders, or anyone else who had a genuine interest in organizational success.

ACTION SUMMARY

Reread the learning objectives that follow. Each objective is followed by questions. Answering these questions accurately will help you retain the most important concepts discussed in this chapter. After answering each question, check your answer with the answer key at the end of this chapter. (*Hint:* If you have doubt regarding the correct response, consult the page whose number follows the answer.)

Circle: ***From studying this chapter, I will attempt to acquire:***

1. An understanding of the term *corporate social responsibility.*

T, F a. According to Davis, since business has certain power over society, society can and must hold business responsible for social conditions that result from the exercise of this power.

a, b, c, d, e b. Major social responsibility areas in which business can become involved include all of the following except: (a) urban affairs; (b) consumer affairs; (c) pollution control; (d) natural resource conservation; (e) all of the above are areas of potential involvement.

2. An appreciation for the arguments both for and against business assuming social responsibilities.

T, F a. Some argue that since business is an influential member of society, it has the responsibility to help maintain and improve the overall welfare of society.

a, b, c, d, e b. Milton Friedman argues that business cannot be held responsible for performing social responsibility activities. He does *not* argue that: (a) doing so has the potential to cause the demise of American business as we know it today; (b) doing so is in direct conflict with the organizational objectives of business firms; (c) doing so would cause the nation to creep toward socialism, which is inconsistent with American business philosophy; (d) doing so is unethical because it requires business managers to spend money that rightfully belongs to the firm's investors; (e) doing so ultimately would either reduce returns to the firm's investors or raise prices charged to consumers.

3. Useful strategies for increasing the social responsiveness of an organization.

a, b, c, d, e a. When using the flowchart approach in social responsibility decision making, one of the following questions is out of appropriate sequential order: (a) Can we afford this action? (b) Does a social responsibility actually exist? (c) Does the firm have a right to undertake this action? (d) Does an assessment of all interests indicate that the act is desirable? (e) Do benefits outweigh costs?

T, F b. The social obligation approach to performing social responsibility activities is concerned primarily with complying with existing legislation on the topic.

4. Insights on the planning, organizing, influencing, and controlling of social responsibility activities.

T, F a. Organizational policies should be established for social responsibility matters in the same manner as, for example, for personnel relations problems.

a, b, c, d, e b. Companies should take social responsibility measurements in all of the following areas except: (a) economic utility area; (b) economic function area; (c) quality-of-life area; (d) social investment area; (e) problem-solving area.

5. A practical plan for how society can help business meet its social obligations.

T, F a. Ultimately, the citizens in a society must pay for the social responsibility activities of business by paying higher prices or higher taxes or both.

a, b, c, d, e b. The following is *not* one of the responsibilities that society has to business, as listed by Jerry McAfee: (a) setting rules that are clear and concise; (b) making rules prospective, not retroactive; (c) making rules goal-setting, not procedure-prescribing; (d) making rules that are subjective, not objective; (e) making sure the rules are economically feasible.

6. An understanding of the relationship between ethics and management.

T, F a. The utilitarian principle suggests that managers should act in such a way that the action taken under the circumstances could be a universal law, or rule, of behavior.

a, b, c, d, e b. Management might strive to encourage ethical behavior in organizations in order to: (a) be morally correct; (b) gain a business advantage by having employees perceive their company as ethical; (c) gain a business advantage by having customers perceive the company as ethical; (d) avoid possible costly legal fees; (e) all of the above.

T, F c. Once developed, a company's code of ethics generally does not have to be monitored or revised for at least two years.

T, F d. Some managers create a special "office of ethics" to show employees the critical importance of ethics.

INTRODUCTORY CASE WRAP-UP

"Larami Corporation 'Super Soaks' Society?" (p. 51) and its related back-to-the-case sections were written to help you better understand the management concepts contained in this chapter. Answer the following discussion questions about this introductory case to further enrich your understanding of the chapter content:

1. Do you think that Larami management has a responsibility to somehow modify the situation involving the Super Soaker so that this product does not encourage youth violence? Explain.
2. Assuming that Larami management has such a responsibility, under what conditions could they commit the company to assume that responsibility?
3. Assuming that Larami management has such a responsibility, when would it be relatively difficult for them to get the company to live up to it?

ISSUES FOR REVIEW AND DISCUSSION

1. Define *corporate social responsibility.*
2. Explain three of the major propositions in the Davis model of corporate social responsibility.
3. Summarize three arguments that support business pursuing social responsibility objectives.
4. Summarize Milton Friedman's arguments against business pursuing social responsibility objectives.
5. What is meant by the phrase *performing required social responsibility activities?*
6. What is meant by the phrase *voluntarily performing social responsibility activities?*
7. List five positive and five negative outcomes a business could experience as a result of performing social responsibility activities.
8. What is the difference between social responsibility and social responsiveness?
9. Discuss the decision-making process that can help managers increase the social responsiveness of a business.
10. In your own words, explain the main differences among Sethi's three approaches to meeting social responsibilities.
11. Which of Sethi's approaches has the most potential for increasing the social responsiveness of a management system? Explain.
12. What is the overall relationship between the four main management functions and performing social responsibility activities?
13. What suggestions does this chapter make about planning social responsibility activities?
14. Describe the process of turning social responsibility policy into action.
15. How do organizing and influencing social responsibility activities relate to planning social responsibility activities?
16. List and define four main areas in which any management system can take measurements to control social responsibility activities.
17. What is a social audit? How should the results of a social audit be used by management?
18. How can society help business meet its social responsibilities?
19. What is the relationship between ethics and social responsibility?
20. Explain how managers can try to judge if a particular action is ethical.
21. What steps can managers take to make their organizations more ethical workplaces?

ACTION SUMMARY ANSWER KEY

1. a. T, p. 52
b. e, p. 54
2. a. T, p. 54
b. c, p. 55

3. a. a, p. 62
b. T, p. 64
4. a. T, p. 65
b. a, p. 69

5. a. T, p. 72
b. d, pp. 71–72

6. a. F, p. 75
b. e, p. 75
c. F, p. 75
d. T, p. 75

CASE STUDY

Procter & Gamble: A Socially Responsible Company

CHERYL MACON
Butler County Community College

Procter & Gamble (P&G) manufactures disposable diapers under both the Pampers and Luvs labels. Disposable diapers are not biodegradable and account for a large percentage of landfill waste. This creates a major concern among environmentally conscious individuals.

Many parents choose disposable diapers because they are easy to use and less messy than cloth diapers. Recently more emphasis has been placed on the environmental effects of these products. Since this has become a pressing issue, P&G's research and development division has been exploring ways to develop a diaper that will prove environmentally safe. Technological advancements have allowed major reductions in packaging and diaper bulk over the past six years. P&G is currently searching for a way to manufacture a biodegradable diaper. The ultimate goal is to keep disposable diapers and other waste out of landfills. Both disposable and cloth diapers have drawbacks; it seems to be a toss-up between landfill waste of disposables and the water usage involved with the cleaning of cloth diapers. In its development of disposable diapers, P&G has shown a sincere concern for not only monetary profits but also social responsibility.

There are varying degrees of social responsibility. Many companies opt to minimize involvement by undertaking only that which is legally required of them, while others select the social responsibility or responsiveness approach. P&G is in business to provide the consumer with the best product available, but the company also takes social responsiveness seriously. P&G places a strong emphasis on environmental impact, not only for today's world but in the future; it has a well known and respected reputation to uphold.

P&G has a detailed Environmental Quality Policy. It states the company's commitment to the safety of its employees, consumers, and the environment. P&G has taken a leading role in reducing environmental impact caused by the company's operations whenever possible. P&G makes it a point to meet or exceed all environmental laws and regulations which govern company operations.

P&G openly provides information about the environmental quality of its products, packaging and operations. For example, P&G provides a brochure of its policies and achievements in the area of environmental safety, as well as a toll-free number listed on its products' packaging to ensure its commitment to meeting consumers' needs. All of the company's plastic bottles are coded for recycling. The hair care products it manufactures are all pumps rather than aerosols. P&G now offers concentrated detergents and "ultra" fabric softeners to cut volume, packaging, and waste, as well as transportation and production energies. Secret and Sure deodorants now have no carton packaging, which saves 3.4 million pounds of waste per year. P&G recycles paperboard, plastic, cardboard, and various metals. Although no government regulations currently require such measures, the company has initiated the effort on its own.

P&G's actions have proven to have a positive community influence, thus providing the company with a strategy acceptable to its stakeholders while allowing for sizable profitability as well. These broad community impacts illustrate that private actions can have important social consequences. Failure to take positive action can prove detrimental to the company and to the business system as a whole.

Today's society requires corporate businesses to consider social responsibility involvement with the same degree of professional competence traditionally used in managing other aspects of business. The manner and extent of social responsibility P&G chooses to undertake has a direct impact not only on its stakeholders, but also on its costs, profits, and reputation. Considering the extensive research it has done and continues to do, P&G appears to be among those companies that take this social obligation seriously.

DISCUSSION QUESTIONS

1. What are the key principles P&G can use to cope with society's view of the company's stance on social responsibility?
2. Do you feel Milton Friedman's theoretical viewpoint would prove successful to P&G in today's business world?
3. How can we as consumers help P&G accomplish its social obligations?
4. Which of Sethi's three social responsibility approaches do you feel P&G is using?

CNN VIDEO CASE

Promoting Cosmetics with a Conscience

ANITA RODDICK
Body Shop International

"I hate the beauty business. [It] sells unattainable dreams. It lies, it cheats, it exploits women. . . ." As the founder and CEO of the Body Shop, Anita Roddick has definite ideas about the industry her company is part of. She has guided her company in a socially responsive approach of the highest order.

Body Shop International PLC (Proprietary Limited Corporation, in England) sees itself as a force to help change the world. Founded in 1976 as a single shop, the company now is a huge cosmetics chain with shops in over forty countries. The first step toward this size and presence occurred in the first year, with the opening of the first franchises and an expansion into Belgium. In 1984, eight years after its start, the Body Shop went public. Selling shares in the company allowed Roddick to raise $10 million. By 1991 the Body Shop had about 620 shops in thirty nine countries. This included forty seven shops in the United States, with many more planned to open here over the following several years.

Anita Roddick sells her Body Shop products to people who respond to the fact that her products are made and sold honestly and ethically.

The ingredients for the Body Shop's cosmetics often come from natural resources in third-world countries. Early in her adult life, Anita Roddick had jobs that required travel in other lands—Polynesia, New Caledonia, Australia, and Africa. She learned how people used locally grown plants and foods to wash and protect their skin and hair.

Roddick doesn't just go into a country and take the ingredients out. She makes sure that the people who live there get fair market value for the ingredients and for the work they do for the Body Shop. She ensures a fair trade of goods and value.

The message about the Body Shop's social conscience often gets relayed in news coverage by the general press. Also, the Body Shop's own T-shirts, window displays, and printed matter support its messages. With such socially activist literature, the company educates its customers.

Potential employees are screened for their feelings about global issues. Roddick's 8,500 employees worldwide can be rallied for demonstrations, such as to protest the burning of the rain forests (a major source of natural cosmetic ingredients). Body Shop employees devote one day a month to community projects. They may take three-week paid leaves of absence for charitable work. All employees, even those who do not work in the shops, must talk with customers on a regular basis.

The Body Shop's containers are returnable for refills, and the packaging is made with recycled and recyclable materials. Body Shop profits are in large part given away to causes.

Profits are also used in alternative testing of product performance and safety. Roddick wishes all the cosmetic industry would lobby together to continue such testing. She says it's much more than putting on the label "not tested on animals"; the industry needs to go beyond that to replace an outmoded system that was set up in the 1940s. It requires changing the law, and the Body Shop is putting enormous funding into making that happen.

Roddick's business philosophy? Business, she says, is "trading—buying and selling—and making a product so good that people don't mind giving you a profit for it. And it's conversations, it's making an environment that is so exciting and so full of electricity that people want to come." Anita Roddick keeps her focus on the people who allow her business to exist and on the people who use the products precisely because they are made and sold honestly and ethically.

VIDEO CASE QUESTIONS

1. The Davis model of corporate social responsibility says that social responsibility arises from social power. What social power did Roddick have when she opened her first shop?
2. List three ways the Body Shop is a socially responsive business.
3. How do you think Anita Roddick would answer Milton Friedman's arguments against business performing social responsibility actions? (See page 55.)
4. Classify Body Shop activities mentioned in the case according to the categories of social responsibility listed in Table 3.1.

CNN VIDEO EXERCISE

Making Ethical Decisions for the Body Shop

EXERCISE GOAL: Learn to evaluate whether actions are ethical, using accepted standards of ethics.

Use the ethics standards on pages 75-76 to help you decide what to do in the following hypothetical situation.

You are the head of a very small export firm in South America. Your biggest contract is selling nuts to the Body Shop, which uses oils from the nuts in various products. Your contract stipulates that the nuts are organic. The contract also stipulates that the people who gather nuts, mostly indigenous peoples living in isolated parts of the rain forest, receive a fair wage for their work. Without their wages, the people who work in cooperatives would have to leave the rain forest to the miners and the lumber companies.

You have just learned that the latest shipment of nuts to arrive from the cooperatives was contaminated by a pesticide while being loaded for transport on riverboats. Do you ship the nuts to the Body Shop?

Write three defenses for shipping the nuts. Write three reasons for not shipping. Considering ethical standards, what should you do?

Reasons for shipping the contaminated nuts:

1. ______________________________

____

2. ______________________________

____

3. ______________________________

____

Reasons for not shipping the contaminated nuts:

1. ______________________________

____

2. ______________________________

____

3. ______________________________

____

you conclude

☐ to ship the contaminated nuts

or

☐ not to ship the contaminated nuts.

PART 1

INTEGRATIVE CASE

Juan Blanes Wins Hearts as Well as Quality

ROBERT E. KEMPER
Northern Arizona University

"There's a magic to total quality management that inspires people around the world," says manager Juan Blanes Sanchez. "And the values of total quality management—trust, winners, winning teams, no fear, profound knowledge—create an emotional tie that links managers to workplace team members."

Juan Blanes, born to Spanish parents in Mayagüez, Puerto Rico, was a young boy when his parents insisted that he be concerned not only for his own personal well-being, but also for that of others. After high school, Juan enrolled in the Interamerican University of Puerto Rico at the San German campus where he studied business administration. Juan felt that a business degree would give him the most latitude in career choices. "It seemed to me," Juan explains, "that if you are going to get an education, you should focus on an area that will benefit you, your family, and your community."

Juan's business skills and degree earned him a position in the family business after graduation in 1974. He spent four years specializing in financial matters: accounting, payroll, collections, and property management. "It was evident that the family business was trending downward and that the family had an excess of managers," he states. "So I started looking for a manufacturing business niche, and there was men's and boys' shirts." Juan established, in Mayagüez, a tax-exempt sewing factory that manufactured and distributed quality shirts. The shirt firm, *Blanes Industrial Incorporated,* opened in 1978 and started manufacturing its own Caribbean designs under the "Avant" label. Caribbean natives and tourists wanted Avant shirts because they had a sterling reputation for superiority. Sales and profits were doubling every year. Then, in the mid-1980s, giant U.S. and Asian firms moved into the Caribbean boys' and men's-shirt market. These shirts attracted customers because of their price. Instead of responding by marketing a lower-quality shirt, Blanes's company continued to focus on the top end of the market. Blanes's shirts were technically innovative, but failed to appeal to a cost-conscious audience. What is more, Blanes was suffering from high employee-benefit costs that often hamper small businesses.

Juan could see no long-term future as a shirt manufacturer and worried that he could not cover employee retirement benefits established for his employees. "These employees were banking on me to provide them with long-term employment, medical benefits, and retirement security. I was not sure that I could provide these benefits given the state of the shirt market." Juan decided to sell the business, but there were no buyers. Juan's next step was to inform the employees that he was closing the plant. "It was not easy to tell an employee that had been working for me for thirteen years that his job was terminated." He assured employees that he would buy out their retirement funds by giving each a cash settlement based upon the retirement contract. Although this dug deep into Juan's personal wealth, he felt it the ethical thing to do for people who had become like family.

After the employees were "bought out" and Juan had helped each find new employment, and all of Blanes's accounts payables were satisfied, Juan turned his attention to 250 accounts receivables. After notifying these companies about disbanding *Blanes Industrial* and asking for payment in full, Juan determined that the only ways to collect what was due was to meet each retail manager face to face so that there would be an understanding of Juan's dilemma. This face-to-face contact proved to be extremely beneficial. All but one retail company paid the account in full.

"I really had to work hard to collect what was due me and I was impressed that only one account would not be settled." Juan had successfully taken care of his former employees and was out of the shirt business without losing a great deal of money. He was not rich, but he felt he had satisfied his parents' personal values by looking out for his own well-being and that of others.

Juan had a vision of a short period of leisure, but that fantasy ended abruptly when management of the Mayagüez, Puerto Rico, operation of Bristol-Myers Squibb invited him to join the Human Resources Department. Bristol-Myers Squibb, based in the United States, is one of several drug companies with manufacturing plants in Puerto Rico. "My new job was as a human resources specialist," he states. "In 1988, Bristol was expanding its drug production activities in Puerto Rico and wanted to make sure that the cost of hiring employees would pay off with long-term satisfied workers. My job was to find out where the trouble spots were and to recommend changes. Bristol wanted me to place a heavy emphasis on training, security, and safety." The company, forced to think quality because of FDA requirements, began paying attention to workers tied to production and shipping activities.

I told the employees that they were winners only if they had pride in their work and loved their job.

One of the trouble spots for Bristol's Mayagüez operation was the packaging line in the Manufacturing Department. Soon, Bristol's management realized that the solution to the challenge of the packaging line was to promote Juan from the Human Resources Department to supervisor of the packaging section. "My dream was to make the packaging section the most desired place to work by making our employees recognize the importance of each other. I told the employees that they were winners only if they had pride in their work and loved their job. I tried to instill the idea of competing with each other rather than against each other." It was not long before Bristol could see a change in the attitude of the packaging-section employees. Juan had won the hearts of the employees by taking action on their complaints, whether the problem was one of security, engineering, production schedule, or safety. An example of Juan's changes using the "competing with" idea was the raising of a conveyer by twelve inches. For years, workers had complained of back injuries caused by having to lean forward to grab cartons off the line. Previous supervisors did not heed the warnings of workers concerning these injuries. After time passed and nothing was done about the height of the line, the workers simply ignored the problem. Then, Juan Blanes learned of this problem. It was not long before he invited an industrial engineer specializing in ergonomics to the department. She spent four hours with Juan, inspecting and evaluating the line, the employees, and the conveyer. Three days later, Juan received a complete evaluation including alternatives for change. Juan's next step was to work with the maintenance engineers. In one day, the conveyer was raised to a new height. Workers quietly applauded and then began making Juan aware of other problems.

Helping to create a better environment for employees keeps Juan interested. He is not impressed with supervisors who put their own interests above those of their employees. "'I win, you lose' is an awful way of life. You win big and you lose big. The company can get killed by supervisors who only look out for themselves. You have to scan every worker, looking at the organization's needs. Then you have to interpret those needs in terms of your consumers." To Juan, workers are an important resource and, when managers remain true to that philosophy, everybody wins.

DISCUSSION QUESTIONS

1. For which types of management skills—technical skills, human skills, or conceptual skills—has Blanes demonstrated a proficiency?
2. Which career stage would you say Blanes was in when he closed the family business? When he was promoted to supervisor of the Bristol-Myers Squibb, Mayagüez, packaging section?
3. Which of the five approaches to management—the classical approach, the behavioral approach, the contingency approach, or the system approach—has Blanes used in the various management actions he has undertaken?
4. Define corporate social responsibility from Blanes's point of view.

PLANNING

This section provides a thorough explanation of planning. It is the first management function covered because most management theorists agree that planning is the fundamental management function, the one on which all other functions are built.

Planning begins with a discussion of organizational objectives: the relationship between management and organizational objectives, individual versus organizational objectives, operational objectives, and management by objectives. Planning is further emphasized through extended discussion of topics such as strategic planning, the decision-making process, and the various plans and planning tools available. In specific terms, the section offers the following fundamentals: a definition of *planning,* the steps of the planning process, the relationship between planning and the chief executive, the qualifications and duties of planners, and the evaluation of planners. The material on decision making emphasizes the definition of *decision,* important elements of the decision situation, and the use of probability theory and decision trees as tools for making decisions involving risk. The strategic planning material discusses environmental analysis establishing organizational direction, strategy formulation, strategy implementation, and strategic control. It also includes information about the tools managers use to develop organizational strategy: critical question analysis, SWOT, the BCG Growth-Share Matrix, the GE Portfolio Matrix, and Porter's Model for Industry Analysis. Plans and planning tool sections cover the dimensions of a plan, why plans fail, plant facilities planning, human resource planning, forecasting, and scheduling.

As before, the material here is challenging. As you study this section, think about how planning concepts relate to the material you read about in Part 1. Remember, also, that an understanding of this new information is important to the comprehension of the material in the remaining sections of the text.

PART

2

CHAPTER

4

ORGANIZATIONAL OBJECTIVES

STUDENT LEARNING OBJECTIVES

From studying this chapter, I will attempt to acquire:

1. An understanding of organizational objectives.
2. An appreciation for the importance of organizational objectives.
3. An ability to tell the difference between organizational objectives and individual objectives.
4. A knowledge of the areas in which managers should set organizational objectives.
5. An understanding of the development of organizational objectives.
6. Some facility in writing good objectives.
7. An awareness of how managers use organizational objectives and help others to attain the objectives.
8. An appreciation for the potential of a management by objectives (MBO) program.

CHAPTER OUTLINE

INTRODUCTORY CASE
Entrepreneur Suffers Growing Pains at Arkansas Freightways

GENERAL NATURE OF ORGANIZATIONAL OBJECTIVES

Definition of Organizational Objectives

GLOBAL HIGHLIGHT
Asea Brown Boveri

Importance of Organizational Objectives

TYPES OF OBJECTIVES IN ORGANIZATIONS

Organizational Objectives
Individual Objectives

AREAS FOR ORGANIZATIONAL OBJECTIVES

ETHICS HIGHLIGHT
IBM France

WORKING WITH ORGANIZATIONAL OBJECTIVES

Establishing Organizational Objectives

QUALITY HIGHLIGHT
American Management Association

DIVERSITY HIGHLIGHT
The Department of Transportation

Guidelines for Establishing Quality Objectives
Guidelines for Making Objectives Operational
Attainment of Objectives
How to Use Objectives

MANAGEMENT BY OBJECTIVES (MBO)

Factors Necessary for a Successful MBO Program
MBO Programs: Advantages and Disadvantages

CASE STUDY
Planning for Survival at Brant Manufacturing

VIDEO CASE
The Essence of Essence Communications: Edward Lewis, Essence Magazine

VIDEO EXERCISE
Setting Organizational Goals, Means, and Measures for *Essence*

INTRODUCTORY CASE

Entrepreneur Suffers Growing Pains at Arkansas Freightways

Last July, Sheridan Garrison got the news that countless entrepreneurs secretly crave: His biggest competition, Jones Truck Lines, had gone out of business. Fast-growing Arkansas Freightways Corporation, which Mr. Garrison founded, seemingly stood to make a fortune as hundreds of shippers scrambled for someone to haul their goods. Mr. Garrison quickly signed up as many customers as he could. But instead of a windfall, he got a nightmare.

Overloaded with business, the regional trucking firm's terminals that service hauling to ten states from Texas to Illinois to Tennessee were backed up for days, infuriating old customers. Some took business elsewhere. The crisis forced the Harrison, Arkansas, concern into costly emergency measures, from paying overtime to renting more trucks. As a result, the company reported a 22 percent drop in net income for the fourth quarter of the year — the first such reversal since Mr. Garrison formed the firm in 1982.

The extra business would bring the company $40 million in annual revenue, but Mr. Garrison soon realized that he had taken on more than he could handle.

The day after Jones failed, Mr. Garrison's company was flooded with orders from its former competitor's customers. "They came to us and said, 'Do you want the business we were giving to Jones?' " Mr. Garrison says. "We're pretty aggressive. We weren't going to turn them down."

In 24 hours, Arkansas Freightways' volume rose 20 percent. The extra business would bring the company $40 million in annual revenue, but Mr. Garrison soon realized he had taken on more than he could handle. At one point, nearly a quarter of all Arkansas Freightways shipments were running behind schedule, up from 5% in normal times. In Dallas and Oklahoma City, two of the company's busiest terminals, shipments that were supposed to be delivered overnight were backed up for days. "That's something I've never experienced before," Mr. Garrison says, "and we'd sold ourselves on service."

He rented 500 trailers and farmed out work to other carriers and to the railroads. Employees labored overtime until the company finished hiring 700 more workers. Office personnel, including senior executives, helped out on the docks, and dock workers became drivers.

Some solutions led to new problems. Packing more goods into each shipment meant trucks took longer to load and unload. The trailers that Arkansas Freightways rented not only required more maintenance but also were much larger than the kind the company normally used, further increasing the time needed for loading. It took five months to overcome such obstacles, but Arkansas Freightways seems back on course. Mr. Garrison says 97 percent of its shipments are arriving on time, partly with the help of a new mainframe computer that supplies a daily analysis of activity at each of the company's 116 terminals. Profit growth, too, has been restored. In the first quarter, net more than doubled to $1.7 million on a 48 percent increase in sales to $57.7 million.

"While we bent some, we never did break," Mr. Garrison says. "But when that company closed its doors, we really had to scramble."

Trucking companies must be ready to deal with the competitive economic environment. Arkansas Freightways found that it took five months, costly emergency measures, and some creative scrambling to assimilate all the new business that it was able to acquire when a rival trucking firm went out of business.

From Michael Selz, "Benefiting from a Rival's Failure May Take Restraint," *Wall Street Journal* (May 19, 1992), B2. Reprinted by permission of Wall Street Journal, © 1992 Dow Jones & Company, Inc. All Rights Reserved Worldwide.

WHAT'S AHEAD Managers such as Sheridan Garrison, the chief executive officer of Arkansas Freightways, must recognize that too much of a focus on one organizational objective like growth can cause an organization serious problems. This chapter can help a manager like Garrison gain a broad appreciation of how managers can use objectives to appropriately guide organizations to success. This chapter discusses (1) the general nature of organizational objectives, (2) different types of organizational objectives, (3) various areas in which organizational objectives should be set, (4) how managers actually work with organizational objectives, and (5) management by objectives (MBO).

GENERAL NATURE OF ORGANIZATIONAL OBJECTIVES

Definition of Organizational Objectives

Organizational objectives are the targets toward which the open management system is directed. They flow from organizational purpose or mission.

The **organizational purpose** is what the organization exists to do, given a particular group of customers and customer needs.

Organizational objectives are the targets toward which the open management system is directed. Organizational input, process, and output, discussed in chapter 2, all exist to reach organizational objectives (see Figure 4.1). Properly developed organizational objectives reflect the purpose of the organization; that is, they flow naturally from the organizational purpose. The **organizational purpose** is what the organization exists to do, given a particular group of customers and customer needs. Table 4.1 contains several statements of organizational purpose, or mission, as developed by actual companies. If an organization is accomplishing its objectives, it is simultaneously accomplishing its purpose and thereby justifying its reason for existence.

Organizations exist for various purposes and thus have various types of objectives. A hospital, for example, may have the primary purpose of providing high-quality medical services to the community. Therefore, its primary objective is furnishing this assistance. The primary purpose of a business organization, in contrast, usually is to make a profit. The primary objective of the business organization, therefore, is to concentrate on making that profit. To illustrate, the primary organizational objective of the Lincoln Electric Company is profit-oriented and has been stated as follows:

> The goal of the organization must be this—to make a better and better product to be sold at a lower and lower price. Profit cannot be the goal. Profit must be a by-product. This is a state of mind and a philosophy. Actually, an organization doing this job as it can be done will make large profits which must be properly divided between user, worker, and stockholder. This takes ability and character.[1]

In a classic article, John F. Mee has suggested that organizational objectives for businesses can be summarized in three points:

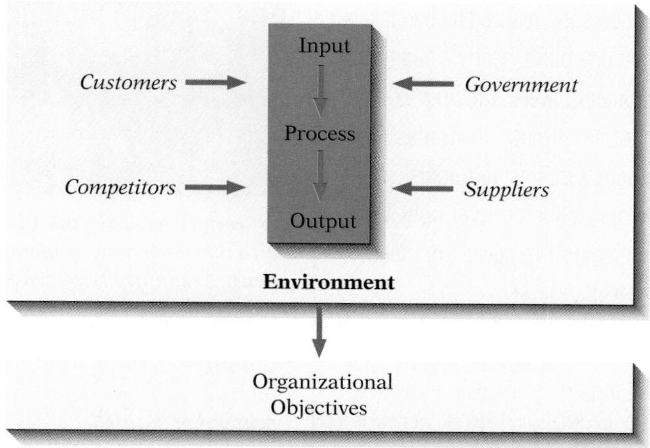

FIGURE 4.1 Existence of open management system to reach organizational objectives

TABLE 4.1 Examples of statements of organizational purpose

Organization name	*Organizational Purpose (Mission)*
DuPont	DuPont is a multinational high-technology company that manufactures and markets chemically related products. It services a diversified group of markets in which proprietory technology provides the competing edge.
Polaroid	Polaroid manufactures and sells photographic products based on its inventions in the field of one-step instant photography and light-polarizing products. Utilizing its inventions in the field of polarized light, the company considers itself to be engaged in one line of business.
Central Soya	The basic mission of Central Soya is to be a leading producer and merchandiser of products for the worldwide agribusiness and food industry.
General Portland Cement	It has long been a business philosophy of Central Portland that "we manufacture and sell cement, but we market concrete." The company sees its job as manufacuring top-quality cement and working with customers to develop new applications for concrete while expanding current uses.

1. Profit is the motivating force for managers.
2. Service to customers by the provision of desired economic values (goods and services) justifies the existence of the business.
3. Social responsibilities do exist for managers in accordance with ethical and moral codes established by the society in which the industry resides.[2]

One of the most important actions managers take is to decide on the objectives for an organization. Unrealistically high objectives are frustrating for employees, and objectives that are too low do not push employees to maximize their potential. Managers should establish performance objectives that they know from experience are within reach for employees, but not within *easy* reach.[3]

GLOBAL HIGHLIGHT
Asea Brown Boveri Decides on Global Objectives

An important part of being a manager is deciding on the objectives to formulate for an organization. Management at ASEA Brown Boveri (ABB) has decided to set the objective to grow in international business.

ABB is the world's largest manufacturer of railway vehicles, the world's leading equipment supplier to the electric power industry, and a major contender in robotics and worldwide pollution control equipment. ABB, winner of R&D magazine's Corporation of the Year award, is a Swiss-Swedish corporation established in 1988. ABB is fast becoming a model for how to manage globally. One of ABB's secrets in accomplishing its objective to grow globally is that the company delegates large amounts of authority to managers around the world but still maintains influence in their important decisions regarding its business. Managers at ABB understand that reaching global objectives involves much more than generating international sales. A company like ABB must use management training sessions to stress the development of global management skills. These skills should include the ability to negotiate more effectively with people from other cultures, the ability to interpret market factors in different countries, and the ability to understand foreign politics. Such training will give a company like ABB a labor force that can compete anywhere in the world.

These Asea Brown Boveri managers now have more autonomy in conducting international business. The company found that it was able to accomplish its objective to grow globally by delegating large amounts of authority to managers in other countries.

Importance of Organizational Objectives

Setting an organizational objective is like identifying the North Star—you sight your compass on it and then use it as the means of getting back on track when you tend to stray.[4] Organizational objectives give managers and all other organization members important guidelines for action in such areas as decision making, organizational efficiency, organizational consistency, and performance evaluation.

Guide for Decision Making

A significant portion of managerial responsibility involves making decisions that inevitably influence the everyday operation and existence of the organization and of organization members. Once managers have a clear understanding of organizational objectives, they know the direction in which the organization must move. It then becomes their responsibility to make decisions that move the organization toward the achievement of its objectives.

Guide for Organizational Efficiency

Because inefficiency results in a costly waste of human effort and resources, managers strive to increase organizational efficiency whenever possible. Efficiency is defined in terms of the total amount of human effort and resources that an organization uses to achieve organizational aims. Therefore, before organizational efficiency can improve, managers must have a clear understanding of organizational goals. Only then are they able to use the limited resources at their disposal as efficiently as possible.

Guide for Organizational Consistency

Organization members often need work-related directives. If organizational objectives are used as the basis for these directives, the objectives serve as a guide to consistent encouragement of such things as productive activity, quality decision making, and effective planning.

Guide for Performance Evaluation

Periodically, the performance of all organization members is evaluated to assess individual productivity and to determine what might be done to increase it. Organizational goals are the guidelines or criteria that should be used as the basis for these evaluations. The individuals who contribute most to the attainment of organizational goals should be considered the most productive. Specific recommendations for increasing productivity should include suggestions about what individuals can do to help the organization move toward goal attainment.[5]

BACK TO THE CASE

The above discussion of organizational objectives gives managers such as Sheridan Garrison, the chief operating officer of Arkansas Freightways, useful insights on how a company can be put on the right track and kept there. The introductory case revealed that Garrison recently focused almost solely on one objective, company growth. He used this objective of growth as a guide for making decisions about taking on the business of a failed competitor and promoting organizational consistency regarding how various company terminals should handle this new business. The case implies that, in order to achieve his objective of growth, Garrison monitored his terminals in various cities and focused on improving their effectiveness in handling new business.

From a management viewpoint, these steps that Garrison took to pursue and reach his growth objective were logical. Although, when considering the shorter run, it is debatable if Garrison made a sound decision to pursue the growth objective to such an extent, it seems that, as a longer term result of Garrison's decision, profits have been restored and even increased.

TYPES OF OBJECTIVES IN ORGANIZATIONS

Objectives can be separated into two categories: organizational and individual. Recognizing the two categories and reacting appropriately to each is a challenge for all modern managers.

Organizational Objectives

Organizational objectives are the formal targets of the organization and are set to help the organization accomplish its purpose. They concern such areas as organizational efficiency, productivity, and profit maximization.

Y.K. Shetty conducted a study to determine the nature and pattern of corporate objectives as they actually exist in organizations. Shetty analyzed 193 companies in four basic industrial groups: (1) chemicals and drugs, (2) packaging materials, (3) electricity and electronics, and (4) food processing.[6] The results of his study indicate that the most common organizational objectives relate to profitability, growth, and market share. Social responsibility and employee welfare objectives are also common and probably reflect a change in managerial attitude over a period of years. Still important but less commonly used objectives, according to the Shetty study, relate to efficiency, research and development, and financial stability.

Individual Objectives

Individual objectives, which also exist within organizations, are the personal goals each organization member would like to reach through activity within the organization. These objectives might include high salary, personal growth and development, peer recognition, and societal recognition.

Individual objectives are personal goals that each organization member would like to reach as a result of personal activity in the organization.

A management problem arises when organizational objectives and individual objectives are not compatible.[7] For example, a professor may have an individual goal of working at a university primarily to gain peer recognition. Perhaps she pursues this recognition primarily by channeling most of her energies into research. This professor's individual objective could make a significant contribution to the attainment of organizational objectives if she were at a university whose organizational objectives emphasized research. Her individual objective might contribute little or nothing to organizational goal attainment, however, if she were employed at a teaching-oriented university. Rather than improving her general teaching ability and the quality of her courses, as the university goals would suggest, she would be secluded in the library writing research articles.

One alternative managers have in situations of this type is to structure the organization so that individuals have the opportunity to accomplish individual objectives while contributing to organizational goal attainment. For example, the teaching-oriented university could take steps to ensure that good teachers received peer recognition—for example, by offering an "excellence in teaching" award. In this way, professors could strive for their personal peer recognition goal while also contributing to the university's organizational objective of good teaching.

An objective, or goal, integration model can assist managers trying to understand and solve problems related to conflict between organizational and individual objectives. Jon Barrett's model, presented in Figure 4.2, depicts a situation in which the ob-

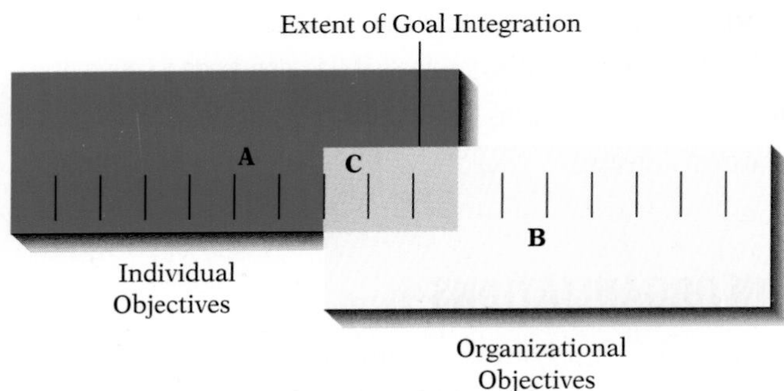

FIGURE 4.2 Goal integration model

Goal integration is compatibility between individual and organizational objectives. It occurs when organizational and individual objectives are the same.

jectives in area C are the only individual ones (area A) compatible with organizational ones (area B). Area C represents the extent of **goal integration.**

Managers should keep two things in mind about the situation depicted in this figure: The individual will tend to work for goals in area C without much managerial encouragement, because the attainment of these goals will result in some type of reward the individual considers valuable. And the individual will usually not work for goals outside area A without some significant type of managerial encouragement, because the attainment of these goals holds little promise of any reward the individual considers valuable. Barrett suggests that "significant types of managerial encouragement" could be (1) modifications to existing pay schedules, (2) considerate treatment from superiors, and (3) additional opportunities to engage in informal social relationships with peers.

BACK TO THE CASE Finding a common ground between organizational objectives and individual objectives often is no easy task, and conflict between these two types of objectives can spell trouble for an organization. Perhaps part of the past success that Garrison has had in accomplishing growth at Arkansas Freightways is the compatibility between organizational and individual objectives. For example, key managers of company terminals as well as drivers at Arkansas Freightways could have individual objectives of national visibility and recognition within the trucking industry. Assuming that they believe that company growth can contribute to the satisfaction of these two individual needs, they would do all they can to help Garrison to achieve the organizational goal of company growth. In this type of situation, a significant degree of goal integration should help Garrison to achieve company growth.

AREAS FOR ORGANIZATIONAL OBJECTIVES

Peter F. Drucker, one of the most influential management writers of modern times, indicates that the very survival of a management system may be endangered if managers emphasize only a profit objective. This single-objective emphasis encourages managers to take action that will make money today with little regard for how a profit will be made tomorrow.[8]

In practice, managers should strive to develop and attain a variety of objectives in all management system areas where activity is critical to the operation and success of the system. Following are the eight key areas in which Drucker advises managers to set management system objectives:

1. *Market standing.* Management should set objectives indicating where it would like to be in relation to its competitors.

2. *Innovation.* Management should set objectives outlining its commitment to the development of new methods of operation.
3. *Productivity.* Management should set objectives outlining the target levels of production.
4. *Physical and financial resources.* Management should set objectives with regard to the use, acquisition, and maintenance of capital and monetary resources.
5. *Profitability.* Management should set objectives that specify the profit the company would like to generate.
6. *Managerial performance and development.* Management should set objectives that specify rates and levels of managerial productivity and growth.
7. *Worker performance and attitude.* Management should set objectives that specify rates of worker productivity as well as the attitudes workers possess.
8. *Public responsibility.* Management should set objectives that indicate the company's responsibilities to its customers and society and the extent to which the company intends to live up to those responsibilities. An example of public or social responsibility objectives can be seen in the "Ethics Highlight."

According to Drucker, since the first five goal areas relate to tangible, impersonal characteristics of organizational operation, most managers would not dispute their designation as key areas. Designating the last three as key areas could arouse some managerial opposition, however, since these areas are more personal and subjective. Regardless of potential opposition, an organization should have objectives in all eight areas to maximize its probability of success.

PARTAGER
LES SERINGUES
SIDA
C'EST RISQUER
LE SIDA

A leaflet in French warns of the danger of acquiring AIDS from shared needles. One corporation, IBM France, has undertaken action to educate employees and their families about ways to help prevent the spread of AIDS.

ETHICS HIGHLIGHT
IBM France Fights AIDS

In France, IBM has set clearly focused objectives of social responsibility. According to Patrick Vienot, the health and safety manager for IBM France, employers have a responsibility to help preserve the general health of society. Vienot feels that companies can help to enhance the health of society by fighting the spread of acquired immune deficiency syndrome (AIDS) through educating employees and their families.

Worldwide, IBM openly and publicly discusses AIDS to educate its employees and the general public about preventing and coping with the illness. IBM tries to protect its 400,000 employees worldwide by providing leaflets about the disease, and by providing small kits for traveling employees. These kits include needles and syringes in case employees need medical treatment in countries where contaminated medical equipment is a serious risk. IBM has stated publicly that it will not ostracize employees who have AIDS. ▶

WORKING WITH ORGANIZATIONAL OBJECTIVES

Appropriate objectives are fundamental to the success of any organization. Theodore Levitt states that some leading industries may be on the verge of facing the same financial disaster as did the railroads, because their objectives are inappropriate for their organizations.[9] Managers, therefore, should approach the development, use, and modification of organizational objectives with utmost seriousness. In general, an organization should have (1) **short-term objectives** (targets to be achieved in one year or less), (2) **intermediate-term objectives** (targets to be achieved in one to five years), and (3) **long-term objectives** (targets to be achieved in five to seven years).

Short-term objectives are targets to be achieved in one year or less.

Intermediate-term objectives are targets to be achieved within one to five years.

Long-term objectives are targets to be achieved within five to seven years.

The **principle of the objective** is a management guideline that recommends that before managers initiate any action, organizational objectives should be clearly determined, understood, and stated.

The necessity of predetermining appropriate organizational objectives has led to the development of what is called the **principle of the objective.** The principle is that before managers initiate any action, organizational objectives should be clearly determined, understood, and stated.[10]

Establishing Organizational Objectives

Setting objectives increasingly is becoming a required and important part of a manager's job. Managers commonly are being asked to establish objectives for themselves, their departments, and their employees.[11] The three main steps that managers must take to develop a set of working organizational objectives are (1) determine the existence of any environmental trends that could significantly influence the operation of the organization, (2) develop a set of objectives for the organization as a whole, and (3) develop a hierarchy of organizational objectives. These three steps are interrelated and usually require input from several people at different levels and operational sections of the organization. Each step is further developed in the paragraphs that follow.

Analyzing Trends

The first step in setting organizational objectives is to list major trends that have existed in the organizational environment over the past five years and to determine if these trends have had a noticeable impact on organizational success. Conceivably, the trends could include such factors as changing customer needs,[12] marketing innovations of competitors, government controls, and social trends such as decreasing family size. Management should then decide which present and future trends are likely to affect organizational success over the next five years. This decision will determine what kinds of objectives are set at various levels of the organization.

QUALITY HIGHLIGHT
American Management Association: "Management Values Trend Influences Product Quality Objectives"

Many different kinds of trends can influence the types of objectives set within an organization. Changes in managers' values over time is one such trend.

According to a recent study by the American Management Association, United States managers today have significantly different values than they had ten years ago. As one example, managers of today place more value on product quality and customers than managers of ten years ago. As a result, a greater proportion of today's managers are setting product quality and customer service objectives than did managers of the past. Customer service objectives are usually explained as a means of enhancing overall product quality within the organization.

A 1991 study by the American Management Association revealed that quality and customer service were organizational objectives given the highest priorities by managers at all levels.

The study focused on almost 1,100 American Management Association numbers. The 1991 Study of the Values of American Managers was undertaken exactly ten years after AMA's first study of values among AMA members. During the 1980s, few managers believed that quality and customer service were important enough to be singled out explicitly as organizational goals. However, when studied as part of the 1991 survey, the objectives of quality and customer service were given the highest priorities by managers at all levels.

The study further indicated that managers' values have changed most significantly regarding the balance between work and home demands. In 1981, more than 62 percent said that they would attend a job-related function rather than an important home function. In 1991, this percentage fell to 45 percent. In light of this change in values regarding the balance of work and home demands, it will be interesting to see what type of organizational objectives managers will encourage over the next few years. ▶

Developing Objectives for the Organization as a Whole

After analyzing environmental trends, management should develop objectives that reflect this analysis for the organization as a whole. For example, the analysis may show that a major competitor has been continually improving its products over the past five years and, as a result, is gaining an increasingly large share of the market. In reaction to this trend, management should set a product improvement objective in an effort to keep up with competitors. This objective would result directly from identification of a trend within the organizational environment and from the organizational purpose of profit. The paragraphs that follow illustrate how management might set financial objectives, product-market mix objectives, and functional objectives for the organization as a whole.

DIVERSITY HIGHTLIGHT
Diversity: Objective for the Whole Organization at the Department of Transportation

Managers at the Department of Transportation (DOT), a major department within the U.S. government, appreciate the role that a properly managed, diverse work force can play in making an organization successful. In fact, management has established an objective for DOT as a whole that focuses on building the contribution that a diverse work force can make to organizational success.

DOT has set the objective of creating a work environment that fully values and uses the talents and capabilities of all employees, including employees of different cultures and colors. Several specific actions have been taken at DOT to try to accomplish this diversity objective. Management began by holding sessions with DOT employees to hear their suggestions on how to best create a diversity-sensitive environment. Building upon this employee input, DOT held a diversity summit that was attended by over 650 DOT executives from across the country. The purpose of the summit was to pinpoint and explore diversity-related challenges and opportunities that confront DOT today. DOT has also assembled a team of human resources management professionals to work full-time on promoting diversity. This team works closely with managers throughout DOT to create, plan, and implement diversity initiatives and ensure that diversity issues are emphasized in all facets of department operations. DOT also publishes a diversity newsletter to help employees understand diversity issues, to provide them with information about department initiatives in the area of diversity, and to explain how diversity issues can be confronted in the workplace. ▶

Creating a work environment that fully values and uses the talents of all its employees is one objective of the Department of Transportation. To accomplish this, DOT held a diversity summit, attended by over 650 DOT executives throughout the country. Its purpose was to pinpoint and explore diversity-related challenges and opportunities facing the department.

Financial objectives are organizational targets relating to monetary issues. They are influenced by return on investment and financial comparison with competitors.

Establishing Financial Objectives. **Financial objectives** are organizational targets relating to monetary issues. In some organizations, government regulations guide management's setting of these objectives. Managers of public utility organizations, for example, have definite guidelines for the types of financial objectives they are allowed to set. In organizations free from government constraints, the setting of financial objectives is influenced mainly by return on investment and financial comparisons with competitors.[13]

Return on investment (ROI) is the amount of money an organization earns in relation to the amount of money invested to keep the organization in operation.[14] Figure 4.3 shows how to use earnings of $50,000 and an investment of $500,000 to calculate a return on investment. If the calculated return is too low, managers can set an overall objective to improve the organization's rate of return.

Information on organizational competition is available through published indexes, such as Dun & Bradstreet's *Ratios for Selected Industries.* These ratios reflect industry averages for key financial areas. Comparing company figures with the industrial averages should tell management about the areas in which new financial objectives probably should be set or the ways in which existing objectives should be modified.[15]

$$\text{Return on Investment} = \frac{\text{Total dollar amount earned}}{\text{Total dollar amount invested to keep organization operating}}$$

$$\text{Return on Investment} = \frac{\$50{,}000 \text{ (earnings)}}{\$500{,}000 \text{ (investment)}} = .10 = 10\% \text{ (rate of return)}$$

FIGURE 4.3 Calculations for return on investment

Product-market mix objectives are objectives that outline which products and the relative number or mix of these products the organization will attempt to sell.

Establishing Product-Market Mix Objectives. **Product-market mix objectives** outline which products—and the relative number or mix of these products—the organization will attempt to sell. Granger suggests the following five steps in formulating product-market mix objectives:[16]

1. Examination of key trends in the business environments of the product-market areas.
2. Examination of growth trends (both market and volume) and profit trends (for the industry and for the company) in the individual product-mix areas.
3. Separation of product-market areas into those that are going to pull ahead and those that are going to drag. For promising areas, these questions need to be asked: How can these areas be made to flourish? Should additional injections of capital, marketing effort, technology, management talent, or the like be used? For the less promising areas, these questions are pertinent: Why is the product lagging? How can this be corrected? If it cannot be corrected, should the product be milked for whatever can be regained, or should it be withdrawn from the market?
4. Consideration of the need or desirability of adding new products or market areas to the mix. In this regard, management should ask these questions: Is there a profit gap to be filled? Based on the criteria of profit opportunity, compatibility, and feasibility of entry, what are possible new areas of interest in order of priority? What sort of programs (acquisitions or internal development) does the company need to develop the desired level of business in these areas?
5. Derivation of an optimum yet realistic product-market mix profile based on the conclusions reached in steps 1–4. This profile embodies the product-market mix objectives, which should be consistent with the organization's financial objectives. Interaction while setting these two kinds of objectives is advisable.

Functional objectives are targets relating to key organizational functions. They should be consistent with financial and product-market mix objectives.

Establishing Functional Objectives. **Functional objectives** are targets relating to key organizational functions, including marketing, accounting, production, and personnel. Functional objectives that are consistent with the financial and product-market mix objectives should be developed for these areas. People in the organization should perform their functions in a way that helps the organization attain its other objectives.[17]

BACK TO THE CASE The information just presented implies that managers such as Garrison should set and strive to achieve objectives in addition to growth objectives. These other objectives should be set in such areas as profitability, market standing, innovation, productivity, physical and financial resources, managerial performance and development, worker performance and attitude, and public responsibility. Naturally, they should be set for the short, intermediate, and long term.

Before developing such objectives, however, Garrison should pinpoint any environmental trends, such as changes in the cost of gasoline or the growth of competitors, that could influence Arkansas Freightways operations. Objectives that reflect such environmental trends could then be set for the organization as a whole. They normally would include financial objectives, such as return on investment, as well as product-market mix objectives, such as the length and size of hauls the company will offer.

Developing a Hierarchy of Objectives

In practice, an organizational objective must be broken down into subobjectives so that individuals of different levels and sections of the organization know what they must do to help reach the overall organizational objective.[18] An organizational objective is attained only after the subobjectives have been reached.

The overall organizational objective and the subobjectives assigned to the various people or units of the organization are referred to as a **hierarchy of objectives.** Figure 4.4 presents a sample hierarchy of objectives for a medium-sized company.

A **hierarchy of objectives** is the overall organizational objectives and the subobjectives assigned to the various people or units of the organization.

Suboptimization exists when subobjectives are conflicting or not directly aimed at accomplishing the overall organizational objective. Figure 4.4 shows that suboptimization could exist within this company between the first subobjective for the finance and accounting department and the second subobjective for the supervisors. Suboptimization would result if supervisors needed new equipment to maintain production and the finance and accounting department couldn't approve the loan without the

Suboptimization is a condition wherein organizational subobjectives are conflicting or not directly aimed at accomplishing overall organizational objectives.

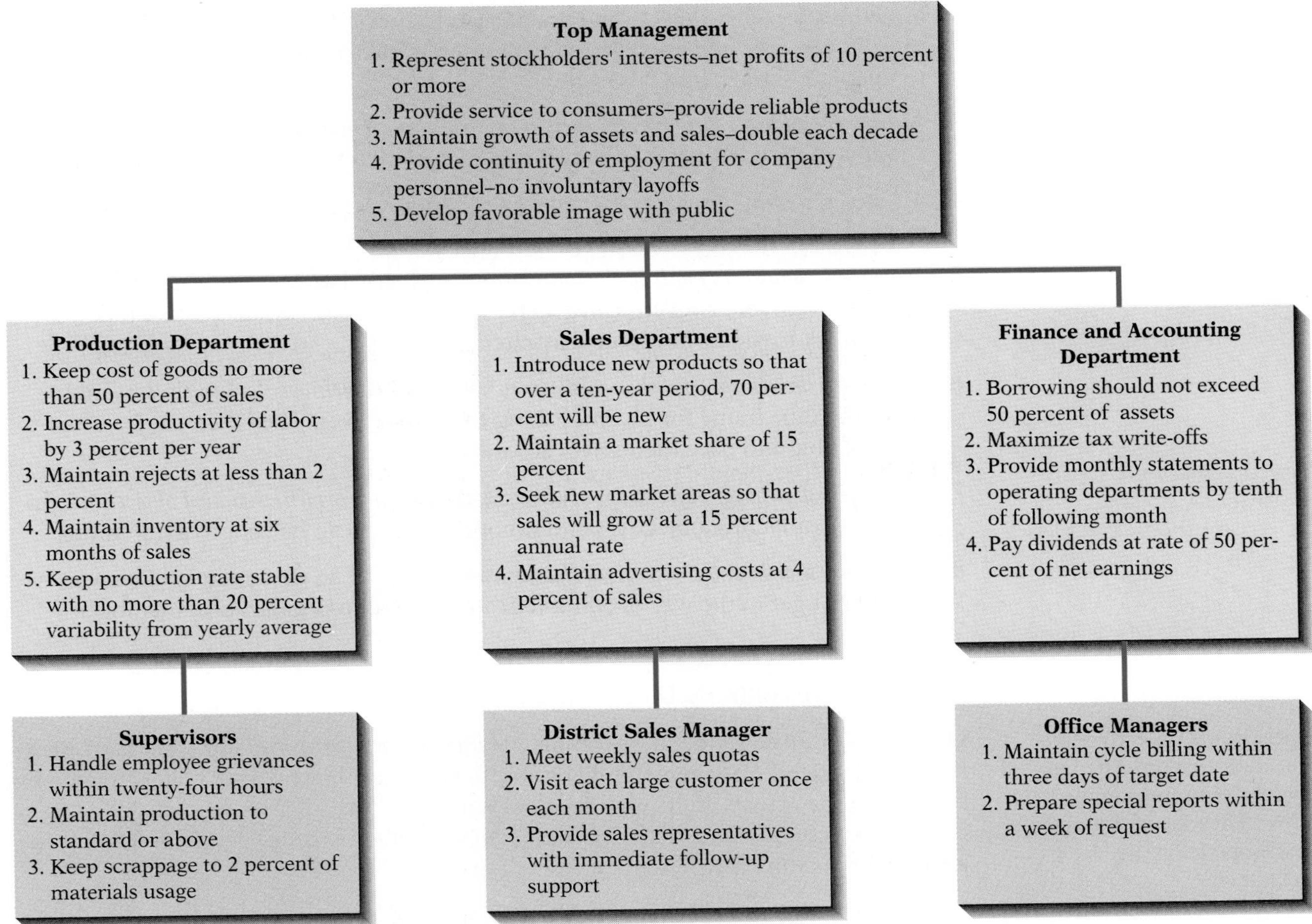

Top Management
1. Represent stockholders' interests–net profits of 10 percent or more
2. Provide service to consumers–provide reliable products
3. Maintain growth of assets and sales–double each decade
4. Provide continuity of employment for company personnel–no involuntary layoffs
5. Develop favorable image with public
Production Department
1. Keep cost of goods no more than 50 percent of sales
2. Increase productivity of labor by 3 percent per year
3. Maintain rejects at less than 2 percent
4. Maintain inventory at six months of sales
5. Keep production rate stable with no more than 20 percent variability from yearly average
Sales Department
1. Introduce new products so that over a ten-year period, 70 percent will be new
2. Maintain a market share of 15 percent
3. Seek new market areas so that sales will grow at a 15 percent annual rate
4. Maintain advertising costs at 4 percent of sales
Finance and Accounting Department
1. Borrowing should not exceed 50 percent of assets
2. Maximize tax write-offs
3. Provide monthly statements to operating departments by tenth of following month
4. Pay dividends at rate of 50 percent of net earnings
Supervisors
1. Handle employee grievances within twenty-four hours
2. Maintain production to standard or above
3. Keep scrappage to 2 percent of materials usage
District Sales Manager
1. Meet weekly sales quotas
2. Visit each large customer once each month
3. Provide sales representatives with immediate follow-up support
Office Managers
1. Maintain cycle billing within three days of target date
2. Prepare special reports within a week of request

FIGURE 4.4 Hierarchy of objectives for a medium-sized organization

company's borrowing surpassing 50 percent of company assets. In this situation, established subobjectives would be aimed in different directions. A manager would have to choose which subobjective would best contribute to obtaining overall objectives and should therefore take precedence.

Controlling suboptimization in organizations is part of a manager's job. Suboptimization can be minimized by developing a thorough understanding of how various parts of the organization relate to one another and by making sure that subobjectives properly reflect these relations.

Guidelines for Establishing Quality Objectives

As with all humanly developed commodities, the quality of goal statements can vary drastically. Managers can increase the quality of their objectives, however, by following some general guidelines:

1. *Managers should let the people responsible for attaining the objectives have a voice in setting them.* Often, the people responsible for attaining the objectives know their job situation better than the managers do and can help to make the objectives more realistic. (They will also be better motivated to achieve them.) Work-related problems that these people face should be thoroughly considered when meaningful objectives are being developed.
2. *Managers should state objectives as specifically as possible.* Precise statements minimize confusion and misunderstanding and ensure that employees have explicit directions for what they should do. Research shows that when objectives are not specific, the productivity of individuals attempting to reach those objectives tends to fluctuate significantly over time.[19]
3. *Managers should relate objectives to specific actions whenever necessary.* In this way, employees do not have to infer what they should do to accomplish their goals.
4. *Managers should pinpoint expected results.* Employees should know exactly how managers will determine whether or not an objective has been reached.
5. *Managers should set goals high enough that employees will have to strive to meet them but not so high that employees give up trying to meet them.* Managers want employees to work hard but not to be frustrated.
6. *Managers should specify when goals are expected to be achieved.* Employees must know the time frame for accomplishing their objectives. They then can be somewhat flexible and pace themselves accordingly.
7. *Managers should set objectives only in relation to other organizational objectives.* In this way, conflicting objectives and suboptimization can be kept to a minimum.
8. *Managers should state objectives clearly and simply.* The written or spoken word should not get in the way of communicating a goal to organization members.

Guidelines for Making Objectives Operational

Operational objectives are objectives that are stated in observable or measurable terms. They specify the activities or operations needed to attain them.

Objectives must be stated in operational terms. That is, if an organization has **operational objectives,** managers should be able to tell if the objectives are being attained by comparing the actual results with the goal statements.[20]

For example, assume that a physical education instructor has set the following objectives for his students:

1. Each student will strive to develop a sense of balance.
2. Each student will attempt to become flexible.

3. Each student will try to become agile.
4. Each student will try to become strong.
5. Each student will work on becoming powerful.
6. Each student will strive to become durable.

These objectives are not operational because the activities and operations a student must perform to attain them are not specified. Additional information, however, could easily make the objectives operational. For example, the fifth physical education objective could be replaced with: Each student will strive to develop the power to do standing broad jumps the distance of his or her height plus one foot. Table 4.2 lists four basically nonoperational objectives and then shows how each can be made operational.

BACK TO THE CASE Once managers have set overall objectives for their organization, the next step is to develop a company hierarchy of objectives. The development of this hierarchy entails breaking down the organization's overall objectives into subobjectives so that all organization members know what they must do to help the company reach its overall objectives.

At Arkansas Freightways, although a hierarchy of objectives probably exists, it may not include a wide array of objectives. Most employees probably understand that the company places a serious emphasis on developing new business, maintaining terminals and driving schedules that support this growth, and know what their particular roles regarding this emphasis actually are. In addition, the company should be sure to address the setting and accomplishment of objectives in other areas, such as social responsibility, employee welfare, and diversification.

In establishing a hierarchy of objectives, Garrison must be careful not to suboptimize, or establish objectives or subobjectives that conflict with one another. Suboptimization is probably a problem at Arkansas Freightways, since growth objectives seem in conflict with objectives such as profitability and high-quality service. In most organizations, confusion about issues such as not knowing what organizational objectives and subobjectives actually exist can make it difficult for managers to recognize when suboptimization is occurring.

Other guidelines for establishing useful objectives at a company like Arkansas Freightways include making the objectives clear, consistent, challenging, and specific. Perhaps most important of all, organizational objectives should be operational. These are certainly good guidelines for Garrison to follow in formulating organizational objectives for Arkansas Freightways. In addition, if Garrison allows workers to participate in establishing organizational objectives, he can ensure that company objectives are realistic and that organization members are committed to reaching them.

TABLE 4.2 Nonoperational objectives versus operational objectives

Nonoperational Objectives	*Operational Objectives*
1. Improve product quality	1. Reduce quality rejects to 2 percent
2. Improve communications	2. Hold weekly staff meetings and initiate a newsletter to improve communications
3. Improve social responsibility	3. Hire fifty hard-core unemployed each year
4. Issue monthly accounting reports on a more timely basis	4. Issue monthly accounting reports so they are received three days following the close of the accounting period

Attainment of Objectives

The attainment of organizational objectives is the obvious goal of all conscientious managers. Managers quickly discover, however, that moving the organization toward goal attainment requires taking appropriate actions within the organization to reach the desired ends. This process is called means–ends analysis.

Means–ends analysis is the process of outlining the means by which various objectives, or ends, in the organization can be achieved.

Basically, **means–ends analysis** entails "(1) starting with the general goal to be achieved; (2) discovering a set of means, very generally specified, for accomplishing this goal; and (3) taking each of these means, in turn, as a new subgoal and discovering a more detailed means for achieving it."[21]

Table 4.3 illustrates means–ends analysis for three sample goals for a hotel: increased market share, financial stability, and owner satisfaction. The goal of increased market share includes two means: good service, and employee morale/loyalty. These two means are subgoals that the hotel manager must focus on attaining in order to reach the goal of increased market share. The last column of the table lists the measures that can be taken to operationalize the subgoals.

Effective managers are aware of the importance not only of setting organizational objectives but also clearly outlining the means by which these objectives can be attained. They know that means–ends analysis is important for guiding their own activities as well as those of their subordinates. The better everyone within the organization understands the means by which goals are to be attained, the greater the probability that the goals actually will be reached.

How to Use Objectives

As stated previously, organizational objectives flow naturally from organizational purpose and reflect the organization's environment. Managers must have a firm understanding of the influences that mold organizational objectives, because as these influences change, the objectives themselves must change. Objectives are not un-

TABLE 4.3 Sample goals, means, and measures for a hotel

Goals	*Means*	*Measures*
Increased market share	Good service	Ratio of repeat business Occupancy Informal feedback
	Employee morale and loyalty	Turnover Absenteeism Informal feedback
Financial stability	Image in financial markets	Price-earnings ratio Share price
	Profitability	Earnings per share Gross operating profit Cost trends Cash flow
	Strength of management team	Turnover Divisional profit Rate of proportion Informal feedback
Owner satisfaction	Adequate cash flow	Occupacy Sales Gross operating profit Departmental profit

changeable directives. In fact, a significant managerial responsibility is to help the organization change objectives when necessary.

MANAGEMENT BY OBJECTIVES (MBO)

Some managers find organizational objectives such an important and fundamental part of management that they use a management approach based exclusively on them. This management approach, called **management by objectives (MBO),** has been popularized mainly through the writings of Peter Drucker.[22] Although mostly discussed as a valuable tool for managers of profit-oriented companies, MBO should also be considered a valuable management tool for managers of nonprofit organizations like libraries or community clubs.[23] The MBO strategy has three basic parts:

Management by objectives (MBO) is a management approach that uses organizational objectives as the primary means by which to manage organizations.

1. All individuals within an organization are assigned a specialized set of objectives that they try to reach during a normal operating period. These objectives are mutually set and agreed upon by individuals and their managers.
2. Performance reviews are conducted periodically to determine how close individuals are to attaining their objectives.
3. Rewards are given to individuals on the basis of how close they come to reaching their goals.[24]

The MBO process contains five steps (see Figure 4.5):

1. *Review organizational objectives.* The manager gains a clear understanding of the organization's overall objectives.
2. *Set worker objectives.* The manager and worker meet to agree on worker objectives to be reached by the end of the normal operating period.
3. *Monitor progress.* At intervals during the normal operating period, the manager and worker check to see if the objectives are being reached.
4. *Evaluate performance.* At the end of the normal operating period, the worker's performance is judged on the extent to which the worker reached the objectives.
5. *Give rewards.* Rewards are given to the worker on the basis of the extent to which the objectives were reached.

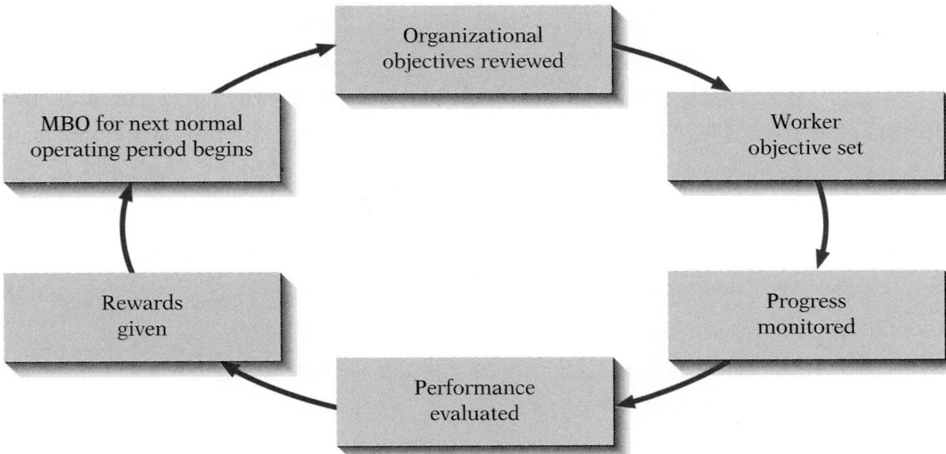

FIGURE 4.5 The MBO Process

Factors Necessary for a Successful MBO Program

Certain key factors are necessary for an MBO program to be successful. First, top management must be committed to the MBO process and set appropriate objectives for the organization.[25] All individual MBO goals are based on these overall objectives. If overall objectives are inappropriate, individual MBO objectives also are inappropriate; and the related individual work activity is nonproductive. Second, managers and subordinates together must develop and agree on each individual's goals. Both managers and subordinates must feel that the individual objectives are just and appropriate if each party is to use them seriously as a guide for action. Third, employee performance should be conscientiously evaluated on the basis of established objectives.[26] This evaluation helps determine whether the objectives are fair and if appropriate means are being used to attain them. Fourth, management must follow through on the employee performance evaluations and reward employees accordingly.[27]

If employees are to continue to strive to reach their MBO program objectives, managers must reward those employees who reach or surpass their objectives more than those who perform short of their objectives. Managers must be careful, however, not to conclude that employees have produced at an acceptable level merely because they have reached their objectives. The objectives set for the employees may have been too low in the first place, and managers failed to recognize it at the time.[28]

MBO Programs: Advantages and Disadvantages

Experienced MBO managers say that there are two advantages to the MBO approach. First, MBO programs continually emphasize what should be done in an organization to achieve organizational goals. Second, the MBO process secures employee commitment to attaining organizational goals. Because managers and subordinates have developed objectives together, both parties are more interested in working to reach those goals.

Managers also admit that MBO programs have disadvantages.[29] One disadvantage is that, because organization members develop objectives together, they actually have less time in which to do their work.[30] Also, elaborate written goals, careful communication of goals, and detailed performance evaluations naturally increase the volume of paperwork in an organization.

Most managers seem to think, however, that MBO's advantages outweigh its disadvantages. Overall, they find MBO programs beneficial.[31]

BACK TO THE CASE

In addition to making sure that an appropriate set of objectives has been developed for an organization, management must also clearly outline for employees the means by which these objectives can be attained. Although Garrison may have done this for the objective of growth, he probably did not follow such guidelines when he quickly took on the extra business created by the failure of his biggest competitor, Jones Truck Lines. Growing too fast caused serious problems, such as difficulties in meeting delivery schedules.

To avoid this problem of growing too fast, Garrison might want to consider clarifying company growth objectives through a management by objectives program. If he did so, each employee would develop with her or his manager a set of mutually agreed upon objectives that would focus on company growth. Performance reviews would give employees feedback on progress in reaching their growth-related objectives, and rewards would be given to the employees who made the most progress. Focusing on growth through an MBO process would let Garrison see immediately if he was considering a growth-related action that would place too much strain on company resources.

ACTION SUMMARY

Reread the learning objectives that follow. Each objective is followed by questions. Answering these questions accurately will help you retain the most important concepts discussed in this chapter. After answering each question, check your answer with the answer key at the end of this chapter. (*Hint:* If you have doubt regarding the correct response, consult the page whose number follows the answer.)

Circle: ***From studying this chapter, I will attempt to acquire:***

1. An understanding of organizational objectives.

T, F **a.** Organizational objectives should reflect the organization's purpose.

a, b, c, d, e **b.** The targets toward which an open management system is directed are referred to as: (a) functional objectives; (b) organizational objectives; (c) operational objectives; (d) courses of action; (e) individual objectives.

2. An appreciation for the importance of organizational objectives.

a, b, c, d, e **a.** Organizational objectives serve important functions in all of the following areas except: (a) making performance evaluations useful; (b) establishing consistency; (c) increasing efficiency; (d) improving wages; (e) decision making that influences everyday operations.

T, F **b.** Implied within organizational objectives are hints on how to define the most productive workers in the organization.

3. An ability to tell the difference between organizational objectives and individual objectives.

a, b, c, d, e **a.** The following is considered to be an individual objective: (a) peer recognition; (b) financial security; (c) personal growth; (d) b and c; (e) all of the above.

a, b, c, d, e **b.** When goal integration exists: (a) there is a positive situation, desired by management; (b) managers will not see conflict between organizational and personal objectives; (c) the individual will work for goals without much managerial encouragement; (d) additional opportunities to engage in informal social relationships with peers will not be necessary to encourage the individual; (e) all of the above.

4. A knowledge of the areas in which managers should set organizational objectives.

a, b, c, d, e **a.** The eight key areas in which Peter F. Drucker advises managers to set objectives include all of the following except: (a) market standing; (b) productivity; (c) public responsibility; (d) inventory control; (e) manager performance and development.

T, F **b.** Long-term objectives are defined as targets to be achieved in one to five years.

5. An understanding of the development of organizational objectives.

a, b, c, d, e **a.** The following factor would not be considered in analyzing trends: (a) marketing innovations of competitors; (b) projections for society; (c) government controls; (d) known existing and projected future events; (e) product-market mix.

a, b, c, d, e **b.** The following factor would not be considered in the "developing objectives for the organization as a whole" stage of setting organizational objectives: (a) establishing a hierarchy of objectives; (b) establishing product-market mix objectives; (c) establishing financial objectives; (d) establishing return-on-investment objectives; (e) establishing functional objectives.

6. Some facility in writing good objectives.

a, b, c, d, e **a.** The following is an objective stated in nonoperational terms: (a) reduce customer complaints by 9 percent; (b) make great progress in new product development; (c) develop a new customer; (d) increase profit before taxes by 10 percent; (e) reduce quality rejects by 2 percent.

T, F **b.** An example of a good operational objective is: "Each student in this class will try to learn how to manage."

7. An awareness of how managers use organizational objectives and help others to attain the objectives.

T, F **a.** Means–ends analysis implies that the manager is results-oriented and discovers a set of means for accomplishing a goal.

a, b, c, d, e **b.** Managers should use the following guidelines in changing objectives: (a) objectives should not be changed; (b) adapt objectives when the organization's environmental influences change; (c) change objectives to create suboptimization as needed; (d) adapt objectives so that they are nonoperational; (e) all of the above are valid guidelines.

8. An appreciation for the potential of a management by objectives (MBO) program.

T, F **a.** Both performance evaluations and employee rewards should be tied to objectives assigned to individuals when the firm is using MBO.

a, b, c, d, e **b.** A method under which a manager is given specific objectives to achieve and is evaluated according to the accomplishment of these objectives is: (a) means–ends analysis; (b) operational objectives; (c) individual objectives; (d) management by objectives; (e) management by exception.

INTRODUCTORY CASE WRAP-UP

"Entrepreneur Suffers Growing Pains at Arkansas Freightways" (p. 89) and its related back-to-the-case sections were written to help you better understand the management concepts discussed in this chapter. Answer the following discussion questions about this introductory case to further enrich your understanding of the chapter content:

1. If you were Garrison, what objectives besides growth would you develop for Arkansas Freightways? Discuss the importance of each objective to the success of the company.
2. Explain how Garrison's preoccupation with growth caused problems in the company. List several of these problems, explain how they were created, and discuss how they could be eliminated in the future.
3. As a manager, what strengths does Garrison have? What weaknesses does he have?

ISSUES FOR REVIEW AND DISCUSSION

1. What are organizational objectives and how do they relate to organizational purpose?
2. Explain why objectives are important to an organization.
3. List four areas in which organizational objectives can act as important guidelines for performance.
4. Explain the difference between organizational objectives and individual objectives.
5. What is meant by goal integration?
6. List and define eight key areas in which organizational objectives should be set.
7. How do environmental trends affect the process of establishing organizational objectives?
8. How does return on investment relate to setting financial objectives?
9. Define *product-market mix objectives*. What process should a manager go through to establish them?
10. What are functional objectives?
11. What is a hierarchy of objectives?
12. Explain the purpose of a hierarchy of objectives.
13. How does suboptimization relate to a hierarchy of objectives?

14. List eight guidelines a manager should follow to establish quality organizational objectives.
15. How does a manager make objectives operational?
16. Explain the concept of means–ends analysis.
17. Should a manager ever modify or change existing organizational objectives? If no, why? If yes, when?
18. Define *MBO* and describe its main characteristics.
19. List and describe the factors necessary for an MBO program to be successful.
20. Discuss the advantages and the disadvantages of MBO.

ACTION SUMMARY ANSWER KEY

1. a. T, p. 90
b. b, p. 90
2. a. d, p. 92
b. T, p. 92
3. a. e, p. 93
b. e, p. 94
4. a. d, pp. 94–95
b. F, p. 95
5. a. e, p. 96
b. a, p. 97
6. a. b, pp. 100–101
b. F, p. 101
7. a. T, p. 102
b. b, pp. 102–103
8. a. T, p. 103
b. d, p. 103–104

CASE STUDY

Planning for Survival at Brant Manufacturing

TONY ORTEGA
California State University, Bakersfield

Brant Manufacturing produces airline seats and seat replacement parts. The company sees the possibility of increasing its profitability by 25 percent if they meet the current demand for new, state-of-the-art equipment.

Airlines are seeking seats that are stronger and lighter in weight than current seats and that have greater capability for passenger comfort and convenience. To keep passengers entertained or busy during the flight, the airlines want to make each seat an entertainment center with features added to make each into a workstation. Providing a telephone, facsimile machine, and a power outlet for a laptop computer, and a small writing table will allow passengers to spend their time aloft productively. The idea of providing a local area network capability that readily connects all or some of the computers, telephones, and fax machines in the aircraft cabin to each other or to ground-based work stations is potentially lucrative.

Brant is small, with approximately 125 employees. Ten people—executives, administrators, design engineers, and production engineers—make up top management. All are English speaking with a very limited ability in Spanish. The workforce are local, skilled Hispanic workers who have limited English-speaking abilities. Although communication is constrained, the workers are eager to learn; they consistently work hard to meet production deadlines. Top management is pleased with the workers because they learn quickly and are productive and highly reliable. The work environment is relaxed, yet busy, because workers are courteous and cooperative. Morale is high.

The most senior and most skilled worker, Emilio Morales, has been with the company since it was founded. He speaks only Spanish. He is a strong leader and can perform all jobs. His major achievement to date is that he reduced maintenance costs by training a small group of workers to perform all maintenance operations on existing machinery. He has turned down a promotion to a supervisory position so that he can continue to train employees who are new to the company or who are moving up to higher paying jobs that require greater skills.

The company has been conducting research and development on a haphazard basis. Morales has been the leader in developing improved production methods and has been effective in developing new ideas for product improvement. Since the skill level and productivity of the workforce has improved significantly, managers have been encouraged to seriously consider improving production methods and formalizing their research and development program.

They recognize, however, that some critical challenges must be resolved before the company can move forward. The production floor must be redesigned to provide isolated work areas where workers can safely use toxic materials; special worker protection measures must be defined, designed, and installed; the implementation of robots and the highly automated, computer-driven production tools that handle highly toxic materials will require a significant capital outlay; training programs must be developed in English and Spanish and instructors must be bilingual; all workers must be trained and tested; adequate bilingual signs for worker safety must be designed; appropriate disposal technology and methods for toxic wastes must be installed; significant time and expense must be spent to obtain the licenses the company needs for permission to purchase, transport, use, and dispose of toxic materials.

Top managers are convinced that Brant's workforce can take on the production of seats made of advanced, lightweight, composite materials that require complex processes. They believe that workers can be trained to deal with toxic production materials and that trained maintenance workers can assemble the electronic components of the new seats. The need for new production tooling is an important cost factor in their strategic planning. If their workers can produce the new seats, then company profitability will increase at least 25 percent. Management is defining company objectives for the next five years.

DISCUSSION QUESTIONS

1. What company strengths and weaknesses do you see?
2. What factors should the company consider before deciding whether to produce the new types of seats?
3. What are some of the problems top management can expect to encounter?
4. What are some reasonable objectives for the company?

CNN VIDEO CASE

The Essence of Essence Communications

EDWARD LEWIS
Essence Magazine

Edward Lewis, the chairman, founder, and guiding light of Essence Communications, built his company from a $130,000 stake into a $38 million operation in little more than twenty years. Lewis's primary objective has been to provide a print voice for black women in America through *Essence* magazine. In addition, Essence has branched into other media, including mail-order catalogue sales, sewing patterns, an eyewear line, and even television. Essence is now one of the top twenty black-owned businesses in the United States.

When Lewis and his partner Clarence Smith founded Essence Communications, they saw an opportunity to fill a niche, as there were no other magazines addressing the needs of black women. Filling this niche led to their mission: to focus on and deal with a trilogy of needs — jobs, housing, and education — from a black woman's perspective. "I think that's how we survive," Lewis says, "because we deal with real issues. At the same time, we take into consideration [that] she has to work, she's also beautiful, she's also intelligent, she wants to look good and we try to make her feel good through the pages of *Essence*." Of course, *Essence*'s broader mission is to achieve all of this while being profitable.

Edward Lewis founded Essence *magazine to fill a marketing niche by addressing a trilogy of needs of African-American women: jobs, housing, and education.*

The development of *Essence*'s profitability is revealed by the growth in its advertising income. The first issue, in May 1970, included 13 pages of ads; the twentieth anniversary issue carried 124 pages of ads. With this many advertisers, and with a monthly circulation of 850,000 readers, the magazine is making money.

Essence's success has given Ed Lewis the opportunity to attain personal goals through business achievement. His generous *Essence* salary enables him to live comfortably and support a household in New York City. He enjoys national recognition and is occasionally seen hobnobbing with Jesse Jackson.

Lewis has not always been successful, though. Despite receiving an alumnus award from his alma mater, the University of New Mexico, academic success was out of reach early in his career. In fact, he acknowledges that academic failures have goaded him on to succeed in business: "It was very difficult because, not having failed before [after failing law school], I began to realize that in life you have your ups and downs and you've got to pick yourself up."

Ed Lewis picked himself up more than twenty years ago and began to define his personal goals: "to speak loud against injustices and really never stop talking, from the standpoint of doing what's right." Lewis sees *Essence* as representative of and as giving voice to the black community in general, as well as to black women in particular. Further, *Essence* offers an innovative product of unquestionable value, combining serious cultural and life-style issues with a sales approach more typical of women's beauty magazines.

Essence Communications provides an excellent example of how an entrepreneur can combine individual and organizational objectives to emerge successful. The growing circulation of *Essence*, the annual *Essence* awards, and the financial growth and diversification of Essence Communications all show that — whether personally or in his business — Ed Lewis continually moves forward.

VIDEO CASE QUESTIONS

1. What is the organizational purpose of *Essence* magazine?
2. Based on the video material, how do you think organizational objectives of *Essence* influence decisions regarding advertising?
3. How do the organizational purpose and organizational objectives of Essence Communications differ? What about Ed Lewis's individual objectives?
4. The text lists eight key areas that Drucker recommends emphasizing as areas for organizational objectives. Which of these does Lewis seem most concerned with, and why?

CNN VIDEO EXERCISE

Setting Organizational Goals, Means, and Measures for *Essence*

EXERCISE GOAL: Learn how a manager can reach stated organizational goals and measure how well those particular means are working.

Your instructor will break the class into groups of three to five members. (Alternatively, this exercise may be done on an individual basis outside of class.) Imagine that your group works as a marketing team for Ed Lewis of *Essence* magazine. The company has given you your marketing goals: 1) increase market share by 5 percent in the women's magazine market, and 2) realize a 10 percent increase in advertising dollars. Groups (or individuals) are to brainstorm and come up with a list of at least three things that the company could do to achieve each of these goals. Then, think in terms of how to measure how well the company is doing in terms of reaching the stated goals. You should devise an appropriate measure for each of the means in your list in order to provide feedback to the company. See Table 4.3 for examples of means and ends measures.

GOAL 1: Increase market share by 5 percent

Suggested Means

(For example, mail a free issue to 50,000 potential subscribers and offer them a 10 percent discount.)

1. ____________________

2. ____________________

3. ____________________

Suggested Measures

(Number of subscribers obtained by this mailing; if successful, repeat the mailing to another 50,000 potential customers.)

1. ____________________

2. ____________________

3. ____________________

GOAL 2: Realize a 10 percent increase in advertising dollars

Suggested Means

(For example, contact four new potential advertisers per week per sales representative.)

1. ____________________

2. ____________________

3. ____________________

Suggested Measures

(Number of new advertisers obtained from contacts.)

1. ____________________

2. ____________________

3. ____________________

CHAPTER

5

FUNDAMENTALS OF PLANNING

STUDENT LEARNING OBJECTIVES

From studying this chapter, I will attempt to acquire:

1. A definition of planning and an understanding of the purposes of planning.
2. A knowledge of the advantages and potential disadvantages of planning.
3. Insights on how the major steps of the planning process are related.
4. An understanding of the planning subsystem.
5. A knowledge of how the chief executive relates to the planning process.
6. An understanding of the qualifications and duties of planners and how planners are evaluated.
7. Guidelines on how to get the greatest return from the planning process.

CHAPTER OUTLINE

INTRODUCTORY CASE
Poor Planning at Weyerhaeuser Kills a Good Product

GENERAL CHARACTERISTICS OF PLANNING

Defining Planning
Purposes of Planning

GLOBAL HIGHLIGHT
SmithKline Beecham

Planning: Advantages and Potential Disadvantages
Primacy of Planning

STEPS IN THE PLANNING PROCESS

DIVERSITY HIGHLIGHT
Johnson & Johnson

THE PLANNING SUBSYSTEM

Quaker Oats Company
Sun Oil Company

PLANNING AND THE CHIEF EXECUTIVE

THE PLANNER

Qualifications of Planners
Duties of Planners
Evaluation of Planners

MAXIMIZING THE EFFECTIVENESS OF THE PLANNING PROCESS

Top Management Support

ETHICS HIGHLIGHT
Shell Oil Company

An Effective and Efficient Planning Organization
An Implementation-Focused Planning Orientation
Inclusion of the Right People

QUALITY HIGHLIGHT
Sun Microsystems

CASE STUDY
Planning for the Pizza Hut Distribution Challenge

VIDEO CASE
Mapping the Future for Amex:
Jim Jones, Amex

VIDEO EXERCISE
Planning Globally for the American Stock Exchange

INTRODUCTORY CASE

Poor Planning at Weyerhaeuser Kills a Good Product

At Wegmans Food Markets, musical videos showed happy babies cooing because a new diaper called UltraSofts kept them dry while it saved their parents money.

Samples and discount coupons were mailed to 50,000 shoppers near the Rochester, N.Y., chain. The hype "was unprecedented," recalls Mary Ellen Burris, Wegmans' consumer affairs director.

Wegmans introduced the product with a huge promotion and advertising campaign last winter. With the $1-off coupon mailed to homes, the bag of 32 large- sized diapers sold for $8.39, or about $1.60 less than the leading brands.

"We've got about 20 problems in the manufacturing process. Many are simple. Some need significant work."

And consumers liked the product. Juanita Gerringer has tried all three national brands but chose UltraSofts for her three-year-old granddaughter, Tina. The toddler is more comfortable in UltraSofts, she says, and they cost at least 10 percent less. "I wouldn't change over to anything else," says the Honeoye, N.Y., consumer.

Such testimonials made the company optimistic. But problems were brewing at its Bowling Green, Kentucky, plant. The system that sprayed the superabsorbent material into the pad didn't work very well. Too much of the material missed the diaper and got into the production line's electronic parts, causing them to corrode. Transformers on the line overheated. The pulp-grinding process, when operated at high speeds, began to burn. Says Bobby Abraham, president of Weyerhaeuser's personal care products division, "We've got about 20 problems in the manufacturing process. Many are simple. Some need significant work."

In addition, Weyerhaeuser couldn't offer suppliers long-term contracts when buying materials needed for the diapers. Without those agreements, the suppliers, who had been manufacturing on a pilot scale, wouldn't expand production of key items like the diaper lining. In turn, production slowed on the UltraSofts line. Instead of full-time production, the Bowling Green plant was making the diapers only once or twice a month, supplying just enough for Wegmans.

Making matters worse, Weyerhaeuser increased UltraSofts' price to retailers 22% to cover the expense of its manufacturing problems. Wegmans says it kept the retail price at $9.39 a bag but couldn't offer nearly as many promotions. The retailer's profits on the diaper have declined because of the price increase, although they won't say by how much.

But, ten months later, UltraSofts is just about dead. Manufacturing problems — including fires and breakdowns on the plant floor that snarled production and triggered a sharp price increase to retailers — have killed Weyerhaeuser Co.'s dream of taking the diaper nationwide. "It's been a disappointment," says Abraham.

The UltraSofts case shows how even the best product innovation can die from poor planning and unexpected problems.

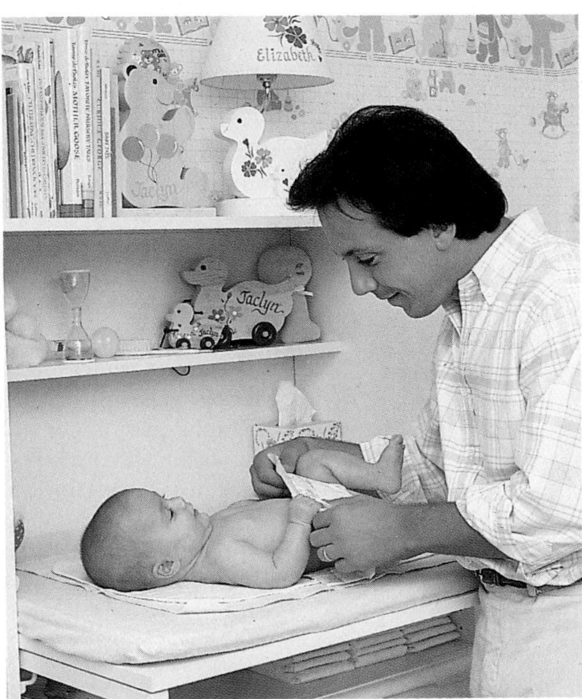

Even satisfied customers willing to buy the product, such as this child's parents, cannot rescue a company from financial disaster when operations problems and poor planning disrupt production.

From Alecia Swasy, "Diaper's Failure Shows How Poor Plans, Unexpected Woes Can Kill New Products," *Wall Street Journal,* October 9, 1990, B1, B4. Reprinted by permission of *Wall Street Journal,* © 1990 Dow Jones & Company, Inc. All Rights Reserved Worldwide.

WHAT'S AHEAD The introductory case discusses the introduction of a new product, UltraSofts baby diapers, by the Weyerhaeuser Company. The case suggests that poor planning can cause the introduction of a new and good product to fail. Concepts in this chapter will help managers such as those at Weyerhaeuser to understand why planning is so important, not only for a new-product-introduction situation, but also for carrying out virtually any other organizational activity. This chapter describes the fundamentals of planning: (1) the general characteristics of planning, (2) steps in the planning process, (3) the planning subsystem, (4) the relationship between planning and the chief executive, (5) the qualifications and duties of planners and how planners are evaluated, and (6) how to maximize the effectiveness of the planning process.

GENERAL CHARACTERISTICS OF PLANNING

Defining Planning

Planning is the process of determining how the management system will achieve its objectives. In other words, it determines how the organization can get where it wants to go.

Planning is the process of determining how the organization can get where it wants to go. Chapter 4 emphasized the importance of organizational objectives and explained how to develop them. Planning is the process of determining exactly what the organization will do to accomplish its objectives. In more formal terms, planning is "the systematic development of action programs aimed at reaching agreed business objectives by the process of analyzing, evaluating, and selecting among the opportunities which are foreseen."[1]

Planning is a critical management activity regardless of the type of organization being managed. Modern managers face the challenge of sound planning in small and relatively simple organizations as well as in large, more complex organizations.[2] In addition, planning challenges confront managers of nonprofit organizations such as libraries[3] as much as they do managers of organizations such as General Motors.

Purposes of Planning

Over the years, management writers have presented several different purposes of planning. For example, C. W. Roney indicates that organizational planning has two purposes: protective and affirmative. The protective purpose of planning is to minimize risk by reducing the uncertainties surrounding business conditions and clarifying the consequences of related management action. The affirmative purpose is to increase the degree of organizational success.[4] For an example of this affirmative purpose, consider Whole Foods Market, a health-food chain in Texas. This company uses planning to ensure success as measured by the systematic opening of new stores. Company head John Mackey believes that increased company success is not an accident, but a direct result of careful planning.[5] Still another purpose of planning is to establish a coordinated effort within the organization. An absence of planning is usually accompanied by an absence of coordination and, therefore, usually contributes to organizational inefficiency.

The fundamental purpose of planning, however, is to help the organization reach its objectives. As stated by Koontz and O'Donnell, the primary purpose of planning is to "facilitate the accomplishment of enterprise and objectives."[6] All other purposes of planning are simply spin-offs of this fundamental purpose.

GLOBAL HIGHLIGHT
The Purposes of Planning and SmithKline Beecham

SmithKline Beckman and Beecham were two large global pharmaceutical companies that recently merged to form a new, even larger global company called SmithKline Beecham. Planning surrounding the merger fulfilled both protective and affirmative purposes.

Global pharmaceutical mergers have helped spread the huge costs of research and have enabled companies to expand their markets to new countries. When SmithKline Beckman and Beecham merged to form SmithKline Beecham, a planning effort was initiated that focused on virtually every aspect of how the new company business should be conducted and how new company resources should be used. To accomplish this planning, over 150 planning teams were established and organized into five major planning groups. Each of three of these groups focused on one of the three major businesses of the newly formed company: pharmaceuticals, over-the-counter health-care products, and animal-care products. The fourth planning group focused on corporate-level procedures and policies, while the fifth group concentrated on how corporate systems should operate. The results of this planning provided substantial benefits for the organization. For example, SmithKline Beecham benefited from significant cost savings by planning for the elimination of activities that both firms had originally performed. Out of this planning process also emerged a plan for how the scientific research resources should be combined into one efficient and effective unit. Overall, this planning effort clearly focused on minimizing risk surrounding the merger situation and increasing the success of the newly-formed SmithKline Beecham. ▶

When pharmaceutical companies SmithKline Beckman and Beecham merged to form SmithKline Beechan, planning teams focused on the three major businesses of the newly formed company, corporate level procedures and policies, and corporate systems.

Planning: Advantages and Potential Disadvantages

A vigorous planning program has many benefits. One is that it helps managers to be future-oriented. They are forced to look beyond their normal everyday problems to project what may confront them in the future.[7] Decision coordination is a second advantage of a sound planning program. No decision should be made today without some idea of how it will affect a decision that might have to be made tomorrow. The planning function helps managers coordinate their decisions. A third advantage to planning is that it emphasizes organizational objectives. Since organizational objectives are the starting points for planning, managers are constantly reminded of exactly what their organization is trying to accomplish.

Overall, planning is very advantageous to an organization. According to a recent survey, as many as 65 percent of all newly-started businesses are not around to celebrate a fifth anniversary. This high failure rate seems primarily caused by inadequate planning within the new businesses. Successful businesses have an established plan, a formal statement that outlines the objectives the organization is attempting to achieve. Planning does not eliminate risk, but it can help managers identify and eliminate organizational problems before they arise.[8]

If the planning function is not well executed within the organization, planning can have several disadvantages. For example, an overemphasized planning program can take up too much managerial time. Managers must strike an appropriate balance between time spent on planning and time spent on organizing, influencing, and controlling. If they don't, some activities that are extremely important to the success of the organization may be neglected. Usually, the disadvantages of planning result from the planning function's being used incorrectly. Overall, the advantages of planning definitely outweigh the disadvantages.

Primacy of Planning

Planning is the primary management function—the function that precedes and is the foundation for the organizing, influencing, and controlling functions of managers. Only after managers have developed their plans can they determine how they want to structure their organization, place their people, and establish organizational controls. As discussed in chapter 1, planning, organizing, influencing, and controlling are interrelated. Planning is the foundation function and the first function to be performed. Organizing, influencing, and controlling are based on the results of planning. Figure 5.1 shows this interrelationship.

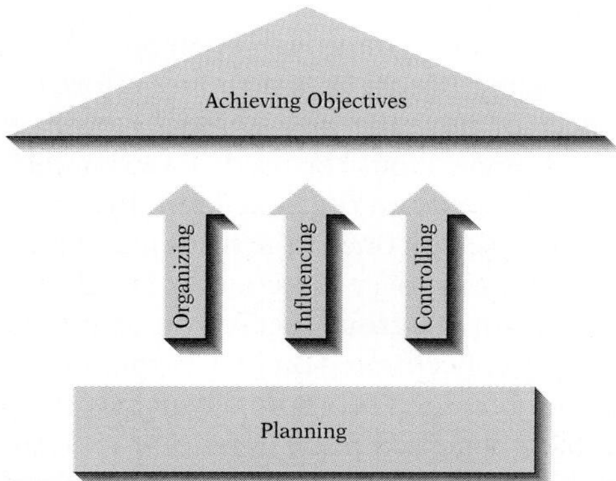

FIGURE 5.1 Planning as the foundation for organizing, influencing, and controlling

BACK TO THE CASE From the facts presented in the introductory case, one may conclude that Weyerhaeuser managers did not plan adequately for the introduction of its new UltraSofts baby diaper product. The process used to determine what Weyerhaeuser should do in fields such as manufacturing and building supplier relations in order to reach its objective of introducing UltraSofts was obviously deficient.

Because of the many related benefits of planning, Weyerhaeuser managers should make certain that the planning process for its next new product introduction is much more thorough and comprehensive. One particularly notable benefit is the probability of increased profits. To gain the benefits of planning, however, Weyerhaeuser managers must be careful that the planning function is well executed and not overemphasized.

Weyerhaeuser management should also keep in mind that planning is the primary management function. Thus, as managers, they should not begin to organize, influence, or control when introducing a new product like UltraSofts until the planning process is complete. Planning is the foundation management function on which all other functions at Weyerhaeuser should be based.

STEPS IN THE PLANNING PROCESS

The planning process contains the following six steps:

1. *State organizational objectives.* A clear statement of organizational objectives is necessary for planning to begin, since planning focuses on how the management system will reach those objectives.[9] In essence, objectives stipulate those areas in which organizational planning must occur.[10] Chapter 4 discusses how the objectives themselves are developed.

2. *List alternative ways of reaching objectives.* Once organizational objectives have been clearly stated, a manager should list as many available alternatives as possible for reaching those objectives.

3. *Develop premises on which to base each alternative.* To a large extent, the feasibility of using any one alternative to reach organizational objectives is determined by the **premises,** or assumptions, on which the alternative is based. For example, two alternatives a manager could generate to reach the organizational objective of increasing profit might be: (a) increase the sale of products presently being produced, or (b) produce and sell a completely new product. Alternative a would be based on the premise that the organization could get a larger share of an existing market. Alternative b would be based on the premise that a new product would

Premises are assumptions on which alternative ways of accomplishing objectives are based.

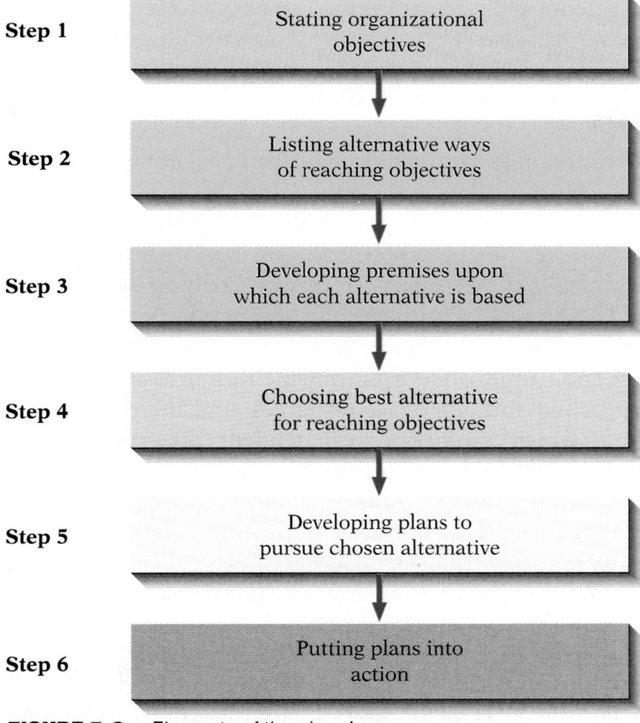

FIGURE 5.2 Elements of the planning process

capture a significant portion of a new market. A manager should list all of the premises for each alternative.

4. *Choose the best alternative for reaching objectives.* An evaluation of alternatives must include an evaluation of the premises on which the alternatives are based. A manager usually finds that the premises on which some of the alternatives are based are unreasonable and can therefore be excluded from further consideration. This elimination process helps determine which alternative would be best to accomplish organizational objectives. The decision making required for this step is discussed more fully in chapter 6.

5. *Develop plans to pursue the chosen alternative.* After an alternative has been chosen, a manager begins to develop strategic (long-range) and tactical (short-range) plans.[11] More information about strategic and tactical planning is presented in chapter 6.

6. *Put the plans into action.* Once plans have been developed, they are ready to be put into action. The plans should furnish the organization with both long-range and short-range direction for activity. Obviously, the organization does not directly benefit from the planning process until this step is performed.

Figure 5.2 shows how the six steps of the planning process relate to one another.

DIVERSITY HIGHLIGHT
Johnson & Johnson Plans to Keep Good Employees by Focusing on Family Diversity

Like many major companies, Johnson & Johnson is developing plans to better attract and retain employees. The Johnson & Johnson philosophy aims to attract and retain employees in the future by taking better care of them today. In addition to

This Johnson & Johnson day care facility is only a part of the family-friendly action that the company has taken to implement a plan to meet the diverse needs of various families within its workforce.

gaining better recruitment and retention figures, the company hopes to see a return in the form of increased productivity, decreased absenteeism, and increased goodwill.

One way that Johnson & Johnson is planning to take better care of its employees today is by improving how the workplace responds to diverse family needs. A modern workforce is represented by many different family structures like single-parent working mothers or fathers, or dual career couples with children; as well as families with responsibilities for elder care.

In 1989, Johnson & Johnson instituted the Balancing Work and Family Program to increase the family-friendly character of its workplace. Balancing Work and Family includes the key management initiative of Manager/Supervisor Training designed to increase sensitivity to work and family issues and policies. In addition to benefits traditionally offered by major companies (family care leave, flexible benefits packages, relocation services), Balancing Work and Family offers a nationwide Resource and Referral Program to help employees find child and elder care resources, and the option of a Dependent Care Account through which employees pay dependent care expenses on a pre-tax basis. Although some Johnson & Johnson facilities have on-site child care centers, the Balancing Work and Family Program encourages managers to arrange for employees with family responsibilities to work at home or during non-standard hours where appropriate.

At Johnson & Johnson as in any company, in order for organizational planning to be successful in creating a family-friendly work environment, top management must solidly support the family-friendly philosophy and its implementation, and employees must be educated as to how organizational success may hinge on meeting the diverse needs of various family types within the workforce. ▶

THE PLANNING SUBSYSTEM

Once managers understand the basics of planning, they can take steps to implement the planning process in their organization. This implementation is the key to a successful planning process. Even though managers might be experts on facts related to planning and the planning process, if they cannot transform this understanding into appropriate action, they are not able to generate useful organizational plans.

A **subsystem** is a system created as part of the process of the overall management system. The planning subsystem increases the effectiveness of the overall management system.

One way of approaching this implementation is to view planning activities as an organizational subsystem. A **subsystem** is a system created as part of the process of the overall management system. Figure 5.3 illustrates this relationship between the overall management system and a subsystem. Subsystems help managers organize the overall system and enhance its success.

Figure 5.4 presents the elements of the planning subsystem. The purpose of this subsystem is to increase the effectiveness of the overall management system through more effective planning. The planning subsystem helps managers to identify planning activities within the overall system and to guide and direct these activities.

Obviously, only a portion of organizational resources is used as input in the planning subsystem. This input is allocated to the planning subsystem and transformed into output through the steps of the planning process.

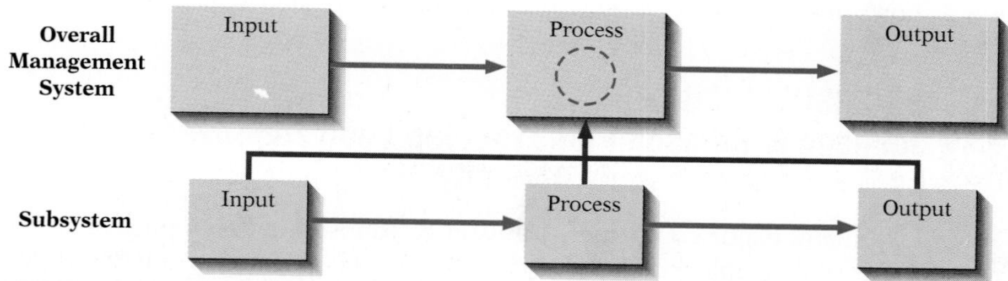

FIGURE 5.3 Relationship between overall management system and subsystem

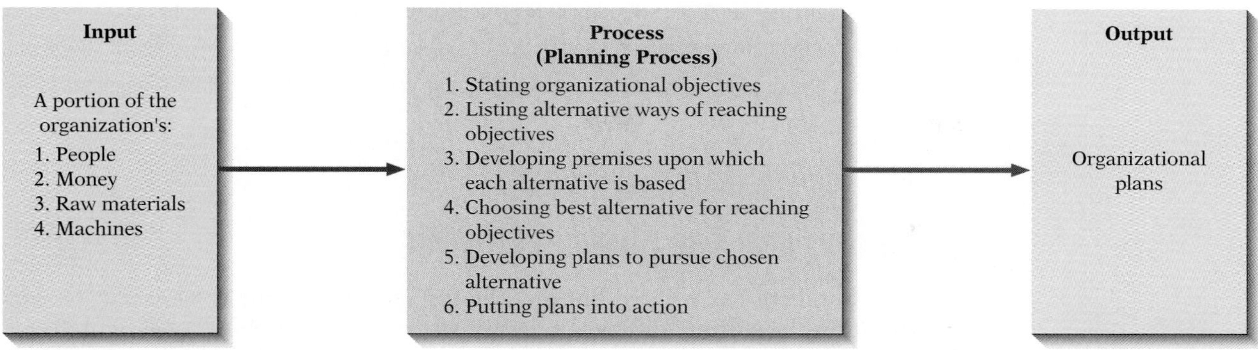

FIGURE 5.4 The planning subsystem

How planning subsystems are organized in the industrial world can be exemplified by the rather informal planning subsystem at the Quaker Oats Company and the more formal planning subsystem at the Sun Oil Company.[12]

Quaker Oats Company

At Quaker Oats, speculations about the future are conducted, for the most part, on an informal basis. To help anticipate particular social changes, the company has opened communication lines with various groups believed to be the harbingers of change. To spearhead this activity, the company has organized a "non-committee," whose members represent a diversity of orientations. They listen to what is going on—monitor social changes—and thus augment the company's understanding of social change. Many companies throughout the world plan in an informal way like Quaker Oats does.[13]

Sun Oil Company

Several groups within Sun Oil Company are engaged in formal business planning and forecasting. Operational planning with a five-year horizon is done annually. The planning activity with the longest time horizon exists within the Sun Oil Company of Pennsylvania, the corporation's refining, transportation, and marketing arm. A centralized planning group, reporting to the vice president of development and planning, is responsible for helping top management set the company's long-term objectives, develop plans to achieve these objectives, and identify likely consumer needs and market developments of the future that might indicate business areas for diversification. Current efforts focus on discussions of a series of long-range issues with the executive committee, a planning process designed to generate a restatement of long-term objectives.

BACK TO THE CASE

For the next new product introduction at Weyerhaeuser, management should design and implement a more useful plan. The process of developing this plan should consist of six steps, beginning with a statement of an organizational objective to successfully introduce the new product and ending with guidelines for putting organizational plans into action.

To implement a planning process at Weyerhaeuser appropriately, management should view planning as a subsystem that is part of the process of the overall management system. They should use a portion of all the organizational resources available at Weyerhaeuser for the purpose of organizational planning. Following our new-product-introduction example, the output of this subsystem would be the actual plans to be used to introduce a new product. Topics such as refining a manufacturing process for the new product and ensuring that suppliers can furnish needed components of the product would be emphasized. Naturally, a comprehensive planning effort at Weyerhaeuser would focus on many other organizational areas besides new product introduction, such as obtaining needed funds and fighting competitors for established products.

PLANNING AND THE CHIEF EXECUTIVE

Henry Mintzberg has pointed out that the top managers—the chief executives—of organizations have many different roles to perform.[14] As organizational figureheads, they must represent their organizations in a variety of social, legal, and ceremonial matters. As leaders, they must ensure that organization members are properly guided in relation to organizational goals. As liaisons, they must establish themselves as links between their organizations and factors outside their organizations. As monitors, they must assess organizational progress. As disturbance handlers, they must settle disputes between organization members. And as resource allocators, they must determine where resources will be placed to benefit their organizations best.

In addition to these many varied roles, chief executives have the final responsibility for organizational planning. As the scope of planning broadens to include a larger portion of the management system, it becomes increasingly important for chief executives to become more involved in the planning process.

As planners, chief executives seek answers to the following broad questions:

1. In what direction should the organization be going?
2. In what direction is the organization going now?
3. Should something be done to change this direction?
4. Is the organization continuing in an appropriate direction?[15]

Keeping informed about social, political, and scientific trends is of utmost importance in helping chief executives to answer these questions.

Given the importance of top management's participating in organizational planning and performing other time-consuming roles, more and more top managers obtain planning assistance by establishing a position for an organization planner.[16] Just as managers can ask others for help and advice in making decisions, they can involve others in formulating organizational plans.[17]

Chief executives of most substantial organizations need help to plan.[18] The remainder of this chapter, therefore, assumes that the organization planner is an individual who is not the chief executive of the organization. The planner is presented as a manager inside the organization who is responsible for giving assistance to the chief executive on organizational planning issues.[19] If, by chance, the planner and the chief executive are the same person in a particular organization, the following discussion relating to the planner can be modified slightly to apply also to the chief executive.

THE PLANNER

Perhaps the most important input in the planning subsystem is the planner. This individual combines all other input and influences the subsystem process so that effective organizational plans become subsystem output. The planner is responsible not only for the plans that are developed but also for advising management about what action should be taken in relation to those plans. Regardless of who actually does the planning or of the organization in which the planning is being done, the qualifications and duties of planners and how planners are evaluated are very important considerations in increasing the effectiveness of the planning subsystem.

Qualifications of Planners

Planners should have four primary qualifications. First, they should have considerable practical experience within their organization. Preferably, they should have been executives in one or more of the organization's major departments. This experience will help them develop plans that are both practical and tailor-made for the organization.

Second, planners should be able to replace any narrow view of the organization (probably acquired while holding other organizational positions) with an understanding of the organization as a whole. They must know how all parts of the organization function and interrelate. In other words, they must possess an abundance of the conceptual skills mentioned in chapter 1.

Third, planners should have some knowledge of and interest in the social, political, technical, and economic trends that could affect the future of the organization. They must be skillful in defining these trends and have the expertise to determine how the organization should react to the trends to maximize success. This particular qualification cannot be overemphasized.

The fourth and last qualification is that planners should be able to work well with others. They inevitably will work closely with several key members of the organization and should possess personal characteristics that are helpful in collaborating and advising effectively. The ability to communicate clearly, both orally and in writing, is one of the most important of these characteristics.[20]

Duties of Planners

Organizational planners have at least three general duties to perform: (1) overseeing the planning process, (2) evaluating developed plans, and (3) solving planning problems.[21]

Overseeing the Planning Process

First, and perhaps foremost, planners must see that planning gets done. To this end, they establish rules, guidelines, and planning objectives that apply to themselves and others involved in the planning process. In essence, planners must develop a plan for planning.

Simply described, a **plan for planning** is a listing of all of the steps that must be taken to plan for an organization. It generally includes such activities as evaluating an organization's present planning process in an effort to improve it, determining how much benefit an organization can gain as a result of planning, and developing a planning timetable to ensure that all of the steps necessary to plan for a particular organization are performed by some specified date.

A **plan for planning** is a listing of all steps that must be taken to plan for an organization. It ensures that planning gets done.

Evaluating Developed Plans

The second general duty of planners is to evaluate plans that have been developed. Planners must decide if plans are sufficiently challenging for the organization, if they are complete, and if they are consistent with organizational objectives. If the developed plans do not fulfill these three requirements, they should be modified appropriately.

Solving Planning Problems

Planners also have the duty to gather information that will help solve planning problems.[22] Sometimes, they may find it necessary to conduct special studies within the organization to obtain this information. They can then recommend what the organization should do in the future to deal with planning problems and forecast how the organization might benefit from related opportunities.

For example, a planner may observe that production objectives set by the organi-

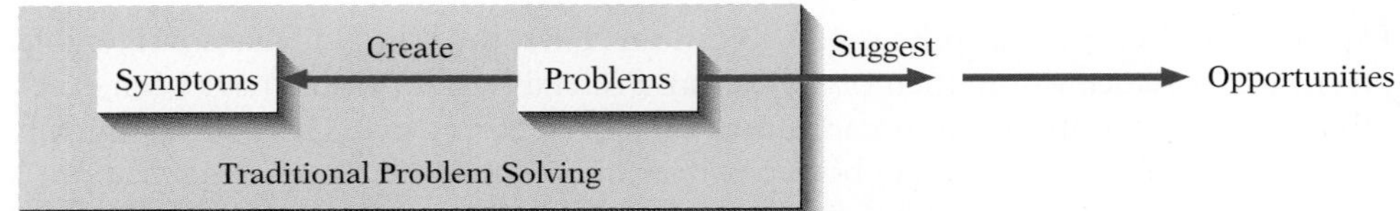

FIGURE 5.5 Relationships among symptoms, problems, and opportunities that face the planner

zation are not being met. This is a symptom of a planning problem. The problem causing this symptom might be that objectives are unrealistically high or that plans developed to achieve production objectives are inappropriate. The planner must gather information pertinent to the problem and suggest to management how the organization can solve its problem and become more successful.

Other symptoms that could signify planning problems are weakness in dealing with competition, declining sales volume, inventory levels that are either too high or too low, high operating expenses, and too much capital being invested in equipment.[23]

King and Cleland have presented the relationships among problems, symptoms, and opportunities in Figure 5.5.

The three duties of planners just discussed—overseeing the planning process, evaluating developed plans, and solving planning problems—are general comments on planners' activities. Table 5.1 lists the specific responsibilities of an organization planner at a large manufacturing company. As this list implies, the main focus of the planner's activities is to advise management on what should be done in the future. The planner helps management not only determine appropriate future action but ensure that the timing of that action is appropriate. In the end, the possibility always exists that the manager may not accept the planner's recommendations.

Evaluation of Planners

As with all other organization members, it is very important that the performance of planners is evaluated against the contribution they make toward helping the organization achieve its objectives.[24] The quality and appropriateness of the system for planning and the plans that the planners develop for the organization should be the primary considerations in this evaluation. Because the organizing, influencing, and controlling functions of the manager are based on the fundamental planning function, the evaluation of planners becomes critically important.

Although the assessment of planners is somewhat subjective, a number of objective indicators do exist. For example, the use of appropriate techniques is one objective indicator. If a planner is using appropriate techniques, it is probable that the planner is doing an acceptable job. The degree of objectivity displayed by the planner is another indicator. To a great extent, the planner's advice should be based on a rational analysis of appropriate information.[25] This is not to say that subjectivity and judgment should be excluded by the planner. Typically, however, opinions should be based on specific and appropriate information.

Malik suggests that objective evidence that a planner is doing a reputable job exists if—

1. The organizational plan is in writing.
2. The plan is the result of all elements of the management team working together.
3. The plan defines present and possible future business of the organization.
4. The plan specifically mentions organizational objectives.
5. The plan includes future opportunities and suggestions on how to take advantage of them.
6. The plan emphasizes both internal and external environments.

TABLE 5.1 Responsibilities of an organization planner

The planner has the responsibility to—

1. Provide information to help management formulate long- and short-range goals and plans of the company. Also assist in the updating of these goals and generally monitor their progress toward attainment.
2. Coordinate activities and prepare special studies centering on acquisitions, disposals, joint endeavors, manufacturing rights, and patents.
3. Serve as resource for determining the acquisition, disposal, and movement of physical properties.
4. Encourage the stimulation of ideas from management toward broadening company operations. Extract these ideas and follow up on possibilities.
5. Develop, recommend, and obtain management approval of plans, procedures, and policies to be followed in implementing a diversification program.
6. Perform basic research on diversification, using such sources as the American Management Association, National Industrial Conference Board, Research Institute of America, and others.
7. Perform internal and external economic studies to secure necessary information for overall planning.
8. Utilize staff service personnel plus line and committee persons in accumulating and evaluating data.
9. Analyze the company's physical properties and personnel capabilities to determine production spans.
10. In conjunction with staff services, periodically survey performance capabilities of sales, engineering, manufacturing, and service components of the company.
11. Conduct an initial survey of the manufacturing organization's physical properties (facilities, equipment, and tools) and keep information current.
12. Investigate and determine possibilities of other significant use for basic products.
13. Assist in communicating and implementing the diversification decisions of management during transition periods.
14. Prepare necessary reports to keep management informed.

7. The plan describes the attainment of objectives in operational terms when possible.
8. The plan includes both long- and short-term recommendations.[26]

These eight conditions furnish managers with some objective guidelines for evaluating the performance of planners. This evaluation, however, should never be completely objective. More subjective considerations include how well planners get along with key members of the organization, the amount of organizational loyalty they display, and their perceived potential.

BACK TO THE CASE

Technically, the chief executive officer (CEO) at Weyerhaeuser is responsible for planning for the organization as a whole and for performing such related time-consuming functions as keeping abreast of internal and external trends that could affect the future of the company. Because planning requires so much time, and because the chief executive officer of Weyerhaeuser has many other responsibilities within the company, the CEO might want to consider appointing a director of planning.

The director of planning at Weyerhaeuser would need certain qualities. Ideally, the planner should have some experience at Weyerhaeuser, be able to see the company as an entire organization, have some ability to gauge and react to major trends that probably will affect the company's future, and be able to work well with others. The planner must oversee the planning process, evaluate developed plans, and solve planning problems. An evaluation of Weyerhaeuser's organization planner would be based on both objective and subjective appraisals of his performance. Perhaps the first problem a company planner at Weyerhaeuser should address is the historically poor planning for the introduction of new products like UltraSofts.

MAXIMIZING THE EFFECTIVENESS OF THE PLANNING PROCESS

Success in implementing a planning subsystem is not easily attainable. As the size of the organization increases, the planning task becomes more complicated, requiring more people, more information, and more complicated decisions.[27] Several safeguards, however, can ensure the success of an organizational planning effort. These safeguards include (1) top management support, (2) an effective and efficient planning organization, (3) an implementation-focused planning orientation, and (4) inclusion of the right people.

Top Management Support

Top management in an organization must support the planning effort, or other organization members may not take the planning effort seriously.[28] Whenever possible, top management should actively help to guide and participate in planning activities. Furnishing the planner with whatever resources are needed to structure the planning organization, encouraging planning as a continuing process (not as a once-a-year activity), and preparing people for the changes that usually result from planning are clear signs that top management is solidly behind the planning effort. The chief executive must give continual and obvious attention to the planning process if it is to be successful.[29] He or she must not be so concerned about other matters that planning is not given the emphasis it deserves.[30]

ETHICS HIGHLIGHT
Top Management Supports Environmental Protection Planning at Shell Oil Company

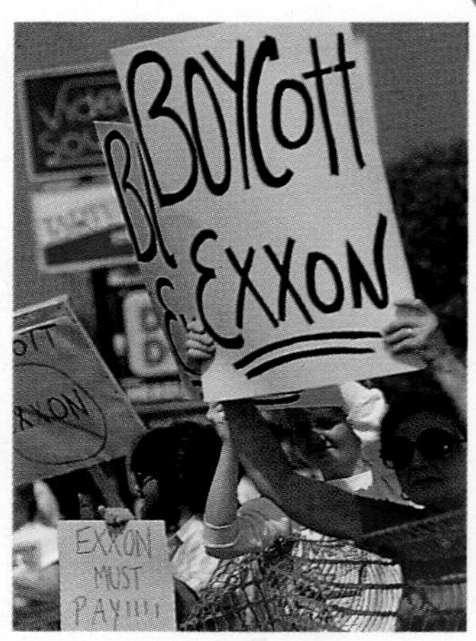

Public pressure from "green groups" have helped to convince top managers at Shell that a pro-environmental policy is an important investment in the company's future.

The Shell Oil Company produces and sells various chemical and petroleum products such as gasoline and oil. In an effort to have all organization members take environmental planning seriously, top management at Shell solidly supports environmental planning within the company.

Top management at Shell has begun supporting environmental planning over the last several years primarily because in the last decade there has been a radical change in public attitudes toward the environment. Most of this change in attitude is credited to pressure groups—called "green groups" who constantly push business as well as society in general to strive to protect the environment. This attitude change has helped companies such as Shell to develop an appreciation for the environment. Given the pro-environment attitudes of society and potential customers, companies such as Shell must now look at environmental protection not as a cost, but as an investment in the future. At Shell, environmental planning is a factor in every business venture. Issues such as health, safety, and environmental considerations are fundamental at every planning stage in the development of a project or product.

Shell continues to strive for improved response to accidents involving oil, gas, chemical, and any other business in which it is engaged. Shell has developed a system of management guidelines that uses environmental audits to determine whether a company activity actually complied with internal environmental standards. ▶

An Effective and Efficient Planning Organization

A well-designed planning organization is the primary vehicle by which planning is accomplished and planning effectiveness is determined. The planner must take the time to design a planning organization as efficient and effective as possible.

The planning organization should have three built-in characteristics. First, it should be designed to use established management systems within the company. As expressed by Paul J. Stonich:

> Many organizations separate formal planning systems from the rest of the management systems that include organization, communication, reporting, evaluating, and performance review. These systems must not be viewed as separate from formal planning systems. Complex organizations need a comprehensive and coordinated set of management systems, including formal planning systems to help them toward their goals.[31]

Second, the planning organization should be simple, yet complex enough to ensure a coordinated effort of all planning participants. Planning can be a complicated process requiring a somewhat large planning organization. The planner should strive to simplify the planning organization and make its complex facets as clearly understood as possible.

Last, the planning organization should be flexible and adaptable. Planning conditions are constantly changing, and the planning organization must be able to respond to these changing conditions.

An Implementation-Focused Planning Orientation

Because the end result of the planning process is some type of action that will help achieve stated organizational objectives, planning should be aimed at implementation.[32] As Peter Drucker points out, a plan is effective only if its implementation helps attain organizational objectives.[33] Plans should be developed and scrutinized after the planner has looked ahead to when they are to be implemented.[34] Ease of implementation is a positive feature of a plan that should be built in whenever possible.

The marketing plan for the Edsel automobile introduced by Ford in the 1950s is an example of how a sound plan can become unsuccessful simply because of ineffective implementation.[35] The rationale behind the Edsel was complete, logical, and defensible. Three consumer trends at that time solidly justified the automobile's introduction: (1) a trend toward the purchase of higher-priced cars, (2) a general income increase that resulted in all income groups purchasing higher-priced cars, and (3) owners of lower-priced Fords trading them in on Buicks, Oldsmobiles, or Pontiacs after they became more affluent. Conceptually, these trends were so significant that Ford's plan to introduce the larger and more expensive Edsel appeared virtually risk-free.

Two factors in the implementation of this plan, however, turned the entire Edsel situation into a financial disaster. First, the network of controllers, dealers, marketing managers, and industrial relations managers created within Ford to get the Edsel to the consumer became very complicated and inefficient. Second, because Ford pushed as many Edsels as possible onto the road immediately after introduction, the quality of the Edsel suffered, and consumers were buying poorly manufactured products. Although the plan to make and market the Edsel was defensible, the long-run influence of the organization and manufacturing processes created to implement the plan doomed it to failure.

Inclusion of the Right People

Planning must include the right people. Whenever possible, planners should obtain input from the managers of the functional areas for which they are planning. These managers are close to the everyday activity of their segments of the organization and can provide planners with invaluable information. They probably also will be involved in implementing whatever plan develops and will be able to furnish the planner with feedback on how easily various plans are being implemented. In general, managers who are to be involved in implementing plans should also be involved in developing the plans.[36]

Input from individuals who will be directly affected by the plans also can be helpful to planners. The individuals who do the work in the organization can give opinions on how various plans will influence work flow. Although it is extremely important that planners involve others in the planning process, not all organization members can or should be involved. The kinds of decisions and types of data needed should dictate the choice of who is involved in what aspects of planning within an organization.[37]

QUALITY HIGHLIGHT
Including the Right People in Planning Enhances Quality at Sun Microsystems

Sun Microsystems uses the team approach to planning as they develop new software products. The team consists of representatives from design engineering, manufacturing, customer service, finance, and marketing.

Sun Microsystems, Inc., is an integrated portfolio of businesses that supply computing technologies, products and services. Its computing solutions include networked workstations and multiprocessing servers, operating system software, silicon designs and other value-added technologies.

Management at Sun Microsystems has developed a team approach to planning. The planning team, known within the company as the business team, is used at Sun primarily during the introduction of a new product. The business team consists of representatives from design engineering, manufacturing, customer service, finance, and marketing.

The business team follows a very specific process. The business team creates a formal plan for a new product that is submitted to an executive-level committee within the corporation. This plan, known as the Product Initiation Form (PIF), is essentially a business plan for a single, new product. Once the executive committee approves a PIF, implementation proceeds by establishing an implementation team, as with the business team, comprised of a number of individuals representing several different operational areas.

Overall, through this cross-functional deployment of individuals in both business and implementation teams, Sun Microsystems has achieved more effective planning. This improved planning has also enhanced overall product quality in the company by contributing to more on-time delivery of products, better product designs, and a higher proportion of products meeting established quality standards when finally manufactured.

BACK TO THE CASE Regardless of who actually ends up having primary responsibility for planning at Weyerhaeuser, a number of safeguards can be taken to ensure that the planning efforts of this person will be successful. First, top executives should actively encourage planning activities and show support for the planning process. Second, the planning organization designed to implement the planning process should use established systems at Weyerhaeuser, be simple yet complex, and be flexible and adaptable. Third, the entire planning process at Weyerhaeuser should be oriented toward easing the implementation of generated plans. Finally, all key people at Weyerhaeuser should be included in the planning process. These safeguards should help Weyerhaeuser management ensure that there will be sound planning for future new-product introductions as well as for all other organizational areas.

ACTION SUMMARY

Reread the learning objectives that follow. Each objective is followed by questions. Answering these questions accurately will help you retain the most important concepts discussed in this chapter. After answering each question, check your answer with the answer key at the end of this chapter. (*Hint:* If you have doubt regarding the correct response, consult the page whose number follows the answer.)

Circle ***From studying this chapter, I will attempt to acquire:***

1. A definition of planning and an understanding of the purposes of planning.

T, F **a.** The affirmative purpose of planning is to increase the degree of organizational success.

a, b, c, d, e **b.** The following is *not* one of the purposes of planning: (a) systematic; (b) protective; (c) affirmative; (d) coordination; (e) fundamental.

2. A knowledge of the advantages and potential disadvantages of planning.

a, b, c, d, e **a.** The advantages of planning include all of the following except: (a) helping managers to be future-oriented; (b) helping coordinate decisions; (c) requiring proper time allocation; (d) emphasizing organizational objectives; (e) all of the above are advantages of planning.

a, b, c, d, e **b.** The following is a potential disadvantage of planning: (a) too much time may be spent on planning; (b) an inappropriate balance between planning and other managerial functions may occur; (c) some important activities may be neglected; (d) incorrect use of the planning function could work to the detriment of the organization; (e) all of the above.

3. Insights on how the major steps of the planning process are related.

a, b, c, d, e **a.** The first major step in the planning process, according to the text, is: (a) developing premises; (b) listing alternative ways of reaching organizational objectives; (c) stating organizational objectives; (d) developing plans to pursue chosen alternatives; (e) putting plans into action.

a, b, c, d, e **b.** The assumptions on which alternatives are based are usually referred to as: (a) objectives; (b) premises; (c) tactics; (d) strategies; (e) probabilities.

4. An understanding of the planning subsystem.

T, F **a.** A subsystem is a system created as part of the process of the overall management system.

a, b, c, d, e **b.** The purpose of the planning subsystem is to increase the effectiveness of the overall management system through which of the following: (a) systematizing the planning function; (b) more effective planning; (c) formalizing the planning process; (d) integrating the planning process; (e) none of the above.

5. A knowledge of how the chief executive relates to the planning process.

T, F **a.** The responsibility for organizational planning rests with middle management.

a, b, c, d, e **b.** The final responsibility for organizational planning rests with: (a) the planning department; (b) the chief executive; (c) departmental supervisors; (d) the organizational planner; (e) the entire organization.

6. An understanding of the qualifications and duties of planners and how planners are evaluated.

T, F **a.** The performance of planners should be evaluated with respect to the contribution they make toward helping the organization achieve its objectives.

a, b, c, d, e **b.** The organizational planner's full responsibilities are: (a) developing plans only; (b) advising about action that should be taken relative to the plans that the chief executive developed; (c) advising about action that should be taken relative to the plans of the board of directors; (d) selecting the person who will oversee the planning process; (e) none of the above.

7. Guidelines on how to get the greatest return from the planning process.

T, F **a.** Top management should encourage planning as an annual activity.

a, b, c, d, e **b.** The following is not a built-in characteristic of an effective and efficient planning organization: (a) it should be designed to use established systems within a company; (b) it should be simple, yet complex enough to ensure coordinated effort; (c) it should cover an operating cycle of not more than one year; (d) it should be flexible and adaptive; (e) all of the above are characteristics of an effective and efficient planning organization.

INTRODUCTORY CASE WRAP-UP

"Poor Planning at Weyerhaeuser Kills a Good Product" and its related back-to-the-case sections were written to help you better understand the management concepts contained in this chapter. Answer the following questions about this introductory case to further enrich your understanding of chapter content:

1. What evidence do you see that Weyerhaeuser's planning needs to improve? Explain.
2. What problems will Weyerhaeuser managers face in trying to make the company stronger in the planning function?
3. Based upon information in the case, who do you think was excluded but should not have been absent from the planning for the introduction of UltraSofts? Explain.

ISSUES FOR REVIEW AND DISCUSSION

1. What is planning?
2. What is the main purpose of planning?
3. List and explain the advantages of planning.
4. Why are the disadvantages of planning called *potential* disadvantages?
5. Explain the phrase *primacy of planning*.
6. List the six steps in the planning process.
7. Outline the relationships between the six steps in the planning process.
8. What is an organizational subsystem?
9. List the elements of the planning subsystem.
10. How do the many roles of a chief executive relate to his or her role as organization planner?
11. Explain the basic qualifications of an organization planner.
12. Give a detailed description of the general duties an organization planner must perform.
13. How would you evaluate the performance of an organization planner?
14. How can top management show its support of the planning process?
15. Describe the characteristics of an effective and efficient planning organization.
16. Why should the planning process emphasize the implementation of organizational plans?
17. Explain why the Edsel automobile failed to generate consumer acceptance.
18. Which people in an organization typically should be included in the planning process? Why?

ACTION SUMMARY

1. a. T, p. 114
b. a, p. 114
2. a. c, p. 115
b. e, p. 115
3. a. c, p. 116
b. b, p. 116
4. a. T, p. 118
b. b, p. 118
5. a. F, p. 120
b. b, p. 120
6. a. T, p. 122
b. e, pp. 122–123
7. a. F, p. 125
b. c, p. 125

CASE STUDY

Planning for the Pizza Hut Distribution Challenge

DR. LESLIE A. TOOMBS
University of Texas at Tyler

Pizza Hut is the number one chain of pizza restaurants in the world. The company has grown by leaps and bounds since PepsiCo acquired it in 1977. PepsiCo's ownership of KFC, Pizza Hut, and Taco Bell makes it America's largest restaurateur in terms of number of outlets. In fact, fast food was PepsiCo's largest revenue-generating segment in 1991, contributing 36.3 percent of total sales. This growth is expected to continue because PepsiCo has vowed to double the size of its restaurant business before the end of the decade. The company plans to achieve this growth by locating food outlets where people congregate, such as at shopping malls, airports, and college student centers.

PepsiCo's growth rate of 7.7 percent in 1991 was about half of 1990's rate. Even though the company lost some momentum, growth was still above the industry rate of 5.4 percent. A decline in growth was also experienced at Pizza Hut. Pizza Hut had an 8.2 percent rate of sales growth in 1991, down from 20 percent in 1990. Executives at Pizza Hut realized that the rapid growth in delivery business may not be enough to offset the decline in performance at the company's five thousand sit-down restaurants.

Since 1985, dine-in pizza has seen no growth. The five thousand outlets are caught somewhere between full-service and fast-food restaurants. Powerful competitors have emerged at both ends. Dominos and Little Caesar's compete strongly in the delivery and take-out market. Upscale chains, such as the Olive Garden, provide powerful competition in the full-service market.

Several strategies are being pursued to enhance Pizza Hut's competitive position. Pizza Hut Café—a new concept which would feature pastas, desserts, and gourmet pizzas—is being explored. However, some feel that this idea comes too late to a market where mid-range pasta shops have already been developed. The company also announced an addition of 25 percent more toppings on the "Lovers" line of pizzas. This strategy was developed to increase sales without decreasing price. The company seems to have concluded that long-term differentiation on the basis of price is impossible. Thus, it is competing on the basis of product superiority.

To further expand its restaurant operations in the United States, PepsiCo acquired a significant minority share of Carts of Colorado, Inc., a producer of mobile carts. At least two-thirds of restaurant expansion is expected to occur in the form of small units over the next five years. PepsiCo has determined that mobile units cost 5 to 10 percent less than traditional units and are 45 to 90 percent as profitable. The mobile units also involve less risk. These units can be installed or removed immediately depending upon traffic flow. PepsiCo plans to expand its current U.S. base of five hundred carts to more than ten thousand in the next decade. The company also plans to set up more than one hundred thousand units abroad. Implementation activities have already begun. Pizza Hut carts are being tested in Arizona supermarkets. Also, negotiations are underway to locate these carts in Wal-Mart stores.

In addition to these strategies to stimulate the domestic market, Pizza Hut executives are trying to capitalize on growth opportunities outside of the United States. Many obstacles and complications have arisen, yet the company has established a presence in Latin America. Pizza Hut International has 110 franchises from Chile to Mexico and hopes to increase this number to five hundred. Further, there are more than fifteen Pizza Huts in Thailand; more than four million Thai customers now eat at Pizza Hut every year To break into the Russian and Chinese markets, the company formed partnerships with local firms. Two Pizza Huts have opened in Moscow and one in Beijing. The company hopes that tourists and foreign residents, as well as members of the bureaucratic elite, will keep the restaurants profitable until more residents have the income and desire to become regular customers. This plan seems to be working, especially in Moscow, where the average waiting time in line to be served has increased from two to three hours.

DISCUSSION QUESTIONS

1. What are Pizza Hut's organizational objectives?
2. What are two alternatives that you believe Pizza Hut executives listed to reach these objectives? Explain the premises on which they are based.
3. How important is the coordination of management teams is to Pizza Hut's plans? Why?
4. Based on the evidence presented in this case, list possible long- and short-term recommendations made by Pizza Hut planners.

CNN VIDEO CASE

Mapping the Future for Amex

JIM JONES
Amex

In 1989 the Board of Governors of the American Stock Exchange (Amex) gave Jim Jones a big assignment: "They said to develop a strategic plan to take the American Stock Exchange into the 1990s."

Jim Jones's background was politics and Washington, D.C. As Jones describes that arena he comments, "While there's a general understanding of what the securities industry is about among policy makers in Washington, I would say very few have an intricate understanding of the industry or of Wall Street and what the purpose of financial markets is." Even so, coming to Wall Street didn't scare Jones, because he had "Main Street" in his experience. And during his time in Congress, he had developed an expertise in international trade and had headed the budget committee. Jones believes that his training and work outside the financial arena prepared him to bring a fresh perspective to his new job as chair of Amex.

Jim Jones of the American Stock Exchange took immediate steps to ensure that goals are set routinely and that plans are in place to reach those goals.

An overall objective of the American Stock Exchange is to develop alliances and joint ventures that will make Amex a participant in the global community, not just in the United States. Another objective is to be a customer-driven institution—focusing on the needs of the stockbrokers—rather than a member-driven institution—focusing more on the needs of the listing companies (the companies registered with the exchange).

In meeting his assignment from the board of governors, and understanding the criteria for a good service organization in the 1990s, Jones took immediate steps that have gained him a reputation for shaking things up. In the drive to turn Amex into a customer-driven institution, he did not replace managers who left; instead, he flattened management and empowered the employees. He hired talented, creative people and unleashed them, telling them to "create new opportunities for growth companies to expand their horizons and their visibility to the financial markets." In a total quality program to measure customer satisfaction, Jones has ensured that goals are set and that compensation and promotions are based on reaching those goals.

One way Amex plans to meet its objectives is through its Emerging Company Marketplace (ECM), opened in 1992. ECM, Jim Jones plans, will be the vehicle by which Amex becomes the premier growth-company equity marketplace, one of its stated goals. ECM nurtures small but growing companies that would otherwise not qualify for listing. It is designed to foster capital for mid-sized companies. Jones admits to being partial to the concept of the entrepreneur, and so he is comfortable with this focus on growth of companies formerly held back by lack of ready funds. "These are the kinds of companies," notes Jones, "that will make the United States competitive in the future."

As part of ensuring a quality marketplace to both the issuers (members) and the investors (customers), Amex offers services that include investor and public relations, advice on pension plans, and so on. Adding such services has meant an increase in revenue for Amex, which makes its money from fees for such services as well as from its stock transactions and dissemination of information. In addition to increasing revenues, however, adding new services has increased management responsibilities in areas other than stock trading. So, a lot of change has occurred at the American Stock Exchange in a very short time as it moves through the 1990s with a focus on the customer, whether inside or outside the United States. Thorough and thoughtful planning will continue to play a critical role at Amex.

VIDEO CASE QUESTIONS

1. Describe the two major planning assignments given Jim Jones by the Board of Governors of the Stock Exchange.
2. Are the purposes of Jones's planning assignments protective or affirmative? Explain your answer.
3. Why does Jones describe his lack of business experience as a benefit in planning Amex's future?
4. Which of the roles of a top manager do you think Jim Jones will be required to play most often to meet the goal of developing global alliances? Explain your answer.

CNN VIDEO EXERCISE

Planning Globally for the American Stock Exchange

EXERCISE GOAL: Learn to use the steps of the planning process as you develop alternatives and premises for a given objective.

Imagine that Jim Jones has given you, a member of the senior management team of Amex, the mission to develop plans to make Amex a participant in a major joint venture with the European Community. Review the steps in the planning process on pages 116–117. Then develop two alternative methods to achieve your objective. Develop premises for each alternative.

Now choose the better alternative for reaching the objective and explain your choice in a memo to Jim Jones.

Objective: Make Amex a participant in the European Community.

Alternative 1: ____________________

____

____

____

Premise a: ____________________

____

____

____

Premise b: ____________________

____

____

____

Alternative 2: ____________________

____

____

____

Premise a: ____________________

____

____

____

Premise b: ____________________

____

____

____

Now choose the better alternative for reaching the objective and explain your choice in a memo to Jim Jones.

CHAPTER

6

MAKING DECISIONS

STUDENT LEARNING OBJECTIVES

From studying this chapter, I will attempt to acquire:

1. A fundamental understanding of the term *decision.*
2. An understanding of each element of the decision situation.
3. An ability to use the decision-making process.
4. An appreciation for the various situations in which decisions are made.
5. An understanding of probability theory and decision trees as decision-making tools.

CHAPTER OUTLINE

INTRODUCTORY CASE
Iacocca Makes a Wrong Decision at Chrysler?

FUNDAMENTALS OF DECISIONS

Definition of a Decision
Types of Decisions

DIVERSITY HIGHLIGHT
U.S. Office of Personnel

The Responsibility for Making Organizational Decisions

ELEMENTS OF THE DECISION SITUATION

State of Nature
The Decision Makers

GLOBAL HIGHLIGHT
United Technologies

Goals to Be Served
Relevant Alternatives
Ordering of Alternatives
Choice of Alternatives

THE DECISION-MAKING PROCESS

Identifying an Existing Problem
Listing Alternative Problem Solutions

ETHICS HIGHLIGHT
Pharmacy Industry

Selecting the Most Beneficial Alternative
Implementing the Chosen Alternative
Gathering Problem-Related Feedback

DECISION-MAKING CONDITIONS

Complete Certainty Condition
Complete Uncertainty Condition
Risk Condition

QUALITY HIGHLIGHT
PepsiCo

DECISION-MAKING TOOLS

Probability Theory
Decision Trees

CASE STUDY
GM: Which Way Is Up?

VIDEO CASE
Making Decisions that Count: John Georges, International Paper

VIDEO EXERCISE
Team Decision Making at International Paper

INTRODUCTORY CASE

Iacocca Makes a Wrong Decision at Chrysler?

Lee Iacocca has been extensively discussed and written about throughout his career. Although recently retired as chairman of Chrysler Corporation, his experiences at Chrysler continue to depict classic examples from which management students of today can learn. The following case is based on one such experience near the very end of Iacocca's career at Chrysler that provides valuable insights concerning how managers make decisions.

"If I made a mistake it was following other companies. And maybe those were grandiose schemes."

When R. S. Miller, Jr., vice chairman of Chrysler Corp., addressed a dinner meeting of company managers a couple of years ago, he concluded by inviting questions from the floor. The first to raise a hand was Mr. Miller's wife, Maggie, who had accompanied him to the event. Would Mr. Miller run Chrysler differently, she asked, if he were chairman instead of Lee Iacocca?

The question startled Mr. Miller, but he quickly recovered. His first move, he replied, would be to bar spouses from corporate meetings. The group broke up in laughter.

Nowadays, though, the question isn't so funny. Lots of people, both inside and outside Chrysler, wonder how the company would be doing without Mr. Iacocca. That's because Chrysler is doing so badly *with* him.

Mr. Iacocca vows to stay the course and lead Chrysler out of its problems. But with remarkable candor, he concedes that he is to blame for many of the company's woes. "I'm confessing my sins here," declares Mr. Iacocca, who turns 66 next month.

His big sin, Mr. Iacocca says, was trying to diversify. His decision put the company into the aerospace and defense businesses but siphoned management attention and money from the crucial task of producing new vehicles. Now Chrysler has sold, or is trying to sell, those businesses. Meanwhile, it hasn't brought to market a single new car whose development was begun after Mr. Iacocca arrived in 1978. Chrysler's current lineup still derives from the decade-old K-car.

In fairness to Mr. Iacocca, say his admirers, his wish to diversify was understandable. Chrysler is being sorely pressed by Japanese competition, which notably doesn't exist in the aerospace and defense businesses. General Motors Corp. and Ford Motor Co. made similar moves. Ford, like Chrysler, is selling those businesses, though GM is sticking with them.

"If I made a mistake it was following other companies. And maybe those were grandiose schemes," says Mr. Iacocca.

Although he is now viewed as a role model who made effective decisions, Lee Iacocca admits that his decision to diversify the company into the aerospace and defense businesses was a bad one because it took needed management and money away from the central task of producing automobiles.

From Paul Ingrassia and Bradley A. Stertz, "With Chrysler Ailing Lee Iacocca Concedes Mistakes in Managing," *Wall Street Journal* (September 17, 1990), Al, A8. Reprinted by permission of *Wall Street Journal,* © 1990 Dow Jones & Company, Inc. All Rights Reserved Worldwide; Raymond Serafin, "It's Lee's Last Hurray as Chrysler Pitchman" *Advertising Age,* Vol. 63, Issue 37.(September 14, 1992) pp. 1, 74, 76.

WHAT'S AHEAD According to the introductory case, Lee Iacocca admitted that his decision to diversify by entering the aerospace and defense businesses was a poor decision for Chrysler. The information in this chapter discusses specifics surrounding a decision-making situation and provides insights about the steps a manager such as Iacocca might take in making such a decision. This chapter discusses: (1) the fundamentals of decisions, (2) the elements of the decision situation, (3) the decision-making process, (4) various decision-making conditions, and (5) decision-making tools. These topics are critical to managers and other individuals who make decisions.

FUNDAMENTALS OF DECISIONS

Definition of a Decision

A **decision** is a choice made between two or more available alternatives.

A **decision** is a choice made between two or more available alternatives. Choosing the best alternative for reaching objectives—the fourth step of the planning process (presented in chapter 5)—is, strictly speaking, making a decision. Although decision making is covered in the planning section of this text, a manager also must make decisions when performing the other three managerial functions: organizing, controlling, and influencing.

Everyone is faced with decision situations each day. A decision situation may involve simply choosing among studying, swimming, or golfing as ways of spending the day. It does not matter which alternative is chosen, only that a choice is actually made.[1]

On a daily basis, managers are concerned with making decisions and communicating them to other organization members.[2] Not all of the decisions are of equal significance to the organization. Some affect a large number of organization members, cost much money to carry out, or have a long-term effect on the organization. These significant decisions can have a major impact not only on the management system itself but on the career of the manager. Other decisions are fairly insignificant, affecting only a small number of organization members, costing little to carry out, and having only a short-term effect on the organization.

Types of Decisions

Decisions can be categorized by how much time a manager must spend in making them, what proportion of the organization must be involved in making them, and the organizational functions on which they focus.[3] Probably the most generally accepted method of categorizing decisions, however, is based on computer language and divides the decisions into two basic types: programmed and nonprogrammed.[4]

Programmed decisions are decisions that are routine and repetitive, and that typically require specific handling methods.

Programmed decisions are routine and repetitive, and the organization typically develops specific ways to handle them. A programmed decision might involve determining how products will be arranged on the shelves of a supermarket. This is a routine and repetitive problem for the organization, and standard arrangement decisions typically are made according to established management guidelines.

DIVERSITY HIGHLIGHT

Nonprogrammed Decision at U.S. Office of Personnel Management Includes a Focus on Severely Disabled Workers

The U.S. Office of Personnel Management is in the process of making a nonprogrammed decision concerning whether to employ home-based workers. Recognizing the needs of the diverse work force of the 1990s, this government office is examining the utility and feasibility of offering home-based positions as a tool for improving employee recruitment, retention, and other aspects of personnel management.

Individuals who presently work at home range from entrepreneurs who work for themselves and have multiple clients to people who are regular company employees.

Research indicates that home-based employee programs work especially well with severely disabled workers. Overall, such programs have been not only cost-effective from a company viewpoint, but also personally satisfying for the workers themselves. Experience shows that proper planning can greatly enhance the success of these home-based employee programs. One area on which such planning should focus relates to the workstation itself. Workstations in the home should be equivalent to those designed for in-office employees. Furnishing lesser equipped offices for home-based workers normally causes worker frustration, and, as a result, less productive workers. Planning should also include ensuring that home-based workers, in order to fit into a company properly, have initial training and orientation relating to their work role and have ongoing contact with support groups to help handle special problems that might arise as a result of working at home. Planning should also include providing home-based workers with the same benefits, status, promotion opportunities, and rights as in-office workers. ▶

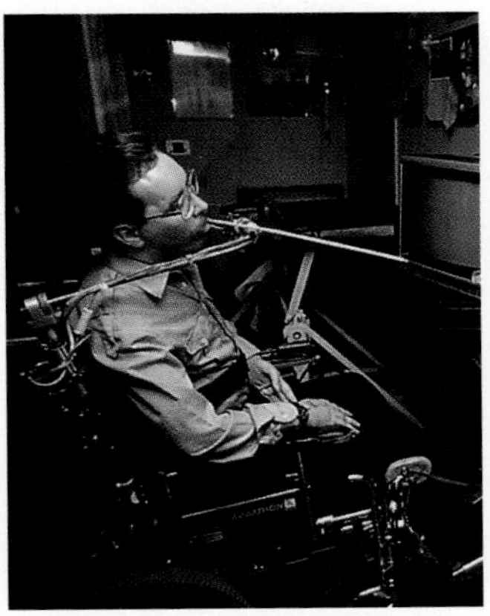

Home-based employee programs work especially well when severely disabled workers are employed. Such programs are not only cost effective from a company viewpoint, but are personally satisfying for the workers themselves.

Nonprogrammed decisions, in contrast, typically are one-shot occurrences and are usually less structured than programmed decisions. One example of a nonprogrammed decision that many managers have had to make in recent years is whether to close a plant.[5] Another example would be a decision focusing on whether a supermarket should carry an additional type of bread. In making this decision, the manager must consider whether the new bread will stabilize bread sales by competing with existing bread carried in the store or increase bread sales by offering a choice of breads to customers who have never before bought bread in the store. These types of issues must be dealt with before the manager can finally decide whether to offer the new bread. Table 6.1 shows traditional and modern ways of handling programmed and nonprogrammed decisions.

Nonprogrammed decisions are decisions that typically are one-shot occurrences and usually are less structured than programmed decisions.

Programmed and nonprogrammed decisions should be thought of as being at opposite ends of a programming continuum, as shown in Figure 6.1. The continuum also indicates that some decisions clearly may not be either programmed or nonprogrammed but some combination of the two.

TABLE 6.1 Traditional and modern ways of handling programmed and nonprogrammed decisions

	Decision-Making Techniques	
Types of Decisions	*Traditional*	*Modern*
Programmed: Routine, repetitive decisions Organization develops specific processes for handling them	1. Habit 2. Clerical routine: Standard operating procedures 3. Organization structure: Common expectations A system of subgoals Well-defined information channels	1. Operations research: Mathematical analysis Models Computer simulation 2. Electronic data processing
Nonprogrammed: One-shot, ill-structured, novel policy decisions Handled by general problem-solving processes	1. Judgment, intuition, and creativity 2. Rules of thumb 3. Selection and training of executives	1. Heuristic problem-solving techniques applied to: Training human decision makers Constructing heuristic computer programs

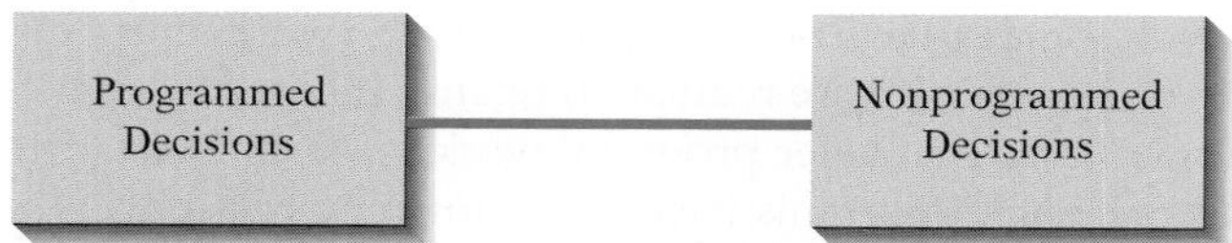

FIGURE 6.1 Continuum of extent of decision programming

The Responsibility for Making Organizational Decisions

Many different kinds of decisions must be made within an organization—such as how to manufacture a product, how to maintain machines, how to ensure product quality, and how to establish advantageous relationships with customers. With varied decisions of this sort, some type of rationale must be developed to stipulate who within the organization has the responsibility for making which decisions.

The **scope of the decision** is the proportion of the total management system that a particular decision will affect. The broader the scope of a decision, the higher the level of the manager responsible for making that decision.

One such rationale is based primarily on two factors: the scope of the decision to be made and the levels of management. The **scope of the decision** is the proportion of the total management system that the decision will affect. The greater this proportion, the broader the scope of the decision is said to be. *Levels of management* are simply lower-level management, middle-level management, and upper-level management. The rationale for designating who makes which decisions is this: The broader the scope of a decision, the higher the level of the manager responsible for making that decision. Figure 6.2 illustrates this rationale.

One example of this decision-making rationale is the manner in which E.I. DuPont de Nemours and Company handles decisions related to the research-and-development function.[6] As Figure 6.3 shows, this organization makes relatively narrow-scope research-and-development decisions, such as "which markets to test" (made by lower-

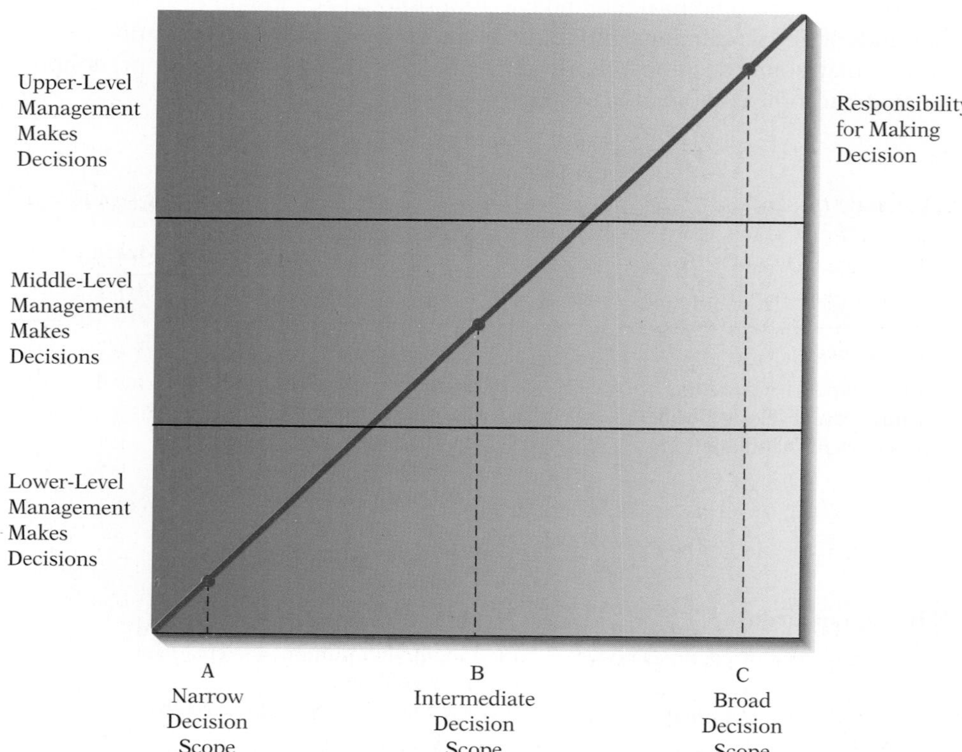

FIGURE 6.2 Level of managers responsible for making decisions as decision scope increases from *A* to *B* to *C*

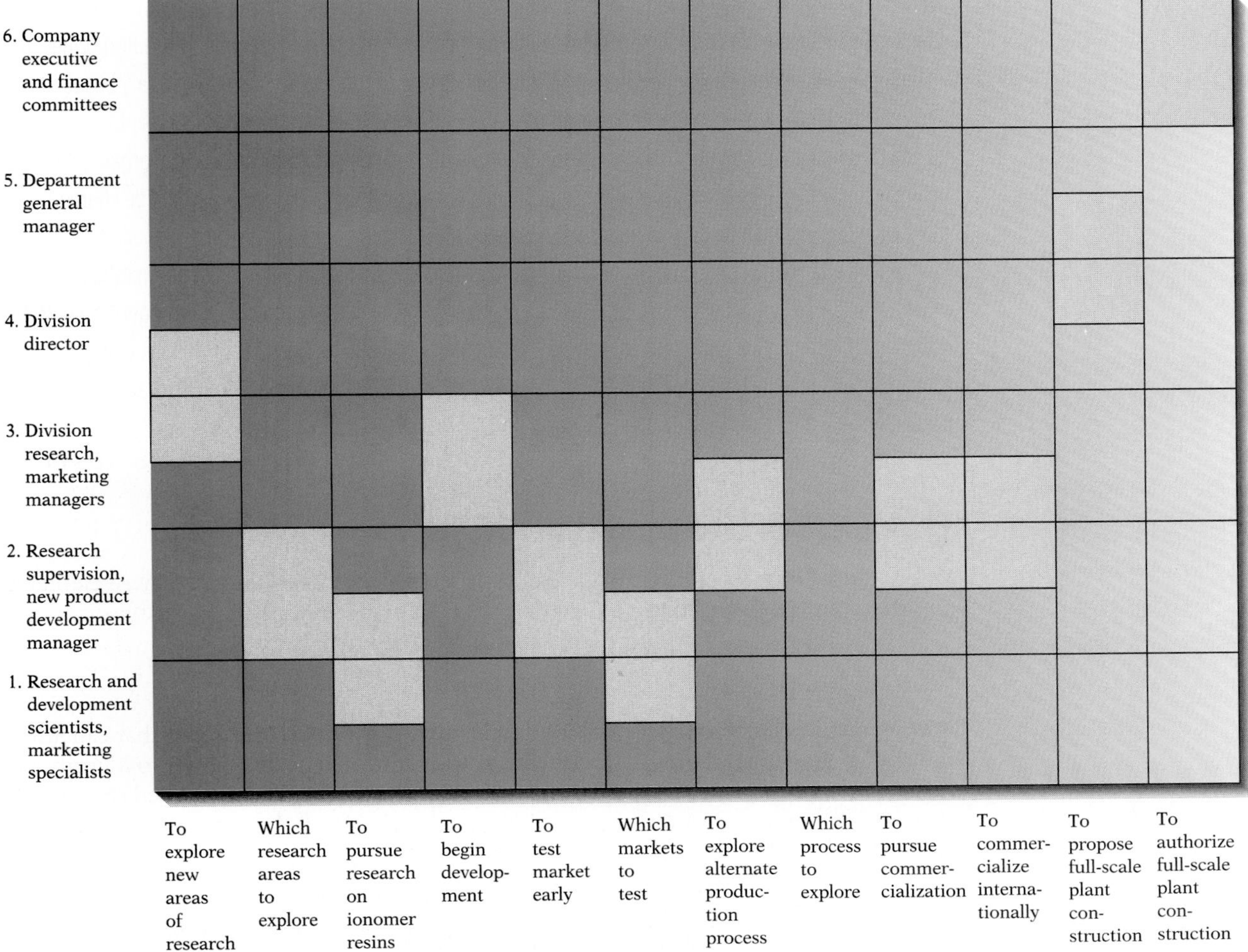

FIGURE 6.3 How scope of decision affects management level making decision at DuPont

level managers), and relatively broad-scope research-and-development decisions, such as "authorize full-scale plant construction" (made by upper-level managers).

Even the manager who has the responsibility for making a particular decision can ask the advice of other managers or subordinates. In fact, some managers advise having groups make certain decisions.

Consensus is one method a manager can use in getting a group to arrive at a particular decision.[7] **Consensus** is agreement on a decision by all the individuals involved in making the decision. It usually occurs after lengthy deliberation and discussion by members of the decision group, who may be either all managers or a mixture of managers and subordinates.[8]

Consensus is agreement on a decision by all individuals involved in making the decision.

Although asking individuals to arrive at a consensus decision is an option available to a manager, the manager must keep in mind that some individuals simply may not be able to arrive at such a decision. Lack of technical skill or poor interpersonal relations within a group may be barriers to arriving at a consensus decision. When individuals arrive at a stalemate in making a decision together, it's probably time for managers to offer assistance in making the decision or simply to make the decision themselves.

Decisions through consensus have both advantages and disadvantages. One advantage is that managers can focus "several heads" on the decision. Another is that individuals in the decision group are more likely to be committed to implementing a decision if they helped make it. The main disadvantage to decisions through consensus is that discussions relating to the decisions tend to be lengthy and therefore costly.

BACK TO THE CASE If Lee Iacocca, former top manager at Chrysler, were forced to confront an issue such as how to design and manufacture automobiles that would have fewer Japanese competitors than the ones he was producing, he would definitely be faced with a formal decision situation, one requiring that he decide upon one of a number of possible solutions. Iacocca would need to scrutinize his decision carefully because of its significance to the organization and to him. Technically, this decision would be nonprogrammed in nature and therefore would be characterized more by judgment than by simple quantitative data.

As the top manager at Chrysler, Iacocca would probably have had the ultimate responsibility for making such a broad-scope decision. This does not mean, however, that Iacocca would have to make the decision by himself. He could ask for advice from other Chrysler employees and perhaps even appoint a group of managers and employees to arrive at a consensus on which of the decision alternatives he should implement.

ELEMENTS OF THE DECISION SITUATION

Wilson and Alexis isolate six basic elements in the decision situation.[9] These elements and their definitions follow.

State of Nature

State of nature refers to the aspects of the decision maker's environment that can affect the choice. Robert B. Duncan conducted a study in which he attempted to identify the environmental characteristics that influenced decision makers. He grouped the characteristics into two categories: the internal environment and the external environment (see Table 6.2).[10]

TABLE 6.2 Environmental factors that can influence managerial decision making

Internal Environment	External Environment
1. Organizational personnel component a. Educational and technological background and skills b. Previous technological and managerial skill c. Individual member's involvement and commitment to attaining system's goals d. Interpersonal behavior styles e. Availability of human resources for utilization within the system 2. Organizational functional and staff units component a. Technological characteristics of organizational units b. Interdependence of organizational units in carrying out their objectives c. Intraunit conflict among organizational functional and staff units d. Interunit conflict among organizational functional and staff units 3. Organizational level component a. Organizational objectives and goals b. Integrative process integrating individuals and groups into contributing maximally to attaining organizational goals c. Nature of the organization's product service	4. Customer component a. Distributors of product or service b. Actual users of product or service 5. Supplier component a. New materials suppliers b. Equipment suppliers c. Product parts suppliers d. Labor supply 6. Competitor component a. Competitors for suppliers b. Competitors for customers 7. Sociopolitical component a. Government regulatory control over the industry b. Public political attitude toward industry and its particular product c. Relationship with trade unions with jurisdiction in the organization 8. Technological component a. Meeting new technological requirements of own industry and related industries in production of product or service b. Improving and developing new products by implementing new technological advances in the industry

The Decision Makers

Decision makers are the individuals or groups who actually make the choice among alternatives.[11] According to Dale, weak decision makers can have four different orientations: receptive, exploitation, hoarding, and marketing.[12]

Decision makers who have a receptive orientation believe that the source of all good is outside themselves, and therefore they rely heavily on suggestions from other organization members. Basically, they want others to make their decisions for them.

Decision makers with an exploitation orientation also believe that good is outside themselves, and they are willing to take ethical or unethical steps to steal ideas necessary to make good decisions. They build their organization on the ideas of others and typically extend little or no credit for the ideas to anyone but themselves.

The hoarding orientation is characterized by decision makers who preserve the status quo as much as possible. They accept little outside help, isolate themselves from others, and are extremely self-reliant. These decision makers emphasize maintaining their present existence.

Marketing-oriented decision makers consider themselves commodities that are only as valuable as the decisions they make. They try to make decisions that will enhance their value and are therefore conscious of what others think of their decisions.

The ideal decision-making orientation is one that emphasizes trying to realize the potential of the organization as well as of the decision maker. Ideal decision makers try to use all of their talents and are influenced mainly by reason and sound judgment. They do not possess the qualities of the four undesirable decision-making orientations just described.

GLOBAL HIGHLIGHT
Executives at United Technologies Detect a Weakness in Japanese Decision Makers

United Technologies is a company that designs, manufactures, and sells high-technology products, such as radar equipment and rocket motors. Executives at United Technologies think that they have identified a common weakness in Japanese multinational decision makers that Western firms can profitably exploit.

According to United Technologies managers, in most Japanese companies, important corporate decisions regarding activities in foreign operations are made by top management Japanese nationals who are quick to tell their foreign customers and managers that there is only one way to handle the design or delivery of a product or service—the way it is done in Japan. These Japanese decision makers seem to base their decisions primarily on Japanese business custom at the home office rather than on the elements of the decision situation itself. Such a practice makes Japanese operations in foreign countries particularly vulnerable to competition from those Western manufacturers that can achieve Japanese standards of excellence in production plus adjust to local adaptability and choice. In the 1990s, United Technologies will strive for those Japanese standards of excellence in production, all the while treating its foreign managers and partners with respect, even deference. ▶

United Technologies designs and manufactures high technology equipment like this sophisticated radar equipment. United Technologies strives for Japanese standards of excellence in production but believes in using a different approach in its management.

Goals to Be Served

The goals that decision makers seek to attain are another element of the decision situation. In the case of managers, these goals should most often be organizational objectives. (Chapter 4 discusses specifics about organizational objectives.)

Relevant Alternatives

Relevant alternatives are alternatives that are considered feasible for implementation and for solving an existing problem.

The decision situation is usually composed of at least two relevant alternatives. A **relevant alternative** is one that is considered feasible for implementation and for solving an existing problem. Alternatives that cannot be implemented or will not solve an existing problem are irrelevant alternatives and should be excluded from the decision-making situation.

Ordering of Alternatives

The decision situation must have a process or mechanism that ranks alternatives from most desirable to least desirable. The process can be subjective, objective, or some combination of the two. Past experience of the decision maker is an example of a subjective process, and the rate of output per machine is an example of an objective process.

Choice of Alternatives

The last element of the decision situation is an actual choice between available alternatives. This choice establishes the fact that a decision is made. Typically, managers choose the alternative that maximizes long-term return for the organization.

BACK TO THE CASE As Iacocca was making his decision about whether to diversify into aerospace and defense businesses, he would need to be aware of all the elements in the decision situation. Both the internal and external environments of Chrysler would be one focus of Iacocca's analysis. For example: Does Chrysler have the internal financial resources and expertise to diversify into these areas? Externally, is there a market for aerospace and defense products that Chrysler would offer? Reason and sound judgment must characterize Iacocca's orientation as a decision maker. Iacocca would have to keep Chrysler's organizational objectives in mind and list relevant alternatives in addition to aerospace or defense businesses. For example, other relevant alternatives might be to design and manufacture earth-moving equipment or farm machinery. In addition, Iacocca would need to list relevant alternatives in some order of desirability before choosing an alternative objective to implement. According to the case, Iacocca admitted that the alternative he chose in this decision situation was inappropriate. The case does not tell us which other alternatives he may have had or why he chose the one that he did.

THE DECISION-MAKING PROCESS

The **decision-making process** is the steps a decision maker takes to make a decision.

A decision is a choice of one alternative from a set of available alternatives. The **decision-making process** is the steps the decision maker takes to choose an alternative. The process that a manager uses to make decisions has significant impact on the quality of decisions made. If managers use an organized and systematic process, the probability that their decisions will be sound is higher than if the process is disorganized and unsystematic.[13]

A model of the decision-making process that is recommended for managerial use is presented in Figure 6.4. In order of occurrence, the decision-making steps this model depicts are (1) identify an existing problem, (2) list possible alternatives to solve the problem, (3) select the most beneficial of these alternatives, (4) put the selected alternative into action, and (5) gather feedback to find out if the implemented alternative is solving the identified problem. The paragraphs that follow elaborate upon each of these steps and explain their interrelationships.[14]

This model of the decision-making process is based on three primary assumptions.[15] First, the model assumes that humans are economic beings with the objective of maximizing satisfaction or return. Second, it assumes that within the decision-making situation all alternatives and their possible consequences are known. The last assumption is that decision makers have some priority system that allows them to rank the desirability of each alternative. If each of these assumptions is met in the decision-

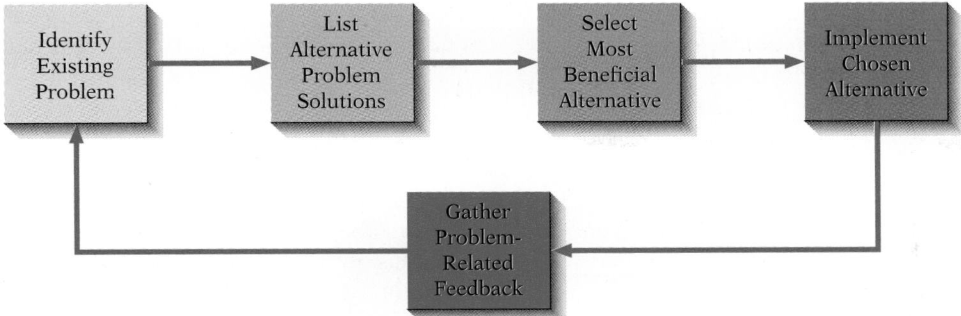

FIGURE 6.4 Model of the decision-making process

making situation, decision makers probably will make the best possible decision for the organization. In reality, one or more of the assumptions often are not met, and related decisions, therefore, are usually something less than the best possible ones for the organization.

Identifying an Existing Problem

Decision making is essentially a problem-solving process that involves eliminating barriers to organizational goal attainment. Naturally, the first step in this elimination process is identifying exactly what the problems or barriers are. Only after the barriers have been adequately identified can management take steps to eliminate them. Several years ago, Molson, a Canadian manufacturer of beer as well as cleaning and sanitizing products, faced a barrier to success: a free-trade agreement that threatened to open Canadian borders to U.S. beer. Although the borders were not due to open for another five years, Molson made a decision to overcome the barrier of increased beer competition from the United States by increasing production and sales of its specialty chemical products. Within four years, Molson's chemical sales were greater than its beer sales. The company essentially eliminated the barrier—the threat of increased U.S. competition for beer sales—by emphasizing sales in a different division.[16] Chester Barnard has stated that organizational problems are brought to the attention of managers mainly through (1) orders issued by managers' supervisors, (2) situations relayed to managers by their subordinates, and (3) the normal activity of the managers themselves.[17]

Listing Alternative Problem Solutions

Once a problem has been identified, managers should list the various possible solutions. Very few organizational problems can be solved in only one way. Managers must search out the many alternative solutions that exist for most organizational problems.

Before searching for solutions, managers must be aware of five limitations on the number of problem-solving alternatives available: (1) authority factors (for example, a manager's superior may have told the manager that the alternative was not feasible); (2) biological or human factors (for example, human factors within the organization may be inappropriate for implementing the alternatives); (3) physical factors (for example, the physical facilities of the organization may be inappropriate for certain alternatives to be seriously considered); (4) technological factors (for example, the level of organizational technology may be inadequate for certain alternatives); and (5) economic factors (for example, certain alternatives may be too costly for the organization).[18]

Figure 6.5 presents additional factors that can limit managers' decision alternatives. This diagram uses the term *discretionary area* to designate feasible alternatives available to managers. Factors that limit this area are legal restrictions, moral and ethical norms, formal policies and rules, and unofficial social norms.[19]

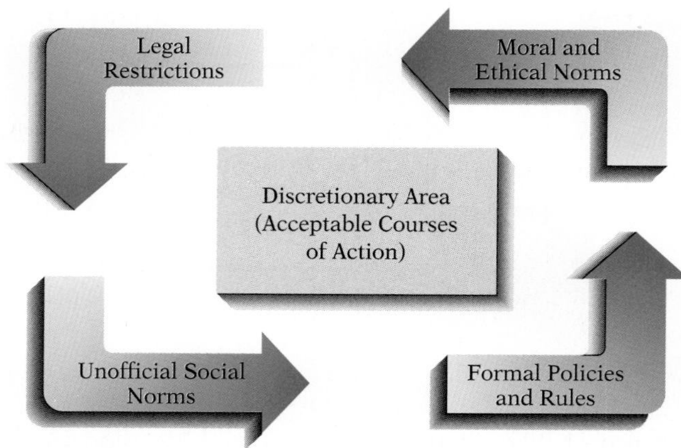

FIGURE 6.5 Additional factors that limit a manager's number of acceptable alternatives

ETHICS HIGHLIGHT
Pharmacy Industry Sells Cigarettes?

Knowing the dangers of tobacco smoking, pharmacy managers face the ethical question of whether to sell tobacco products to the public. A recent survey revealed that 35 percent of pharmacy managers have decided not to sell tobacco products at all and 90 percent will not sell to minors.

Disagreement about what ethical norms actually exist in a decision situation can cause significant differences in the way different managers react to the same decision situation. Pharmacy managers face the dilemma of determining what ethical norms exist in decisions about whether to sell tobacco products to the public. A recent survey of pharmacy managers regarding this issue uncovered ethical foundations both for selling and for curtailing sales, and there appeared to be no consensus. Only 35 percent of those surveyed decided *not* to sell the products. However, 9 out of 10 pharmacy managers surveyed said that they would not sell tobacco products to minors and would ask for proof of age when in doubt. Most of the pharmacy managers who made the decision to sell cigarettes think that adults should have the right to decide if they wish to consume tobacco products at risk to their health. Pharmacy managers choosing *not* to sell the products believe that a pharmacy manager has an ethical responsibility to protect society from products harmful to it. In this situation, because pharmacy managers have interpreted ethical norms regarding the sale of cigarettes much differently, they have made different decisions regarding whether to sell tobacco products. ▶

Selecting the Most Beneficial Alternative

Decision makers can select the most beneficial solution only after they have evaluated each alternative very carefully. This evaluation should consist of three steps. First, decision makers should list, as accurately as possible, the potential effects of each alternative as if the alternative had already been chosen and implemented. Second, a probability factor should be assigned to each of the potential effects. This would indicate how probable the occurrence of the effect would be if the alternative were implemented. Third, keeping organizational goals in mind, decision makers should compare each alternative's expected effects and their respective probabilities.[20] The alternative that seems to be most advantageous to the organization should be chosen for implementation.

Implementing the Chosen Alternative

The next step is to put the chosen alternative literally into action. Decisions must be supported by appropriate action if they are to have a chance of being successful.

Gathering Problem-Related Feedback

After the chosen alternative has been implemented, decision makers must gather feedback to determine the effect of the implemented alternative on the identified problem.

If the identified problem is not being solved, managers need to search out and implement some other alternative.

BACK TO THE CASE Assume that Lee Iacocca is facing a decision to increase product safety. He first would need to identify the problem. He would need to find out if customer injury resulted from faulty parts, inadequate safety devices, or poor operating instructions. Once he identified the problem, he would have to list all possible problem solutions; for example: Can the quality of parts be improved? Can additional safety devices be invented? Would better operating instructions reduce the risk of injury?

After eliminating nonfeasible solutions, Iacocca would have to evaluate all remaining solutions, select one, and implement it. If operating instructions were unreliable because of customer error, or if better quality parts were too expensive to manufacture, the best alternative might be to create new safety devices for Chrysler products. Iacocca would then have to initiate appropriate action within the company so that such devices could be designed and manufactured. Problem-related feedback would be extremely important once the safety devices were added. Iacocca would need to find out if the new devices in fact did reduce customer injury. If they did not, he would need to decide what additional action should be taken to improve product safety.

DECISION-MAKING CONDITIONS

In most instances, it is impossible for decision makers to be sure of exactly what the future consequences of an implemented alternative will be. The word *future* is the key in discussing decision-making conditions. For all practical purposes, because organizations and their environments are constantly changing, future consequences of implemented decisions are not perfectly predictable.

In general, there are three different conditions under which decisions are made. Each of these conditions is based on the degree to which the future outcome of a decision alternative is predictable. These conditions are (1) complete certainty, (2) complete uncertainty, and (3) risk.[21] Figure 6.6 shows these three conditions on a continuum of predictability of the organizational environment, with complete certainty at one end and complete uncertainty at the other.

Complete Certainty Condition

The **complete certainty condition** exists when decision makers know exactly what the results of an implemented alternative will be. In this condition, managers have complete knowledge about a decision. All they have to do is list outcomes for alternatives and then choose the outcome with the highest payoff for the organization. For example, the outcome of an investment alternative based on buying government bonds is, for all practical purposes, completely predictable because of established government interest rates. Deciding to implement this alternative essentially would be making a decision in a complete certainty situation. Unfortunately, most organizational decisions are made outside the complete certainty situation.

The **complete certainty condition** is the decision-making situation in which the decision maker knows exactly what the results of an implemented alternative will be.

FIGURE 6.6 Continuum of decision-making conditions

Complete Uncertainty Condition

The **complete uncertainty condition** is the decision-making situation in which the decision maker has absolutely no idea what the results of an implemented alternative will be.

The **complete uncertainty condition** exists when decision makers have absolutely no idea what the results of an implemented alternative will be. The complete uncertainty condition would exist, for example, if there were no historical data on which to base a decision. Not knowing what happened in the past makes it difficult to predict what will happen in the future. In this situation, decision makers usually find that sound decisions are merely a matter of chance. An example of a decision made in a complete uncertainty situation would be choosing to pull the candy machine lever labeled "Surprise of the Day" rather than the lever that would deliver a candy bar that is familiar. It is fortunate that few organizational decisions need to be made in the complete uncertainty condition.

Risk Condition

The **risk condition** is the decision-making situation in which the decision maker has only enough information to estimate how probable the outcome of implemented alternatives will be.

The primary characteristic of the **risk condition** is that decision makers have only enough information about the outcome of each alternative to estimate how probable the outcome will be if the alternative is implemented.[22] Obviously, the risk condition is somewhere between complete certainty and complete uncertainty. The manager who hires two extra salespeople to increase annual organizational sales is deciding in a risk situation. He may believe that the probability is high that these two new salespeople will increase total sales, but it is impossible for him to know for sure. Some risk is associated with this decision.

In reality, *degrees* of risk can be associated with decisions made in the risk situation. The lower the quality of information related to the outcome of an alternative, the closer the situation is to complete uncertainty and the higher is the risk of choosing that alternative. Most decisions made in organizations have some amount of risk associated with them. The following highlight illustrates PepsiCo's highly effective system for handling risk in decision making.

QUALITY HIGHLIGHT
PepsiCo Teaches Risk Taking

PepsiCo feels that making risky decisions well is a very important part of maintaining a desirable level of product quality—so important, in fact, that teaching managers how to take risks is a critical component of PepsiCo's management training program.

PepsiCo has the most sophisticated and comprehensive U.S. system for turning bright young people into strong managers. The company's chief executive officer, Wayne Calloway, describes the process as taking eagles and teaching them to fly in formation. In a recent survey, PepsiCo ranks first in attracting and developing talented people. As part of their training, managers are encouraged to make decisions on their own, to make them fast, and to get used to taking risks related to their decisions. Calloway indicates that wrong decisions are more likely to be tolerated if the person who made the decision calculated the risk carefully and accurately. PepsiCo teaches its managers that the best time to make relatively more risky decisions is when the company is being successful; the time for more conservative and less risky decisions is when competition is strong and the business seems somewhat less successful. ▶

Teaching managers how to take risks is a critical component of PepsiCo's management training program. CEO Wayne Calloway likens the process to taking eagles and teaching them to fly in formation.

BACK TO THE CASE The introductory case reveals that Lee Iacocca faced a decision regarding how to handle increased competition, especially from the Japanese. Iacocca's decision-making condition for such a situation is somewhere between complete certainty and complete uncertainty about the outcome of his alternatives. He could decide, for example, to lower Chrysler's prices or to increase advertising to fight off the competition, but he has no guarantee that such measures would produce the desired results. He *does* know, however, what has worked in the past to stop competitors, and thus he is not dealing with a complete unknown. Therefore, any decision that Iacocca would make about handling increased competition would be made under the risk condition. In other words, Iacocca would have to determine the outcome probability for each of his alternatives and base his decision on the alternative that looked most advantageous.

DECISION-MAKING TOOLS

Most managers develop intuition about what decisions to make. This intuition is a mostly subjective feeling, developed from years of experience in a particular organization or industry, that gives managers insights about making a decision.[23] Although intuition can be an important part of making a decision, most managers tend to emphasize more objective decision-making tools, such as linear programming, queuing or waiting-line methods, and game theory.[24] Perhaps the two most widely used of the objective decision-making tools are probability theory and decision trees.

Probability Theory

Probability theory is a decision-making tool used in risk situations—situations wherein decision makers are not completely sure of the outcome of an implemented alternative. Probability refers to the likelihood that an event or outcome will actually occur and allows decision makers to calculate an expected value for each alternative. The **expected value (EV)** for an alternative is the income (I) it would produce multiplied by its probability of making that income (P). In formula form, EV = I × P. Decision makers generally choose and implement the alternative with the highest expected value.[25]

Probability theory is a decision-making tool used in risk situations—situations in which the decision maker is not completely sure of the outcome of an implemented alternative.

Expected value (EV) is the measurement of the anticipated value of some event, determined by multiplying the income an event would produce by its probability of making that income (EV = I × P).

An example will clarify the relationship of probability, income, and expected value. A manager is trying to decide where to open a store that specializes in renting surfboards. She is considering three possible locations (A, B, and C), all of which seem feasible. For the first year of operation, the manager has projected that, under ideal conditions, she would earn $90,000 in Location A, $75,000 in Location B, and $60,000 in Location C. After studying historical weather patterns, however, she has determined that there is only a 20 percent chance, or a .2 probability, of ideal conditions during the first year of operation in Location A. Locations B and C have a .4 and a .8 probability, respectively, for ideal conditions during the first year. Expected values for each of these locations are as follows: Location A—$18,000; Location B—$30,000; Location C—$48,000. Figure 6.7 shows the situation this decision maker

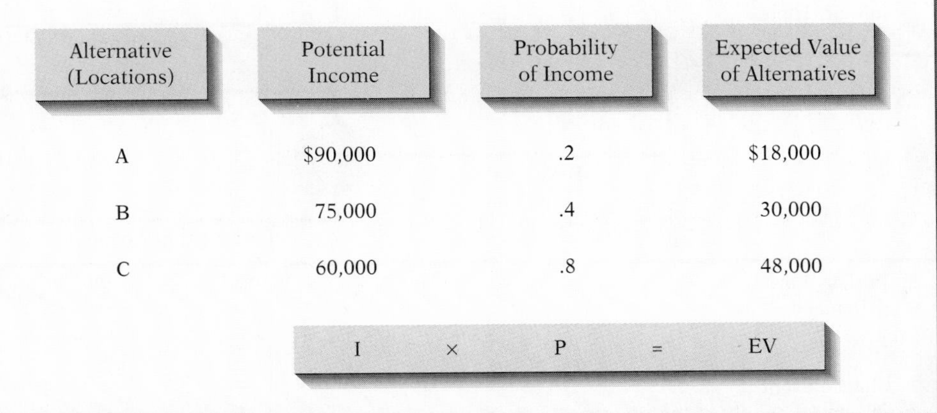

Alternative (Locations)
Potential Income
Probability of Income
Expected Value of Alternatives
A
$90,000
.2
$18,000
B
75,000
.4
30,000
C
60,000
.8
48,000
I × P = EV

FIGURE 6.7 Expected values for locating surfboard rental store in each of three possible locations

faces. According to her probability analysis, she should open a store in Location C, the alternative with the highest expected value.

Decision Trees

A **decision tree** is a graphic decision-making tool typically used to evaluate decisions containing a series of steps.

In the previous section, probability theory was applied to a relatively simple decision situation. Some decisions, however, are more complicated and involve a series of steps. These steps are interdependent; that is, each step is influenced by the step that precedes it. A **decision tree** is a graphic decision-making tool typically used to evaluate decisions containing a series of steps.[26]

John F. Magee has developed a classic illustration that outlines how decision trees can be applied to a production decision.[27] In his illustration (see Figure 6.8), the Stygian Chemical Company must decide whether to build a small or a large plant to manufacture a new product with an expected life of ten years. This figure clearly shows that management must decide whether to build a small plant or a large one (Decision Point 1). If the choice is to build a large plant, the company could face high or low average product demand or high initial and then low demand. If, however, the choice is to build a small plant, the company could face either initially high or initially low product demand. If the small plant is built and high product demand exists during an initial two-year period, management could then choose whether to expand the plant (Decision Point 2). Whether the decision is made to expand or not to expand, management could then face either high or low product demand.

Now that various possible alternatives related to this decision have been outlined, the financial consequence of each different course of action must be compared. To adequately compare these consequences, management must (1) study estimates of investment amounts necessary for building a large plant, for building a small plant, and

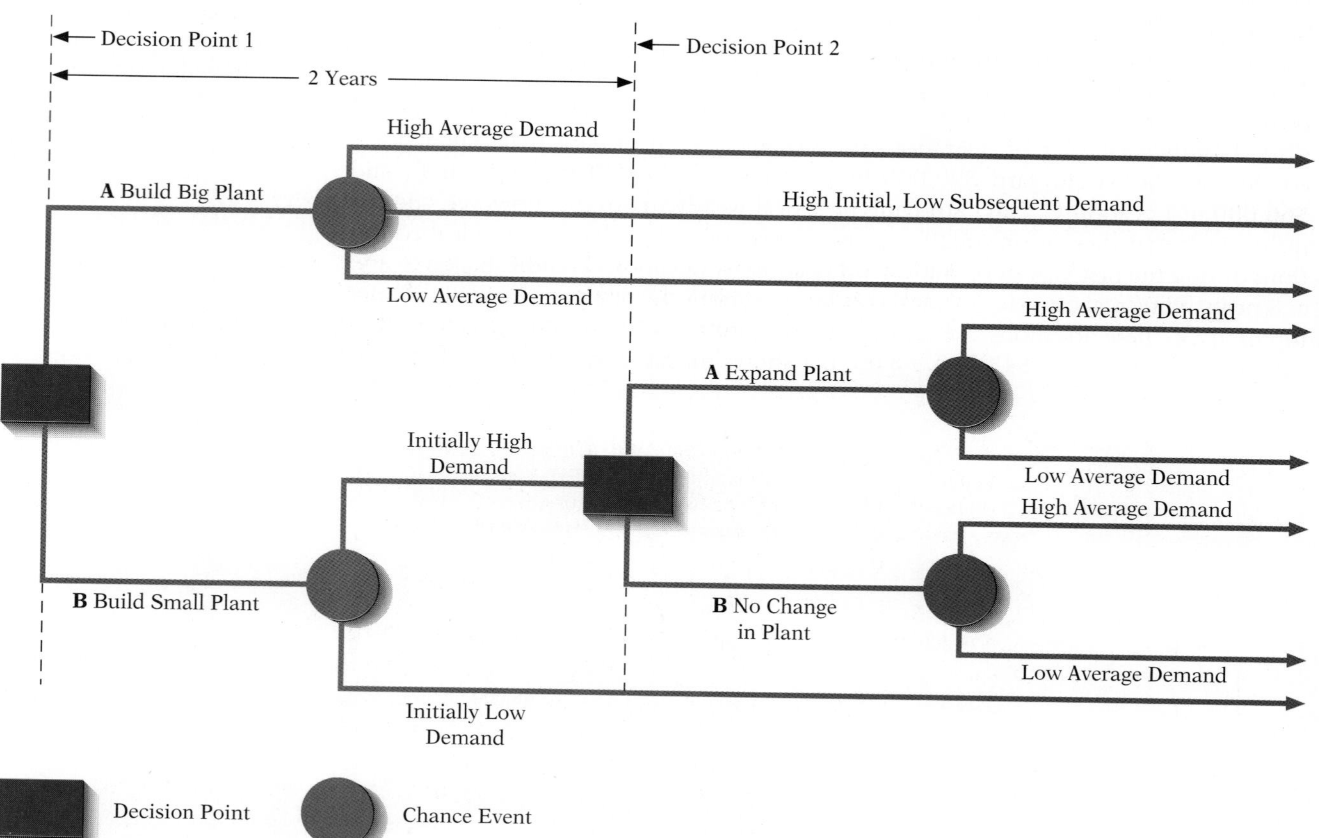

FIGURE 6.8 A basic decision tree illustrating the decision facing Stygian management
(Copyright © 1964 by the President and Fellows of Harvard College; all rights reserved.)

for expanding a small plant; (2) weigh the probabilities of facing different product demand levels for various decision alternatives; and (3) consider projected income yields for each decision alternative.

Analysis of the expected values and net expected gain for each decision alternative helps management to decide on an appropriate choice. *Net expected gain* is defined in this situation as the expected value of an alternative minus the investment cost. For example, if building a large plant yields the highest net expected gain, Stygian management should decide to build the large plant.

BACK TO THE CASE

Lee Iacocca had two tools available to make better decisions at Chrysler. First, he could have used probability theory to obtain an expected value for various decision alternatives and then implemented the alternative with the highest expected value. For example, in determining a tactic for meeting Japanese competition, Iacocca or his successor may need to decide whether to devote more of the company's resources to making higher quality automobiles or initiating more effective advertising for his present products. This decision would depend on such factors as manufacturing costs of quality improvements and expected impact of new advertising.

Second, in making a decision about choices that involve a series of steps related to each alternative, Iacocca could have used a decision tree to help him picture and evaluate each alternative. For example, to meet the Japanese competition he could have chosen to design an entirely new solar-powered automobile or devote more resources to the improvement of existing automobiles. Either of these alternatives would indicate different decision-making steps.

Iacocca and his successors must remember that business judgment is an essential adjunct to the effective use of any decision-making tool. The purpose of the tool is to improve the quality of the judgment, not to replace it. They not only must choose alternatives with the help of probability theory and a decision tree, but they must use their own good judgment in deciding what is best for Chrysler.

ACTION SUMMARY

Reread the learning objectives that follow. Each objective is followed by questions. Answering these questions accurately will help you retain the most important concepts discussed in this chapter. After answering each question, check your answer with the answer key at the end of this chapter. (*Hint:* If you have doubt regarding the correct response, consult the page whose number follows the answer.)

Circle: ***From studying this chapter, I will attempt to acquire:***

1. A fundamental understanding of the term *decision*.

T, F **a.** A decision is a choice made between two or more alternatives.

a, b, c, d, e **b.** Decision making is involved in the following function: (a) planning; (b) organizing; (c) controlling; (d) influencing; (e) all of the above.

2. An understanding of each element of the decision situation.

a, b, c, d, e **a.** The following type of decision-making orientation involves the belief that the source of all good is outside oneself and that, therefore, one must rely heavily on suggestions from other organizational members: (a) exploitation; (b) hoarding; (c) marketing; (d) natural; (e) receptive.

a, b, c, d, e **b.** According to Wilson and Alexis, all of the following are elements of the decision situation except: (a) the state or nature of the decision environment; (b) the decision makers; (c) the goals to be served; (d) the timeliness of the decision; (e) the relevant alternatives.

3. An ability to use the decision-making process.

a, b, c, d, e **a.** After identifying an existing problem, the next major step in the decision-making process is: (a) defining the terminology in the problem statement; (b) listing possible alternatives to solve the problem; (c) investigating possible alternatives to determine their effect on the problem; (d) determining what parties will participate in the problem-solving process; (e) identifying sources of alternatives to solve the problem.

a, b, c, d, e **b.** After going through the decision-making process, if the identified problem is not being solved as a result of the implemented alternative, the manager should: (a) attempt to redefine the problem; (b) turn attention to another problem; (c) search out and implement some other alternative; (d) attempt to implement the alternative until the problem is solved; (e) accept the fact that the problem cannot be solved.

4. An appreciation for the various situations in which decisions are made.

T, F **a.** The risk condition exists when decision makers have absolutely no idea of what the results of an implemented alternative will be.

T, F **b.** When operating under the complete uncertainty condition, decision makers usually find that sound decisions are a matter of chance.

5. An understanding of probability theory and decision trees as decision-making tools.

a, b, c, d, e **a.** Expected value is determined by using the formula: (a) $EV = I \times P$; (b) $EV = I/P$; (c) $EV = I + P$; (d) $EV = P - I$; (e) $EV = 2P \times I$.

a, b, c, d, e **b.** In the case of the Stygian Chemical Company, the problem was solved through the use of: (a) executive experience; (b) decision tree technique; (c) queuing theory; (d) linear programming; (e) demand probability.

INTRODUCTORY CASE WRAP-UP

"Iacocca Makes a Wrong Decision at Chrysler?" (p. 133) and its related back-to-the-case sections were written to help you better understand the management concepts contained in this chapter. Answer the following discussion questions about this introductory case to further enrich your understanding of chapter content:

1. List three alternatives that Iacocca might have considered in meeting Japanese competition before making a decision to diversify into aerospace and defense businesses.
2. What information would Iacocca need to evaluate these three alternatives?
3. Do you think that you would enjoy making the kinds of decisions at Chrysler that Iacocca must make? Explain.

ISSUES FOR REVIEW AND DISCUSSION

1. What is a decision?
2. Describe the difference between a significant decision and an insignificant decision. Which would you rather make? Why?
3. List three programmed and three nonprogrammed decisions that the manager of a nightclub would probably have to make.
4. Explain the rationale for determining which managers in the organization are responsible for making which decisions.
5. What is the consensus method of making decisions? When would you use it?
6. List and define the six basic elements of the decision-making situation.
7. How does the receptive orientation for decision making differ from the ideal orientation for decision making?
8. List as many undesirable traits of a decision maker as possible. (They are implied within the explanations of the receptive, exploitation, hoarding, and marketing orientations to decision making.)
9. What is a relevant alternative? An irrelevant alternative?

10. Draw and describe in words the decision-making process presented in this chapter.
11. What is meant by the term *discretionary area?*
12. List the three assumptions on which the decision-making process presented in this chapter is based.
13. Explain the difference between the complete certainty and complete uncertainty decision-making situations.
14. What is the risk decision-making situation?
15. Are there degrees of risk associated with various decisions? Why?
16. How do decision makers use probability theory? Be sure to discuss expected value in your answer.
17. What is a decision tree?
18. Under what conditions are decision trees usually used as decision-making tools?

ACTION SUMMARY ANSWER KEY

1. **a.** T, p. 134
   b. e, p. 134
2. **a.** e, p. 139
   b. d, pp. 138–140
3. **a.** b, p. 141
   b. c, p. 142–143
4. **a.** F, p. 144
   b. T, p. 144
5. **a.** a, p. 145
   b. b, pp. 146–147

CASE STUDY

GM: Which Way Is Up?

TONY ORTEGA
California State University Bakersfield

Top management at General Motors has been unable to decide which are the right things to do. In 1991, the big three automakers together—General Motors (GM), Ford, and Chrysler—lost a total of $10 billion on their North American business.

GM's recent history includes a series of crucial ups and downs that triggered key strategic decisions. In 1979, the company launched its front-wheel-drive cars. In 1980, General Motors suffered its worst year since 1921, posting a $763 million dollar loss. When Japan yielded to pressure and agreed to limit its auto shipments to the United States, GM, like the other U.S. automakers, reveled in windfall profits. However, instead of investing in its core business, the company sought higher returns by investing the money elsewhere. Among other things, GM bought almost half of Britain's Lotus.

In 1984, GM undertook a massive reorganization. Under the new structure, Chevrolet-Pontiac-Canada would develop, manufacture, and market small cars while Buick-Oldsmobile-Cadillac would concentrate on big ones. To create a corporate look, GM designed its cars to resemble one another. Consequently, GM built the first look-alike cars: Buick Somerset, Oldsmobile Calais, and Pontiac Grand Am. Unfortunately, buyers could not tell an Oldsmobile from a Buick and had a hard time telling a $9,000 Pontiac from a $25,000 Cadillac. This was great for Pontiac, but a disaster for Cadillac. In 1985, GM bought Hughes for $5 billion and posted a record $96.4 billion in sales. GM slipped from 16th to 109th on *Fortune*'s Most Admired list. In 1987, GM took a hit on its market share. GM's share of car sales dropped to 36.6 percent, a decline of nearly five points in a single year. In 1989, GM bought half of Saab for $600 million. In 1990, Robert Stempel succeeded Roger Smith, CEO since 1981, and the Saturn arrived on the consumer market with production problems. GM negotiated a generous contract with the United Auto Workers because Stempel was eager to avoid a strike, and he believed that GM could improve quality faster if workers weren't worried about layoffs. Rather than cut production, GM kept its factories running. The company slashed retail prices and increased its scarcely profitable wholesale deliveries to fleet customers to move its product.

It was at this time that the economy started to weaken. In 1991, GM posted a $4.5 billion loss, although fleet sales peaked at 20 percent of total market. Notably, GM offered a $2,500 incentive on the Cadillac Brougham. Finally, in 1992, problems at GM came to a head. The two car groups that were created in 1984 had quickly blossomed into bureaucracies, adding a layer of management and a duplication of marketing and engineering staffs. GM had violated a basic management precept: instead of flattening the organization and getting closer to the customer, it had done just the reverse, but GM executives blamed the 1984 reorganization for high costs, indifferent quality, inefficient coordination, brand erosion, and loss of market share. In 1993, the outside directors—led by John Smale—demoted the president, Robert Stempel, and put Jack Smith in charge. Smith immediately began to undo the reorganization because the structure was not working. He began by combining all the passenger-car divisions into a single North American Organization. He replaced the group executives and their separate staffs with a skeleton staff of three hundred people.

General Motors remains at a crossroads. Global automobile markets are growing and competition in the automotive industry is getting keener. The largest single group of affluent consumers in history, the baby boomers, are maturing, and they are redefining their transportation needs and wants. Lifestyles are changing. Population growth has generated a fresh push for the development of mass transit. Environmental considerations are having a profound impact on automotive engineering. Automobiles using alternate fuels have been mandated. The automotive industry as we have known it is changed. Top management at GM must make some fundamental choices.

DISCUSSION QUESTIONS

1. What should be the technical core of GM business? What business should the company be in?
2. What should be the most important objective for the company's immediate recovery?
3. What is a reasonable strategy for achieving the objective?
4. What factors should be considered in evaluating the current automobile market?

Making Decisions That Count

John Georges
International Paper

As chief executive officer of the largest paper company in the world, John Georges has weathered some challenging times and has made some difficult decisions. He's used his decision-making skills to survive an industrywide depression and a brutal labor strike, and he's come out on top in both situations.

International Paper (IP) produces lumber, grocery bags, juice cartons, and all sorts of products created from wood, in addition to paper. It is a $9.5 billion enterprise, and John Georges has made it one of the thirty blue-chip companies on the Dow-Jones Industrial Average.

Nonetheless, money is not all that matters to Georges; he has a very personal attitude toward being CEO. He believes in working with each employee according to his or her skills and abilities, and he works with each one differently. He treats each employee according to individual needs, desires, and talents.

John Georges meets problems squarely. He harvests as much information and advice as he can, makes a decision, and takes action to get the job done.

When Georges became IP's president in 1981, the company's mills were not doing well. The economy was in a recession, and the paper industry was hard hit. Earnings were poor, and the short-term outlook throughout the industry was bleak. Mills were shutting down, and workers were being laid off. In the face of this, Georges and his management team decided to spend $7 billion to modernize their operations.

Their decision was not made lightly. Georges and his managers discussed at length whether it was appropriate, in light of the paper industry's troubles, to reinvest in IP's old plants, or whether they should move on to new products and new challenges. However, they kept coming back to the same decision: to do what they knew how to do and build up their base business. If they could succeed, then at some point in the future, they would have the luxury to expand into new areas as well. The decision was the right one. IP experienced ten percent growth per year in the decade from 1979 to 1989, in the face of industry losses. In 1988 alone, IP showed an 82 percent increase.

To gain as they did, Georges and his team had to make other tough decisions when it came to labor problems. Union management saw the opportunity to combine workers from many mills in a strike that would bring potentially crippling pressure to bear on IP, thereby gaining a major bargaining advantage in contract negotiations. IP management locked out over 2,000 workers at one of the mills in response to the strike and hired replacements for them. When three other mills struck, they hired replacement workers there, too. Over 2,000 people lost permanent jobs as a result of that strike, but IP prevailed.

In addition, John Georges's long-term decisions on behalf of IP must reflect a concern for environmental issues. Trees, the prime ingredient of IP's products, are only a renewable resource if properly managed. For each tree IP cuts, five new ones are planted. The new trees are hybrids created through IP's genetic research programs. They have increased pest and disease resistance, as well as generally faster growth rates than naturally occurring trees. As a result, the replacement trees are more likely to survive and thrive and can usually be harvested at an earlier age than natural forests.

IP's policy also forbids harvesting trees along roadsides, rivers, and lakeshores. There is an obvious public relations profit in not exposing the public to the devastating appearance of raw cutting, but there is a more important gain for IP in the long run. To cut in these sites would expose reforestation areas and natural water supplies to environmental stresses that would eventually cause a reduction of future harvests. Thus, simple conservation techniques such as saving forested belts along a lakeshore benefit IP twice: a short-term public relations gain and a long-term financial gain. These benefits are balanced against the one-time benefit of harvesting the existing trees in those protected areas—Georges clearly made another right decision.

John Georges's attitude toward problems is to meet them squarely. He harvests as much information and advice as he can and then makes a decision. In the end, as he says, you've got to get on with the job.

VIDEO CASE QUESTIONS

1. Give an example of a nonprogrammed decision made by John Georges and the IP management team.
2. Plot the steps in the decision-making process that led to IP's choice of plant modernization.
3. Describe the scope of the decisions Georges and his team made regarding modernization at IP, and also regarding labor problems that they confronted.
4. According to the text, what style of decision-making process was used in choosing the modernization plan?

CNN VIDEO EXERCISE

Team Decision Making at International Paper

EXERCISE GOAL: Practice each stage of the decision-making process.

Imagine that you work at International Paper as a manager in the Recycled Paper division. Further imagine that International Paper has not been able to meet consumer demand for recycled paper products because only one of its plants has the necessary machinery. You are part of the decision-making team that must decide how many IP plants should be retooled to produce recycled products. Complete the following activities:

1. Define the decision that must be made, and state whether the decision is a programmed or non-programmed decision.

____

____

____

____

2. List two possible alternatives for solving the problem faced by IP.

1. ______________________________

____

____

2. ______________________________

____

____

3. Work with a student next to you to identify any alternatives either of you has included that are not feasible due to your lack of authority.

____

____

____

____

4. In order to list the potential benefits and effects of any of your alternatives, what information do you require? List as many kinds of information as you can. Then work with a student next to you to add to both of your lists.

1. ______________________________

2. ______________________________

3. ______________________________

4. ______________________________

5. ______________________________

6. ______________________________

7. ______________________________

5. Decide how many plants to retool.

CHAPTER

7

STRATEGIC PLANNING

STUDENT LEARNING OBJECTIVES

From studying this chapter, I will attempt to acquire:

1. Definitions of both strategic planning and strategy.
2. An understanding of the strategy management process.
3. A knowledge of the impact of environmental analysis on strategy formulation.
4. Insights on how to use critical question analysis and SWOT analysis to formulate strategy.
5. An understanding of how to use business portfolio analysis and industry analysis to formulate strategy.
6. Insights on what tactical planning is and on how strategic and tactical planning should be coordinated.

CHAPTER OUTLINE

INTRODUCTORY CASE
Sea World Plots a New Competitive Course

STRATEGIC PLANNING

Fundamentals of Strategic Planning
Strategy Management

ETHICS HIGHLIGHT
Quaker Oats

GLOBAL HIGHLIGHT
The Limited, Inc.

QUALITY HIGHLIGHT
Lutheran General Health System

DIVERSITY HIGHLIGHT
Methodist Hospital

TACTICAL PLANNING

COMPARING AND COORDINATING STRATEGIC AND TACTICAL PLANNING

PLANNING AND LEVELS OF MANAGEMENT

CASE STUDY
EPI Products

VIDEO CASE
Spicing up Sales: Charles McCormick, McCormick and Company

VIDEO EXERCISE
Strategic Planning at McCormick Spice

INTRODUCTORY CASE

Sea World Plots a New Competitive Course

Walking through the cavernous passenger loading area of Sea World's new simulator ride, park president Bill Davis fires a question at one of the ride's testers. "Is this thing going to work?" he asks, stepping over construction debris.

"I sure hope so," the employee says.

Davis chuckles. While there is considerable cleaning, landscaping, and fine-tuning to be done, he is confident that *Mission: Bermuda Triangle* will be ready for guests May 22, in time for the Memorial Day weekend.

"Anheuser-Busch knows the value of putting a major thrill ride in its parks. It has seen the impact new roller coasters have had."

"I rode it three or four times on Monday and it was great," Davis said Wednesday. "The one thing we are not going to do is open an attraction that is not ready to open."

Mission: Bermuda Triangle will simulate an underwater dive. Passengers will seemingly plunge a mile below the ocean's surface, where they will view deep-sea flora and fauna and, as their journey continues, learn why the area has been called the "graveyard of the Atlantic."

The ride is part of $48 million of new exhibits and improvements planned this year at the Sea World and Busch Gardens park owned by Anheuser-Busch Companies, the St. Louis brewer.

Mission: Bermuda Triangle is the first ride installed at the Orlando park. In its 19-year history, Sea World has concentrated on marine animal shows rather than edge-of-the-seat experiences.

The new ride is likely to help the park compete against its neighbors, Universal Studios Florida and Walt Disney World, which already have simulator rides, said John Gerner, an attractions industry consultant in Richmond, Va.

The ride might also help Sea World attract thrill-seeking teenagers and boost attendance by 5 percent to 15 percent this year, Gerner said. Attendance last year was 3.9 million.

"Anheuser-Busch knows the value of putting a major thrill ride in its parks," Gerner said. "It has seen the impact new roller coasters have had" when installed at Busch Gardens parks in Tampa and Williamsburg, Va.

Earlier this week, the hum of construction machinery could be heard at the new ride. Lights flashed off and on as the electrical system was tested. Employees puzzled over a stubborn, sticking door.

Bright orange and yellow submersibles that were used in undersea exploration are on loan to Sea World from oceanographic institutes, and are on display at the entrance of the ride.

Guests entering the attraction will see a pre-show hosted by ABC journalist Hugh Downs. They will then be belted into one of three "submersibles"—the Neptune, Skipjack or Barracuda.

The cabins are attached to motion bases that pitch, shake, and tilt in sync with a film. The motion and video duplicate what people would actually feel on an underwater exploration.

"Early in the ride, it's very smooth, much like you're floating in the water," said Davis, standing near one of the several-ton motion bases. "Then, at the appropriate time, it really starts jostling you. There's a lot of motion."

To ensure that the cabins can withstand constant use, each will be run for a continuous 24 hours before the ride opens to guests, said Rick Waterhouse, the park's vice president of design and engineering.

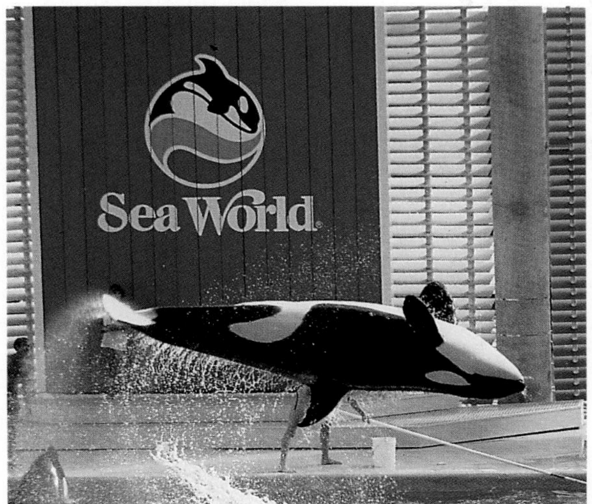

Sea World is best known for its entertaining and informative marine animal shows and exhibits. However, in order to compete with the many theme parks in Orlando and the surrounding area, Sea World has made a strategic decision to add simulation rides such as a simulated underwater dive.

From Susan G. Strother, "Sea World Plots Competitive Course 1st Ride," *Orlando Sentinel* (May 15, 1992), C1, C6. Reprinted by permission.

WHAT'S AHEAD The introductory case highlights the new competitive course taken by Bill Davis, president of Sea World. Developing a new course of this sort is actually part of Sea World's strategic planning process. The material in this chapter explains how developing a competitive strategy fits into strategic planning and discusses the strategic planning process as a whole. Major topics included in this chapter are (1) strategic planning, (2) tactical planning, (3) comparing and coordinating strategic and tactical planning, and (4) planning and levels of management.

STRATEGIC PLANNING

For managers to be successful strategic planners, they must understand the fundamentals of strategic planning and how to formulate strategic plans.

Fundamentals of Strategic Planning

Defining Strategic Planning

Strategic planning is long-term planning that focuses on the organization as a whole.

Strategic planning is long-range planning that focuses on the organization as a whole.[1] Managers consider the organization as a total unit and ask themselves what must be done in the long term to attain organizational goals. *Long range* is usually defined as a period of time extending about three to five years into the future. Hence, in strategic planning, managers try to determine what their organization should do to be successful at some point three to five years in the future. The most successful managers tend to be those who are able to encourage innovative strategic thinking within their organizations.[2]

The **commitment principle** is a management guideline that advises managers to commit funds for planning only if they can anticipate, in the foreseeable future, a return on planning expenses as a result of the long-range planning analysis.

Managers may have a problem trying to decide exactly how far into the future they should extend their strategic planning. As a general rule, they should follow the **commitment principle**, which states that managers should commit funds for planning only if they can anticipate, in the foreseeable future, a return on planning expenses as a result of the long-range planning analysis. Realistically, planning costs are an investment and therefore should not be incurred unless a reasonable return on that investment is anticipated.

Defining Strategy

Strategy is a broad and general plan developed to reach long-term organizational objectives; it is the end result of strategic planning.

Strategy is defined as a broad and general plan developed to reach long-term objectives. Organizational strategy can, and generally does, focus on many different organizational areas, such as marketing, finance, production, research and development, personnel,[3] and public relations.[4]

Actually, strategy is the end result of strategic planning. Although larger organizations tend to be more precise in their development of organizational strategy than smaller organizations,[5] every organization should have a strategy of some sort.[6] For a strategy to be worthwhile, however, it must be consistent with organizational objectives, which in turn must be consistent with organizational purpose. Table 7.1 illustrates this relationship between organizational objectives and strategy by presenting sample organizational objectives and strategies for three well-known business organizations.

Strategy management is the process of ensuring that an organization possesses and benefits from the use of an appropriate organization strategy.

Strategy Management

Strategy management is the process of ensuring that an organization possesses and benefits from the use of an appropriate organizational strategy. Within this definition, an appropriate strategy is a strategy best suited to the needs of an organization at a particular time.

TABLE 7.1 Examples of organizational objectives and related strategies for three organizations in different business areas

Company	*Type of Business*	*Sample Organization Objectives*	*Strategy to Accomplish Objectives*
Ford Motor Company	Automobile manufacturing	1. Regain market share recently lost to General Motors 2. Regain quality reputation that was damaged because of Pinto gas tank explosions	1. Resize and downsize present models 2. Continue to produce sub-intermediate, standard, and luxury cars 3. Emphasize use of programmed combustion engines instead of diesel engines.
Burger King	Fast food	Increase productivity	1. Increase people efficiency 2. Increase machine efficiency
CP Railroad	Transportation	1. Continue company growth 2. Continue company profits	1. Modernize 2. Develop valuable real estate holdings 3. Complete an appropriate railroad merger

The strategy management process is generally thought to consist of five sequential and continuing steps: (1) environmental analysis, (2) establishing organizational direction, (3) strategy formulation, (4) strategy implementation, and (5) strategic control.[7] The relationships among these steps are illustrated in Figure 7.1.

BACK TO THE CASE

In developing a plan to compete with other theme parks, management at Sea World would normally begin by thinking strategically. That is, management should try to determine what can be done to ensure that Sea World will be successful with its theme park at some point three to five years in the future. Naturally, developing a theme park that best suits the marketplace is part of this thinking. Sea World management must be careful, however, to spend funds on strategic planning only if they can anticipate a return on these expenses in the foreseeable future.

The result of Sea World's overall strategic planning will be a strategy—a broad plan that outlines what must be done to reach long-range objectives and carry out the organizational purpose of the company. This strategy will focus on many organizational areas, one of which will be competing with other theme parks. Once the strategy has been formulated using the results of an environmental analysis, Sea World management must conscientiously carry out the remaining steps of the strategy management process: strategy implementation and strategic control.

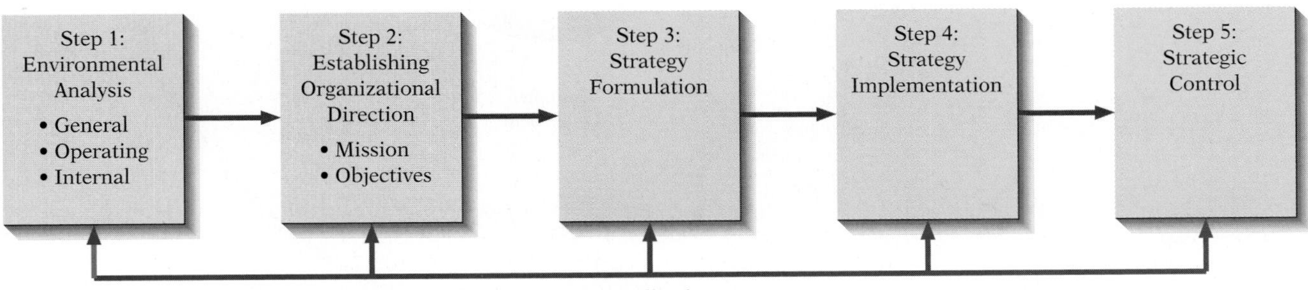

FIGURE 7.1 Steps of the strategy management process

Environmental Analysis

The first step of the strategy management process is environmental analysis. Chapter 2 presented organizations as open management systems that are constantly interacting with their environments. In essence, an organization can be successful only if it is appropriately matched to its environment. **Environmental analysis** is the study of the organizational environment to pinpoint environmental factors that can significantly influence organizational operations. Managers commonly perform environmental analyses to help them understand what is happening both inside and outside their organizations and to increase the probability that the organizational strategies they develop will appropriately reflect the organizational environment.

Environmental analysis is the study of the organizational environment to pinpoint environmental factors that can significantly influence organizational operations.

In order to perform an environmental analysis efficiently and effectively, a manager must thoroughly understand how organizational environments are structured.[8] For purposes of environmental analysis, the environment of an organization is generally divided into three distinct levels: the general environment, the operating environment, and the internal environment.[9] Figure 7.2 illustrates the relative positions of these levels to one another and to the organization; it also shows the important components of each level. Overall, managers must be aware of these three environmental levels, understand how each level affects organizational performance, and then formulate organizational strategies in response to this understanding.

The **general environment** is the level of an organization's external environment that contains components normally having broad long-term implications for managing the organization; its components are economic, social, political, legal, and technological

The General Environment. The level of an organization's external environment that contains components normally having broad long-term implications for managing the organization is the **general environment**. The components normally considered part of the general environment are economic, social, political, legal, and technological.

The *economic component* is the part of the general environment that indicates how resources are being distributed and used within the environment. This component is

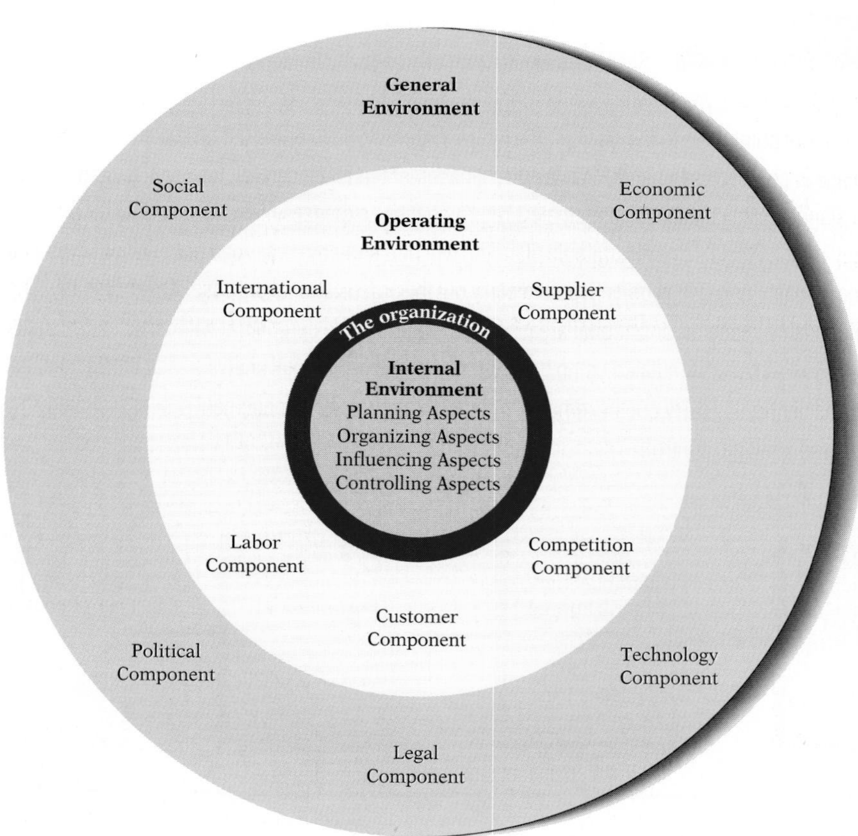

FIGURE 7.2 The organization, the levels of its environment, and the components of those levels

based on **economics,** the science that focuses on understanding how people of a particular community or nation produce, distribute, and use various goods and services. Important issues considered in an economic analysis of an environment generally include the wages paid to labor, inflation, the taxes paid by labor and businesses, the cost of materials used during the production process, and the prices at which produced goods and services are sold to customers.[10]

Economics is the science that focuses on understanding how people of a particular community or nation produce, distribute, and use various goods and services.

Economic issues such as these can significantly influence the environment in which a company operates and the ease or difficulty the organization experiences in attempting to reach its objectives. For example, it should be somewhat easier for an organization to sell its products at higher prices if potential consumers in the environment are earning relatively high wages and paying relatively low taxes than if these same potential customers are earning relatively low wages and have significantly fewer after-tax dollars to spend.

Naturally, organizational strategy should reflect the economic issues in the organization's environment. To build on the preceding example, if the total amount of after-tax income that potential customers earn has significantly declined, an appropriate organizational strategy might be to lower the price of goods or services to make them more affordable. Such a strategy should be evaluated carefully, however, because it could have a serious impact on organizational profits.

The *social component* is the part of the general environment that describes the characteristics of the society in which the organization exists. Two important features of a society commonly studied during environmental analysis are demographics and social values.[11]

Demographics are the statistical characteristics of a population. The characteristics include changes in numbers of people and income distribution among various population segments. These changes can influence the reception of goods and services within the organization's environment and thus should be reflected in organizational strategy.

Demographics are the statistical characteristics of a population. Organizational strategy should reflect demographics.

For example, the demand for retirement housing probably would increase dramatically if both the number and the income of retirees in a particular market area doubled. Effective organizational strategy would include a mechanism for dealing with such a probable increase in demand within the organization's environment.

An understanding of demographics also can be helpful in developing a strategy aimed at recruiting new employees to fill certain positions within an organization. Knowing that only a small number of people have a certain type of educational background, for example, would indicate to an organization that it should compete more intensely to attract these people. To formulate a recruitment strategy, managers need a clear understanding of the demographics of the groups from which employees eventually will be hired.

Social values are the relative degrees of worth that society places on the ways in which it exists and functions. Over time, social values can change dramatically, causing obvious changes in the way people live. Table 7.2 offers several brief examples of how changes in social values can cause changes in the way people live. These changes alter the organizational environment and, as a result, have an impact on organizational strategy. It is important for managers to remember that although changes in the values of a particular society may come either slowly or quickly, they are inevitable.[12] The following Ethics Highlight shows how Quaker Oats responded to changing societal values.

Social values are the relative degrees of worth society places on the manner in which it exists and functions.

ETHICS HIGHLIGHT
Quaker Oats Cashes in on Fitness Fad

As values of our society have shifted toward exercising and maintaining better physical health, Quaker Oats intensified its marketing of Gatorade, a drink touted as an after-exercise refreshment that effectively and efficiently replaces body nutrients lost through exercise. Recently, however, Quaker Oats has come under some attack.

TABLE 7.2 Examples of how social values can affect strategy

- For many years, people were opposed to gambling. This has changed in some places, such as Las Vegas and Atlantic City. A number of states have legalized state-run lotteries. But legalized gambling was voted down in Miami, Florida. The social value that gambling is immoral has special relevance for such firms as Resorts International and Holiday Inns.
- At one time, it was thought that families should have two to four children. Today, not all accept this norm, and the new standards have a big impact on P&G (Pampers), Gerber (baby food), builders (houses versus condominiums), Mattel (toys), and others.
- It used to be common for retired people, single people, widows, and widowers to live with relatives. Now there is a trend toward living alone, and this has a big impact on builders, appliance manufacturers, food packers, magazine publishers, and others.
- For years, most married women stayed home. Now, most work. This has caused problems for firms that sold door-to-door (Avon and Fuller Brush) and has increased business for a variety of firms, such as nursery schools, prepared food firms, restaurants (two-employee families eat out more frequently), and home security systems, to name a few.
- At one time, people lived in one place all their lives. Now, there are thousands of people who are nomads. They live in campers and motor homes and move from place to place as jobs open up or as the spirit moves them. This provides opportunities for and threats to firms.
- Increased education has led to new attitudes on the part of employees about how many hours they wish to work, the quality of life they expect at work, and the kind of supervisory style they expect, which can affect how strategies are developed and implemented. New benefits programs are also needed for new lifestyles.
- After the Three Mile Island nuclear plant incident, when an accident at the plant caused a release of radiation, more people started to question the safety of nuclear power. New plant construction and uranium mining in Canada, the United States, and Australia have been cut drastically, while coal operators are seeing new opportunities.

Quaker Oats has recently come under attack for promoting Gatorade as an effective way to replenish body nutrients lost during exercise when ordinary water does just as well.

Scientific analyses have shown that Gatorade is really no more effective than water in replenishing body fluids. Some might say that it is unethical for Quaker Oats to present Gatorade as a worthwhile product. The company could argue, however, that as with other image products, merely consuming the drink gives a person a special athletic self-image that makes him or her feel better.

Gatorade has the largest show of any product in the so-called sports drink market in the United States and is Quaker Oats' biggest brand. Competitors estimate Gatorade spends about $100 million a year on marketing the drink. Many companies have tried to win market share from Gatorade, but none have been very successful. ▶

The *political component* is the part of the general environment that contains the elements related to government affairs. Examples include the type of government in existence, the government's attitude toward various industries, lobbying efforts by interest groups, progress on the passage of laws, and political party platforms and candidates. Recent events such as the reunification of the Federal Republic of Germany and the German Democratic Republic and the shift from a Marxist-Socialist government in the Soviet Union illustrate how the political component of an organization's general environment can change at the international level.

The *legal component* is the part of the general environment that contains passed legislation. Simply stated, this component is the rules or laws that society's members must follow. Some examples of legislation specifically aimed at the operation of organizations are the Clean Air Act of 1963 (most recently amended in 1990) that focuses on minimizing air pollution, the Occupational Safety and Health Act of 1970 (most recently amended in 1984) that aims at maintaining a safe workplace, the Comprehensive Environmental Response, Compensation, and Liability Act of 1980 (most recently amended in 1988) that emphasizes controlling hazardous waste sites, and the Consumer Products Safety Act of 1972 (most recently amended in 1988) that upholds the notion that businesses must provide safe products for consumers. Naturally, overtime, new laws are passed and some old ones are eliminated.

The *technology component* is the part of the general environment that includes new approaches to producing goods and services. These approaches can include new procedures as well as new equipment. The trend toward exploiting robots to improve productivity is an example of the technology component. The increasing use of robots in the next decade should vastly improve the efficiency of U.S. industry.

The Operating Environment. The level of an organization's external environment that contains components normally having relatively specific and more immediate implications for managing the organization is the **operating environment.** As Figure 7.2 shows, major components of this environmental level are generally thought to include customers, competition, labor, suppliers, and international issues.

The **operating environment** is the level of the organization's external environment that contains components normally having relatively specific and immediate implications for managing the organization.

The *customer component* is the operating environment segment that is composed of factors relating to those who buy goods and services provided by the organization. Profiles—detailed descriptions—of those who buy organizational products are commonly created by businesses. Developing such profiles helps management generate ideas for improving customer acceptance of organizational goods and services.

The *competition component* is the operating environment segment that is composed of those with whom an organization must battle in order to obtain resources. Overall, strategy involves the search for a plan of action that will give one organization an advantage over its competitors.[13] Because understanding competitors is a key factor in developing effective strategy, understanding the competitive environment is a fundamental challenge to management. Basically, the purpose of competitive analysis is to help management understand the strengths, weaknesses, capabilities, and likely strategies of existing and potential competitors.[14]

The *labor component* is the operating environment segment that is composed of factors influencing the supply of workers available to perform needed organizational tasks. Issues such as skill levels, trainability, desired wage rates, and average age of potential workers are important to the operation of the organization. Another important but often overlooked issue is the potential workers' desire to work for particular organizations.

The *supplier component* is the operating environment segment that entails all variables related to the individuals or agencies that provide organizations with resources needed to produce goods or services. The individuals or agencies are called **suppliers.** Issues such as how many suppliers offer specified resources for sale, the relative quality of the materials offered by suppliers, the reliability of supplier deliveries, and the credit terms offered by suppliers all become important in managing an organization effectively and efficiently.

Suppliers are individuals or agencies that provide organizations with resources needed to produce organizational goods and services.

GLOBAL HIGHLIGHT
The Limited Inc. Plans Global Manufacturing

The Limited Inc. is one of the largest purchasers of women's clothing in the world. More than 50 percent of its merchandise is manufactured overseas. Vital to the company's success is its international supplier network. Managing such a complex network and integrating them into their vast retailing operation requires tremendous planning.

Limited Chairman Leslie Wexner took control of that network in 1978, when he purchased Mast Industries, Limited Inc.'s major supplier. Today, Mast coordinates production with more than 300 manufacturers, and more than 6,000 suppliers. Most are in the Far East. The network allows production at the lowest possible cost, both because labor in these countries is cheaper than in the United States and because Limited Inc. orders in such large volume.

Integrating the international supplier network—including 300 manufacturers and 6,000 suppliers—into its vast retailing operation is vital to The Limited's continued success.

One drawback to the existing system is that it can be difficult to control quality.

Because the company orders in such large volume, one supplier often cannot fill the entire order. One style of shorts, for instance, can be manufactured in three or four countries, with varying levels of quality.

"Great-quality factories don't grow on trees," says Martin Trust, Mast's president. "If I could, I'd make everything in one country."

On evaluating the situation, Mast developed a strategic plan to take more control of production quality: Mast has formed joint ventures with manufacturers. With Limited Inc.'s financial backing, these manufacturers build and operate factories in countries that are not subject to U.S. apparel import restrictions. ▶

The *international component* is the operating environment segment that is composed of all the factors relating to the international implications of organizational operations. Although not all organizations must deal with international issues, the number is increasing dramatically and continually. Significant factors in the international component include other countries' laws, culture, economics, and politics.[15] Important variables within each of these four categories are presented in Table 7.3.

The **internal environment** is the level of an organization's environment that exists inside the organization and normally has immediate and specific implications for managing the organization.

The Internal Environment. The level of an organization's environment that exists inside the organization and normally has immediate and specific implications for managing the organization is the **internal environment.** In broad terms, the internal environment includes marketing, finance, and accounting. From a more specifically management viewpoint, it includes planning, organizing, influencing, and controlling within the organization. Table 7.4 contains these more management-specific factors in the internal environment and sample questions that managers can ask in exploring them.

TABLE 7.3 Important aspects of the international component of the organization's operating environment

Legal Environment	Cultural Environment
Legal tradition	Customs, norms, values, beliefs
Effectiveness of legal system	Language
Treaties with foreign nations	Attitudes
Patent and trademark laws	Motivations
Laws affecting business firms	Social institutions
	Status symbols
Economic Environment	Religious beliefs
Level of economic development	
Population	**Political System**
Gross national product	Form of government
Per capita income	Political ideology
Literacy level	Stability of government
Social infrastructure	Strength of opposition parties and groups
Natural resources	Social unrest
Climate	Political strife and insurgency
Membership in regional economic blocks (EEC, LAFTA, etc.)	Government attitude toward foreign firms
Monetary and fiscal policies	Foreign policy
Nature of competition	
Currency convertibility	
Inflation	
Taxation system	
Interest rates	
Wage and salary levels	

TABLE 7.4 Several management-specific aspects of an organization's internal environment and questions related to exploring them

Planning Aspects
- Are organizational plans clearly linked to organizational goals?
- Is the sequencing for the performance of specific tasks appropriate?
- Are plans developed for both the short term and the long term?

Organizing Aspects
- Are tasks assigned to the right people?
- Do organizing efforts put plans into action?
- Are tasks appropriately assigned to either individuals or groups?

Influencing Aspects
- Do the rewards offered employees actually motivate them?
- Are organization members encourgaed to do work that actually contributes to organizational goal attainment?
- Is communication within the organization effective and efficient?

Controlling Aspects
- Is information gathered to measure recent performance?
- Is present performance compared to preestablished standards?
- Are organizational characteristics modified when necessary to ensure that preestablished standards are met?

BACK TO THE CASE

As part of the strategy development process, Sea World management should spend time analyzing the government in which the organization exists. Naturally, managers should focus on Sea World's general, operating, and internal environments. Environmental factors that probably would be important for them to consider as they pursue strategic planning include the number of theme parks with which Sea World competes and knowing whether this number will be increasing or decreasing. Other factors might include the strengths and weaknesses of their theme park when compared to competing parks, the reasons that people pay to go to theme parks, and the methods that competitors such as Disney World and Universal Studios are using to promote their products to their customers. Obtaining information about environmental issues such as these will increase the probability that any strategy developed for Sea World will be appropriate for its environment and will help the company achieve success in the long term.

Establishing Organizational Direction

The second step of the strategy management process is establishing organizational direction. Through an interpretation of information gathered during environmental analysis, managers can determine the direction in which an organization should move. Two important ingredients of organizational direction are organizational mission and organizational objectives.

Determining Organizational Mission. The most common initial act in establishing organizational direction is determining an organizational mission. **Organizational mission** is the purpose for which—the reason why—an organization exists. In general, the firm's organizational mission reflects such information as what types of products or services the organization produces, who its customers tend to be, and what important values it holds. Organizational mission is a very broad statement of organizational direction and is based upon a thorough analysis of information generated through environmental analysis.[16]

The **organizational mission** is the purpose for which or the reason why an organization exists.

A **mission statement** is a written document developed by management, normally based upon input by managers as well as nonmanagers, that describes and explains what the mission of an organization actually is.

Developing a Mission Statement. A **mission statement** is a written document developed by management, normally based on input by managers as well as nonmanagers, that describes and explains what the mission of an organization actually is. Normally, the mission is expressed in writing to ensure that all organization members have easy access to it and thoroughly understand exactly what the organization is trying to accomplish. Sample mission statements for three different organizations are contained in Table 7.5.

The Importance of Organizational Mission. An organizational mission is normally very important to an organization because it usually helps management to increase the probability that an organization will be successful. This probability is increased for several reasons. First, the existence of an organizational mission helps management to focus human effort in a common direction. The mission makes explicit the major targets the organization is trying to reach and helps managers keep these targets in mind as they make decisions. Second, the existence of an organizational mission helps managers because it serves as a sound rationale for allocating resources. A properly developed mission statement gives managers general but useful guidelines about how resources should be used to best accomplish organizational purpose. Third, the existence of a mission statement can help managers because it pinpoints broad but important job areas within an organization. A well-developed mission generally helps management define critical jobs that must be accomplished.[17]

QUALITY HIGHLIGHT
Lutheran General Health System's Mission Emphasizes Quality

Stephen Ummel, president and CEO of Lutheran General Health System, created a task force to develop a mission statement that could be used to coordinate the efforts of the company's various operating units. The resulting mission statement emphasizes quality of health care services.

A mission statement should emphasize the organizational values that are important in managing a particular organization. The Lutheran General Health System now has a mission statement that emphasizes quality of services provided as an important value that managers should respond to in managing the organization.

Lutheran General Health System is a multiregional, multicorporate network of health and human service organizations, including the 742-bed Lutheran General Hospital. According to Richard L. Phillips, M.D., chairperson of Lutheran General Health System's board of directors, the most important job of the board is to review and define the mission and related core values of the organization as a whole. During the 1980s, each of the company's seven separate health care facilities had a separate mission statement and a different strategic direction. As a result, the company had very little coordination among its operating units in areas such as quality, long-term care, and substance abuse treatment. Stephen L. Ummel, the company's president and CEO, created an 18-member task force to develop a mission statement containing important values for the company as a whole. The task force was charged with exploring the company's core values and drafting a common mission statement for all of Lutheran's operating units. The task force recently completed its project and the company's board has approved the final mission statement. The newly approved mission statement has already been instrumental in providing a basis for Lutheran's push toward total quality management in all of its operating units. ▶

The Relationship Between Mission and Objectives. Organizational objectives were defined in chapter 4 as the targets toward which the open management system is directed. Sound organizational objectives reflect and flow naturally from the purpose of the organization. The purpose of an organization is contained in its mission statement. As a result, useful organizational objectives must reflect and flow naturally from an organizational mission that, in turn, was designed to reflect and flow naturally from the results of an environmental analysis.

TABLE 7.5 Mission statements for three different organizations

The Crummer School[1]
The mission of the Crummer School is to improve general management through formal education programs stressing an administrative point of view, research and publication involving new knowledge and teaching materials, and relationships with businesses and the community. In fulfilling this mission the School is committed to programs that emphasize high quality, innovation, problem solving, and the application of management theory. The emphasis of the Crummer School is on the full-time MBA program. The primary target market for this core business is the national pool of applicants, with or without an academic background in business, but including those who have business experience.
IBM[2]
IBM Corporation is in the business of applying advanced information technology to help solve the problems of business, government, science, space exploration, defense, education, medicine, and other areas of human activity. IBM offers customers solutions that incorporate information processing systems, software, communications systems, and other products and services to address specific needs. These solutions are provided by IBM's worldwide marketing organizations, as well as through the company's business partners, including authorized dealers and remarketers.
Federal Express[3]
Federal Express is committed to our People-Service-Profit philosophy. We will produce outstanding financial returns by providing totally reliable, competitively superior, global air-ground transportation of high-priority goods and documents that require rapid, time-certain delivery. Equally important, positive control of each package will be maintained utilizing real time electronic tracking and tracing systems. A complete record of each shipment and delivery will be presented with our request for payment. We will be helpful, courteous, and professional to each other and the public. We will strive to have a completely satisfied customer at the end of each transaction.

Strategy Formulation

After managers involved in the strategic management process have analyzed the environment and determined organizational direction through the development of a mission statement and organizational objectives, they are ready to formulate strategy. **Strategy formulation** is the process of determining appropriate courses of action for achieving organizational objectives and thereby accomplishing organizational purpose.

A **strategy formulation** is the process of determining appropriate courses of action for achieving organizational objectives and thereby accomplishing organizational purpose.

Tools for Developing Organizational Strategies. Managers formulate strategies that reflect environmental analysis, lead to the fulfillment of organizational mission, and result in the reaching of organizational objectives. Special tools that managers can use for assistance in formulating strategies include (1) critical question analysis, (2) SWOT analysis, (3) business portfolio analysis, and (4) Porter's Model for Industry Analysis.

Strategy development tools include critical question analysis, SWOT analysis, business portfolio analysis, and Porter's Model for Industry Analysis.

The four strategy development tools are related but distinct. Managers should use which one tool or combination of tools seems most appropriate for them and their organizations.

1. *Critical Question Analysis.* A synthesis of the ideas of several contemporary management writers suggests that formulating appropriate organizational strategy is a process of **critical question analysis**—answering the following four basic questions.[18]

Critical question analysis is a strategy development tool composed mainly of four questions:

What are the purposes and objectives of the organization?

What are the purposes and objectives of the organization? The answer to this question states where the organization wants to go. As indicated earlier, appropriate strategy reflects organizational purpose and objectives. By answering this question during strategy formulation, managers are likely to remember this important point and thereby minimize inconsistencies among purposes, objectives, and strategies.

Where is the organization presently going?

Where is the organization presently going? The answer to this question can tell managers if an organization is achieving organizational goals and, if so, whether the level of such progress is satisfactory. Whereas the first question focuses on where the organization wants to go, this one focuses on where the organization is actually going.

In what kind of environment does the organization exist?

In what kind of environment does the organization now exist? Both internal and external environments—factors both inside and outside the organization—are covered in this question. For example, assume that a poorly trained middle-management team and a sudden influx of competitors in a market are factors that exist respectively in the internal and external environments of an organization. Any strategy formulated, if it is to be appropriate, should deal with these factors.

What can be done to better achieve organizational objectives in the future?

What can be done to better achieve organizational objectives in the future? The answer to this question actually results in the strategy of the organization. The question should be answered, however, only after managers have had adequate opportunity to reflect on the answers to the previous three questions. Managers can develop appropriate organizational strategy only if they have a clear understanding of where the organization wants to go, where the organization *is* going, and in what environment the organization exists.

SWOT analysis is a strategy-development tool that matches internal organizational strengths and weaknesses with external opportunities and threats.

2. *SWOT Analysis.* **SWOT analysis** is a strategic planning tool that matches internal organizational strengths and weaknesses with external opportunities and threats.[19] (SWOT is an acronym for a firm's Strengths and Weaknesses and its environmental Opportunities and Threats.) SWOT analysis is based on the assumption that if managers carefully review such strengths, weaknesses, opportunities, and threats, a useful strategy for ensuring organizational success will become evident. Table 7.6 contains several key considerations that managers should cover in performing a SWOT analysis.

Business portfolio analysis is the development of business-related strategy that is based primarily on the market share of businesses and the growth of markets in which businesses exist.

3. *Business Portfolio Analysis.* Business portfolio analysis is another strategy development tool that has gained wide acceptance.[20] **Business portfolio analysis** is an organizational strategy formulation technique that is based on the philosophy that organizations should develop strategy much as they handle investment portfolios. Just as sound financial investments should be supported and unsound ones should be discarded, sound organizational activities should be emphasized and unsound ones deemphasized. Two business portfolio tools are the BCG Growth-Share Matrix and the GE Multifactor Portfolio Matrix.

The BCG Growth-Share Matrix. The Boston Consulting Group (BCG), a leading manufacturing consulting firm, developed and popularized a portfolio analysis tool that helps managers develop organizational strategy based upon market share of businesses and the growth of markets in which businesses exist.[21]

A **strategic business unit (SBU)** is, in business portfolio analysis, a significant organizational segment that is analyzed to develop organizational strategy aimed at generating future business or revenue. SBUs vary in form but have four common characteristics.

The first step in using the BCG Growth-Share Matrix is identifying strategic business units (SBUs) that exist within an organization. A **strategic business unit** is a significant organization segment that is analyzed to develop organizational strategy aimed at generating future business or revenue. Exactly what constitutes an SBU varies from organization to organization. In larger organizations, an SBU could be a company division, a single product, or a complete product line. In smaller organizations, it might be the entire company. Although SBUs vary drastically in form, each has the characteristics of (a) being a single business or collection of related businesses, (b) having its own

TABLE 7.6 Important considerations for SWOT analysis

Internal		External	
Strengths	*Weaknesses*	*Opportunities*	*Threats*
A distinctive competence? Adequate financial resources? Good competitive skills? Well thought of by buyers? Quality of product/service? An acknowledged market leader? Well-conceived functional area strategies? Access to economies of scale? Insulated (at least somewhat) from strong competitive pressures? Proprietary technology? Cost advantages? Competitive advantages? Product innovation abilities? Proven management? Other?	No clear strategic direction? A deteriorating competitive position? Obsolete facilities? Subpar profitability because . . .? Lack of quality product/service? Lack of managerial depth and talent? Missing key skills or competencies? Poor track record in implementing strategy? Plagued with internal operating problems? Vulnerable to competitive pressures? Falling behind in R&D? Too narrow a product line? Weak market image? Competitive disadvantages? Below-average marketing skills? Inability to finance needed changes in strategy? Other?	Enter new markets or segments? Add to product line? Diversify into related products? Add complementary products? Integrate vertically? Integrate horizontally? Able to move to better strategic group? Complacency among rival firms? Faster market growth? Other?	Likely entry of new competitors? Rising sales of substitute products? Slower market growth? Adverse government policies? Growing competitive pressures? Vulnerability to business cycles? Growing bargaining power of customers or suppliers? Changing buyer needs and tastes? Adverse demographic changes? Other?

competitors, (c) having a manager who is accountable for its operation, and (d) being an area that can be independently planned for within the organization.[22]

After SBUs have been identified for a particular organization, the next step in using the BCG Matrix is to categorize them as being within one of the following four matrix quadrants (see Figure 7.3):

a. *Stars.* SBUs that are "stars" have a high share of a high-growth market and typically need large amounts of cash to support their rapid and significant growth. Stars also generate large amounts of cash for the organization and are usually areas in which management can make additional investments and earn attractive returns.

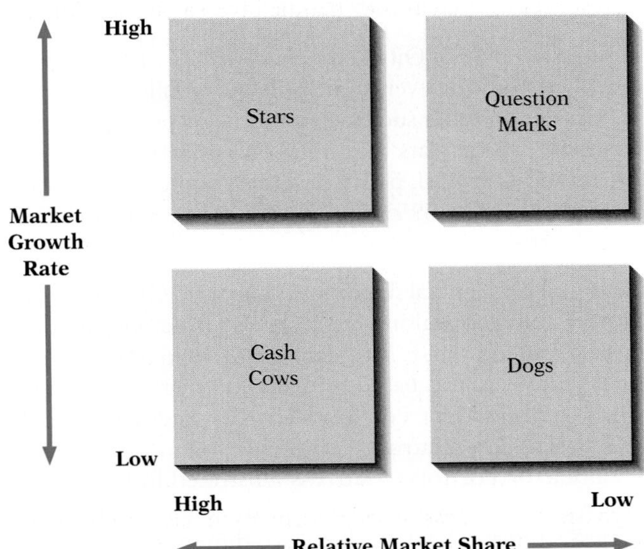

FIGURE 7.3 The BCG Growth-Share Matrix

"Good evening, cash flow fans."

USA Today, August 30, 1990, 2B. Copyright 1990, *USA Today*. Reprinted with permission.

b. *Cash cows.* SBUs that are cash cows have a large share of a market that is growing only slightly. Naturally, these SBUs provide the organization with large amounts of cash. Since the market is not growing significantly, however, the cash is generally used to meet the financial demands of the organization in other areas, such as in the expansion of a star SBU. The cartoon on this page humorously makes the point that managers typically find cash cows very desirable. Perhaps the main reason for this desirability is the financial flexibility that a cash cow provides a manager.

c. *Question marks.* SBUs that are "question marks" have a small share of a high-growth market. They are called question marks because it is uncertain whether management should invest more cash in them to get a larger share of the market or should deemphasize or eliminate them because such an investment would be ineffective. Naturally, through further investment, management attempts to turn question marks into stars.

d. *Dogs.* SBUs that are "dogs" have a relatively small share of a low-growth market. They may barely support themselves, or they may even drain cash resources that other SBUs have generated. Examples of dogs are buggy whips and slide rules.

Companies such as Westinghouse and Shell Oil have used the BCG Matrix in their strategy management processes. There are, however, some possible pitfalls in this technique. For example, the matrix does not consider such factors as (a) various types of risk associated with product development, (b) threats that inflation and other economic conditions can create in the future, and (c) social, political, and ecological pressures.[23] Managers must remember to weigh such factors carefully when designing organizational strategy based on the BCG Matrix.

The GE Multifactor Portfolio Matrix. The General Electric Company (GE), with the help of McKinsey and Company, a leading consulting firm, has also developed a popular portfolio analysis tool. This tool, called the GE Multifactor Portfolio Matrix, helps managers develop organizational strategy that is based primarily on market attractiveness and business strengths. The GE Multifactor Portfolio Matrix was designed to be more complete than the BCG Growth-Share Matrix.

The basic use of the GE Multifactor Portfolio Matrix is illustrated in Figure 7.4. Each of the organization's businesses or SBUs is plotted on a matrix in two dimensions: industry attractiveness and business strength. Each of these two dimensions is actually

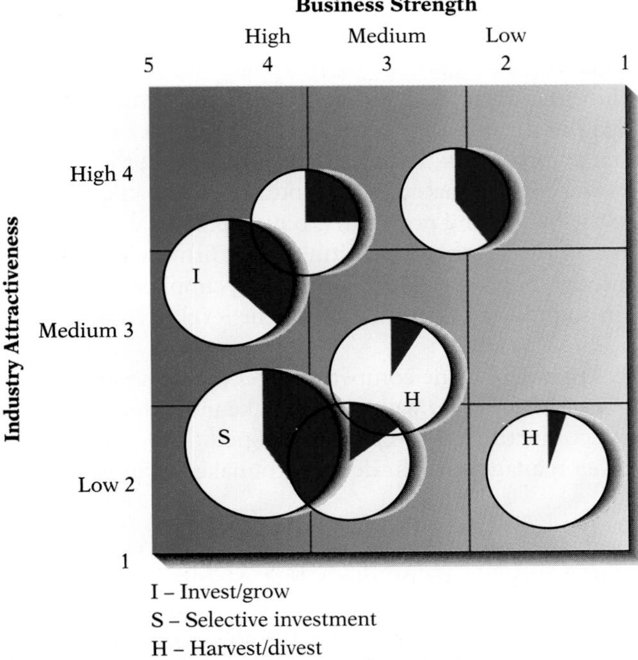

FIGURE 7.4 GE's Multifactor Portfolio Matrix

a composite of a variety of factors that each firm must determine for itself given its own unique situation. As examples, industry attractiveness might be determined by factors such as the number of competitors in an industry, the rate of industry growth, and the weakness of competitors within an industry. Business strengths might be determined by factors such as a company's financially solid position, its good bargaining position over suppliers, and its high level of technology use.

Several circles appear on the GE Multifactor Portfolio Matrix. Each circle represents a company line of business or SBU. Circle size indicates the relative market size for each line of business. The shaded portion of a circle represents the proportion of the total SBU market that a company has captured.

Specific strategies for a company are implied by where their businesses (represented by circles) fall on the matrix. Businesses falling in the cells that form a diagonal from lower left to upper right are medium-strength businesses that should be invested in only selectively. Businesses above and to the left of this diagonal are the strongest and the ones that the company should invest in and help to grow. Businesses in the cells below and to the right of the diagonal are low in overall strength and are serious candidates for divestiture.

Overall, portfolio models provide graphic frameworks for analyzing relationships among the businesses of an organization, and they can provide useful strategy recommendations. However, no such model yet devised provides a universally accepted approach for dealing with these issues. Portfolio models should never be applied in a mechanistic fashion, and any conclusions they suggest must be carefully considered in the light of sound managerial judgment and experience.

4. *Porter's Model for Industry Analysis.* Perhaps the most well known tool for formulating strategy is a model developed by Michael E. Porter, an internationally acclaimed strategic-management expert.[24] Essentially, Porter's model outlines the primary forces that determine competitiveness within an industry and illustrates how the forces are related. Porter's model suggests that in order to develop effective organizational strategies, managers must understand and react to those forces

within an industry that determine an organization's level of competitiveness within that industry.

Porter's model is presented within Figure 7.5 on this page. According to the model, competitiveness within an industry is determined by the following: new entrants or new companies within the industry; products that might act as a substitute for goods or services that companies within the industry produce; the ability of suppliers to control issues like costs of materials that industry companies use to manufacture their products; the bargaining power that buyers possess within the industry; and the general level of rivalry or competition among firms within the industry. According to the model, buyers, product substitutes, suppliers, and potential new companies within an industry all contribute to the level of rivalry among industry firms.

Understanding the forces that determine competitiveness within an industry should help managers develop strategies that will tend to make individual companies within the industry more competitive. Porter has developed three generic strategies to illustrate those that managers might develop to make organizations more competitive:

Differentiation is a strategy that focuses on making an organization more competitive by developing a product or products that customers perceive as being different from products offered by competitors.

Differentiation. **Differentiation** is a strategy that focuses on making an organization more competitive by developing a product or products that customers perceive as being different from products offered by competitors. Products might be offered to customers as different because of uniqueness in areas like product quality, design, or level of service after a sale. Examples of products that customers commonly purchase because they are perceived as being different include Nike's Air Jordan shoes, because of their high-technology "air" construction, and Honda automobiles, because of their high reliability.

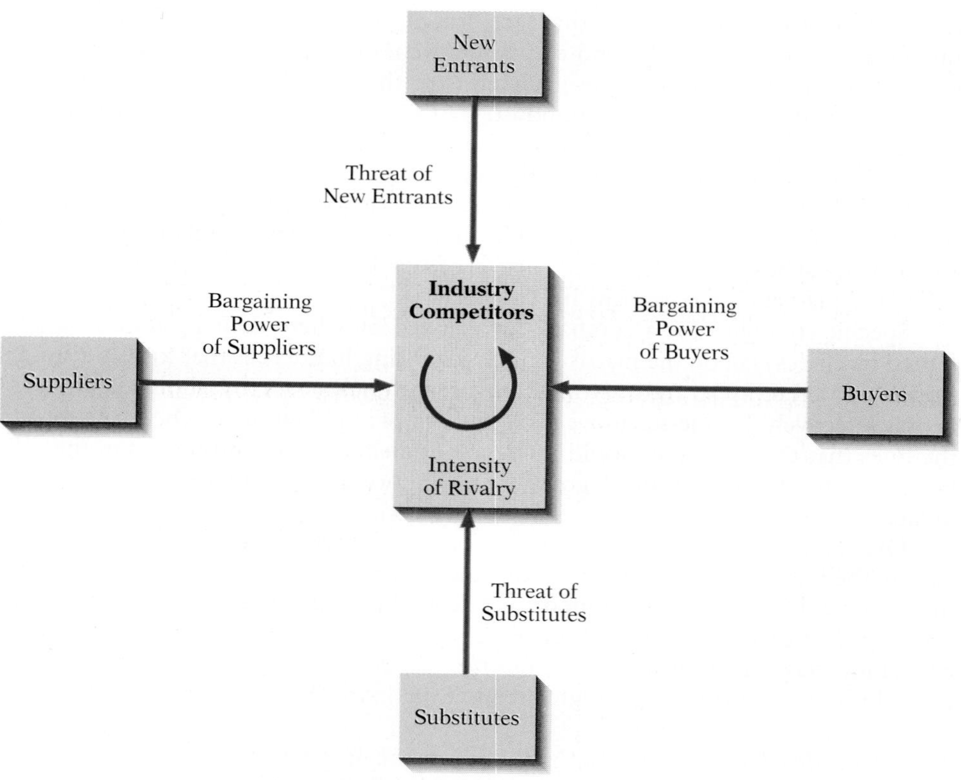

FIGURE 7.5 Porter's model of factors that determine competitiveness within an industry

Cost Leadership. **Cost leadership** is a strategy that focuses on making an organization more competitive by producing its products more cheaply than competitors can. According to the logic behind this strategy, by producing products more cheaply than competitors, organizations can offer products to customers at lower prices than the competitors', and thereby hope to increase market share. Examples of tactics managers might use to gain cost leadership include obtaining lower prices for product parts purchased from suppliers and using technology like robots to increase organizational productivity.

Cost leadership is a strategy that focuses on making an organization more competitive by producing its products more cheaply than competitors can.

Focus. **Focus** is a strategy that emphasizes making an organization more competitive by targeting a particular customer. Magazine publishers commonly use a focus strategy in offering their products to specific customers. *Working Woman* and *Ebony* are examples of magazines that are aimed respectively at the target markets of employed women and African Americans.

Focus is a strategy that emphasizes making an organization more competitive by targeting a particular customer.

Sample Organizational Strategies. Analyzing the organizational environment and applying one or more of the strategy tools—critical question analysis, SWOT analysis, business portfolio analysis, and Porter's model—give managers a foundation on which to formulate an organizational strategy. Four of the organizational strategies that can evolve are growth, stability, retrenchment, and divestiture. The following discussion of sample organizational strategies features business portfolio analysis as the tool used to arrive at the strategy, but the same strategies could also result from critical question analysis, SWOT analysis, or Porter's model.

Growth. **Growth** is a strategy adopted by management to increase the amount of business that an SBU is currently generating. The growth strategy is generally applied to star SBUs or question mark SBUs that hold the potential of becoming stars. Management generally invests substantial amounts of money to implement this strategy and may even sacrifice short-term profit to build long-term gain.[25]

Growth is a strategy adopted by management to increase the amount of business that a strategic business unit is currently generating.

Managers can also encourage growth by purchasing an SBU from another organization. For example, Black & Decker, not satisfied with being an international power in power tools, purchased General Electric's small-appliance business. Through this purchase, Black & Decker hoped that the amount of business it did would grow significantly over the long term.[26] Similarly, President Enterprises, the largest food company in Taiwan, recently bought the American Famous Amos brand of chocolate chip cookies. Despite a downturn in the U.S. cookie market, management at President saw the purchase as important for company growth because it gave the company a nationally recognized product line in the U.S.[27]

Stability. **Stability** is a strategy adopted by management to maintain or slightly improve the amount of business that an SBU is generating. This strategy is generally applied to cash cows, since these SBUs are already in an advantageous position. Management must be careful, however, that the strategy doesn't turn cash cows into dogs.

Stability is a strategy adopted by management to maintain or slightly improve the amount of business a strategic business unit is generating.

Retrenchment. In this section, *retrench* is used in the military sense: to defend or fortify. Through **retrenchment** strategy, management attempts to strengthen or protect the amount of business an SBU is generating. The strategy is generally applied to cash cows or stars that begin to lose market share.

Retrenchment is a strategy adopted by management to strengthen or protect the amount of business a strategic business unit is currently generating.

Douglas D. Danforth, the chief executive of Westinghouse, is convinced that retrenchment is an important strategy for his company. According to Danforth, bigger profits at Westinghouse depend not only on fast-growing new products but also on the revitalization of Westinghouse's traditional businesses of manufacturing motors and gears.[28]

Divestiture. **Divestiture** is a strategy generally adopted to eliminate an SBU that is not generating a satisfactory amount of business and that has little hope of doing so in

Divestiture is a strategy adopted to eliminate a strategic business unit that is not generating a satisfactory amount of business and has little hope of doing so in the future.

the near future. In essence, the organization sells or closes down the SBU in question. This strategy is generally applied to SBUs that are dogs or question marks that have failed to increase market share but still require significant amounts of cash. Divestiture means discarding or getting rid of something.

DIVERSITY HIGHLIGHT
Strategic Planning at Methodist Hospital Stresses Diversity

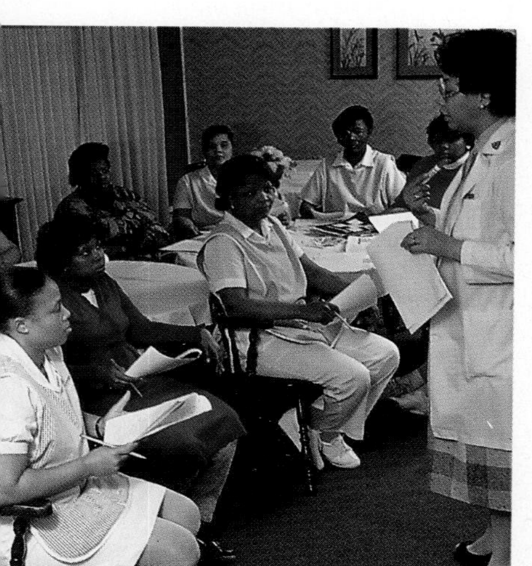

Several hospitals' strategic plans include an emphasis accommodating a workforce composed of workers from diverse backgrounds. One element of the diversity focus of these plans is continuing education for workers.

Strategic planning can focus on many different organizational issues. In today's modern organizational environment, one such issue is diversity.

As an example of such a special diversity focus in strategic planning, several hospitals are now developing a new strategic planning emphasis on accommodating a changing, twenty-first century diverse workforce, a workforce that will be dominated by women, minorities, and immigrants. Methodist Hospital in Indianapolis, Indiana, is an obvious leader in the area of including such a diversity focus in strategic planning.

Strategic planning at Methodist Hospital has clearly been adjusted to emphasize the diverse needs, values, expectations, and languages of today's diverse workforce. Since management at Methodist Hospital recognizes that continued education for workers is a critical component of developing a productive, diversified workforce in the future, the new strategic focus includes an emphasis on diversification-related education of employees. The new strategic focus also calls for identifying new and improved ways to help the emerging diverse workforce fill the hospital's labor needs. For example, management might be able to redesign certain jobs so that they are better suited to the special skills of a diverse workforce.

Methodist Hospital's strategic focus on diversity also includes special steps for attracting and retaining a diverse workforce. These steps include the establishment of special workplace policies such as allowing employees to design flexible work schedules. Another such step might be to establish special benefit packages that focus on the special needs of this diverse workforce; for example, employees with children might be easier to attract and retain if Methodist Hospital provided day care. ▶

Strategy Implementation

Strategy implementation, the fourth step of the strategy management process, is putting formulated strategy into action.

Strategy implementation, the fourth step of the strategy management process, is putting formulated strategies into action. Without success in strategy implementation, valuable and worthwhile strategies that managers have developed are virtually worthless.[29]

The successful implementation of strategy requires four basic skills[30]:

Interacting skill is the ability to manage people during implementation. Managers who have the ability to understand the fears and frustrations that others feel during the implementation of a new strategy tend to be the best implementers. These managers are also able to show empathy for organization members and bargain for the best way to put a strategy into action.

Allocating skill is the ability to provide organizational resources necessary to implement a strategy. Successful implementers have talent to schedule jobs, budget time and money, and allocate other resources that are critical for implementation.

Monitoring skill is the ability to use information to determine whether a problem has arisen that is blocking implementation. Good strategy implementers set up feedback systems that constantly give them information about the status of strategy implementation.

Organizing skill is the ability to create throughout the organization a network of people who can help to solve implementation problems when they occur. Good implementers customize this network to include those people who can solve the special types of problems that will characterize the implementation of a particular strategy.

Overall, the successful implementation of a strategy requires a focus on handling people appropriately, allocating resources necessary for implementation, monitoring implementation progress, and solving implementation problems when they occur. Perhaps the most important requirements are to know which people can solve specific implementation problems and to be able to involve them when those problems arise.

Strategic Control

Strategic control, the last step of the strategy-management process, is monitoring and evaluating the strategy-management process as a whole in order to make sure that it is operating properly.[31] Strategic control focuses on the activities involved in environmental analysis, organizational direction, strategy formulation, strategy implementation, and strategic control itself—ensuring that all steps of the strategy management process are appropriate, compatible, and functioning properly.[32] Strategic control is a special type of organizational control. Organizational control is featured in chapters 17, 18, and 19.

Strategic control, the last step of the strategy management process, is monitoring and evaluating the strategy management process as a whole in order to make sure that it is operating properly.

BACK TO THE CASE

Based upon the above information, after Sea World has performed its environmental analysis, it must determine the direction in which the organization will move to maintain its competitive position. Issues such as adding ride-oriented attractions will naturally surface. Developing a mission statement with related objectives would be a clear signal to all Sea World employees about the role of new ride attractions in the organization's future. Sea World management has several tools available to assist them in formulating strategy. If they were to be effective in this area, however, they must use the tools in conjunction with environmental analysis. One of the tools, critical question analysis, would require management to analyze the purpose of Sea World, the direction in which Sea World is going, the environment in which it exists, and how its goals might be better achieved.

SWOT analysis, another strategy development tool, would require management to generate information regarding the internal strengths and weaknesses of Sea World, as well as the opportunities and threats that exist within Sea World's environment. Management probably would classify the products of competitors, such as new movie-related rides and attractions at the Universal Studios theme park in Orlando, as threats—significant factors to be considered in Sea World's strategy development process.

Business portfolio analysis would suggest that Sea World management classify each major attraction (SBU) in the park as a star, cash cow, question mark, or dog, depending on the growth rate of the market interested in the attraction and the market share that the Sea World attraction possesses. By categorizing *Mission: Bermuda Triangle* and the other Sea World attractions as units for SBU analysis, managers could develop growth, stability, retrenchment, or divestiture strategies for each attraction that they offer. Sea World managers should use whichever strategy development tools they think would be most useful. Their objective in this case, of course, is to determine the appropriate strategy for the development of Sea World's attractions.

To successfully execute the chosen strategy, managers at Sea World must apply their interacting skill, allocating skill, monitoring skill, and organizing skill. In addition, they must be able to improve the strategy management process when necessary.

TACTICAL PLANNING

Tactical planning is short-range planning that emphasizes current operations of various parts of the organization.

Tactical planning is short-range planning that emphasizes the current operations of various parts of the organization. *Short range* is defined as a period of time extending only about one year or less into the future. Managers use tactical planning to outline what the various parts of the organization must do for the organization to be successful at some point one year or less into the future.[33] Tactical plans usually are developed for organizations in the areas of production, marketing, personnel, finance, and plant facilities.

COMPARING AND COORDINATING STRATEGIC AND TACTICAL PLANNING

In striving to implement successful planning systems within organizations, managers must remember several basic differences between strategic planning and tactical planning. First, because upper-level managers generally have a better understanding of the organization as a whole than do lower-level managers, and since lower-level managers generally have a better understanding of the day-to-day organizational operations than do upper-level managers, strategic plans usually are developed by upper-level management and tactical plans by lower-level management. Second, because strategic planning emphasizes analyzing the future and tactical planning emphasizes analyzing the everyday functioning of the organization, facts on which to base strategic plans are usually more difficult to gather than are facts on which to base tactical plans.

A third difference between strategic and tactical planning involves the amount of detail in the final plans. Because strategic plans are based primarily on a prediction of the future and tactical plans on known circumstances that exist within the organization, strategic plans generally are less detailed than tactical plans. Last, because strategic planning focuses on the long term and tactical planning on the short term, strategic plans cover a relatively long period of time whereas tactical plans cover a relatively short period of time. All of these major differences between strategic and tactical planning are summarized in Table 7.7 below.

In spite of their differences, tactical and strategic planning are integrally related. As Russell L. Ackoff states, "We can look at them separately, even discuss them separately, but we cannot separate them in fact."[34] In other words, managers need both tactical and strategic planning programs, but these programs must be closely related to be successful. Tactical planning should focus on what to do in the short term to help the organization achieve the long-term objectives determined by strategic planning.

TABLE 7.7 Major differences between strategic and tactical planning

Area of Difference	*Strategic Planning*	*Tactical Planning*
Individuals involved	Developed mainly by upper-level management	Developed mainly by lower-level management
Facts on which to base planning	Facts are relatively difficult to gather	Facts are relatively easy to gather
Amount of detail in plans	Plan contain relatively little detail	Plans contain substantial amounts of detail
Length of time plans cover	Plans cover long periods of time	Plans cover short periods of time

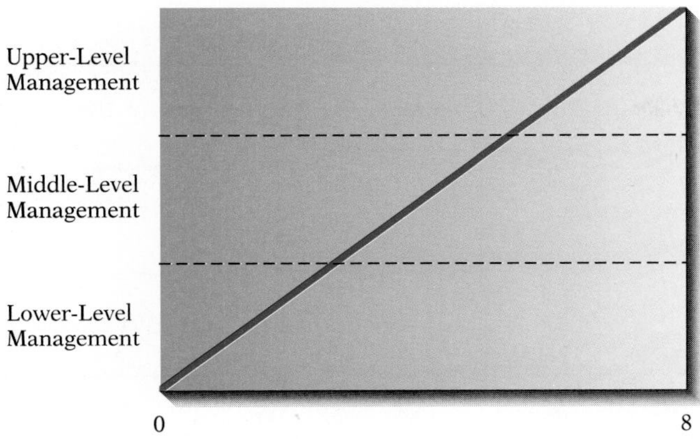

FIGURE 7.6 Increase in planning time as manager moves from lower-level to upper-level management positions

PLANNING AND LEVELS OF MANAGEMENT

Top management of an organization has the primary responsibility for seeing that the planning function is carried out. Although all levels of management typically are involved in the planning process, upper-level managers usually spend more time planning than do lower-level managers. Lower-level managers are highly involved with the everyday operations of the organization and therefore normally have less time to contribute to planning than does top management. Middle-level managers usually spend more time planning than lower-level managers but less time than upper-level managers. Figure 7.6 shows the increase in planning time spent as managers move from lower-level to upper-level management positions. In small as well as large organizations, deciding on the amount and nature of the work that managers should handle personally is extremely important.

The type of planning managers do also changes as the managers move up in the organization. Typically, lower-level managers plan for the short term, middle-level managers plan for a somewhat longer term, and upper-level managers plan for an even longer term. The expertise of lower-level managers in everyday operations makes them the best planners for what can be done in the short term to reach organizational objectives—in other words, tactical planning. Upper-level managers usually have the best understanding of the organizational situation as a whole and are therefore better equipped to plan for the long term—or to develop strategic plans. Figure 7.7 shows that as managers move from lower to upper management, they spend more time on strategic planning and less time on tactical planning. The total amount of time spent on strategic planning by lower-level managers, however, has been increasing.[35]

BACK TO THE CASE In addition to developing strategic plans for its organization, Sea World management should consider tactical, or short-range, plans that would complement its strategic plans. Tactical plans for Sea World should emphasize what can be done within approximately the next year to reach the organization's three- to five-year objectives and to stem competition from other theme parks. For example, Sea World could devote more resources to aggressive, short-range marketing campaigns or increase visitors to the park by enhancing the overall visual attractiveness of its park.

In addition, Sea World management must closely coordinate strategic and tactical planning within the company. They must keep in mind that strategic planning and tactical planning are different types of activ-

	Today	One Week Ahead	One Month Ahead	Three to Six Months Ahead	One Year Ahead	Two Years Ahead	Three to Four Years Ahead	Five to Ten Years Ahead
President	1%	2%	5%	17%	15%	25%	30%	5%
Vice President	2%	4%	10%	29%	20%	20%	13%	2%
Works Manager	4%	8%	15%	38%	20%	10%	5%	
Superintendent	6%	10%	20%	43%	10%	9%	2%	
Department Manager	10%	10%	25%	39%	10%	5%	1%	
Section Supervisor	15%	20%	25%	37%	3%			
Group Supervisor	38%	40%	15%	5%	2%			

FIGURE 7.7 Movement of planning activities from a short-range to a long-range emphasis as a manager moves from a lower-level to an upper-level management position

ities that may involve different people within the organization and result in plans with different degrees of detail. Yet they must also remember that these two types of plans are interrelated. While lower-level managers would be mostly responsible for developing tactical plans, upper-level managers would mainly spend time on long-range planning and developing strategic plans that reflect company goals.

ACTION SUMMARY

Reread the learning objectives that follow. Each objective is followed by questions. Answering these questions accurately will help you retain the most important concepts discussed in this chapter. After answering each question, check your answer with the answer key at the end of this chapter. (*Hint:* If you have doubt regarding the correct response, consult the page whose number follows the answer.)

Circle: ***From studying this chapter, I will attempt to acquire:***

1. Definitions of both strategic planning and strategy.

T, F **a.** Strategic planning is long-range planning that focuses on the organization as a whole.

a, b, c, d, e **b.** Strategy: (a) is a specific, narrow plan designed to achieve tactical planning; (b) is designed to be the end result of tactical planning; (c) is a plan designed to reach long-range objectives; (d) is timeless, and the same strategy can meet organizational needs anytime; (e) is independent of organizational objectives and therefore need not be consistent with them.

2. An understanding of the strategy-management process.

a, b, c, d, e — **a.** Which of the following is not one of the steps in strategy management: (a) strategy formulation; (b) strategy implementation; (c) strategy control; (d) environmental analysis; (e) all of the above are steps.

T, F — **b.** The steps of the strategy management process are sequential but usually not continuing.

3. A knowledge of the impact of environmental analysis on strategy formulation.

T, F — **a.** Environmental analysis is the strategy used to change an organization's environment to satisfy the needs of the organization.

a, b, c, d, e — **b.** All of the following are factors to be considered in environmental analysis except: (a) suppliers; (b) economic issues; (c) demographics; (d) social values; (e) none of the above.

4. Insights on how to use critical question analysis and SWOT analysis to formulate strategy.

a, b, c, d, e — **a.** The following is *not* one of the four basic questions used in critical question analysis: (a) Where has the organization been? (b) Where is the organization presently going? (c) What are the purposes and objectives of the organization? (d) In what kind of environment does the organization now exist? (e) What can be done to better achieve organizational objectives in the future?

T, F — **b.** SWOT is an acronym for "Strengths and Weaknesses, Objectives and Tactics."

5. An understanding of how to use business portfolio analysis to formulate strategy.

a, b, c, d, e — **a.** Use of the BCG Matrix considers the following factors: (a) types of risk associated with product development; (b) threats that economic conditions can create in the future; (c) social factors; (d) market shares and growth of markets in which products are selling; (e) political pressures.

a, b, c, d, e — **b.** When using the BCG Matrix, products that capture a high share of a rapidly growing market are sometimes known as: (a) cash cows; (b) milk products; (c) sweepstakes products; (d) stars; (e) dog products.

T, F — **c.** Use of the GE Multifactor Portfolio Matrix considers total market size for an SBU but generally does not consider the amount of that market that the SBU has won.

6. Insights on what tactical planning is and on how strategic and tactical planning should be coordinated.

T, F — **a.** Tactical plans generally are developed for one year or less and usually contain fewer details than strategic plans.

a, b, c, d, e — **b.** The following best describes strategic planning: (a) facts are difficult to gather, and plans cover short periods of time; (b) facts are difficult to gather, and plans cover long periods of time; (c) facts are difficult to gather, and plans are developed mainly by lower-level managers; (d) facts are easy to gather, and plans are developed mainly by upper-level managers; (e) facts are easy to gather, and plans are developed mainly by lower-level managers.

INTRODUCTORY CASE WRAP-UP

"Sea World Plots a New Competitive Course" (p.155) and its related back-to-the-case sections were written to help you better understand the management concepts contained in this chapter. Answer the following discussion questions about this introductory case to further enrich your understanding of chapter content:

1. Is Sea World management's response to its theme park competitors—adding a new ride—a strategic management issue? Explain.
2. Give three factors in Sea World's internal environment that management should be assessing in deter-

mining the company's organizational direction. Why are these factors important?

3. Using the business portfolio matrix, categorize *Mission: Bermuda Triangle* as a dog, question mark, star, or cash cow. From a strategic planning viewpoint, what do you recommend that Sea World management do as a result of this categorization? Why?

ISSUES FOR REVIEW AND DISCUSSION

1. What is strategic planning?
2. How does the commitment principle relate to strategic planning?
3. Define *strategy* and discuss its relationship with organizational objectives.
4. What are the major steps in the strategy management process? Discuss each step fully.
5. Why is environmental analysis an important part of strategy formulation?
6. List one major factor from each environmental level that could have significant impact on specific strategies developed for an organization. How could the specific strategies be affected by each factor?
7. Discuss the significance of the questions answered during critical question analysis.
8. Explain in detail how SWOT analysis can be used to formulate strategy.
9. What is business portfolio analysis?
10. Discuss the philosophy on which business portfolio analysis is based.
11. What is an SBU?
12. Draw and explain the BCG Growth-Share Matrix.
13. What potential pitfalls must managers avoid in using this matrix?
14. Explain three major differences in using the GE Multifactor Portfolio Matrix to develop organizational strategy as opposed to the BCG Matrix.
15. Draw and explain Porter's model of factors that determine competitiveness within an industry. What is the significance of this model in regard to developing organizational strategy?
16. List and define four sample strategies that can be developed for organizations.
17. What is tactical planning?
18. How do strategic and tactical planning differ?
19. What is the relationship between strategic and tactical planning?
20. How do time spent planning and scope of planning vary as management level varies?

ACTION SUMMARY ANSWER KEY

1. a. T, p. 156
b. c, p. 156
2. a. e, p. 157
b. F, p. 157
3. a. F, p. 158
b. e, p. 158
4. a. a, pp. 165–166
b. F, p. 166
5. a. d, pp. 166–167
b. d, pp. 167–168
c. F, pp. 168–169
6. a. F, p. 174
b. b, p. 174

CASE STUDY

EPI Products

LESLIE TOOMBS
University of Texas at Tyler, and Leslie Brunetta

In 1988, it looked as though the Krok sisters had it made. Within two years of founding EPI Products, Inc., they'd hit $100 million sales on the strength of their original product alone. With the introduction of a new range of EPI products, they predicted they would triple that figure in 1989. Instead, they filed for bankruptcy. What went wrong? Industry analysts say the Kroks' catastrophic failure was due to a fatal lack of planning by these business world beginners.

The story had started happily enough. Solomon Krok, a South African pharmaceutical company owner, bought United States' marketing rights to an Israeli hair-removal product called "Epilady." Epilady works by somewhat comfortably pulling hairs out by their roots; this offers women who shave their legs an opportunity to throw away their razors. Solomon gave marketing rights and start-up money to three of his daughters. The sisters established EPI Products in California, with Arlene as President, Loren as head of East Coast operations, and Sharon as head of advertising.

In July 1987, the Kroks launched Epilady in many prestigious department stores, including Bloomingdale's and Marshall Field. Within five months, Epilady was the top-selling department store item of any kind.

However, Remington Products, Inc., which is one of the nation's leading manufacturers of shaving products, soon posed a daunting challenge to the Kroks: it announced the impending introduction of Smooth & Silky, a product that would do the same job as Epilady but would be available in more stores for less money. So the Kroks came up with a plan: they would market a deluxe edition of the original Epilady, packaged with luxury accessories, to be sold at top-dollar prices in high-end department stores. Then, about six months later, they would start selling the original Epilady model, with no deluxe packaging or accessories, at sharply discounted prices in the same mass-market stores Remington had targeted. This way, they could maintain the high profit margins they garnered at the top stores while competing in the mass market with Remington.

When the Kroks had first announced plans to move the original Epilady to the mass-market, many of the more exclusive store executives had been furious. They worried that the strategy would detract from Epilady's prestige and thereby slow sales in their stores. Despite these fears, EPI product sales at these department stores were strong during the 1988 Christmas season—traditionally the peak sales time for personal grooming appliances—and the executives backed down.

During 1989, Epilady seemed to be working faster and smoother for the Kroks than they or the industry analysts had ever anticipated. That year, EPI Products racked up $200 million in sales. However, in the spring of 1990, the Kroks' glittering new company began to fall apart quickly. Profits from EPI product sales couldn't keep up with the pace at which the Kroks were spending money to keep their company expanding. By autumn, EPI Products, Inc., had filed for Chapter 11 bankruptcy.

Industry analysts who once marveled at the Kroks' success began to conduct the EPI Products autopsy. They called the Kroks' advertising strategy unsophisticated and not worthy of a company of EPI's size. Also, the Kroks' original strategy to outwit Remington was a drastic mistake, analysts added. Customers were bound to figure out that they could buy essentially the same product sold in top-drawer department stores for less money in mass-market stores. This both sliced into EPI's profit margins and cheapened its image.

By the end of 1990, the Kroks had hired professional managers to try to pull EPI Products out of bankruptcy, but many analysts predicted that it was too late to turn the company around.

DISCUSSION QUESTIONS

1. In considering the general environment within which EPI Products functions, how do you think social values affected Epilady sales, and how should these have been taken into account in planning future sales strategies?
2. In considering the operating environment, understanding competition is essential to good strategic planning. What major competitive advantage did Remington's Soft and Silky have over Epilady? What major advantage did Epilady have?
3. As a small business unit (SBU) of EPI Products, Epilady should be characterized as which of the following—a star? a cash cow?
4. Do you think the Kroks engaged in strong strategic planning? In strong tactical planning? Why or why not?

CNN VIDEO CASE

Spicing up Sales

CHARLES McCORMICK
McCormick and Company

McCormick and Company is one of the oldest spice merchants in the United States. It was founded in 1889 by Willoughby McCormick, who started by making flavorings and syrups in his basement and who had seven nephews working for him, one of whom he fired seven times. That boy later became president of the company, and he was the present chairman's father. Uncle Willoughby believed in making the decisions and telling his staff what to do; the staff was not invited to comment. In the process of growth under Willoughby McCormick, the company branched into liniment and insecticides and other products far removed from the spice industry.

Uncle Willoughby's nephew-successor disagreed with his uncle's management style. When young McCormick's turn came to run the show, he instituted a new philosophy, called "multiple management," which continues at McCormick's today.

McCormick wrote a one-paragraph mission statement for his company which focused on what would give the highest returns.

In 1987 the company elected a team in Chairman Charles "Buzz" McCormick and President Bailey Thomas, who continue the multiple management philosophy. As Buss McCormick explains it, the system gives employees "a chance to participate with any ideas they want about any subject in the business; and it throws the salesman in with the accountant, with the lawyer, with the computer expert, and these folks come up with ideas and then they are presented to top management and, in most cases, accepted." The system is made up of middle management boards that meet every other week. In this way, employees are cross-trained. They understand company operations better, and they provide each other with more support than occurs in companies less encouraging of interdepartmental communication.

The strategic plan instituted by McCormick and Thomas was to bring focus to the company. (Remember Uncle Willoughby's excursion into insecticides?) "We felt," says McCormick, "that maybe we were trying to run with too many ideas at once. We wrote a one-paragraph mission statement for the company and we really, division by division, focused on what was going to give us the largest returns. . . . Basically, this meant supporting the winners and getting rid of the losers."

McCormick & Co. is streamlining its operations and abandoning plans to continue diversifying into non-spice business. Its employees are concentrating on the manufacture of spices, seasonings, and flavors. Their market includes grocery sales, industrial flavorings, and snack-food seasonings. Getting their products on supermarket shelves is a very competitive activity because a supermarket usually handles only one major brand of spices. Because spices are an important part of a supermarket's sales picture, however, continuing to seek shelf space is worth the effort.

McCormick's stock value, profits, and market share have been increasing steadily. In 1991 the company's revenues were $1.4 billion, representing 43 percent of the market share. McCormick's goal is closer to 70 percent. The means by which they plan to achieve this goal include having better packaging than their competition, having the best products, and having the best people—people who are working harder to meet the goal. "It's our *only* business," stresses Buzz McCormick, "and we feel it's *our* business. We look at it on a worldwide basis and we've just got all kinds of growth in front of us."

VIDEO CASE QUESTIONS

1. Why did McCormick and Company need a strategic plan? What was the major purpose of the plan adopted by McCormick? What actions have McCormick and Thomas taken to institute the plan?
2. Review the definition of demographics and social values on page 159 of your textbook. How might these considerations affect planning at McCormick and Company?
3. Explain how McCormick and Thomas could have used a BCG Growth-Share Matrix to help create their strategic plan.
4. Would McCormick's system of multiple management be better used in developing the company's strategic plans or tactical plans?

CNN VIDEO EXERCISE

STRATEGIC PLANNING AT McCORMICK SPICE

EXERCISE GOAL: Learn how to use SWOT analysis to formulate strategy.

Your instructor will divide the class into groups of three to five members. Imagine that your group of managers has been asked by Buzz McCormick to apply SWOT analysis techniques to McCormick and Company. He expects to use the results of your analysis to help in strategic planning for the late 1990s. Review Table 7.6. Then create your own table for McCormick, followed by a list of at least three recommendations for strategic planning based on the results of your analysis. Recommendations should either suggest ways to counteract internal weaknesses or external threats or utilize internal strengths and develop external opportunities.

Firm Strengths

1. ______________________________
2. ______________________________
3. ______________________________

Firm Weaknesses

1. ______________________________
2. ______________________________
3. ______________________________

Firm Opportunities

1. ______________________________
2. ______________________________
3. ______________________________

Firm Threats

1. ______________________________
2. ______________________________
3. ______________________________

Recommendations for Strategic Planning

1. ______________________________
2. ______________________________
3. ______________________________

CHAPTER

8

PLANS AND PLANNING TOOLS

STUDENT LEARNING OBJECTIVES

From studying this chapter, I will attempt to acquire:

1. A complete definition of a plan.
2. Insights regarding various dimensions of plans.
3. An understanding of various types of plans.
4. Insights on why plans fail.
5. A knowledge of various planning areas within an organization.
6. A definition of forecasting.
7. An ability to see the advantages and disadvantages of various methods of sales forecasting.
8. A definition of scheduling.
9. An understanding of Gantt charts and PERT.

CHAPTER OUTLINE

INTRODUCTORY CASE
Fiat Plans Car Production

PLANS

Plans: A Definition

ETHICS HIGHLIGHT
Toyota Motor Corporation

Dimensions of Plans
Types of Plans

DIVERSITY HIGHLIGHT
Security Pacific Bank

Why Plans Fail
Planning Areas: Input Planning

GLOBAL HIGHLIGHT
Mexico

QUALITY HIGHLIGHT
Toyota Motor Corporation

PLANNING TOOLS

Forecasting
Scheduling

CASE STUDY
Carol Kirby of Baskin-Robbins:
Planning a New Image

VIDEO CASE
A Lucky Star: James Kinnear, Texaco

VIDEO EXERCISE
Creating a PERT Network for James Kinnear

INTRODUCTORY CASE

Fiat Plans Car Production

Automobile group Fiat, shrugging off the slowdown in European car demand, plans to build a major car plant in Basilicata, southern Italy, and expand and remodel an existing parts factory at Avellino, near Naples.

The decision involves investments totaling five trillion lire ($4.5 billion) over a three year period.

The Basilicata car plant will produce 1,800 cars a day and employ 7,000 workers, while the Avellino parts plant will be transformed into a factory producing 3,600 engines a day and employing 1,300 people.

"The move is a little bit surprising, given that they have announced production cutbacks."

The company is going ahead with the plan despite having cut back production because of slack European demand. [Recently,] Fiat doubled the number of workers temporarily laid off to 70,000 as part of a program of plant closures that cut planned output by about 90,000 cars. As a result, Fiat expects to produce about 2,150,000 cars a year worldwide, down from a level of about 2,250,000 sustained in previous years.

Susanne Oliver, European automotive analyst at London brokerage firm Hoare Govett, said the move was unexpected in the current depressed state of the market. "The move is a little bit surprising, given that they have announced production cutbacks. And that in the medium term there is no sign of an upswing in demand," she said.

"Obviously, it takes some years to bring the plants on stream . . . , nevertheless, capacity is being underutilized," she added. The Basilicata plant will have a theoretical capacity of almost 400,000 cars a year, working an average 220 days a year. Avellino could produce 790,000 engines a year.

Fiat will be eligible for hefty state aid on both plants. The company declined to put a figure on the subsidies, but a [spokesperson] said, "We have asked the government for the maximum the law allows—nothing special, but the maximum."

An official of the ministry dealing with Italy's depressed South, the Mezzogiorno, said state grants of 15 percent were available on large productive investments of this type. On this calculation, Fiat could receive a subsidy of about 750 billion lire, though not all funds invested may be eligible.

In addition, soft loans, at 60 percent of prime rate, are available to cover 30 percent of the investment cost, and reductions will also be given on social security payments for workers. Extra subsidies may also be available because the plants are in zones that sustained earthquake damage in 1980.

Fiat, which already has ambitious production plans in Poland, is calculating that European car demand will sustain a further increase in capacity. "We think Europe will continue to absorb cars—maybe not at the record level of the past two to three years, but the market is healthy," a [spokesperson] said.

Despite the slowdown in European car demand, Fiat has invested five trillion lire ($4.5 billion) in auto and parts factories.

From Guy Collins, "Fiat Will Build, Expand in Italy's Depressed South," *Wall Street Journal*, November 29, 1990, A9. Reprinted by permission of *Wall Street Journal*, (c) 1990 Dow Jones & Company, Inc. All Rights Reserved Worldwide.

WHAT'S AHEAD The introductory case describes Fiat's plans to build one new plant and to increase the capacity of another. This chapter emphasizes several fundamental issues about plans that should be useful to managers like those at Fiat who are involved in planning. This chapter describes what plans are and discusses several valuable tools that can be used in actually developing plans.

PLANS

The first half of the chapter covers the basic facts about plans. It (1) defines what a plan is, (2) outlines the dimensions of a plan, (3) lists various types of plans, (4) discusses why plans fail, and (5) explains two major organizational areas in which planning usually takes place.

Plans: A Definition

A **plan** is a specific action proposed to help the organization achieve its objectives.

A **plan** is a specific action proposed to help the organization achieve its objectives. A critical part of the management of any organization is developing logical plans and then taking necessary steps to put the plans into action.[1] Regardless of how important experience-related intuition may be to managers, successful management actions and strategies typically are based on reason. Rational managers are extremely important to the development of an organizational plan.

ETHICS HIGHLIGHT
Toyota Uses Philanthropy Plan to Aim at General Motors

The Toyota Motor Company, a Japanese company, is one of the largest automobile manufacturers in the world. Toyota's top management has recently outlined a philanthropy plan to help the company in its efforts to better compete with General Motors.

Toyota has designed a comprehensive company plan that includes both domestic and overseas components. The plan outlines an enormous undertaking that calls for annual automobile production and sales of more than 6 million units within three to five years. Toyota president Shoichiro Toyoda, believing that the world automobile market has plenty of room to grow, is determined to move past General Motors as the world's largest automaker by the end of this century.

Although GM's output and sales have declined in recent years and Toyota's output and sales have increased, some industry analysts have expressed doubt about Toyota's ability to develop a marketing effort that will enable the company to catch GM. Toyota's management team, however, insists that company aspirations to overtake GM are realistic. One reason for Toyota's optimism is the company's philanthropy plan, which channels corporate profits into local communities, enhancing Toyota's public image and thus boosting sales. Over the last few years, Toyota has channeled about 1.5 percent of its profits into philanthropy programs. In the near future, the company's level of philanthropy will probably remain about the same or increase. ▶

Toyota president Shoichiro Toyoda hopes to overtake GM as the world's largest auto maker. The plan involves a marketing effort to develop a positive image by channeling corporate profits into a philanthropy plan for local communities.

Dimensions of Plans

In planning, managers should consider:
the **repetitiveness dimension,** the extent to which the plan is to be used over and over again;

Kast and Rosenzweig identify a plan's four major dimensions: (1) repetitiveness, (2) time, (3) scope, and (4) level.[2] Each dimension is an independent characteristic of a plan and should be considered during plan development.[3]

The **repetitiveness dimension** describes the extent to which a plan is used time after time. Some plans are specially designed for one situation that is relatively short-term in nature. Plans of this sort are essentially nonrepetitive. Other plans, however, are designed to be used time after time for situations that continue to occur over the long term. These plans are basically repetitive in nature.

The **time dimension** of a plan is the length of the time period the plan covers. In chapter 7, strategic planning was defined as being long-term in nature, and tactical planning was defined as being short-term. It follows, then, that strategic plans cover relatively long periods of time and tactical plans cover relatively short periods of time.

the **time dimension,** the length of time to plan covers;

The **scope dimension** describes the portion of the total management system at which the plan is aimed. Some plans are designed to cover the entire open management system: the organizational environment, inputs, process, and outputs. A plan for the management system as a whole is often referred to as a master plan. Other plans, however, are developed to cover only a portion of the management system. An example would be a plan developed to cover the recruitment of new workers—a portion of the organizational input segment of the management system. The greater the portion of the management system that a plan covers, the broader the scope of the plan is said to be.

the **scope dimension,** the portion of the total management system at which the plans are aimed;

The **level dimension** of a plan indicates the level of the organization at which the plan is aimed. Top-level plans are those designed for the top-management level of the organization, whereas middle-level and lower-level plans are designed for middle-level and lower-level management, respectively. Because all parts of the management system are interdependent, however, plans for any level of the organization have some effect on all other levels.

and the **level dimension,** the level of the organization at which the plan is aimed.

Figure 8.1 illustrates the four dimensions of an organizational plan. This figure stresses that when managers develop a plan, they should consider the degree to which it will be used over and over again, the period of time it will cover, the parts of the management system on which it focuses, and the organizational level at which it is aimed.

BACK TO THE CASE In developing plans for a company like Fiat, management is actually developing recommendations for future actions. As such, plans should be action-oriented. Plans should state precisely what Fiat is going to do in order to achieve its goals.

In developing the plans, managers like those at Fiat should consider how often the plans will be used and the length of time they will cover. Will a plan be implemented only once or be used on a long-term basis to handle an ongoing issue such as maintaining product quality? Obviously, a plan to build a new factory would not be used very often by most companies and would be designed to cover a specific amount of time.

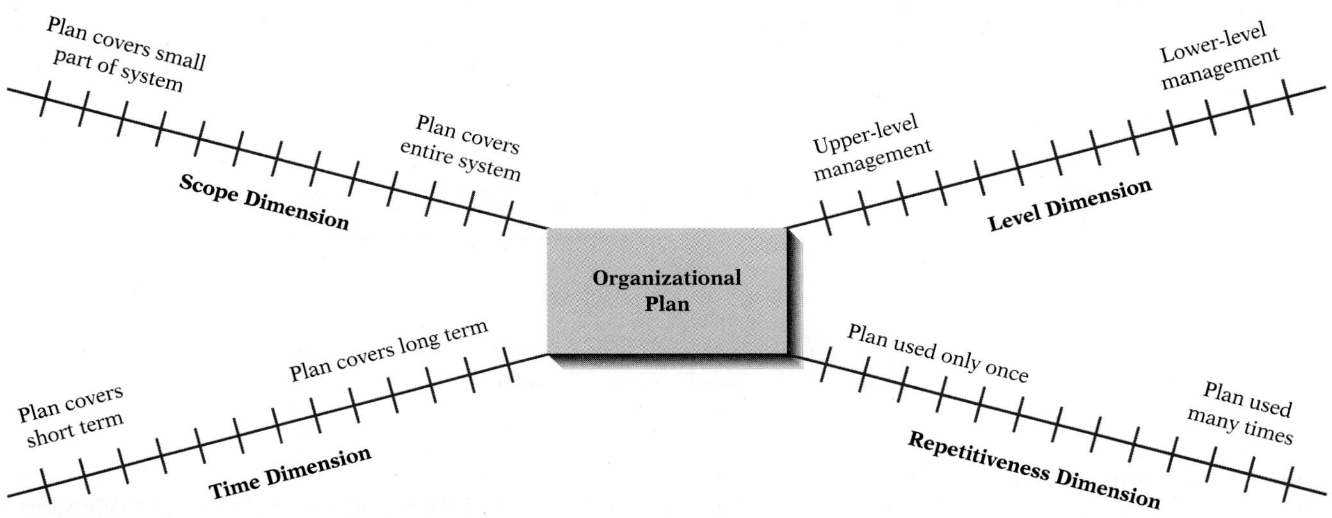

FIGURE 8.1 Four major dimensions to consider when developing a plan

Managers like those at Fiat should consider at which part of the organization to aim the plans that they develop and on which level the plans will focus. For example, a plan to cut costs may encompass all Fiat operations, whereas a plan to improve product quality may affect only one part of the production process. Similarly, a plan to cut costs may be aimed at top-level management, whereas a product quality plan may be aimed toward lower-level management and the auto assemblers themselves. Of course, managers like those at Fiat must realize that, because management systems are interdependent, any plans they implement will affect the system as a whole.

Types of Plans

Standing plans are plans that are used over and over because they focus on organizational situations that occur repeatedly.

Single-use plans are plans that are used only once or several times because they focus on organizational situations that do not occur repeatedly.

With the repetitiveness dimension as a guide, organizational plans usually are divided into two types: standing and single-use. **Standing plans** are used over and over again because they focus on organizational situations that occur repeatedly. **Single-use plans** are used only once or several times, because they focus on relatively unique situations within the organization. Figure 8.2 illustrates that standing plans can be subdivided into policies, procedures, and rules and that single-use plans can be subdivided into programs and budgets.

Standing Plans: Policies, Procedures, and Rules

A **policy** is a standing plan that furnishes broad guidelines for channeling management thinking in specified directions.

A **policy** is a standing plan that furnishes broad, general guidelines for channeling management thinking toward taking action consistent with reaching organizational objectives. For example, an organizational policy relating to personnel might be worded as follows: "Our organization will strive to recruit only the most talented employees." This policy statement is very broad, giving managers only a general idea of what to do in the area of employment. The policy is intended to display the extreme importance management has attached to hiring competent employees and to guiding action accordingly.

A **procedure** is a standing plan that outlines a series of related actions that must be taken to accomplish a particular task.

A **procedure** is a standing plan that outlines a series of related actions that must be taken to accomplish a particular task. In general, procedures outline more specific actions than do policies. Organizations usually have many different sets of procedures covering the various tasks to be accomplished. The sample procedure in Table 8.1 lists the series of steps that recruiters take to interview prospective academic employees at Indiana State University.

A **rule** is a standing plan that designates specific required action.

A **rule** is a standing plan that designates specific required action. In essence, a rule indicates what an organization member should or should not do and allows no room for interpretation. An example of a rule that many companies are now establishing is No Smoking.[4] The concept of rules may become clearer if one thinks about the purpose and nature of rules in such games as Scrabble and Monopoly.

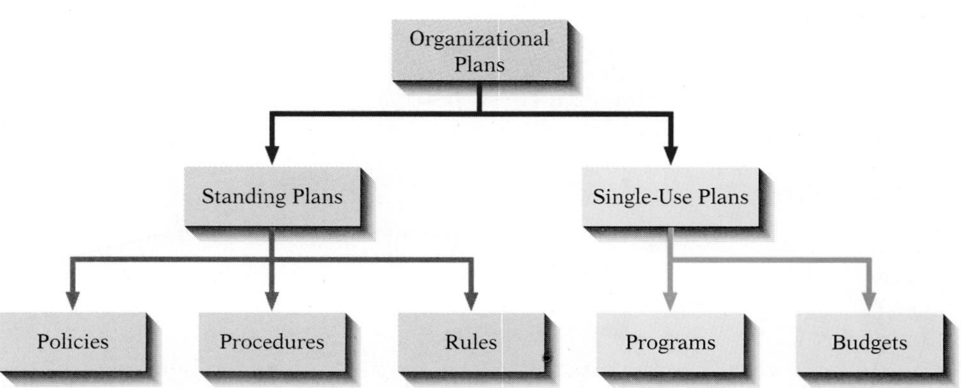

FIGURE 8.2 Standing plans and single-use plans

TABLE 8.1 Procedure for interviewing prospective academic employees at Indiana State University

1. Any candidate brought to campus for an interview should be a best prospect of at least three qualified persons whose credentials have been examined. Personnel supply in an academic field may reduce the number of possible candidates.
2. Before an invitation is extended to a candidate who must travel a distance greater than 500 miles to reach Terre Haute, the department chairperson should:
   a. ascertain the existence of the vacancy or authorization by a call to the assistant vice president for academic affairs.
   b. forward to the dean and assistant vice president credentials that should include, if possible, parts d, e, f, and g, Item 6, below.
3. Any administrative person who is scheduled to interview a candidate should be forwarded credentials for the candidate prior to the interview.
4. Interviews with administrative personnel should be scheduled as follows:

   A candidate whose probable academic rank will be instructor or assistant professor should talk with the dean prior to the assistant vice president. A candidate whose academic rank should probably be associate professor should be scheduled for an interview with the vice president for academic affairs in addition to the dean and assistant vice president. In addition to the above, a candidate for appointment as professor or department chairperson should also be scheduled for a meeting with the president.
5. Although courtesy to the candidate may demand that the interview schedule be maintained, the vice president, at his or her discretion or in agreement with the suggestion by the chairperson, dean, or assistant vice president, may cancel the interview for the candidate with the president.
6. A recommendation for appointment should contain the following:
   a. a letter from the department chairperson (or dean) setting forth the recommendation and proposing the academic rank and salary.
   b. a statement from the dean if the recommendation letter is prepared by the department chairperson.
   c. the completed university résumé form. This can be completed by the candidate when on campus or returned to the chairperson by mail later, but must be included.
   d. vitae information.
   e. placement papers.
   f. official transcripts (especially important if placement papers are not current or were prepared by a university bureau).
   g. as many as three letters of recommendation, one or two of these reflecting the candidate's current assignment. These letters are necessary if the placement materials have not been updated to contain current recommendations.
   h. a written report on any telephone conversations concerning the candidate made by the department chairperson.
7. Because of the difficulty in arranging interviews on Saturday, campus visits should occur during the week.
8. Whenever possible, accommodations at the Hulman Center should be limited to one overnight. The university cannot accept any charge for hotel accommodations other than at the Hulman Center. "Hotel accommodations" are defined to be lodging only, and not food, telephone, or other personal services.
9. Travel can be reimbursed in one of the following ways:
   a. a candidate traveling in-state will have mileage paid, at the rate of 25 cents per mile. The official Indiana map is used to compute mileage rather than a speedometer reading.
   b. a candidate traveling from out of state can claim the cost of airfare (tourist class) or train fare (coach class).
   c. a candidate who may choose to drive from out of state cannot be paid a mileage cost. Instead, airfare and train-fare amounts are determined and the lesser of the two is paid as an automobile mileage reimbursement.

Although policies, procedures, and rules are all standing plans, they are different from one another and have different purposes within the organization. As Figure 8.3 on page 188 illustrates, however, for the standing plans of an organization to be effective, policies, procedures, and rules must be consistent and mutually supportive.

Single-Use Plans: Programs and Budgets

A **program** is a single-use plan designed to carry out a special project within an organization. The project itself typically is not intended to be in existence over the entire life of the organization. However, the program exists to achieve some purpose that, if accomplished, will contribute to the organization's long-term success.

A **program** is a single-use plan designed to carry out a special project in an organization. Programs aid success indirectly.

A common example is the management development program found in many organizations. This program exists to raise the skill levels of managers in regard to one or

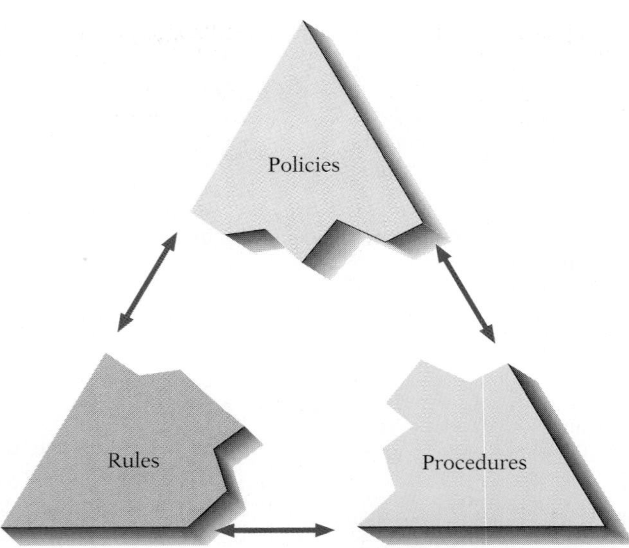

FIGURE 8.3 A successful standing plan program with mutually supportive policies, procedures, and rules

more of the skills mentioned in chapter 1: technical skills, conceptual skills, or human skills. Increasing the skill levels, however, is not an end in itself. The purpose of the program is to produce competent managers who are equipped to help the organization be successful over the long term. Once managerial skills have been raised to a desired level, the management development program can be deemphasized. Areas on which modern management development programs commonly focus include understanding and using the computer as a management tool, handling international competition, and planning for a major labor shortage by the year 2000.[5]

DIVERSITY HIGHLIGHT
Program at Security Pacific Bank Emphasizes Diversity

Diversity in the workforce is a reality—and an opportunity—facing organizations in the 1990s. A first step in implementing a successful diversity program is to research and learn from other organizations that have successfully organized and implemented such an effort. Security Pacific Bank is one such organization.

In order for diversity-in-the-workforce programs to be successful, organizations must realize that diversity must become part of the essence of the way the organization operates.

In studying this company's diversity program, several insights concerning how to be successful in such an effort become apparent. First, diversity programs in organizations must be designed to be appropriate for the organization's size, customers, available financial and staff resources, community expectations, management styles, and company culture. A diversity program that is too costly for an organization to support, for example, is doomed to failure. Second, if a diversity program is to be successful, the organization must have sound business reasons for advancing the program. Building a more productive workforce in an organization would be one such reason. Third, a successful diversity program requires the full support of top management. Without this support, organization members will not take the program seriously, and it will not realize its full potential. Fourth, if a diversity program is to be successful, management must make a long-term commitment to it. Building a productive, diverse workforce may take a number of years and adequate time must be allocated to designing and implementing the program. Last, the organization itself—not simply top management—must own and be in charge of the program. Organization members must realize that diversity is not just a fad; it must become part of the very essence of the organization and the way it operates. ▶

A **budget** is a single-use financial plan that covers a specified length of time.[6] It details how funds will be spent on labor, raw materials, capital goods, information systems, marketing, and so on, as well as how the funds will be obtained.[7] Although budgets are planning devices, they are also strategies for organizational control. They are covered in more detail in chapter 18.

A **budget** is a control tool that outlines how funds in a given period will be spent, as well as how they will be obtained.

Why Plans Fail

If managers know why plans fail, they can take steps to eliminate the factors that cause failure and thereby increase the probability that their plans will be successful. A study by K. A. Ringbakk determined that plans fail when:[8]

1. Corporate planning is not integrated into the total management system.
2. There is a lack of understanding of the different steps of the planning process.
3. Management at different levels in the organization has not properly engaged in or contributed to planning activities.[9]
4. Responsibility for planning is wrongly vested solely in the planning department.
5. Management expects that plans developed will be realized with little effort.
6. In starting formal planning, too much is attempted at once.
7. Management fails to operate by the plan.
8. Financial projections are confused with planning.
9. Inadequate inputs are used in planning.
10. Management fails to see the overall planning process.

Planning Areas: Input Planning

As discussed earlier, organizational inputs, process, outputs, and environment are major factors in determining how successful a management system will be. Naturally, a comprehensive organizational plan should focus on each of these factors. The following two sections cover planning in two areas normally associated with the input factor: plant facilities planning and human resource planning. Planning in areas such as these normally is called **input planning**—the development of proposed action that will furnish sufficient and appropriate organizational resources for reaching established organizational objectives.

Input planning is the development of proposed action that will furnish sufficient and appropriate organizational resources for reaching established organizational objectives.

Plant Facilities Planning

Plant facilities planning involves determining the type of buildings and equipment an organization needs to reach its objectives. A major part of this determination is called **site selection**—deciding where a plant facility should be located.[10] Table 8.2 shows several major areas to be considered in plant site selection, and it gives sample questions that can be asked when these areas are to be explored. Naturally, the specifics of site selection vary from organization to organization.[11]

Plant facilities planning is input planning that involves developing the type of work facility an organization will need to reach its objectives. One facet of plant facilities planning is site selection.

Site selection is determining where a plant facility should be located. It may involve a weighting process to compare site differences.

GLOBAL HIGHLIGHT
Mexico as an Attractive Manufacturing Site

For several years, United States' companies have been building and running manufacturing plants just across the Mexican border. The mere existence of these plants—called *maquiladoras*—is evidence that, over the years, Mexico has become an

As U.S. manufacturers find ways to enhance the productivity of the workers in the maquiladora industry, Mexico will become an even more attractive site for foreign manufacturing plants.

extremely attractive foreign manufacturing site for U.S. companies. The low cost of Mexican labor—significantly less than that in the United States—is the main reason for the success of the *maquiladora* industry. Accompanying these lower labor costs, however, are several challenges that U.S. managers of *maquiladoras* must face: In general, the Mexican labor force associated with the *maquiladora* industry is young, inexperienced, and unskilled; because the labor force is mainly from rural Mexico, there are significant cultural differences between Mexican workers and U.S. owners or managers; Mexican labor laws seem to be more protective of workers than are U.S. labor laws. As U.S. manufacturers find ways to improve the productivity of the Mexican labor force through special training for young, unskilled workers, they are gaining a real appreciation for the Mexican culture and learning to manage effectively within the limits of Mexican labor laws. U.S. manufacturers can overcome the challenges of the *maquiladora* industry, improve the productivity of the Mexican labor force, and make Mexico an even more appealing site for foreign manufacturing plants. ▶

One factor that can significantly influence site selection is whether a site is being selected in a foreign country. In a foreign country, management may face such issues as foreign governments taking different amounts of time to approve site purchases and political pressures slowing down or preventing the purchase of a site. For example, when Japanese investors locate businesses in the United States, they select those states that have low unionization rates, low employment rates, relatively impoverished populations, and the highest educational levels possible. Japanese managers believe that such dimensions ensure the success of Japanese business at a foreign site.[12]

Many organizations use a weighting process to compare site differences among

TABLE 8.2 Major areas of consideration when selecting a plant site, and sample exploratory questions

Major Areas for Consideration in Site Selection	*Sample Question to Begin Exploring Major Areas*
Profit	
Market location	Where are our customers in relation to the site?
Competition	What competitive situation exists at the site?
Operating costs	
Suppliers	Are materials available near the site at reasonable cost?
Utilities	What are utility rates at the site? Are utilities available in sufficient amounts?
Wages	What wage rates are paid in comparable organizations near the site?
Taxes	What are tax rates on income, sales, property, and so on for the site?
Investment costs	
Land/development	How expensive is land and construction at the site?
Others	
Transportation	Are airlines, railroads, highways, and so on available to the site?
Laws	What laws exist related to zoning, pollution, and so on that influence operations if the site is chosen?
Labor	Does an adequate labor supply exist around the site?
Unionization	What degree of unionization exists in the site area?
Living conditions	Are housing, schools, and so on appropriate around the site?
Community relations	Is the community supportive of the organization moving into the area?

foreign countries. Basically, this process involves (1) deciding on a set of variables that are critical to obtaining an appropriqte site; (2) assigning each of these variables a weight, or rank, of relative importance; and (3) ranking alternative sites, depending on how they reflect these different variables.

As an example, Table 8.3 shows the results of such a weighting process for seven site variables and six countries. In this table, "living conditions" are worth 100 points and are the most important variable; "effect on company reputation" is worth 35 points and is the least important variable. Also in this table, various countries are given a number of points for each variable, depending on the importance of the variable and how it exists within the country. The illustration shows that, given the established set of weighted criteria, Japan, Mexico, and France received more points and therefore are more desirable sites than Chile, Jamaica, and Australia.

QUALITY HIGHLIGHT
Toyota Motor Corporation Plans a Smooth Move

When Toyota considered locating its Camry automobile plant in Georgetown, Kentucky, many factors were used to decide if the site would be appropriate. The nonunion, abundant labor force was one consideration. Others were Kentucky's central location, which makes shipping easier, the success of other Japanese car manufacturers that had located in Kentucky, and the availability of land in neighboring states for Japanese suppliers who would make the move with Toyota. State officials also offered a $125 million incentive package.

Early in the selection process, Toyota began meeting regularly with Georgetown Mayor Tom Prather to hear community concerns about the proposed plant overburdening local services, including the school system. In addition, some townspeople frankly expressed fear of the Japanese because they were unfamiliar.

To stem anxiety, Toyota invested in the local community, giving Georgetown $1 million for a community center, roughly $8.5 million to the local school district, and $1 million to the University of Kentucky Library. Also, many of the company's Japanese managers participated in community events, joining the local Chamber of Commerce, Rotary Club, and United Way. Although it could not eliminate all the anti-Japanese, antidevelopment feelings in Georgetown, Toyota's early recognition of problems, thorough planning, and substantial financial investment in the region won over much of the community.

Toyota's move to Georgetown has progressed smoothly from groundbreaking to an efficiently run plant. The positive feelings of the community and the high morale of the workers ensure the production of high-quality automobiles. ▶

Before beginning to build this Georgetown, Kentucky, Camry automobile plant, Toyota Motor Corporation worked hard and made substantial investments to ensure positive feelings within the local community and to promote high morale among workers.

TABLE 8.3 Results of weighing seven site variables for six countries

Criteria	Maximum Value Assigned	Sites					
		Japan	*Chile*	*Jamaica*	*Australia*	*Mexico*	*France*
Living conditions	100	70	40	45	50	60	60
Accessibility	75	55	35	20	60	70	70
Industrialization	60	40	50	55	35	35	30
Labor availability	35	30	10	10	30	35	35
Economics	35	15	15	15	15	25	25
Community capability and attitude	30	25	20	10	15	25	15
Effect on company reputation	35	25	20	10	15	25	15
Total	370	260	190	165	220	275	250

BACK TO THE CASE Managers such as those at Fiat would normally use both standing plans and single-use plans in a company. Standing plans include policies, procedures, and rules, and should be developed for situations that occur repeatedly. One such policy Fiat management could develop might focus on the degree of product quality the managers want to emphasize with employees.

Single-use plans include programs and budgets and should be developed to help manage situations that occur less often. The Fiat example implies that Fiat management has worked on a budget that allows it to renovate an existing plant in Avellino, Italy. In developing such plans, managers like those at Fiat should thoroughly understand the reasons why plans can fail and take steps to avoid those pitfalls.

Planning plant facilities and human resource planning are two types of planning that managers commonly perform. In Fiat's case, planning plant facilities entails designing the types of factories that the company needs to reach its objectives. The company developed plans to build a new plant in Basilicata and to expand and remodel an existing parts factory near Avellino. An influential part of the decision to develop these plans most certainly was the financial support package offered the company by the government.

Human resource planning involves obtaining or developing the personnel an organization needs to reach its objectives. Fiat management certainly must have considered the numbers and kinds of employees needed to run the new and renovated factories. Such discussion inevitably had to have focused on issues such as when such employees would be needed, how they would be obtained, and how they would be trained appropriately after joining the Fiat company.

Human Resource Planning

Human resources are another area of concern to input planners. Organizational objectives cannot be attained without appropriate personnel.[13] Future needs for human resources are influenced mainly by employee turnover, the nature of the present work force, and the rate of growth of the organization.[14]

Personnel planners should try to answer such questions as: (1) What types of people does the organization need to reach its objectives? (2) How many of each type are needed? (3) What steps for the recruitment and selection of these people should the organization take? (4) Can present employees be further trained to fill future needed positions? (5) At what rate are employees lost to other organizations? These are not the only questions personnel planners should ask, but they are representative.

Human resource planning is input planning that involves obtaining the human resources necessary for the organization to achieve its objectives.

Figure 8.4 shows the human resource planning process developed by Bruce Coleman. According to his model, **human resource planning** involves reflecting on organizational objectives to determine overall human resource needs, comparing these needs to the existing human resource inventory to determine net human resource needs, and, finally, seeking appropriate organization members to meet the net human resource needs.

PLANNING TOOLS

Planning tools are techniques managers can use to help develop plans.

Planning tools are techniques managers can use to help develop plans. The remainder of this chapter discusses forecasting and scheduling, two of the most important of these tools.

Forecasting

Forecasting is a planning tool used to predict future environmental happenings that will influence the operation of the organization.

Forecasting is the process of predicting future environmental happenings that will influence the operation of the organization. Although sophisticated forecasting techniques have been developed only rather recently, the concept of forecasting can be

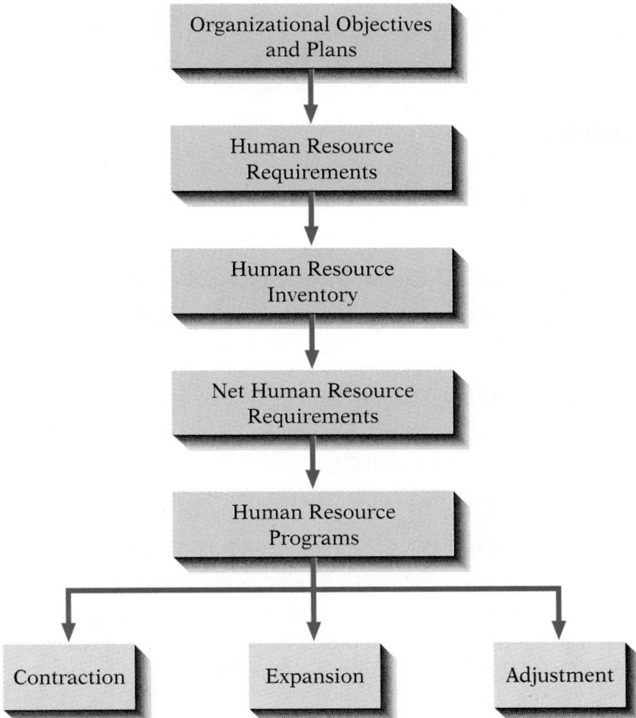

FIGURE 8.4 The human resource planning process

traced at least as far back in the management literature as Fayol.[15] The importance of forecasting lies in its ability to help managers understand the future makeup of the organizational environment, which in turn helps them formulate more effective plans.[16]

William C. House, in describing the Insect Control Services Company, has developed an excellent illustration of how forecasting works. Table 8.4 lists the primary factors the company attempts to measure in developing its forecast. In general, Insect Control Services forecasts by attempting to:[17]

1. Establish relationships between industry sales and national economic and social indicators.
2. Determine the impact of government restrictions concerning the use of chemical pesticides on the growth of chemical, biological, and electromagnetic energy pest-control markets.
3. Evaluate sales growth potential, profitability, resources required, and risks involved in each of its market areas (commercial, industrial, institutional, governmental, and residential).
4. Evaluate the potential for expansion of marketing efforts in geographical areas of the United States as well as foreign countries.
5. Determine the likelihood of technological breakthroughs that would make existing product lines obsolete.

In addition to the more general process of organizational forecasting illustrated by Insect Control Services are specialized types of forecasting, such as economic forecasting, technological forecasting, social trends forecasting, and sales forecasting. Although a complete organizational forecasting process can and usually should include all of these types of forecasting, sales forecasting is typically cited as the key organizational forecast. A *sales forecast* is a prediction of how high or how low sales will be over the period of time under consideration. It is the key forecast because it serves as the

TABLE 8.4 Primary factors measured during Insect Control Services' forecasting process

Gross National Product

Measure of total dollars available for industrial, commercial, institutional, and residential purchases of insect control units.

Personal Consumption Expenditures

Measure of dollars available for consumer purchases of:

1. *Services*—affect potential contract insect control services.
2. *Durables*—affect market potential for residential units.
3. *Nondurables*—affect sales of food, drugs, and other products that influence expansion of industrial and commercial users of insect control equipment.

Governmental Purchases of Goods, Services

Measure of spending for hospitals, government food services, other institutions that purchase insect control equipment.

Gross Private Domestic Investment in New Plant and Equipment

A measure of business expansion that indicates the size and nature of market potential for industrial and commercial purchases of insect control units in new or expanded existing establishments.

Industrial Production for Selected Industries

Measure of expansion of industrial output for industries that are users, potential users of insect control units, or materials suppliers for insect control services. Such expansion (or contraction) of output will likely affect:

1. Industrial and commercial purchases of insect control units.
2. Availability of materials used to manufacture insect control units.

Employment and Unemployment Levels

Indicates availability or scarcity of human resources available to augment Insect Control Services' human resources pool.

Consumer, Wholesale Prices

Measure of ability, willingness of homeowners to purchase residential units, and availability and cost of raw materials and component parts.

Corporate Profits

Indicates how trends in prices, unit labor costs, and productivity affect corporate profits. Size of total corporate profits indicates profit margins in present and potential markets and funds available for expansion.

Business Borrowings, Interest Rates

Measures of the availability and cost of borrowed funds needed to finance working capital needs and plant and equipment expansion.

fundamental guideline for planning within the organization. Once the sales forecast has been completed, managers can decide, for example, if more salespeople should be hired, if more money for plant expansion must be borrowed, or if layoffs are upcoming and cutbacks in certain areas are necessary. The following section describes various methods of sales forecasting.

Methods of Sales Forecasting

The **jury of executive opinion method** is a method of predicting future sales levels primarily by asking appropriate managers to give their opinions on what will happen to sales in the future.

Jury of Executive Opinion Method. The **jury of executive opinion method** of sales forecasting is straightforward. A group of managers within the organization assemble to discuss their opinions on what will happen to sales in the future. Since these discussion sessions usually revolve around the hunches or experienced guesses of each of the managers, the resulting forecast is a blend of expressed opinions.

A more recently developed forecasting method, similar to the jury of executive opinion method, is called the *delphi method*.[18] This method also gathers, evaluates, and summarizes expert opinions as the basis for a forecast.[19] The basic delphi method employs the following steps:

Step 1: Various experts are asked to answer independently, in writing, a series of questions about the future of sales or whatever other area is being forecasted.

Step 2: A summary of all the answers is then prepared. No expert knows how any other expert answered the questions.

Step 3: Copies of the summary are given to the individual experts with the request that they modify their original answers if they think they should.

Step 4: Another summary is made of these modifications, and copies again are distributed to the experts. This time, however, expert opinions that deviate significantly from the norm must be justified in writing.

Step 5: A third summary is made of the opinions and justifications, and copies are distributed to the experts. Justification for all answers is now required in writing.

Step 6: The forecast is generated from all of the opinions and justifications that arise from step 5.

Sales Force Estimation Method. The **sales force estimation method** is a sales forecasting technique that predicts future sales by analyzing the opinions of salespeople. Salespeople interact with customers and use this interaction as the basis for predicting future sales. As with the jury of executive opinion method, the resulting forecast normally is a blend of the views of the salespeople as a group.

The **sales force estimation method** is a method of predicting future sales levels primarily by asking appropriate salespeople for their opinions of what will happen to sales in the future.

The sales force estimation method is generally considered a very valuable management tool and is commonly used in business and industry throughout the world. Although the accuracy of sales forecasts using this method are mostly satisfactory, managers have found that accuracy can be improved by such simple steps as providing salespeople with sufficient time to forecast and offering incentives for accurate forecasts. Some companies even offer special training to help salespeople become better forecasters by helping them to better interpret their interactions with customers.[20]

Times Series Analysis Method. The **time series analysis method** predicts future sales by analyzing the historical relationship between sales and time. Information showing the relationship between sales and time typically is presented on a graph, as in Figure 8.5. This presentation clearly displays past trends, which can be used to predict future sales.

The **time series analysis method** is a method of predicting future sales levels by analyzing the historical relationship in an organization between sales and time.

The actual number of years included in a time series analysis will vary from company to company. As a general rule, managers should include as many years as necessary

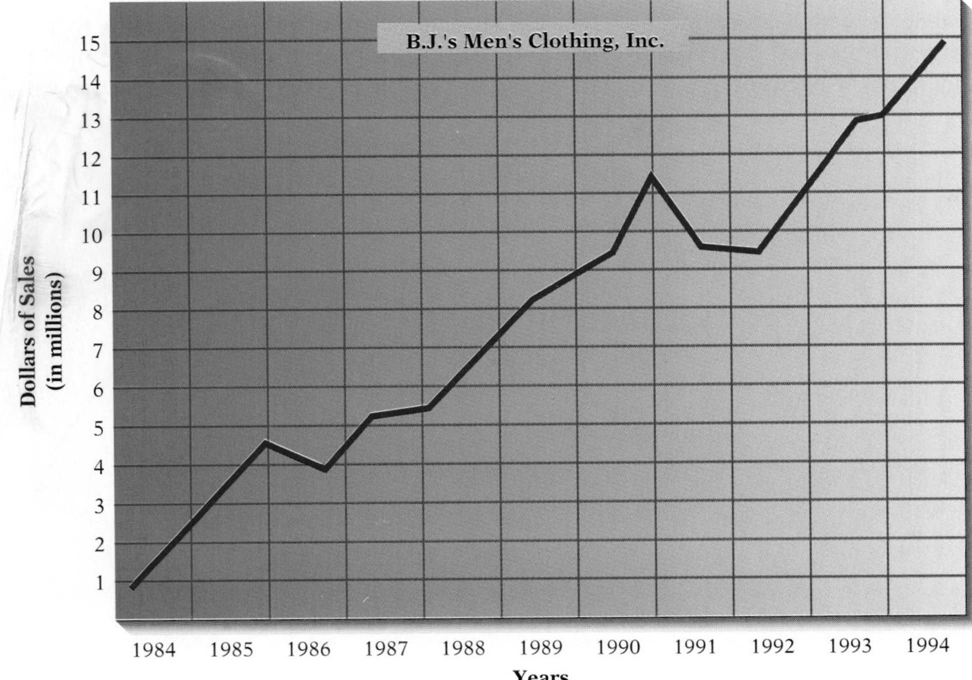

FIGURE 8.5 Time series analysis method

to make sure that important sales trends do not go undetected. At the Coca-Cola Company, for example, management believes that in order to validly predict the annual sales of any one year, it must chart annual sales in each of the ten successive previous years.[21]

The time series analysis in Figure 8.5 indicates steadily increasing sales over time. However, since, in the long term, products generally go through what is called a product life cycle, the predicted increase probably is overly optimistic. A **product life cycle** is the five stages through which most new products and services pass. The stages are introduction, growth, maturity, saturation, and decline.

A **product life cycle** is the five stages through which most new products and services pass: introduction, growth, maturity, saturation, and decline.

Figure 8.6 shows how these five stages are related to product sales over a period of time. In the introduction stage, a product is brand new, and sales are just beginning to build. In the growth stage, because the product has been in the marketplace for some time and is now becoming more accepted, product sales continue to climb. During the maturity stage, competitors enter the market; and while sales are still climbing, they normally climb at a slower rate than in the growth stage. After the maturity stage comes the saturation stage, when nearly everyone who wanted the product has it. Sales during the saturation stage typically are due to replacements of a worn-out product or to population growth. The last product life cycle stage—decline—finds the product being replaced by a competing product.

Managers may be able to keep some products out of the decline stage through improvements in product quality, or innovations. Other products, such as scissors, may never reach this last stage because of the lack of competing products.

Evaluating Sales Forecasting Methods

The sales forecasting methods just described are not the only ones available to managers. Other more complex methods include the statistical correlation method and the computer simulation method.[22] The methods just discussed, however, do provide a basic foundation for understanding sales forecasting.

In practice, managers find that each sales forecasting method has advantages and disadvantages, as shown in Table 8.5. Before deciding to use a particular sales forecasting method, a manager must carefully weigh the advantages and disadvantages as they relate to a particular organization. The decision may be to use a combination of methods rather than just one. Whatever method is finally adopted, the framework should be logical, fit the needs of the organization, and be capable of adaptation to changes in the environment.

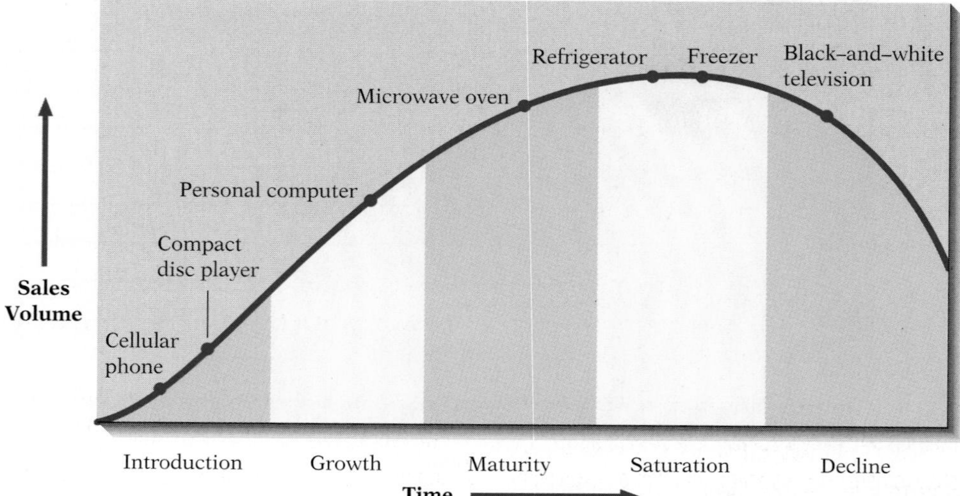

FIGURE 8.6 Stages of the product life cycle

TABLE 8.5 Advantages and disadvantages of three methods of sales forecasting

Sales Forecasting Method	*Advantages*	*Disadvantages*
Jury of executive opinion	1. Can provide forecasts easily and quickly 2. May not require the preparation of elaborate statistics 3. Pools a variety of specialized viewpoints for experience and judgment 4. May be the only feasible means of forecasting, especially in the absence of adequate data	1. Is inferior to a more factual basis of forecasting, since it is based so heavily on opinion 2. Requires costly executive time 3. Is not necessarily more accurate, because opinion is averaged 4. Disperses responsibility for accurate forecasting 5. Presents difficulties in making breakdowns by products, time intervals, or markets for operating purposes
Sales force estimation	1. Uses specialized knowledge of people closest to the market 2. Places responsibility for the forecast in the hands of those who must produce the results 3. Gives sales force greater confidence in quotas developed from forecasts 4. Tends to give results greater stability because of the magnitude of the sample 5. Lends itself to the easy development of product, territory, customer, or sales representatives' breakdowns	1. Sales representatives of some firms may be poor estimators, being either more optimistic or more pessimistic than conditions warrant 2. If estimates are used as a basis for setting quotas, sales representatives are inclined to understate the demand to make the goal easier to achieve 3. Sales representatives are often unaware of the broad economic patterns shaping future sales and are thus incapable of forecasting trends for extended periods 4. Since sales forecasting is a subsidiary function of the sales force, sufficient time may not be made available for it 5. Requires an extensive expenditure of time by executives and sales force 6. Elaborate schemes are sometimes necessary to keep estimates realistic and free from bias
Time series analysis	1. Forces the forecaster to consider the underlying trend, cycle, and seasonal elements in the sales series 2. Takes into account the particular repetitive or continuing patterns exhibited by the sales in the past 3. Provides a systematic means of making quantitative projections	1. Assumes the continuation of historical patterns of change in sales components without considering outside influences that may affect sales in the forecast period 2. Is often unsatisfactory for short-term forecasting, since, for example, the pinpointing of cyclical turning points by mechanical projections is seldom possible 3. May be difficult to apply in cases where erratic, irregular forces disrupt or hide the regularity of component patterns within a sales series 4. Requires technical skill, experience, and judgment

BACK TO THE CASE

One of the planning tools available to Fiat management is forecasting, which involves predicting future environmental events that could influence the operation of the company. Although various specific types of forecasting—such as economic, technological, and social trends forecasting—are available to it, Fiat management would probably use sales forecasting as its key forecast since that method will predict for managers how high or low their sales will be during the time period they are considering. According to the information we have, Fiat managers made a sales forecast, and the results of this forecast were used to help make the decision to construct a new factory and expand an existing one.

In order to forecast sales, managers like those at Fiat could follow the jury of executive opinion method by having Fiat executives discuss their opinions of future sales. This method would be quick and easy to use, and assuming that Fiat executives have a good feel for product demand, might be as valid as any other method that the company might use.

Fiat management could also ask its auto retailers (sales force) for opinions on predicted sales. Although the opinions of car dealers may not be completely reliable, these salespeople are closest to the market and must ultimately make the sales.

Finally, Fiat management could use the time series analysis method and analyze the relationship between sales and time. Although this method takes into account the cyclical patterns and past history of sales, it also assumes the continuation of these patterns in the future without considering outside influences, such as economic downturns, that could cause the patterns to change.

Because each sales forecasting method has both advantages and disadvantages, managers at Fiat should carefully analyze each of the methods before deciding which method alone or in combination should be used in their company.

Scheduling

Scheduling is the process of formulating detailed listings of activities that must be performed to accomplish a task, allocating resources necessary to complete the task, and setting up and following timetables for completing the task.

The **Gantt chart** is a scheduling tool composed essentially of a bar chart with time on the horizontal axis and the resource to be scheduled on the vertical axis. The Gantt chart is used for scheduling resources.

Scheduling is the process of formulating a detailed listing of activities that must be accomplished to attain an objective. This listing is an integral part of an organizational plan. Two scheduling techniques are Gantt charts and the program evaluation and review technique (PERT).

Gantt Charts

The **Gantt chart,** a scheduling device developed by Henry L. Gantt, is essentially a bar graph with time on the horizontal axis and the resource to be scheduled on the vertical axis. Possible resources to be scheduled include management system inputs, such as human resources and machines.

Figure 8.7 shows a completed Gantt chart for a work period entitled "Workweek 28." The resources scheduled over the five workdays on this chart were human resources: Wendy Reese and Peter Thomas. During this workweek, both Reese and Thomas were scheduled to produce ten units a day for five days. Actual units produced, however, show a deviation from this planned production. There were days when each of the two workers produced more than ten units, as well as days when each produced fewer than ten units. Cumulative production on the chart shows that Reese produced forty units and Thomas produced forty-five units over the five days.

Although the Gantt chart may seem quite simple, it has many valuable uses for managers. First, managers can use the chart as a summary overview of how organizational resources are being used. From this summary, they can detect such facts as which

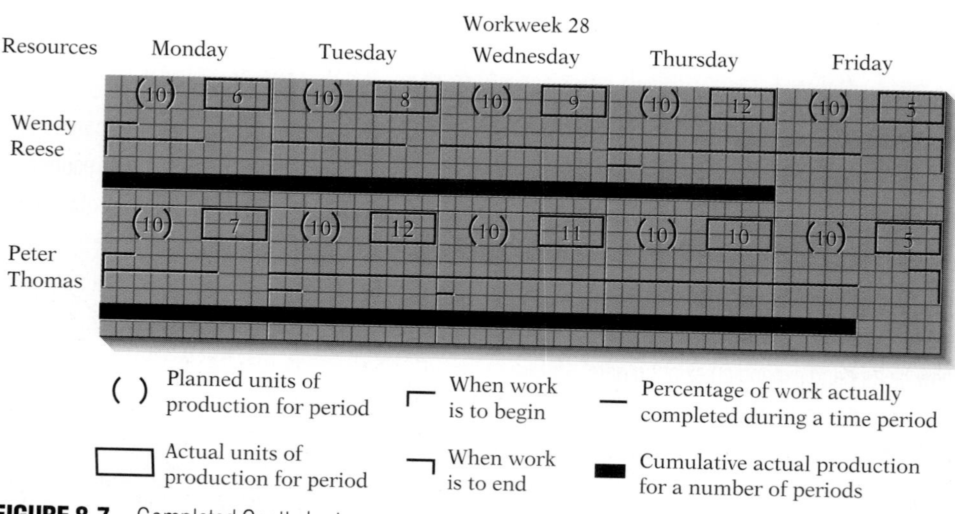

FIGURE 8.7 Completed Gantt chart

resources are consistently contributing to productivity. Second, managers can use the Gantt chart to help coordinate organizational resources. The chart can show which resources are not being used during specific periods, thereby allowing the resources to be scheduled for work on other production efforts. Third, the chart can be used to establish realistic worker output standards. For example, if workers are completing scheduled work too quickly, output standards may need to be raised so that workers are scheduled for more work per time period.

Program Evaluation and Review Technique (PERT)

The main weakness of the Gantt chart is that it does not contain any information about the interrelationship of tasks to be performed. All tasks to be performed are listed on the chart, but there is no way of telling if one task must be performed before another can be completed. The program evaluation and review technique (PERT), a technique that evolved in part from the Gantt chart, is a scheduling tool designed to emphasize the interrelationship of tasks.

Defining PERT. **PERT** is a network of project activities showing both the estimates of time necessary to complete each activity within the project and the sequential relationships among activities that must be followed to complete the project. PERT was developed in 1958 for use in designing the Polaris submarine weapon system.[23] The individuals involved in managing this project found Gantt charts and other existing scheduling tools of little use because of the complicated nature of the Polaris project and the interdependence of its tasks.[24]

The **program evaluation and review technique (PERT)** is a scheduling tool that is essentially a network of project activities showing estimates of time necessary to complete each activity and the sequential relationship of activities that must be followed to complete the project.

The PERT network contains two primary elements: activities and events. **Activities** are specified sets of behavior within a project, and **events** are the completions of major project tasks. Within the PERT network, each event is assigned corresponding activities that must be performed before the event can materialize.[25]

Activities and events are the primary elements of a PERT network. **Activities** are specified sets of behavior within a project. **Events** are completions of major project tasks.

A sample PERT network designed for the building of a house is presented in Figure 8.8. In this figure, events are symbolized by circles and activities are symbolized by arrows. To illustrate, the figure indicates that after the event "Foundation

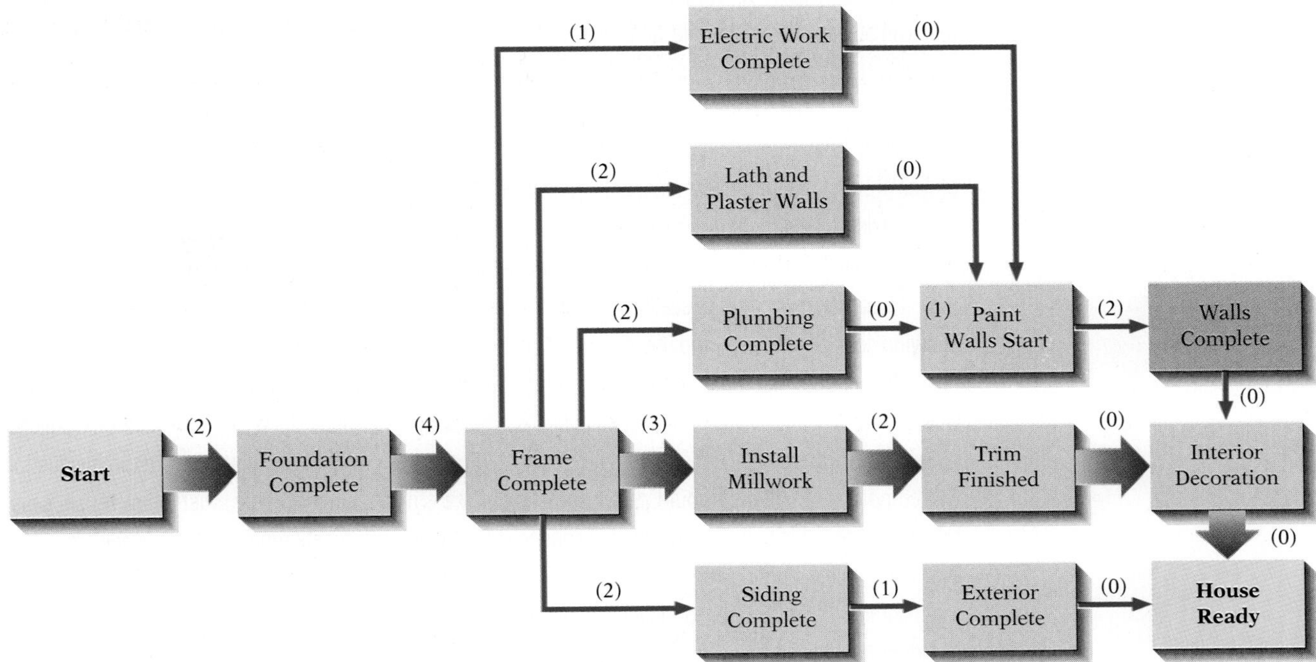

FIGURE 8.8 PERT network designed for building a house

Complete" (represented by a circle) has materialized, certain activities (represented by an arrow) must be performed before the event "Frame Complete" (represented by another circle) can materialize.

Two other features of the network shown here also should be emphasized. First, the left-to-right presentation of events shows how the events interrelate or the sequence in which they should be performed. Second, the numbers in parentheses above each arrow indicate the units of time necessary to complete each activity. These two features should help managers ensure that only necessary work is being done on a project and that no project activities are taking too long.

A **critical path** is the sequence of events and activities within a program evaluation and review technique (PERT) network that requires the longest period of time to complete.

Critical Path. Close attention should be paid to the **critical path** of a PERT network—the sequence of events and activities requiring the longest period of time to complete. The path is called the critical path because a delay in the time necessary to complete this sequence results in a delay for the completion of the entire project. The critical path in Figure 8.8 is indicated by thick arrows; all other paths are indicated by thin arrows. Managers try to control a project by keeping it within the time designated by the critical path. The critical path can help managers predict which features of a schedule will become unrealistic. It can provide insights concerning how the issues might be eliminated.[26]

Steps in Designing a PERT Network. When designing a PERT network, managers should follow four primary steps:[27]

Step 1: List all the activities/events that must be accomplished for the project and the sequence in which these activities/events should be performed.

Step 2: Determine how much time will be needed to complete each activity/event.

Step 3: Design a PERT network that reflects all of the information contained in steps 1 and 2.

Step 4: Identify the critical path.

BACK TO THE CASE

Scheduling is another planning tool available to Fiat management. It involves the detailed listing of activities that must be accomplished to reach an objective. For example, if Fiat's goal is to have all of its employees working proficiently on updated equipment in its planned renovated factory within two years, management needs to schedule activities such as installing the equipment, training the employees, and establishing new output standards.

Two scheduling techniques available to Fiat management are Gantt charts and PERT. To schedule employee production output, Fiat managers might want to use Gantt charts—bar graphs with time on the horizontal axis and the resources to be scheduled on the vertical axis. Managers also might find these charts helpful for evaluating workers' performance and setting new production standards.

If Fiat managers want to see the relationships among tasks, they can use PERT to develop a flowchart showing activities, events, and the amount of time necessary to complete each task. For example, a PERT network would be helpful in scheduling the installation of new machines, because this type of schedule would indicate which equipment needed to be installed first, the amount of time each installation would require, and how other activities in renovating an existing factory would be affected before the installation was completed. PERT also would demonstrate to Fiat the critical path managers must follow for successful installation. This path represents the sequence of activities and events requiring the longest amount of time to complete, and it determines the total time the project will need to finish. If, for example, new welding machinery takes longer to install than other types of equipment, Fiat management should target the completion of the entire equipment installation on the basis of this component's installation time.

ACTION SUMMARY

Reread the learning objectives that follow. Each objective is followed by questions. Answering these questions accurately will help you retain the most important concepts discussed in this chapter. After answering each question, check your answer with the answer key at the end of this chapter. (*Hint:* If you have doubt regarding the correct response, consult the page whose number follows the answer.)

Circle: ***From studying this chapter, I will attempt to acquire:***

1. A complete definition of a plan.

a, b, c, d, e — **a.** A plan is: (a) the company's buildings and fixtures; (b) a specific action proposed to help the company achieve its objectives; (c) a policy meeting; (d) a projection of future sales; (e) an experiment to determine the optimal distribution system.

a, b, c, d, e — **b.** The following is generally *not* an important component of a plan: (a) the evaluation of relevant information; (b) the assessment of probable future developments; (c) a statement of a recommended course of action; (d) a statement of manager intuition; (e) strategy based on reason or rationality.

2. Insights regarding various dimensions of plans.

T, F — **a.** Most plans affect top management only.

a, b, c, d, e — **b.** The following is one of the four major dimensions of a plan: (a) repetitiveness; (b) organization; (c) time; (d) a and c; (e) b and c.

3. An understanding of various types of plans.

a, b, c, d, e — **a.** Standing plans that furnish broad guidelines for channeling management thinking in specified directions are called: (a) procedures; (b) programs; (c) single-use plans; (d) policies; (e) rules.

a, b, c, d, e — **b.** Programs and budgets are examples of: (a) single-use plans; (b) standing rules; (c) procedures; (d) Gantt chart components; (e) critical paths.

4. Insights on why plans fail.

a, b, c, d, e — **a.** The following is a reason that plans fail: (a) adequate inputs are used in planning; (b) corporate planning is integrated into the total management system; (c) management expects that plans developed will be realized with little effort; (d) management operates by the plan; (e) responsibility for planning is vested in more than just the planning department.

T, F — **b.** The confusion of planning with financial projections will have no effect on the success of the plans.

5. A knowledge of various planning areas within an organization.

T, F — **a.** Input planning includes only site selection planning.

a, b, c, d, e — **b.** Personnel planners who reflect on organizational objectives to determine overall human resource needs and compare needs to existing human resource inventory are engaging in a type of planning called: (a) process layout; (b) plant facilities; (c) input; (d) life cycle; (e) delphi.

6. A definition of forecasting.

T, F — **a.** Forecasting is the process of setting objectives and scheduling activities.

a, b, c, d, e — **b.** According to the text, the following product is in the growth stage of the product life cycle: (a) microwave oven; (b) cellular phone; (c) black-and-white television; (d) personal computer; (e) refrigerator.

7. An ability to see the advantages and disadvantages of various methods of sales forecasting.

a, b, c, d, e — **a.** The sales forecasting technique that utilizes specialized knowledge based on interaction with customers is: (a) jury of executive opinion; (b) sales force estimation; (c) time series analysis; (d) a and b; (e) b and c.

T, F **b.** One of the advantages of the jury of executive opinion method of forecasting sales is that it may be the only feasible means of forecasting, especially in the absence of adequate data.

8. A definition of scheduling.

T, F **a.** Scheduling can best be described as: (a) the evaluation of alternative courses of action; (b) the process of formulating goals and objectives; (c) the process of formulating a detailed listing of activities; (d) the calculation of the break-even point; (e) the process of defining policies.

a, b, c, d, e **b.** Scheduling is the process of predicting future environmental happenings that will influence the operations of the organization.

9. An understanding of Gantt charts and PERT.

a, b, c, d, e **a.** The following is not an acceptable use of a Gantt chart: (a) as a summary overview of how organizational resources are being used; (b) to help coordinate organizational resources; (c) to establish realistic worker output standards; (d) to determine which resources are consistently contributing to productivity; (e) none of the above (all are acceptable uses of Gantt charts).

a, b, c, d, e **b.** In a PERT network, the sequence of events and activities requiring the longest period of time to complete is: (a) called the network; (b) indicated by thin arrows; (c) the path that managers avoid; (d) the critical path; (e) eliminated from the rest of the project so the project will not take too long.

INTRODUCTORY CASE WRAP-UP

"Fiat Plans Car Production" (p. 183) and its related back-to-the-case sections were written to help you better understand the management concepts contained in this chapter. Answer the following discussion questions about this introductory case to further enrich your understanding of chapter content:

1. Should Fiat's plant facilities planning be related to its human resource planning? Explain.
2. Explain this statement: "The quality of Fiat's decision to build another factory and to expand and renovate another is largely determined by the validity of the company's sales forecast."
3. What sales forecasting method(s) do you think Fiat management should have used as the basis for making its plant facilities decision? Explain.

ISSUES FOR REVIEW AND DISCUSSION

1. What is a plan?
2. List and describe the basic dimensions of a plan.
3. What is the difference between standing plans and single-use plans?
4. Compare and contrast policies, procedures, and rules.
5. What are the two main types of single-use plans?
6. Why do organizations have programs?
7. Of what use is a budget to managers?
8. Summarize the ten factors that cause plans to fail.
9. What is input planning?
10. Evaluate the importance of plant facilities planning to the organization.
11. What major factors should be involved in site selection?
12. Describe the human resource planning process.
13. What is a planning tool?
14. Describe the measurements usually employed in forecasting. Why are they taken?
15. Draw and explain the product life cycle.
16. Discuss the advantages and disadvantages of three methods of sales forecasting.

17. Elaborate on the statement that all managers should spend some time scheduling.
18. What is a Gantt chart? Draw a simple chart to assist you in your explanation.
19. How can information related to the Gantt chart be used by managers?
20. How is PERT a scheduling tool?
21. How is the critical path related to PERT?
22. List the steps necessary to design a PERT network.

ACTION SUMMARY ANSWER KEY

1. **a.** b, p. 184
b. d, p. 184
2. **a.** F, p. 185
b. d, pp. 184–185
3. **a.** d, p. 186
b. a, p. 186
4. **a.** c, p. 189
b. F, p. 189
5. **a.** F, p. 189
b. c, p. 192
6. **a.** F, p. 192
b. d, p. 196
7. **a.** b, p. 195
b. T, p. 197
8. **a.** c, p. 198
b. F, p. 198
9. **a.** e, pp. 198–199
b. d, p. 200

CASE STUDY

Carol Kirby of Baskin-Robbins: Planning a New Image

SAMUEL C. CERTO
Rollins College

Carol Kirby was first invited to Baskin-Robbins in 1984 as a marketing consultant to conduct a strategic study of the famous ice cream firm. Although a 1984 survey found Baskin-Robbins the favorite fast-food chain for the second consecutive year and profits continued to grow at a steady pace, management realized that there was a change taking place in the industry and they could ill afford to sit back and watch it happen. They knew they should be able to capitalize on their excellent product awareness and product preference but realized that they would need a plan to compete against the many new entries in the ice cream market. Yuppie tastes for the new premium ice creams plus a growing trend toward health-conscious eating seemed likely to erode Baskin-Robbins' profits.

Indeed, in her study, Kirby found that many adults tended to think of Baskin-Robbins as a place they used to go, or as a place where they would go only for children's birthday parties. Although the famous and off-beat Baskin-Robbins' flavors such as "Bubble Gum" and "Lunar Cheesecake" might keep the young customers happy and coming back, they would no longer be enough to attract adults as well. It was clear that a plan to change the company's image was necessary.

After the initial study ended, Kirby was invited to stay on as marketing chief. She knew that planning an updated company image would be her biggest task and that more research would be needed. She conducted focus groups, telephone interviews, and direct mail surveys to determine potential customers' perceptions and found that many people perceived Baskin-Robbins as being out of step with the times. Young adults watching their weight and people of all ages concerned about cholesterol wanted a healthier alternative to ice cream. Kirby decided not to tamper with their premium ice cream in order to compete with the new super-rich Haagen-Dasz and Frusen-Gladje. Instead, she decided to expand into a neglected niche—lighter desserts. She proposed new products for health-conscious consumers. In 1988 she introduced frozen yogurt; in 1989, sugar-free ice cream; in 1990, low-fat ice cream. In each case, a variety of interesting flavors were offered. To shop owners who were reluctant to invest in new equipment, Kirby presented her plan as a challenge and was able to win them over.

To help customers recognize the change in the Baskin-Robbins product line, a whole new look was needed for their retail stores. Kirby initiated a softer, more "up-scale" store decor with a more adult atmosphere to replace the pink and brown carnival stripes. Natural wood furniture replaced the school desks that adults found so uncomfortable, and sleek new store signs promoting Baskin-Robbins Ice Cream and Frozen Yogurt were added.

When the whole package was in place, a series of television spots focused on the new health-oriented products. The new line, "Now there's more to love us for, " summarized the new image.

The planned, new image seems to have taken hold. "The market was calling out for lower-calorie, lower-fat desserts," says Kirby. "Now 25 percent of our sales come from those products, products we didn't even have four years ago."

DISCUSSION QUESTIONS

1. Evaluate Kirby's plan for Baskin-Robbins's new image in terms of repetitiveness, time, scope, and level.
2. What specific steps did Kirby take to ensure that the plan would not fail?
3. Which of the sales forecasting options described in the chapter would be most useful to Kirby in forecasting ice cream and frozen yogurt sales?
4. Prepare a PERT chart to plan and implement the image changes Kirby formulated for Baskin-Robbins.

CNN VIDEO CASE

A Lucky Star

JAMES KINNEAR

Texaco

Generations of Americans have grown up hearing that they can trust their cars to the man who wears the Texaco star. In the 1960s James Kinnear, then a budding Texaco executive, had a vision of Texaco's future: "I was of the view, with the way the modern motorist goes down the interstate highways, we wanted a simple, identifiable symbol, that he would know that there was a Texaco service station. And so more and more, rather than using the printed word, we decided to concentrate on the star."

Kinnear could imagine automobile travel growing, speeds increasing, and interstate highway systems expanding, and by imagining these changes, he knew that in the future, Texaco would need a symbol that could be identified quickly, easily, from a distance.

Kinnear's team created a leaner structure for the entire company. "We had a plan," says Kinnear, "we had our objectives, and we proceeded towards that plan."

Kinnear began pumping gas and washing cars in 1954, a trainee just home from the Korean War. His training led him to the oil fields of Texas and then, in 1959, to the new state of Hawaii to start operations in a new territory for Texaco.

At Texaco, Kinnear has never been bored or unhappy. Nonetheless, he must have had some doubts when, in January of 1987, he became CEO of a company in turmoil. In 1985, Texaco had lost a historic legal judgment to a small wildcatting oil company, Pennzoil; Pennzoil claimed that Texaco's 1984 purchase of Getty Oil had breached a prior purchase agreement between Pennzoil and Getty. The courts ordered Texaco to pay $10.5 billion to Getty, and Texaco faced insolvency. On April 12, 1987, Kinnear announced that Texaco had filed for reorganization under Chapter 11. "We can answer to our shareholders and our employees," Kinnear stated. "And that answer is that today's action had to be taken to safeguard tomorrow's future."

As CEO of a company in reorganization, Kinnear still faced a tremendous challenge, but with one advantage. The protection offered by Chapter 11 of the Internal Revenue Code enabled Texaco to design a plan for the future without fear of immediate suffocation at the hands of creditors. Kinnear's new plans were soon threatened from another side, though.

During the 1980s, Carl Icahn carried out a series of flamboyant and generally successful takeovers of publicly held companies. Within a year of Texaco's filing, Icahn began buying Texaco stock. He soon became Texaco's largest shareholder—and, although Kinnear had achieved some degree of safety from creditor actions, he and his management team were still ultimately responsible to their shareholders.

Texaco's objective was not only to become profitable once again, but also to use this opportunity to reorder and streamline its operations. Corporate raiders—takeover experts such as Icahn—frequently have a more short-range view. Long-term profitability is often seen as secondary to an immediate opportunity to realize profits and sell off assets. Kinnear wanted to preserve Texaco, but to hold off Icahn's takeover bid, he knew he would have to move quickly to increase dividends and restore profits. He succeeded; in June of 1989, Icahn withdrew from contention for Texaco. Dividends were up; stock prices were up; and company morale was once again high. On January 29, 1990, Texaco emerged from Chapter 11.

James Kinnear credits Texaco's management team with the successful reorganization. While he held off the takeover bid, just as he had fended off the press in April of 1987, his team created a leaner structure for the entire company. "We had a plan," says Kinnear; "we had our objectives, and we proceeded toward that plan. And the fact that it's worked out so well for us and, I must say, for our stockholders certainly makes me very, very proud. And I'm really proud of the people in this company that, through the organizational structure that we have, enabled them to continue to run the business while we fought the wars."

In 1993, Kinnear retired, leaving the reigns to Alfred C. DeCrane, who had worked closely with Kinnear during the restructuring period.

VIDEO CASE QUESTIONS

1. How do the four dimensions of repetitiveness, time, scope, and level relate to James Kinnear's plans for the reorganization of Texaco while it was under Chapter 11 bankruptcy?
2. Review the list of reasons for plan failure. Were any of these responsible for Texaco's loss to Pennzoil? Why?
3. When Kinnear was a trainee with Texaco, oil consumption per capita was increasing in the United States. During the 1970s, when oil became more expensive, consumption dropped. Suggest special projects for which Kinnear might have designed single-use plans in each situation.
4. When James Kinnear forecasts the future for Texaco's oil interests, what factors will he be looking at? List one possible consideration in each of the following categories: economic, technological, social trends, sales.

CNN VIDEO EXERCISE

Creating a PERT Network for James Kinnear

EXERCISE GOAL: Learn to create a PERT network to allow employees to perform their jobs at home.

Imagine that Texaco, like many other corporations in the United States, has decided that many of its workers can perform their jobs at home as telecommuters. Eliminating a need for in-office employees reduces overhead and flattens the number of middle managers needed to funnel information.

At-home employees require state-of-the-art equipment: personal computers, fax machines, laptop computers. Employees may be linked by a leased phone line. Your boss tells you to set up the system. After you gulp a few times, you start working on a PERT network to see what is needed. Several stops are listed below. You may add or subtract steps as needed to make a logical PERT network. You may shorten the wording as needed to fit your chart.

START

IDENTIFY POSSIBLE DEPARTMENTS

IDENTIFY PERSONNEL WITHIN DEPARTMENTS

TRAIN PERSONNEL ON COMPUTER SYSTEM

OBTAIN HARDWARE BIDS

PURCHASE HARDWARE

HOLD MEETINGS TO SOUND OUT PERSONNEL

DETERMINE WHAT FILES/OTHER INFORMATION EACH EMPLOYEE MUST HAVE

SET UP COMPUTER SYSTEM

CREATE ACCESS TO NEEDED INFORMATION VIA COMPUTER

CREATE INFORMATION FLOW NETWORK

CREATE/MODIFY SOFTWARE

SYSTEM READY

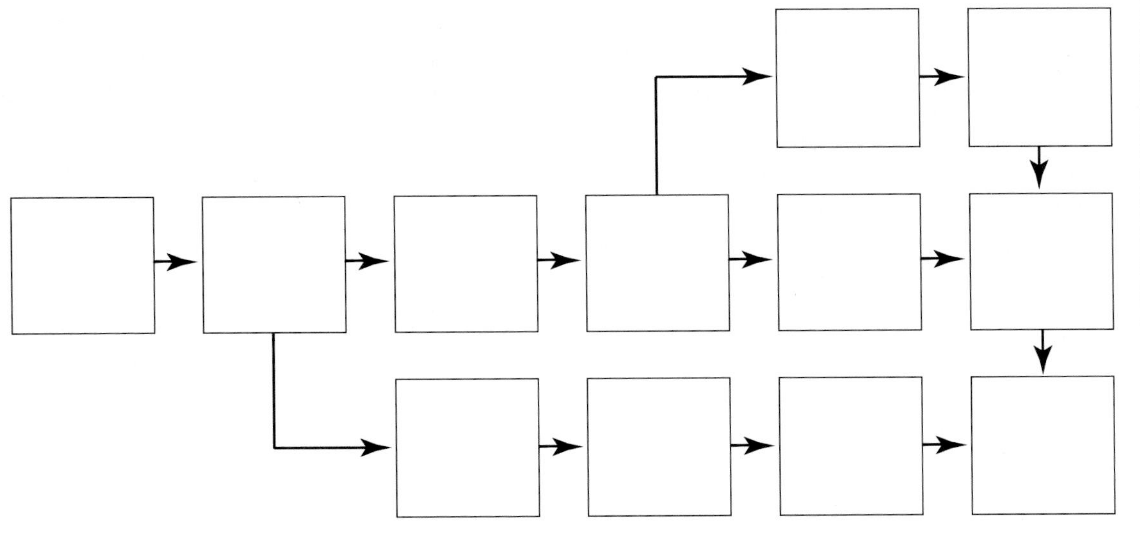

PART 2
INTEGRATIVE CASE

Planning for World-Class Performance Transformation at Bristol-Myers Squibb, Mayagüez

ROBERT E. KEMPER
Northern Arizona University

At Bristol-Myers Squibb, Mayagüez, Puerto Rico, top management defined "success" as the accomplishment of two goals: (1) leaving a permanent legacy for Puerto Ricans and (2) providing bread for over five hundred Puerto Rican families. Unfortunately, said some Bristol employees—who would later become members of the Bristol's World-Class Performance Task Force (WCPTF)—"those are antiquated versions of success, and until Bristol makes a major commitment to master the fundamentals of world-class performance, Bristol will not gain competitive standing in the global marketplace."

More to the point, the WCPTF announced, in a presentation to Carl Robbins, president of Bristol-Myers Squibb's Pharmaceutical Division, "Puerto Ricans need to understand that the world they live in has changed. The effortless economic superiority that the U.S. enjoyed in the aftermath of World War II is gone. What Puerto Ricans must do is determined decreasingly by what they wish to do and increasingly by the best practices of others."

Early in 1990, the WCPTF recognized that the past success of Bristol in Mayagüez was driven by two people, the general manager and the director of human resources. Further, they recognized that, if a transformation from a successful Puerto Rican division to a world-class division was to happen, these two people must be persuaded to start the transformation. WCPTF members found that the two people had invested their life in the Bristol Mayagüez operation. Luis A. Battistini began his career at Bristol Mayagüez and moved quickly to the top. In 1992, he completed his twenty-second year as general manager. The director of human resources began his business career as an operator at Bristol Mayagüez and remains with the company after twenty-two years. The WCPTF agreed that both have made great commitments to the Mayagüez operation, but that their visions, "leaving a Puerto Rico legacy" and "providing bread for five hundred Puerto Rican families" no longer apply to current marketplace realities.

In response to this situation, and with the backing of the parent company, Bristol's Puerto Rican operation turned its focus toward planning to become a world-class performer. For Bristol, a world-class performer is one that possesses a culture of continual change; stays out of the complacency zone; looks for continuous improvement; searches for ways to reduce manufacturing costs; demonstrates leadership by taking risks; makes quality and the customer top priorities; empowers all workers; demonstrates social responsibility; and possesses a company-wide vision for excellence.

The world-class performance (WCP) transformation process began in September 1990 with presentations to all Bristol Mayagüez directors. Directors were asked to support the WCP idea and to establish policies and budgets to integrate the process throughout the Bristol Mayagüez operation. In April 1991, Bristol's managers selected a team of employees to attend an R. D. Garwood World Class Performance Seminar. By mid-1991, a core team was studying the Garwood ideas. In November, General Manager Luis A. Battistini acknowledged his participation in the WCP transformation process by presiding over the initial WCPTF meeting. Battistini and the Bristol directors formally addressed all Bristol Mayagüez employees in February 1992. Bristol's mission statement, with emphasis on world-class performance, was presented and discussed.

By the end of 1992, it was clear to WCPTF members that the key success factors for the WCP were senior executive leadership, people empowerment through education and task forces, rewards and recognition of employees, standards for world-class performance, and management by facts. The concepts of lower costs, higher quality, better service, increased manufacturing flexibility, reduced process cycles, and reduced set-up times gave focus to the standards for world-class performance.

When Bristol turned its company-wide focus to world-class performance, the WCPTF established a plan of action for the company. Task forces worked on business strategy and assessment of goals and performance objectives. All directors and managers attended the World Class Seminar in Atlanta. The Return-on-Investment Task Force determined costs and benefits of WCP and found that ranking activities and expenditures had a significant benefit. The Objectives and Strategies Implementation Task Force is applying its guidelines to a global market by prioritizing payback activities and determining resources required to implement the program.

To ensure that those in leadership roles understood the overall concepts of WCP and how to facilitate and implement change, nineteen managers attended a facilitators' course at the University of Puerto Rico, Mayagüez. The goal was to help managers to plan internationally for Bristol's operational efficiencies, but to execute locally through existing personnel. Software training was provided to teach personnel about the specific software tools and their use. Every employee was given a summary of the WCP and allowed to raise questions, concerns, and issues. The WCPTF wanted employees to use what they knew about competition and innovation and to tap into technologies that already existed. Secretaries learned the ideas of WCP and how the WCP would affect their jobs.

When Bristol turned its company-wide focus to world class performance, the WCPTF established a plan of action for the company.

The WCPTF visualized four transformational stages of WCP. Before the program began, Bristol was in the first-stage, unconscious incompetence, meaning that the company was unaware of the benefits of WCP. As the program progressed, Bristol reached the conscious incompetence stage, where it became aware of the benefits of WCP but was not able to implement them. At the conscious competence stage, Bristol began to implement programs to improve performance. The final stage, unconscious competence, is where WCP becomes second nature for the company. That is, WCP must become a way of life for all Bristol employees. The WCPTF's plan of action focuses on achieving a level of unconscious competence for all employees by identifying task-force leaders, objectives, and achievements.

"We keep hearing that, as Americans, we need to invest in our future," says Roberto Rodriguez, Bristol Mayagüez world class coordinator. "The world-class process is such an investment. We know that the pace of technological and global change is not going to slow down. Economic activity is only going to become more international as time goes on. And since it is not likely that consumers will suddenly stop buying specialized and sophisticated products, we have to do all we can to ensure that our manufacturing personnel have the skills to compete. We want our employees to not only help stop any erosion of Puerto Rican jobs, but to create new ones as well."

DISCUSSION QUESTIONS

1. What steps did Bristol-Myers Squibb, Mayagüez, take to ensure the effectiveness of the plan to become a world-class performer?
2. Consider the decision-making process defined in chapter 6. How does Bristol's World Class Performance Task Force correlate to that plan?
3. Discuss a SWOT analysis for Bristol-Myers Squibb, Mayagüez, as it plans to become a world-class performer. List at least three items in each category.
4. Was Bristol's plan to become a world-class performer a standing plan, a single-use plan, or a policy? Explain.

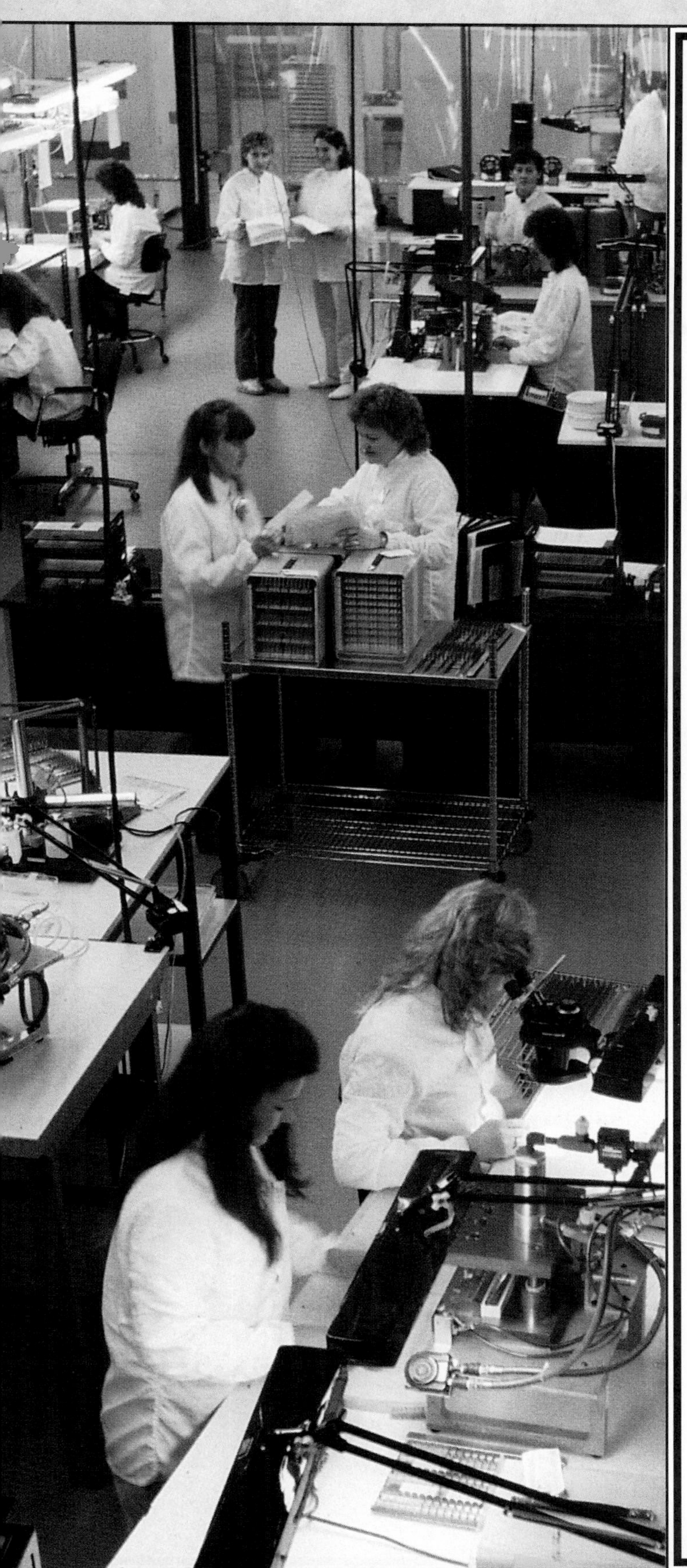

ORGANIZING

PART

3

This section discusses the second major management function—organizing. Organizing naturally follows planning, discussed in the previous section, because it is the primary mechanism by which managers put plans into action.

This section covers the fundamentals of organizing, responsibility, authority, delegation, managing human resources, and organizational change and stress. More specifically, it covers several organizing fundamentals, including the definition of *organizing,* the five main steps involved in organizing, and the classical principles that influence the organizing process.

The material will focus on responsibility as a fundamental ingredient in the organizing process and will indicate that delegating authority is an important component of organizing. In addition, the point will be made that an organization can be centralized or decentralized, depending on the amount of authority its management delegates. The discussion of managing human resources will emphasize the tasks of furnishing the organization with people who will make desirable contributions toward the attainment of organizational objectives and the tasks of utilizing the processes of recruitment, selection, training, and performance evaluation. Finally, the section will explain that organizational change is often necessary in order to increase organizational effectiveness and that the success of a particular change is based on the collective influence of such issues as how and what type of changes are made. This discussion also will address the relationship between stress and organizational change and will emphasize the importance of studying and managing stress.

One important point to remember is that organizing naturally follows planning. Organizing concepts discussed here will be challenging and will relate to concepts discussed in previous sections. Understanding organizing is important to understanding the remainder of the text.

CHAPTER

9

FUNDAMENTALS OF ORGANIZING

STUDENT LEARNING OBJECTIVES

From studying this chapter, I will attempt to acquire:

1. An understanding of the organizing function.
2. An appreciation for the complications of determining appropriate organizational structure.
3. Insights on the advantages and disadvantages of division of labor.
4. A working knowledge of the relationship between division of labor and coordination.
5. An understanding of span of management and the factors that influence its appropriateness.
6. An understanding of scalar relationships.

CHAPTER OUTLINE

INTRODUCTORY CASE
MCI Communications Organizes to Be More Competitive

A DEFINITION OF ORGANIZING

The Importance of Organizing
The Organizing Process
The Organizing Subsystem

CLASSICAL ORGANIZING THEORY

Structure

DIVERSITY HIGHLIGHT
The Banking Industry

GLOBAL HIGHLIGHT
Crown Cork & Seal Company

ETHICS HIGHLIGHT
Gerber Products Company

Division of Labor

QUALITY HIGHLIGHT
Mercedes-Benz

Span of Management
Scalar Relationships

CASE STUDY
Organizing the Sedona Fire Department

VIDEO CASE
Organizing a Family Business: Stanley and Edwin Shulman, Alixandre Furs

VIDEO EXERCISE
Creating an Organizational Structure at Alixandre Furs

INTRODUCTORY CASE

MCI Communications Organizes to Be More Competitive

MCI Communications Corporation, headquartered in Washington, D.C., provides a wide spectrum of domestic and international voice and data communication services. For residential customers, the company offers long distance opportunities like PrimeTime and SuperSaver. For business customers, communication opportunities provided by MCI enable businesspeople to strengthen relationships between customers and suppliers and to eliminate the traditional communications barriers of time and distance. MCI is the only telecommunications services company offering a full spectrum of voice, data messaging, and fax services with international capability. MCI, facing vigorous competition and a sluggish economy, recently announced that it is restructuring operations and may lay off 1,500 employees nationwide over the next six months.

The streamlining is intended to allow managers to react more swiftly to competition.

The long-distance company is revamping operations along commercial and residential lines, setting up a Business Markets unit and a Consumer Markets unit. The business unit will have four divisions, pared down from seven. In addition, a Network Services organization is being set up to meet new demands of both the business and consumer units.

The streamlining, which gives MCI a structure more like AT&T's, is intended to allow managers to react more swiftly to competition and position the company for growth. The previous structure, with seven regions corresponding to the seven regional Bell companies, has proven unwieldy as AT&T has sharpened efforts to stem further erosion of its market share. That share has dropped to around 70 percent of the $50 billion to $55 billion long-distance market.

Bert C. Roberts, Jr., MCI president, said the reorganization is being driven by "our recognition of the changing conditions that most businesses are experiencing" and the demands of a more competitive marketplace. He said that MCI expects to grow more rapidly than the overall market for long-distance service.

From Mary Lu Carnevale, "MCI to Revamp Units, May Cut 1,500 Staffers," *Wall Street Journal,* November 16, 1990, A3. Reprinted by permission of *Wall Street Journal,* © 1990 Dow Jones & Company, Inc. All Rights Reserved Worldwide.

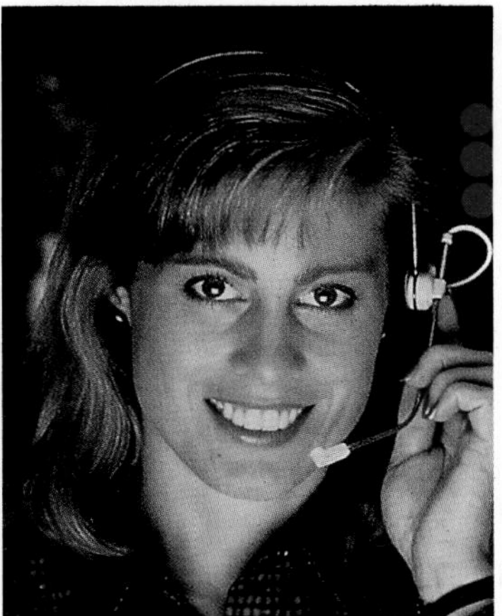

This communications worker provides a part of MCI Communications Corporation's full spectrum of telecommunications services. The company offers long distance opportunities such as PrimeTime and SuperSaver to residential customers and a full range of telecommunications services including voice, data messaging, and fax services to business customers.

WHAT'S AHEAD The introductory case describes, in general, how MCI is being organized in order to be more competitive. Information in this chapter would be useful to a manager like Bert C. Roberts, Jr., in contemplating organizing issues. This chapter emphasizes both a definition of organizing and principles of classical organizing theory that can be useful in actually organizing a company.

A DEFINITION OF ORGANIZING

Organizing is the process of establishing orderly uses for all resources in the organization.

Organizing is the process of establishing orderly uses for all resources within the management system. These uses emphasize the attainment of management system objectives and assist managers not only in making objectives apparent but also in clarifying which resources will be used to attain them.[1] A primary focus of organizing includes determining both what individuals will do in an organization and how their individual efforts should best be combined to contribute to the attainment of organizational objectives.[2] *Organization* refers to the result of the organizing process.

In essence, each organizational resource represents an investment from which the management system must get a return. Appropriate organization of these resources increases the efficiency and effectiveness of their use. Henri Fayol developed sixteen general guidelines for organizing resources:[3]

1. Judiciously prepare and execute the operating plan.
2. Organize the human and material facets so that they are consistent with objectives, resources, and requirements of the concern.
3. Establish a single competent, energetic guiding authority (formal management structure).
4. Coordinate all activities and efforts.
5. Formulate clear, distinct, and precise decisions.
6. Arrange for efficient selection so that each department is headed by a competent, energetic manager and all employees are placed where they can render the greatest service.
7. Define duties.
8. Encourage initiative and responsibility.
9. Offer fair and suitable rewards for services rendered.
10. Make use of sanctions against faults and errors.
11. Maintain discipline.
12. Ensure that individual interests are consistent with the general interests of the organization.
13. Recognize the unity of command.
14. Promote both material and human coordination.
15. Institute and effect controls.
16. Avoid regulations, red tape, and paperwork.

The Importance of Organizing

The organizing function is extremely important to the management system, because it is the primary mechanism with which managers activate plans. Organizing creates and maintains relationships between all organizational resources by indicating which resources are to be used for specified activities and when, where, and how they are to be used. A thorough organizing effort helps managers to minimize costly weaknesses, such as duplication of effort and idle organizational resources.

Some management theorists consider the organizing function so important that they advocate the creation of an organizing department within the management system. Typical responsibilities of this department would include developing (1) reorganization plans that make the management system more effective and efficient,[4] (2) plans to improve managerial skills to fit current management system needs, and (3) an advantageous organizational climate within the management system.[5]

The Organizing Process

The five main steps of the organizing process, as presented in Figure 9.1, are (1) reflecting on plans and objectives,[6] (2) establishing major tasks, (3) dividing major tasks into subtasks, (4) allocating resources and directives for subtasks, and (5) evaluating the results of implemented organizing strategy.[7] As the figure implies, managers should continually repeat these steps. Through repetition they obtain feedback that will help them improve the existing organization.

The management of a restaurant can illustrate how the organizing process might work. The first step the manager would take to initiate the organizing process would be to reflect on the restaurant's plans and objectives. Because planning involves determining how the restaurant will attain its objectives, and organizing involves determining how the restaurant's resources will be used to activate plans, the restaurant manager must start to organize by understanding planning.

The second and third steps of the organizing process focus on tasks to be performed within the management system. The manager must designate major tasks or jobs to be performed within the restaurant. Two such tasks might be serving customers and cooking food. Then the tasks must be divided into subtasks. For example, the manager might decide that serving customers includes the subtasks of taking orders and clearing tables.

The fourth organizing step is determining who will take orders, who will clear the tables, and what the details of the relationship between these individuals will be. The size of tables and how the tables are to be set also are factors to be considered at this point.

In the fifth step, evaluating the results of a particular organizing strategy, the manager gathers feedback on how well the implemented organizing strategy is working.

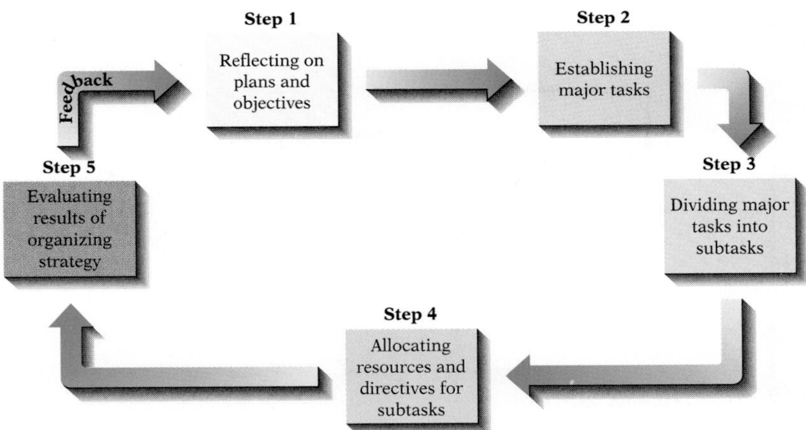

FIGURE 9.1 Five main steps of the organizing process

This feedback should furnish information that can be used to improve the existing organization. For example, the manager may find that a particular type of table is not large enough and that larger ones must be purchased if the restaurant is to attain its goals.

The Organizing Subsystem

The organizing function, like the planning function, can be visualized as a subsystem of the overall management system (see Figure 9.2). The primary purpose of the organizing subsystem is to enhance the goal attainment of the general management system by providing a rational approach for using organizational resources. Figure 9.3 presents the specific ingredients of the organizing subsystem. The input is a portion of the total resources of the organization, the process is the steps involved in the organizing function, and the output is organization.

BACK TO THE CASE In contemplating how MCI should be organized, Bert C. Roberts can focus on answering several important questions. These questions should be aimed at establishing an orderly use of MCI's organizational resources. Because these resources represent an investment on which he must get a return, Roberts's questions should be geared toward gaining information that will be used to maximize this return. Overall, such questions should focus on determining the use of MCI's resources that will best accomplish its goals. Some preliminary questions might be as follows:

1. What organizational objectives exist at MCI? For example, does MCI want to focus on international markets as well as domestic markets? Does MCI want to grow or to maintain its present size?
2. What plans does MCI have to accomplish these objectives? Is MCI going to open more offices abroad? Are additional training programs being added to enable employees to understand how best to work abroad?
3. What are the major tasks MCI must go through to offer message and voice products? For example, how many steps are involved in developing needed fax equipment and making it available to appropriate customers?

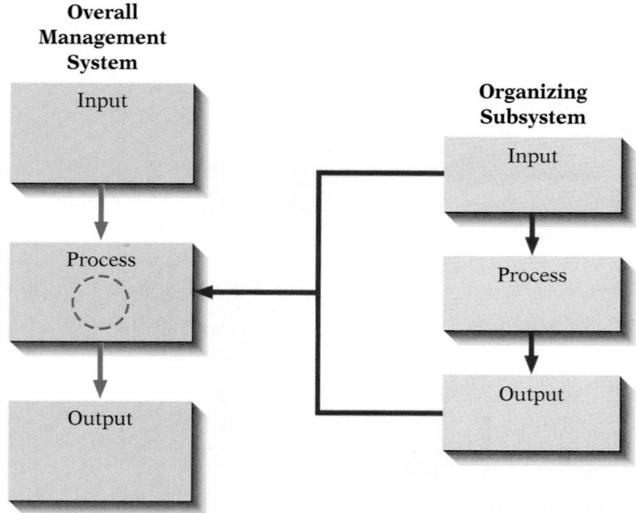

FIGURE 9.2 Relationships between overall management system and organizing subsystem

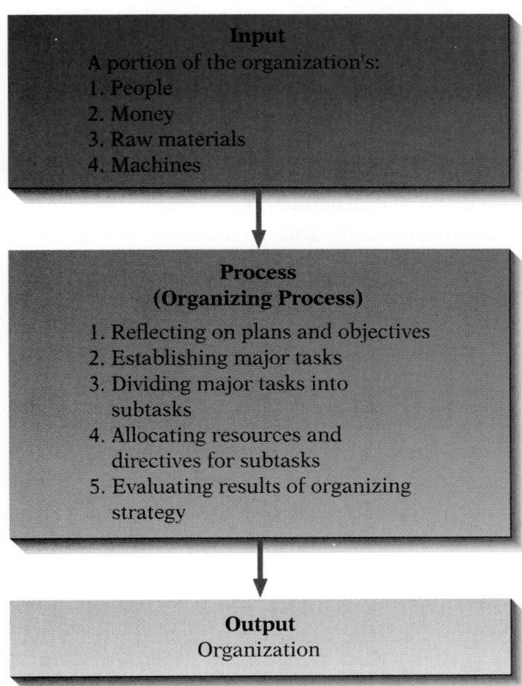

FIGURE 9.3 Organizing subsystem

4. What resources does MCI have to run its operations? Answers to this question focus on such issues as the number of employees, financial resources available, equipment being used, and so on.

Roberts also should begin thinking of some mechanism for evaluating the organizing strategy he develops. Once the strategy is implemented, Roberts must be able to get feedback on how all of MCI's resources are functioning so he can improve his organizing efforts. For example, Roberts may find that in order for MCI to become more competitive he needs greater voice-messaging capability in one country than in another and more employees in the Consumer Markets unit. With appropriate feedback, Roberts can continually improve MCI's existing organizational system.

CLASSICAL ORGANIZING THEORY

Classical organizing theory is the cumulative insights of early management writers on how organizational resources can best be used to enhance goal attainment. The writer who probably had the most profound influence on classical organizing theory was Max Weber.[8] According to Weber, the main components of an organizing effort are detailed procedures and rules, a clearly outlined organizational hierarchy, and, mainly, impersonal relationships among organization members.

Classical organizing theory is the cumulative insights of early management writers on how organizational resources can best be used to enhance goal attainment. Max Weber used the term **bureaucracy** to describe a management system with detailed procedures and rules, a clearly outlined organizational hierarchy, and, mainly, impersonal relationships among organization members.

Weber used the term **bureaucracy** to label the management system that contains these components. Although Weber firmly believed in the bureaucratic approach to organizing, he became concerned when managers seemed to overemphasize the merits of a bureaucracy.[9] He cautioned that a bureaucracy is not an end in itself but a means to the end of management system goal attainment. The main criticism of Weber's bureaucracy, as well as the concepts of other classical organizing theorists, is the obvious lack of concern for the human variable within the organization. Considerable discussion on this variable is presented in chapters 13 through 16.

The rest of this chapter summarizes four main considerations of classical organizing theory that all modern managers should include in their organizing efforts. They are (1) structure, (2) division of labor, (3) span of management, and (4) scalar relationships.

Structure

Structure is designated relationships among resources of the management.

In any organizing effort, managers must choose an appropriate structure. **Structure** refers to designated relationships among resources of the management system. Its purpose is to facilitate the use of each resource, individually and collectively, as the management system attempts to attain its objectives.[10]

An **organization chart** is a graphic representation of organizational structure.

Organization structure is represented primarily by means of a graphic illustration called an **organization chart.** Traditionally, an organization chart is constructed in pyramid form, with individuals toward the top of the pyramid having more authority and responsibility than individuals toward the bottom.[11] The relative positioning of individuals within boxes on the chart indicates broad working relationships, and lines between boxes designate formal lines of communication between individuals.

Figure 9.4 is an example of an organization chart. Its dotted line is not part of the organization chart but has been added to illustrate the pyramid shape of the chart. The positions close to the restaurant manager's involve more authority and responsibility; the positions farther away involve less authority and responsibility. The locations of positions also indicate broad working relationships. For example, the positioning of the head chef over the three other chefs indicates that the head chef has authority over them and is responsible for their productivity. The lines between the individual chefs and the restaurant manager indicate that formal communication from chef 1 to the restaurant manager must go through the head chef.

Historically speaking, pyramidal organization structures are probably modeled on the structure of military command; in the western world, the structure of organized religion has also been hierarchical, with authority derived from the top. Some researchers have found that women are not comfortable with this type of hierarchical structure. As more and more women enter the management field, a new model may need to be created. In *The Female Advantage: Women's Ways of Leadership,* author Sally Helgesen postulates that women create networks or "webs" of authority and that women's leadership styles are relational rather than hierarchical and authoritarian.[12] Management writer Tom Peters suggests that, in the 1990s, these styles will become inherently better suited to new kinds of organizational structures, required for a competitive global environment, that will feature teamwork and participative management.[13]

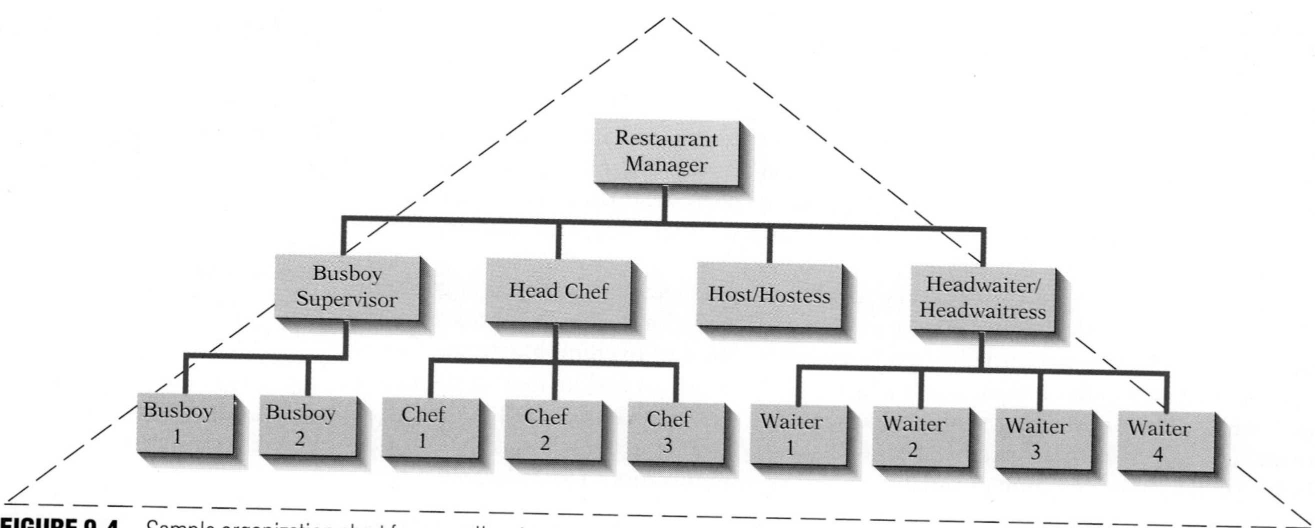

FIGURE 9.4 Sample organization chart for a small restaurant

Formal and Informal Structure

In reality, two basic types of structure exist within management systems: formal and informal. **Formal structure** is defined as the relationships among organizational resources as outlined by management. It is represented primarily by the organization chart.

Informal structure is defined as the patterns of relationships that develop because of the informal activities of organization members. It evolves naturally and tends to be molded by individual norms, values, or social relationships. In essence, informal structure is a system or network of interpersonal relationships that exists within, but is not usually identical to, an organization's formal structure.[14] The primary focus of this chapter is formal structure. More details on informal structure are presented in chapter 16.

Formal structure is defined as the relationships among organizational resources as outlined by management.

Informal structure is defined as the patterns of relationships that develop because of the informal activities of organization members.

Departmentalization and Formal Structure: A Contingency Viewpoint

The most common method of instituting formal relationships among resources is by establishing departments. Basically, a **department** is a unique group of resources established by management to perform some organizational task. The process of establishing departments within the management system is called **departmentalization.** These departments typically are based on, or contingent on, such situational factors as the work functions being performed, the product being assembled, the territory being covered, the customer being targeted, and the process designed for manufacturing the product. (For a quick review of the contingency approach to management, see p. 39.)

A **department** is a unique group of resources established by management to perform some organizational task.

Departmentalization is the process of establishing departments in the management system.

DIVERSITY HIGHLIGHT
Banks Must Build Diverse Departments into Teams

Many banks have traditionally been organized into departments, such as trusts, real estate, and consumer loans. A growing challenge for bank managers is how to build each department, with its highly diverse mix of personnel, into an effective and efficient work team.

A recent study by the Hudson Institute, entitled "Workforce 2000," estimates that 85 percent of the net increase in the labor pool by 2000 will consist of women, African Americans, Hispanic Americans, Asian Americans, and other minority groups. In building department personnel into effective and efficient teams, banks cannot rely on changes and enlightenment in society to eliminate the prejudices of its employees. Instead, banks themselves must design and implement training programs that focus on diversity. To be effective, such diversity training should include all levels of bank personnel: top management, middle managers, department managers, and all other staff. In addition, banks should initiate special programs aimed at helping the members of this diverse workforce eliminate personal distractions and concentrate more on doing their work well and reaching their full potential as employees. Such programs could include providing on-site day care for workers' dependents and establishing appropriate work-at-home alternatives.

A bank's focus on building productive, diverse work teams should be ongoing. The efforts of supervisors and managers at all levels of the organization to manage cultural diversity should be an open topic. Conducting focus group discussions can help management gather feedback indicating whether all employees feel that they are indeed a valued part of the organization. In addition, bank managers at all levels should be held accountable for hiring and promoting qualified minorities and women.

Banks need to initiate special programs aimed at helping members of a diverse workforce reach their full potential as employees.

Perhaps the most widely used base for establishing departments within the formal structure is the type of *work functions* (activities) being performed within the management system.[15] The major categories into which the functions typically are divided are

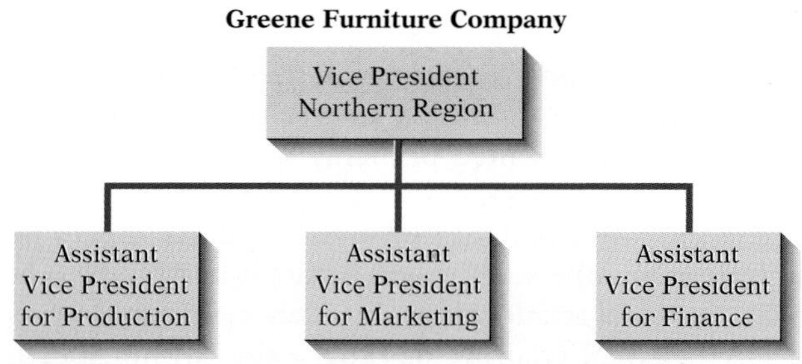

Greene Furniture Company
Vice President Northern Region
Assistant Vice President for Production
Assistant Vice President for Marketing
Assistant Vice President for Finance

FIGURE 9.5 Organization structure based primarily on function

marketing, production, and finance. Figure 9.5 is an organization chart showing structure based primarily on function for a hypothetical organization, Greene Furniture Company.

Organization structure based primarily on *product* departmentalizes resources according to the products being manufactured. As more and more products are manufactured, it becomes increasingly difficult to coordinate activities across them. Organizing according to product allows managers to logically group the resources necessary to produce each product. Figure 9.6 is a Greene Furniture Company organization chart showing structure based primarily on product.

Structure based primarily on *territory* departmentalizes according to the place where the work is being done or the geographic market area on which the management system is focusing. As market areas and work locations expand, the physical distance between places can make the management task extremely cumbersome. The distances can range from a relatively short span between two points in the same city to a relatively long span between two points in the same state, in different states, or even in different countries.[16] To minimize the effects of distances, resources can be departmentalized according to territory. Figure 9.7 is a Greene Furniture Company organization chart based primarily on territory.

Greene Furniture Company
Production Superintendent
Recliner Chairs
Beds
Kitchen Tables

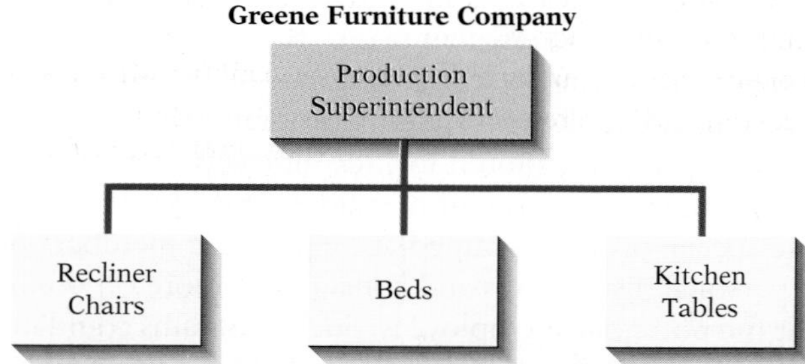

FIGURE 9.6 Organization structure based primarily on product

Greene Furniture Company
President
Vice President Western Region
Vice President Northern Region
Vice President Eastern Region

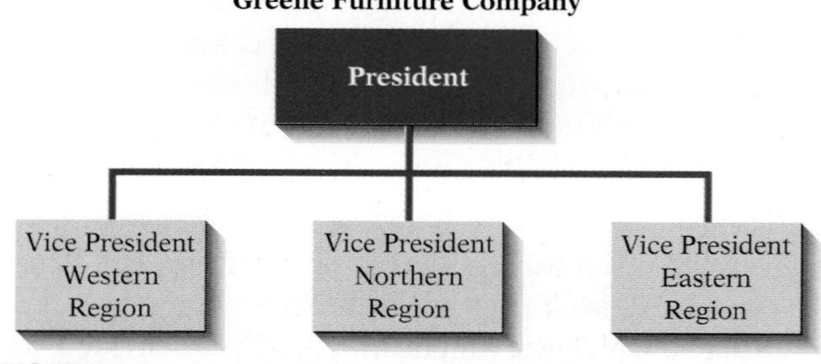

FIGURE 9.7 Organization structure based primarily on territory

GLOBAL HIGHLIGHT
Crown Cork & Seal Company Organizes by Territory to Boost International Expansion

The Crown Cork & Seal Company, headquartered in Philadelphia, Pennsylvania, manufactures and sells a variety of food and beverage packaging containers as well as packaging machinery. The company has designed its structure to ensure its continued international growth.

Recently, the company has experienced substantial international growth. In just the last three years, the firm has virtually doubled its global sales to an estimated $3.8 billion. Overall, Crown Cork & Seal has 141 plants in thirty-two countries. When John F. Connelly took it over in 1956, the company had worldwide sales of $100 million, but a heavy debt load had it close to collapse. By 1962, Crown was relatively debt-free and positioned for growth, with the beverage industry as its main target. To help ensure its continued success in its second century, Connelly has restructured the company into two basic divisions: North America and International. Such a structure should help focus organizational resources and efforts to continue organizational growth in the global arena. The company's present international efforts focus on Hong Kong, the Peoples' Republic of China, Korea, Venezuela, and Saudi Arabia. ▶

Crown Cork & Seal, like many American companies, looks to global expansion in areas such as Hong Kong to insure growth.

Structure based primarily on the *customer* establishes departments in response to the organization's major customers. This structure, of course, assumes that major customers can be identified and divided into logical categories. Figure 9.8 is a Greene Furniture Company organization chart based primarily on customers. Greene Furniture obviously can clearly identify its customers and divide them into logical categories.

Structure based primarily on *manufacturing process* departmentalizes according to the major phases of the process used to manufacture products. In the case of Greene Furniture Company, the major phases are woodcutting, sanding, gluing, and painting. Figure 9.9 is the organization chart that reflects these phases.

If the situation warrants it, individual organization charts can be combined to

FIGURE 9.8 Organization structure based primarily on customers

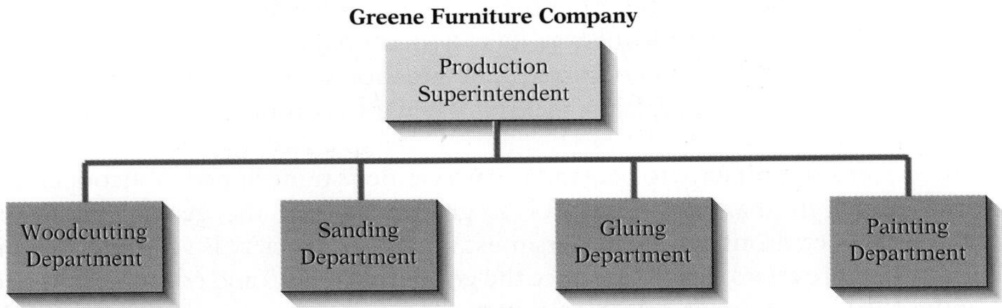

FIGURE 9.9 Organization structure based primarily on manufacturing process

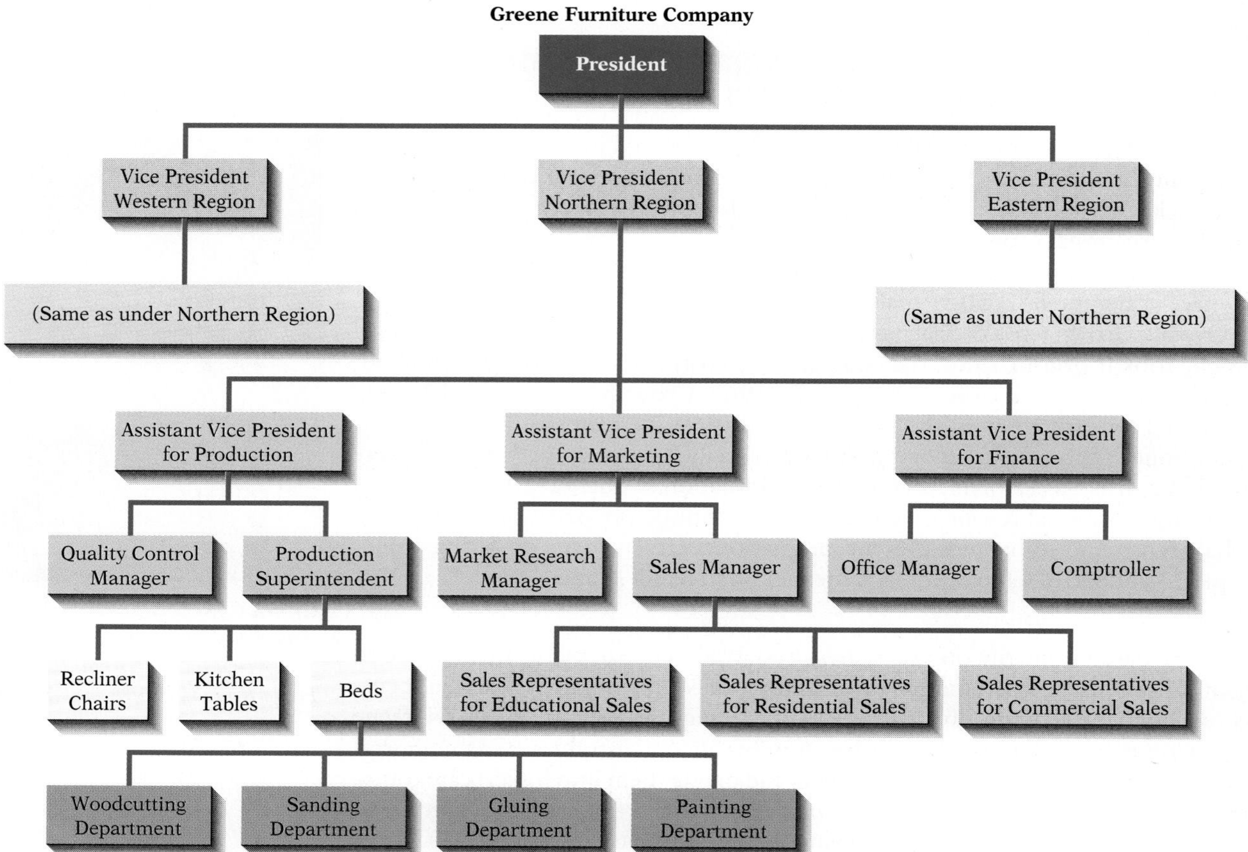

FIGURE 9.10 Organization structure based primarily on function, product, territory, customers, and manufacturing process

show all five of these factors. Figure 9.10 shows how all the factors are included on the same organization chart for Greene Furniture Company.

ETHICS HIGHLIGHT
Gerber Products Company's Structure Fails to Perform

Recent happenings at the Gerber Products Company indicate that managers should also study and communicate about the manufacturing process from a more nontraditional, socially responsible viewpoint. When a woman found a chip of ceramic in some Gerber baby food and reported it to the firm, it was considered a routine consumer complaint and the company spent no time reflecting on the manufacturing process used to produce the food. After the media found out about the chip, however, Gerber's social responsibility focus was quickly questioned. The general public was outraged that such an event had occurred. The situation escalated into a crisis as executives fought a barrage of complaints that translated into consumer pressure for a total recall of the product.

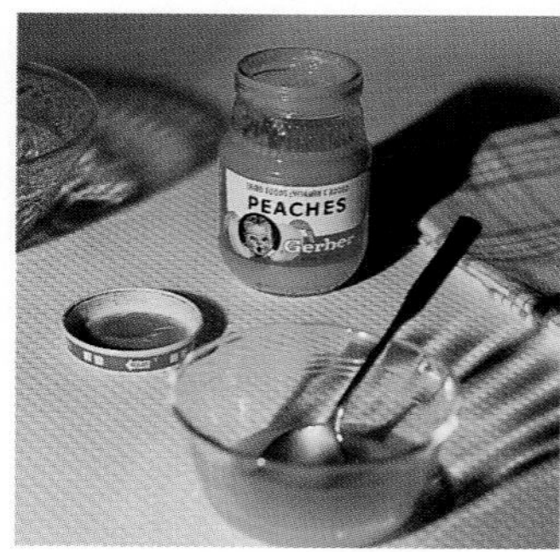

Gerber Products' mishandling caused a crisis that could have been averted by open communication.

The situation didn't have to become a crisis. Gerber's tight-lipped, noncooperative responses about its manufacturing process greatly alarmed the general public. In today's business environment, managers must realize that society is very interested in manufacturing processes used to produce the goods that it buys and consumes. As a result of the way Gerber handled this situation, the company's image was tarnished in the eyes of consumers and society as a whole, which almost inevitably would have a negative impact on an organization's profits. ▶

Forces Influencing Formal Structure

According to Shetty and Carlisle, the formal structure of a management system is continually evolving. Four primary forces influence this evolution: (1) forces in the manager, (2) forces in the task, (3) forces in the environment, and (4) forces in the subordinates.[17] The evolution of a particular organization is actually the result of a complex and dynamic interaction among these forces, as Figure 9.11 illustrates.

Forces in the manager are the unique way in which a manager perceives organizational problems.[18] Naturally, background, knowledge, experience, and values influence the manager's perception of how formal structure should exist or be changed. Forces in the task include the degree of technology involved in the task and the complexity of the task. As task activities change, a force is created to change the existing organization. Forces in the environment include the customers and suppliers of the management system, along with existing political and social structures. Forces in the subordinates include the needs and skill levels of subordinates. Obviously, as the environment and subordinates vary, forces are created simultaneously to change the organization.

BACK TO THE CASE In order to develop a sound organizing effort, a manager should take classical organizing theory into consideration. Of the four major elements of classical organizing theory, the first to be considered here is structure. Roberts's considerations regarding the structure of MCI would be aimed at creating working relationships among all MCI employees. In order to develop an effective organizational structure, Roberts must analyze situational factors in the company, such as functions, products, geographic locations, customers, and processes involved in offering its products to customers.

Information within the case suggests that Roberts's new organization structure for MCI is based primarily on customers. For example, the case informs us that the long distance company is revamping its operations along commercial and residential lines; the company is setting up a Business Markets unit (business customers) and a Consumer Markets unit (residential customers). According to Roberts's concept, the Business Markets unit will have four different divisions. In addition, Roberts's organizing strategy includes a Network Services unit that will be set up to meet the new demands of both the Business Markets and the Consumer Markets units.

A manager like Roberts typically uses an organization chart to represent organization structure. Such a chart would not only allow Roberts to see the lines of authority and responsibility at MCI, but also to understand the broad working relationships among his employees.

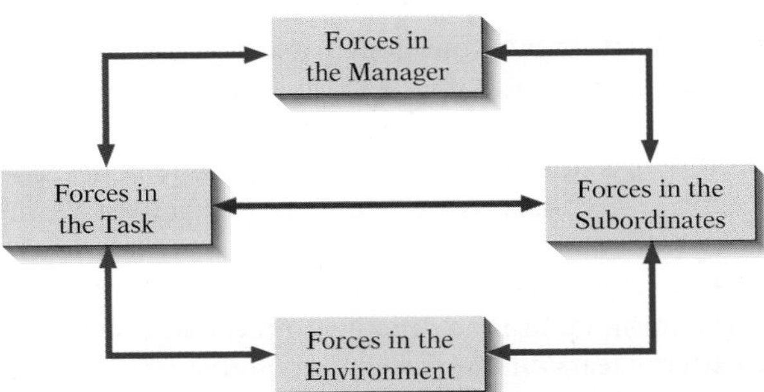

FIGURE 9.11 Forces influencing the evolution of organization structure

Division of Labor

Division of labor is the assignment of various portions of a particular task among a number of organization members. Division of labor calls for specialization.

The second main consideration of any organizing effort is how to divide labor. The **division of labor** is the assignment of various portions of a particular task among a number of organization members. Rather than one individual's doing the entire job, several individuals perform different parts of it. Production is divided into a number of steps, with the responsibility for completion of various steps assigned to specific individuals. In essence, individuals specialize in doing part of the task rather than the entire task.

A commonly used illustration of division of labor is the automobile production line. Rather than one individual assembling an entire car, specific portions of the car are assembled by various individuals. The following sections discuss the advantages and disadvantages of division of labor and the relationship between division of labor and coordination.

Advantages and Disadvantages of Division of Labor

Several generally accepted explanations have been offered for why division of labor should be employed. First, because workers specialize in a particular task, their skill for performing that task tends to increase. Second, workers do not lose valuable time in moving from one task to another. Because they typically have one job and one place in which to do it, time is not lost changing tools or locations. Third, because workers concentrate on performing only one job, they naturally try to make the job easier and more efficient. Last, division of labor creates a situation in which workers need only to know how to perform their part of the work task rather than the process for the entire product. The task of understanding their work, therefore, typically does not become too much of a burden.

Arguments also have been presented to discourage the use of extreme division of labor.[19] Overall, these arguments stress that the advantages of division of labor focus solely on efficiency and economic benefit and overlook the human variable. Work that is extremely specialized tends to be boring and therefore usually causes production rates to go down. Clearly, some type of balance is needed between specialization and human motivation. How to arrive at this balance is discussed further in chapter 15.

Division of Labor and Coordination

Coordination is the orderly arrangement of group effort to provide unity of action in the pursuit of a common purpose. It involves encouraging the completion of individual portions of a task in an appropriate, synchronized order.

In a division of labor situation with different individuals doing portions of a task, the importance of effective coordination becomes obvious. Mooney has defined **coordination** as "the orderly arrangement of group effort to provide unity of action in the pursuit of a common purpose."[20] Coordination involves encouraging the completion of individual portions of a task in a synchronized order that is appropriate for the overall task. Groups cannot maintain their productivity without coordination.[21] Part of the synchronized order for assembling an automobile entails installing seats only after the floor has been installed; adhering to this order of installation is an example of coordination.

Establishing and maintaining coordination may, but does not always, involve close supervision of employees. Managers can also establish and maintain coordination through bargaining, formulating a common purpose, or improving on specific problem solutions.[22] Each of these efforts is considered a specific management tool. Managers should try to break away from the idea that coordination is achieved only through close employee supervision.

Mary Parker Follett has furnished concerned managers with valuable advice on how to establish and maintain coordination within the organization. First, Follett says that coordination can be attained with the least difficulty through direct horizontal relationships and personal communications. When a coordination problem arises, speaking with peer workers may be the best way to solve it. Second, Follett suggests that coordination be a discussion topic throughout the planning process. In essence, managers should plan for coordination. Third, maintaining coordination is a continuing process and should be treated as such. Managers cannot assume that because their management system shows coordination today it will show coordination tomorrow. Follett also notes that managers should not leave the existence of coordination to chance. Coordination can be achieved only through purposeful management action. Last, according to Follett, the importance of the human element and the communication process should be considered in any attempt to encourage coordination. Employee skill levels and motivation levels are primary considerations, as is the effectiveness of the human communication process used during coordination activities.[23]

QUALITY HIGHLIGHT
Mercedes-Benz Improves Coordination to Improve Product Quality

Improving coordination can improve the effectiveness and efficiency of the workforce in virtually any organization. Mercedes-Benz executives focus on improving coordination to in turn improve product quality.

One of the ways Mercedes-Benz demonstrates its commitment to product quality is through a plan designed to improve coordination among three different manufacturing and assembly plants.

Acknowledging that new competitors such as Lexus and Infinity have made an impact in the upscale automobile business, Mercedes-Benz executives are neither discouraged nor digressing from decades-old objectives. The company remains committed to the needs and wants of the upscale-but-unpretentious buyer who is looking for a vehicle that balances style and performance with form and function.

As in the past, the company will compete by remaining firmly committed to improving the overall quality of its products. Klaus-Dieter Vohringer, a member of the Mercedes-Benz top management team, says the company will demonstrate this commitment to product quality through a plan focusing on improving coordination among three different manufacturing and assembly plants. This major restructuring of the manufacturing process at Mercedes-Benz is projected to result not only in better product quality, but also more productive uses of existing facilities, quicker response to changing customers' needs and competitive products, and lowered product costs. According to Vohringer, over the years, Mercedes-Benz has developed a sophisticated understanding of its customers. In order to maintain a high level of customer satisfaction, the company must be constantly on the alert for new methods of improving product quality; better coordination in the manufacturing process should help Mercedes-Benz achieve its quality goals. ▶

BACK TO THE CASE In developing the most appropriate way to organize MCI employees, Roberts can reflect on the second major element in classical organizing theory: division of labor. Roberts could decide, for example, that instead of having one person do all the work involved in servicing a business customer, the labor could be divided so that, for each business customer, one person would make the initial contact, one person would assess communication needs of the organization, and yet another person would explore various alternative MCI ways of meeting those needs. In this way, employees could work more quickly and could specialize in one area of business customer relations, such as assessing business needs or meeting needs of business customers.

In considering the appropriateness of division of labor at MCI, Roberts could also consider a mechanism for enhancing coordination. In order to develop such a mechanism, Roberts must have a thorough understanding of how various MCI business processes occur so he can split up various tasks and maintain coordination within the various MCI divisions. In addition, Roberts must stress communication as a prerequisite for coordination. Without having MCI employees continually communicate with one another, coordination will be virtually impossible. In taking action aimed at enhancing organizational coordination, Roberts must also plan for and take action toward maintaining such coordination.

Span of Management

The **span of management** is the number of individuals a manager supervises.

The third main consideration of any organizing effort is **span of management**—the number of individuals a manager supervises. The more individuals a manager supervises, the greater the span of management. Conversely, the fewer individuals a manager supervises, the smaller the span of management. The span of management has a significant effect on how well managers can carry out their responsibilities.[24] Span of management is also called span of control, span of authority, span of supervision, and span of responsibility.

The central concern of span of management is a determination of how many individuals a manager can supervise effectively. To use human resources effectively, managers should supervise as many individuals as they can best guide toward production quotas. If they are supervising too few individuals, they are wasting a portion of their productive capacity. If they are supervising too many, they lose part of their effectiveness.

Designing Span of Management: A Contingency Viewpoint

As reported by Harold Koontz, several important situational factors influence the appropriateness of the size of an individual's span of management.[25]

Similarity of Functions. The degree to which activities performed by supervised individuals are similar or dissimilar. As the similarity of subordinates' activities increases, the span of management appropriate for the situation becomes wider. The converse is also generally accurate.

Geographic Contiguity. The degree to which subordinates are physically separated. In general, the closer subordinates are physically, the more of them managers can supervise effectively.

Complexity of Functions. The degree to which workers' activities are difficult and involved. The more difficult and involved the activities are, the more difficult it is to manage a large number of individuals effectively.

Coordination. The amount of time managers must spend to synchronize the activities of their subordinates with the activities of other workers. The greater the amount of time managers must spend on coordination, the smaller their span of management should be.

Planning. The amount of time managers must spend developing management system objectives and plans and integrating them with the activities of their subordinates. The more time managers must spend on planning activities, the fewer individuals they can manage effectively.

Table 9.1 summarizes the factors that tend to increase and decrease span of management.

TABLE 9.1 Major factors that influence the span of management

Factor	*Factor Has Tendency to Increase Span of Management when—*	*Factor Has Tendency to Decrease Span of Management when—*
1. Similarity of functions	1. Subordinates have similar functions	1. Subordinates have different functions
2. Geographic contiguity	2. Subordinates are physically close	2. Subordinates are physically distant
3. Complexity of functions	3. Subordinates have simple tasks	3. Subordinates have complex tasks
4. Coordination	4. Work of subordinates needs little coordination	4. Work of subordinates needs much coordination
5. Planning	5. Manager spends little time planning	5. Manager spends much time planning

TABLE 9.2 Geometric increase of possible manager-subordinate relationships

Number of Subordinates	*Number of Relationships*
1	1
2	6
3	18
4	44
5	100
6	222
7	490
8	1,080
9	2,376
10	5,210
11	11,374
12	24,708
18	2,359,602

Graicunas and Span of Management

Perhaps the best-known contribution to span-of-management literature was made by V.A. Graicunas, a management consultant.[26] His contribution was the development of a formula for determining the number of *possible* relationships between a manager and subordinates when the number of subordinates is known. **Graicunas's formula** is as follows:

Graicunas's formula is a formula that makes the span-of-management point that as the number of a manager's subordinates increases arithmetically, the number of possible relationships between the manager and the subordinates increases geometrically.

$$C = n\left(\frac{2^n}{2} + n - 1\right)$$

C is the total number of possible relationships between manager and subordinates, and n is the known number of subordinates. Table 9.2 shows what happens to the total possible number of manager-subordinate relationships as the number of subordinates increases from 1 to 18. As the number of subordinates increases arithmetically, the number of possible relationships between the manager and those subordinates increases geometrically. Figure 9.12 (p. 228) illustrates the six possible relationships between a manager and two subordinates.

A number of criticisms have been leveled at Graicunas's work. Arguments that Graicunas did not take into account a manager's relationships outside the organization and that he considered only potential relationships rather than actual relationships have some validity. The real significance of Graicunas's work, however, does not lie within the realm of these criticisms. His main contribution was pointing out that span of management is an important consideration that can have a far-reaching organizational impact.[27]

Height of Organization Chart

A **flat organization chart** is an organization chart characterized by few levels and relatively large spans of management; a **tall organization chart** is an organization chart characterized by many levels and relatively small spans of management. A broad span of management indicates a flat organization chart; a narrow span indicates a tall organization chart.

A definite relationship exists between span of management and the height of an organization chart. Normally, the greater the height of the organization chart, the smaller the span of management. It also follows that the lower the height of the organization chart, the greater the span of management. Organization charts with little height are usually referred to as **flat;** those with much height are usually referred to as **tall.**

Figure 9.13 is a simple example of the relationship between organization chart height and span of management. Organization chart A has a span of management of six, and organization chart B has a span of management of two. As a result, chart A is flatter than chart B. Both charts have the same number of individuals at the lowest level. The larger span of management in A is reduced in B merely by adding a level to B's organization chart.

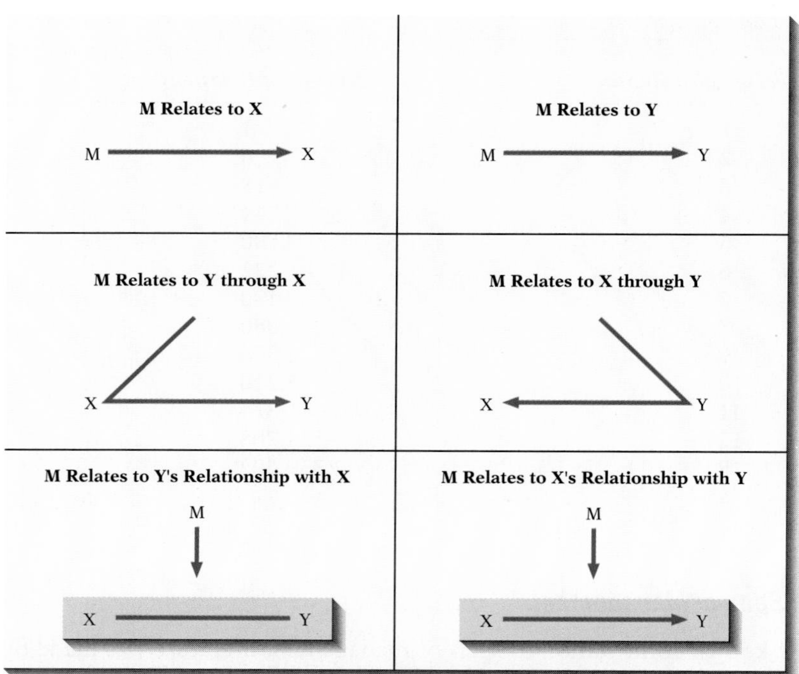

FIGURE 9.12 Six possible relationships between manager M and two subordinates, X and Y

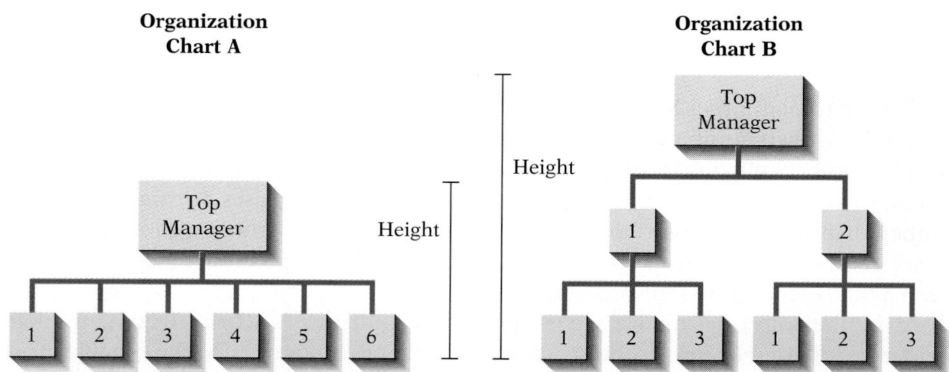

FIGURE 9.13 Relationship between organization chart height and span of management

An organization's structure should be built from top to bottom to ensure that appropriate spans of management are achieved at all levels. Increasing spans of management merely to eliminate certain management positions and thereby reduce salary expenses may be very shortsighted.[28] Increasing spans of management for objectives such as increasing the speed of organizational decision making or building a more flexible organization seems more appropriate for helping the organization achieve success in the longer run.[29]

Scalar Relationships

Scalar relationships refer to the chain-of-command positioning of individuals on an organization chart.

The fourth main consideration of any organizing effort is **scalar relationships**—the chain of command. Organization is built on the premise that the individual at the top possesses the most authority and that other individuals' authority is scaled downward according to their relative position on the organization chart. The lower an individual's position on the organization chart, the less authority possessed.

The scalar relationship, or chain of command, is related to the unity of command.

Unity of command means that an individual should have only one boss. If too many bosses give orders, the probable result is confusion, contradiction, and frustration, a situation that usually results in ineffectiveness and inefficiency. Although the unity of command principle first appeared in more modern management literature well over seventy-five years ago, it is still discussed today as a critical ingredient of successful, contemporary organizations.[30]

Unity of command is a management principle that recommends that an individual have only one boss.

Fayol has indicated that strict adherence to the chain of command is not always advisable.[31] Figure 9.14 serves to explain Fayol's rationale. If individual F needs information from individual G and follows the concept of chain of command, F has to go through individuals D, B, A, C, and E before reaching G. The information would get back to F only by going from G through E, C, A, B, and D. Obviously, this long and involved process can be very expensive for the organization in terms of time spent getting the information.

To decrease this expense, Fayol has recommended that in some situations a bridge, or **gangplank,** be used to allow F to go directly to G for information. This bridge is represented in Figure 9.14 by the dotted line that goes directly from F to G. Managers should use these organizational bridges with great care, however, because although F might get the information from G more quickly and cheaply, individuals D, B, A, C, and E are left out of the communication channel. The lack of information caused by Fayol's bridge might be more costly in the long run than would going through the established chain of command. If managers do use an organizational bridge, they must be extremely careful to inform all other appropriate individuals within the organization of the information they receive.

A **gangplank** is a communication channel extending from one organizational division to another but not shown in the lines of communication outlined on an organization chart. Use of Fayol's gangplank may be quicker, but it could be costly in the long run.

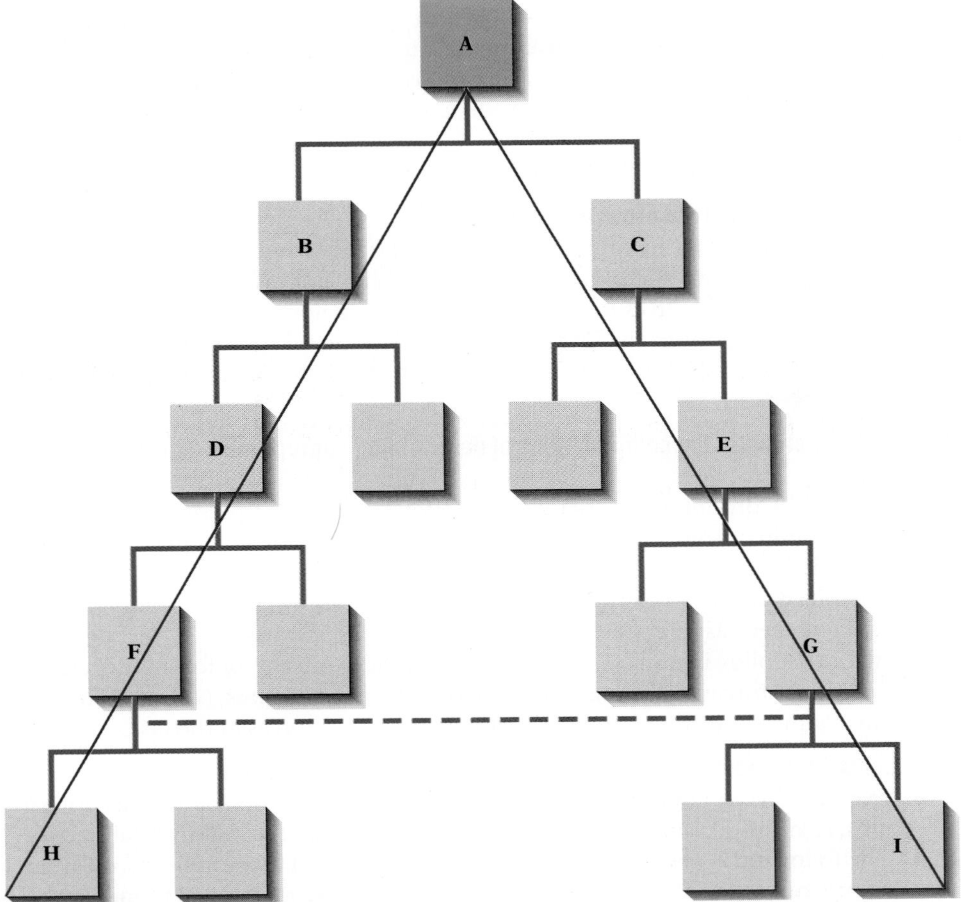

FIGURE 9.14 Sample organization chart showing that to always adhere to the chain of command is not advisable

BACK TO THE CASE The last two major elements in classical organizing theory that a manager could reflect on are span of management and scalar relationships. For Roberts, span of management focuses on the number of subordinates that managers in various roles at MCI can successfully supervise. In thinking about span of management, Roberts might explore several important situational factors, such as similarities among various MCI activities, the extent to which MCI workers being managed are physically separated, and the complexity of various MCI work activities.

For example, Roberts should consider that merely signing up a business customer as a long-distance user is fairly simple and that installing a special equipment network within a company is much more difficult. Therefore, the span of management for workers doing the signing up should generally be larger than the span of management for workers doing the installation. Two other important factors Roberts should consider in determining spans of management for various MCI managers are the amount of time managers must spend coordinating workers' activities and the amount of time managers spend planning. With all of this information, Roberts should be quite capable of determining appropriate spans of management for MCI managers.

ACTION SUMMARY

Reread the learning objectives that follow. Each objective is followed by questions. Answering these questions accurately will help you retain the most important concepts discussed in this chapter. After answering each question, check your answer with the answer key at the end of this chapter. (*Hint:* If you have doubt regarding the correct response, consult the page whose number follows the answer.)

Circle: ***From studying this chapter, I will attempt to acquire:***

1. An understanding of the organizing function.

a, b, c, d, e — **a.** Of the five steps in the organizing process, the following is grossly out of order: (a) reflect on plans and objectives; (b) establish major tasks; (c) allocate resources and directives for subtasks; (d) divide major tasks into subtasks; (e) evaluate results of the implemented organizational strategy.

T, F — **b.** Proper execution of the organizing function normally results in minimal duplication of effort.

2. An appreciation for the complications of determining appropriate organizational structure.

a, b, c, d, e — **a.** The XYZ Corporation is organized as follows: it has (1) a president, (2) a vice president in charge of finance, (3) a vice president in charge of marketing, and (4) a vice president in charge of human resources management. This firm is organized on the: (a) functional basis; (b) manufacturing process basis; (c) customer basis; (d) territorial basis; (e) production basis.

a, b, c, d, e — **b.** All of the following forces are influences on the evolution of formal structure except: (a) forces in the manager; (b) forces in subordinates; (c) forces in the environment; (d) forces in the division of labor; (e) forces in the task.

3. Insights on the advantages and disadvantages of division of labor.

a, b, c, d, e — **a.** Extreme division of labor tends to result in: (a) human motivation; (b) boring jobs; (c) nonspecialized work; (d) decreased work skill; (e) all of the above.

a, b, c, d, e — **b.** The following is *not* a generally accepted advantage of division of labor within an organization: (a) workers' skills in performing their jobs tend to increase; (b) workers need to know only how to perform their specific work tasks; (c) workers do not waste time in moving from one task to another; (d) workers naturally tend to try to make their individual tasks easier and more efficient; (e) none of the above (all are advantages of the division of labor).

4. A working knowledge of the relationship between division of labor and coordination.

T, F **a.** Effective coordination is best achieved through close employee supervision.

T, F **b.** Mary Parker Follett has contended that managers should plan for coordination.

5. An understanding of span of management and the factors that influence its appropriateness.

a, b, c, d, e **a.** Of the factors listed, the following would have a tendency to increase (expand) the span of management: (a) subordinates are physically distant; (b) subordinates have similar functions; (c) subordinates have complex tasks; (d) subordinates' work needs close coordination; (e) manager spends much time in planning.

a, b, c, d, e **b.** The concept of span of management concerns: (a) seeing that managers at the same level have equal numbers of subordinates; (b) employee skill and motivation levels; (c) supervision of one less than the known number of subordinates; (d) a determination of the number of individuals a manager can effectively supervise; (e) a and d.

6. An understanding of scalar relationships.

a, b, c, d, e **a.** The management concept that recommends that employees should have one and only one boss is termed: (a) departmentalization; (b) function; (c) unity of command; (d) scalar relationship; (e) none of the above.

T, F **b.** According to Fayol, under no circumstances should a gangplank be used in organizations.

INTRODUCTORY CASE WRAP-UP

"MCI Communications Organizes to Be More Competitive" (p. 213) and its related back-to-the-case sections were written to help you better understand the management concepts contained in this chapter. Answer the following discussion questions about this introductory case to further enrich your understanding of the chapter content:

1. Does it seem reasonable that Roberts is attempting to better organize MCI in order to remain more competitive? Explain.
2. List all the questions you can think of that Roberts should ask himself in exploring how to best organize MCI.
3. Explain why it would be important for Roberts to ask each of the questions you listed.

ISSUES FOR REVIEW AND DISCUSSION

1. What is organizing?
2. Explain the significance of organizing to the management system.
3. List the steps in the organizing process. Why should managers continually repeat these steps?
4. Can the organizing function be thought of as a subsystem? Explain.
5. Fully describe what Max Weber meant by the term *bureaucracy*.
6. Compare and contrast formal structure with informal structure.
7. List and explain three factors that management structure is based on, or contingent on. Draw three sample portions of organization charts that illustrate the factors you listed.
8. Describe the forces that influence formal structure. How do these forces collectively influence structure?
9. What is division of labor?
10. What are the advantages and disadvantages of employing division of labor within a management system?

11. Define *coordination.*
12. Does division of labor increase the need for coordination? Explain.
13. Summarize Mary Parker Follett's thoughts on how to establish and maintain coordination.
14. Is span of management an important management concept? Explain.
15. Do you think that similarity of functions, geographic contiguity, complexity of functions, coordination, and planning influence appropriate span of control in all management systems? Explain.
16. Summarize and evaluate Graicunas's contribution to span-of-management literature.
17. What is the relationship between span of management and *flat* and *tall* organizations?
18. What are scalar relationships?
19. Explain the rationale behind Fayol's position that always adhering to the chain of command is not necessarily advisable.
20. What caution should managers exercise when they use the gangplank Fayol described?

ACTION SUMMARY ANSWER KEY

1. **a.** c, p. 215
   b. T, p. 215
2. **a.** a, pp. 219–220
   b. d, p. 223
3. **a.** b, p. 224
   b. e, p. 224
4. **a.** F, p. 224
   b. T, pp. 224–225
5. **a.** b, p. 226
   b. d, p. 226
6. **a.** c, p. 229
   b. F, p. 229

CASE STUDY

Organizing the Sedona Fire Department

ROBERT E. KEMPER

South of Flagstaff, Arizona, lies the picture-postcard town of Sedona. Combining the best of frontier style and contemporary materials, Sedona is a testament to an active, concerned community. In this land of red-rock mesas and pillars, the town is in harmony with its setting.

Through the center of town runs a county line, so the community was historically represented by two separate fire districts: the Sedona–Red Rock Fire District in Yavapai County and the Sedona–Oak Creek Fire District in Coconino County. These districts functioned separately from their inception until July 1, 1985, when they agreed to form the Sedona Fire Department (SFD). Although their activities are now combined, Arizona law prevents total merger.

The SFD serves a region of 120 square miles, including the city of Sedona (incorporated in 1988) and some outlying areas. Eight fire stations, four in each district, protect the region. Volunteer members of the SFD are assigned to the station nearest their individual residences.

Members from both original districts govern the Sedona Fire Department. Each district has a five-member board that votes not only on district matters but also on matters concerning the SFD. Together, the boards hire a fire chief, who serves as the executive officer of the SFD and is responsible for general management and day-to-day operations.

The SFD consists of 121 volunteers and 24 full-time employees. An organizational chart located in the fire chief's office shows eleven divisions: (1) fire chief/deputy chief, (2) administrative, (3) fire marshall, (4) personnel, (5) repair and maintenance, (6) communications, (7) resources, (8) suppression, (9) emergency medical services (EMS), (10) nondivisional, and (11) finance. All division heads report to the chief. However, Chapter 1 of the SFD "Organization and Rules and Regulations" describes only two divisions, the Fire Division and the EMS Division. These are supported by six subcenters: administrative services section, communications division, fire prevention, repair-and-maintenance division, public-information section, and resource division.

The Fire Division suppresses and assists in the prevention of hostile fires and hazardous situations within the SFD's boundaries. EMS provides emergency medical patient care, rescue, and transportation within those boundaries. The six subcenters are charged with providing appropriate support for those two primary functions.

Job descriptions exist for some of the volunteer and paid employee positions, but not for some key full-time and volunteer positions. The job descriptions in use are generally outdated and may either not describe actual duties performed or not encompass other legitimate duties belonging to the job.

Full-time employees receive performance evaluations. They are evaluated on strengths and weaknesses but not on specifics of job performance. If an employee does not agree with the evaluation, there is little recourse. Existing grievance procedures deal with disciplinary actions and terminations.

No SFD employee has ever received a bad performance evaluation. The previous fire chief's attitude toward personnel was more than benign; pay raises and promotions were automatic. As a result, some employees fill posts for which they are not qualified, and some volunteers respond to emergency calls only after determining which full-time supervisor is on duty. Morale is low.

The new fire chief wants to modernize job descriptions, performance evaluations, and grievance procedures. He has identified the following needs: (1) updated performance evaluation forms for each job description to evaluate the actual work required; (2) grievance procedures for performance evaluations, disciplinary actions, and terminations; (3) personnel guidelines on how to document, evaluate, and discipline employees; (4) a program to train the personnel manager and supervisors on use of personnel guidelines; and (5) a systematic program to assist the personnel manager to create an updated personnel handbook.

DISCUSSION QUESTIONS

1. Based on the list of needs prepared by the chief, evaluate his understanding of the five steps in the organizing process. How does he plan to organize personnel management for the Sedona Fire Department?
2. Evaluate the organizational structure of the Sedona Fire Department.
3. The organizational structure of the SFD is based primarily on work functions. Is it based on territory in any way? How?
4. How do the concepts of division of labor and span of management relate to the problems described at SFD?

CNN VIDEO CASE

Organizing a Family Business

STANLEY AND EDWIN SHULMAN
Alixandre Furs

In 1927, at the brink of the Depression, Russian immigrant Samuel Shulman founded a company in his adopted home town of New York—Alixandre Furs. From the beginning, his company targeted a clientele that demanded high quality, and that clientele has carried Alixandre Furs through the Depression and through good times, through "Republican cloth coats" and through antifur activism. Samuel Shulman determined that his company would always buy the best-quality pelts and would sew to the specifications of the best fur designers—and Alixandre Furs dominates the quality fur market now as it did fifty years ago.

Stanley Schulman and his brothers run Alixandre Furs, not from the top down, but through mutual communication.

Stanley Shulman joined the family business in 1952 after completing a master's program in finance at Columbia University. He had planned to go to work on Wall Street, but his father told him that was unacceptable, so Stanley Shulman, like everyone else in his family, obeyed his father. Now he is president of the most successful fur business in the United States.

It was not easy for Stanley Shulman to abandon his dream of becoming a Wall Street wizard, and he harbored great resentment: "My brother Edwin and I—who had preceded me in the business—both worked in the factory at first. And we used to look in the showroom and I used to kick him and say, 'We'll never get in the showroom. . .' and he used to kick me and say, 'Keep quiet, put your head down, work. We'll get there someday.' And the someday happened." Stanley Shulman is now king of the most glamorous showroom in the fur industry.

Edwin Shulman, vice president and treasurer of Alixandre Furs, is in charge of what he calls "the dirty end" of the business. He manages production, from the purchasing and preparation of pelts through sewing the designer labels into finished garments. Over almost forty years in business together, he and his brother have become good partners. "We both understand each other and we respect each other, and we have different facets of the business which we are now bringing third generation in[to], to teach."

However, Stanley and Edwin Shulman's children have not been coerced into their fathers' business as their fathers were before them. They have been exposed to Alixandre all their lives and have been taught that it is a business and must be nurtured as a business by a devoted team. Having chosen to join the team, three sons are now learning that business from the inside out.

"It's extremely important that much thought be given to the relationships among the principals of the firm and the children," says Stanley Shulman. "We run this business very much as if it were a team and that third generation is like . . . the junior varsity, and during these years they fill these niches and find out where they're comfortable also. It isn't something that comes down from on top. It's done mutually." Shulman is particularly proud of what he has learned working with his son Brett. When Stanley Shulman and his father disagreed, they didn't communicate; when Brett Shulman and his father disagree, they concentrate on resolving the business issue rather than on their relationship—"and it saves so much anguish and pain and wasted time that it's tremendous."

Together, Stanley and Edwin Shulman control the most glamorous, and the largest, fur business in the United States, with contracts overseas as well. Their mutual respect and their solid professional relationship has been key to ensuring Alixandre Fur's continued domination of the high-end fur market. They learned how to manage a fur business from their father, but they have learned to manage a family business by considering the needs of the business separately from the needs of the family. "There were ways of doing things," Stanley Shulman learned, "and if you couldn't do it in the best possible way, you shouldn't do it; you should get out and do something else."

VIDEO CASE QUESTIONS

1. How do environmental forces of family relationships affect management at Alixandre Furs in this generation? How did they affect management in the past?
2. Consider Figures 9.5 through 9.8 on pp. 220–221. Which of these department formulas applies to Alixandre Furs?
3. The text states that a primary focus of organizing human resources is not merely assigning jobs, but also determining how each person's efforts can best be combined with the efforts of others to reach organizational objectives. Based on the case material, how does Stanley Shulman support this statement?
4. Based on the information in this case, does use of Fayol's "gangplank" concept to bypass time lost communicating up and down the chain of command seem to be a good idea for Alixandre Furs?
5. Give two examples of ways in which problems with coordination of labor might cause tremendous difficulties at Alixandre Furs.

CNN VIDEO EXERCISE

Creating an Organizational Structure at Alixandre Furs

ACTION GOAL: Create one formal chain of command for a company organized by departments, and another for the same company organized by product teams.

The president of Alixandre Furs is Stanley Shulman, and his brother Edwin is vice president and treasurer. Using information from the video case, draw a simple organization chart for Alixandre Furs.

Now imagine that the Shulmans decide to reorganize Alixandre Furs into two basically autonomous product divisions. One division will produce coats; the other division will produce jackets, vests, and other garments. Each division needs buyers, designers, cutters, stitchers, and marketers, as well as fulfillment and accounting services. Draw an organization chart showing the new divisions, assuming that the divisions will share the services of fulfillment and accounting

Organization by Departments

Organization by Product Divisions

CHAPTER

10

RESPONSIBILITY, AUTHORITY, AND DELEGATION

STUDENT LEARNING OBJECTIVES

From studying this chapter, I will attempt to acquire:

1. An understanding of the relationship of responsibility, authority, and delegation.
2. Information on how to divide and clarify job activities of individuals within an organization.
3. Knowledge of the differences among line authority, staff authority, and functional authority.
4. An appreciation for the issues that can cause conflict in line and staff relationships.
5. Insights on the value of accountability to the organization.
6. An understanding of how to delegate.
7. A strategy for eliminating various barriers to delegation.
8. A working knowledge of when and how an organization should be decentralized.

CHAPTER OUTLINE

INTRODUCTORY CASE
"Famous" Amos: The Organizing Challenge

RESPONSIBILITY

Dividing Job Activities

QUALITY HIGHLIGHT
Motorola

Clarifying Job Activities of Managers

AUTHORITY

Types of Authority

ETHICS HIGHLIGHT
General Electric

Accountability

DIVERSITY HIGHLIGHT
Procter & Gamble

DELEGATION

Steps in the Delegation Process
Obstacles to the Delegation Process
Eliminating Obstacles to the Delegation Process
Centralization and Decentralization

GLOBAL HIGHLIGHT
Levi Strauss & Company

CASE STUDY
Empowerment at Iomega

VIDEO CASE
Working Patterns: John Lehmann, Butterick Company

VIDEO EXERCISE
Delegating Responsibilities at Butterick

INTRODUCTORY CASE

"Famous" Amos: The Organizing Challenge

Wally "Famous" Amos, a pioneer of the now burgeoning \$450–million-a-year gourmet cookie industry, . . . is an entrepreneur who is famous not only for his delicious chocolate chip cookies but [also] for his upbeat take on life in general. This former William Morris Talent Agency employee, the first [African American] ever hired by the agency to be a talent agent, founded his company in 1975 with \$24,000 (in exchange for 25 percent of stock) lent by celebrity friends Helen Reddy, her husband Jeff Wald, and singer Marvin Gaye. Amos had been baking cookies since he was a teenager (his Aunt Della got him started) and he regularly used them as a "hook" to charm the producers and other Hollywood executives he met during his fourteen years as an agent. People kept telling Amos he should sell his cookies, but it wasn't until he took a downturn as an agent that he decided he wanted a more stable business of his own to run.

He traded in his tailored suits for Hawaiian-style shirts, baggy pants, and a panama hat.

Amos opened his first store, which an artist friend designed, on Sunset Boulevard. He traded in his tailored suits for Hawaiian-style shirts, baggy pants, and a panama hat. Then he had himself photographed and put on each package of Famous Amos cookies. For the opening, he sent out 2,500 invitations to the press, and, as a band played, poured champagne and dispensed cookies to his willing publicity pawns. By the next morning, lines formed outside his door as people tried to purchase part of L.A.'s latest media event.

The Famous Amos Chocolate Chip Cookie Company quickly grew to [include] stores in Santa Monica and Hawaii. The company grossed \$300,000 in its first year, \$4 million in 1979, and \$10 million in 1987. Today, there are twenty seven "fresh-baked" retail outlets across the country, and Famous Amos cookies line the shelves of thousands of grocery stores and supermarkets worldwide.

From CNN Cable News Network "Pinnacle" interview, September 24, 1988 and Dennis P. Kimbro, "Dreamers: Black Sales Heros and Their Secrets," *Success* 37 (May 1990), 40–41.

Recently, Amos sold his company to Denver real estate investors and entrepreneurs Jeffrey and Ronald Baer. Wally Amos remains a director and a shareholder of the company that he has sold. The outstanding initial success of "Famous" Amos Cookies is primarily based upon the ability of Amos to see a market and to sell his vision. One of the most pressing challenges that the company must now meet is how to professionally manage the company that has evolved. Meeting ever present management challenges like how to best organize the efforts of employees throughout the company will be a prerequisite to company success in the future.

The challenge facing the Famous Amos Chocolate Chip Cookie Company is to organize the efforts of employees throughout the company.

WHAT'S AHEAD The introductory case describes how Wally Amos initiated and built his "Famous" Amos Cookie Company, which he eventually sold to Jeffrey and Ronald Baer. The case ends with the implication that the company has gone beyond an initial fledgling phase and must now focus more on meeting normal management challenges if the company is to maintain its existence. The case indicates that one such challenge is how best to organize the efforts of employees throughout the company. The information in this chapter, organizing the job activities of individuals within an organization, should be of great value to managers like Amos and the Baers. Three major elements of organizing—(1) responsibility, (2) authority, and (3) delegation—are presented.

Chapter 9 has discussed how to apply principles of organizational structure, division of labor, span of management, and scalar relationships to establish an orderly use of resources within the management system. Productivity within any management system, however, results from specific activities performed by individuals within that organization. An effective organizing effort therefore includes not only a rationale for the orderly use of management system resources but also three other elements of organizing that specifically channel the activities of organization members. These three elements are responsibility, authority, and delegation.

RESPONSIBILITY

Responsibility is the obligation to perform assigned activities.

Perhaps the most fundamental method of channeling the activity of individuals within an organization, **responsibility** is the obligation to perform assigned activities. It is the self-assumed commitment to handle a job to the best of one's ability. The source of responsibility lies within the individual. A person who accepts a job agrees to carry out a series of duties or activities or to see that someone else carries them out.[1] The act of accepting the job means that the person is obligated to a superior to see that job activities are successfully completed. Because responsibility is an obligation that a person *accepts*, there is no way it can be delegated or passed on to a subordinate.

A **job description** is a listing of specific activities that must be performed to accomplish some task or job.

A summary of an individual's job activities within an organization is usually in a formal statement called a **job description**—a listing of specific activities that must be performed by whoever holds the position.[2] Unclear job descriptions can confuse employees and may cause them to lose interest in their jobs.[3] When properly designed, job descriptions communicate job content to employees, establish performance levels that employees must maintain, and act as a guide that employees can follow to help the organization reach its objectives.[4]

Job activities are delegated by management to enhance the accomplishment of management system objectives. Management analyzes its objectives and assigns specific duties that will lead to reaching those objectives. A sound organizing strategy includes specific job activities for each individual within the organization. As objectives and other conditions within the management system change, however, individual job activities within the organization may have to be changed.

Three areas related to responsibility are (1) dividing job activities, (2) clarifying job activities of managers, and (3) being responsible. Each of these topics is discussed in the sections that follow.

Dividing Job Activities

Because many individuals work within a given management system, organizing necessarily involves dividing job activities among a number of people. One individual cannot be obligated or responsible for performing all of the activities within an organization. Some method of distributing job activities and thereby channeling the activities of several individuals is needed.

The seven main organizational responsibility relationships described by this tool are listed in Table 10.1. Once organization members decide which of these relationships exist within their organization, they define the relationships between these responsibilities.

Being Responsible

Managers can be described as responsible if they perform the activities they are obligated to perform.[8] Because managers typically have more impact on an organization than nonmanagers, responsible managers are a prerequisite for management system success. Several studies have shown that responsible management behavior is highly valued by top executives, because the responsible manager guides many other individuals within the organization in performing their duties appropriately.

The degree of responsibility that managers possess can be determined by analysis of managers' (1) attitude toward and conduct with subordinates, (2) behavior with upper management, (3) behavior with other groups, and (4) personal attitudes and values. Table 10.2 summarizes what each of these dimensions includes for the responsible manager.

BACK TO THE CASE

In organizing the activities of employees, Amos and the Baers must recognize, for example, that a department manager's job activities within the company, as well as those of his or her subordinates, are a major factor in company success. Because actions of department managers have an impact on all personnel within the department, a department manager's job activities must be well defined. From the viewpoint of company divisions, one department manager's job activities should be coordinated with the activities of other departments. Amos and the Baers might choose to use the management responsibility guide process to achieve this coordination of responsibilities.

Over all, for managers within the Famous Amos Cookie Company to be responsible managers, they must perform the activities that they are obligated to perform. They must also respond appropriately to their subordinates, their superiors in the company, and their peers in other departments in the division.

TABLE 10.1 Seven responsibility relationships among managers, as used in the management responsibility guide

1. *General Responsibility*—The individual guides and directs the execution of the function through the person accepting operating responsibility.
2. *Operating Responsibility*—The individual is directly responsible for the execution of the function.
3. *Specific Responsibility*—The individual is responsible for executing a specific or limited portion of the function.
4. *Must Be Consulted*—The individual, if the decision affects his or her area, must be called on before any decision is made or approval is granted, to render advice or relate information, but not to make the decision or grant approval.
5. *May Be Consulted*—The individual may be called on to relate information, render advice, or make recommendations.
6. *Must Be Notified*—The individual must be notified of action that has been taken.
7. *Must Approve*—The individual (other than persons holding general and operating responsibility) must approve or disapprove.

TABLE 10.2 Four key dimensions of responsible management behavior

Behavior with Subordinates	*Behavior with Upper Management*	*Behavior with Other Groups*	*Personal Attitudes and Values*
Responsible managers— 1. Take complete charge of their work groups 2. Pass praise and credit along to subordinates 3. Stay close to problems and activities 4. Take action to maintain productivity and are willing to terminate poor performers if necessary	Responsible managers— 1. Accept criticism for mistakes and buffer their groups from excessive criticism 2. Ensure that their groups meet management expectations and objectives	Responsible managers make sure that any gaps between their areas and those of other managers are securely filled	Responsible managers— 1. Identify with the group 2. Put organizational goals ahead of personal desires or activities 3. Perform tasks for which there is no immediate reward but that help subordinates, the company, or both 4. Conserve corporate resources as if the resources were their own

AUTHORITY

Individuals are assigned job activities to channel their behavior appropriately. Once they have been given the assignments they must be given a commensurate amount of authority to perform the obligations.[9]

Authority is the right to perform or command.

Authority is the right to perform or command. It allows its holders to act in certain designated ways and to directly influence the actions of others through orders. It also allows its holder to allocate the organization's resources in order to achieve the objectives of the organization.[10]

The following example illustrates the relationship between job activities and authority. Two primary tasks for which a particular service station manager is responsible are pumping gasoline and repairing automobiles. The manager has the complete authority necessary to perform either of these tasks. If he or she chooses, however, the activity of automobile repair can be delegated to the assistant manager. Along with the activity of repairing, however, the assistant also should be delegated the authority to order parts, to command certain attendants to help, and to do anything else necessary to perform the repair jobs. Without this authority, the assistant manager may find it impossible to complete the delegated job activities.

Practically speaking, authority is a factor that only increases the probability that a specific command will be obeyed.[11] The following excerpt emphasizes that authority does not always exact obedience:

> People who have never exercised power have all kinds of curious ideas about it. The popular notion of top leadership is a fantasy of capricious power: the top man [*or woman*] presses a button and something remarkable happens; he [*or she*] gives an order as the whim strikes him [*or her*], and it is obeyed. Actually, the capricious use of power is relatively rare except in some large dictatorships and some small family firms. Most leaders are hedged around by constraints—tradition, constitutional limitations, the realities of the external situation, rights and privileges of followers, the requirements of team work, and most of all, the inexorable demands of large-scale organization, which does not operate on capriciousness. In short, most power is wielded circumspectly.[12]

As chapter 9 showed, the positioning of individuals on an organization chart indicates the relative amount of authority delegated to each individual. Individuals toward the top of the chart possess more authority than individuals toward the bottom. Chester Barnard writes, however, that in reality the source of authority is determined not by decree from the formal organization but by whether or not authority is accepted by those existing under it. According to Barnard, authority exists and will exact obedience only if it is accepted.

In line with this rationale, Barnard defines *authority* as the character of communication by which an order is accepted by an individual as governing the actions the individual takes within the system. Barnard maintains that authority will be accepted only if the individual (1) can understand the order being communicated, (2) believes the order is consistent with the purpose of the organization, (3) sees the order as compatible with personal interests, and (4) is mentally and physically able to comply with the order. The fewer of these four conditions that exist, the smaller the probability that authority will be accepted and that obedience will be exacted.

Barnard also offers some guidance on what action managers can take to raise the odds that their commands will be accepted and obeyed. According to Barnard, more and more of a manager's commands will be accepted over the long term if:[13]

1. Formal channels of communication are used by the manager and are familiar to all organization members.
2. Each organization member has an assigned formal communication channel through which orders are received.
3. The line of communication between manager and subordinate is as direct as possible.
4. The complete chain of command is used to issue orders.
5. Managers possess adequate communication skills.
6. Managers use formal communication lines only for organizational business.
7. A command is authenticated as coming from a manager.

BACK TO THE CASE

Amos and the Baers must be sure that any individuals within their company who are delegated job activities also are delegated a commensurate amount of authority to give related orders and to accomplish their obligated activities. Company managers must recognize that authority must be accepted if obedience is to be exacted. To increase the probability of acceptance, care should be taken to ensure that individuals understand internal orders and see orders as being consistent with the objectives of both the department they work in as well as the company. Employees should perceive that the orders that they are given are compatible with their individual interests, and they should see themselves as being mentally and physically able to follow the orders.

Types of Authority

Three main types of authority can exist within an organization: (1) line authority, (2) staff authority, and (3) functional authority. Each type exists only to enable individuals to carry out the different types of responsibilities with which they have been charged.

Line and Staff Authority

Line authority, the most fundamental authority within an organization, reflects existing superior–subordinate relationships. It is the right to make decisions and to give orders concerning the production-, sales-, or finance-related behavior of subordinates. Over all, line authority pertains to matters directly involving management system production, sales, and finance and, as a result, the attainment of objectives. Individuals directly responsible for these areas within the organization are delegated line authority to assist them in performing their obligated activities.

Line authority is the right to make decisions and to give orders concerning the production-, sales-, or finance-related behavior of subordinates.

Whereas line authority involves giving orders concerning production activities, **staff authority** is the right to advise or assist those who possess line authority and other

Staff authority is the right to advise or assist those who possess line authority.

staff personnel. Staff authority exists to enable those responsible for improving the effectiveness of line personnel to perform their required tasks. Examples of organization members with staff authority are members of accounting and human resource departments. Obviously, line and staff personnel must work closely together to maintain the efficiency and effectiveness of the organization. To help ensure that line and staff personnel work together productively, a manager must be sure that both groups understand the organizational mission, have specific objectives to strive for, and understand how they act as partners to help the organization reach its objectives.[14]

Size is perhaps the most significant factor in determining whether or not staff personnel are used within an organization. Generally, the larger the organization, the greater the need and ability to pay for staff personnel. As an organization grows, management generally finds a greater need for more expertise in more diversified areas. Although small organizations may also need this expertise, they may find that hiring part-time consultants when a need arises may be more practical than hiring a full-time staff individual who may not always be kept busy.

Figure 10.2 shows how line-staff relationships can be presented on an organization chart. The plant manager on this chart has line authority over each immediate subordinate—human resource manager, production manager, and sales manager. The human resource manager also has staff authority in relation to the plant manager. This simply means that the human resource manager possesses the right to advise the plant manager on human resource matters. Final decisions concerning human resource matters, however, are in the hands of the plant manager, the individual holding line authority. Similar relationships exist between the sales manager and the sales research specialist, as well as between the production manager and the quality control manager. To carry the example of the human resource manager's staff authority one step further, Table 10.3 contains a detailed listing of the types of decision areas over which a human resource manager generally has jurisdiction. These decision areas are not directly related to production but could ultimately have a favorable influence on it.

Roles of Staff Personnel. Harold Stieglitz has pinpointed the following three roles that staff personnel typically perform to assist line personnel:[15]

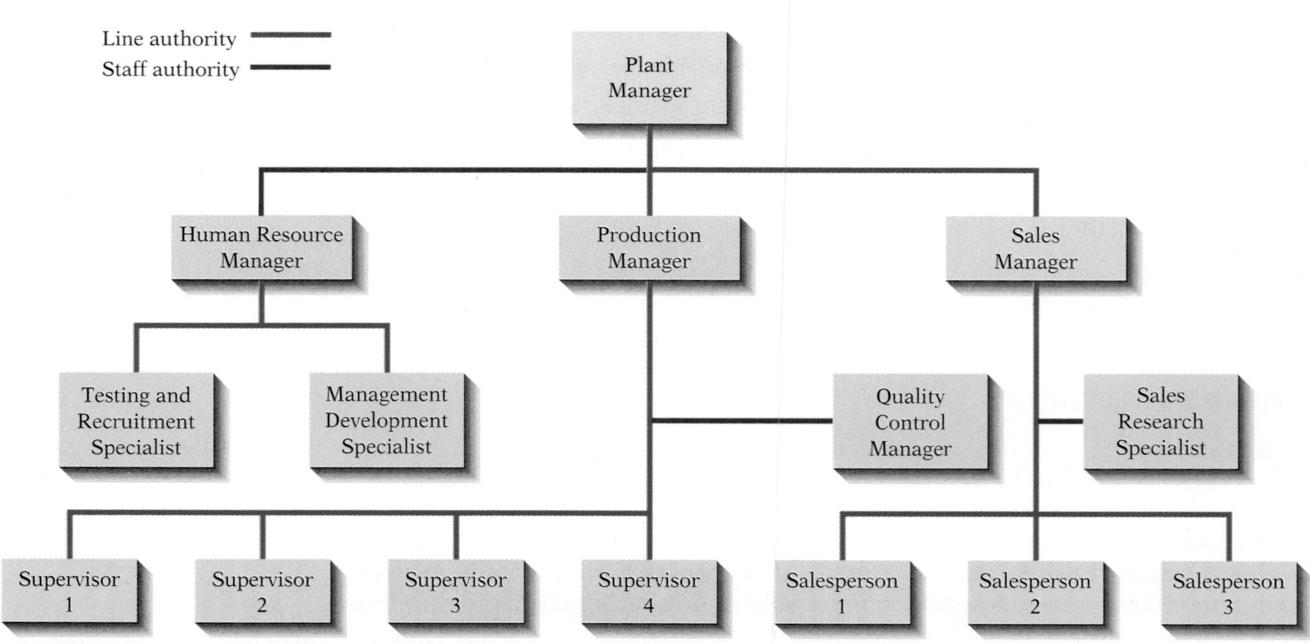

FIGURE 10.2 Possible line-staff relationships in selected organizational areas

TABLE 10.3 Typical decision areas for a human resource director

Human resource records/reports
Human resource research
Insurance benefits administration
Unemployment compensation administration
EEO compliance/affirmative action

Wage/salary/administration
Workers' compensation administration
Tuition aid/scholarships
Job evaluation
Health/medical services

Retirement preparation programs
Preemployment testing
Vacation/leave processing
Induction/orientation
Promotion/transfer/separation processing

Counseling/employee assistance programs
Pension/profit-sharing plan administration
College recruiting
Recreation/social/recognition programs
Recruiting/interviewing/hiring

Attitude surveys
Union/labor relations
Complaint/disciplinary procedures
Relocation services administration
Supervisory training

Employee communications/publications
Executive compensation administration
Human resource planning
Safety programs/OSHA compliance
Management development

Food services
Performance evaluation, nonmanagement
Community relations/fund drives
Suggestion systems
Thrift/savings plan administration

Security/plant protection
Organization development
Management appraisal/MBO
Stock plan administration
Skill training, nonmanagement

Public relations
Administrative services (mail, PBX, phone, messengers, fax, photocopying, etc.)
Payroll processing
Travel/transportation services administration
Library
Maintenance/janitorial services

1. *The advisory or counseling role.* The professional expertise of staff personnel in this role is aimed at solving organizational problems. The staff personnel are seen as internal consultants, with the relationship between line and staff being similar to that between a professional and a client. An example of this role might be the staff quality control manager who advises the line production manager on possible technical modifications to the production process that will help maintain the quality of products produced.
2. *The service role.* Staff personnel in this role provide services that can more efficiently and effectively be provided by a single centralized staff group than by many individuals within the organization attempting to provide the services themselves. This role can probably best be understood by our viewing staff personnel as suppliers and line personnel as customers. For example, members of a human resource department recruit, employ, and train workers for all organizational departments. In essence, they are the suppliers of workers; and the various organizational departments needing workers are their customers.
3. *The control role.* In this role, staff personnel help establish a mechanism for evaluating the effectiveness of organizational plans. Staff personnel exercising this role are seen as representatives, or agents, of top management.

These three are not the only roles performed by staff personnel within organizations, but they are the main ones. In the final analysis, the role of staff personnel in any organization should be specially designed to best meet the needs inherent within that organization. It is entirely possible that to meet the needs of a particular organization, staff personnel must perform some combination of the three main roles.

ETHICS HIGHLIGHT
General Electric Staff Organizes Renovation

At General Electric, a social responsibility project was recently organized and managed by one of its staff personnel, Bob Hess, a marketing specialist. As part of a sales meeting, G.E. salespeople renovated San Diego's Vincent de Paul Joan Kroc urban center for the homeless. The project was part of a company program in which tired buildings used by a worthy nonprofit organization are selected and then renovated by its employees. At the beginning of the renovation day, G.E. workers formed teams, each having a captain, a safety expert, and a task expert. In about eight hours, G.E. work teams completed 95 percent of the job, renovating space for 400 beds and preparing space for 200 additional beds.

The handling of sales training at General Electric reflects a very progressive management attitude. Through staff activities, the company has been able to demonstrate a desire and ability to make a worthwhile contribution to society.

Corporate work teams are organized to renovate buildings for worthy nonprofit organizations.

Conflict in Line-Staff Relationships. Most management practitioners readily admit that a noticeable amount of conflict usually centers around line-staff relationships.[16] From the viewpoint of line personnel, conflict is created between line and staff personnel because staff personnel tend to assume line authority, do not give sound advice, steal credit for success, do not keep line personnel informed, and do not see the whole picture. From the viewpoint of staff personnel, conflict is created between line and staff personnel because line personnel do not make proper use of staff personnel, resist new ideas, and do not give staff personnel enough authority.

To overcome these potential conflicts, staff personnel must strive to emphasize the objectives of the organization as a whole, encourage and educate line personnel in the appropriate use of staff personnel, obtain needed skill if it is not already possessed, and deal with resistance to change rather than view this resistance as an immovable barrier. Line personnel's effort in minimizing line-staff conflict should include using staff personnel wherever possible, making proper use of the abilities of staff personnel, and keeping staff personnel appropriately informed.[17]

BACK TO THE CASE

Assuming that a main objective of the Famous Amos Cookie Company is to produce the highest quality cookie possible, Famous Amos personnel who are directly responsible for achieving this objective should possess line authority to perform their responsibilities. For example, individuals responsible for purchasing ingredients for cookies must be given the right to do everything necessary to obtain cookie ingredients that will result in the best possible cookies.

This organization may need one or more individuals charged with the responsibility of assisting the line through a staff position. Perhaps such individuals could be responsible for advising Famous Amos management through the results of various surveys focusing on issues such as how the consumer rates the quality of Famous Amos Cookies relative to that of a competitor (Mrs. Fields' Cookies, for example), or how employees should be trained to become more productive. Anyone responsible for advising the line should be delegated appropriate staff authority.

As in all organizations, the potential for conflict between Famous Amos Cookie Company line personnel and staff personnel probably would be significant. Company management should be aware of this potential and encourage both line and staff personnel to minimize it.

Functional Authority

Functional authority is the right to give orders within a segment of the management system in which the right is normally nonexistent.

Functional authority is the right to give orders within a segment of the organization in which this right is normally nonexistent. This authority usually is assigned to individuals to complement the line or staff authority they already possess. Functional authority generally covers only specific task areas and is operational only for designated amounts of time. It typically is possessed by individuals who, in order to meet their responsibilities, must be able to exercise some control over organization members in other areas.

The vice president for finance in a particular organization is an example of someone with functional authority. Among his or her basic responsibilities, this manager is obligated to monitor the financial situation within the management system. To accomplish this monitoring, however, he or she must have appropriate financial information continually flowing in from various segments of the organization. The vice president for finance usually is delegated the functional authority to order various departments to furnish the kinds and amounts of information he or she needs to perform an analysis. In reality, the functional authority this manager possesses allows him or her to give orders to personnel within departments in which he or she normally cannot give orders.

From the previous discussion on line authority, staff authority, and functional authority, it is reasonable to conclude that although authority can exist within an organization in various forms, these forms should be used in a combination that will best enable individuals to carry out their assigned responsibilities and thereby best help the management system accomplish its objectives. When trying to decide what authority combination is best for a particular organization, managers must keep in mind that the use of each type of authority naturally has both advantages and disadvantages (see Table 10.4). Figure 10.3 is an organization chart that shows how the three types of authority could be combined for the overall benefit of a hospital management system.

Accountability

Accountability is the management philosophy whereby individuals are held liable, or accountable, for how well they use their authority and live up to their responsibility of performing predetermined activities.[18] The concept of accountability implies that if predetermined activities are not performed, some type of penalty, or punishment, is justifiably forthcoming. One company executive has summed up the punishment theme of accountability with the statement, "Individuals who do not perform well simply will not be around too long."[19] Also implied in the accountability concept, however, is the notion that some kind of reward follows if predetermined activities are performed well.

Accountability is the management philosophy that individuals are held liable, or accountable, for how well they use their authority or live up to their responsibility of performing predetermined activities.

TABLE 10.4 Advantages and disadvantages of line authority, staff authority, and functional authority

Advantages	*Disadvantages*
Line Authority	
Maintains simplicity	Neglects specialists in planning
Makes clear division of authority	Overworks key people
Encourages speedy action	Depends on retention of a few key people
Staff Authority	
Enables specialists to give expert advice	Confuses organization if functions are not clear
Frees line executive of detailed analysis	Reduces power of experts to put recommendations into action
Affords young specialists a means of training	Tends toward centralization of organization
Functional Authority	
Relieves line executives of routine specialized decisions	Makes relationships more complex
Provides framework for applying expert knowledge	Makes limits of authority of each specialist a difficult coordination problem
Relieves pressure of need for large numbers of well-rounded executives	Tends toward centralization of organization

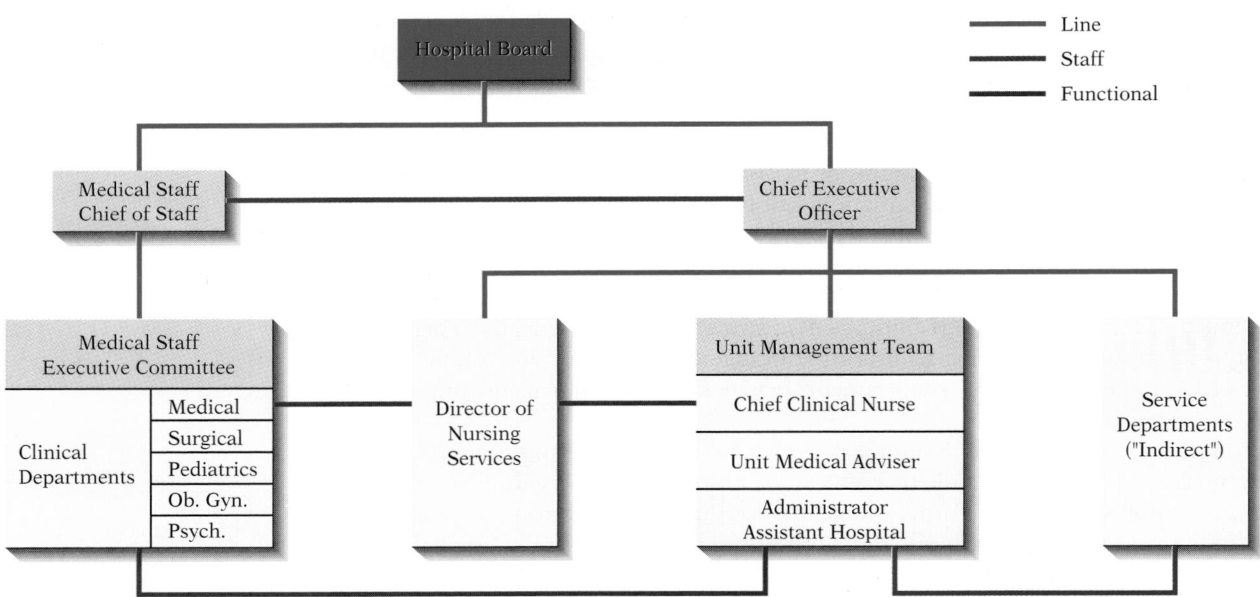

FIGURE 10.3 Proposed design for incorporating three types of authority in a hospital

DIVERSITY HIGHLIGHT
Procter & Gamble's Managers Held Accountable for Advancement of Minorities

Chairman Edwin L. Artzt believes that Procter & Gamble must be able to harness the energies of a diverse workforce in order for the company to compete on a global basis.

Organizations commonly hold managers accountable for performance issues such as earning higher profits, developing new products, and keeping work environments safe. At Procter & Gamble, managers are also held accountable for a somewhat uncommonly used performance variable, the advancement of minority workers.

Edwin L. Artzt, the chairman of Procter & Gamble, aims to build a tougher, faster, more global Procter & Gamble. According to Artzt, Procter & Gamble must be able to harness the energies of a diverse workforce if this objective is to be accomplished. Artzt has instituted a system to track minority employees' advancement and to hold managers accountable for their progress. P&G's participative approach to decision making, use of teams in accomplishing company projects, and formulation and assignment of company goals will be useful only if the company is successful in building its workforce—which will inevitably become progressively more diverse—into a productive, dedicated work unit.

As with any company, however, diversity is not the only issue at Procter & Gamble. Artzt is also taking other steps to build a faster, tougher company. For example, Artzt is demanding that managers consistently beat the competition to market with the latest products. Many inside the company, however, think that Artzt is pushing this first-to-market agenda too hard. Artzt is also being criticized for seemingly focusing too much on financial results in the short term. Critics think that such a focus seems contrary to building a truly faster, tougher company. Artzt can easily counter this criticism of short-term focus, however, by pointing out his record of new product development. In building Procter & Gamble for the longer term, Artzt has spent $400 million this past year on developing new products. This spending on new products is up 50 percent from recent yearly averages. ▶

BACK TO THE CASE

Functional authority and accountability are two additional factors that Amos and the Baers must consider when organizing employee activities within the Famous Amos Cookie Company. Some employee may have to be delegated functional authority to supplement the line or staff authority already possessed. For example, the accountant, a staff person who advises management on financial affairs, may need to gather financial results of various company retail outlets throughout the country. Functional authority would enable staff individuals to command that this information be channeled to them.

In organizing employee activity, Amos and the Baers should also stress the concept of accountability—that living up to assigned responsibilities brings rewards, and not living up to them has negative consequences.

DELEGATION

Previous sections of this chapter have discussed responsibility and authority as complementary factors that channel activity within the organization. **Delegation** is the actual process of assigning job activities and corresponding authority to specific individuals within the organization. This section focuses on (1) steps in the delegation process, (2) obstacles to the delegation process, (3) elimination of obstacles to the delegation process, and (4) centralization and decentralization.

Delegation is the process of assigning job activities and related authority to specific individuals in the organization.

Steps in the Delegation Process

According to Newman and Warren, there are three steps in the delegation process, any of which may be either observable or implied.[20] The first of the three steps is assigning specific duties to the individual. In all cases, the manager must be sure that the subordinate has a clear understanding of what these duties entail.[21] Whenever possible, the activities should be stated in operational terms so the subordinate knows exactly what action must be taken to perform the assigned duties. The second step of the delegation process involves granting appropriate authority to the subordinate. The subordinate must be given the right and power within the organization to accomplish the duties assigned. The last step of the delegation process involves creating the obligation for the subordinate to perform the duties assigned. The subordinate must be aware of the responsibility to complete the duties assigned and must accept that responsibility. Table 10.5 offers several suggestions that managers can follow to ensure the success of the delegation process.

Obstacles to the Delegation Process

Obstacles that can make delegation within an organization difficult or even impossible can be classified in three general categories: (1) obstacles related to the supervisor, (2) obstacles related to subordinates, and (3) obstacles related to organizations.

One supervisor-related obstacle to delegation is that some supervisors resist delegating their authority to subordinates because they find using their authority very satisfying. The cartoon on page 250 characterizes a manager who seems to delegate simply because he enjoys exercising authority. Two other such obstacles are that supervisors may be afraid that their subordinates will not do a job well or that surrendering some of their authority may be seen by others as a sign of weakness. Also, if supervisors are insecure in their job or see specific activities as being extremely important to their personal success, they may find it difficult to put the performance of these activities into the hands of others.

Even if supervisors wish to delegate to subordinates, they may encounter several subordinate-related roadblocks. First, subordinates may be reluctant to accept dele-

TABLE 10.5 Guidelines for making delegation effective

- Give employees freedom to pursue tasks in their own way.
- Establish mutually agreed-upon results and performance standards related to delegated tasks.
- Encourage an active role on the part of employees in defining, implementing, and communicating progress on tasks.
- Entrust employees with completion of whole projects or tasks whenever possible.
- Explain relevance of delegated tasks to larger projects or to department or organization goals.
- Give employees the authority necessary to accomplish tasks.
- Allow employees not ordinarily available access to information, people, and departments necessary to perform delegated task.
- Provide training and guidance necessary for employees to complete delegated tasks satisfactorily.
- When possible, delegate tasks on basis of employee interests.

gated authority for fear of failure, a lack of self-confidence, or because of a feeling that the supervisor doesn't have confidence in him or her.[22] These obstacles probably will be especially apparent if subordinates have not experienced the use of delegated authority previously. Other obstacles include the feeling that the supervisor will not be available for guidance once the delegation is made or that being a recipient of additional authority may complicate comfortable working relationships.

Characteristics of the organization itself also may make delegation difficult. For example, a very small organization may present the supervisor with only a minimal number of activities to be delegated. In addition, if few job activities and little authority have been delegated over the history of the organization, an attempt to initiate the delegation process could make individuals reluctant and apprehensive. In essence, the supervisor would be introducing a change in procedure that some members of the organization might resist very strongly.

Wall Street Journal, March 9, 1990, A13.

Eliminating Obstacles to the Delegation Process

Delegation usually results in several organizational advantages, thus the elimination of obstacles to delegation is important to managers. Advantages of delegation include improved subordinate involvement and interest, more free time for the supervisor to accomplish tasks, and, as the organization gets larger, assistance from subordinates in completing tasks the manager simply wouldn't have time for otherwise.[23] Although delegation also has potential disadvantages, such as the possibility of the manager losing track of the progress of a task once it has been delegated,[24] the potential advantages of some degree of delegation generally outweigh the potential disadvantages.

What can managers do to eliminate obstacles to the delegation process? First of all, they must continually strive to uncover any obstacles to delegation that exist in their organization. Next, they should approach specific action to eliminate these obstacles with the understanding that the obstacles may be deeply ingrained and may therefore require long-term time and effort. Specific managerial actions usually necessary to overcome obstacles include building subordinate confidence in the use of delegated authority, minimizing the impact of delegated authority on established working relationships, and helping the delegatee with problems whenever necessary.[25]

Koontz, O'Donnell, and Weihrich say that for managers to overcome the obstacles to delegation, they must possess certain critical characteristics. These characteristics include the willingness to consider seriously the ideas of others, the insight to allow subordinates the free rein necessary to carry out their responsibilities, trust in the abilities of subordinates, and the ability to allow people to learn from their mistakes without suffering unreasonable penalties for making them.[26]

BACK TO THE CASE

To delegate effectively within the Famous Amos Cookie Company, managers must assign specific duties to individuals, grant corresponding authority to these individuals, and create the awareness within these individuals that they are obligated to perform these activities.

In encouraging the use of delegation within their company, Amos and the Baers must be aware that obstacles to delegation may exist within managers, their subordinates, or the departments within which they work. They must be sure that managers meet the delegation challenge: discovering which delegation obstacles exist within their work environments and then taking steps to eliminate them. If Famous Amos managers are to be successful delegators, they also must be willing to consider the ideas of their subordinates, allow them the free rein necessary to perform their assigned tasks, trust them, and help them learn from their mistakes without suffering unreasonable penalties.

Centralization and Decentralization

Noticeable differences exist in the relative number of job activities and the relative amount of authority delegated to subordinates from organization to organization. In practice, it is not a case of delegation either existing or not existing within an organization. Delegation exists in most organizations but in varying degrees.

The terms **centralization** and **decentralization** describe the general degree to which delegation exists within an organization. These terms can be visualized at opposite ends of a delegation continuum (see Figure 10.4). From this figure, it is apparent that centralization implies that a minimal number of job activities and a minimal amount of authority have been delegated to subordinates by management, whereas decentralization implies the opposite.

Centralization is the situation in which a minimal number of job activities and a minimal amount of authority are delegated to subordinates.

Decentralization is the situation in which a significant number of job activities and a maximum amount of authority are delegated to subordinates.

The problems that practicing managers usually face are determining whether to further decentralize an organization and deciding how to decentralize if that course of action is advisable. The section that follows contains practical suggestions on whether an organization should be decentralized and how decentralization should take place.

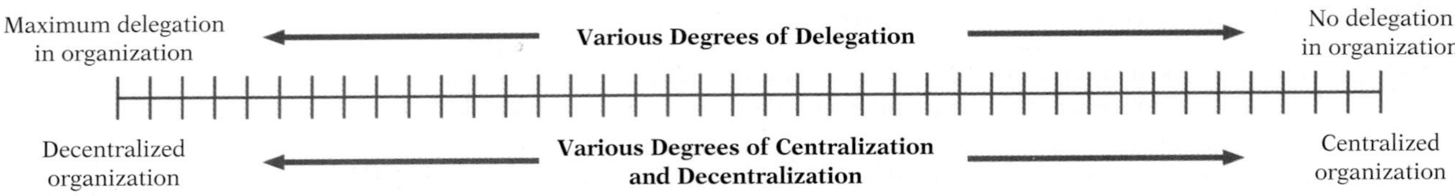

FIGURE 10.4 Centralized and decentralized organizations on delegation continuum

Decentralizing an Organization: A Contingency Viewpoint

The degree of decentralization that managers should employ depends on, or is contingent on, their own unique organizational situations. Specific questions to determine the amount of decentralization appropriate for a situation include:

1. *What is the present size of the organization?* As stated earlier, the larger the organization, the greater the likelihood that decentralization will be advantageous. As an organization increases in size, managers have to assume more and more responsibility and different types of tasks. Delegation is typically an effective means of helping managers keep up with this increased work load.
2. *Where are the organization's customers located?* As a general rule, the more physically separated the organization's customers are, the more viable a significant amount of decentralization is. Decentralization places appropriate management resources close to the customers and thereby allows for quick customer service. J.C. Penney, for example, decentralized its purchasing activities to give managers the ability to buy merchandise best suited to customers of their individual stores.[27]
3. *How homogeneous is the product line of the organization?* As the product line becomes more heterogeneous, or diversified, the appropriateness of decentralization generally increases. Different kinds of decisions, talents, and resources are needed to manufacture different products. Decentralization usually minimizes the potential confusion that can result from diversification by separating organizational resources by product and keeping pertinent decision making close to the manufacturing process.
4. *Where are organizational suppliers?* The location of raw materials from which the organization's products are manufactured is another important consideration. Time loss and perhaps even transportation costs associated with shipping raw materials over great distances from supplier to manufacturer could support the need for decentralizing certain functions.

   For example, the wood necessary to manufacture a certain type of bedroom set may be available only from tree growers in certain northern states. If the bedroom set is an important enough product line for a furniture company and if the costs of transporting the lumber are substantial, a sound basis for a decision to decentralize probably exists. The effect of this decision might be the building of a plant that produces only bedroom sets in a northern state close to where the necessary wood is readily available. The advantages of such a costly decision, of course, would accrue to the organization only over the long term.
5. *Is there a need for quick decisions in the organization?* If there is a need for speedy decision making within the organization, a considerable amount of decentralization is probably in order. Decentralization avoids red tape and allows the subordinate to whom authority has been delegated to make on-the-spot decisions if necessary. This delegation is advisable only if the potential delegatees have the ability to make sound decisions. If they don't, the increased decision-making speed via delegation has no advantage. Quick or slow, a decision cannot reap benefits for the organization if it is unsound.

6. *Is creativity a desirable feature of the organization?* If creativity is desirable, then some decentralization probably is advisable. Decentralization allows delegatees the freedom to find better ways of doing things. The mere existence of this freedom can encourage the incorporation of new and more creative techniques within the task process.[28]

GLOBAL HIGHLIGHT
Decentralization Makes Levi Strauss a Strong Global Competitor

Decentralization involves delegating authority to others. Management at Levi Strauss & Company has found that its organization can remain competitive at the international level by delegating significant amounts of authority to its managers in other countries.

Levi, best known for its denim clothing products, is the only U.S. apparel maker that is truly global in its operations. Levi's success turns on its ability to develop a global strategy that does not stifle local initiative. Implementation of this strategy is delicate but often includes delegating to foreign managers the authority needed to adjust their tactics to meet the changing tastes of their home markets. To protect its brand identity and quality, Levi has organized its foreign operations as subsidiaries that run mostly independently; the company now uses computers to track sales and manufacturing in various countries. As the U.S. denim jeans market continues to shrink, foreign sales are driving Levi's growth. Foreign consumers seem willing to avoid trendy apparel and invest in time-proven and stable denim products. In recent months, about 39 percent of the company's total revenues and 60 percent of its pretax profit before interest and corporate expenses has come from abroad. Although the denim jeans market overall seems to be shrinking, Levi jeans sales continues to grow. Overall, Levi is experiencing faster growth than many of its foreign rivals. ▶

Managers at Levi Strauss & Company have found that one way to remain competitive at the international level is to delegate authority to foreign managers. For instance, Japanese managers can readily respond to the clothing tastes of Japanese consumers.

BACK TO THE CASE Centralization implies that few job activities and little authority have been delegated to subordinates; decentralization implies that many job activities and much authority have been delegated. Managers within the Famous Amos Cookie Company will have to determine the best degree of delegation for their individual situations. For guidelines, Famous Amos managers can use the rules of thumb that greater degrees of delegation probably will be appropriate for the company as departments become larger, as retail outlets become more dispersed and diversified, and as the need for quick decision making and creativity increases.

Decentralization at Massey-Ferguson: A Classic Example

Positive decentralization is decentralization that is advantageous for the organization in which it is being implemented; negative decentralization is the opposite. One way to ascertain how an organization should be decentralized is to study a classic example of an organization with positive decentralization: Massey-Ferguson.[29]

Massey-Ferguson is a worldwide farm equipment manufacturer that has enjoyed noticeable success with decentralization over the past several years.[30] The company has three guidelines for determining the degree of decentralization of decision making that is appropriate for a situation:[31]

1. The competence to make decisions must be possessed by the person to whom authority is delegated. A derivative of this is that the superior must have confidence in the subordinate to whom authority is delegated.
2. Adequate and reliable information pertinent to the decision is required by the person making the decision. Decision-making authority therefore cannot be

pushed below the point at which all information bearing on the decision is available.

3. If a decision affects more than one unit of the enterprise, the authority to make the decision must rest with the manager accountable for the most units affected by the decision.

Massey-Ferguson also encourages a definite attitude toward decentralization. The company's organization manual indicates that delegation is not delegation in name only but a frame of mind that includes both what a supervisor says to subordinates and the way the supervisor acts toward them. Managers at Massey-Ferguson are encouraged to allow subordinates to make a reasonable number of mistakes and to help subordinates learn from these mistakes.

Another feature of the positive decentralization at Massey-Ferguson is that decentralization is complemented by centralization:

> The organization plan that best serves our total requirements is a blend of centralized and decentralized elements. Marketing and manufacturing responsibilities, together with supporting service functions, are located as close as possible to local markets. Activities that determine the long-range character of the company, such as the planning and control of the product line, the planning and control of facilities and money, and the planning of the strategy to react to changes in the patterns of international trade, are highly centralized.[32]

Massey-Ferguson management recognizes that decentralization is not necessarily an either/or decision and uses the strengths of both centralization and decentralization to its advantage.

Not all activities at Massey-Ferguson, however, are eligible for decentralization consideration. Only management is allowed to follow through on the following responsibilities:[33]

1. The responsibility for determining the overall objectives of the enterprise.
2. The responsibility for formulating the policies that guide the enterprise.
3. The final responsibility for the control of the business within the total range of the objectives and policies, including control over any changes in the nature of the business.
4. The responsibility for product design where a product decision affects more than one area of accountability.
5. The responsibility for planning for the achievement of overall objectives and for measuring actual performance against those plans.
6. The final approval of corporate plans or budgets.
7. The decisions pertaining to the availability and the application of general company funds.
8. The responsibility for capital investment plans.

BACK TO THE CASE The Massey-Ferguson decentralization situation could give Amos and the Baers many valuable insights on what characteristics the decentralization process within the company should assume. First, Famous Amos managers should use definite guidelines to decide whether their situation warrants added decentralization. In general, additional delegation would be warranted within the company as the competence of subordinates increases, as Famous Amos managers' confidence in their subordinates increases, and as more adequate and reliable decision-making information within the company becomes available to subordinates. For delegation to be advantageous for the Famous Amos Cookie Company, company managers must help subordinates learn from their mistakes. Depending on their situations, individual Famous Amos managers may want to consider supplementing decentralization with centralization.

ACTION SUMMARY

Reread the learning objectives that follow. Each objective is followed by questions. Answering these questions accurately will help you retain the most important concepts discussed in this chapter. After answering each question, check your answer with the answer key at the end of this chapter. (*Hint:* If you have doubt regarding the correct response, consult the page whose number follows the answer.)

Circle: ***From studying this chapter, I will attempt to acquire:***

1. An understanding of the relationship of responsibility, authority, and delegation.

T, F **a.** Responsibility is a person's self-assumed commitment to handle a job to the best of his or her ability.

a, b, c, d, e **b.** The following element is *not* an integral part of an effective organizing effort: (a) rationale for the orderly use of management system resources; (b) responsibility; (c) authority; (d) delegation; (e) none of the above (they are all important).

2. Information on how to divide and clarify job activities of individuals within an organization.

a, b, c, d, e **a.** The following is *not* one of the four basic steps for dividing responsibility by the functional similarity method: (a) designing specific jobs by grouping similar activities; (b) examining management system objectives; (c) formulating management system objectives; (d) designating appropriate activities that must be performed to reach objectives; (e) making specific individuals responsible for performing activities.

a, b, c, d, e **b.** A management responsibility guide can assist organization members in the following way: (a) by describing the various responsibility relationships that exist in their organization; (b) by summarizing how the responsibilities of various managers within the organization relate to one another; (c) by identifying manager work experience; (d) a and b; (e) none of the above.

3. Knowledge of the differences among line authority, staff authority, and functional authority.

a, b, c, d, e **a.** The production manager has mainly: (a) functional authority; (b) staff authority; (c) line authority; (d) a and c; (e) all of the above.

T, F **b.** An example of functional authority is the vice president of finance being delegated the authority to order various departments to furnish him or her with the kinds and amounts of information needed to perform an analysis.

4. An appreciation for the issues that can cause conflict in line and staff relationships.

a, b, c, d, e **a.** From the viewpoint of staff personnel, one reason for line-staff conflict is that line personnel: (a) do not make proper use of staff personnel; (b) resist new ideas; (c) do not give staff personnel enough authority; (d) a and c; (e) all of the above.

a, b, c, d, e **b.** From the viewpoint of line personnel, conflicts between line and staff can occur for the following reason: (a) staff may assume line authority; (b) staff may not offer sound advice; (c) staff may steal credit for success; (d) staff may fail to keep line informed; (e) all of the above.

5. Insights on the value of accountability to the organization.

T, F **a.** Accountability is how well individuals live up to their responsibility for performing predetermined activities.

a, b, c, d, e **b.** Rewarding employees for good performance is most closely related to: (a) simplicity; (b) a clear division of authority; (c) centralization; (d) decentralization; (e) accountability.

6. An understanding of how to delegate.

T, F **a.** The correct ordering of the steps in the delegation process is the assignment of duties, the creation of responsibility, and the granting of authority.

a, b, c, d, e **b.** The following are obstacles to the delegation process: (a) obstacles related to supervisors; (b) obstacles related to subordinates; (c) obstacles related to the organization; (d) all of the above; (e) none of the above.

7. A strategy for eliminating various barriers to delegation.

a, b, c, d, e **a.** Eliminating obstacles to delegation usually results in which of the following advantages: (a) improved subordinate involvement and interest; (b) more free time for the supervisor; (c) assistance for the supervisor to accomplish tasks he or she wouldn't be able to do otherwise; (d) all of the above; (e) none of the above.

T, F **b.** Generally, the potential advantages of some degree of delegating outweigh the disadvantages.

8. A working knowledge of when and how an organization should be decentralized.

a, b, c, d, e **a.** A high degree of centralization within an organization would be most advisable under which of the following conditions: (a) the organization is relatively small; (b) the organization is relatively large; (c) creativity is important to the firm's success; (d) the delegatees have the ability to make sound decisions; (e) the product line is diversified.

T, F **b.** According to the management philosophy that exists at Massey-Ferguson, the responsibility for formulating the policies that guide the organization should be highly decentralized.

INTRODUCTORY CASE WRAP-UP

"'Famous' Amos: The Organizing Challenge" (p. 237) and its related back-to-the-case sections were written to help you better understand the management concepts contained in this chapter. Answer the following discussion questions about this introductory case to further enrich your understanding of the chapter content:

1. What first step would you recommend that Amos and the Baers take in organizing the activities of individuals within their company? Why?
2. Discuss the roles of responsibility, authority, and accountability in organizing the activities of individuals within the Famous Amos company.
3. At this time, do you think that the company should be more centralized or more decentralized? Why?

ISSUES FOR REVIEW AND DISCUSSION

1. What is responsibility, and why does it exist in organizations?
2. Explain the process a manager would go through to divide responsibility within an organization.
3. What is a management responsibility guide, and how is it used?
4. List and summarize the four main dimensions of responsible management behavior.
5. What is authority, and why does it exist in organizations?
6. Describe the relationship between responsibility and authority.

7. Explain Barnard's notion of authority and acceptance.
8. What steps can managers take to increase the probability that subordinates will accept their authority? Be sure to explain how each of these steps increases the probability.
9. Summarize the relationship that generally exists between line and staff personnel.
10. Explain three roles that staff personnel can perform in organizations.
11. List five possible causes of conflict in line-staff relationships and suggest appropriate action to minimize the effect of these causes.
12. What is functional authority?
13. Give an example of how functional authority actually works in an organization.
14. Compare the relative advantages and disadvantages of line, staff, and functional authority.
15. What is accountability?
16. Define *delegation* and list the steps of the delegation process.
17. List three obstacles to the delegation process and suggest action for eliminating them.
18. What is the relationship between delegation and decentralization?
19. What is the difference between decentralization and centralization?

ACTION SUMMARY ANSWER KEY

1. **a.** T, p. 238
   b. e, p. 238
2. **a.** c, p. 239
   b. d, p. 240
3. **a.** c, pp. 243–244
   b. T, pp. 246–247
4. **a.** e, p. 246
   b. e, p. 246
5. **a.** F, p. 247
   b. e, p. 247
6. **a.** F, p. 249
   b. d, pp. 249–250
7. **a.** d, p. 251
   b. T, p. 251
8. **a.** a, p. 252
   b. F, p. 254

CASE STUDY

Empowerment at Iomega

STEPHEN M. BECKSTEAD
Utah State University

Iomega Corporation, founded in 1980, manufactures removable data storage and drive systems for IBM PC compatibles, the Apple Macintosh, and other computers. The company employs approximately 1,100 employees and, in 1991, had annual sales exceeding $136 million.

Fred Wenninger, a Ph.D. physics and former division manager at the Fort Collins division of Hewlett-Packard, became president of Iomega in 1989. Under his management, there was far more participation by all employees in the everyday functioning of the company. The new environment was one of total quality management. Authority was delegated down to the operating level—to those who actually did the work.

The production areas were reorganized to function as teams. The role of the manager was changed from controller and director to facilitator. The teams were empowered to structure themselves the best way they determined. Members of the team could, without management supervision, assign tasks and rotate jobs within their own teams. They could change the layout of the production line or workstation to improve productivity or to make their jobs easier. Traditional management decisions were now being made by hourly employees.

Some groups at Iomega have become more productive by using the authority and responsibility given them. For example, when Wenniger became president, he changed the format for the executive staff meeting. Whereas his predecessor used a dictatorial style, Wenninger allows each member of his executive team to offer input prior to making important decisions. The members of the executive team now feel they can help shape the future of the company.

Once a decision is reached at the executive level, Wenninger provides the freedom for executive team members to accomplish their tasks. One good example of this is Iomega's expansion into Europe. The executive staff decided to expand the European operations of Iomega. A vice president of European operations was hired and given the resources required for the expansion. With this level of empowerment, a new European headquarters has been secured and the expansion is well under way. This is all a direct result of the support, empowerment, and authority granted by Mr. Wenninger to the executive staff.

The Research and Development (R&D) group has also met with success under Wenninger's new management style. With resources under their control, the R&D group introduced three new products in 1992: (1) a 150 megabyte (MB) removable hard drive; (2) a 250 MB tape drive; and (3) a 21 MB floptical drive (a floppy disk drive that can hold 21 MB of data). The 150 MB removable hard drives were developed and introduced in a record development time for Iomega. Although Wenninger has been very supportive of these operations, he has also expected the best from them. Managers and employees alike have done well under the increased empowerment and accountability.

This transition to decentralized decision making has not been without its problems. Some who have responsibility are hesitant to use the authority given them by Wenninger. Others have tended to abuse this authority.

One adverse effect of the delegation of authority is the increase in frivolous spending throughout the company. Although the individual amounts are immaterial, the frequency is alarming. One group completed a project on time and as a reward they went to dinner with their spouses or dates at the most expensive restaurant in the state. This cost Iomega almost $100 per person. Executive perks are also on the rise. With this new authority, executive staff members have managed to attend one all-expense-paid meeting with their partners in Europe and another meeting—several weeks long—in Australia. These expensive trips are hard to justify given the benefits received. Although delegation and authority have been pushed down the organization and managers feel they are better able to do their jobs, it has been difficult to hold managers to their approved budgets and many things are flowing "under the bridge" without restraint.

DISCUSSION QUESTIONS

1. When Wenniger became president of Iomega, he decentralized decision making. In your opinion, was he successful? Why or why not?
2. How did the executive staff and R&D group respond to Wenninger's decentralization of authority and responsibility?
3. Why are some people or groups hesitant to accept authority delegated to them?
4. What could Wenninger do to hold his managers accountable for meeting their approved budgets?

CNN VIDEO CASE

Working Patterns

JOHN LEHMANN
Butterick Company

Responsibility, authority, and delegation are everyday concepts to John Lehmann, chairman of Butterick Company. Butterick, best known for its tissue-paper patterns for home sewers, is also the publisher of seven magazines and a line of greeting cards. The company's annual revenues are about $120 million, and its profit picture now is about three times what it was almost ten years ago, when Butterick was owned by American Can.

In 1983, John Lehmann and other top executives at Butterick united to buy the company back from American Can. They felt that the company had become mired in a bureaucracy and was often held back from acting on its needs quickly enough. As an example, Lehmann says, "If we wanted to buy a new printing press, we would have to go through six different departments, and three or four months later get approval." Also, for fifteen years as part of American Can, Butterick never had the same president longer than two years. Clearly, as long as Butterick was part of the large parent company, the executives at Butterick had little authority to follow up on their own problem-solving activities.

When John Lehmann delegates a task he not only gives the employee the authority to get the job done, but he also gives that person the training he or she needs.

With control back in Butterick's own hands, John Lehmann remembers the pitfalls of having responsibility but no authority, of having jobs to do but no authority to get them done. He gives his employees not only the authority but also the training to support it. To ensure that Butterick's executives understand their market, Lehmann and his executives learned how to sew; then they personally followed a Butterick pattern for a woman's blouse, so that they could be exposed to the problems of the home sewer.

We asked how a man can run a business targeted to women, Lehmann responds, "Have the right women in the right jobs." He adds that about half of Butterick's vice presidents are women and that all the patterns are designed by women. Butterick Company has eleven hundred people, and John Lehmann knows most of them by their first names. Two qualities that Lehmann has brought to Butterick are the work ethic and a commitment to the idea that work needs to be fun. The combination of these two qualities has resulted in an almost-zero turnover rate. Lehmann sees the job of delegation as meaning more than delegating assignments and the authority to do them. He knows it is his job also to promote an uplifting atmosphere throughout the company. "I bring it to the executives, and then they take it further into the company. We have a happy group."

This commitment makes it doubly hard for Lehmann to tell someone when he thinks it's time for them to leave the company. He notes, "I don't do it soon enough because I'm emotional. I think, 'What is he going to do? Is she going to find something soon?' It's very difficult because when you fire someone, you don't hurt one person. You hurt that person, you hurt the children, the mother-in-law that lives with them. It's a domino effect when you let someone go."

The next change Lehmann anticipates to boost sales at Butterick Company is a change in fashion, which has not occurred for several years and which needs to occur to sell more patterns. One other idea Lehmann has—and he calls it his greatest idea although he has never been able to follow through on it—is this: "I'd like to be able to have a pattern self-destruct. Statistically, all patterns are used two and a half times." Certainly, consumers won't be crying out for a pattern that can only be used once!

VIDEO CASE QUESTIONS

1. How does Butterick help ensure that its employees will accept authority?
2. How does Butterick's history illustrate the need for decentralization?
3. Explain how some of the problems experienced at Butterick under American Can were due to responsibility gaps.
4. Based on the information in the case, how much do you think Butterick is decentralized? Which of Butterick's functions require decentralization?

CNN VIDEO EXERCISE

Delegating Responsibilities at Butterick

EXERCISE GOAL: Begin to understand the lines between responsibility, authority, and delegation in working relationships.

Imagine that John Lehmann has just hired you to manage his group of high-fashion designers. This group is well known both for the wide appeal of its patterns and for its temperamental nature. Other managers you have talked with have warned you that this group is made up of "difficult employees." Although you have a strong background in merchandising in the women's wear industry, your experience with the pattern business is admittedly limited. Before you meet with your new staff for a planning session, you decide to identify the issues you think can be delegated completely to fashion designers, which issues involve shared authority, and which remain your sole responsibility as a manager. You have made a list of some of these issues.

Possible issues: (a) determine type of apparel to design (blouses, slacks, suits, etc.), (b) choose colors, patterns (checks, stripes, etc.), (c) assess productivity of design team members, (d) assess clarity of pattern directions, (e) create ensembles or single items of clothing, (f) promote group design versus individual design, (g) communicate with upper management, (h) identify problems that impact schedules or objectives.

Your next step is to assign each issue to one of the categories below. Be prepared to explain your choices.

Although your first few meetings with the fashion design team go well, after the fourth team conference, you encounter a problem. A particularly talented member of the team asks to speak with you privately. In your office she complains about your management of the team. She says, "I want artistic freedom and latitude for innovation. I want to set fashion direction, not lag behind the market. I need creative autonomy and control of my projects. I am an artist. I do not want my ideas diluted or changed, and I do not want to have compromise by working jointly with other designers."

You know that your response is important in setting the tone for future relations between yourself and your staff. How do you respond?

Delegated Responsibility	Shared Authority	Manager's Responsibility

CHAPTER

11

MANAGING HUMAN RESOURCES

STUDENT LEARNING OBJECTIVES

From studying this chapter, I will attempt to acquire:

1. An overall understanding of how appropriate human resources can be provided for the organization.
2. An appreciation for the relationship among recruitment efforts, an open position, sources of human resources, and the law.
3. Insights on the use of tests and assessment centers in employee selection.
4. An understanding of how the training process operates.
5. A concept of what performance appraisals are and how they best can be conducted.

CHAPTER OUTLINE

INTRODUCTORY CASE
Getting the Right People for Universal Studios

DEFINING APPROPRIATE HUMAN RESOURCES

STEPS IN PROVIDING APPROPRIATE HUMAN RESOURCES

Recruitment
Selection

GLOBAL HIGHLIGHT
Compaq Computer Company

Training

QUALITY HIGHLIGHT
Aetna Life & Casualty Company

Performance Appraisal

DIVERSITY HIGHLIGHT
US West

ETHICS HIGHLIGHT
Mobil Chemical Company

CASE STUDY
Managing Diversity at Levi Strauss

VIDEO CASE
The American Workforce: Retraining to Stay Competitive

VIDEO EXERCISE
Keeping Frigidaire Cool through Job Analysis

INTRODUCTORY CASE

Getting the Right People for Universal Studios

The new Universal Studios Florida (Orlando), which opened in 1990, is a combination film production center and tourist attraction. In anticipation of hiring employees for the grand opening of the tourist park section of the operation, the company ran an ad in a local paper.

Management found that some people will do almost anything to get a job at Universal Studios Florida. One job seeker paid for an airplane to tow a banner over the studio tour's office in Orlando to get attention. A man who applied for an advertising position sent a wedding-cake ornament, complete with bride and groom figurines. He said he and Universal would be a "match made in heaven." Another aspiring publicist sent a shoe box with one shoe inside. He said he wanted to get his foot in the door.

The tourist park . . . received more than 30,000 resumes for 2,500 positions.

In response to the ad and other recruiting efforts, the tourist park operation received more than 30,000 resumes for the 2,500 positions it needed to fill. Interest in Universal's jobs continues to build, and the company's human resources department recently reported that it receives about 250 applications and dozens of telephone inquiries each day.

The studio tour itself is not in the business of hiring performers and technicians who work on movies and TV shows—that's the job of film producers who lease sound stages from Universal. Universal Studios Florida is a joint venture between MCA, Inc., which also owns Universal Studios Hollywood in Universal City, California, and The Rank Organisation PLC in London.

In fact, most of the jobs at Universal Studios Florida have little to do with Hollywood. Jobs such as cooks, cashiers, parking attendants, security officers, and ride operators can be found at most other tourist attractions in Central Florida.

When Universal receives an application, it enters the information into its "applicant tracking system" computer and then mails postcards with E.T.'s picture, thanking applicants for their interest. In some instances, an applicant will be called in for an interview. But usually prospects are told that limited job opportunities are available.

From "Movie Theme Park Is Rehearsal for Foreign Venture," *Marketing News* 24 (July 9, 1990), 5; Adam Yeomans, "Job Seekers Go All Out at Universal," *The Orlando Sentinel,* September 27, 1989, C1, C6.

In hiring employees for Universal Studios — mostly for positions like cooks, cashiers, parking attendants, security officers, and ride operators — managers look, not just for workers, but for the right workers. *Universal Studios wants to hire individuals who will make a valuable contribution toward meeting the company's organizational objectives. The hiring process includes four basic steps: recruitment, selection, training, and performance appraisal.*

WHAT'S AHEAD The introductory case discusses an unusually high interest shown by people in working for the tourist park segment of Universal Studios Florida. The task of hiring not just people, but the *right* people is part of managing human resources in an organization. This chapter discusses the process of managing human resources within an organization and illustrates how hiring the right employees fits within this process. This chapter focuses on the process by first defining appropriate human resources and then examining the steps to be followed in providing them.

The emphasis in chapter 10 has been on organizing the activity of individuals within the management system. To this end, responsibility, authority, and delegation were discussed in detail. This chapter continues to explore the relationship between individuals and organizing by discussing how appropriate human resources can be provided for the organization.

DEFINING APPROPRIATE HUMAN RESOURCES

Appropriate human resources are the individuals in the organization who make a valuable contribution to management system goal attainment.

The phrase **appropriate human resources** refers to the individuals within the organization who make a valuable contribution to management system goal attainment. This contribution, of course, is a result of productivity in the positions they hold. The phrase *inappropriate human resources* refers to organization members who do not make a valuable contribution to the attainment of management system objectives. In essence, these individuals are ineffective in their jobs.

Productivity in all organizations is determined by how human resources interact and combine to use all other management system resources. Such factors as background, age, job-related experience, and level of formal education all have some role in determining the degree of appropriateness of the individual to the organization. Although the process of providing appropriate human resources for the organization is involved and somewhat subjective, the following section offers insights on how to increase the success of this process.

STEPS IN PROVIDING APPROPRIATE HUMAN RESOURCES

To provide appropriate human resources to fill either managerial or nonmanagerial openings, managers follow four sequential steps: (1) recruitment, (2) selection, (3) training, and (4) performance appraisal. Figure 11.1 illustrates these steps.

Recruitment

Recruitment is the initial attraction and screening of the total supply of prospective human resources available to fill a position.

Recruitment is the initial attraction and screening of the total supply of prospective human resources available to fill a position. Its purpose is to narrow a large field of prospective employees to a relatively small group of individuals from which someone eventually will be hired. To be effective, recruiters must know (1) the job they are trying to fill, (2) where potential human resources can be located, and (3) how the law influences recruiting efforts.

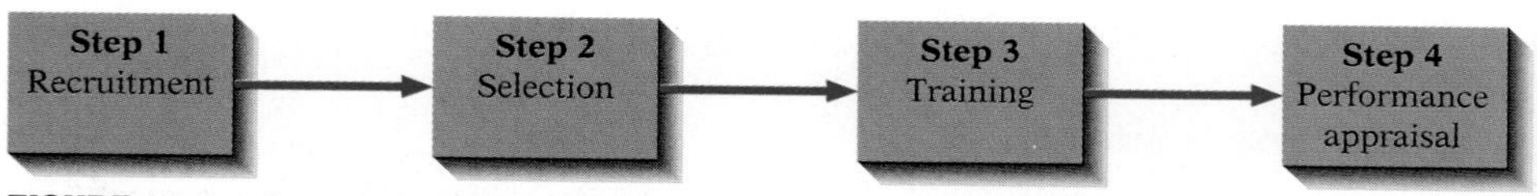

FIGURE 11.1 Four sequential steps to provide appropriate human resources for an organization

Knowing the Job

Recruitment activities must begin with a thorough understanding of the position to be filled so the broad range of potential employees can be narrowed intelligently. **Job analysis** is a technique commonly used to gain an understanding of a position. Basically, job analysis is aimed at determining a **job description** (the activities a job entails)[1] and a **job specification** (the characteristics of the individual who should be hired for the job). Figure 11.2 shows the relationship of job analysis to job description and job specification.

Job analysis is a technique commonly used to gain an understanding of what a task entails and the type of individual who should be hired to perform the task.

The U.S. Civil Service Commission has developed a procedure for performing a job analysis (see Table 11.1).[2] As with all job analysis procedures, the Civil Service procedure uses information gathering as the primary means of determining what workers do and how and why they do it. Naturally, the quality of the job analysis depends on the accuracy of information gathered.[3] This information is used to develop both a job description and a job specification.

A **job description** is a list of specific activities that must be performed to accomplish some task or job.

A **job specification** is a list of characteristics of the individual who should be hired to perform a specific task or job.

BACK TO THE CASE In hiring new employees for an operation like Universal Studios Florida, management must be careful to emphasize hiring not just workers, but the *right* workers. For Universal Studios Florida, appropriate human resources are those people who will make a valuable contribution to the attainment of Universal's organizational objectives. In hiring cooks, cashiers, parking attendants, security officers, and ride operators, management should consider only those people who will best help the organization become successful. In finding appropriate human resources, management at Universal Studios Florida has to follow four basic steps: (1) recruitment, (2) selection, (3) training, and (4) performance appraisal.

Basically, recruitment would entail the initial screening of individuals available to fill open positions at Universal. For recruitment efforts to be successful at a company such as Universal, recruiters have to know the jobs they are trying to fill, where potential human resources can be located, and how the law influences recruiting efforts.

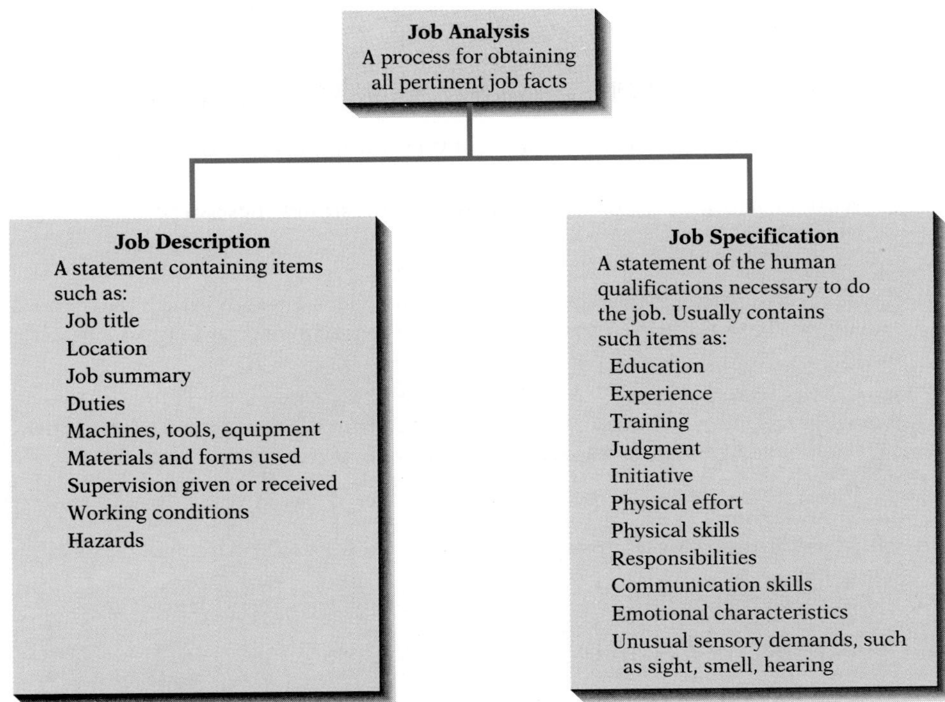

FIGURE 11.2 Relationship of job analysis, job description, and job specification

TABLE 11.1 Information to obtain when performing a job analysis

Identifying Information (such as):
Name of incumbent
Organization/unit
Title and series
Date
Interviewer

Brief Summary of Job:
(This statement will include the primary duties of the job. It may be prepared in advance from class specifications, job descriptions, or other sources. However, it should be checked for accuracy using the task statements resulting from the analysis.)

Job Tasks:
What does the worker do? How does the worker do it? Why? What output is produced? What tools, procedures, aids are involved? How much time does it take to do the task? How often does the worker perform the task in a day, week, month, or year?

Knowledge, Skills, and Abilities Required:
What does it take to perform each task in terms of the following?

1. Knowledge required
   a. What subject matter areas are covered by the task?
   b. What facts or principles must the worker have an acquaintance with or understand in these subject matter areas?
   c. Describe the level, degree, and breadth of knowledge required in these areas or subjects.
2. Skills required
   a. What activities must the worker perform with ease and precision?
   b. What are the manual skills required to operate machines, vehicles, equipment, or to use tools?
3. Abilities required
   a. What is the nature and level of language ability, written or oral, required of the worker on the job?
   Are there complex oral or written ideas involved in performing the task, or simple instructional materials?
   b. What mathematical ability must the worker have? Will the worker use simple arithmetic, complex algebra?
   c. What reasoning or problem-solving ability must the worker have?
   d. What instructions must the worker follow? Are they simple, detailed, involved, abstract?
   e. What interpersonal abilities are required? What supervisory or managing abilities are required?
   f. What physical abilities such as strength, coordination, and visual acuity must the worker have?

Physical Activities:
Describe the frequency and degree to which the incumbent is engaged in such activities as: pulling, pushing, throwing, carrying, kneeling, sitting, running, crawling, reaching, climbing.

Environmental Conditions:
Describe the frequency and degree to which the incumbent will encounter working under such conditions as these: cramped quarters, moving objects, vibration, inadequate ventilation.

Typical Work Incidents:

1. Situations involving the interpretation of feelings, ideas, or facts in terms of personal viewpoint.
2. Influencing people in their opinions, attitudes, or judgments about ideas or things.

Recruiters could acquire an understanding of open positions at a company like Universal by performing a job analysis. The job analysis would force them to determine the job description of the open position—the activities of a cook, parking attendant, or security officer, for example—and the job specification of the position, including the type of individual who should be hired to fill that position.

Knowing Sources of Human Resources

Besides a thorough knowledge of the position the organization is trying to fill, recruiters must be able to pinpoint sources of human resources. A barrier to this pinpointing is the fact that the supply of individuals from which to choose is continually changing; there are times when finding appropriate human resources is much harder than at other times. An article published in 1977 discussed just such a change in the human resources supply—an expected surplus of qualified managers: "For the past couple of years, a few thoughtful observers of new business trends have been warning that a glut of corporate executives is imminent. The reason, of course, is the U.S. baby boom of the late 1940s and 1950s."[4] Overall, sources of human resources available to fill a position can be categorized in two ways: (1) sources inside the organization and (2) sources outside the organization.

Sources Inside the Organization. The existing pool of employees in an organization is one source of human resources. Individuals already in an organization may be well qualified for an open position. Although existing personnel sometimes are moved laterally within an organization, most internal movements are usually promotions. Promotion from within typically has the advantages of building morale, encouraging employees to work harder in hopes of being promoted, and helping individuals decide to stay with a particular organization because of possible future promotions.[5] Companies such as Exxon and General Electric find it very rewarding to train managers themselves for upward movement within the organization.[6]

Some type of **human resource inventory** usually is helpful to a company to keep current with possibilities for filling a position from within. The inventory should indicate which individuals in the organization would be appropriate for filling a position if it became available. Walter S. Wikstrom suggested three types of records that can be combined to maintain a useful human resource inventory in an organization.[7] Although Wikstrom focused on filling managerial positions, slight modifications to his inventory forms would make his records equally applicable to nonmanagerial positions. Many organizations computerize records like the ones Wikstrom suggests in order to make a human resource inventory system as efficient and effective as possible.

The first of Wikstrom's three record-keeping forms for a human resource inventory is a **management inventory card** (see Figure 11.3 on page 268). The card in the figure has been completed for a fictional manager named Mel Murray. It indicates Murray's age, year of employment, present position and length of time it has been held, performance ratings, strengths and weaknesses, the positions to which Murray might move, when he would be ready to assume these positions, and additional training he would need to fill the positions. In short, this card is both an organizational history of Murray and an explanation of how he might be used in the future.

Figure 11.4 on page 268 shows Wikstrom's second human resource inventory form—a **position replacement form.** This form focuses on maintaining position-centered information, rather than the people-centered information on the management inventory card. The form in the figure indicates little about Murray as a person but much about individuals who could replace him. The position replacement form is helpful in determining what would happen to Murray's present position if Murray were selected to be moved within the organization or if he left the organization altogether.

Wikstrom's third human resource inventory form is called a **management manpower replacement card** (see Figure 11.5 on page 269). This chart presents a composite view of the individuals who management considers significant for human

A **human resource inventory** is an accumulation of information concerning the characteristics of the organization members; this information focuses on the past performance of organization members as well as on how they might be trained and best used in the future.

The **management inventory card** is a form used in compiling a human resource inventory—containing an organizational history of an individual and an explanation of how the individual might be used in the future.

The **position replacement form** is a form used in compiling a human resource inventory—summarizing information about organization members who could fill a position should it open.

A **management manpower replacement chart** is a form used in compiling a human resource inventory—people-oriented and presenting a total composite view of individuals whom management considers significant to human resource planning.

Name Murray, Mel	**Age** 47	**Employed** 1985
Present Position Manager, Sales (House Fans Division)		On Job 6 years
Present Performance Outstanding—exceeded sales goal in spite of stiffer competition		
Strengths Good planner—motivates subordinates very well—excellent communication.		
Weaknesses Still does not always delegate as much as situation requires. Sometimes does not understand production problems.		
Efforts to Improve Has greatly improved in delegating in last two years; also has organized more effectively after taking a management course on own time and initiative.		
Could Move to Vice President, Marketing		**When** 1997
Training Needed More exposure to problems of other divisions (attend top staff conference?). Perhaps university program stressing staff role of corporate marketing versus line sales.		
Could Move to Manager, House or Industrial Fans Division		**When** 1998 1999
Training Needed Course in production management; some project working with production people; perhaps a good business game somewhere.		

FIGURE 11.3 Management inventory card

Position	Manager, Sales (House Fans Division)			
Performance Outstanding	**Incumbent** Mel Murray	**Salary** $44,500	**May Move** 1 Year	
Replacement 1 Earl Renfrew		**Salary** $39,500	**Age** 39	
Present Position Field Sales Manager, House Fans		**Employed:** Present Job 3 years	Company 10 years	
Training Needed Special assignment to study market potential for air conditioners to provide forecasting experience.			**When ready** now	
Replacement 2 Bernard Storey		**Salary** $38,500	**Age** 36	
Present Position Promotion Manager, House Fans		**Employed:** Present Job 4 years	Company 7 years	
Training Needed Rotation to field sales. Marketing conference in fall.			**When ready** 2 years	

FIGURE 11.4 Position replacement form

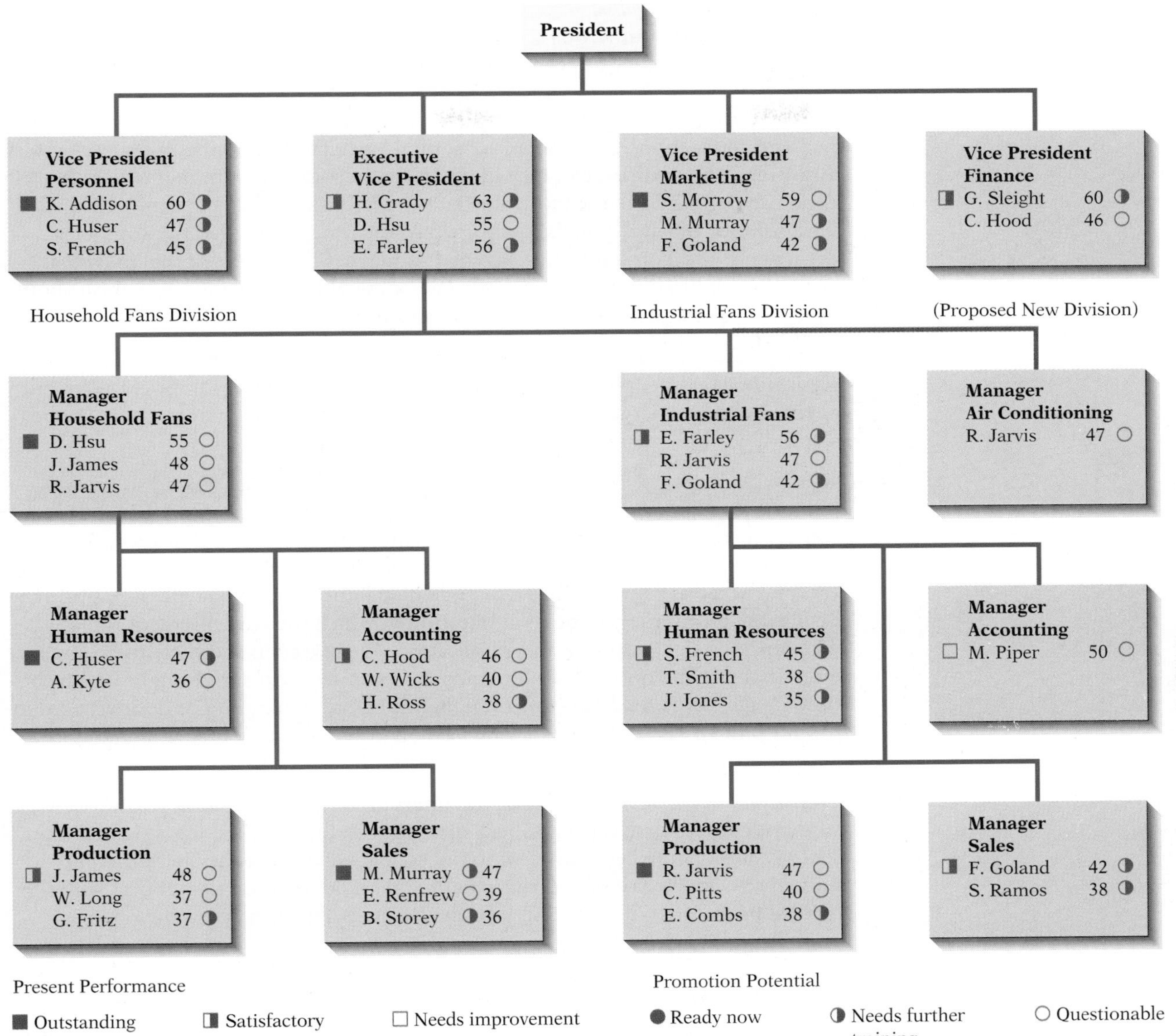

FIGURE 11.5 Management manpower replacement chart

resource planning. The performance rating and promotion potential of Murray can easily be compared with those of other employees when the company is trying to determine which individual would most appropriately fill a particular position.

The management inventory card, the position replacement form, and the management manpower replacement chart are three separate record-keeping devices for a human resource inventory. Each form furnishes different data on which to base a hiring-from-within decision. The questions these forms help answer are (1) What is the organizational history of an individual, and what potential does the person possess (management inventory card)? (2) If a position becomes vacant, who might be eligible to fill it (position replacement form)? (3) What are the relative merits of one individual filling the position as compared to another (management manpower replacement chart)? Considering the answers to these three questions collectively should help to ensure the success of hiring-from-within decisions. Computer software is available to help managers keep track of complex human resource inventories and to make resultingly better decisions about how people should be best deployed and developed.[8]

Sources Outside the Organization. If a position cannot be filled by someone presently in the organization, numerous sources of prospective human resources are available outside the organization. They include:

1. *Competitors.* One commonly tapped external source of human resources is competing organizations. Since there are several advantages to luring human resources away from competitors, this type of piracy has become a common practice. Among the advantages are (1) the individual knows the business, (2) the competitor will have paid for the individual's training up to the time of hire, (3) the competing organization will probably be weakened somewhat by the loss of the individual, and (4) once hired the individual becomes a valuable source of information about how to best compete with the other organization.
2. *Employment agencies.* Employment agencies help people find jobs and help organizations find people. They can be either public or private. Public employment agencies do not charge fees, whereas private ones collect a fee from either the person hired or the organization, once a hiring has been finalized.
3. *Readers of certain publications.* Perhaps the most widely addressed source of potential human resources is the readership of certain publications. To tap this source, recruiters simply place an advertisement in a suitable publication. The advertisement describes the open position in detail and announces that the organization is accepting applications from qualified individuals. The type of position to be filled determines the type of publication in which the advertisement is placed. The objective is to advertise in a publication whose readers are likely to be interested in filling the position. An opening for a top-level executive might be advertised in *The Wall Street Journal,* a training director opening might be advertised in the *Journal of Training and Development,* and an educational opening might be advertised in the *Chronicle of Higher Education.*
4. *Educational institutions.* Several recruiters go directly to schools to interview students close to graduation. Liberal arts schools, business schools, engineering schools, junior colleges, and community colleges all have somewhat different human resources to offer. Recruiting efforts should focus on the schools with the highest probability of providing human resources appropriate for the open position.

Knowing the Law

The **Equal Employment Opportunity Commission (EEOC)** is an agency established to enforce the laws that regulate recruiting and other managerial practices.

Modern legislation has a major impact on organizational recruitment practices, and a recruitment effort must reflect the laws that govern it. The Civil Rights Act passed in 1964 and amended in 1972 created the **Equal Employment Opportunity Commission (EEOC)** to enforce the laws established to prohibit discrimination on the basis of race, color, religion, sex, and national origin in recruitment, hiring, firing, layoffs, and all other employment practices. The EEOC report was amended in 1978 to include the Pregnancy Discrimination Act, which required employees to treat pregnancy as any other form of medical disability, as far as leave and insurance.

Equal opportunity legislation protects the right of a citizen to work and to get a fair wage based primarily on merit and performance. The EEOC seeks to maintain the existence of this right by holding labor unions, private employers, educational institutions, and government bodies responsible for its continuance. The four steps usually followed by the EEOC to hold organizations accountable are presented in Table 11.2.

Affirmative action programs are programs in the area of equal employment opportunity whose basic purpose is to eliminate barriers against and increase opportunities for underutilized or disadvantaged individuals.

In response to equal opportunity legislation, many organizations have **affirmative action programs.** Translated literally, *affirmative action* can be defined as positive movement. "In the area of equal employment opportunity, the basic purpose of positive movement or affirmative action is to eliminate barriers and increase opportunities for the purpose of increasing the utilization of underutilized and/or disadvantaged individuals."[9] The organization can judge how well it is eliminating these barriers by (1)

TABLE 11.2 Four steps followed by the EEOC to uphold equal opportunity legislation

1. The EEOC receives a charge alleging employment discrimination. Such a charge can be filed by an individual, by a group on behalf of an individual, or by any of the EEOC commissioners. Primary consideration for processing the charge is given to an approved state or local employment practices agency, if one exists. This agency has 60 days in which to act on the charge (120 days if the agency has been in operation less than a year). In the absence of such an agency, the EEOC is responsible for processing the charge. If neither the local agency nor the EEOC has brought suit within 180 days of the official filing date, the charging party may request a right-to-sue letter by which to initiate private civil action.
2. The EEOC investigates the charge to gather sufficient facts to determine the precise nature of the employer or union practice. If these facts show *probable cause* to believe that discrimination exists, the EEOC initiates step 3.
3. The EEOC conciliates or attempts to persuade the employer to voluntarily eliminate the discrimination. In this regard, the EEOC will provide extensive technical aid to any employer or union in voluntary compliance with the law. If conciliation fails, the EEOC initiates step 4.
4. The EEOC files suit in federal court (or the aggrieved parties may initiate their own private civil action). Court-ordered compliance with Title VII usually results in large expenses for the employer, often exceeding the cost of voluntary affirmative action.

determining how many minority and disadvantaged individuals it presently employs, (2) determining how many minority and disadvantaged individuals it should employ according to EEOC guidelines, and (3) comparing the numbers obtained in steps 1 and 2. If the two numbers are close to the same, employment practices within the organization probably should be maintained; if the numbers are not about the same, employment practices should be modified accordingly.

Modern management writers recommend that managers follow the guidelines of affirmative action not because they are mandated by law, but primarily because of the characteristics of today's labor supply.[10] According to these writers, more than one-half of the U.S. work force now consists of minorities, immigrants, and women. Because the overall work force is diverse in its makeup, employees in today's organizations will tend to be more diverse. Modern managers face the challenge of developing a productive work force from an increasingly diverse labor pool. This task is more formidable than simply complying with affirmative action laws.

BACK TO THE CASE

A successful recruitment effort at Universal requires recruiters to know where to locate the available human resources to fill open positions. These sources may be both within Universal and outside it. Because Universal Studios Florida is relatively new, sources within the company would be limited to other divisions already operating, such as Universal Studios Hollywood.

When making plans to open an operation like Universal Studios Florida, management had to plan for obtaining needed appropriate human resources along with other resources like equipment and real estate. To do this, management kept current on the possibilities of filling positions from within by maintaining some type of human resource inventory. This inventory helped management organize information about (1) the organizational histories and potential of various Universal employees, (2) the employees at other Universal locations who might be eligible to fill the positions needed to complete the work force in Florida, and (3) the relative abilities of various Universal employees to fill the necessary openings. Other sources of potential human resources outside Universal are competitors, public and private employment agencies, the readers of industry-related publications, and various types of educational institutions.

Universal management must also be aware of how the law influences its recruitment efforts. Basically, the law says that Universal recruitment practices cannot discriminate on the basis of race, color, religion, sex, or national origin. If recruitment practices at Universal are found to be discriminatory, the company is subject to prosecution by the Equal Employment Opportunity Commission.

Selection

Selection is choosing an individual to hire from all of those who have been recruited.

The second major step involved in managing human resources for the organization is **selection**—choosing an individual to hire from all those who have been recruited.[11] Hence, selection is dependent on and follows recruitment. The cartoon below lightheartedly illustrates the importance of selecting the right people for an organization.

The selection process typically is represented as a series of stages through which prospective employees must pass to be hired.[12] Each stage reduces the total group of prospective employees until, finally, one individual is hired. Figure 11.6 lists the specific stages of the selection process, indicates reasons for eliminating prospective employees at each stage, and illustrates how the group of potential employees is narrowed down to the individual who ultimately becomes the employee. Two tools often used in the selection process are testing and assessment centers.

"How many times do I have to tell Personnel we want a hip young crowd buying our products, not working for us?"

Stages of the Selection Process

Preliminary screening from records, data sheets, etc.
Preliminary interview

Intelligence tests
Aptitude tests

Personality tests
Performance references

Diagnostic interview

Physical examination
Personal judgment

Reasons for Elimination

Lack of adequate educational and performance record
Obvious misfit from outward appearance and conduct
Failure to meet minimum standards
Failure to have minimum necessary aptitude
Negative aspects of personality
Unfavorable or negative reports on past performance
Lack of necessary innate ability, ambition, or other qualities
Physically unfit for job
Remaining candidate placed in available position

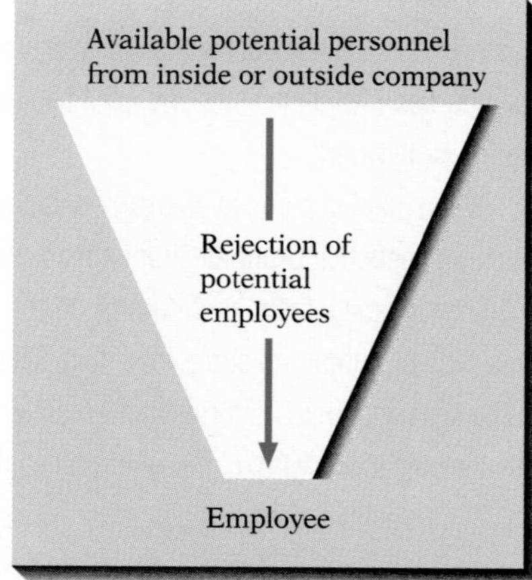

FIGURE 11.6 Summary of major factors involved in the selection process

GLOBAL HIGHLIGHT
Compaq Computer Company's International Selection Slipups

At times, managers must handle situations involving selection mistakes—hiring individuals who quickly leave the company voluntarily or are fired. The company's expenses in areas such as recruitment and selection are essentially lost when such a person leaves a company.

Growth at Compaq Computer Company, a computer manufacturer in Houston, Texas, has been phenomenal over recent years. The nine-year-old firm has recently had annual sales of $2.1 billion with $225 million in net profit. The company's expansion into international markets has been a significant reason for its success. Selection mistakes in this international arena are likely to be more expensive for the company than selection mistakes in the domestic arena. This expense difference exists simply because foreign assignments are usually more expensive for an American company like Compaq to set up and maintain than domestic assignments. Expenses incurred by a company with employees posted to a foreign country include salary based on the value of the U.S. dollar in that country, housing allowance, cost-of-living adjustments, transportation allowances, and tuition for children's private schools. ▶

If Compaq Computer Company were to make a selection error in assigning an employee to this plant in Singapore, it would be more expensive for the company than if the same selection error were made in the home office in Houston.

Testing

Testing is examining human resources for qualities relevant to performing available jobs.[13] Although many different kinds of tests are available for organizational use, they generally can be divided into four categories.[14]

1. *Aptitude tests.* Tests of aptitude measure the potential of an individual to perform a task. Some aptitude tests measure general intelligence, and others measure special abilities, such as mechanical, clerical, or visual abilities.
2. *Achievement tests.* Tests that measure the level of skill or knowledge an individual possesses in a certain area are called achievement tests. This skill or knowledge may have been acquired through various training activities or through experience in the area. The skill tests may include typing or keyboarding tests.
3. *Vocational interest tests.* Tests of vocational interest attempt to measure an individual's interest in performing various kinds of jobs and are administered on the assumption that certain people perform jobs well because the job activities are interesting to them. The basic purpose of this type of test is to help select the individuals who find certain aspects of an open position interesting.
4. *Personality tests.* Personality tests attempt to describe an individual's personality dimensions in such areas as emotional maturity, subjectivity, honesty,[15] and objectivity. Personality tests can be used advantageously if the personality characteristics needed to do well in a particular job are well defined and if individuals possessing those characteristics can be pinpointed and selected.

Several guidelines should be observed when tests are used as part of the selection process. First, care should be taken to ensure that the test being used is both valid and reliable. A test is *valid* if it measures what it is designed to measure and *reliable* if it measures similarly time after time.[16] Second, test results should not be used as the sole source of information to determine whether to hire someone. People change over time, and someone who doesn't score well on a particular test might still develop into a productive employee. Such factors as potential and desire to obtain a position should be assessed subjectively along with test scores in the final selection decision. A third guideline is that care should be taken to determine that the tests used are nondiscriminatory in nature; many tests contain language or cultural biases that may discriminate against minorities. This third guideline is especially important in that the EEOC has the authority to prosecute organizations that use discriminatory testing practices.

Assessment Centers

An **assessment center** is a program in which participants engage in and are evaluated on a number of individual and group exercises constructed to simulate important activities at the organizational levels to which these participants aspire.

Another tool often used to help increase the success of employee selection is the **assessment center.** Although the assessment center concept is discussed in this chapter primarily as an aid to selection, it also has been used as an aid in such areas as human resource training and organization development. The first industrial use of the assessment center is usually credited to AT&T.[17] Since AT&T's initial efforts, the assessment center concept has been growing quickly and today is used not only as a means for identifying individuals to be hired from outside an organization, but also for identifying individuals from inside the organization who should be promoted. Corporations that have used assessment centers extensively include J.C. Penney, Standard Oil of Ohio, and IBM.[18]

An assessment center has been defined as a program, not a place, in which participants engage in a number of individual and group exercises constructed to simulate important activities at the levels to which participants aspire.[19] These exercises might include such activities as participating in leaderless discussions, giving oral presentations, or leading a group in solving some assigned problem. Individuals performing the activities are observed by managers or trained observers who evaluate both their ability and their potential. In general, participants are assessed on the basis of (1) leadership, (2) organizing and planning ability, (3) decision making, (4) oral and written communication skills, (5) initiative, (6) energy, (7) analytical ability, (8) resistance to stress, (9) use of delegation, (10) behavior flexibility, (11) human relations competence, (12) originality, (13) controlling, (14) self-direction, and (15) overall potential.[20]

BACK TO THE CASE

After the initial screening of potential human resources, Universal Studios Florida was faced with the task of selecting the individuals to be hired from those who had been screened. Two tools that Universal could use in this selection process are testing and assessment centers. After screening potential employees for positions at Universal, management could administer aptitude tests, achievement tests, vocational interest tests, or personality tests to see which of the individuals screened had the qualities necessary to work a specific job. In using these tests, however, management had to make sure that the tests were both valid and reliable, that they were not the sole basis on which a selection decision was made, and that they were nondiscriminatory.

Universal can also use assessment centers to simulate the tasks necessary to perform jobs that workers will be performing. Individuals who performed well on these tasks would probably be more appropriate for the positions than would those who did poorly. The use of assessment centers might be particularly appropriate in evaluating applicants for positions such as ride attendant. Simulating this job would help give management an idea of how prospective attendants might interact with customers during actual rides.

Training

Training is the process of developing qualities in human resources that will enable them to be more productive.

After recruitment and selection, the next step in providing appropriate human resources for the organization is training. **Training** is the process of developing qualities in human resources that ultimately will enable them to be more productive and thus to contribute more to organizational goal attainment. The purpose of training is to increase the productivity of individuals in their jobs by influencing their behavior. Table 11.3 provides an overview of the types and popularity of training being offered by organizations.

The training of individuals is essentially a four-step process: (1) determining training needs, (2) designing the training program, (3) administering the training program,

TABLE 11.3 Types and popularity of training offered by organizations

Types of Training	*Percentage of Surveyed Companies That Offer This Type of Training*
1. Management skills and development	74.3
2. Supervisory skills	73.4
3. Technical skills/knowledge updating	72.7
4. Communication skills	66.8
5. Customer relations/services	63.8
6. Executive development	56.8
7. New methods/procedures	56.5
8. Sales skills	54.1
9. Clerical/secretarial skills	52.9
10. Personal growth	51.9
11. Computer literacy/basic computer skills	48.2
12. Employee/labor relations	44.9
13. Disease prevention/health promotion	38.9
14. Customer education	35.7
15. Remedial basic education	18.0

and (4) evaluating the training program. These steps are presented in Figure 11.7. Each of these steps is described in more detail in the sections that follow.

Determining Training Needs

The first step of the training process is determining the organization's training needs.[21] **Training needs** are the information or skill areas of an individual or group that require further development to increase the organizational productivity of that individual or group. Only if training focuses on these needs can it be of some productive benefit to the organization.

Training needs are information or skill areas of an individual or group that require further development to increase the organizational productivity of the individual or group.

The training of organization members is typically a continuing activity. Even individuals who have been with an organization for some time and who have undergone initial orientation and skills training need continued training to improve skills.

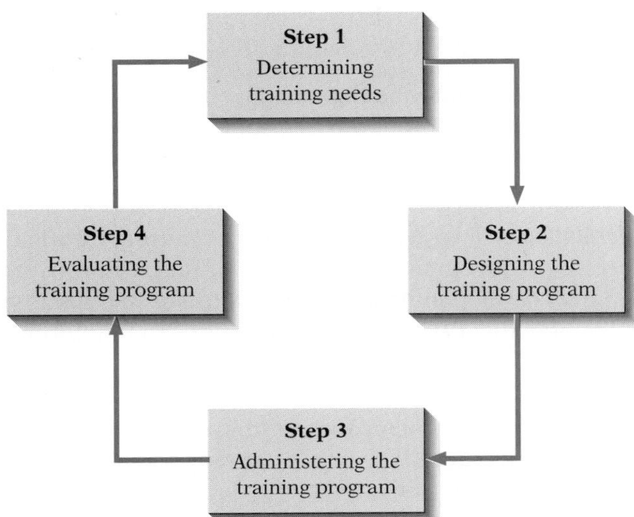

FIGURE 11.7 Steps of the training process

Several methods of determining which skills to focus on for more established human resources are available. The first method is evaluating the production process within the organization. Such factors as excessive rejected products, deadlines that are not met, and high labor costs are clues to existing levels of production-related expertise. Another method for determining training needs is direct feedback from employees on what they believe are the organization's training needs. Organization members may be able to verbalize clearly and accurately exactly what types of training they need to help them do a better job. A third way of determining training needs involves looking into the future. If the manufacture of new products or the use of newly purchased equipment is foreseen, some type of corresponding training almost certainly will be needed.

Designing the Training Program

Once training needs have been determined, a training program aimed at meeting those needs must be designed. Basically, designing a program entails assembling various types of facts and activities that will meet the established training needs. Obviously, as training needs vary, the facts and activities designed to meet those needs vary.

BACK TO THE CASE

After hiring, Universal Studios Florida must train new employees to be productive organization members. To train effectively, Universal must determine training needs, design a corresponding training program, and administer and evaluate the training program.

Designing a training program requires that Universal assemble facts and activities that address specific company training needs: information or skill areas that must be further developed in Universal employees in order to make them more productive. As time goes on, Universal should focus on training more established employees as well as newly hired employees.

As mentioned in the case, Universal Studios Florida is a new operation. In this situation, management should try to learn as much as possible from similar training programs that the company operates in other locations such as Universal Studios Hollywood. Knowing strengths and weaknesses of training programs at such company locations would help management at Universal Studios Florida design efficient and effective training programs for its operation.

Administering the Training Program

The next step of the training process is administering the training program, or actually training the individuals. Various techniques exist for both transmitting necessary information and developing needed skills in training programs. Several of these techniques are discussed in the sections that follow.

Techniques for Transmitting Information. Two techniques for transmitting information in training programs are lectures and programmed learning. Although it probably could be argued that these techniques develop some skills in individuals as well as transmit information to them, they are primarily devices for the dissemination of information.

A **lecture** is primarily a one-way communication situation in which an instructor trains by orally presenting information to an individual or group.

1. *Lectures.* Perhaps the most widely used technique for transmitting information in training programs is the lecture. The **lecture** is a primarily one-way communication in which an instructor orally presents information to a group of listeners. The instructor typically does most of the talking in this type of training situation. Trainees participate primarily through listening and note taking.

   An advantage of the lecture is that it allows the instructor to expose trainees to a maximum amount of information within a given time period. The lecture, however, also has its disadvantages:

> The lecture generally consists of a one-way communication: the instructor presents information to the group of passive listeners. Thus, little or no opportunity exists to clarify meanings, to check on whether trainees really understand the lecture material, or to handle the wide diversity of ability, attitude, and interest that may prevail among the trainees. Also, there is little or no opportunity for practice, reinforcement, knowledge of results, or overlearning. . . . Ideally, the competent lecturer should make the material meaningful and intrinsically motivating to his or her listeners. However, whether most lectures achieve this goal is a moot question. . . . These limitations, in turn, impose further limitations on the lecture's actual content. A skillful lecturer may be fairly successful in transmitting conceptual knowledge to a group of trainees who are ready to receive it; however, all the evidence available indicates that the nature of the lecture situation makes it of minimal value in promoting attitudinal or behavioral change.[22]

QUALITY HIGHLIGHT
Aetna Life & Casualty Company Trains via TV

When Aetna Life & Casualty Company evaluated its employee training program, it found that the key problem was not the quality of the instructors, the tools and styles of program presentations, the content, or even the materials that supplement the workshops. Instead, Aetna found that the key problem in the training program was enabling large numbers of geographically distributed trainees to attend programs given at a central location and providing rooms large enough for programs at additional locations.

Aetna realized that if it wanted to provide high-quality service to its customers, it had to train more than a select few of its employees who were able to travel to the program locations. Aetna's goal was to dramatically increase the number of its employees involved in training, thereby enhancing the quality of the service they could provide to their customers. Aetna executives and training personnel brainstormed ideas for disseminating their employee training more widely and came up with a plan to offer interactive training via television.

Aetna has developed the Aetna Television Network, which links 235 field offices with the home office. The Aetna Television Network enables the company to extend the use of its training programs by making them available throughout the country to office locations that normally would be unable to take advantage of them. As an example, over the past few years 810 Aetna employees have participated in a business-writing workshop in person, whereas over 3,000 have participated in them on Aetna's television network.

To reach its goal of providing high-quality service to its customers, Aetna uses the Aetna Television Network to provide interactive training for its employees.

Training employees via television is gaining in popularity throughout the business world. Television networks established for business training enable training programs to be extremely flexible. The same workshop can be heard by employees throughout a company at the same time or at different times as schedules allow. The trend toward using television as a vehicle for increasing the quality of training should continue to grow in the future. ▶

2. *Programmed Learning.* Another commonly used technique for transmitting information in training programs is called programmed learning. **Programmed learning** is a technique for instructing without the presence or intervention of a human instructor.[23] Small parts of information that require related responses are presented to individual trainees. The trainees can determine from the accuracy of their responses whether their understanding of the obtained information is accurate. The types of responses required of trainees vary from situation to situation but usually are multiple-choice, true-false, or fill-in-the-blank. Figure 11.8 on page 278 shows a portion of a programmed learning training package that could be

Programmed learning is a technique for instructing without the presence of a human instructor—small pieces of information requiring responses are presented to individual trainees. It has advantages and disadvantages.

Frame 3[24]

Program evaluation and review technique, PERT, is performed on a set of time-related activities and events which must be accomplished to reach an objective. The evaluation gives the expected completion time and the probability of completing the total work within that time. By means of PERT, it is possible not only to know the exact schedule, but also to control the various activities on a daily basis. Overlapping and related activities are reviewed. PERT is more practical for jobs involving a one-time effort than for repeat jobs. It is a planning-controlling medium designed to: (1) focus attention on key components, (2) reveal potential problem areas, (3) provide a prompt reporting on accomplishments, and (4) facilitate decision making.

The time-related activities and events are set forth by means of a PERT network (see figure 17). In this illustration, the circles represent events that are sequential accomplishment points; the arrows represent activities or the time-consuming elements of the program. In this type of network, an arrow always connects two activities. All of the activities and events must be accomplished before the end objective can be attained. The three numbers shown for each arrow or activity represent its estimated times, respectively, for the optimistic, most likely, and pessimistic times. The program starts with event no.1 and ends with event no.12. From calculations for the time required for each path from no.1 to no.12, it is found that path 1-2-4-8-11-12 requires the *longest time* and, hence, is the *critical path* because it controls the time required to complete the program. Toward it, managers would direct their attention in order to: (1) ensure that no breakdowns occur in it; (2) better the current times required, if possible; and (3) trade off time from the noncritical paths to the critical path, if the net effect is to reduce total time of the critical path.

Figure 17

PERT Network

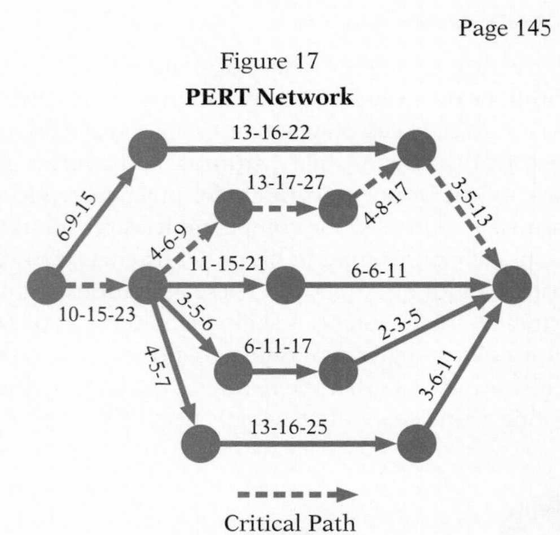

Indicate whether each of the following statements is true or false by writing "T" or "F" in the space provided.

__1. PERT centers its attention on social constraints.
__2. PERT is best applied to assembly-line operations.
__3. In PERT, the *critical path* is the path that requires the longest time.
__4. In the PERT network, circles represent events and the arrows represent activities.

Now turn to Answer Frame 3[24], page 146.

Answer frame 3[24]

1. False. PERT centers its attention on *time* constraints.
2. False. PERT is more practical for jobs involving a one-time effort than for repeat jobs.
3. True. In PERT, the critical path is the path that requires the *longest* time. If this path can be shortened, the program can be completed in a shorter time period.
4. True. Circles represent events that are sequential accomplishment points, and arrows represent activities or the time-consuming elements for the program.

You have completed chapter 24. Now turn to chapter 25.

FIGURE 11.8 Portion of a programmed learning training package featuring PERT

used to familiarize trainees with PERT (program evaluation and review technique).

As with the lecture method, programmed learning has both advantages and disadvantages. Among the advantages are that it can be computerized and students can learn at their own pace, know immediately if they are right or wrong, and participate actively. The primary disadvantage of this method is that no one is present to answer questions for the learner.

Techniques for Developing Skills. Techniques for developing skills in training programs can be divided into two broad categories: on-the-job and classroom. Techniques for developing skills on the job usually are referred to as **on-the-job training.** These techniques reflect a blend of job-related knowledge and experience and include coaching, position rotation, and special project committees. Coaching is direct critiquing of how well an individual is performing a job. Position rotation involves moving an individual from job to job to enable the person to obtain an understanding of the organization as a whole. Special project committees involve assigning a particular task to an individual to furnish him or her with experience in a designated area.[24]

On-the-job training is a training technique that blends job-related knowledge with experience in using that knowledge on the job.

Classroom techniques for developing skills also reflect a blend of job-related knowledge and experience. The skills addressed through these techniques can range from technical skills, such as computer programming, to interpersonal skills, such as leadership. Specific classroom techniques aimed at developing skills include various types of management games and role-playing activities. The most common format for management games requires small groups of trainees to make and then evaluate various management decisions. The role-playing format typically involves acting out and then reflecting on some people-oriented problem that must be solved in the organization.

Contrary to the typical one-way-communication role in the lecture situation, the skills instructor in the classroom encourages high levels of discussion and interaction among trainees, develops a climate in which trainees learn new behavior from carrying out various activities, acts as a resource person in clarifying related information, and facilitates learning through job-related knowledge and experience in applying that knowledge.[25] The difference between the instructional role used in information dissemination and the instructional role used in skill development is dramatic.[26]

Evaluating the Training Program

After the training program has been completed, management should evaluate its effectiveness.[27] Because training programs represent a cost investment—costs include materials, trainer time, and production loss while the individuals are being trained rather than doing their jobs—a reasonable return is required.

Basically, management must evaluate the training program to determine if it meets the needs for which it was designed. Answers to questions such as the following help determine training program effectiveness:

1. Has the excessive reject rate declined?
2. Are deadlines being met more regularly?
3. Are labor costs per unit produced decreasing?

If the answer to such questions is yes, the training program is at least somewhat successful, but perhaps its effectiveness could be enhanced through certain selective changes. If the answer is no, some significant modification to the training program is warranted.

In a recent survey of business people, 50 percent of the respondents thought that there would be no change in their sales per year if training programs for experienced salespeople were halted.[28] Such feedback should be scrutinized very closely to see if the sales training as it presently exists in respondents' companies should be discontinued, modified slightly, or drastically altered in an effort to make it more valuable. Based on the results of this survey, the training will probably be changed significantly to make it valuable to experienced salespeople. This survey illustrates the importance of gathering feedback aimed at making training more effective and efficient.

BACK TO THE CASE After training needs at Universal Studios Florida are determined and programs have been designed to meet those needs, the programs must be administered. In administering its training programs, Universal might use both the lecture technique and the programmed learning technique for transmitting information to trainees. For developing skills in trainees, Universal could use on-the-job-training methods, such as coaching, position rotation, or special project committees. For developing skills in a classroom setting, Universal could use instructional techniques such as role-playing activities. For example, waiters could be asked to handle customers who display various kinds of attitudes and have different-sized families. These situations then could be videotaped and reviewed as often as necessary from the standpoint of improving waiter-customer relationships.

Once a Universal training program has been completed, it must be evaluated to determine if it has met the training need for which it was designed. Training programs aimed at specific motor skills such as cash-register operating would be much easier to evaluate than training programs aimed at interpersonal skills such as developing customer relations. The evaluation of any training program at Universal, of course, should emphasize how to improve the program the next time it is implemented.

Performance Appraisal

Performance appraisal is the process of reviewing past productive activity to evaluate the contribution individuals have made toward attaining management system objectives.

Even after individuals have been recruited, selected, and trained, the task of making them productive within the organization is not finished. The fourth step in the process of providing appropriate human resources for the organization is **performance appraisal**—the process of reviewing individuals' past productive activity to evaluate the contribution they have made toward attaining management system objectives.[29] As with training, performance appraisal is a continuing activity that focuses on the more established human resources within the organization as well as on the relatively new ones. A main purpose is to furnish feedback to organization members about how they can become more productive and to help the organization in its quest for quality.[30] Performance appraisal also has been called performance review and performance evaluation. Table 11.4 describes several methods of performance appraisal.

DIVERSITY HIGHLIGHT
Performance Appraisal at US West Includes Diversity Focus

This manager at U.S. West is a part of the overall, companywide effort to encourage diversity. U.S. West's efforts resulted in the company receiving the Personnel Journal's Optima award.

US West is a telecommunications company that services much of the midwest and the Rocky Mountains. The company considers diversity to be so important to its future that evaluations of managerial performance include a focus on diversity.

To ensure that US West managers throughout the company fully support and encourage diversity within the company, top management has developed a "Pluralism Performance Menu" (PPM). The PPM is essentially a vehicle for appraising the top 125 corporate officers based on how well they promote diversity as a productive element within their operational units. As an example, through the PPM, managers are evaluated based on the overall performance of their units as well as on how accurately their units are representative of the labor force in their geographic areas. In New Mexico, for instance, 50 percent of US West employees are Hispanic. If managers hire and promote only white males from such a diverse employee population base, or otherwise fail to show support for the company's diversity efforts, their salaries may be reduced or they may lose their annual bonuses.

US West has recently received *Personnel Journal*'s Optimas Award for its outstanding efforts to promote workforce diversity. The award is given annually to companies that display excellence in human resource management in any one of ten categories, ranging from quality of life to global outlook. Two benchmarks used to describe US West's recent progress in promoting diversity are that women hold 52 per-

TABLE 11.4 Descriptions of several methods of performance appraisal

Name of Appraisal Method	*Description*
Rating scale	Individuals appraising performance use a form containing several employee qualities and characteristics to be evaluated (e.g., dependability, initiative, leadership). Each evaluated factor is rated on a continuum or scale ranging, for example, from 1 to 7 or more points.
Employee comparisons	Appraisers rank employees according to such factors as job performance and value to the organization. Only one employee can occupy a particular ranking.
Free-form essay	Appraisers simply write down their impressions of employees in paragraph form.
Critical-form essay	Appraisers write down particularly good or bad events involving employees as these events occur. Records of all documented events for any one employee are used to evaluate that person's performance.

cent of the management jobs and that 13 percent of the managers are African American. ▶

Why Use Performance Appraisals?

Most firms in the United States use some type of performance appraisal system.[31] Douglas McGregor has suggested the following three reasons for using performance appraisals in an organization:[32]

1. They provide systematic judgments to support salary increases, promotions, transfers, and sometimes demotions or terminations.
2. They are a means of telling subordinates how they are doing and of suggesting needed changes in behavior, attitudes, skills, or job knowledge; they let subordinates know where they stand with the boss.
3. They also are being used increasingly as a basis for the coaching and counseling of individuals by superiors.

Handling Performance Appraisals

If performance appraisals are not handled well, their benefits to the organization are minimized. Several guidelines can assist in increasing the appropriateness with which the appraisals are conducted.[33] The first guideline is that performance appraisals should stress both the performance within the position the individual holds and the success with which the individual is attaining objectives. Performance and objectives should become inseparable topics of discussion during performance appraisals. The second guideline is that appraisals should emphasize the individual in the job, not the evaluator's impression of observed work habits. In other words, emphasis should be more on an objective analysis of performance than on a subjective evaluation of habits. The third guideline is that the appraisal should be acceptable to both the evaluator and the subject. Both individuals should agree that the appraisal can be of some benefit to the organization and to the worker. The fourth, and last, guideline is that performance appraisals should be used as the basis for improving individuals' productivity within the organization[34] by making them better equipped to produce.

Potential Weaknesses of Performance Appraisals

To maximize the potential payoff of performance appraisals to the organization, managers must avoid several potential weaknesses of the appraisal process. Some of these potential weaknesses are (1) individuals involved in performance appraisals could view them as a reward-punishment situation, (2) the emphasis of performance appraisal could be put on completing paperwork rather than on critiquing individual performance, (3) individuals being evaluated could view the process as being unfair or biased, and (4) some type of negative reaction from a subordinate could be generated when the evaluator offers any unfavorable comments.[35]

To avoid these potential weaknesses, supervisors and employees should view the performance appraisal process as an opportunity to increase the worth of the individual through constructive feedback, not as a means of rewarding or punishing individuals through positive or negative comments. Paperwork should be seen only as an aid in providing this feedback, not as an end in itself. Also, care should be taken to make appraisal feedback as tactful and objective as possible to help minimize any negative reactions of the subject.

ETHICS HIGHLIGHT
Mobil Chemical Company Employee Challenges Performance Appraisal

Mobil Chemical and its former environmental affairs manager ended up in a federal courtroom, allowing a jury to decide whether the company wrongfully discharged the employee. Improper use of the performance process can subject a company to litigation by its employees.

Valcar Bowman, Jr., a former environmental affairs manager for Mobil Chemical, is suing the company that fired him. According to Bowman, a recent performance appraisal listed him as uncooperative, without specifying the form taken by his lack of cooperation. Shortly thereafter, Bowman was dismissed. Bowman claims that he was fired unjustly because he refused to falsify government environmental assessment reports.

Bowman was hired to manage Mobil's environmental affairs; at the time, the company assured Bowman that it was committed to a program of environmental excellence. Bowman says that he came to believe otherwise. As one of the last significant events while Bowman was still employed by Mobil, Bowman's staff was ordered to give to a company attorney an environmental report that the staff had written concerning Mobil's Bakersfield, California, plant. Bowman believes that this action was taken to keep the report out of the hands of the government's Environmental Protection Agency.

This case emphasizes the importance of management's properly using the performance appraisal process. Had they specifically documented legitimate ways in which Bowman had been uncooperative, they would have been in a stronger legal position.

The case will be heard by a jury in the U.S. District Court in Newark, New Jersey. If the court finds that Bowman's allegations are true, he will probably be able to recover substantial damages, because improper use of the performance appraisal process could subject the company to litigation initiated by employees. In addition, the company would probably find itself the target of additional investigations by the government regarding the validity and distribution of reports that it has generated. ▶

BACK TO THE CASE The final step in providing appropriate human resources at Universal Studios Florida is performance appraisal. This means that the contributions that Universal employees make to the attainment of management system objectives must be evaluated. Although in the next few years all employees having their performances appraised at Universal would be relatively new employees, ultimately the performance appraisal process at Universal should focus as well on more established employees.

It would be difficult to visualize a Universal employee who could not benefit from a properly conducted performance appraisal. Such an appraisal would stress activities on the job and effectiveness in accomplishing job objectives. An objective appraisal would provide Universal employees with tactful, constructive criticism that should help to increase their productivity. Handled properly, Universal's appraisals would not be a reward or a punishment in themselves, but rather an opportunity to increase employees' value to the company and help employees become more productive over time rather than being without guidance and perhaps moving toward an inevitable outcome of dismissal.

ACTION SUMMARY

Reread the learning objectives that follow. Each objective is followed by questions. Answering these questions accurately will help you retain the most important concepts discussed in this chapter. After answering each question, check your answer with the answer key at the end of this chapter. (*Hint:* If you have doubt regarding the correct response, consult the page whose number follows the answer.)

Circle: ***From studying this chapter, I will attempt to acquire:***

1. An overall understanding of how appropriate human resources can be provided for the organization.

T, F — **a.** An appropriate human resource is an individual whose qualifications are matched to job specifications.

a, b, c, d, e — **b.** The term *appropriate human resources* refers to: (1) finding the right number of people to fill positions; (b) individuals being satisfied with their jobs; (c) individuals who help the organization achieve management system objectives; (d) individuals who are ineffective; (e) none of the above.

2. An appreciation for the relationship among recruitment efforts, an open position, sources of human resources, and the law.

a, b, c, d, e — **a.** The process of narrowing a large number of candidates to a smaller field is: (a) rushing; (b) recruitment; (c) selection; (d) enlistment; (e) enrollment.

a, b, c, d, e — **b.** The characteristics of the individual who should be hired for the job are indicated by the: (a) job analysis; (b) job specification; (c) job description; (d) job review; (e) job identification.

3. Insights on the use of tests and assessment centers in employee selection.

a, b, c, d, e — **a.** The level of skill or knowledge an individual possesses in a particular area is measured by: (a) aptitude tests; (b) achievement tests; (c) acuity tests; (d) assessment tests; (e) vocational interest tests.

a, b, c, d, e — **b.** The following guideline does *not* apply when tests are being used in selecting potential employees: (a) the tests should be both valid and reliable; (b) the tests should be nondiscriminatory in nature; (c) the tests should not be the sole source of information for determining whether someone is to be hired; (d) such factors as potential and desire to obtain a position should not be assessed subjectively; (e) none of the above—all are important guidelines.

4. An understanding of how the training process operates.

a, b, c, d, e — **a.** Four steps involved in training individuals are: (1) designing the training program, (2) evaluating the training program, (3) determining training needs, (4) administering the training program. The correct sequence for these steps is:
(a) 1, 3, 2, 4
(b) 3, 4, 1, 2
(c) 2, 1, 3, 4

(d) 3, 1, 4, 2
(e) none of the above

T, F **b.** The lecture offers learners an excellent opportunity to clarify meanings and ask questions, since communication is two-way.

5. A concept of what performance appraisals are and how they best can be conducted.

a, b, c, d, e **a.** Performance appraisals are important in an organization because they: (a) provide systematic judgments to support promotions; (b) provide a basis for coaching; (c) provide a basis for counseling; (d) let subordinates know where they stand with the boss; (e) all of the above.

a, b, c, d, e **b.** To achieve the maximum benefit from performance evaluations, a manager should: (a) focus only on the negative aspects of performance; (b) punish the worker with negative feedback; (c) be as subjective as possible; (d) focus only on the positive aspects of performance; (e) use only constructive feedback.

INTRODUCTORY CASE WRAP-UP

"Getting the Right People for Universal Studios" (p. 263) and its related back-to-the-case sections were written to help you better understand the management concepts contained in this chapter. Answer the following discussion questions about this introductory case to further enrich your understanding of chapter content:

1. How important to an organization such as Universal Studios Florida is the training of employees? Explain.
2. What actions besides training must an organization such as Universal take to make employees as productive as possible? Why?
3. Based upon information in the case, what do you think will be the biggest challenge for Universal management in successfully providing appropriate human resources for the organization? Explain.

ISSUES FOR REVIEW AND DISCUSSION

1. What is the difference between appropriate and inappropriate human resources?
2. List and define the four major steps in providing appropriate human resources for the organization.
3. What is the purpose of recruitment?
4. How are job analysis, job description, and job specification related?
5. List the advantages of promotion from within.
6. Compare and contrast the management inventory card, the position replacement form, and the management manpower replacement chart.
7. List three sources of human resources outside the organization. How can these sources be tapped?
8. Does the law influence organizational recruitment practices? If so, how?
9. Describe the role of the Equal Employment Opportunity Commission.
10. Can affirmative action programs be useful in recruitment? Explain.
11. Define *selection*.
12. What is the difference between aptitude tests and achievement tests?
13. Discuss three guidelines for using tests in the selection process.
14. What are assessment centers?
15. List and define the four main steps of the training process.
16. Explain two possible ways of determining organizational training needs.
17. What are the differences between the lecture and programmed learning as alternative methods of transmitting information in the training program?
18. On-the-job training methods include coaching, position rotation, and special project committees. Explain how each of these methods works.
19. What are performance appraisals, and why should they be used?
20. If someone asked your advice on how to conduct performance appraisals, describe in detail what you would say.

ACTION SUMMARY ANSWER KEY

1. a. F, p. 264
b. c, p. 264
2. a. b, p. 264
b. b, p. 265
3. a. b, p. 273
b. d, pp. 273–274
4. a. d, pp. 274–275
b. F, pp. 276–277
5. a. e, p. 281
b. e, p. 282

CASE STUDY

Managing Diversity at Levi Strauss

MARY S. THIBODEAUX
University of North Texas

Among a growing number of progressive companies taking steps to recognize and value differences among workers is Levi Strauss. Levi Strauss may be said to have come a long way. For under its famous logo dated 1908 was the proclamation "None but white women and girls are employed." According to *Business Week,* Levi is now recognized as among the most culturally and ethnically diverse companies in the U.S., with 56 percent of its 23,000 employees belonging to minority groups. Fifteen percent of top management are non-white and 30 percent are women.

How has Levi Strauss made these strides? Several programs have been underway. Since the mid 1980s, CEO Robert Haas has taken the lead in working to eliminate the "glass ceiling" that often prevents women and minorities from being promoted rapidly (if at all) through the ranks. As of 1992, the company was spending $5 million a year on three-and-one-half day "valuing diversity" workshops for all senior managers; other managers are required to attend shorter versions. Blacks, Hispanics, lesbians and gay men are supported in their in-house networking efforts. In addition to a diversity council, a portion of managers' bonuses is even tied to meeting the goals in its "Aspiration Statement." This statement firmly and clearly states that employees aspire to appreciate diversity.

Diversity training will not change lifetime attitudes overnight. Its purpose is to make managers aware of the constellation of issues and needs involved. Although no two programs will be identical, many will involve the following components: (1) behavior awareness, (2) acknowledgment of biases and stereotypes, (3) focus on job performance, (4) avoidance of assumptions, and (5) modification of policy and procedure manuals.

Have these efforts paid off for Levi Strauss? Executives at this company clearly believe that the diversity program has. They say that "good intentions make good business," and that companies that want to hire the best people must seek to hire them without limitations because of such factors as race, gender, and ethnicity. Loraine Binion, internal audits manager and a black female says that there is an opportunity for anyone at Levi Strauss because of the mix that one sees in the executive ranks. Other executives believe that the diversity program has helped its product design and marketing efforts. The company credits one of its Argentine employees with thinking up the ideas for its very successful line of Dockers casual wear. While it is difficult for Levi Strauss to determine the exact bottom-line effect of this or any similar program, the company has been profitable for each of the years that it has implemented a diversity program.

Despite their advantages, diversity programs can lead to internal problems and strife. Levi has seen disagreements increase—some executives and other employees have even left the company over issues raised by the diversity program. It has also been the subject of a boycott by the Boy Scouts and some Christian groups because of its stand on homosexuality. But overall, Levi's executives believe that the diversity program's advantages outweigh its disadvantages. The message sent is a strong and long lasting one.

DISCUSSION QUESTIONS

1. How does managing diversity differ from affirmative action? Are affirmative action programs becoming things of the past?
2. In a company, such as Levi Strauss, that emphasizes recruiting a diverse work force, which aspect of job analysis would likely be adjusted to meet that emphasis? Why?
3. Were the problems that Levi Strauss experienced to be expected? Could they have been prevented?
4. What may be some indirect means of measuring the effectiveness of diversity programs?

CNN VIDEO CASE

The American Workforce: Retraining to Stay Competitive

In 1992, the United States government was spending $4 billion in retraining programs. Private industry was spending $40 billion. Indeed, a lot of money is being used to retrain U.S. workers, but—on a per-worker comparison basis—the small country of Germany spent twice the amount we spent. Retraining the American workforce requires a tremendous commitment by business and government alike if the country is to remain competitive in the global marketplace. Notes one expert, "Although we are still the most productive nation in the world, our productivity growth has slowed and is now lower than nearly all other industrialized nations." The same expert, speaking about the two-thirds of the American workforce

In the average U.S. company a manager supervises five people. Motorola's investment in worker training has allowed each one of its managers to supervise 23 workers.

that is not college-educated, adds, "An estimated 40 million workers need remedial and upgrade training in order [for the United States] to be fully internationally competitive."

It is predicted that more than 60 percent of new jobs will require *better* than a high-school education. However, 70 percent of people entering the workforce won't even have high-school diplomas. In addition to needing basic skills in reading, language, and math, workers need to be computer literate. With more emphasis on teamwork in many jobs, communication skills are essential. And, as workers are being increasingly empowered to make more decisions on the job, they are performing certain aspects of jobs that used to rest with management. Thus, some critical thinking and leadership skills are also necessary qualifications.

Some businesses have training programs for their workers. The programs range widely in their coverage and are usually job-specific, although some include basic general skills instruction as well. A full 98 percent of manufacturers with on-site training programs consider them to be effective.

At Frigidaire Company, in Edison, New Jersey, about one half of the company's fourteen hundred employees have taken part in the company program. "The classroom is like a lab," remarks one employee, "and when you're out on the floor working, it's like you're doing a forty-hour lab." Another employee emphasizes the broadening viewpoint gained through such additional education: "It's an opportunity for me to learn why this company or any other company does things that regular employees don't understand." Frigidaire offers classes from technical skills and safety to management and supervision.

At Motorola University, two hundred twenty-five instructors teach one hundred thirty-four courses year-round, and each of Motorola's hundred thousand employees worldwide must spend five days each year in the school. This cost Motorola $70 million in 1991, but the investment has paid off in productivity. At one Motorola cellular phone factory, productivity quadrupled; now one manager supervises twenty-three workers compared to most other U.S. factories, where one manager supervises only five people. This is an example of workers taking on many management functions themselves. One worker remembers: "When I first started at Motorola, I was on a line forty hours a week. I never did anything else—it was always production. As they encouraged me to take charge, I got involved with doing graphs, following goals, and from there it just kept building."

There is a causal relationship between a reputation for excellence and retraining. Companies known for excellence *all* have retraining programs to match their reputations; these companies consistently devote time and resources to building workers' skills. Nevertheless, employees of Fortune 500 companies spend a little more than 2 percent of their worktime in training, and that training is directed chiefly at managers, with line workers rarely receiving special training. Many small companies simply don't retrain.

VIDEO CASE QUESTIONS

1. Why do changing work styles require additional skills from employees?
2. Why is retraining the current workforce important to employers? Give at least two reasons.
3. Describe at least two alternatives to retraining.
4. Why do you think smaller companies are less likely to institute retraining programs?

CNN VIDEO EXERCISE

Keeping Frigidaire Cool through Job Analysis

ACTION GOAL: Prepare a job analysis for a position at Frigidaire, as part of an overall evaluation of the company's training program.

Imagine that, as part of an evaluation of its ongoing training operation, Frigidaire is preparing a detailed job analysis for each position within the company. Complete the following job analysis for the position of secretary to the executive vice president. The primary duties of the job are given. Use your knowledge and experience of secretarial work in other settings to consider the knowledge, skills, and abilities required for an executive secretary to organize and prepare a monthly operating report.

Job Analysis: Secretary to the Executive Vice President

Identifying Information:

Secretary to the Executive Vice President
Administration Unit
Date: ____________

Brief Summary of Job:
Secretary prepares all correspondence, memos, reports. Secretary initiates monthly reports and tabulates operating information. Secretary heads team of administration secretaries to coordinate work on annual, semi-annual, and monthly reports, including budgets and spreadsheets. Secretary makes appointments, travel arrangements, etc. Must maintain confidentiality.

Knowledge, Skills, and Abilities Required to Prepare Monthly Report

1. Knowledge Required

a. What subject matter areas are covered by the task?

____

b. What facts or principles must the secretary understand in these subject matter areas?

____

c. Describe the level, degree, and breadth of knowledge required in these areas or subjects.

____

2. Skills Required

a. What activities must the secretary perform with ease and precision?

____

b. What are the manual skills required to operate machines or to use tools?

____

3. Abilities Required

a. What is the nature and level of written and oral language ability required of the secretary?

____

b. What mathematical ability must the secretary have?

____

c. What reasoning or problem-solving ability must the secretary have?

____

d. What instructions must the secretary follow?

____

e. What interpersonal abilities are required? What supervisory or managing abilities?

____

CHAPTER

12

ORGANIZATIONAL CHANGE AND STRESS

STUDENT LEARNING OBJECTIVES

From studying this chapter, I will attempt to acquire:

1. A working definition of *changing an organization.*
2. An understanding of the relative importance of change and stability to an organization.
3. Some ability to know what kind of change should be made within an organization.
4. An appreciation for why individuals affected by a change should be considered when the change is being made.
5. Some facility in evaluating change.
6. An understanding of how organizational change and stress are related.

CHAPTER OUTLINE

INTRODUCTORY CASE
PepsiCo Reorganizes Pizza Hut and Taco Bell

FUNDAMENTALS OF CHANGING AN ORGANIZATION

Defining "Changing an Organization"
Change versus Stability

GLOBAL HIGHLIGHT
Banco Español de Credito

FACTORS TO CONSIDER WHEN CHANGING AN ORGANIZATION

The Change Agent

QUALITY HIGHLIGHT
Hutchinson Technology

Determining What Should Be Changed

ETHICS HIGHLIGHT
Sonoco

The Kind of Change to Make

DIVERSITY HIGHLIGHT
McDonald's Corporation

Individuals Affected by the Change
Evaluation of Change

CHANGE AND STRESS

Defining Stress
The Importance of Studying Stress
Managing Stress in Organizations

CASE STUDY
Managing Change in Transition: Kathleen A. Cote of ComputerVision

VIDEO CASE
Spirit under Stress: Susie Thompkins, Esprit de Corps

VIDEO EXERCISE
Effecting Change at Esprit de Corps

INTRODUCTORY CASE

PepsiCo Reorganizes Pizza Hut and Taco Bell

PepsiCo Inc. manufactures, sells, and distributes soft drink concentrates, syrups, and snack foods. The company also operates and develops franchise restaurants such as Pizza Hut and Taco Bell.

PepsiCo Inc., seeking to pump more expertise into its rapidly growing international restaurants, recently announced that it is combining the operations of its businesses abroad with those of its more mature domestic chains.

Under the realignment, PepsiCo turned to two executives who have propelled its restaurants above competitors amid the depressed U.S. fast-food business. Steve Reinemund, forty-two-year-old president and chief executive officer of Pizza Hut's U.S. business, and John Martin, forty-five, his counterpart at Taco Bell, now also are responsible for the overseas operations of their respective chains.

The reorganization underscores the growing importance of PepsiCo's overseas restaurants.

Those international divisions previously were run under a separate PepsiCo division, PepsiCo Food Service International, which also supplied PepsiCo's U.S. and Canadian restaurants with items such as straws, napkins, and cups.

The reorganization underscores the growing importance of PepsiCo's overseas restaurants, which have been quietly building sales at a 33 percent clip in recent years. Since 1980, under PepsiCo Food Service, Taco Bell and Pizza Hut have boosted annual sales overseas to more than $1 billion, while spreading to sixty-two countries from its original eighteen.

"Our international restaurant business has really come of age in the last few years," said Wayne Calloway, chairman and chief executive officer of PepsiCo, in a statement. A spokesman at PepsiCo, based in Purchase, New York, wouldn't say whether the reorganization involved an increase in spending abroad.

Some industry observers said the moves may have been spurred by the slumping U.S. fast-food market even though PepsiCo's restaurants, which also include Kentucky Fried Chicken, have generally outperformed the industry. "In the current climate [in the United States] it's better to be positioned more globally," says Ron Paul, president of Technomic Inc., a food-service consulting company.

The PepsiCo spokesman said the changes had been under consideration since 1986, when PepsiCo acquired Kentucky Fried Chicken. That chain has had a structure under which the international and domestic businesses reported to one executive. And PepsiCo's other divisions—soft drinks and snack foods—have a similar structure.

PepsiCo also said that Graham Butler, fifty-one, who was president of PepsiCo Food Service, would head his reorganized division, PepsiCo Food Systems Worldwide Distribution. The division will now serve as the distribution arm of supplies for PepsiCo's global restaurants.

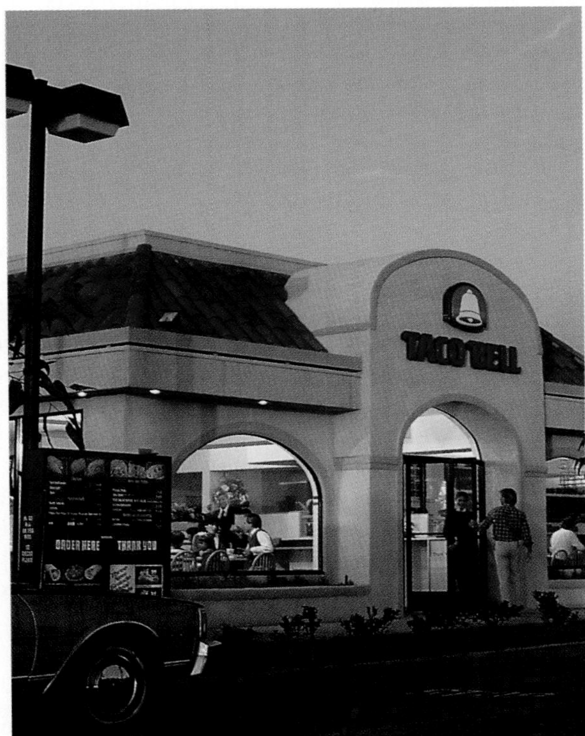

PepsiCo has recently undergone a reorganization in which the company's international restaurants, including Taco Bell and Pizza Hut—previously run by a separate PepsiCo international division—will now be run as part of the domestic operations of the chains.

From Michael J. McCarthy, "PepsiCo to Consolidate Its Restaurants, Combining U.S. and Foreign Operations," Wall Street Journal, October 30, 1990, A4.

WHAT'S AHEAD In essence, in the introductory case, Wayne Calloway, the PepsiCo chairman and chief executive officer, has decided to make certain changes within his company. Managers like Calloway ultimately are held accountable for making such changes successfully. As a result, Calloway and other managers undergoing the task of modifying an organization pay careful attention to the kinds of topics featured in this chapter. Topics such as the fundamental effects of changing an organization, the factors to consider when changing an organization, and stresses attending organizational changes must be faced thoughtfully and planned for carefully by managers responsible for those changes.

FUNDAMENTALS OF CHANGING AN ORGANIZATION

Thus far, discussion in this "Organizing" section of the text has centered on the fundamentals of organizing, furnishing appropriate human resources for the organization, authority, delegation, and responsibility. This chapter focuses on changing an organization.

Defining "Changing an Organization"

Changing an organization is the process of modifying an existing organization to increase organizational effectiveness.

Changing an organization is the process of modifying an existing organization. The purpose of organizational modifications is to increase organizational effectiveness—that is, the extent to which an organization accomplishes its objectives. These modifications can involve virtually any organizational segment and typically include changing the lines of organizational authority, the levels of responsibility held by various organization members, and the established lines of organizational communication.

Most managers agree that if an organization is to be successful, it must change continually in response to significant developments, such as customer needs, technological breakthroughs, and government regulations. The study of organizational change is extremely important because all managers at all organizational levels are faced throughout their careers with the task of changing their organization. Managers who determine appropriate changes to make in organizations and then can implement such changes enable their organizations to be more flexible and innovative.[1] Because change is such a fundamental and necessary part of organizational existence, managers who can successfully implement change are very important to organizations of all kinds.

Many managers consider change to be so critical to the success of the organization that they encourage employees to continually search for areas in which beneficial organizational change can be made. In a classic example, General Motors has provided employees with a "think list" to encourage them to develop ideas for organizational change and to remind them that change is important to the continued success of GM. The think list contained the following questions.[2]

1. Can a machine be used to do a better or faster job?
2. Can the fixture now in use be improved?
3. Can handling of materials for the machine be improved?
4. Can a special tool be used to combine the operations?
5. Can the quality of the part being produced be improved by changing the sequence of the operation?
6. Can the material used be cut or trimmed differently for greater economy or efficiency?
7. Can the operation be made safer?

8. Can paperwork regarding this job be eliminated?
9. Can established procedures be simplified?

Change versus Stability

In addition to organizational change, some degree of stability is a prerequisite for long-term organizational success.[3] Figure 12.1 presents a model developed by Hellriegel and Slocum that shows the relative importance of change and stability to organizational survival. Although these authors use the word *adaptation* in their model rather than *change*, the two terms are essentially synonymous. This model stresses that the greatest probability of organizational survival and growth exists when both stability and adaptation are high within the organization (number 3 on the model). The organization without stability to complement or supplement change is at a definite disadvantage. When stability is low, the probability for organizational survival and growth declines. Change after change without stability typically results in confusion and employee stress.[4]

GLOBAL HIGHLIGHT
Banco Español de Credito: Too Much Change at a Spanish Bank?

Too much change without stability can be a problem for the United States as well as for foreign organizations. Mario Conde, chairman of the Spanish bank *Banco Español de Credito (Banesto),* has recently been the target of considerable criticism. Simply stated, critics indicate that Conde has failed to revive quickly enough the sluggish, old-fashioned Spanish bank that he took over in 1987. Conde responds to such criticism by saying that, by the end of the century, *Banesto* will be the largest and most

Banco Español de Credito *will be the largest and most profitable group in Spain by the end of the century according to Mario Conde, chairman.*

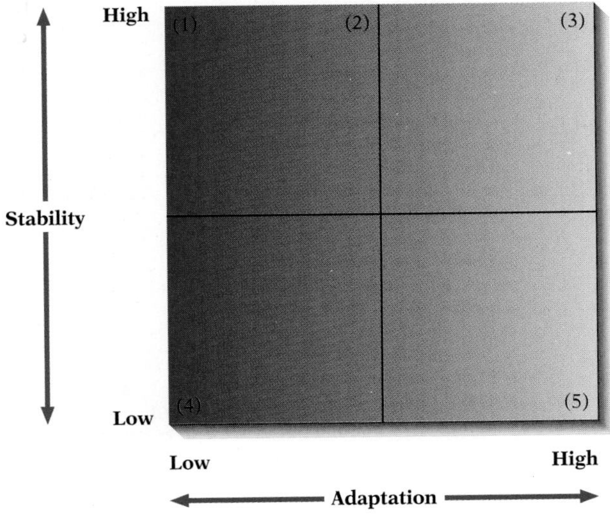

(1) High death probability (slow)
(2) High survival probability
(3) High survival and growth probability
(4) Certainty of death (quick)
(5) Certainty of death (quick)

FIGURE 12.1 Adaptation, stability, and organizational survival profitable industrial group in Spain. Conde does not believe that he has been slow in turning *Banesto* around; a turnaround of this nature simply takes time. If too many changes are made too quickly in a financial institution such as *Banesto,* a crisis can result. Employees need time to get used to one change before another change is made. While Conde wants *Banesto* to be a successful international bank, he is careful not to create organizational problems by making the timetable for achieving success too short. ▶

BACK TO THE CASE The foregoing information provides several insights about how Calloway should make a decision like changing PepsiCo's organization structure as it relates to Pizza Hut and Taco Bell. As an example, Calloway should evaluate such a change in relation to the degree that the changes would better enable PepsiCo to accomplish its objectives. Calloway should understand that making such changes is extremely important; if PepsiCo is to have continued success over the long run, such changes will probably have to be made a number of times. In fact, appropriate change is so important to a company like PepsiCo that Calloway may want to consider initiating some type of program that would encourage employees to submit their ideas on how to change the company in order to increase its effectiveness. When considering possible changes, however, Calloway will have to keep in mind that some level of stability is also necessary if his company is to survive and grow over the long term.

FACTORS TO CONSIDER WHEN CHANGING AN ORGANIZATION

How managers deal with the major factors to be considered when changing an organization determines to a great extent how successful an organizational change will be. These factors are (1) the change agent, (2) determining what should be changed, (3) the kind of change to make, (4) individuals affected by the change, and (5) evaluation of change. Although the following sections discuss each of these factors individually, Figure 12.2 makes the point that their collective influence ultimately determines the success of a change.

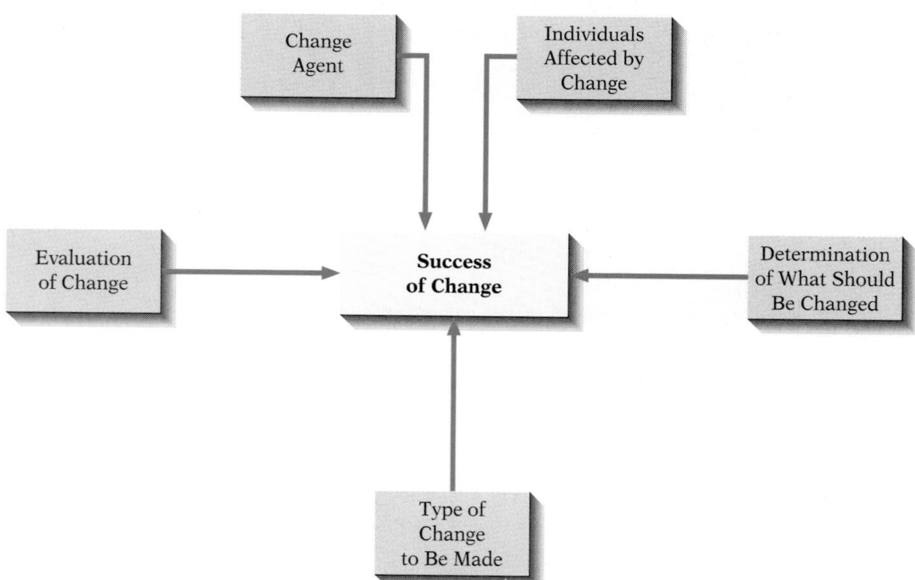

FIGURE 12.2 The collective influence of five major factors on the success of changing an organization

The Change Agent

Perhaps the most important factor to be considered by managers when changing an organization is determining who will be the **change agent**—anyone inside or outside the organization who tries to effect change.[5] The change agent might be a self-designated manager within the organization or possibly an outside consultant hired because of a special expertise in a particular area. Although in reality the change agent may not be a manager, the terms *manager* and *change agent* are used synonymously throughout this chapter.

A **change agent** is an individual inside or outside the organization who tries to modify an existing organizational situation.

Several special skills are necessary for success as a change agent, including the ability to determine how a change should be made, to solve change-related problems, and to use behavioral science tools to influence people appropriately during the change. Perhaps the most overlooked skill of successful change agents is the ability to determine how much change employees can withstand.[6]

Over all, managers should choose change agents who possess the most expertise in the areas suggested by the necessary special skills. A potentially beneficial change for the organization might not result in any advantages if the wrong person is designated to make the change.

QUALITY HIGHLIGHT
Outside Change Agent Brings Quality to Hutchinson Technology

Change agents can come from either inside or outside the organization. The Hutchinson Technology company used a change agent from outside the company to raise the quality of products the company produced.

About ten years ago, Hutchinson Technology Inc. (HTI), a manufacturer of precision computer components, hired Rath & Strong, a management consulting firm, to introduce quality management into its manufacturing operations. HTI management was very interested in the quality movement and wanted to reap the benefits of producing quality products. The process was so successful that HTI management decided to expand programs initiated by Rath & Strong to include non-manufacturing departments like marketing and human resources. Hutchinson was so excited with the results of Rath & Strong's programs that HTI management invited the consultants to return simply to see the significant improvements to the original process that had materialized.

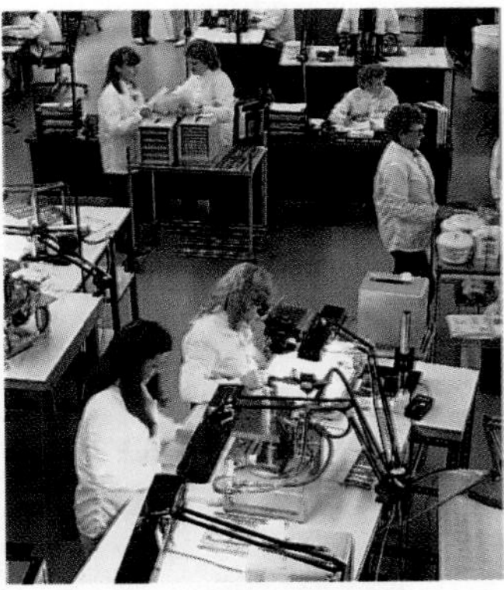

Hutchinson Technology Inc., a manufacturer of precision computer components, employed a change agent company to introduce quality management into its manufacturing operations.

Rath & Strong were so successful as outside change agents for quality that they enlarged and refined the Hutchinson process and began to offer it to other clients as Internal Product Quality (IPQ). The relationship between HTI and Rath & Strong continues to evolve: the two companies share discoveries they make in improvements to the quality management process. Such practices exemplify how rewarding outside change agents can be to a company. According to Dan Ciampa, president of Rath & Strong, his change agent company uses IPQ to help companies improve the way they work when they are not facing a crisis. IPQ allows them to work at their own pace and to learn about themselves, their products, and their internal clients and providers. ▶

BACK TO THE CASE Because Wayne Calloway undoubtedly had the main role in deciding to make the Taco Bell/Pizza Hut change at PepsiCo as well as actually implementing the change, for this particular change Calloway is the change agent. Calloway probably designated himself change agent because of his ability to determine if and how this particular type of change within PepsiCo should be made. After all, Calloway is probably the one manager in the company best suited to evaluate the advantages and disadvantages of having a separate international restaurant division for Pizza Huts and Taco Bells, as opposed to having every restaurant in a particular chain report to a single U.S. manager regardless of the restaurant's location.

As change agent, Calloway must have the ability to use behavioral science tools to influence organization members during the implementation of the Pizza Hut/Taco Bell change. Examples: Calloway must determine how much change these PepsiCo employees can withstand. He must influence his staff so its members learn to work together in their new divisions. And he must implement his changes gradually, so that employees will not be overwhelmed. Over all, the ability to use behavioral science tools will help Calloway to be successful in implementing his Pizza Hut/Taco Bell change at PepsiCo.

Determining What Should Be Changed

Another major factor managers should consider is exactly what should be changed within the organization. In general, managers should make changes that increase organizational effectiveness.

It has been generally accepted for many years that organizational effectiveness is the result primarily of organizational activities centering around three main classes of factors: (1) people, (2) structure, and (3) technology. **People factors** are attitudes, leadership skills, communication skills, and all other characteristics of the human resources within the organization. Organizational controls, such as policies and procedures, constitute **structural factors.** And **technological factors** are any types of equipment or processes that assist organization members in the performance of their jobs.

People factors are attitudes, leadership skills, communication skills, and all other characteristics of the organization's employees.

Structural factors are organizational controls, such as policies and procedures.

Technological factors are any types of equipment or processes that assist organization members in the performance of their jobs.

For an organization to maximize effectiveness, appropriate people must be matched with appropriate technology and appropriate structure. Thus, people factors, technological factors, and structural factors are not independent determinants of organizational effectiveness. Instead, as Figure 12.3 shows, organizational effectiveness is determined by the relationship of these three factors.

ETHICS HIGHLIGHT
Attitude Change is the Key to Sonoco Establishing a Socially Responsible Position on Job Safety

Progressive companies seriously pursue the challenge of establishing a safe environment in which their employees work. They pursue this challenge not only because fewer accidents means a more productive workforce, but also because companies have a serious responsibility to society to provide a workplace in which employees can be free from harm. The Sonoco Products Company, an organization that produces primarily paperboard packaging, had to change employee attitudes in order to reshape its company into one that is appropriately responsible to society for job safety.

The Sonoco Products Company had to change its employees' attitudes in order to work toward higher standards of job safety. This socially responsible attitude has helped to ensure the company's success.

The Corrugating Department of Sonoco Products Company's Paper Division in Hartsville, South Carolina, recently reached a milestone when its employees completed their first year of injury-free work. As a result, the Paper Division was presented the annual Best Safety Record award by the Southern Pulp & Paper Safety Association. In order to achieve such an accomplishment, management had to instill in employees the attitude that job safety is important and deserves serious attention from everyone at Sonoco. This new attitude was established primarily through a company program called STOP—Safety Training Observation Program. STOP is a program designed and implemented to make employees understand the importance of job safety and to help them develop safe work habits. STOP was successful at Sonoco because, during the program, management continually stressed job safety as an area of importance to the company, employees and management shared responsibility for creating a safe work environment, and management and workers constantly focused on being safe in the workplace. Once organization members at Sonoco developed the attitude that a safe

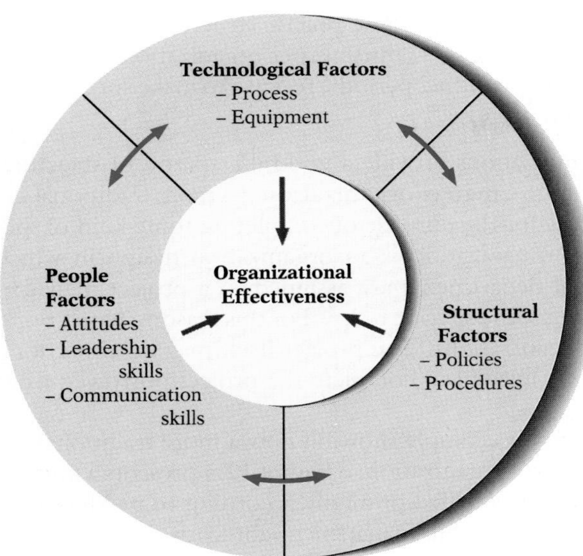

FIGURE 12.3 Determination of organizational effectiveness by the relationship of people, technological, and structural factors

work environment is indeed important, actually establishing such an environment became a realistic objective for management. ▶

The Kind of Change to Make

The kind of change to make is a third major factor that managers should consider when changing an organization. Although managers can choose to change an organization in many different ways, most changes can be categorized as one of three kinds: (1) technological change, (2) structural change, or (3) people change. These three kinds obviously correspond to the three main determinants of organizational effectiveness. Each kind of change is named for the one determinant that the change emphasizes over the other two.

For example, **technological change** emphasizes modifying the level of technology within a management system. Because technological change often involves outside experts and highly technical language, structural change and people change are the two kinds discussed in more detail here.

Technological change is a type of organizational change that emphasizes modifying the level of technology in the management system.

Structural Change

Structural change emphasizes increasing organizational effectiveness by changing controls that influence organization members during the performance of their jobs. The following sections further describe this approach and discuss matrix organizations (organizations modified to complete a special project) as an example of structural change.

Describing Structural Change. **Structural change** is change aimed at increasing organizational effectiveness through modifications to the existing organizational structure. These modifications can take several forms: (1) clarifying and defining jobs; (2) modifying organizational structure to fit the communication needs of the organization; and (3) decentralizing the organization to reduce the cost of coordination, increase the controllability of subunits, increase motivation, and gain greater flexibility.[7] Although structural change must include some consideration of people and technology to be successful, its primary focus is obviously on changing organizational structure. In general, managers choose to make structural changes within the organization if information they have gathered indicates that the present organizational structure is

Structural change is a type of organizational change that emphasizes modifying an existing organizational structure.

the main cause of organizational ineffectiveness. The precise structural change managers make varies from situation to situation, of course. After organizational structure has been changed, management should conduct periodic reviews to make sure that the change is accomplishing its intended purpose.[8]

A **matrix organization** is a traditional organizational structure that is modified primarily for the purpose of completing some type of special project.

Matrix Organizations. Matrix organizations provide a good illustration of structural change. According to C. J. Middleton, a **matrix organization** is a more traditional organization that is modified primarily for the purpose of completing some kind of special project.[9] In essence, a matrix organization is an organization design in which individuals from various functional departments are assigned to a project manager, who is responsible for accomplishing some specific task.[10] For this reason, matrix organizations are also called project organizations. The project itself may be either long term or short term, with employees needed to complete the project borrowed from various organizational segments.

John F. Mee has developed a classic example showing how a more traditional organization can be changed into a matrix organization.[11] Figure 12.4 presents a portion of a traditional organizational structure divided primarily according to product line. Although this design could be generally useful, managers might learn that it makes it impossible for organization members to give adequate attention to three government projects of extreme importance to long-term organizational success.

Figure 12.5 presents one way of changing this more traditional organizational structure into a matrix organization to facilitate completion of the three government projects. A manager would be appointed for each of the three projects and allocated personnel with appropriate skills to complete the project. The three project managers would have authority over the employees assigned to them and be accountable for the performance of those people. Each of the three project managers would be placed on the chart in Figure 12.5 in one of the three boxes labeled Venus Project, Mars Project, and Saturn Project. As a result, work flow related to each project would go from right to left on the chart. After the projects were completed, the organization chart could be changed back to its original design, if that design is more advantageous.

There are several advantages and disadvantages to making structural changes such as those reflected by the matrix organization. Among the major advantages are that such structural changes generally result in better control of a project, better customer relations, shorter project development time, and lower project costs. Accompanying

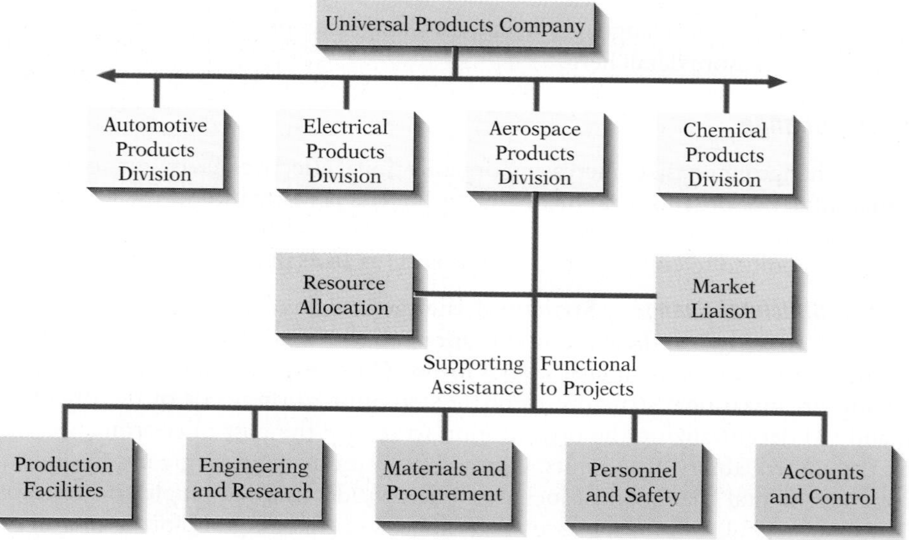

FIGURE 12.4 Portion of a traditional organizational structure based primarily on product

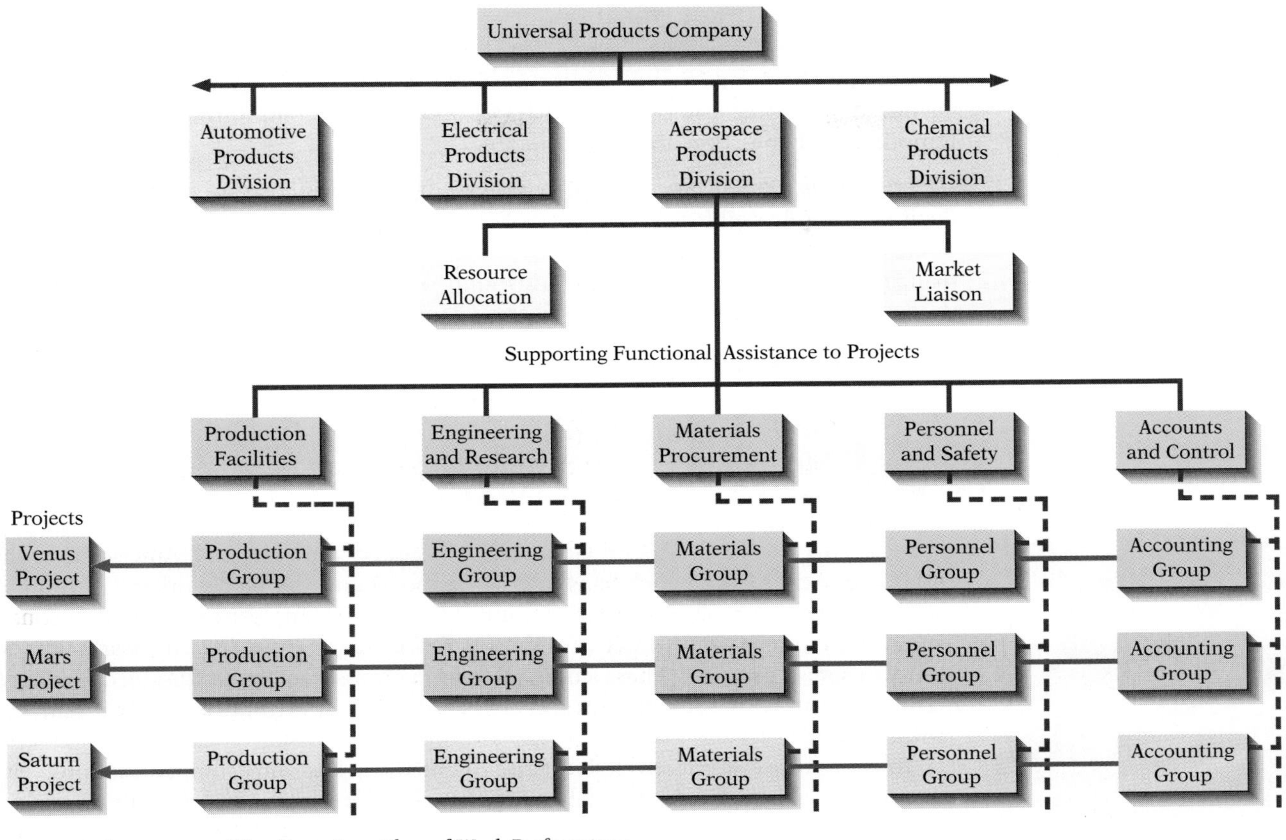

FIGURE 12.5 Traditional organization chart transformed into matrix organization

these advantages, however, are the disadvantages that such structural changes also generally create more complex internal operations, which commonly cause conflict, encourage inconsistency in the application of company policy, and result in a more difficult situation to manage.[12] One point, however, is clear. For a matrix organization to be effective and efficient, organization members must be willing to learn and execute somewhat different organizational roles.[13] The significance of the advantages and disadvantages relative to the success of changing a specific organization obviously varies from situation to situation.

BACK TO THE CASE There are different types of changes that a manager like Wayne Calloway can make in an organization. As examples, such managers can change technological factors, people factors, and structural factors in order to increase organizational effectiveness. Calloway's change regarding Pizza Hut and Taco Bell restaurants focuses mainly on structural factors. Before the change, restaurant managers of Pizza Huts and Taco Bells in foreign countries reported to the head of a special division that existed just for them. Meanwhile, managers of Pizza Huts and Taco Bells in the United States reported to a different U.S. division head. As a result of Calloway's change, all Pizza Hut managers throughout the world will report to a designated division head, and all Taco Bell managers throughout the world will report to a different division head. Both of these new division heads will be headquartered in the United States.

People Change

Although successful people change also involves some consideration of structure and technology, the primary emphasis is on people. The following sections discuss people change and examine grid organization development, one commonly used means of attempting to change organization members.

People change is changing certain aspects of organization members to increase organizational effectiveness.

Describing People Change. **People change** emphasizes increasing organizational effectiveness by changing certain aspects of organization members. The focus of this kind of change is on such factors as employees' attitudes and leadership skills. In general, managers should attempt to make this kind of change when human resources are shown to be the main cause of organizational ineffectiveness.

DIVERSITY HIGHLIGHT
McDonald's Corporation Is Changing the Way Employees Think about Disabled Workers

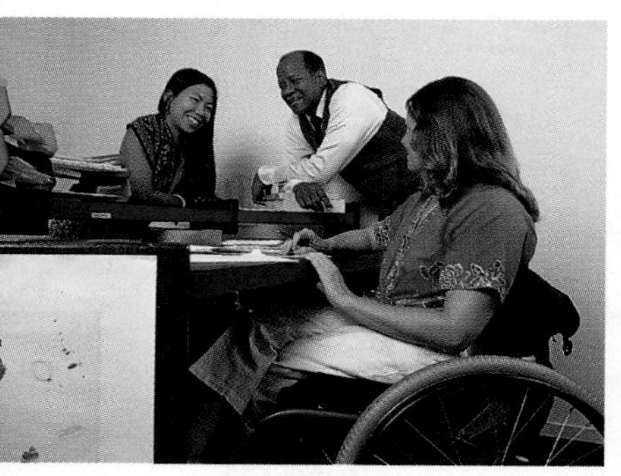

Many companies, including McDonald's, have developed specific programs designed to help employees learn to appropriately interact with workers who are diabled. The 1990 Americans with Disabilities Act created some mandates to prevent discrimination against people who are disabled.

In 1990, President George Bush signed into law the Americans with Disabilities Act (ADA), which bans discrimination against disabled workers. Although some employers may be concerned about hiring the disabled, history shows that companies like DuPont and Target Stores have found that employing the disabled is a sound business practice. These companies have found that many disabled workers make loyal, enthusiastic employees and provide valuable contributions in obtaining organizational goals.

In order to most effectively integrate disabled workers into companies, however, some managers have found that they must change the way that employees think of disabled workers. As a result, these managers have developed specific programs to prepare their current employees for appropriate interaction with disabled workers. For example, McDonald's Corporation sponsors awareness training for its employees, which allows them to role-play as disabled workers. Such training allows employees to experience how disabled workers may actually feel, and how they may react to other employees' statements concerning them or attitudes about them. Following the advice of companies with a successful history of employing the disabled, however, such awareness training should avoid prejudging the disabled's limitations. Often, employees who have not had direct experience with disabled workers overestimate their limitations. As a result, disabled workers may not be challenged as much as they should be.

Overall, hiring disabled employees can provide significant benefits, including obtaining loyal and productive workers and managers. In addition, hiring disabled employees can result in important consumer-related benefits: consumers commonly develop a deep sense of respect for companies that hire the disabled. ▶

Organization development (OD) is the process that emphasizes changing an organization by changing organization members and bases these changes on an overview of structure, technology, and all other organizational ingredients.

The process of people change can be referred to as **organization development (OD).** Although OD focuses mainly on changing certain aspects of people, these changes are based on an overview of structure, technology, and all other organizational ingredients. Figure 12.6 demonstrates this organizational overview approach by showing both overt and covert organizational components considered during OD efforts. Overt factors are generally easily detectable and pictured as the tip of an organizational iceberg; covert factors are usually more difficult to assess and therefore are displayed as the part of the organizational iceberg that is "under water."

Grid organization development (grid OD) is a commonly used organization development technique based on a theoretical model called the managerial grid.

Grid OD. One commonly used OD technique for changing people in organizations is called **grid OD.**[14] The **managerial grid** is a basic model describing various managerial styles; it is used as the foundation for grid OD. The managerial grid is based on the premise that various managerial styles can be described by means of two primary atti-

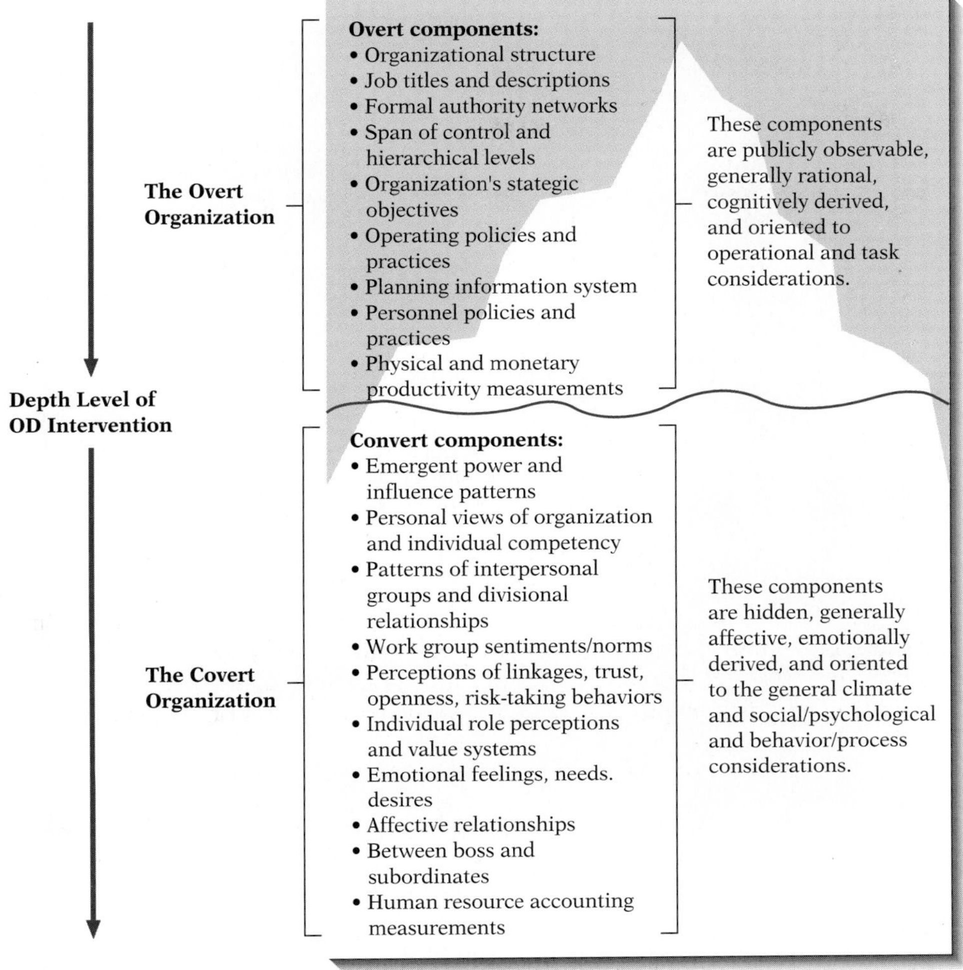

Overt components:
• Organizational structure
• Job titles and descriptions
• Formal authority networks
• Span of control and hierarchical levels
• Organization's stategic objectives
• Operating policies and practices
• Planning information system
• Personnel policies and practices
• Physical and monetary productivity measurements
These components are publicly observable, generally rational, cognitively derived, and oriented to operational and task considerations.
The Overt Organization
Depth Level of OD Intervention
Convert components:
• Emergent power and influence patterns
• Personal views of organization and individual competency
• Patterns of interpersonal groups and divisional relationships
• Work group sentiments/norms
• Perceptions of linkages, trust, openness, risk-taking behaviors
• Individual role perceptions and value systems
• Emotional feelings, needs. desires
• Affective relationships
• Between boss and subordinates
• Human resource accounting measurements
These components are hidden, generally affective, emotionally derived, and oriented to the general climate and social/psychological and behavior/process considerations.
The Covert Organization

FIGURE 12.6 The organizational iceberg

tudes of the manager: concern for people and concern for production. Within this model, each attitude is placed on an axis, which is scaled 1 through 9, and is used to generate five managerial styles. Figure 12.7 on page 302 shows the managerial grid, its five managerial styles, and the factors that characterize each of these styles.

A **managerial grid** is a theoretical model based on the premise that concern for people and corncern for production are the two primary attitudes that influence management style.

The central theme of this managerial grid is that 9,9 management (as shown on the grid) is the ideal managerial style. Managers using this style have high concern for both people and production. Managers using any other style have lesser degrees of concern for people or production and are thought to reduce organizational success accordingly. The purpose of grid OD is to change organization managers so they will use the 9,9 management style.

How is a grid OD program conducted? The program has six main training phases for all managers within the organization. The first two phases focus on acquainting managers with the managerial grid concept and assisting them in determining which managerial style they most commonly use. The last four phases of the grid OD program concentrate on encouraging managers to adopt the 9,9 management style and showing them how to use this style within their specific job situation. Emphasis throughout the program is on developing teamwork within the organization.

Some evidence suggests that grid OD is useful because it is effective in enhancing profit, positively changing managerial behavior, and positively influencing managerial attitudes and values.[15] Grid OD probably will have to undergo more rigorous testing

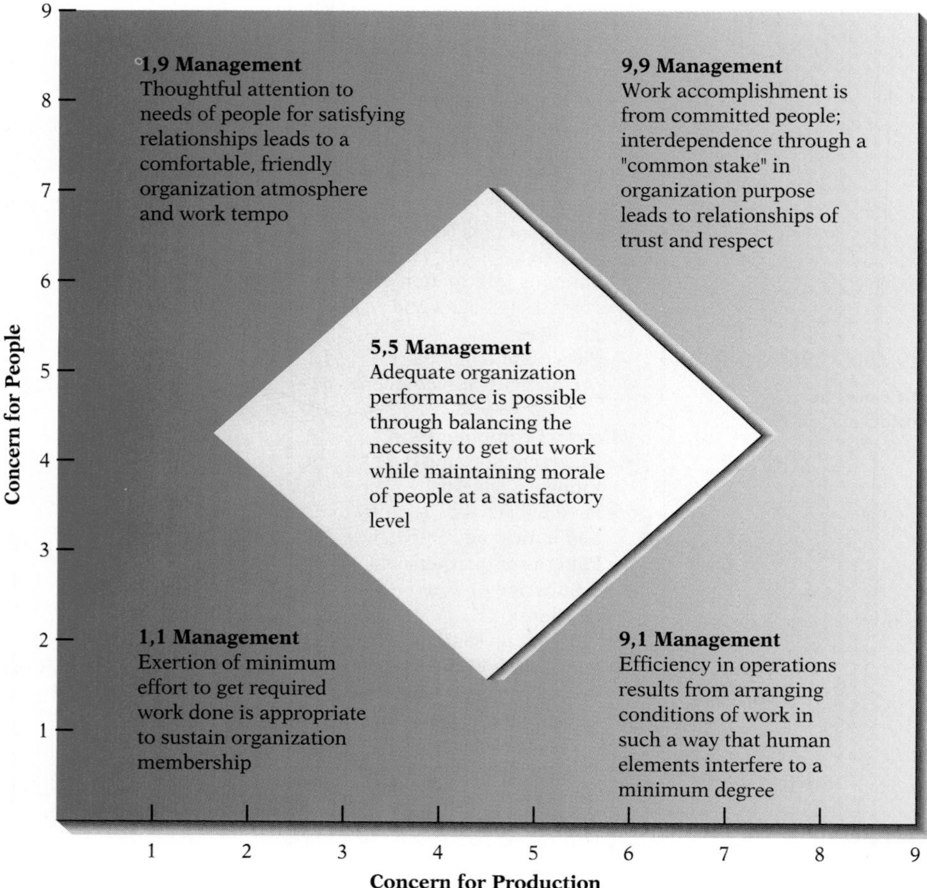
1,9 Management
Thoughtful attention to needs of people for satisfying relationships leads to a comfortable, friendly organization atmosphere and work tempo
9,9 Management
Work accomplishment is from committed people; interdependence through a "common stake" in organization purpose leads to relationships of trust and respect
5,5 Management
Adequate organization performance is possible through balancing the necessity to get out work while maintaining morale of people at a satisfactory level
1,1 Management
Exertion of minimum effort to get required work done is appropriate to sustain organization membership
9,1 Management
Efficiency in operations results from arranging conditions of work in such a way that human elements interfere to a minimum degree
Concern for People
Concern for Production
1 2 3 4 5 6 7 8 9

FIGURE 12.7 The managerial grid

for an extended period of time, however, before conclusive statements about it can be made.

The Status of Organization Development. If the entire OD area is taken into consideration, changes that emphasize both people and the organization as a whole seem to have inherent strength. There are, however, several commonly voiced weaknesses of OD efforts. These weaknesses indicate that (1) the effectiveness of an OD program is difficult to evaluate, (2) OD programs are generally too time consuming, (3) OD objectives are commonly too vague, (4) the total costs of an OD program are difficult to pinpoint at the time the program starts, and (5) OD programs are generally too expensive.[16]

These weaknesses, however, should not eliminate OD but should indicate areas to perfect within it. Managers can improve the quality of OD efforts by (1) systematically tailoring OD programs to meet the specific needs of the organization, (2) continually demonstrating as part of the program exactly how people should change their behavior, and (3) conscientiously changing organizational reward systems so organization members who change their behavior as suggested by the OD program are rewarded.[17]

Managers have been using OD techniques for several decades. The broad and useful applications of these techniques continue to be documented in the more recent management literature. OD techniques are being applied to business organizations as well as many other types of organizations such as religious organizations.[18]

In addition, OD applications are being documented throughout the world, with increasing use being reported in countries like Hungary, Poland, and the United Kingdom.[19]

BACK TO THE CASE Wayne Calloway's Pizza Hut/Taco Bell change would not be classified as people change. Although the people involved in the change must be considered to some extent, the main emphasis of the change is on structural change. If, however, Calloway had found that problems with human resources were the main cause of organizational ineffectiveness in foreign Pizza Huts and Taco Bells, he might have proposed organization development rather than structural change. In fact, Calloway may find at any time that he needs to use a grid OD in order to modify management styles and produce more cooperative team effort now that the proposed structural changes have been implemented.

Individuals Affected by the Change

A fourth major factor to be considered by managers when changing an organization is the people affected by the change. A good assessment of what to change and how to make the change probably will be wasted if organization members do not support the change. To increase the chances of employee support, managers should be aware of (1) the usual employee resistance to change, (2) how this resistance can be reduced, and (3) the three phases usually present when behavioral change occurs.

Resistance to Change

Resistance to change within an organization is as common as the need for change. After managers decide on making some organizational change, they typically meet with employee resistance aimed at preventing the change from occurring.[20] This resistance generally exists because organization members fear some personal loss, such as a reduction in personal prestige, a disturbance of established social and working relationships, and personal failure because of an inability to carry out new job responsibilities.

Reducing Resistance to Change

Because resistance typically accompanies proposed change, managers must be able to reduce the effects of this resistance to ensure the success of needed modifications. Resistance usually can be reduced by means of the following guidelines:[21]

1. *Avoid surprises.* People need time to evaluate a proposed change before management implements it. Elimination of time to evaluate how the change may affect individual situations usually results in automatic opposition to it. Whenever possible, individuals who will be affected by a change should be kept informed of the kind of change being considered and the probability that the change will be adopted.
2. *Promote real understanding.* When fear of personal loss related to a proposed change is reduced, opposition to the change is reduced.[22] Most managers would agree that having organization members thoroughly understand a proposed change is a major step in reducing this fear. This understanding may even generate support for the change by focusing attention on possible individual gains that could materialize as a result of it. Individuals should receive information that will help them answer the following change-related questions that invariably will be asked:
   - Will I lose my job?
   - Will my old skills become obsolete?
   - Am I capable of producing effectively under the new system?
   - Will my power and prestige decline?
   - Will I be given more responsibility than I care to assume?
   - Will I have to work longer hours?
   - Will it force me to betray or desert my good friends?[23]

3. *Set the stage for change.* Perhaps the most powerful tool for reducing resistance to change is management's positive attitude toward change. This attitude should be displayed openly by top and middle management as well as by lower management. In essence, management should demonstrate its appreciation for change as one of the basic prerequisites for a successful organization. Management also should strive to be seen as encouraging change only to increase organizational effectiveness, not just for the sake of trying something new. To emphasize this attitude toward change, some portion of organizational rewards should be earmarked for the organization members who are most instrumental in implementing constructive change.
4. *Make tentative change.* Resistance to change also can be reduced by making changes on a tentative basis. This approach establishes a trial period during which organization members spend some time working under a proposed change before voicing support or nonsupport of it. Tentative change is based on the assumption that a trial period during which organization members live under a change is the best way of reducing feared personal loss. Judson has summarized the benefits of using the tentative approach:
   - Those involved are able to test their reactions to the new situation before committing themselves irrevocably.
   - Those involved are able to acquire more facts on which to base their attitudes and behavior toward the change.
   - Those involved with strong preconceptions are in a better position to regard the change with greater objectivity. Consequently, they could review their preconceptions and perhaps modify some of them.
   - Those involved are less likely to regard the change as a threat.
   - Management is better able to evaluate the method of change and make any necessary modifications before carrying it out more fully.[24]

The Behavioral Side of Change

Almost any change requires that organization members modify the way in which they are accustomed to behaving or working. Therefore, managers must not only be able to decide on the best people–structure–technology relationship for the organization but also to make corresponding changes in such a way that related human behavior is changed most effectively. Positive results of any change will materialize only if organization members change their behavior as necessitated by the change.

Kurt Lewin, a German social scientist, pioneered the study of field theory. According to Lewin, behavioral change is caused by three distinct but related conditions experienced by an individual: (1) unfreezing, (2) changing, and (3) refreezing.[25]

Unfreezing is the state in which individuals experience a need to learn new behaviors.

The first condition, **unfreezing,** is the state in which individuals become ready to acquire or learn new behaviors—they experience the ineffectiveness of their present mode of behavior and are ready to attempt to learn new behavior that will make them more effective. It may be especially difficult for individuals to "thaw out" because of positive attitudes they traditionally associate with their past behavior.

Changing is the state in which individuals begin to experiment with performing new behaviors.

Changing, the second of Lewin's conditions, is the situation in which individuals, now unfrozen, begin experimenting with new behaviors. They try the new behaviors that they hope will increase their effectiveness. According to Edgar Schein, this changing is best effected if it involves both identification and internalization.[26] *Identification* is the process in which individuals performing new behaviors pattern themselves after someone who already has expertise in those behaviors—that is, individuals model themselves after an expert. *Internalization* is the process in which individuals performing new behaviors attempt to use those behaviors as part of their normal behavioral pattern. In other words, individuals consistently try to make the new behaviors useful over an extended period of time.

Refreezing, the third of Lewin's conditions, is the situation in which individuals see that the new behavior they have experimented with during "changing" is now part of themselves. They have developed attitudes consistent with performing the new behavior and see that behavior as part of their normal mode of operations. The rewards individuals receive as a result of performing the new behavior are instrumental in refreezing.

Refreezing is the state in which an individual's experimentally performed behaviors become part of the person.

For managers to increase their success as change agents, they must be able to make their changes in such a way that individuals who will be required to modify their behavior as a result of the change live through Lewin's three conditions. Here is an example: A middle-level manager named Sara Clark has gathered information indicating that Terry Lacey, a lower-level manager, must change his technique for transmitting memos. Clark knows that Lacey firmly believes he can save time and effort by writing out his intracompany memos rather than having them typed, proofread, corrected if necessary, and then sent out. Lacey also believes that an added benefit to this strategy is the fact that it frees his secretary to do other kinds of tasks.

Clark, however, has been getting several requests for help in reading Lacey's sometimes illegible handwriting and knows that some of Lacey's memos are written so poorly that words and sentences are misinterpreted. Obviously, some change is necessary. As Lacey's superior, Clark could simply mandate change by telling Lacey to write more clearly or to have his memos typed. This strategy, however, might not have enough effect to cause a lasting behavioral change and could conceivably result in the additional problem of personal friction between the two managers.

Clark could increase the probability of Lacey's changing his behavior in a more lasting way if she helps Lacey experience unfreezing, changing, and refreezing. To encourage unfreezing, Clark could direct all questions she receives about Lacey's memos back to Lacey himself and make sure that Lacey is aware of all misinterpretations and resulting mistakes. This should demonstrate to Lacey that there is some need for change.

Once Lacey recognizes the need for changing the way in which he writes his memos, he will be ready to try alternative memo-writing methods. Clark could then suggest methods to Lacey, taking special care to give him examples of what others do to write intracompany memos (identification). Over time, Clark could also help Lacey develop the method of transmitting memos that best suits his talents (internalization).

After Lacey has developed an effective method of writing memos, Clark should take steps to ensure that positive feedback about his memo writing reaches Lacey. This feedback, of course, will be instrumental in refreezing Lacey's new method. The feedback can come from Clark, from Lacey's subordinates and peers, and from Lacey's own observations.

Evaluation of Change

As with all other actions, managers should spend some time evaluating the changes they make. The purpose of this evaluation is not only to gain insights into how the change itself might be modified to further increase organizational effectiveness but also to determine whether the steps taken to make the change can be modified to increase organizational effectiveness the next time they are used.

According to Margulies and Wallace, making this evaluation may be difficult, because data from individual change programs may be unreliable.[27] Regardless of the difficulty, however, managers must do their best to evaluate change to increase the organizational benefit from the change.

Evaluation of change often involves watching for symptoms that indicate that further change is necessary. For example, if organization members continue to be oriented more to the past than to the future, if they recognize the obligations of rituals more than the challenges of current problems, or if they owe allegiance more to departmental goals than to overall company objectives, the probability is relatively high that further change is necessary.[28]

A word of caution is needed at this point. Although symptoms such as those listed in the preceding paragraph generally indicate that further change is warranted, this is not always the case. The decision to make additional changes should not be made solely on the basis of symptoms; more objective information also should be considered. In general, additional change is justified if it (1) further improves the means for satisfying someone's economic wants, (2) increases profitability, (3) promotes human work for human beings, or (4) contributes to individual satisfaction and social well-being.[29]

BACK TO THE CASE

Wayne Calloway must realize that even though he has formulated a change that would be beneficial to PepsiCo, his attempt to implement this change could prove unsuccessful if he does not appropriately consider the people affected by the change. For example, because Calloway is implementing new reporting lines to the United States for foreign Pizza Huts and Taco Bells, foreign organization members may fear that this change will diminish their control over their jobs. As a result, they may subtly resist the change.

To overcome such resistance, Calloway could use strategies like giving foreign Pizza Hut and Taco Bell employees enough time to fully evaluate and understand the change, presenting a positive attitude about the change, and, if resistance is very strong, suggesting that the proposed change will be tentative until it is fully evaluated. In addition, Calloway probably would find Lewin's unfreezing–changing–freezing theory helpful in implementing the proposed change.

Calloway's changes at PepsiCo need to be evaluated after implementation to discover whether further organizational change is necessary and whether the process used by Calloway to make the change might be improved for future use. This evaluation process could result, for example, in a suggestion that PepsiCo change back to its former organization structure, because the new structure does not allow enough independent tailoring of products to meet foreign tastes in individual countries, or that future implementations should focus more on allowing individuals affected by a change to experience unfreezing, changing, and refreezing.

CHANGE AND STRESS

This chapter focuses on changing an organization to make it more effective, efficient, and successful. When managers implement changes, they should be concerned about the stress they may be creating. Such stress could be significant enough to eliminate the improvement that was intended to be the result of the change. In fact, stress could result in the organization being less effective than it was before the change was attempted. This section defines stress and discusses the importance of studying and managing stress.

Defining Stress

Stress is the bodily strain that an individual experiences as a result of coping with some environmental factor.

The bodily strain that an individual experiences as a result of coping with some environmental factor is **stress.** Hans Selye, an early authority on this subject, said that stress is essentially the factors affecting wear and tear on the body.[30] In organizations, this wear and tear is caused primarily by the body's unconscious mobilization of energy when an individual is confronted with organizational or work demands.[31]

The Importance of Studying Stress

There are several sound reasons for studying stress.[32] First, stress can have damaging psychological and physiological effects on employees' health and on employees' contributions to the effectiveness of the organization. It can cause heart disease, and it can keep employees from being able to concentrate or to make decisions. A second important reason to study stress is that it is a major cause of employee absenteeism and turnover. Certainly, such factors severely limit the potential success of an organization. A third reason to study stress is that stress experienced by an employee can affect the safety of other workers or even the public. Another important reason for studying stress is that it represents a very significant cost to organizations. Some estimates put the cost of stress-related problems in the U.S. economy at $150 billion a year. As examples of these costs, many modern organizations spend a great deal of money treating stress-related employee problems through medical programs, and they must absorb expensive legal fees related to handling stress-related lawsuits.

Managing Stress in Organizations

Because stress is felt by virtually all employees in all organizations, insights about managing stress are valuable to all managers. This section is built on the assumption that in order to appropriately manage stress in organizations, managers must (1) understand how stress influences worker performance, (2) identify where unhealthy stress exists in organizations, and (3) help employees handle stress.

Understanding How Stress Influences Worker Performance

To deal with stress in an organization, managers must understand the relationship between the amount of stress felt by a worker and the worker's performance. This relationship is shown in Figure 12.8. According to this figure, extremely high and extremely low levels of stress tend to have negative effects on production. Additionally, increasing stress tends to increase performance up to some point (Point A in the figure). If the level of stress increases beyond this point, performance will begin to deteriorate. In sum, from a performance viewpoint, having individuals experience some stress is generally considered advantageous because it tends to increase production. However, having individuals feel too much or too little stress is generally considered disadvantageous, because it tends to decrease production. The cartoon on page 308 lightheartedly illustrates the profound negative effect that too much stress can have on job performance.

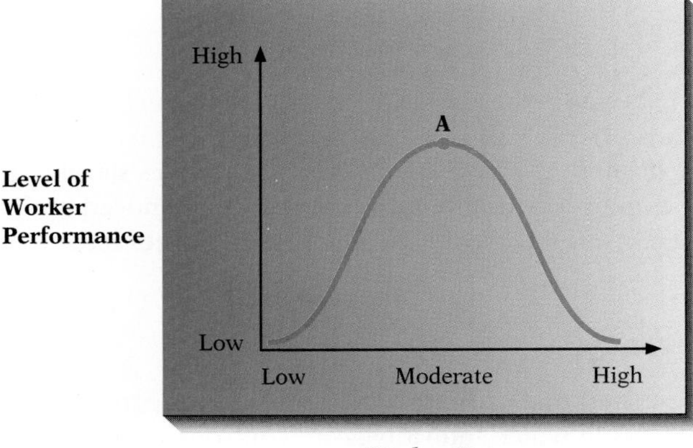

FIGURE 12.8 The relationship between worker stress and the level of worker performance

Keller is a good man but totally lacking in stress-management skills.

Harvard Business Review (July/August 1987), 64.
© Lee Lorenz 1989.

Identifying Unhealthy Stress in Organizations

After managers understand the impact of stress on performance, they must be able to identify where stress exists within the organization.[33] Once the existence of stress is pinpointed, the managers must determine whether the stress is at an appropriate level or if it is too high or too low. Because most stress-related organizational problems involve too much stress rather than too little, the remainder of this section focuses on undesirably high levels of stress.

It can be difficult for managers to identify the people in the organization who are experiencing detrimentally high levels of stress. Part of the difficulty is that people often respond to high stress in different ways. Another part of the difficulty is that physiological reactions to stress are hard, if not impossible, for managers to observe and monitor. Such reactions include high blood pressure, pounding heart, and gastrointestinal disorders.

Despite the difficulty, there are several observable symptoms of undesirably high stress levels that managers can recognize.[34] These symptoms are as follows:[35]

- Constant fatigue
- Low energy
- Moodiness
- Increased aggression
- Excessive use of alcohol
- Temper outbursts
- Compulsive eating
- High levels of anxiety
- Chronic worrying

Managers who observe one or more of these symptoms in employees should investigate further to determine if employees exhibiting the symptoms are indeed under too much stress. If so, the managers should attempt to help the employees reduce or handle their stress.

Helping Employees Handle Stress

A **stressor** is an environmental demand that causes people to feel stress.

A **stressor** is an environmental demand that causes people to feel stress. Stressors are common in organizational situations in which individuals are confronted by circumstances for which their usual behaviors are inappropriate or insufficient and where negative consequences are associated with their not properly dealing with the situation.[36] Organizational change is an obvious stressor, but as Figure 12.9 indicates, many other

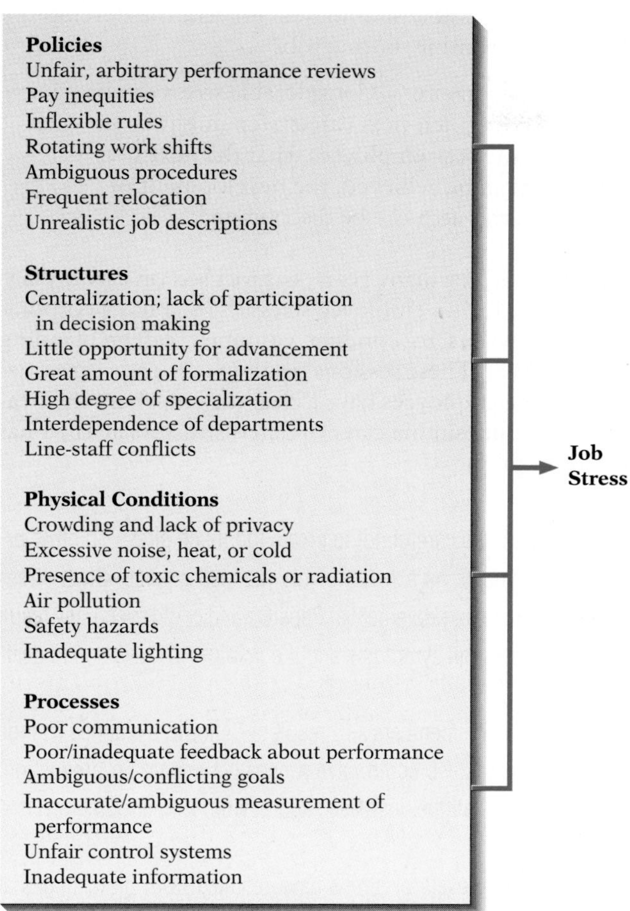

Policies
Unfair, arbitrary performance reviews
Pay inequities
Inflexible rules
Rotating work shifts
Ambiguous procedures
Frequent relocation
Unrealistic job descriptions
Structures
Centralization; lack of participation in decision making
Little opportunity for advancement
Great amount of formalization
High degree of specialization
Interdependence of departments
Line-staff conflicts
Physical Conditions
Crowding and lack of privacy
Excessive noise, heat, or cold
Presence of toxic chemicals or radiation
Air pollution
Safety hazards
Inadequate lighting
Processes
Poor communication
Poor/inadequate feedback about performance
Ambiguous/conflicting goals
Inaccurate/ambiguous measurement of performance
Unfair control systems
Inadequate information
Job Stress

FIGURE 12.9 Additional organizational stressors

factors related to organizational policies, structure, physical conditions, and processes can also act as stressors.[37]

In general, stress is not reduced significantly until the stressors causing it have been coped with satisfactorily or withdrawn from the environment. For example, if too much organizational change is causing undesirably high levels of stress, management may be able to reduce stress by improving organizational training that is aimed at preparing workers to deal with the job demands resulting from the change. Management might also deal with such stress by not making further organizational changes.[38] Such action would be aimed at reducing the significance of organizational change as a stressor and thereby reducing stress levels.

In addition to working in a focused manner on organizational change and other organizational stressors after they are observed, management can adopt several strategies to help prevent the development of unwanted stressors in organizations. Three such strategies follow:[39]

1. *Create an organizational climate that is supportive of individuals.* Organizations commonly seem to evolve into large bureaucracies with formal, inflexible, impersonal climates. This setup leads to considerable job stress. Making the organizational environment less formal and more supportive of employee needs will help prevent the development of unwanted organizational stressors.
2. *Make jobs interesting.* In general, routine jobs that do not allow employees some degree of freedom often result in undesirable employee stress. Management's

focus on making jobs as interesting as possible should help prevent the development of unwanted stressors related to routine, boring jobs.

3. *Design and operate career counseling programs.* Considerable stress can be generated when employees do not know what their next career step might be or when they might take it. If management can show employees what the next step will probably be and when it realistically can be achieved, the development of unwanted organizational stressors in this area can be discouraged.

IBM is an example of a company that, for many years, has focused on career planning for its employees as a vehicle for reducing employee stress.[40] IBM has a corporationwide program to encourage supervisors to conduct voluntary career planning sessions with employees on an annual basis. These sessions result in one-page career action plans. At the end of the sessions, the employees have a clear idea of where their careers are headed. The development of undesirable career-related stressors at IBM has been discouraged as a result of this program.

BACK TO THE CASE Calloway should be careful not to create too much stress on other organization members as a result of his planned change. Such stress could be significant enough to eliminate any planned improvement at PepsiCo and could eventually result in such stress-related effects on employees as physical symptoms and the inability to make sound decisions.

Although some additional stress on organization members as a result of Calloway's planned change at PepsiCo could enhance productivity, too much stress could have a negative impact on production. Signs that Calloway could look for include constant fatigue, increased aggression, temper outbursts, and chronic worrying.

If Calloway determines that undesirably high levels of stress have resulted from his changes at PepsiCo, he should try to reduce the stress through training organization members to execute their new job demands resulting from the change. Or he may want to simply slow the rate of his planned change.

Naturally, it would be wise for Calloway to take action to prevent unwanted stressors from developing as a result of his planned change. Toward this end, Calloway can work to ensure that the organizational climate at PepsiCo is supportive of individual needs and that jobs resulting from the planned change are as interesting as possible.

ACTION SUMMARY

Reread the learning objectives that follow. Each objective is followed by questions. Answering these questions accurately will help you retain the most important concepts discussed in this chapter. After answering each question, check your answer with the answer key at the end of this chapter. (*Hint:* If you have doubt regarding the correct response, consult the page whose number follows the answer.)

Circle: ***From studying this chapter, I will attempt to acquire:***

1. A working definition of ***changing an organization.***

T, F **a.** The purpose of organizational modifications is to increase the extent to which an organization accomplishes its objectives.

a, b, c, d, e **b.** Organizational modifications typically include changing: (a) overall goals and objectives; (b) established lines of organizational authority; (c) levels of responsibility held by various organization members; (d) b and c; (e) all of the above.

2. An understanding of the relative importance of change and stability to an organization.

a, b, c, d, e **a.** According to the Hellriegel and Slocum model, the following is the most likely outcome when both adaptation and stability are high: (a) high probability of slow death; (b) high survival probability; (c) high survival and growth probability; (d) certainty of quick death; (e) possibility of slow death.

T, F **b.** According to Hellriegel and Slocum, repeated changes in an organization without stability typically result in employees with a high degree of adaptability.

3. Some ability to know what kind of change should be made within an organization.

T, F **a.** Although managers can choose to change an organization in many ways, most changes can be categorized as one of three kinds: (1) people change, (2) goal or objective change, and (3) technological change.

a, b, c, d, e **b.** Decentralizing an organization is a structural change aimed at: (1) reducing the cost of coordination; (b) increasing the controllability of subunits; (c) increasing motivation; (d) all of the above; (e) a and b.

4. An appreciation for why individuals affected by a change should be considered when the change is being made.

a, b, c, d, e **a.** The following is not an example of personal loss that organization members fear as a result of change: (a) possibility of a reduction in personal prestige; (b) disturbance of established social relationships; (c) reduction in overall organizational productivity; (d) personal failure because of an inability to carry out new job responsibilities; (e) disturbance of established working relationships.

T, F **b.** Support for a proposed change may be altered by focusing attention on possible individual gains that could materialize as a result of the change.

5. Some facility in evaluating change.

a, b, c, d, e **a.** Symptoms indicating that further change is necessary are that organization members: (a) are oriented more to the future than to the past; (b) recognize the challenge of current problems more than the obligations of rituals; (c) owe allegiance more to overall company goals than to departmental goals; (d) none of the above; (e) a and b.

T, F **b.** Change is an inevitable part of management and considered so important to organizational success that some managers encourage employees to suggest needed changes.

6. An understanding of how organizational change and stress are related.

T, F **a.** Stress is simply the rate of wear and tear on the body.

T, F **b.** From a managerial viewpoint, stress on employees can be either too high or too low.

T, F **c.** Stressors are the factors within an organization that reduce employee stress.

INTRODUCTORY CASE WRAP-UP

"PepsiCo Reorganizes Pizza Hut and Taco Bell" (see p. 291) and its related back-to-the-case sections were written to help you better understand the management concepts contained in this chapter. Answer the following discussion questions about this introductory case to further enrich your understanding of chapter content:

1. Would it be difficult to reorganize Pizza Hut and Taco Bell as discussed in the case? Explain your answer.
2. Do you think that certain employees will subtly resist Calloway's changes? Why or why not?
3. What elements of Calloway's plan would cause organization members to experience stress, and what could Calloway do to help alleviate this stress? Be specific.

ISSUES FOR REVIEW AND DISCUSSION

1. What is meant in this chapter by the phrase *changing an organization?*
2. Why do organizations typically undergo various changes?
3. Does an organization need both change and stability? Explain.
4. What major factors should a manager consider when changing an organization?
5. Define *change agent* and list the skills necessary to be a successful change agent.
6. Explain the term *organizational effectiveness* and describe the major factors that determine how effective an organization will be.
7. Describe the relationship between "determining what should be changed within an organization" and "choosing a kind of change for the organization."
8. What is the difference between structural change and people change?
9. Is matrix organization an example of a structural change? Explain.
10. What is the difference between the overt and covert factors considered during organizational development?
11. Draw and explain the managerial grid.
12. Is grid OD an example of a technique used to make structural change? Explain.
13. What causes resistance to change?
14. List and explain the steps managers can take to minimize resistance to change.
15. Explain the significance of unfreezing, changing, and refreezing to changing the organization.
16. How and why should managers evaluate the changes they make?
17. Define *stress* and explain how it influences performance.
18. List three stressors that could exist within an organization. For each stressor, discuss a specific management action that could be aimed at eliminating the stressor.
19. What effect can career counseling have on employee stress? Explain.

ACTION SUMMARY ANSWER KEY

1. a. T, p. 292
b. d, p. 292
2. a. c, p. 293
b. F, p. 293
3. a. F, p. 296
b. d, p. 297
4. a. c, p. 303
b. T, p. 303
5. a. d, pp. 305–306
b. T, p. 292
6. a. T, p. 306
b. T, p. 307
c. F, p. 308

CASE STUDY

Managing Change in Transition: Kathleen A. Cote of ComputerVision

SYLVIA KEYES
Bridgewater State College

The past few years have brought a lot of changes to Massachusetts-based ComputerVision, Inc. (formerly Prime Computer), a manufacturer of minicomputer and midrange computer systems. Kathleen Cote, as president and general manager of ComputerVision Service, the service division of the company, has helped both her employees and the organization as a whole to adjust to those changes.

Prior to joining ComputerVision in 1986, Kathleen Cote had experienced many changes at Wang Laboratories, another Massachusetts computer firm. A few years after coming to Wang as a senior production manager, she was asked to serve as project manager for relocating some of the manufacturing functions to a new plant. A year later, she took on another plant start-up, this time from the beginning.

Shortly after that plant was up and running, the computer industry experienced an industrywide downturn; Cote was asked to downsize and later close the facility. She said, "If I think what I am most proud of in my life, it's starting up that facility; and when I think about the thing that is most disappointing for me, it was having to close down that facility two years later. The facility, the operation, the people all had the highest quality and lowest cost production operation; we had an excellent culture, a diverse work force, and we were all very proud of what we had accomplished. So it was very, very hard to have to lay people off and close the facility."

Kathleen Cote joined ComputerVision as Vice President of Manufacturing in 1986. However, in March of 1988, big changes soon occurred when there was a hostile takeover attempt, and 10 percent of the work force was laid off. In October of 1988, a so-called friendly takeover occurred; the company was restructured into five separate strategic business units, and an additional 20 percent of the work force was laid off. The new administration asked Cote if she would like to leave manufacturing and run ComputerVision Service. "It's about a $600 million business. . . . So I decided that would be an opportunity to expand my general management experience."

After the reorganization, ComputerVision, along with the entire mini-computer industry, faced some very difficult times. It was unable to reduce its debt and continued to lose money. The external forces of economics, the global economy, instability in Europe during the Eastern bloc transition, and Japan's slowdown all contributed to very difficult business conditions.

To what then does Cote attribute the ongoing success of the service business? She claims that ComputerVision Service became very good at managing change. While the sweeping changes to the industry did impact ComputerVision Service, the company was constantly able to figure out ways to bring in new kinds of revenues, cut costs, consolidate, and shift its attention to new areas. ComputerVision Service became good at reacting, "downsizing" the operation, consolidating functions, and reducing costs.

In spite of all the difficulties both externally and internally, the people in the front line of the services organization are the ones who really made a difference in keeping the customer base. Cote says that ComputerVision Service has strengthened in the process of changing. All of the pain has forced the company to focus on its financial performance—and probably has made the difference between the company's failing and moving forward.

Cote claims that while the employees do indeed face stress, so does she. The difference is that her stress is self-imposed. "I feel responsible for every person in the organization and the success of the organization. I want to bring people and their careers again to a place where they can continue." Cote realizes that she is not going to be able to do that for everybody, so the best that she can do is try to deliver performance while encouraging each person to do his or her best.

DISCUSSION QUESTIONS

1. Where would you place Cote on Blake and Mouton's managerial grid?
2. Explain how Kurt Lewin's refreezing applies to ComputerVision.
3. List four types of stress that would make employees resistant to change after layoffs have occurred even though those employees have been kept on.
4. What stress management techniques would you attempt to use if you were in Cote's position?

CNN VIDEO CASE

Spirit under Stress

SUSIE TOMPKINS
Esprit de Corps

Few companies can do better than Esprit de Corps in testing the stick-to-itiveness or durability of its employees, not to mention its fashion selections. This near-billion-dollar clothing company in San Francisco has its roots in a mid-sixties clothing line called "Plain Jane," designed by Jane Tice. Co-founder of the company was Susie Tompkins, Tice's friend and assistant. By 1967, the Plain Jane company had a strong presence in New York Department stores, thanks to an aggressive salesman named Allan Schwartz. By 1970, the company had earned a name for itself and was grossing over $1 million a year.

Things started changing when Susie Tompkins's husband, Doug Tompkins, sold his own stores (devoted to mountaineering) and decided to put his energy into the Plain Jane company,

Susie Tompkins felt a sense of responsibility to her partners and employees to maintain the company culture and to keep the company growing.

to the distress of Schwartz and Tice. Under Doug Tompkins's influence, the name was changed in 1971 to Esprit de Corp. The next several years saw continually increasing revenues, more and more employees, and two expansions into new and larger headquarters. Although the Tompkins's combined share of the company was 45 percent—compared to Schwartz and Tice's 55 percent—the Tompkinses exerted more control on the overall business planning and management. In 1976 Schwartz left, and in 1979 Tice left. Doug Tompkins became director of image, and Susie Tompkins, head of design.

Unexpectedly in 1986, a sad song started playing for the company, due to overexpansion into retailing (leaving the wholesale business undermanaged), a failed fall fashion line (suddenly out of touch with the Esprit customer), and marital problems between Susie and Doug. Attempts to bring the business back under control included cutbacks in personnel and the sale of a warehouse. Morale plummeted, despite the fact that headquarters was called Little Utopia, employee perks included gourmet food and free kayaking lessons, and private lives were open to company consideration because the employee's total involvement was the norm.

In 1988, the Tompkinses hired a Board of Directors to rescue their company. The Board fired both of them as CEO (Doug) and Design Director (Susie), but kept Doug as head of Esprit International and gave Susie the hollow title of "Fashion Consultant." Susie started a legal battle and, for two years, employees wondered who would prevail, or if the company would even survive. Finally, on May 31, 1990, Doug agreed to sell to Susie. She comments, "We had a lot of responsibility to our other partners and to our employees to keep the culture and keep the company growing. We couldn't be selfish; we had to give this company a chance to survive."

On returning, Susie rejected the self-indulgent employee perks of the eighties. She lent Esprit $10 million for an employee stock ownership plan, to thank the people she regarded more as family than as work force. She started focusing more attention on social consciousness, for instance, by rewarding employees for efforts supportive of education and the environment.

With 1991 sales estimated over $900 million and with the company regaining a sense of purpose, Esprit de Corps seemed to be coming back strong. However, on April 15 Corrado Federico resigned as CEO, after having been with Esprit for ten years and helping it through the battles. Chairman Isaac Stein filled in until Fritz Ammann became CEO in April 1992. In July of that year, a little more than a year after Stein referred to her as "spiritual head of the company," Susie Tompkins resigned as Esprit's creative director. Although she maintains an ownership position and plans to stay involved in the product, she looks forward to having more time to pursue socially conscious activities in the community.

VIDEO CASE QUESTIONS

1. Identify the major outside change agent at work during the history of Esprit de Corps.
2. How might a long-term Esprit employee have reacted to the 1986 cutbacks? How would the unfreezing conditions of behavioral change apply?
3. What types of stress related to policies and processes most likely affected employees while Susie and Doug Tompkins battled for control of the company?

CNN VIDEO EXERCISE

Effecting Change at Esprit de Corps

ACTION GOAL: Consider how an Esprit manager might have helped employees change their behavior during the period of cutbacks and corporate dissension beginning in 1986.

Imagine that you are the manager of an Esprit warehouse in 1987. You must make some major changes in procedures due to company cutbacks and the sale of one warehouse.

Inventory clerks are accustomed to physically counting merchandise once a week. They usually enjoy this part of their job; they can be on the move in the large warehouse, and they get to see and touch the merchandise. However, with the increased flow of merchandise and with the personnel cutbacks, the inventory clerks are overworked. The physical count sometimes takes an entire day, and such a long count is physically grueling.

You have decided to eliminate the physical count by having all incoming merchandise tagged with a scannable label. Floor clerks will perform the physical count daily, using scanners, and inventory clerks will not perform physical counts at all. What strategies can you use to help your inventory clerks change their behavior as necessitated by your decision? Review the section "The Behavioral Side of Change" on pages 304–305. Then briefly describe your strategies in outline format.

Strategies to Facilitate Behavioral Change

I. Unfreezing

____

____

____

____

____

____

II. Changing

____

____

____

____

____

____

III. Refreezing

____

____

____

____

____

____

PART 3

INTEGRATIVE CASE

USAir: Begins with You, but Where Does It End?

CHERYL MACON
Butler County Community College

USAir makes every effort to uphold its customer service policy, "USAir begins with YOU." The company plans to continue with its successful formula, developed over the years, of making the customer the top priority.

USAir, formerly All American Airlines, began as a mail carrier in 1939. In 1945, after the war, it became certified to carry passengers. In 1946, the company changed its name to Allegheny Airlines, which today is a separate branch providing only commuter flights. Allegheny merged with Lake Central in 1968 and in 1972 it acquired Mohawk Airlines. Finally, in 1978 it became USAir, more than doubling its size by virtue of two mergers with Pacific Southwest and Piedmont. With the acquisition of Piedmont, USAir began flying to Europe; the number of USAir employees has since doubled. New geographical areas have been added and still more are sought. In 1993, British Airways invested in USAir and now shares in the computer reservations of some of the seats.

Today, USAir is the dominant carrier in Pittsburgh. It spends $1.1 billion in Pennsylvania on payroll, fuel, taxes, and other items. The recent building of the Pittsburgh International Airport included a great deal of input from USAir officials. The airline operates solely out of two of the four terminals, controls fifty of the seventy-five gates, and services 88 percent of Pittsburgh's passenger traffic. USAir also dominates the cargo area, with 65,000 square feet set aside for the company's use.

In order to continue to provide an efficient and effective means of delivering customer service, USAir's organizational strategies at every level of the company are key. These strategies must also accommodate the recent growth as well as plans for further expansion.

In accordance with strict government regulations, USAir operates under a formal organizational structure. The company departmentalizes according to functions such as aircraft maintenance, flight operations, marketing, finance, legal, and customer service. Due to the nature of the business, USAir is highly specialized and has a broad span of management within a very tall organizational structure. USAir operates primarily by the unity of command principle, although situations do arise which require employees to answer to more than one boss.

USAir, as the dominant carrier in Pittsburgh, is the second largest employer in southwest Pennsylvania, with over twelve thousand employees in this region alone. In order to recruit and maintain workers for such a large company, there are very specific personnel practices in place.

USAir provides to each employee detailed job descriptions for each position. Because of the company's size, managers often delegate authority. For the most part, the accountability of the delegated task remains with the supervisor and is not passed along to the subordinate. USAir has a line/staff organization which, for the most part, is centralized. However, the corporation is split geographically, with operations based in Pittsburgh but the financial, legal, marketing, and headquarters staff based in Washington, D.C.

USAir makes every effort to promote from within and is an equal opportunity employer. It is a government contractor, and therefore maintains a strict affirmative action policy. USAir has a strong commitment to complying with government regulations. Policies and procedures for the hiring and transferring of employees are clearly spelled out in the corporate policy manual. Records are kept and affirmative action progress is monitored in order to fulfill legal reporting requirements and to assure that the most qualified candidates fill vacant positions.

Depending on the area of employment, there may be certain selection tests or requirements before employment is granted, i.e., eye exam, height and weight restrictions, and/or a physical. Drug testing is now mandatory for all USAir employees.

USAir offers varied training programs. The amount and length of a program is directly dependent upon the type of job being sought. All new hires receive training. Some jobs, such as flight attendant, pilot and mechanic positions, require recurrent training in order to update employees' knowledge of federal mandates, operations, and new technology. USAir has a performance appraisal system which differs among departments. Pilots and flight attendants are observed in the performance of their duties by both company personnel and Federal Aviation Administration representatives.

Upper management feels that most personnel have adapted well to recent changes brought about by mergers and growth. Some resistance, however, has been felt since the mergers because of geographic factors. For example, Piedmont was primarily a southern carrier, while USAir was dominant in the northern states, and some employees were forced to move or denied promotions if they refused to move. The merger process is continually being evaluated within each department and among upper management officials. While these mergers have been deemed successful by upper management, the decline in worldwide economic conditions has significantly affected the company.

[USAir] plans to continue with its successful formula . . . of making the customer the top priority.

In order to help employees deal with the changes, USAir offers an employee-assistance program which has been expanded to include stress management. This program covers all employees and their family members, for any problem that might affect job performance or health. USAir does not believe that a certain amount of stress is advantageous or serves as a motivator, therefore the company attempts to deal with such problems before they escalate.

The economy—and particularly the economics of the airline industry—will probably have the most influence on the eventual success or failure of USAir. However, the company has grown and expanded in a difficult market by keeping its focus on the customer, by assisting its employees through transitions, and by carefully planning and organizing.

DISCUSSION QUESTIONS

1. Is the formal organizational structure in place at USAir appropriate? Why or why not?
2. The case states that when authority at USAir is delegated, the accountability for the delegated task is generally retained by the supervisor. What are the pros and cons of such a practice?
3. What steps does USAir take to ensure that the employees it recruits are the best qualified people for the positions, while meeting federal EEOC guidelines?
4. Do you believe USAir is wise in attempting to avoid job-related stress? Why or why not?

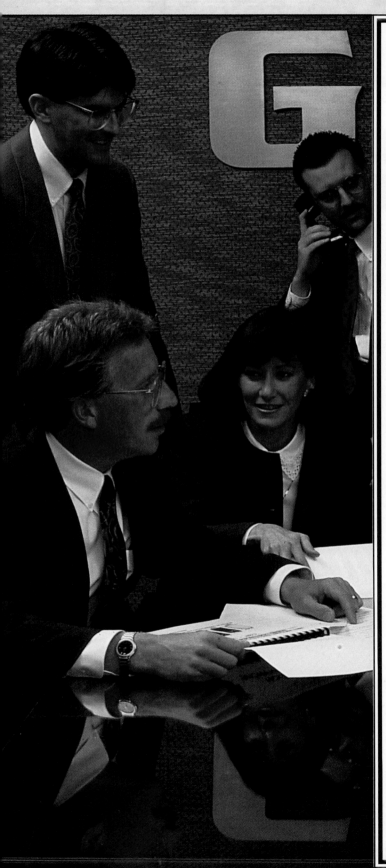

INFLUENCING

PART

4

Influencing is the third of the four major management functions that must be performed for organizations to have long-term success. The last two sections of the text focused on how managers plan and organize resources in order to reach organizational objectives. This section discusses important people-oriented issues that managers must consider in influencing workers to become and remain productive.

In general, the most important influencing tasks are communication, leadership, motivation, and groups and corporate culture.

The discussion of the fundamentals of influencing and communication defines *influencing* and presents it as a subsystem of the overall management system. Within this subsystem, communication is an important issue. It involves specific elements and processes, can be successful or unsuccessful, and can take various forms, such as verbal or nonverbal and formal or informal. The explanation of leadership will include the definition of *leadership,* specific leadership strategies that relate to decision making, the level of follower maturity, and the process of engineering situations to fit leadership styles.

This section will also include the definition of *motivation* and a discussion of several models that are used to describe it. It will describe theories that focus on human needs as an integral part of motivation theory and several strategies that managers can use to motivate organization members.

Finally, the discussion on groups and corporate culture will stress that, for managers to influence organization members, they must be able to manage groups of people. This discussion will define *groups,* distinguish between formal and informal groups, and suggest ways that managers can maximize group effectiveness. Discussion also focuses on corporate culture as a variable in managing groups.

CHAPTER

13

FUNDAMENTALS OF INFLUENCING AND COMMUNICATION

STUDENT LEARNING OBJECTIVES

From studying this chapter, I will attempt to acquire:

1. An understanding of influencing.
2. An understanding of interpersonal communication.
3. A knowledge of how to use feedback.
4. An appreciation for the importance of nonverbal communication.
5. Insights on formal organizational communication.
6. An appreciation for the importance of the grapevine.
7. Some hints on how to encourage organizational communication.

CHAPTER OUTLINE

INTRODUCTORY CASE
Eaton Managers Concentrate on Influencing People

FUNDAMENTALS OF INFLUENCING

Defining "Influencing"
The Influencing Subsystem

COMMUNICATION

Interpersonal Communication

GLOBAL HIGHLIGHT
Compression Labs

DIVERSITY HIGHLIGHT
Bull Worldwide Information Services

Interpersonal Communication in Organizations

ETHICS HIGHLIGHT
Dow Corning

QUALITY HIGHLIGHT
Holiday Inn

CASE STUDY
The Wal-Mart Influence

VIDEO CASE
PG&E's Master Communicator: Richard Clarke, Pacific Gas and Electric

VIDEO EXERCISE
Mastering Communication at PG&E

INTRODUCTORY CASE

Eaton Managers Concentrate on Influencing People

It's 7:30 a.m., time for the morning quiz at Eaton Corp.'s factory. Ten union workers, each representing work teams, sit around a boardroom table. "What were our sales yesterday?" asks a supervisor at the head of the table. A worker, glancing at a computer printout, replies that they were $625,275. "And in the month?" From another worker comes the response: $6,172,666. . . .

Eaton may not be a household name, and its products—including gears, engine valves, truck axles and, at Lincoln, Nebraska, circuit breakers—aren't glamorous. But its success in raising productivity and cutting costs throws plenty of doubt on recent handwringing about unmotivated American workers and flaccid American corporations. . . .

Getting people to think for themselves—and work in teams—is important to Eaton.

Getting people to think for themselves—and work in teams—is important to Eaton. The company starts by hiring managers who aren't autocratic and training them to accept encroachments on their authority. Not everyone can hack it: When engineers at Lincoln were evicted from their office enclave and the department was moved out onto the shop floor, the department chief and a colleague quit in protest.

Managers who adjust, however, tend to stay at one plant a long time. Mr. Kelly has been plant manager at Lincoln since 1980. The Kearney manager, Nebraskan Robert Dyer, is an area native who was hired as a machine operator in 1969, when the plant opened. That, too, isn't unusual: twenty-three of Lincoln's salaried staff of fifty-seven came up from the rank and file. . . .

Management shares extensive financial data with employees at the two plants to underscore the link between their performance and the factory's. At Kearney, a TV monitor in the cafeteria indicates how specific shifts and departments did the previous day against their cost and performance goals. Lincoln gets the message out via computer printouts. "It gives you a sense of direction," says Ricky Rigg, a metal fabricator, "and makes you appreciate what you do more."

At Kearney, where workers labor amid the noise and heat of hot forged metal, bonuses are based on the entire plant's performance compared with the prior year. In the first quarter, for instance, Kearney topped the year-earlier profit and cost criteria by 7 percent—and workers got a quarterly bonus of 7 percent, or about $500 each. Kearney employees have earned a bonus every quarter since the system was introduced six years ago.

There's noncash recognition as well. On a recent Wednesday, the Kearney plant held a lunchtime barbecue to mark the first shift's 365th consecutive day without any injuries. Plant Manager Dyer and his staff prepared the meal—hamburgers, hot dogs, potato salad and baked beans—while the first shift chowed down.

"Bob personifies what I look for in a plant manager," says George Dettloff, general manager of Eaton's engine-components division and Mr. Dyer's boss. "He manages, but he gives people freedom."

That style was evident a year ago, when Kearney was looking for a human-resources manager to replace one who had resigned. A joint labor-management committee of eighteen people whittled the field down to three candidates. But when it came time for a final decision, Mr. Dyer asked the committee to decide on its own.

These team workers at Eaton Corporation are planning and evaluating their own work. The company provides them with the financial information and other data they need to make their own decisions.

From Thomas F. O'Boyle, "A Manufacturer Grows Efficient by Soliciting Ideas From Employees," *Wall Street Journal* (June 5, 1992), A1, A4. Reprinted by permission of *Wall Street Journal*, © 1992 Dow Jones & Company, Inc. All Rights Reserved Worldwide.

BACK TO THE CASE In the introductory case, Eaton Corporation's recent success in enhancing company productivity and efficiency is credited largely to how its managers manage people. According to the case, Eaton managers manage by taking steps such as encouraging employees to think for themselves, to make decisions about who is hired at Eaton, and to make changes in the company that will result in improvements. The information in this chapter emphasizes the value of managers such as those at Eaton and offers insights into what additional steps might be taken. The chapter is divided into two main parts: fundamentals of influencing and communication.

FUNDAMENTALS OF INFLUENCING

The four basic managerial functions—planning, organizing, influencing, and controlling—were introduced in chapter 1. *Influencing* follows *planning* and *organizing*, to be the third of these basic functions covered in this text. A definition of *influencing* and a discussion of the influencing subsystem follow.

Defining "Influencing"

Influencing is the process of guiding the activities of organization members in appropriate directions, involving the performance of four primary management activities: (1) leading, (2) motivating, (3) considering groups, and (4) communicating.

Influencing is the process of guiding the activities of organization members in appropriate directions. Appropriate directions, of course, are those that lead to the attainment of management system objectives. Influencing involves focusing on organization members as people and dealing with such issues as morale, arbitration of conflicts, and the development of good working relationships among individuals. Influencing is a critical part of a manager's job. The ability of a manager to influence others is a primary determinant of how successful a manager will be.[1]

The Influencing Subsystem

As with the planning and organizing functions, the influencing function can be viewed as a subsystem that is part of the overall management system process (see Figure 13.1). The primary purpose of the influencing subsystem is to enhance the attainment of management system objectives by guiding the activities of organization members in appropriate directions.

Figure 13.2 on page 323 shows the specific ingredients of the influencing subsystem. The input of this subsystem is composed of a portion of the total resources of the

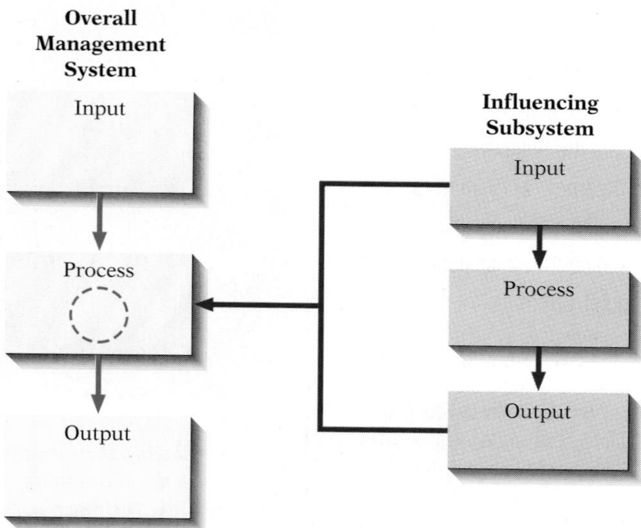

FIGURE 13.1 Relationship between overall management system and influencing subsystem

overall management system, and the output is appropriate organization member behavior. The process of the influencing subsystem involves the performance of four primary management activities: (1) leading, (2) motivating, (3) considering groups, and (4) communicating. Managers transform a portion of organizational resources into appropriate organization member behavior mainly by performing these four activities.

As Figure 13.2 shows, leading, motivating, and considering groups are related influencing activities, each of which is accomplished, to some extent, by managers communicating with organization members. For example, managers decide what kind of a leader they should be only after they analyze the characteristics of various groups with which they will interact and determine how these groups can best be motivated. Then, regardless of the strategy they adopt, their leading, motivating, and working with groups will be accomplished, at least to some extent, by communication with other organization members.

In fact, as Figure 13.3 implies, all management activities are accomplished at least in part through communication or communication-related endeavors.[2] Because communication is used repeatedly by managers, communication skills are often referred to as the fundamental management skill.

Supporting the notion that communication is the fundamental management skill are the results of a recent survey of chief executives. The results (which appear in Table 13.1, p. 324) show communication skill as the most important skill (along with interpersonal skills) to be taught to management students.

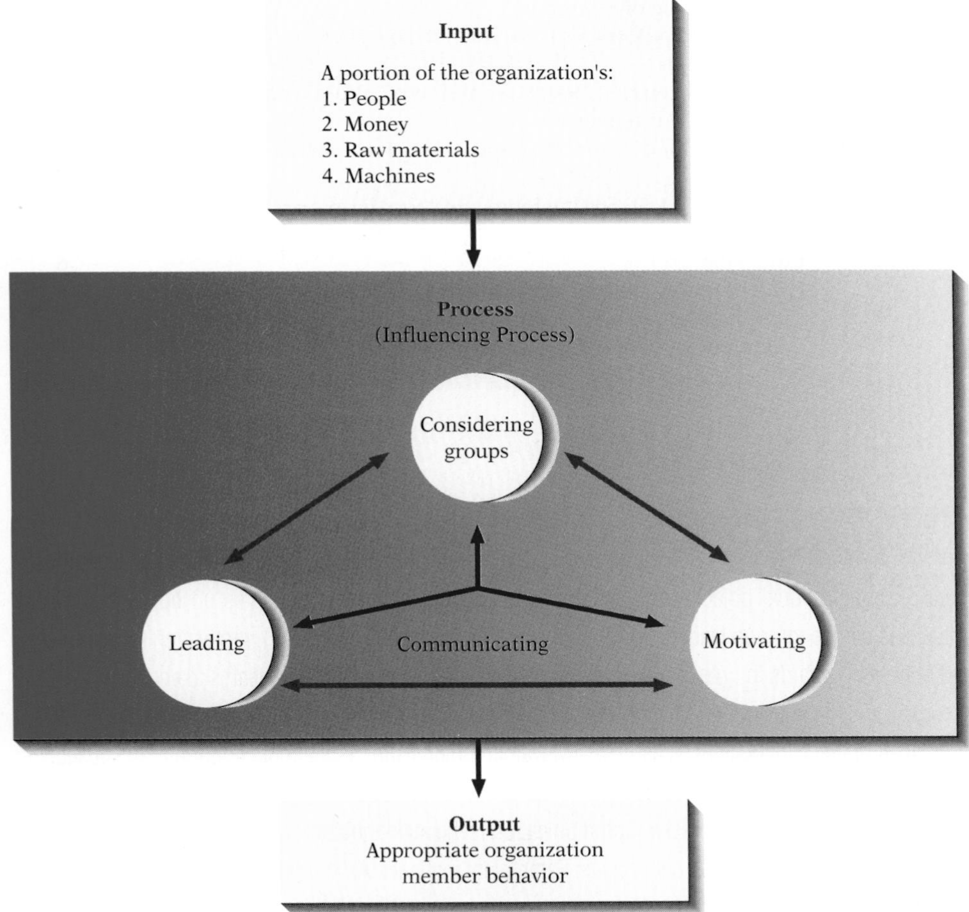

FIGURE 13.2 The influencing subsystem

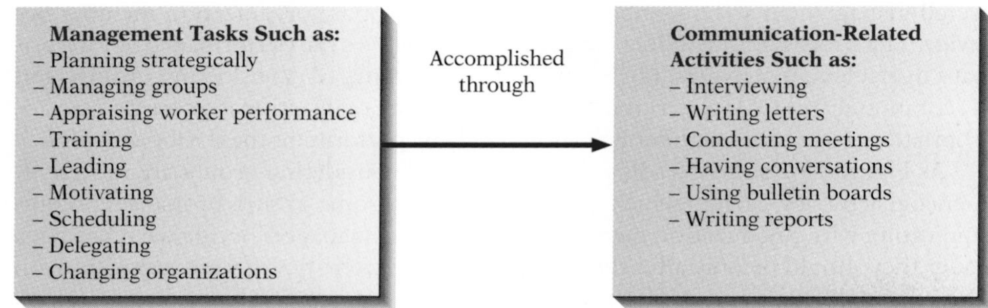

FIGURE 13.3 Management tasks and possible communication-related behavior used to help accomplish those tasks

TABLE 13.1 Chief executives rank importance of skills to be taught to management students

*Rank**	*Key Learning Area*	*Frequency Indicated*
1	Oral and written communication skills	25
1	Interpersonal skills	25
3	Financial/managerial account skills	22
4	Ability to think, be analytical, and make decisions	20
5	Strategic planning and goal setting—concern for long-term performance	13
6	Motivation and commitment to the firm—to give 110%	12
7	Understanding of economics	11
8	Management information systems and computer applications	9
8	To know all you can about your business, culture, and overall environment	9
8	Marketing concept (the customer is king) and skills	9
11	Integrity	7
11	To know yourself: Setting long- and short-term career objectives	7
13	Leadership skills	6
13	Understanding of the functional areas of the business	6
13	Time management: Setting priorities—how to work smart, not long or hard	1

*1 is most important.

BACK TO THE CASE

One of the primary functions of Eaton's management is influencing—guiding the activities of Eaton employees to enhance the accomplishment of organizational objectives. Illustrations in the case give clear examples on how the company influences people through leadership (hiring managers who aren't autocratic), motivation (granting cash and non-cash rewards for jobs done well), managing groups (operating work teams to enhance company success), and communicating (giving workers feedback on exactly how well they are doing).

Of all of these influencing activities, however, communication is the most important. In subsequent back-to-the-case sections, discussion will focus on communication as it relates to Robert Dyer, Eaton's plant manager in Lincoln, Nebraska. Communication is the main tool through which Dyer should, at least to some extent, accomplish his duties as an Eaton plant manager. As mentioned in the introductory case, through communication Dyer spreads the message of how well the plant is performing, what problems and challenges it faces, and how these problems and challenges will be addressed. Almost any work that Dyer plans to do at Eaton (planning, organizing, or controlling) will require him to communicate with other Eaton employees. In essence, Dyer must be a good communicator if he is to be a successful plant manager.

Communication is discussed further in the rest of this chapter. Leading, motivating, and considering groups are discussed in chapters 14, 15, and 16, respectively.

COMMUNICATION

Communication is the process of sharing information with other individuals. Information, as used here, is any thought or idea that managers desire to share with other individuals. In general, communication involves one individual projecting a message to one or more others that results in all people arriving at a common understanding of the message.[3] Because communication is a commonly used management skill and is often cited as the one ability most responsible for a manager's success, prospective managers must learn how to communicate.[4]

Communication is the process of sharing information with other individuals.

The communication activities of managers generally involve interpersonal communication—sharing information with other organization members. The following sections feature both the general topic of interpersonal communication and the more specific topic of interpersonal communication in organizations.

Interpersonal Communication

To be a successful interpersonal communicator, a manager must understand (1) how interpersonal communication works, (2) the relationship between feedback and interpersonal communication, and (3) the importance of verbal versus nonverbal interpersonal communication.

How Interpersonal Communication Works

Interpersonal communication is the process of sharing information with other individuals.[5] To be complete, the process must have the following three basic elements:

1. *The source/encoder.* The **source/encoder** is the person in the interpersonal communication situation who originates and encodes information to be shared with another person. Encoding is the process of putting information in a form that can be received and understood by another individual. Putting thoughts into a letter is an example of encoding. Until information is encoded, it cannot be shared with others. (From here on, the source/encoder will be referred to simply as the source.)

The **source/encoder** is the person in the interpersonal communication situation who originates and encodes information that the person wants to share with others.

2. *The signal.* Encoded information that the source intends to share constitutes a **message.** A message that has been transmitted from one person to another is called a **signal.**

A **message** is encoded information that the source/encoder intends to share with others. The **signal** is a message that has been transmitted from one person to another.

GLOBAL HIGHLIGHT
Compression Labs Sends Messages via Videoconferencing

The dissemination of messages becomes a greater technical challenge as businesses expand into the international arena. According to Carl Marszewski of Compression Labs, Inc., the increased need to compete with other businesses on the international level has driven organizations to look for new and better ways of projecting communication signals. As with Compression Labs, a growing number of businesses are using international videoconferencing, conferences via television, as an economical yet effective way to communicate about topics like new areas for organizational research, reviewing budgets, and overall organizational problem solving. In gen-

A growing number of global businesses are using international videoconferencing as an effective way to communicate about topics such as new areas for organizational research, reviewing budgets, and overall problem solving.

eral, organizations have met with some difficulty in providing videoconferences across national borders. Issues like a lack of coordination between the United States and other countries has made the process challenging. Given the intense competition among firms at the global level along with the effectiveness and efficiency of videoconferencing, aggressive firms will undoubtedly find ways to overcome any difficulties relating to the videoconferencing process. A rapid growth in the area of international videoconferencing is forecasted for the future. ▶

The **decoder/destination** is the person or people in the interpersonal communication situation with whom the source/encoder attempts to share information.

3. *The decoder/destination.* The **decoder/destination** is the person with whom the source is attempting to share information. This individual receives the signal and decodes, or interprets, the message to determine its meaning. Decoding is the process of converting messages back into information. In all interpersonal communication situations, message meaning is a result of decoding. (From here on, decoder/destination will be referred to as the destination.)

The classic work of Wilbur Schramm helps us understand the role played by each of the three elements of the interpersonal communication process. As implied in Figure 13.4, the source determines what information to share, encodes this information in the form of a message, and then transmits the message as a signal to the destination. The destination decodes the transmitted message to determine its meaning and then responds accordingly.

A manager who desires to assign the performance of a certain task to a subordinate would use the communication process in the following way: First, the manager would determine exactly what task he or she wanted the subordinate to perform. Then the manager would encode and transmit a message to the subordinate that would accurately reflect this assignment. The message transmission itself could be as simple as the manager telling the subordinate what the new responsibilities include. Next, the subordinate would decode the message transmitted by the manager to ascertain its meaning and then would respond to it appropriately.

Successful communication is an interpersonal communication situation in which the information the source/encoder intends to share with the decoder/destination and the meaning the decoder/destination derives from the transmitted message are the same.

Unsuccessful communication is an interpersonal communication situation in which the information the source/encoder intends to share with the decoder/destination and the meaning the decoder/destination derives from the transmitted message are different.

Successful and Unsuccessful Interpersonal Communication. **Successful communication** is an interpersonal communication situation in which the information the source intends to share with the destination and the meaning the destination derives from the transmitted message are the same. Conversely, **unsuccessful communication** is an interpersonal communication situation in which the information the source intends to share and the meaning the destination derives from the transmitted message are different.

To increase the probability that communication will be successful, the message must be encoded to ensure that the source's experience with the way a signal should be decoded is equivalent to the destination's experience of the way it should be decoded. If this situation exists, the probability is high that the destination will interpret the signal as intended by the source. Figure 13.5 on page 327 illustrates these overlapping fields of experience that ensure successful communication.

Barriers to Successful Interpersonal Communication. Factors that decrease the probability that communication will be successful commonly are called communication barriers. A clear understanding of these barriers is helpful to managers in their

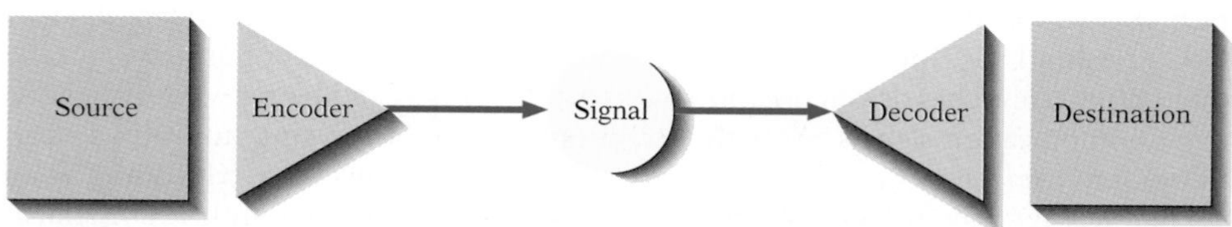

FIGURE 13.4 Role of the source, signal, and destination in the communication process

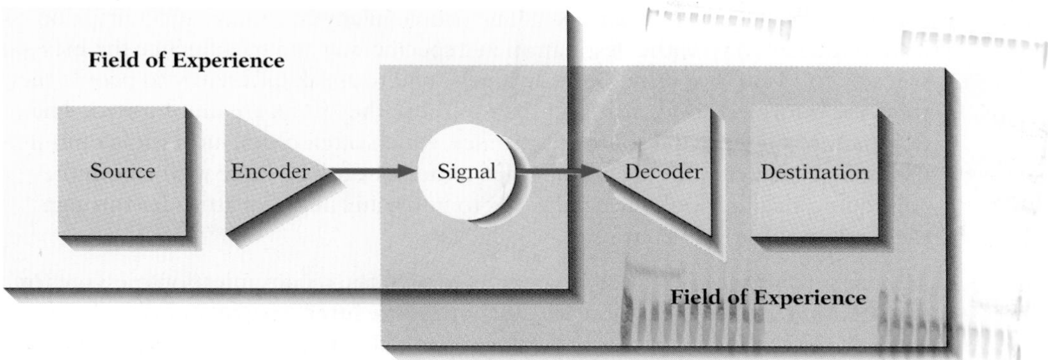

FIGURE 13.5 Overlapping fields of experience that ensure successful communication

attempt to maximize communication success. The following sections discuss both communication macrobarriers and communication microbarriers.

Communication macrobarriers are factors that hinder successful communication in a general communication situation.[6] These factors relate primarily to the communication environment and the larger world in which communication takes place. Among the macrobarriers are the following:[7]

Communication macrobarriers are factors that hinder successful communication and that relate primarily to the communication environment and the larger world in which communication takes place.

1. *The increasing need for information.* Because society is constantly and rapidly changing, individuals have a greater and greater need for information. This increased need tends to overload communication networks, thereby distorting communication. To minimize the effects of this barrier, managers should take steps to ensure that organization members are not overloaded with information. Only information critical to the performance of their jobs should be transmitted to them.

2. *The need for increasingly complex information.* With today's rapid technological advances, most people are faced with complex communication situations in their everyday lives. If managers take steps to emphasize simplicity in communication, the effects of this barrier can be lessened. Also, furnishing organization members with adequate training to deal with more technical areas might be another strategy for overcoming this barrier.

3. *The reality that individuals in the United States are increasingly coming in contact with individuals using languages other than English.* As business becomes international in scope and as organization members travel more, the need to know other languages increases. The potential communication barrier of this multilanguage situation is obvious. Moreover, individuals who deal with foreigners need to be familiar not only with their languages but also with their cultures. Knowledge of a foreign language may be of little value if individuals don't know which words, phrases, and actions are culturally acceptable.

4. *The need for learning decreases time available for communication.* Many managers feel pressured to learn new and important concepts that they have not had to know in the past. Issues like learning about the intricacies of international business as well as computer usage continue to use significant amounts of managerial time. Many managers believe that because of the increased demands on their time called for by the need to train, less time is available for communicating with other organization members.

Communication microbarriers are factors that hinder successful communication in a specific communication situation.[8] These factors relate directly to such variables as the communication message, the source, and the destination. Among the microbarriers are the following:[9]

Communication microbarriers are factors that hinder successful communication and that relate primarily to such variables as the communication message, the source, and the destination.

1. *The source's view of the destination.* The source in any communication situation has a tendency to view the destination in a specific way and to influence the messages by this view. For example, individuals tend to speak differently to people they think are informed about a subject than to those they think are uninformed. The destination can sense the source's attitudes, which often block successful communication. Managers should keep an open mind about the people with whom they communicate and should be careful not to imply any negative attitudes through their communication behavior.

Message interference is stimuli that compete with the communication message for the attention of the decoder/destination.

2. *Message interference.* Stimuli that compete with the communication message for the attention of the destination are called **message interference,** or noise.[10] An example of message interference is a manager talking to an office worker while the worker is trying to input data into a word processor. Inputting data is message interference because it competes with the manager's communication message for the office worker's attention. Managers should attempt to communicate only when they have the total attention of the individuals with whom they wish to share information. A lighthearted example of message interference is shown in the cartoon below.

3. *The destination's view of the source.* The destination can have certain attitudes toward the source that also can hinder successful communication. If, for example, a destination believes that the source has little credibility[11] in the area about which the source is communicating, the destination may filter out much of the source's message and only slightly consider the part of the message actually received. When communicating, managers should attempt to consider the worth of messages transmitted to them independent of their personal attitudes toward the source. They may lose many valuable ideas if personal feelings toward others influence which messages they listen to carefully.

Perception is the interpretation of a message as observed by an individual.

4. *Perception.* **Perception** is an individual's interpretation of a message. Different individuals can perceive the same message in very different ways. The two primary factors that influence the way in which a stimulus is perceived are the destination's education level and the destination's amount of experience. To minimize the negative effects of this perceptual factor on interpersonal communication, managers should try to send messages with precise meanings. Ambiguous words generally tend to magnify negative perceptions.

5. *Multimeaning words.* Because many words in the English language have several different meanings, a destination may have difficulty deciding which meaning should be attached to the words of a message. A manager should not assume that a word means the same thing to all people who use it.

Reprinted with special permission of King Features Syndicate, Inc.

A classic study by Lydia Strong substantiates this point. Strong concluded that for the 500 most common words in our language, there are 4,070 different dictionary definitions. On the average, each of these words has over 18 usages. The word *run* is an example:[12]

Babe Ruth scored a *run*.
Did you ever see Jesse Owens *run*?
I have a *run* in my stocking.
There is a fine *run* of salmon this year.
Are you going to *run* this company or am I?
You have the *run* of the place.
What headline do you want to *run*?
There was a *run* on the bank today.
Did he *run* the ship aground?
I have to *run* (drive the car) downtown.
Who will *run* for president this year?
Joe flies the New York–Chicago *run* twice a week.
You know the kind of people they *run* around with.
The apples *run* large this year.
Please *run* my bath water.

When encoding information, managers should be careful to define the terms they use whenever possible and never use obscure meanings for words when designing messages.[13] They also should try to use words in the same way they see their destination using them.

DIVERSITY HIGHLIGHT
Different Languages in Manufacturing Facility Create Special Challenge at Bull Worldwide Information Services

In certain situations, language can be considered a formidable communication microbarrier. In the modern industrial world, for example, a diverse work force can mean that a manager must deal with many different languages within the same manufacturing facility.

Hard work and a commitment to change helped Joel Beck reach his current position as vice president of U.S. manufacturing for Bull Worldwide Information Services. Beck, a thirty-two-year veteran of the plant and a former production worker, places a great deal of emphasis on people. Integrity and fairness are the keys to good leadership. Beck advises managers who are setting out on the same path as he is on that they cannot lead out of fear. Rather, managers should worry about what they can control. A manager must also demonstrate commitment.

Beck believes that, once managers accept work-force diversity as a factor to be managed, they must accept the equality of all people, and adopt a sensitivity to other races and creeds. According to Beck, a primary objective for the manager must be to figure out how to exploit a diverse work force for the benefit of the organization as well as the individuals themselves.

For Beck, communication is an issue that illustrates how difficult and challenging working with a diverse work force might be. There are twenty-four different languages spoken at his plant, including sign language. Dealing with such language differences has given Beck a great deal of experience dealing with work-force diversity. ▶

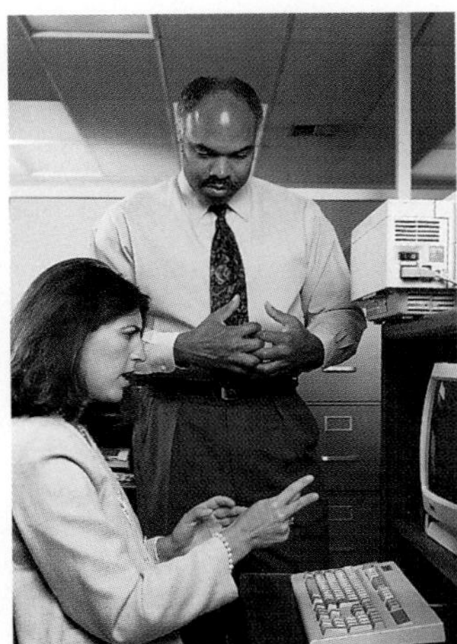

Managers of a diverse workforce must meet the difficult challenge of communicating with all workers. Here, a manager and employee communicate through sign language.

BACK TO THE CASE

In discussing Robert Dyer's ability to communicate, we are actually discussing his ability to share ideas with other Eaton employees. For Dyer to be a successful communicator, he must concentrate on the three essential elements of the communication process. The first element is the source—the individual who wishes to share information with another. In this case, the source is Dyer. The second element is the signal—the message transmitted by Dyer. The third element is the destination—the Eaton employee with whom Dyer wishes to share information. Dyer should communicate with Eaton employees by determining what information he wants to share, encoding the information, and then transmitting the message. The subordinates would then interpret the message and respond accordingly. Dyer's communication would be successful if subordinates interpreted messages as he intended.

If Dyer is to be a successful communicator, he must minimize the impact of numerous communication barriers. These barriers include (1) Eaton employees' need to have more information and more complex information to do their jobs, (2) message interference, (3) Dyer's view of the destination as well as the destination's view of Dyer, (4) the perceptual process of the people involved in the communication attempt, and (5) multimeaning words.

Feedback and Interpersonal Communication

Feedback is, in the interpersonal communication situation, the decoder/destination's reaction to a message.

Feedback is the destination's reaction to a message. In general, feedback can be used by the source to ensure successful communication.[14] For example, if the destination's message reaction is inappropriate, the source can conclude that communication was not successful and that another message should be transmitted. If the destination's message reaction is appropriate, the source can conclude that communication was successful. This, of course, assumes that the appropriate reaction did not happen merely by chance. Because of the potentially high value of feedback, managers should encourage feedback whenever possible and evaluate it carefully.[15]

Feedback can be either verbal or nonverbal.[16] To gather verbal feedback, the source could simply ask the destination pertinent message-related questions. The destination's answers would probably indicate to the source whether the message was perceived as intended. To gather nonverbal feedback, the source may have to observe the destination's nonverbal response to a message. An example is a manager who has transmitted a message to a subordinate indicating new steps that must be taken in the normal performance of the subordinate's job. Assuming that no other problems exist, if the steps are not followed accurately, the manager has nonverbal feedback indicating the need for clarification of the initial message.

Robert S. Goyer has suggested other uses for feedback besides determining whether a message is perceived as intended.[17] For example, over time a source can use feedback to evaluate his or her personal communication effectiveness by determining the proportion of the destination's message reactions that he or she actually intended. A formula illustrating how this evaluation, the **communication effectiveness index,** can be calculated is shown in Figure 13.6. The higher this proportion, the greater the communication effectiveness of the source.

A **communication effectiveness index** is the intended message reactions divided by the total number of transmitted messages.

If managers discover that their communication effectiveness index is relatively low over an extended period of time, they should assess their situation to determine how to improve their communication skill. One problem they may discover is that they are repeatedly using a vocabulary confusing to the destination. For example, a study conducted by Group Attitudes Corporation found that if managers used certain words repeatedly in communication with steelworkers, the steelworkers almost certainly

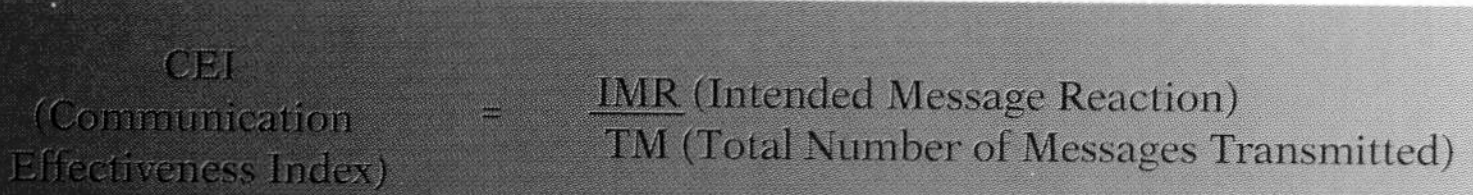

CEI
(Communication
Effectiveness Index)
=
IMR (Intended Message Reaction)
TM (Total Number of Messages Transmitted)

FIGURE 13.6 Calculation of communication effectiveness index

would become confused.[18] Words causing confusion include accrue, contemplate, designate, detriment, magnitude, and subsequently.

Besides analyzing their vocabulary, managers should attempt to increase their communication effectiveness by following the "ten commandments of good communication" as closely as possible. These commandments are as follows:[19]

1. *Seek to clarify your ideas before communicating.* The more systematically you analyze the problem or idea to be communicated, the clearer it becomes. This is the first step toward effective communication. Many communications fail because of inadequate planning. Good planning must consider the goals and attitudes of those who will receive the communication and those who will be affected by it.

2. *Examine the true purpose of each communication.* Before you communicate, ask yourself what you really want to accomplish with your message—obtain information, initiate action, change another person's attitude? Identify your most important goal and then adapt your language, tone, and total approach to serve that specific objective. Don't try to accomplish too much with each communication. The sharper the focus of your message, the greater its chances of success.

3. *Consider the total physical and human setting whenever you communicate.* Meaning and intent are conveyed by more than words alone. Many other factors influence the overall impact of a communication, and managers must be sensitive to the total setting in which they communicate. Consider, for example, your sense of timing, that is, the circumstances under which you make an announcement or render a decision; the physical setting—whether you communicate in private or otherwise, for example; the social climate that pervades work relationships within the company or a department and sets the tone of its communications; custom and practice—the degree to which your communication conforms to, or departs from, the expectations of your audience. Be constantly aware of the total setting in which you communicate. Like all living things, communication must be capable of adapting to its environment.

4. *Consult with others, when appropriate, in planning communications.* Frequently, it is desirable or necessary to seek the participation of others in planning a communication or in developing the facts on which to base the communication. Such consultation often lends additional insight and objectivity to your message. Moreover, those who have helped you plan your communication will give it their active support.

5. *Be mindful, while you communicate, of the overtones rather than merely the basic content of your message.* Your tone of voice, your expression, your apparent receptiveness to the responses of others—all have a significant effect on those you wish to reach. Frequently overlooked, these subtleties of communication often affect a listener's reaction to a message even more than its basic content. Similarly, your choice of language—particularly your awareness of the fine shades of meaning and emotion in the words you use—predetermines in large part the reactions of your listeners.

6. *Take the opportunity, when it arises, to convey something of help or value to the receiver.* Consideration of the other person's interests and needs—trying to look at things from the other person's point of view—frequently points up opportunities to convey something of immediate benefit or long-range value to the other person. Subordinates are most responsive to managers whose messages take the subordinates' interests into account.

7. *Follow up your communication.* Your best efforts at communication may be wasted, and you may never know whether you have succeeded in expressing your true meaning and intent if you do not follow up to see how well you have put your message across. You can do this by asking questions, by encouraging the

receiver to express his or her reactions, by follow-up contacts, and by subsequent review of performance. Make certain that every important communication has feedback so that complete understanding and appropriate action result.

8. *Communicate for tomorrow as well as today.* Even though communications may be aimed primarily at meeting the demands of an immediate situation, they must be planned with the past in mind if they are to maintain consistency in the receiver's view. Most important, however, communications must be consistent with long-range interests and goals. For example, it is not easy to communicate frankly on such matters as poor performance or the shortcomings of a loyal subordinate, but postponing disagreeable communications makes these matters more difficult in the long run and is actually unfair to your subordinates and your company.

9. *Be sure your actions support your communications.* In the final analysis, the most persuasive kind of communication is not what you say, but what you do. When your actions or attitudes contradict your words, others tend to discount what you have said. For every manager, this means that good supervisory practices—such as clear assignment of responsibility and authority, fair rewards for effort, and sound policy enforcement—serve to communicate more than all the gifts of oratory.

10. *Last, but by no means least: Seek not only to be understood but also to understand—be a good listener.* When you start talking, you often cease to listen, at least in that larger sense of being attuned to the other person's unspoken reactions and attitudes. Even more serious is the occasional inattentiveness you may be guilty of when others are attempting to communicate with you. Listening is one of the most important, most difficult, and most neglected skills in communication. It demands that you concentrate not only on the explicit meanings another person is expressing, but also on the implicit meanings, unspoken words, and undertones that may be far more significant.[20]

Verbal and Nonverbal Interpersonal Communication

Verbal communication is the sharing of ideas through words.

Nonverbal communication is the sharing of ideas without the use of words.

Interpersonal communication is generally divided into two types: verbal and nonverbal. Up to this point, the chapter has emphasized **verbal communication**—communication that uses either spoken or written words to share information with others.

Nonverbal communication is sharing information without using words to encode thoughts. Factors commonly used to encode thoughts in nonverbal communication are gestures, vocal tones, and facial expressions. In most interpersonal communication, verbal and nonverbal communications are not either-or occurrences. Instead, the destination's interpretation of a message generally is based not only on the words in the message but also on such images as the source's gestures and facial expressions.

In an interpersonal communication situation in which both verbal and nonverbal factors are present, nonverbal factors may have more influence on the total effect of a message than verbal factors. Over two decades ago, Albert Mehrabian developed a formula that showed the relative contributions of both verbal and nonverbal factors to the total effect of a message. This formula is as follows: Total message impact = .07 words + .38 vocal tones + .55 facial expressions.[21] Of course, both vocal tones and facial expressions are nonverbal factors. Besides vocal tones and facial expressions, gestures,[22] gender,[23] and dress[24] can influence the effect of a verbal message. Given the great potential influence of nonverbal factors on the effect of a message, managers should use nonverbal message ingredients to complement verbal message ingredients whenever possible.[25]

Nonverbal messages also can be used to add new content to verbal messages. To this end, a head might be nodded or a voice might be toned to show either agreement or disagreement.

Regardless of how managers decide to combine verbal and nonverbal factors, they must be sure that the two do not present contradictory messages. For instance, the words of a message might express approval, whereas the nonverbal factors express disapproval. This type of situation creates message ambiguity and leaves the destination frustrated.

BACK TO THE CASE

The employees' reactions to Dyer's messages can provide Dyer with perhaps his most useful tool in making communication successful—feedback. When feedback does not seem appropriate, Dyer should transmit another message to clarify the meaning of his first message. Dyer must be alert to both verbal and nonverbal feedback. Over time, if feedback indicates that Dyer is a relatively unsuccessful communicator, he should analyze his situation carefully to improve his communication effectiveness. Dyer might find, for instance, that he is using a vocabulary that is generally inappropriate for certain employees or that he is not following one or more of the ten commandments of good communication.

In addition, Dyer must remember that he can communicate to others without using words. His facial expressions, gestures, and even the tone of his voice say things to people. Most of Dyer's communication situations involve both verbal and nonverbal messages to Eaton employees. Because the impact of a message may be generated mostly by its nonverbal components, Dyer must be certain that his nonverbal messages complement his verbal messages.

Interpersonal Communication in Organizations

To be effective communicators, managers must understand not only general interpersonal communication concepts but also the characteristics of interpersonal communication within organizations, called **organizational communication.** Organizational communication directly relates to the goals, functions, and structure of human organizations.[26] Organizational success, to a major extent, is determined by the effectiveness of organizational communication.

Organizational communication is interpersonal communication within organizations.

Although organizational communication often was referred to by early management writers, the topic began to receive systematic study and attention only after World War II. From World War II to the 1950s, organizational communication as a discipline made significant advances in such areas as mathematical communication theory and behavioral communication theory.[27] Since the 1970s emphasis on organizational communication has grown in colleges of business throughout the nation.[28] The following information focuses on three fundamental organizational communication topics: (1) formal organizational communication, (2) informal organizational communication, and (3) the encouragement of formal organizational communication.

Formal Organizational Communication

In general, organizational communication that follows the lines of the organization chart is called **formal organizational communication.**[29] As discussed in chapter 9, the organization chart depicts relationships of people and jobs and shows the formal channels of communication among them.

Formal organizational communication is organizational communication that follows the lines of the organization chart.

ETHICS HIGHLIGHT
A Lack of Formal Organizational Communication Impacts Ethical Practices at Dow Corning

The Dow Corning Corporation is a company that manufacturers various kinds of silicone-based products and medical implants, including reconstructive and cosmetic breast implants. Management at Dow recently discovered that formal organizational communication must flow freely and openly if the company is to maintain ethical practices.

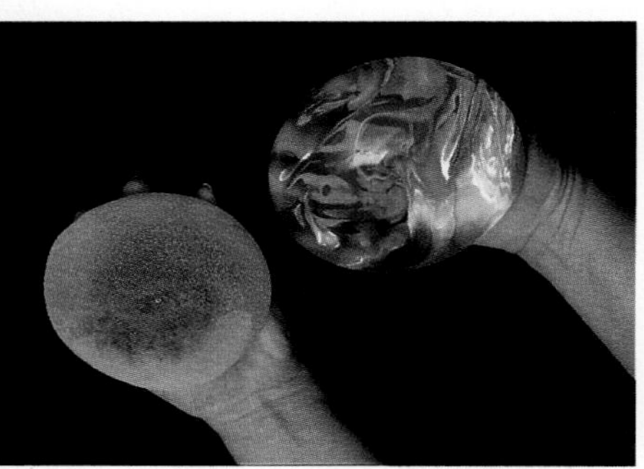

Some silicon breast implants have been found to be faulty and potentially dangerous. For instance, the implant on the left has become infected and bacteria laden.

Dow Corning has long been recognized as a pioneer in corporate ethics. It was one of the first companies to establish an ethics program, which many believe to be the most elaborate in corporate America. Recent controversy surrounding Dow Corning, however, exposes the limitations of this program. This controversy should also serve to remind other companies that even the best ethics programs and plans are not a guarantee against lapses or some unethical events occurring within companies.

Dow has recently been very busy defending itself from allegations that it sold breast implants knowing that the implants were faulty and that there was possible danger associated with their use. In addition, there is some evidence that certain organization members at Dow Corning took measures to prevent potential problems associated with implant use from becoming public knowledge.

Over fifteen years ago, Dow Corning launched its ethics program by beginning a series of audits to monitor compliance and to communicate with employees about ethics. The audits were conducted through group meetings by a Business Conduct Committee, which was made up of company executives. Some ethicists believe that the ethics program at Dow Corning failed to discover the breast implant problems because few managers are likely to speak openly about moral issues in a room filled with many employees, including the managers' supervisors. ▶

Types of Formal Organizational Communication. In general, there are three basic types of formal organizational communication: (1) downward, (2) upward, and (3) lateral.

Downward organizational communication is communication that flows from any point on an organization chart downward to another point on the organization chart.

Downward organizational communication is communication that flows from any point on an organization chart downward to another point on the organization chart. This type of formal organizational communication relates primarily to the direction and control of employees. Job-related information that focuses on what activities are required, when the activities should be performed, and how the activities should be coordinated with other activities within the organization must be transmitted to employees. This downward communication typically includes a statement of organizational philosophy, management system objectives, position descriptions, and other written information relating to the importance, rationale, and interrelationships of various departments.[30]

Upward organizational communication is communication that flows from any point on an organization chart upward to another point on the organization chart.

Upward organizational communication is communication that flows from any point on an organization chart upward to another point on the organization chart.[31] This type of organizational communication contains primarily the information managers need to evaluate the organizational area for which they are responsible and to determine if something is going wrong within the organization. Techniques that managers commonly use to encourage upward organizational communication include informal discussions with employees, attitude surveys, the development and use of grievance procedures, suggestion systems, and an "open-door" policy that invites employees to come in whenever they would like to talk to management.[32] Organizational modifications based on this feedback enable the organization to be more successful in the future.

Lateral organization communication is communication that flows from any point on an organization chart horizontally to another point on the organization chart.

Lateral organizational communication is communication that flows from any point on an organization chart horizontally to another point on the organization chart. Communication that flows across the organization usually focuses on coordinating the activities of various departments and developing new plans for future operating periods. Within the organization, all departments are related to all other departments. Only through lateral communication can these departmental relationships be coordinated well enough to enhance the attainment of management system objectives.

Patterns of Formal Organizational Communication. By nature, organizational communication creates patterns of communication among organization members. These patterns evolve from the repeated occurrence of various serial transmissions of information. According to Haney, a **serial transmission** involves passing information from one individual to another. It occurs when

A **serial transmission** is the passing of information from one individual through a series of individuals.

> *A* communicates a message to *B*; *B* then communicates *A*'s message (or rather his or her interpretation of *A*'s message) to *C*; *C* then communicates his or her interpretation of *B*'s interpretation of *A*'s message to *D*; and so on. The originator and the ultimate recipient of the message are separated by middle people.[33]

Of course, one of the obvious weaknesses of a serial transmission is that messages tend to become distorted as the length of the serial transmission increases. Research has shown that message details may be omitted, altered, or added in a serial transmission.[34]

As presented in a classic article by Alex Bavelas and Dermot Barrett,[35] the potential inaccuracy of transmitted messages is not the only weakness of a serial transmission. Serial transmissions can also influence morale, the emergence of a leader, the degree to which individuals involved in the transmissions are organized, and their efficiency. Three basic organizational communication pattern studies and their corresponding effects on the variables just mentioned are shown in Figure 13.7.

QUALITY HIGHLIGHT
Enhanced Formal Communication Contributes to Improving Quality at Holiday Inn

Improving the flow of communication that follows the organization chart can be of immense benefit to an organization. Holiday Inn found that improving the flow of such communication improves the quality of customer service.

Marketing and product quality were the themes at a recently held Holiday Inn Worldwide Franchise Conference. Through this conference, Holiday Inn was able to eliminate skepticism Holiday Inn operators were feeling toward the company itself. Individual Holiday Inn operators seemed more confident in the company after the announcement of a newly developed plan to improve the customer service as well as customer attitudes toward Holiday Inn through an improvement in Holiday Inn's formal

Holiday Inn will be able to improve the quality of service offered to customers by improving its formal communications system.

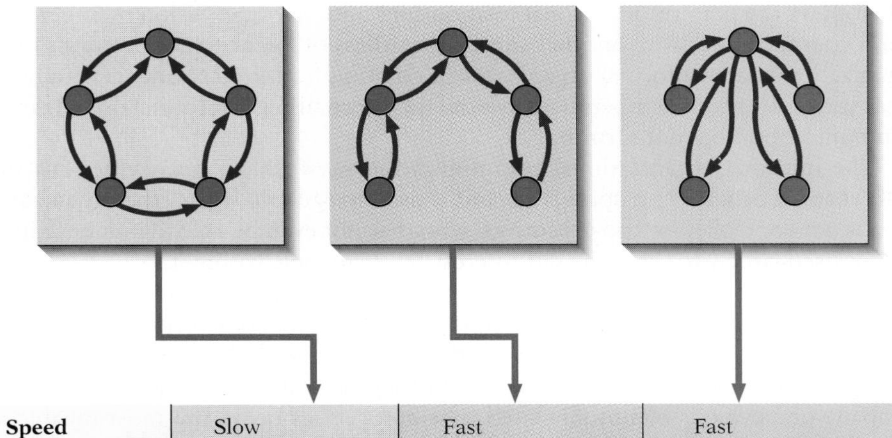

Speed	Slow	Fast	Fast
Accuracy	Poor	Good	Good
Organization	No stable form of organization	Slowly emerging but stable organization	Almost immediate and stable organization
Emergence of Leader	None	Marked	Very pronounced
Morale	Very good	Poor	Very poor

FIGURE 13.7 Relationship between three patterns of organizational communication and group characteristics of speed, accuracy, organization, emergence of leader, and morale

communication system. The company announced plans to extend its satellite communication system into Europe. This expansion will allow more efficient communication of hotel room rate information between North America and Europe, thus improving the quality of service offered to customers.

Mike Leven, president of the Holiday Inn franchise division, said that over time franchisees have watched the process of growth and have seen Holiday Inn's commitment to maintaining the quality of the company's service. Holiday Inn chairman Bryan Langton believes that this focus on quality has helped the company in recent years to outperform the industry in occupancy. ▶

BACK TO THE CASE As plant manager at Eaton, Robert Dyer must strive to understand the intricacies of organizational communication—interpersonal communication as it takes place within the organization. The success of organizational communication at Eaton is an important factor in determining the company's level of success. Dyer can communicate with his people in two basic ways: formally and informally.

In general, Dyer's formal communication should follow the lines on the organization chart. Dyer can communicate downward to, for example, a department head, or upward to, for example, George Dettloff, Eaton's engine components division general manager and Dyer's boss mentioned in the case. Dyer's downward communication will commonly focus on the activities subordinates are performing. His upward communication will commonly illustrate how the company is performing. Dyer can get advice on problems and improve coordination by communicating laterally with other plant managers like Mr. Kelly, the manager at Eaton's Lincoln, Nebraska, plant. A manager like Dyer should take steps to ensure that lateral communication also occurs at other organizational levels to enhance planning and coordination within his plant.

Informal organizational communication is organizational communication that does not follow the lines of the organization chart.

The **grapevine** is the network of informal organizational communication.

Informal organizational communication is organizational communication that does not follow the lines of the organization chart. This type of communication typically follows the pattern of personal relationships among organization members. One friend communicates with another friend, regardless of their relative positions on the organization chart. Informal organizational communication networks generally exist because organization members have a desire for information that formal organizational communication does not furnish.

The informal organizational communication network, or **grapevine,** has three main characteristics: (1) it springs up and is used irregularly within the organization; (2) it is not controlled by top executives, who may not even be able to influence it; and (3) it is used largely to serve the self-interests of the people within it.

Understanding the grapevine is a prerequisite for a complete understanding of organizational communication. Some estimates indicate that 70 percent of all communication in organizations follows organizational grapevines.[36] Not only do grapevines carry great amounts of communication, but they carry it at very rapid speeds.[37] The company grapevine is commonly cited by employees as being the most reliable and credible source of information about company events.[38]

As with formal organizational communication, informal organizational communication uses serial transmissions. Organization members involved in these transmissions, however, are more difficult for managers to identify than are those in the formal communication network. Keith Davis's classic article that appeared in the *Harvard Business Review* has been a significant help to managers over the years in understanding how organizational grapevines exist and operate. Figure 13.8 contains the four grapevine patterns outlined by Davis that tend to exist in organizations.[39]

1. *The single-strand grapevine.* *A* tells *B*, who tells *C*, who tells *D*, and so on. This type of grapevine tends to distort messages more than any other.

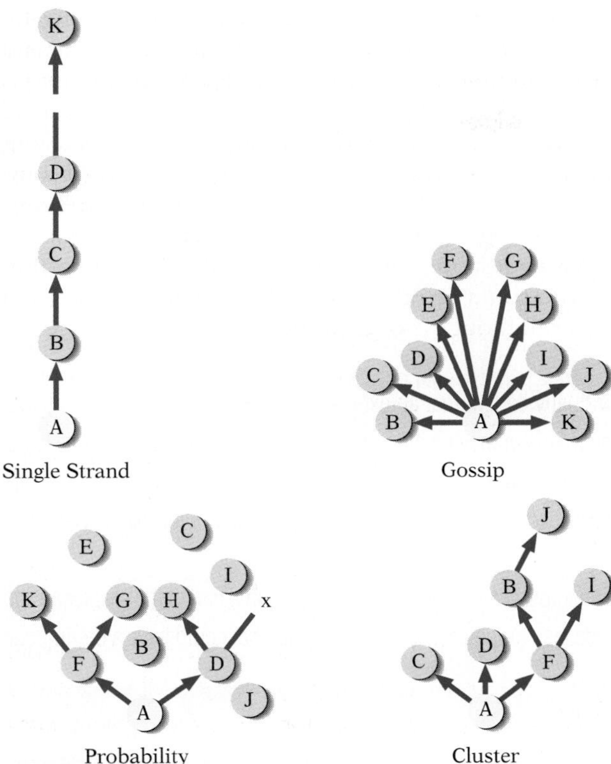

FIGURE 13.8 Four types of organizational grapevines
(Copyright © 1953 by the President and Fellows of Harvard College: all rights reserved.)

2. *The gossip grapevine.* *A* informs everyone else on the grapevine.
3. *The probability grapevine.* *A* communicates randomly, for example, to *F* and *D*. *F* and *D* then continue to inform other grapevine members in the same way.
4. *The cluster grapevine.* *A* selects and tells *C*, *D*, and *F*. *F* selects and tells *I* and *B*, and *B* selects and tells *J*. Information in this grapevine travels only to selected individuals.

Clearly, grapevines are a factor managers must deal with because they can, and often do, generate rumors that can be detrimental to organizational success.[40] On the other hand, when employees have what they view as sufficient organizational information, it seems to build their sense of belonging to the organization and their level of productivity. Grapevines could be used to help managers to maximize information flow to employees.[41] Some writers argue that managers should encourage the development of grapevines and strive to become grapevine members to gain feedback that could be very valuable in improving the organization.[42] Exactly how individual managers should deal with the grapevine, of course, depends on the specific organizational situation in which the managers find themselves.

Encouraging Formal Organizational Communication. Organizational communication often is called the nervous system of the organization. The organization acts only in the way that its nervous system, or organizational communication, directs it. Since formal organizational communication is generally the more important type of communication that takes place within the organization, managers must encourage its free flow if the organization is to be successful.

Managers can use many different strategies to encourage the flow of formal organizational communication. One strategy is listening attentively to messages that come through formal channels. Listening shows organization members that managers are interested in what subordinates have to say and encourages employees to use formal communication channels in subsequent situations. General guidelines for listening are presented in Table 13.2. Another managerial strategy is to support the flow of clear and concise statements through formal communication channels. Receiving an ambiguous message through a formal organizational communication channel can discourage members from using that channel again. A third strategy managers can use is taking care to ensure that all organization members have free access to the use of formal communication channels within the organization. Obviously, organization members cannot communicate formally within the organization if they don't have access to the formal communication network. A fourth strategy is assigning specific communication responsibilities to staff personnel who could be of enormous help to line personnel in spreading important information throughout the organization.

BACK TO THE CASE It is virtually certain that an extensive grapevine exists in Dyer's plant. Although this grapevine must be dealt with, Dyer may not be able to influence it significantly. Eaton employees at the plant, as well as employees for any company, typically are involved in grapevines for self-interest and because the formal organization has not furnished them with the information they believe they need.

By developing various social relationships, Dyer could conceivably become part of the grapevine and obtain valuable feedback from it. Also, because grapevines generate rumors that could have a detrimental

TABLE 13.2 Ten commandments for good listening

1. *Stop talking!*
   You cannot listen if you are talking.
   Polonius *(Hamlet):* "Give every man thine ear, but few thy voice."
2. *Put the talker at ease.*
   Help the talker feel free to talk.
   This is often called a permissive environment.
3. *Show the talker that you want to listen.*
   Look and act interested. Do not read your mail while he or she talks.
   Listen to understand rather than to oppose.
4. *Remove distractions.*
   Don't doodle, tap, or shuffle papers.
   Will it be quieter if you shut the door?
5. *Empathize with the talker.*
   Try to put yourself in the talker's place so that you can see his or her point of view.
6. *Be patient.*
   Allow plenty of time. Do not interrupt the talker.
   Don't start for the door or walk away.
7. *Hold your temper.*
   An angry person gets the wrong meaning from words.
8. *Go easy on argument and criticism.*
   This puts the talker on the defensive. He or she may "clam up" or get angry.
   Do not argue: even if you win, you *lose*.
9. *Ask questions.*
   This encourages the talker and shows you are listening.
   It helps to develop points further.
10. *Stop talking!*
    This is first and last, because all other commandments depend on it.
    You just can't do a good listening job while you are talking.

Nature gave us two ears but only one tongue,
which is a gentle hint that we should listen more than we talk.

effect on the success of Dyer's plant, he should try to ensure that personnel at his plant are given all the information they need to do their jobs well through formal organizational communication, thereby reducing the need for a grapevine.

Because formal organizational communication is vitally important to Dyer's plant, he should try to encourage its flow as much as possible. He can do this by listening intently to messages that come to him over formal channels, supporting the flow of clear messages through formal channels, and making sure that all employees at his plant have access to formal communication channels.

ACTION SUMMARY

Reread the learning objectives that follow. Each objective is followed by questions. Answering these questions accurately will help you retain the most important concepts discussed in this chapter. After answering each question, check your answer with the answer key at the end of this chapter. (*Hint:* If you have doubt regarding the correct response, consult the page whose number follows the answer.)

Circle: ***From studying this chapter, I will attempt to acquire:***

1. An understanding of influencing.

T, F — **a.** The influencing function can be viewed as forcing the activities of organization members in appropriate directions.

a, b, c, d, e — **b.** The following activity is *not* a major component of the influencing process: (a) motivating; (b) leading; (c) communicating; (d) correcting; (e) considering groups.

2. An understanding of interpersonal communication.

a, b, c, d, e — **a.** Communication is best described as the process of: (a) sharing emotion; (b) sharing information; (c) sending messages; (d) feedback formulation; (e) forwarding information.

a, b, c, d, e — **b.** The basic elements of interpersonal communication are: (a) source/encoder, signal, decoder/destination; (b) sender/message, encoder, receiver/decoder; (c) signal, source/sender, decoder/destination; (d) signal, source/decoder, encoder/destination; (e) source/sender, signal, receiver/destination.

3. A knowledge of how to use feedback.

T, F — **a.** Feedback is solely verbal.

a, b, c, d, e — **b.** Robert S. Goyer suggested using feedback: (a) as a microbarrier; (b) as a way for sources to evaluate their communication effectiveness; (c) to ensure that instructions will be carried out; (d) to evaluate the decoder; (e) all of the above.

4. An appreciation for the importance of nonverbal communication.

T, F — **a.** In interpersonal communication, nonverbal factors may play a more influential role than verbal factors.

T, F — **b.** Nonverbal messages can contradict verbal messages, which can create frustration in the destination.

5. Insights on formal organizational communication.

a, b, c, d, e — **a.** The following is *not* upward communication: (a) cost accounting reports; (b) purchase order summary; (c) production reports; (d) corporate policy statement; (e) sales reports.

a, b, c, d, e — **b.** The primary purpose served by lateral organizational communication is: (a) coordinating; (b) organizing; (c) direction; (d) evaluation; (e) control.

6. An appreciation for the importance of the grapevine.

a, b, c, d, e — **a.** The following statement concerning the grapevine is *not* correct: (a) grapevines are irregularly used in organizations; (b) a grapevine can and often does generate harmful rumors; (c) the grapevine is used largely to serve the self-interests of the people within it; (d) some managers use grapevines to their advantage; (e) in time, and with proper pressure, the grapevine can be eliminated.

T, F **b.** The grapevine is much slower than formal communication channels.

7. Some hints on how to encourage organizational communication.

a, b, c, d,e **a.** To encourage formal organizational communication, managers should: (a) support the flow of clear and concise statements through formal channels; (b) ensure free access to formal channels for all organization members; (c) assign specific communication responsibilities to staff personnel; (d) a and b; (e) all of the above.

T, F **b.** Since formal organizational communication is the most important type of communication within an organization, managers must restrict its flow if the organization is to be successful.

INTRODUCTORY CASE WRAP-UP

"Eaton Managers Concentrate on Influencing People" (p. 321) and its related back-to-the-case sections were written to help you better understand the management concepts contained in this chapter. Answer the following discussion questions about this introductory case to further enrich your understanding of chapter content:

1. List three problems that could be caused at Eaton's Kearney plant if Robert Dyer were a poor communicator.
2. Explain *how* the problems you listed in number 1 can be caused by Dyer's inability to communicate.
3. Assuming that Dyer is a good communicator, discuss three ways that he is positively impacting Eaton's Kearney plant as a result of this communication expertise.

ISSUES FOR REVIEW AND DISCUSSION

1. What is influencing?
2. Describe the relationship between the overall management system and the influencing subsystem.
3. What factors make up the input, process, and output of the influencing subsystem?
4. Explain the relationship between the factors that compose the process section of the influencing subsystem.
5. What is communication?
6. How important is communication to managers?
7. Draw the communication model presented in this chapter and explain how it works.
8. How does successful communication differ from unsuccessful communication?
9. Summarize the significance of field of experience to communication.
10. List and describe three communication macrobarriers and three communication microbarriers.
11. What is feedback, and how should managers use it when communicating?
12. How is the communication effectiveness index calculated, and what is its significance?
13. Name the ten commandments of good communication.
14. What is nonverbal communication? Explain its significance.
15. How should managers use nonverbal communication?
16. What is organizational communication?
17. How do formal and informal organizational communication differ?
18. Describe three types of formal organizational communication, and explain the general purpose of each type.
19. Can serial transmissions and other formal communication patterns influence communication effectiveness and the individuals using the patterns? If so, how?
20. Draw and describe the four main types of grapevines that exist in organizations.
21. How can managers encourage the flow of formal organizational communication?

ACTION SUMMARY ANSWER KEY

1. **a.** F, p. 322
   b. d, pp. 322–323
2. **a.** b, p. 325
   b. a, pp. 325–326
3. **a.** F, p. 330
   b. b, p. 330
4. **a.** T, p. 332
   b. T, pp. 332–333
5. **a.** d, p. 334
   b. a, p. 334
6. **a.** e, pp. 336–337
   b. F, p. 336
7. **a.** e, pp. 337–338
   b. F, p. 338

CASE STUDY

The Wal-Mart Influence

ROBERT E. KEMPER
Northern Arizona University

Wal-Mart Stores Incorporated operates an expanding chain of modern retail outlets, marketing merchandise through discount department stores, wholesale clubs, deep-discount drugstores, supercenters, and hypermarkets. By February 1993, these included 1,853 Wal-Mart Discount Cities, 256 Sam's Warehouse Clubs, 4 Hypermart USAs, and 30 Supercenters. Wal-Mart plans to open 150 new stores every year.

Wal-Mart's distribution facilities are a major key to its success. Centers rely on laser scanners to route goods coming off company trailers along conveyer belts up to eleven miles long. The technology is standard—mechanized conveyers, bar coding, and computer inventory—but no one else operates it this effectively. The average Wal-Mart store is a one-stop shopping center, typically serving a community of about 150,000 people, although many of its new stores are opening in large cities such as Houston, Denver, and Phoenix. Wage costs are held at eight percent of total sales. There are 470,000 employees and 120,000 stockholders. Insiders own forty-four percent of common stock.

Wal-Mart does everything it can to make its people feel part of a family. It hires locally, trains its people, encourages them to ask questions, and generously praises them. David Glass, Wal-Mart's boss, prides himself on being a visible, accessible leader, much in the same image as Wal-Mart's founder, the late Sam Walton. Wal-Mart prides itself on being fair in its dealings with the public—this was the core of Sam Walton's philosophy. Glass spends the better part of each year visiting the stores personally. At the stores, Glass's style consists largely of breezing along the aisles, notebook in hand, and asking questions.

Even when Glass is not visiting stores, he maintains communication through a six-channel satellite system that gives the remote Wal-Mart headquarters a computer-communications-complex appearance worthy of the U.S. Defense Department. Its goal is to link every location in the Wal-Mart empire by voice and video, facilitating store-to-store and store-to-home-office communications. The satellite system also gathers store data for the chain's master computers, and it reduces time and dollars spent on credit card checks, flashing back responses in four or five seconds.

By satellite, Wal-Mart executives can talk to every store at the same time as often as they like, or they can direct communications to only a few. However, the biggest advantage is in sharing merchandise information. A buyer can go on video and announce, "These are the new items for Department 16. Here is how you should display them."

Wal-Mart people are motivated and productive, and high productivity lends itself to low overhead. Employees operate in an environment where ideas and change are encouraged. For example, if a store associate makes suggestions regarding mechandising ideas that would create significant sales gains for an item, or improvements to existing procedures that would result in cost savings, these ideas can be quickly disseminated by the satellite system. With 470,000 associates to make suggestions, this leads to substantial sales gains, cost reductions, and improved productivity.

Also, there are award programs on top of award programs for those associates: regional all-star teams, an all-star departmental honor roll, VPI (volume-producing item) contests, a departmental sales honor roll, and a shrinkage incentive program. Names and pictures of award winners are run in the company magazine, *Wal-Mart World*.

Visitors say that Wal-Mart is particularly adept at striking that delicate balance needed to convince shoppers its prices are low but its stores are not too cheap. David Glass and Wal-Mart's 120,000 stockholders certainly would not disagree, nor will Kmart executives, who must watch from the sidelines as Wal-Mart sees retail sales increase 10 percent, while number two Kmart sees increases of only 2.4 percent for stores open a year or more. Wal-Mart certainly seems to have a happy influence on both its associates and its clientele.

DISCUSSION QUESTIONS

1. What effect do you think the satellite system has had on formal communication at Wal-Mart? Why?
2. What effect do you think David Glass's appearances at Wal-Mart stores has on informal communication at Wal-Mart? Why?
3. Sam Walton died in 1992. What effect do you think his departure has had on communication at Wal-Mart? Why?
4. What management tasks does the company magazine *Wal-Mart World* accomplish?

CNN VIDEO CASE

PG&E's Master Communicator

RICHARD CLARKE
Pacific Gas and Electric

In 1945, while president of his high-school student body, Richard Clarke was invited to be a guest at the opening of the United Nations. At the luncheon afterward, he sat at the same table as Madam Chiang Kai-shek and engaged in conversation about what the United Nations meant, from one high-school student's perspective.

Clarke was not a typical high-school student any more than he is a typical CEO. One of the concepts he believes in—enough to follow through on personally—is the importance of communicating with *all* employees in the organization. The organization is Pacific Gas & Electric (PG&E), the nation's largest public utility. How can one possibly try to communicate at any real level with its twenty-six thousand employees? Clarke has what he calls "brown-bag lunches." These lunches, held monthly, are attended by two hundred or more employees; they are invited to stand up and ask their CEO any question they want. In addition to these lunches, Clarke also makes a point of getting out in the field and talking with employees while they are on the job.

Richard Clarke invites PG&E employees to a monthly brown-bag lunch where they are invited to stand up and ask him any question they like.

This obvious caring by management helps explain why PG&E was able to respond quickly when a 7.1 Richter-scale earthquake hit San Francisco in 1987 and left 1.5 million customers in the dark. Reports Clarke, "There's a tradition in our company, a sense of commitment and loyalty, that when something happens, our people just report to work. They're not called. They just know." This response by its employees helped PG&E to put in twenty miles of new gas mains in about three weeks, as part of its rebuilding after the earthquake. PG&E also showed community responsibility by bringing in blankets, flashlights, and portable hot-water showers to help lessen people's discomfort after the disaster.

In another form of communication, PG&E has a policy of seeking conversations and joint projects with environmental groups, believing that environmentalism will be a worldwide force in this decade. The utility company had to learn this lesson the hard way. In its construction of two nuclear power plants in Diablo Canyon, California, a process that spanned fourteen years, PG&E made some mistakes. Among them, the company ignored seismological studies when it built only two miles from an earthquake fault, and it made a major engineering error that resulted in the suspension of its license by the Nuclear Regulatory Commission. In 1987 PG&E had to write off $1 billion due to mismanagement of the Diablo Canyon project.

Since then, PG&E has learned its lesson well and has developed an alliance with the environmentalists. As Clarke explains, "This part of California is so rich in its environmental features, and our company has been here since the Gold Rush. We went back to our roots and came forward with an environmental awareness and a consciousness." PG&E could anticipate that the nation's energy resource plans would increasingly include the component of energy efficiency. The company has worked out an arrangement with the environmentalists and the state of California whereby profits will be helped if the company produces and sells less energy and if the customers use less. PG&E's advertising is now geared to these goals. The company provides rebates to customers to cover some of the customers' costs in converting to energy-efficient lighting, for example; in a few years, the customers' lower energy bills offset the costs of the new lighting.

Richard Clarke would like to be remembered, he says, "as the one who brought PG&E from the era of a utility monopoly to a competitive, innovative, environmentally super-conscious company that was extremely effective up to the turn of the century."

VIDEO CASE QUESTIONS

1. In what ways has Clarke been able to influence employees and others.
2. How does Clarke use communication to create employee responsibility?
3. How do you think unsuccessful communication may account for PG&E's mistakes at Diablo Canyon?
4. What microbarrier did Clarke overcome in order to communicate successfully with environmentalists? Explain in terms of source and destination.

CNN VIDEO EXERCISE

Mastering Communication at PG&E

EXERCISE GOAL: Learn how to resolve a difficult communication problem with an employee.

In chapter 11 you learned that performance appraisals must be handled well to be of value to the company. Imagine that you are a manager at PG&E and that three months ago you hired a new employee. Although her credentials were excellent and she interviewed well, her work habits are very poor. She comes in late, leaves early, and takes long lunches. She has insulted several members of the clerical and support staff.

You must meet with this employee and explain what she must do to meet company expectations. You also are going to put her on a three-month probationary period. You want the employee to agree that she has been at fault, and you want her to agree to the terms of her probation. You want to hear any explanations, problems, or questions that she may have.

Now follow these steps:

1. Write what you hope to communicate and accomplish by meeting with this employee. Think about how you will approach the meeting to achieve your goals.
2. In class, you will be part of either the "employees" group or the "employers" group. If you are an employee, play the full role: you do not understand company expectations; you refuse to admit you have done anything wrong; you insist that you are doing great work; and so on. Show any number of emotions, including anger, sorrow, and disbelief.
3. Begin the role-plays.
4. While you watch other students conduct their role-plays, complete the following appraisal sheet for each employer.

Communication Role-Play Appraisal Sheet

Name of student playing employer: ______________________________

1. Does the "employer" put the "employee" at ease? What else might the employer have done to put the employee at ease?

____

____

____

2. Were there distractions during the meeting? What were they? How might the employer have avoided them?

____

____

____

3. Did the employer get the employee to admit that she was at fault? What else might the employer have done to accomplish this goal?

____

____

____

4. By the end of the meeting, did the employee have a clear understanding of her employer's expectations?

____

____

____

5. Did the employer maintain composure throughout the meeting?

____

____

____

6. Did the employer demonstrate good listening skills?

____

____

____

CHAPTER

14

LEADERSHIP

STUDENT LEARNING OBJECTIVES

From studying this chapter, I will attempt to acquire:

1. A working definition of leadership.
2. An understanding of the relationship between leading and managing.
3. An appreciation for the trait and situational approaches to leadership.
4. Insights about using leadership theories that emphasize decision-making situations.
5. Insights about using leadership theories that emphasize more general organizational situations.
6. An understanding of alternatives to leader flexibility.
7. An appreciation of both transformational and substitute leadership theory.

CHAPTER OUTLINE

INTRODUCTORY CASE
Liz Claiborne: The Wizard of Working Women's Fashion

DEFINING LEADERSHIP

LEADER VERSUS MANAGER

THE TRAIT APPROACH TO LEADERSHIP

THE SITUATIONAL APPROACH TO LEADERSHIP: A FOCUS ON LEADER BEHAVIOR

GLOBAL HIGHLIGHT
China

Leadership Situations and Decisions

ETHICS HIGHLIGHT
NBC News

Leadership Behaviors

QUALITY HIGHLIGHT
Potlatch Corporation

RECENT EMPHASIS ON LEADERSHIP

Transformational Leadership
Substitutes for Leadership
Women as Leaders
Ways Women Lead

DIVERSITY HIGHLIGHT
Corning

CASE STUDY
Al Scott's Vision of Quality for Wilson Sporting Goods

VIDEO CASE
When Inexperience Paid Off:
Richard Branson, The Virgin Group

VIDEO EXERCISE
Planning an Executive Retreat for Virgin Atlantic Airways

INTRODUCTORY CASE

Liz Claiborne: The Wizard of Working Women's Fashion

By listening to women and giving them the fashions that they want to wear, Elisabeth Claiborne has built America's top-selling women's clothing label—Liz Claiborne. The fashions are simple, straightforward garments for career women. Claiborne believed that women did not want or need outrageous or exciting fashions but were looking for clothing that would give them style, quality, fit, and value.

Elisabeth Claiborne (who retired from Liz Claiborne in 1989) was a fashion designer who had earned her respect designing women's clothing. As more women entered the work force in the early 1970s, she saw a gap in the women's fashion industry. Between the casual slacks and jeans look and the boardroom-career-suit look was a huge market for relaxed, yet functional and coordinated, separates that career women could mix and match. Claiborne talked to real working women, designed clothing to fit their life-styles, and built a whole wardrobe around them.

Claiborne led by teaching her designers, not by doing the designing for them.

In 1975, with this vision of the working woman in mind—and with $50,000 in savings and $200,000 as seed money from family and friends—Elisabeth Claiborne and her husband, Arthur Ortenberg, launched Liz Claiborne. One year later, sales had reached $200 million and the fashion industry was already referring to her as "visionary" and "the great pathfinder."

Claiborne and her husband decided from the start that Liz Claiborne employees should feel themselves part of the company. To foster team spirit, she spent a part of each day working with a different division. Her upbeat manner shaped positive relationships with her employees. Claiborne offered her employees both credit and responsibility for the tasks they performed. They took responsibility for mistakes, learned, and then went forward. Claiborne led by teaching her designers, not by doing the designing for them. She let them know, however, that she could do it as well as they could, or better.

From Joan E. Rigdon, "Using Lateral Moves to Spur Employees," *Wall Street Journal* (May 26, 1992), B1, B9. Reprinted by permission of *Wall Street Journal*, © 1992 Dow Jones & Company, Inc. All Rights Reserved Worldwide.

In 1989, Liz Claiborne and Arthur Ortenberg turned over the reins of the $2 billion-plus fashion empire to Jerome Chazen, an original partner in the firm. By having laid the groundwork from the beginning for company spirit and a staff of capable employees, Claiborne and Ortenberg were prepared to turn the company over to the new management. The years of leading, teaching, correcting, and guiding will pay off because the Liz Claiborne team style will be perpetuated through Elisabeth Claiborne's successors.

At Liz Claiborne's clothing company, employees work as a team; they learn to take responsibility and receive credit for their performance.

WHAT'S AHEAD Liz Claiborne, the founder and leader of the company which bears her name, has been deeply concerned with perpetuating her company. Although she apparently is a "natural" at visionary leadership, most of us must learn how to be effective leaders. This chapter discusses (1) how to define leadership, (2) the difference between a leader and a manager, (3) the trait approach to leadership, (4) the situational approach to leadership, and (5) recent emphasis on leadership.

DEFINING LEADERSHIP

Leadership is the process of directing the behavior of others toward the accomplishment of objectives.

Leadership is the process of directing the behavior of others toward the accomplishment of some objective. Directing, in this sense, means causing individuals to act in a certain way or to follow a particular course. Ideally, this course is perfectly consistent with such factors as established organizational policies, procedures, and job descriptions. The central theme of leadership is getting things accomplished through people. As indicated in chapter 13, leadership is one of the four main interdependent activities of the influencing subsystem and is accomplished, at least to some extent, by communicating with others. It is extremely important that managers have a thorough understanding of what leadership entails. Leadership has always been considered a prerequisite for organizational success. Given issues such as the increased capability afforded by enhanced communication technology and the rise of international business, leadership is more important now than ever before.[1]

LEADER VERSUS MANAGER

Leading is not the same as managing. Many executives do not understand the difference between leading and managing, and are therefore under a misapprehension about how to carry out their organizational duties.[2] Although some managers are leaders and some leaders are managers, leading and managing are not identical activities.[3] According to Theodore Levitt, management consists of

> the rational assessment of a situation and the systematic selection of goals and purposes (what is to be done); the systematic development of strategies to achieve these goals; the marshalling of the required resources; the rational design, organization, direction, and control of the activities required to attain the selected purposes; and, finally, the motivating and rewarding of people to do the work.[4]

Leadership, as one of the four primary activities of the influencing function, is a subset of management. Managing is much broader in scope than leading and focuses on behavioral as well as nonbehavioral issues. Leading emphasizes mainly behavioral issues. Figure 14.1 makes the point that, although not all managers are necessarily leaders, the most effective managers, over the long term, are leaders.

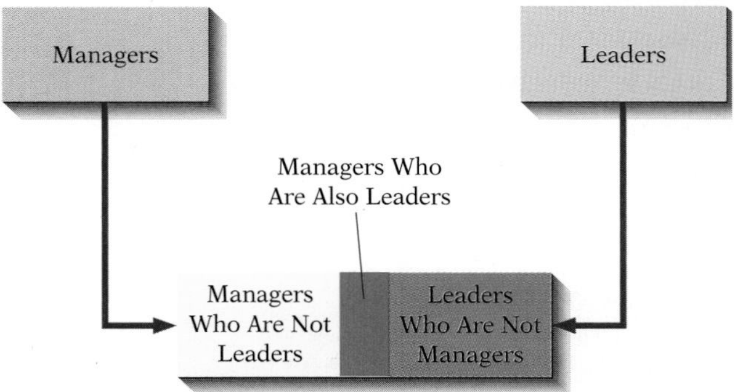

FIGURE 14.1 Most effective managers over the long term are also leaders

Merely possessing management skills is no longer sufficient for an executive to be successful in today's business world. Modern executives need a fundamental understanding of the difference between management and leading and how both activities must be combined to achieve organizational success. A manager makes sure that a job gets done and a leader cares about and focuses on the people who do the job.[5] To combine management and leadership, modern executives should demonstrate a calculated and logical focus on organizational processes (management) along with a genuine concern for workers as people (leadership).[6]

THE TRAIT APPROACH TO LEADERSHIP

The **trait approach to leadership** is based on early leadership research that seemed to assume that a good leader is born, not made. The mainstream of this research attempted to describe successful leaders as precisely as possible. The reasoning was that, if a complete profile of the traits of a successful leader could be summarized, it would be fairly easy to pinpoint the individuals who should and should not be placed in leadership positions.

The **trait approach to leadership** is an outdated view of leadership that sees the personal characteristics of an individual as the main determinants of how successful the individual could be as a leader.

Many of the early studies that attempted to summarize the traits of successful leaders have been documented.[7] One of these summaries concludes that successful leaders tend to possess the following characteristics:[8]

1. Intelligence, including judgment and verbal ability.
2. Past achievement in scholarship and athletics.
3. Emotional maturity and stability.
4. Dependability, persistence, and a drive for continuing achievement.
5. The skill to participate socially and adapt to various groups.
6. A desire for status and socioeconomic position.

An evaluation of a number of these trait studies, however, concludes that their findings tend to be inconsistent.[9] One researcher says that fifty years of study have failed to produce one personality trait or set of qualities that can be used consistently to discriminate leaders from nonleaders.[10] It follows, then, that no trait or combination of traits guarantees that a leader will be successful. Leadership is apparently a much more complex issue.

Contemporary management writers and practitioners generally agree with the notion that leadership ability cannot be explained by an individual's traits or inherited characteristics. More popular current thought supports the notion that individuals can be trained to be good leaders. Thousands of employees each year are sent through leadership training programs in support of the idea that leaders can be and are being developed through instructional programs.[11]

BACK TO THE CASE

From the preceding material, a manager such as Elisabeth Claiborne, founder of Liz Claiborne, should understand that leadership activities are those activities within the company that involve directing the behavior of organization members so that company goals are reached. A manager such as Claiborne should also understand that leading and managing are not the same thing. When managing, Claiborne is involved with planning, organizing, influencing, and controlling within the company. When leading, she is performing an activity that is part of the influencing function of management. To maximize her long-term success, Claiborne should strive to be both a manager and a leader.

In assessing her leadership ability, Claiborne should not fall into the trap of trying to increase her leadership success by changing her personal traits or attitudes to mirror those of successful leaders that she might know. Studies based on the trait approach to leadership should indicate to Claiborne that merely changing her characteristics will not guarantee her success as a leader.

THE SITUATIONAL APPROACH TO LEADERSHIP: A FOCUS ON LEADER BEHAVIOR

The **situational approach to leadership** is a relatively modern view of leadership that suggests that successful leadership requires a unique combination of leaders, followers, and leadership situations.

The emphasis of leadership study has shifted from the trait approach to the situational approach. Leadership style must be appropriately matched to the situation the leader faces. The more modern **situational approach to leadership** is based on the assumption that the instances of successful leadership are somewhat different and require a unique combination of leaders, followers, and leadership situations. This interaction commonly is expressed in formula form: SL = f (L,F,S). In this formula, SL is *successful leadership,* f stands for *function of,* and L,F, and S are, respectively, the *leader,* the *follower,* and the *situation.*[12] A translation of this formula would be that successful leadership is a function of the leader, the follower, and the situation. In other words, the leader, the follower, and the situation must be appropriate for one another if a leadership attempt is to be successful.

GLOBAL HIGHLIGHT China's Leadership Style

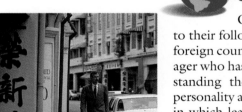

For a U.S. manager with a position of leadership within a Chinese organization, it is critical to understand the Chinese value system and working style.

One leadership challenge commonly faced by U.S. managers is how to react to their followers as well as to the particular situation appropriately when leading in a foreign country. As an example, consider the leadership challenge faced by a U.S. manager who has a position of leadership in a Chinese organization. For this leader, understanding the Chinese value system and working styles is critical. The Chinese personality and working style is presently dominated by a more traditional value system in which leaders must demonstrate strength and expertise. A leader in China is expected to build trust and personal relationships with followers. Terminating irresponsible workers is generally discouraged because such a discharged worker would lose too much "face." The Chinese are used to working at a relatively slow pace characterized by much leader patience and control. Chinese leaders commonly give employees gifts to show concern openly and offer encouragement, but they never criticize employees openly.

Leading in a Chinese organization would normally require somewhat different leadership tactics than leading in a U.S. organization. In general, U.S. managers should assess and react to situational leadership variables based on the social norms and customs of the country in which they are managing rather than on their own. ▶

Leadership Situations and Decisions

The Tannenbaum and Schmidt Leadership Continuum

Tannenbaum and Schmidt wrote one of the first and perhaps most well-quoted articles on the situational approach to leadership. The authors emphasize situations in which a leader makes decisions.[13] Since one of the most important tasks of a leader is making sound decisions, practical and legitimate leadership thinking should contain some emphasis on decision making. Figure 14.2 presents Tannenbaum and Schmidt's model of leadership behavior, which contains such a decision-making emphasis.

The model presented in the figure is actually a continuum, or range, of leadership behavior available to managers in making decisions. Each type of decision-making behavior in this model has both a corresponding degree of authority used by the manager and a related amount of freedom available to subordinates. Management behavior at

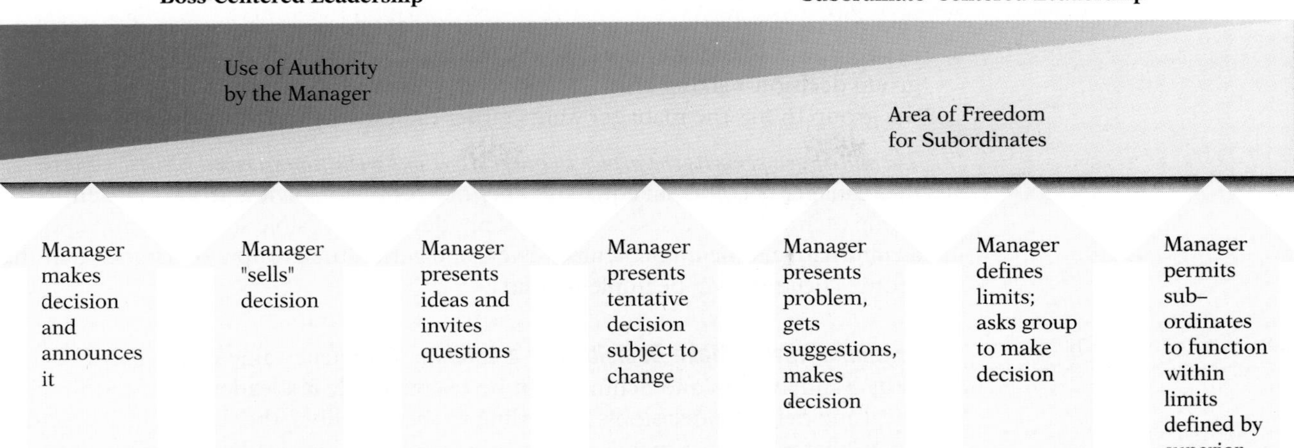

FIGURE 14.2 Continuum of leadership behavior that emphasizes decision making

the extreme left of the model characterizes the leader who makes decisions by maintaining high control and allowing little subordinate freedom. Behavior at the extreme right characterizes the leader who makes decisions by exercising little control and allowing much subordinate freedom and self-direction. Behavior between the extreme left and right reflects a gradual change from autocratic to democratic leadership, or vice versa. Managers displaying leadership behavior toward the right of the model are more democratic and are called *subordinate-centered* leaders. Managers displaying leadership behavior toward the left of the model are more autocratic and are called *boss-centered* leaders. Each type of leadership behavior in this model is explained in more detail in the following list:

1. *The manager makes the decision and announces it.* This behavior is characterized by the manager (a) identifying a problem, (b) analyzing various alternatives available to solve the problem, (c) choosing the alternative that will be used to solve the problem, and (d) requiring followers to implement the chosen alternative. The manager may or may not use coercion, but the followers have no opportunity to participate directly in the decision-making process.
2. *The manager "sells" the decision.* As before, the manager identifies the problem and independently arrives at a decision. Rather than announce the decision to subordinates for implementation, however, the manager tries to persuade subordinates to accept the decision.
3. *The manager presents ideas and invites questions.* Here, the manager makes the decision and attempts to gain acceptance through persuasion. One additional step is taken, however; subordinates are invited to ask questions about the decision.
4. *The manager presents a tentative decision that is subject to change.* The manager allows subordinates to have some part in the decision-making process but retains the responsibility for identifying and diagnosing the problem. The manager then arrives at a tentative decision that is subject to change on the basis of subordinate input. The final decision is made by the manager.
5. *The manager presents the problem, gets suggestions, and then makes the decision.* This is the first leadership activity described thus far that allows subordinates the opportunity to offer problem solutions before the manager does. The manager still identifies the problem in the first place.
6. *The manager defines the limits and asks the group to make a decision.* This behavior is characterized by the manager first defining the problem and setting the bound-

aries within which a decision must be made. The manager then sets up a partnership with subordinates to arrive at an appropriate decision. However, if the group of subordinates does not perceive the manager as genuinely desiring a serious group decision-making effort, it will tend to arrive at conclusions that reflect what the group thinks the manager wants rather than what the group actually wants.

7. *The manager permits the group to make decisions within prescribed limits.* Here the manager becomes an equal member of a problem-solving group. The entire group identifies and assesses the problem, develops possible solutions, and chooses an alternative to be implemented. Everyone within the group understands that the group's decision will be implemented.

Determining How to Make Decisions as a Leader. The true value of the model developed by Tannenbaum and Schmidt can be realized only if a leader can use it to make practical and desirable decisions. According to these authors, the three primary factors, or forces, that influence a manager's determination of which leadership behavior to use in making decisions are (1) forces in the manager, (2) forces in subordinates, and (3) forces in the leadership situation.

1. *Forces in the Manager.* Managers should be aware of four forces within themselves that influence their determination of how to make decisions as a leader. The first force is the manager's values, such as the relative importance to the manager of organizational efficiency, personal growth, the growth of subordinates, and company profits. For example, if subordinate growth is valued highly, the manager may want to give the group members the valuable experience of making a decision, even though he or she could have made the decision much more quickly and efficiently alone.

   The second influencing force within the manager is the level of confidence in subordinates. In general, the more confidence a manager has in subordinates, the more likely the style of decision making will be democratic, or subordinate-centered. The reverse is also true. The less confidence a manager has in subordinates, the more likely the style of decision making will be autocratic, or boss-centered.

   The third influencing force within the manager is personal leadership strengths. Some managers are more effective in issuing orders than in leading a group discussion, and vice versa. A manager must be able to recognize personal leadership strengths and capitalize on them.

   The fourth influencing force within the manager is tolerance for ambiguity. The move from a boss-centered style to a subordinate-centered style means some loss of certainty about how problems should be solved. If this reduction of certainty is disturbing to a manager, it may be extremely difficult for the manager to be successful as a subordinate-centered leader.

BACK TO THE CASE The situational approach to leadership affords us more insights into why Liz Claiborne is successful than does the trait approach. The situational approach suggests that the successful leadership of Claiborne is determined by the appropriate combination of these factors: (1) Claiborne's role as leader; (2) Liz Claiborne employees' roles as followers; and (3) the situations within the company that Liz Claiborne has faced. Each of the factors has played a significant role in determining the success of Liz Claiborne as a leader.

One of the most important activities Claiborne performs as a leader is making decisions. She can make decisions in any number of ways, ranging from authoritarian to democratic. For example, Claiborne made the decision to branch out into retailing by opening factory-outlet stores that sell out-of-season merchandise and stand-alone stores that sell current merchandise. Reaching that decision, Claiborne could have announced to her employees that the company would open new stores. Or, she could have defined several possible alternatives for entering retailing, discussed them with the appropriate employees, and allowed staff members to come up with their own suggestions on retailing alternatives. Or, she could have suggested to appropriate staff workers that the company would like to branch out into retailing, asked them to develop their own ideas about where and what type of stores should be opened, and then made the decision on the basis of her own ideas and those of staff. In that situation, the outcome might have been that stand-alone or factory stores were not chosen as the best solution for how to branch out into retailing.

2. *Forces in Subordinates.* A manager also should be aware of forces within subordinates that influence the manager's determination of how to make decisions as a leader.[14] To understand subordinates adequately, a manager should keep in mind that subordinates are both somewhat different and somewhat alike. Any cookbook approach for deciding how to lead all subordinates is therefore impossible. Generally speaking, however, a manager could increase success as a leader by allowing subordinates more freedom in making decisions when:[15]
   - The subordinates have a relatively high need for independence. (People differ greatly in the amount of direction they desire.)
   - They have a readiness to assume responsibility for decision making. (Some see additional responsibility as a tribute to their ability. Others see it as someone above them "passing the buck.")
   - They have a relatively high tolerance for ambiguity. (Some employees prefer to have clear-cut directives given to them. Others prefer a wider area of freedom.)
   - They are interested in the problem and believe it is important.
   - They understand and identify with goals of the organization.
   - They have the necessary knowledge and experience to deal with the problem.[16]
   - They have learned to expect to share in decision making. (People who have come to expect strong leadership and then suddenly are confronted with the request to share more fully in decision making are often upset by this new experience. People who have enjoyed a considerable amount of freedom resent the boss who begins to make all the decisions alone.)

   If these characteristics of subordinates do not exist in a particular situation, a manager probably should move toward a more autocratic, or boss-centered, approach to making decisions.

3. *Forces in the Situation.* The last group of forces that influence a manager's determination of how to make decisions as a leader are forces in the leadership situation. The first such situational force involves the type of organization in which the leader works. Such organizational factors as the size of working groups and their geographical distribution become especially important in deciding how to make decisions as a leader. Extremely large work groups or a wide geographic separation of work groups, for example, could make a subordinate-centered leadership style impractical.

   The second situational force is the effectiveness of group members working together. To this end, a manager should evaluate such issues as the experience of the group in working together and the degree of confidence group members have in their ability to solve problems as a group. As a general rule, a manager should assign decision-making responsibilities only to effective work groups.

   The third situational force is the problem to be solved. Before acting as a subordinate-centered leader, a manager should be sure that the group possesses the expertise necessary to make a decision about the existing problem. If it doesn't

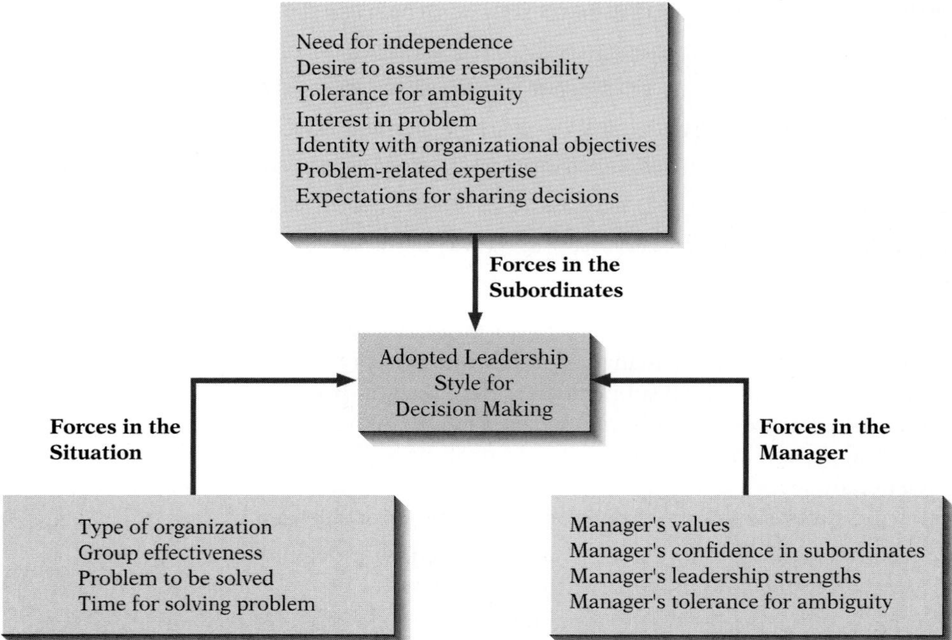

FIGURE 14.3 Collective influence of forces in the manager, the subordinates, and the situation on the leadership style adopted for decision making

have the necessary expertise, the manager should move toward more boss-centered leadership.

The fourth situational force involves the time available to make a decision. As a general guideline, the less time available, the more impractical it becomes to have the decision made by a group. Typically, it takes a group more time than an individual to reach a decision.

Figure 14.3 summarizes the main forces that influence a manager's determination of how to make decisions as a leader and stresses that this determination is the result of the collective influence of all of these forces. As the situational approach to leadership implies, a manager will be successful as a decision maker only if the method used to make those decisions appropriately reflects the leader, the followers, and the situation.

Determining How to Make Decisions as a Leader: An Update. Tannenbaum and Schmidt's original article on leadership decision making was so widely accepted that the two authors were invited by *Harvard Business Review* to update their original work.[17] This update stressed that in modern organizations the relationship among forces within the manager, subordinates, and situation had become more complex and more interrelated than ever. As the relationship becomes increasingly complicated, it obviously becomes more difficult for the leader to determine how to lead.

The update also stresses both societal and organizational environments as more modern forces to consider in determining how to lead. Such societal and organizational values as affirmative action and pollution control should have some influence on the decision making of leaders.

The Vroom-Yetton-Jago Model

Another major decision-focused theory of leadership that has gained widespread attention was first developed in 1973[18] and refined and expanded in 1988.[19] This theory, which we will call the "Vroom-Yetton-Jago (VYJ) Model" after its three major contributors, focuses on how much participation to allow subordinates in the decision-making process. The VYJ Model is built on two important premises: (1) organizational decisions should be of high quality (should have a beneficial impact on performance), and (2) subordinates should accept and be committed to organizational decisions that are made.

Overall, the VYJ Model suggests that there are five different decision styles or ways that leaders can make decisions. These decision styles range from the leader's being autocratic (the leader makes the decision) to consultative (the leader makes the decision after interacting with the followers) to group-focused (the manager meets with the group, and the group makes the decision). All five decision styles within the VYJ Model are described in Figure 14.4.[20]

The VYJ Model, presented in Figure 14.5, is actually a method for determining when a leader should use which decision style. As you can see, the model is a type of decision tree.[21] In order for a leader to determine which decision style to use in a particular situation, the leader starts at the left of the decision tree by stating an organizational problem being addressed. After the problem has been stated, the leader asks a series of questions about the problem as determined by the structure of the decision tree until a decision style appropriate for the situation is determined at the far right side of the model. For example, consider the very bottom path of the decision tree. After stating an organizational problem, the leader determines that a decision related to that problem has a low quality requirement, that it is important that subordinates are committed to the decision, and it is very uncertain that if the leader made the decision by himself or herself that subordinates would be committed to the decision. As a result of these factors, the model suggests that the leader uses the GII decision style, the leader meets with the group to discuss the situation, and the group makes the decision.

The VYJ Model seems promising. Research dealing with an earlier version of this model has yielded some evidence that decisions which managers make that are consistent with the model tend to be more successful than are decisions managers make that are inconsistent with the model.[22] The model tends to be somewhat complex, however, and therefore difficult for practicing managers to apply.

Decision Style	Definition
AI	Manager makes the decision alone.
AII	Manager asks for information from subordinates but makes the decision alone. Subordinates may or may not be informed about what the situation is.
CI	Manager shares the situation with individual subordinates and asks for information and evaluation. Subordinates do not meet as a group, and the manager alone makes the decision.
CII	Manager and subordinates meet as a group to discuss the situation, but the manager makes the decision.
GII	Manager and subordinates meet as a group to discuss the situation, and the group makes the decision.

A = autocratic; C = consultative; G = group

FIGURE 14.4 The five decision styles available to a leader according to the Vroom-Yetton-Jago Model

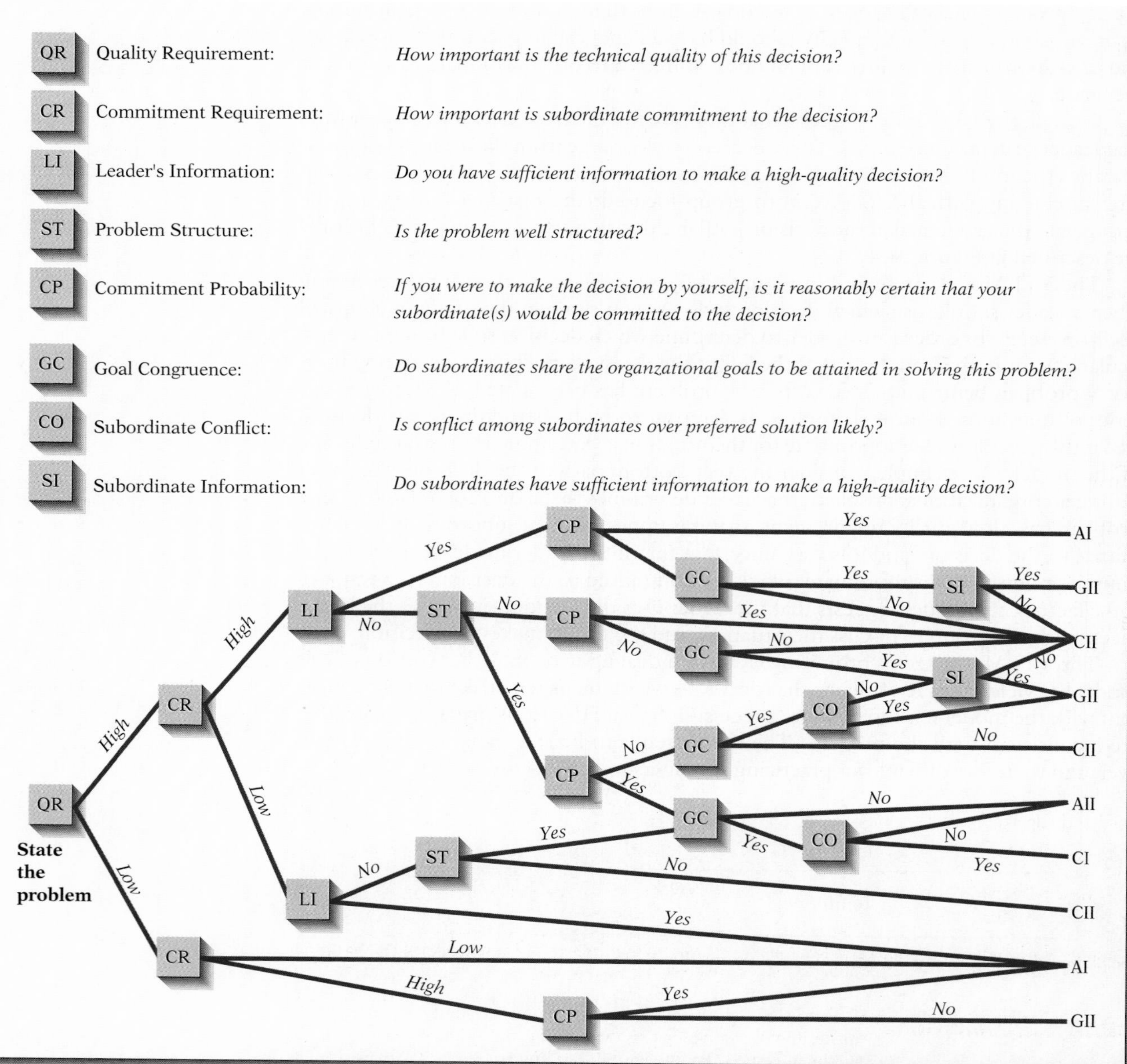

QR Quality Requirement: How important is the technical quality of this decision?
CR Commitment Requirement: How important is subordinate commitment to the decision?
LI Leader's Information: Do you have sufficient information to make a high-quality decision?
ST Problem Structure: Is the problem well structured?
CP Commitment Probability: If you were to make the decision by yourself, is it reasonably certain that your subordinate(s) would be committed to the decision?
GC Goal Congruence: Do subordinates share the organzational goals to be attained in solving this problem?
CO Subordinate Conflict: Is conflict among subordinates over preferred solution likely?
SI Subordinate Information: Do subordinates have sufficient information to make a high-quality decision?
State the problem

FIGURE 14.5 The Vroom-Yetton-Jago Model

ETHICS HIGHLIGHT
Leader of NBC News Resigns over Ethical Debacle

Michael Gartner, the leader of NBC News for most of the last five years, has never been immune to criticism. He was blamed for every problem faced by NBC News—cutting the budget, botching the coverage of the San Francisco earthquake, bungling the transition from Jane Pauley to Deborah Norville, and naming the rape victim in the William Kennedy Smith trial—but he still managed to survive. However, his resignation was the result of having aired two newscasts of questionable validity that most people say he was unaware of until after the fact.

The most critical problem centered on NBC's commissioning a safety-analysis firm to conduct a crash test on the controversial Chevrolet truck with the gas tanks mounted outside the truck-bed walls.

This firm purchased two previously owned GM pickups. One had a non-standard gas cap on the fuel tank, which a previous owner had bent to fit as a replacement for the original gas cap that had been lost. It was this vehicle that burst into a fifteen-second flame-out caused by toy rocket motors that were set to ignite upon impact from a driverless vehicle.

Three weeks later, Tom Brokaw, the anchor of NBC News had to make another public apology for misleading news coverage on logging practices in the Pacific northwest. This incident involved the use of "inappropriate video" on the problems of clear cutting forests. The video showed what was purported to be fish killed by stream damage precipitated by clear cut logging. The fish had actually been stunned for testing purposes as part of an environmental study. Some dead fish were videotaped at a location other than the forest in question. The clear cutting damage was filmed in another state and was a result of a forest fire rather than poor logging practices.

In business, a leader can make several errors in judgment and survive. Making ethical mistakes is catastrophic to one's leadership status. ▶

Michael Gartner of NBC News finally resigned after having been blamed for a host of problems and controversies.

BACK TO THE CASE In trying to decide exactly how to make decisions as leaders, Claiborne and Chazen, have had to look at forces within themselves, such as their values, confidence in subordinates, and personal leadership strengths. If Chazen believes that he is more knowledgeable about the fashion industry than his staff is, he will be likely to make boss-centered decisions. Claiborne recognized many years ago that forces in her subordinates—such as the need for independence, the readiness to assume responsibility, and the knowledge of and interest in the issues to be decided—affect her decisions as a leader. She recognized that her staff was relatively independent and responsible and consequently allowed some of her employees to make important decisions with respect to the design of an entire clothing line.

Forces within the company which must be considered include the number of people making decisions and the problem to be solved. If the staff of the Claiborne company remains small, the democratic decision-making style will more than likely be used. This style of leadership allows employees to become involved in decisions as to what a particular clothing line should look like. The subordinate-centered leadership style will likely be used if the Claiborne staff is knowledgeable about the problem at hand.

The VYJ model suggests that Chazen should try to make decisions in such a fashion that the quality of decisions is enhanced and followers are committed to the decisions. Decisions should be made by matching leadership style (autocratic, consultative, or group) to the particular situation faced at the time.

Leadership Behaviors

The lack of success in trying to identify predictive leadership traits led researchers to look at other variables in order to explain leadership success or failure. Rather than looking at traits leaders should possess, the behavioral approach looked at what good leaders do. Are they concerned with getting a task done or do they concentrate on interpersonal skills such as keeping their followers happy and maintaining high morale?

Two major studies were involved in identifying leadership behavior. One series was conducted by the Bureau of Business Research at Ohio State University and is referred to as the OSU study. A second series was conducted about the same time at the University of Michigan and is referred to as the Michigan study.

The OSU Studies

Structure behavior is leadership activity that (1) delineates the relationship between the leader and the leader's followers or (2) establishes well-defined procedures that the followers should adhere to in performing their jobs.

The OSU studies are a series of leadership investigations that concluded that leaders exhibit two main types of behavior. The first type, called **structure behavior,** is any leadership activity that delineates the relationship between the leader and the leader's followers or establishes well-defined procedures that followers should adhere to in performing their jobs. Overall, structure behavior limits the self-guidance of followers in the performance of their tasks. Although it would be correct to conclude that structure behavior can be, and sometimes is, relatively firm, it would be incorrect to assume that it is rude and malicious.[23]

Structure behavior can be useful to leaders as a means of minimizing follower activity that does not significantly contribute to organizational goal attainment. Leaders must be careful, however, that they do not discourage follower activity that will contribute to organizational goal attainment.

Consideration behavior is leadership behavior that reflects friendship, mutual trust, respect, and warmth in the relationship between the leader and the followers.

Leadership style is the behavioral pattern a leader establishes while guiding organization members in appropriate directions.

The second main type of leadership behavior described by the OSU studies, **consideration behavior,** is leadership behavior that reflects friendship, mutual trust, respect, and warmth in the relationship between the leader and the followers. Consideration behavior generally is aimed at developing and maintaining a more human relationship between the leader and the followers.

The OSU studies resulted in a model that depicts four fundamental leadership styles. A **leadership style** is the behavior a leader exhibits while guiding organization members in appropriate directions. Each of the four leadership styles in Figure 14.6 is a different combination of structure behavior and consideration behavior. For example, the high structure/low consideration leadership style is that of a leader who emphasizes structure behavior and deemphasizes consideration behavior. The OSU studies have made a significant contribution to the understanding of leadership. The central thoughts and ideas generated by these studies still serve as the basis for modern leadership thought and research.[24]

The Michigan Studies

At about the same time that the OSU Leadership Studies were being conducted, researchers at the University of Michigan, led by Rensis Likert, were also performing a series of historically significant leadership studies.[25] Analyzing information based upon interviews of both leaders and followers or managers and subordinates, the Michigan Studies pinpointed two basic types of leader behavior: job-centered behavior and employee-centered behavior.

Job-centered behavior is leader behavior through which the leader focuses primary attention on the work a subordinate is doing.

Job-Centered Behavior. **Job-centered behavior** is leader behavior through which the leader focuses primary attention on the work a subordinate is doing. Such behavior indicates that the leader is very interested in the work the subordinate is performing and how well the subordinate is doing the work.

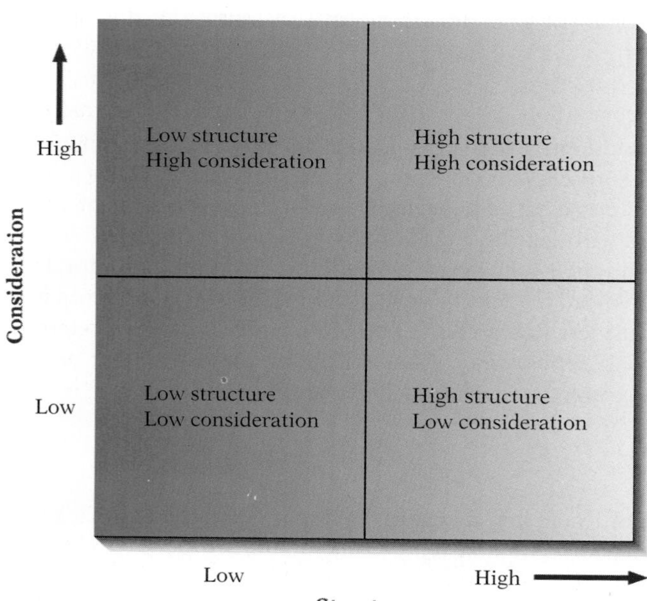

FIGURE 14.6 Four fundamental leadership styles based on structure behavior and consideration behavior

Employee-Centered Behavior. **Employee-centered behavior** is leader behavior through which the leader focuses primary attention on subordinates as people. Such behavior indicates that the leader is very attentive to the personal needs of subordinates and is interested in building cooperative work teams that are satisfying to subordinates and advantageous for the organization.

Employee-centered behavior is leader behavior through which the leader focuses primary attention on subordinates as people.

The results of the OSU studies and the Michigan Studies are very similar. Both research efforts indicated two primary dimensions of leader behavior: a work dimension (structure behavior/job-centered behavior) and a people dimension (consideration behavior/employee-centered behavior). The following section focuses, given these two primary dimensions of leader behavior, on determining the most advisable leadership style for a manager to adopt.

Effectiveness of Various Leadership Styles

An early investigation of high school superintendents concluded that desirable leadership behavior seems to be associated with high leader emphasis on both structure and consideration and that undesirable leadership behavior tends to be associated with low leader emphasis on both dimensions.[26] Similarly, the managerial grid covered in chapter 12 implies that the most effective leadership style is characterized by high consideration and high structure. Results of a more recent study indicate that high consideration is always preferred by subordinates.[27]

One should be cautious about concluding that any single leadership style is more effective than any other.[28] The leadership situation is so complex that pinpointing one leadership style as the most effective is an oversimplification. In fact, a successful leadership style for managers in one situation may be ineffective in another situation. Recognizing the need to link leadership styles to appropriate situations, in a classic article A.K. Korman says that a worthwhile contribution to leadership literature would be a rationale for systematically linking appropriate styles with various situations so as to ensure effective leadership.[29] The life cycle theory of leadership, which is covered in the next section, provides such a rationale.

The Hersey-Blanchard Life Cycle Theory of Leadership

The **life cycle theory of leadership** is a rationale for linking leadership styles with various situations so as to ensure effective leadership. This theory uses essentially the same two types of leadership behavior as the OSU leadership studies, but it calls the dimensions "task" rather than "structure" and "relationships" rather than "consideration."

The **life cycle theory of leadership** is a leadership concept that hypothesizes that leadership styles should reflect primarily the maturity level of the followers.

The life cycle theory is based primarily on the relationship of follower maturity, leader task behavior, and leader relationship behavior. In general terms, according to this theory, leadership style should reflect the maturity level of the followers. **Maturity** is defined as the ability of the followers to perform their job independently, their ability to assume additional responsibility, and their desire to achieve success. The more of each of these characteristics that followers possess, the more mature they are said to be. Maturity here is not necessarily linked to chronological age.

As used in the life cycle theory of leadership, **maturity** is an individual's ability to independently perform the job, to assume additional responsibility, and to desire success.

Figure 14.7 shows the life cycle theory of leadership model. The curved line in this model indicates the maturity level of the followers. As the maturity curve runs from right to left, the followers' maturity level increases. In more specific terms, the theory indicates that effective leadership behavior should shift from (1) high-task/low-relationships behavior to (2) high-task/high-relationships behavior to (3) high-relationships/low-task behavior to (4) low-task/low-relationships behavior, as one's followers progress from immaturity to maturity.[30]

The theory suggests, therefore, that a style of leadership will be effective only if it is appropriate for the maturity level of the followers. Table 14.1 describes how each of the four main leadership styles is perceived when it is both effective and ineffective, or appropriate and inappropriate, for followers' maturity levels.

There are some exceptions to the general philosophy of the life cycle theory. For example, if there is a short-term deadline to meet, a leader may find it necessary to

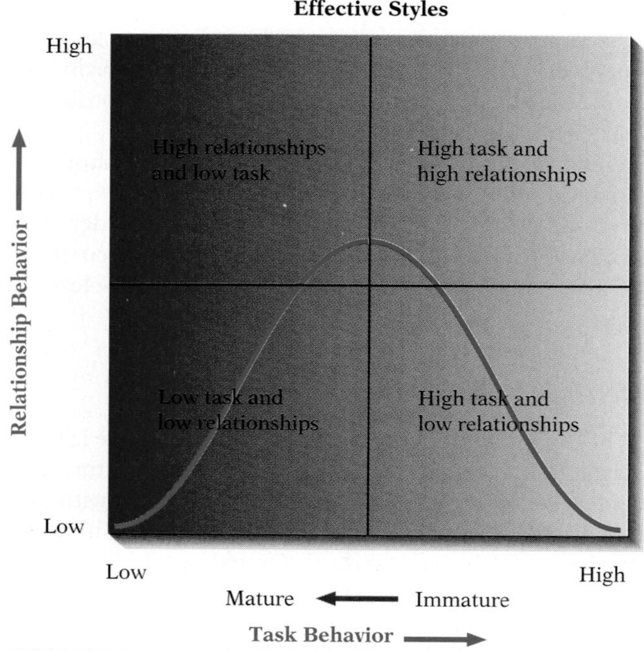

FIGURE 14.7 The life cycle theory of leadership model

accelerate production through a high-task/low-relationships style, rather than a low-task/low-relationships style, even if the followers are mature. A high-task/low-relationships leadership style carried out over the long term with such followers, however, typically results in a poor working relationship of the leader and followers.

Following is an example of how the life cycle theory applies to a leadership situation: A man has just been hired as a salesperson in a men's clothing store. At first, this individual is extremely immature — that is, unable to solve task-related problems independently. According to the life cycle theory, the appropriate style for leading this sales-

TABLE 14.1 How basic leadership styles are perceived by others as effective and ineffective

Basic Styles	*Effective*	*Ineffective*
High task and low relationships	Often seen as knowing what he or she wants and imposing personal methods for accomplishing this without creating resentment	Often seen as having no confidence in others, unpleasant, and interested only in short-term output
High task and high relationships	Often seen as satisfying the needs of the group for setting goals and organizing work, but also providing high levels of socioemotional support	Often seen as initiating more structure than is needed by the group and spending more time on socioemotional support than necessary
High relationships and low task	Often seen as having implicit trust in people and as being concerned primarily with developing their talents	Often seen as interested primarily in harmony and being seen as "a good person," and being unwilling to risk disruption of a relationship to accomplish a task
Low task and low relationships	Often seen as appropriately permitting subordinates to decide how the work should be done and playing only a minor part in their social interaction	Often seen as uninvolved and passive, as a "paper shuffler" who cares little about the task at hand or the people involved

person at his level of maturity is high task/low relationships. The leader should tell the salesperson exactly what should be done and how it should be done. The salesperson should be shown how to make cash and charge sales and how to handle merchandise returns. The leader also should begin laying some of the groundwork for developing a personal relationship with the salesperson. Too much relationship behavior at this point, however, should be avoided, since it easily can be misinterpreted as permissiveness.

As time passes and the salesperson increases somewhat in job-related maturity, the next appropriate style for leading him is high task/high relationships. Although the salesperson's maturity has increased somewhat, the leader needs to watch him closely, because he still needs some guidance and direction at various times. The main difference between this leadership style and the first leadership style is the amount of relationship behavior displayed by the leader. Building on the groundwork laid during the period of the first leadership style, the leader is now ready to start developing an atmosphere of mutual trust, respect, and friendliness between her and the salesperson.

As more time passes, the salesperson's maturity level increases still further. The next style appropriate for leading this individual is high relationships/low task. The leader can now deemphasize task behavior, because the salesperson is now of above-average maturity in his job and usually can solve job-related problems independently. As with the previous leadership style, the leader still emphasizes the development of a human relationship with her follower.

As the salesperson's maturity level reaches its maximum, the appropriate style for leading him is low task/low relationships. Again, the leader can deemphasize task behavior, because the follower is thoroughly familiar with the job. The leader also can deemphasize relationship behavior, because she now has a good working relationship with the follower. Here, task behavior is seldom needed, and relationship behavior is used primarily to nurture the good working rapport that has developed between the leader and the follower. The salesperson, then, is left to do his job without close supervision, knowing that he has a positive working relationship with a leader who can be approached for additional guidance.

The acceptance of the life cycle approach is more than likely due to its intuitive appeal.[31] Although at first glance it seems like a worthwhile leadership concept, some care probably should be exercised in its application because of the lack of scientific investigation verifying its worth.[32]

QUALITY HIGHLIGHT
Jim Pattillo: Potlatch Corporation's St. Maries Complex General Manager

The Potlatch Corporation, headquartered in San Francisco, California, is among the ten largest wood- and paper-product companies in the United States. Included in the company's Western Regional Wood Products Division is the St. Maries complex in St. Maries, Idaho. Jim Pattillo has been general manager of this plywood and lumber facility for over six years. During that time he has used his leadership and understanding of quality management principles to develop a culture within the operation in which employees at all levels trust both management and each other. He has done this by showing that he believes in the people who work for the organization and is willing to empower people to take charge of their processes.

Pattillo has invested heavily in training across a wide spectrum of quality tools and techniques. Within the past two years, every manager and supervisor at the St. Maries complex has attended on-site education courses in quality principles such as teamwork, statistical process control, quality planning, and cycle time reduction. He has insisted that these people take their training back to the plant floor to share with the operators and line personnel. Together, they have worked to improve processes throughout the facility. Employees have formed teams to attack a wide variety of problems, including machine downtime in the sawmill. There, through the use of such tools as flow charts

A worker in a paper mill checks the quality of a roll of paper. The Potlatch Corporation of San Fransisco has used quality management priciples to improve customer satisfaction and shorted manufacturing lead times.

and Pareto analysis, this downtime has been reduced by more than 75 percent in the past six months.

When Pattillo took over at St. Maries, there were few instances of employees making suggestions for improvement. Now, through Pattillo's leadership, employees' input and involvement are paying huge dividends for the division. The work that Jim and his staff have been doing to improve customer satisfaction and shorten manufacturing lead times is making a positive impact on the rest of the organization. More important, Potlatch's St. Maries complex is well on its way to becoming a true learning organization, with employees at all levels continually striving to improve their processes in order to consistently provide quality products and services to all customers, internal and external. ▶

BACK TO THE CASE The OSU leadership studies furnish managers like Claiborne and Chazen with insights on leadership behavior in general situations. According to the OSU studies, Claiborne and Chazen can exhibit two general types of leadership behavior: structure and consideration. Structure behavior will be used if Liz Claiborne employees are told what to do — for example, to use certain designs and fabrics. Consideration behavior will be used if these leaders attempt to build human rapport with employees by discussing their concerns and developing friendships with them.

Of course, depending on how Claiborne and Chazen emphasize these two behaviors, a number of outcomes are possible. Leadership style can reflect a combination of structure and consideration ranging from high structure/low consideration to low structure/high consideration. For example, if giving orders to employees is stressed and developing relationships de-emphasized, the resulting style will be high structure/low consideration. If good rapport with staff is emphasized and members of the organization are allowed a lot of independence the style is called low structure/high consideration.

Although no single leadership style is more effective than any other in all situations, the life cycle theory of leadership furnishes Claiborne and Chazen with a strategy for using various styles in various situations. According to this theory, the selected style should be consistent with the maturity level of Liz Claiborne employees. As employees progress from immaturity to maturity, leadership style should shift systematically from (1) high-task/low-relationships behavior, to (2) high-task/high-relationships behavior, to (3) high-relationships/low-task behavior, to (4) low-task/low-relationships behavior.

Fiedler's Contingency Theory

Leader flexibility is the ability of leaders to change their leadership styles.

Situational theories of leadership, such as life cycle theory, are based on the concept of **leader flexibility**—the idea that successful leaders must change their leadership styles as they encounter different situations. Can leaders be so flexible as to span all major leadership styles? The only answer to this question is that some leaders can be flexible and some cannot. After all, a leadership style may be so ingrained in a leader that it takes years to even approach flexibility. Also, some leaders may have experienced such success in a basically static situation that they believe flexibility is unnecessary. Unfortunately, there are numerous obstacles to leader flexibility.

One strategy, proposed by Fred Fiedler, for overcoming these obstacles is changing the organizational situation to fit the leader's style, rather than changing the leader's style to fit the organizational situation.[33] Relating this thought to the life cycle theory of leadership, one finds that it may be easier to shift various leaders to situations appropriate for their leadership styles than to expect leaders to change styles as situations change. It probably would take three to five years to train managers to effectively use a concept such as life cycle theory.[34] Changing the situation a particular leader faces, however, can be done in the short term simply by exercising organizational authority.

According to Fiedler and his **contingency theory of leadership,** leader-member relations, task structure, and the position power of the leader are the three primary factors that should be used for moving leaders into situations appropriate for their leadership styles. *Leader-member relations* is the degree to which the leader feels accepted by the followers. *Task structure* is the degree to which the goals—the work to be done—and other situational factors are outlined clearly. *Position power* is determined by the extent to which the leader has control over the rewards and punishments the followers receive. How these three factors can be arranged in eight different combinations is presented in Table 14.2. Each of these eight combinations is called an octant.

The **contingency theory of leadership** is a leadership concept that hypothesizes that, in any given leadership situation, success is determined primarily by (1) the degree to which the task being performed by the followers is structured, (2) the degree of position power possessed by the leader, and (3) the type of relationship that exists between the leader and the followers.

Figure 14.8 shows how effective leadership varies among the eight octants. From an organizational viewpoint, this figure implies that management should attempt to match permissive, passive, and considerate leaders with situations reflecting the middle of the continuum containing the octants. The figure also implies that management should try to match a controlling, active, and structuring leader with the extremes of this continuum. Possible actions that Fiedler suggests to modify the leadership situation are as follows:[35]

1. In some organizations, we can change the individual's task assignment. We may assign to one leader very structured tasks which have implicit or explicit instructions telling him what to do and how to do it, and we may assign to another the tasks that are nebulous and vague. The former are the typical production tasks; the latter are exemplified by committee work, by the development of policy, and by tasks which require creativity.
2. We can change the leader's position power. We not only can give him a higher rank and corresponding recognition, we also can modify his position power by giving him subordinates who are equal to him in rank and prestige or subordinates who are two or three ranks below him. We can give him subordinates who are experts in their specialties or subordinates who depend upon the leader for guidance and instruction. We can give the leader the final say in all decisions affecting his group, or we can require that he make decisions in consultation with his subordinates, or even that he obtain their concurrence. We can channel all directives, communications, and information about organizational plans through the leader alone, giving him expert power, or we can provide these communications concurrently to all his subordinates.
3. We can change the leader-member relations in this group. We can have the leader work with groups whose members are very similar to him in attitude, opinion,

TABLE 14.2 Eight combinations, or octants, of three factors: leader-member relations, task structure, and leader position power

Octant	*Leader-Member Relations*	*Task Structure*	*Leader Position Power*
I	Good	High	Strong
II	Good	High	Weak
III	Good	Weak	Strong
IV	Good	Weak	Weak
V	Moderately poor	High	Strong
VI	Moderately poor	High	Weak
VII	Moderately poor	Weak	Strong
VIII	Moderately poor	Weak	Weak

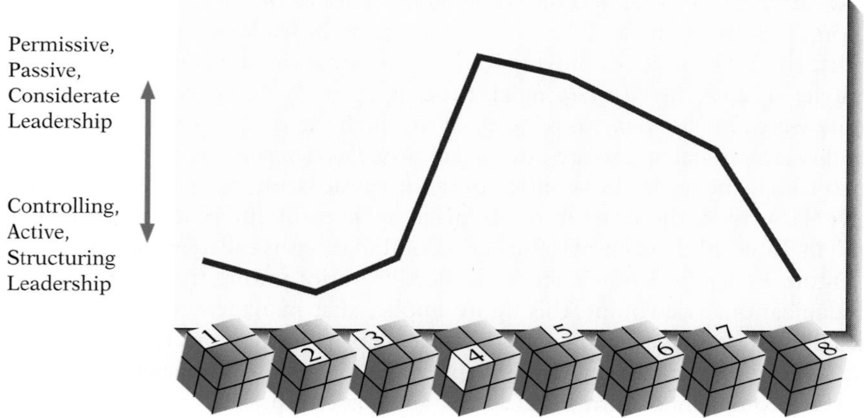

Leader-Member Relations	Good	Good	Good	Good	Poor	Poor	Poor	Poor
Task Structure	**Structured**		**Unstructured**		**Structured**		**Unstructured**	
Leader Position Power	Strong	Weak	Strong	Weak	Strong	Weak	Strong	Weak

FIGURE 14.8 How effective leadership style varies with Fiedler's eight octants

> technical background, race, and cultural background. Or we can assign him subordinates with whom he differs in any one or several of these important aspects. Finally, we can assign the leader to a group in which the members have a tradition of getting along well with their supervisors or to a group that has a history and tradition of conflict.

Overall, Fiedler's work helps destroy the myths that there is one best leadership style and that leaders are born, not made. Further, Fiedler's work supports the theory that almost every manager in an organization can be a successful leader if placed in a situation appropriate for the person's leadership style. This, of course, assumes that someone in the organization has the ability to assess the characteristics of the organization's leaders and of other important organizational variables and then to match the two accordingly.[36] Fiedler's model, like any theoretical model, has its limitations and criticisms. Although it may not provide any concrete answers, it does emphasize the contention that situational variables are very important in determining leadership effectiveness. It may actually be easier to change the leadership situation or move the leader to a more favorable situation than to try to change a leader's style.[37]

Path-goal theory of leadership is a theory of leadership that suggests the primary activity of a leader should be to make desirable and achievable rewards available to organization members as a result of attaining organizational goals and to clarify the kinds of behavior that must be performed to earn those rewards.

The Path-Goal Theory of Leadership

The **path-goal theory of leadership** suggests that the primary activity of a leader should be to make desirable and achievable rewards available to organization members as a result of attaining organizational goals and to clarify the kinds of behavior that must be performed to earn those rewards.[38] In essence, the leader outlines the goals that followers should aim for and clarifies how (the path that followers take) to earn those goals. Overall, the path-goal theory indicates that managers can facilitate job performance by showing employees how their performance directly affects their receiving desired rewards.

According to the path-goal theory of leadership, leaders perform four primary types of behavior:

1. *Directive behavior.* Directive behavior is leader behavior aimed at telling followers what to do and how to do it. The leader indicates what performance goals exist and precisely what must be done to achieve them.
2. *Supportive behavior.* Supportive behavior is leader behavior aimed at being friendly with followers and showing interest in them as human beings. Through supportive behavior, the leader shows sensitivity to the personal needs of followers.
3. *Participative behavior.* Participative behavior is leader behavior in which suggestions from the follower are sought regarding business operations with the result that followers are involved in making important organizational decisions. Consistent with this type of leader behavior, followers often help to determine the rewards that will be available to them in organizations and what must be done to earn those rewards.
4. *Achievement behavior.* Achievement behavior is leader behavior aimed at setting challenging goals for followers to reach and expressing and demonstrating confidence that followers will meet the challenge. This leader behavior focuses on making goals difficult enough so that employees find achieving them challenging but not so difficult that followers view them as impossible and therefore give up trying to achieve them.

As with other situational theories of leadership, the path-goal theory proposes that leaders can be successful if they are able to match appropriately these four types of behavior to situations that they face. For example, assuming that inexperienced followers do not have a thorough understanding of a job, a manager may appropriately use more directive behavior to develop this understanding and to ensure that serious job-related problems are avoided. For more experienced followers, assuming that they have a more complete understanding of a job, directive behavior would probably be inappropriate and might create interpersonal problems between the leader and the followers. If jobs are very structured, with little room for employee interpretation of how the work should be done, directive behavior is probably less needed than if there is much room for employees to determine how work might get done. If followers are getting much personal satisfaction and encouragement, and support from members of a work group, supportive behavior by the leader is probably not as important as when followers are getting little or no satisfaction from personal relationships in the work group.

The primary focus of the path-goal theory of leadership is on how leaders can increase employee effort and productivity by clarifying performance goals and the path to be taken to achieve those goals.[39] Over time, the path-goal theory of leadership has gained increased acceptance. Research suggests that the path-goal theory holds promising potential for helping managers to enhance employee commitment to achieving organizational goals and thereby gives managers a key for increasing the probability that organizations will be successful.[40] It should be pointed out the majority of the research has been conducted on parts of the model rather than on the complete model.[41]

RECENT EMPHASIS ON LEADERSHIP

As with any academic area, the area of leadership is continually evolving. Topics that have recently been getting more attention in the leadership literature are transformational leadership, trust, substitutes for leadership, women as leaders, and ways women lead. This section relates each of these topics to leadership.

Transformational Leadership

Transformational leadership is leadership that inspires organizational success by profoundly affecting followers' beliefs in what an organization should be, as well as followers' values like justice and integrity.

Transformational leadership is leadership that inspires organizational success by profoundly affecting followers' beliefs in what an organization should be, as well as followers' values, such as justice and integrity.[42] Transformational leadership creates a sense of duty within an organization, encourages new ways of handling problems, and promotes learning for all organization members. Transformational leadership is closely related to concepts like charismatic leadership or inspirational leadership.

Perhaps transformational leadership is receiving more attention recently because of the dramatic changes that many organizations are going through and the critical importance of transformational leadership in "transforming" or changing organizations successfully. Lee Iacocca is often used as an example of a successful transformational leader because of his successful efforts in transforming Chrysler Corporation from a floundering company into a much more successful company that could avoid bankruptcy.

Transformational leaders perform several important tasks. Transformational leaders raise followers' awareness of organizational issues and their consequences.[43] Organization members must understand the high-priority issues that exist for an organization and what will happen if the issues are not faced successfully. Transformational leaders also create a vision of what the organization should be, build commitment to that vision throughout the organization, and facilitate changes throughout the organization that support the vision.[44] In essence, transformational leadership is consistent with strategy developed through an organization's strategic management process.

Managers of the future will continue to face the challenge of significantly changing organizations. The accelerating trend toward positioning organizations to be more competitive in a global business environment will be a primary contributor to the need to change organizations significantly in the future. As a result, transformational leadership will probably get increasing attention in leadership literature. Although there is much practical appeal and interest in the topic of transformational leadership, more research is needed to develop insights about how to be a successful transformational leader.

Substitutes for Leadership

There are times when leaders do not have to lead, or, for one reason or another, cannot lead. Situational substitutes can sometimes have as much influence on employees as any leader.[45] Many of you have heard or observed situations in which the leader had little or no impact on the situation. This could be due to a number of reasons, including factors beyond the leader's control.

Because so many factors can affect a situation, some people argue that leadership is actually irrelevant to many organization outcomes.[46] Because of various conditions—such as strong subordinates, knowledge of the task, and organizational constraints—subordinates may not need or even want leadership.[47] Substitute leadership theory attempts to identify situations in which the input of leader behavior is canceled out or made less significant by the subordinate. As examples: a subordinate may have such high levels of ability, experience, education, and internal motivation that little or no leadership is required or desired; task characteristics may be so routine that the subordinate does not require much, if any, leadership; organizational characteristics such as group cohesion and a high degree of formalization may reduce the need for leadership. In our earlier discussion of life cycle theory we also saw the situation in which the leader does not have to lead: when the leader delegates tasks to highly mature followers in a low-task/low relationship situation.

Throughout this chapter, attention has been given to a number of factors affecting leadership effectiveness. Much of this attention has centered on leadership characteristics, situations, and leader behavior. Substitute theory tends to downplay the importance of these dimensions. What could account for this? Meindl and Ehrlich[48] suggest one possible answer: we have had a tendency throughout history to romanticize leadership, treating it as more important than it actually is. But substitute theory reminds us that, in some situations with some people in some organizations, things just seem to get done regardless of the quality of leadership.

Women as Leaders

One can read Stogdill's *Handbook of Leadership* (1974) and barely find any reference to women in leadership except as a subject deserving further research.[49] This is probably because, in 1970, only 15 percent of all managers were women. By 1989, this figure had risen to more than 40 percent.[50] By 1995, women will make up about 63 percent of the total workforce.[51] Just how many of these women will become leaders in their companies or industries remains to be seen. Currently, only three of every one hundred top jobs in the largest U.S. companies are held by women, about the same number as a decade ago.[52] A Labor Department study showed that the glass ceiling keeps many women from moving up in management and leadership positions.[53] The "glass ceiling" is the subtle barrier of negative attitudes and prejudices that prevents women from reaching seemingly attainable top management and leadership positions.

Ways Women Lead

Women who have broken through the glass ceiling have found that effective leaders don't come from one mold. In the past, women leaders have modeled their leadership styles after successful male managers.[54] Women often describe their leadership styles as transformational—getting workers to transform or subordinate their individual self-interests into group consensus directed toward a broader goal.[55] This leadership style attributes power to personal characteristics such as charisma, personal contacts, and interpersonal skills rather than to the organizational structure.[56]

Men, on the other hand, are more likely to characterize their leadership as transactional.[57] They see their jobs as involving a series of transactions between themselves and their subordinates. This leadership style involves exchanging rewards for services or dispensing punishment for inadequate performance.

DIVERSITY HIGHLIGHT
For James G. Kaiser of Corning, Being Employee-Centered Includes a Focus on Diversity

James G. Kaiser is a senior vice president at Corning Inc. Kaiser is responsible for keeping the Technical Products Division competitive in the global marketplace and for masterminding the strategic planning for his division's operations. In addition, Kaiser oversees research and development for new products and is responsible for seeking business partners with whom the company can pursue joint ventures. Lastly, Kaiser is in charge of a series of export and sales offices in several locations.

James G. Kaiser, senior vice-president at Corning, Inc., takes a leadership role in managing people from different cultures. As president of Corning's Leadership Council, Kaiser focuses on cultural diversity issues and offers guidance to other up-and-coming African-American executives.

Kaiser considers himself to be a people-oriented manager. He is an African-American manager who sees his race as an asset in managing people from different cultures because it enables him to have a broader perspective on the differences among various types of employees. Kaiser focuses formally on cultural diversity at Corning largely through the Executive Leadership Council, a group with the mission of offering guidance and leadership to other up-and-coming African-American executives. As president of Corning's Executive Leadership Council, Kaiser has helped provide minority executives with a network and a discussion forum that helps them to understand what the achievement of excellence actually means within and for the African-American community and how excellence can be accomplished.

Because Kaiser is an African-American leader, one could argue that he has special insights for advising and helping minority employees to be successful leaders. For their own long-run success, however, leaders like Kaiser must be careful not to become "specialists" in dealing with only one culture, but to become "generalists" in developing the skills to successfully manage people from many different cultures. ▶

BACK TO THE CASE The life cycle theory suggests that a leader should be flexible enough to behave as the situation requires. As suggested by Fiedler, if Claiborne's leadership style is high task in nature, she generally will be a more successful leader in situations best described by octants 1, 2, 3, and 9 in Table 14.2 and Figure 14.8. If, however, Claiborne's leadership style is more relationship oriented, she will probably be a more successful leader in situations represented by octants 4, 5, 6, and 7. Overall, Fiedler's work can provide Claiborne and Chazen with insights on how to orchestrate situations at Liz Claiborne to match their particular leadership styles.

The path-goal theory of leadership suggests that Claiborne should emphasize clarification of what rewards are available to followers in the organization, how those rewards can be earned, and elimination of barriers that could prohibit followers from earning those rewards. Claiborne can use directive behavior, supportive behavior, participative behavior, and achievement behavior in implementing the path-goal theory.

Claiborne has always focused on being a transformational leader, a leader who inspires followers to focus seriously on achieving organizational objectives. As a transformational leader, she does and should continue to encourage new ideas, create a sense of duty, and encourage employees to learn and grow. As a company like Liz Claiborne undergoes more and more significant change, the importance of the leader being a transformational leader increases.

Liz Claiborne's leaders must always keep in mind that regardless of the type of leader he or she may be, there are and will be situations that one just cannot control and on which leadership ability will have little or no impact.

ACTION SUMMARY

Reread the learning objectives that follow. Each objective is followed by questions. Answering these questions accurately will help you retain the most important concepts discussed in this chapter. After answering each question, check your answer with the answer key at the end of this chapter. (*Hint:* If you have doubt regarding the correct response, consult the page whose number follows the answer.)

Circle: ***From studying this chapter, I will attempt to acquire:***

1. A working definition of leadership.

a, b, c, d, e **a.** The process of directing others toward the accomplishment of some objective is: (a) communication; (b) controlling; (c) leadership; (d) managing; (e) none of the above.

a, b, c, d, e **b.** Directing must be consistent with: (a) organizational policies; (b) procedures; (c) job descriptions; (d) none of the above; (e) all of the above.

2. An understanding of the relationship between leading and managing.

T, F **a.** Leading and managing are the same process.

a, b, c, d, e **b.** In the relationship between managers and leaders, one could say that: (a) all managers are leaders; (b) all leaders are managers; (c) some leaders are not managers; (d) managers cannot be leaders; (e) management is a subset of leadership.

3. An appreciation for the trait and situational approaches to leadership.

a, b, c, d, e **a.** The following is true about the conclusions drawn from the trait approach to leadership: (a) the trait approach identifies traits that consistently separate leaders from nonleaders; (b) there are certain traits that guarantee that a leader will be successful; (c) the trait approach is based on early research that assumes that a good leader is born, not made; (d) leadership is a simple issue of describing the traits of successful leaders; (e) none of the above.

a, b, c, d, e **b.** The situational approach to leadership takes into account: (a) the leader; (b) the follower; (c) the situation; (d) a and b; (e) a, b, and c.

4. Insights about using leadership theories that emphasize decision-making situations.

a, b, c, d, e **a.** Forces in the manager that determine leadership behavior include: (a) the manager's values; (b) the manager's confidence in subordinates; (c) the manager's strengths; (d) the manager's tolerance for ambiguity; (e) all of the above.

a, b, c, d, e **b.** Limiting the self-guidance of the follower and specifically defining procedures for the follower's task performance is called: (a) initiating behavior; (b) structure behavior; (c) maturity behavior; (d) consideration behavior; (e) relationship behavior.

T, F **c.** The VYJ model suggests that a leader should match one of five decision-making styles to the particular situation that the leader faces.

5. Insights about using leadership theories that emphasize more general organizational situations.

a, b, c, d, e **a.** The ability of followers to perform their jobs independently and to assume additional responsibility in their desire to achieve success is called: (a) maturity; (b) authority; (c) aggressiveness; (d) assertiveness; (e) consideration.

a, b, c, d, e **b.** Usually upon entrance into an organization, an individual is unable to solve task-related problems independently. According to the life cycle theory, the appropriate style of leadership for this person is: (a) high task/low relationships; (b) high task/high relationships; (c) high relationships/low task; (d) low task/low relationships; (e) none of the above.

T, F **c.** According to the path-goal theory of leadership, a leader should carefully inform followers of the rewards that are available to them in the organization and then allow them to pick their own methods of earning the rewards.

6. An understanding of alternatives to leader flexibility.

a, b, c, d, e **a.** According to Fiedler, the three primary factors that should be used as a basis for moving leaders into more appropriate situations are: (a) task behavior, consideration behavior, maturity; (b) maturity, job knowledge, responsibility; (c) the worker, the leader, the situation; (d) leader-member relations, task structure, position power; (e) task structure, leadership style, maturity.

T, F **b.** Fiedler's studies have proven true the myths that leaders are born, not made, and that there is one best leadership style.

7. An appreciation of both transformational leadership and substitute leadership theory.

T, F **a.** Transformational leaders modify organizations by precisely carrying out strategic plans and emphasizing only slightly the values that followers may have.

T, F **b.** Transformational leadership might be called charismatic or inspirational leadership.

T, F **c.** There are situations in which a leader has very little influence because many of the variables are out of his/her control.

T, F **d.** Even though there are situations in which a leader has little or no impact on the outcome, the leader is nevertheless an important part of management.

INTRODUCTORY CASE WRAP-UP

"Liz Claiborne" (p. 347) and its related back-to-the-case sections were written to help you better understand the leadership concepts contained in this chapter. Discuss the following questions about this case to further enrich your understanding of chapter content.

1. Will Liz Claiborne's successor inherit any special leadership problems? If so, list the problem(s) you see. If none, why not?
2. If a strong personality and value system are considered to be leadership traits, how do you overcome or follow the personality of Liz Claiborne? Do you have to worry about this?

ISSUES FOR REVIEW AND DISCUSSION

1. What is leadership?
2. How does leadership differ from management?
3. Explain the trait approach to leadership.
4. What relationship exists between successful leadership and leadership traits?
5. Explain the situational approach to leadership.
6. Draw and explain Tannenbaum and Schmidt's leadership model.
7. List the forces in the manager, the subordinates, and the situation that ultimately determine how a manager should make decisions as a leader.
8. How is the VYJ Model similar to the Tannenbaum and Schmidt Model? How is it different?
9. What contribution did the OSU studies make to leadership theory?
10. Can any one of the major leadership styles resulting from the OSU studies be called more effective than the others? Explain.
11. Compare the results of the OSU studies with the results of the Michigan Studies.
12. What is meant by *maturity* as it is used in the life cycle theory of leadership?
13. Draw and explain the life cycle theory of leadership model.
14. What is meant by *leader flexibility*?
15. Describe some obstacles to leader flexibility.
16. In general, how might obstacles to leader flexibility be overcome?
17. In specific terms, how does Fiedler suggest that obstacles to leader flexibility be overcome?
18. Based upon the path-goal theory of leadership, how would you advise a friend to lead?
19. Describe three challenges that a transformational leader must face.
20. List three situations in which you think a leader should delegate tasks.

ACTION SUMMARY

1. **a.** c, p. 348
   b. e, p. 348
2. **a.** F, p. 348
   b. c, p. 348
3. **a.** c, p. 349
   b. e, p. 350
4. **a.** e, p. 352
   b. b, p. 357
   c. T, pp. 354–355
5. **a.** a, p. 359
   b. a, pp. 359–361
   c. F, p. 364
6. **a.** d, p. 363
   b. F, p. 364
7. **a.** F, p. 366
   b. T, p. 366
   c. T, p. 366
   d. F, p. 366

CASE STUDY

Al Scott's Vision of Quality for Wilson Sporting Goods

STEPHEN M. BECKSTEAD
Utah State University

Every weekday morning at 9:00, Al Scott, plant manager at Wilson Sporting Goods in Humboldt, Tennessee, meets with his staff to discuss the business of "manufacturing the world's finest golf balls." Named one of the "Best Plants in America" by *Industry Week* magazine, the Humboldt plant produces some 96-million-dozen golf balls each year, and the volume is growing.

Things were not always so rosy at the Humboldt plant. In 1985, the Wilson Humboldt facility was considered to be one of the least effective plants within the corporation. In addition to losing money each year, the plant had severe deficiencies in quality, safety, productivity, morale, and housekeeping. But Scott's vision of Wilson was not limited by the poor performance. Scott wanted to manufacture the best golf ball and have the finest golf ball production facilities in the world. His vision was reflected in the mission statement he drafted which states, "Our mission is to be recognized . . . as the premier manufacturer of golf balls." To become the best, Scott crafted five guiding philosophies that were to direct the plant's activities: employee involvement, continuous improvement, just-in-time manufacturing, total quality management, and lowest total cost manufacturer.

Scott knew that to be successful he would have to get the right people in each department. Managers and supervisors were made coaches, while employees were called associates. Everyone was asked to change his or her old ways. Rather than using the excuse that "we have always done it this way," all associates were empowered to find new solutions to old problems. A just-in-case mentality was refocused to a just-in-time approach. A "we can't afford to do it" response was changed to "we can't afford *not* to do it."

On January 12, 1987, Scott formed "Team Wilson"—". . . the formal program that allows associates to participate in problem-solving groups that will deal with issues concerning quality, productivity, housekeeping, and safety." Teams were to focus their efforts on reducing operating expenses, improving cash flow, reducing inventory, and improving safety and housekeeping.

The employees responded to Scott's vision and new style of management. Managers started coaching and encouraging employee participation. By 1992, 66 percent of the workers had formed voluntary teams. Each team represented a specific plant area and created its own unique logo, T-shirts, and poster, which hung in the plant. Many of the teams were headed by hourly associates, with team members composed of both hourly associates and coaches. Each team was empowered to spend up to $500 for each project they selected without management approval. This meant that authority and management responsibility usually reserved for managers and supervisors was pushed down to the operations level.

To help associates make good managerial decisions, they received training, directed and coordinated by an in-house trainer. Associate training included interaction training, life enrichment training (such as team building, self-esteem, time management, and attitude training), as well as training in the tools to total quality management (statistical process control, cause and effect analysis, etc.).

With vision, changes in leadership style, and employee involvement, Scott turned the Humboldt facility into one of the best in the United States. During Scott's tenure at Wilson, market share has increased from two to seventeen percent. During the same time frame annual inventory turns increased from 6.5 to 85, while inventory was slashed by two-thirds. Manufacturing losses caused by scrap and rework were reduced by 67 percent. Productivity has increased a whopping 121 percent.

Scott knows that without the high associate involvement in Team Wilson teams, Wilson would not have become one of the best plants in America. To show appreciation to all Wilson associates, Wilson holds several cookouts, picnics, and parties each year. To recognize team accomplishments, three Team Wilson teams are chosen each quarter for awards.

DISCUSSION QUESTIONS

1. Where does Scott fall on the Tannenbaum and Schmidt Leadership Continuum? Please explain.
2. Given the information in the case, would you say Scott focused on job-centered behavior or employee-centered behavior? Please explain.
3. Scott transformed the Wilson, Humboldt plant from the worst in the corporation to the best. Comment on Scott's transformational leadership skills.
4. Discuss what Scott did to build trust between the employees at Wilson and himself.

CNN VIDEO CASE

When Inexperience Paid Off

RICHARD BRANSON
The Virgin Group

Britain's ninth richest citizen, Richard Branson, was a high-school dropout, a claim many successful entrepreneurs can make. Displaying classic entrepreneurial characteristics, Branson describes his approach: "I'm best at starting companies, getting them up and running, finding good people and hopefully motivating those people. I love immersing myself completely in a new venture, learning all about it. And then, generally speaking, I move on and start something else and leave other good people there to run it."

The first business Richard Branson started was an alternative magazine. Branson soon gave this up in favor of selling records, an activity he first engaged in to raise money for the magazine. From a little store in central London, the record company grew into a record-store chain. With that success, Branson decided to *make* records as well as sell them, so he started Virgin Music. The Virgin label—for all of Branson's enterprises—connotes his personal inexperience in each enterprise as he begins it. Branson's inexperience must be a positive force: in 1992, Virgin Music was sold to Thorn EMI for $880 million, with Branson's share coming to $540 million. In the twenty years since he started the record company, Branson never really thought he would sell it, but he knew that if he did sell it, he would not sell it cheap; and he certainly didn't. Nevertheless the decision to sell was difficult, since he had started the business in his youth. "I remember [after the sale] running back to my home . . . tears streaming down my face."

Richard Branson believes that companies need to be run from the bottom up—a receptionist's job must be considered as important as the top manager's job.

With the money from the sale, however, Richard Branson is expanding his biggest enterprise, Virgin Atlantic Airways, and maintaining his retail operation, Virgin Megastores. Branson's twist on the airline business is to provide an airline focused on customer service and limited to about fourteen major cities in the world. "I knew when we started it, there's no small airline in the world that has ever survived." He hopes that, by targeting fewer cities, Virgin Atlantic Airways will be able to keep its focus on customer service, which will differentiate the airline enough for it to succeed. Branson also learned what *not* to do, from advice given him by British entrepreneur Freddie Laker, whose own small airline Skytrain went defunct two years before Virgin Atlantic started.

Why get into such a tough business? "Well," says Branson, "it is an enormous challenge in that it's not an easy business to be in and it's enormously romantic . . . and it helps promote other businesses you're doing." (Branson hopes to have the airline's destinations coincide with cities where he has Virgin Megastores.)

Branson's management style has not changed much, either as he has aged or has run different kinds of businesses. He still believes that companies should be run from the bottom up; that is, the receptionist's job should be considered as important as the top manager's job. This builds loyalty. Also, Branson chooses people he likes on the personal level. He says, "If you've got likable people, then they'll be good with their staff and then the staff will flourish." This, according to Branson, will bring the kind of success he has managed. "The staff should come first, the customers second, and shareholders third."

VIDEO CASE QUESTIONS

1. What is the main characteristic that makes Richard Branson more a leader than a manager?
2. Show evidence that Branson is a transformational leader.
3. The Ohio State University studies of leaders identify two types of leadership behavior: structure behavior and consideration behavior. Which type of behavior does Richard Branson seem to exhibit?
4. Where in Table 14.1 would you place Richard Branson's basic style?

CNN VIDEO EXERCISE

Planning an Executive Retreat for Virgin Atlantic Airways

ACTION GOAL: Draft a memo using an assigned leadership style.

Imagine that, as director of personnel for Virgin Atlantic Airways, you have been planning an executive retreat during which the top managers will work to improve their interpersonal and interdepartmental relations. Draft a brief memo announcing your decision to plan a retreat. In the memo, describe the need for such a retreat, state what you hope it will accomplish, and explain the particulars of time, place, and expenses. Modify the information as needed to fit the leadership style you use in your memo.

Write the memo using a leadership style from the Tannenbaum and Schmidt Leadership Continuum on page 351. If your last name begins with one of the letters A–C, use style 1; letters D–F, style 2; letters G–I, style 3; letters J–L, style 4, letters M–P, style 5; letters Q–T, style 6; letters U–Z, style 7.

When all classmates have presented their plan, discuss the leadership behaviors. Which kind of leader would you be willing to work for? Happy to work for? How can employees work with employers whose leadership style is stifling or authoritarian?

TO:

FROM:

DATE:

CHAPTER

15

MOTIVATION

STUDENT LEARNING OBJECTIVES

From studying this chapter, I will attempt to acquire:

1. A basic understanding of human motivation.
2. Insights on various human needs.
3. An appreciation for the importance of motivating organization members.
4. An understanding of various motivation strategies.

CHAPTER OUTLINE

INTRODUCTORY CASE
American Greetings Motivates through Lateral Moves

THE MOTIVATION PROCESS

Defining Motivation
Process Theories of Motivation
Content Theories of Motivation: Human Needs

GLOBAL HIGHLIGHT
Maslow's Hierarchy

MOTIVATING ORGANIZATION MEMBERS

The Importance of Motivating Organization Members
Strategies for Motivating Organization Members

DIVERSITY HIGHLIGHT
Greyhound

QUALITY HIGHLIGHT
Apple Computer

ETHICS HIGHLIGHT
Government

CASE STUDY
Motivation at America West Airlines

VIDEO CASE
Motivating through Intrapreneurship

VIDEO EXERCISE
Analyzing Motivation at Federal Express

INTRODUCTORY CASE

American Greetings Motivates through Lateral Moves

With few promotions to give out, companies are trying to motivate employees by shifting them sideways instead of up.

Consider American Greetings Corp., the Cleveland greeting card and licensing concern. The company recently redesigned about 400 jobs in its creative division and asked workers and managers to reapply. Everyone was guaranteed a position, and no one took a pay cut, company officials say.

When the restructuring is completed later this year, employees will develop products in teams instead of assembly-line fashion. And they'll be free to transfer back and forth among teams that make different products, instead of working on just one product line, as they have in the past.

Traditionally, lateral moves have smacked of demotion, because they derailed what seemed like inevitable promotions.

As a result, people who have spent careers specializing in Christmas and Easter cards will be able to sign up to work on birthday ribbons, humorous mugs and Valentine's Day gift bags all in the same year. And artists whose only job was choosing dyes will be trying their hands at illustration and lettering.

"It unleashes a lot of their creative potential," says Dennis Chupa, a division vice president, who engineered the shakeup. Adds an employee: "A lot of people think it's a good time to make a change or work for someone different."

The main purpose of the restructuring is to cut production time by as much as half for some products, especially greeting cards that play on fleeting fads. But at the same time, American Greetings is addressing an increasingly common problem: how to light fires under workers at a time when few promotions or pay raises are on the horizon.

Unless companies act now, workers whose eyes have glazed over during the recession will leave "so damn fast when the economy turns up that they're going to leave burn marks on the carpet," says Marilyn Moats Kennedy, editor of the newsletter "Kennedy's Career Strategist." Lateral moves that require new skills may be companies' "only hope" for retaining talent, she says.

Traditionally, lateral moves have smacked of demotion, because they derailed what seemed like inevitable promotions. The moves make more sense now that more hands are grabbing for fewer rungs on the corporate ladder. "If the channel above you is clogged, moving sideways can get you out of the traffic jam," says Robert Kelley, a business professor at Carnegie Mellon University who has written about nontraditional career paths.

The greeting card industry utilizes the diverse talents of many creative individuals. American Greetings Corporation recently restructured its operation to allow employees to work in teams and to transfer back and forth between different kinds of products, in order to cut production time and keep employees motivated and creative.

From Joan E. Rigdon, "Using Lateral Moves to Spur Employees," *Wall Street Journal* (May 26, 1992), B1, B9. Reprinted by permission of *Wall Street Journal*, © 1992 Dow Jones & Company, Inc. All Rights Reserved Worldwide.

WHAT'S AHEAD Dennis Chupa, the division vice president at American Greetings in the introductory case, has engineered a reorganization of company workers. This reorganization is partially aimed at motivating workers at a time when few company promotions or pay raises are on the horizon. The material in this chapter discusses insights about why managers such as Chupa should focus on motivating workers and how this might be accomplished. This chapter addresses two major topics: 1) the motivation process, and 2) motivating organization members.

THE MOTIVATION PROCESS

Motivation is the inner state that causes an individual to behave in a way that ensures the accomplishment of some goal.

To be successful in working with other people, managers first need a thorough understanding of the motivation process. To this end, a definition of **motivation,** various motivation models, and descriptions of people's needs are the main topics of discussion in this section of the chapter.

Defining Motivation

Motivation is the inner state that causes an individual to behave in a way that ensures the accomplishment of some goal.[1] In other words, motivation explains why people behave the way they do. The more managers understand organization members' behavior, the better able they should be to influence that behavior and make it more consistent with the accomplishment of organizational objectives. Since productivity is a result of the behavior of organization members, influencing this behavior is a manager's key to increasing productivity.

Process theories of motivation are explanations of motivation that emphasize how individuals are motivated.

Content theories of motivation are explanations of motivation that emphasize internal characteristics of people.

Over the years, several different theories about motivation have been proposed. In general, these theories have been categorized into two basic types: process theories and content theories. **Process theories of motivation** are explanations of motivation that emphasize how individuals are motivated. In essence, the process theories focus on the steps that occur when an individual is motivated. **Content theories of motivation** are explanations of motivation that emphasize internal characteristics of people. The main focus of the content theories is understanding the needs that people possess and how they can be satisfied. The following sections discuss both important process and content theories of motivation and establish a relationship between them that can be useful to managers in motivating organization members.

Process Theories of Motivation

Four important theories that describe how motivation occurs are (1) the needs-goal theory, (2) the Vroom expectancy theory, (3) the equity theory, and (4) the Porter-Lawler theory. These theories build on one another to furnish a description of the motivation process that begins at a relatively simple and easily understood level and culminates at a somewhat more intricate and realistic level.

The Needs-Goal Theory of Motivation

The **needs-goal theory** is a motivation model that hypothesizes that felt needs cause human behavior.

The **needs-goal theory** of motivation (see Figure 15.1) is the most fundamental of the motivation theories discussed in this chapter. As the figure indicates, motivation begins with an individual feeling a need. This need is then transformed into behavior directed at supporting, or allowing, the performance of goal behavior to reduce the felt need. Theoretically, a goal-supportive behavior and goal behavior continue until the felt need has been reduced significantly.

For example, when an individual feels hunger (a need), this need typically is transformed first into behavior directed at supporting the performance of the goal behavior of eating. This supportive behavior could include such activities as buying, cooking, and serving the food to be eaten. The goal-supportive behaviors and the goal behavior

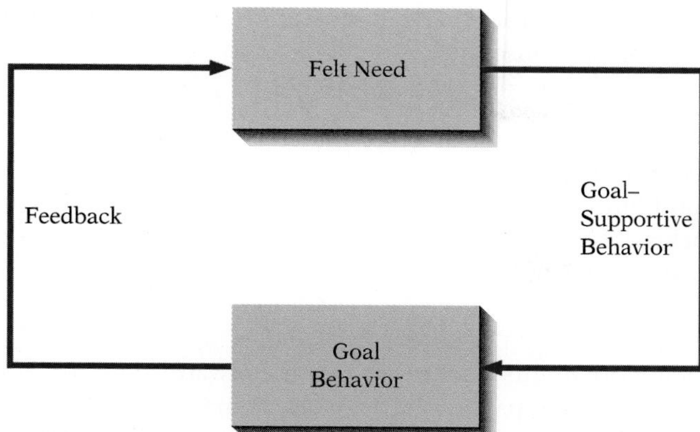

FIGURE 15.1 The needs-goal theory of motivation

itself—eating—typically continue until the individual's hunger substantially subsides. Once the individual experiences the hunger again, however, the entire cycle is repeated.

If managers are to have any success in motivating employees, they must understand the personal needs that employees possess.[2] When managers offer rewards to employees that are not relevant to the personal needs of employees, the employees will not be motivated. For example, if a top executive is already in the highest income tax bracket, more money is not likely to be an effective motivator. Instead, a more meaningful incentive—perhaps a higher-level title or offer of partnership in the firm—would be a more effective motivator. Managers must be familiar with needs that employees possess and offer rewards to employees that can satisfy these needs.[3]

The Vroom Expectancy Theory of Motivation

In reality, the motivation process is more complex than is depicted by the needs-goal theory. The **Vroom expectancy theory** of motivation handles some of the additional complexities.[4] As with the needs-goal theory, the Vroom expectancy theory is based on the premise that felt needs cause human behavior. In addition, however, the Vroom theory addresses the issue of **motivation strength**—an individual's degree of desire to perform a behavior. As this desire increases or decreases, motivation strength is said to fluctuate correspondingly.

The **Vroom expectancy theory** is a motivation theory that hypothesizes that felt needs cause human behavior and that motivation strength depends on an individual's degree of desire to perform a behavior.

Motivation strength is an individual's degree of desire to perform a behavior.

Vroom's expectancy theory is shown in equation form in Figure 15.2. According to this theory, motivation strength is determined by the perceived value of the result of performing a behavior and the perceived probability that the behavior performed will cause the result to materialize. As both of these factors increase, the motivation strength, or the desire to perform the behavior, increases. In general, individuals tend to perform the behaviors that maximize personal rewards over the long term.

An illustration of how Vroom's theory applies to human behavior could be a college student who has been offered the summer job of painting three houses at the rate of $200 a house. Assuming that the student has a need for money, her motivation strength, or desire, to paint the houses is determined by two major factors: her perceived value of $600 and the perceived probability that she actually can paint the houses satisfactorily and, thus, receive the $600. As the perceived value of the $600 re-

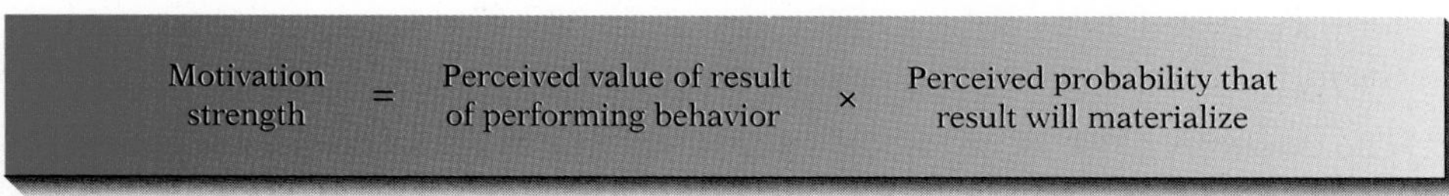

FIGURE 15.2 Vroom's expectancy theory of motivation in equation form

ward and the probability that the houses can be painted satisfactorily increase, the student's motivation strength to paint the houses increases.

Equity Theory of Motivation

Equity theory of motivation is an explanation of motivation that emphasizes an individual's perceived fairness of an employment situation and how perceived inequities can cause certain behaviors.

The work of J. Stacy Adams, **equity theory,** looks at an individual's perceived fairness of an employment situation and finds that perceived inequities can lead to changes in behavior. When individuals believe that they have been treated unfairly compared with coworkers, Adams found that they will react in one of the following ways to attempt to bring the inequity into balance:[5]

1. Some will try to change their work inputs to better match the rewards they are receiving. If they believe they are being paid too little, workers may tend to work less hard. On the other hand, if they believe that they are being paid more than their coworkers, they will increase their work outputs to match their rewards.
2. Some will try to change the compensation they receive for their work by asking for a raise or through legal action.
3. Some will try to change the perception of an inequality if attempts to change the actual inequality are unsuccessful. This can be accomplished by attempting to distort the status of certain jobs or by rationalizing that the inequity does not really exist.
4. Some will leave the situation rather than try to change it. People who feel they are being treated unfairly may decide to quit rather than to face the inequitable situation.

Perceptions of inequities can arise in any number of management situations such as work assignments, promotions, ratings reports, and office assignments, but they occur most often in terms of money. They are emotionally charged issues that deal with human beings, and even a minor inequity in the mind of a manager can be important in the minds of those affected. Effective managers attempt to keep equity issues in balance because the steps that a worker will take to try to balance the scales are not always the best for the organization.[5]

The Porter-Lawler Theory of Motivation

The **Porter-Lawler theory** is a motivation theory that hypothesizes that felt needs cause human behavior and that motivation strength is determined primarily by the perceived value of the result of performing the behavior and the perceived probability that the behavior performed will cause the result to materialize.

Intrinsic rewards are rewards that come directly from performing a task.

Extrinsic rewards are rewards that are extraneous to the task accomplished.

Porter and Lawler developed a motivation theory that presents a more complete description of the motivation process than either the needs-goal theory or the Vroom expectancy theory.[6] The **Porter-Lawler theory** of motivation (see Figure 15.3) is consistent with the prior theories in that it accepts the premises that felt needs cause human behavior and that effort expended to accomplish a task is determined by the perceived value of rewards that will result from the task and the probability that the rewards will materialize. In addition, however, the Porter-Lawler motivation theory stresses three other characteristics of the motivation process:

1. The perceived value of a reward is determined by both intrinsic and extrinsic rewards that result in need satisfaction when a task is accomplished. **Intrinsic rewards** come directly from performing a task, and **extrinsic rewards** are extraneous to the task. For example, when a manager counsels a subordinate about a personal problem, the manager may get some intrinsic reward in the form of personal satisfaction simply from helping another individual. In addition to this intrinsic reward, however, the manager also would receive an extrinsic reward in the form of the overall salary the manager is paid.[7]
2. The extent to which an individual effectively accomplishes a task is determined primarily by two variables: the individual's perception of what is required to perform the task and the individual's ability to perform the task. Naturally, the effec-

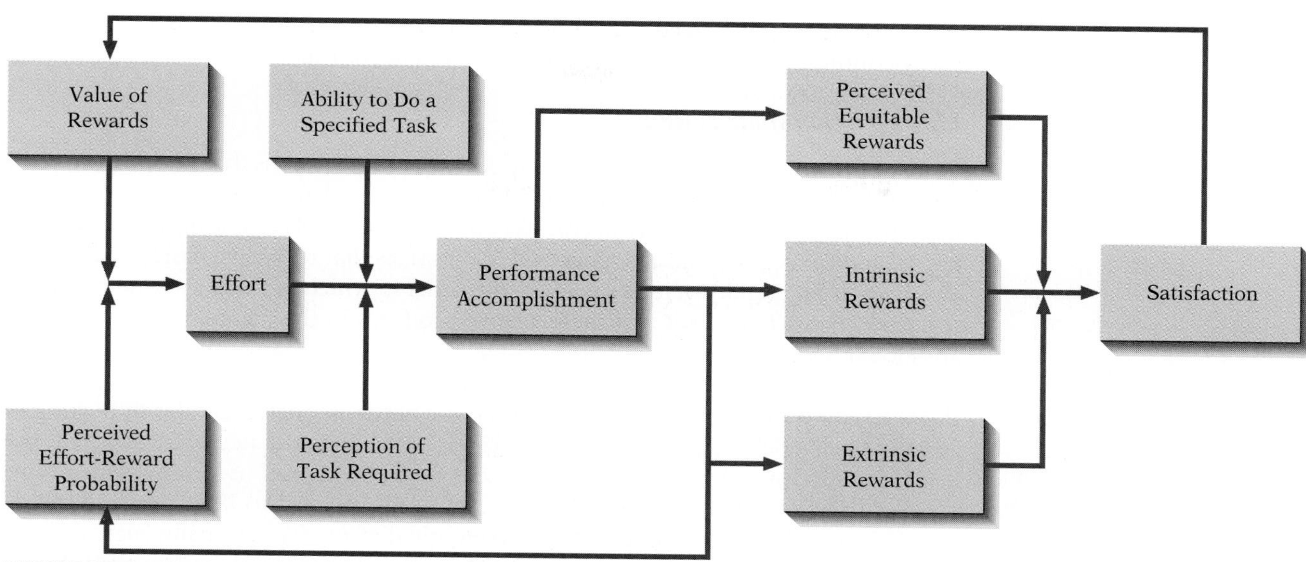

FIGURE 15.3 The Porter-Lawler theory of motivation

tiveness at accomplishing a task increases as the perception of what is required to perform the task becomes more accurate and as the ability to perform the task increases.

3. The perceived fairness of rewards influences the amount of satisfaction produced by those rewards. In general, the more equitable an individual perceives the rewards to be, the greater the satisfaction the individual will experience as a result of receiving them.

BACK TO THE CASE Motivation is an inner state that causes individuals to act in certain ways that ensure the accomplishment of some goal. Dennis Chupa in the introductory case seems to have an accurate understanding of the motivation process in that he is focusing on influencing the behavior of his employees to make it consistent with American Greetings objectives. That is, he is encouraging employees within the company to be creative and efficient in performing their jobs. The reorganization emphasizing lateral job moves that Chupa designed should be a valuable tool in making this encouragement effective.

To motivate employees, Chupa must keep five specific principles of human motivation clearly in mind: (1) felt needs cause behavior aimed at reducing those needs; (2) the degree of desire to perform a particular behavior is determined by an individual's perceived value of the result of performing the behavior and the perceived probability that the behavior will cause the result to materialize; (3) the perceived value of a reward for a particular behavior is determined by both intrinsic and extrinsic rewards that result in need satisfaction when the behavior is accomplished; (4) individuals can effectively accomplish a task only if they understand what the task requires and have the ability to perform the task; and (5) the perceived fairness of a reward influences the degree of satisfaction generated when the reward is received.

Content Theories of Motivation: Human Needs

The motivation theories discussed thus far imply that an understanding of motivation is based on an understanding of human needs. There is some evidence that people in general possess strong needs for self-respect, respect from others, promotion, and psychological growth.[8] Although pinpointing all human needs is impossible, several theories have been developed to help managers better understand these needs: (1)

Maslow's hierarchy of needs, (2) Alderfer's ERG theory, (3) Argyris's maturity-immaturity continuum, and (4) McClelland's acquired needs theory.

Maslow's Hierarchy of Needs

Perhaps the most widely accepted description of human needs is the hierarchy of needs concept developed by Abraham Maslow.[9] Maslow states that human beings possess five basic needs: (1) physiological needs, (2) security needs, (3) social needs, (4) esteem needs, and (5) self-actualization needs. He theorizes that these five basic needs can be arranged in a hierarchy of importance—the order in which individuals generally strive to satisfy them. The needs and their relative positions in the hierarchy of importance are shown in Figure 15.4.

Physiological needs are Maslow's first set of human needs—for the normal functioning of the body, including the desires for water, food, rest, sex, and air.

Security, or **safety, needs** are Maslow's second set of human needs—reflecting the human desires to keep free from physical harm.

Physiological needs relate to the normal functioning of the body. They include the needs for water, rest, sex, and air. Until these needs are met, a significant portion of an individual's behavior is aimed at satisfying them. Once the needs are satisfied, behavior is aimed at satisfying the security needs on the next level of Maslow's hierarchy.

Security, or **safety, needs** are the needs individuals feel to keep themselves free from harm, including both bodily and economic disaster. Traditionally, management has probably best helped employees satisfy their physiological and security needs through adequate employee wages or salaries. It is with these salaries that employees purchase such things as food and housing in order to satisfy basic human needs.

A relatively new issue regarding employee safety needs is the threat of terrorism. The possibility of terrorism has placed executives working in international settings and in certain jobs or industries within the United States in uncomfortable situations. As a result of this threat to employee safety, many companies are developing special security and safety programs for their employees in international settings.[10]

Security is a basic human need. According to Maslow's hierarchy, as security needs are satisfied, behavior tends to be aimed at satisfying social needs.

Social needs are Maslow's third set of human needs—reflecting the human desires to belong, including the desire for friendship, companionship, and love.

Esteem needs are Maslow's fourth set of human needs—including the desires for self-respect and respect from others.

Self-actualization needs are Maslow's fifth set of human needs—reflecting the human desire to maximize potential.

Social needs include the desire for love, companionship, and friendship. These needs reflect a person's desire to be accepted by others. As the needs are satisfied, behavior shifts to satisfying esteem needs.

Esteem needs are the desire for respect. They generally are divided into two categories: self-respect and respect for others. Once esteem needs are satisfied, the individual emphasizes satisfying self-actualization needs.

Self-actualization needs are the desire to maximize whatever potential an individual possesses. For example, in the nonprofit public setting of a high school, a principal who seeks to satisfy self-actualization needs would strive to become the best principal possible. Self-actualization needs are the highest level of Maslow's hierarchy.

Although many management theorists admit that Maslow's hierarchy can be use-

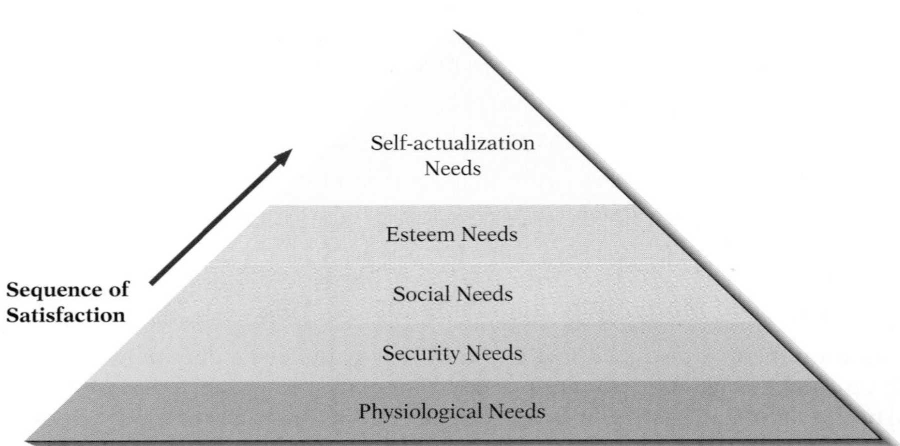

FIGURE 15.4 Maslow's hierarchy of needs

ful in understanding human needs, they have also expressed concern about the hierarchy. Maslow himself has said:

> I of all people should know just how shaky this foundation for the theory is as a final foundation. My work on motivation came from the clinic, from a study of neurotic people. The carryover of this theory to the industrial situation has some support from industrial studies, but certainly I would like to see a lot more studies of this kind before feeling finally convinced that this carryover from the study of neurosis to the study of labor in factories is legitimate. The same thing is true of my studies of self-actualizing people— there is only this one study of mine available. There were many things wrong with the sampling, so many in fact that it must be considered to be, in the classical sense anyway, a bad or poor or inadequate experiment. I am quite willing to concede this— because I'm a little worried about this stuff which I consider to be tentative being swallowed whole by all sorts of enthusiastic people who really should be a little more tentative in the way that I am.[11]

Traditionally there have been concerns related to Maslow's hierarchy that are based on its lack of a research base,[12] a questioning of whether Maslow has accurately pinpointed five basic human needs,[13] and some doubt as to whether human needs actually are arranged in a hierarchy.[14] Despite such concerns, Maslow's hierarchy is probably the most popular conceptualization of human needs to date, and it continues to be positively discussed in management literature.[15] The concerns do indicate, however, that Maslow's hierarchy should be considered more a subjective statement than an objective description of human needs.

GLOBAL HIGHLIGHT
Maslow's Hierarchy and Japanese, Chinese, and U.S. Workers

Companies such as Motorola and Digital Equipment International commonly experience the challenge of understanding the human needs of workers from different cultures. Research shows that, because people from different cultures normally place different values on the various human needs in Maslow's hierarchy, management has a special challenge in understanding how the hierarchy of needs might vary from country to country.

For an organization to function effectively, managers must motivate subordinates to take consistent action toward company goals. In global companies like Digital or Motorola, managers must understand the link between motivation and the changing importance of various human needs from country to country. For example, consider how Maslow's hierarchy of needs might be applied differently to workers in Japan, China, and the United States. Research indicates that when attempting to motivate Chinese workers, managers should focus on the esteem and social needs of organization members. On the other hand, when attempting to motivate Japanese workers, managers should focus more on safety, social, esteem, and self-actualization needs of organization members. When attempting to motivate United States workers, managers should emphasize the esteem and self-actualization needs of organization members. ▶

Research indicates that, when attempting to motivate Japanese workers, managers should focus on safety, social, esteem, and self-actualization needs of organization members.

Alderfer's ERG Theory

Clayton Alderfer responded to some of the criticisms of Maslow's work with his own study of human needs.[16] He identified three basic categories of needs: (1) existence needs—the need for physical well-being, (2) relatedness needs—the need for satisfying interpersonal relationships, and (3) growth needs—the need for continuing personal growth and development. The first letters of these needs form the acronym ERG by which the theory is now known.

Alderfer's ERG theory is an explanation of human needs that divides them into three basic types: existence needs, relatedness needs, and growth needs.

Alderfer's ERG theory is similar to Maslow's theory except in three major respects: He identified only three orders of human needs, compared to Maslow's five orders of needs. In contrast to Maslow, Alderfer found that workers may sometimes activate their higher-level needs before they have completely satisfied all of the lower-level needs. Alderfer also found that movement in his hierarchy in satisfying human needs is not always upward. He found, reflected in his frustration-regression principle, that a worker frustrated by failing to satisfy an upper-level need might regress by trying to fulfill an already satisfied lower-level need. Alderfer's work, in conjunction with Maslow's work, has implications for management. Job-enrichment strategies can help an individual to meet the higher-order needs. If an employee is frustrated by work that fails to provide the opportunity for growth or development on the job, he or she might spend more energy trying to make more money, thus regressing to a lower level.

Argyris's Maturity-Immaturity Continuum

Argyris's maturity-immaturity continuum is a concept that furnishes insights on human needs by focusing on an individual's natural growth progress from immaturity to maturity.

Argyris's maturity-immaturity continuum also furnishes insights on human needs.[17] This continuum concept focuses on the personal and natural development of people to explain how needs exist.[18] According to Argyris, as people naturally progress from immaturity to maturity, they move:

1. From a state of passivity as an infant to a state of increasing activity as an adult.
2. From a state of dependence on others as an infant to a state of relative independence as an adult.
3. From being capable of behaving only in a few ways as an infant to being capable of behaving in many different ways as an adult.
4. From having erratic, casual, shallow, and quickly dropped interests as an infant to having deeper interests as an adult.
5. From having a short time perspective as an infant to having a much longer time perspective as an adult.
6. From being in a subordinate position as an infant to aspiring to occupy an equal or superordinate position as an adult.
7. From a lack of awareness of self as an infant to awareness and control over self as an adult.

Thus, according to Argyris's continuum, as individuals mature, they have increasing needs for more activity, enjoy a state of relative independence, behave in many different ways, have deeper interests, consider a relatively long time perspective, occupy an equal position with other mature individuals, and have more awareness of themselves and control over their own destiny. Unlike Maslow's needs, Argyris's needs are not arranged in a hierarchy. Like Maslow's hierarchy, however, Argyris's continuum represents primarily a subjective position on the existence of human needs.

McClelland's Acquired-Needs Theory

McClelland's acquired-needs theory is an explanation of human needs that focuses on desires for achievement, power, and affiliation as needs that people develop as a result of their life experiences.

Another theory about human needs, called **McClelland's acquired-needs theory,** focuses on the needs that people develop through their life experiences—acquired needs. This theory, formulated by David C. McClelland in the 1960s, focuses on three of the many needs humans develop in their lifetimes: (1) the need for achievement (*nAch*)—the desire to do something better or more efficiently than it ever has been done before; (2) the need for power (*nPower*)—the desire to control, influence, or be responsible for others; and (3) the need for affiliation (*nAff*)—the desire to maintain close, friendly, personal relationships. A person's early life experiences determine which of these needs will be highly developed and therefore dominate the personality.

McClelland's studies of these acquired human needs have significant implications for management.

McClelland claims that, in some business people, the need to achieve is so strong that it is more motivating than a quest for profits.[19] To maximize their satisfaction, individuals with high achievement needs tend to set goals for themselves that are challenging yet achievable.[20] Although these individuals do not avoid risk completely, they assess it very carefully. Individuals motivated by the need to achieve do not want to fail and will avoid tasks that involve too much risk. Individuals with a low need for achievement generally avoid challenges, responsibilities, and risk.

People with a high need for power are highly motivated to try to influence other people and to be responsible for subordinate behavior. They are likely to seek advancement and to assume increasingly responsible work activities. Power-oriented managers are comfortable in competitive situations and with their decision-making roles. Managers with a high need for affiliation, on the other hand, tend to have a cooperative, team-centered style of management in which a task is completed through team efforts. However, a high need for affiliation could also sacrifice a manager's effectiveness when the need for social approval and friendship interferes with the manager's ability to make managerial decisions.[21]

BACK TO THE CASE

Chupa undoubtedly understands the basic motivation principle that felt needs cause behavior. Before managers like Chupa can have maximum impact on motivating their organization members, however, they must also meet the more complex challenge of being thoroughly familiar with various individual human needs of their employees.

According to Maslow, people generally possess physiological needs, security needs, social needs, esteem needs, and self-actualization needs arranged in a hierarchy of importance. Argyris suggests that as people mature, they have increasing needs for activity, independence, flexibility, deeper interests, analyses of longer time perspectives, a position of equality with other mature individuals, and control over personal destiny. McClelland believes that the need for achievement—the desire to do something better or more efficiently than it has ever been done before—is a strong human need.

Guaranteeing every worker a position with no pay cuts as part of Chupa's reorganization focused on satisfying employee physiological and safety needs. Other features complementing Chupa's reorganization, like management development programs or a "best card verse of the month" program, could further motivate Chupa's employees by satisfying other needs that they might have.

MOTIVATING ORGANIZATION MEMBERS

People are motivated to perform behavior to satisfy personal needs. Therefore, from a managerial viewpoint, motivation is the process of furnishing organization members with the opportunity to satisfy their needs by performing productive behavior within the organization. As discussed in chapter 13, motivation is one of the four primary interrelated activities of the influencing function performed by managers to guide the behavior of organization members toward attainment of organizational objectives. The following sections discuss the importance of and strategies for motivating organization members.

The Importance of Motivating Organization Members

Figure 15.5 makes the point that unsatisfied needs of organization members can lead to either appropriate or inappropriate member behavior. Managers who are successful at motivating organization members minimize inappropriate behavior and maximize

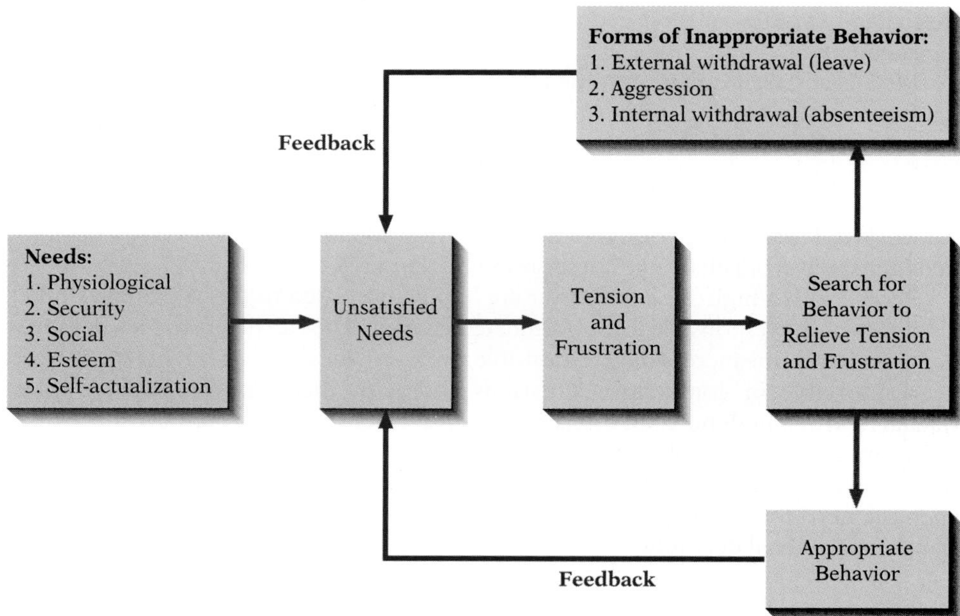

FIGURE 15.5 Unsatisfied needs of organization members resulting in either appropriate or inappropriate behavior

appropriate behavior. Correspondingly, these managers raise the probability that productivity will increase and lower the probability that productivity will decrease.

Strategies for Motivating Organization Members

Managers have various strategies for motivating organization members. Each strategy is aimed at satisfying people's needs (consistent with those described by Maslow's hierarchy of needs, Alderfer's ERG theory, Argyris's maturity-immaturity continuum, and McClelland's acquired needs theory) through appropriate organizational behavior. These managerial motivation strategies are (1) managerial communication, (2) Theory X–Theory Y, (3) job design, (4) behavior modification, (5) Likert's management systems, (6) monetary incentives, and (7) nonmonetary incentives. The strategies are discussed in the sections that follow.

It is important to remember that no single strategy will necessarily always be more effective for a manager than any other. In fact, a manager may find that some combination of these strategies is the most effective strategy in the organizational situation.

Managerial Communication

Perhaps the most basic motivation strategy for managers is simply to communicate well with organization members. This manager–subordinate communication can satisfy such basic human needs as recognition, a sense of belonging, and security. For example, such a simple action as a manager's attempting to become better acquainted with subordinates could contribute substantially to the satisfaction of each of these three needs. As another example, a message from a manager to a subordinate that praises the subordinate for a job well done can help satisfy the subordinate's recognition and security needs. As a general rule, managers should strive to communicate often with other organization members, not only because communication is the primary means of conducting organizational activities but also because it is a basic tool for satisfying the human needs of organization members.

Theory X–Theory Y

Another motivation strategy involves managers' assumptions about the nature of people. Douglas McGregor identified two sets of assumptions: **Theory X** involves negative assumptions about people that McGregor believes managers often use as the basis for dealing with people. **Theory Y** represents positive assumptions that McGregor believes managers should strive to use.[22] Theory X and Theory Y assumptions are presented in Table 15.1.

Theory X is a set of essentially negative assumptions about the nature of people.

Theory Y is a set of essentially positive assumptions about the nature of people.

McGregor implies that managers who use Theory X assumptions are "bad" and that those who use Theory Y assumptions are "good." Reddin, however, argues that production might be increased by using either Theory X or Theory Y assumptions, depending on the situation the manager faces: "Is there not a strong argument for the position that any theory may have desirable outcomes if appropriately used? The difficulty is that McGregor had considered only the ineffective application of Theory X and the effective application of Theory Y.[23]

Reddin proposes a **Theory Z**—an effectiveness dimension that implies that managers who use either Theory X or Theory Y assumptions when dealing with people can be successful, depending on their situation. Figure 15.6 shows Z as an effectiveness dimension relating to Theory X and Theory Y.

Theory Z is the effectiveness dimension that implies that managers who use either Theory X or Theory Y assumptions when dealing with people can be successful, depending on their situation.

The basic rationale for using Theory Y rather than Theory X in most situations is that managerial activities that reflect Theory Y assumptions generally are more successful in satisfying the human needs of most organization members than are managerial activities that reflect Theory X assumptions. Therefore, the activities based on Theory Y assumptions generally are more successful in motivating organization members than are the activities based on Theory X assumptions.

BACK TO THE CASE Once a manager such as Chupa understands that felt needs cause behavior and is aware of people's different types of needs, he is ready to apply this information to motivating his work force. From Chupa's viewpoint, motivating employees means furnishing them with the opportunity to satisfy their human needs by performing their jobs. This is a very important notion because successful motivation tends to increase employee productivity. If Chupa does not furnish his employees with an opportunity to satisfy their human needs while working, low morale

TABLE 15.1 McGregor's X–Theory Y assumptions about the nature of people

Theory X Assumptions	*Theory Y Assumptions*
The average person has an inherent dislike for work and will avoid it if he or she can.	The expenditure of physical and mental effort in work is as natural as play or rest.
Because of this human characteristic of dislike of work, most people must be coerced, controlled, directed, and threatened with punishment to get them to put forth adequate effort toward the achievement of organizational objectives.	People will exercise self-direction and self-control in the service of objectives to which they are committed.
	Commitment to objectives is a function of the rewards associated with achievement.
The average person prefers to be directed, wishes to avoid responsibility, has relatively little ambition, and wants security above all.	The average person learns, under proper conditions, not only to accept but to seek responsibility.
	The capacity to exercise a relatively high degree of imagination, ingenuity, and creativity in the solution of organizational problems is widely, not narrowly, distributed in the population.

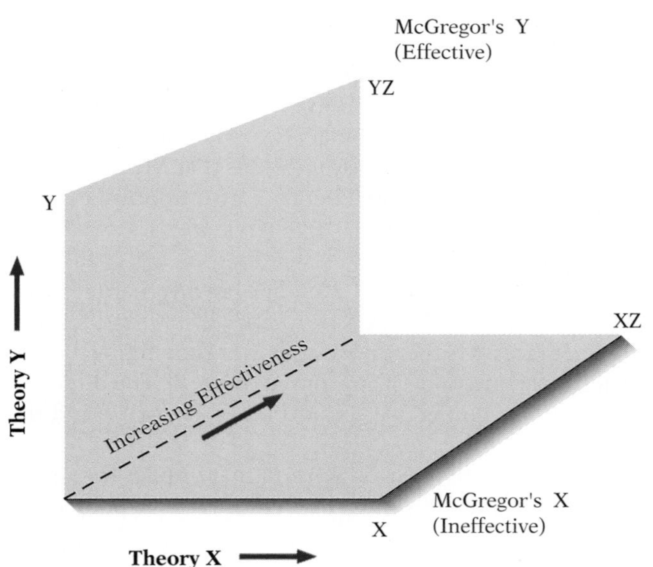

FIGURE 15.6 Theory X, Theory Y, and the effectiveness dimension Z

within the company will probably eventually develop. Signs of this low morale might be only a few employees initiating new ideas, people avoiding the confrontation of tough situations, and employees resisting innovation.

What does the above information recommend that Chupa actually do to further motivate American Greetings workers? One strategy he might follow is merely taking time to communicate with his employees. Manager–employee communication can help satisfy employee needs for recognition, belonging, and security. Another of Chupa's strategies might be based on McGregor's Theory X–Theory Y concept. In following this concept when dealing with employees, Chupa should assume that work is as natural as play; that employees can be self-directed in goal accomplishment; that the granting of rewards encourages the achievement of American Greetings objectives; that employees seek and accept responsibility; and that most employees are creative, ingenious, and imaginative. The adoption of such assumptions by Chupa can lead to the satisfaction of many of the needs defined by Maslow, Argyris, and McClelland.

Job Design

A third strategy managers can use to motivate organization members involves the design of jobs that organization members perform. The following two sections discuss earlier and more recent job design strategies.

Earlier Job Design Strategies. A movement has existed in American business to make jobs simpler and more specialized so as to increase worker productivity. Theoretically, this movement is aimed at making workers more productive by enabling them to be more efficient. Perhaps the best example of this movement is the development of the automobile assembly line. A negative result of work simplification and specialization, however, is job boredom. As work becomes simpler and more specialized, it typically becomes more boring and less satisfying to the individuals performing the jobs. As a result, productivity suffers.

Job rotation is the process of moving individuals from one job to another and not requiring individuals to perform only one job over the long term.

Perhaps the earliest major attempt to overcome job boredom was **job rotation**—moving individuals from job to job and not requiring individuals to perform merely one simple and specialized job over the long term. For example, a gardener would do more than just mow lawns; he might also trim bushes, rake grass, and sweep sidewalks. Although job rotation programs have been known to increase organizational profitability, they typically are ineffective, because, over time, individuals become bored with all the jobs they are rotated into.[24] Job rotation programs, however, usually are more effective in achieving other objectives, such as training, by providing individuals with an overview of how the various units of the organization function.

DIVERSITY HIGHLIGHT
Job Rotation for Managers Enhances Motivation and Diversity at Greyhound Financial Corporation

Recent turbulence in the U.S. business environment has led to something of a motivational crisis among corporate managers, who have experienced increased competition, tightening budget constraints, and changing demographics influencing both customer potential and work-force productivity. To ensure organizational survival in spite of these factors, organizations have been downsizing (becoming a more appropriate size given the marketplace and competitors) and adopting flatter organizational structures.

Greyhound Financial Corporation (GFC) has sought to maintain top-managerial motivation despite these discouraging factors through a unique form of job rotation for managers called the "Muscle Building" program. Basically, this program involves managers periodically changing jobs with one another in order to learn more about other areas of the organization. Since the program helps managers to become generalists rather than specialists about company operations, the program helps prevent career gridlock. In essence, as a result of the program, managers are qualified to be promoted to several different segments of the organization.

The rotation program also helps managers to develop the skills they need to manage a diverse work force. As managers switch jobs, they work with several different types of employees from many different backgrounds. Other hidden benefits of the program include building increased loyalty from the firm's highest potential executive material, and increasing confidence of managers in their abilities to accept new and totally different career responsibilities. ▶

Greyhound Financial Corp. uses a job rotation program for managers —"Muscle Building"— to help maintain top managerial motivation and to encourage diversity within the organization.

Job enlargement is another strategy developed to overcome the boredom of more simple and specialized jobs. **Job enlargement** means increasing the number of operations an individual performs and, in theory, thereby increasing the individual's satisfaction in work. According to the job enlargement concept, the gardener's job would become more satisfying as such activities as trimming bushes, raking grass, and sweeping sidewalks were added to the gardener's initial activity of mowing grass. Some research supports[25] the theory that job enlargement makes jobs more satisfying, and some does not.[26] Job enlargement programs, however, generally have been more successful in increasing job satisfaction than have job rotation programs.

Job enlargement is the process of increasing the number of operations an individual performs in a job.

More Recent Job Design Strategies. A number of other job design strategies have evolved since the development of job rotation and job enlargement programs. Two of these more recent strategies are job enrichment and flextime.

1. *Job Enrichment.* Frederick Herzberg has concluded from his research that the degrees of satisfaction and dissatisfaction that organization members feel as a result of performing a job are two different variables determined by two different sets of items.[27] The items that influence the degree of job dissatisfaction are called **hygiene,** or **maintenance, factors**. The items that influence the degree of job satisfaction are called motivating factors, or motivators. Hygiene factors relate to the work environment, and motivating factors relate to the work itself. The items that make up Herzberg's hygiene and motivating factors are presented in Table 15.2.

Hygiene, or **maintenance, factors** are items that influence the degree of job dissatisfaction.

Motivating factors are items that influence the degree of job satisfaction.

Herzberg has indicated that if hygiene factors are undesirable in a particular job situation, organization members will become dissatisfied. Making these factors more desir-

TABLE 15.2 Herzberg's hygiene factors and motivators

Dissatisfaction: Hygiene or Maintenance Factors	*Satisfaction: Motivating Factors*
1. Company policy and administration	1. Opportunity for achievement
2. Supervision	2. Opportunity for recognition
3. Relationship with supervisor	3. Work itself
4. Relationship with peers	4. Responsibility
5. Working conditions	5. Advancement
6. Salary	6. Personal growth
7. Relationship with subordinates	

able by, for example, increasing salary generally will not motivate people to do a better job, but it will keep them from becoming dissatisfied. In contrast, if motivating factors are high in a particular job situation, organization members generally are motivated to do a better job. In general, people tend to be more motivated and productive as more motivators are built into their job situation.

Job enrichment is the process of incorporating motivators into a job situation.

The process of incorporating motivators into a job situation is called **job enrichment.** Earlier reports indicated that companies such as Texas Instruments[28] and Volvo[29] had notable success in motivating organization members through job enrichment programs. More recent reports continue to support the value of job enrichment,[30] but experience indicates that, for a job enrichment program to be successful, it must be carefully designed and administered.[31] An outline of a successful job enrichment program is presented in Table 15.3.

Herzberg's overall findings indicate that the most productive organization members are involved in work situations characterized by desirable hygiene factors and motivating factors. The needs on Maslow's hierarchy of needs that desirable hygiene factors and motivating factors generally satisfy are shown in Figure 15.7. Esteem needs can be satisfied by both types of factors. An example of esteem needs satisfied by a hygiene factor could be a private parking space—a status symbol and a working condition evidencing the importance of the organization member. An example of esteem needs

TABLE 15.3 Outline of successful job enrichment program

Specific Changes Aimed at Enriching Jobs	*"Motivators"—These Changes Are Aimed at Incrasing:*
1. Removing some controls while retaining accountability	Responsibility and personal achievement
2. Increasing the accountability of individuals for own work	Responsibility and recognition
3. Giving a person a complete natural unit of work (module, division, area, and so on)	Responsibility, achievement, and recognition
4. Granting additional authority to an employee in his or her activity; job freedom	Responsibility, achievement, and recognition
5. Making periodic reports directly available to the worker rather than to the supervisor	Internal recognition
6. Introducing new and more difficult tasks not previously handled	Growth and learning
7. Assigning individuals specific or specialized tasks, enabling them to become expert	Responsibility, growth, and advancement

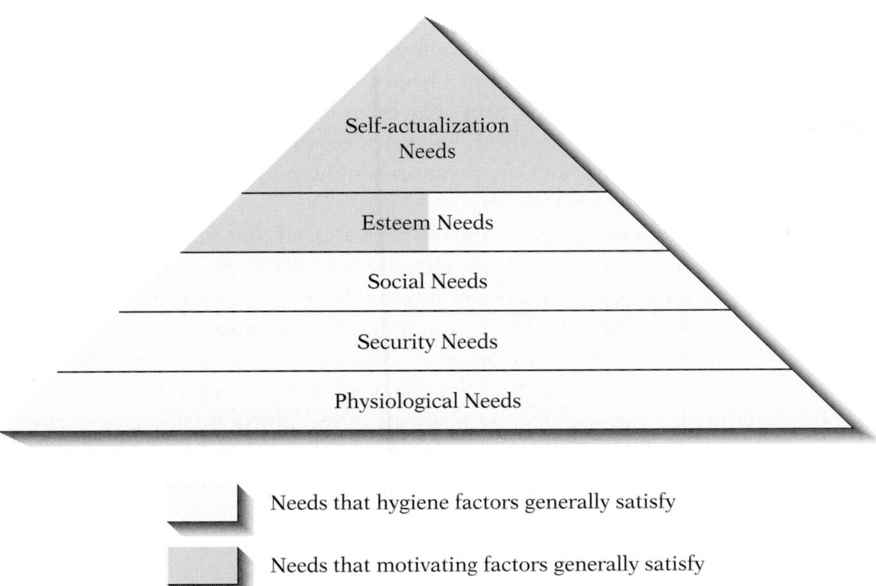

FIGURE 15.7 Needs on Maslow's hierarchy that desirable hygiene factors and motivating factors generally satisfy

satisfied by a motivating factor could be an award received for outstanding performance—a display of importance through recognition of a job well done.

QUALITY HIGHLIGHT
Apple Computer's Job Enrichment Excels

Apple Computer has attempted to provide both hygiene factors and motivating factors for its employees. Apple executives firmly believe that highly motivated, satisfied employees produce high-quality products. Apple's job enrichment program serves as a good example of how management can take steps to enrich a work environment.

Creating the right work environment—pleasant but challenging—is a key to encouraging people to be productive at Apple. For example, management at Apple strives to incorporate award systems for employees, such as recognition for jobs well done and opportunities for growth and advancement. In addition to these motivators, hygiene factors have been made acceptable to employees, and Apple management takes pride in providing sufficiently generous salaries to valued employees.

As one example of the recognition programs at Apple, the company announces new products and projects through the employees who developed them instead of through a public relations office. This announcement process gives recognition to hardworking employees and makes them feel as though they are making valuable contributions to the company. At Apple, rewards and recognition are an ongoing and constant part of company life. Such aspects of corporate life should help management ensure the quality of its products, such as the Macintosh and Apple computers. ▶

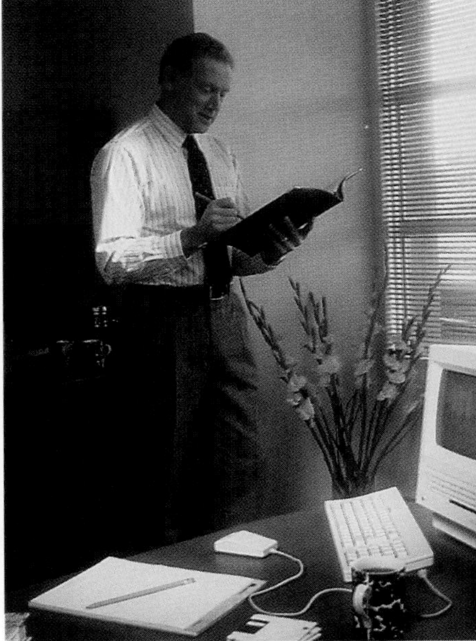

Apple executives believe that motivated, satisfied employees produce high quality products. Creating the right work environment—pleasant but challenging—is a key to encouraging people to be productive at Apple Computer.

2. *Flextime.* Another more recent job design strategy for motivating organization members is based on a concept called flextime. Perhaps the most common traditional characteristic of work in the United States is that jobs are performed within a fixed eight-hour workday. Recently, however, this tradition has been challenged. Faced with motivation problems and absenteeism, many managers have turned to scheduling innovations as a possible solution.[32]

   The main purpose of these scheduling innovations is not to reduce the total number of work hours but to provide workers with greater flexibility in the exact

Flextime is a program that allows workers to complete their jobs within a workweek of a normal number of hours that they schedule themselves.

hours during which they must perform their jobs. The main thrust of **flextime,** or flexible working hours programs, is that it allows workers to complete their jobs within a workweek (of a normal number of hours) that they arrange themselves.[33] The choices of starting and finishing times can be as flexible as the organizational situation allows. To ensure that flexibility does not become counterproductive within the organization, many flextime programs include a core period during which all employees must be on the job.

Various kinds of organizational studies have indicated that flextime programs have some positive organizational effects. Douglas Fleuter, for example, has reported that flextime contributes to greater job satisfaction, which typically results in greater productivity.[34] Other research concludes that flextime programs can result in higher motivation levels of workers.[35] Because organization members generally find flextime programs to be desirable, such programs can help management to better compete with other organizations in recruiting qualified new employees.[36] (A listing of the advantages and disadvantages of flextime programs appears in Table 15.4.) Although many well-known companies, such as Scott Paper, Sun Oil, and Samsonite, have adopted flextime programs,[37] more research must be conducted to conclusively assess flextime's true worth.

BACK TO THE CASE

Chupa can use two major job design strategies to motivate his employees at American Greetings. With job enrichment, Chupa can incorporate into employee jobs such motivating factors as opportunities for achievement, recognition, and personal growth. Chupa's allowing workers to transfer back and forth among work teams and work on more than one product can be viewed as a type of job enrichment, allowing workers opportunities for personal growth. However, for maximum success, hygiene factors at American Greetings—company policy and administration, supervision, salary, and working conditions, for example—also should be perceived as desirable by employees.

The second major job design strategy that Chupa can use to motivate his employees is flextime. With flextime, the employees would have some freedom in scheduling the beginning and ending of workdays.

TABLE 15.4 Advantages and disadvantages of using flextime programs

Advantages	*Disadvantages*
Improved employee attitude and morale	Lack of supervision during some hours of work
Accommodation of working parents	Key people unavailable at certain times
Decreased tardiness	Understaffing at times
Fewer traffic problems —workers can avoid congested streets and highways	Problem of accommodating employees whose output is the input for other employees
Accommodation of those who wish to arrive at work before interruptions begin	Employee abuse of flextime program
Increased production	Difficulty in planning work schedules
Facilitation of employee scheduling of medical, dental, and other types of appointments	Problem of keeping track of hours worked or accumulated
Accommodation of leisure-time activities of employees	Inability to schedule meetings at convenient times
Decreased absenteeism	Inability to coordinate projects
Decreased turnover	

Of course, this freedom would be somewhat limited by such organizational factors as seasonal demand or peak selling seasons.

Behavior Modification

A fourth strategy that managers can use in motivating organization members is based primarily on a concept known as behavior modification. As stated by B.F. Skinner, the Harvard psychologist considered by many to be the "father" of behavioral psychology, **behavior modification** focuses on encouraging appropriate behavior as a result of the consequences of that behavior.[38] According to the law of effect,[39] behavior that is rewarded tends to be repeated, and behavior that is punished tends to be eliminated. Although behavior modification programs typically involve the administration of both rewards and punishments, rewards generally are emphasized, because they are more effective than punishments in influencing behavior. Obviously, the main theme of behavior modification is not new.

Behavior modification is a program that focuses on managing human activity by controlling the consequences of performing that activity.

Behavior modification theory asserts that if managers want to modify subordinates' behavior, they must ensure that appropriate consequences occur as a result of that behavior.[40] **Positive reinforcement** is a desirable consequence of a behavior, and **negative reinforcement** is the elimination of an undesirable consequence of a behavior. If a worker's arriving on time is positively reinforced, or rewarded, the probability increases that the worker will arrive on time more often. In addition, if the worker experiences some undesirable outcome on arriving late for work, such as a verbal reprimand, the worker is negatively reinforced when this outcome is eliminated by on-time arrival. According to behavior modification theory, positive reinforcement and negative reinforcement are both rewards that increase the likelihood that behavior will continue.

Positive reinforcement is a reward that is a desirable consequence of behavior.

Negative reinforcement is a reward that is the elimination of an undesirable consequence of behavior.

Punishment is the presentation of an undesirable behavioral consequence or the removal of a desirable behavioral consequence that decreases the likelihood of the behavior continuing.[41] Extending the earlier example, managers could punish employees for arriving late for work by exposing them to some undesirable consequence, such as a verbal reprimand, or by removing a desirable consequence, such as their wages for the amount of time they are late.[42] Although this punishment probably would quickly cause workers to come to work on time, it might be accompanied by undesirable side effects, such as high levels of absenteeism and turnover, if it were emphasized over the long term.

Punishment is the presentation of an undesirable behavioral consequence or the removal of a desirable one that decreases the likelihood of the behavior continuing.

Behavior modification programs have been applied both successfully and unsuccessfully in a number of organizations.[43] The behavior modification efforts of Emery Air Freight Company, now called Emery Worldwide, resulted in the finding that the establishment and use of an effective feedback system is important in making a behavior modification program successful.[44] This feedback should be aimed at keeping employees informed of the relationship between various behaviors and their consequences. Other ingredients that successful behavior modification programs include are (1) giving different levels of rewards to different workers depending on the quality of their performances, (2) telling workers what they are doing wrong, (3) punishing workers privately in order not to embarrass them in front of others, and (4) always giving rewards and punishments when earned to emphasize that management is serious about behavior modification efforts.[45]

ETHICS HIGHLIGHT
Government's Ethical Expectations?

Behavior is likely to be modified if it is appropriately encouraged through positive reinforcement, negative reinforcement, and punishment. The lack of ethical behavior in government, for example, may be the result of a perception by government employees that acting ethically will not result in any meaningful consequences.

Since there is no clearly defined system of rewards and punishments for ethical and unethical behavior in government, government employees may receive the message that unethical behavior will go unpunished.

The federal government's ethical standards are stated clearly in the Ethics in Government Act and in established criminal laws. However, it is questionable whether there is a clearly defined reward system tied to established ethical standards. In addition, because there are very few official violators of ethical standards who have been legally prosecuted and an even smaller number of severe penalties or punishments for violations, it is not surprising that ethical violations in government continue to occur. The lack of negative reinforcement and of punishment allows unethical behavior in government to continue without significant discouraging. According to the behavior modification concept, it seems somewhat unrealistic to expect government leaders to follow a set of ethical guidelines without a system of positive reinforcement, negative reinforcement, and punishment to encourage their following the guidelines. ▶

Likert's Management Systems

Another strategy that managers can use for motivating organization members is based on the work of Rensis Likert, a noted management scholar.[46] As a result of studying several types and sizes of organizations, Likert has concluded that management styles in organizations can be categorized into the following systems:[47]

System 1. This style of management involves having no confidence or trust in subordinates. Subordinates do not feel free to discuss their jobs with superiors and are motivated by fear, threats, punishments, and occasional rewards. Information flow is directed primarily downward, and upward communication is viewed with great suspicion. The bulk of all decision making is at the top of the organization.

System 2. This style of management involves condescending confidence and trust (such as master to servant) in subordinates. Subordinates do not feel very free to discuss their jobs with superiors and are motivated by rewards and some actual or potential punishment. Information flows mostly downward, and upward communication may or may not be viewed with suspicion. Although policies are made primarily at the top of the organization, decisions within a prescribed framework are made at lower levels.

System 3. This style of management involves having substantial, but not complete, confidence in subordinates. Subordinates feel fairly free to discuss their jobs with superiors and are motivated by rewards, occasional punishment, and some involvement. Information flows both upward and downward. Upward communication is often accepted but at times may be viewed with suspicion. Although broad policies and general decisions are made at the top of the organization, more specific decisions are made at lower levels.

System 4. This style of management involves having complete trust and confidence in subordinates. Subordinates feel completely free to discuss their jobs with superiors and are motivated by such factors as economic rewards based on a compensation system developed through participation and involvement in goal setting. Information flows upward, downward, and horizontally. Upward communication is generally accepted. However, if it is not, related questions are asked candidly. Decision making is spread widely throughout the organization and is well coordinated.

Likert has suggested that as the management style moves from system 1 to system 4, the human needs of individuals within the organization tend to be more effectively satisfied over the long term. Thus, as the organization moves toward system 4, it tends to become more productive over the long term.

Figure 15.8 illustrates the comparative long- and short-term effects of both system 1 and system 4 on organizational production. Managers may increase production in the short term by using a system 1 management style, because motivation by fear, threat, and punishment is generally effective in the short term. Over the long term, however, this style usually causes production to decrease, primarily because of the long-

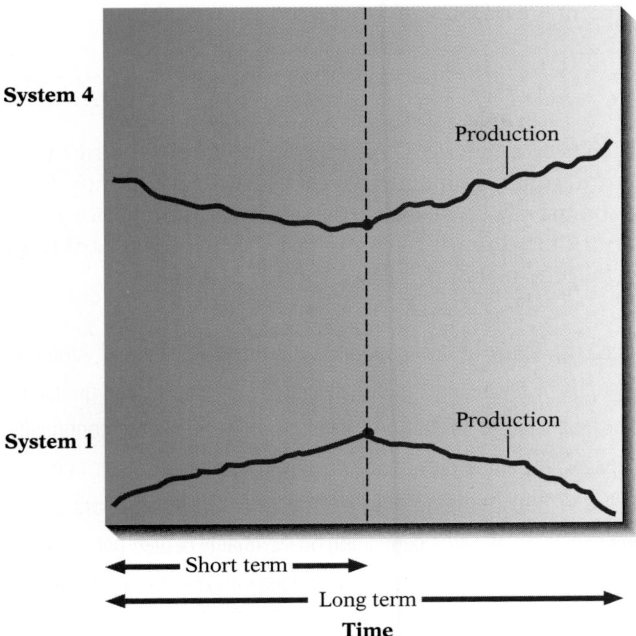

FIGURE 15.8 Comparative long-term and short-term effects of system 1 and system 4 on organizational production

term nonsatisfaction of organization members' needs and the poor working relationships between managers and subordinates.

Conversely, managers who initiate a system 4 management style probably face some decline in production initially, but an increase in production over the long term. The short-term decline occurs because managers must implement a new system to which organization members must adapt. The production increase over the long term materializes as a result of organization members' adjustment to the new management system, greater satisfaction of the human needs of organization members, and the good working relationships that tend to develop between managers and subordinates. This long-term production increase can also be related to decision making under the two management systems. Because decisions reached in system 4 are more likely to be thoroughly understood by organization members than decisions reached in system 1, decision implementation is more likely to be efficient and effective in system 4 than in system 1.

Likert has offered his **principle of supportive relationships** as the basis for management activity aimed at developing a system 4 management style. This principle states:

> The leadership and other processes of the organization must be such as to ensure a maximum probability that in all interactions and in all relationships within the organization, each member in light of his or her background, values, desires, and expectations will view the experience as supportive and one which builds and maintains his or her sense of personal worth and importance.[48]

The **principle of supportive relationships** is a management guideline that indicates that all human interaction with an organization should build and maintain the sense of personal worth and the importance of those involved in the interaction.

Monetary Incentives

A number of firms make a wide range of money-based compensation programs available to their employees as a form of motivation.[49] For instance, employee stock ownership plans (ESOPs) motivate the employee to boost production by offering shares of company stock as a benefit. Other incentive plans include lump-sum bonuses—one-time cash payments and gain-sharing—a plan by which members of a team receive a bonus when that team exceeds an expectation. All of these plans link the amount of pay closely to performance. By putting more of the employees' pay at risk, firms are able to keep more of the wages as a percentage of sales and therefore controllable in a downturn.[50]

Nonmonetary Incentives

A firm also has the opportunity to keep employees committed and motivated by other, nonmonetary means. For instance, some companies have a policy of promoting from within. They go through an elaborate process of advertising jobs within before going to the outside to fill vacancies. Another example is to emphasize quality. It is hard to be happy in a job when you know that the work produces a shoddy product.[51]

BACK TO THE CASE Chupa can apply behavior modification to his situation at American Greetings by rewarding appropriate employee behavior and punishing inappropriate employee behavior. Punishment has to be used very carefully, however. If used continually, the working relationship between Chupa and his employees can be destroyed. For the behavior modification program to be successful, Chupa has to furnish employees with feedback on which behaviors are appropriate and inappropriate, give workers different rewards depending on the quality of their performance, tell workers what they are doing wrong, punish workers privately, and consistently give rewards and punishments when earned.

To use Likert's system 4 management style to motivate employees over the long term, Chupa has to demonstrate complete confidence in his workers and encourage workers to feel completely free to discuss problems with him. In addition, communication at American Greetings has to flow freely in all directions within the organization structure, with upward communication generally discussed candidly. Chupa's decision-making process under system 4 has to involve many employees. Chupa can use the principle of supportive relationships as the basis for his system 4 management style. No single strategy mentioned in this chapter for motivating organization members would necessarily be more valuable to managers such as Chupa than any other of the strategies. In reality, Chupa will probably find that some combination of all of these strategies is most useful in motivating the work force at American Greetings.

ACTION SUMMARY

Reread the learning objectives that follow. Each objective is followed by questions. Answering these questions accurately will help you retain the most important concepts discussed in this chapter. After answering each question, check your answer with the answer key at the end of this chapter. (*Hint:* If you have doubt regarding the correct response, consult the page whose number follows the answer.)

Circle: ***From studying this chapter, I will attempt to acquire:***

1. A basic understanding of human motivation.

a, b, c, d, e **a.** An individual's inner state that causes him or her to behave in such a way as to ensure accomplishment of a goal is: (a) ambition; (b) drive; (c) motivation; (d) need; (e) leadership.

T, F **b.** According to the needs-goal theory of motivation, a fulfilled need is motivator.

a, b, c, d, e **c.** The following most comprehensively describes how motivation takes place: (a) the Vroom expectancy theory; (b) the needs-goal theory; (c) the Porter-Lawler theory; (d) all of the above; (e) none of the above.

2. Insights on various human needs.

a, b, c, d, e **a.** The following is a rank-ordered listing of Maslow's hierarchy of needs from lowest to highest: (a) self-actualization, social, security, physiologic, esteem; (b) social, security, physiologic, self-actualization; (c) esteem, self-actualization, security, social, physiologic; (d) physiologic, security, social, esteem, self-actualization; (e) physiologic, social, esteem, security, self-actualization.

a, b, c, d, e **b.** According to Argyris, as individuals mature, they have an increasing need for: (a) greater dependence; (b) a shorter-term perspective; (c) more inactivity; (d) deeper interests; (e) youth.

a, b, c, d, e **c.** The desire to do something better or more efficiently than it has ever been done before is known as the need for: (a) acceleration; (b) achievement; (c) acclamation; (d) actualization; (e) none of the above.

3. An appreciation for the importance of motivating organization members.

T, F **a.** From a managerial viewpoint, motivation is the process of furnishing organization members with the opportunity to satisfy their needs by performing productive behavior within the organization.

T, F **b.** The concepts of motivation and appropriate behavior are closely related.

4. An understanding of various motivation strategies.

a, b, c, d, e **a.** The following is a Theory Y assumption: (a) the average person prefers to be directed; (b) most people must be threatened and coerced before they will put forth adequate effort; (c) commitment to objectives is a function of the rewards associated with achievement; (d) the average person seeks no responsibility; (e) all of the above.

a, b, c, d, e **b.** The process of incorporating motivators into the job situation is called: (a) job enlargement; (b) flextime; (c) satisfying; (d) job enrichment; (e) Theory X.

a, b, c, d, e **c.** Successful behavior modification programs can include: (a) giving rewards and punishments when earned; (b) giving rewards according to performance quality; (c) telling workers what they are doing wrong; (d) punishing workers privately; (e) all of the above.

INTRODUCTORY CASE WRAP-UP

"American Greetings Motivates through Lateral Moves" (p. 375) and its related back-to-the-case sections were written to help you better understand the management concepts contained in this chapter. Answer the following discussion questions about this introductory case to further enrich your understanding of chapter content:

1. Do you think it would be unusual for a manager like Chupa to spend a significant portion of his time motivating his work force? Explain.
2. Which of the needs on Maslow's hierarchy of needs would the restructuring at American Greetings probably help satisfy? Why? If you have omitted one or more of the needs, explain why the reorganization probably would not satisfy those needs.
3. Is it possible for Chupa's restructuring to be successful in both cutting production time and motivating workers? Explain fully.

ISSUES FOR REVIEW AND DISCUSSION

1. Define *motivation* and explain why managers should understand it.
2. Describe the difference between process and content theories of motivation.
3. Draw and explain a model that illustrates the needs-goal theory of motivation.
4. Explain Vroom's expectancy theory of motivation.
5. List and explain three characteristics of the motivation process contained in the Porter-Lawler motivation theory that are not contained in either the needs-goal or Vroom's expectancy theories.
6. What is the main theme of the equity theory of motivation?

7. What does Maslow's hierarchy of needs tell us
8. What concerns have been expressed about Maslow's hierarchy of needs?
9. What are the similarities and differences between Maslow's hierarchy of needs and Alderfer's ERG theory?
10. Explain Argyris's maturity-immaturity continuum.
11. What is the need for achievement?
12. Summarize the characteristics of individuals who have high needs for achievement.
13. Explain "motivating organization members."
14. Is the process of motivating organization members important to managers? Explain.
15. How can managerial communication be used to motivate organization members?
16. What are Theory X, Theory Y, and Theory Z? What does each of these theories tell us about motivating organization members?
17. What is the difference between job enlargement and job rotation?
18. Describe the relationship of hygiene factors, motivating factors, and job enrichment.
19. Define *flextime;* define *behavior modification.*
20. What basic ingredients are necessary to make a behavior modification program successful?
21. In your own words, summarize Likert's four management systems.
22. What effect do Likert's systems 1 and 4 generally have on organizational production in both the short and long terms? Why do these effects occur?
23. List three nonmonetary incentives that you personally would find desirable as an employee within an organization. Why would these incentives be desirable to you?

ACTION SUMMARY ANSWER KEY

1. **a.** c, p. 376
   b. F, pp. 376–377
   c. c, pp. 378–379

2. **a.** d, pp. 380–381
   b. d, p. 382
   c. b, p. 382

3. **a.** T, p. 383
   b. T, pp. 383–384

4. **a.** c, p. 385
   b. d, p. 388
   c. e, p. 391

CASE STUDY

Motivation at America West Airlines

SAMUEL C. CERTO
Rollins College

When the airline industry was deregulated in the United States in 1978, Edward Beauvais and Michael Conway began to amass the capital to create their own low-cost yet high-quality airline. In 1983, they initiated service of America West Airlines (AWA) with three aircraft and 280 employees. Today, the airline employs over 11,800 people and dominates service through Arizona. The airline consistently ranks first in on-time performance and high in customer satisfaction. At the root of AWA's success, say Beauvais and Conway, is its focus on its number one asset—its employees.

When Beauvais and Conway established AWA, they set out to create an atmosphere that would foster strong morale and a high degree of involvement among employees. They were convinced that a highly motivated work force would be the key to successful operation, so they implemented an employee ownership program that would spur motivation. In the first year of employment, all employees are required to purchase (at a discount) shares of company stock equal to 20 percent of that year's salary. Owner-pilots tend to baby their aircraft, and all owner-employees are on the lookout to save money and improve service.

Another spur to motivation that Beauvais and Conway identified is an atmosphere of respect. To foster this environment, AWA has one rule: No Rules. Everyone is treated as an individual, and employees are responsible for performing jobs their own way, without having to seek management approval. By delegating authority, management has given theultimate compliment to their workers—they are trusted to solve problems capably. Managers are available to coach employees, to help them shape ideas, and to encourage them to develop and to try new solutions along the way.

Beauvais and Conway are convinced that AWA's open-door policy and open system of communications also contribute to a highly motivated work force. Employee advisory boards representing pilots, technicians, customer service representatives, and several other work groups meet regularly with all levels of management to discuss work-related issues and to share ideas for cutting costs or improving operations. Beauvais spends about a quarter of his 50- to 70-hour workweek in visits with employees. He asks sharp questions, is a good listener, and really cares about the employees. AWA's open-door policy dictates that any employee can have access to anyone at any level of the corporate structure without fear of reprisals.

The AWA work environment is also designed to allow maximum productivity on the job. An attractive package of benefits includes on-site child care, eldercare, maternity leave, on-site medical care, and an employee assistance program that offers confidential counseling on issues ranging from personal financial management to substance abuse difficulties to interpersonal relationship problems. AWA also offers employees the opportunity to share jobs or, in some cases, to work at home. All this helps to free workers from day-to-day worries so they can concentrate on doing the best job they can.

America West also has a system of rewards and special bonuses in place, to keep workers enthusiastic about the company. Guest passes and heavily discounted tickets to special events are offered to employees with perfect attendance. Managers asking "What is perfect?" are told to give as many passes as they can justify. "Don't look at the five percent who abuse the system," they are advised. "Look at the 95 percent of the people who are motivated by it." Another reward is the anniversary prepayment plan available every four years: An employee can draw a quarter of his or her annual salary in advance, allowing the employee to take a special trip or make a major purchase or perhaps simply to earn extra interest by investing the money.

Beauvais and Conway are in the airline business for the long haul. By managing employees in the way they would choose to be managed themselves, these executives are continually creating and re-creating the kind of high-energy, motivated work force that is essential to success.

DISCUSSION QUESTIONS

1. Maslow's hierarchy of needs suggests a sequence of satisfactions. How do Beauvais and Conway seek to meet employee needs?
2. Would you characterize Beauvais and Conway as Theory X, Theory Y, or Theory Z managers?
3. According to Rensis Likert, management styles can be characterized as System 1, 2, 3, or 4. How would Likert characterize the management system at AWA? Why do you think so?
4. Why do you think Beauvais and Conway feel AWA's management style is so important?

CNN VIDEO CASE

Motivating through Intrapreneurship

"Customer satisfaction begins with job satisfaction. And, if the employees are partaking in some aspect of their job, making decisions and coming up with solutions, and the solutions are being acted on, they'll feel a little more satisfied, and take the responsibility to see that the plan is more successful because they designed it." Bill Schoffield, a vice president at Federal Express, thus summarizes some major motivating factors at work in his company.

The road to successful employee motivation at Federal Express was not totally smooth. When one facility found itself without managers for a while, Federal Express allowed the eager employees to continue without managers. The employees soon discovered, however, that without the managers as a support mechanism, it was nearly impossible for them to concentrate on and succeed in their own jobs. There was too much interference from other tasks.

To help build employee motivation at the AT&T Credit Corporation, each self-managing work group sets its own targets and monitors its own budgets

Now Federal Express uses "quality action teams," in which workers participate, within the scope of their own jobs, to suggest solutions to their own problems; then the managers enable them to fix the problems.

Giving workers more freedom boosts productivity. When entrepreneurial qualities are encouraged within a company, that company is encouraging *intrapreneurship.* The quality action teams at Federal Express are one example. Another is 3M, where technical workers are encouraged to devote 15 percent of their time to their own projects. If 3M likes a project, the workers who had the idea often take charge of the new effort and run it as their own business within 3M.

Another example of intrapreneurship takes place in self-managing groups at the AT&T Credit Corporation. Each group sets its own goals and monitors its own budgets. The group members even evaluate each other's performance.

Intrapreneurship allows companies to leverage people's creative energies, to do things that are unique but still within the vision and scope of the particular company. At the same time, there are some difficulties. Some managers do not want to give up control. Other managers may be too busy, after their companies downsized, to hear new ideas that could further complicate their jobs. Also, the parent company itself may expect results too quickly. Notes Patricia Koch, Bell Atlantic's Executive Director of Intrapreneurship, sometimes a company needs to "swallow a patience pill." It takes time for a company to develop the right atmosphere and the most appropriate support structures for intrapreneuring. Sometimes, too, it is difficult for intrapreneurs to hear that the company has decided not to pursue their particular ideas; some people may continue working on their ideas anyway.

Despite the difficulties, intrapreneurship has a foothold in business today, because it motivates. Two famous products developed through intrapreneurship programs: 3M's Post-it Notes and Gillette's Sensor razor.

VIDEO CASE QUESTIONS

1. How does the experience of Federal Express employees in working without managers relate to the Vroom expectancy theory of motivation?
2. How did Federal Express work to correct the hygiene factors that created employee dissatisfaction when employees worked without supervisors?
3. Which need identified in Maslow's hierarchy does intrapreneurship fulfill in ways that other management work styles do not?
4. What problems would confront a manager at Federal Express whose assumptions about the nature of people tended toward McGregor's Theory X?

CNN VIDEO EXERCISE

Analyzing Motivation at Federal Express

ACTION GOAL: Use Herzberg's research on hygiene factors and motivation to analyze Federal Express's quality action teams as a motivator.

Review the material on pages 387–389 about Herzberg's description of hygiene factors and motivating factors. Then complete the chart below, using information from the video case to outline factors at Federal Express that caused dissatisfaction and to show how intrapreneurship increased satisfaction among workers. You will not have information for each factor.

After completing the chart, decide which of the motivating factors is most important at Federal Express. Write a brief essay explaining why that factor is significant.

Dissatisfaction:
Hygiene or Maintenance Factors

1. Company policy and administration: ____________________

____

2. Supervision: ____________________

____

3. Relationship with supervisor: ____________________

____

4. Relationship with peers: ____________________

____

5. Working conditions: ____________________

____

6. Salary: ____________________

____

Satisfaction:
Motivating Factors

1. Opportunity for achievement: ____________________

____

2. Opportunity for recognition: ____________________

____

3. Work itself: ____________________

____

4. Responsibility: ____________________

____

5. Advancement: ____________________

____

6. Personal growth: ____________________

____

CHAPTER

16

GROUPS AND CORPORATE CULTURE

STUDENT LEARNING OBJECTIVES

From studying this chapter, I will attempt to acquire:

1. A definition of the term *group* as used within the context of management.
2. A thorough understanding of the difference between formal and informal groups.
3. Knowledge of the types of formal groups that exist in organizations.
4. An understanding of how managers can determine which groups exist in an organization.
5. An appreciation for how managers must evaluate formal and informal groups simultaneously to maximize work group effectiveness.
6. Insights about managing corporate culture to enhance organizational success.

CHAPTER OUTLINE

INTRODUCTORY CASE
Groups Are Important to Progress at Rolls-Royce

DEFINING GROUPS

KINDS OF GROUPS IN ORGANIZATIONS

Formal Groups

DIVERSITY HIGHLIGHT
Equitable

ETHICS HIGHLIGHT
Calvary Hospital

QUALITY HIGHLIGHT
Standard Steel

Informal Groups

MANAGING WORK GROUPS

Determining Group Existence
Understanding the Evolution of Informal Groups
Maximizing Work Group Effectiveness

GLOBAL HIGHLIGHT
Mazda

CORPORATE CULTURE

CASE STUDY
Rewards in a Self-Managed Work Team at Boeing

VIDEO CASE
Building a Group Culture:
Kay Unger, Gillian Group

VIDEO EXERCISE
Making Decisions by Committee at the Gillian Group

INTRODUCTORY CASE

Work Groups Are Important to Progress at Rolls-Royce

In Crewe, England, Dennis Jones lifts a long slice of stainless steel and peers down the edge, squinting one eye as if aiming a rifle. He likes what he sees.

The piece is slightly bowed, he explains, to create the illusion from a distance of a straight line, "like a column on the Parthenon." It's perfect for a Rolls-Royce radiator grill," says Mr. Jones, who has built the units for 22 years in a shop at the company's factory here. "We can't afford to make many mistakes," he concedes.

Workers now . . . get pulled off the floor for "brown-paper sessions," in which engineers and workers sit together dissecting and critiquing production processes on long sheets of brown paper taped to the wall.

Indeed, that could be the motto for the whole company these days. Rolls-Royce Motor Cars Ltd., maker of one of the world's ultimate status symbols, has fallen on hard times and is scrambling to recover. Battered by recession and a shift in tastes that makes its cars seem excessively opulent even to some millionaires, the company had a loss of $54.5 million last year and appears set to splash into red ink again this year. Worldwide sales recently fell nearly by half, to 1,722 cars.

Peter Ward, Rolls-Royce's normally affable forty-six-year-old chairman, bristles at the constant rumors about the imminent takeover. "It isn't as urgent as some commentators tend to make it seem," he says.

Mr. Ward has his own ideas about turning the company around. And as odd as it may seem for one of the world's last bastions of handcrafted auto manufacturing, many of his plans are adaptations of the lean manufacturing concepts originated by high-volume Japanese car makers.

Over the past several years, Mr. Ward has installed a computer-controlled production system, slashed 1,300 jobs and reorganized workers into Japanese-style teams. Rolls-Royce now has its own version of such Japanese innovations as just-in-time parts delivery and continuous quality improvement.

"We've really gone further than the Japanese," Mr. Ward asserts. He adds that some of the moves are only bringing Rolls-Royce closer to its original structure. Before World War II, the car maker used a much more open system, with workers learning a variety of skills and having a closer contact with management and engineers. This faded during the 1960s and 1970s, says Mr. Ward, as unions sharply defined workers' tasks and the shop floor became more insulated from the management suite.

Not that any change is easy in a company as tradition-bound as Rolls-Royce, where workers are often second- or third-generation employees. The changes also are grating against Britain's class structure. Workers now routinely get pulled off the floor for "brown-paper sessions," in which engineers and workers sit together, dissecting and critiquing production processes on long sheets of brown paper taped to the wall. Company officials say some of the best worker input still comes, however, from yellow notes stuck on by workers when no one else is around.

To cope with an $54.5 million trading loss, Rolls-Royce has installed a computer-controlled production system and reorganized workers at its main plant in Crewe, England.

From Timothy Aeppel, "Rolls-Royce Tries to Restore Luster as Car Sales Fade," *Wall Street Journal* (May 26, 1992), B3. Reprinted by permission of *Wall Street Journal,* © 1992 Dow Jones & Company, Inc. All Rights Reserved Worldwide.

WHAT'S AHEAD The introductory case highlights the important role that new work groups or teams are playing in solving problems at Rolls-Royce. The material in this chapter should help a manager like Peter Ward, Rolls-Royce's chairman, to gain some insight into the broad area of work group management. This chapter (1) defines groups, (2) discusses the kinds of groups that exist in organizations, and (3) explains what steps managers should take to manage groups appropriately.

The previous chapters in this section have dealt with three primary activities of the influencing function: (1) communication, (2) leadership, and (3) motivation. This chapter focuses on managing groups, the last major influencing activity to be discussed in this text. As with the other three activities, managing work groups requires guiding the behavior of organization members in order to increase the probability of reaching organizational objectives.

DEFINING GROUPS

A **group** is any number of people who (1) interact with one another, (2) are psychologically aware of one another, and (3) perceive themselves to be a group.

To deal with groups appropriately, managers must have a thorough understanding of the nature of groups in organizations.[1] As used in management-related discussions, a **group** is not simply a gathering of people. Rather it is "any number of people who (1) interact with one another, (2) are psychologically aware of one another, and (3) perceive themselves to be a group."[2] Groups are characterized by their members' communicating with one another over time and being small enough that each member is able to communicate with all other members on a face-to-face basis.[3] As a result of this communication, each group member influences and is influenced by all other group members.

The study of groups is important to managers, because the most common ingredient of all organizations is people and the most common technique for accomplishing work through these people is dividing them into work groups. In a classic article, Cartwright and Lippitt list four additional reasons for studying groups:[4]

1. Groups exist in all kinds of organizations.
2. Groups inevitably form in all facets of organizational existence.
3. Groups can cause either desirable or undesirable consequences within the organization.
4. An understanding of groups can help managers increase the probability that the groups with which they work will cause desirable consequences within the organization.

KINDS OF GROUPS IN ORGANIZATIONS

Groups that exist in organizations typically are divided into two basic types: formal and informal.

Formal Groups

A **formal group** is a group that exists in an organization by virtue of management decree to perform tasks that enhance the attainment of organizational objectives.

A **formal group** is a group that exists within an organization, by virtue of management decree, to perform tasks that enhance the attainment of organizational objectives.[5] Figure 16.1 is an organization chart showing a formal group. The placement of organization members in such areas as marketing departments, personnel departments, or production departments involves establishing formal groups.

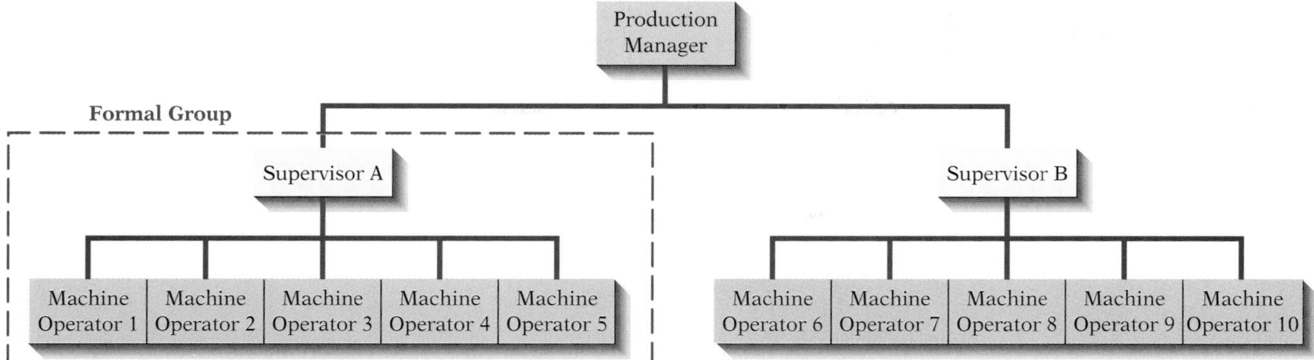

FIGURE 16.1 A formal group

Organizations actually are made up of a number of formal groups that exist at various organizational levels. The coordination of and communication among these groups is the responsibility of managers, or supervisors, commonly called "linking pins." Figure 16.2 shows the various formal groups that can exist within an organization and the linking pins associated with those groups. The linking pins are organization members who belong to two formal groups.

DIVERSITY HIGHLIGHT
Managing a Diverse Sales Force Takes Special Insight at Equitable

An example of a formal group that must be managed in many organizations is a sales force. According to José S. Suquet, manager of Equitable Life Assurance Company's South Florida agency, managing a sales force in a multicultural, multiethnic environment requires special insight and understanding. Suquet says that the key to management success is not to overcompensate for cultural diversity, but to be consistent across the board. Suquet's experience suggests that regardless of culture, employees need to feel that they are treated fairly and that managers do not have "favorites" who get special treatment.

Experience also indicates that the first critical step in managing a successful, diverse sales force is recruiting. Managers should look beyond cloning themselves and attempt to recruit people who reflect the market. Managers should struggle to build a sales force that represents the diverse ethnic market segments the company wishes to penetrate. Building such a sales force should help to ensure that salespeople are able to com-

To successfully manage a diverse salesforce a manager must first recruit employees who reflect the company's market, and then treat all employees fairly without giving some "favorite" special treatment.

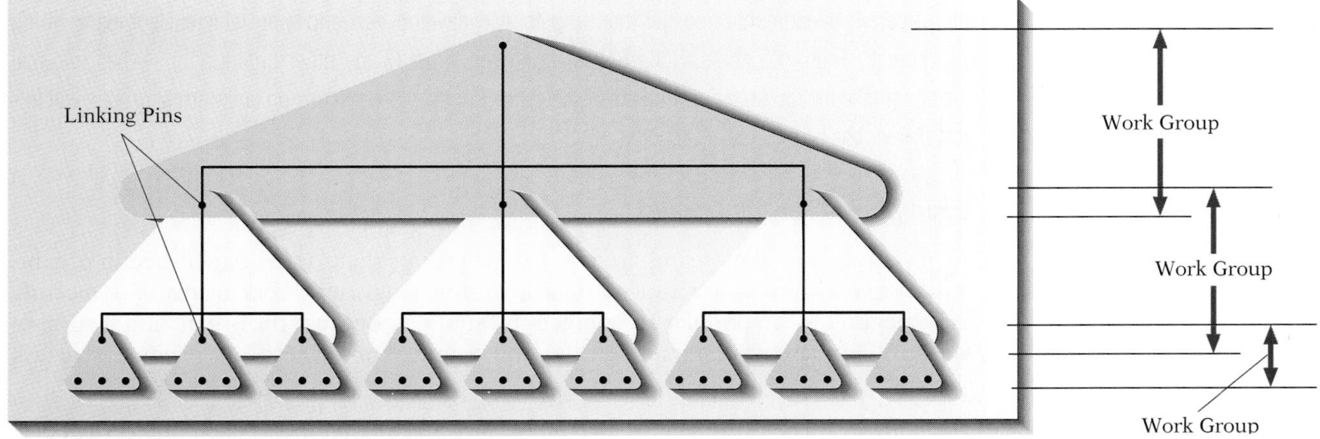

FIGURE 16.2 Formal groups and related linking pins

municate successfully with customers. Managers should determine such things as the language or languages that salespeople may need to speak, and should be sensitive to customs, jargon, and individual needs that are relevant to a particular organizational situation. When managing a diverse sales force, managers should also keep in mind that, simply because two or more people have the same ethnic and cultural backgrounds, they will not necessarily have the same opinions about organizational issues, approach problems in the same way, or be motivated by the same organizational incentives. ▶

Formal groups are clearly defined and structured. The following sections discuss (1) the basic kinds of formal groups, (2) examples of formal groups as they exist in organizations, and (3) the four stages of formal group development.

Kinds of Formal Groups

A **command group** is a formal group that is outlined in the chain of command on an organization chart. Command groups handle routine activities.

A **task group** is a formal group of organization members who interact with one another to accomplish mostly nonroutine organizational tasks. (Members of any one task group can and often do come from various levels and segments of an organization.)

Formal groups commonly are divided into command groups and task groups. **Command groups** are formal groups that are outlined on the chain of command on an organization chart. They typically handle the more routine organizational activities.

Task groups are formal groups of organization members who interact with one another to accomplish most of the organization's nonroutine tasks. Although task groups commonly are considered to be made up of members on the same organizational level, they can consist of people from different levels of the organizational hierarchy. For example, a manager could establish a task group to consider the feasibility of manufacturing some new product. Representatives from various levels of such organizational areas as production, market research, and sales probably would be included as members.

BACK TO THE CASE In order for a manager such as Ward to be able to manage work groups at Rolls-Royce, he needs to understand the definition of the term *group* and the idea that there are several types of groups that exist in organizations. A *group* at Rolls-Royce — or any other organization — is any number of people who interact, are psychologically aware of each other, and who perceive themselves as a group. A company like Rolls-Royce is made up of formal groups — the groups that appear on the company's organization charts — such as the marketing department. Managers of groups act as the "linking pins" among departments. The ability of managers at Rolls-Royce to coordinate and communicate with these groups, as well as their success in dealing with their own departments, is certainly important to the future success of Rolls-Royce as a whole.

At times, managers at Rolls-Royce can form new groups to handle some of the more nonroutine challenges. For example, management can form a task group; that is, they could choose two people from several different departments and get them together to develop new and more efficient company hiring procedures. Then, of course, Rolls-Royce — as with virtually any other organization — has informal groups (those that do not appear on the organization chart). More discussion on informal groups will follow in later back-to-the-case sections.

Examples of Formal Groups

Committees and work teams are two formal groups that can be established in organizations. Committees are a more traditional formal group. Work teams only recently have begun to gain popular acceptance and support. Because the organizing section of this text emphasized command groups, the examples in this section will emphasize task groups.

A **committee** is a task group that is charged with performing some type of specific activity. Committees are established for specific reasons.

Committees. A **committee** is a group of individuals that has been charged with performing some type of activity. Therefore, it usually is classified as a task group. From a managerial viewpoint, the major reasons for establishing committees are (1) to allow organization members to exchange ideas, (2) to generate suggestions and recommendations that can be offered to other organizational units, (3) to develop new ideas for solving existing organizational problems, and (4) to assist in the development of organizational policies.[6]

Committees typically exist within all organizations and at all organizational levels. As Figure 16.3 suggests, the larger the organization, the greater the probability that committees will be used within that organization on a regular basis. The following two sections discuss why managers should use committees and what makes committees successful.

ETHICS HIGHLIGHT
Calvary Hospital Forms Ethics Committees

Results of a survey conducted at Calvary Hospital in the Bronx, New York, indicate that managers are commonly using committees in hospitals to help make ethical decisions. Health care professionals today are faced with many different and significant ethical dilemmas. As an example, should patients be denied treatment because they cannot afford to pay for it or they do not have appropriate medical insurance? As another example, which patients should receive transplant organs first from donors? In order to better handle such ethical dilemmas, hospital administrators are commonly establishing and seeking input from hospital ethics committees. In order to get worthwhile views from these committees, representatives from many different areas of health care are being asked to serve. Not only physicians, but nurses are being included on the committees; nurses are heavily involved in patient care, and their input in making ethical decisions can be extremely valuable. Naturally, the primary purpose of these committees is to help managers (hospital administrators and other health care professionals) to ensure that appropriate decisions are made in response to ethical dilemmas being faced. Organization members seem willing to participate in ethics committees because this participation allows them to express to management various ethical concerns they may have about the work situation.

The hospital ethics committee at Calvary Hospital in the Bronx, New York, includes members from many different areas of health care. The committee considers ethical medical dilemmas such as whether or not to deny treatment to patients who cannot afford to pay.

1. *Why Managers Should Use Committees.* Managers generally agree that committees have several uses in organizations. One is that committees can improve the quality of decision making.[7] As more people become involved in making a decision, the strengths and weaknesses of that decision tend to be discussed in more detail, and the quality of the decision tends to increase.

   Another reason for committees is that they encourage honest opinions.

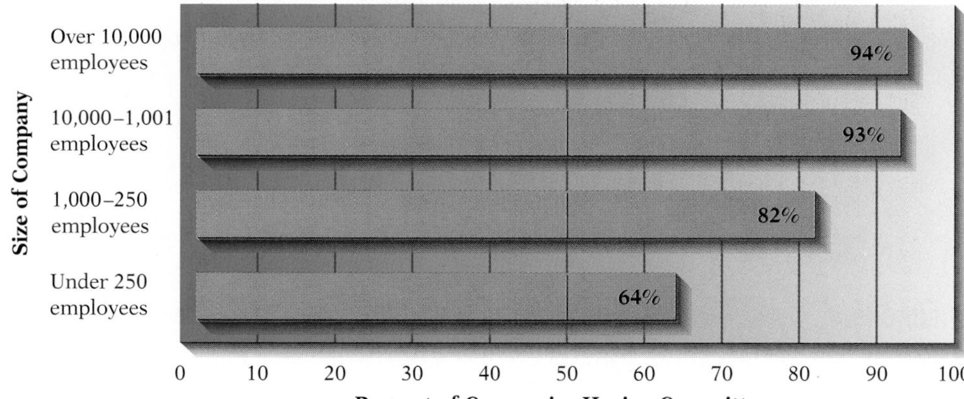

FIGURE 16.3 Percent of companies having committees, by size of company

Committee members feel protected because the group output of a committee logically cannot be totally associated with any one member of that group.

Committees also tend to increase organization member participation in decision making and thereby enhance support of committee decisions. Also, as a result of this increased participation, committee work creates the opportunity for committee members to satisfy their social or esteem needs.

Finally, committees ensure the representation of important groups in the decision-making process. Managers must choose committee members wisely, however, to achieve this representation. When a committee does not appropriately represent various interest groups, a committee decision will quite possibly exclude the interests of other important organizational groups.

Executives vary somewhat in their opinions about using committees in organizations. A study reported by McLeod and Jones indicates that most executives favor using committees in organizations.[8] According to this study, executives claim to get significantly more information from organizational sources other than committees. However, they find that the information from committees is more valuable to them than the information from any other source (see Figure 16.4). However, some top executives show only qualified acceptance of committees as work groups, and others express negative feelings. In general, the executives who are negative about using committees are fewer in number than those who are positive about them or who display qualified acceptance of them.

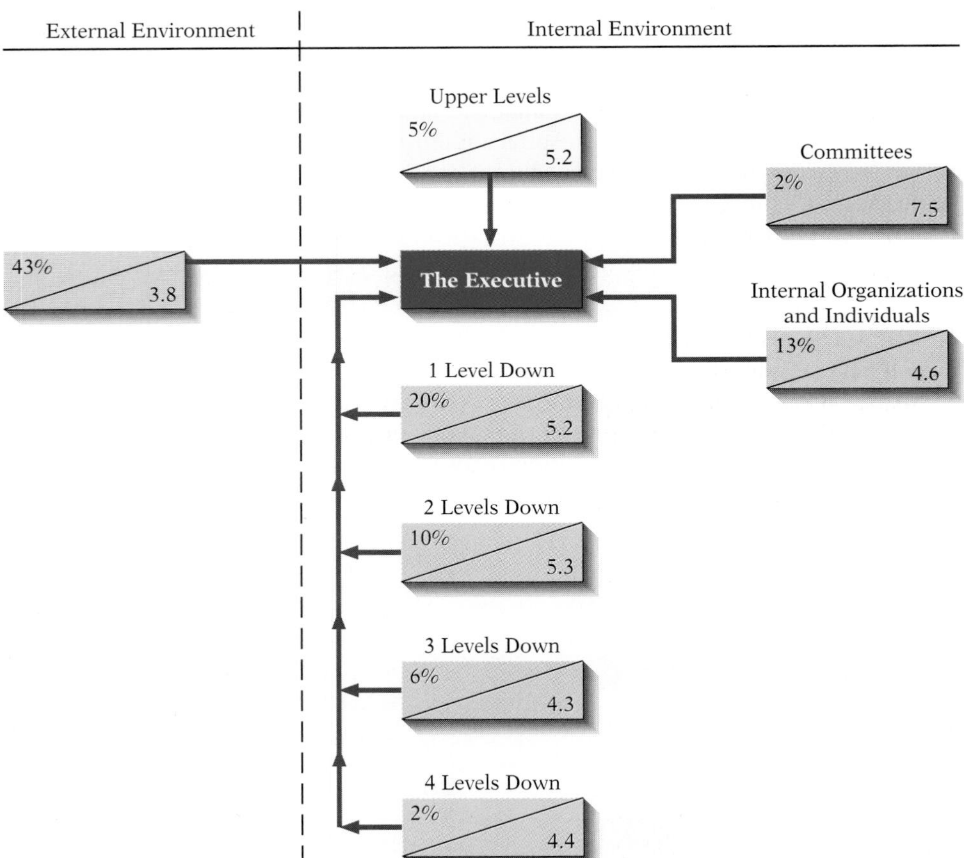

FIGURE 16.4 Comparing volume and value of information to executives from several organizational sources. *In each rectangle, the number above the diagonal is the percentage of overall volume for that source. The number* below *the diagonal is the average value, from 0 (no value) to 10 (maximum value), assigned the transaction. Amounts may not total 100 percent because of rounding.*

2. *What Makes Committees Successful.* Although committees have become a commonly accepted management tool, managerial action taken to establish and run committees is a major variable in determining their degree of success. Procedural steps that can be taken to increase the probability that a committee will be successful are the following:[9]

   a. The committee's goals should be clearly defined, preferably in writing. This focuses the committee's activities and reduces the time devoted to discussing what the committee is supposed to do.

   b. The committee's authority should be specified. Can the committee merely investigate, advise, and recommend, or is it authorized to implement decisions?

   c. The optimum size of the committee should be determined. With fewer than five members, the advantages of group work may be diminished. With more than ten or fifteen members, the committee may become unwieldy. Although size varies with the circumstances, the ideal number of committee members for many tasks seems to range from five to ten.

   d. A chairperson should be selected on the basis of the ability to run an efficient meeting—that is, the ability to keep the participation of all committee members from getting bogged down in irrelevancies and to see that the necessary paperwork gets done.

   e. Appointing a permanent secretary to handle communications is often useful.

   f. The agenda and all supporting material for the meeting should be distributed before the meeting. When members have a chance to study each item beforehand, they are likely to stick to the point and be ready with informed contributions.

   g. Meetings should be started on time, and the time at which they will end should be announced at the outset.

   In addition to these procedural steps, managers can follow a number of more people-oriented guidelines to increase the probability of committee success. In this regard, a manager can increase the quality of discussion in committees by:[10]

   a. *Rephrasing ideas already expressed.* This rephrasing makes sure that the manager as well as other individuals on the committee have a clear understanding of what has been said.

   b. *Bringing a member into active participation.* All committee members represent possible sources of information, and the manager should serve as a catalyst to spark individual participation whenever appropriate.

   c. *Stimulating further thought by a member.* The manager should encourage committee members to think ideas through carefully and thoroughly. Only this type of analysis generates high-quality committee output.

   Managers should also help the committee avoid a phenomenon called "groupthink."[11] **Groupthink** is the mode of thinking that people engage in when seeking agreement becomes so dominant in a group that it tends to override the realistic appraisal of alternative problem solutions. Groups operate under groupthink when their members are so concerned with being too harsh in their judgments of other group members that objectivity in problem solving is lost. Such groups tend to adopt a softer line of criticism and to seek complete support on every issue, with little conflict generated to endanger the "we-feeling" atmosphere.[12]

Groupthink is the mode of thinking that people engage in when seeking agreement becomes so dominant in a group that it tends to override the realistic appraisal of alternate problem solutions.

Work Teams. **Work teams** are another example of task groups used in organizations. Work teams in the United States have evolved from the problem-solving teams—based on Japanese-style quality circles—that were widely adopted in the 1970s. Problem-solving teams consist of five to twelve volunteer members from different areas of the department who meet weekly to discuss ways to improve quality and efficiency.

A **work team** is a task group used in organizations to achieve greater organizational flexibility or to cope with rapid growth. Work teams help organizations to be flexible and to cope with rapid growth.

Special-purpose teams developed in the early to middle 1980s out of the problem-solving teams. Special-purpose teams typically involve both workers and union representatives who meet together to collaborate on operational decisions at all levels, creating an atmosphere for quality and productivity improvements.

The special-purpose teams laid the foundation for the self-managing work teams of the 1990s that appear to be the wave of the future.[13] These self-managing teams consist of five to fifteen employees who work together to produce an entire product. Members learn all the tasks and rotate from job to job on the project. The teams even take over such managerial duties as scheduling work and vacations and ordering materials. The concept of the work team is a fundamental change in how work is organized, giving the employees control over their jobs.

By employing work teams, the firm draws upon the talent and creativity of all its employees, not just a few maverick inventors or top executives, to make important decisions.[14] As product quality becomes more and more important, managers will need to rely more and more on the team approach in order to stay competitive.[15] Consider a recent situation at Yellow Freight Systems, a shipping company, in which management had a serious concern for enhancing the excellence of service that its customers received.[16] Management established, in essence, a work team to address this concern. The work team was made up of members from many different parts of the company including marketing, sales, operations, and human resources. Over all, the task of the work team was to manage an excellence-in-service campaign that management had initiated.

QUALITY HIGHLIGHT
Work Teams Focus on Quality at Standard Steel

Over the years, organizations have used work teams in many different ways. The Standard Steel Company in Burnham, Pennsylvania, is using work teams to focus on improving product quality.

Steelmill employees use teamwork as a way to ensure a quality product. Standard Steel has instituted a program to build quality into every operation of the company.

Recently, Standard Steel has been undergoing a major rehabilitation in an effort to improve its financial position and bring greater stability to its fluctuating performance. Standard Steel management has instituted, as the primary vehicle for achieving this rehabilitation, a program to build better quality into every operation the company performs. Currently, the program is in its very early stages and is concentrating on educating every employee about the company's new focus on quality.

The program at Standard Steel teaches employees in work teams to evaluate quality issues by using specific, objective, data-gathering and problem-solving techniques. The program emphasizes that, to assess how product quality can be improved, employees should look at every single system in the company.

In addition to manufacturing systems, Standard's program also looks at the way management and workers interact with one another when discussing and solving quality-related problems. The program is built on the concept that positive working relationships between management and workers will ultimately improve the ways in which the company analyzes and solves quality-related problems. Standard Steel's industrial relations vice president, Joseph E. Wapner, says that perhaps the most important system instituted for quality improvement is the company's less antagonistic way of dealing with employees and the union. ▶

BACK TO THE CASE Rolls-Royce management could decide to form a committee to achieve some specific goal. A committee might be formed, for example, on how to enhance the quality of automobiles offered by Rolls-Royce. Such a committee could allow various Rolls-Royce departments to exchange quality improvement ideas and generate related suggestions to management. Such a committee could improve Rolls-Royce decision making in general by encouraging honest feedback from employees about quality issues in the organization. Such a committee can also be used to get fresh ideas about enhancing product quality, and can encourage Rolls-Royce employees to participate more seriously in improving the quality of automobiles offered by the company. Also, such a committee can help Rolls-Royce management to ensure that all appropriate departments are represented in important quality decisions. When Rolls-Royce takes action to improve the quality of its automobiles, for example, every important angle must be considered, including design, production, marketing, sales, and so on.

In managing such a quality committee at Rolls-Royce, management should encourage quality committee members to take certain steps which can help the committee be successful. After all, while committees *can* be useful, a poorly run committee wastes a lot of time. As an example of such steps, the committee should develop a clear definition of its goals and the limits of its authority. Is the committee just going to come up with quality improvement ideas, or should it also take the initial steps toward implementing those ideas?

In addition, the quality committee should not have too few or too many members. Issues must be addressed such as appointing an administrator to handle communications and appointing a chairperson who is good with people-oriented issues. A quality committee needs someone who can rephrase ideas clearly to ensure that everyone understands and who can get members to participate and think about the issues while avoiding groupthink. A company like Rolls-Royce wants original ideas to come out of committees, not a unanimous opinion that evolved because everyone was avoiding conflict.

Stages of Formal Group Development

Another facet of managing formal groups is understanding the stages of formal group development. In a classic book, Bernard Bass has suggested that group development is a four-stage process influenced primarily by groups learning how to use their resources.[17] Although these stages may not occur sequentially, for the purpose of clarity the discussion that follows assumes that they do. The four stages can be labeled and defined as follows:

1. *The acceptance stage.* It is relatively common for members of a new group initially to mistrust each other somewhat. The acceptance stage occurs only after the initial mistrust within the group has been transformed into mutual trust and the general acceptance of group members by one another.

2. *The communication and decision-making stage.* Once the acceptance stage has been passed, group members are better able to communicate frankly with one another. This frank communication provides the basis for effectively establishing and using some type of group decision-making mechanism.

3. *The group solidarity stage.* Group solidarity comes naturally as the mutual acceptance of group members increases and communication and decision making continue within the group. This stage is characterized by members becoming more involved in group activities and cooperating, rather than competing, with one another. Group members find being a member of the group extremely satisfying and are committed to enhancing the group's overall success.

4. *The group control stage.* A natural result of group solidarity is group control. This stage involves group members attempting to maximize group success by matching individual abilities with group activities and by assisting one another. Flexibility and informality tend to characterize this stage.

In general terms, as a group passes through each of these four stages, it tends to become more mature and more effective — and therefore more productive. The group that reaches maximum maturity and effectiveness is characterized by:[18]

1. *Members functioning as a unit.* The group works as a team. Members do not disturb one another to the point of interfering with their collaboration.
2. *Members participating effectively in group effort.* Members work hard when there is something to do. They usually do not loaf even if they get the opportunity to do so.
3. *Members being oriented toward a single goal.* Group members work for common purposes and thereby do not waste group resources by moving in different directions.
4. *Members having the equipment, tools, and skills necessary to attain the group's goals.* Group members are taught the various parts of their jobs by experts and strive to acquire whatever resources are needed to attain group objectives.
5. *Members asking and receiving suggestions, opinions, and information from one another.* A member who is uncertain about something stops working and asks another member for information. Group members generally talk to one another openly and frequently.

BACK TO THE CASE Managers in companies like Rolls-Royce must be patient and understand that it's going to take some time for a new group to develop into a productive working unit. The members in any new work group must start by trusting and accepting one another and then begin communicating and exchanging ideas. Once acceptance and communication increase, group solidarity and control come naturally. In other words, the group members get involved, cooperate, and try to maximize the group's success.

This is true also with the quality committee that is being used as an example. Rolls-Royce management must be patient and let the quality committee mature before management can expect maximum effectiveness and productivity. If given time to grow, the group will likely function as a unit, members will participate willingly and effectively, and the group will reach valuable decisions about what needs to be done to improve the quality of automobiles that Rolls-Royce offers.

Informal Groups

An **informal group** is a collection of individuals whose common work experiences result in the development of a system of interpersonal relations that extends beyond those established by management.

Informal groups, the second major kind of group that can exist within an organization, are groups that develop naturally as people interact. An **informal group** is defined as a collection of individuals whose common work experiences result in the development of a system of interpersonal relations that extend beyond those established by management.[19] As Figure 16.5 shows, informal group structures can deviate significantly from formal group structures. As in the case of Supervisor A in the figure, an organization member can belong to more than one informal group at the same time. In contrast to formal groups, informal groups typically are not highly structured in terms of procedure and are not formally recognized by management.

The following sections discuss (1) various kinds of informal groups that can exist in organizations, (2) the benefits usually reaped by membership in informal groups, and (3) encouraging the development of informal groups.

Kinds of Informal Groups

An **interest group** is an informal group that gains and maintains membership primarily because of a special concern each member possesses about a specific issue.

Informal groups generally are divided into two types: interest groups and friendship groups. **Interest groups** are informal groups that gain and maintain membership primarily because of a special concern each member possesses about a specific issue. An example is a group of workers pressing management for better pay or working

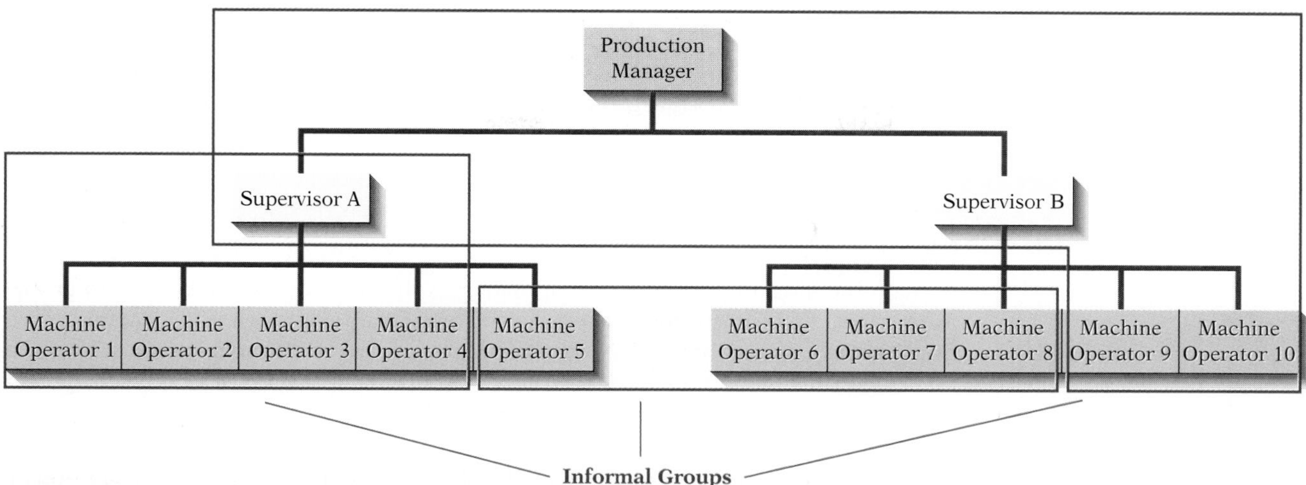

FIGURE 16.5 Three informal groups that deviate significantly from formal groups within the organization

conditions. Once the interest or concern that causes an informal group to form has been eliminated, the group tends to disband.

As its name implies, **friendship groups** are informal groups that form in organizations because of the personal affiliation members have with one another. Personal factors such as personal interests, race, gender, and religion serve as foundations for friendship groups. As with interest groups, the membership of friendship groups tends to change over time. Here, however, group membership changes as friendships dissolve or new friendships are made.

A **friendship group** is an informal group that forms in organizations because of the personal affiliation members have with one another.

Benefits of Informal Group Membership

Informal groups tend to develop in organizations because of various benefits that group members obtain. These benefits include (1) perpetuation of social and cultural values that group members consider important, (2) status and social satisfaction that might not be enjoyed without group membership, (3) increased ease of communication among group members, and (4) increased desirability of the overall work environment.[20] These benefits may be one reason that employees who are on fixed shifts or who continually work with the same groups are sometimes more satisfied with their work than employees whose shifts are continually changing.[21]

BACK TO THE CASE There are also issues regarding informal groups that could impact the success of work groups at Rolls-Royce. Employee groups get together at times because of certain issues. For example, certain minority employees could get together as a group to increase the opportunities for their professional growth at Rolls-Royce. And, of course, employees form friendship groups, which ease communication and provide feelings of satisfaction in a company. In general, such informal groups can improve the work environment for everyone involved; encouraging their development can therefore be very advantageous for management.

Perhaps Rolls-Royce management can accelerate the development of a quality committee into a productive unit by placing individuals on this committee who already know and trust one another through membership in one or more informal groups at Rolls-Royce. As an example, some members of the newly formed quality committee might know and trust one another immediately as a result of membership on a company bowling or softball team. Under such circumstances, a trust developed among employees through past informal group affiliations could help the formal quality committee to develop into a productive group more quickly.

MANAGING WORK GROUPS

To manage work groups effectively, managers must simultaneously consider the effect of both formal and informal group factors on organizational productivity. This consideration requires three steps: (1) determining group existence, (2) understanding the evolution of informal groups, and (3) maximizing work group effectiveness.

Determining Group Existence

Sociometry is an analytical tool that can be used to determine what informal groups exist in an organization and who the members of those groups are.

A **sociogram** is a sociometric diagram that summarizes the personal feelings of organization members about the people in the organization with whom they would like to spend free time.

Perhaps the most important step that managers should take in managing work groups is determining what groups exist within the organization and who their members are. **Sociometry** is an analytical tool that managers can use to help determine such information. It can also provide information on the internal workings of an informal group, such as the group leader, the relative status level of various members within the group, and the group's communication networks.[22] This information on informal groups, along with an understanding of the established formal groups as shown on an organization chart, gives managers a complete picture of the group structure.

The procedure involved in performing a sociometric analysis in an organization is quite basic. Various organization members simply are asked, through either an interview or a questionnaire, to name several other organization members with whom they would like to spend some of their free time. A sociogram then is constructed to summarize the informal relationships among group members. **Sociograms** are diagrams that visually link individuals within the group according to the number of times they were chosen and whether the choice was reciprocal.

Figure 16.6 shows two sample sociograms based on a classic study of two groups of boys in a summer camp—the Bulldogs and the Red Devils.[23] An analysis of these sociograms results in several interesting observations. For example, more boys within the Bulldogs than within the Red Devils were chosen as being desirable to spend time with. This probably implies that the Bulldogs are a closer-knit informal group than the Red Devils. Also, communication between L and most other Red Devils members is likely to occur directly, whereas communication between C and other Bulldogs is likely to pass through other group members. Last, the greater the number of times an individual is chosen, the more likely that individual will be the group leader. Thus individuals C and E would tend to be Bulldog leaders, and individuals L and S would tend to be Red Devil leaders.

Sociometric analysis can give managers many useful insights on the informal groups within an organization. Although managers may not want to perform a formal sociometric analysis, they can casually gather information that would indicate what form a sociogram might take in a particular situation. This information can be gathered through inferences made in normal conversations that managers have with other organization members and through observations of how various organization members relate to one another.

Understanding the Evolution of Informal Groups

Obviously, knowing what groups exist within an organization and what characterizes the membership of those groups is an important prerequisite for managing groups effectively. A second prerequisite is understanding how informal groups evolve, because this gives managers some insights on how to encourage informal groups to develop appropriately within an organization. Naturally, encouraging these groups to develop and maintaining good relationships with work group members can help ensure that organization members support management in the process of attaining organizational objectives.[24]

Perhaps the most widely accepted framework for explaining the evolution of informal groups was developed by George Homans.[25] Figure 16.7 broadly summarizes his

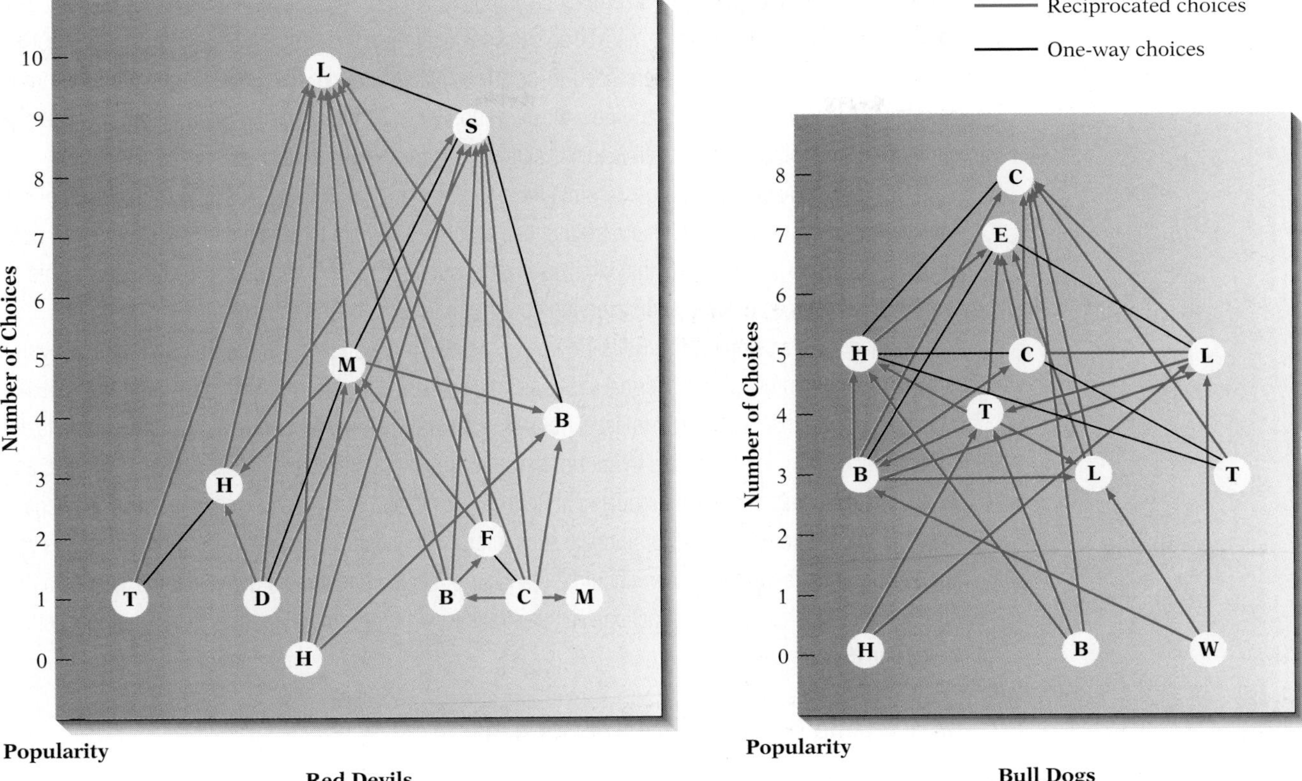

FIGURE 16.6 Sample sociograms

theory. According to Homans, the sentiments, interactions, and activities that emerge as part of an informal group result from the sentiments, interactions, and activities that exist within a formal group. In addition, the informal group exists to obtain the consequences of satisfaction and growth for its members. Feedback on whether the consequences are achieved can result in forces that attempt to modify the formal group in order to increase the probability that the informal group will achieve the consequences.

An example to illustrate Homans's concept involves twelve factory workers who are members of a formal work group that manufactures toasters. According to Homans, as these workers interact to assemble toasters, they might discover common personal interests that encourage the evolution of informal groups. In turn, these informal groups will tend to maximize the satisfaction and growth of their members. Once established, the informal groups will probably resist changes or established segments of informal groups that threaten the satisfaction and growth of the informal group's members.

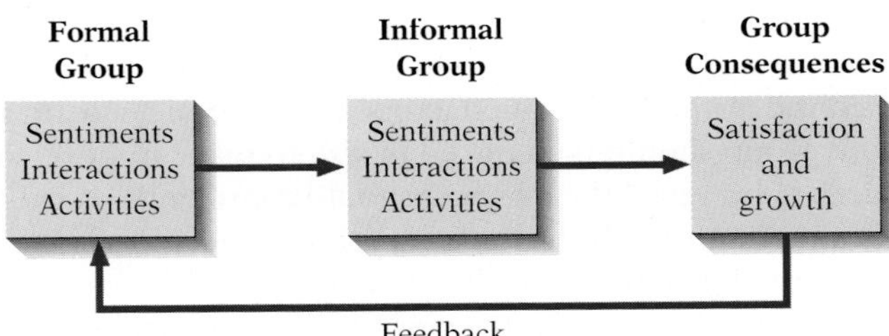

FIGURE 16.7 Homans's ideas on how informal groups develop

BACK TO THE CASE In order for a company such as Rolls-Royce to be successful, managers must be able to consider how both formal and informal groups affect organizational productivity. Managers need to determine what informal groups exist and who the group members are, as well as understand how these groups form. Armed with this information, managers in companies like Rolls-Royce can strive to make their work groups more effective.

One way management can get information about the groups at Rolls-Royce is to use sociometry. Managers can design a questionnaire asking their employees whom they spend time with and then construct a sociogram to summarize this information. Of course, managers can do a more casual analysis by just talking to their employees and observing how they interact with one another.

Managers in a company like Rolls-Royce should also try to understand how informal groups evolve and realize that an organization's formal structure influences how the informal groups develop within it. For example, assume that in one department at Rolls-Royce there are thirty people who work on automobile design. Many of them are interested in sports, have become friends because of this common interest, and work well together as a result. If a manager at Rolls Royce needed to make some changes in such a department, he or she should try to accommodate such informal friendship groups to keep group members satisfied. Only with very good reason should a manager of such a department damage the existence of the productive friendship group with actions such as transferring one or more informal group members out of the design department.

Maximizing Work Group Effectiveness

Once managers determine which groups exist within an organization and understand how informal groups evolve, they should strive to maximize work group effectiveness. As the following discussion emphasizes, maximizing work group effectiveness requires that managers continue to consider both formal and informal dimensions of the organization.

Figure 16.8 indicates the four factors primarily responsible for collectively influencing work group effectiveness: (1) size of work group, (2) cohesiveness of work group, (3) work group norms, and (4) status of work group members. (The terms *work group* and *formal group* are used synonymously in the sections that follow.)

Size of Work Group

As work group size (the number of members in a work group) increases, forces usually are created within that group that can either increase or decrease its effectiveness.[26] The ideal number of members for a work group depends primarily on the group's purpose.[27] For example, the ideal size for a fact-finding work group usually is set at about fourteen members, and the maximum size for a problem-solving work group is approximately seven members.[28]

Work group size is a significant determinant of group effectiveness because it has considerable impact on three major components of a group: (1) leadership, (2) group members, and (3) group processes. A summary of how these factors can be influenced by group size is presented in Table 16.1.

Managers attempting to maximize group effectiveness by modifying formal group size also should consider informal group factors. For example, a manager may decide that a formal work group should be reduced in size to make it more effective. Before making this reduction, however, the manager should consider the existence of informal groups within the formal group. If the manager reduces the size of the formal group by transferring the informal group leader, the effectiveness of the work group could diminish considerably. The slight ineffectiveness of the overly large formal work group might be more advantageous than the greater ineffectiveness that could result from reducing the formal group size and possibly transferring the informal group leader.

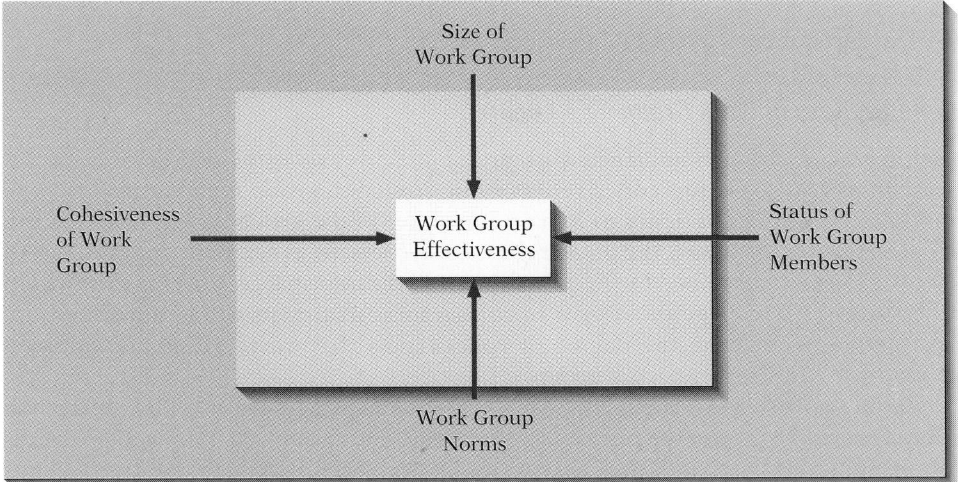

FIGURE 16.8 Primary determinants of work group effectiveness

GLOBAL HIGHLIGHT: Mazda's Work Group System

At Mazda, management has found that some jobs would require work groups that would be so large and therefore so unproductive that the company has engineered a work group system to handle a job rather than a single work group. According to Sarah Griffin of Mazda Motor Manufacturing (USA), management at the Flat Rock, Michigan, plant has designed and implemented a plan using a series of work groups to better control job injuries within its facility. This work group system involves a department work group for each department at the plant as well as a central work group that monitors, controls, and coordinates the activities of the department work groups. Thus far, this work group system has identified fifty-two jobs that pose significant safety risk to workers because of the excessive bending, reaching, and lifting motions that the jobs require. Joe Galusha, Mazda's safety and health specialist, is encouraged by the initial results of the work groups' system in identifying and eliminating "injury risk" positions within the company. He stresses, however, that the job of

This work group at Mazda Motor Manufacturing's Flat Rock, Michigan, assembly plant is a part of a work group system that controls job injuries within its facility.

TABLE 16.1 Possible effects of group size on group leadership, group members, and group processes

Dimensions	*Group Size* 2–7 *Members*	8–12 *Members*	13–16 *Members*
Leadership			
1. Demand on leader	Low	Moderate	High
2. Differences between leader and members	Low	Low to moderate	Moderate to high
3. Direction of leader	Low	Low to moderate	Moderate to high
Members			
4. Tolderance of direction from leader	Low to high	Moderate to high	High
5. Domination of group interaction by a few members	Low	Moderate to high	High
6. Inhibition in participation by ordinary members	Low	Moderate	High
Group processes			
7. Formalization of rules and proceedures	Low	Low to moderate	Moderate to high
8. Time required for reaching decisions	Low to moderate	Moderate	Moderate to high
9. Tendency for subgroup to form	Low	Moderate to high	High

the work group system will never really end. Instead, he views the functioning of the work group system as a continuing effort. ▶

Cohesiveness of Work Group

Group cohesiveness is the attraction group members feel for one another in terms of the desire to remain a member of a group and to resist leaving it.

Another factor that can influence work group effectiveness is the degree of cohesiveness of the group. **Group cohesiveness** is the attraction group members feel for one another in terms of the desire to remain a member of the group and to resist leaving it.[29] The greater the desire, the greater the cohesiveness. In general, the cohesiveness of a work group is determined by the cohesiveness of the informal groups that exist within it. Therefore, to manage the degree of cohesiveness that exists within a work group, managers must manage the degree of cohesiveness that exists within the informal groups that constitute the work group.

Group cohesiveness is extremely important to managers because the greater the cohesiveness, the greater the probability the group will accomplish its objectives. In addition, some evidence indicates that groups whose members have positive feelings toward one another tend to be more productive than groups whose members have negative feelings toward one another.[30]

Indicators of high group cohesiveness include the following:[31]

1. The members have a broad, general agreement on the goals and objectives of the informal group.
2. A significant amount of communication and interaction is evident among participating members.
3. There is a satisfactory level of homogeneity in social status and social background among the members.
4. Members are allowed to participate fully and directly in the determination of group standards.
5. The size of the group is sufficient for interaction but is not so large as to stymie personal attention. Normally, the optimum size range of an informal group is from four to seven members.
6. The members have a high regard for their fellow members.
7. The members feel a strong need for the mutual benefits and protection the group appears to offer.
8. The group is experiencing success in the achievement of its goals and in the protection of important values.

Because the cohesiveness of informal groups is such an influential determinant of the cohesiveness of work groups and, as a result, of work group effectiveness, management should assist in the development of informal group cohesiveness whenever possible. (This, of course, assumes that the informal group is attempting to make a constructive contribution to organizational goal attainment.) To this end, managers should attempt to enhance the prestige of existing informal group members, design the overall organization to encourage informal group development, and eliminate organizational barriers to continuing informal group membership over an extended period of time.

If, however, managers determine that an informal group is attempting to attain objectives that are counterproductive to those of the organization, an appropriate strategy would be to attempt to reduce informal group cohesiveness. For example, managers could take action to limit the prestige of existing group members and design the overall organization to discourage further group cohesiveness. This type of action, however, could result in a major conflict between management and various informal groups that exist within the organization. Over all, managers must keep in mind that the greater the cohesiveness of informal groups with nonproductive objectives, the greater the probability that those nonproductive objectives will be attained.

Work Group Norms

Group norms are a third major determinant of work group effectiveness. In this chapter, **group norms** apply only to informal groups. These norms are appropriate or standard behavior that is required of informal group members. Therefore, they significantly influence the behavior of informal group members in their formal group. According to Hackman, group norms (1) are structured characteristics of groups that simplify the group-influence processes; (2) apply only to behavior, not to private thoughts and feelings of group members; (3) generally develop only in relation to the matters that most group members consider important; (4) usually develop slowly over time; and (5) sometimes apply only to certain group members.[32]

Group norms are appropriate or standard behavior that is required of informal group members.

Systematic study of group norms has revealed that there is generally a close relationship between those norms and the profitability of the organization of which the group is a part.[33] Although it would be impossible to state all possible norms that might develop in a group, most group norms relate to one or more of the following: (1) organizational pride, (2) performance, (3) profitability, (4) teamwork, (5) planning, (6) supervision, (7) training, (8) innovation, (9) customer relations, and (10) honesty or security.

Norms usually are divided into two general types: negative and positive. **Negative norms** are required informal group behavior that limits organizational productivity. **Positive norms** are required informal group behavior that contributes to organizational productivity. Examples of negative norms might include stopping work fifteen minutes before quitting time, taking extended coffee breaks, or not rushing to finish work because more will be assigned. Examples of positive norms include doing work correctly the first time and not wasting expensive company materials.

Negative norms are informal group standards that limit organizational productivity.

Positive norms are informal group standards that contribute to organizational productivity.

Some managers consider group norms to be of such great importance to the organization that they develop profiles of group norms to assess the norms' organizational impact. Figure 16.9 shows a normative profile developed by one company manager. This particular profile is characterized by a number of norm differences. For example, a high level of organizational pride and good customer relations contrast

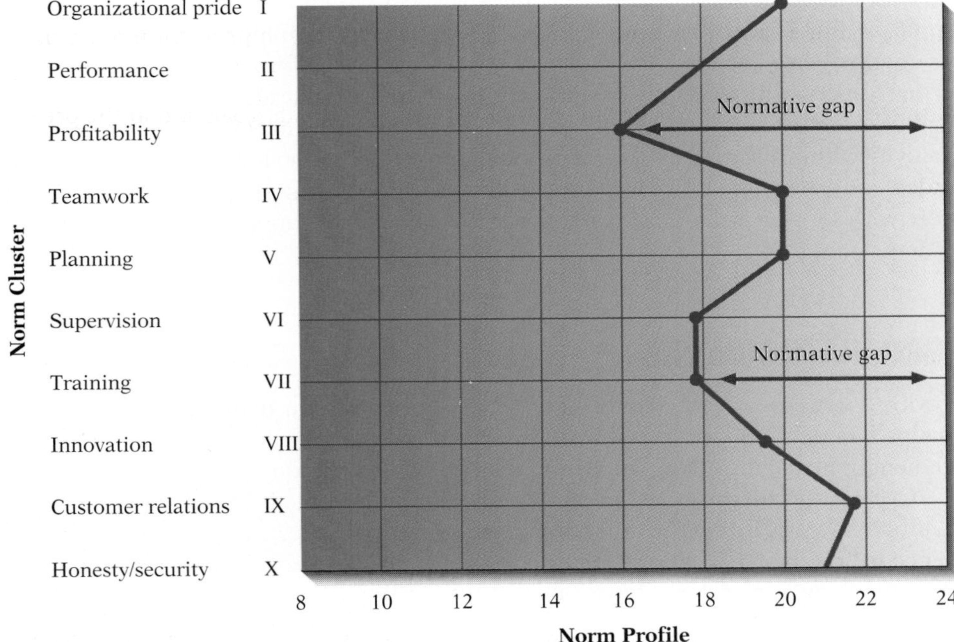

FIGURE 16.9 Sample normative profile

with a lower concern for profitability. What actually happened in this company was that employees placed customer desires at such a high level that they were significantly decreasing organizational profitability to please customers. Once these norms were discovered, management took steps to make the situation more advantageous to the organization.

As the preceding information suggests, a key to managing behavior within a formal work group is managing the norms of the informal groups that exist within the formal group. More specifically, Homans's framework for analyzing group behavior indicates that informal group norms are mainly the result of the characteristics of the formal work group of which the informal group is a part. As a result, changing the existing norms within an informal group means changing the characteristics of the formal work group of which the informal group is a part.

For example, an informal group could have the negative norm: Don't rush the work—they'll just give you more to do. For a manager to change this norm, the factor in the formal work group from which the norm probably arose should be eliminated. The manager might find that this norm is a direct result of the fact that workers are formally recognized within the organization through pay and awards regardless of the amount of work performed. Changing the formal policy so the amount of work accomplished is considered in formal organizational recognition should help dissolve this negative norm. In some situations, norms may be difficult, if not impossible, to change.

Status of Work Group Members

Status is the positioning of importance of a group member in relation to other group members.

Status is the position of a group member in relation to other group members. Overall, an individual's status within a group is determined not only by the person's work or role within the group but by the nonwork qualities the individual brings to the group. Work-related determinants of status include titles, work schedules, and perhaps most commonly, amounts of pay group members receive.[34] Nonwork-related determinants of status include education level, race, age, and sex. Table 16.2 on page 419 shows an entertaining but realistic treatment of how status symbols vary within the formal groups of an organizational hierarchy. These status symbols generally are used within formal work groups to reward individual productivity and to show the different levels of organizational importance.

To maximize the effectiveness of a work group, managers also should consider the status of members of the informal groups that exist within the formal group. For example, within a formal group, the formal group leaders have higher status than other group members. The informal groups that exist within the formal group also have informal leaders, who generally are different from the formal leader and of higher status than other informal group members. Management usually finds that, to increase productivity within a formal work group, the support of both the formal and the informal leaders must be gained. In fact, some evidence suggests that production is associated more with support from informal group leaders than with support from formal group leaders.[35]

CORPORATE CULTURE

Previous sections of this chapter have focused primarily on managing smaller work groups. This section, on the other hand, discusses corporate culture as an important ingredient in managing all organization members as a total group.

Corporate culture is a set of shared values and beliefs that organization members have regarding the functioning and existence of their organization.

Corporate culture is defined as a set of shared values and beliefs that organization members have regarding the functioning and existence of their organization.[36] The evidence for the type of corporate culture present in any organization can be found by studying its own special combination of status symbols, traditions, history, and physical environment. By understanding the significance of this evidence of corporate culture, management can help to develop a culture that is beneficial to the firm. For

TABLE 16.2 How status symbols vary with various levels of the organizational hierarchy

Visible Appurtenances	*Top Dogs*	*VIPs*	*Brass*	*No. 2s*	*Eager Beavers*	*Hoi Polloi*
Briefcases	None—they ask the questions	Use backs of envelopes	Someone goes along to carry theirs	Carry their own—empty	Daily—carry their own—filled with work	Too poor to own one
Desks, office	Custom made (to order)	Executive style (to order)	Type A, "Director"	Type B, "Manager"	Castoffs from No. 2s	Yellow oak—or castoffs from eager beavers
Tables, office	Coffee tables	End tables or decorative wall tables	Matching tables, type A	Matching tables, type B	Plain work table	None—lucky to have own desk
Carpeting	Nylon—one-inch pile	Nylon—one-inch pile	Wool-twist (twist pad)	Wool-twist (without pad)	Used wool pieces—sewed	Asphalt tile
Plant stands	Several—kept filled with strange, exotic plans	Several—kept filled with strange, exotic plans	Two—repotted whenever they take a trip	One medium-sized—repotted annually during vacation	Small—repotted when plant dies	May have one in the department or bring their own from home
Vacuum water bottles	Silver	Silver	Chromium	Plain painted	Coke machine	Water fountains
Library	Private collective	Autographed or complimentary books and reports	Selected references	Impressive titles on covers	Books everywhere	Dictionary
Parking space	Private—in front of office	In plant garage	In company garage—if enough seniority	In company properties—somewhere	On the parking lot	Anywhere they can find a space—if they can afford a car

example, by looking at the status symbols—the visible, external signs of one's social position that are associated with the various positions in the firm—one can get a feeling for the social hierarchy in the organization. Status symbols such as size and location of one's office, use of executive clubs, and reserved parking are all indicators of the status level of a job.

Traditions and history developed over time in a firm can determine the special way that workers in that particular firm act on a daily basis. Typically, the traditions can help workers know exactly what is expected of them. By developing traditions, managers can therefore help to steer the everyday behaviors that go on.

The firm's physical environment makes a statement about the firm's type of corporate culture. For instance, offices that are closed with few common areas for organization members to meet creates an image of a closed form of culture. A building with open offices and considerable common areas for the employees to interact indicates a more open culture. Whether the doors are consistently closed or open is another clue as to the type of formality that exists in an organization.

The significance of corporate culture for management is that it influences the behavior of everyone within an organization, and, if carefully crafted, can have a positive and significant effect on organizational success.[37] If not properly managed, however, corporate culture can help doom an organization to failure. Typically, top management as well as other present or past organizational leaders in an organization are the key agents for influencing corporate culture.

Advice about the way managers should handle corporate culture issues commonly appears in the current management literature.[38] One example of such advice that seems especially practical and helpful suggests that managers can use five primary mechanisms to help develop and reinforce a desired corporate culture. These mechanisms are[39]

1. *What leaders pay attention to, measure, and control.* Leaders can communicate very effectively what their vision of the organization is and what they want done by consistently emphasizing the same issues in meetings, in casual remarks and questions, and in strategy discussions. For example, if product quality is the dominant value to be inculcated in employees, leaders may consistently inquire about the effect of any proposed changes in product quality.

2. *Leaders' reactions to critical incidents and organizational crises.* The manner in which leaders deal with crises can create new beliefs and values and reveal underlying organizational assumptions. For example, when a firm faces a financial crisis but does not lay off any employees, the message may be that the organization sees itself as a "family" that looks out for its members.

3. *Deliberate role modeling, teaching, and coaching.* The behaviors that leaders perform in both formal and informal settings have an important effect on employee beliefs, values, and behaviors. For example, if the CEO regularly works very long hours and on weekends, other managers may respond to spending more of their time at work, too.

4. *Criteria for allocation of rewards and status.* Leaders can quickly communicate their priorities and values by consistently linking rewards and punishments to the behaviors they are concerned with. For example, if a weekly bonus is given for exceeding production or sales quotas, employees may recognize the value placed on these activities and focus their efforts on them.

5. *Criteria for recruitment, selection, promotion, and retirement of employees.* The kinds of people who are hired and who succeed in an organization are those who accept the organization's values and behave accordingly. For example, if managers who are action oriented and who implement strategies effectively consistently move up the organizational ladder, the organization's priorities should come through loud and clear to other managers.

The corporate culture discussion suggests that managers can influence the type of culture that exists within organizations. In general, a manager must first determine the characteristics of a culture that would be appropriate for an organization and then take calculated and overt steps to encourage the establishment, growth, and maintenance of that culture. Merely allowing corporate culture to develop without planned management influence can result in the appearance of an inappropriate corporate culture that ultimately limits the degree of success that an organization can attain.

BACK TO THE CASE

In managing groups, managers in a company such as Rolls-Royce should consider the four major factors that influence work group effectiveness. First of all, the size of the work group can be important to its productivity. A twenty-person quality committee would be somewhat large and probably would hamper the group's effectiveness. However, managers should consider informal groups before making changes in group size. The quality committee could end up being less productive without one or more of its respected members than it would be if it were slightly too large.

Another important factor that influences work group effectiveness at a company such as Rolls-Royce is a group cohesiveness. Because a more cohesive group will tend to be more effective, Rolls-Royce managers should try to increase the cohesiveness of the company's work groups. Again, informal groups are very important here. Rolls-Royce managers can probably increase the cohesiveness of their formal groups by such actions as allowing members to take breaks together or rewarding informal group members for a job well done.

The group norms, or appropriate behaviors required within the informal group, are a third factor that affects the productivity of formal group behavior at a company such as Rolls-Royce. Because these norms affect company profitability, managers must be aware of them and understand how to influence them within the formal group structure. For example, assume that a smaller informal group of workers within a larger department is installing automobile interiors and really cares about the quality of the interiors installed. Unfortunately, because of its quality norm, the informal group's members are taking too much time installing each interior. Management could try to improve this norm by giving bonuses to group members who produce the best-quality interiors in the shortest amount of time. This reward would probably increase the formal group productivity while encouraging a positive norm within the informal group.

Status within the informal groups also affects work group productivity in a company such as Rolls-Royce. For example, if Rolls-Royce managers want to increase production for some group, management should try to encourage the informal group's leaders, as well as the group's formal supervisor. Chances are that a targeted group will become more productive only if its informal high-status members support that objective.

Overall, if a company like Rolls-Royce wants to maximize work group effectiveness, management must remember both the formal and informal dimensions of its work groups while considering the four main factors that influence work group productivity.

ACTION SUMMARY

Reread the learning objectives that follow. Each objective is followed by questions. Answering these questions accurately will help you retain the most important concepts discussed in this chapter. After answering each question, check your answer with the answer key at the end of this chapter. (*Hint:* If you have doubt regarding the correct response, consult the page whose number follows the answer.)

Circle: ***From studying this chapter, I will attempt to acquire:***

1. A definition of the term *group* as used within the context of management.

T, F — **a.** A group is made up of people who interact with one another, perceive themselves to be a group, and are primarily physically aware of one another.

a, b, c, d, e — **b.** According to Cartwright and Lippit, it is *not* true to say that: (a) groups exist in all kinds of organizations; (b) groups inevitably form in all facets of organizational existence; (c) groups cause undesirable consequences within the organization, so their continued existence should be discouraged; (d) understanding groups can assist managers in increasing the probability that the groups with which they work will cause desirable consequences within the organization; (e) all of the above are true.

2. A thorough understanding of the difference between formal and informal groups.

T, F — **a.** An informal group is a group that exists within an organization by virtue of management decree.

T, F — **b.** A formal group is one that exists within an organization by virtue of interaction among organization members in proximity to one another.

3. Knowledge of the types of formal groups that exist in organizations.

a, b, c, d, e — **a.** The type of group that generally handles more routine organizational activities is the: (a) informal task group; (b) informal command group; (c) formal task group; (d) formal command group; (e) none of the above.

a, b, c, d, e — **b.** Managers should be encouraged to take the following steps to increase the success of a committee: (a) clearly define the goals of the committee; (b) rephrase ideas that have already been expressed; (c) select a chairperson on the basis of ability to run an efficient meeting; (d) a and b; (e) a, b, and c.

4. An understanding of how managers can determine which groups exist in an organization.

T, F — **a.** The technique of sociometry involves asking people whom they would like to manage.

a, b, c, d, e — **b.** A sociogram is defined in the text as: (a) a letter encouraging group participation; (b) a diagram that visually illustrates the number of times that the individuals were chosen within the group and whether the choice was reciprocal; (c) a composite of demographic data useful in determining informal group choices; (d) a computer printout designed to profile psychological and sociological characteristics of the informal group; (e) none of the above.

5. An appreciation for how managers must evaluate formal and informal groups simultaneously to maximize work group effectiveness.

a, b, c, d, e — **a.** Which of the following factors has the least influence on the effectiveness of a work group: (a) age of the work group; (b) size of the work group; (c) cohesiveness of the work group; (d) norms of the work group; (e) a and d.

T, F — **b.** Knowing what informal groups exist within an organization and how informal groups evolve are prerequisites for managing groups effectively.

6. Insights about managing corporate culture to enhance organizational success.

T, F — **a.** The concept of corporate culture usually does not include the set of beliefs that organization members have about their organization and its functioning.

a, b, c, d, e — **b.** Mechanisms that managers can use to influence corporate culture include: (a) what leaders pay attention to; (b) criteria that leaders use to make organizational awards; (c) criteria leaders use to select new employees; (d) all of the above; (e) none of the above.

INTRODUCTORY CASE WRAP-UP

"Groups are Important to Progress at Rolls-Royce" (p. 401) and its related back-to-the-case sections were written to help you better understand the management concepts contained in this chapter. Answer the following discussion questions about this introductory case to further enrich your understanding of chapter content:

1. What kind of group would the Japanese-style work teams at Rolls-Royce be classified as? Explain.
2. What advice would you give to a Rolls-Royce manager who is managing such a work team?

ISSUES FOR REVIEW AND DISCUSSION

1. How is the term *group* defined in this chapter?
2. Why is the study of groups important to managers?
3. What is a formal group?
4. Explain the significance of linking pins to formal groups in organizations.
5. List and define two types of formal groups that can exist in organizations.
6. Why should managers use committees in organizations?
7. What steps can managers take to ensure that a committee will be successful?
8. Explain how work teams can be valuable to an organization.
9. Describe the stages a group typically goes through as it becomes more mature.
10. What is an informal group?
11. List and define two types of informal groups in organizations.
12. What benefits generally accrue to members of informal groups?
13. What is the relationship between work teams and informal groups?
14. Are formal groups more important to managers than informal groups? Explain.
15. Describe the sociometric procedure used to study informal group membership. What can the results of a sociometric analysis tell managers about members of an informal group?
16. Explain Homans's concept of how informal groups develop.
17. List and define the primary factors that influence work group effectiveness.
18. What is the relationship among formal groups, informal groups, and work group effectiveness?
19. Define corporate culture. Can managers actually build corporate culture? Explain.

ACTION SUMMARY ANSWER KEY

1. **a.** F, p. 402
   b. c, p. 402
2. **a.** F, p. 402
   b. F, p. 402
3. **a.** d, p. 404
   b. e, p. 407
4. **a.** F, p. 412
   b. b, p. 412
5. **a.** a, p. 414
   b. T, p. 412
6. **a.** F, p. 418
   b. d, p. 420

CASE STUDY

Rewards in a Self-Managed Work Team at Boeing

MARY S. THIBODEAUX
University of North Texas

In 1987 a new plant of a wholly-owned subsidiary of Boeing was opened in a north Texas facility located near Denton, Texas. The plant now employs approximately 400 workers.

These workers are divided into five functional areas: material, production, human resources, quality control, and engineering. Roughly one-half of the employees are classified as production payroll; the remainder are classified as support payroll.

What is unique about this plant is that it started with, and is still operated around, the concept of self-managed work teams. These teams are involved in the operations of the plant in all stages from the selection of employees to company-wide evaluations to scheduling to discipline.

Boeing's philosophy clearly reflects its attitude toward a high-empowerment, high-involvement environment. According to public documents, "Boeing believes that people work best when they: are in and feel a part of a team where they can be trusted and trust each other to do their jobs; share leadership and make decisions; are accepted and respected; resolve issues with sensitivity and understanding; have the opportunity to accomplish challenging goals and contribute to continuing improvement."

There are no first-level supervisors in this plant. Team members are trained and expected to take responsibility for the day-to-day operations of their teams. The goal is to have 20 percent of labor time devoted to indirect labor activities. Each team member is responsible for learning the technical tasks involved in his or her job and is expected to assume a leadership responsibility that contributes to team operations. Team members receive training in these roles from either the current holder of the role or a support team member (trainer) or a combination of both. Leadership responsibilities are rotated annually.

Candidates for hiring must pass an aptitude test and go through a special evaluation process. They then go through a rigorous four-to-six-week training period. This training represents the first- or core-level courses in the "pay-for-knowledge" technical skills plan. This system rewards employees with increases in pay for learning specified skills and concepts at designated times.

After completing training, new employees receive a raise at the end of ninety days; if they cannot successfully complete training, they are terminated. Although they have been trained in both technical and leadership skills, the new employees usually are not given leadership responsibilities during the first six months. They are allowed to concentrate on learning technical skills and becoming more comfortable in the "Boeing environment." After 180 days the employees receive another raise.

During the second six months, team members are given a leadership assignment to perform. Working in conjunction with a career planner, team members also begin the process of developing a career plan which identifies the technical courses they will learn during the next six months. The process is repeated as team members move from one step to the next in their pay-for-knowledge plan until they reach what is called "team rate" at step six.

Is this program a success? Boeing reports improved flexibility—"allowing us to move people in order to adjust to changing business conditions"; fewer job classifications than would be expected; a low absenteeism rate (4.1 percent in 1991); a low turnover rate (10 percent); and high overall morale of the employees.

This program also presents some challenges. It is expensive in terms of time, money, and dedication to the objective. Scheduling has presented a "real challenge"; business needs must be matched with training needs, and instructors, trainees, and classroom facilities must be coordinated. Keeping track of present and future training requires a great deal of record keeping. And some employees find working under this system especially stressful.

DISCUSSION QUESTIONS

1. How do self-managed teams differ from other work groups?
2. What primary factors should be considered in forming an effective work team at the Boeing plant?
3. Discuss the motivational effects of a pay-for-knowledge pay system.
4. What information provided in the case indicates that the leadership at Boeing is developing and reinforcing a strong participative culture?

CNN VIDEO CASE

Building a Group Culture

KAY UNGER
Gillian Group

Kay Unger perceives herself as a group member; as a woman, as a designer, as an entrepreneur, as a family member, her life is in many ways defined by the groups of which she feels herself a part. In 1972, she and partner John Levy founded a fashion design and merchandising concern called "St. Gillian," later renamed the Gillian Group. That change reflects a great deal of Unger's view of her work and of her coworkers.

In the first year, St. Gillian's corporate revenues totaled $1.2 million. By 1990, corporate revenues topped $125 million. During a period when recession caused problems throughout the fashion industry, the Gillian Group grew and prospered.

Kay Unger, chief designer, works with teams of designers, drapers, seamstresses, and models to create fashions for the Gillian Group.

During that same time, many small design firms appeared and disappeared, just as hemlines rose and fell. The fashions acceptable to American women, and in particular to American working women, were undergoing tremendous upheaval.

Women had finally made inroads into corporate boardrooms and were unwilling to "dress for success" in pinstripe suits, plain white blouses, and foulard ties any longer. Designs from the haute couture houses of Paris did not suit a working woman's life-style, nor did the extremes they represented.

Enter Kay Unger. "I know what women who work need. I know the comfort level," she says of her clientele, because "I'm one of *her.* I know who *she* is." That knowledge of her market led Unger to create the sort of clothing working women demanded while other designers were scrambling to adapt to the notion that real clothes could not afford to take their cue from haute couture any longer. Unger's designs have made the Gillian Group one of the forty largest women-owned businesses in the United States. Membership in the club of working women was a key to Gillian's success.

Unger sees another difference, too, in the way working women interact with their coworkers:

> They approach business and get the job done in the same way [as men]; it's their approach to people, I think, that's different. . . . They're really great listeners—I think it's a female thing—and they're extremely organized. Perhaps it's from organizing homes or maybe it's something that's been ingrained in women from times past, but there is a sense of organization that's different. And there are no rules.

Operating outside the bounds of strict policies and rules is also, Unger believes, a common characteristic of entrepreneurs. Unlike businesspeople who work in traditional roles, such as Unger's investment-banker father, she feels that entrepreneurs are more flexible in the routes they chart to success. This helps them to avoid the internal politics and rivalry that many ambitious businesspeople on the rise encounter in established organizational environments. In Unger's opinion, the desire for independence, rather than a specific corporate goal, is key to this group: "We each make our own set of rules."

At the Gillian Group, the rules in the design area have been made by Kay Unger. Every two weeks, the designers meet to establish a new "color story"—that is, a block of related or integrated colors that form the core of the new set of clothing designs to be created. After the colors are chosen, the design group breaks into smaller teams centered around designers—Kay Unger herself is the chief designer of the Gillian Group. Those teams are made up of designers, drapers, seamstresses, and models on whom the garments are tried; staff from other areas of the company, such as purchasing and marketing, may also be consulted at this stage. Finally, with creative input from the entire group, specific designs are sketched, and prototypes are created.

Kay Unger's employees work in a creative environment, where they are encouraged to express their creativity and explore their talents. On the other hand, when employees don't work out for the Gillian Group, Unger does not hesitate to fire them. John Levy describes her as "sincere, demanding, and tough"; she demands a great deal from herself, and the people working for her learn to follow her example. Her criteria are clear: Do the best work you can, and give extra time and effort. Most important, be flexible in the face of a business that never slows down. To be a success in Kay Unger's world, employees must agree with her when she says, "I love chaos."

VIDEO CASE QUESTIONS

1. Are design teams at the Gillian Group formal or informal groups? What specific type?
2. Give an example of how groupthink affects sales in the fashion industry. Give an example of how it might negatively affect design at a fashion house such as the Gillian Group.
3. Based on the case, name three mechanisms you believe Kay Unger uses to reinforce the corporate culture at the Gillian Group.
4. Which group would you expect to use more status symbols at Gillian—production, design, or corporate management? Why?

CNN VIDEO EXERCISE

Making Decisions by Committee at the Gillian Group

ACTION GOAL: Learn how to plan a successful committee meeting by role-playing some of the people-oriented behaviors that improve the quality of a group interaction.

Imagine that Kay Unger has decided to invite all members of the Gillian Group to meet in committees to examine several possibilities she is considering for the company. In the first meeting, Ms. Unger wants all employees to discuss frankly the problems that might result from expanding into new types of fashion, including fragrances and accessories. She wants employees to brainstorm about the new equipment and the new personnel that such new products would necessitate. Employees will meet in groups drawn from throughout the organization, so some employees may not know one another well.

Review the information on committees on pages 404–407 and complete the following activities as if you were Kay Unger.

1. Write a brief statement of the goals for the committees and specify the level of authority the committees will have.

____

____

____

____

2. Write a brief agenda for the first meeting of the groups. In a small group, assign the following roles (each group needs each role to be played): designer, textile purchaser, secretary, data-processing clerk, model, publicist, receptionist, and counter. The counter has a special assignment during the meeting: to list each member of the group and to note each time a member of the group shows one of the following types of behavior:
   - rephrasing ideas already expressed
   - bringing a member into active participation
   - stimulating further thought by a member

____

____

____

____

Meetings should last at least fifteen minutes. Follow one of the agendas group members have created. Each person in the group should think of at least one suggestion. At the end of the meeting, discuss how easy or how difficult it was to use the counted behaviors.

PART 4

INTEGRATIVE CASE

The Navajo Arts and Crafts Enterprise: Bringing Together Culture and Business

ROBERT E. KEMPER
Northern Arizona University

The 1990 U.S. Census lists more than 100,000 Native American Indians living on the 25,000 square mile continuous Navajo reservation that covers parts of Arizona, New Mexico, and Utah, and on the three checkerboard-patterned reservations in northern New Mexico. According to tribal custom, the Navajo people are tied together by *matrilineal clans,* extended family groups linked through the mothers. Women remain the official heads of more than a quarter of Navajo households.

The people feel strong ties to their land; more than 80 percent have always lived on the reservation. However, reservation life is hard: Winters are long and bitter, distances are vast, and water is always in short supply. About 50 percent of reservation homes don't have piped-in water; only 25 percent have central heat. At twenty-five years of age or older, two-thirds of Navajos are not high school graduates. More than half live below the U.S. poverty line, and unemployment is very high.

Although all U.S. citizens are subject to federal law, Navajos on the reservations are not subject to state laws. The Navajo nation is administered by an elected president and Navajo Tribal Council, with its capital in Window Rock, Arizona. Traditionally, there has been little need for formal government structures; the culture strictly defines appropriate behaviors. Respect for the harmony of living things with each other and their environment is paramount, and respectful, polite behavior is the norm. A Navajo who is ill can be brought back into harmony through traditional healing procedures, although bodily illness is treated by medical methods as well. In government as in medicine, traditions and the new ways have been integrated—not always with success.

The Navajo Arts and Crafts Enterprise (NACE) and the Window Rock Inn are the only corporations to maintain profitable operation under tribal management. The NACE store in Window Rock displays excellent works of weaving, silverwork, basketry, woodwork, and paintings that are in demand worldwide. NACE's goal is to further the educational, social, and economic development of the people through development and marketing of traditional tribal arts and crafts. It is administered by a board of directors appointed by the tribal council; a general manager is hired by the board. During the late 1970s and early 1980s, the tribal council employed consultants from Arthur Andersen to advise NACE and general manager Raymond Smith about personnel and financial practices, to maximize profitability.

Smith had been a member of the famed "Navajo Code Talkers" of World War II and had served on the tribal council for twenty years prior to taking the NACE job. He was well liked by employees and well respected among the Navajo people. Following Arthur Andersen's evaluation of NACE, Smith and his staff were trained in the use of appropriate personal computer accounting systems.

Personnel management systems were not so simple, however. Arthur Andersen produced an eighty-page personnel manual, covering every item from hiring and firing to the use of nonexistent corporate credit cards and vehicles. The manual was a generic one, not customized to meet NACE's very specific needs. Nonetheless, Smith adhered to the policies for day-to-day operations, and when he found fault with a particular policy—for example, a sick-leave procedure that did not allow for traditional healing ceremonies—he would ignore it. Generally, his slighting of procedure favored his employees.

However, in the summer of 1986, in accordance with NACE bylaws, Smith refused to purchase some handicrafts from a board member. The board retaliated: rather than issue Smith's new employment contract scheduled to begin in October, his old contract was extended for a period of ninety days only. During that ninety-day period, Smith was to use his best efforts to achieve the following objectives: (1) to prepare revised employee personnel policies, focusing specifically on leave policies; (2) to prepare written employee evaluations, discuss them with the employees, and submit them to the board; and (3) to develop a written plan for NACE operations, including memoranda setting forth different types of decisions confronting NACE and recommendations for the level at which approval should be made.

NACE's goal is to further the educational, social, and economic development of the people...

Smith met with a local attorney to discuss NACE's difficulties and the board's action. They agreed that the problems concerning personnel procedures and evaluations appeared to stem from the generic Arthur Andersen manual. NACE needed clearly defined policies that could be applied universally, not ignored, but that would be appropriate and fair based on Navajo cultural expectations. The sick-leave policy must incorporate a time allowance for healing ceremonies, for example; appraisal and penalization policies must be modified to work in light of the Navajo's traditional aversion toward confrontation as disrespectful and impolite. In short, the generic personnel policies would only work within the culture for which they were designed. NACE, and all tribal-managed businesses, would need Navajo personnel policies in order to succeed.

DISCUSSION QUESTIONS

1. A major goal of tribally administered businesses on the Navajo reservations is employment of Navajos. Given this goal, do you think a store like NACE's run by the tribe should be run differently than an arts-and-crafts store somewhere else, such as Phoenix?
2. Do you think Raymond Smith acted appropriately in suspending written sick-leave policies to allow those employees who desire it time for traditional healing ceremonies (generally a few days)? Was this the act of a leader or a manager? How might you have handled the situation differently?
3. It is considered rude, a sort of imposition, among the Navajo to touch a stranger. Imagine you are an Arthur Andersen consultant visiting NACE for the first time, and you immediately shake hands with each employee you meet. What impact do you think this might have on your work there?
4. Consider the following motivating strategies: promotion from within, salary bonuses, flextime options, and inclusion in an employee advisory group. Which do you think would work well for NACE employees? Which would not?

CONTROLLING

PART

5

This section introduces controlling, the fourth and last major management function. The previous three sections showed that managers must be able to plan, organize, and influence organizational variables. This section will explain that managers must also control these variables in order for their organizations to achieve long-term success. The section will discuss the principles of controlling, the fundamentals of production management and control, and how information relates to the control function.

The discussion of the principles of controlling will open with a definition of *control function.* It will then present the three main steps in controlling and discuss the three main types of control. In addition, it will address the job of a controller and the elements necessary for managers to successfully perform the control function.

Production is an area that requires careful control. Therefore, the discussion of the fundamentals of production management and control will emphasize operations management, productivity, and control tools that relate directly to production control. These tools include management by exception, breakeven analysis, materials requirements planning, and quality control. Quality is discussed from the viewpoints of enhancing productivity and maintaining product excellence.

The section explains how information relates to the control function and how managers can use computers for generating and analyzing information using two information-related systems: the management information system (MIS) and the management decision support system (MDSS).

As you study this new material, think about how the other functions of management relate to the process of controlling. Once you understand this last major function, you should have a thorough knowledge of how controlling must interact with planning, organizing, and influencing if organizations are to achieve long-term success.

CHAPTER

17

PRINCIPLES OF CONTROLLING

STUDENT LEARNING OBJECTIVES

From studying this chapter, I will attempt to acquire:

1. A definition of *control.*
2. A thorough understanding of the controlling subsystem.
3. An appreciation for various kinds of control and for how each kind can be used advantageously by managers.
4. Insights on the relationship between power and control.
5. Knowledge of the various potential barriers that must be overcome for successful control.
6. An understanding of steps that can be taken to increase the quality of a controlling subsystem.

CHAPTER OUTLINE

INTRODUCTORY CASE
A Lack of Control at *USA Today*

FUNDAMENTALS OF CONTROLLING

Defining Control
Defining Controlling

GLOBAL HIGHLIGHT
Euro Disneyland

QUALITY HIGHLIGHT
Modern of Marshfield Inc.

Types of Control

ETHICS HIGHLIGHT
Propane Appliances

DIVERSITY HIGHLIGHT
Cosmetics Industry

THE CONTROLLER AND CONTROL

The Job of the Controller
How Much Control Is Needed?

POWER AND CONTROL

A Definition of Power
Total Power of a Manager
Steps for Increasing Total Power

PERFORMING THE CONTROL FUNCTION

Potential Barriers to Successful Controlling
Making Controlling Successful

CASE STUDY
Measuring Performance at Texaco

VIDEO CASE
In the Driver's Seat: Frank Olson, Hertz

VIDEO EXERCISE
Controlling Costs at Hertz

INTRODUCTORY CASE

A Lack of Control at USA Today

Read a copy of *USA Today* lately? A lot has changed since the paper first hit the newsstands in 1982. In those days, its video-age "fast format" and relentless optimism made it the butt of industry jokes. But under editor Peter Prichard, stories have gotten longer and the tone less reflexively upbeat—and *USA Today* has even produced highly regarded series on such unpalatable subjects as the S&L crisis and the wobbly insurance industry. Across the country, its authoritative sports coverage and nanosecond response to breaking events and lifestyle trends have prompted many editors to rethink their own papers' priorities. Circulation continues to grow, too, reaching 1.81 million in 1991, second to the *Wall Street Journal*. . . .

USA Today is still dogged by the perception among would-be advertisers and the media elite that it remains News Lite, a triumph of marketing over substance.

Yet, for all its improvements and impact on American journalism, the colorful McPaper is still in the red, largely because many advertisers haven't warmed to it. Analysts estimate that *USA Today* has lost a staggering $800 million since 1982; the 1991 figure is reportedly about $20 million. Although *USA Today* publisher Thomas Curley says "We have to do better—and will," some industry experts say the paper's huge production costs and inability to compete for local advertising could doom the paper to, at best, marginal profitability for years. "If you can't do it in a decade, you're clearly not going to make money from ads," contends Robert M. Johnson, the publisher of *Newsday*. And while the other major journalistic innovation of the 1980s, Ted Turner's CNN, has won respect, *USA Today* is still dogged by the perception among many would-be advertisers and the media elite that it remains News Lite, a triumph of marketing over substance. . . .

Is *USA Today* destined to remain a money loser? Smith Barney analyst John Reidy points to an obvious solution: raising the price from fifty to seventy-five cents, which would gross an additional $65 million a year. Curley rejects that idea for now, saying circulation could drop sharply. He says the *Wall Street Journal*'s newsstand sales dipped after it hiked its price to seventy-five cents—and *USA Today* is much more dependent on single-copy sales. Curley insists the paper can be profitable by "selling one-half page more advertising a day." He says that will happen when the recession eases, and he's planning aggressive strategies—like targeting Japanese companies, which so far have viewed *USA Today* as unprestigious, and increasing regional-ad sales, which have grown from zero to $15 million in two years. Even if the paper doesn't break through, virtually nobody expects Gannett to pull the plug on *USA Today* any time soon. "The paper has made Gannett a company to be reckoned with," says Lou Heldman, chairman of the American Society of Newspaper Editors' Future of Newspapers Committee. But at $800 million and counting, the price for respectability remains expensive indeed.

For all of its improvements and impact on American journalism, USA Today *is in the red largely because many advertisers have not warmed to it.*

From Joshua Hammer, "The McPaper Route," *Newsweek* (April 27, 1992), 58–59. © 1992 Newsweek, Inc. All rights reserved. Reprinted by permission.

WHAT'S AHEAD The introductory case implies that huge production costs are a factor at *USA Today* that could doom the paper to marginal profitability at best for years to come. The management function called "control" can help managers such as those at *USA Today* to reduce the negative impact of high production costs. The material in this chapter explains why *USA Today*'s high production costs would be categorized as a control issue at the company, and elaborates on the control function as a whole. Major topics in this chapter are (1) fundamentals of controlling, (2) the controller and control, (3) power and control, and (4) performing the control function.

FUNDAMENTALS OF CONTROLLING

As the scale and complexity of modern work organizations grow, the problem of control in organizations gains significance.[1] Prospective managers need a working knowledge of the essentials of the controlling function.[2] To this end, the following sections provide a definition of control, a definition of controlling, and a discussion of the various types of control that can be used in organizations.

Defining Control

Control is making something happen the way it was planned to happen.

Stated simply, **control** is making something happen the way it was planned to happen.[3] As implied in this definition, planning and control are virtually inseparable.[4] In fact, the two have been called the Siamese twins of management. According to Robert L. Dewelt:

> The importance of the planning process is quite obvious. Unless we have a soundly charted course of action, we will never quite know what actions are necessary to meet our objectives. We need a map to identify the timing and scope of all intended actions. This map is provided through the planning process.
>
> But simply making a map is not enough. If we don't follow it or if we make a wrong turn along the way, chances are we will never achieve the desired results. A plan is only as good as our ability to make it happen. We must develop methods of measurement and control to signal when deviations from the plan are occurring so that corrective action can be taken.[5]

Murphy's Law is a lighthearted observation about organizations indicating that anything that can go wrong will go wrong.

Overall, managers should continually control, check to make sure that organizational activities and processes are going as planned. Murphy's Law is a lighthearted concept that makes the serious point that managers should continually control. According to **Murphy's Law,** anything that can go wrong will go wrong.[6] This law implies that managers must continually be alert for possible problems within the management system. Even if a management system is operating well one day, the system might erode somewhat over time. Managers must constantly seek feedback that indicates the level at which a system is performing and make corrective changes in the system when they become necessary.

Defining Controlling

Controlling is the process the manager goes through to control.

Controlling is the process managers go through to control. According to Robert Mockler, controlling is

> a systematic effort by business management to compare performance to predetermined standards, plans, or objectives to determine whether performance is in line with these standards and presumably to take any remedial action required to see that human and other corporate resources are being used in the most effective and efficient way possible in achieving corporate objectives.[7]

For example, production workers generally have production goals they must achieve per day and week. At the end of each working day, the number of units produced by each worker is recorded so weekly production levels can be determined. If the weekly totals are significantly below the weekly goals, the supervisor must take action to ensure that actual production levels are equivalent to planned production levels. If production goals are met, the supervisor probably should allow work to continue as it has in the past.

The following sections discuss the controlling subsystem and provide more details about the control process itself.

BACK TO THE CASE The above information supports the notion that *USA Today*'s cost problem actually should be categorized as a control problem. In essence, control is making things happen at *USA Today* in a way they were planned to happen. In this case, because profit levels are obviously not reaching planned levels, management should take action aimed at reducing production costs. This action would help to ensure that profits achieved in the future are more in line with planned profit levels. In essence, *USA Today*'s control must be closely linked to its planning activities.

Controlling at *USA Today* is the steps that management takes in order to control. Ideally, this process at *USA Today*, as within any company, would include determining the plans, standards, and objectives for publishing the newspaper; then action can be taken to eliminate organizational characteristics that caused deviation from these factors.

The Controlling Subsystem

As with the planning, organizing, and influencing functions described in earlier chapters, controlling can be viewed as a subsystem that is part of the overall management system. The purpose of the controlling subsystem is to help managers enhance the success of the overall management system through effective controlling. Figure 17.1 shows the specific ingredients of the controlling subsystem.

The Controlling Process

As the process (controlling process) segment of Figure 17.2 on page 436 implies, the three main steps of the controlling process are (1) measuring performance, (2) comparing measured performance to standards, and (3) taking corrective action.

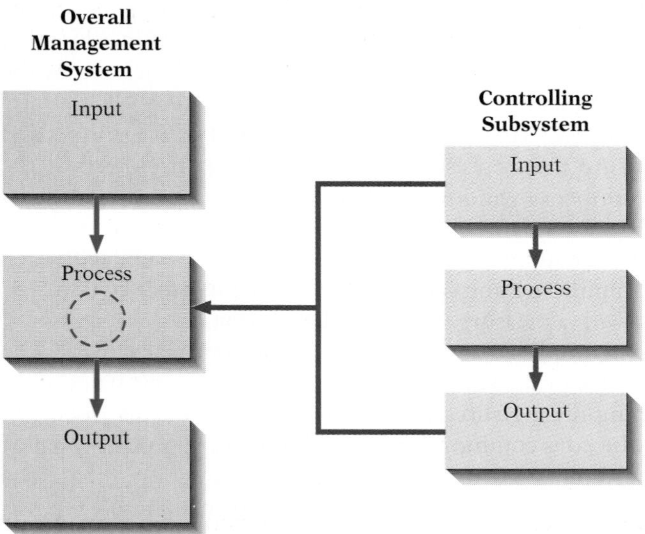

FIGURE 17.1 Relationship between overall management system and controlling subsystem

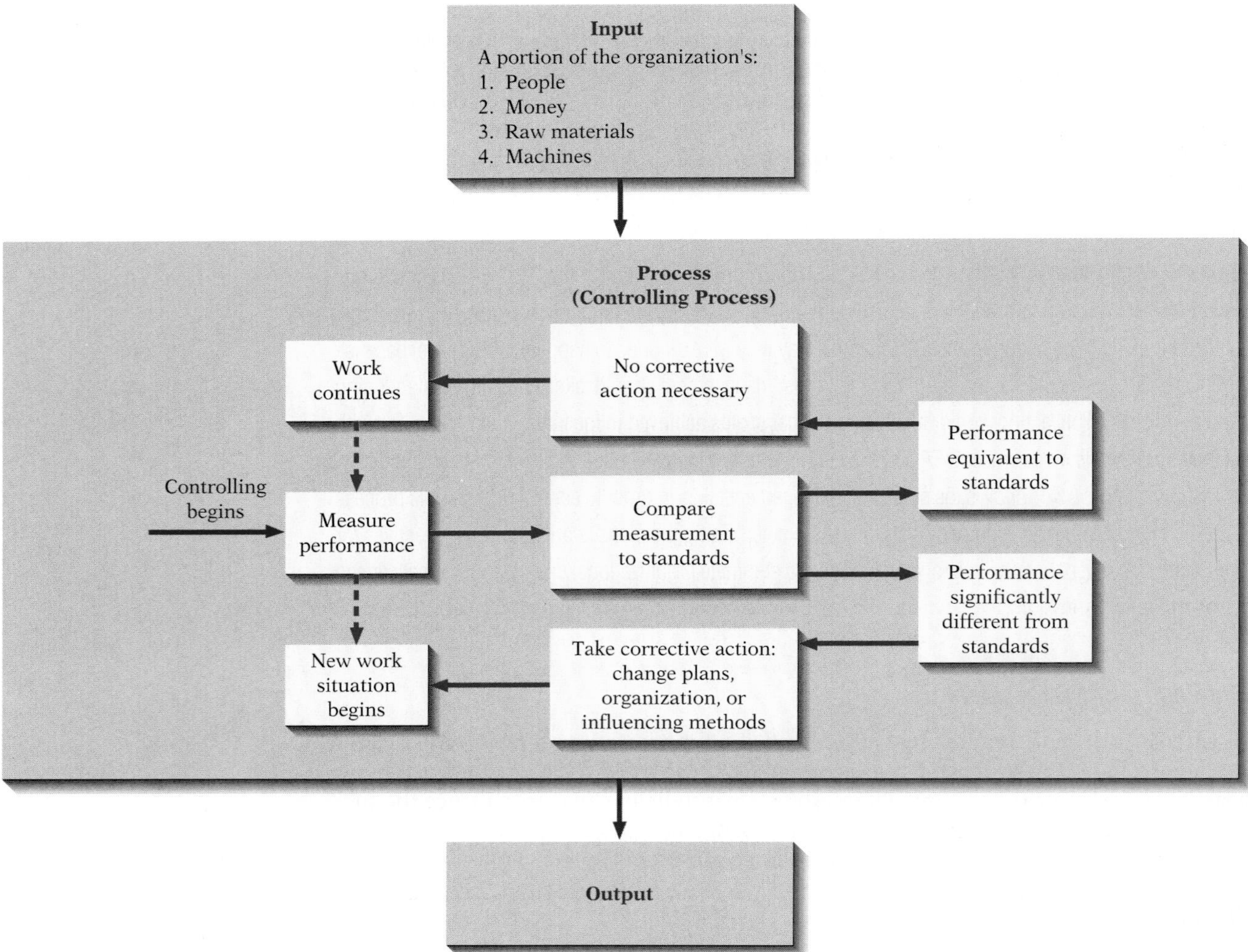

FIGURE 17.2 The controlling subsystem

Measuring Performance. Before managers can determine what must be done to make an organization more effective and efficient, they must measure current organizational performance.[8] And before such a measurement can be taken, some unit of measure that gauges performance must be established and the quantity of this unit generated by the item whose performance is being measured must be observed.

For example, a manager who wants to measure the performance of five janitors first has to establish units of measure that represent janitorial performance, such as the number of floors swept, the number of windows washed, or the number of light bulbs changed. After designating these units of measures for janitorial performance, the manager then has to determine the number of each of these units associated with each janitor. This process of determining the units of measure and the number of units per janitor furnishes the manager with a measure of janitorial performance.

Managers also must keep in mind that a wide range of organizational activities can be measured as part of the control process. For example, the amounts and types of inventory kept on hand are commonly measured to control inventory, and the quality of goods and services being produced is commonly measured to control product quality. Performance measurements also can relate to various effects of production, such as the degree to which a particular manufacturing process pollutes the atmosphere.

As one might suspect, the degree of difficulty in measuring various types of organizational performance is determined primarily by the activity being measured. For example, the degree of difficulty in measuring the performance of a highway maintenance worker would differ greatly from the degree of difficulty in measuring the performance of a student enrolled in a college-level management course.

GLOBAL HIGHLIGHT
Controlling Finances at Euro Disneyland

One area in which performance measurements are commonly taken involves the financial affairs of an organization. Certified public accountant Judson Green left the Arthur Young accounting firm to join Walt Disney World in Florida. Today, Green is a senior vice president at Disney and working at Euro Disneyland outside Paris. The French government has extended unprecedented hospitality to Euro Disneyland by offering favorable land deals, tax breaks, and loans with advantageous payback provisions. In addition, decisions that affect the financial affairs of Euro Disney are commonly made by Green in conjunction with people in cities like London and Brussels. In the near future, Disney's focus will shift to developing hotels outside the theme park as well as planning and initiating the building of a second theme park in Europe. A major responsibility of Green's is to monitor or measure the effects of various financial decisions being made for Euro Disney. From such measurements he will encourage company actions that meet or exceed profitability standards while discouraging such actions that do not meet or are below the standards. In essence, Green is responsible for controlling financial activities at Euro Disney. ▶

Now that Euro Disneyland is open, the strategic focus is shifting to the development of hotels nearby and to initiating plans for a second theme park in Europe.

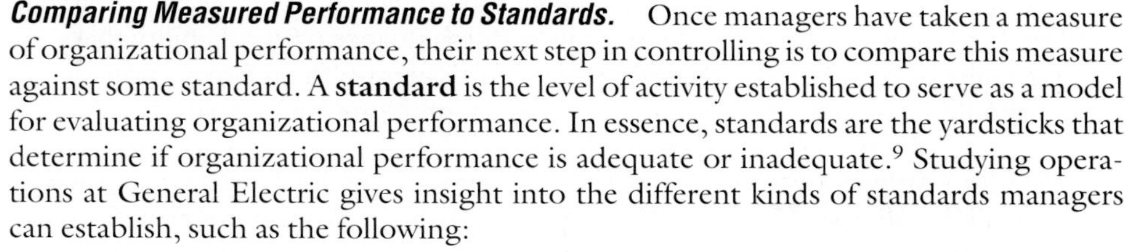

Comparing Measured Performance to Standards. Once managers have taken a measure of organizational performance, their next step in controlling is to compare this measure against some standard. A **standard** is the level of activity established to serve as a model for evaluating organizational performance. In essence, standards are the yardsticks that determine if organizational performance is adequate or inadequate.[9] Studying operations at General Electric gives insight into the different kinds of standards managers can establish, such as the following:

A **standard** is the level of activity established to serve as a model for evaluating organizational performance.

1. *Profitability standards.* In general, these standards indicate how much money General Electric would like to make as profit over a given time period—that is, its return on investment. More and more, General Electric is using computerized preventative maintenance on its equipment to help maintain profitability standards. Such maintenance programs at General Electric help to reduce labor costs and equipment downtime and thereby help to raise company profits.[10]

2. *Market position standards.* These standards indicate the share of total sales in a particular market that General Electric would like to have relative to its competitors. As an indication of market position standards at General Electric, John F. Welch, Jr., company chairman, announced in 1988 that any product his company offers must have the highest or second highest market share when compared against all products offered by competitors.[11]

3. *Productivity standards.* How much various segments of the organization should produce is the focus of these standards. Management at General Electric has found that one of the most successful methods of convincing organization members to be committed to increasing company productivity is simply to treat them with dignity and make them feel they are part of the General Electric team.[12]

4. *Product leadership standards.* General Electric would like to assume one of the lead positions in its field in product innovation. Product leadership standards indicate what must be done to attain such a position. Reflecting this interest in innovation, General Electric has been a pioneer in developing synthetic diamonds for industrial use. In fact, General Electric is considered by most a leader in this area,

having recently found a method for making synthetic diamonds at a purity of 99.9 percent. In all probability, such diamonds will eventually be used as a component of super-high-speed computers.[13]

5. *Personnel development standards.* Standards in this area indicate the type of training programs to which General Electric personnel should be exposed to develop appropriately. General Electric's commitment to sophisticated training technology is an indication of the seriousness with which the company pursues personnel development standards. Company training sessions are commonly supported by sophisticated technology like large-screen projection systems, computer-generated visual aids, combined video and computer presentations, and laser videos.[14]
6. *Employee attitudes standards.* These standards indicate the types of attitudes that General Electric management should strive to develop in its employees. Building attitudes in employees toward enhancing product quality reflects a modern employee attitude standard that General Electric and many other companies are presently striving to achieve.[15]
7. *Social responsibility standards.* General Electric recognizes its responsibility to make a contribution to society. Standards in this area outline the level and types of contributions that should be made. One recent activity at General Electric that reflects social responsibility standards is a renovation of San Diego's Vincent de Paul Joan Kroc center for the homeless. Work teams made up of General Electric employees painted, cleaned, and remodeled a building to create a better facility for a number of San Diego's disadvantaged citizens.[16]
8. *Standards reflecting relative balance between short- and long-range goals.* General Electric recognizes that short-range goals exist to enhance the probability that long-range goals will be attained. These standards express the relative emphasis that should be placed on attaining various short- and long-range goals.[17]

American Airlines has set two very specific standards for appropriate performance of airport ticket offices: (1) at least 95 percent of the flight arrival times posted should be accurate in that actual arrival times do not deviate more than fifteen minutes from posted times, and (2) at least 85 percent of the customers coming to the airport ticket counter do not wait more than five minutes to be serviced. As a general guideline, successful managers pinpoint all important areas of organizational performance and establish corresponding standards in each area.[18]

BACK TO THE CASE

In theory, *USA Today*'s management should view controlling activities within the company as a subsystem of the organization's overall management system. For management to achieve organizational control, *USA Today*'s controlling subsystem requires a portion of the people, money, raw materials, and machines available within the company.

The process portion of the controlling subsystem at *USA Today* involves management taking three steps: (1) measuring the performance levels of various productive units, (2) comparing these performance levels to predetermined performance standards for these units, and (3) taking any corrective action necessary to make sure that planned performance levels are consistent with actual performance levels.

Based upon information in the introductory case, one area in which management at *USA Today* should develop standards is desired profitability level of the newspaper. According to the case, there seem to be two main reasons why the newspaper is presently not very profitable: huge production costs and an inability to compete for local advertising. Because the newspaper is not earning a desirable level of profits, management should control by taking steps to lower production costs and compete for more local advertising revenue.

Taking Corrective Action. Once managers have measured actual performance and compared this performance with established performance standards, they should take corrective action if necessary. **Corrective action** is managerial activity aimed at bringing organizational performance up to the level of performance standards. In other words, corrective action focuses on correcting the mistakes in the organization that are hindering organizational performance. Before taking any corrective action, however, managers should make sure that the standards being used were properly established and that the measurements of organizational performance are valid and reliable.

Corrective action is managerial activity aimed at bringing organizational performance up to the level of performance standards.

At first glance, it seems fairly simple to state that managers should take corrective action to eliminate **problems**—factors within organizations that are barriers to organizational goal attainment. In practice, however, it may be difficult to pinpoint the problem causing some undesirable organizational effect. For example, a performance measurement may indicate that a certain worker is not adequately passing on critical information to fellow workers. If the manager is satisfied that the communication standards are appropriate and that the performance measurement information is valid and reliable, corrective action should be taken to eliminate the problem causing this substandard performance.

Problems are factors within organizations that are barriers to organizational goal attainment.

However, what exactly is the problem causing substandard communication? Is it that the individual is not communicating because he or she doesn't want to communicate? Or is the person not communicating because the job makes communication difficult? Does the person have the training needed to enable him or her to communicate in an appropriate manner? The manager must determine whether the individual's lack of communication is a problem in itself or a **symptom**—a sign that a problem exists.[19] For example, the individual's lack of communication could be a symptom of inappropriate job design or a cumbersome organizational structure.

A **symptom** is a sign that a problem exists.

Once an organizational problem has been identified, necessary corrective action can focus on one or more of the three primary management functions of planning, organizing, and influencing. Correspondingly, corrective action can include such activities as modifying past plans to make them more suitable for future organizational endeavors, making an existing organizational structure more suitable for existing plans and objectives, or restructuring an incentive program to make sure that high producers are rewarded more than low producers. In addition, because planning, organizing, and influencing are closely related, there is a good chance that corrective action taken in one area will necessitate some corresponding change in one or both of the other two areas.

A study by Y.K. Shetty surveyed 171 managers from *Fortune's* list of the thirteen hundred largest U.S. industrial and nonindustrial companies.[20] One purpose of the study was to investigate the types of corrective action programs managers use and the frequency with which they are used. Table 17.1 presents the results of this study. The

TABLE 17.1 Corrective action programs commonly used by managers and frequency of use

Corrective Action Program	*Frequency of Program Use*
Cost reduction	2.3
Employee participation	3.1
Productivity incentives	3.3
Goal setting with productivity focus	3.5
Increased automation	3.8
Quality improvement	3.9
Increased employee training	4.7
Better labor-management relations	4.9
Increased research and development	5.3

Note: The lower the frequency, the higher the relative use of the program.

corrective action programs listed in the table are only a sample of such programs, not an exhaustive list.

QUALITY HIGHLIGHT
Modern of Marshfield Inc. Capitalizes on CATS

The work of a quality improvement team can monitor organizational performance in many different areas and can implement corrective action aimed at solving identified organizational problems.

Managers commonly face situations in which they must take corrective actions to improve organizational performance. Although sometimes managers may need to take the corrective action themselves, in some situations, it may be more advantageous or simply necessary to have other organization members take the action, either individually or as a group. For example, William J. Mork, president of Modern of Marshfield Inc. (a custom sofa-sleeper manufacturer in Marshfield, Wisconsin), successfully takes corrective action through groups of organization members. Mork credits 80 to 90 percent of the company's $6 million profits to the impact made by its twelve Corrective Action Teams (CATS). In essence, CATS are small control groups within the company. The groups monitor organizational performance in many different areas and implement corrective action aimed at solving identified organizational problems. A small group of organization members called a Quality Improvement Team oversees and coordinates the efforts of CATS. Mork believes that the success of CATS has had many beneficial effects on the organization, for example: (1) the company has been financially able to pay each employee a bonus, (2) the company has been able to make payments out of profits to debtors and thereby significantly reduce company debt, and (3) company profits have resulted in more cash on hand that the company could use to finance everyday operations. Over all, because Mork believes that having groups take corrective action within his company has contributed significantly to recent organizational success, he will probably continue with his CATS program in the future. ▶

BACK TO THE CASE In determining that corrective action is necessary at *USA Today,* management must be certain that the action is aimed at organizational problems rather than at symptoms of problems. For example, if production costs are too high because workers are not trained well enough to operate their equipment properly, the symptom of high production costs will disappear as a result of the corrective action: improving training of production workers.

Inevitably, corrective action at *USA Today* such as improved worker training must focus on further planning, organizing, or influencing efforts. As examples, how must *USA Today*'s plans change if production workers are being more carefully trained? Will the company still need the same number of production supervisors if workers become more competent as a result of improved training?

Types of Control

There are three types of management control: (1) precontrol, (2) concurrent control, and (3) feedback control. The type is determined primarily by the time period in which the control is emphasized in relation to the work being performed.

Precontrol

Precontrol is control that takes place before some unit of work is actually performed.

Control that takes place before work is performed is called **precontrol,** or feed-forward control.[21] In this regard, management creates policies, procedures, and rules aimed at eliminating behavior that will cause undesirable work results. For example, the manager of a small record shop may find that a major factor in developing return customers is having salespeople discuss various records with customers. This manager might use precontrol by establishing a rule that salespeople cannot talk to one another while a customer is in the store. This rule is a precontrol because it is aimed at eliminating anticipated problems with salespeople before the salespeople are faced with a customer. Precontrol focuses on eliminating predicted problems.

Concurrent Control

Control that takes place as work is being performed is called **concurrent control.** It relates not only to human performance but also to such areas as equipment performance and department appearance. For example, most supermarkets have rigid rules about the amount of stock that should be placed on the selling floor. In general, these stores want to display generous amounts of all products on the shelves, with no empty spaces. A concurrent control aimed at ensuring that shelves are stocked as planned could be a stock manager's making periodic visual checks throughout a work period to evaluate the status of the sales shelves and, correspondingly, the performance of the stock crew.[22]

Concurrent control is control that takes place as some unit of work is being performed.

Feedback Control

Control that concentrates on past organizational performance is called **feedback control.** Managers exercising this type of control are attempting to take corrective action within the organization by looking at organizational history over a specified time period. This history may concentrate on only one factor, such as inventory levels, or on the relationships among many factors, such as net income before taxes, sales volume, and marketing costs.

Feedback control is control that takes place after some unit of work has been performed.

Figure 17.3 is an example of a report, developed for an oil company, that can serve as the basis for feedback control. This particular report contains graphs that show various trends over a number of years as well as handwritten notes that highlight major trends. Management would use this report to compare actual organizational performance with planned organizational performance and then to take whatever corrective action is necessary to bring together actual and planned performance. Of course, the structures of such reports vary from organization to organization, depending on the various types and forms of information needed to present an overview of specific organizational activities.

ETHICS HIGHLIGHT
Feedback Control for Product Safety in Propane Appliances

Feedback control is a technique that managers can use to ensure that they are carrying out their ethical responsibility to provide consumers with products that are indeed safe to use. Information generated through feedback control regarding the safe use of propane appliances, for example, can give managers insights into how to make their products safer to use.

Propane appliance accidents are not uncommon. According to the Consumer Product Safety Commission, more than 400 home fires each year are caused by gas grills alone. Nearly every propane fire or explosion is prefaced by an uncontrolled and accidental release of propane gas. The question is whether something can be done to control inadvertent propane leakage. In general, analysis suggests that propane appliance parts are not manufactured to guard against the flow of excess gas while consumers are attempting to light these appliances. Based on this information, propane appliance manufacturers can take specific steps to improve product safety, including researching methods of controlling propane flow during the lighting of such appliances. Management must keep in mind that not only is the company responsible to society to design and manufacture products that are safe, but also safer products, if marketed appropriately, could result in increased sales. ▶

Management for companies manufacturing gas grills must keep in mind that not only are they responsible to society to engineer and manufacture products that are safe, but also that safer products could result in increased sales.

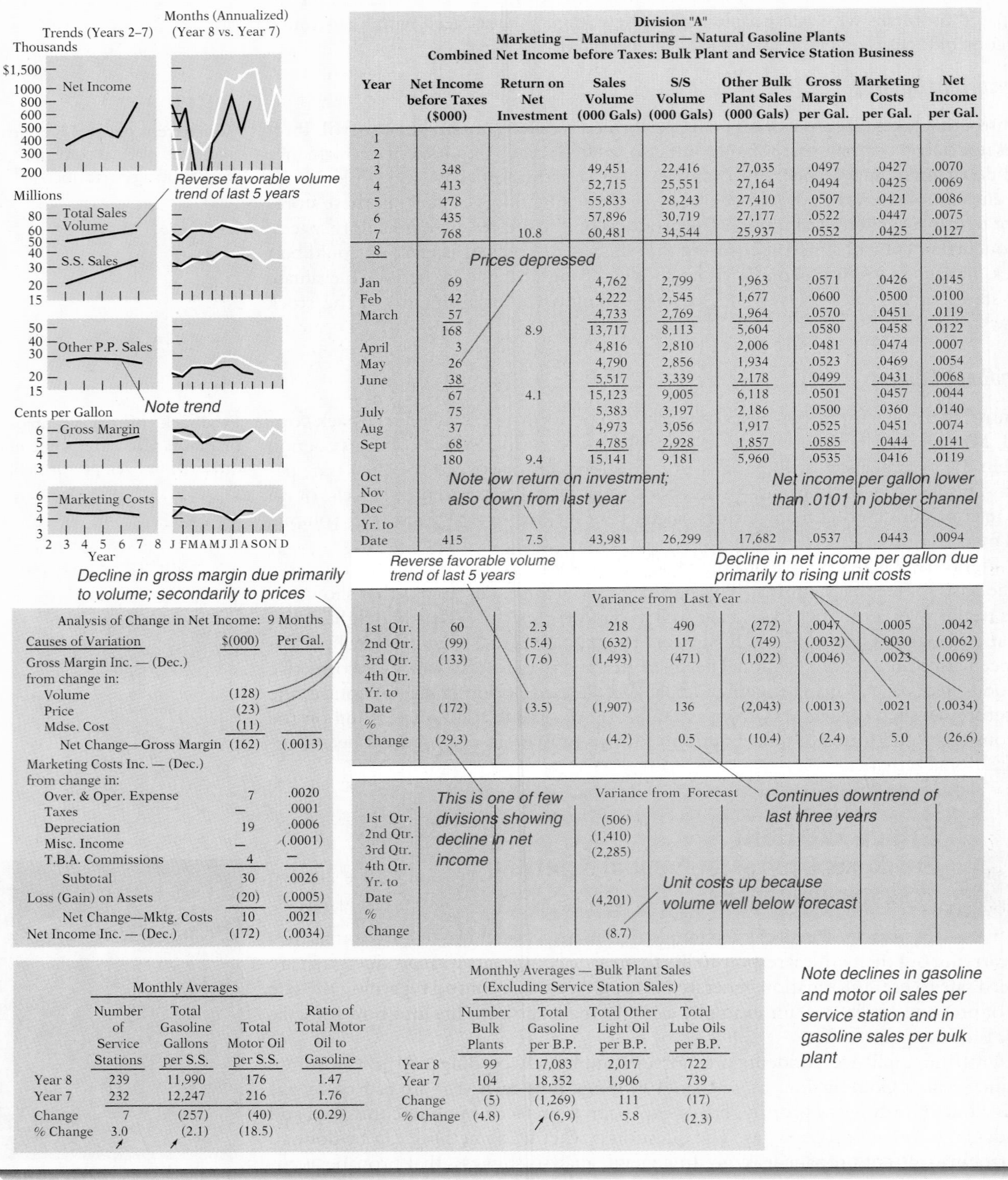

Division "A"
Marketing — Manufacturing — Natural Gasoline Plants
Combined Net Income before Taxes: Bulk Plant and Service Station Business

Year	Net Income before Taxes ($000)	Return on Net Investment	Sales Volume (000 Gals)	S/S Volume (000 Gals)	Other Bulk Plant Sales (000 Gals)	Gross Margin per Gal.	Marketing Costs per Gal.	Net Income per Gal.
1								
2								
3	348		49,451	22,416	27,035	.0497	.0427	.0070
4	413		52,715	25,551	27,164	.0494	.0425	.0069
5	478		55,833	28,243	27,410	.0507	.0421	.0086
6	435		57,896	30,719	27,177	.0522	.0447	.0075
7	768	10.8	60,481	34,544	25,937	.0552	.0425	.0127
8								
Jan	69		4,762	2,799	1,963	.0571	.0426	.0145
Feb	42		4,222	2,545	1,677	.0600	.0500	.0100
March	57		4,733	2,769	1,964	.0570	.0451	.0119
	168	8.9	13,717	8,113	5,604	.0580	.0458	.0122
April	3		4,816	2,810	2,006	.0481	.0474	.0007
May	26		4,790	2,856	1,934	.0523	.0469	.0054
June	38		5,517	3,339	2,178	.0499	.0431	.0068
	67	4.1	15,123	9,005	6,118	.0501	.0457	.0044
July	75		5,383	3,197	2,186	.0500	.0360	.0140
Aug	37		4,973	3,056	1,917	.0525	.0451	.0074
Sept	68		4,785	2,928	1,857	.0585	.0444	.0141
	180	9.4	15,141	9,181	5,960	.0535	.0416	.0119
Oct								
Nov								
Dec								
Yr. to Date	415	7.5	43,981	26,299	17,682	.0537	.0443	.0094

Variance from Last Year

1st Qtr.	60	2.3	218	490	(272)	.0047	.0005	.0042
2nd Qtr.	(99)	(5.4)	(632)	117	(749)	(.0032)	.0030	(.0062)
3rd Qtr.	(133)	(7.6)	(1,493)	(471)	(1,022)	(.0046)	.0023	(.0069)
4th Qtr.								
Yr. to Date	(172)	(3.5)	(1,907)	136	(2,043)	(.0013)	.0021	(.0034)
% Change	(29.3)		(4.2)	0.5	(10.4)	(2.4)	5.0	(26.6)

Variance from Forecast

1st Qtr.			(506)					
2nd Qtr.			(1,410)					
3rd Qtr.			(2,285)					
4th Qtr.								
Yr. to Date			(4,201)					
% Change			(8.7)					

Analysis of Change in Net Income: 9 Months

Causes of Variation	$(000)	Per Gal.
Gross Margin Inc. — (Dec.) from change in:		
Volume	(128)	
Price	(23)	
Mdse. Cost	(11)	
Net Change—Gross Margin	(162)	(.0013)
Marketing Costs Inc. — (Dec.) from change in:		
Over. & Oper. Expense	7	.0020
Taxes	–	.0001
Depreciation	19	.0006
Misc. Income	–	(.0001)
T.B.A. Commissions	4	–
Subtotal	30	.0026
Loss (Gain) on Assets	(20)	(.0005)
Net Change—Mktg. Costs	10	.0021
Net Income Inc. — (Dec.)	(172)	(.0034)

Monthly Averages

	Number of Service Stations	Total Gasoline Gallons per S.S.	Total Motor Oil per S.S.	Ratio of Total Motor Oil to Gasoline
Year 8	239	11,990	176	1.47
Year 7	232	12,247	216	1.76
Change	7	(257)	(40)	(0.29)
% Change	3.0	(2.1)	(18.5)	

Monthly Averages — Bulk Plant Sales (Excluding Service Station Sales)

	Number Bulk Plants	Total Gasoline per B.P.	Total Other Light Oil per B.P.	Total Lube Oils per B.P.
Year 8	99	17,083	2,017	722
Year 7	104	18,352	1,906	739
Change	(5)	(1,269)	111	(17)
% Change	(4.8)	(6.9)	5.8	(2.3)

FIGURE 17.3 Example of a report that can serve as the basis for feedback control
(Copyright © 1957 by the President and Fellows of Harvard College: all rights reserved.)

DIVERSITY HIGHLIGHT
Feedback Control Shows Cosmetics Industry Developing New Products for Diverse Population Segments

For years, the cosmetics industry has operated on the assumption that cosmetics sales are not influenced by recessions. As a result, companies like Maybelline Company and Fashion Fair have historically developed company plans with little regard to the United States economy.

Through feedback control, however, cosmetics companies are starting to conclude that economic downturns indeed can influence cosmetics sales. A focus on most recent operating periods in the industry indicates that the $4-billion-a-year cosmetics market has gone soft. Further, industry analysts conclude that the latest recession is the main reason.

Feedback control includes taking corrective action to try to reignite cosmetics sales. The cosmetics industry has finally recognized the needs of a previously underserved diverse population—African American, Asian, Hispanic, and Native American women—that has not been able to wear mainstream makeup lines, the colors and formulations of which were developed specifically for white skin. New products developed specially for such ethnic customers are expected to give the previously "recession-proof" business a boost. Cosmetics industry consultant Allan Mottus estimates that makeup for women of color accounts for approximately 10 percent of the market. Overall, makeup companies are addressing cultural diversity by either introducing separate, new brand lines aimed specifically at ethnic customers, or expanding present mainstream product lines to include wider shade ranges. ▶

Based on information received through feedback control, the cosmetics industry has developed new products for a previously underserved diverse population—African American, Asian, Hispanic, and Native American women.

In controlling at *USA Today*, management should use an appropriate combination of precontrol, concurrent control, and feedback control. Precontrol would emphasize the elimination of the factors at *USA Today* that could cause poor annual profitability of the newspaper before the year actually begins. Through concurrent control, management would be able to assess the profitability of *USA Today* during a particular operating period. Lastly, feedback control at *USA Today* would enable management to control at the end of some operating period. With feedback control, management would improve future performance by analyzing a segment of history of *USA Today*.

Some use of each of these types of control could increase the probability of *USA Today* eliminating profitability problems before they become too overwhelming. *USA Today* management must not make the commonly made mistake of emphasizing feedback control to the exclusion of concurrent control and precontrol.

THE CONTROLLER AND CONTROL

Organization charts developed for medium- and large-sized companies typically contain a position called controller. The sections that follow explain more about controllers and their relationship to the control function by discussing the job of the controller and how much control is needed within an organization.

The **controller** is the staff individual whose basic responsibility is assisting line managers with the controlling function by gathering appropriate information and generating necessary reports that reflect this information.

The Job of the Controller

The **controller** (also sometimes called the comptroller) is usually a staff person who gathers information that helps managers control. From the preceding discussion, it is clear that managers have the responsibility of comparing planned and actual performance and of taking corrective action when necessary. In smaller organizations, managers may be completely responsible for gathering information about various aspects of the organization and developing necessary reports based on this information. In medium- or large-sized companies, however, the controller handles much of this work. The controller's basic responsibility is assisting line managers with the controlling function by gathering appropriate information and generating reports that reflect this information.[23] The controller usually works with information about the following financial dimensions of the organization: (1) profits, (2) revenues, (3) costs, (4) investments, and (5) discretionary expenses.[24]

The sample job description of a controller in Table 17.2 shows that the controller is responsible for generating information on which a manager can base the exercising of control. Because the controller generally is not directly responsible for taking corrective action within the organization but instead advises a manager of what corrective action should be taken, the controller position is primarily a staff position.

How Much Control Is Needed?

As with all organizational endeavors, control activities should be pursued if the expected benefits of performing such activities are greater than the costs of performing them.[25] The process of comparing the cost of any organizational activity with the expected benefit of performing the activity is called **cost-benefit analysis.** In general,

Cost-benefit analysis is the process of comparing the cost of some activity to the benefit or revenue that results from the activity to determine the total worth of the activity to the organization.

TABLE 17.2 Sample job description for a controller in a large company

Objectives

The controller (or comptroller) is responsible for all accounting activities within the organization.

Functions

1. *General accounting.* Maintain the company's accounting books, accounting records, and forms. This includes:
   a. Preparing balance sheets, income statements, and other statements and reports.
   b. Giving the president interim reports on operations for the recent quarter and fiscal year to date.
   c. Supervising the preparation and filing of reports to the SEC.
2. *Budgeting.* Prepare a budget outlining the company's future operations and cash requirements.
3. *Cost accounting.* Determine the cost to manufacture a product and prepare internal reports to management of the processing divisions. This includes:
   a. Developing standard costs.
   b. Accumulating actual cost data.
   c. Preparing reports that compare standard costs to actual costs and highlight unfavorable differences.
4. *Performance reporting.* Identify individuals in the organization who control activities and prepare reports to show how well or how poorly they perform.
5. *Data processing.* Assist in the analysis and design of a computer-based information system. Frequently, the data-processing department is under the controller, and the controller is involved in management of that department as well as other communications equipment.
6. *Other duties.* Other duties may be assigned to the controller by the president or by corporate bylaws. Some of these include:
   a. Tax planning and reporting.
   b. Service departments such as mailing, telephone, janitors, and filing.
   c. Forecasting.
   d. Corporate social relations and obligations.

Relationships

The controller reports to the vice president for Finance.

managers and controllers should collaborate to determine exactly how much controlling is justified in a given situation.

Figure 17.4 below shows controlling activity over an extended period of time. According to this figure, controlling costs increase steadily as more and more controlling activities are performed. In addition, because the controlling function requires start-up costs, controlling costs at first usually are greater than the income generated from increased controlling. As controlling starts to correct major organizational errors, however, the income from increased controlling eventually equals controlling costs (point X_1 on the graph) and ultimately surpasses them by a large margin.

As more and more controlling activity is added beyond X_1, however, controlling costs and the income from increased controlling eventually become equal again (point X_2 on the graph). As more controlling activity is added beyond X_2, controlling costs again surpass the income from increased controlling. The main reason this last development takes place is that major organizational problems probably have been detected much earlier, and corrective measures taken now are aimed primarily at smaller and more insignificant problems.

BACK TO THE CASE

The job of a controller at *USA Today* would be to gather information for reports that management could use to take corrective action. The controller would not take any corrective action at the company, but would simply advise management as to what corrective action should be taken.

In operating properly, *USA Today* management determines, with the advice of the controller, exactly how much control is necessary at the company; that is, which newspaper production costs seem the most detrimental and how these expenses are to be reduced. Management should continue to increase controlling at *USA Today* as long as the benefit from the control activities (enhanced profitability) exceeds their cost. *USA Today* management should keep in mind, however, that too much control can cause excessive paperwork in the company and slow decision making to an undesirable level.

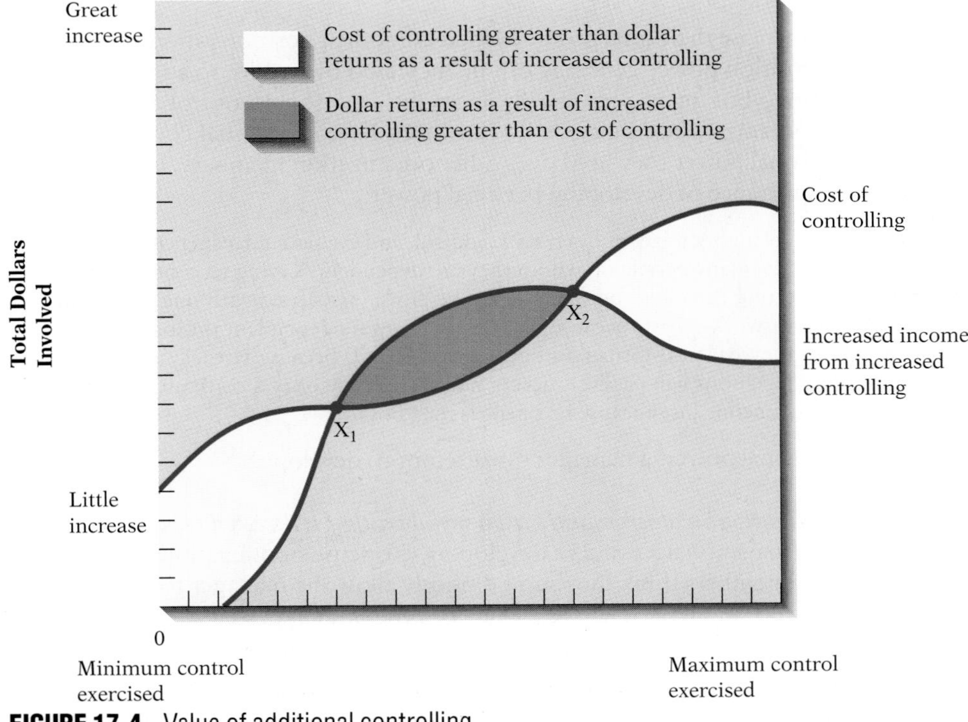

FIGURE 17.4 Value of additional controlling

POWER AND CONTROL

To control successfully, managers must understand not only the control process itself but also how organization members relate to it. Up to this point, the chapter has emphasized nonhuman variables of controlling. This section focuses on power, perhaps the most important human-related variable in the control process. The following sections discuss power by (1) presenting its definition, (2) elaborating on the total power of managers, and (3) listing the steps managers can take to increase their power over other organization members.

A Definition of Power

Power is the extent to which an individual is able to influence others so that they respond to orders.

Perhaps the two most often confused terms in management are *power* and *authority*. Authority was defined in chapter 10 as the right to command or give orders. The extent to which an individual is able to influence others so that they respond to orders is called **power.** The greater this ability, the more power an individual is said to have.

Obviously, power and control are closely related. To illustrate, after a manager compares actual performance with planned performance and determines that corrective action is necessary, orders usually are given to implement this action. Although the orders are issued through the manager's organizational authority, they may or may not be followed precisely, depending on how much power the manager has over the individuals to whom the orders are addressed.

Total Power of a Manager

Total power is the entire amount of power an individual in an organization possesses, mainly the amount of position power and the amount of personal power possessed by the individual.

The **total power** a manager possesses is made up of two different kinds of power: position power and personal power.[26] **Position power** is power derived from the organizational position a manager holds. In general, moves from lower-level management to upper-level management accrue more position power for a manager. **Personal power** is power derived from a manager's human relationships with others.[27]

Steps for Increasing Total Power

Position power is power derived from the organizational position that one holds.

Personal power is the power derived from the relationship that one person has with another.

Managers can increase their total power by increasing their position power or their personal power. Position power generally can be increased by a move to a higher organizational position, but managers usually have little personal control over moving upward in an organization. Managers do, however, have substantial control over the amount of personal power they hold over other organization members. John P. Kotter stresses the importance of developing personal power:

> To be able to plan, organize, budget, staff, control, and evaluate, managers need some control over the many people on whom they are dependent. Trying to control others solely by directing them and on the basis of the power associated with one's position simply will not work—first, because managers are always dependent on some people over whom they have no formal authority, and second, because virtually no one in modern organizations will passively accept and completely obey a constant stream of orders from someone just because he or she is the "boss."[28]

To increase personal power, a manager can attempt to develop:[29]

1. *A sense of obligation in other organization members that is directed toward the manager.* If a manager is successful in developing this sense of obligation, other organization members think they should rightly allow the manager to influence them within certain limits. The basic strategy generally suggested to create this sense of obligation is to do personal favors for people.
2. *A belief in other organization members that the manager possesses a high level of expertise within the organization.* In general, a manager's personal power increases as organization members perceive that the manager's level of expertise is increas-

ing. To increase the perceived level of expertise, the manager must quietly make significant achievement visible to others and rely heavily on a successful track record and respected professional reputation.

3. *A sense of identification that other organization members have with the manager.* The manager can strive to develop this identification by behaving in ways that other organization members respect and by espousing goals, values, and ideals commonly held by them. The following description illustrates how a certain sales manager took steps to increase the degree to which his subordinates identified with him:

    One vice-president of sales in a moderate-sized manufacturing company was reputed to be so much in control of his sales force that he could get them to respond to new and different marketing programs in a third of the time taken by the company's best competitors. His power over his employees was based primarily on their strong identification with him and what he stood for. Emigrating to the United States at age seventeen, this person worked his way up "from nothing." When made a sales manager in 1965, he began recruiting other young immigrants and sons of immigrants from his former country. When made vice-president of sales in 1970, he continued to do so. In 1975, 85 percent of his sales force was made up of people whom he hired directly or who were hired by others he brought in.[30]

4. *The perception in other organization members that they are dependent on the manager.* Perhaps the main strategy the manager should adopt in this regard is a clear demonstration of the amount of authority the manager possesses over organizational resources. Action taken in this regard should emphasize not only influence over resources necessary for organization members to do their jobs but also influence over resources organization members personally receive in such forms as salaries and bonuses. This strategy is aptly reflected in the managerial version of the Golden Rule: "He who has the gold makes the rules."

BACK TO THE CASE

For *USA Today* management to be successful in controlling they have to be aware not only of the intricacies of the control process itself but also of how to deal with people as they relate to the control process. With regard to people and control, *USA Today* management has to consider the amount of power they hold over organization members—that is, their ability to encourage workers to follow orders. Based on the introductory case, many of these orders would probably be related to implementing new and better methods for producing the newspaper as well as improved techniques for selling advertising.

The total amount of power that *USA Today* management possesses comes from the positions they hold and from their personal relationships with other organization members. As an example, *USA Today*'s top managers already have more position power than any other managers in the organization. Therefore, to increase their total power, they would have to develop their personal power. Top management might attempt to do this by developing (1) a sense of obligation in other organization members toward them, (2) the belief in other organization members that top management has a high level of task-related expertise, (3) a sense of identification that other organization members have with them, and (4) the perception in organization members that they are dependent on top management.

PERFORMING THE CONTROL FUNCTION

Controlling can be a detailed and intricate process, especially as the size of the organization increases. The two sections that follow furnish valuable guidelines for successfully executing this potentially complicated controlling function. These sections discuss potential barriers to successful controlling and making controlling successful.

Potential Barriers to Successful Controlling

Managers should take steps to avoid the following potential barriers to successful controlling:[31]

1. *Control activities can create an undesirable overemphasis on short-term production as opposed to long-term production.* As an example, in striving to meet planned weekly production quotas, a manager might "push" machines in a particular area and not allow these machines to be serviced properly. This kind of management behavior would ensure that planned performance and actual performance are equivalent in the short term but may cause the machines to deteriorate to the point that long-term production quotas are impossible to meet.

2. *Control activities can increase employee frustration with their jobs and thereby reduce morale.* This reaction tends to occur primarily when management exerts too much control. Employees get frustrated because they perceive management as being too rigid in its thinking and not allowing the freedom necessary to do a good job.[32] Another feeling that employees may have from overcontrol is that control activities are merely a tactic to pressure workers to higher production.

3. *Control activities can encourage the falsification of reports.* Employees may perceive management as basing corrective action solely on department records with no regard to extenuating circumstances. If this is the case, employees may feel pressured to falsify reports so that corrective action regarding their organizational unit will not be too drastic. For example, actual production may be overstated in order that it will look good to management, or it may be understated to create the impression that planned production is too high, thereby tricking management into thinking that a lighter work load is justified.

   A well-publicized example of individuals falsifying control reports involved the Federal Aviation Administration (FAA) and Eastern Airlines.[33] The FAA is a government organization charged with controlling airlines' safety. Part of the controlling process established by the FAA involves airline companies filling out service reports and returning them to the FAA for monitoring and evaluation. Prior to the end of Eastern's existence as a company, Eastern and senior maintenance executives were charged by a federal grand jury with conspiring to falsify aircraft maintenance records and returning improperly maintained aircraft to passenger service. The indictment charged that company managers signed off or coerced aircraft mechanics and mechanics supervisors to sign off on maintenance that had not been completed on fifty-two different occasions. Management may have seen the falsification of maintenance reports as one way of reducing maintenance costs and thereby helping to alleviate Eastern's poor profit performance. In essence, the pressure of poor profits at Eastern Airlines may have caused certain company managers to falsify service reports, making it impossible for the FAA to properly control the airline company.

4. *Control activities can cause the perspective of organization members to be too narrow for the good of the organization.* Although controls can be designed to focus on relatively narrow aspects of an organization, managers must keep in mind that any corrective action should be considered not only in relation to the specific activity being controlled but also in relation to all other organizational units.

   For example, a manager may determine that actual and planned production are not equivalent in a specific organizational unit because of various periods when a low inventory of needed parts causes some production workers to pursue other work activities instead of producing a product. Although the corrective action to be taken in this situation would seem to be simply raising the level of inventory, this probably would be a very narrow perspective of the problem. The manager should seek to answer questions such as the following before any corrective action is taken: Is there enough money on hand to raise current inventory levels? Are there sufficient personnel presently in the purchasing department to effect a necessary increase? Who will do the work the production workers presently are doing when they run out of parts?

5. *Control activities can be perceived as the goals of the control process rather than the means by which corrective action is taken.* Managers must keep in mind that information should be gathered and reports should be designed to facilitate the taking of corrective action within the organization. In fact, these activities can be justified only if they yield some organizational benefit that extends beyond the cost of performing them.

Making Controlling Successful

In addition to avoiding the potential barriers to successful controlling mentioned in the previous section, managers can perform certain activities to make the control process more effective. In this regard, managers should make sure that:

1. *Various facets of the control process are appropriate for the specific organizational activity being focused on.* As an example, standards and measurements concerning a line worker's productivity are much different from standards and measurements concerning a vice president's productivity. Controlling ingredients related to the productivity of these individuals, therefore, must be different if the control process is to be applied successfully.
2. *Control activities are used to achieve many different kinds of goals.* According to Jerome, control can be used for such purposes as standardizing performance, protecting organizational assets from theft and waste, and standardizing product quality.[34] Managers should keep in mind that the control process can be applied to many different facets of organizational life and that, for the organization to receive maximum benefit from controlling, each of these facets should be emphasized.
3. *Information used as the basis for taking corrective action is timely.*[35] Some time necessarily elapses as managers gather control-related information, develop necessary reports based on this information, decide what corrective action should be taken, and actually take the corrective action. However, information should be gathered and acted on as promptly as possible to ensure that the situation, as depicted by this information, has not changed and that the organizational advantage of corrective action will, in fact, materialize.
4. *The mechanics of the control process are understandable to all individuals who are in any way involved with implementing the process.*[36] Managers should take steps to ensure that people know exactly what information is necessary for a particular control process, how that information is to be gathered and used to compile various reports, what the purposes of various reports actually are, and what corrective actions are appropriate given various possible types of reports. The lesson here is simple: For control to be successful, all individuals involved in controlling must have a working knowledge of how the control process operates.[37]

BACK TO THE CASE In addition to understanding the intricacies of control and how people fit into the control process, *USA Today* management must be aware of the potential barriers to successful controlling and the action they could take to increase the probability that controlling activities would be successful—that is, that factors like new and improved production techniques introduced within the company will be performed efficiently, effectively, and without resistance.

To overcome the potential control-related barriers at *USA Today,* management must balance its emphasis on short-term versus long-term objectives, minimize the negative influence controlling can have on the morale of *USA Today* organization members, eliminate forces that can lead to the falsification of control-related reports, implement a control perspective that has appropriately combined narrow and broad organizational focuses, and stress controlling as a means rather than an end.

With regard to the action that can be taken to increase the probability of effective controlling activities, *USA Today* management must be sure that various facets of its controlling subsystem are appropriate for company activities, that components of the controlling subsystem are flexible and suited to many purposes, that corrective action is based on timely information, and that the controlling subsystem is understood by all organization members involved in its operation.

ACTION SUMMARY

Reread the learning objectives that follow. Each objective is followed by questions. Answering these questions accurately will help you retain the most important concepts discussed in this chapter. After answering each question, check your answer with the answer key at the end of this chapter. (*Hint:* If you have doubt regarding the correct response, consult the page whose number follows the answer.)

Circle: ***From studying this chapter, I will attempt to acquire:***

1. A definition of *control*.

a, b, c, d, e — **a.** Managers must develop methods of measurement to signal when deviations from standards are occurring so that: (a) the plan can be abandoned; (b) quality control personnel can be notified; (c) the measurement standards can be checked; (d) corrective action can be taken; (e) none of the above.

T, F — **b.** Control is making something happen the way it was planned to happen.

2. A thorough understanding of the controlling subsystem.

a, b, c, d, e — **a.** The main steps of the controlling process include all of the following *except:* (a) taking corrective action; (b) establishing planned activities; (c) comparing performance to standards; (d) measuring performance; (e) all of the above are steps in controlling.

T, F — **b.** Standards should be established in all important areas of organizational performance.

3. An appreciation for various kinds of control and for how each kind can be used advantageously by managers.

a, b, c, d, e — **a.** The following is *not* one of the basic types of management control: (a) feedback control; (b) precontrol; (c) concurrent control; (d) exception control; (e) all are basic types of control.

a, b, c, d, e — **b.** An example of precontrol established by management would be: (a) rules; (b) procedures; (c) policies; (d) budgets; (e) all of the above are examples.

4. Insights on the relationship between power and control.

T, F — **a.** According to Kotter, controlling others solely on the basis of position power will not work.

a, b,c, d, e — **b.** The extent to which an individual is able to influence others to respond to orders is: (a) power; (b) sensitivity; (c) authority; (d) communication skills; (e) experience.

5. Knowledge of the various potential barriers that must be overcome for successful control.

a,b,c,d,e — **a.** Potential barriers to successful controlling can result in: (a) an overemphasis on short-term production as opposed to long-term production; (b) employees' frustration with their jobs and thereby reduced morale; (c) the falsification of reports; (d) causing the perception of organization members to be too narrow for the good of the organization; (e) all of the above.

T, F **b.** Control activities should be seen as the means by which corrective action is taken.

6. An understanding of steps that can be taken to increase the quality of a controlling subsystem.

a, b, c, d, e **a.** All of the following are suggestions for making controlling successful *except:* (a) managers should make sure the mechanics of the control process are understood by organization members involved with controlling; (b) managers should use control activities to achieve many different kinds of goals; (c) managers should ensure that control activities are supported by most organization members; (d) managers should make sure that information used as the basis for taking corrective action is timely; (e) all of the above are suggestions.

T, F **b.** The standards and measurements concerning a line worker's productivity are much the same as the standards and measurements concerning a vice president's productivity.

INTRODUCTORY CASE WRAP-UP

"A Lack of Control at USA Today" (p. 433) and its related back-to-the-case sections were written to help you better understand the management concepts contained in this chapter. Answer the following discussion questions about this introductory case to further enrich your understanding of chapter content:

1. List four areas in which standards should be developed at *USA Today*. Why would standards in these areas be important to company success?
2. Assume that *USA Today* has a controller. From what the case tells about this company, describe five important duties of this controller. Be as specific as you can about how the activities relate to this particular company.
3. Would power be important for *USA Today* management to possess in ensuring the success of new programs aimed at reducing production costs and increasing the sales of advertising space? Explain.

ISSUES FOR REVIEW AND DISCUSSION

1. What is control?
2. Explain the relationship between planning and control.
3. What is controlling?
4. What is the relationship between the controlling subsystem and the overall management system?
5. Draw and explain the controlling subsystem.
6. List and discuss the three main steps of the controlling process.
7. Define the term *standards.*
8. What is the difference between a symptom and a problem? Why is it important to differentiate between a symptom and a problem in controlling?
9. What types of corrective action can managers take?
10. List and define the three basic types of control that can be used in organizations.
11. What is the relationship between controlling and the controller?
12. What basis do managers use to determine how much control is needed in an organization?
13. What is the difference between power and authority? Describe the role of power within the control process.
14. What determines how much power a manager possesses?
15. How can a manager's personal power be increased?
16. Describe several potential barriers to successful controlling.
17. What steps can managers take to ensure that control activities are successful?

ACTION SUMMARY ANSWER KEY

1. **a.** d, p. 434
   b. T, p. 434
2. **a.** b, p. 435
   b. T, pp. 437–438
3. **a.** d, p. 440
   b. e, p. 440
4. **a.** T, p. 446
   b. a, p. 446
5. **a.** e, pp. 448–449
   b. T, p. 449
6. **a.** c, p. 449
   b. F, p. 449

CASE STUDY

Measuring Performance at Texaco

SAMUEL C. CERTO
Rollins College

Texaco's newest gasoline product, System 3, a patented blend of gasoline and seven additive components, is designed to remove the deposits that build up on a car's intake valves; the product is intended to improve the engine's performance. Texaco claims that drivers can improve the performance of their cars by using System 3 gasoline. Texaco's advertising campaign for the product urges drivers to test System 3 by purchasing five tankfuls of the product to see the change in performance for themselves. In order for this campaign to be effective, Texaco realized that the product the customer receives at gasoline pumps throughout the country must be of a consistent quality.

Star Enterprise and Texas Refining and Marketing Inc. (TRMI), two of Texaco's refining and marketing entities, began an extensive testing program to ensure that the gasoline sold at Texaco pumps is the System 3 gasoline that was developed. The testing program also checks to see that the product sold has the proper posted octane and that it is free from any degradation or contamination that might have occurred in the distribution process.

With some 16,000 outlets nationwide, checking the product from every pump nozzle is a staggeringly difficult job, so Star Enterprises and TRMI turned to Southwest Research Institute, an independent nationally recognized testing company for help. Southwest's hundreds of testers across the country visit randomly selected outlets to collect half-gallon samples of each grade of gasoline in specially prepared and identified galvanized metal containers. The samples are then delivered overnight to Southwest Research's San Antonio, Texas laboratories for chemical analysis and computerized sorting of the data collected. The data are then immediately transferred electronically to Star Enterprise or TRMI field offices. If the test data reveal a problem, testers go back to the problem area, sample the wholesaler's other stations, and investigate to see where the problem originated. If a particular retailer or distributor is at fault, Texaco immediately brings any discrepancy to their attention. If the problem originated at one of Texaco's refineries or somewhere in the distribution system, Texaco's refinery managers are notified, and prompt corrective action is taken.

This product-testing program is only part of Texaco's introduction of a carefully planned quality-improvement program announced in Texaco's 1989 annual report. Texaco's goal is to ensure that things are "done right, on time, every time, in line with customer expectation." Texaco has also set up an oversight committee with representatives from refineries, various marketing groups, transporters, and Texaco's legal department to plan what each department should be doing to control product quality. Potential for problems can occur during the refining and blending process; in any shipment, whether by tanker, barge, pipeline, or truck; as well as at any of the storage facilities. For instance, although the refinery may be turning out the proper product, contamination or commingling may have occurred from another batch of gasoline that preceded the System 3 in the pipeline. The oversight committee meets regularly to find these potential weak links in the chain and to plan ways to ensure the product's integrity.

Texaco's wholesalers and dealers cooperate with and endorse the quality-testing program. Bedford Mitchell, one of Texaco's station dealers, makes the following point: "Reputable Texaco wholesalers and dealers don't have any problem with the program. It's good for them. It also assures Texaco customers that they're getting the quality the company advertises." In fact, the wholesale managers encourage even more feedback, good and bad. They want to know whether there are problems and, if so, where they are, so that they can ensure the highest possible product quality.

DISCUSSION QUESTIONS

1. Does Texaco use precontrol, concurrent control, or feedback control measures in their total product quality assurance program?
2. How does the testing program help Texaco measure performance, compare the performance to established standards, and then take corrective action?
3. What barriers did Texaco have to overcome in order to implement their testing program?
4. What steps did Texaco take to ensure that its control process was successful?

CNN VIDEO CASE

In the Driver's Seat

FRANK OLSON
Hertz

When I started I was a garage man, I was a rental agent, I was a station manager, I was an office manager, I was a salesman, I was a marketing executive. I worked in finance and I worked in operations. And I think that you can come up in any channel in the organization and grow to become the chief executive. I think you need to sprinkle your career with different responsibilities.

This is the road Frank Olson took to the top at Hertz, the world's largest car rental firm. Like many other American corporate leaders, Olson is convinced that an executive can best chart the company's future by knowing its history and its workings from personal experience.

Frank Olson identifies a lack of communication, in terms of both feedback and quality control, as one of the central control problems at Hertz.

Olson started with Hertz at the age of 18 behind the car-rental counter, and he maintains that like each job he has held, the rental counter left its mark on him. He knows what issues will affect the customer and whether the issues are realistic. In the case of advertised prices, for example, Olson argues that generally the prices charged by Hertz end up being as low as those charged by many smaller competitors. However, the competitors advertise low rates and then tack on extra fees once the customer has rented the car. "If you bundled up the aftercharges that occur at these off-airport car loan companies and you compared those to the Hertzes and the Avises, you'd find that the price was no different," he says. "So the perception, in this case, is more important than reality."

Hertz has chosen to build a clientele based on a reputation for reliability and high-quality service, with an underlying assumption that most customers will not be swayed simply by advertised low rates. Large corporate accounts and seasoned business travelers—the vast bulk of rental-car business in the United States—have fallen in line with this strategy, and despite the proliferation of competitors, Hertz remains number one in its industry.

A reputation can be tarnished, however, and goodwill, once lost, is difficult to regain. That is why Frank Olson was devastated by fraud charges brought against his company in 1988. Apparently, customers who returned damaged rental cars had been overcharged on a regular basis for repair work done by or for Hertz. Luckily, Hertz management had located the problem and refunded many of the overcharges before the bad publicity struck, so they were able to mitigate some of the damaging effects. Nonetheless, the company faced $20 million in fines and a difficult time in the press.

Olson learned a lot from that experience:

> What you have to do is constantly reinforce what's right and what's wrong. And you do that by communication directly to the employees from the very top of the organization. You do that by meetings with management to explain to them real-life issues that can occur in business and how it should be handled. You do that by encouraging whistle-blowing, so that if somebody is told to do something wrong, they feel the freedom to raise their hand without fear of reprisal.

Olson identified the problem that cost Hertz so much in money and goodwill as arising from a lack of communication, in terms of both feedback and quality control. Appropriate policies had been in place all along for managing repairs, but management had not involved itself in reviewing actual operations. The policies were not adhered to, and employees were apparently unwilling or afraid to blow the whistle on fellow employees or supervisors.

So, the next issue facing Olson and his now-privately held company is to ensure that operations are appropriately controlled, not simply outlined. He sees Hertz's fall in this case as a mere aberration, and most travel writers agree with him, but there are bigger problems in the industry. Olson is a champion of the move to regulate car-rental advertising to do away with hidden aftercharges and bait-and-switch ploys. He knows that Hertz can stand up to the challenge.

Customer service is the cornerstone of Hertz's success and accounts for double-digit growth figures annually throughout the past thirty years. Frank Olson maintains the respect of his workers by identifying with them, by knowing all aspects of their work, and by being perceived as knowledgeable and honest. He hopes that Hertz will continue to be perceived by its customers as that same sort of leader.

VIDEO CASE QUESTIONS

1. What sort of standard do you think truth-in-advertising regulations represent?
2. In what way do you think Frank Olson's career development increases his total power at Hertz?
3. Rate the following standards in terms of their relative values at Hertz: employee attitude standards, market-position standards, product-leadership standards, and social-responsibility standards.
4. How can the problem of overcharging for repairs described in the case be avoided in the future?

CNN VIDEO EXERCISE

Controlling Costs at Hertz

EXERCISE GOAL: Design a controlling subsystem to control costs.

As the manager of the Hertz Repair Division, you have started to see labor invoices that you know are out of line with current prices. You have promised Frank Olson that you will develop a procedure to ensure that car repair costs will be monitored and held to a certain standard. Using Figure 17.2, The Controlling Subsystem, on page 436, design a controlling subsystem for Hertz by filling in the information in the diagram.

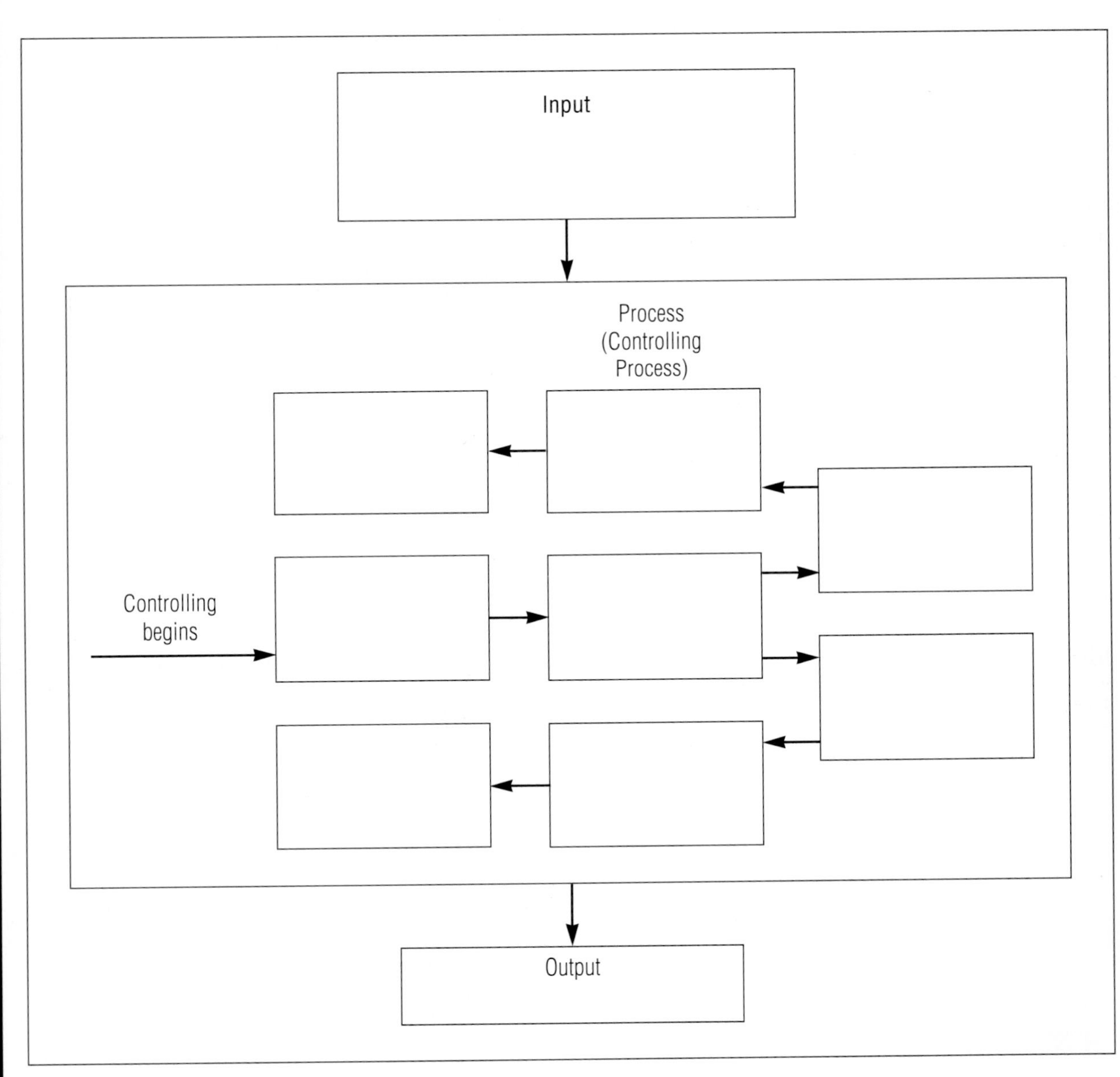

CHAPTER

18

PRODUCTION MANAGEMENT AND CONTROL

STUDENT LEARNING OBJECTIVES

From studying this chapter, I will attempt to acquire:

1. Definitions of production, productivity, and quality.
2. An understanding of the importance of operations and production strategies, systems, and processes.
3. Insights on the role of operations management concepts in the workplace.
4. An understanding of how operations control procedures can be used to control production.
5. Insights concerning operations control tools and how they evolve into a continual improvement approach to production management and control.

CHAPTER OUTLINE

INTRODUCTORY CASE
Bridgestone (USA): Eliminating the Fire and Building Bridges of Quality

PRODUCTION

Defining Production
Productivity
Quality and Productivity

QUALITY HIGHLIGHT
Adidas USA

Automation

GLOBAL HIGHLIGHT
GMFanuc

Strategies, Systems, and Processes

OPERATIONS MANAGEMENT

Defining Operations Management
Operations Management Considerations

ETHICS HIGHLIGHT
Firestone

DIVERSITY HIGHLIGHT
Americans with Disabilities Act

OPERATIONS CONTROL

Just-in-Time Inventory Control
Maintenance Control
Cost Control
Budgetary Control
Ratio Analysis
Materials Control

SELECTED OPERATIONS CONTROL TOOLS

Using Control Tools to Control Organizations
Inspection
Management by Exception
Management by Objectives
Breakeven Analysis
Other Broad Operations Control Tools

CASE STUDY
Caterpillar's Factory, a Star

VIDEO CASE
Profits and People: Robert Rich of Rich Products

VIDEO EXERCISE
Computing a Breakeven Analysis for Rich Products

INTRODUCTORY CASE

Bridgestone (USA): Eliminating the Fire and Building Bridges of Quality

Bridgestone Corporation is Japan's largest tiremaker. Along with its two plants in Tennessee—LaVergne and Warren County—it operates twelve plants in Japan and others in Thailand, Taiwan, Indonesia, and Australia. Bridgestone ranks third in worldwide tire production, after Goodyear and Michelin. Before moving to Tennessee, Bridgestone had already established a reputation for quality in the United States. Its motto "Serving society with products of superior quality" did more than pay lip service to that credo. The company had won the Deming Prize in 1968, and its quality department was called the "Deming Plan Promotion Department." Twice each year, the company invited winning quality circles from each of its plants around the world to two intense days of presentations. In 1987, LaVergne hosted the first such presentation in the United States.

[Bridgestone's] quality department was called the "Deming Plan Promotion Department."

Bridgestone came to Tennessee because of a $52 million purchase of the truck tire plant previously owned by Akron Ohio's Firestone Tire and Rubber Company. The purchase was a "friendly merger." Bridgestone's $2.6 billion payment was then the largest sale in history of a U.S. firm to a Japanese corporation. The news was enthusiastically received by most of Firestone's 53,500 employees. The enthusiasm of the employees had its base in the operating results during the period 1983–1987 at LaVergne: a 200 percent increase in the output of the plant and achievement of a 2.2 incidence rate for injuries relative to 14.0 for the industry. A capital outlay of $500 million was used to deal with quality problems. The changes that produced the results were cost-cutting measures that ranged from modification of machinery to worker involvement. Workers who had lived in fear of losing their jobs were suddenly drawn into a giant renewal effort. Firestone had lost the enthusiasm of its workers and Bridgestone won them back with the drive of Deming's philosophy.

An example of Bridgestone's style is illustrated in the following quality story: "In a tire plant, the unit that cleans and changes the two-ton iron molds that fit into presses and givethe tire its distinctive tread is the *mold shop.* A team from Bridgestone's passenger tire mold shop had become adept at the plant's simplified problem-solving format." The team undertook several projects, one of which is described here:

> The team chose to improve in/down loader adjustment, the means by which the mold was loaded and lowered into the pres. It required too much time to load each of the thirty-nine presses. The process involved using a large wrench to turn a threaded bolt to the proper setting, located by trial-and-error because often bolts became worn and rusty and therefore had to be adjusted. Sometimes the person changing the mold had difficulty finding the wrench. The method had been used for seventeen years, but the group believed that there had to be a better way. When the project began, in February, the shop averaged four loader adjustments per day. The team hoped to reduce the adjustment time by 75 percent by May 31. The threaded shaft was replaced with a bar with set holes and a pin. The person changing the mold could move the bar up and down to the proper position and lock it in place with a pin. Gone was the wrench. The team went through the Plan-Do-Check-Act cycle again and decided to attach a limit switch to the loader, which further reduced the time. The adjustment now showed a 95-percent improvement. The team met its May target date, working four months.

Bridgestone's purchase of Firestone Tire and Rubber Company was, in 1988, the largest sale in history of a U.S. firm to a Japanese corporation.

From Mary Walton, *Deming Management at Work: Six Successful Companies that Use the Quality Principles of the World-Famous W. Edwards Deming* (New York: G. P. Putnam's Sons, 1991), 187–188; Kathleen Morris, "A Bridge Far Enough: Four Years after Buying Firestone, Bridgestone Finally Gets Tough," *Financial World.* (June 9, 1992), pp. 52–54.

WHAT'S AHEAD The introductory case profiles the transformation of the Firestone management philosophy to the Bridgestone management philosophy. The case reports on the phases that Bridgestone used to transform a manufacturing disaster into a manufacturing success. This chapter can help a manager gain a broad appreciation of how operations management concepts and operations control can be used to guide organizations appropriately to success.

Production control ensures that an organization produces goods and services as planned.

This chapter emphasizes the fundamentals of **production control**—ensuring that an organization produces goods and services as planned. The primary discussion areas in the chapter are (1) production, (2) operations management, (3) operations control, and (4) selected operations control tools.

PRODUCTION

To reach organizational goals, all managers must plan, organize, influence, and control to produce some type of goods or services. Naturally, these goods and services may vary significantly from organization to organization. This section of the chapter defines production and productivity and discusses the relationship between quality and productivity, and automation.

Defining Production

Production is the transformation of organizational resources into products.

Production is the transformation of organizational resources into products.[1] In this definition, *organizational resources* are all assets available to a manager to generate products, *transformation* is the set of steps necessary to change these resources into products, and *products* are various goods or services aimed at meeting human needs. Figure 18.1 on page 459 contains examples of organizational resources (inputs), transformation processes, and goods and services produced (outputs) for each of three different types of organizations.

Productivity

Productivity is an important consideration in designing, evaluating, and improving modern production systems.

Defining Productivity

Productivity is the relationship between the amount of goods or services produced and the organizational resources needed to produce them.

Productivity is the relationship between the total amount of goods or services being produced (output) and the organizational resources needed (input) to produce them. This relationship is usually expressed by the following equation:[2]

$$\text{Productivity} = \frac{\text{Outputs}}{\text{Inputs}}$$

The higher the value of the ratio of outputs to inputs, the higher the productivity of the operation.

Although managers should continually strive to make their production processes as productive as possible, it is no secret that over the last twenty years the rate of productivity growth related to production management and innovation in manufacturing within the United States has lagged significantly behind that of countries such as Japan, West Germany, and France.[3] Some of the more traditional strategies for increasing productivity include (1) improving the effectiveness of the organizational workforce through training, (2) improving the production process through automation, (3) improving product design to make products easier to assemble, (4) improving the production facility by purchasing more modern equipment, and (5) improving the quality of workers hired to fill open positions.

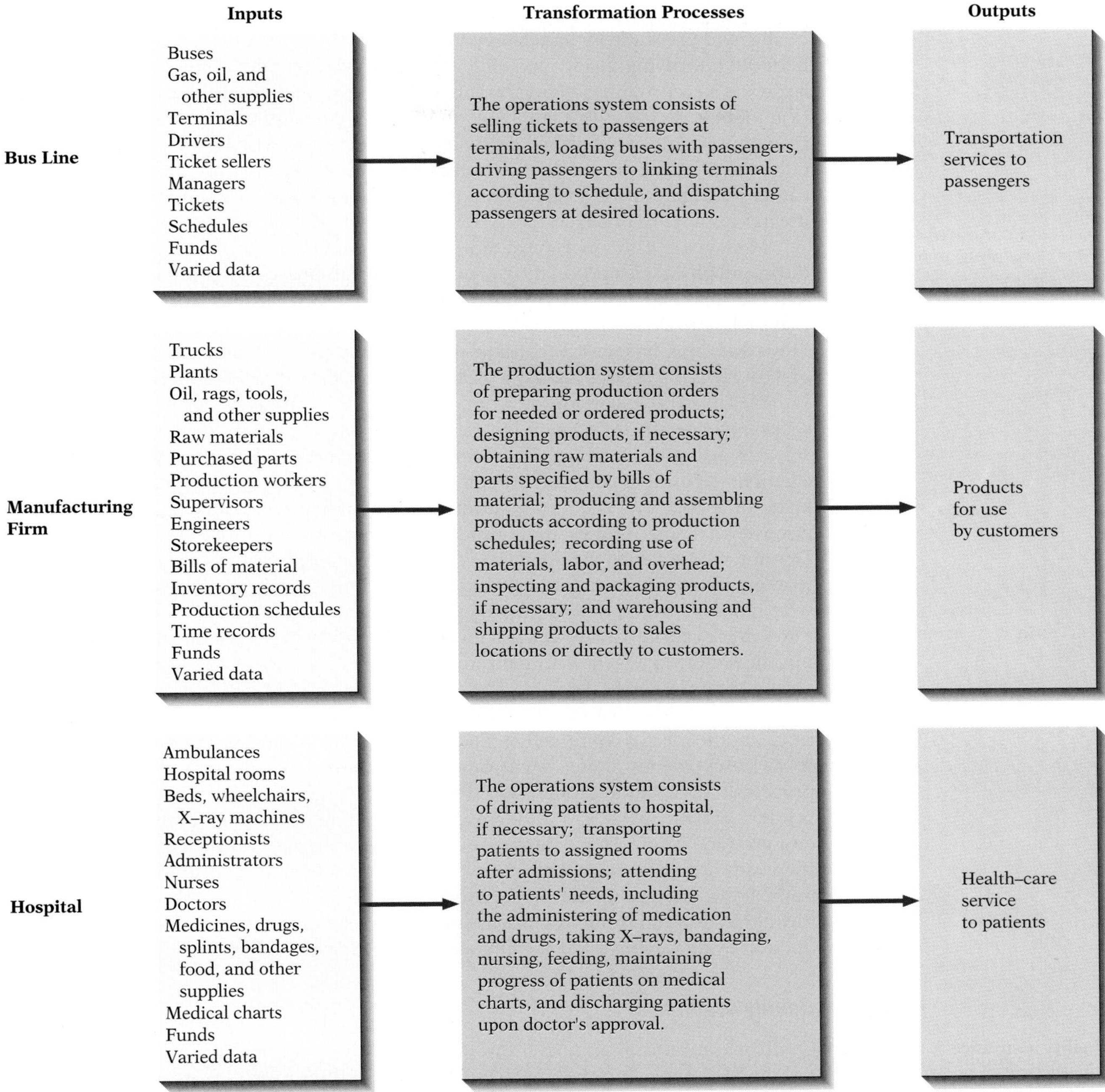

FIGURE 18.1 Inputs, transformation processes, and outputs for three different types of organizations

Quality and Productivity

Quality can be defined as how well a product does what it is intended to do—how closely it satisfies the specifications to which it is built. In a broad sense, quality is a degree of excellence on which products or services can be ranked on the basis of selected features or characteristics. Quality is a characteristic that makes something what it is. Product quality determines an organization's reputation. It is the customer who determines what quality is. Customers define quality in terms of appearance, performance, availability, flexibility, and reliability.

Quality is the extent to which a product reliably does what it is intended to do.

During the last several years, managerial thinking about the relationship between quality and productivity has changed drastically. Managers once saw little relationship between improving quality and increasing productivity. Improving quality was viewed largely as a controlling activity that took place somewhere near the end of the production process. Because this emphasis on improving quality typically resulted in merely rejecting a number of finished products that could otherwise be offered to customers, efforts to improve product quality were generally believed to lower productivity. Many earlier managers chose to achieve higher levels of productivity simply by producing a greater number of products given some fixed level of available resources.

Management theorists have more recently found that improving product quality during all phases of a production process actually improves the productivity of the system that manufactures the product.[4] As early as 1948, Japanese companies observed that such improvements in product quality normally resulted in improved productivity. How does this happen? According to Dr. W. Edwards Deming, a world-renowned quality expert, a serious and consistent quality focus normally reduces nonproductive variables like the reworking of products, production mistakes, delays and production snags, and poor use of time and materials.

According to Deming, for continual improvement to become a way of life, management needs to understand the company and its operations. Most managers feel they know their company and its operations, but when they begin drawing flowcharts, they discover that their understanding of strategy, systems, and processes is not complete. Deming recommends that managers question every aspect of an operation and involve workers in discussion before improving operations. Deming believes that a manager who seriously focuses on improving product quality throughout all phases of a production process initiates a set of chain reactions that benefits not only the organization but the society in which the organization exists.[5] A complete set of organizational variables appears in Figure 18.2.

Deming's flow diagram introduces the customer to the operations process and introduces the idea of continually refining knowledge, design, and inputs to the process so as to constantly increase customer satisfaction. The diagram shows the whole process as an integrated operation. From the first input to actual use of the finished product, it is one process; a problem at the beginning will impact on the whole and the end product. There are no barriers between the company and the customer, between the customer and its suppliers, between the company and its people. The process is unified: the greater the harmony among all components, the better the results. The following sections continue the discussion of the relationship between quality and production by discussing quality assurance and quality circles.

Quality Assurance

Quality assurance is an operational activity aimed at achieving the organization's quality objectives.

Quality assurance is an operations process involving a broad group of activities that are aimed at achieving the organization's quality objectives. An organization's interpretation of quality is expressed in its strategies. Although the precise activities involved in quality assurance vary from organization to organization, activities like determining the safest system for delivering goods to customers and maintaining the quality of parts or materials purchased from suppliers are included in most quality assurance efforts.

Statistical quality control is a process used to determine how many products from a larger number should be inspected to calculate a probability that the total number of products meets organizational quality standards.

Quality assurance is a much broader concept than statistical quality control. **Statistical quality control** is the process used to determine how many products from a larger number should be inspected to calculate a probability that the total number of products meets organizational quality standards.

Quality assurance is a continuum of activities that start when quality standards are set and end when quality goods and services are delivered to the customer. An effective quality assurance strategy reduces the need for quality control and subsequent corrective actions.

Quality assurance is best when a "no rejects" philosophy is adopted by manage-

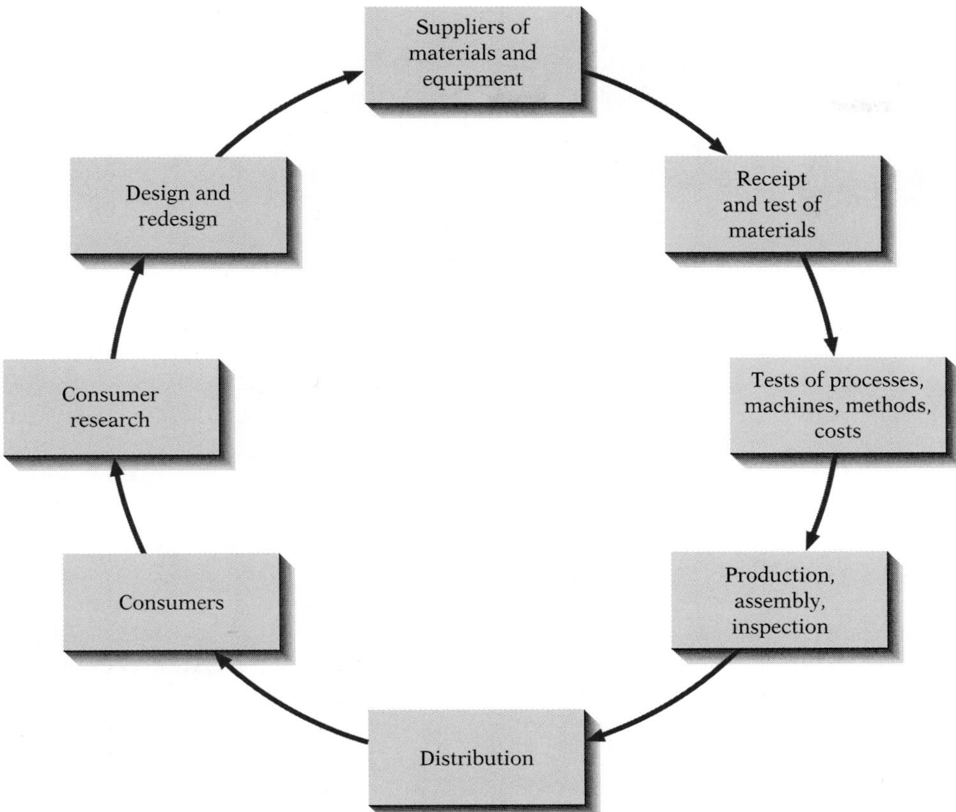

FIGURE 18.2 Deming's flow diagram for improving product quality

ment. Unfortunately, for most mass-produced products, this is not economically feasible. Employees should approach production with a "do not make the same mistake once" mind-set. Mistakes are costly. Detecting defective products in the final quality control inspection is too late and too expensive. Emphasizing quality in the early stages—during product and process design—will reduce rejects.

Quality Circles

Recently, managers have involved all of a company's employees in quality control. In general, management solicits the ideas of employees in judging and maintaining product quality. This trend toward more involvement of employees in quality control developed from a control system originating in Japan called quality circles. Although many corporations are now moving beyond the concept of the quality circle to the concept of the work team, as discussed in chapter 16, many of the ideas generated from quality circles continue to be valid. **Quality circles** are simply small groups of workers who meet to discuss a particular project in terms of quality assurance. Solutions to the problems are communicated directly to management at a formal presentation session. Figure 18.3 shows the quality circle problem-solving process.

Quality circles are small groups of workers that meet with management to discuss quality related problems.

Most quality circles are similar in the way they operate. Each circle is usually under eight members in size, and leaders of the circles are not necessarily the members' supervisors. Members may be outsiders or task members. The focus is on operational problems rather than interpersonal ones. Although the problems to be discussed are sometimes assigned by management, they can also be uncovered by the group itself.[6]

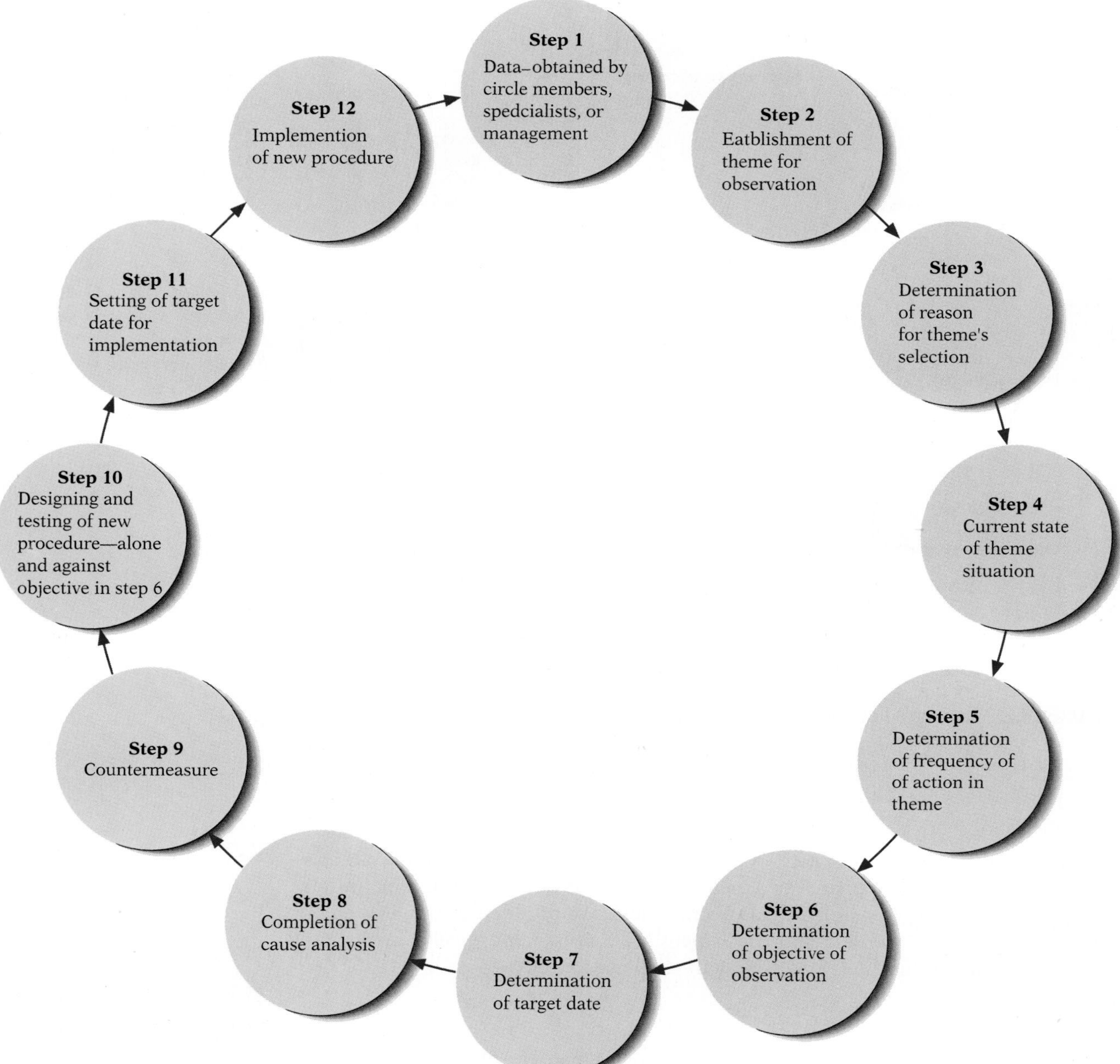

FIGURE 18.3 The quality circle problem-solving process

QUALITY HIGHLIGHT
Focusing on Quality at Adidas USA

Adidas USA is an athletic apparel company perhaps best known for its athletic footwear. Recent events at Adidas illustrate that, without proper control aimed at enhancing profit, an organization may not exist long enough to have an opportunity to focus on enhancing product quality.

Although over the last few years, Adidas USA Inc. has lost significant amounts of money, the company recently reported a profit rather than a loss. The company went from a $63-million loss in 1989 to a $2-million profit in 1990. This profit, although small, is particularly significant because it was earned despite an 11 percent drop in revenues, to $249 million. Staff reductions and a focus on collecting overdue receivables were important control measures that helped to produce the turnaround in earnings. The company also exercised control by analyzing product lines weekly to assess and increase contributions to profit that each line was making.

Adidas's chief financial officer, Andrew P. Hines, concedes that cost reduction measures taken by the company are primarily one-time control measures. According to Hines, now that the company is becoming more profitable, its real challenge is to build lasting quality in both its staff and its products. Adidas USA dominated the U.S. market for athletic footwear in the 1970s, but strong competition and internal problems in the 1980s caused its market share to dwindle from more than 60 percent to 4 percent. Hines believes that measures such as creating a new pay-for-performance plan, clarifying and documenting job responsibilities, and instituting critical training programs will significantly contribute to Adidas building more quality into its staff as well as its products.

In 1992, Adidas was acquired by Britain's Pentland Group, which plans to invigorate the Adidas brand name by upgrading products, improving distribution, and signing up more big-name endorsers. ▶

The challenge for Adidas USA is to enhance profit through control measures for long enough to have the opportunity to enhance product quality.

Automation

Preceding material introduced the topic of productivity within organizations. Automation—including **robots,** mechanical devices built to perform repetitive tasks efficiently, and **robotics,** an area of study dealing with the development and use of robots—shows promising signs of increasing organizational productivity in a revolutionary way.

Robots are mechanical devices built to perform repetitive tasks efficiently.

Robotics is the study of the development and use of robots.

Over the past twenty years, a host of advanced manufacturing systems have been developed and implemented to support operations. Most of these advanced systems are automated systems that combine hardware-industrial robots and computers—and software.

Automation means that electro-mechanical devices replace human effort. Human effort in operations includes welding, materials handling, design, drafting, and decision making.

The goals of new automation include reduced inventories, higher productivity, and faster billing and product distribution cycles. The Asian countries appear to be doing the best job of making optimal use of company resources through automation. Five levels of automation are presented in Table 18.1.

GLOBAL HIGHLIGHT
GMFanuc Focuses on Robotics

Managers face situations that may allow them to increase productivity through the use of robotics. In addition to enhancing productivity, the application of robots to work situations may be a critical factor in enabling organizations to compete with Japanese firms in the future.

Although robots were invented in the United States and although the country still leads in advanced robotics research, Japan leads in the practical use of robots. Japanese companies of all sizes use robots because they make it easier to quickly alter a production line in order to make several different models of a product. One of the few profitable U.S. robot companies is GMFanuc, a joint venture between General Motors (GM) and Fanuc, a Japanese robot manufacturer. According to GMFanuc officials, robots are more than a substitute for human labor because robots can perform some jobs better than people can. As electronics components become smaller and smaller, robots

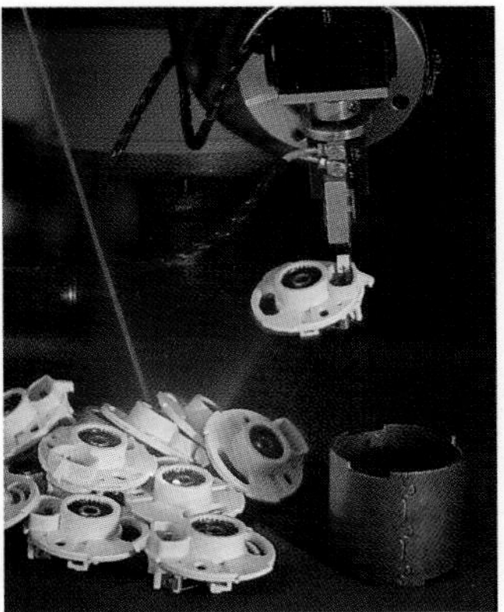

One key to competing with Japanese manufacturers is for U.S. companies to find appropriate uses for robots in manufacturing situations that maximize the investments they have made in robotics.

TABLE 18.1 The state of automation

Levels of Automation	*Description of Operations*
Level 1	Firms attempt to make optimal use of company resources without additional or updated automation. They do this by simplifying manufacturing procedures and reorganizing the shop or service floor. Asian countries generally excel at this level. Companies in the United States have adopted such techniques but have had difficulty with implementation. Western European companies lag behind both Asian and U.S. companies.
Level 2	Firms at the second level use robots, computers, operations management (OM) tools, advanced shop-floor systems, and flexible manufacturing processes to perform repetitive, menial work in specific areas. These resources are used widely in Japan and the United States. The Japanese companies are the leaders. European countries lag far behind the United States and Japan.
Level 3	Firms at the third level use shared hierarchical or object-oriented computer data bases to link specific automated areas to one another and to computer-aided design techniques. Many U.S. manufacturers have implemented this automation step, but these techniques have been most widely adopted by non-unionized smaller companies. Japanese companies are slightly ahead of U.S. companies at this level, while the European companies lag far behind.
Level 4	Firms automate the complex steps of production scheduling and diagnostics through the use of artificial computer intelligence, computer-aided design, and object-oriented computer software. U.S. companies are the most progressive in implementing these techniques. Few Japanese companies have adopted these techniques, but those that have are more effective than the U.S. companies.
Level 5	Firms create a computer-integrated enterprise where everything from product planning to customer service is determined by expanded artificial intelligence (AI) and object-oriented techniques. This factory of the future remains beyond the capabilities of most companies, but consultants paint a rosy picture of an environment where new computer-designed products zip from computer terminal to machines on the factory floor and production lines switch at a moment's notice from making television sets to making personal computers.

are becoming an essential ingredient for the production of such items as watches and videocassette recorders. Overblown expectations for the use of robots in manufacturing situations as well as higher return requirements for dollars invested in robots are two primary reasons why robotics has not been as popular in the United States as in Japan. The key to competing with Japanese manufacturers in the future may be to find better uses of robots in various manufacturing situations. ▶

Strategies, Systems, and Processes

According to Kemper and Yehudai, an effective and efficient operations manager is skilled not only in management, production, and productivity but also in strategies, systems, and processes. A strategy is a plan of action. A system is a particular linking of organizational components that facilitates carrying out a process. A process is a flow of interrelated events toward a goal purpose or end. Strategies create interlocking systems and processes when they are comprehensive, functional, and dynamic—when they designate responsibility and provide criteria by which to measure output.[7]

BACK TO THE CASE

Firestone had not ignored quality assurance and statistical quality control. Far from it. The company had eighteen "roving inspectors" whose jobs were to do nothing but check for quality. A statistical quality control supervisor reported information, dealt with discrepancies, and tried to make sure components in noncompliance (in terms of length, depth, width, bias angle, etc.) were not used in production. However, little cooperation and coordination existed among marketing, operations, and research and development. Inspectors checked machines for pressures and settings and went over the finished product. Nevertheless, there was insufficient emphasis on preventing defects.

After the inspectors had collected the requisite data, they would give a supervisor the results and expect him to make corrections. Often the supervisor did not know any more than anyone else about what to do. Workers regarded the inspectors as company cops. Workers were told what they were doing wrong, but management gave little help.

The statistical quality controllers felt some responsibility to try to control quality, but it was difficult. The quality assurance process was not the result of input from production workers—the only people who could literally build quality into the product. This was the Firestone system.

Bridgestone, on the other hand, wanted people with sufficient education concerning quality assurance and they wanted people who had demonstrated an ability to work in teams. The Firestone men and women who stayed with Bridgestone received training in the basics of charting and teamwork. In a two-year period, Bridgestone devoted some 50,000 man-hours to training. Prospective employees each took twenty hours of unpaid training as part of the evaluation process.

The Bridgestone operations strategy was to involve everybody in quality assurance. Self-directed work teams offered an environment in which continuous improvement was a way of life. Working on teams was natural. Quality circles were low priority, for everybody in the plant was on a team. Not 20 but 100 percent of the people were members of a team.

OPERATIONS MANAGEMENT

Operations management deals with managing the production of goods and services in organizations. The sections that follow define *operations management* and discuss various strategies that managers can use to make production activities more effective and efficient.

Defining Operations Management

According to Chase and Aquilano, **operations management** is the performance of the managerial activities entailed in selecting, designing, operating, controlling, and updating production systems.[8] Figure 18.4 describes these activities and categorizes them as being either periodic or continual. The distinction between periodic and continual activities is based on the relative frequency of their performance: Periodic activities are performed from time to time, and continual activities are performed essentially without interruption.

Operations management is the systematic direction (strategy) and control of operations processes that transform resources into finished goods and services; it is getting things done by working with or through other people.

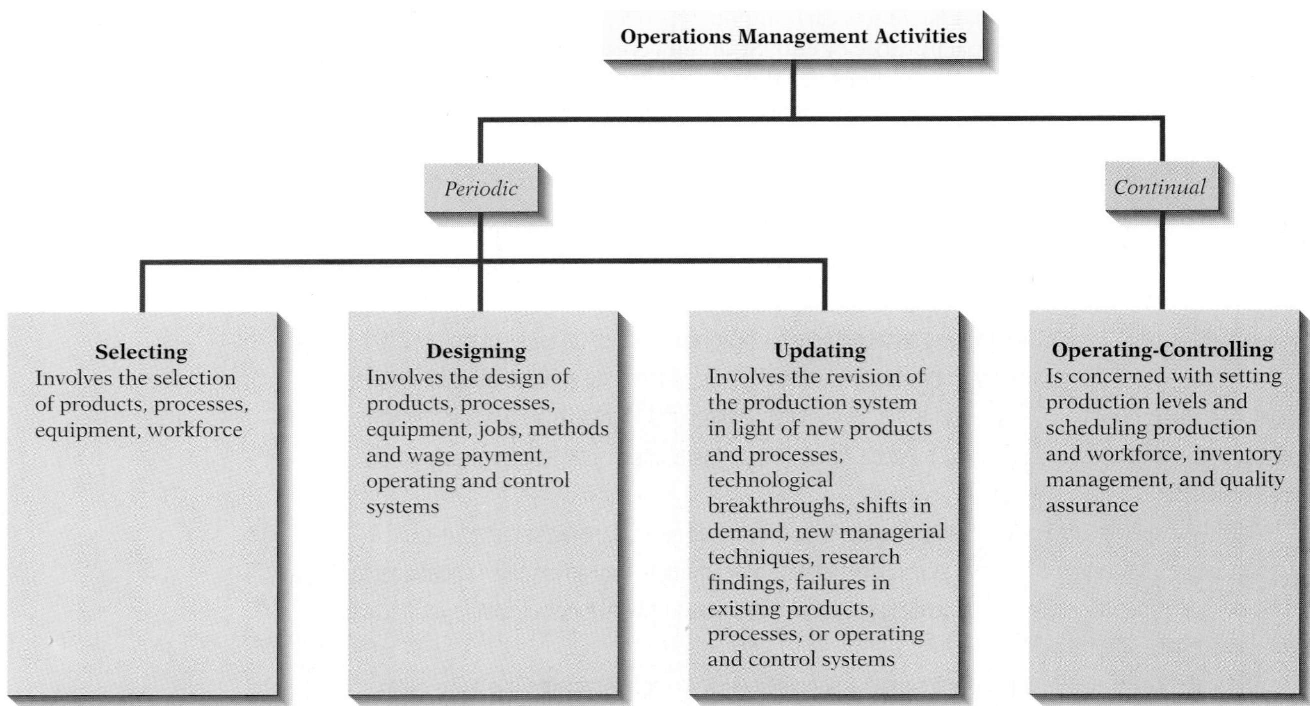

FIGURE 18.4 Major activities performed to manage production

Operations Management Considerations

Overall, *operations management* is the systematic direction and control of operations processes that transform resources into finished goods and services. The concept conveys three key notions: First, operations management involves managers, people who get things done by working with or through other people. Second, operations management takes place within the context of objectives and policies that drive the organization's strategic plans. Third, the criteria relevant for judging the actions taken as a result of operations management are standards for effectiveness and efficiency. **Effectiveness** is the degree to which managers attain organizational objectives: "doing the right things." **Efficiency** is the degree to which organizational resources contribute to productivity: "doing things right." A review of organizational performance based on these standards is essential to enhancing the success of any organization.

Effectiveness is the degree to which managers attain organizational objectives; it is doing the right things.

Efficiency is the degree to which organizational resources contribute to production; it is doing things right.

Operations strategies—capacity, location, product, process, layout, and *human resources*—are specific plans of action designed to assure that resources are obtained and used effectively and efficiently. An *operational strategy* is implemented by people who get things done with and through people. It is achieved in the context of objectives and policies derived from the organization's strategic plan.

Capacity Strategy

Capacity strategy is an operational plan of action aimed at providing the organization with the right facilities to produce the needed output at the right time.

Capacity strategy is a plan of action aimed at providing the organization with the right facilities to produce the needed output at the right time. The output capacity of the organization determines its ability to meet future demands for goods and services. *Insufficient capacity* results in loss of sales that in turn affects profits. *Excess capacity* results in higher production costs. The *optimal capacity strategy,* where quantity and timing are in balance, provides an excellent basis for minimizing operating costs and maximizing profits.

Capacity flexibility enables the company to deliver its goods and services to its customers in a shorter time than its competitors. Capacity flexibility is part of capacity strategy and includes having flexible plants and processes, broadly trained employees, and easy and economical access to external capacity such as suppliers.

Managers use capacity strategy to balance the costs of overcapacity and undercapacity. The inability to accurately forecast long-term demand makes the balancing task difficult and risky. Modifying long-range capacity decisions while in production is difficult and costly. In a highly competitive environment, construction of a new high-tech facility might take longer than the life cycle of the product. In the case of overcapacity, closing a plant saddles management with a high economic cost and an even higher social cost. Closing a plant is a tremendous burden on employees and the community in which the plant operates. These high social costs will have an adverse effect on the firm.

Traditionally, the concept of economies of scale has led to large plants that tried to do everything. More recently, the concept of the focused facility has suggested that better performance can be achieved if the plant is more specialized, concentrates on fewer tasks, and is therefore smaller.

A five-step process can aid management in making sound strategic capacity decisions: (1) measure the capacity of currently available facilities; (2) estimate future capacity needs based on demand forecasts; (3) compare future capacity needs and available capacity to determine whether capacity must be increased or decreased; (4) identify ways to accommodate long-range capacity changes (expansion or reduction); and (5) select the best alternative based on a quantitative and qualitative evaluation.

Location Strategy

Location strategy is a plan of action that provides the organization with a competitive location for its headquarters, manufacturing, service, and distribution activities. A competitive location results in lower transportation and communication costs among the various facilities, costs that may run as high as 20 to 30 percent of a product's selling price. These costs greatly affect the volume of sales and amount of profit generated by a particular product. Additionally, many other quantitative and qualitative factors are important when formulating location strategy.

Location strategy is an operational plan of action that provides the organization with a competitive location for its headquarters, manufacturing, services, and distribution activities.

A successful location strategy requires a company to consider the following major location factors in its location study: the nearness to market and distribution centers; the nearness to vendors and resources; the requirements of federal, state, and local governments; the character of direct competition; the degree of interaction with the rest of the corporation; the quality and quantity of labor pools; the environmental attractiveness of the area; the requirements of taxes and financing; the kinds of existing and potential transportation; and the quality of utilities and services. The dynamic nature of these factors could make what is a competitive location today an undesirable location in five years.

ETHICS HIGHLIGHT
Firestone Exits LaVergne

Firestone built its radial truck tire plant in LaVergne in 1972. After a decade in LaVergne, Tennessee, with demand less than anticipated, a hostile local union, and quality problems, Firestone announced that it was planning to either sell the LaVergne plant or close it if a buyer could not be found. Firestone had shut down seven of its seventeen plants, and it was clear that the company planned to go ahead with the closure of the LaVergne plant, and the workers at Lavergne would lose their jobs. Had Firestone taken seriously what some believe to be an obligation to the community and employees?

When Bridgestone negotiated the purchase of this Firestone radial tire plant in La Vergne, Tennessee, it developed what many hope will be a long-range ethical commitment to the community and workers in La Vergne.

Bridgestone wanted to locate in Tennessee. Tennessee was openly wooing Japanese companies—Nissan was in Smyrna, Komatsu, in Chattanooga, Sharp, in Memphis, and Toshiba, in the tiny town of Lebanon. Bridgestone had ample reason for buying the LaVergne plant and had entered negotiations with Firestone. Bridgestone sent negotiators to LaVergne to arrange to buy the plant. Bridgestone sought a purchase that was contingent on a contract with the union. The union leadership seemed to view the negotiations as an opportunity to win concessions, not make them. Both sides dug in their heels. Then, in a moment of ill-advised bravado, the local union president told the Japanese that they could just go back to Japan. Had the union taken seriously its obligation to its members and, some might ask, to the community?

Bridgestone's negotiators went home. Soon the local union's officers were summoned to Akron to meet with Firestone's top management and officers of the International Rubber Workers Union. This union and management discussion resulted in an invitation for Bridgestone negotiators to come back to the bargaining table. This time both sides made commitments. Bridgestone pledged to recall laid-off workers. The union eased work rules and promised to lobby for ratification. The $52 million sale went through.

The social relationships that the employees, the community, and Firestone became involved in are believed by many to be legitimate expectations that were left unstated in the agreement Firestone made when it located in LaVergne. Bridgestone, on the other hand, developed what many hope will be a long-range ethical commitment to the community and workers. A successful location strategy requires that a company not only consider major location factors, but also long-range ethical and cultural factors as well. ▶

Product Strategy

Product strategy is an operational plan of action that determines which goods and services an organization will produce and market.

Product strategy is a plan of action outlining which goods and services an organization will produce and market. Product strategy is a main component of the operations strategy and the link between the operations strategy and the other functional strategies, especially marketing and research and development. In essence, product, marketing, and research and development strategies fit together to build an effective overall operations strategy. The product strategy and the operations strategy of the business should take into account the strengths and weaknesses of operations, which are primarily internal, as well as those of other functional areas which deal more with external opportunities and threats.

Cooperation and coordination among marketing, operations, and research and development from the inception of a new product is beneficial to the company. At the very least, it ensures a smooth transition from research and development to production. Operations people are able to contribute to the quality of the total product, not just attempt to improve the quality of the components. Even the most sophisticated product can be designed so that it is relatively simple to produce, reducing the number of units that must be scrapped or reworked during production and reducing the need for highly trained and highly paid employees. The product's price competitiveness or profits can thus increase.

Process Strategy

Process strategy is an operational plan of action that determines which means and methods the organization will use to transform resources into goods and services.

Process strategy is a plan of action outlining the means and the methods that the organization uses to transform resources into goods and services. Materials, labor, information, equipment, and managerial skills are resources that must be transformed. A competitive process strategy will ensure the most efficient and effective use of the organization's resources.

Manufacturing processes may be grouped into three different types. The first type is the *continuous process,* a product-oriented high volume, low-variety process, used, for example, in producing chemicals, beer, and petroleum products. The second type is the *repetitive process,* a product-oriented production process that uses modules, used for producing items in large lots. This mass-production or assembly-line process is used in the auto and appliance industries. The third manufacturing process is used to produce small lots of custom-designed products such as furniture and is commonly known as the *job-shop process,* a high variety, low volume system. The production of one-of-a-kind items is included in this type of process, as is unit production. Spaceship and weapons system production are considered job-shop activities. It is common for an organization to use more than one type of manufacturing process at the same time and in the same facility.

Process strategy is directly linked to product strategy. The decision to select a particular process strategy may be the result of external market opportunities or threats. When this is true, the product takes center stage and the process becomes a function of the product. The corporation decides what it wants to produce then it selects a process strategy to produce it.

The function of process strategy is to determine what equipment will be used, what maintenance will be necessary, and what level of automation will be most effective and efficient. The type of employees and the level of employee skills needed are a direct result of the process strategy.

BACK TO THE CASE

After changing the product strategy, Bridgestone's management developed a new process strategy for workers at the LaVergne plant. Managers considered what equipment would be used, what maintenance was necessary, what level of automation would be most effective and efficient, and what workers could do to improve the product and process. The idea was that people could observe a process, even those who were strangers to it. Impartial observers saw things that closely involved workers did not. Worker suggestions were helpful. Inviting people to observe one process resulted in many improvements that reduced the changeover time in treads on the quad cold tuber by 80 percent.

Worker observations at the LaVergne facility began with the study of machine processes, but then quickly spread to capacity, product, and process activities. Workers soon found other applications. When a worker suffered a partial loss of two fingers while using new machinery, few figured that the fault lay with the equipment. New machines are supposed to be safe! Workers observed other workers using the equipment. Firestone's approach would have been to tell workers that the body ply cutter was new and nothing could be wrong with it. Firestone's management would have said that the injured worker had not been following the proper procedures and that the accident was the worker's fault. Bridgestone's management, however, wanted to know the hazards a worker faced when using the equipment. Further, management wondered what other ways the cutter might present a hazard.

About a dozen people gathered on the midnight shift, divided the machine into four sectors, and conducted a four-hour, safety-sensitivity training class. Workers found no less than sixty-three potential dangers, including six places where the absence of machine guards could allow a worker to injure fingers.

The watchers gathered afterward to list their observations and assign priorities and countermeasures. Since then, workers have conducted many observations of production and operations activities. Some observations have included follow-ups to earlier ones. Usually, top managers are invited as well, to become familiar with activities in the plant.

Layout Strategy

Layout strategy is a plan of action that outlines the location and flow of all organizational resources around, into, and within production and service facilities. A cost-effective and cost-efficient layout strategy is one that minimizes the cost of processing, transporting, and storing materials throughout the production and service cycle.

Layout strategy is an operational plan that determines the location and flow of organizational resources around, into, and within production and service facilities.

A layout strategy is closely linked, directly and indirectly, to the rest of the components of operations strategy—capacity, location, product, process, and human resource. The layout strategy is usually one of the last to be formulated. It must target capacity and process requirements. It must satisfy the organization's product design, quality, and quantity requirements. Finally, it must target facility and location require-

Layout is the overall arrangement of equipment, work areas, service areas, and storage areas within a facility that produces goods or provides services.

Product layout is a layout designed to accommodate a limited number of different products that require high volumes, highly specialized equipment, and narrow employee skills.

Process (functional) layout is a layout pattern based primarily on grouping together similar types of equipment.

Fixed position layout is a layout plan appropriate for organizations involved in a large number of different tasks that require low volumes, multipurpose equipment, and broad employee skills.

ments. An effective layout strategy will be compatible with the organization's available quality of work life.

A **layout** is the overall arrangement of equipment, work areas, service areas, and storage areas within a facility that produces goods or provides services. The three basic types of layouts for manufacturing facilities are product, process, and fixed position.

1. A **product layout** is appropriate for organizations that produce and service a limited number of different products. It is not appropriate for an organization that is involved with constant or frequent changes of products. A product layout is most appropriate when production volumes are high, equipment is highly specialized, and the employees' skills are narrow.
2. A **process (functional) layout** is appropriate for organizations involved in a large number of different tasks. It best serves an organization whose production volumes are low, equipment is multipurpose, and employees' skills are broad.
3. The **fixed position layout** is most appropriate for an organization whose product is stationary while resources flow. A *group technology layout* is a cell of a product layout within a larger process layout. It benefits organizations that require both types of layout.

Most manufacturing facilities are a combination of two or more different types of layouts. Various techniques assist in designing an efficient and effective layout that meets the required specifications. Figure 18.5 illustrates each of the three basic layout patterns.

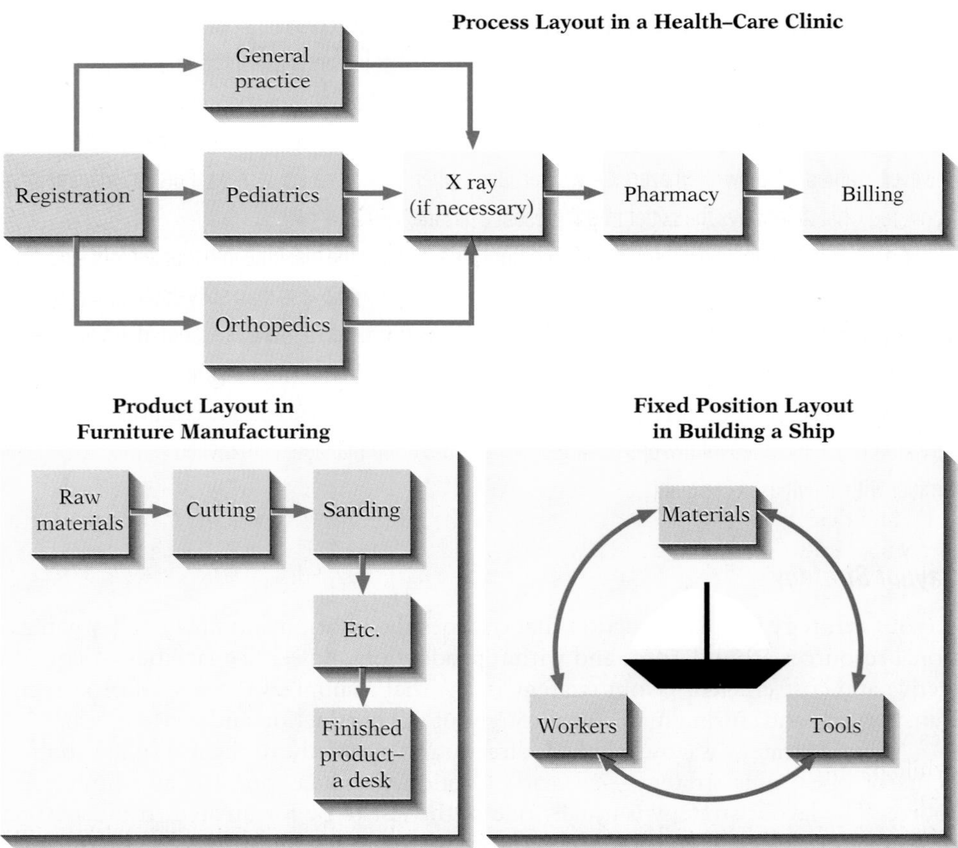

FIGURE 18.5 Three basic layout patterns

Human Resources Strategy

Human resources are individuals engaged in any of the organization's activities. There are two human resource imperatives: (1) the need to optimize individual, group, and organizational effectiveness; and (2) the need to enhance the quality of organizational life. A **human resources strategy** is a plan to use the organization's human resources effectively and efficiently while maintaining or improving the quality of work life.

Human resources strategy is an operational plan to use the organization's human resources effectively and efficiently.

As discussed in Chapter 11, human resource management is about employees. Employees are the means of enhancing organizational effectiveness. Whereas financial management attempts to increase organizational effectiveness through the allocation and conservation of financial resources, human resource management (personnel management) attempts to increase organizational effectiveness through factors like the establishment of personnel policies, education and training, and procedures.

Manpower planning is an operational plan that focuses on hiring the right employees for a job and training them to be productive.

Operations management attempts to increase organizational effectiveness by the methods used in the manufacturing and service processes. Human resources, one such factor, must be compatible with operations tasks.

Manpower planning is the primary focus of the operations human resource strategy. Hiring the right employees for a job and training them to be productive is a lengthy and costly process. Fair treatment and trust are the basis of a human resource strategy. The employee, not operations, takes center stage.

Job design is an operational plan that determines who will do a specific job and how and where the job will be done.

Job design is concerned with who will do a specific job and with how and where the job will be done. The goal of job design is to facilitate productivity. Successful job design takes into account efficiency and behavior. Job design must also guarantee that working conditions are safe and that the health of the employees will not be jeopardized in the short or long run.

Work methods analysis is an operational tool used to improve productivity and ensure the safety of workers.

Motion study techniques are operational tools that are used to improve productivity.

Work methods analysis is used to improve productivity and can be performed for new or existing jobs. **Motion study techniques** are also used to improve productivity.

Work measurement methods are operational tools that are used to establish labor standards.

Work measurement methods are used to establish labor standards. These standards can be used for planning, control, productivity improvements, costing and pricing, bidding, compensation, motivation, and financial incentives.

DIVERSITY HIGHLIGHT
Including Workers Who Are Disabled in the Production Process

Effective July 1992, the Americans with Disabilities Act (ADA) requires all companies with twenty-five or more employees to begin hiring qualified people with disabilities if reasonable accommodations can be made without undue hardship. Statistics compiled by government agencies, research firms, and companies that employ the disabled show that workers who are disabled are just as productive as their peers who are not physically challenged and that they are more punctual and less transient.

The Americans with Disabilities Act requires that all companies with 25 or more employees must hire qualified people with disabilities providing that reasonable accommodations can be made without undue hardship.

The design and implementation of new training programs will help organization members understand what the law means by "disabled." Under the ADA, persons are considered disabled if they have a physical or mental impairment that substantially limits one or more major life activities, or if they have a record of impairment. According to the law, under special circumstances, an individual can also be considered disabled if he or she has a relationship or association with a person who is disabled.

Because of this new law, companies should begin at once reviewing how employees who are disabled can be included within the organizational production process while maintaining or improving productivity. To be better equipped to meet this challenge, management should take steps such as assessing how to best design job application forms and other hiring procedures so that job candidates with disabilities can be adequately evaluated for a job. Management should also evaluate the role of preemployment physicals when considering such job candidates and determine whether established training programs should be redesigned when considering them as trainees. In order to attract and retain only the most productive workers, management should evaluate the effectiveness of existing benefits packages in meeting the needs of workers who are disabled. Management should also evaluate organizational career opportunities as they relate to the advancement of all workers, including those with disabilities. ▶

OPERATIONS CONTROL COMPONENTS

Once a decision is made to design an operational plan of action, resource allocations are considered. After the functional operations strategy has been determined using marketing and financial plans of action, specific tasks to accomplish the functional objectives are considered. This is known as operations control.

Operations control is an operational plan that specifies the operational activities of an organization.

Operations control is making sure that operations activities are carried out as planned. Major components of operations control include *just-in-time inventory control, maintenance control, cost control, budget control, ratio analysis control and, materials control.* Each of these components is discussed in detail in the following sections.

Just-in-Time Inventory Control

Just-in-time (JIT) inventory control is an inventory control technique that reduces inventories to a minimum by arranging for components to be delivered to the production facility just in time to be used.

Just-in-time (JIT) inventory control is control that reduces inventories to a minimum by arranging for them to be delivered to the production facility "just in time" to be used. The concept, developed primarily by the Toyota Motor Company of Japan,[9] is also called "zero inventory" and "kanban"—the latter a Japanese term referring to purchasing raw materials by using a special card ordering form.

JIT is based on the management philosophy that products should be manufactured when customers need them and in the quantities customers need in order to minimize levels of raw materials and finished goods inventories kept on hand.[10] Overall, JIT emphasizes maintaining operations within a company by using only the resources that are absolutely necessary to meet customer demand.

JIT works best in companies that manufacture relatively standardized products and that have consistent product demand. Such companies can comfortably order materials from suppliers and assemble products in several small, continuous batches. The result is a smooth, consistent flow of purchased materials and assembled products and little inventory buildup. Companies that manufacture nonstandardized products that have sporadic or seasonal demand generally must face more irregular purchases of raw materials from suppliers, more uneven production cycles, and greater accumulations of inventory.

If implemented successfully, JIT can enhance organizational performance in several important ways. First, it can reduce unnecessary labor expenses generated by products manufactured but not sold. Second, it can minimize the tying up of monetary resources needed to purchase production related materials that do not result in sales on a timely basis.[11] Third, it can help management minimize expenses normally associated with maintaining an inventory—for example, storage and handling costs. Better inventory management and improved control of labor costs are two of the most commonly cited benefits of JIT.[12]

Experience indicates that successful JIT programs tend to have certain common characteristics:[13]

1. *Closeness of suppliers.* Manufacturers using JIT find it beneficial to have suppliers of raw materials within short distances of them. As companies begin to order smaller quantities of raw materials, suppliers sometimes must be asked to make one or more deliveries per day. Short distances make multiple deliveries per day feasible.

2. *High quality of materials purchased from suppliers.* Manufacturers using JIT find it difficult to overcome problems caused by defective materials purchased from suppliers. Since the materials inventory is kept small, defective materials may mean that the manufacturer must wait until the next delivery from the supplier before the production process can continue. Such production slowdowns can be disadvantageous, causing late delivery to customers or lost sales because finished products are unavailable.
3. *Well-organized receiving and handling of materials purchased from suppliers.* Companies using JIT must be able to receive and handle raw materials effectively and efficiently. Such materials must be available for the production process where and when they are needed. Naturally, if the materials are not available, extra costs are built into the production process.
4. *Strong management commitment.* Management must be strongly committed to the concept of JIT. The system takes time and effort to plan, install, and improve—and is therefore expensive to implement. Management must be willing to commit funds to initiate the JIT system and to support it once it is functioning.

Maintenance Control

Maintenance control is control aimed at keeping the organization's facility and equipment functioning at predetermined work levels. In the planning stage, managers must select a strategy that will direct personnel to fix equipment before it malfunctions or after it malfunctions. Fixing equipment before it malfunctions is referred to as a **pure-preventive maintenance policy**. At the other end of the maintenance continuum is the **pure-breakdown policy**—fixing equipment after it malfunctions.

Pure-preventive maintenance policy is a policy that assures that machine adjustments, lubrication, cleaning, parts replacement, painting, and needed repairs and overhauls are performed before malfunction of facilities or machines occurs.

Pure-breakdown (repair) policy is a policy whereby machine adjustments, lubrication, cleaning, parts replacement, painting, and needed repairs and overhaul are performed after malfunction of facilities or machines occurs.

Most organizations implement a maintenance strategy somewhere in the middle of the maintenance continuum. Management faces a trade-off situation. An attempt is made to select a level and a frequency of maintenance that minimizes the cost of preventive maintenance and of breakdowns (repair). Since no level of preventive maintenance can eliminate breakdowns completely, repair is always an important activity. Whether management decides on a pure-preventive or pure-breakdown policy, or something in between, the prerequisite for a successful maintenance program is the availability of maintenance parts and supplies or replacement (standby) equipment. Some organizations choose to keep standby machines to protect themselves against the consequences of breakdowns. Plants that use special-purpose equipment are more likely to invest in standby equipment than plants that have general-purpose equipment.

Cost Control

Cost control is broad control aimed at keeping all organizational costs at planned levels. Since cost control relates to all organizational costs, it emphasizes activities in all organizational areas, such as research and development, operations, marketing, and finance. If an organization is to be successful, managers must control costs in all organizational areas. Cost control, therefore, is an important responsibility of all managers in an organization.

Operations activities are very cost intensive—perhaps the most cost intensive of all organizational activities. As a result, when significant cost savings are realized in organizations, they are generally realized at the operations level.

Overall, operations managers are responsible for controlling the cost of goods or services sold. Since producing goods and services at or below planned cost levels is the primary objective of operations managers, they are commonly evaluated primarily on the basis of cost control. When operations costs consistently are above planned levels, a change in operations management may be necessary.

The more general cost control process involves four stages: 1) establishing standard or planned cost amounts, 2) measuring actual costs incurred, 3) comparing planned costs to incurred costs, and 4) making needed changes to reduce actual costs to planned cost when necessary. Following these stages for more specific operations cost control, the operations manager must first establish planned costs or cost standards for operations activities like labor, materials, and overhead. Next, the operations manager must actually measure or calculate the costs incurred for these activities. Third, the operations managers must compare actual operations costs to planned operations costs. Fourth, the operations manager must take steps to reduce actual operations costs to planned levels if necessary.

Budgetary Control

A **budget** is a control tool that outlines how funds will be obtained and spent in a given period.

As described in chapter 8, a budget is a single-use financial plan that covers a specified length of time. The **budget** of an organization is the financial plan outlining how funds in a given period will be obtained and spent.

In addition to being a financial plan, however, a budget can be the basis for *budgetary control,* making sure that income and expenses occur as planned.[14] As managers gather information on actual receipts and expenditures within an operating period, significant deviations from budgeted amounts may be uncovered. In such a case, managers can develop and implement a control strategy aimed at making actual performance more consistent with planned performance. This, of course, assumes that the plan contained in the budget is appropriate for the organization. The following sections discuss potential pitfalls of budgets and people considerations in using budgets.

Potential Pitfalls of Budgets

To maximize the benefits of using budgets, managers must be able to avoid several potential pitfalls. These pitfalls include:

1. *Placing too much emphasis on relatively insignificant organizational expenses.* In preparing and implementing a budget, managers should allocate more time for dealing with significant organizational expenses and less time for relatively insignificant organizational expenses. For example, the amount of time managers spend on developing and implementing a budget for labor costs typically should be much more than the amount of time managers spend on developing and implementing a budget for office supplies.
2. *Increasing budgeted expenses year after year without adequate information.* It does not necessarily follow that items contained in last year's budget should be increased this year. Perhaps the best-known method developed to overcome this potential pitfall is zero-base budgeting.[15] Zero-base budgeting is the planning and budgeting process that requires managers to justify their entire budget requests in detail rather than simply to refer to budget amounts established in previous years.[16]

   Zero-base budgeting requires managers to justify their entire budget request in detail rather than simply referring to budget amounts established in previous years.

   Some management theorists believe **zero-base budgeting** is a more complete management tool than more traditional budgeting, which simply starts with the budget amount established in the prior year,[17] because more focused identification and control of each budget item is emphasized. This tool, however, will be implemented successfully only if management is able to explain adequately what zero-base budgeting is and how it will be used within a particular organization.[18] One of the earliest and most commonly cited successes in implementing a zero-base budgeting program was in the Department of Agriculture's Office of Budget and Finance.[19]
3. *Ignoring the fact that budgets must be changed periodically.* Managers should recognize that such factors as costs of materials, newly developed technology, and product demand constantly are changing and that budgets should be reviewed and modified periodically in response to these changes. A special type of budget called a variable budget is sometimes used to determine automatically such needed

changes in budgets. **Variable budgets** outline various levels of resources to be allocated for each organizational activity, depending on the level of production within the organization. It follows, then, that a variable budget automatically indicates increases or decreases in the amount of resources allocated for various organizational activities, depending on whether production levels increase or decrease. Variable budgets also have been called flexible budgets.

Variable budgets are budgets that outline various levels of resources to be allocated for each organizational activity, depending on the level of production within the organization. Also called flexible budgeting.

People Considerations in Using Budgets

Many managers believe that although budgets are valuable planning and control tools, they can result in major human relations problems in an organization. For example, in a classic article by Chris Argyris, budgets are shown to build pressures that unite workers against management, cause harmful conflict between management and factory workers, and create tensions that result in worker inefficiency and worker aggression against management.[20] Depending on the severity of such problems, budgets may result in more harm to the organization than good.

Several strategies have been suggested to minimize the human relations problems caused by budgets. The most often recommended strategy is to design and implement appropriate human relations training programs for finance personnel, accounting personnel, production supervisors, and all other key people involved in the formulation and use of budgets. These training programs should be designed to emphasize both the advantages and disadvantages of applying pressure on people through budgets and the possible results of using budgets to imply organization member success or failure.[21]

Ratio Analysis

Another type of control uses ratio analysis.[22] A *ratio* is a relationship between two numbers that is calculated by dividing one number into the other. **Ratio analysis** is the process of generating information that summarizes the financial position of an organization through the calculation of ratios based on various financial measures that appear on the organization's balance sheet and income statements.[23] The ratios available to managers for controlling organizations typically are divided into four categories, as shown in Table 18.2: (1) liquidity ratios, (2) leverage ratios, (3) activity ratios, and (4) profitability ratios.

Ratio analysis is a control tool that summarizes the financial position of an organization by calculating ratios based on various financial measures.

Using Ratios to Control Organizations

Managers can use ratio analysis in three ways to control an organization.[24] First, managers should evaluate all ratios simultaneously. This strategy ensures that managers will

TABLE 18.2 Four categories of ratios

Type	*Example*	*Calculation*	*Interpretation*
Profitability	Return on investment (ROI)	$\frac{\text{Profit after taxes}}{\text{Total assets}}$	Productivity of assets
Liquidity	Current ratio	$\frac{\text{Current assets}}{\text{Current liabilities}}$	Short-term solvency
Activity	Inventory turnover	$\frac{\text{Sales}}{\text{Inventory}}$	Efficiency of inventory management
Leverage	Debt ratio	$\frac{\text{Total debt}}{\text{Total assets}}$	How a company finances itself

develop and implement a control strategy appropriate for the organization as a whole rather than one that suits only one phase or segment of the organization.

Second, managers should compare computed values for ratios in a specific organization with the values of industry averages for those ratios. (The values of industry averages for the ratios can be obtained from Dun & Bradstreet; Robert Morris Associates, a national association of bank loan officers; the Federal Trade Commission; and the Securities and Exchange Commission.) Managers can increase the probability of formulating and implementing appropriate control strategies by comparing their financial situation to that of competitors.

Third, managers' use of ratios to control an organization also should involve trend analysis. Managers must remember that any set of ratio values is actually only a determination of relationships that exist in a specified time period, perhaps a year. To use ratio analysis to its maximum advantage, values for ratios should be accumulated for a number of successive time periods to uncover specific organizational trends. Once these trends are uncovered, managers can formulate and implement appropriate strategies for dealing with them.

Materials Control

Materials control is an operational activity that determines the flow of materials from vendors through an operations system to customers.

Materials control is control that supports the flow of materials from vendors through an operations system to customers. The ability to achieve the desired level of product cost, quality, availability, dependability, and flexibility depends heavily on the effective and efficient flow of materials. In its broadest form, materials management activities can be organized into six groups or functions: purchasing, receiving, inventorying, floor controlling, trafficking, and shipping and distributing. This structure is a result of a long process of organizational evolution.

Over 50 percent of the expenditures of a typical manufacturing company are spent on procurement of materials, including raw materials, parts, sub-assemblies, and supplies, and the purchasing department is engaged in several activities. Purchasing of production materials is largely automated and linked to a resources requirement planning system. Purchasing of all other materials is based on a requisition from the user. Purchasing does not end with the placement of an order; order follow-up is equally crucial.

Receiving activities may include unloading, identifying, inspecting, reporting, and storing inbound shipments. Shipping and distribution activities are similar to receiving. They may include preparing documents, packaging, labeling, loading, and directing outbound shipments to customers and to distribution centers.

Shipping and receiving activities are sometimes organized as one unit. A traffic manager's main activities include selection of the transportation mode, coordination of arrival and departure of shipments, and audit of freight bills.

Inventory control activities ensure the continuous availability of purchased materials. Work-in-process and finished-goods inventory are inventory control subsystems. Inventory control specifies what, when, and how much to buy. Held inventories buffer a variety of uncertainties that can disrupt supply. Since holding inventory is costly, an optimal inventory control policy must provide a predetermined level of certainty of supply at the lowest possible cost.

Shop-floor control activities include input/output control, scheduling, sequencing, routing, dispatching, and expediting.

While many materials management activities can be programmed, it is the human factor that is the key to a competitive performance. Skilled and motivated employees are crucial.

BACK TO THE CASE

What a morale booster for a guy on the midnight to 8 A.M. shift to have the vice president for production there. Having a vice president observing workers had not been possible at Firestone because workers did not trust the bosses and suspected that the observations were merely a device to find fault with workers. That is not the case at Bridgestone; in addition to the vice president, four observers were present—a plant visitor, a member of the human resources staff, a chemist, and a project manager.

"Write down anything," the supervisor said over the roar of machines. The observers wrote things such as, "This guy is walking too much," or "Looks like he's not handling the knife right." The observers did not ask questions of the two men on the machine, but watched silently as the workers did their jobs.

For eighteen minutes the group watched and took notes, focusing principally on one worker who scurried about changing computerized machine settings for the new lot, slicing off the old stock with a knife, and prying its remains from the tuber with a crowbar.

Then the observers reassembled in a conference room above the factory floor. The supervisor quickly scrawled three headings across a broad sheet of paper: "Problem/Countermeasure/Who."

He went around the observers one by one, asking for their input. Someone said that one worker seemed to spend a lot of time flipping through a book of computer codes looking for the correct one. Someone suggested that the codes be flagged. Another noted that the paperwork involved with the die change was more difficult when the worker wore gloves. The supervisor assigned a countermeasure: "Do as much paperwork before change as possible."

Each countermeasure was assigned to a person in the "who" list. The supervisor promised to send out a copy to everyone involved and ask for dates when changes could be made. In a week, the supervisor called back to check on the suggested changes. Another observation was scheduled for two weeks later to see if the changes had helped. Such involvement by top management helps workers. Instead of saying "Why's everything so screwed up?" bosses now say, "I know why Mark's having that problem. I saw it myself, and I've got to get him some resources to help."

When Bridgestone began the observations, the countermeasures considered worthwhile were those that saved ten minutes. Now Bridgestone is looking at improving operations that take only two minutes.

SELECTED OPERATIONS CONTROL TOOLS

In addition to understanding production, operations management, and operations control, managers also should be aware of various operations control tools that can be used within an operations facility. A **control tool** is a specific procedure or technique that presents pertinent organizational information in a way that helps managers and workers develop and implement appropriate control strategy. That is, a control tool helps managers and workers pinpoint the organizational strengths and weaknesses on which a useful control strategy must focus. This section discusses specific control tools for day-to-day operations as well as for larger run operations.

Control tool is a specific procedure or technique that presents pertinent organizational information in such a way that a manager is aided in developing and implementing an appropriate control strategy.

Using Control Tools to Control Organizations

Continual improvement of operations is not theoretical. On a daily basis, organizations struggle with new ways of doing things. Organizations have different goals and strategies, but in many respects they are the same. The goal of continual improvement applies not just to money-making enterprises, but to those with other missions as well.

On the one hand, organizational leaders are continually changing systems and personal styles of management. And on the other, everyone within the organization is learning to live with change. Continuous improvement is nothing but the development and use of better methods.

Inspection

Traditionally, managers believed that if you wanted good quality, you hired many inspectors. These inspectors made sure an operation was producing at the quality level expected. Inspectors simply examined and graded finished products or components, parts, or services at any stage of operation by measuring, tasting, touching, weighing, disassembling, destroying, and testing. The goal of inspection was to detect unacceptable quality levels before a bad product or service reached a customer. When inspectors found more defects they blamed the workers and increased the number of inspectors.

Today, managers know that inspection will not catch problems built into the system. The traditional inspection process is not improvement and does not guarantee quality. Inspection, according to Deming, is a limited, grossly overused, and often misused tool.[25] Further, Deming recommends that management stop relying on mass inspection to achieve quality. Deming advocates either 100 percent inspection in those cases where defect-free work is impossible or no inspection where the level of defects is acceptably small.

Management by Exception

Management by exception is a control tool that allows only significant deviations between planned and actual performance to be brought to the manager's attention.

Management by exception is a control technique that allows only significant deviations between planned and actual performance to be brought to a manager's attention.[26] Actually, management by exception is based on the exception principle, a management principle that appears in early management literature.[27] The exception principle recommends that subordinates handle all routine organizational matters, leaving managers to handle only nonroutine, or exceptional, organizational issues.

Although exceptional issues might be uncovered when managers themselves detect significant deviation between standards and performance, some managers establish rules to ensure that exceptional issues surface as a matter of normal operating procedure. It is important to establish the rules carefully, so that a true deviation is always brought to the manager's attention. Two examples of such rules are the following:[28]

1. A department manager must immediately inform the plant manager if actual weekly labor costs exceed estimated weekly labor costs by more than 15 percent.
2. A department manager must immediately inform the plant manager if actual dollars spent plus estimated dollars to be spent on a special project exceed the funds approved for the project by more than 10 percent.

These two rules focus on production-related expenditures. However, such rules can be established in virtually any organizational area.

If appropriately administered, management by exception yields the added advantage of ensuring the best use of a manager's time. Because it brings only significant issues to the manager's attention, the possibility that the manager will spend valuable time working on relatively insignificant issues is automatically eliminated.

Of course, the significant issues brought to the manager's attention could be organizational strengths as well as organizational weaknesses. The manager should try to eliminate the weaknesses and reinforce the strengths.

Management by Objectives

Management by objectives, as discussed in chapter 4, is a control tool in which the manager assigns a specialized set of objectives and action plans to the workers and then rewards the individuals on the basis of how close they come to reaching their goals. It is a control technique that has been implemented successfully in some corporations in order to use an employee-participative means to improve productivity.

Breakeven Analysis

Another production-related control tool commonly used by managers is breakeven analysis. **Breakeven analysis** is the process of generating information that summarizes various levels of profit or loss associated with various levels of production. The following sections discuss (1) the basic ingredients of breakeven analysis, (2) the types of breakeven analysis available to managers, and (3) the relationship between breakeven analysis and controlling.

Breakeven analysis is a control tool that summarizes the various levels of profit or loss associated with various levels of production.

Basic Ingredients of Breakeven Analysis

Breakeven analysis typically includes reflection, discussion, reasoning, and decision making relative to the following seven major ingredients:

1. *Fixed costs.* **Fixed costs** are expenses incurred by the organization regardless of the number of products produced. Some examples are real estate taxes, upkeep to the exterior of a business building, and interest expenses on money borrowed to finance the purchase of equipment.
2. *Variable costs.* Expenses that fluctuate with the number of products produced are called **variable costs.** Some examples are costs of packaging a product, costs of materials needed to make the product, and costs associated with packing products to prepare them for shipping.
3. *Total costs.* **Total costs** are simply the sum of fixed costs and variable costs associated with production.
4. *Total revenue.* **Total revenue** is all sales dollars accumulated from selling manufactured products or services. Naturally, total revenue increases as more products are sold.
5. *Profits.* **Profits** are defined as the amount of total revenue that exceeds the total costs of producing the products sold.
6. *Loss.* **Loss** is the amount of the total costs of producing a product that exceeds the total revenue gained from selling the product.
7. *Breakeven point.* The **breakeven point** is the situation wherein the total revenue of an organization equals its total costs—that is, the point at which the organization is generating only enough revenue to cover its costs. The company is neither gaining a profit nor incurring a loss.

Fixed costs are expenses incurred regardless of the number of products produced.

Variable costs are expenses that fluctuate with the number of products produced.

Total costs are the sum of fixed costs and variable costs.

Total revenue is all sales dollars accumulated from selling goods or services that are produced.

Profits are the amount of total revenue that exceeds total costs.

Loss is the amount of the total costs of producing a product that exceeds the total revenue.

The **breakeven point** is the situation wherein the total revenue of an organization equals its total costs.

Types of Breakeven Analysis

There are two somewhat different procedures for determining the same breakeven point for an organization: algebraic breakeven analysis and graphic breakeven analysis.

Algebraic Breakeven Analysis. The following simple formula is commonly used to determine the level of production at which an organization breaks even:

$$BE = \frac{FC}{P - VC}$$

where—

BE = the level of production at which the firm breaks even

FC = total fixed costs of production

P = price at which each individual unit is sold to customers

VC = variable costs associated with each product manufactured and sold

Two sequential steps must be followed in using this formula to calculate a breakeven point. First, the variable costs associated with producing each unit must be subtracted from the price at which each unit will sell. The purpose of this calculation is to determine how much of the selling price of each unit sold can go toward covering total fixed costs incurred from producing all products. The second step is to divide the remainder calculated in the first step into total fixed costs. The purpose of this calculation is to determine how many units must be produced and sold to cover fixed costs. This number of units is the breakeven point for the organization.

For example, a book publisher could face the fixed costs and variable costs per paperback book presented in Table 18.3. If the publisher wants to sell each book for $12, the breakeven point could be calculated as follows:

$$BE = \frac{\$88,800}{\$12 - \$6}$$

$$BE = \frac{\$88,800}{\$6}$$

$$BE = 14,800 \text{ copies}$$

This calculation indicates that if expenses and selling price remain stable, the book publisher will incur a loss if book sales are fewer than 14,800 copies, will break even if book sales equal 14,800 copies, and will make a profit if book sales exceed 14,800 copies.

Graphic Breakeven Analysis. Graphic breakeven analysis entails the construction of a graph that shows all the critical elements in a breakeven analysis. Figure 18.6 is a breakeven graph for the book publisher. Note that in a breakeven graph, the total revenue line starts at zero.

Using the Algebraic and Graphic Breakeven Methods. Both the algebraic and the graphic methods of breakeven analysis for the book publisher result in the same breakeven point—14,800 books produced and sold. However, the processes used to arrive at the point are quite different.

The situation managers face usually determines which breakeven method they should use. For example, if managers simply desire a quick yet accurate determination of a breakeven point, the algebraic method generally suffices. If they prefer a more complete picture of the cumulative relationships between the breakeven point, fixed costs, and escalating variable costs, the graphic breakeven method probably is more useful. The book publisher could quickly and easily see from Figure 18.6 the cumulative relationships of fixed costs, escalating variable costs, and potential profit and loss associated with various levels of production.

Control and Breakeven Analysis

Breakeven analysis is a useful control tool because it helps managers understand the relationships between fixed costs, variable costs, total costs, and profit and loss within an organization. Once these relationships are understood, managers can take steps to

TABLE 18.3 Fixed costs and variable costs for a book publisher

Fixed Costs (Yearly Basis)		*Variable Costs per Book Sold*	
1. Real estate taxes on property	$ 1,000	1. Printing	$2.00
2. Interest on loan to purchase equipment	5,000	2. Artwork	1.00
3. Building maintenance	2,000	3. Sales commission	.50
4. Insurance	800	4. Author royalties	1.50
5. Salaried labor	80,000	5. Binding	1.00
Total fixed costs	$88,800	Total variable costs per book	$6.00

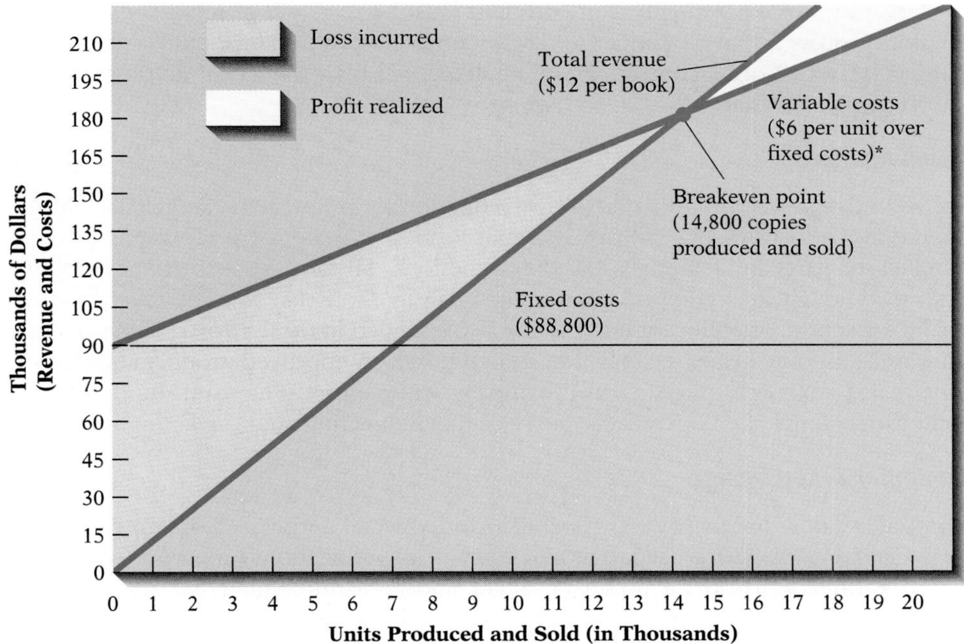

*Note that drawing the variable costs line on top of the fixed costs line means that variable costs have been added to fixed costs. Therefore, the variable costs line also represents total costs.

FIGURE 18.6 Breakeven analysis for a book publisher

modify one or more of the variables to reduce significant deviation between planned and actual profit levels.[29] Increasing costs or decreasing selling prices has the overall effect of increasing the number of units an organization must produce and sell to break even. Conversely, the managerial strategy for decreasing the number of products an organization must produce and sell to break even entails lowering or stabilizing fixed and variable costs or increasing the selling price of each unit. The exact breakeven control strategy a particular manager should develop and implement is dictated primarily by the manager's unique organizational situation.

Other Broad Operations Control Tools

Some of the best-known and most commonly used operations control tools are listed below.[30] The primary purpose of these tools is to control the production of organizational goods and services.[31]

Decision-tree Analysis

Decision-tree analysis, as discussed in chapter 6, is a statistical and graphical multiphase decision-making technique containing a series of steps. Decision trees allow a decision maker to deal with uncertain events by determining the relative expected value of each alternative course of action. The probabilities of different possible events are known, as are the monetary payoffs that result from a particular alternative and a particular event. Decision trees are best used where capacity decisions involve several capacity expansion alternatives and where the selection of the alternative with the highest expected profit or the lowest expected cost is necessary.

Decision-tree analysis is a statistical and graphical multiphased decision-making technique that shows the sequence and interdependence of decisions.

Process Control

Statistical process control, known as **process control,** is a technique that assists in monitoring production processes. Production processes must be monitored continuously in order to assure that the quality of their output will be acceptable. An early detection of a faulty production process is preferred. It is less costly than the detection of

Process control is a technique that assists in monitoring production processes.

parts that do not meet quality standards and must be scrapped or reworked. If a production process is out of control or shows unstable performance, corrective action must be taken. Process control can be implemented with the aid of graphical charts known as control charts.

Value Analysis

Value analysis is a cost control and cost reduction technique that examines all the parts, materials, and functions of an operation.

Value analysis is a cost-control and cost-reduction technique that can help to control operations by focusing primarily on material costs. The analysis is performed by examining all the parts and materials, and their functions. The analysis is aimed at reducing costs through cheaper components and materials in a way that will not affect product quality or appeal. Simplification of parts is also included in these efforts. Value analysis can result not only in cost savings, but sometimes in an improved product at the same time. Value analysis requires a team (company-wide) effort. The team should at least include personnel from operations, purchasing, engineering, and marketing.

Computer-Aided Design

Computer-aided design (CAD) is a computerized technique for designing new products or modifying existing ones.

Computer-aided design **(CAD)** systems include several automated design technologies. *Computer graphics* is used to design geometric specifications for parts. *Computer-aided engineering (CAE)* is used to evaluate and perform engineering analyses on a part. CAD also includes technologies that are used in process design. CAD can function to assure the quality of a product by assuring the quality of parts in the product as well as the appropriateness of product design for establishing product quality.

Computer-Aided Manufacturing

Computer-aided manufacturing (CAM) is a technique using computers to plan and program production equipment in the production of manufactured items.

CAM can help to control operations through Computer-controlled machine tools and computer-aided inspection. CAD and CAM processes can be linked through a computer, which can be very beneficial when production processes must be altered. The linkage enables design changes to be implemented in a very short period of time because CAD and CAM systems have the ability to share information easily.

BACK TO THE CASE Bridgestone used the same basic workforce as Firestone. One of the first decisions the Bridgestone management made was to change the Firestone control strategy. Firestone's management used a force of roving inspectors and statisticians who used a stack of data to achieve quality assurance. Workers were constantly testing to confirm or recheck production that was first considered to be abnormal. Authority and responsibility for quality assurance at Firestone were centered in Akron. When a tire failed, a second one was checked. If the second failed, the lot was held until a decision to resume came from Akron.

Defects at Firestone routinely surfaced in the final inspection area. For years, workers had told management about the problem, but, until many truck companies started sending back tires and dropping accounts, Firestone's management did little to correct the operations system. Management blamed the workers.

Bridgestone's management stressed that everyone was part of a team. Executives who had once had reserved parking spots took their chances with everyone else. The only people who wore ties were the computer consultants and buyers. Engineers' offices were moved to the factory floor. And in the offices of the support staff, the walls came tumbling down. Meeting areas were located throughout, and at any given time a visitor could see animated groups of people clustered around tables, going over charts or drawings. When Bridgestone (USA) moved into corporate offices in a handsome, flower-bordered pink granite building on the outskirts of Nashville, the same thing happened. Walls were ripped down and replaced with partitions.

Walls and management-originated control tools were barriers. Some managers missed their offices and the air of superiority over the subordinates. But once the former Firestone managers became accustomed to the new control strategy, they learned to cope. While there were more interruptions working in an open space with other people, the new strategy brought workers and control tools closer together with a mutual respect for each other.

ACTION SUMMARY

Reread the learning objectives that follow. Each objective is followed by questions. Answering these questions accurately will help you retain the most important concepts discussed in this chapter. After answering each question, check your answer with the answer key at the end of this chapter. (*Hint:* If you have doubt regarding the correct response, consult the page whose number follows the answer.)

Circle: ***From studying this chapter, I will attempt to acquire:***

1. Definitions of production, productivity, and quality.

a, b, c, d, e **a.** *Production* is defined simply as the transformation of organizational resources into: (a) profits; (b) plans; (c) forecasts; (d) processes; (e) products.

a, b, c, d, e **b.** *Productivity* is the relationship between the amount of goods or services produced and: (a) profits; (b) the organizational resources needed to produce them; (c) quality; (d) operations management activities; (e) advanced manufacturing support.

T, F **c.** *Quality* is the extent to which a product reliably does what it is intended to do.

2. An understanding of the importance of operations and production strategies, systems, and processes.

a, b, c, d **a.** The flow of interrelated events moving toward a goal, purpose, or end is: (a) a system; (b) a process; (c) a strategy; (d) a plan.

a, b, c, d **b.** A particular linking of mission, goals, strategies, policies, rules, people, and raw materials that facilitates carrying out a process is: (a) a system; (b) a process; (c) a strategy; (d) a plan.

3. Insights on the role of operations management concepts in the workplace.

T, F **a.** The criteria relevant for judging the actions taken as a result of operations management are effectiveness and efficiency.

a, b, c, d **b.** An operations strategy is achieved in a context of objectives and policies derived from the organization's: (a) capacity strategy; (b) product strategy; (c) strategic plan; (d) human resource strategy.

a, b, c, d **c.** The reputation of an organization is determined by: (a) its size; (b) its style of management; (c) its profits; (d) its product quality.

4. An understanding of how operations control procedures can be used to control production.

T, F **a.** Just-in-time inventory control is an inventory control technique that is based on the management philosophy that products should be manufactured when customers need them.

a, b, c, d, e **b.** Potential pitfalls of using budgets as control tools include: (a) too much emphasis placed on relatively insignificant organizational expenses; (b) changing budgets periodically; (c) increasing budgeted expenses year after year without adequate information; (d) a and c; (e) a and b.

a, b, c, d **c.** Managers can use ratio analysis in the following way to control an organization:

a. Evaluate all ratios simultaneously in order to look at the organization as a whole.
b. Compare computed values for ratios with values of industry averages.
c. Accumulate values for ratios for successive time periods to uncover specific organizational trends.
d. a, b, and c.

5. **Insights concerning operations control tools and how they evolve into a continual-improvement approach to production management and control.**

T, F a. By using inspection, managers can expect to catch any problems that are built into the system.

T, F b. Management by exception is a control technique that allows only significant deviations between planned and actual performance to be brought to the manager's attention.

a, b, c, d, e c. The overall effect on the breakeven point of increasing costs or decreasing selling prices is that: (a) the number of products an organization must sell to break even increases; (b) the amount of profit a firm will receive at a fixed number of units sold increases; (d) the number of products an organization must sell to break even decreases; (d) a and b; (e) there is no effect on the breakeven point.

INTRODUCTORY CASE WRAP-UP

"Bridgestone (USA): Eliminating the Fire and Building Bridges of Quality" (p. 457) and its related back-to-the-case sections were written to help you better understand the management concepts contained in this chapter. Answer the following discussion questions about this introductory case to further enrich your understanding of chapter content:

1. What were the most important changes Bridgestone's management made to improve management/worker relationships?
2. What is the risk that Bridgestone's management must face when employees make operations changes based on Deming's cycle of continual improvement?
3. What is the relationship between production quality and Bridgestone's emphasis on everyone being part of a team?

ISSUES FOR REVIEW AND DISCUSSION

1. Define both *production* and *production control.*
2. Thoroughly explain the equation used to define productivity.
3. Discuss the relationship between quality and productivity.
4. What questions come to mind when looking at Deming's flow diagram for improving product quality?
5. What is quality assurance, and what is its relationship to statistical quality control?
6. Discuss how quality circles normally operate. What purpose do they serve?
7. Discuss the importance of automation in building productive organizations in the future.
8. Explain the term *operations management* as well as the major managerial activities involved in operations management.
9. List the three key concepts conveyed in the discussion of operations management.
10. List the six operations strategies and explain how each can continue to increase productivity.
11. What steps are recommended to aid management in making sound strategic capacity decisions?
12. Discuss the three types of manufacturing processes.
13. Name the three basic types of layout patterns and give an example of each.
14. Discuss the two human resources strategy imperatives and the definition of a human resource strategy.
15. Discuss the management philosophy behind just-in-time inventory control.
16. Explain the difference between a pure-preventive maintenance policy and a pure-breakdown (repair) policy.

17. Explain why cost control is an important responsibility of every manager.
18. Define *budget*. How can managers use a budget to control an organization?
19. List three potential pitfalls of budgets.
20. What is ratio analysis?
21. What guidelines would you recommend to managers using ratio analysis to control an organization?
22. What is materials control, and how can it aid in production control?
23. What is a control tool?
24. Define *management by exception* and describe how it can help managers control production.
25. List and define seven major ingredients of breakeven analysis.
26. How can managers use breakeven analysis as an aid in controlling production?
27. List and define five other control tools.

ACTION SUMMARY ANSWER KEY

1. **a.** e, p. 458
   b. b, p. 458
   c. T, p. 459
2. **a.** b, p. 465
   b. a, pp. 464–465
3. **a.** T, p. 466
   b. c, p. 466
   c. d, p. 459
4. **a.** T, p. 472
   b. d, p. 474
   c. d, pp. 475–476
5. **a.** F, p. 478
   b. T, p. 478
   c. a, p. 481

CASE STUDY

Caterpillar's Factory, a Star

MARY S. THIBODEAUX
University of North Texas

According to a recent *Fortune* article, many U.S. companies have relegated their factories to the status of "just another cost center," but for Caterpillar ("Cat"), the world's largest producer of earth-moving construction equipment, the factory is a star. In an effort to recover from financial problems experienced in the 1980s, Cat is hard at work training employees to work with new robots, computerized assembly machinery, and new ways of thinking and behaving. Materials handling equipment is now broken into thirteen profit centers (down from twenty-two plants) and has brought together on the factory floor the design engineers and marketing and pricing personnel to work alongside production workers. Cat is now able to focus its "three key aspects of manufacturing"—people, process, and design—all together. The new factory design is called "PWAF (pee-waf)," for plant with a future.

What is so different about PWAF? Consider the old plants: Bins of parts sat in work-in-process inventory for weeks at a time. Parts were shuttled back and forth between buildings, losing time and money. The process seemed haphazard at best. PWAF plans are based on cell production.

In a nonrefurbished section of one transmission factory stands an assembly line of thirty-five machine tools, each with at least one operator. Only one kind of case can be worked on at a time, with a two- to forty-eight-hour setup time for each new casing. On the other side of the plant, the cellular system is in use. Each cell does its own milling, drilling, sorting, etc. However, because the cells are designed to handle several different cases, the setup time per case is reduced to a few seconds. Pierre Guerindon, creator of PWAF, says the work time to produce each transmission has been cut from ninety days down to fifteen!

To assist with installing the changes, Caterpillar has established corporate manufacturability teams, including representatives from purchasing, manufacturing, and engineering; the teams meet monthly. Simplification is emphasized in product designs, manufacturing processes, and operating procedures. It costs less. Competition from companies such as Komatsu puts pressure on Caterpillar to get things right the first time and to get the most out of scarce resources. Cat is now simplifying virtually all areas of its operations.

In an industry where most companies are organized by function, Cat's new system requires multifunctionalized interaction. At Cat, team building across function lines closely resembles a matrix organizational philosophy.

Suppliers are also involved in the process from an early stage of product design. This is because new inventory controls are based on just-in-time (JIT) methods; trust and commitment are necessary between Cat and suppliers. The relationship is solidified by the Caterpillar Supplier Certification program begun in the late 1970s. Certification can take as long as two years, and is under continuous review.

Caterpillar is not known traditionally as an industry pacesetter, as it allows its competitors to lead in both product design and customer complaints. Once technology has been developed and problems ironed out by trial and error elsewhere, Caterpillar introduces trouble-free products that enhance the company's reputation for high quality. Products must not only be high in quality, but also capital intensive and capable of benefiting from high technology, and they must fit into Cat's distribution system.

Company officials assert that Caterpillar has committed itself to a long-term point of view and will continue with its plant modernization program. They expect to realize major benefits from a new emphasis on product design and annual quality-improvement programs—and from simplification.

DISCUSSION QUESTIONS

1. In moving from a traditional American system of manufacturing to a flexible, JIT/Japanese style, do you think Caterpillar is trying to do too much too quickly based on the information presented? Why or why not?
2. Which layout pattern did the old Caterpillar system of manufacture most closely resemble? What about the PWAF system?
3. Describe the JIT system, and explain how it benefits Caterpillar's PWAFs.
4. Consider the algebraic equation for breakeven analysis:

$$BE = \frac{\text{Fixed costs}}{\text{(Price minus Variable Costs)}}.$$

How do you think Caterpillar's PWAF system will lower the breakeven point of manufacture most directly in the long run?

CNN VIDEO CASE

Profits and People

ROBERT RICH
Rich Products

Robert Rich, although only in his forties, is the president of Rich Food Products, Inc., one of the largest industries in Buffalo, New York. He is a second-generation leader; the company was founded in 1945 by his father, Robert Rich, Sr., who continues to serve as its chair.

Like many children in family businesses, Rich was set to work learning the business from the ground up. He recalls,

> I've worked in every phase of the business. I used to work loading trucks in the summertime and I've worked in the plant several summers as well. I think it's literally impossible for anyone to make decisions about any part of a business if they haven't worked in that part of the business.

Robert Rich oversees the tight controls over all aspects of production at Rich Products, from just-in-time shipping of raw materials to servicing floor machinery.

However, the part of the business he enjoys most is the sound of the shop floor: "It's very loud out here, but this sounds to me like jobs for the people in the community." With calculated and well-managed expansion through both growth strategies and new acquisitions, Rich Food Products has grown and created many new jobs in Buffalo and around the country. Rich Products now operates thirty-eight production facilities, all dedicated to processing and packaging frozen and preserved food products that range from Coffee Rich—the company's first and flagship product—to barbecued beef and bakery products.

The Riches made a commitment to automation early in the corporation's development and have continued to invest in the latest technology available for food processing, packaging, and shipping. Measuring, mixing, wrapping, and labeling are all tasks that can be handled more quickly by machines than by people. In Rich's factories, machines do the cooking, and people run the machines. Materials-requirement planning is especially important to a company involved with food products because spoilage is a crucial consideration when inventories of perishable raw materials are involved.

Therefore, planning ahead to identify necessary quantities and factory shelf life of raw materials or ingredients is a high priority for all thirty-eight Rich Food Products facilities. Scheduling the purchases, shipping, delivery, and timely off-loading is also crucial. Just-in-time (JIT) inventory control methods could have been invented for the business of processing food products.

Another important aspect of JIT methods is the factory shelf life of the finished product. Even deep-frozen food has a limited life span before it begins deteriorating, and Robert Rich does not want his name associated with freezer-burned or tasteless food. JIT inventory control systems can continue to be useful after production, too, because they can be designed to make production schedules as well as raw-material orders conform to advance sales projections.

Tight controls over all aspects of production, from JIT shipping of raw materials to carefully selected servicing down-time for shop floor machinery, are integral to the success of Rich Food Products. Like many successful businesspeople, Robert Rich is impatient with people and with systems that do not recognize the need for these controls:

> I think that most people in business are used to having a timetable, moving along, maybe even being arbitrary at times to get things done. . . . I think the best thing that our company, for example, can do politically is do what we do best and provide jobs for our area, and that's the life blood of business. I think that's the goal of business.

Rich is a leader who prides himself on developing not only new opportunities and jobs, but also the capabilities of his employees. His pride in his community and in his company is evident to them, and that in turn motivates them to be proud of what they do. Pride in a high-quality product is a great spur to productivity—one Rich knows from personal experience. Pride in personal achievement is another spur he wants his people to feel, too. "One of my major objectives is to . . . be there when people need me, but make sure that they're being given the decision-making power, that they're being paid to perform."

VIDEO CASE QUESTIONS

1. A primary goal for Rich Food Products is to provide new jobs through organizational growth. Deming's chain reaction shows providing new jobs as a final outcome of improving quality. Give two examples of ways in which a Rich factory might improve quality to achieve this goal.
2. List three possible uses for robotics in one of the Rich Products facilities.
3. Assume that Rich Food Products has just acquired a major producer of bakery products. In the weeks immediately following this acquisition, how do you think the current ratio, the quick ratio, and the debt ratio will be affected?
4. When Rich Products upgrades the automation in a production facility, the fixed costs for that facility increase. In order to maintain the same breakeven point, what changes can be made in other aspects of the facility's business? What would you recommend?

CNN VIDEO EXERCISE

Computing a Breakeven Analysis for Rich Products

EXERCISE GOAL: Learn to work out an algebraic breakeven analysis.

Suppose that Robert Rich is considering adding an herb salad dressing mix to his line of food products. Rich wants to sell the mix to stores at a case price of $15.00 each. From the list of costs below, determine the total variable costs per case, the total fixed costs, and complete an algebraic breakeven analysis to determine how many units (cases) of salad dressing mix need to be sold to break even.

Costs

Rent—$15,000.00
Raw materials (herbs and spices)—$3.25
Packages and labels—$1.25
Insurance—$4,000.00
Interest on packaging equipment loan—$2,000.00
Shipping cartons—$.50
Sales commission—$1.35
Utilities—$4,500.00
Salaried labor—$120,000.00
Packaging labor (piece rate)—$2.65

Fixed Costs	Amounts
______________	______________
______________	______________
______________	______________
______________	______________
______________	______________
Total fixed costs:	______________

Variable Costs	Amounts
______________	______________
______________	______________
______________	______________
______________	______________
______________	______________
Total variable costs:	______________

$$BE = \frac{\$\_\_\_\_\_\_}{\$\_\_\_\_\_\_} = \_\_\_\_\_\_ \text{ cases}$$

CHAPTER

19

INFORMATION

STUDENT LEARNING OBJECTIVES

From studying this chapter, I will attempt to acquire:

1. An understanding of the relationship between data and information.
2. Insights on the main factors that influence the value of information.
3. Knowledge of some potential steps for evaluating information.
4. An appreciation for the role of computers in handling information.
5. An understanding of the importance of a management information system (MIS) to an organization.
6. A feasible strategy for establishing an MIS.
7. Information about what a management decision support system is and how it operates.

CHAPTER OUTLINE

INTRODUCTORY CASE
Sam Walton Taught Others at Wal-Mart to Use Information

ESSENTIALS OF INFORMATION

Factors Influencing the Value of Information
Evaluating Information
Computer Assistance in Using Information

ETHICS HIGHLIGHT
Burroughs Wellcome

THE MANAGEMENT INFORMATION SYSTEM (MIS)

GLOBAL HIGHLIGHT
Pohang Iron & Steel Company

Describing the MIS

DIVERSITY HIGHLIGHT
Target

QUALITY HIGHLIGHT
Nashua

Establishing an MIS

THE MANAGEMENT DECISION SUPPORT SYSTEM (MDSS)

CASE STUDY
Mainframes Are Not Dead at 3Com Corporation

VIDEO CASE
The Shape of the World:
Caleb Dean Hammond III, Hammond, Inc.

VIDEO EXERCISE
Improving the MIS at Hammond, Inc.

INTRODUCTORY CASE

Sam Walton Taught Others at Wal-Mart to Use Information

Samuel Moore Walton, who died in 1992 at 74 after a long fight with cancer, did not invent the discount department store, although it hardly seems possible that he didn't. Mr. Sam grabbed hold of the leading edge of retailing in 1962 and never let go, creating a value-powered merchandising machine that seems certain to outlive his memory. . . .

Wal-Mart is ultimately a monument to consumers: It has saved them billions. Walton's perpetual obsession with lowering the cost to consumers forced prices down elsewhere—in department stores, for example. Recalls Kurt Barnard, president of the Retail Marketing Report and a Walton friend: "He always said, 'Nothing happens until a customer walks into a store with a purpose, buys something, and walks out.' That was his philosophy. Satisfy the customer." . . .

Managers suck in information from Monday to Thursday, exchange ideas on Friday and Saturday, and implement decisions in the stores on Monday.

His vision was apparent in 1956 as a Ben Franklin variety store owner. To lure one of his first store managers, Bob Bogle, away from the state health department, Walton showed him the books and offered to pay him 25 percent of the store's net profit in addition to salary. "Sam Walton was honest to the core," says Bogle. In the early years Walton would show his books to just about anyone he thought could help him. Today the company still shares information, right down to single-store results, with the associates—as Wal-Mart calls its employees. Profit sharing, equal to 5 percent to 6 percent of an associate's earnings, extends to the lowest levels. Says Bogle, one of the many people Walton made wealthy: "That profit sharing is the yeast that keeps this thing going."

Once an Army intelligence officer, Walton had an insatiable hunger for information, which in turn equipped Wal-Mart for speedy decision-making. He collected ideas and numbers on his famous yellow pads and converted them to merchandising action using the most rapid means available. At first this was a heavily laden, beat-up Plymouth that Walton would drive—and none too well, say all who knew him—from the Bentonville store to outlying branches.

That demand for information, and its creative use, is just as evident today. Wal-Mart is deep into information systems, and not because Walton loved computers—he didn't. His people insisted on serious crunching ability, and Mr. Pickup Truck listened—another Walton trait—and then signed the check. So, long before its rivals, Wal-Mart had enough computer and satellite capacity to track a space shuttle or towel sales in Tuscaloosa. Walton's memorial service was broadcast to every store over the company's satellite system.

Wal-Mart today converts information to action virtually immediately, a remarkable achievement for a $44-billion-a-year company. Managers suck in information from Monday to Thursday, exchange ideas on Friday and Saturday, and implement decisions in the stores on Monday. This bias toward action left a big impression on General Electric CEO Jack Welch. As he said to a *Fortune* conference: "Everybody there has a passion for an idea, and everyone's ideas count. Hierarchy doesn't matter. They get eighty people in a room and understand how to deal with each other without structure. I have been there three times now. Every time you go to that place in Arkansas, you can fly back to New York without a plane. The place actually vibrates."

Sam Walton's first store—Walton's 5 and 10 in Bentonville, Arkansas—is, aptly, a Wal-Mart museum. This is appropriate since Sam Walton's perpetual obsession—to lower the cost to consumers—forced prices down elsewhere.

From Bill Saporito, "What Sam Walton Taught America," *Fortune* (May 4, 1992), 104-105. © 1992 Time Inc. All rights reserved.

WHAT'S AHEAD The introductory case discusses how Sam Walton, a former army intelligence officer, had an insatiable hunger for information. In addition, the case discusses how information, the computer, and an information system are all used together at Wal-Mart in order to help managers make quicker and better decisions. This chapter presents material that should be useful to managers like those at Wal-Mart who are attempting to better use information in organizations. Major topics in this chapter are 1) essentials of information, 2) the management information system (MIS), and (3) the management decision support system (MDSS).

Controlling is the process of making things happen as planned. Of course, managers cannot make things happen as planned if they lack information on the manner in which various events in the organization occur. This chapter discusses the fundamental principles of handling information in an organization by first presenting the essentials of information and then examining both the management information system (MIS) and the management decision support system (MDSS).

ESSENTIALS OF INFORMATION

Data are facts or statistics.

Information is the set of conclusions derived from data analysis.

The process of developing information begins with the gathering of some type of facts or statistics, called **data.** Once gathered, data typically are analyzed in some manner. In general terms, **information** is the conclusions derived from data analysis. In management terms, information is the conclusions derived from the analysis of data that relate to the operation of an organization. As examples to illustrate the relationship between data and information, managers gather data regarding pay rates that individuals are receiving within industries to develop information about how to develop competitive pay rates,[1] data regarding hazardous-materials accidents in order to gain information about how to improve worker safety,[2] and data regarding customer demographics in order to gain information about product demand in the future.[3]

The information that managers receive heavily influences managerial decision making, which in turn determines the activities that will be performed within the organization, which in turn dictate the eventual success or failure of the organization.[4] Some management writers consider information to be of such fundamental importance to the management process that they define *management* as the process of converting information into action through decision making.[5] The following sections discuss (1) factors that influence the value of information, (2) how to evaluate information, and (3) computer assistance in using information.

Factors Influencing the Value of Information

Some information is more valuable than other information.[6] The value of information is defined in terms of the benefit that can accrue to the organization through the use of the information. The greater this benefit, the more valuable the information.

Four primary factors determine the value of information: (1) information appropriateness, (2) information quality, (3) information timeliness, and (4) information quantity. In general, management should encourage the generation, distribution, and use of organizational information that is appropriate, of high quality, timely, and of sufficient quantity. Following this guideline will not necessarily guarantee sound decisions, but it will ensure that important resources necessary to make such decisions are available.[7] Each of the factors that determine information value is discussed in more detail in the paragraphs that follow.

Information Appropriateness

Information appropriateness is defined in terms of how relevant the information is to the decision-making situation faced by the manager. If the information is quite relevant, then it is said to be appropriate. Generally, as the appropriateness of information increases, the value of that information increases.

Information appropriateness is the degree to which information is relevant to the decision-making situation that faces the manager.

Figure 19.1 shows the characteristics of information appropriate for the following common decision-making situations: (1) operational control, (2) management control, and (3) strategic planning.[8]

Operational control decisions relate to assuring that specific organizational tasks are carried out effectively and efficiently. Management control decisions relate to obtaining and effectively and efficiently using the organizational resources necessary to reach organizational objectives. Strategic planning decisions relate to determining organizational objectives and designating the corresponding action necessary to reach them.

As Figure 19.1 shows, characteristics of appropriate information change as managers shift from making operational control decisions to making management control decisions to making strategic planning decisions. Strategic planning decision makers need information that focuses on the relationship of the organization to its external environment, emphasizes the future, is wide in scope, and presents a broad view. Appropriate information for this type of decision is usually old and not completely accurate.

Information appropriate for making operational control decisions has dramatically different characteristics than information appropriate for making strategic planning decisions. Operational control decision makers need information that focuses for the most part on the internal organizational environment, emphasizes the performance history of the organization, and is well defined, narrow in scope, and detailed. In addition, appropriate information for this type of decision is both highly current and highly accurate.

Information appropriate for making management control decisions generally has characteristics that fall somewhere between the extreme characteristics of appropriate operational control information and appropriate strategic planning information.

Information Quality

The second primary factor that determines the value of information is **information quality**—the degree to which information represents reality. The more closely information represents reality, the higher the quality and the greater the value of the information. In general, the higher the quality of information available to managers, the better equipped the managers are to make appropriate decisions and the greater the probability that the organization will be successful over the long term. Perhaps the most significant factor in producing poor-quality information is data contamination. An issue like inaccurate data gathering can result in information that is of very low quality—a poor representation of reality.[9]

Information quality is the degree to which information represents reality.

Information Timeliness

Information timeliness, the third primary factor that determines the value of information, is the extent to which the receipt of information allows decisions to be made and action to be taken so the organization can gain some benefit from possessing the information. Information received by managers at a point when it can be used to the advantage of the organization is said to be timely.

Information timeliness is the extent to which the receipt of information allows decisions to be made and action to be taken so the organization can gain some benefit from possessing the information.

For example, a product may be selling poorly because its established market price is significantly higher than that of competitive products. If this information is received by management after the product has been discontinued, the information will be un-

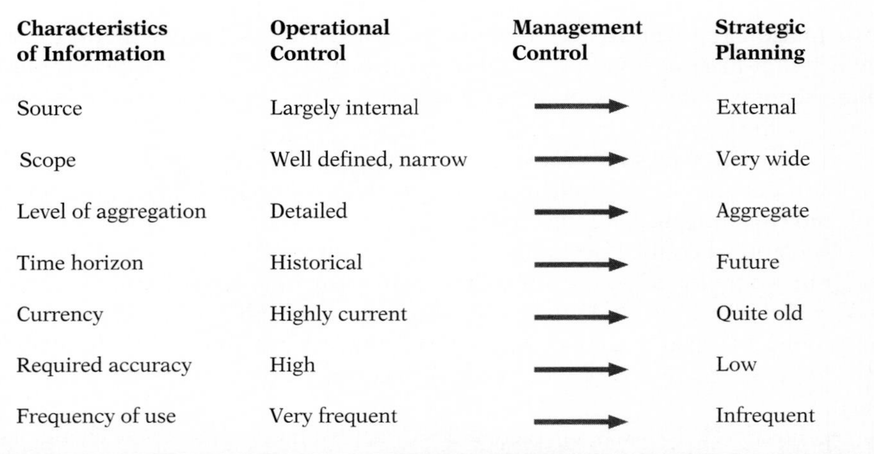

Characteristics of Information	Operational Control	Management Control	Strategic Planning
Source	Largely internal	→	External
Scope	Well defined, narrow	→	Very wide
Level of aggregation	Detailed	→	Aggregate
Time horizon	Historical	→	Future
Currency	Highly current	→	Quite old
Required accuracy	High	→	Low
Frequency of use	Very frequent	→	Infrequent

FIGURE 19.1 Characteristics of information appropriate for decisions related to operational control, management control, and strategic planning

timely. If, however, it is received soon enough to adjust the selling price of the product and thereby significantly increase sales, it will be timely.

Information Quantity

Information quantity is the amount of decision-related information a manager possesses.

The fourth and final determinant of the value of information is **information quantity**—the amount of decision-related information managers possess. Before making a decision, managers should assess the quantity of information they possess that relates to the decision being made. If this quantity is judged to be insufficient, more information should be gathered before the decision is made. If the amount of information is judged to be as complete as necessary, managers can feel justified in making the decision.

Evaluating Information

Evaluating information is the process of determining whether the acquisition of specified information is justified. As with all evaluations of this kind, the primary concern of management is to weigh the dollar value of benefit gained from using some quantity of information against the cost of generating that information.

According to the flowchart in Figure 19.2, the first major step in evaluating organizational information is to determine the value of that information by pinpointing the data to be analyzed and then determine the expected value or return to be received from obtaining perfect information based on these data. Next, this expected value should be reduced by the amount of benefit that will not be realized because of deficiencies and inaccuracies expected to appear in the information.

Then the expected value of organizational information should be compared with the expected cost of obtaining that information. If the expected cost does not exceed the expected value, the information should be gathered. If it does exceed the expected value, managers either must increase the information's expected value or decrease its expected cost before the information gathering can be justified. If neither of these objectives is possible, management cannot justify gathering the information.

One generally accepted strategy for increasing the expected value of information is to eliminate the characteristics of the information that tend to limit its usefulness. Table 19.1 lists some of these characteristics and the possible actions management can take to eliminate them.

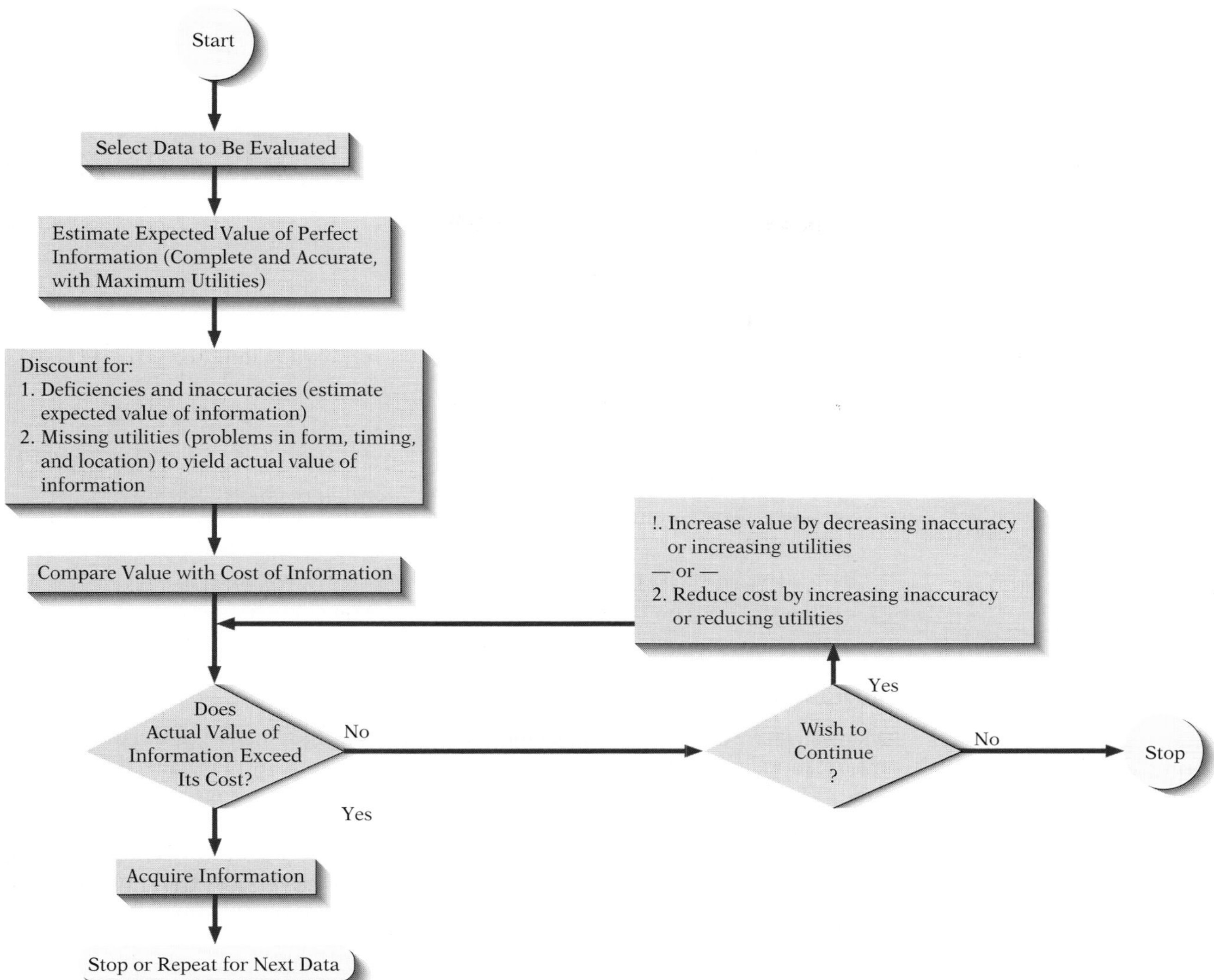

FIGURE 19.2 Flowchart of main activities in evaluating information

BACK TO THE CASE

According to the above material, information at Wal-Mart can be defined as the conclusions derived from the analysis of data relating to the way in which the company operates. The case implies that managers at Wal-Mart are better able to make sound decisions, including better control decisions, because of the successful data handling achieved by the company's information system.

One important factor in evaluating the overall worth of Wal-Mart's information handling system would be the overall impact of the system on the value of information that company managers receive. Evidently, Sam Walton determined, probably through a process of gathering feedback from other Wal-Mart managers, that investing in computers, satellites, and other data-handling devices would enhance the value of information that organization members would receive, and at a reasonable cost. That is, for a reasonable cost, equipment such as computers would enhance the appropriateness, quality, timeliness, and quantity of information that Wal-Mart managers would be able to use. Overall, Sam Walton believed that the benefits of making investments in computers and information systems would outweigh the costs of the equipment; he therefore had Wal-Mart invest in the equipment.

TABLE 19.1 Characteristics that tend to limit the usefulness of information and how to eliminate them

Characteristics That Tend to Limit the Usefulness of Information	*Possible Actions to Eliminate These Characteristics**
Language or format not understood	Translate, revise, or change format
Volume excessive: time required to examine information exceeds the intuitive estimate of the value of the contents	Condense
Received before need perceived	Store for possible future need
Received after needed	Ensure against future occurrence
Inaccessible	Create access
Time or cost of access excessive	Relocate data, change access
No right of use, or closed communication channels because of conflicting subunit goals, authority relationships, and so forth	Relocate information; alter or open transmission channels; change relationships

*The organization will incur some additional cost by taking one or more of these actions.

Computer Assistance in Using Information

A **computer** is an electronic tool capable of accepting data, interpreting data, performing ordered operations on data, and reporting on the outcome of these operations. Computers are extremely helpful in generating information from raw data.

Managers have an overwhelming amount of data to gather, analyze, and transform into information before making numerous decisions. In fact, many managers in the United States as well as in the United Kingdom and other foreign countries are currently complaining that they are overloaded with information.[10] A computer is a tool managers can use to assist in the complicated and time-consuming task of generating this information. A **computer** is an electronic tool capable of accepting data, interpreting data, performing ordered operations on data, and reporting on the outcome of these operations. Computers give managers the ability to store vast amounts of financial, inventory, and other data so that the data will be readily accessible for making day-to-day decisions. Table 19.2 lists several specific computer operations for handling information.

The sections that follow discuss the main functions of computers and possible pitfalls in using computers.

Main Functions of Computers

The five main functions of computers are:

1. The **input function**—computer activities through which the computer enters the data to be analyzed and the instructions to be followed to analyze the data appropriately.

2. The **storage function**—computer activities involved with retaining the material entered into the computer during the performance of the input function.

A computer function is a computer activity that must be performed to generate organizational information. Computers perform five main functions: (1) input, (2) storage, (3) control, (4) processing, and (5) output. The relationships among these functions are shown in Figure 19.3 on page 498.

The **input function** consists of computer activities through which the computer enters the data to be analyzed and the instructions to be followed to analyze the data appropriately. As Figure 19.3 shows, the purpose of the input function is to provide data and instructions to be used in the performance of the storage, processing, control, and output functions.

The **storage function** consists of computer activities involved with retaining the material entered into the computer during the performance of the input function. The storage unit, or memory, of a computer is similar to the human memory in that various facts can be stored until they are needed for processing. In addition, facts can be stored, used in processing, and then restored as many times as necessary. As Figure 19.3 demonstrates, the storage, processing, and control activities are dependent on one another and ultimately yield computer output.

TABLE 19.2 Computer operations that assist management in handling information

Operation	*How a Computer Can Aid Managers*
Billing	Control of buying, inventory, selling; rapid paying cycle; improved cash position; data about customers, products, items, costs, prices, sales representatives, sales statistics
Accounts receivable	Shorten average collections of accounts receivables; highlight past-due statements, improve cash flow, invoice summary
Sales analysis	Review sales volume on the basis of profit contributions as well as gross profit contribution; compute sales representatives' commission plans; pinpoint sales improvement for customers and sales representatives
Inventory	Provide control of inventory, generation of distribution-by-value report—that is, quantity sold annual sales are accumulated and printed as percentage of total number of items and total annual sales; pinpoint marginal items; segment inventory; establish order quantities and order points; cycle reviewing of vendor lines
Payroll	Construct payroll accounting system; produce reports to management, employees, government agencies; reduce peak work loads, strengthen managerial control over human resources
Materials planning	Determine components requirements; plan inventory per item by time period; determine how change in order quantity or delivery will affect production schedule; consolidate requirements of multiple-use items; reduce materials planning costs
Purchasing	Provide performance figures by item, supplier, and buyer in terms of cost, quality, and delivery; achieve tangible savings by meeting discount dates through faster processing of invoices; simplify analysis of historical data, expedite purchase orders based on production shortages and late deliveries
Dispatching and shop floor control	Reduce expediting costs because job status records are current; give early notification of exceptions requiring corrective action plus daily revisions of order priority by machine group
Capacity planning and operation scheduling	Make available labor requirements by time period in time to take corrective action; provide immediate information about effect of changes on work orders, simplified planning on availability of tools, realistic order release dates

ETHICS HIGHLIGHT
Burroughs Computerizes Benefits Information

Managers commonly face the situation of storing data in computers. One issue that must be faced in this situation is the ethical consideration of how management will keep private and personal data about organization members from being accessed by inappropriate individuals. Burroughs Wellcome, a large pharmaceutical company in North Carolina, has successfully dealt with this issue of maintaining employee privacy in its system of computer data storage.

At Burroughs Wellcome, rather than dedicating a large portion of the human resource department staff to answering routine questions about company benefits on a regular basis, management uses a computer-based system to answer such employee queries. Questions are answered consistently and accurately, twenty-four hours a day, seven days a week. More personal questions from employees can focus on specific questions regarding wages and wage rates as well as medical benefits. More general ques-

Answers to many human resources questions can be obtained from a computer-based system.

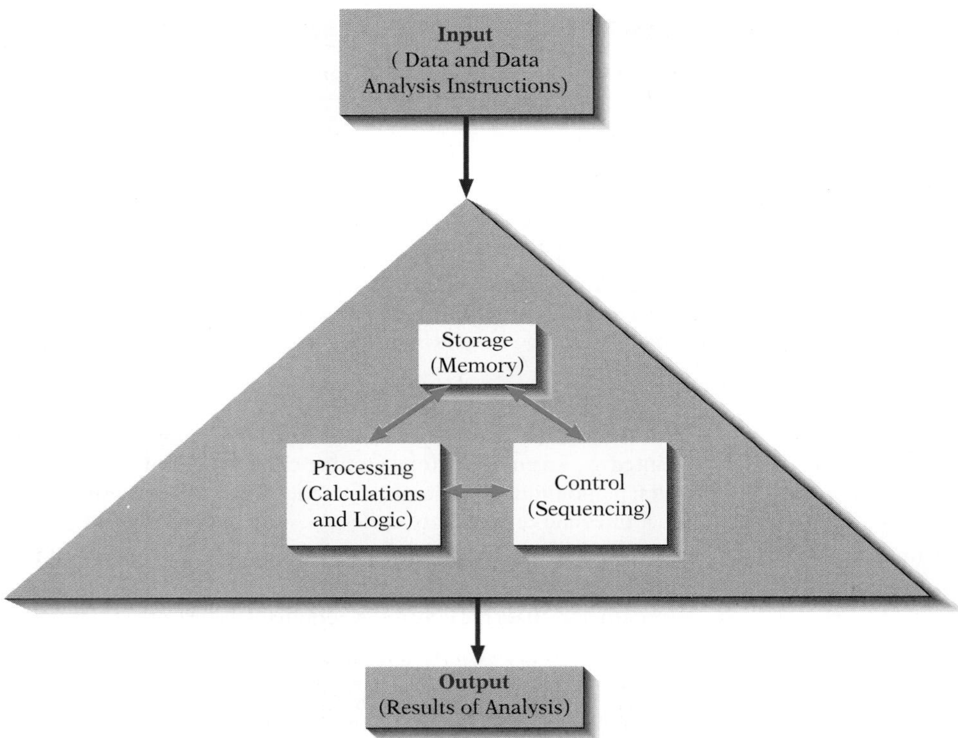

FIGURE 19.3 Relationships among the five main functions of a computer

(Copyright © 1969 by the President and Fellows of Harvard College: all rights reserved.)

tions can also be asked regarding issues like job openings that exist within the company, weather-related plant closings, and holiday schedules. This system used at Burroughs even has a voice-response capability so that employee questions can get an oral response. The voice-response system is sophisticated enough to select, retrieve, and report responses from a large pool of data, yet simple enough to be accessed by a touch-tone telephone. Concern about the ethical issue of employee privacy is adequately addressed in the Burroughs system. Employees are issued personal identification numbers. No one can ask or access information about a specific employee without using the identification number issued to that employee. ▶

3. The **processing function**—computer activities involved with performing the logic and calculation steps necessary to analyze data appropriately.

The **processing function** consists of the computer activities involved with performing both logic and calculation steps necessary to analyze data appropriately. Calculation activities include virtually any numeric analysis. Logic activities include such analysis as comparing one number to another to determine which is larger. Data, as well as directions for processing the data, are furnished by input and storage activities.

4. The **control function**—computer activities that dictate the order in which other computer functions are performed.

Computer activities that dictate the order in which other computer functions are performed compose the **control function.** Control activities indicate (1) when data should be retrieved after storage, (2) when and how the data should be analyzed, (3) if and when the data should be restored after analysis, (4) if and when additional data should be retrieved, and (5) when output activities (described in the next paragraph) should begin and end.

5. The **output function**—computer activities that take the results of input, storage, processing, and control functions and transmit them outside the computer.

The **output function** comprises the activities that take the results of the input, storage, processing, and control functions and transmits them outside the computer. These results can appear in such diverse forms as data on magnetic tape or characters typed on paper. Obviously, the form in which output appears is determined primarily by how the output is to be used. Output that appears on magnetic tape, for example, can be used as input for another computer analysis but is of little value for analysis by human beings.

Possible Pitfalls in Using Computers

The computer is a sophisticated management tool with the potential of making a significant contribution to organizational success. For this potential to materialize, however, the following possible pitfalls should be avoided:

1. *Thinking that a computer is capable of independently performing creative activities.* A computer does not lessen the organization's need for a manager's personal creative ability and professional judgment.[11] A computer is capable only of following precise and detailed instructions provided by the computer user. The individual using the computer must tell the computer exactly what to do, how to do it, and when to do it. Computers are simply pieces of equipment that must be directed very precisely by computer users to perform some function.
2. *Spending too much money on computer assistance.*[12] In general, computers can be of great assistance to managers. The initial cost of purchasing a computer as well as updating it when necessary, however, can be very high.[13] Managers need to keep comparing the benefit obtained from computer assistance with the cost of obtaining this assistance. In essence, an investment in a computer should be expected to help the organization generate enough added revenue to not only finance the computer, but also contribute an acceptable level of net profit.[14]
3. *Overestimating the value of computer output.* Some managers fall into the trap of assuming that they have "the answer" once they have received information generated by computer analysis. The cartoon below illustrates problems that can arise when organization members think that computers generate "the answer." Managers must recognize that computer output is only as good as the quality of data and directions for analyzing the data that human beings have put into the computer. Inaccurate data or inappropriate computer instructions yield useless computer output. A commonly used phrase to describe such an occurrence is "garbage in, garbage out."

Sorry, but according to our brand-new $40,000 computer, we don't have any paintbrushes — and if we did, it wouldn't know how much to charge for one.
Orlando Sentinel *(May 1, 1989).*

BACK TO THE CASE Sam Walton recognized the value of the computer as an important aid in making management decisions. The computer at Wal-Mart can accept data within the company, such as daily sales levels of various products, perform operations on the data, such as percentage increases of various product sales on a daily or weekly basis, and quickly distribute the results of this analysis to managers. In order for such results to be distributed to management, data must be put into Wal-Mart computers, stored, and appropriately controlled and processed.

In addition to providing such valuable decision-related information as this sales volume report, computers at a company like Wal-Mart can perform many other functions. As examples, computers can generate and track bills to Wal-Mart customers, generate payroll checks to Wal-Mart employees, and write orders for products as they are needed from product wholesalers. Despite Sam's intense interest in computers, he knew very well that computers, like any other management tool, have limitations. As an example, Sam knew that computer assistance at Wal-Mart, as in any company, is only as good as the people running the computers, and that managers should not expect computers to independently perform creative activities.

THE MANAGEMENT INFORMATION SYSTEM (MIS)

A **management information system (MIS)** is a network established in an organization to provide managers with information that will assist them in decision making. An MIS gets information to where it is needed.

In simple terms, a **management information system (MIS)** is a network established within an organization to provide managers with information that will assist them in decision making.[15] The following, more complete definition of an MIS was developed by the Management Information System Committee of the Financial Executives Institute:

> An MIS is a system designed to provide selected decision-oriented information needed by management to plan, control, and evaluate the activities of the corporation. It is designed within a framework that emphasizes profit planning, performance planning, and control at all levels. It contemplates the ultimate integration of required business information subsystems, both financial and nonfinancial, within the company.[16]

The title of the specific organization member responsible for developing and maintaining an MIS varies from organization to organization. In smaller organizations, a president or vice president may possess this responsibility. In larger organizations, an individual with a title such as "director of information systems" may be solely responsible for appropriately managing an entire MIS department. The term *MIS manager* is used in the sections that follow to indicate the person within the organization who has the primary responsibility for managing the MIS. The term *MIS personnel* is used to designate the nonmanagement individuals within the organization who possess the primary responsibility of actually operating the MIS. Examples of nonmanagement individuals are computer operators and computer programmers. The sections that follow describe an MIS more fully and outline the steps managers take to establish an MIS.

Managers at Pohang Iron & Steel Company in South Korea developed a complex management information system to monitor the 60,000 items that are critical in controlling production costs.

GLOBAL HIGHLIGHT
Pohang Iron & Steel Company Needs a Complex MIS

Managers face situations involving the use of a management information system in managing activities at virtually all levels of an organization. This description implies that although an MIS may be relatively simple, some managers also have to face a situation of developing and using a very complex MIS, especially if their organizations are of significant size.

Management at the Pohang Iron & Steel Company in Korea faced the challenge of developing a complex MIS in order to manage its organizational activities efficiently and effectively. A complex MIS was needed primarily as a result of the large size of the company and the complexity of the activities involved in manufacturing steel. The company's MIS permits managers to monitor any phase of the steel production process. In addition, the system continually monitors about 60,000 items that are critical in controlling production costs and, at specified intervals, automatically updates the status of these items. To best interpret and react to information that flows on its MIS, management uses regularly scheduled video conferences with organization members in different locations. Pohang is the only Korean company to use regularly scheduled video conferences in this fashion. Pohang was founded in 1973 by the government of the Republic of Korea and is now the second largest and most competitive steel maker in the world. The company's success is largely credited to its development and use of its sophisticated MIS. ▶

Describing the MIS

The MIS is perhaps best described by a summary of the steps necessary to properly operate an MIS[17] and by a discussion of the different kinds of information various managers need to make job-related decisions.

Operating the MIS

MIS personnel generally perform six sequential steps to properly operate an MIS.[18] (Figure 19.4 summarizes the steps and indicates the order in which they are performed.) The first step is to determine what information is needed within the organization,[19] when it will be needed, and in what form it will be needed. Because the basic purpose of the MIS is to assist management in making decisions, one way to begin determining management information needs is to analyze (1) decision areas in which management makes decisions, (2) specific decisions within these decision areas that

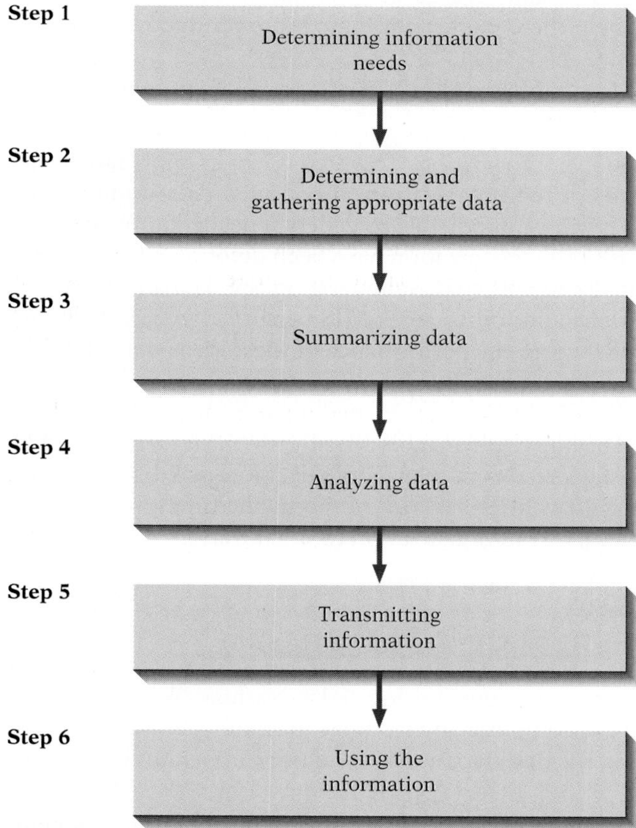

FIGURE 19.4 The six steps necessary to operate an MIS properly in order of their performance

management actually must make, and (3) alternatives that must be evaluated to make these specific decisions. Table 19.3 presents such an analysis for a manager making decisions related to production and operations management.

DIVERSITY HIGHLIGHT
Target's MIS Focuses on Hispanic Workers

Target, a mass market discount retailer, is monitoring changing demographics in the area surrounding its stores and is attempting to build a work force that reflects the diversity of that population.

According to Target's vice president of public and consumer affairs, George Hite, and president, Warren Feldberg, Target Stores is implementing aggressive expansion plans. Target, a consumer products retailer, has gained its success primarily by designing its merchandise programs to reflect societal life-style trends. Company success has been significant enough to yield plans to add about 300 new stores over the next three years. Target management is being prepared for expansion through comprehensive planning and a strong emphasis on management development.

Several MIS challenges face a company as substantial as Target. For example, management must have certain information: how competitive Target must be in order to hire adequate numbers of workers; current trends in technology that might help Target to become more efficient; financial results that the company is generating; continuing education necessary to built a productive work force; international factors, such as purchasing cheaper products abroad; and the level of work-force diversity that the company possesses and should aspire to.

The MIS at Target has provided management with a foundation of information upon which to make diversity-related decisions. As an example, in southern California, the company is monitoring changing demographics of the population surrounding stores in the area and attempting to build a work force that reflects the diversity of that population. As a result, in southern California, Target is hiring a greater proportion of Hispanic workers. In order to help these workers become more productive, Target is offering them free English classes.

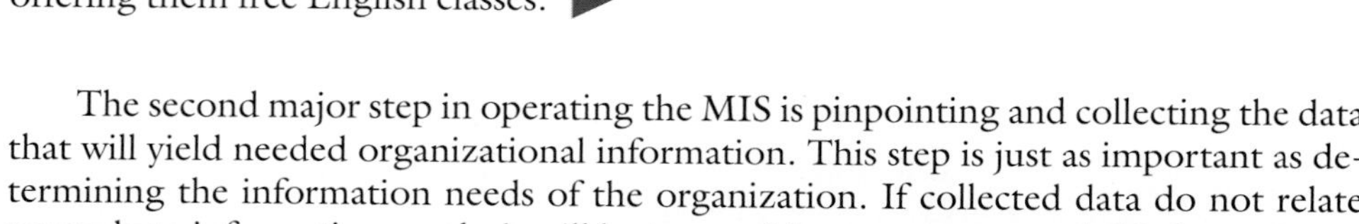

The second major step in operating the MIS is pinpointing and collecting the data that will yield needed organizational information. This step is just as important as determining the information needs of the organization. If collected data do not relate properly to information needs, it will be impossible to generate needed information.

After the information needs of the organization have been determined and appropriate data have been pinpointed and gathered, summarizing the data and analyzing the data are, respectively, the third and fourth steps MIS personnel generally should take to properly operate an MIS. It is in the performance of these steps that MIS personnel find computer assistance of great benefit.

The fifth and sixth steps are transmitting the information generated by data analysis to appropriate managers and having the managers actually use the information. The performance of these last two steps results in managerial decision making. Although each of the six steps is necessary if an MIS is to run properly, the time spent on performing each step naturally will vary from organization to organization.

QUALITY HIGHLIGHT
Nashua Operates Its MIS to Enhance Quality

The Nashua Corporation is a company located in Nashua, New Hampshire and involved in the manufacture of computer and facsimile machine supplies. Recently, Nashua has focused on changing the design of its MIS and how it operates in an effort to enhance product quality.

Making changes to improve product quality is nothing new at Nashua. The company has been involved in making such changes since the late 1970s. Until recently, the changes have primarily emphasized developing more efficient and effective product de-

TABLE 19.3 Decision areas, decisions, and alternatives related to production and operation management

Decision Areas	*Decisions*	*Alternatives*
Plant and equipment	Span of process	Make or buy
	Plant size	One big plant or several smaller ones
	Plant location	Locate near markets or locate near materials
	Investment decisions	Invest mainly in buildings, or equipment, or inventories, or research
	Choice of equipment	General-purpose or special-purpose equipment
	Kind of tooling	Temporary, minimum tooling or "production tooling"
Production planning and control	Frequency of inventory taking	Few or many breaks in production for buffer stocks
	Inventory size	High inventory or a lower inventory
	Degree of inventory control	Control in great detail or in lesser detail
	What to control	Controls designed to minimize machine downtime, or labor cost, or time in process, or to maximize output of particular products or material usage
	Quality control	High reliability and quality or low costs
	Use of standards	Formal, or informal, or none at all
Labor and staffing	Job specialization	Highly specialized or not highly specialized
	Supervision	Technically trained first-line supervisors or nontechnically trained supervisors
	Wage system	Many job grades or few job grades; incentive wages or hourly wages
	Supervision	Close supervision or loose supervision
	Industrial engineers	Many or few industrial engineers
Product design/ engineering	Size of product line	Many customer specials, or few specials, or none at all
	Design stability	Frozen design or many engineering change orders
	Technological risk	Use of new processes unproved by competitors or follow-the-leader policy
	Engineering	Complete packaged design or design-as-you-go approach
	Use of manufacturing engineering	Few or many manufacturing engineers
Organization and management	Kind of organization	Functional, or product focus, or geographical, or other
	Executive use of time	High involvement in investment, or production planning, or cost control, or quality control, or other activities
	Degree of risk assumed	Decisions based on much or little information
	Use of staff	Large or small staff group
	Executive style	Much or little involvement in detail; authoritarian or nondirective style; much or little contact with organization

velopment techniques. Now, Nashua management is focusing on changing the role of information systems as a means of maintaining or increasing product quality. MIS personnel within the company are involved in designing and implementing a new role for MIS that will better contribute to Nashua's quest for product quality.

The development of this new MIS role was initiated by Nashua's director of management information systems, Tim Gallagher. Under the old MIS design, the system only focused on gathering and processing data that all divisions in the company could use in some way. The newly developing MIS design is quite different. This design reflects the company's overall philosophy of pushing quality improvement decisions down in the organization to the point where the work is actually being performed rather than having quality-related decisions made by an organization member who is far removed from where the work is being done. In the past, there was one centralized MIS department for Nashua as a whole. The newly evolving MIS plan entails building nine data centers located throughout the company. Each data center can focus on providing different and individualized information to organization members who

A management information system design can influence product quality.

are involved in making very different decisions about improving quality within the company. ▶

Different Managers Need Different Kinds of Information

For maximum benefit, an MIS must collect relevant data, transform that data into appropriate information, and transmit that information to the appropriate managers. Appropriate information for one manager within an organization, however, may not be appropriate information for another. Robert G. Murdick suggests that the degree of appropriateness of MIS information for a manager depends on the activities for which the manager will use the information, the organizational objectives assigned to the manager, and the level of management at which the manager functions.[20] All of these factors, of course, are closely related.

Murdick's thoughts on this matter are best summarized in Figure 19.5. As can be seen from this figure, because the overall job situations of top managers, middle managers, and first-line managers are significantly different, the kinds of information these managers need to satisfactorily perform their jobs also are significantly different.

Organizational Level	Type of Management	Manager's Organizational Objectives	Appropriate Information from MIS	How MIS Information Is Used
1. Top management	CEO, president, vice president	Survival of the firm, profit growth, accumulation and efficient use of resources	Environmental data and trends, summary reports of operations, "exception reports" of problems, forecasts	Corporate objectives, policies, constraints, decisions on strategic plans, decisions on control of the total company
2. Middle management	Middle managers such as marketing, production, and financial	Allocation of resources to assigned tasks, establishment of plans to meet operating objectives, control of operations	Summaries and exception reports of operating results, corporate objectives, policies, constraints, decisions on strategic plans, relevant actions and decisions of other middle managers	Operating plans and policies, exception reports, operating summaries, control procedures, decisions on resource allocations, actions and decisions related to other middle managers
3. First-line management	First-line managers whose work is closely related	Production of goods to meet marketing needs, supplying budgets, estimates of resource requirements, movement and storage of materials	Summary reports of transactions, detailed reports of problems, operating plans and policies, control procedures, actions and decisions of related first-line managers	Exception reports, progress reports, resource requests, dispatch orders, cross-functional reports

FIGURE 19.5 Appropriate MIS information under various sets of organizational circumstances

BACK TO THE CASE

In order for a company like Wal-Mart to get maximum benefit from its computer assistance, management must appropriately build each main ingredient of its MIS. A company's MIS is the organizational network established to provide managers with information that helps them make job-related decisions. Such a system at a major company such as Wal-Mart would necessitate the use of several MIS personnel who would help determine information needs at the company, help determine and collect appropriate Wal-Mart data, summarize and analyze these data, transmit analyzed data to appropriate Wal-Mart managers, and generally help managers in interpreting received MIS information.

In order to make sure that managers get appropriate information, MIS personnel must appreciate that different managers at a company like Wal-Mart need different kinds of information. As an example, a top manager such as Sam Walton would normally need information that summarizes trends such as consumer tastes, competitor moves, and summary reports for the company as a whole. Middle managers at Wal-Mart would normally need information that focuses more on specific operating divisions or units within the company like all stores in the state of Alabama. More lower-level managers, perhaps store managers or department supervisors, would normally need information such as daily sales figures by departments within a store, or number of errors made in handling customers at the checkout counter.

Establishing an MIS

The process of establishing an MIS involves four stages: (1) planning for the MIS, (2) designing the MIS, (3) implementing the MIS, and (4) improving the MIS.

Planning for the MIS

The planning stage is perhaps the most important stage of establishing an MIS. Commonly cited factors that make planning for the establishment of an MIS an absolute necessity are the typically long periods of time needed to acquire MIS-related data-processing equipment and to integrate it within the operation of the organization, the difficulty of hiring competent operators of the equipment, and the major amounts of financial and managerial resources typically needed to operate an MIS.[21]

The specific types of plans for an MIS vary from organization to organization. However, a sample plan for the establishment of an MIS at General Electric is shown in Figure 19.6 on page 506. This particular plan, of course, is abbreviated. Much more detailed outlines of each of the areas in this plan would be needed before it could be implemented. It is interesting to note that this plan includes a point (about a third of the way down the figure) at which management must decide if there is enough potential benefit to be gained from the existence of the MIS to continue the process of establishing it. This particular plan specifies that if management decides there is not sufficient potential benefit to be gained by establishing the MIS, given its total costs, the project should be terminated.

Designing the MIS

Although data processing equipment is normally an important ingredient of management information systems, the designing of an MIS should not begin with a comparative analysis of the types of such equipment available. Many MIS managers mistakenly think that data processing equipment and an MIS are synonymous.

Stoller and Van Horn indicate that, because the purpose of an MIS is to provide information that will assist managers in making better decisions, the designing of an MIS should begin with an analysis of the kinds of decisions the managers actually make in a particular organization.[22] These authors suggest that designing an MIS should consist of four steps: (1) defining various decisions that must be made to run an organization, (2) determining the types of existing management policies that may influence the ways

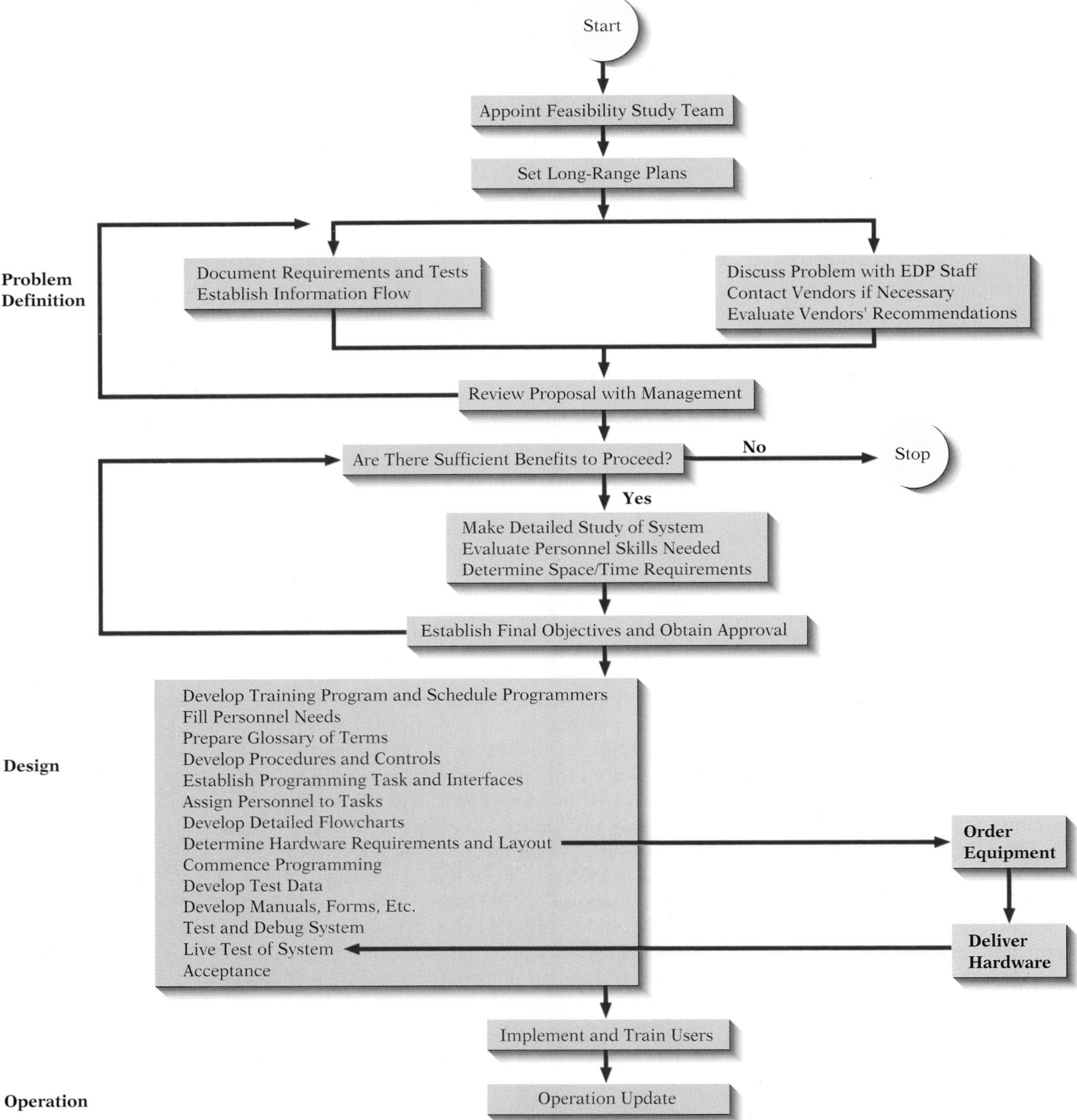

FIGURE 19.6 Plan for establishing an MIS at General Electric

in which these decisions should be made, (3) pinpointing the types of data needed to make these decisions, and (4) establishing a mechanism for gathering and appropriately processing the data to obtain needed information.

Implementing the MIS

The third stage in the process of establishing an MIS within an organization is implementation—that is, putting the planned for and designed MIS into operation. In this stage, the equipment is acquired and integrated into the organization. Designated data are gathered, analyzed as planned, and distributed to appropriate managers within the organization. Line managers make decisions based on the information they receive from the MIS.

Management of the implementation process of the MIS can determine the ultimate success or failure of the system.[23] To help ensure that this process will be successful, management can attempt to find an executive sponsor—a high-level manager who understands and supports the MIS implementation process. The support of such a sponsor will be a sign to all organization members that the MIS implementation is important to the organization and that all organization members should cooperate in making the implementation process successful. In addition, making sure that the MIS is as simple as possible and serves information needs of management is critical in making successful the implementation of an MIS. If the MIS is overly complicated or does not meet information needs of management, the implementation will meet with much resistance and will probably have only limited success.

Improving the MIS

Once the MIS is operating, MIS managers should continually strive to maximize its value. The two sections that follow provide insights on how MIS improvements might be made.

Symptoms of Inadequate MIS. To improve an MIS, MIS managers must first find symptoms or signs that the existing MIS is inadequate. A list of such symptoms, developed by Bertram A. Colbert, a principal of Price Waterhouse & Company, is presented in Table 19.4.[24]

Colbert divides the symptoms into three types: (1) operational, (2) psychological, and (3) report content. Operational symptoms and psychological symptoms relate, respectively, to the operation of the organization and the functioning of organization members. Report content symptoms relate to the actual makeup of the information generated by the MIS.

TABLE 19.4 Symptoms of an inadequate MIS

Operational	*Psychological*	*Report Content*
Large physical inventory adjustments	Surprise at financial results	Excessive use of tabulations of figures
Capital expenditure overruns	Poor attitude of executives about usefulness of information	Multiple preparation and distribution of identical data
Inability of executives to explain changes from year to year in operating results	Lack of understanding of financial information on part of nonfinancial executives	Disagreeing information from different sources
Uncertain direction of company growth	Lack of concern for environmental changes	Lack of periodic comparative information and trends
Cost variances unexplainable	Executive homework reviewing reports considered excessive	Lateness of information
No order backlog awareness		Too little or excess detail
No internal discussion of reported data		Inaccurate information
Insufficient knowledge about competition		Lack of standards for comparison
Purchasing parts from outside vendors when internal capability and capacity to make is available		Failure to identify variances by cause and responsibility
Record of some "sour" investments in facilities, or in programs such as R&D and advertising		Inadequate externally generated information

Although the symptoms in the table are clues that an MIS is inadequate, the symptoms themselves may not actually pinpoint MIS weaknesses. Therefore, after such symptoms are detected, MIS managers usually must gather additional information to determine what MIS weaknesses exist. Answering questions such as the following would be of some help to MIS managers in determining these weaknesses:[25]

1. Where and how do managers get information?
2. Can managers make better use of their contacts to get information?
3. In what areas is managers' knowledge weakest, and how can managers be given information to minimize these weaknesses?
4. Do managers tend to act before receiving information?
5. Do managers wait so long for information that opportunities pass them by and the organization becomes bottlenecked?

Typical Improvements to an MIS. MIS inadequacies vary from situation to situation, depending on such factors as the quality of an MIS plan, the appropriateness of an MIS design, and the kinds of individuals operating an MIS. However, several activities have the potential of improving the MIS of most organizations:

1. *Building cooperation among MIS personnel and line managers.*[26] Cooperation of this sort encourages line managers to give MIS personnel honest opinions of the quality of information being received. Through this type of interaction, MIS designers and operators should be able to improve the effectiveness of an MIS.
2. *Constantly stressing that MIS personnel should strive to accomplish the purpose of the MIS—providing managers with decision-related information.* In this regard, it probably would be of great benefit to hold line managers responsible for continually educating MIS personnel on the types of decisions organization managers make and the corresponding steps taken to make these decisions. The better MIS personnel understand the decision situations that face operating managers, the higher the probability that MIS information will be appropriate for decisions these managers must make.
3. *Holding, wherever possible, both line managers and MIS personnel accountable for MIS activities on a cost-benefit basis.*[27] This accountability reminds line managers and MIS personnel that the benefits the organization receives from MIS functions must exceed the costs. In effect, this accountability emphasis helps increase the cost consciousness of both line managers and MIS personnel.
4. *Operating an MIS in a "people conscious" manner.* An MIS, like the formal pyramidal organization, is based on the assumption that organizational affairs can and should be handled in a completely logical manner. Logic, of course, is important to the design and implementation of an MIS. In addition, however, MIS activities also should include people considerations.[28] After all, even if MIS activities are well thought out and completely logical, an MIS can be ineffective simply because people do not use it as intended.

According to Dickson and Simmons, several factors can cause people to resist using an MIS.[29] A summary of these factors according to working groups is presented in Table 19.5. This table implies that for managers to improve MIS effectiveness, they may have to take steps to reduce such factors as threats to power and status that might be discouraging MIS use.

BACK TO THE CASE

Assume that Wal-Mart has just decided to establish an MIS within the company. Wal-Mart, like any other company, would probably gain significantly by carefully planning the way in which its MIS would be established. For example, perhaps the following questions during the planning stage of Wal-Mart's MIS would be useful: Is an appropriate

TABLE 19.5 Causes for four different working groups' resistance to an MIS

	Operating (Nonclerical)	*Operating (Clerical)*	*Operating Management*	*Top Management*
Threats to economic security		X	X	
Threats to status or power		X	X*	
Increased job complexity	X		X	X
Uncertainty or unfamiliarity	X	X	X	X
Changed interpersonal relations or work patterns		X*	X	
Changed superior-subordinate relationships		X*	X	
Increased rigidity or time pressure	X	X	X	
Role ambiguity		X	X*	X
Feelings of insecurity		X	X*	X*

X = The reason is possibly the cause of resistance to MIS development.
X* = The reason has a strong possibility of being the cause of resistance.

computer-based system being acquired and integrated? Does the company need new MIS personnel or will present personnel require further training in order to operate the new MIS? Will managers need additional training in order to operate the new MIS?

About the design and implementation stages of Wal-Mart's new MIS, management should seek answers to such questions as: How do we design the new MIS based upon managerial decision making? How can we ensure that the new MIS as designed and implemented will be functional?

Concerning the new MIS at Wal-Mart, managers as well as MIS personnel should continually try to improve it. All users of the new MIS should be aware of the symptoms of an inadequate MIS and should constantly attempt to pinpoint and eliminate corresponding MIS weaknesses. Suggestions for improving the new MIS could include: (1) building additional cooperation between MIS managers, MIS personnel, and line managers; (2) stressing that the purpose of the MIS is to provide managers with decision-related information; (3) using cost-benefit analysis to evaluate MIS activities; and (4) ensuring that the MIS operates in a people-conscious manner.

THE MANAGEMENT DECISION SUPPORT SYSTEM (MDSS)

Traditionally, the MIS that uses electronic assistance in gathering data and providing related information to managers has been invaluable. This MIS assistance has been especially useful in areas where programmed decisions (see chapter 6) are necessary, because the computer continually generates the information that helps managers make these decisions. An example is using the computer to track cumulative labor costs by department. The computer can be used to automatically gather and update the cumulative labor costs per department, compare the costs to corresponding annual budgets, and calculate the percentage of the budget that each department has reached to date. Such information would normally be useful in controlling departmental labor costs.

Closely related to the MIS is the **management decision support system (MDSS)**—an interdependent set of decision aids that help managers make nonprogrammed decisions (see chapter 6).[30] Figure 19.7 illustrates possible components of the MDSS and describes what they do. The MDSS is typically characterized by the following:[31]

A **management decision support system (MDSS)** is an interdependent set of computer-oriented decision aids that help managers make nonprogrammed decisions.

1. Corporate databases. A **database** is a reservoir of corporate facts consistently organized to fit the information needs of a variety of organization members.

1. *One or more corporate databases.* A **database** is a reservoir of corporate facts consistently organized to fit the information needs of a variety of organization members. These databases (also termed corporate databases) tend to contain facts about all of the important facets of company operations, including financial as well

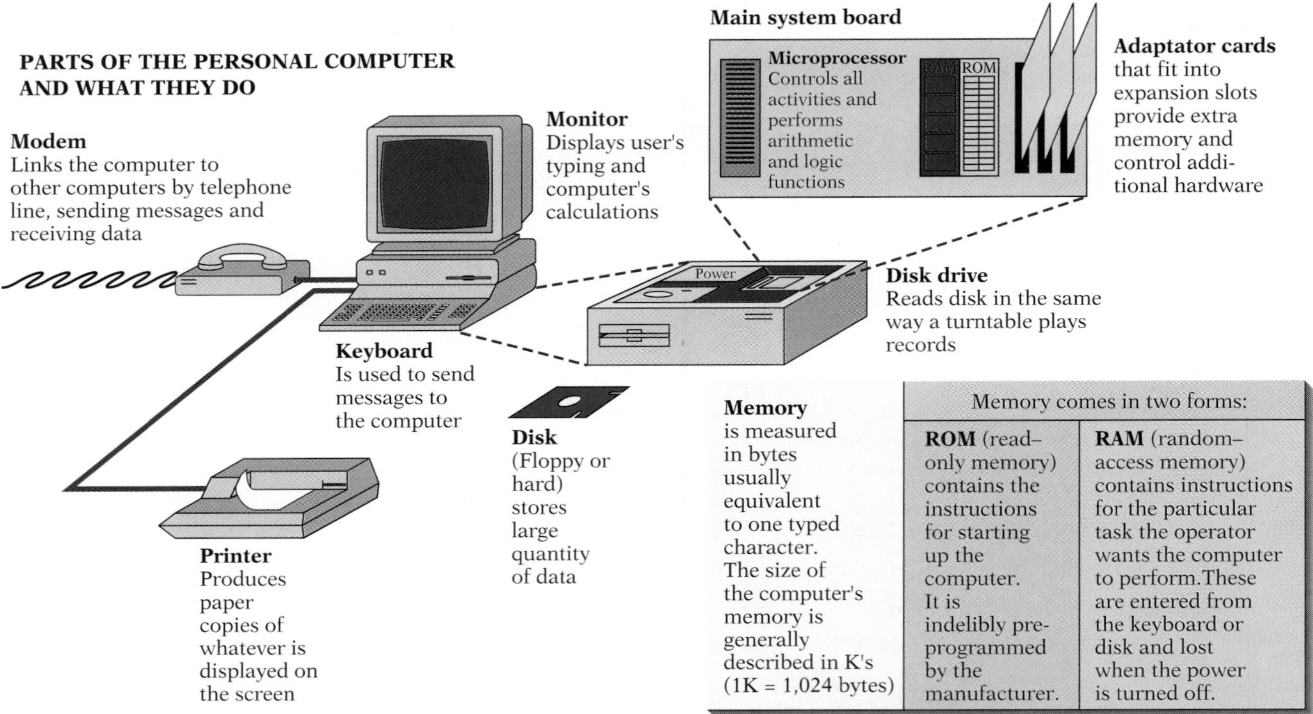
PARTS OF THE PERSONAL COMPUTER AND WHAT THEY DO
Main system board
Microprocessor Controls all activities and performs arithmetic and logic functions
RAM
ROM
Adaptator cards that fit into expansion slots provide extra memory and control additional hardware
Modem Links the computer to other computers by telephone line, sending messages and receiving data
Monitor Displays user's typing and computer's calculations
Power
Disk drive Reads disk in the same way a turntable plays records
Keyboard Is used to send messages to the computer
Disk (Floppy or hard) stores large quantity of data
Memory is measured in bytes usually equivalent to one typed character. The size of the computer's memory is generally described in K's (1K = 1,024 bytes)
Memory comes in two forms:
ROM (read-only memory) contains the instructions for starting up the computer. It is indelibly preprogrammed by the manufacturer.
RAM (random-access memory) contains instructions for the particular task the operator wants the computer to perform. These are entered from the keyboard or disk and lost when the power is turned off.
Printer Produces paper copies of whatever is displayed on the screen

FIGURE 19.7 Possible components of a management decision support system (MDSS) and what they do

as nonfinancial information. These facts are used to explore issues important to the corporation. For example, a manager might find it helpful to use facts from the corporate database to forecast profits for each of the next three years.

2. User databases. A **user database** is a database developed by an individual manager or other user.

2. *One or more user databases.* In addition to the corporate database, an MDSS tends to contain several additional user databases. A **user database** is a database developed by an individual manager or other user. These databases may be derived from but are not necessarily limited to the corporate database. They tend to address specific issues peculiar to the individual users. For example, a production manager might be interested in exploring the specific issue of lowering production costs. To do so, the manager might build a simple user database that includes departmental facts about reject rates of materials purchased from various suppliers. The manager might be able to lower production costs by eliminating the materials from the suppliers with the highest reject rates.

3. Model databases. A **model base** is a collection of quantitative computer programs that can assist management decision support system (MDSS) users in analyzing data within databases.

"What if" analysis is the simulation of a business situation over and over again using somewhat different data for selected decision areas.

3. *A set of quantitative tools stored in a model base.* A **model base** is a collection of quantitative computer programs that can assist MDSS users in analyzing data in databases. For example, the production manager discussed in item 2 might use a correlation analysis program stored in a model base to accurately determine any relationships that might exist between reject rates and the materials from various suppliers.

One desirable feature of a model base is its ability to allow the user to perform **"what if" analysis**—the simulation of a business situation over and over again using somewhat different data for selected decision areas. For example, a manager might first determine the profitability of a company under present conditions. The manager might then ask *what* would happen *if* materials costs increased by 5 percent. Or *if* products were sold at a different price. Popular programs such as Lotus 1-2-3 and the Interactive Financial Planning System (IFPS)[32] allow managers to ask as many "what if's" as they want to and to save their answers without changing their original data.

4. *A dialogue capability.* The ability of an MDSS user to interact with an MDSS is **dialogue capability.** Such interaction typically involves extracting data from a database, calling various models stored in the model base, and storing analysis results in a file. How this dialogue capability interacts with other MDSS ingredients is depicted in Figure 19.8.

4. Dialogue capability. A **dialogue capability** is the ability of a management decision support system (MDSS) user to interact with a management decision support system.

The continued technological developments related to microcomputers have made the use of the MDSS concept feasible and its application available to virtually all managers. In addition, the continued development of extensive software to support information analysis related to more subjective decision making is contributing to the popularity of MDSS.

BACK TO THE CASE

The above information about MDSS implies that Wal-Mart managers could use their own software to tap into corporate databases. In order for Wal-Mart to gain maximum advantage from an MIS, its managers should be able to use an MDSS efficiently and effectively. If Wal-Mart managers are not familiar with the MDSS concept, they can undergo training aimed at understanding and using the MDSS. Wal-Mart managers could use the MDSS to help them make both programmed and nonprogrammed decisions.

In building and using the most advantageous MIS possible, management at a company like Wal-Mart should ensure that MIS users within the company have adequate equipment to operate and use an MDSS, adequate access to a corporate database, are properly employing user databases, have appropriate model bases available, and have adequate dialogue capability within the company's MDSS. If management at a company like Wal-Mart is successful in ensuring that these issues reflect MDSS use within the company, then the probability is high that the company MDSS is being properly used. If, on the other hand, management is not successful in ensuring these issues reflect MDSS use within the company, management would probably be able to improve operations by encouraging organization members to appropriately use an MDSS.

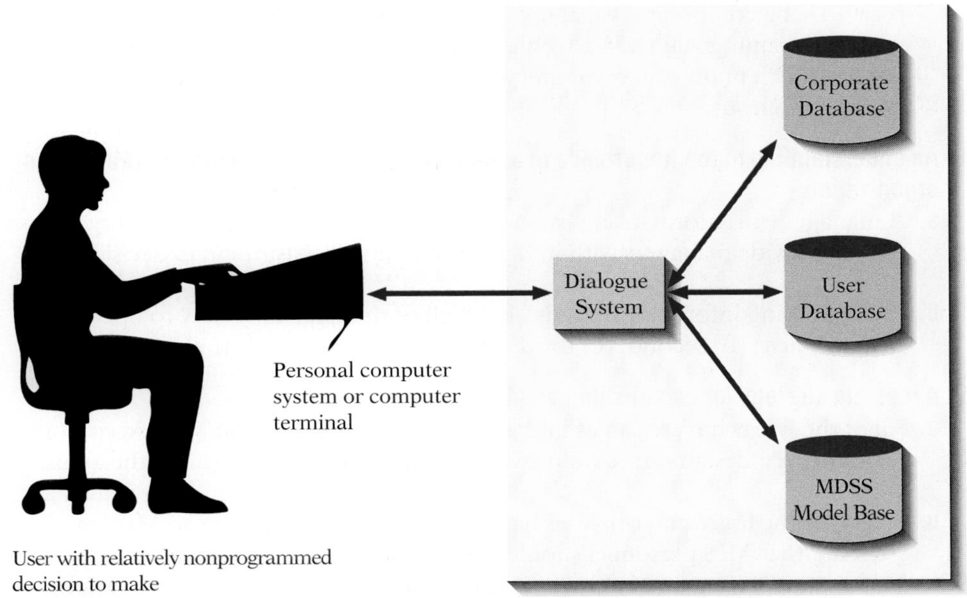

FIGURE 19.8 How dialogue capability interacts with other MDSS ingredients

ACTION SUMMARY

Reread the learning objectives that follow. Each objective is followed by questions. Answering these questions accurately will help you retain the most important concepts discussed in this chapter. After answering each question, check your answer with the answer key at the end of this chapter. (*Hint:* If you have doubt regarding the correct response, consult the page whose number follows the answer.)

Circle: ***From studying this chapter, I will attempt to acquire:***

1. An understanding of the relationship between data and information.

a, b, c, d, e **a.** Data can be: (a) information; (b) opinion; (c) premises; (d) facts; (e) gossip.

a, b, c, d, e **b.** Information can be defined as conclusions derived from: (a) data analysis; (b) opinion; (c) premises; (d) gossip; (e) none of the above.

2. Insights on the main factors that influence the value of information.

a, b, c, d, e **a.** All of the following are primary factors determining the value of information except: (a) appropriateness; (b) expense; (c) quality; (d) timeliness; (e) quantity.

T, F **b.** The appropriateness of the information increases as the volume of the information increases.

3. Knowledge of some potential steps for evaluating information.

a, b, c, d, e **a.** All of the following are main activities in evaluating information except: (a) acquiring information; (b) comparing value with cost of information; (c) selecting data to be evaluated; (d) using information in decision making; (e) discounting expected value for deficiencies and inaccuracies.

T, F **b.** The primary concern of management in evaluating information is the dollar value of the benefits gained compared to the cost of generating the information.

4. An appreciation for the role of computers in handling information.

a, b, c, d, e **a.** All of the following are main computer functions except: (a) input; (b) storage; (c) control; (d) heuristic; (e) output.

a, b, c, d, e **b.** All of the following are possible pitfalls in using the computer except: (a) thinking that a computer is independently capable of creative activities; (b) failing to realize that a computer is capable only of following precise and detailed instructions; (c) training and retraining all computer operating personnel; (d) spending too much money on computer assistance; (e) overestimating the value of computer output.

5. An understanding of the importance of a management information system (MIS) to an organization.

T, F **a.** A management information system is a network established within an organization to provide managers with information that will assist them in decision making.

a, b, c, d, e **b.** "Determining information needs" is which of the steps necessary to operate an MIS: (a) first; (b) second; (c) third; (d) fourth; (e) none of the above.

6. A feasible strategy for establishing an MIS.

a, b, c, d, e **a.** All of the following are stages in the process of establishing an MIS except: (a) planning; (b) designing; (c) improving; (d) implementing; (e) all of the above are stages.

a, b, c, d, e **b.** Which of the following activities has the potential of improving an MIS: (a) stressing that MIS personnel should strive to accomplish the purpose of an MIS; (b) operating an MIS in a "people-conscious" manner; (c) encouraging line managers to continually request additional information through the MIS; (d) a and b; (e) all of the above.

7. Information about what a management decision support system is and how it operates.

T, F **a.** A management decision support system is a set of decision aids aimed at helping managers make nonprogrammed decisions.

T, F **b.** There is basically no difference between a corporate database and a user database.

T, F **c.** Dialogue capability allows the MDSS user to interact with an MIS.

INTRODUCTORY CASE WRAP-UP

"Sam Walton Taught Others at Wal-Mart to Use Information" (p. 491) and its related back-to-the-case sections were written to help you better understand the management concepts contained in this chapter. Answer the following discussion questions about this introductory case to further enrich your understanding of chapter content:

1. If you were a store manager at Wal-Mart, what three functions would you use a computer to perform? Be as specific as possible.
2. List three decisions that an MDSS could help the manager of a Wal-Mart garden supplies department to make. For each decision, describe the data that must be in the database in order to provide such help.
3. The main steps of the controlling process are measuring performance, comparing performance to standards, and taking corrective action. Discuss a possible role of an MIS at Wal-Mart in each of these steps.

ISSUES FOR REVIEW AND DISCUSSION

1. What is the difference between data and information?
2. List and define four major factors that influence the value of information.
3. What are operational control decisions and strategic planning decisions? What characterizes information appropriate for making each of these decisions?
4. Discuss the major activities involved in evaluating information.
5. What factors tend to limit the usefulness of information, and how can these factors be overcome?
6. Is a computer a flexible management tool? Explain.
7. How do the main functions of a computer relate to one another?
8. Summarize the major pitfalls managers must avoid when using a computer.
9. Define *MIS* and discuss its importance to management.
10. What steps must be performed to operate an MIS properly?
11. What major steps are involved in establishing an MIS?
12. Why is planning for an MIS such an important part of establishing an MIS?
13. Why does the designing of an MIS begin with analyzing managerial decision making?
14. How should managers use the symptoms of an inadequate MIS as listed in Table 19.4?
15. How could building cooperation between MIS personnel and line managers improve an MIS?
16. How can management use cost-benefit analysis to improve an MIS?
17. Describe five possible causes of resistance to using an MIS. What can managers do to ensure that these causes do not affect their organization's MIS?
18. How does an MDSS differ from an MIS? Define *"what if" analysis* and give an illustration of how a manager might use it.

ACTION SUMMARY ANSWER KEY

1. **a.** d, p. 492
   b. a, p. 492
2. **a.** b, p. 492
   b. F, p. 493
3. **a.** d, pp. 494–495
   b. T, p. 494
4. **a.** d, pp. 496–498
   b. c, p. 499
5. **a.** T, p. 500
   b. a, p. 501
6. **a.** e, p. 505
   b. d, p. 508
7. **a.** T, p. 509
   b. F, pp. 509–510
   c. F, p. 511

CASE STUDY

Mainframes Are Not Dead at 3Com Corporation

ROBERT E. KEMPER
Northern Arizona University

3Com Corporation, a computer connecting firm based in Santa Clara, California, offers complete, broad-based, integrated computer solutions and databases for its customers. Its services include analyzing the client's software and hardware needs, defining what databases the company already has access to and determining what additional databases are needed, designing the appropriate network system to get the information efficiently to the proper workers in the company, and providing the service needed to keep the whole system up and running. 3Com has grown for over twenty years and provides global communications solutions to customers located in Europe, Australia, Hong Kong, and Japan, as well as in the United States. 3Com is a half-billion-dollar company with over seventeen hundred employees worldwide.

The computer technology that allows companies and individuals to capture, handle, and distribute the information needed to do business continues to change. New technologies continually offer advances that allow companies to change the way they do things. As PCs (personal computers) have become more and more powerful, operators at workstations are able to do more and more of the analytical, accounting, and operational work that was formerly done by the mainframe computers. At 3Com, however, the mainframe concept is not dead. Mainframes still carry the huge, predetermined loads—the databanks and repositories of industry information compiled from many different sources that would overwhelm a PC's capabilities. At the PCs and workstations, operators are able to gain access to the information stored and processed in the mainframes and still maintain the flexibility of running their own programs and applications on their own PCs.

By 1992, 3Com had reached the point where it needed to improve the capabilities available to its customers. 3Com was looking for a truly user-accessible repository of many types of industry data that could interact with a wide range of computer environments. Most 3Com customers already have users outfitted with PCs and Macintosh computers that are networked with highly customized packages and Hewlett-Packard mainframe computers. But these users also need convenient access to business information.

3Com's vision was to create an information environment that would enhance the decision-making process. The solution had to satisfy four major principles of information access:

1. access to information in corporate databases with easily understood data content and intuitive information access tools.
2. The ability to maintain the existing desktop environment consisting of 3,000 Apples, Macintoshes, and IBM PCs, as well as decision support tools like Microsoft Excel.
3. The ability to connect existing Hewlett-Packard mainframe computers and the 3Com network environment, which features 3Com's mission to provide global data networking infrastructures that allow people to use data proactively and efficiently through sophisticated networks.
4. Global access to worldwide information within the corporate database repositories.

With these goals in mind, 3Com sent out a request to five major database vendors asking for bids on a total solution—one that would include connection to the 3Com network and Hewlett-Packard mainframe computers. Finalists were selected on criteria that included how well the system functioned overall, degree of integration with PCs and databases already in use, system cost, and vendor qualifications. The final selection included a combination of mainframe and operating systems, a database, and various information access tools.

Following the selection, there was a three-month installation period, during which the new system was connected to the current environment. Later, an application prototype based on 3Com's worldwide sales reporting system was created. It was a challenge, but an integrated PC cross-network, cross-mainframe communication system was achieved.

DISCUSSION QUESTIONS

1. In the context of this case, what is the difference between data and information?
2. Define information access and discuss its importance to management.
3. What steps must be performed to develop a user-accessible database?
4. Why does the selection of computer hardware begin with analyzing managerial decision making?

CNN VIDEO CASE

The Shape of the World

CALEB DEAN HAMMOND III

Hammond, Inc.

Caleb Dean Hammond III is the president of Hammond, Inc., a company that has produced maps and atlases since 1900. His father serves the company as chair of the board; his wife Kathy is vice president and chief operating officer. Nonetheless, the almost century-long family orientation of this company does not mean that it is slow to adapt. Indeed, in the map business, quick changes and flexibility are part of everyday life.

In 1990, following the Iraqi invasion of Kuwait, the world's interest centered on the Middle East. U.S. service personnel from all over the globe were being sent to an area of which they and their families had only passing knowledge. The Hammonds responded immediately, preparing a *Middle East Crisis Atlas* to help introduce and guide them, to give "a true graphic sense of where they are and, hopefully, what they are doing there," as Dean Hammond relates.

Dean Hammond relies on computer assistance not only for preparation of maps for the atlases, but also to run divisions, track prospect lines, and control inventories.

To publish pictures of a rapidly changing world as quickly as possible is a challenge that all map- and atlas-makers face. In recent years, this aspect of their business has been changed by computer aids. Although artists and graphic designers are still integral to the business of cartography, mathematicians, physicists, and engineers have now joined the team as well. Political and factual changes are now easily made by inputting updated data into computer databases. Hammond has invested in a highly sophisticated database and map-drawing system that contains the equivalent of 150 person-years of information. Raw data is entered in terms of latitudes and longitudes, and the computer prepares a map based on that data; information can be provided about such disparate values as population statistics, volumes of rainfall or river flow, and political shifts.

The ease of updating provided by the computer system is particularly important to the preparation of atlases, which generally reflect a great deal of population-oriented information. An atlas may include as many as 8,000 changes from one edition to the next; regular updating of the computer database makes most of these changes fairly painless to accomplish. Dean Hammond says,

> The fact for me that is the most exciting, I believe, is the transfer of information to the electronic side of things because we are now able to deliver far better data in all languages in digital as well as print media, and there's an enormous market out there.

In addition, computer assistance is important to more than just the speedy updating of geographical information. Hammond, Inc., also relies on information systems to run other corporate divisions. Hammond's salespeople, for example, use the systems to track prospect lists and client information, including contacts, dates of sales calls and follow-up timings, past order history, and so on.

Others use computer databases to track inventories, compare inventories to sales orders, order new printings when necessary, and schedule deliveries. Tight inventory control is especially important to a company such as Hammond because the world is always changing. Maps and atlases must be timely in order to be salesworthy; a large inventory of outdated publications represents a waste of money.

"People are watching world events," says Dean Hammond, "and we have to respond and, in some cases, to lead the understanding of what those events mean." As a thoroughly modernized company in the old-world science of cartography, Hammond, Inc., stands ready and willing to meet that challenge.

VIDEO CASE QUESTIONS

1. Give two examples of how Hammond managers might use the what-if capabilities of MDSS software.
2. How do you think Hammond, Inc., justified the expense of a computerized map-making system such as the one they purchased to their shareholders?
3. Of the following four factors—appropriateness, quality, timeliness, and quantity—affecting the value of information, which do you think is (are) most important to Hammond, Inc.? Why?

CNN VIDEO EXERCISE

Improving the MIS at Hammond, Inc.

EXERCISE GOAL: Learn to assess the amount and kinds of information needed for an MIS.

Imagine that you are planning to make some major changes in the MIS at Hammond, Inc. As a beginning step in your planning, consider the kinds of work done by each of the employees listed in the chart below. There are many kinds of information to which these employees should have immediate access through their computers. Think of as many kinds of information as you can; list them in the chart in the appropriate columns.

Share your completed chart in a small group. Discuss which information and files used by the cartographer should always be accessible to the head of Cartographic Services and to the personnel director. Which files, if any, of the regional sales manager should always be accessible to the personnel director?

As a group, create a statement about which kinds of files an employee may keep privately, which kinds of files should be constantly available to others, and which kinds of files an employee may use independently until a project is ready to be turned over to another group.

	Cartographer for European Division	Head of Cartographic Services	Regional Sales Manager	Personnel Director
Kinds of Information Needed on Immediate Basis				

PART 5

INTEGRATIVE CASE

Buy Me a Light—A Mag Light

ROBERT E. KEMPER
Northern Arizona University

Tony Maglica decided to build the perfect flashlight. With his name (or part of it) on every one, his ego would accept no less. There was an unanswered need for a flashlight that people could rely on to work whenever they turned it on, and Tony Maglica responded. He created a market niche—high-quality flashlights with a sleek appearance that speaks of good design.

The Maglight is, by any measure, the best flashlight there is, a state-of-the-art flashlight. "The light had to be distinguished, beautiful, a showpiece," Maglica says. "I wanted people to be proud to give it as a gift. Besides, if you are designing something to last a long time, you have to build it so that people are willing to look at it for a long time." Not surprisingly, Maglight prices are state-of-the-art as well.

Each year, thanks to word of mouth and consistent quality, the number of people who recognize the Mag name increases. Magazines like *Fortune* include Mag on its list of the best U.S.-made products, and the Maglight has appeared in books that celebrate the best of U.S. design. It has become a status symbol.

Maglights are sold through independent representatives. The company's best-seller, the Mini-Mag, retails for about \$16.95, double the price of a typical flashlight. Their top-of-the-line model, complete with AC converter, battery pack, and wall mounting bracket, can run as high as \$150. Of necessity, Maglica deals exclusively with high-end salespeople who specialize in explaining why this product should cost more than the alternatives.

In designing the initial flashlight, Maglica required an extremely close tolerance to ensure the parts would fit together well. He also specified safeguards to eliminate some traditional reasons for flashlight failure. For example, batteries leak over time and the corrosive battery acid eventually dissolves most on-off switches, rendering the flashlight useless. In his prototype, Maglica created a switch that rubs off the battery-acid buildup every time the light is flicked on or off.

The design was clever, but there was no manufacturing equipment on the market to meet Mag's specifications. To meet his quality requirements, Maglica had to build his own equipment, which meant an investment of time and money. Nonetheless, everywhere you look at Mag Instruments, Inc., you find a commitment to quality production, to strict quality control—and Mag did \$70 million worth of business in 1989.

Just inside the Mag Instruments factory door are open boxes marked "Scrap"; they are first to catch your eye. They are full of flashlights that Mag's quality inspectors have rejected—some days, up to \$80,000 worth. Perhaps the flashlights work, but their housings are loose—scrap the entire batch. Surely this commitment to quality must pay off.

The keys to Mag's success are its unique design and its manufacturing process. Both are patent protected, and Maglica has employed an army of attorneys to keep them from being duplicated. Since 1983, Maglica has spent \$16 million in lawyers' fees on suits against not only copycat companies but also retailers who sold the copies. Mag constantly searches the marketplace for imitators.

In fact, with its commitment to upscale design and high-quality production, Mag has to some extent painted itself into a corner. To allow competition, to change its marketing strategy, or to downgrade its market position would risk everything Maglica has created since entering business in 1978. So Maglica and his wife Claire live and breathe their business. Married for ten years, they take separate vacations so there will always be a Maglica minding the store. No one can be hired without being approved first by Tony Maglica—these people will determine his company's reputation, and he wants to meet them.

Mag Instruments pays an average \$1 more per hour than their employees could make at similar jobs. Yet even so, it is hard to attract workers. "Working with screw machines is becoming a dying trade," says Maglica. So now the company has set up a training school for unskilled but willing workers. Maglica has no idea what the program will cost, however: "That would be the wrong way of looking at it. The question I ask myself is, what will this cost me if I do not do it?"

Of course, the Maglicas did not know the cost of their

quality vigilance when Tony Maglica designed his first flashlight. They only knew they wanted to build the best flashlight the world had ever seen. That plan might have been fatal—what if they had built the perfect light, and no one cared? "We all take pride in what we are doing," says Claire Maglica. "Maybe it's our naïveté, but we define success as putting out the best products we can." For now, their commitment is paying off; people are willing to pay for the best.

Everywhere you look at Mag Instruments, Inc., you find a commitment to quality production, to strict quality control. . .

DISCUSSION QUESTIONS

1. Give examples of each type of control (precontrol, concurrent control, and feedback control) used at Mag Instruments, Inc., to ensure the market position of Maglights.
2. If you were to perform cost-benefit analysis at Mag Instruments, where on the curve of payback do you think controlling might fall, according to the case? Why?
3. Consider the principle of Deming's chain reaction discussed in Chapter 18. How do you think this applies to the Maglica's new training program?
4. The Maglicas evidently rely on inspection as a major form of quality control. How might they use quality circles in their factory? Do you think this would be helpful?
5. The acquisition of information can be very costly. Scouring the marketplace for possible patent infringement, for example, must cost Mag Instruments a fair amount of money annually. Is the cost of acquiring this information justified? Why or why not?

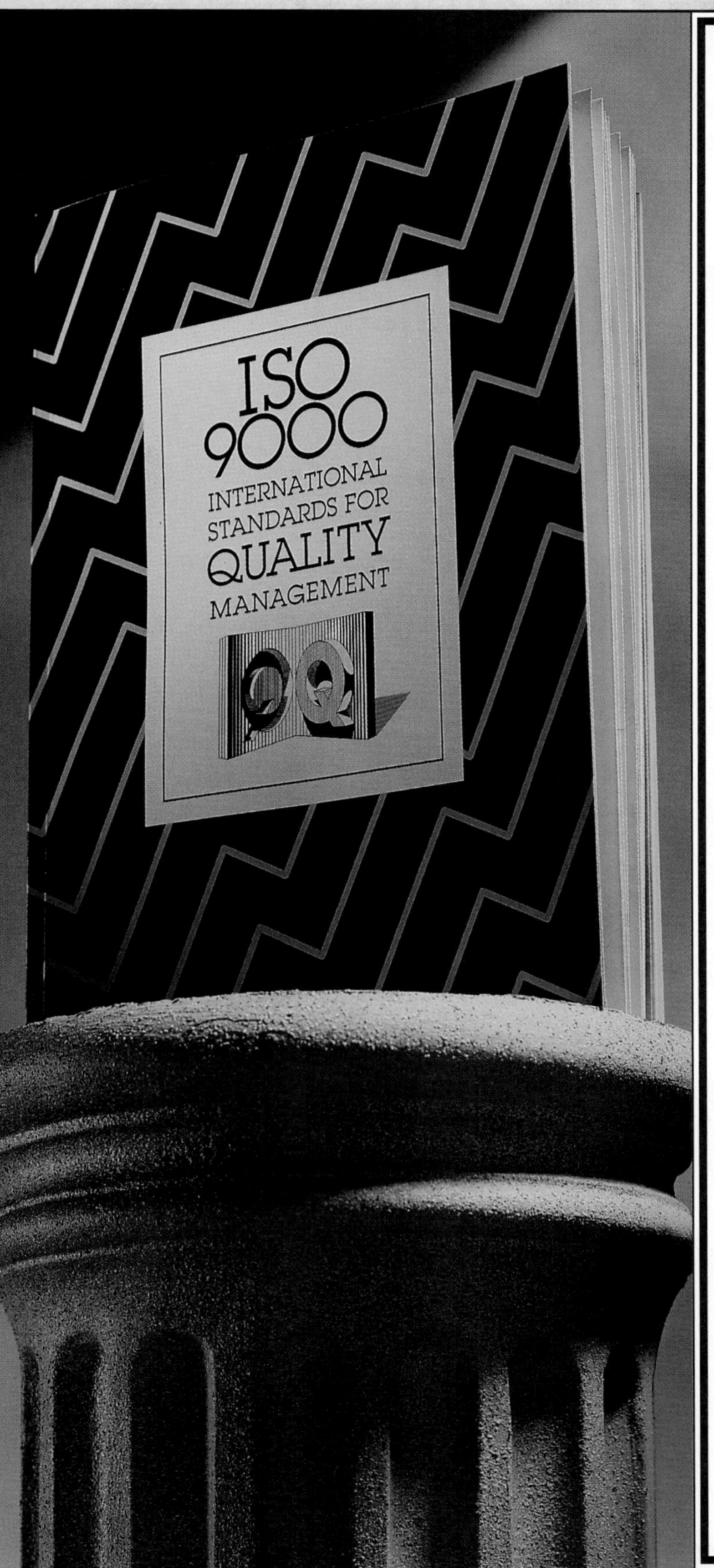

TOPICS FOR SPECIAL EMPHASIS

PART

6

The first five sections of this text introduced the subject of management and presented discussions of the four major management functions. This section emphasizes topics that present challenges for modern managers. This last section covers international management, quality as a means of building competitive organizations, and diversity.

The discussion of international management defines *international management* and *multinational corporations,* explains the complexities and risks involved in managing internationally, and examines, through a study of Japanese management techniques, how the four management functions and the process of comparative management relate to the field of international management. The increasing importance of international management is emphasized.

Quality is discussed from the viewpoint of maintaining organizational competitiveness through total quality management (TQM), building excellence into all functions performed by an organization. This section discusses the importance of a quality focus within an organization and presents advice on how to achieve TQM from internationally recognized experts like Philip B. Crosby, W. Edwards Deming, and Joseph M. Juran. Diversity is discussed in terms of helping managers understand the advantages of a diverse workforce and then presenting strategies to help managers promote diversity in organizations.

Keep this text in your professional library as a reference book that can help you meet the many challenges you will face throughout your management career.

CHAPTER

20

INTERNATIONAL MANAGEMENT

STUDENT LEARNING OBJECTIVES

From studying this chapter, I will attempt to acquire:

1. An understanding of international management and its importance to modern managers.
2. An understanding of what constitutes a multinational corporation.
3. Insights concerning the risk involved in investing in international operations.
4. Knowledge about planning and organizing in multinational corporations.
5. Knowledge about influencing and controlling in multinational corporations.
6. Insights about what comparative management is and how it might help managers do their jobs better.
7. Ideas on how to be a better manager through the study of Japanese management techniques.

CHAPTER OUTLINE

INTRODUCTORY CASE
Estée Lauder's Moscow Perfumery Plans for Expansion

FUNDAMENTALS OF INTERNATIONAL MANAGEMENT

THE MULTINATIONAL CORPORATION

Defining the Multinational Corporation

ETHICS HIGHLIGHT
Hazardous Waste

Complexities of Managing the Multinational Corporation

GLOBAL HIGHLIGHT
U.S. Companies in China

Risk and the Multinational Corporation

MANAGEMENT FUNCTIONS AND MULTINATIONAL CORPORATIONS

Planning for Multinational Corporations
Organizing Multinational Corporations

DIVERSITY HIGHLIGHT
European Organization Structures

Influencing People in Multinational Corporations
Controlling Multinational Corporations

COMPARATIVE MANAGEMENT: AN EMPHASIS ON JAPANESE MANAGEMENT

Defining Comparative Management

QUALITY HIGHLIGHT
The Deming Prize

Insights from Japanese Motivation Strategies
Insights from Japanese Management Practices: Theory Z

CASE STUDY
The Jolly Green Giant's Maquiladora

VIDEO CASE
International Joint Venturing: Sharing Risks and Benefits

VIDEO EXERCISE
Risks and Rewards of International Joint Ventures

INTRODUCTORY CASE

Estée Lauder's Moscow Perfumery Plans for Expansion

An elegant, well-stocked boutique stands on Moscow's Tverskaya Street (formerly Gorky Street), one block from the Kremlin and Red Square. That makeup, moisturizers, and fragrances can be bought with rubles, and that current sales exceed $15 million are startling: "The average Russian worker earns 200 rubles a month and a bottle of Tuscany, a male cologne, sells in the store for 120 rubles," notes Jeanette Wagner, president of Estée Lauder's international division.

As globalization continues to change the world's business practices, American international management modes must change.

Shortly before the breakup of the Soviet Union and after sixteen years of experience supplying cosmetics—sold for dollars and other hard currencies in government-controlled special tourist shops and for rubles in a limited number of ruble shops and company stores—Estée Lauder opened its perfumery.

The shop—open twelve hours a day, seven days a week—serves 2,000 customers a day. They often wait in line for six hours to part with two weeks' salary for cosmetics. In January 1992, alone, the shop sold 10,000 bottles of Lauder's fragrance, Beautiful. "There are obviously a lot of rubles around and people do understand value," says Wagner, even though a devalued ruble and price increases of 600 percent were introduced in February, 1992. A quality-hungry Russian economy is responsible for Lauder's business not being hurt.

Russian retailers and their staffs must be taught to value customers and to provide service. The store's newly enlarged staff of twenty-four women, specially trained by Kira Zamaryonov, a Russian-born U.S. retail management expert from Saks Fifth Avenue, to offer personalized service is a completely new concept to the Russian consumer. Consumer classes teaching skin care and makeup application are planned. Other novelties include optional product gift wrapping and the use of attractive shopping bags. In April 1992, Mossoviet, the store's actual owner, limited access to the store to employees of Moscow enterprises only. This policy helps preserve limited supplies for Muscovites, while turning away outside visitors.

Lauder's plans for expansion include adding more selling space at Gum department store facing Red Square in Moscow, opening a new shop at St. Petersburg's Nevsky Prospect, establishing a store in the Czech Republic, and garnering 80 percent ownership of a cosmetic boutique in Budapest. Lauder products are currently imported from their manufacturing plants in England, Belgium, and Switzerland, but plans to set up production facilities in Russia are being considered.

As globalization continues to change the world's business practices, American international management modes must change in order to remain competitive while honoring local traditions. Managing in multinational organizations requires balancing complex strategies needed to extend home country strengths abroad, adjusting organization to these strategies as well as to a worldwide presence, staffing and training across national boundaries, and establishing effective operating controls to encourage optimum results.

Personalized service, consumer classes, and attractive packaging are new concepts to the Russian cosmetic consumers who are willing to wait in line for six hours in order to part with two weeks' salary for cosmetics.

From Peter Gumbel, "Perfume Follows the Scent of Dollars along Twisted Path," *Wall Street Journal,* November 17, 1989, B13E(F); Lisa I. Fried, "Beauty May Be Skin Deep in Moscow," *Management Review* (March 1990), 33–34; Francine Parnes, "Lauder to Add Stores," *We/*Mb/ (March 1992), 12.

WHAT'S AHEAD The introductory case illustrates the expansion of Estée Lauder, an American-based cosmetics organization, into the international management arena of an emerging free enterprise economy—once the communist Soviet Union, a group of fifteen republics under central control. Russia, the dominant republic, recognizes the need to attract foreign investment, and foreign investors recognize its attractive entrepreneurial market opportunities.

Major topics that will be covered are fundamentals of international management, the multinational corporation, management functions and multinational corporations, and comparative management.

FUNDAMENTALS OF INTERNATIONAL MANAGEMENT

International management is performing management activities across national borders.

International management is simply the performance of management activities across national borders. International management entails reaching organizational objectives by extending management activities to include an emphasis on organizations in foreign countries.

In practice, this emphasis may take any of several different forms and can vary from simply analyzing and fighting competition in foreign markets to establishing a formal partnership with a foreign company. AMP, Inc., for an example, is a company fighting competition in a foreign market. AMP, Inc., a manufacturer of electrical parts, is headquartered in Harrisburg, Pennsylvania. Overall, the company is profitable and efficient, and has achieved outstanding success by gaining control of 15 to 20 percent of its multinational market. The company has factories in seventeen countries because experience showed that competitors could best be beaten in foreign markets by a company's actually producing products within market areas. For AMP, Inc., each overseas subsidiary is staffed entirely by local citizens.[1] An example of a formal partnership is National Steel, a U.S. company that has formed an equal partnership with Nippon Kokan, a Japanese steel company, in an effort to gain a competitive advantage over other world steel producers.[2]

Outstanding progress in areas such as transportation, communication, and technology makes access to foreign countries more feasible and attractive as time passes. As a result, many modern managers face numerous international issues that can have a direct and significant effect on organizational success. For example, the following situation was facing managers at Xerox.

> Xerox corporation is racing to meet deadlines at once. It must slim its copier business fast enough to beat the Japanese. Japanese competition in small copiers, a nagging worry since the mid-1970s, has shrunk Xerox's market share in America to roughly half of total copier revenue. In Europe, its other big market, Xerox has only a quarter of the revenues. Xerox has had to accept slimmer profit margins to stop the rot.[3]

The notable trend that already exists in the United States and other countries toward developing business relationships in and with foreign countries is expected to accelerate even more in the future.[4] As Figures 20.1 and 20.2 indicate, U.S. investment in foreign countries and investment by foreign countries in the United States has been growing since 1970 and is expected to continue growing, with only slight slowdowns or setbacks in recessionary periods. Information of this nature has caused many management educators as well as practicing managers to voice the opinion that an understanding of international management is necessary for a thorough and contemporary understanding of the fundamentals of management.[5]

BACK TO THE CASE As the introductory case shows, Estée Lauder is an organization involved in international management. The firm experienced substantial sales abroad even before Estée Lauder entered the Russian market. Managers within Estée Lauder perform management activities such as planning, organizing, influencing, and controlling across national borders

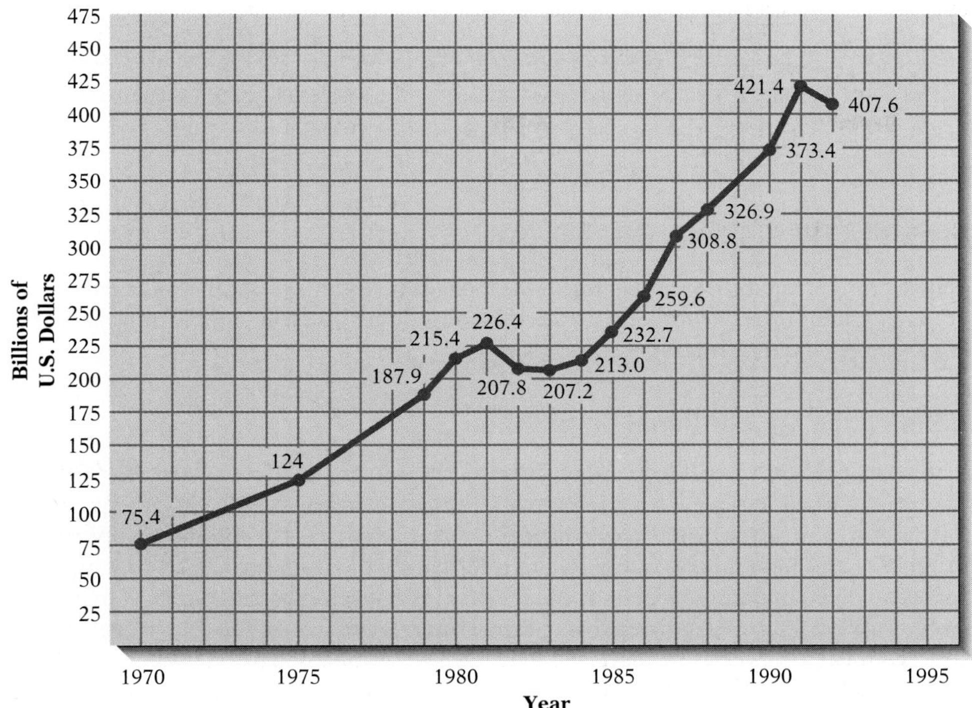

FIGURE 20.1 Growth in U.S. investment (Author forecast based on past data)

Note: Method of compiling U.S. direct investment abroad and foreign direct investment in the U.S. was changed in 1991

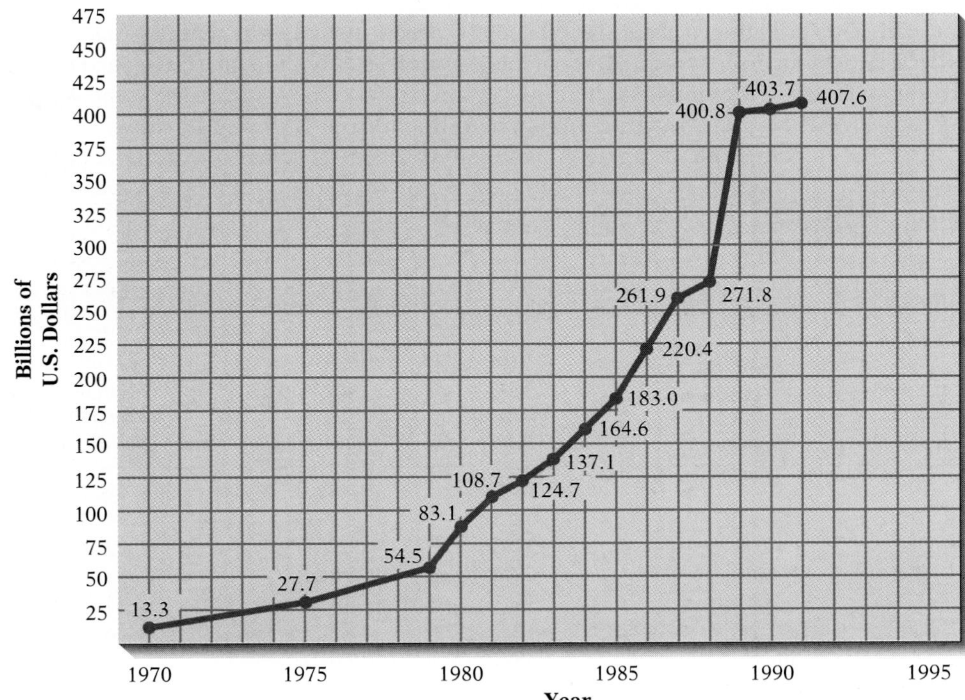

FIGURE 20.2 Growth in foreign investment in the United States (Author forecast based on past data)

Note: Method of compiling U.S. direct investment abroad and foreign direct investment in the U.S. was changed in 1991 to the north, south, east, and west. Given the international trend toward greater foreign investment, Estée Lauder is likely to continue to emphasize global expansion, particularly in eastern Europe, and the trend will no doubt be characterized by foreign firms attempting to compete with Estée Lauder in the United States.

THE MULTINATIONAL CORPORATION

This section presents more specifics about managing organizations in the international arena by defining *multinational corporation* and discussing the complexities and risks of managing the multinational corporation.

Defining the Multinational Corporation

A **multinational corporation (MNC)** is a company that has significant operations in more than one country.

The term *multinational corporation* first appeared in the dictionary about 1970 and has been defined in several ways in conversation and textbooks alike. For the purposes of this text, a **multinational corporation** is a company that has significant operations in more than one country. In essence, a multinational corporation is an organization that is involved in doing business at the international level. It carries out its activities on an international scale that disregards national boundaries and on the basis of a common strategy from a corporation center.[6]

A list of the ten largest multinationals in this country (see Table 20.1) includes four corporations whose major business is energy, including Exxon, Mobil, Texaco, and Chevron. As the table implies, foreign revenue, related profit, and foreign assets owned can be significant for multinational organizations.

A list of the ten largest foreign investments in the United States (See Table 20.2) includes such well-known organizations as Seagram, Shell, BP, A & P (Tengelmann), Hardee's (Imasco), Smith Corona and Ground Round (Hanson), Sony, and Burger King and Pillsbury (Grand Metropolitan). Although a worldwide recession lasting into the early 1990s reduced multinational direct investment in the United States, the North American Free Trade Agreement between the United States, Canada, and Mexico will make the northern hemisphere the largest free-trade zone in the world, surely a strong magnet attracting foreign investment from Europe and Asia.

Neil H. Jacoby explains that companies go through six stages to reach the highest degree of multinationalization (see Table 20.3). As the table indicates, companies can range from slightly multinationalized organizations that simply export products to a

TABLE 20.1 The effect of foreign operations on the ten largest U.S. multinationals

1991 Rank	*Company*	*Foreign Revenue as Percent of Total*	*Foreign Profit as Percent of Total Profits*	*Foreign Assets as Percent of Total Profits*
1	Exxon	75.9	84.2	58.4
2	IBM	62.3	P–D	54.3
3	General Motors	31.8	P–D	23.4
4	Mobil	68.1	86.3	56.6
5	Ford Motor	39.1	35.9	31.6
6	Texaco	49.9	57.6	28.6
7	Chevron	38.2	87.4	31.3
8	EI du Pont	44.8	52.7	39.8
9	Citicorp	52.9	P–D	43.2
10	Philip Morris	27.4	25.4	25.6

P–D: Profit to deficit

TABLE 20.2 The ten largest foreign investments in the United States

1991 Rank	*Foreign Investor*	*Country*	*Total Revenue (in millions of dollars)*	*Assets (in millions of dollars)*
1	Seagram Co. Ltd.	Canada	42,003	45,432
2	Royal Dutch/Shell Group	Netherlands/UK	22,201	27,998
3	British Petroleum Plc	UK	15,829	N/A
4	Tengelmann Group	Germany	11,591	3,213
5	B.A.T. Industries Plc/Imasco Ltd.	UK/Canada	9,300	N/A
6	Petroleos de Venezuela	Venezuela	8,922	3,262
7	Unilever NV/Unilever Plc	Netherlands/UK	8,855	9,056
8	Hanson Plc	UK	8,788	17,592
9	Sony Corp.	Japan	8,337	N/A
10	Grand Metropolitan Plc	UK	8,033	8,289

N/A: Not available

TABLE 20.3 Six stages of multinationalization

Stage 1	*Stage 2*	*Stage 3*	*Stage 4*	*Stage 5*	*Stage 6*
Exports its products to foreign countries	Establishes sales organizations abroad	Licenses use of its patterns and know-how to foreign firms that make and sell its products	Establishes foreign manufacturing facilities	Multinationalizes management from top to bottom	Multinationalizes ownership of corporate stock

foreign country to highly multinationalized organizations that have some of their owners in other countries.

In general, the larger the organization, the greater the likelihood that it participates in international operations of some sort. Companies such as General Electric, Lockheed, and du Pont, which have annually accumulated over $1 billion from export sales, support this generalization. Exceptions, however, also exist. BRK Electronics, for example, a small firm in Aurora, Illinois, has won a substantial share of world sales of smoke detectors. By setting up local distributors in Italy, France, and England, BRK caused its export sales to climb from $124,000 in one year to $4 million five years later.[7] An increasing number of smaller organizations are becoming involved in international operations.

Some U.S. companies send large quantities of hazardous waste materials to Mexico and other less-developed countries for disposal by Mexican companies.

ETHICS HIGHLIGHT
U.S. Companies Send Hazardous Waste to Mexico

The export of hazardous wastes by companies in more developed countries to companies in less-developed countries is becoming commonplace. For example, U.S. companies commonly send large quantities of such waste to Mexico for disposal by Mexican companies. Although accidents related to this business could cause extensive environmental damage and even result in a loss of human life in one or more countries, useful international legislation governing this type of business is virtually nonexistent.

Perhaps partly in response to the absence of such legislation, public controversy surrounding international trade in the disposal of hazardous wastes emphasizes ethical issues. Individuals demonstrating against the disposal of hazardous wastes in their areas insist that they have a right to a livable environment that is free of hazardous waste disposal sites. Citizens of underdeveloped countries charge that the dumping of hazardous wastes in their countries by developed countries is simply another means of racism and should be halted immediately.

In facing this international hazardous waste disposal situation, managers should ensure that interests of domestic and foreign societies are protected along with interests of their organizations. Although much of this protection may be voluntary at this time, the evolution of legislation in this area will undoubtedly require such protection in the future. For example, the Japanese have developed a one hundred-year plan, New Earth 21, to develop ecologically efficient technology to provide clean energy to the world. ▶

Complexities of Managing the Multinational Corporation

The definition of *international management* and the discussion of what constitutes a multinational corporation clearly demonstrate that international management and domestic management are quite different. International management differs from domestic management because it involves operating:[8]

1. Within different national sovereignties.
2. Under widely disparate economic conditions.
3. Among people living within different value systems and institutions.
4. In places experiencing the industrial revolution at different times.
5. Often over greater geographical distance.
6. In national markets varying greatly in population and area.

GLOBAL HIGHLIGHT
U.S. Companies in China

China is a country in which U.S. managers typically find special challenges, from developing interpersonal working relationships to simply living in the general environment. American managers indicate the most significant barrier to the development of personal relationships with Chinese employees seems to be fear and suspicion of the foreign managers by the Chinese. To compound the challenges and frustrations in the workplace, U.S. managers report that simply living in China is difficult due to a lack of privacy, problems of arranging for personal travel, and even a lack of entertainment outside of work.

American managers in China have difficulty adjusting to the lack of privacy, obstacles to personal travel, and the lack of entertainment in off-work hours.

However, because "China has now become the world's fastest growing economy, with GDP expected to jump by nearly 12 percent this year . . . demand from the U.S. is obviously playing a significant part of that growth . . . making China the source of America's second largest bilateral trade deficit, after Japan," American business must learn to cope with the trade restrictions imposed by both governments as well as the issues of human rights and the environment.

Overall, U.S. managers abroad are faced with the challenges of managing and living in a foreign society. Most U.S. managers undergo special training in programs designed and implemented to more successfully handle these challenges, in China as well as in other countries. ▶

Risk and the Multinational Corporation

Naturally, developing a multinational corporation requires a substantial investment in foreign operations. Normally, managers who make foreign investments believe that such investments (1) reduce or eliminate high transportation costs; (2) allow participation in the rapid expansion of a market abroad; (3) provide foreign technical, design, and marketing skills; and (4) earn higher profits.[9]

Many managers decide to internationalize their companies, however, without having an accurate understanding of the risks involved in making such a decision.[10] For example, political complications involving the **parent company** (the company investing in the international operations) and various factions within the **host country** (the country in which the investment is made) could keep the desirable outcomes in the preceding paragraph from materializing. Table 20.4 lists various possible sources of political risk, several groups within the host country that might generate the risk, and possible effects of the risk on the investing organization.

The **parent company** is the company investing in international operations.

The **host country** is the country in which an investment is made by a foreign company.

The likelihood of desirable outcomes related to foreign investments probably always will be somewhat uncertain and will vary from country to country. Nevertheless, managers faced with making a foreign investment must assess this likelihood as accurately as possible. Obviously, a poor decision to invest in another country can cause serious financial problems for the organization.

BACK TO THE CASE

In essence, Estée Lauder is a multinational corporation—an organization with significant operations in more than one country. International management at Estée Lauder is a complex matter due to the separation by distance of its headquarters from its various subsidiaries. Management does recognize that the global market consists of individual nations, all with their own cultures, life-styles, economies, and governments. Dealing with the bureaucracy in Russia and the other newly independent republics with economies in shambles and new, untried governments presents a dilemma to Estée Lauder. But U.S. companies need to pursue business ventures in eastern Europe because the needs of the people have not been met. Though difficult initially, business can

TABLE 20.4 Political risk in investing in a foreign country

Sources of Political Risk	*Groups through Which Political Risk Can Be Generated*	*Political Risk Effects: Types of Influence on Business Operations*
Competing political philosophies (nationalism, socialism, communism)	Government in power and its operating strategies	Confiscation: Loss of assets without compensation
Social unrest and disorder	Nonparliamentary opposition groups (e.g., anarchist or guerilla movement working from within or outside of country)	Expropriation with compensation: Loss of freedom to operate
Vested interests of local business groups	Nonorganized common interest groups: students, workers, peasants, minorities, and so forth	Operational restrictions: Market shares, product characteristics, employment policies, locally shared ownership, and so forth
Recent and impending political independence	Foreign governments or intergovernment agencies such as the European Economic Community	Loss of transfer freedom: Financial (e.g., dividends, interest payments), goods, personnel, or ownership rights
Armed conflicts and internal rebellions for political power	Foreign governments willing to enter into armed conflict or to support internal rebellion	Breaches or unilateral revisions in contracts and agreements
New international alliances		Discrimination, such as taxes or compulsory subcontracting
		Damage to property or personnel from riots, insurrections, revolutions, and wars

succeed—as Estée Lauder has illustrated—and the prospect of substantial increased return from foreign operations makes the risk tolerable.

MANAGEMENT FUNCTIONS AND MULTINATIONAL CORPORATIONS

The sections that follow discuss the four major management functions—planning, organizing, influencing, and controlling—as they occur at multinational corporations.

Planning for Multinational Corporations

Planning was defined in chapter 5 as determining how the management system will achieve its objectives. This definition is applicable to the management of both domestic and multinational organizations. In general, such management tools as policies, procedures, rules, budgets, forecasting, Gantt charts, and the program evaluation and review technique (PERT) are equally valuable in planning for either domestic or multinational organizations.

Perhaps the primary difference between planning in multinational versus domestic organizations involves strategic planning. Organizational strategy for the multinational organization must include provisions that focus on the international arena, whereas such strategy for a domestic organization does not. Increased environmental uncertainties along with a growing sense of international competition are causing more and more managers to carefully evaluate internationalization as an organizational strategy. The most significant challenge facing modern managers may be how to plan strategically in order to survive in a multinational business world.[11]

To develop appropriate international strategies, managers explore issues such as (1) establishing a new sales force in a foreign country, (2) developing new manufacturing plants in other countries through purchase or construction, (3) financing international expansion, and (4) determining which countries represent the most suitable candidates for international expansion. Although international strategies vary, most include some emphasis on one or more of the following areas: imports/exports, license agreements, direct investing, and joint ventures.

Imports/Exports

Importing is buying goods or services from another country. **Exporting** is selling goods or services to another country.

Strategy in imports/exports emphasizes reaching organizational objectives by **importing** (buying goods or services from another country) or **exporting** (selling goods or services to another country).

Organizations of all sizes are importing and exporting. On the one hand, there are very small organizations, such as People's Car Company, which is made up basically of two people who import cars from Mexico to be sold to American dealers for resale.[12] On the other hand, there are extremely large and complex organizations, such as Eastman Kodak, which exports photographic products to a number of foreign countries.[13]

License Agreements

A **license agreement** is a right granted by one company to another to use its brand name, technology, product specifications, and so on, in the manufacture or sale of goods and services.

A **license agreement** is a right granted by one company to another to use its brand name, technology, product specifications, and so on in the manufacture or sale of goods and services. Naturally, the company to which the license is extended pays some fee for the privilege. International strategy in this area involves reaching organizational objectives through either the purchase or sale of licenses at the international level.

For example, Ohio Mattress Company, a relatively small mattress manufacturer, has generated outstanding profits by making and selling Sealy bedding in Ohio, Texas, and Puerto Rico. A license purchased by Ohio Mattress from Sealy gives Ohio Mattress the right to manufacture and sell Sealy's well-known products.[14]

Direct Investing

Direct investing is using the assets of one company to purchase the operating assets (for example, factories) of another company. International strategy in this area emphasizes reaching organizational objectives through the purchase of operating assets of a company in another country.

Direct investing is using the assets of one company to purchase the operating assets of another company.

For example, Robinson Nugent, Inc., of New Albany, Indiana, manufactures sophisticated electronic parts that are used in other products assembled by high-tech manufacturers throughout the world. The company opened a manufacturing facility in Delemont, Switzerland, in an effort to maintain its share of the European market. Overall, the company believes that this Swiss plant has had a good effect on European sales and has even increased demand for exports from the United States to Europe by 40 percent.[15]

Joint Ventures

An **international joint venture** is a partnership formed by a company in one country with a company in another country for the purpose of pursuing some mutually desirable business undertaking. International strategy that includes joint ventures emphasizes the attainment of organizational objectives through partnerships with foreign companies.

An **international joint venture** is a partnership formed by a company in one country with a company in another country for the purpose of pursuing some mutually desirable business undertaking.

Joint ventures between car manufacturers in Europe are becoming more and more common as companies strive for greater economies of scale and higher standards in product quality and delivery. Renault, for example, formulated a network of deals for diesel engines from Fiat, gasoline engines from Volvo, forgings and castings from Peugeot, and gearboxes from Volkswagen.[16]

Organizing Multinational Corporations

Organizing was defined in chapter 9 as the process of establishing orderly uses for all resources within the organization. This definition applies equally to the management of either domestic or multinational organizations. Two organizing topics regarding multinational corporations, however, bear further discussion. These topics are organization structure and the selection of managers.

Organization Structure

Organization structure was defined in chapter 8 as established relationships among resources within the management system, and the *organization chart* is the graphic illustration of organization structure. Chapter 9 also noted that departments shown on organization charts are most commonly established according to function, product, territory, customers, or manufacturing process. Internationally oriented organizations also normally establish structure based on these five areas (see Figure 20.3 on p. 532).

As with domestic organizations, there is no best way to organize all multinational corporations. Instead, managers of these organizations must analyze the multinational circumstances that confront them and develop an organization structure that best suits the circumstances.

DIVERSITY HIGHLIGHT
European Organization Structures Are Becoming More Diverse

An organization structure is specifically designed to carry out established organizational plans. Recently, many European firms have begun purposely designing organization structures to carry out plans to build more diverse working units. These

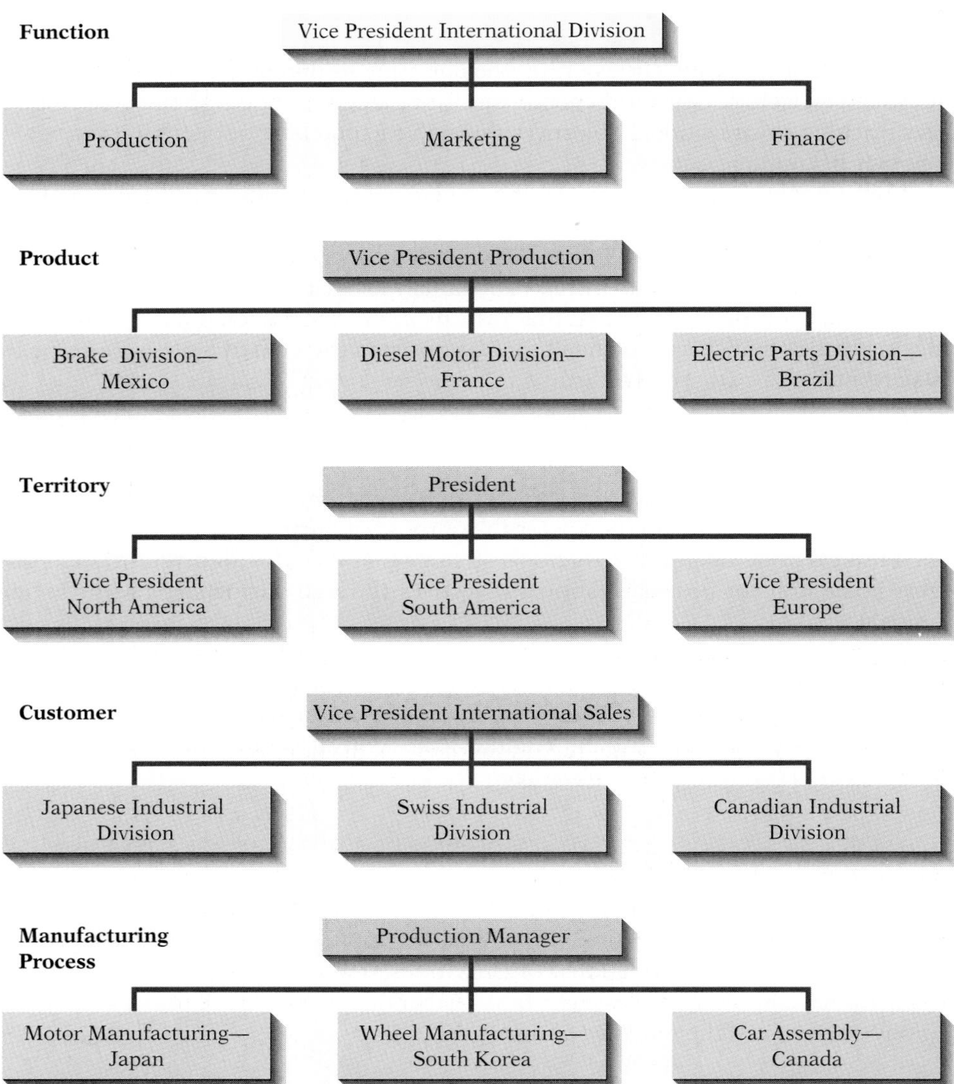

FIGURE 20.3 Partial multinational organization charts based on function, product, territory, customers, and manufacturing process

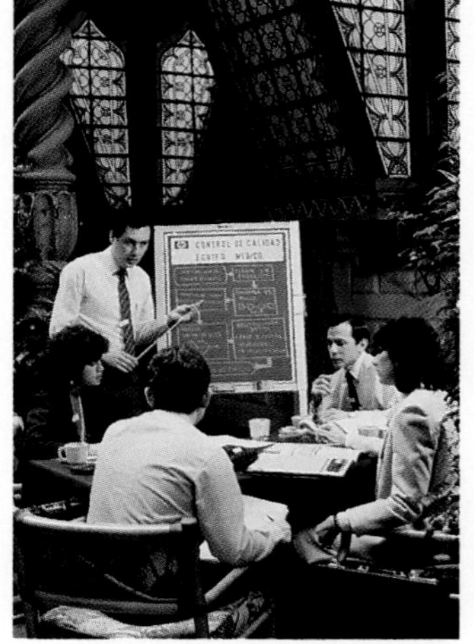

Hewlett Packard of Spain has taken concrete steps to incorporate more women professionals from other countries into its organization structure.

companies see the development of such diversity as essential to becoming top European and global competitors.

One trend reflecting European companies' building more diverse structures is the increased hiring of workers from other countries. European human resource directors predict that this trend will become even more significant as hiring workers across national borders in Europe becomes more accepted. Nobody seems to know, however, exactly how significant this trend will become. In order for this trend to benefit European companies, management will have to be competent in handling people from a number of countries.

Several noteworthy European companies are creating organizational structures that include individuals from various countries. At Mars Inc., for example, where international transfers are now simply called transfers, the general manager is English, the finance manager French, and the personnel director Swiss. Hewlett-Packard of Spain has taken concrete steps to incorporate more women professionals from other countries into its organization structure. ▶

Selection of Managers

For multinational organizations to thrive, they must of course have competent managers. One important characteristic that is believed to be a primary determinant of how competently managers can guide multinational organizations is their attitude toward how such organizations should operate.

Over the years, management theorists have identified three basic managerial attitudes toward the operations of multinational corporations: ethnocentric, polycentric, and geocentric.[17] The **ethnocentric attitude** reflects a belief that multinational corporations should regard home country management practices as superior to foreign country management practices. Managers with an ethnocentric attitude seem prone to making the mistake of stereotyping home country management practices as sound and reasonable and foreign management practices as faulty and unreasonable.[18] The **polycentric attitude** reflects a belief that because foreign managers are closer to foreign organizational units, they probably understand them better, and therefore foreign management practices should generally be viewed as more insightful than home country management practices. Managers with a **geocentric attitude** believe that the overall quality of management recommendations, rather than the location of managers, should determine the acceptability of management practices used to guide multinational corporations.

The **ethnocentric attitude** is the attitude that reflects a belief that multinational corporations should regard home country management practices as superior to foreign country management practices.

The **polycentric attitude** is the attitude that reflects a belief that, because foreign managers are closer to foreign organizational units, they probably understand them better—and therefore foreign management practices generally should be viewed as more insightful than home country management practices.

The **geocentric attitude** is the attitude that reflects a belief that the overall quality of management recommendations, rather than the location of managers, should determine the acceptability of management practices used to guide multinational corporations. The geocentric attitude generally is considered most appropriate for long-term organizational success.

Understanding the potential worth of these three attitudes within multinational corporations is extremely important. The ethnocentric attitude, although perhaps having the advantage of keeping the organization simple, generally causes organizational problems, because feedback from foreign operations is eliminated. In some cases, the ethnocentric attitude even causes resentment toward the home country within the foreign society. The polycentric attitude can create the advantage of tailoring the foreign organizational segment to its culture, but it can lead to the sizable disadvantage of creating numerous individually run, relatively unique, and therefore difficult-to-control foreign organizational segments.

The geocentric attitude is generally thought to be the most appropriate for managers in multinational corporations. This attitude promotes collaboration between foreign and home country management and encourages the development of managerial skill regardless of the organizational segment or country in which managers operate. An organization characterized by the geocentric attitude generally incurs high travel and training expenses, and many decisions are made by consensus. Although risks such as the wide distribution of power in such an organization are real, payoffs such as better-quality products, worldwide utilization of the best human resources, increased managerial commitment to worldwide organizational objectives, and increased profit generally outweigh potential harm. Overall, managers with a geocentric attitude create organizations that contribute more to the long-term success of the multinational corporation. Table 20.5 compares in more detail the types of organizations generally created by managers who possess ethnocentric, polycentric, and geocentric attitudes.

Influencing People in Multinational Corporations

Influencing was defined in chapter 13 as guiding the activities of organization members in appropriate directions through such activities as communicating, leading, motivating, and managing groups. Influencing people in a multinational corporation, however, is more complex and challenging than in a domestic organization.

The factor that probably contributes most to this increased complexity and challenge is culture. **Culture** is the total characteristics of a given group of people and their environment. Factors generally designated as important components of a culture include customs, beliefs, attitudes, habits, skills, state of technology, level of education, and religion. As a manager moves from a domestic corporation involving basically one culture to a multinational corporation involving several, the task of influencing usually becomes progressively more difficult.

Culture is the total characteristics of a given group of people and their environment.

TABLE 20.5 Different organizational characteristics typical of ethnocentric, polycentric, and geocentric management

Organizational Characteristics	Managerial Attitudes		
	Ethnocentric	*Polycentric*	*Geocentric*
Complexity of organization	Complex in home country, simple in subsidiaries	Varied and independent	Increasingly complex and interdependent
Authority, decision making	High in headquarters	Relatively low in headquarters	Aim for a collaborative approach between headquarters and subsidiaries
Evaluation and control	Home standards applied for persons and performance	Determined locally	Find standards that are universal and local
Rewards and punishments, incentives	High in headquarters, low in subsidiaries	Wide variation; can be high or low for subsidiary performance	International and local executives rewarded for reaching local and worldwide objectives
Communicating, information flow	High volume to subsidiaries: orders, commands, advice	Little to and from headquarters, little between subsidiaries	Both ways and between subsidiaries; heads of subsidiaries part of management team
Identification	Nationality of owner	Nationality of host country	Truly international company but identifying with national interests
Perpetuation (recruiting, staffing, development)	Recruit and develop people of home country for key positions everywhere in the world	Develop people of local nationality for key positions in their own country	Develop best people everywhere in the world for key positions everywhere in the world

To successfully influence people, managers in multinational corporations should:

1. *Acquire a working knowledge of the languages used in countries that house foreign operations.* Multinational managers attempting to operate without such knowledge are prone to making costly mistakes.
2. *Understand the attitudes of people in countries that house foreign operations.* An understanding of these attitudes can help managers design business practices that are suitable for unique foreign situations. For example, Americans generally accept competition as a tool to encourage people to work harder. As a result, U.S. business practices that include some competitive aspects seldom create significant disruption within organizations. Such practices, however, could cause disruption if introduced in either Japan or the typical European country.
3. *Understand the needs that motivate people in countries housing foreign operations.* For managers in multinational corporations to be successful in motivating people in different countries, they must present these individuals with the opportunity to satisfy personal needs while being productive within the organization. In designing motivation strategies, multinational managers must understand that people in different countries often have different personal needs. For example, people in Switzerland, Austria, Japan, and Argentina tend to have high security needs, whereas people in Denmark, Sweden, and Norway tend to have high social needs. People in Great Britain, the United States, Canada, New Zealand, and Australia tend to have high self-actualization needs.[19] Thus, to be successful at influencing, multinational managers must understand their employees' needs and mold such organizational components as incentive systems, job design, and leadership style to correspond to these needs.

Controlling Multinational Corporations

Controlling was defined in chapter 17 as making something happen the way it was planned to happen. As with domestic corporations, control in multinational corporations requires that standards be set, performance be measured and compared to standards, and corrective action be taken if necessary. In addition, control in such areas as labor costs, product quality, and inventory is important to organizational success regardless of whether the organization is domestic or international.

Control of a multinational corporation has additional complexities. First, there is the problem of different currencies. Management must decide how to compare profit generated by organizational units located in different countries and therefore expressed in terms of different currencies.

Another complication is that organizational units in multinational corporations are generally more geographically separated. This increased distance normally makes it difficult for multinational managers to keep a close watch on operations in foreign countries.

One action managers are taking to help overcome the difficulty of monitoring geographically separated foreign units is to carefully design the communication network or management information system that links them. A significant part of this design is to require all company units to acquire and install similar MIS equipment in all offices, both foreign and domestic, in an effort to ensure the likelihood of network hookups when communication becomes necessary. In addition, such standardization of MIS equipment seems to provide the advantages of facilitating communication among all foreign locations as well as making MIS equipment repair and maintenance problems more understandable, more easily solved, and therefore less expensive.[20]

BACK TO THE CASE

Planning tools such as policies, procedures, and budgets are equally valuable at Estée Lauder in managing either domestic or foreign operations. The company's strategies abroad, however, must focus on its international sector, including: joint ventures (a partnership between Estée Lauder and an eastern European partner); exporting (production of Estée Lauder products in one country and shipment of the finished goods to another country for sale); licensing (selling the rights to a foreign company to reproduce and sell Estée Lauder products for a fee or royalty); direct investment, possibly in Russia (to take advantage of low labor costs to produce, sell, and/or export Estée Lauder cosmetics); and countertrade (necessitated by difficulties in currency exchange).

When organizing a multinational operation such as Estée Lauder, structure should be based on one or more of the important variables of function, product, territory, or manufacturing process. Estée Lauder's management considers each variable within the situation confronting them and designs the appropriate organization structure from the company's New York headquarters.

Managers selected for multinational positions are those possessing geocentric attitudes, as opposed to polycentric or ethnocentric attitudes. Influencing at Estée Lauder requires managers who understand the culture of the people in each country in which the company operates. Fluency in the language of the country and an understanding of the attitudes and personal needs that motivate those within the foreign work force are required. Without reliable secondary data to refer to, it may be difficult for Estée Lauder to learn how to adequately reward Russian workers in order to motivate them. Rewards used to motivate Russian employees may need to be much different from rewards used to motivate British workers.

The control process at Estée Lauder requires that standards, measurements, and needed corrective action be involved to achieve efficiency and economies of scale, just as in a domestic firm. The significant distances and different currencies and exchange controls contribute to making control more complicated for Estée Lauder abroad.

COMPARATIVE MANAGEMENT: AN EMPHASIS ON JAPANESE MANAGEMENT

Perhaps the most popular international management topic today is comparative management. The sections that follow define *comparative management* and provide insights on Japanese management practices that can be of value to U.S. managers.

Defining Comparative Management

Comparative management is the study of the management process in different countries to examine the potential of management action under different environmental conditions.

Comparative management is the study of the management process in different countries to examine the potential of management action under different environmental conditions. Whereas international management focuses on management activities across national borders,[21] comparative management analyzes management practices in one country for their possible application in another country.[22]

The sections that follow discuss motivation and management practice insights that were formulated by analysis of Japanese management methods. These insights currently are being applied by many U.S. managers.

QUALITY HIGHLIGHT
The Deming Prize—No Longer a Stranger at Home

The prestigious Japanese quality assurance award—the Deming Prize, honoring American W. Edwards Deming—was awarded to an American company for the first time when, in 1989, Florida Power and Light made history by winning the prize.

Japan's most prestigious quality assurance award, the Deming Prize, honors the American, W. Edwards Deming. Deming is a statistician and quality control expert. Deming's work in statistical quality measures created a devotion to quality control that has become ingrained in Japanese industrial culture. Until recently, however, Deming's native country ignored his work. His namesake prize had eluded U.S. companies until Florida Power and Light (FPL) made history by winning the Deming Prize in 1989.

Established in 1951 by the Japanese Union of Scientists and Engineers, the Deming Prize goes to organizations that demonstrate a successful, companywide quality control program. The award has helped establish total quality techniques in nearly every aspect of Japanese industry. Many Japanese organizations enter the grueling application procedure to streamline and upgrade internal quality procedures to a level worthy of securing the award. This nationwide acceptance has resulted in the massive improvements in manufacturing quality that have helped Japanese industry take giant strides in the global market.

The Deming has three categories: Japanese individuals, Japanese organizations, and overseas companies. The third category was a response, in 1986, to the growing non-Japanese interest in quality.

FPL learned from Japan's Kansai Electric Power Company, the first service firm to win a Deming in 1984. FPL launched an all-out effort to win the prize after CEO John J. Hudiburg and a team of FPL managers visited Kansai and other Japanese firms. According to Donald F. Borgschulte, FPL's director of systems and programming, completing the grueling challenge process was satisfaction enough. "Just being in the competition vastly improved the company's quality improvement process," Borgschulte said. "The challenge for the Deming Prize has accelerated a new management process from two years to six to ten months. The outcome was almost irrelevant."

American manufacturers acknowledge that they lag behind their Japanese rivals in dedication to quality. In 1987, the U.S. Commerce Department established the Malcolm Baldrige National Quality Award, named for its late secretary. The award recognizes firms which exhibit world-class business management as well as satisfy the needs of their customers.[23]

U.S. industry is adopting Japanese management techniques to cut unit-production and inventory costs utilizing benchmarking—copying and improving a competitor's product or strategy. For example, a prestigious American mail-order firm, L. L. Bean, Inc., is recognized as a highly efficient organization utilizing "problem solving at the worker level"; such industrial giants as Xerox and Chrysler have adopted Bean's order and distribution methods. Identifying partners willing to share efficient business practices is "fast becoming a condition of survival."[24] ▶

Insights from Japanese Motivation Strategies

The one country studied the most from a comparative management viewpoint is Japan. Before World War II, huge industrial conglomerates called *zaibatsus* controlled the Japanese economy. The *zaibatsus* were outlawed after the war, and a variation known as *keiretsus* emerged, collections of a number of major business organizations,[25] whose managers effectively motivate organization members.

Japanese managers seem to be able to motivate their subordinates by:

1. *Hiring employees for life rather than for some shorter period of time.* A close relationship between workers and the organization is built through this lifetime employment. Because workers know that they have a guaranteed job and that their future is therefore heavily influenced by the future of the organization, they are willing to be flexible and cooperative.[26]
2. *Elevating employees to a level of organizational status equal to that of management.* In Japanese factories, employees at all levels wear the same work clothes, eat in the same cafeteria, and use the same restrooms.[27]
3. *Making employees feel that they are highly valued by management and that the organization will provide for their material needs.*[28] New workers and their relatives attend a ceremony at which the company president welcomes them to the firm. The newcomers often live in company-built housing for several years until they can afford to buy their own housing. Also, much employee life outside work is spent in company social clubs, with weddings and receptions often being held in company facilities. Some Japanese companies even help pay for wedding expenses.

Japanese managers obviously go to great lengths to build positive working relationships with their employees. In addition, there is some evidence that similar actions have been applied successfully by Japanese managers in motivating American employees at the Nissan plant in Smyrna, Tennessee. Because the general Japanese culture has been shown to be a significant factor influencing the success of Japanese management,[29] however, managers of other countries should imitate Japanese actions with extreme caution.[30] After all, what Japanese workers find desirable or need-satisfying may not be the same as what workers from other countries find desirable or need-satisfying.[31]

Insights from Japanese Management Practices: Theory Z

Given the success of organizations such as Nissan and Toshiba, many U.S. management writers have been carefully analyzing Japanese organizations and comparing them to American organizations. The purpose is to make recommendations about how Japanese management practices can be used to improve the operation of American organizations.

One such recommendation, called Theory Z, was introduced by William Ouchi in 1981.[32] **Theory Z** suggests that significant management practices in the United States and Japan be combined into one middle-ground, improved framework. Ouchi studied the following management practices in U.S. and Japanese organizations: (1) the length of time workers were employed, (2) the way decisions were made, (3) where responsibility existed, (4) the rate at which employees were evaluated and promoted, (5) the

Theory Z is the effectiveness dimension that implies that managers who use either Theory X or Theory Y assumptions when dealing with people can be successful, depending on their situation.

type of control tools used, (6) the degree to which employees had specialized career paths, and (7) the type of concern shown for employees. Figure 20.4 summarizes Ouchi's findings about how management practices differ in U.S. and Japanese organizations.

In addition, the figure contains Ouchi's suggestions for how to integrate American and Japanese management practices to develop a new, more successful American organization, called a Type Z organization. According to Ouchi, the Type Z organization is characterized by the "individual responsibility" of American organizations as well as the "collective decision making, slow evaluation and promotion, and holistic concern for employees" of Japanese organizations. The length of employment, control, and career path characteristics of the Type Z organization are essentially compromises between American and Japanese organizations.

In a very short time, Ouchi's Theory Z concept gained popularity not only among management theoreticians but also among practicing managers.

As indicated by Organization Type J, employee participation in decision making involved the evolution of teamwork or work teams, effectively introduced in the 1980s by such U.S. multinational organizations as Ford, Digital Equipment, General Electric, Champion International, and Boeing. Similarly, flexible work practices and cross-trained workers, the basis of teamwork as practiced in Japan, were introduced by Japanese operators of U.S. subsidiaries. The evolution of worker participation in the United States is illustrated in Figure 20.5.

Japanese management has taught U.S. business to consider new approaches to compete with the Japanese high standard of industrialization. For example, leading American management consultants are developing and proposing future changes for U.S managers' consideration in the areas of strategies, organization, group cooperation, and competitive advantage.[33]

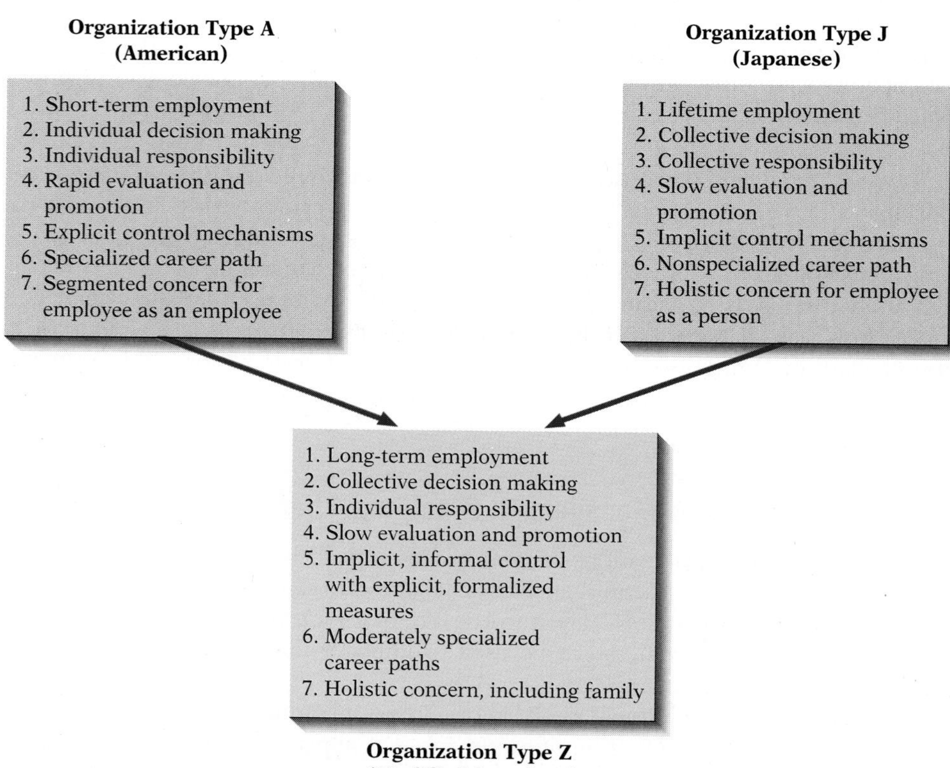

FIGURE 20.4 Combining significant American and Japanese management practices to form the Type Z organization

	Problem-Solving Teams	Special-Purpose Teams	Self-Managing Teams
Structure and function	■ Consist of 5 to 12 volunteers, hourly and salaried, drawn from different areas of a department. Meet one to two hours a week to discuss ways of improving quality, efficien– cy, and work environment. No power to implement ideas	■ Duties may include designing and introducing work reforms and new technology, meeting with suppliers and customers, linking seperate functions. In union shops, labor and manage– ment collaborate on operational decisions at all levels	■ Usually 5 to 15 employees who produce an entire product instead of subunits. Members learn all tasks and rotate from job to job. Teams take over managerial duties, including work and vacation scheduling, ordering materials, etc.
Results	■ Can reduce costs and im– prove product quality. But do not organize work more effi– ciently or force managers to adopt a participatory style. Tend to fade away after a few years	■ Involve workers and union representatives in decisions at ever–higher levels, creating atmosphere for quality and productivity improvements. Create a foundation for self– managing work teams	■ Can increase productivity 30 percent or more and substantially raise quality. Fundamentally change how work is organized, giving employees control over their jobs. Create flatter organization by eliminating supervisors
When introduced	■ Small–scale efforts in 1920's and 1930's. Widespread adoption in late 1970's based on Jap– anese Quality Circles	■ Early to middle 1980's, grow– ing out of problem–solving ap– proach. Still spreading, especially in union sectors	■ Used by a few companies in 1960's and 1970's. Began rapid spread in mid–to–late 1980's, and appear to be wave of future

FIGURE 20.5 The Evolution of Worker Participation in the U.S.

BACK TO THE CASE Management at Estée Lauder, a privately held rather than public corporation, is undoubtedly involved with comparative management, most closely with Organization Type A's strong centralized management. For most of the twentieth century, Russian and eastern European societies have labored under communism—command economies governed by virtual dictatorships—where employees were not motivated by rewards. Instead, they struggled toward the achievement of long-term, often-unattainable economic goals set by officials unfamiliar with the non-competitive attitude of the workers. Perhaps even some of the features of Organization Type J—such as lifetime employment, collective responsibility, implicit control mechanisms, and a nonspecified career path—relate to certain aspects of the communistic work ethic.

As "the stirrings of a market economy are appearing just as the old centrally planned economy totters toward collapse,"[34] and due to the limitations of Russia's infrastructure, it might well be to Estée Lauder's advantage to blend the American and Japanese management practices by implementing features of Organization Type Z. Adoption of the promise of long-term employment, which may lead to increased control of subordinates by management, limited collective decision making, individual responsibility, slow evaluation and promotion, and informal control but with explicit formalized measures may be advantageous to Estée Lauder. Russia and its neighboring republics offer some of the best investment opportunities in the world to these companies—like Estée Lauder—willing and able to handle the management challenges presented.

As of September 30, 1992, *East European Investment Magazine* reported that the United States had taken the lead in investments in Eastern Europe with "219 acquisitions, joint ventures, and startups valued at nearly $8 billion" in the past year.[35]

ACTION SUMMARY

Reread the learning objectives that follow. Each objective is followed by questions. Answering these questions accurately will help you retain the most important concepts discussed in this chapter. After answering each question, check your answer with the answer key at the end of this chapter. (*Hint:* If you have doubt regarding the correct response, consult the page whose number follows the answer.)

Circle: ***From studying this chapter, I will attempt to acquire:***

1. An understanding of international management and its importance to modern managers.

T, F **a.** To reach organizational objectives, management may extend its activities to include an emphasis on organizations in foreign countries.

a, b, c, d, e **b.** The U.S. multinational corporation with the highest net profit in 1991 was: (a) IBM; (b) Citicorp; (c) Exxon; (d) General Motors; (e) Mobil.

2. An understanding of what constitutes a multinational corporation.

a, b, c, d, e **a.** According to Jacoby, the first stage in a corporation's multinationalization is when the corporation: (a) multinationalizes ownership of corporate stock; (b) multinationalizes management from top to bottom; (c) establishes foreign manufacturing facilities; (d) establishes sales organizations abroad; (e) exports its products.

T, F **b.** In general, the smaller the organization, the greater the likelihood that it participates in international operations of some sort.

3. Insights concerning the risk involved in investing in international operations.

a, b, c, d, e **a.** Managers who make foreign investments believe that such investments: (a) reduce or eliminate high transportation costs; (b) allow participation in the rapid expansion of a market abroad; (c) provide foreign technical, design, and marketing skills; (d) earn higher profits; (e) a, b, c, and d.

T, F **b.** A manager's failure to understand the different national sovereignties, disparate national conditions, and different national values and institutions can lead to poor investment decisions.

4. Knowledge about planning and organizing in multinational corporations.

T, F **a.** The primary difference between planning in multinational versus domestic organizations probably involves operational planning.

a, b, c, d, e **b.** The attitude that multinational corporations should regard home country management practices as superior to foreign country practices is known as a(n): (a) egocentric attitude; (b) ethnocentric attitude; (c) polycentric attitude; (d) geocentric attitude; (e) isocentric attitude.

5. Knowledge about influencing and controlling in multinational corporations.

a, b, c, d, e **a.** The factor that probably contributes most to the increased complexity and challenge of influencing in multinational organizations is: (a) language; (b) attitudes; (c) personal needs; (d) culture; (e) none of the above.

T, F **b.** The standardization of MIS equipment is a major factor in facilitating communication and control among a multinational organization's foreign locations.

6. Insights about what comparative management is and how it might help managers do their jobs better.

T, F **a.** Comparative management emphasizes analyzing management practices in one country to determine how to best counteract the effectiveness of a foreign competitor.

a, b, c, d, e **b.** A successful Japanese technique involved copying and improving a competitor's strategy and product. The similar U.S. technique is known as: (a) problem solving; (b) benchmarking; (c) toeing the mark; (d) *keiretsus;* (e) none of the above.

7. Ideas on how to be a better manager through the study of Japanese management techniques.

T, F **a.** Since the Japanese have been so successful and there is little relationship between their culture and their success, American management would be wise to immediately implement the Japanese techniques.

a, b, c, d, e **b.** Which of the following is *not* one of the significant management practices that Ouchi studied in American and Japanese organizations: (a) the length of time workers were employed; (b) the way in which decisions were made; (c) the type of incentive plan used; (d) where responsibility existed within the organization; (e) the rate at which employees were evaluated and promoted.

INTRODUCTORY CASE WRAP-UP

"Estée Lauder's Moscow Perfumery Plans for Expansion: (p. 523) and its related back-to-the-case sections were written to help you better understand the management concepts contained in this chapter. Answer the following discussion questions about this introductory case to further enrich your understanding of the chapter content:

1. Do you think that at some point in your career you will become involved in international management? Explain.
2. If you were involved in managing an Estée Lauder perfumery in Russia, what challenges do you think would be the most difficult to meet? Why?
3. Evaluate the following statement: Estée Lauder can learn how to better plan and organize expansion in eastern Europe by studying the management of other successful retail operations in the USSR before the breakup.

ISSUES FOR REVIEW AND DISCUSSION

1. Define *international management.*
2. How significant is the topic of international management to the modern manager? Explain fully.
3. What is meant by the term *multinational corporation?*
4. List and explain four factors that contribute to the complexity of managing multinational corporations.
5. Choose an organization and describe how it has become multinational by progressing through two or more stages of Jacoby's six stages of multinationalization.
6. List and define four areas in which managers can develop internationally oriented strategies.
7. What is the difference between direct investing and joint ventures at the international level?
8. Draw segments of organization charts that organize a multinational corporation on the basis of product, function, and customers.
9. Is there one best way to organize all multinational corporations? Explain fully.
10. What are the differences between ethnocentric, polycentric, and geocentric attitudes? Describe advantages and disadvantages of each.
11. How does culture affect the international management process?
12. Discuss three suggestions that would be helpful to a manager attempting to influence organization members in different countries.
13. What effect will the emergence of the new eastern European republics have on the management strategies of multinational organizations? Discuss.
14. How can comparative management help managers of today?
15. What insights can be learned from Japanese managers about ways to motivate people? Should caution be exercised by a Canadian manager in applying these insights? Explain.
16. As a result of studying Japanese management, U.S. worker participation in decision making evolved from problem-solving to special-purpose to self-managing teams. Discuss the positive results affecting international management of the last team.

ACTION SUMMARY

1. **a.** T, p. 524
   b. c, p. 526
2. **a.** e, p. 527
   b. F, p. 527
3. **a.** e, p. 529
   b. T, pp. 528–529
4. **a.** F, p. 530
   b. b, p. 533
5. **a.** d, p. 533
   b. T, p. 535
6. **a.** F, p. 536
   b. b, pp. 536–537
7. **a.** F, p. 537
   b. c, pp. 537–538

CASE STUDY

The Jolly Green Giant's Maquiladora

MARY S. THIBODEAUX
University of North Texas

Andy Brooks, an unemployed worker in southern California, is very disturbed about the thousands of maquiladoras springing up in Mexico. Because of them, the managers of Green Giant closed his plant, laid off the workers making from nine to twelve dollars per hour, and moved the facility to Juarez, Mexico, where workers are paid approximately one dollar per hour.

The Mexican word *maquiladora* (also referred to as *twin-plant*) is derived from a Spanish word used in colonial Mexico. Today, *maquiladora* is used to mean a production facility that operates in Mexico and manufactures, assembles, or produces goods with raw materials that have been temporarily imported into Mexico. Because the parts are generally used to manufacture goods for export, the imported parts are placed "in-bond" to avoid taxes. When these finished products are exported from Mexico, no export fee or value-added tax is charged by the Mexican government. Many U.S. companies have been establishing operations in Mexico since the mid-1960s, and the number is expected to increase when the North American Free Trade Agreement wins final approval. The door was opened when Mexico liberalized export restrictions to allow for more maquiladoras.

The main attraction for U.S. companies is simply the availability of cheap labor. Other strategic and competitive advantages of the maquiladora program include improved logistics and transportation, as well as the availability of skilled personnel. Many well-known companies such as General Motors, General Electric, Ford, Eastman Kodak, Chrysler, and International Telephone and Telegraph participate in these programs. Firms from Britain, Finland, Spain, France, Japan, and the Netherlands also participate in such programs.

Green Giant denies that it went to Mexico for the low wages there. Rather it says it was attracted by the proximity to its eastern U.S. markets and by the year-round growing season.

In a "Green Giant Fact Sheet" sent to the *Wall Street Journal* in 1992, Green Giant publicly extolled the treatment, pay, and benefits of its Irapuato, Mexico, workers. Green Giant said it paid all employees in Irapuato wages that averaged "25 percent to 30 percent in excess of the prevailing wage in the area," and provided "life insurance, major medical insurance and emergency care as based on need to each employee." The Mexican government praises the "Jolly Green Giant" as being a good citizen because it provides jobs. Likewise, the company believes that it is meeting its social responsibility because the payroll for its 1,200 Irapuato workers is about $5 million annually and because it pays an additional $11 million a year to growers of broccoli.

Susan Valtierra, a 22-year-old who makes $6.70 per day, feels that her job at Green Giant is a good one. While Susan voices the attitude of many workers, other employees are suspicious of many of Green Giant's claims. They talk about the fact that American companies, including Green Giant, enjoy huge labor savings when they come to Mexico. They also mention the fact that a worker may remain a "temporary" worker for many years, allowing the company to avoid some of the required benefits paid to full-time employees. A recent survey by Wharton Econometric Forecasting Associates in Pennsylvania showed that the average maquiladora wage equaled $1.73 per hour, compared with $2.17 an hour for Mexican manufacturers. But maquiladora operators argue that, if hidden paycheck items such as free transportation, meals, and food baskets are included, the maquiladora pay scale more closely approximates Mexican wages.

Officials of the Teamsters Union, which represents the nearly two hundred U.S. workers who lost their jobs as a result of Green Giant's transfer from Watsonville, California, to Irapuato, calculate that Green Giant is saving $4 million in yearly labor costs. The union members believe that the primary motivation for the move was the labor savings.

Do the pluses outweigh the minuses? Green Giant thinks so, but the debate remains.

DISCUSSION QUESTIONS

1. Does a company have a legal and/or ethical obligation to meet the requirements of a host country? Should a company go beyond the requirements that have been established in a developing country?
2. What are some possible benefits and costs to American companies of engaging in free trade with Mexico?
3. Values differ from country to country; should a multinational company follow its own management practices or those of the host country?
4. What are the risks and benefits for multinational companies running maquiladoras in Mexico?

CNN VIDEO CASE

International Joint Venturing: Sharing Risks and Benefits

IBM, America's biggest computer company; Siemens, a pacesetting microelectronics firm in Germany; and Toshiba, Japan's biggest computer company—what do they have in common besides success in the field of technology? They are all trying to develop a silicon circuit that will revolutionize consumer electronics, *and* they are not racing against each other to do this; they are working together, in a joint venture relationship.

There are risks and costs, as well as benefits, to being part of a joint venture, international or otherwise. One risk is the possibility of giving up a technology that might have belonged solely to one company (or country) but that now will be shared with others. But former competitors working together may do a better job developing and marketing that technology than any single company could. Another way joint ventures have overcome this risk of giving up a particular technology is by joining the efforts of two companies that are not in direct competition with each other. Sharp (Japan) does not make microprocessors, but Intel (U.S.A.) does; Intel does not make some semiconductors that Sharp makes.

IBM, Siemens, and Toshiba are working together in a joint venture to develop a silicon circuit that will revolutionize consumer electronics.

Even when a company does have a particular technology, if the company for one reason or another cannot exploit that technology, then "there's no point in having it," says Kathryn Harrigan, professor of Strategic Management at Columbia Business School. "Sometimes, you need *help* in order to get the benefits of that investment out to the marketplace."

Anticipated benefits in the three-way venture by IBM, Siemens, and Toshiba include innovation, quality, and speed to market. Anticipated by Intel in its joint venture with Sharp are additional capital ($700 million provided by Sharp), additional markets ("it's easier to sell to Japan if you've got a partner"), and specialized technology (extensive knowledge and training of Sharp employees to help develop the processes and do the necessary product R&D).

A properly structured legal agreement is critical to the success of any joint venture. All partners must perceive the agreement as benefitting them enough to stay in it. Points out one expert, "The secret of a good deal is that everybody puts their desires on the table, their limits to what they can accept and not accept, and they're very honest about what they see as potential pitfalls. Then you address those up front and you get on with the cross-cultural exchange."

In international joint venturing, an important aspect is the physical location of the manufacturing plant. In the venture of IBM, Siemens, and Toshiba, the plant will be in the U.S. In the venture of Intel and Sharp, the plant will be in Japan. Because Intel is a huge exporter from the U.S., the company is not worried about locating this particular job outside the country. Plus, the location was an important factor in convincing Sharp to participate. At the same time, Intel needed to integrate its product designs into Sharp products as quickly as possible. Since American manufacturers have not been able to hold onto the consumer electronics business in the United States, Intel's future may rest on achieving integration of its products with the foreign products that will be selling here.

Professor Harrigan points out that the Japanese may be better at using strategic alliances because they work harder at it. Because of their culture, they are better at working in teams. "But," says Harrigan, "it can be learned. We can improve, and we are improving."

VIDEO CASE QUESTIONS

1. How does a joint venture differ from a partnership or a subsidiary relationship?
2. Is a geocentric managerial attitude appropriate for a joint venture such as that among IBM, Siemens, and Toshiba? Explain.
3. What does Intel stand to gain from its joint venture with Sharp?
4. Why might the American viewpoint on competition prove to be a disadvantage in an international joint venture?

CNN VIDEO EXERCISE

Risks and Rewards of International Joint Ventures

ACTION GOAL: Learn to assess attitudes—ethnocentric, polycentric, and geocentric—of multinational corporations toward their branches in other countries.

Work with two other students to role-play a meeting among managers from IBM, Toshiba, and Siemens to plan the location of the silicon circuit plant. The agenda of the meeting should include a discussion of three sites: one each in the United States, Germany, and Japan. The discussion should focus on the consideration of available workers and available managers.

Review the discussion of basic managerial attitudes toward the operation of multinational corporations on pages 533–534. For the first five minutes of the role-play, all three participants should adopt an ethnocentric attitude. For the next five minutes, all three should adopt a polycentric attitude. For the final five minutes, all three should adopt a geocentric attitude.

At the end of the role-plays, discuss what problems each attitude created in the discussion. Then discuss what training most American managers require before they can adopt a geocentric attitude.

1. Describe an ethnocentric attitude.

____

____

____

____

2. Describe a polycentric attitude.

____

____

____

____

3. Describe a geocentric attitude.

____

____

____

____

4. Briefly note problems created by each attitude.

____

____

____

____

5. What training would you suggest to bring about a geocentric attitude among managers.

____

____

____

____

CHAPTER

21

QUALITY: BUILDING COMPETITIVE ORGANIZATIONS

STUDENT LEARNING OBJECTIVES

From studying this chapter, I will attempt to acquire:

1. An understanding of the relationship between quality and total quality management.
2. An appreciation of the importance of quality.
3. Insight about how to achieve quality.
4. An understanding of how strategic planning can be used to promote quality.
5. Knowledge about the quality improvement process and reengineering.

CHAPTER OUTLINE

INTRODUCTORY CASE
IOMEGA Corporation: Success Built on Continuous Improvement

FUNDAMENTALS OF QUALITY

Defining Total Quality Management

QUALITY HIGHLIGHT
Ford Motor Company

The Importance of Quality
The Quality Awards
Achieving Quality

ETHICS HIGHLIGHT
American Marketing Association

QUALITY THROUGH STRATEGIC PLANNING

Environmental Analysis and Quality
Establishing Organizational Direction and Quality
Strategy Formulation and Quality
Strategy Implementation and Quality
Strategic Control and Quality

GLOBAL HIGHLIGHT
U.S. Lagging on ISO 9000

THE QUALITY IMPROVEMENT PROCESS

The Incremental Improvement Process
Reengineering Improvements

DIVERSITY HIGHLIGHT
Digital Equipment Corporation

CASE STUDY
JAS's Trackmaster: The Result of Total Quality Management

VIDEO CASE
Quality in the Auto Industry: GM's Saturn Keeps Orbiting

VIDEO EXERCISE
Will Success Spoil Saturn?

INTRODUCTORY CASE

IOMEGA Corporation: Success Built on Continuous Improvement

Many experts consider IOMEGA Corporation to be one of the world's leading manufacturers of computer removable mass storage devices, including Floptical, Magneto Optical, and Tape products as well as the popular Bernoulli Box. IOMEGA's products are on the leading edge of technology and have acquired an international reputation for quality.

In recognition of its successful commitment to quality, productivity, and customer satisfaction, IOMEGA was awarded the prestigious Shingo Prize for Excellence in American Manufacturing in 1992. It is interesting that this recognition came only a few years after the company's vital signs warned of impending disaster.

> **IOMEGA's strategy became one of customer satisfaction through the application of unique technology in the production and delivery of [its] products.**

After some initial success following its founding in 1980, IOMEGA experienced serious difficulties in the mid-1980s. Some of these difficulties could be attributed to general conditions in the U.S. computer industry at that time. However, enough of the difficulties were directly attributable to the company's management that, in 1987, new senior managers were appointed to try to rescue the company.

IOMEGA's strategy became one of customer satisfaction through the application of unique technology in the production and delivery of profitable, high-quality, leading-edge products. At the end of 1992, IOMEGA employed more than eleven hundred people worldwide and, to date, has shipped almost a million disk drives and eight million removable disks. What's more, the company now appears financially healthy.

Examples of improvement initiatives include company-wide efforts to

- establish a clear direction and values, being sure that every employee, customer, supplier, and shareholder clearly understands these commitments,
- eliminate wasted effort and cost,
- improve product quality to the point of consistent defect-free production,
- reduce cycle time from customer order to product delivery,
- empower spontaneous (self-appointed) quality improvement teams,
- improve information systems and communication networks,
- train, retrain, and cross train employees, and to take full advantage of individual employee knowledge and expertise,
- continuously improve everything.

The effects of these and other similar management initiatives have resulted in remarkable improvements in performance. Some quantitative evidence from 1992 of IOMEGA's world-class performance includes the following:

- Almost 80 percent of sales are to repeat buyers
- Almost 99 percent overall of customers would recommend IOMEGA products to a friend (100 percent for some products and no less than 98 percent for any product)
- Less than 0.4 percent overall product defect rate
- Up to 95 percent reduction in cycle time

Such performance, resulting from an uncompromising commitment to customer satisfaction, quality, and productivity places IOMEGA among the elite of American manufacturers.

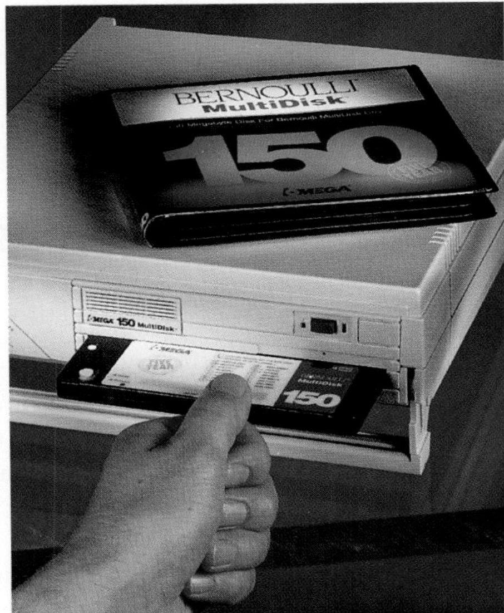

Company-wide quality initiatives at IOMEGA have led to customer satisfaction and financial success for the company through the production and delivery of high quality, yet profitable, products such as the Bernoulli box.

WHAT'S AHEAD The introductory case focuses on how IOMEGA is on the leading edge in its commitment to quality. The remainder of this chapter presents useful information for managers like those at IOMEGA who are interested in emphasizing quality throughout their organizations. This chapter (1) defines quality and total quality management, (2) explains the importance of quality, (3) discusses how to achieve quality, (4) describes how strategic planning can improve quality, and (5) outlines skills useful in achieving quality.

FUNDAMENTALS OF QUALITY

Quality is the extent to which a product does what it is supposed to do—how closely and reliably it satisfies the specifications to which it is built.

Quality was defined earlier in this text as how well a product does what it is supposed to do—how closely and reliably it satisfies the specifications to which it is built. In general, quality was presented as the degree of excellence on which products or services can be ranked. This chapter expands the subject of product quality.

Defining Total Quality Management

Total quality management (TQM) is the continuous process of involving all organization members in ensuring that every activity related to the production of goods and services has an appropriate role in establishing product quality.

Total quality management (TQM) is the continuous process of involving all organization members in ensuring that every activity related to the production of goods or services has an appropriate role in establishing product quality.[1] In essence, all organization members emphasize the appropriate performance of activities throughout the company in order to maintain the quality of products offered by the company. Under the TQM concept, all organization members work both individually and collectively to maintain the quality of products offered to the marketplace.

Although the TQM movement actually began in the United States, the establishment, growth, and development of the movement throughout the world is largely credited to the Japanese. The Japanese believe that a TQM program should be company-wide and must include the cooperation of all people within a company. Top managers, middle managers, supervisors, and workers throughout a company must strive together to ensure that all phases of company operations appropriately affect product quality. Such operations include areas like market research, research and development, product planning, design, production, purchasing, vendor management, manufacturing, inspection, sales, after-sales customer care, financial control, personnel administration, and company training and education.

QUALITY HIGHLIGHT
"Quality is Job 1" at Ford

Ford Motor Company has advertised for a number of years that "quality is Job 1." Symbolic of that commitment is the company's refusal, a few years ago, to release its new Thunderbird model in time for *Motor Trend's* Car of the Year competition; Ford chose to delay the Thunderbird's release because some quality problems had not been solved. The Thunderbird was the leading contender for the award that year, which would have meant millions of dollars in additional sales and some highly visible publicity.

Because of such commitment, Ford has led the way among American automobile manufacturers in meeting the Japanese quality challenge. Consequently, American auto manufacturers are regaining market share, largely due to improved quality. ▶

Ford Motor Company's commitment to quality has helped Ford lead the way to meeting Japanese quality.

The TQM concept has been adopted by a majority of firms throughout Japan. In fact, TQM is generally credited with being a major factor in Japan's undeniable success in establishing that country as a major competitor in the world marketplace. Although

U.S. firms seem to be moving somewhat toward accepting and implementing the TQM concept, there are some basic differences between the traditional (U.S.) and Japanese positions on establishing and maintaining total quality. Table 21.1 demonstrates some of these basic differences.

In essence, TQM is a means to the end of product quality. The excellence or quality of all management activities (planning, organizing, influencing, and controlling) inevitably influences the quality of final goods or services offered by organizations to the marketplace. In general, the more effective a TQM program within an organization, the higher the quality of goods and services that an organization can offer to the marketplace. The Quality Highlight feature has been used throughout this text to illustrate that quality is related to planning, organizing, influence, and controlling issues.

TABLE 21.1 Comparison of traditional and TQM approaches to quality

Traditional	*TQM*
Quality is a function of how well the product or service meets the specifications.	Same as the traditional position.
Quality depends on all departments—from purchasing to engineering design to production to shipping to service.	Same as the traditional position.
The quality goal is to reach a present percentage of defectives.	Accept no defects—insist on perfection.
Quality goals are set one fiscal year at a time.	Strive to improve quality consistently, not once a year, but all the time.
There is an optimal level of quality. Customers will not pay for a higher level.	Increasing quality all the time will increase market share and spur new market demand.
Quality control is done through inspections during production and through final inspection of completed lots.	Every production worker is responsible for inspection, even if this means stopping the assembly line to correct an observed defect.
Use statistical sampling methods to inspect large lots of completed products.	Inspect each piece as it is produced to catch defects before a whole lot is poorly made. Keep inventory low, using the just-in-time concept.
Set acceptable quality levels (AQL) based on sampling tables. These levels are stated in number of defects per 100 units produced.	Reject sampling tables, because no level of defects is acceptable. Express defects in number of defects per 1,000,000 units produced.
Use a random sample, typically of size $n = 5$, to check for process stability.	Use a sample of $n = 2$, consisting of the first piece and last piece produced in each lot to assure stability.
The quality control (QC) department is responsible for testing and inspection.	The QC department monitors quality, but also teaches and spreads QC information. Actual inspection by workers.
Rework of defective units is done on a separate rework line with its own staff.	Workers or groups correct their own errors, even if they have to stay late. (In reality, very few reworks are needed because of total quality control.)
Janitors keep workplaces clean.	Workers themselves are responsible for housekeeping of their work areas.

The Importance of Quality

Many managers and management theorists believe that organizations without high-quality products will be unable to compete in the world marketplace of today. A writer in *Business Week* supports this belief:[2]

> Quality. Remember it? American manufacturing has slumped a long way from the glory days of the 1950s and '60s when "Made in the U.S.A." proudly stood for the best that industry could turn out. . . . While the Japanese were developing remarkably higher standards for a whole host of products, from consumer electronics to cars and machine tools, many U.S. managers were smugly dozing at the switch. Now, aside from aerospace and agriculture, there are few markets left where the U.S. carries its own weight in international trade. For American industry, the message is simple: Get Better or Get Beat.

Producing high-quality products is not an end in itself. Successfully offering high-quality goods and services to the marketplace typically results in three important benefits for the organization: a positive company image, lower costs and higher market share, and decreased product liability costs.

Positive Company Image

To a significant extent, an organization's reputation for high quality results in a positive image for the organization.

Overall, organizations gain many advantages from having a positive company image. A positive image, for example, can be instrumental in recruiting valuable new employees, accelerating sales of a product newly offered to the marketplace, and obtaining needed loans from financial institutions. To summarize, high-quality products generally result in a positive company image, which in turn results in numerous organizational benefits.

Lower Costs and Higher Market Share

Activities that support product quality benefit the organization by yielding lower costs and greater market share. Figure 21.1 on page 547 illustrates this point. According to the top half of this figure, greater market share or gain in product sales is a direct result of customer perception of improved product quality. According to the bottom half of the figure, activities within an organization that contribute to product quality result in such benefits as increased productivity, lower rework and scrap costs, and lower warranty costs, which in turn result in lower manufacturing costs and lower costs of servicing products after they are sold. The figure also makes the important point that both greater market share and lower costs attributed to high quality normally result in greater organizational profits.

Decreased Product Liability Costs

Product manufacturers are increasingly facing legal suits over damages caused by faulty products. Organizations that design and produce faulty products are being held liable in the courts for damages resulting from the use of such products. As a dramatic example, Pfizer, a company that develops mechanical heart valves, has recently settled an estimated 180 lawsuits by heart-implant patients claiming that valves used in their implants were faulty.[3] Successful TQM efforts typically result in improved products and product performance. Naturally, the normal result of improved products and product performance is lower product liability costs.

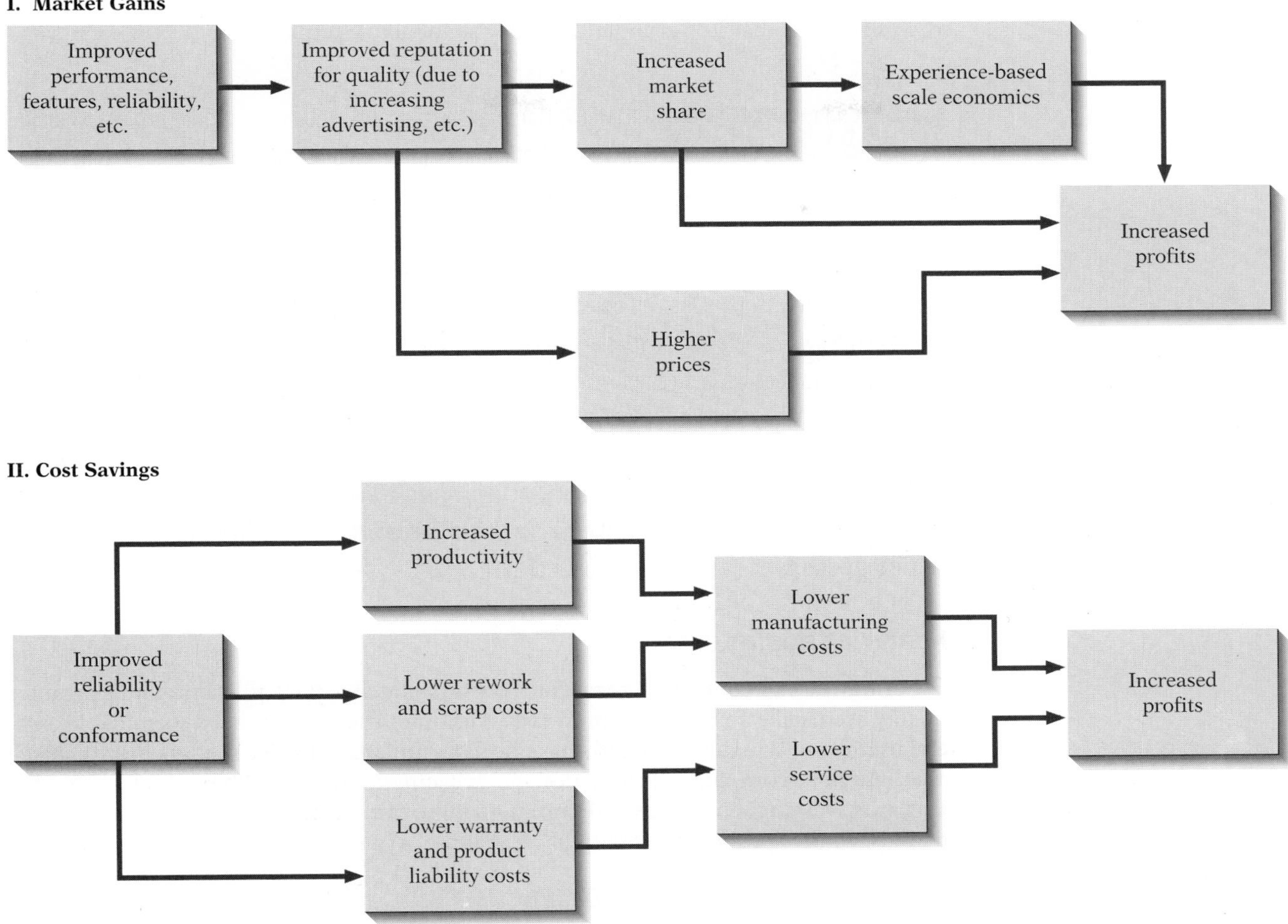

FIGURE 21.1 TQM typically results in lower costs and greater market share

The Quality Awards

Recognizing these benefits of quality, companies in recent years have increased their emphases on manufacturing high-quality products. Several major awards have been established to recognize those organizations producing exceptionally high quality products and services.

The most prestigious international award is the Deming Award, established in Japan in honor of W. Edwards Deming, who introduced Japanese firms to statistical quality control and quality improvement techniques after World War II.

The most widely known award in the United States is the **Malcolm Baldrige National Quality Award,** awarded by the American Society of Quality and Control. This award was established in 1988.

Malcolm Baldrige National Quality Award National awards given in the United States to companies doing exemplary work in the area of quality.

A few major awards recognize outstanding quality in particular industries. One example is the Shingo Prize for Excellence in American Manufacturing, sponsored by several industry groups, including the Association for Manufacturing Excellence and the National Association of Manufacturers, and administered by Utah State University. Another example, in the health-care industry, is the Healthcare Forum/Witt Award: Commitment to Quality.

The president of the United States and several states also have established a variety of quality awards. NASA gives an award for outstanding quality to its exceptional subcontractors.

As these examples suggest, quality is an increasingly important element in an organization's ability to compete in today's global marketplace.

BACK TO THE CASE IOMEGA Corporation has defined quality as "conformance to requirements." Meeting all requirements but one (even if that is only one of hundreds or thousands) still results in a defective product. The company's commitment to quality demands defect-free products and services for every customer, every time.

Whether in a company brochure or in interviews with management and employees, the statement is the same: "Quality is more than an objective. It is a way of life." All IOMEGA employees—not just production employees—are trained in total quality management and improvement techniques. Accountants, secretaries, and housekeeping employees learn similar techniques to establish and maintain world-class performance in their respective responsibilities. Many employees even describe how their personal lives have been improved by using total quality management techniques at home and in community activities.

IOMEGA's experience supports a quotation from Aristotle that "quality is a habit." A university professor stated recently, only half jokingly, that the United States will regain its preeminent economic position in the world when its highways are clear of litter.

Achieving Quality

Ensuring that all company operations play a productive role in maintaining product quality seems like an overwhelming task. Although the task is indeed formidable, several useful and valuable guidelines have been formulated to make the task more achievable. Advice from three internationally acclaimed experts—Philip B. Crosby, W. Edwards Deming, and Joseph M. Juran—on how to achieve product quality is summarized in the sections that follow.[4]

Crosby's Advice on Achieving Quality

Philip B. Crosby is generally known throughout the world as an expert in the area of quality and is accepted as a pioneer of the quality movement in the United States.[5] Crosby's work provides managers with valuable insights regarding how to achieve product quality: According to Crosby, an organization must be "injected" with certain ingredients relating to integrity, systems, communications, operations, and policies. By adding these ingredients to an organization, the organization should be able to achieve significant progress in achieving product quality. Crosby calls these ingredients the "vaccination serum" that prevents the disease of low company-wide quality. The ingredients of Crosby's vaccination serum are presented in Table 21.2.

Deming's Advice on Achieving Quality

W. Edwards Deming was originally trained as a statistician and began teaching statistical quality control in Japan shortly after World War II. He is recognized internationally as a primary contributor to Japanese quality-improvement programs. Deming advocates that the way to achieve product quality is to continuously improve the design of a product and the process used to manufacture it. According to Deming, top management has the primary responsibility for achieving product quality. Deming advises that management follow fourteen points to achieve a high level of success in improving and maintaining product quality:[6]

Dr. Deming's 14 Points

1. Create and publish to all employees a statement of the aims and purposes of the company or other organization. The management must demonstrate constantly their commitment to this statement.

TABLE 21.2 Crosby's vaccination serum for preventing poor total quality management

Integrity

A. The chief executive officer is dedicated to having the customer receive what was promised, believes that the company will prosper only when all employees feel the same way, and is determined that neither customers nor employees will be hassled.
B. The chief operating officer believes that management performance is a complete function requiring that quality be "first among equals"—schedule and cost.
C. The senior executives, who report to those in A and B, take requirements so seriously that they can't stand deviations.
D. The managers, who work for the senior executives, know that the future rests with their abilities to get things done through people—right the first time.
E. The professional employees know that the accuracy and completeness of their work determines the effectiveness of the entire work force.
F. The employees as a whole recognize that their individual commitments to the integrity of requirements are what make the company sound.

Systems

A. The quality management function is dedicated to measuring conformance to requirements and reporting any differences accurately.
B. The quality education system (QES) ensures that all employees of the company have a common language of quality and understand their personal roles in causing quality to be routine.
C. The financial method of measuring nonconformance and conformance costs is used to evaluate processes.
D. The use of the company's services or products by customers is measured and reported in a manner that causes corrective action to occur.
E. The companywide emphasis on defect prevention serves as a base for continual review and planning using current and past experience to keep the past from repeating itself.

Communications

A. Information about the progress of quality improvement and achievement actions is continually supplied to all employees.
B. Recognition programs applicable to all levels of responsibility are a part of normal operations.
C. Each person in the company can, with very little effort, identify error, waste, opportunity, or any concern to top management quickly—and receive an immediate answer.
D. Each management status meeting begins with a factual and financial review of quality.

Operations

A. Suppliers are educated and supported in order to ensure that they will deliver services and products that are dependable and on time.
B. Procedures, products, and systems are qualified and proven prior to implementation and then continually examined and officially modified when the opportunity for improvement is seen.
C. Training is a routine activity for all tasks and is particularly integrated into new processes and procedures.

Policies

A. The policies on quality are clear and unambiguous.
B. The quality function reports on the same level as those functions that are being measured and has complete freedom of activity.
C. Advertising and all external communications must be completely in compliance with the requirements that the products and services must meet.

© 1979. Crosby: *Quality without Tears.* Reprinted with permission from McGraw-Hill.

2. Learn the new philosophy, top management and everybody.
3. Understand the purpose of inspection, for improvement of processes and reduction of cost.
4. End the practice of awarding business on the basis of price tag alone.

5. Improve constantly and forever the system of production and service.
6. Institute training.
7. Teach and institute leadership.
8. Drive out fear. Create trust. Create a climate for innovation.
9. Optimize toward the aims and purposes of the company the efforts of teams, groups, staff areas.
10. Eliminate exhortations for the work force.
11. a. Eliminate numerical quotas for production. Instead, learn and institute methods for improvement.

    b. Eliminate M. B. O. Instead, learn the capabilities of processes, and how to improve them.
12. Remove barriers that rob people of pride of workmanship.
13. Encourage education and self-improvement for everyone.
14. Take action to accomplish the transformation.

ETHICS HIGHLIGHT
American Marketing Association Promotes "Zero Defects" Ethics

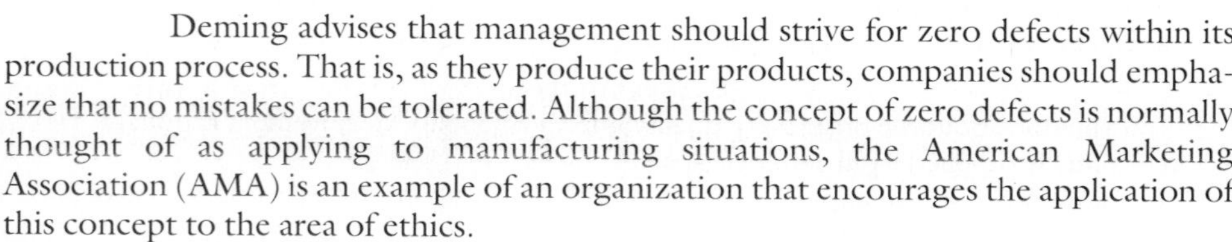

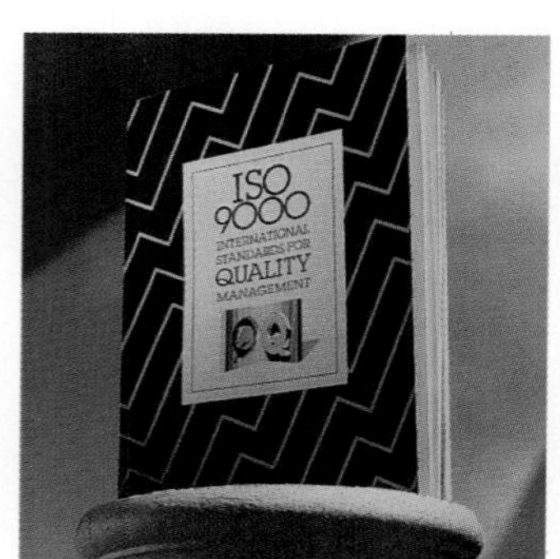

Companies that adopt codes of conduct for their employees must also take responsibility for communicating those codes to their members. The American Marketing Association's code of ethics describes the responsibilities of managers and the rights and duties of individuals involved in the marketing process.

Deming advises that management should strive for zero defects within its production process. That is, as they produce their products, companies should emphasize that no mistakes can be tolerated. Although the concept of zero defects is normally thought of as applying to manufacturing situations, the American Marketing Association (AMA) is an example of an organization that encourages the application of this concept to the area of ethics.

The AMA is a professional organization established and maintained to meet the needs of professional marketing managers. The AMA recently adopted a new code of ethics that describes the responsibilities of such managers and the rights and duties of individuals involved in the marketing process. As with any code of ethics, the AMA Code will have impact only if managers understand it, become committed to it, and comply with it. If the AMA had its way, a company or person would be deemed reputable only by having high standards for quality products and services and demonstrating constant emphasis on maintaining high ethical practices.

The AMA's philosophy about ethics indicates that an emphasis on high-quality ethics should be a component of every quality program. Naturally, maintaining high ethical practices within an organization is not an easy task to accomplish. One philosophy that can help managers to accomplish this task, however, is to adopt a zero-defects philosophy about ethical practices. That is, managers will strive to eliminate every ethical practices mistake in their organizations. ▶

Juran's Advice on Achieving Quality

Joseph M. Juran taught quality concepts to the Japanese and has been a significant force in the quality focus throughout the world. Juran's philosophy emphasizes that management should pursue the mission of quality improvement and maintenance on two levels: (1) the mission of the firm as a whole to achieve and maintain high quality; and (2) the mission of individual departments within the firm to achieve and maintain high quality.

According to Juran, quality improvement and maintenance is a clear process.

Managers must be involved with studying symptoms of quality problems, pinpointing the quality problems implied by the symptoms, and applying solutions to these problems. For maximum effect of a quality effort, strategic planning for quality should be similar to an organization's strategic planning for any other organizational issue like finance, marketing, or human resources; that is, strategic planning for quality should include setting short-term and long-term quality goals, comparing quality results with quality plans, and integrating quality plans with other corporate strategic areas. More discussion on the relationship between quality and strategic planning follows.

Shingo's Advice on Achieving Quality

The late Shigeo Shingo served as president of Japan's Institute of Management Improvement and distinguished himself as one of the world's leading experts on improving the manufacturing process. He and Taiichi Ohno are credited with the creation of the revolutionary Toyota Production Systems.

Shingo first learned quality production techniques from the Americans, who advocated statistical techniques. He later broke with this approach, however, in favor of what he called "mistake-proofing," or in Japanese, *poka yoke*.

The essence of *poka yoke* is that production systems should be made mistake-proof, so that it is impossible for a system to produce anything except good product. Previously, quality was governed primarily by inspecting work after it was done, to catch and then fix defects, if possible. Even statistical quality control is dependent upon inspecting products to diagnose problems with production systems. Shingo recognized the wasted effort and cost of inspections, so he developed methods to assure that products are produced correctly the first time, every time.

Figure 21.2 shows an example of a *poka yoke* device to prevent errors in a brake wire clamp mounting.[7] Before the improvement, the mounting bridge would accommodate either left or right parts, regardless of the one needed. This confusion often caused the wrong part to be installed. A *poka yoke* bridge was devised on mounts to assure that only the correct part could be inserted.

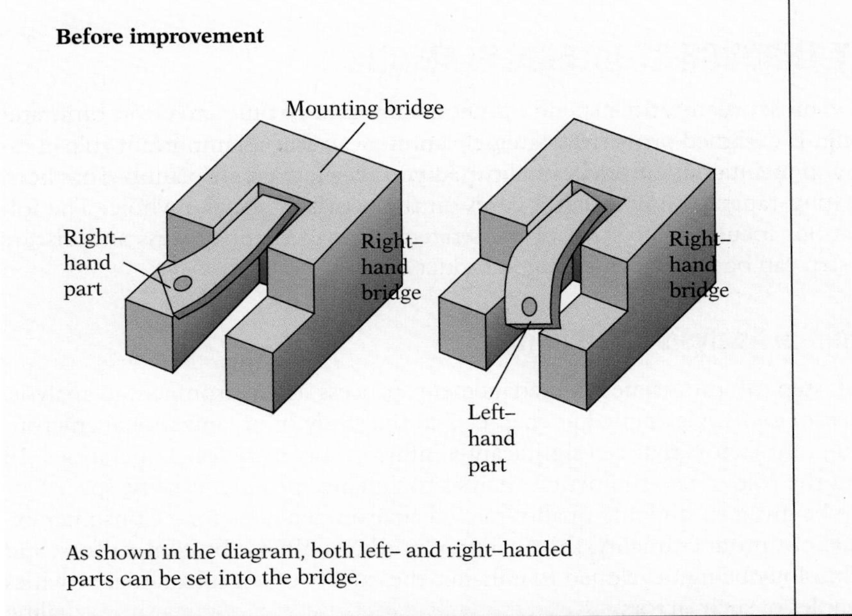

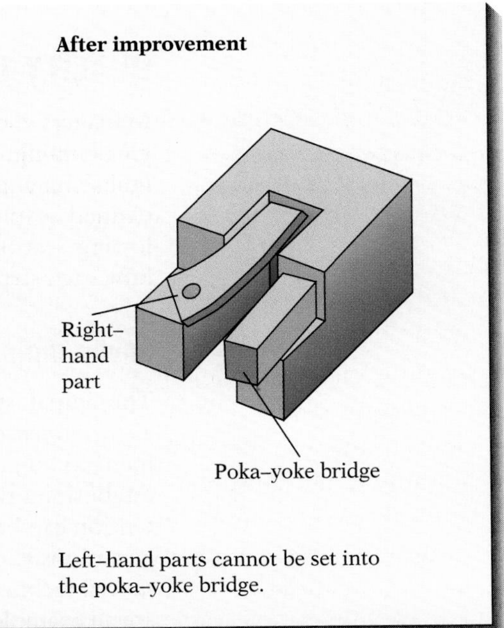

Effects: Confusion of left and right parts was reduced to zero.

FIGURE 21.2 *Poka yoke* device

Feigenbaum's Advice on Achieving Quality

Armand V. Feigenbaum is credited with originating the term "total quality control," today more often referred to "total quality management," or TQM. The basic idea of TQM is that every operation in an organization can benefit from the application of quality improvement principles. Defects are costly and unacceptable throughout any organization, not just on the manufacturing floor.

BACK TO THE CASE When asked how to achieve quality, experts consistently advise making improvement and not stopping until everything is improved, and then doing it all over again and again and again. . . .

In the November 30, 1992, issue of *Business Week,* Fred Wenninger, chief executive officer of IOMEGA Corporation, responded to the question, "Where should a beginner start?" with these comments:

- "Find your main bottleneck and attack it relentlessly."
- The problem and its solution should be easy for everyone to understand.
- Some improvement should show up relatively quickly.
- The problem should be "cheap" to fix.

With these criteria in mind, IOMEGA chose to attack cycle time first. In 1989, production time for a drive was twenty-eight days. By the end of 1992, it took only one and a half days, an almost 95 percent improvement.

Wenninger continued, "Step two is to repeat the problem-solving cycle, and keep repeating it, until the process improves to the point where something else surfaces as the biggest bottleneck—then go after that." This process led IOMEGA to other improvements, including: major reductions in inventories (too costly to maintain and too difficult to control defects); "mistake-proofing" of the production system rather than inspection of finished products for defects; and certification of suppliers to improve the quality of materials going into production. Today, the improvement process at IOMEGA continues.

QUALITY THROUGH STRATEGIC PLANNING

Managers in most organizations spend significant amounts of time and effort on strategic planning. If designed properly, strategic planning can play an important role in establishing and maintaining product quality.[8] As you recall, strategic planning has been defined as long-range planning that focuses on the organization as a whole. The following sections focus on the steps of the strategic management process and discuss how each step can be used to encourage product quality.

Environmental Analysis and Quality

The initial step of the strategic management process is environmental analysis. *Environmental analysis* is defined in chapter 7 as the study of organizational environment to pinpoint factors that can significantly influence organizational operations. In establishing the role of environmental analysis to enhance product quality, special attention can be given to studying quality-related environmental factors. Consumer expectations about product quality, the quality of products offered by competitors, and special technology being developed to enhance the quality of organizational activities are all examples of such factors.

Suppliers are often given special attention during environmental analysis by managers who stress quality. Suppliers are those companies that sell materials to be used in the final assembly of a product by another company. As an example, General Motors has many suppliers who furnish the company with parts that are then used in the final assembly of GM automobiles. Basically, the satisfactory performance of a final product will be only as good as the quality of parts obtained from company suppliers. Defective parts from suppliers can result in delayed delivery schedules, reduced sales, and reduced productivity. Special study of suppliers during environmental analysis can alert management to suppliers who can help to improve product quality through the quality of the parts that they furnish.

Establishing Organizational Direction and Quality

In this step of the strategic management process the results of environmental analysis are used as the basis for determining the path that the organization will take in the future. This path is then documented and distributed throughout the organization in the form of a mission statement and related objectives. Assuming that environmental analysis results indicate that product quality is important for an organization, a manager can use an organizational mission statement and its related objectives to give general direction to organization members regarding the organization's focus on product quality. The following is an example of a mission statement used to encourage total quality by Charles Steinmetz, president of All America Inc., the largest privately owned pest control company in the United States:[9]

> All America Termite & Pest Control, Inc., operating as Sears Authorized Termite & Pest Control, was founded to provide the residential market a once-a-year pest control service as well as premium termite protection.
>
> The purpose of our company is to provide our customers the highest quality of customer service available in our industry while providing unlimited personal and financial potential to our employees.
>
> We will commit the time, energy, expertise, and resources needed to provide premier customer service. Furthermore, we realize there are no other choices, options, or alternatives in our pursuit of quality.
>
> This requires us to give each customer full value for his or her money and to provide that value the first time and every time we have an opportunity to be of service.
>
> We will resolve any customer problems quickly, whether real and apparent or hidden or imaginary. If for any reason we cannot satisfy any customer, we will stand behind our satisfaction or money-back guarantee.
>
> Our commitment to our employees is no less important. We will provide all employees with the training necessary for them to become proficient at their job as well as proper equipment, safe materials, and a safe working environment.
>
> We will provide ample personal and family benefits to provide reasonable security and offer unlimited compensation, significant opportunity for advancement, and an environment that limits success only by the limits of each employee's hard work, dedication, and capabilities.

In studying how different companies establish the direction of a product quality focus, it becomes apparent that different companies define product quality in different ways. For example, at some companies product quality is defined as a stronger product that will last longer, or as a heavier, more durable product. At other companies, product quality can be the degree to which a product conforms to design specifications, or product excellence at an acceptable price and at an acceptable cost. In still other companies, quality is defined as the degree to which a product meets consumer requirements. Whatever management decides that its definition of product quality might be, this definition must be communicated to all organization members in order that they might work together in a focused and efficient way to achieve predetermined product quality.

Strategy Formulation and Quality

After determining organizational direction, the next step of the strategic management process is strategy formulation—deciding what steps should be taken to best deal with competitors. Incorporating the issue of product quality as part of the focus of a SWOT analysis (Strengths, Weaknesses, Opportunities, Threats) can help managers develop quality-based strategies. As an example, it may be pointed out as a result of a SWOT analysis that organization members are not adequately trained to deal with certain product quality issues. Naturally, a strategy based on this organizational weakness would be to improve quality-oriented training.[10]

Several management strategies have proven especially successful in improving and maintaining high quality operations and products. These include the following:

Value Adding. All assets and effort should, as much as possible, directly add value to the product or service. All activities, processes, and costs that do not directly add value to the product should, as much as possible, be eliminated. Non-value-adding costs are wasteful and can be very costly. This particular strategy is largely responsible for the drastic reductions in staff positions in most large organizations in recent years. As an example, investment analysis does not add value to the product coming off the production line. Therefore, many companies are simplifying their investment strategies and placing greater emphasis on production processes.

Leadership. The traditional vision of "The Boss," with whip in hand, *driving* lazy, reluctant workers to ever-higher production goals set from on high by management, is disappearing. In quality-focused organizations, "associates" (no longer called "workers" in many quality-focused organizations) are *led*. Management establishes vision and organizational values, and works with the associates to perfect the production process.

Empowerment. Associates are organized into self-directed teams and empowered to do and improve their jobs, even to change work processes. They are trained, retrained, and cross trained in a variety of jobs. "Facilitators" (formerly called "supervisors") work with the associates to provide the resources necessary to meet customer needs.

Partnering. The organization establishes what are described as "partnerships" with suppliers and customers, i.e., actively working with suppliers and customers to find ways to improve the quality of products and services. Efforts are made to reduce the number of suppliers as much as possible to only those that can meet two requirements:

1. Suppliers must prove themselves reliable and cost-effective.
2. Suppliers must prove the sustained quality of their products.

Many quality-focused companies formally certify their suppliers.

The Right Information Right Now. Today's competitiveness requires such attention to production processes. The new global marketplace is exacting and unsympathetic. There simply is no longer the time to wait for indirect traditional financial reports of performance to make the decisions required to compete successfully.

There isn't the time to wade through mountains of tables, reports, and other documents to find the right information. Consequently, in a quality management environment, information systems are required that provide immediate access to critical nonfinancial and financial information, specifically tailored to the needs of the manager.

Computerized information systems are answering this need. Everyone is trained in computers, from executive management through production staff.

Computer terminals are now as commonplace on factory floors as they are in offices.

Continuous Improvement and Innovation. The clarion themes of the quality movement are continuous improvement and constant innovation. Last year's best performance is not good enough today, and today's best practices will not be good enough perhaps even next month.

Tom Peters reported in *Thriving on Chaos: Handbook for a Management Revolution* that in 1982 Toyota, the company establishing the model for quality in automobile manufacturing, was implementing an average of five thousand employee suggestions (i.e., improvements) every day.[11] That number does not include improvements initiated by management. Peters further advocated, "as a starting point," companies should target the percentage of revenues stemming from new products and services introduced in the previous twenty-four months at 50 percent.[12] While these numbers might seem extreme—and perhaps they are for some companies—they clearly suggest the rapidly changing market place in which today's organizations compete.

Strategy Implementation and Quality

When the results of environmental analysis indicate that product quality is important for an organization, that product quality direction has been established through its mission statement and related objectives, and that strategy has been developed for achieving or maintaining product quality, management is ready to implement its product quality strategy. Implementation merely requires putting product quality strategy into action.

Although implementing product quality strategy seems like a straightforward step, in reality it is quite complex. In order for managers to succeed at implementing product quality strategy, they must meet challenges such as being sensitive to the fears and frustrations of employees in implementing new strategy, providing organizational resources needed to implement the strategy, monitoring implementation progress, and creating and using a network of individuals throughout the organization who can be helpful in overcoming implementation barriers.

Two tools managers commonly use to implement product quality strategy are policies and organizational structure. Each of these tools is discussed further in the following sections.

Policies for Quality. A policy is defined in chapter 8 as a standing plan that furnishes broad, general guidelines for channeling management thinking toward taking action consistent with reaching *organizational* objectives. A quality-oriented policy is a special type of policy. A **quality-oriented policy** is a standing plan that furnishes broad, general guidelines for channeling management thinking toward taking action consistent with reaching *quality* objectives. Quality-oriented policies can be made in virtually any organizational area and can focus on issues like the quality of new employees recruited, the quality of plans developed within the organization, the quality of decision-related information gathered and distributed within the organization, the quality of parts from suppliers to be used in the final assembly of products, and the quality of training used to prepare employees to work in foreign subsidiaries.

A **quality-oriented policy** is a standing plan that furnishes broad, general guidelines for channeling management thinking toward taking action consistent with reaching quality objectives.

Organizing for Quality Improvement. Juran says that "to create a revolutionary rate of quality improvement requires . . . a special organization structure."[13] He suggests organizing a *"quality council,"* consisting largely of upper managers, to direct and coordinate the company's quality improvement efforts.

The quality council's main job is to establish an appropriate infrastructure, which would include:

1. A process for nominating and selecting improvement projects

2. A process for assigning project improvement teams
3. A process for making improvements
4. A variety of resources, such as time for diagnosis and remedy of problems, facilitators to assist in the improvement process, diagnostic support, and training
5. A process for review of progress
6. A process for dissemination of results and for recognition
7. An appropriate employee merit rating system to reward quality improvement.
8. Extension of business planning to include goals for quality improvement

Juran points out that upper management's role in quality improvement includes active involvement in each element of the infrastructure, including serving on some improvement project teams.

Notice that such a structure involves employees at all levels. All employees, including managers, serve on quality improvement teams. The quality council comprises mostly upper management, but also may include other employees as well.

Strategic Control and Quality

Strategic control emphasizes monitoring the strategic management process to make sure that it is operating properly. In terms of product quality, strategic control would focus on monitoring company activities to ensure that product quality strategies are operating as planned. In achieving strategic control in the area of product quality, management must measure how successful it has become in achieving product quality.

Insights offered by Philip Crosby state that in order to control efforts in achieving product quality, several organizational areas should be monitored. These areas include management's understanding and attitude toward quality, how quality appears within an organization, how organizational problems are handled, the cost of quality as a percentage of sales, quality improvement actions taken by management, and how management summarizes the organization's quality position.

According to Crosby, organizations go through five successive stages of quality maturity as they approach the maximum level of quality in all phases of organizational activity. Each of the stages represents variations of the above monitoring areas. Figure 21.3 depicts Crosby's five stages of quality and the different variations of monitoring areas represented with each stage. Figure 21.3 is actually a rating instrument called the Quality Management Maturity Grid. Strategic control concerning quality would focus on ensuring that an organization evolves to Stage V of the Quality Management Maturity Grid.

ISO 9000: International Standards for Quality Management concentrates on the company's ability to implement quality management and deliver quality goods and services.

GLOBAL HIGHLIGHT
U.S. Lags on Rigorous New Quality Standard

A new international standard of quality is rapidly sweeping the world. It is called ISO 9000—a standard of quality management and quality assurance created in 1987 by the International Organization for Standardization, or ISO, of Geneva, Switzerland.

While the organization has helped bring the world closer together by nudging countries and companies into creating more interchangeable products, it has only recently begun to tackle the plethora of quality programs that have spread over the globe in the last decade. The result is ISO 9000—a series of quality standards and guidelines that sets forth design, manufacturing, inspection, packaging, marketing and other controls associated with producing quality goods and services. ISO 9000 does not focus on individual products. It concentrates on the quality of a company's overall system—its structure, responsibilities, processes and resources for implementing quality management.

QUALITY MANAGEMENT MATURITY GRID

Rater ______________________ Unit ______________________

Measurement Categories	*Stage I: Uncertainty*	*Stage II: Awakening*	*Stage III: Enlightenment*	*Stage IV: Wisdom*	*Stage V: Certainty*
Management understanding and attitude	No comprehension of quality as a management tool. Tend to blame quality department for "quality problems."	Recognizing that quality management may be of value but not willing to provide money or time to make it all happen.	While going through quality improvement program learn more about quality management; becoming supportive and helpful.	Participating. Understand absolutes of quality management. Recognize their personal role in continuing emphasis.	Consider quality management an essential part of company system.
Quality organization status	Quality is hidden in manufacturing or engineering departments. Inspection probably not part of organization. Emphasis on appraisal and sorting.	A stronger quality leader is appointed but main emphasis is still on appraisal and moving the product. Still part of manufacturing or other.	Quality department reports to top management, all appraisal is incorporated, and manager has role in management of company.	Quality manager is an officer of company; effective status reporting and preventive action. Involved with consumer affairs and special assignments.	Quality manager on board of directors. Prevention is main concern. Quality is a thought leader.
Problem handling	Problems are fought as they occur; no resolution; inadequate definition; lots of yelling and accusations.	Teams are set up to attack major problems. Long-range solutions are not solicited.	Corrective action communication established. Problems are faced openly and resolved in an orderly way.	Problems are identified early in their development. All functions are open to suggestion and improvement.	Except in the most unusual cases, problems are prevented.
Cost of quality as % of sales	Reported: unknown Actual: 20%	Reported: 3% Actual: 18%	Reported: 8% Actual: 12%	Reported: 6.5% Actual: 8%	Reported: 2.5% Actual: 2.5%
Quality improvement actions	No organized activities. No understanding of such activities.	Trying obvious "motivational" short-range efforts.	Implementation of the 14-step program with thorough understanding and establishment of each step.	Continuing the 14-step program and starting Make Certain.	Quality improvement is a normal and continued activity.
Summation of company quality posture	"We don't know why we have problems with quality."	"Is it absolutely necessary to always have problems with quality?"	"Through management commitment and quality improvement we are identifying and resolving our problems."	"Defect prevention is a routine part of our operation."	"We know why we do not have problems with quality."

FIGURE 21.3 The Quality Management Maturity Grid

© 1979. Crosby: *Quality without Tears.* Reprinted with permission from McGraw-Hill.

Under ISO 9000, quality is largely a matter of getting products to conform to contractual specifications. It incorporates both the detection and prevention of defects and establishes quality standards that most of the better manufacturers in the world should be able to meet. Five times as many companies in Europe and in the Pacific Rim are certified under ISO 9000 than in the U.S. Illinois, for example, has only twelve sites certified. In the entire United States, there are less than four hundred sites. ▶

BACK TO THE CASE One of the key strategies for quality improvement is the elimination, as much as possible, of every task, activity, cost, or other element of the business that does not directly add value to the product. IOMEGA Corporation discovered early in its quality improvement efforts several non-value-adding—and therefore cost- and time-increasing—problems in its production.

Storage of inventories was a particular nuisance to IOMEGA's quality improvement program. Storage costs included those for warehouse space, inventory management, warehouse employees, security, handling damage, and obsolescence.

Consequently, IOMEGA began producing almost entirely products for which it had firm orders, allowing the company to ship immediately, thereby avoiding inventory costs. Also, by speeding up the production cycle, the company could further reduce its work-in-process inventories. The result was a 75 percent reduction in inventories and a 41 percent reduction in plant space.

THE QUALITY IMPROVEMENT PROCESS

Two approaches may be taken to improve quality. The first is the one advocated by most of the quality experts, such as Deming, Juran, Crosby, and Feigenbaum. This process can be described as "incremental improvement." One thing is improved at a time. Of course, many of these incremental improvements may be undertaken simultaneously throughout an organization. Toyota's average of five thousand improvements per day in 1982 already has been mentioned.

The second approach is advocated by Michael Hammer, who advocates the complete reengineering of a process.[15] This requires starting with what sometimes is described as "a clean sheet of paper." The question is asked, "If we were to start over today, how would we do this?"

The Incremental Improvement Process

A variety of researchers and consultants have advocated a variety of incremental approaches to achieving excellent quality in products and processes. Regardless of their differences, almost all of the plans bear some remarkable similarities. Although a specific improvement process may not precisely follow the outline in Figure 21.4, most such processes at least approximate it.

Step 1: An area of improvement is chosen, which often is called the improvement "theme." This may be chosen by management, or an improvement team may choose the theme. Examples might include:

- a reduction in production cycle time,
- an increase in the percentage of non-defective units produced,
- a reduction in the variability of raw material going into production,
- an increase in on-time deliveries,
- a reduction in machine downtime,
- a reduction in employee absenteeism.

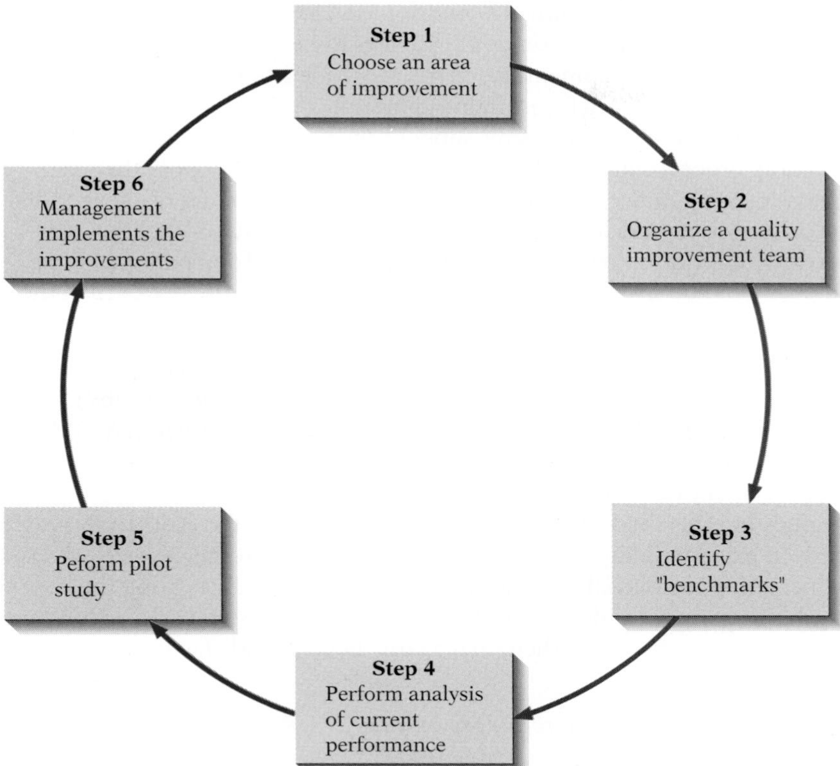

FIGURE 21.4 The quality improvement process

Of course, there are many possible examples, of which these are only a few. The point is that an improvement objective must be chosen.

An example might be taken from a pizza company, whose delivery business is lagging behind its competitors, chiefly because of slow deliveries. The improvement theme in this case may be a reduction in delivery time (i.e., cycle time).

Step 2: If a quality improvement team has not already been organized, one is organized. Members of this team might include:

- one or more associates directly responsible for the work being done
- one or more customers receiving the benefit of the work
- one or more suppliers providing input into the work
- a member of management
- perhaps one or more experts in areas particularly relevant to solving the problem and making the improvement

For the pizza delivery company, the team might include two pizza builders, a driver, a university student customer, a local resident customer, and a store manager.

Step 3: The team "benchmarks" the best performers, that is, the team identifies how much improvement is required in order to match the very best. For example, the pizza company may discover in this step that the benchmark (i.e., in this case, the fastest average time required from the moment an order is taken to the moment of front-door delivery) established by a competitor is twenty minutes.

Suppose current performance of the company is an average of thirty-five minutes compared to the twenty-minute benchmark. There is a minimum possible improvement of fifteen minutes on the average.

Step 4: The team performs an analysis to find out how current performance can be improved to meet, or beat, the benchmark. Factors to be analyzed include potential problems related to equipment, materials, work methods, people, and environmental factors, such as legal constraints, physical conditions, and weather. In the case of the pizza delivery company, suppose the team discovered that the pizza-building process could be shortened by four minutes. Suppose they also found an average lag of five minutes between the time the pizza is ready and the time the delivery van picks it up. Finally, suppose the team discovered that a different oven could shorten cooking time by seven minutes. Total potential time saved, then, would be sixteen minutes, an average of one minute better than the benchmark.

Step 5: The team performs a pilot study to test the selected remedies to the problem. In the pizza case, suppose the team conducted a pilot program for a month. The new pizza-building process was implemented. A new driver and van were added for the month, and a new oven was rented. At the end of the month, suppose actual improvement was seventeen minutes average.

The question then becomes, Is the improvement worth the cost? In this case, the improved pizza-building process can improve other customer service as well, thereby increasing the overall sales capacity of the company. By beating the benchmark, the company's delivery system can become the standard, a significant marketing advantage. Suppose, then, that a cost/benefit study favors the changes.

Step 6: Management implements the improvements.

Many such incremental improvements can greatly enhance a company's competitiveness. Of course, as more and more companies achieve better and better quality, the market becomes more and more demanding. The key, using the incremental approach, is to continually be improving both product and process.

Reengineering Improvements

Hammer argues that significant improvement requires "breaking away from . . . outdated rules and . . . assumptions. . . ." It requires a complete rethinking of the process. He, too, recommends organizing a team representing the functional units involved in the process being reengineered, as well as other units depending upon the process.

One important reason to reengineer is the need to integrate computerized production and information systems, which can be expensive and very difficult to accomplish piecemeal with an incremental approach.

Hammer outlines seven principles of reengineering:

Principle 1. Organize around outcomes, not tasks. Traditionally, work has been organized around different tasks, such as sawing, typing, assembling, and supervising. This first principle of reengineering would have one person or team performing all the steps in a process. The person or team would be responsible for the outcome of the total process.

Principle 2. Have those who use the output of the process perform the process. For example, a production department may do its own purchasing, and even its own cost accounting. This principle would require a broader range of expertise from individuals and teams, and a greater integration of activities.

Principle 3. Subsume information-processing work into the real work that produces the information. Modern computer technology now makes it possible for a work process to process information simultaneously. For example, scanners at checkout counters in grocery stores both process customer purchases and update accounting and inventory records at the same time.

Principle 4. Treat geographically dispersed resources as though they were centralized. Hammer uses Hewlett-Packard as an example of how this principle works. Each of the company's fifty manufacturing units had its own separate purchasing department, which prevented scale discounts. But rather than centralize purchasing, which would have reduced responsiveness, the company simply introduced a corporate unit to coordinate local purchases, so that scale discounts could be achieved. The local purchasing units retained their decentralized authority and thereby preserved the responsiveness to local manufacturing needs.

Principle 5. Link parallel activities instead of integrating their results. Several processes are often required to produce products and services. Too often, companies segregate these processes so that only at the final stage does the product come together. If problems occur in one or more processes, those problems may not become apparent until too late, at the final step. It is better, Hammer says, to link and coordinate the various processes so that such problems are avoided.

Principle 6. Put the decision point where the work is performed, and build control into the process. Traditional bureaucracies place decision authority separate from the work. This new principle suggests that the people doing the work should also make the decisions. The salesman should have the authority and responsibility to approve credit, for example. This principle saves time and helps the organization respond to customer needs.

Some managers worry that such practices would reduce control over the process. Control can, however, be built into the process. In the example, criteria for credit approval can be built into a computer program, giving the salesman specific guidance on the decision.

Principle 7. Capture information once and at the source. Computerized on-line databases help make this principle achievable. Computers now make it easy to collect information when it originates, store it , and send it to those who need it.

Reengineering allows major improvements to be made all at once. While reengineering can be expensive, today's rapidly changing markets sometimes demand such drastic response.

DIVERSITY HIGHLIGHT
A New Quality Culture at Digital Equipment Corporation

The principles and practices of achieving outstanding quality have themselves created a new culture—a quality culture. The diverse workers in today's most successful organizations must adopt this culture, or fail along with their respective organizations.

As an example of the great diversity of workers uniting in individual U.S. plants, Digital Equipment Corporation's Boston factory employs 350 employees who speak nineteen languages and who represent forty-four countries. The plant manager issues written announcements in English, Chinese, French, Spanish, Portuguese, Vietnamese, and Haitian Creole.

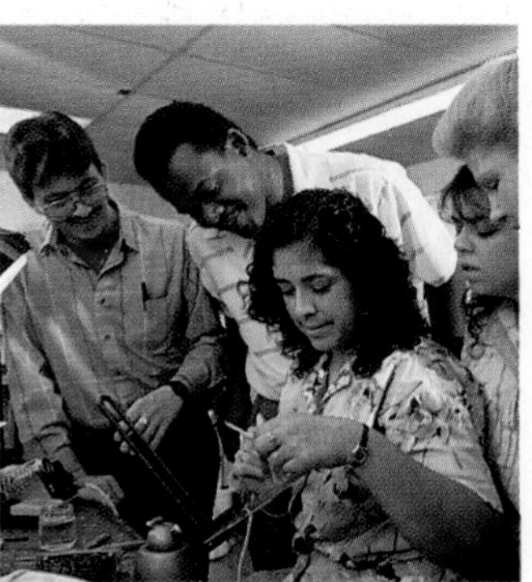

By adopting a culture of diversity, a company fosters the best that each individual can offer from his or her own background and perspective.

Such diversity could make cooperation in a single effort almost impossible without everyone adopting a common culture of the organization. The advantage of adopting the quality culture is that it fosters the best that each individual can offer from his or her unique background and perspective.

An unanswered question is to what extent the quality culture will eventually produce a blend, actually reducing cultural diversity among workers, especially if they transfer the principles of quality to their homes and neighborhoods. ▶

BACK TO THE CASE IOMEGA management adopted W. Edwards Deming's general approach to continuous improvement. This approach is sometimes called the Deming Cycle, although Deming adopted the approach from Walter A. Shewhart, who first introduced statistical quality control techniques in the 1930s.

The approach has four stages:

1. *Plan* what improvement needs to be made and how to do it.
2. *Do* the plan on a small scale to see if it works.
3. *Check* the results.
4. *Act;* that is, implement the indicated improvements in the process; or plan, do, and check again until such improvements are indicated.

This process is called a cycle because it is to be done over and over again, on a continuous basis. IOMEGA applies the Deming Cycle to all improvement activities, whether in production, accounting, marketing, or elsewhere in the company. Management attributes much of IOMEGA's dramatic turnaround to the "turning of the Deming Cycle."

ACTION SUMMARY

Reread the learning objectives that follow. Each objective is followed by questions. Answering these questions accurately will help you to retain most important concepts discussed in this chapter. After answering each question, check your answer with the answer key at the end of the chapter. (*Hint:* If you have doubt regarding the correct response, consult the page whose number follows the answer.)

Circle: ***From studying this chapter, I will attempt to acquire:***

1. An understanding of the relationship between quality and total quality management.

T, F **a.** Overall, product quality and total quality management are the same.

a, b, c, d, e **b.** A TQM program is *not* characterized by: (a) a continual process; (b) efforts by all organization members; (c) a focus on only a few critical work activities; (d) a focus on the production process; (e) efforts to involve organization members.

2. An appreciation of the importance of quality.

T, F **a.** High product quality can result in reduced costs but generally not increased market share.

T, F **b.** Increasing product quality can reduce product liability costs for an organization.

3. Insight about how to achieve quality.

a, b, c, d, e **a.** According to Crosby, in order to achieve quality, an organization must contain critical ingredients relating to: (a) integrity; (b) systems; (c) communications; (d) operations; (e) all of the above.

T, F **b.** According to Deming, a company can improve its product quality by choosing suppliers based on quality and not on price alone.

T, F **c.** According to Juran, a company can improve its product quality by focusing on the quality of the organization as a whole as well as the quality of individual departments.

a, b, c, d, e **d.** According to Shingo, *poka yoke* means (a) production; (b) mistake-proofing; (c) worker commitment; (d) quality; (e) diversity.

T, F **e.** According to Feigenbaum, defects are unacceptable only on the manufacturing floor.

4. An understanding of how strategic planning can be used to promote quality.

T, F **a.** Establishing an appropriate mission statement is important in achieving quality.

T, F **b.** Establishing and using appropriate policies and organization structure are important steps in quality-oriented strategy formulation.

5. Knowledge about the quality improvement process and reengineering.

T, F **a.** The incremental improvement approach involves improving one thing at a time.

a, b, c, d, e **b.** The following is a principle of the reengineering approach to improving quality: (a) organize around outcomes; (b) link parallel activities; (c) put decision points where the work is performed; (d) capture information at the source; (e) all are principles of reengineering for quality.

INTRODUCTORY CASE WRAP-UP

"IOMEGA Corporation: Success Built on Continuous Improvement" (p. 543) and its related back-to-the-case sections were written to help you better understand the management concepts contained in this chapter. Answer the following discussion questions about the introductory case to further enrich your understanding of chapter content:

1. Should a successful quality improvement program at IOMEGA be viewed as an improvement in the company's social performance? If not, why not? If so, how?
2. Does application of the Deming Cycle ensure IOMEGA's competitiveness in the future?
3. Given IOMEGA's success with an incremental improvement approach, what circumstances do you think would call for a step improvement using a reengineering approach, if any?

ISSUES FOR REVIEW AND DISCUSSION

1. What is the difference between product quality and total quality management (TQM)?
2. Is a successful TQM program important to an organization? Explain.
3. Discuss three benefits that are the result of achieving high product quality.
4. What advice does Crosby give on achieving quality?
5. What advice does Deming give on achieving quality?
6. What advice does Juran give on achieving quality?
7. What advice does Shingo give on achieving quality?
8. Discuss how establishment of organizational direction as a step of the strategic management process can be used to improve the success of an effort to raise product quality.
9. Can quality be a significant component of a company's strategy? Explain.
10. Discuss the significance of policies and organization structure as components of an effort to maintain product quality.
11. Based on Crosby's "five successive stages of quality maturity," how would you control TQM efforts in an organization?
12. Discuss how the strategies of partnering and empowerment can improve the quality within an organization.
13. When organizing for quality, which structural changes do you anticipate would make the greatest contributions towards achieving total quality.
14. Under which circumstances do you see the incremental improvement process being used to improve quality?
15. Under which circumstances do you see the reengineering approach to quality improvement being used?
16. Discuss Hammer's principles of reengineering for improvement.
17. Would you be concerned with work-force diversity in a program aimed at enhancing product quality? Why or why not? If you would be concerned, what action would you take?

ACTION SUMMARY ANSWER KEY

1. a. F, p. 544
b. c, p. 544

2. a. F, p. 546
b. T, p. 546

3. a. e, p. 548
b. T, p. 549
c. T, p. 550
d. b, p. 551
e. F, p. 552

4. a. T, p. 553
b. F, pp. 554–555

5. a. T, pp. 558–560
b. e, pp. 560–561

CASE STUDY

JAS's Trackmaster: The Result of Total Quality Management

MILDRED GOLDEN PRYOR
East Texas State University

JAS Manufacturing located in Carrolton, Texas, is a small company that manufactures Trackmaster treadmills. In 1990, JAS management decided to embark on a total quality initiative. Since JAS is a small company, there was no formal quality policy; but pride in workmanship and elements of self-management permeated the work environment. JAS managers benchmarked larger companies—particularly potential customers—to learn how quality systems work. They wrote a policy manual for their quality system which included their quality improvement initiative. They learned the philosophies and methodologies of Drs. Deming, Juran, Ishikawa, and others; and they began applying this knowledge.

Although they achieved some immediate, positive results, they soon learned that work groups needed specific team-building and team-development training in order to become work teams. Managers learned that long-term momentum for total quality cannot be sustained by simply finding problems and eliminating them. The company needed to refine existing systems and processes, as well as establish new systems and processes where none existed or where they were not well defined.

In 1993, JAS conducted a survey of all employees and held interviews to determine peoples' concerns in the work environment. Employees responded positively to the survey and interviews. Where improvements were needed, the employees offered recommendations. Their ideas were not limited to their own processes, but included company policies, strategic management issues, and organizational structure as well.

All employees, from top management down, were trained in a variety of total quality concepts, including process ownership, evaluation, and improvement; team building, development, and facilitation; and strategic management. In the training sessions, mission and vision statements were developed, and all employees learned how to set goals and develop and implement strategies, including quality improvement strategies. Designated process owners identified process constraints and activities which did not add value; where possible, they were eliminated. The CEO flowcharted one of her processes and used the flowchart to teach workers the importance of process evaluation and improvement. For example, she showed employees the impact of the failure to pull the packing slip on the invoice paying process. She asked people to help her refine the invoice paying process; they were surprised at how easy it was. Employees realized that many of their jobs impact the jobs of others and that many times what they do (or fail to do) hinders other processes.

As these internal customer and supplier relationships were established, employees were able to communicate more openly about what they needed to improve their own processes. They also learned the difference between a work group and a work team, as well as how to transform their work groups into work teams. They learned leadership and empowerment concepts and immediately began generating ideas for improvement. Where possible, after consulting with their internal customers and suppliers, workers implemented the ideas themselves. In other cases, they made recommendations to management and helped develop milestone charts for implementation.

At JAS, the total quality initiative is not something employees work at when they have time away from their "real jobs." Total quality is part of their real jobs. Employees do not have to "form a team" to evaluate and improve processes; their work groups *are* their teams. Where cross-functional processes exist, process owners are designated and internal customers and suppliers form their own informal improvement teams. Improvements have been realized in strategy formulation and implementation as well as in process baselines such as safety, quality, and cycle time.

DISCUSSION QUESTIONS

1. What roles did management and employees play in the total quality effort at JAS Manufacturing?
2. Why do hourly workers need to understand the concepts of strategic management and even take part in the development of company strategies?
3. According to the total quality management experts discussed in the chapter, what did JAS management do correctly as they implemented their total quality initiative? What could they have done better?
4. What are the next steps JAS Manufacturing should take?

CNN VIDEO CASE

Quality in the Auto Industry GM's Saturn Keeps Orbiting

When preparing this case, the author used an electronic search service for background information on General Motors's car model Saturn. In response to the author's request for on-line assistance, the representative for the search service typed her answers on the author's computer screen; then, instead of signing off, she typed: "By the way, we've just purchased a Saturn SW1; it's GREAT!"

Word-of-mouth is a wonderful sales tool when a quality product is the topic. That is exactly the kind of user reaction General Motors knows will help sell its Saturn line; this car model was designed and built with quality in mind. Even so, the road to the success story has not been smooth.

General Motors' Saturn was designed and built using W.E. Deming's teaching that the more quality you build into a product the less it will cost in the end.

Launched in the fall of 1990, GM's 1991-model Saturn was three years late, had experienced problems during assembly, and still had recalls after its introduction to the marketplace. Plastic body parts wouldn't fit together quite right, and there was a problem with the seats. GM finally had to recall over a thousand cars in early 1991 because of problems with the cooling system; it recalled another eighteen hundred cars a few months later.

Fixing things after the fact is happening more and more often in the U.S. auto industry. In 1990, domestic cars had 26 percent more defects than Asian imports had. Why? Some analysts believe the problem lies, at least in part, in Japan's ability to change its tooling and designs more rapidly than the United States can; Japan takes only about three years to upgrade its models, compared to five years for the United States. Faster upgrading means earlier improvements in quality.

Still, progress was made during the 1980s, and U.S. cars should start faring better. GM has accepted W. E. Deming's teaching that the more quality you build into a product, the less it will cost in the end. No longer does GM think it's better to wait until a car is assembled to start fixing things; the company is willing now to stop the assembly and fix the problem right there.

Given its own huge bureaucracy, GM had to form a new subsidiary devoted solely to creating the Saturn and doing it right. GM's own layers of jobs and people were getting in the way of efficient processing and new methods of communication and achievement. Workers at the new subsidiary—GM's new Saturn plant in Spring Hill, Tennessee—have little doubt that U.S. cars will start showing great improvements, based on strides being made in management techniques in the industry in general, and, specifically, at their own plant. At the Spring Hill plant, an innovative assembly line runs with teams, not individuals. "It definitely makes it better," says one employee, "when you've got *two* people looking for everything, to make sure every nut and bolt is put together right." Saturn workers call each other "partners," and consensus management rules the day.

Overall these days, GM's strategy is quality. After studying its competition—the Japanese auto industry—GM has developed its own plan of action. Two things the Japanese do very well compared to American companies are training new workers and limiting the number of different job classifications. Better trained workers who are empowered to do more (thus needing fewer categories of jobs) translates to higher quality product. After a rocky start, GM now recognizes that people are key, and communication is a high priority.

Car companies may not even need to worry about proving to anyone that they are quality conscious. As far as many analysts are concerned, simply surviving until 1995 will automatically mean a car manufacturer is producing a quality product.

VIDEO CASE QUESTIONS

1. How does Deming's advice about achieving quality relate to GM's new willingness to stop assembly to correct problems?
2. At what stage in Crosby's five stages of quality maturity would you place GM? Why?
3. What role do you think environmental analysis played in GM's decision to form a new subsidiary to create the Saturn? In what ways do you think Saturn's success will affect the rest of GM?
4. Saturn managers have an exceptional opportunity to exercise system skill. Explain why.

CNN VIDEO EXERCISE

Will Success Spoil Saturn?

ACTION GOAL: Use points from Crosby's Vaccination Serum and Dr. Deming's 14 Points to analyze the effect of the new policies on Saturn's quality commitment.

By the spring of 1993, the Saturn Corporation had made some major changes in its operations in order to meet the high demand for its automobiles. The Spring Hill, Tennessee, plant had been operating on a fifty-hour workweek for more than a year. Many employees who had been laid off from other GM facilities were being hired into Saturn to relieve the situation. And perhaps most significant, the extensive training program that helped the original Saturn work force learn cooperative work methods was reduced by more than half. New workers spend 175 hours in initial training; 700 hours had been the norm. New workers skip the basic skills component of the training program, which covered topics such as conflict management and worker self-management, in favor of on-the-job training.

Saturn's leaders are divided about the changes. Some say that employees will not be able to continue their successful self-management without the proper training. Others, including the personnel chief, say that the company simply cannot afford the time and expense of training.,

What do you think? Analyze the effect that the reduced training might have on quality at GM's Saturn plant in Spring Hill. In your analysis, use at least two points from Crosby's vaccination serum (page 553) and two points from Dr. Deming's 14 points (pages 552–554).

Effect of Reduced Training on Quality

Crosby's Vaccination Serum

1. ______________________________

____

____

2. ______________________________

____

____

Dr. Deming's 14 Points

1. ______________________________

____

____

2. ______________________________

____

____

____

CHAPTER

22

MANAGEMENT AND DIVERSITY

STUDENT LEARNING OBJECTIVES

From studying this chapter, I will attempt to acquire:

1. A definition of diversity and an understanding of its importance in the corporate structure.
2. An understanding of the advantages of a diverse workforce.
3. An awareness of the challenges facing managers within a diverse workforce.
4. An understanding of the strategies for promoting diversity in organizations.
5. Insights into the role of the manager in promoting diversity in the organization.

CHAPTER OUTLINE

INTRODUCTORY CASE
Ortho Pharmaceutical: "Showcase" for Cultural Diversity

DEFINING DIVERSITY

Diversity

QUALITY HIGHLIGHT
Frito-Lay

ADVANTAGES OF DIVERSITY IN ORGANIZATIONS

Keeping and Gaining Market Share
Cost Savings
Increased Productivity and Innovation
Better Quality of Management

DIVERSITY HIGHLIGHT
General Electric

CHALLENGES MANAGERS FACE IN WORKING WITH DIVERSE POPULATIONS

Changing Demographics

GLOBAL HIGHLIGHT
AT&T

Ethnocentrism, Prejudices, Stereotypes, and Discrimination

STRATEGIES FOR PROMOTING DIVERSITY IN ORGANIZATIONS

Workforce 2000
Equal Employment and Affirmative Action

ETHICS HIGHLIGHT
Procter and Gamble

Pluralism

THE ROLE OF THE MANAGER

Planning
Organizing
Influencing
Controlling

MANAGEMENT DEVELOPMENT AND DIVERSITY TRAINING

CASE STUDY
Rebuilding LA

VIDEO CASE
The Glass Ceiling: Shattered or Still in Place?

VIDEO EXERCISE
Taking a SWOT at the Steelcase Ceiling

INTRODUCTORY CASE

Ortho Pharmaceutical: "Showcase" for Cultural Diversity

Few companies can match the cultural diversity record of Ortho Pharmaceutical. The company, part of Johnson & Johnson's $4 billion pharmaceutical manufacturing sector, produces, distributes, and markets women's health-care products, such as Ortho-Novum™ contraceptives and Retin-A™ skin ointment. Ortho is also known as "the most progressive client" of Elsie Cross, of Elsie Y. Cross Associates, a well-known diversity consultant. This company has become her diversity "showcase for the how and why of corporate culture change."

> **". . . if you value differences among people, incorporate those differences into the team and then reward the team, change happens."**

Currently, women and minorities at Ortho Pharmaceutical are being promoted in numbers representative of their numbers within the general workforce. According to an article in the *Los Angeles Times Magazine,* women hold 25 percent of the management positions, up from 22 percent in the year prior to beginning this corporate diversity program. Similarly, African-Americans in managerial positions have increased from 6 percent to 13 percent, while all minorities jumped from 10 percent representation within managerial ranks to 18 percent. Although white males still hold a significant 63 percent of the top positions within the company, Ortho's record of upward mobility for women and minorities is still impressive.

Ortho Pharmaceutical's move toward diversity began when the company contacted the consulting firm of Elsie Y. Cross Associates in 1986. At that time, Gary Parlin, a white male, was Ortho's president. In spite of the affirmative action policies that were in place, Ortho had difficulty retaining women and minority employees. Moreover, the financial costs of such high turnover were extensive. Parlin worked with Cross and her staff to implement an organizational development assessment of the company's systems. Their assessment revealed that white males felt comfortable about their futures in the company, while women and minorities felt stifled, ignored, and saw little opportunity for advancement.

As a result of this assessment, management found that recruiters tended not to seek a diverse pool of candidates. Once hired, women and minorities received little of the feedback, mentoring, or promotions made available to their white male counterparts. After collaborating with the Cross firm and implementing an extensive planned-change effort, management has found that employees now speak very differently of their experiences in the company. After six years, a black marketing-research manager at Ortho was able to say: "This is a safe harbor. . . . Here I can be myself. I can say what I like, do what I like. I can disagree with people. At other companies, just to disagree meant political suicide." The kind of qualitative cultural changes referred to by this manager would be a plus for any corporation.

Although progress has been made, only one woman and one person of color currently sit on the board of directors, the top policy-making body of the company. Responding to these concerns, a company spokesperson said "What we do here isn't easy. But if you value differences among people, incorporate those differences into the team and then reward the team, change happens. Never fast enough, but it happens nonetheless."

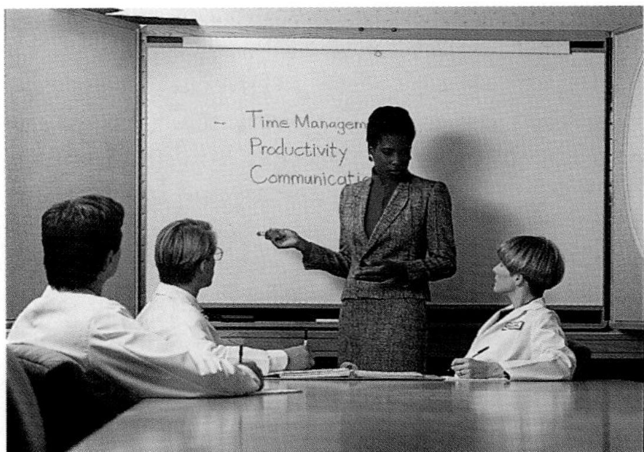

Diversity is valuable to an organization because it enables the organization to draw on all the rich contributions that a multicultural workforce has to offer and enhances the pool of information available for making decisions.

From J. P. White, "Elsie Cross vs. The Suits: One Black Woman Is Teaching White Corporate America to Do the Right Thing," *Los Angeles Times Magazine* (August 9, 1992).

WHAT'S AHEAD How will the increasingly diverse workforce in the United States affect the responsibilities of managers? Is the current attention to diversity somewhat exaggerated? Or, are managers expected to play an ever-increasing role in the kinds of activities occurring at Ortho Pharmaceutical? This chapter can help a manager understand the challenges that a diverse workforce poses for American businesses. This chapter discusses (1) the definition and social implications of diversity, (2) advantages of diversity in organizations, (3) challenges facing managers in working with diverse populations, (4) managerial strategies for promoting diversity in organizations, and (5) the role of the manager in promoting effective workforce diversity.

DEFINING DIVERSITY

Diversity is the degree of basic human differences among a given population. Areas of diversity include gender, race, ethnicity, religion, social class, physical ability, sexual orientation, and age.

Overall, **diversity** refers to characteristics of individuals that shape their identities and the experiences they have in society. This chapter is designed to provide information about workforce diversity and to discuss the strengths and dilemmas of a diverse workforce. The chapter describes some of the organizational strategies for promoting social diversity in organizations. It also explains the specific diversity-related role of the manager in relation to the four management functions. Given the nature of this topic, you will need to integrate information you have learned from other chapters. For example, you will need to consider the legal foundation for developing an inclusive workforce—affirmative action and Equal Employment Opportunity (EEO), discussed in chapter 11, and ideas about organizational change, discussed in chapter 16.

Social Implications of Diversity

Workforce diversity is not a new issue. Historically, immigration of people from specific regions and cultures has been happening since the United States was a colony. The American population has always been a multifaceted mix of individuals and groups who varied by gender, race, ethnicity, religion, social class, physical ability, sexual orientation, and age. These basic human differences are among those comprising what we refer to as diversity. The purpose of exploring diversity issues is to learn how to include members of diverse groups equally, accepting the differences and utilizing the talents of all employees.

A **majority group** is the group of people holding the majority of the positions of decision-making power, control of resources and information, and access to system rewards.

A **minority group** is the smaller in number or lesser in granted rights and status of two groups together representing a whole. The larger group is called the majority group.

Diversity includes understanding the relationships between two groups in organizations: majority groups and minority groups. **Majority group** refers to the group of people holding the majority of the positions of decision-making power, control of resources and information, and access to system rewards. The majority group is not *always* the group representing a numerical majority. The term **minority group** refers to a group of people who lack critical power, resources, acceptance, and social status within the overall organization or system. Together, minority and majority group members form an entire social system. Minority group members are often, but not always, lesser in number than members of the majority group. For example, women are seen as a minority group in most organizations because they do not have the critical power to shape organizational decisions and to control resources. Moreover, women are still working to achieve full acceptance and social status within the workplace. In some instances white males are numerical minorities. For example, in most health-care organizations, women outnumber men. Although men are numerical minorities, they are unlikely to be denied social status because men tend to hold the positions of power in the health care system hierarchy, such as physician and health care administrator.

QUALITY HIGHLIGHT
Frito-Lay Strives to Be the Employer of Choice

Within any company, quality is achieved by being able to attract and retain the best human resources. Frito-Lay intends to do just that by developing a diversity training program to help employees learn to value the diversity of the company's current workforce. Frito-Lay's training program was developed by consultants and is specifically tailored to the needs of employees. First, the training program introduces employees to key terms and concepts. Second, people form relatively homogeneous discussion groups and are encouraged to learn more about their own cultural group. This prepares them to learn about diverse groups. Last, the small groups merge into larger diverse groups of about forty people. As a larger group, employees take part in a variety of planned activities.

A key feature of Frito-Lay's motivation for implementing diversity training is that the company wanted the demographics of its resident workforce to mirror the demographics of the marketplace. Frito-Lay is ultimately striving to be the "employer of choice." By attracting and retaining good employees from all cultural groups, the company will be in a position to maintain high quality in every aspect of the company's services. ▶

In one format for diversity training programs, groups meet to share views and common problems. Then, the small groups are merged into larger diverse groups involved in a variety of planned activities.

ADVANTAGES OF DIVERSITY IN ORGANIZATIONS

Managers are becoming increasingly dedicated to seeking a wide range of talents from every group represented within the nation's culture. As we learned in chapter 16, group decisions can improve the quality of decision making. Work groups or teams, drawing on the rich contributions of a multicultural workforce, gain the advantage of enhancing the pool of information and approaches available to the group.

Ann Morrison, author of *The New Leaders: Guidelines on Leadership Diversity in America*, carried out a comprehensive study of sixteen private and public organizations in the United States. In her book, she outlines the several other advantages of diversity, which follow.[1]

Keeping and Gaining Market Share

Because markets are becoming increasingly diverse, managers must understand their customers' preferences. Failing to do this could result in loss of business in the United States and internationally. Some argue that one of the best ways to ensure that the organization has the ability to capture diverse markets is to include diversity among the organization's decision makers. Diversity among the managerial ranks might enhance company credibility. For example, a manager who is of the same gender or ethnic background as a customer may imply to the customer that his or her day-to-day experiences will be understood. One African-American female manager said that she used her influence to change the name of a product that her company intended to sell at Wal-Mart. "I knew that I had shopped for household goods at Wal-Mart, whereas the CEO of this company, a white, upper-middle-class male, had not. He listened to me and we changed the name of the product."

Morrison's study cites a case in which one company lost an important opportunity for new business in a southwestern city's predominantly Hispanic community. The business ultimately went to a competitor, whose Hispanic manager in charge of the project solicited input from the Hispanic community.

Cost Savings

There are high costs involved in recruiting, training, relocating, and replacing employees and in providing competitive compensation packages. According to Morrison, the cost of Corning Corporation's high turnover among women and people of color, was estimated at $2 to $4 million a year. Many managers in her study felt that personnel expenses associated with turnover (often using as much as two-thirds of an organization's budget) could be cut by instituting diversity practices that would give non-traditional managers more incentive to stay. When non-traditional managers remain with the organization, other non-traditional employees at lower levels feel more committed to the company. In addition to the personnel costs, executives are distressed by legal fees and staggering settlement amounts. For example, $17.65 million in damages was awarded to a woman employed by Texaco who claimed she was passed over for a management promotion because of her gender. Executives are learning that such monies could be better used to promote diversity.

Increased Productivity and Innovation

Many executives in Morrison's study expect greater productivity from employees in organizations that focus on diversity. These managers feel that employees who feel valued, competent, and relaxed in their work setting will enjoy coming to work and will perform at a high level. Morrison also cites a study by Donna Thompson and Nancy DiTomaso which states that a multicultural approach has a positive effect on employees' perception of equity. This in turn, affects their morale, goal setting, effort, and performance. The managers in Morrison's study see innovation as another strength of a diverse workforce.

Better Quality of Management

Morrison's study also found that including non-traditional employees in fair competition for advancement can improve the quality of management by providing a wider pool of talent. According to the research cited in Morrison's study, exposure to diverse

TABLE 22.1 Advantages of a Diverse Workforce

- Improved ability to keep and gain market share
- Cost savings
- Increased productivity
- A more innovative workforce
- Minority and women employees who are more motivated
- Better quality of managers
- Employees who have internalized the message that "different" does not mean "less than"
- Employees who are accustomed to making use of differing worldviews, learning styles, and approaches in the decision-making process and in the cultivation of new ideas
- Employees who have developed multicultural competencies, such as learning to recognize, surface, discuss, and work through work-related issues pertaining to global, cultural, or intergroup differences
- A workforce that is more resilient when faced with change

Source: Adapted from Ann M. Morrison, *The New Leaders: Guidelines on Leadership Diversity in America*. Jossey Bass: San Francisco 1992, pp. 18–27.

colleagues can help managers develop breadth and openness. The quality of management can also be improved by building more effective personnel policies and practices. Once developed, they will eventually benefit all employees in the organization. Morrison's study found that many of the programs initially developed for non-traditional managers resulted in improvements that were later applied throughout the organization. Ideas such as adding training for mentors, improving techniques for developing managers, and improving processes for evaluating employees for promotion (a concept originally developed for nontraditional managers), were later adopted for wider use. (See Table 22.1 for more information on the advantages of a diverse workforce.)

BACK TO THE CASE As previously discussed, a company that uses the diverse talents of a multicultural workforce to its advantage benefits along with the workers. For example, some experts believe that one of the best ways for a company to capture diverse markets is by including diversity among the organization's decision makers. Health-care products such as Ortho Pharmaceutical's contraceptives may require varied marketing strategies to sell successfully in different cultures. By including decision makers who are sensitive to different cultural attitudes about contraceptives, Ortho can work to establish the product and marketing strategies required to meet the needs of various groups.

Ortho Pharmaceutical can expect its productivity to increase when workforce diversity is encouraged because workers who feel valued, competent, and relaxed in their work setting will perform at a higher level than workers who feel that their efforts have little value. Also by providing training to encourage nontraditional managers to remain with the organization, Ortho Pharmaceutical can expect to lower its personnel costs associated with recruiting, training, and replacing employees.

DIVERSITY HIGHLIGHT
General Electric Values Global Sensitivity

General Electric Aircraft Company has developed leadership values which specifically indicate what they view as effectiveness in leadership. According to these guidelines, effective leaders should ". . . have the capacity to develop global brains and global sensitivity." In keeping with this appreciation of global diversity, the company has developed diversity training sessions for everyone in the company.

In keeping with an appreciation of global diversity, many companies are instituting diversity training sessions for all employees.

One innovative approach developed by General Electric Aircraft Company is their program, "Leveraging Differences (Cultural Diversity)," which utilizes an Interactive Video Disk (IVD). This program consists of five components: (1) an introduction explains how a company evolves from "homogeneous, to assimilative, to heterogeneous, and finally to multicultural"; (2) "Walk a Mile in My Shoes" focuses on problems women face in the workplace; (3) "Something I've Always Wanted to Ask You People" gives trainees a chance to express their curiosity about members of other groups, specifically Asians, African Americans, Hispanics, and women; (4) "You Decide" presents the trainee with a variety of problem-solving situations which have implications for diversity; and (5) a summary, with closing remarks by John Rittenhouse, General Electric's senior vice president.

Strengths of these modules are that they are easily understandable by a wide range of employees, available to use on company time, and require responses from the employee. This program reflects the leadership values statement, which includes the following goals: selecting "the most talented team members available"; fully utilizing people "regardless of race, gender, ethnic origin, culture, or age"; and learning to see "the priority of all aspects of diversity to business success." ▶

CHALLENGES MANAGERS FACE IN WORKING WITH DIVERSE POPULATIONS

We have seen that there are compelling reasons for organizations to encourage a diverse work force. However, for managers to fully appreciate the implications of promoting diversity, it is important that they understand some of the challenges facing managers within a diverse workforce. Changing demographics and an array of issues brought to light by these changes will be discussed in the following sections.

Changing Demographics

Demographics, as defined in chapter 7 as the statistical characteristics of a population, are an important tool used by managers to study workforce diversity. According to *Workforce 2000: Work and Workers for the Twenty-First Century,* a report developed for the United States Department of Labor by the Hudson Institute, the contemporary workforce and the jobs it will perform will parallel changes in the economy. This report, published in 1987, projected the following five demographic facts as "most important" in relation to workers and jobs by the year 2000:[2] (1) the population and the workforce will grow more slowly than at any time since the 1930s; (2) the average age of the population and the workforce will rise, and the pool of young workers entering the labor market will shrink; (3) more women will enter the workforce; (4) minorities will make up a larger share of new entrants into the labor force; and (5) immigrants will represent the largest share of the increase in the population and the workforce. The underlying causes and some of the consequences of these trends are summarized in Table 22.2.

This study by the Hudson Institute clearly emphasizes the growth of nonwhites, women, immigrants, and older workers within the workforce. Figure 22.1 on page 580 illustrates the distribution of new entrants in the workforce based on these demographic patterns.

GLOBAL HIGHLIGHT AT&T Connects the World

AT&T offers five consumer services to travelers and consumers living outside the United States: AT&T USADirect, AT&T World Connect, AT&T USADirect Service In-Language, AT&T Calling Card, and AT&T TeleTicket Service. The oldest service, USADirect, introduced in 1985, allows users to call the United States from 113 countries and helps them save on the cost. The newest service, USADirect Service In-Language, is offered to residents in sixteen countries. Using this service, consumers can make calls to the United States through operators who speak their languages. These consumer services are increasing, and with them, the need to understand diversity. Only fifteen months after instituting USADirect Service In-Language, 250 additional Spanish speaking operators were needed. Similar hiring increases occurred when Polish and Hungarian were added.

By providing multilingual telephone services, AT&T hopes to gain a competitive advantage in the global communications market.

African consumers are a large market for the more established USADirect Service. According to Yaw Osei-Amoako, market development manager for Africa in Morristown, New Jersey, the more than fifty thousand USADirect calls per week from Ghana are mostly Ghanians calling their U.S. relatives.

With respect to global diversity, Osei-Amoako, himself a Ghanaian, says: "Patience is the key virtue here. The Europeans understand this better than the Americans because of their colonial experience. Americans want to come in, make a deal, go home. The Africans want to get to know you personally, know all about your family, what you like, what you don't like, where you come from."

The service was initially offered in Liberia and is now available in ten African countries. It is an emerging market that is also being pursued by Sprint and MCI. No one can say for certain, but it seems that skills in global diversity may provide the competitive edge in gaining this market share.

TABLE 22.2 *Workforce 2000:* Current and Projected Demographic Trends

Demographic Trends	*Underlying Demographics*	*Consequences*
1. The population and the workforce will grow more slowly than at any time since the 1930s.	Annual population growth will slump from close to 1.9 percent in the 1950s to only 0.7 percent by 2000. The labor force, which exploded in the 1940s and 1950s will be expanding by only 1 percent annually in the 1990s, down from 2.9 percent in the 1970s.	These slow growth rates will tend to slow down the nation's economic expansion, shifting the economy more toward income-sensitive products and services (e.g., luxury goods and convenience services) Labor markets may tighten forcing employers to use more capital-intensive production systems.
2. The average age of the population and the workforce will rise, and the pool of young workers entering the labor market will shrink.	The average age of the workforce will climb from 36 today to 39 by the year 2000. The number of young workers, age 16–24, will drop by almost 2 million, or 8 percent.	This decline in young people in the labor force will have both positive and negative impacts. The older workforce will be more experienced, stable, and reliable, but may be less adaptable (e.g., less likely to move, to change occupations, or to undertake retraining than are younger ones). Companies that have grown by adding larger numbers of flexible, lower-paid workers will find such workers in short supply in the 1990s.
3. More women will enter the workforce.	Almost two-thirds of the new entrants into the workforce between now and the year 2000 will be women. 61 percent of all women of working age are expected to have jobs by 2000.	Although concentrated in jobs that pay less than those jobs predominated by men, women will be rapidly entering many higher-paying professional and technical fields. This continued "feminization" of work will lead to a boom in the convenience industries due to the heightened need for "instant" products and "delivered-to-the-door" services; increased call for day care, for more time off from work for pregnancy leave and child-rearing duties; increased interest in part-time, flexible, and stay-at-home jobs.
4. Nonwhites will be a larger share of new entrants into the labor force.	Nonwhites will double their current share of the workforce, making up 29 percent of the new entrants into the labor force between now and the year 2000.	Due to the concentration of African Americans in declining central cities and slowly growing occupations, this increased share of a more slowly growing workforce will not necessarily improve the opportunities available to these workers.
5. Immigrants will represent the largest share of the increase in the population and the workforce since the first World War.	Approximately 600,000 legal and illegal immigrants are projected to enter the United States annually between now and the year 2000. Two-thirds or more of immigrants of working age are likely to join the labor force.	Immigrant workers, concentrated in the south and west, are likely to reshape local economies, promoting faster economic growth and labor surpluses.

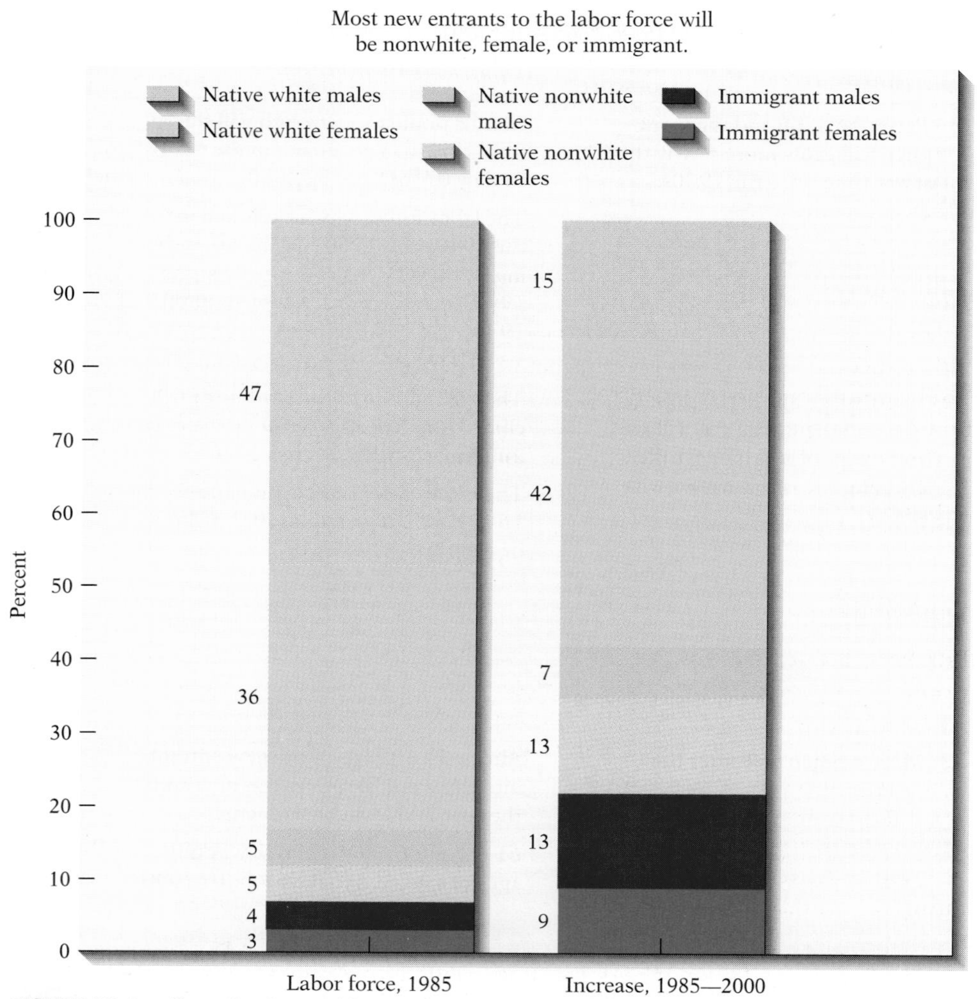

Most new entrants to the labor force will be nonwhite, female, or immigrant.

Native white males
Native white females
Native nonwhite males
Native nonwhite females
Immigrant males
Immigrant females

Percent
100
90
80
70
60
50
40
30
20
10
0

47
36
5
5
4
3

15
42
7
13
13
9

Labor force, 1985
Increase, 1985—2000

FIGURE 22.1 Growth of nonwhites entering the labor force

Ethnocentrism, Prejudices, Stereotypes, and Discrimination

Ethnocentrism is the belief that one's own group, culture, country, or customs are superior to others'.

Prejudices are preconceived judgments, opinions, or assumptions about issues, behaviors, individuals, or groups of people.

Stereotypes are positive or negative assessments or perceived attributes toward members of a group.

Discrimination is the act of treating an issue, person, or behavior unjustly or inequitably.

The changing demographics described by the *Workforce 2000* report set the stage for social dynamics which can interfere with a productive workforce. In order to be successful in diversifying organizations, these dynamics and possible related interference with productivity must be neutralized. Our natural tendency for judging other groups less favorably than our own is one of the problems inherent in coping with diversity. This tendency is the source of **ethnocentrism,** the belief that one's own group, culture, country, or customs are superior to others'. Two related dynamics are **prejudices** and **stereotypes.** A prejudice is a preconceived judgment, opinion or assumption about issues, behaviors, or groups of people.[3] Stereotypes may be positive or negative assessments or perceived attributes toward members of a group. It is important for managers to recognize these ways of perceiving others so that they can monitor their own perceptions and help their employees to view others more accurately.

When verbalized or acted upon, these dynamics can cause discomfort and stress for the judged individual. In some cases, these processes can result in outright **discrimination.** Discrimination refers to treating an issue, person, or behavior unjustly or inequitably. Discrimination often stems from stereotypes and prejudices. For example, consider a disabled person who is turned down for promotion because the boss feels that this employee would not be able to handle the regular travel accompanying this particular job. Prejudging this employee's capabilities based on his or her "difference" and implementing the preconception through differential treatment is considered discrimination.

Discrimination occurs when stereotypes are acted upon in ways that affect hiring, pay, or promotion (for example, steering older employees into less visible job assignments which are unlikely to provide opportunities for advancement). Other challenges facing minorities and women include the pressure to conform to the organization's culture, high penalties for mistakes, and tokenism. **Tokenism**[4] refers to being one of very few members of your group in the organization. "Token" employees experience either very high or very low visibility in the organization. One African-American male employee indicated that he was "discouraged" by his white female manager from participating on voluntary committees and task forces within the company. At the same time, in his performance appraisal he was criticized for being "aloof" and taking a "low-profile approach." In other cases, minorities are seen as representatives or "spokespeople" for all members of their group. Many are subject to high expectations and scrutiny from members of their own group. One Latino male employee described how other Latino employees in the company "looked up to him" for his achievements in the organization. The following sections more fully discuss prejudice, stereotypes and discrimination as related to women, minorities, older workers, and workers with disabilities.

Tokenism refers to being one of very few members of a group in an organization.

Women

Rosabeth Kanter has researched the pressures women managers face from other women in organizations. In her classic study of gender dynamics in organizations, she points to the high expectations women have of other women.[5]

Women in organizations confront **gender-role stereotypes.** Gender-role stereotypes are perceptions about people based on what our society believes are appropriate behaviors for their gender. Both men and women's self expression are constrained by gender role stereotyping. For example, women in organizations are often thought to be good listeners. This attribution is based on our societal view that women are nurturing. Although this is a positive assessment, it is not true of all women or of any woman all the time. Hence, the negative outcome is the expectation that this stereotype creates for women in the workplace. Women professionals often remark that they are frequently sought out by colleagues who want to discuss non-work-related problems. Women managers also describe the subtle sanctioning they experience from both men and women when they do not respond to the expectation that they portray a nurturing component within their management style. In general, ethnocentrism, prejudices, and stereotypes inhibit our ability to accurately process information.

Gender-role stereotypes are perceptions about the sexes based on what society believes are appropriate behaviors for men and women.

A major pattern of discrimination affecting women in organizations is described as the "glass ceiling."[6] **The glass ceiling** refers to an invisible "ceiling," or limit to advancement. This term, originally coined to describe barriers facing women, can also describe the experiences of other minorities. Although both women and men face the need to balance work and family concerns, it is still more common for women to have primary responsibility for household management and their careers. At times they are denied opportunities for advancement based on this stereotype. Sexual harassment is another form of discrimination disproportionately affecting female employees. Sexual harassment is any unwanted sexual language, behavior, or imagery negatively affecting an employee.[7]

The **glass ceiling** is an invisible ceiling or limit that prevents women and minorities from advancing beyond a certain organizational level.

Minorities

Similarly, minorities experience stereotypes about their group. They too encounter misunderstandings and expectations based on ethnic or cultural differences. Members of ethnic or racial minority groups are socialized within their particular culture. Many are socialized as members of two cultural groups—the dominant culture and their racial or ethnic culture. Ella Bell, professor of organizational behavior at MIT, refers to this dual membership as "biculturalism." In her study of African-American women, she identifies the stress of coping with membership in two cultures simultaneously, as

Bicultural stress is the stress of coping with membership in two cultures simultaneously.

Role conflict is the conflict resulting when a person fills competing roles from two cultures.

Role overload is the result of a person having too many expectations to comfortably fulfill.

bicultural stress.[8] She indicates that **role conflict**—competing roles from two cultures—and **role overload**—too many expectations to comfortably fulfill—are common characteristics of bicultural stress. Although these issues can be applied to many minority groups, they are particularly intense for women of color. This is because this group experiences dynamics affecting *both* minorities and women.

Socialization in one's culture of origin can lead to misunderstandings in the workplace. This is particularly true when the manager relies solely on the cultural norms of the majority group. According to these norms, within American culture it is acceptable—even positive—to publicly praise an individual for a job well done. However, in cultures that place primary value on group harmony and collective achievement, this method of rewarding an employee causes emotional discomfort. Employees feel that, if praised publicly, they will "lose face" within their group.

Older Workers

In addition to women and minorities, older workers represent a significant and valuable component of the labor force. The "baby boomers" of the 1950s are now approaching middle age, while the previous generation of workers approaches retirement. Management is faced with significant questions concerning how to tap the rich knowledge and experience base of these workers, and how to help older workers avoid the occupational stagnation of later years. This is especially important given the *Workforce 2000* prediction of the dwindling supply of younger workers, and the consequences of baby boomers reaching the pre-retirement career phase simultaneously. This population bulge could create competition for scarce jobs as many people reach various career phases at the same time.

With respect to diversity, older workers bring some specific challenges for managers. Stereotypes and prejudices of older workers link age with senility, incompetence, and lack of worth in the labor market.[9] Jeffrey Sonnenfeld, an expert on senior executives and older workers, compiled research findings from several studies of older employees. He found that co-workers and managers view older workers as "deadwood," and seek to "weed them out" through pension incentives, biased performance appraisals, or other methods. However, Sonnenfeld's compilation of research indicates that, while older managers were more cautious, less likely to take risks, and less open to change, many are high performers. Studies which tracked individuals' careers over the long term indicate that there is a peak in performance occurring around age forty-five to fifty and a second peak around age fifty-five to sixty. Performance in some fields (e.g., sales) improved with age or did not differ significantly based on the age of the employee.

It is the manager's responsibility to see that older workers are valued for their contribution to the organization and that they are treated fairly. This means that the manager needs some understanding of and sensitivity to the very real physiological and psychological changes that older workers are adjusting to. In order to support older workers, the manager must pay attention to performance appraisal processes, retirement incentives, training programs, blocked career paths, union insurance pensions, and affirmative action goals.[10]

Workers with Disabilities

People with disabilities are also subject to the dynamics that affect minority groups, such as stereotyping, prejudices, and discrimination. For example, one manager confessed that, prior to attending diversity training sessions offered through a nearby university, he felt "uncomfortable" around people who are disabled. One disabled professional indicated that she was always received warmly by phone, and was told that her background was exactly what companies were looking for. When she showed up for job interviews, however, she was not well received and was sometimes told that her credentials were lacking in some way.

This discussion of the dynamics women and minorities experience in organizations is summarized in Figure 22.2. Managers who can recognize these dynamics will be more prepared to address and resolve problems within a diverse workforce.

STRATEGIES FOR PROMOTING DIVERSITY IN ORGANIZATIONS

This section looks at several approaches to diversity and strategies that organizations can consider in their plans for promoting cultural diversity in their organizations. The Hudson Institute, in its *Workforce 2000* report, offers six strategies that corporations can undertake to implement diversity. The EEOC is legally empowered to regulate organizations to insure that management practices enhance diversity. Organizations can move beyond the legal requirements by striving toward pluralism as outlined by Jean Kim's five strategies.

Workforce 2000

Some of the challenges facing American corporations were also discussed in the Hudson Institute's *Workforce 2000* report. According to the authors of this report, six major issues will require the full attention of business leaders: These issues include the need to:

1. *Stimulate balanced world growth.* The United States must pay less attention to its share of world trade and more attention to the growth of the economies of the

Women	Challenges in Common	Minorities
• Gender–role stereotypes –expectations and prejudices • Limits to organizational advancement, i,e., "glass ceiling • High expectations from and scrutiny by other women	• Discrimmination in hiring, pay, and promotions • Pressure to conform to the majority culture at the expense of one's own culture • Hostile or stressful work environment: — too high visibility — too low visibility (e.g., tracked into jobs with low responsibility, status, or opportunity for advancement) • Dynamics of tokenism • Seen as representative spokesperson for all members of one's group •Isolation or lower degree of social acceptance • Lack of opportunities for mentoring and sponsorship	• Racial stereotypes, ethnocentism and prejudices • Bicultural stress • High expectations from and scrutiny by other members of one's group

FIGURE 22.2 Challenges managers face in working with diverse populations

other nations of the world, including those nations in Europe, Latin America, and Asia with whom the U.S. competes.

2. *Accelerate productivity increases in service industries.* Prosperity will depend much more upon how fast output per worker increases in health care, education, retailing, government, and other services, than on gains in manufacturing.

3. *Maintain the dynamism of an aging workforce.* As the average age of American workers climbs toward forty, the nation must insure that its workforce does not lose its adaptability and willingness to learn.

4. *Reconcile the conflicting needs of women, work, and families.* Despite the huge increases in the numbers of women in the workforce, many of the policies and institutions that cover pay, fringe benefits, time away from work, pensions, welfare, and other issues have not yet been adjusted to the new realities.

5. *Fully integrate into the economy African-American and Hispanic workers.* The shrinking numbers of young people, the rapid pace of industrial change, and the rising skill requirements of the emerging economy make the task of fully utilizing minority workers particularly urgent between now and 2000.

6. *Improve the education and skills of all workers.* Human capital—knowledge, skills, organization, and leadership—is key to economic growth and competitiveness.[12]

The *Workforce 2000* report summarizes the key dynamics which will significantly influence modern management. Many of the demographic shifts and the challenges which lie ahead are based upon complex societal issues. Organizations—and, ultimately, their leaders and managers—will find it necessary to clarify their own social values. As discussed in chapter 7, social values refer to the relative worth society places on the way it exists and functions. These six challenges imply the need for organizations to become more inclusive, that is, include a broader mix of employees and to develop an organizational culture that maximizes the value and potential of each worker. As with any major initiative, commitment to developing an inclusive organization begins with those in positions of authority at the top of the organizational hierarchy. However, on a day-to-day operational basis, each manager's level of commitment is critical in determining how well or how poorly the organization's strategies and approaches are implemented.

Equal Employment and Affirmative Action

As you recall from chapter 11, The Equal Employment Opportunity Commission (EEOC) is an agency established to enforce the laws that regulate recruiting and other management practices. Affirmative action was discussed in terms of programs designed to eliminate barriers against and increase opportunities for underutilized or disadvantaged individuals. These programs are intended to be positive steps forward in the area of managing diversity and have created many opportunities for both women and minority groups. However, more can be done. For example, some employees have mixed feelings about EEOC and affirmative action programs. They feel that these programs have been misused to create **reverse discrimination.** Reverse discrimination refers to inequalities affecting members of the majority group as an outcome of programs designed to help underrepresented groups. When an organization stops short of developing a multicultural organization, individuals' feelings and intergroup conflicts continue, even though the organization may have implemented the appropriate legal approaches.

Reverse discrimination is an inequity affecting members of the majority group as an outcome of programs designed to help underrepresented groups.

BACK TO THE CASE As discussed previously, legal approaches alone do not resolve all issues relating to diversity. When Gary Parlin consulted with Cross, his questions were aimed at discovering why his affirmative action policies were failing. His company was investing time, energy, and money in recruiting, hiring, and training women and members of underrepresented groups only to lose them within a relatively short span of time. This is a common problem, and one that often goes unquestioned. Again, the role of the manager in monitoring goal achievement and assessing the effectiveness of policies that are in place is essential to whether affirmative action becomes simply a "paper tool" that does not lead to more effective business practices or whether it is used to select and hire the best employees.

For affirmative action policies to be effective, managers need to be held accountable for their implementation. As with any other organizational policy, these standards can be ignored, misused, or treated as a low priority. Poor recruitment and hiring of women and minorities is commonly cited as one of the misuses of affirmative action. Hiring individuals whose background and training or personal goals are poorly matched to company goals establishes a costly revolving door for the organization. When employees are hired inappropriately due to emphasis on quotas rather than commitment to fair management practices, both the company and the employee lose.

Organizational Commitment to Diversity

Figure 22.3 shows the range of organizational commitment to multiculturalism. The broad base of the bottom of the continuum reflects organizations who have committed resources, planning, and time to the ongoing shaping and sustaining of a multicultural organization. The top of the continuum represents those organizations which are directing very little attention toward managing diversity. Most organizations exist somewhere between the extremes depicted in Figure 22.3

Some organizations make no efforts to promote diversity and do not comply with affirmative action and EEOC standards. Figure 22.3 depicts these companies at the top of the diversity continuum. The lack of attention to diversity needs within such organizations sends a strong message to their employees that the dynamics of difference are not important. Even more detrimental to the organization is the outcome of maintaining exclusionary practices.

Some organizations base their diversity strategy solely on compliance with affirmative action and EEOC policies. They make no attempts to provide education and training for employees or to reinforce managerial commitment through the organization's reward system. Managers in some companies breach company affirmative action and EEOC policies. When top management does not sanction those responsible, the likelihood of costly legal action against the organization increases.

Some organizations, although they comply with the enforcement of affirmative action and EEOC policies, have no organizational supports for education or training for diversity. There is often a lack or an inconsistent managerial commitment toward diversity.

Other organizations may comply with affirmative action and EEOC policies, but the organization's systems and structures may not be adequate to support real organizational change. This could occur if the affirmative action and EEOC policies are narrowly defined, or if the education and training that is available is not ongoing, or if managerial rewards for implementing diversity programs are inconsistent or lacking. Although these programs may be useful, they are unlikely to result in any long term organizational change or any lasting change in making an organization's climate more receptive to diverse groups.

Some organizations effectively implement affirmative action and EEOC policies, providing ongoing education and training programs pertaining to diversity, and tie or-

No diversity efforts:
- noncompliance with affirmative action and EEOC

Diversity efforts based on:
- compliance with affirmative action and EEOC policies
- inconsistent enforcement and implementation (those who breach policies may not be sanctioned unless noncompliance results in legal action)
- support of policies is not rewarded; organization relies on individual managers' interest or commitment

Diversity efforts based on:
- compliance with and enforcement of affimative action and EEOC policies
- No organizational supports with respect to education, training
- Inconsistent or poor managerial commitment

Diversity efforts based on:
- narrowly defined affirmative action and EEOC policies combined with one–shot education and/or training programs
- inconsistent managerial commitment; rewards not tied to effective implementation of diversity programs and goal achievement
- no attention directed toward organizational climate

Diversity efforts based on:
- effective implementation of affirmative action and EEOC policies
- ongoing education and training programs
- managerial commitment tied to organization rewards
- minimal attention directed toward cultivating an inclusive and supportive organizational climate

Broad–based diversity efforts based on:
- effective implementation of affirmative action and EEOC policies
- organization–wide assessment and management's top–down commitment to diversity
- managerial commitment tied to organization rewards
- ongoinig processes of organization assessment and programs for the purpose of creating an organizational climate which is inclusive and supportive of diverse groups

FIGURE 22.3 Organizational diversity continuum

ganizational rewards to managerial commitment and success in meeting diversity goals and addressing diversity issues. However, such companies may be directing only minimal attention toward cultivating an inclusive and supportive organizational climate for diverse populations of employees.

The most effective diversity efforts are based on managerial implementation of affirmative action and EEOC policies that are developed in conjunction with an organization-wide assessment of the company's systems and structures. This is depicted as the bottom of the continuum. Such assessment is necessary to determine how the organization's systems support or hinder diversity goals. Generally, for such a comprehensive assessment to take place, top management must "buy in" to the idea that diversity is important to the company. This support from the top is critical to all successful diversity efforts and underlies tying organizational rewards to managment's commitment to diversity. Ongoing processes of organization assessment and continuing programs are also necessary to create an organizational climate which is inclusive and supportive of diverse groups.

BACK TO THE CASE As mentioned previously, managerial commitment is one of the most significant factors influencing the success of company diversity initiatives. In the case of Ortho Pharmaceutical, it was Gary Parlin's interest in achieving excellence in all areas that promoted him to seek answers to a very costly company problem. Once an organizational assessment and diagnosis were made, Parlin discovered that there was a number of performance breakdowns at the operational level.

He was quick to respond to the finding that problems in the area of recruiting were hindering the hiring of a diverse slate of candidates. Having an overview and diagnosis of company strengths and weaknesses relating to diversity allowed Parlin and his staff of top managers to plan an effective long-term process for the company. Managerial commitment to these organizational plans resulted in a dramatic increase in upward mobility for women and people of color.

ETHICS HIGHLIGHT
Procter & Gamble

Procter & Gamble's (P&G) sense of social responsibility was evident in the simple response one human resource manager gave when asked about the company's motivation to implement diversity training programs: "You need to treat people right." Realizing that social responsibility and the ethics of creating a just community within the organization do not preclude good business sense, this official added that, "If you do diversity correctly you end up ahead. Diverse thinking is required to stay up-to-date and competitive."

P&G follows the rationale that there is a compelling need to remain current in terms of consumer needs as well as employees' needs in today's work force. For this reason, P&G developed a series of programs which range from intensive two- to three-day sessions targeted for managers to shorter electronic media programs targeted for hourly employees. If these programs result in P&G "treating people right," the company may have found just the right approach to integrating corporate ethics with business success.

Many companies are creating programs to help employees learn to integrate business success with the corporate ethics of "treating people right."

Pluralism

Pluralism refers to an environment in which differences are acknowledged, accepted, and seen to be a significant contribution to the whole. A diverse workforce is most effective when managers are able to guide the organization toward achieving pluralism. Approaches, or strategies to achieve effective workforce diversity, can be classified in five major categories, outlined by Jean Kim of Stanford University: (1) the "Golden Rule" approach, (2) assimilation approach, (3) righting the wrongs approach, (4) the culture-specific approach, and (5) the multicultural approach.[13] Each approach is described briefly in the following sections.

Pluralism is an environment in which cultural, group, and individual differences are acknowledged, accepted, and viewed as a significant contribution to the whole.

The "Golden Rule" Approach

The "Golden Rule" approach to diversity relies on the biblical dictate "Do unto others as you would have them do unto you."[14] The major strength of this approach is that it emphasizes individual morality. Its major flaw is that individuals apply the Golden Rule from their own particular frame of reference without knowledge of the cultural expectations, traditions, and preferences of the other person. One African-American male manager recalled a situation in which he was having difficulty scheduling a work-related event. In exasperation, he volunteered to schedule the event on Saturday. He was reminded by another employee that many of the Jewish employees hold religious services on Saturday. He was initially surprised—then somewhat embarrassed—that he had simply assumed that "all people" attended "church" on Sunday.

Assimilation Approach

The assimilation approach advocates shaping organization members to fit the existing culture of the organization. This approach pressures those who are not members of the dominant culture to conform. This must be done at the expense of their own cultures and worldviews. The result is the creation of a homogeneous culture that suppresses the creativity and diversity of views that could benefit the organization. One black woman in middle management said, "I always felt uncomfortable in very formal meetings. I tend to be very animated when I talk, and this is not the norm for the company. Until I became more comfortable with myself and my style, I felt inhibited. I was tempted to try to change my style to fit in."

Righting the Wrongs Approach

"Righting the wrongs" is an approach that addresses past injustices experienced by a particular group. When a group's history places them at a disadvantage to achieving career success and mobility, policies are developed to create a more equitable set of conditions. For example, the original migration of blacks to the United States was forced upon them as slaves. Righting the wrongs includes approaches designed to compensate for damages or disadvantages impacting blacks due to historical and existing inequalities. This approach most closely parallels the affirmative action policies discussed in chapter 11. However, this approach also goes beyond affirmative action in that it emphasizes tapping the unique talents of each group in the service of organizational productivity.

Culture-Specific Approach

The culture-specific approach teaches employees the norms and practices of another culture to prepare them to interact effectively. This approach is often used to assist employees in making the transition for international assignments. However, the approach neglects to give employees a genuine appreciation for the culture they are about to encounter. Stewart Black and Hal Gergerson, in their study of managers on assignment in foreign countries, found that some employees on international assignment identify much more with the parent firm than with the local operation.[15] One male manager, after two years of opening retail outlets throughout Europe, saw the Europeans as "lazy and slow to respond to directives." One can only speculate that the training and preparation he was given failed to help him adjust to the host country or to appreciate its people and culture.

Multicultural Approach

Finally, the multicultural approach provides opportunities for employees to raise their awareness and develop an appreciation of differences of culture or personal characteristics. The focus is on how interpersonal skills and attitudinal changes relate to organizational performance. A strength of this approach is the assumption that individuals —as well as the organization itself—will be required to make changes to accommodate the diversity of the organization's members.[16]

The multicultural approach may be the most effective approach managers can utilize because it advocates change on the part of management, employees, and organization systems and structures. This approach includes the idea that some efforts will have to be directed toward "righting the wrongs" so that underrepresented groups are present throughout the organization.

THE ROLE OF THE MANAGER

Managers play an essential role in tapping the potential capacities of each person within their departments. To do this requires multiple competencies and commitments which are anchored within the four basic management functions of planning, organiing, influencing, and controlling. Planning applies to the manager's role in developing programs to promote diversity, while organizing, influencing, and controlling are involved in the implementation phases.

Planning

Planning is discussed in chapter 8 as a specific action proposed to help the organization achieve its objectives. Planning is an ongoing process that includes troubleshooting and continually defining areas of improvement. Planning for diversity may involve selecting diversity training programs for the organization or setting diversity goals for employees within the department.

Setting recruitment goals for members of underrepresented groups is a key example of planning. If top management has identified Hispanic employees as a group that is underrepresented within the company, each manager will need to collaborate with the human resources department to achieve the goal of higher Hispanic representation. A manager's role might be to establish goals and objectives for the increased representation of this group within five years. To achieve this five-year vision, the manager needs to establish benchmark goals for each year.

Organizing

Organizing is discussed in chapter 9 as the process of establishing orderly uses for all resources within the management system. To achieve a diverse work environment, the manager will need to work with human resource professionals in the areas of recruitment, hiring, and retention, so that the best match is made between the company and the employees it hires. Responsibilities may lead to establishing task forces or committees to explore issues and provide ideas, carefully choosing work assignments to support the career development of all employees, and evaluating the extent to which goals are being achieved.

Once managers begin to hire from a diverse pool of employees, they will need to turn their attention to retaining them. This means paying attention to the many concerns within a diverse workforce. In the case of working women and men with families, skillfully utilizing the organization's resources to support their needs, in areas like daycare for employee dependents, allowing flexible work arrangements in keeping with company policy, and assigning and re-assigning work responsibilities equitably to accommodate family leave usage are all examples of managers applying the organizing function.

Influencing

Chapter 18 calls influencing the process of guiding the activities of organization members in appropriate directions. This management function is integrally tied to an effective leadership style, good communication skills, knowledge about how to motivate others, and an understanding of organizational culture and group dynamics. Influencing organization members with respect to valuing diversity generally requires encouraging and supporting employees in their efforts to participate constructively within a diverse work environment. This necessitates that the manager, too, engage in the career development and training processes that will provide the skills for facilitating smooth operation of a diversive work community.

Managers are also accountable for informing their employees of breaches of organizational policy and etiquette. For example, once top management defines the diversity strategy for the organization, each manager will need to influence the employees within "his" or "her" span of management. Perhaps the diversity strategy selected by top management includes: educating employees about policies relating to diversity (e.g., defining inappropriate behavior when interviewing prospective employees, or making sure that employees understand what constitutes sexual harassment) and educating employees about cultural diversity by providing workshops for employees on specific issues.

The manager's role includes holding employees accountable for learning about policies and complying with them. The manager might accomplish this through regular meetings, consultations with staff, or one-on-one meetings where necessary. To encourage participation in diversity workshops, the manager may need to communicate the importance of this knowledge base, or might choose to tie organizational rewards, where appropriate, to the development of diversity competencies; such rewards could include giving praise or recognition, or providing workers with opportunities to utilize diversity skills on desirable work assignments.

Controlling

Seeing that compliance with the legal stipulations of EEOC and affirmative action occurs is one aspect of the controlling functions associated with managing a diverse work force. Chapter 17 defines the controlling function as the set of activities which make something happen as planned. Hence the evaluation activities necessary to assess diversity efforts are a part of the controlling role that managers play in shaping a multicultural work force. Managers may find this aspect the most difficult to execute. It has been difficult to evaluate planned-change approaches in general and is particularly so when applied to diversity efforts. Many times the most successful diversity approaches simply reveal more problems and issues as employees begin to speak more openly about their concerns. In addition, the subtle attitudinal changes in one group's perception of another group are so difficult to measure. What can be accurately measured are the outcome variables of turnover, representation of underrepresented groups at all levels of the company, and legal problems stemming from inappropriate or illegal behaviors, such as discrimination or sexual harassment.

A manager engaged in the controlling function with respect to diversity will provide ongoing monitoring of how well the unit is doing with respect to goals and standards. The manager will decide what measures to use (e.g., indicators of productivity, turnover, absenteeism, or promotion) and will need to interpret this information in light of diversity goals and standards. For example, the manager will need to assess whether the low rate of promotions for African-American men in the department is due to subtle biases toward this group or poorer performance than others within the organization. The manager might need to explore and understand the current organizational dynamics, as well as provide necessary supports for this group. Supports might include fostering more social acceptance, learning more about the African-American male's bicultural experience in the company, making mentoring or other opportunities available, or providing some specific job-related training.

MANAGEMENT DEVELOPMENT AND DIVERSITY TRAINING

From the complex set of skills needed to promote diversity, it becomes obvious that managers themselves will need organizational support. One important approach utilized by a large number of companies as a component of their diversity strategy is **diversity training.** Diversity training is a learning process implemented to raise managers' awareness and develop competencies concerning the issues and needs involved in managing a diverse work force. Chapter 11 refers to training as the process of developing qualities in human resources that will enable them to be more productive and to contribute more to organizational goal attainment. Some companies develop intensive programs for management and less intensive, more generalized programs for other employees. As stated in chapter 11, such programs generally focus on the following five components or themes: (1) behavioral awareness, (2) acknowledgment of biases and stereotypes, (3) focus on job performance, (4) avoidance of assumptions, and (5) modification of policy and procedure manuals.

Diversity training is a learning process designed to raise managers' awareness and develop competencies of the issues and needs involved in managing a diverse workforce.

Donaldson and Scannell, authors of *Human Resource Development: The New Trainer's Guide,* have developed a four-stage model describing how managers progress in managing a diverse workforce. The first stage is described as "unconscious incompetence," in which individuals are unaware of the behaviors they engage in that are problematic for members of other groups. The second stage, "conscious incompetence" refers to a learning process of discovering (or becoming conscious of) behaviors that create incompetence in interactions with members of diverse groups. The third stage is one of becoming "consciously competent," where individuals learn how to relate with diverse groups and cultures by deliberately thinking about how to interact. The last stage is "unconscious competence," in which the manager has internalized the new behaviors and is so comfortable relating to others different than him or herself that little conscious effort is required.[17]

> Managers who have progressed to the "unconscious competence" stage will be the most effective with respect to interacting in a diverse workforce. Effective interaction is key to carrying out the four management functions previously discussed.

Table 22.3 summarizes the discussion of the challenges facing managers who work with diverse populations. The manager, who is responsible for controlling organizational goals and outcomes, is accountable for understanding these challenges and recognizing the dynamics described. In addition to treating employees fairly, managers must also influence other employees to cooperate with the company's diversity needs and goals.

In order for managers to respond to the challenges of working with diverse populations they must recognize employee difficulties in coping with diversity. These difficulties include resistance to change, ethnocentrism, lack of and misinformation about other groups, as well as prejudices, biases, and stereotypes. Some employees lack the motivation to invest energy in understanding cultural differences. This is because coping with and understanding diversity requires time and energy. At times one must take emotional risks necessary to explore issues of diversity with others who are different.

TABLE 22.3 Organizational Challenges and Supports Related to Managing in a Diverse Workforce

Organizational Challenges	Organizational Supports
Employee difficulties in coping with cultural diversity	*Educational programs and training to assist employees in working through difficulties*
• resistance to change • ethnocentrism • lack of and mis-information • prejudices, biases and stereotypes	*Top-down management support for diversity*
Employee lack of motivation to invest energy in understanding cultural differences due to:	• managers who have diversity skills and competence • education and training • awareness raising • peer support in the workplace • organizational climate that supports diversity • open communication with one's manager about diversity issues • recognition for employee development of diversity skills and competencies • recognition for employee contributions to enhancing diversity goals • organizational rewards for manager's implementation of organizational diversity goals and objectives
• time, energy and emotional risk necessary to explore issues of diversity • lack of social or concrete rewards provided for investing in diversity work (e.g., lack of peer support, absence of monetary rewards, unclear linkage between multicultural competence and career mobility) • interpersonal and intergroup conflicts which arise when diversity issues are either ignored or mismanaged	
Work group problems	
• lack of cohesiveness • communication problems • employee stress	

There are not always social rewards (e.g. peer support and approval) or concrete rewards (e.g. financial compensation or career opportunities). When diversity issues are ignored, however, or when they are mismanaged, interpersonal and intergroup conflicts arise. These conflicts very often affect the functioning of the workgroup, causing a lack of cohesiveness, communications problems, or employee stress.

There are a number of supports available to managers who are facing the challenges of diversity in the workplace. A primary source of support is education and training programs to assist employees in working through difficulties they may encounter in coping with diversity. Managers may recommend such programs to their employees and may themselves participate in available programs.

Another source of support for diversity is managerial support from the top down within the company. When this top–down support exists, the organization is more likely to have, (1) managers who have skills in working within a diverse workforce, (2) effective education and diversity training programs, (3) an organizational climate that is supportive of diversity and which fosters peer support for exploring diversity issues, (4) open communication with one's manager about diversity issues, (5) recognition for employees' development of diversity skills and competencies, (6) recognition for employee contributions to enhancing diversity goals, and (7) organizational rewards for managers' implementation of organizational diversity goals and objectives.

BACK TO THE CASE

As mentioned above, managers are provided with more extensive training than other employees. This is because managers are key in implementing diversity initiatives. Not only do they need to engage effectively in the four management functions, applying these functions to diversity related tasks, but also they need to learn about their own levels of competency with respect to diversity.

By knowing how to interact across cultures and identify groups, managers are more effective as members of the management team and are more effective with employees within their units. Managers with a high level of multicultural competence are more able to support and foster the kind of culture change that occurred at Ortho Pharmaceutical. One African-American market-research manager at Ortho describes the company as a place where he can disagree with others without being penalized. He indicates that he can be himself. One of the major benefits of cultivating diversity within an organization is that the culture becomes safer for the expression of differences, and more open to the kinds of new ideas that surface through disagreement and open communication.

Even though the distribution of women and minorities within Ortho Pharmaceutical is more equitable, such improvements do not necessarily lead to changes in the company's culture. These kinds of subtle changes in an organization's culture take time. To Ortho's credit, top management's promotion of diversity extended beyond increases in the numerical presence of women and minorities at all levels. At least one company spokesperson felt that management genuinely valued differences, incorporated differences into the (management) team, and tied organizational rewards to diversity efforts. This complex long-term strategy is giving Ortho positive results.

ACTION SUMMARY

Reread the learning objectives that follow. Each objective is followed by questions. Answering these questions accurately will help you retain the most important concepts discussed in this chapter. After answering each question, check your answer with the answer key at the end of this chapter. (*Hint:* If you have doubt regarding the correct response, consult the page whose number follows the answer).

Circle: ***From studying this chapter, I will attempt to acquire:***

1. A definition of diversity and an understanding of its importance in the corporate structure.

T, F **a.** Diversity refers to characteristics which shape individuals' identities and the experiences they have in society.

a, b, c, d, e **b.** The following is *not* true of workforce diversity: (a) it is a new issue; (b) it stems from workforce demographics; (c) it involves developing an inclusive organization; (d) it includes age and physical ability; (e) it is a strength that can be built on.

2. An understanding of the advantages of a diverse workforce.

a, b, c, d, e **a.** Advantages of a diverse workforce include all of the following except: (a) employees who develop multicultural competencies; (b) cost savings; (c) similarity in thinking and approaches; (d) increased productivity; (e) improved ability to keep and gain the market share.

T, F **b.** Advantages of a diverse workforce result in a "better quality of management" because managers are recruited from a wider pool of talent.

3. An awareness of the challenges facing managers within a diverse workforce.

a, b, c, d, e **a.** Challenges facing American corporations include all of the following except: (a) the need to look beyond traditional sources of personnel; (b) the need to assess the opportunities inherent in demographic projections; (c) the need to adapt to changes in the structure of the workforce; (d) the need to prepare for the high influx of younger workers; (e) the need to improve the educational preparation of all workers.

a, b, c, d, e **b.** The following is a potential challenge facing American business leaders: (a) reconciling the conflicting needs of women, work, and families; (b) fully assimilating into the economy African-American and Hispanic workers; (c) maintaining the dynamism of an aging workforce; (d) accelerating productivity increases in service industries; (e) all of the above.

a, b, c, d, e **c.** Dynamics of coping with diverse populations include: (a) "the glass ceiling"; (b) tokenism; (c) bicultural stress; (d) ethnocentrism; (e) all of the above.

4. An understanding of the strategies for promoting diversity in organizations.

T, F **a.** Following the appropriate affirmative action and EEOC guidelines will resolve intergroup conflicts and result in an effectively diverse organization.

b. The following is true regarding strategies for promoting diversity in organizations: (a) organizations vary widely with respect to the strategies they employ; (b) all organizations comply with affirmative action and EEOC guidelines; (c) exclusionary practices have no effect on the organization; (d) diversity programs always result in comprehensive culture change; (e) all of the above.

5. Insights into the role of the manager in promoting diversity in the organization.

a, b, c, d, e **a.** A manager who is engaging in the four functions of management with respect to diversity might be involved in all of the following except: (a) establishing hiring goals for specific underrepresented groups; (b) granting family leave time; (c) communicating the importance of diversity training; (d) letting employees know they are not accountable for knowing diversity-related policies; (e) assessing progress toward diversity goals.

a, b, c, d, e **b.** In a diverse organization, the highest level of diversity competence is described as "conscious competence."

INTRODUCTORY CASE WRAP-UP

"Ortho Pharmaceutical 'Showcase' for Cultural Diversity" (page 569) and its related back-to-the-case sections were written to help you better understand the management concepts contained in this chapter. Answer the following discussion questions about this introductory case to further enrich your understanding of chapter content:

1. How important to an organization such as Ortho Pharmaceutical is the implementation of workforce diversity goals? Explain.
2. Based on the facts in the case, what strengths has Ortho Pharmaceutical gained from cultivating diversity within the company?
3. Based on the facts in the case, what organizational challenges does Ortho Pharmaceutical face? Discuss the organizational supports that exist to address these challenges.

ISSUES FOR REVIEW AND DISCUSSION

1. What is diversity?
2. Why is diversity an important contemporary management issue?
3. List the six challenges facing American businesses and organizations.
4. Define pluralism.
5. Describe the five major approaches organizations employ to respond to diversity.
6. List the advantages of a diverse workforce.
7. List the challenges of a diverse workforce.
8. Give a detailed description of the dynamics encountered by diverse populations in the workplace.
9. Outline the organizational supports to help managers address the challenges of a diverse workforce.
10. Describe the range of strategies organizations employ to implement workforce diversity.
11. Explain the concept of reverse discrimination.
12. What is the relationship between the four management functions and the implementation of diversity goals?
13. Why should managers undergo diversity training?
14. What is the meaning of "unconscious competence" and why is it desirable for managers?

ACTION SUMMARY ANSWER KEY

1. **a.** T, p. 570
   b. a, p. 570
2. **a.** c, pp. 571–573
   b. T, p. 572
3. **a.** d, pp. 574–575
   b. e, pp. 579–580
   c. e, pp. 576–578
4. **a.** F, p. 580
   b. a, pp. 581–582
5. **a.** d, p. 585–586
   b. F, p. 587

CASE STUDY

Rebuilding LA

TONY ORTEGA
California State University, Bakersfield

A vivid example of cultures in collision are the riots that occurred in Los Angeles during the spring of 1992. The city of Los Angeles is highly diverse. It is not uncommon, for example, for schools to report that over seventy different languages are spoken in the school yard during recess. Los Angeles boasts of many ethnic enclaves, such as Little Tokyo (Japanese), Chinatown (Chinese), and Watts (African-American). Each of these ethnic groups has become a coherent and vital constituency in its own right. The groups have learned to compete with each other when necessary and to form coalitions when mutually beneficial. They are no longer novices in the political arena.

The riots arose from the videotaped beating of Rodney King in 1992. Mr. King had been speeding and, after a chase, the police pulled him over. The videotape showed Mr. King, an African-American, taking a brutal beating at the hands of white police officers. The police officers involved were charged with using excessive force and brought to trial. There was an expectation that the officers would be found guilty; however, a jury found them innocent. The announcement of the verdict sparked a series of riots, looting episodes, and acts of arson which transformed southeast Los Angeles into a war zone. The riots lasted several days. People of all ethnic backgrounds were involved. There were fifty-three fatalities, 2,383 injuries, 17,000 arrests for looting, arson, and curfew violations, 1,700 businesses were damaged, and over $780 million in losses. Why did the riots happen? Several factors are listed as causes: racism; poverty; little or no communication between government and the governed; a decrease in spending by the U.S. Department of Defense, causing a loss of jobs in local aerospace firms; a sluggish economy with resulting high unemployment; and a rising sense of tension between minorities and the Los Angeles Police Department. While no single factor is dominant, all factors played a part.

The organization charged with leading the revitalization of the destroyed area is called Rebuild LA. Peter Ueberroth, white and from a privileged background, was appointed by the Mayor of Los Angeles to lead the effort. Critics point out that he has not previously shown an interest or competency in dealing with urban dilemmas. But he is a winner; his confidence and ambition are infectious, and he is an outstanding salesperson. Ueberroth was primarily chosen because of his managerial skill in hosting the 1984 Olympic games. It was expected, at first, that the games would cost more than the city could afford, would tie up traffic in knots, and would, perhaps, experience devastating acts of terrorism. Instead, the 1984 games were a tremendous success that charmed millions of spectators from around the world and earned over $150 million in profit for use by succeeding host cities.

Ueberroth is a consummate planner who leads, organizes, and delegates tasks. He determines the right things to do and finds skilled people who will do them right. He creates a vision of the desired final result and then lets people work toward that goal. He has asked for volunteers, receiving them in hastily constructed offices near downtown. Ueberroth intends to meld the volunteers, as he did the Olympics volunteers, into a grass-roots work force that is interracial, productive, and cheerful. In the process, this group may suggest a model of a community life that might come to pass.

The success of Rebuild LA depends on the ability of three elements—community, government, and private business—to work together. To date, the rebuilding of Los Angeles has been slow and erratic. Yet many citizens have high confidence of success. All hope that their confidence is not misplaced.

DISCUSSION QUESTIONS

1. Is Peter Ueberroth the right person to head the Rebuild LA organization? Why? Why not?
2. Who else should participate in leading the Rebuild LA task force? What implications will these decisions have on top management of local companies?
3. What actions should Mr. Ueberroth take first? Why?
4. How will the success or failure of rebuilding Los Angeles impact business? Will the corporate culture of local companies be affected?

CNN VIDEO CASE

The Glass Ceiling: Shattered or Still in Place?

The answer to the above question depends on the company. Even with a particular company in mind, remember that the glass ceiling refers to access to upper-level management positions; no matter how many benefits are available to ease women's load, if the company doesn't have representative female numbers at the top, there's a glass ceiling.

Consider in this video case three major companies. All three companies provide day care for children, all have flexible working hours, all allow for job sharing; in other words, all have family-friendly benefit programs.

Steelcase, in Grand Rapids, Michigan, is a hugely successful office-furniture manufacturer. Its many female employees are happy to work there because Steelcase goes beyond the norm to help its employees balance work and home. In addition, Steelcase employees have access to an on-site wellness center, a referral center for child-care needs, and even take-home birthday cakes. But in its eighty-year history, Steelcase has had only one woman in upper management. Even middle management suffers from a female representation of only 15 percent.

Today, because top management made it a priority, women at Ben & Jerry's represent one-half of top management and two-thirds of middle management.

Xerox, in Rochester, New York, offers the usual family-friendly benefits and recognizes women who work well in its corporate structure. One woman, Tosh Baron, president of an $8 billion division, comments that she values her position in the company and believes she achieved it by enjoying the job rather than by seeking the status per se. It is a mixed blessing, however. "The trade-off is that there are *many* times I really wish I was home; and yet you know you've made the choice."

Ben and Jerry's, an ice cream company in Waterbury, Vermont, is hard at work developing a new way to do business. Only four years ago, there were no women at all in top management at Ben & Jerry's. Today, women represent 50 percent of top management and two thirds of middle management. How could this happen in so short a time? It happened because top management made it a high-priority goal.

Commenting on the process of bringing about a balance, one of the female employees points out. "You have to roll your sleeves up and show your stuff and say 'yeah, we can do this'—we're not these alien creatures and we're really just part of the gang and it's okay." Adds Vice Chairman Jerry Greenfield, "It has worked out great. You can look at the performance of the company [the bottom line] on one hand; but just being there day to day—there's a better feel to the place."

What conclusions may be drawn from the three company examples? Starting with the Steelcase approach, some analysts believe all those benefits are making things too comfortable and are allowing the female employees to become complacent, not willing to climb the corporate ladder to meet the challenges at the top. Whatever the reason, Steelcase has almost no female representation, a situation that will cost the company in the future. Says Jerry Myers, president, "We have some learning to do."

Xerox is doing better at promoting women to top-level positions, yet the women often still feel torn between the demands of home and business. This tension costs the business as well as the family.

Ben and Jerry's, by getting the commitment from top management and following action plans, has the gender balance in place—and the changes just keep coming. Chuck Lacy, president, says, "The next stage of evolution for us is to create a company which realistically adapts to the realities of family life. The more we have both of us [men and women] together, working together as equals, the better place it's going to be for *everyone.*"

VIDEO CASE QUESTIONS

1. In "glass ceiling," explain the meanings of the terms "glass" and "ceiling."
2. Many women feel their careers suffer when they are switched to the "mommy track" for taking time out to have a family. At which company do you think the "mommy track" poses the biggest problem?
3. Describe ways it may be difficult for the first female at Steelcase to "fit in" with the executives.
4. In which company do you think upper-level managers are most committed to influencing employees to help eliminate the glass ceiling? Explain.

CNN VIDEO EXERCISE

Taking a SWOT at the Steelcase Ceiling

EXERCISE GOAL: Prepare a SWOT analysis to guide Steelcase in moving women into middle and upper management.

Imagine that you are personnel director for Steelcase. Jerry Myers, the company president, has asked you to prepare a plan to improve female representation in middle and upper management at Steelcase. As a first step, prepare a SWOT analysis for Steelcase focusing on the work environment for women. Before you begin, review the chapter 7 material (pages 165–167) about SWOT analyses. List at least one issue for each category related to women workers at Steelcase.

Internal		External	
Strengths	Weaknesses	Opportunities	Threats

PART 6

INTEGRATIVE CASE

Global Quality at Federal Express

ROBERT E. KEMPER
Northern Arizona University

Federal Express has a global vision. It does not recognize geographic, political, or trade boundaries and it provides the products and services to match today's global economic needs.

Federal Express is the world's largest air freight company and full-service, all-cargo airline. Every day, Federal Express moves over 1.7 million pieces of freight between destinations in the Far East, Europe, Central and South America, Australia, the United States, the Middle East, and the Caribbean. Federal's state-of-the-art system handles packages and shipments of any size and weight.

One of the most challenging management tasks facing Federal is to build an organization of people from many different cultures into a productive work team that focuses on product quality. Federal Express, from its inception, has put its people first because it is ethically right and because it is good business as well. To build such a work team, Federal's managers stimulate within each organization member an awareness of and appreciation for the culture and heritage of every other organizational member. Cross-cultural training programs build this awareness. Federal Express executives believe that the world is full of good people who come in all shapes, sizes, and colors, and with many levels of skills and knowledge. The secret to managing workforce diversity at Federal Express is reflected in the following six management practices: (1) put employee considerations first; (2) involve each employee as an invaluable team member; (3) be dedicated to promotions from within; (4) enact progressive programs that guarantee fair treatment; (5) provide outstanding wages, benefits, and profit-sharing opportunities; and say thank you and well done—in all languages at every opportunity.

This attention to workforce diversity earned Federal the "Nobel Prize" for quality—the Malcolm Baldrige National Quality Award (MBNQA). Winning the MBNQA is a tribute to the overall consumer satisfaction with Federal Express's domestic and international service. Federal is committed to delivering each shipment entrusted to it on schedule 100 percent of the time. Equally important, Federal maintains 100 percent accuracy of all information pertaining to each item it carries. Federal's objective is to have a 100 percent satisfied customer at the end of each transaction.

Through a quality improvement process focusing on twelve service quality indicators (SQIs)—all tied to customer expectations and articulated at all levels of its international business—the Memphis-based firm continues to set higher standards for service and customer satisfaction. Measuring themselves against a 100-percent service standard, managers and employees strive to improve all aspects of the way Federal Express does business.

To spur progress toward its ultimate target of 100-percent customer satisfaction, Federal Express has set up cross-functional teams for each service component. A senior executive leads each team and assures the involvement of front-line employees, support personnel, and managers from all parts of the corporation, when needed. Two of these corporate-wide teams have a network of over a thousand employees working on improvements.

The company's advanced computer—including the Super Tracker (a hand-held computer used for scanning a shipment's bar code)—and tracking systems gather performance data every time a package changes hands between pick-up and delivery. Rapid analysis of data from the firm's far-flung operations yields daily SQI reports transmitted to workers at all Federal Express sites. Management meets daily to discuss the previous day's performance and tracks weekly, monthly, and annual trends. Analysis of data contained in the company's more than thirty major databases assists quality action teams (QATs) in locating the root causes of problems that surface in SQI reviews. Extensive customer and internal data drive cross-functional teams involved in the company's new product introduction process.

Federal Express's "People-Service-Profit" philosophy guides management policies and actions. The company has a well-developed and thoroughly deployed management evaluation system called SFA (survey/feedback/action), which involves a survey of employees, analysis of each work group's results by the work group's manager, and a discussion between the manager and the work group to develop written action plans to help the manager improve and become more effective. Data from the SFA process are aggregated at all levels of the organization for use in policy making.

Federal's objective is to have a 100 percent satisfied customer at the end of each transaction.

Federal Express's adherence to a management philosophy emphasizes people, service, and profit, in that order, and results in high levels of customer satisfaction. Sales growth has been rapid, too, with annual revenues topping $1 billion within ten years of the company's founding.

The service quality indicator (SQI) measurements directly link the corporate planning process, which begins with the chief executive officer and the chief operations officer and an executive planning committee. SQIs are the basis for corporate executive evaluation. Individual performance objectives are established and monitored. Executive bonuses rest upon the performance of the whole corporation in meeting performance improvement goals. And, in the annual employee survey, if employees do not rate management leadership at least as high as they did the year before, no executive receives a year-end bonus.

Employees are encouraged to be innovative and to make decisions that advance quality goals. Federal Express provides employees with the information and technology they need to continuously improve their performance. An example is the digitally assisted dispatch system (DADS), which communicates to some 35,000 couriers through screens in their vans. The system enables quick response to pick-up and delivery dispatches and allows couriers to manage their time and routes with high efficiency.

Federal Express has a "no-layoff" philosophy and a guaranteed fair-treatment procedure for handling employee grievances worldwide. It is a model for firms in many industries. Employees can participate in a program to qualify front-line workers for management positions. In addition, Federal Express has a well-developed recognition program for team and individual contributions to company performance. Over the last five years, at least 91 percent of employees said they were "proud to work for Federal Express."

Training of front-line personnel is a responsibility of managers and "recurrency training" is a widely used instrument for improvement. Teams regularly assess training needs and a worldwide staff of training professionals devise programs to address those needs. To aid this effort, Federal Express has developed an interactive video system for employee instruction. An internal television network, accessible throughout the company, also serves as an important avenue for employee education.

Other air-express competitors are getting better and, more than in any other year in Federal's twenty-year history, fiscal 1993 demonstrates that Federal Express must constantly strive to improve the system and to find better ways of doing things if it is to keep its leadership position in a global marketplace.

DISCUSSION QUESTIONS

1. Why should a successful domestic corporation such as Federal Express consider entering the global market?
2. As a Malcolm Baldrige National Quality Award winner, what advantage does Federal Express have over its competition? Explain.
3. If Federal Express were faced with a decision that required it to choose between quality and global expansion, which would you recommend? Explain.
4. How important to Federal Express is the implementation of workforce diversity goals? Explain.

The Malcolm Baldrige National Quality Award

A Blueprint for Excellence

"An act to amend the Stevenson-Wydler Technology Innovation Act of 1980, to establish the Malcolm Baldrige National Quality Award with the objective of encouraging American business and other organizations to practice effective quality control in the provision of their goods and services."

That brief paragraph has resulted in nothing less than a quality revolution among United States businesses. As the Japanese challenge of the 1980s spurred U.S. companies to focus their attention on quality improvement, the Malcolm Baldrige National Quality Award is generating similar enthusiasm in the 1990s—and it's providing just the blueprint that companies need to define quality for their organizations, involve all personnel in the quality effort, continuously improve their processes and, above all, keep their customers satisfied.

MALCOLM BALDRIGE NATIONAL QUALITY AWARD CRITERIA (1992)

The Malcolm Baldrige National Quality Award is an annual Award to recognize U.S. companies that excel in quality management and quality achievement.

The Award promotes:

- awareness of quality as an increasingly important element in competitiveness.
- understanding of the requirements for quality excellence, and
- sharing of information on successful quality strategies and the benefits derived from implementation of these strategies.

Award Participation

The Award has three eligibility categories:

- Manufacturing companies

Excerpted from Allyn and Bacon's *Profiles of Malcolm Baldrige Award Winners,* originally published by the Bureau of Business Practice as *Award Winning Quality: Strategies from the Winners of the Malcolm Baldrige National Quality Award* (BBP © 1992). Used with permission of the Bureau of Business Practice (BBP), a division of the Business and Professional Group of Paramount Publishing, a Paramount Communications Company.

- Service companies
- Small businesses

Up to two Awards may be given in each category each year. Award recipients may publicize and advertise their Awards. In addition to publicizing the receipt of the Award, recipients are expected to share information about their successful quality strategies with other U.S. organizations.

Companies participating in the Award process submit applications that include completion of the Award Examination.

Award Examination Review

The Award Examination is based upon quality excellence criteria through a public-private partnership. In responding to these criteria, each applicant is expected to provide information and data on the company's quality processes and quality improvement. Information and data submitted must be adequate to demonstrate that the applicant's approaches could be replicated or adapted by other companies.

The Award Examination is designed not only to serve as a reliable basis for making Awards but also to permit a diagnosis of each applicant's overall quality management.

All applications are reviewed and evaluated by members of the Malcolm Baldrige National Quality Award Board of Examiners. When Board members are assigned to review applications, business and quality expertise is matched to the business of the applicant. Accordingly, applications from manufacturing companies are assigned primarily to Board members with manufacturing expertise, and service company applications are assigned primarily to those with service expertise. Strict rules regarding real and potential conflicts of interest are followed in assigning Board members to review applications.

Applications are reviewed without funding from the United States Government. Review expenses are paid primarily through application fees; partial support for the reviews is provided by the Foundation for the Malcolm Baldrige National Quality Award.

After the Award Examination review, all applicants receive feedback reports prepared by members of the Board of Examiners.

DESCRIPTION OF THE AWARD CRITERIA

Award Criteria Purposes

The Malcolm Baldrige National Quality Award Criteria are the basis for making Awards and providing feedback to applicants. In addition, they have three other important national purposes:

- to help elevate quality standards and expectations;
- to facilitate communication and sharing among and within organizations of all types based upon common understanding of key quality requirements; and
- to serve as a working tool for planning, training, assessment, and other uses.

The Award Criteria are directed toward dual results-oriented goals: To project key requirements for delivering ever-improving value to customers while at the same time maximizing the overall productivity and effectiveness of the delivering organization.

To achieve these results-oriented goals, the Criteria need to be built upon a set of values that together address and integrate the overall customer and company performance requirements.

Core Values and Concepts

The Award Criteria are built upon these core values and concepts:

- Customer-driven quality
- Leadership
- Continuous improvement
- Full participation
- Fast response
- Design quality and prevention
- Long-range outlook
- Management by fact
- Partnership development
- Public responsibility

Brief descriptions of the core values and concepts follow.

Customer-Driven Quality

Quality is judged by the customer. All product and service attributes that contribute value to the customer and lead to customer satisfaction and preference must be addressed appropriately in quality systems. Value, satisfaction, and preference may be influenced by many factors throughout the customer's overall purchase, ownership, and service experiences. This includes the relationship between the company and customers—the trust and confidence in products and services—that leads to loyalty and preference. This concept of quality includes not only the product and service attributes that meet basic requirements. It also includes those that enhance them and differentiate them from competing offerings. Such enhancement and differentiation may include new offerings, as well as unique product-product, service-service, or product-service combinations.

Customer-driven quality is thus a strategic concept. It is directed toward market share gain and customer retention. It demands constant sensitivity to emerging customer and market requirements and measurement of the factors that drive customer satisfaction. It also demands awareness of developments in technology, and rapid and flexible response to customer and market requirements. Such requirements extend well beyond defect and error reduction, merely meeting specifications, or reducing complaints. Nevertheless, defect and effort reduction and elimination of causes of dissatisfaction contribute significantly to the customers' view of quality and are thus also important parts of customer-driven quality. In addition, the company's approach to recovering from defects and errors is crucial to its improving both quality and relationships with customers.

Leadership

A company's senior leaders must create clear and visible quality values and high expectations. Reinforcement of the values and expectations requires their substantial personal commitment and involvement. The leaders must take part in the creation of strategies, systems, and methods for achieving excellence. The systems and methods need to guide all activities and decisions of the company and encourage participation and creativity by all employees. Through their regular personal involvement in visible activities, such as planning, review of company quality performance, and recognizing employees for quality achievement, the senior leaders serve as role models reinforcing the values and encouraging leadership in all levels of management.

Continuous Improvement

Achieving the highest levels of quality competitiveness requires a well-defined and well-executed approach to continuous improvement. Such improvement needs to be part of all operations and of all work unit activities of a company. Improvements may be of several types: (1) enhancing value to the customer through new and improved products and services; (2) reducing errors, defects, and waste; (3) improving responsiveness and cycle time performance; and (4) improving productivity and effectiveness in the use of all resources. Thus, improvement is driven not only by the objective to provide better quality, but also by the need to be responsive and efficient—both conferring additional marketplace advantages. To meet all of these objectives, the process of continuous improvement must contain regular cycles of planning, execution, and evaluation. This requires a basis—preferably a quantitative basis—for assessing progress, and for deriving information for future cycles of improvement.

Full Participation

Meeting the company's quality and performance objectives requires a fully committed, well-trained, and involved work force. Reward and recognition systems need to reinforce full participation in company quality objectives. Factors bearing upon the safety, health, well-being, and morale of employees need to be part of the continuous improvement objectives and activities of the company. Employees need education and training in quality skills related to performing their work and to understanding and solving quality-related problems. Training should be reinforced through on-the-job applications of learning, involvement, and empowerment. Increasingly, training and participation need to be tailored to a more diverse workforce.

Fast Response

Success in competitive markets increasingly demands ever-shorter product and service introduction cycles and more rapid response to customers. Indeed, fast response itself is often a major quality attribute. Reduction in cycle times and rapid response to customers can occur when work processes are designed to meet both quality and response goals. Accordingly, response time improvement should be included as a major focus within all quality improvement processes of work units. This requires that all designs, objectives, and work unit activities include measurement of cycle time and responsiveness. Major improvements in response time may require work processes and paths to be simplified and shortened. Response time improvements often "drive" simultaneous improvements in quality and productivity. Hence it is highly beneficial to consider response time, quality, and productivity objectives together.

Design Quality and Prevention

Quality systems should place strong emphasis on design quality—problem prevention achieved through building quality into products and services and into the processes through which they are produced. Excellent design quality may lead to major reductions in "downstream" waste, problems, and associated costs. Design quality includes the creation of fault-tolerant (robust) processes and products. A major design issue is the design-to-introduction cycle time. To meet the demands of ever-more rapidly changing markets, companies need to focus increasingly on shorter product and service introduction times. Consistent with the theme of design quality and prevention, continuous improvement and corrective actions need to emphasize interventions "upstream"—at the earliest stages in processes. This approach yields the maximum overall benefits of improvements and corrections. Such upstream intervention also needs to take into account the company's suppliers.

Long-Range Outlook

Achieving quality and market leadership requires a future orientation and long-term commitments to customers, employees, stockholders, and suppliers. Strategies, plans, and resource allocations need to reflect these commitments and address training, employee development, supplier development, technology evolution, and other factors that bear upon quality. A key part of the long-term commitment is regular review and assessment of progress relative to long-term plans.

Management by Fact

Meeting quality and performance goals of the company requires that process management be based upon reliable information, data, and analysis. Facts and data needed for quality assessment and quality improvement are of many types, including: customer, product and service performance, operations, market, competitive comparisons, supplier, employee-related, and cost and financial. Analysis refers to the process of extracting larger meaning from data to support evaluation and decision making at various levels within the company. Such analysis may entail using data individually or in combination to reveal information—such as trends, projections, and cause and effect—that might not be evident without analysis. Facts, data, and analysis support a variety of company purposes, such as planning, reviewing company performance, improving operations, and comparing company quality performance with competitors'.

Partnership Development

Companies should seek to build internal and external partnerships, serving mutual and larger community interests. Such partnerships might include those that promote labor-management cooperation with suppliers and customers, and linkages with education organizations. Partnerships should consider longer-term objectives as well as short-term needs, thereby creating a basis for mutual investments. The building of partnerships should address means of regular communication, approaches to evaluating progress, means for modifying objectives, and methods to accommodate to changing conditions.

Public Responsibility

A company's customer requirements and quality system objectives should address areas of corporate citizenship and responsibility. These include business ethics, public health and safety, environment, and sharing of quality-related information in the company's business and geographic communities. Health, safety, and environmental considerations need to take into account the life cycle of products and services and include factors such as waste generation. Quality planning in such cases should address adverse contingencies that may arise throughout the life cycle of production, distribution, and use of products. Plans should include problem avoidance and company response if avoidance fails, including how to maintain public trust and confidence. Inclusion of public responsibility areas within a quality system means not only meeting all local, state, and federal legal and regulatory requirements, but also treating these and related requirements as areas for continuous improvement. In addition, companies should support—within reasonable limits of their resources—national, industry, trade, and community activities to share nonproprietary quality-related information.

Criteria Framework

The core values and concepts are embodied in seven categories, as follows:

1.0 Leadership
2.0 Information and Analysis

3.0 Strategic Quality Planning
4.0 Human Resource Development and Management
5.0 Management of Process Quality
6.0 Quality and Operational Results
7.0 Customer Focus and Satisfaction

The framework connecting and integrating the categories is given in Figure A.1.

The framework has four basic elements:

Driver

Senior executive leadership creates the values, goals, and systems, and guides the sustained pursuit of quality and performance objectives.

System

System comprises the set of well-defined and well-designed processes for meeting the company's quality and performance requirements.

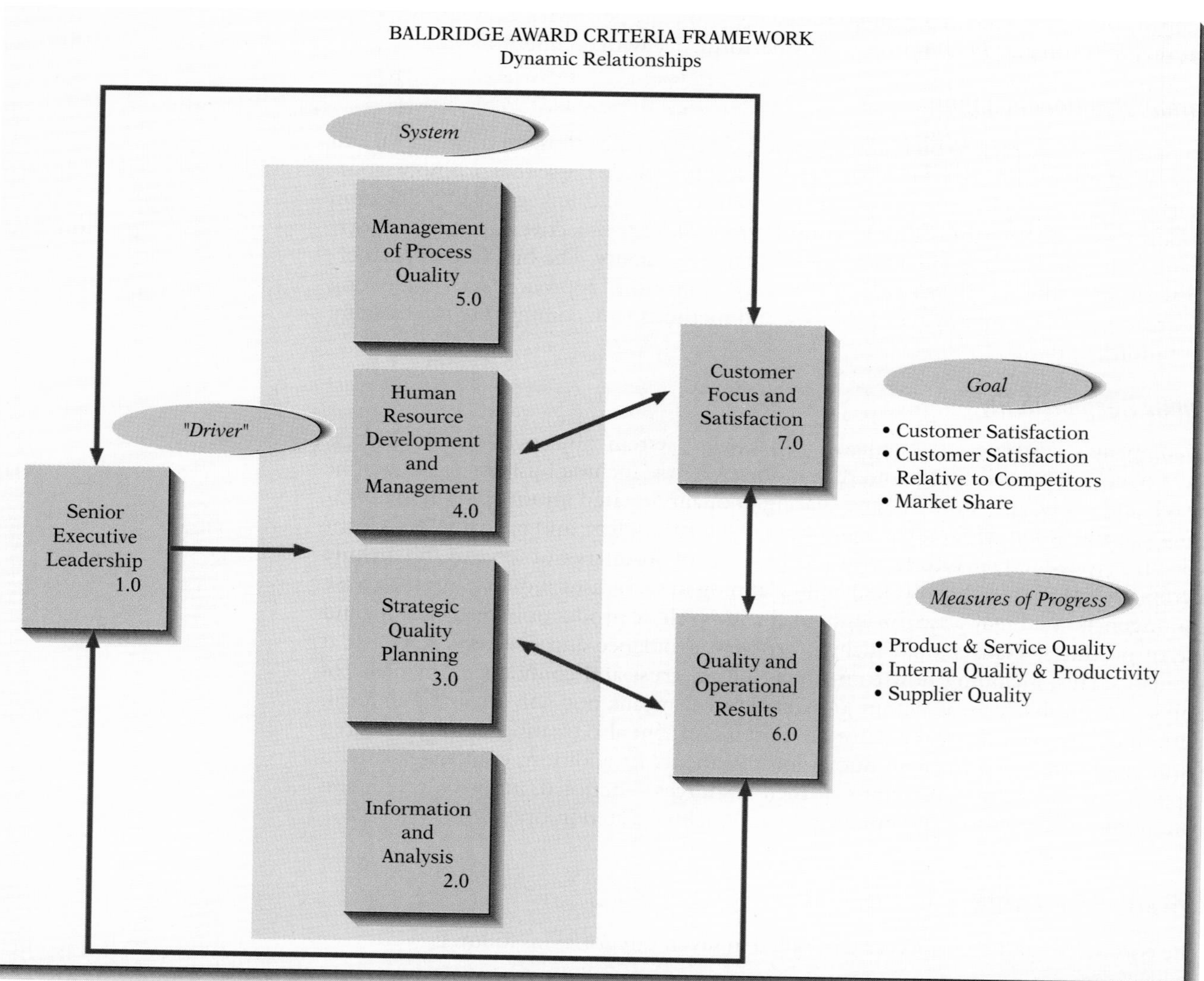

Figure A.1 Baldrige Award Criteria Framework

Measures of Progress

Measures of progress provide a results-oriented basis for channeling actions to delivering ever-improving customer value and company performance.

Goal

The basic aim of the quality process is the delivery of ever-improving value to customers.

THE BOTTOM LINE: CONTINUOUS IMPROVEMENT IS WHAT COUNTS

As you will learn from reading the comprehensive success stories detailed in Quality Modules 2, 3, and 4, achieving award winning quality is a painstaking process. It takes a tremendous amount of commitment and dedication to achieve the level of excellence that fulfills the stringent Malcolm Baldrige National Quality Award criteria, and also to apply for the Award.

Yet every year, thousands and thousands of companies request applications, and dozens of them actually apply for the Award, some going through the difficult application process year after year.

Why do so many companies undertake this monumental effort? Some are encouraged to apply by their customers, who want to do business with only the most quality-effective suppliers. But as these modules illustrate, most companies that participate in the Baldrige process do so with one critical goal in mind: *self-improvement.*

The Baldrige application process—and even the Award itself—will certainly not solve all a company's problems. It is not a panacea, and should never be regarded as such. However, it *is* a sound, thorough blueprint for quality improvement, and it has stimulated interest in quality in the United States as nothing has ever done before. The Baldrige process is helping to bring U.S. companies together to pool their ideas, resources, and strategies for keeping their industries strong and viable.

The bottom line is this: The companies that benefit most from the Baldrige process are the ones that recognize that it's not winning the Award that counts the most; it's developing the discipline, drive, and vision to set their organizations on the path to excellence, and then to keep striving ever onward toward continuous improvement.

True quality winners never rest on their laurels: They recognize that improvement doesn't stop with receiving a Baldrige Award—or any other award, for that matter: It must be an *ongoing* process that never ends.

This commitment to continuous improvement is crucial if a company is to survive—and *thrive*—in today's challenging marketplace. Putting the powerful Baldrige process to work as an improvement tool can help an organization to be a quality winner.

QUALITY MODULE 2

Selected Baldrige Winners from the Manufacturing Companies Award Category

Texas Instruments: A 1992 Winner

If your company applies for the Baldrige Award but doesn't win, should you continue to apply every year? Will the time and money involved be worth the assessments you receive from the Baldrige examiners? This smart company thought so—and its dedication brought the rewards of impressive quality and a Baldrige win in 1992.

Approximately 65 percent of all the air-to-ground "smart weapons" used in Operation Desert Storm were made by Texas Instruments Incorporated's Defense Systems & Electronics Group (DSEG)—a 1992 Malcolm Baldrige National Quality Award winner in the manufacturing category. With 15,000 employees at 10 locations in Texas, DSEG is the first business solely dedicated to defense to win the MBNQA.

DSEG began its quality journey in 1982, so it already had an aggressive quality road map in place when the Baldrige Award was introduced in 1988. However, DSEG leaders believed that the Baldrige criteria might serve as a template to pull their quality process together and keep it focused. So they spent 1988 attending seminars and acquainting themselves and other key people in the Group with the criteria.

By the end of the year, top people at DSEG felt that they had gained the necessary understanding and buy-in of the Baldrige template. So in 1989, says Vice President of Quality Assurance Mike Cooney, "we had people at each of our organizational functions within the Defense Systems and Electronics Group write what we called a 'miniapplication' for their organization." Every group—including Production, Engineering, Human Resources, Contracting, Accounting, and support functions—wrote a miniapplication against the Baldrige criteria.

"We then took those miniapplications, did an internal assessment, and scored ourselves based on our learning of the process in 1988," Cooney recalls. "We wrote feedback reports to each of these organizations, based on their miniapplications. They, in turn, developed action plans to enhance their individual quality improvement plans."

On the basis of the results of these miniapplications, Cooney says, "we felt that we were ready to make a credible challenge against the Baldrige criteria and to make a for-

Excerpted from *Quality Assurance Bulletin,* Number 1610, May 25, 1993 (BBP © 1993) and from Allyn and Bacon's *Profiles of Malcolm Baldrige Award Winners,* originally published by the Bureau of Business Practice as *Award Winning Quality: Strategies from the Winners of the Malcolm Baldrige National Quality Award* (BBP © 1992). Used with permission of the Bureau of Business Practice (BBP), a division of the Business and Professional Group of Paramount Publishing, a Paramount Communications Company.

mal application. So in 1990, we formally applied for the Baldrige Award. Although we did not get a site visit that first year, we did get an extensive feedback report. In some cases, this report correlated with our own internal self-assessment; in other cases, it opened our eyes to areas where we needed to make a more concentrated effort to improve."

As a result of the 1990 feedback report, the DSEG Quality Improvement Team (composed of President Hank Hayes and his staff) developed five thrusts that would allow DSEG to accelerate its quality journey: *Customer Satisfaction, Stretch Goals, Benchmarking, Teamwork/Empowerment,* and *Total Quality.*

After going through the formal application process for the first time and getting feedback from the Baldrige examiners, DSEG leaders had to decide whether to apply again the next year or work on improvements and wait some period of time before making another formal application. "We felt very strongly then—and still feel now—that it is very important to continue the formal application process," says Cooney. "It is a 'forcing function' and it gives you invaluable feedback. Nothing takes the place of making that formal 75-page application and getting that independent assessment of your [organization]. So we felt it was important to continue to apply."

DSEG applied again in 1991 and got a site visit. The examiners' feedback confirmed that DSEG's five improvement thrusts were putting the Group on the right course; however, they advised that DSEG still needed improvement in a few areas. After working diligently to improve these areas, reports Cooney, "we applied for the Baldrige Award for the third time in 1992—and the rest is history."

THE FIVE QUALITY THRUSTS

The five improvement thrusts that DSEG uses to guide its continuous improvement journey have slowly evolved over time. Changes to these quality initiatives are based on feedback reports from Baldrige examiners, as well as training and experimental "aha's" on the part of DSEG leaders. Here's a look at the five thrusts as they have evolved.

1. Customer Satisfaction

One of the critical lessons DSEG learned from Baldrige feedback reports was the tremendous importance of *processes.* Cooney notes that "the continual probing of the Baldrige criteria" made people at DSEG realize that they needed processes for

Understanding customers' concerns
Formal feedback reporting to address those concerns.
Truly assessing how satisfied customers were and identifying and addressing areas where customers *weren't* satisfied.

DSEG began to conduct semiformal customer surveys by participating in various government and industry associations' surveys. Also, a customer satisfaction thrust team worked with a third party to develop and conduct a survey of DSEG's customers. The feedback obtained from this survey (which will be done bianually) is being used to improve the organization's customer service process.

2. Stretch Goals

"One of the weaknesses perceived by the Baldrige examiners was that we needed stretch goals," says Joe Borden, manager of Total Quality Management at DSEG. The Group established two stretch goals:

To Attain Six Sigma Quality for Both Products and Services
(This means achieving a defect rate of no more than 3.4 parts per million.)

"When we established Six Sigma as a goal in 1992, our top management team went to Motorola [where the Six Sigma concept was developed] and attended every seminar it had," Borden says. When the executives returned, they announced that all 15,000 DSEG employees would receive Six Sigma training. DSEG licensed Motorola's training materials and had Motorola managers come to DSEG plants to help implement the training process.

To Improve Cycle Time

(This is an emphasis of the Baldrige Award criteria.) As you study and map your processes to understand the source of defects, you have the opportunity to eliminate non-value-added steps and thus reduce cycle time, notes Borden.

3. Benchmarking

A DSEG quality team went to Xerox to learn its "classic" benchmarking approach. "We now have an extremely active benchmarking network led by a full-time benchmarking champion," Borden reports.

DSEG is benchmarking around 80 different processes at other companies. In turn, DSEG is being benchmarked by an equal number of companies. Companies whose processes DSEG has benchmarked include 3M, Corning, Quaker Oats, and Motorola.

This diversity is noteworthy because at first DSEG only benchmarked its competitors. However, the 1990 Baldrige examiners weren't impressed with this limited scope, and challenged DSEG to also compare its processes with those used by *other types* of organizations. "We realized that one objective of the Baldrige process was to *share* and *learn,* and we could learn from other people besides our direct competitors. This really stimulated our benchmarking thrust and made it successful," Cooney notes.

4. Teaming/Empowerment

"One element of Total Quality Management is *people involvement,*" says Borden. "The primary way we deploy quality policy up and down the organization is through the work of our many types of teams."

DSEG has virtually replaced the traditional hierarchical organizational chart with team charts. The teaming network starts at the very top—President Hank Hayes leads a Quality Improvement Team at the group level. Five members of this team act as leaders for each of the five improvement thrust teams. As of this writing, nearly 1,900 management and employee teams are active within DSEG.

5. Total Quality Integration

Initially, the purpose of the total quality thrust was to define the Baldrige criteria, to integrate them into DSEG's road map, and to deploy them throughout the organization. "We wanted to improve and to *continue to improve* at a faster rate than our competition was doing," Cooney says. "We planned to use the Baldrige criteria to do an annual assessment of how we were progressing on our road map. Having won the Award, we [will] now ensure than an annual assessment *continues* to take place."

MAKING THE MOST OF THE BALDRIGE PROCESS

The first year DSEG applied for the Baldrige Award, the Group had several people gather information, but that changed over the years. Since then, seven members of the Quality Improvement Teams have taken responsibility for the seven categories of the Baldrige criteria *(Leadership, Information and Analysis, Strategic Quality Planning, Human Resource Development and Management, Management of Process Quality, Quality and Operational Results,* and *Customer Focus and Satisfaction).*

"Hank Hayes, our president, took responsibility for category one—Leadership," notes Borden. "Other senior executives assumed responsibility for the other six. We had a team of four to five people who worked with them to write their portions of the application. Then Mike Cooney and I served as the overseers of the process. We were

Training: An Investment in Quality

Going through the Baldrige application process helped Texas Instruments' Defense Systems & Engineering Group gain a new awareness of the importance of employee training. "There was a time when we looked at training as something that was nice to do, but it was considered an expense," concedes Manager of Total Quality Management Joe Borden. "Today, however, because of our five thrusts and our interest in continuous improvement, our management looks at training as an *investment*. This includes training having to do with quality, such as Six Sigma (mentioned earlier), cycle time reduction, and business process management, as well as skills training. We now feel that in one year, a company will more than recover everything that it invests in training."

When DSEG began its initial quality training programs in 1982, top management was exposed to the teachings of such experts as Phil Crosby and Joseph Juran. After the higher-ups received their instruction, the training was cascaded down to other levels of management and employees. Over the past 10 years, quality training has changed dramatically at DSEG. "We still train our management first when everyone is to receive strategic training such as Six Sigma. However, we have evolved into training our natural teams together," explains Borden. "These teams, along with DSEG's suppliers and customers, are getting the same training simultaneously. All training is done internally by [the various groups'] own training organizations." Employees also receive "job enhancement" training, which includes literacy and basic skills training.

To gauge the effectiveness of the various training programs, DSEG managers have begun conducting job needs assessments. These are followed by an evaluation of the employees' skills to see whether there is a knowledge gap (between what employees need to know to work effectively in the various functions and what they actually do know). Whenever gaps are detected, management establishes and administers the required quality and job skills training programs in these areas.

the system integrators." Well over 100 people were involved in writing the application and implementing the improvement actions; Cooney and Borden edited and wrote the final application.

DSEG has enjoyed many positive results since the Group began using the Baldrige criteria. "Over the last five years, we have been able to cut the cost of the HARM missile in half for our customer. This is our largest program," Borden points out. "We have also made major improvements in cycle time. We have shipped 15,000 missiles in the last 10 years on that program, and have *never* missed a delivery. The reliability of that missile is 400 to 500 percent of the customer's specifications and continues to improve every year. We are seeing those kinds of results on most of our programs."

GET ON THE FIELD AND PLAY!

If you're interested in using the Baldrige criteria to improve *your* operation by integrating them into your company's quality process, you need to conduct an internal self-assessment based on the criteria. Then make a formal application immediately afterward, Cooney advises. "It's easy to sit on the sidelines and talk about how good you are, but the only way to *prove it* is to get on the field and play," he says. "Getting on the field and playing is making that formal application."

Borden stresses that "you shouldn't use an outside consultant to write your application for you. When you write the application, you come face-to-face with your weaknesses. If you have a consultant writing the application for you, you will miss a lot of learning opportunities."

One tip for success: Keep in mind that the criteria are universally applicable. "When you begin to understand that the Baldrige criteria are applicable to *any kind* of organization—service or otherwise—you are well along in working [with] the process and integrating it into your organization," Cooney concludes.

Xerox Corporation: A 1989 Winner

Through its comprehensive Leadership Through Quality process, Xerox regained marketplace strength, increased revenues, and won several quality awards—not the least of which was the Malcolm Baldrige National Quality Award, bestowed on the company in 1989.

The Xerox Corporation created the copier industry in 1959, when it introduced the first plain-paper copier. For the next 15 years, Xerox completely dominated the copier/duplicator business because it controlled the patents, and, therefore, the company had no real competition.

However, in the mid-1970s, Federal Trade Commission settlements required Xerox to open international access to key patents. Of course, this also opened the floodgates for the competition. Soon, Japanese companies targeted the low-priced copiers, while IBM and Eastman Kodak competed with the higher-end equipment.

Xerox's period of unchallenged market dominance was over. And the company knew it would have to assure truly superior products and services if it was to retain its edge. By taking its time and developing a proactive Leadership Through Quality process, Xerox not only regained marketplace strength, it also won several quality awards—including the Malcolm Baldrige National Quality Award, in 1989.

BENCHMARKING PROCESS REVEALS AREAS NEEDING IMPROVEMENT

"In 1979, Xerox manufacturing and development units began to try to understand why we were not more competitive in the marketplace," says Sam M. Malone, Jr., project manager, Corporate Communications at Xerox Corporation (Webster, NY). "So these units began a benchmarking process. For Xerox, benchmarking was a process of measuring all procedures and operations against the best *external*—not internal—standards," he explains.

"Benchmarking enabled us to get some insights into strategies and improvements we needed to make in order to be more competitive. For example, through the benchmarking process, we discovered that the Japanese were *selling* their copiers for what it cost Xerox to *manufacture* them." (This enabled the Japanese to control 40 percent of the copier/duplicator market by 1980.)

Benchmarking uncovered other inefficiencies at the company. "As a result of using benchmarks, we found that we had ten times as many suppliers as our Japanese competitors had. We also found that we employed basically twice the number of people and took twice as long to develop new products," Malone points out.

A STRATEGY TO REGAIN THAT CRITICAL COMPETITIVE EDGE

Xerox had been in a joint venture with Fuji Photo Films since 1962, but the division had not been competing effectively on the Japanese market. However, Fuji Xerox adopted a quality process, turned itself around, and won the Deming Award in 1980. David T. Kearns, then chairman and CEO of Xerox, was liaison officer to Fuji Xerox and had made over 20 trips to Japan. He noted this success and recognized that similar success was possible—and was definitely needed—throughout the corporation.

"At this time, Xerox was struggling with losing market shares, struggling with cost pressures, and struggling with not being competitive in the marketplace," recalls Malone. "So Mr. Kearns, having had experience with Fuji Xerox, said, 'Fuji is an allied industry with similar products. If a quality process worked for them, why won't it work for us?'"

This positive, determined attitude—along with the discoveries Xerox made while benchmarking—prompted the company to develop a process that would enable it to assure top quality and delivery and recapture its marketplace position. Here are the steps the company followed in its journey toward total improvement:

Form Quality of Work Life (QWL) Teams

In 1980, Xerox negotiated a contract with its manufacturing union that called for the exploration of a joint problem-solving process. "This process was designed to engage the production staff in ways to make the business more effective and to gather ideas for improvement," reports Malone.

"But those were basically stand-alone efforts in our Webster, New York manufacturing plant and were not related, not integrated, and certainly did not go broad-based across the organization."

Increase the Number of QWL Teams and Decrease the Number of Suppliers

In 1981, the number of Quality of Work Life Teams continued to grow in the manufacturing division. Xerox began reducing its production supplier base, which then numbered 5,000 suppliers.

Xerox also began to conduct seminars across the country for its suppliers to train them in statistical process and quality control. Eventually, fewer than 500 production suppliers were being used by the company.

Start Up Employee Involvement (EI) Groups in Product Development Areas

The following year, in 1982, the employee involvement process spread to the product development organizations in Webster and Henrietta, New York.

Implement the Just in Time (JIT) Process

In less than one year, in 1982, JIT at Xerox was recognized as saving the company $1 million in inventory costs.

Initiate a Quality Leadership Process

Early in 1983, 25 key senior corporate managers at Xerox met in their training center right outside of Washington, D.C. "This group became the designers of the quality process inside Xerox," Malone reports. "That process was titled, 'Leadership Through Quality.'"

This was a long-term process meant to change the way Xerox people worked and managed so they could *continuously improve* the way they met the requirements of their customers.

"There were some fundamental stakes in the ground put down at that meeting," explains Malone. These were the resolutions the group developed concerning Xerox's quality effort:

- It was to be a worldwide process.
- It would involve all employees.
- It would use a common approach to quality improvement and problem-solving.

- Every employee would be thoroughly trained.
- Training would cascade down through the organization, focusing on managers as the training conduits.

This strategy integrated existing QWL and EI teams into a more comprehensive, corporatewide, worldwide effort.

Plan the Quality Process Slowly and Carefully

"The management team spent around a year and a half developing our Leadership Through Quality process," explains Malone. "The old attitude had been, 'ready, fire, aim,' " he concedes. "This time, however, we were really taking care to 'ready, aim, and then fire.' And we didn't fire until we felt sure the aim was right."

With this in mind, the management team was certain of several factors as it worked on its plans:

The quality strategy was going to be a *process*, not a program. Xerox would not call its quality effort a *program*, because a program has a beginning and an end. "We would instead call it a *process*, because a process is ongoing," Malone stresses.

The company was making a *long-term* commitment. "We did not get sick overnight; therefore we did not expect that we would get well overnight," Malone asserts.

"We spent a lot of time researching existing approaches to quality," he continues. "We adopted approaches from others so that they would fit our culture and our needs. Once the elements were agreed upon, the training team designed a training program to meet those needs."

Develop a Specific Quality Policy and Identify Change Mechanisms Necessary to Fulfill It.

During its planning period, the executives developed the Xerox Quality Policy, which says:

Xerox is a quality company. Quality is the basic business principle for Xerox. Quality means providing our external and internal customers with innovative products and services that fully satisfy their requirements. Quality improvement is the job of every Xerox employee.

The management team recognized that fulfilling this policy's requirements would necessitate an enormous change in the Xerox culture. So they laid out a five-year strategy to accomplish this change and identified six change mechanisms they would use to support the cultural change being undertaken:

Management Behavior and Actions. Managers were to lead the change by practicing the principles of Leadership Through Quality *day in and day out.*

Transition Teams. These teams were to guide the changes and to make sure the implementation was consistent across the organization.

Standards and Measurements. These were to provide Xerox people with new ways of assessing and performing their work and solving problems, and it included a nine-step quality improvement process; competitive benchmarking; an emphasis on error prevention and doing things right the first time; and techniques for determining the cost of quality.

Training. Every Xerox staffer was to be given an understanding of Leadership Through Quality and a working knowledge of the tools and techniques for quality improvement. The training would be delivered in "family groups" consisting of a manager and the people who report directly to him or her. It was to include application of the newly learned tools on a work group project. Also, the training was to "cascade" downward throughout the organization.

Recognition and Rewards. To encourage and motivate Xerox people to practice the behaviors of Leadership Through Quality, some form of recognition was to be given. This could be in the form of a simple thank-you or a cash bonus.

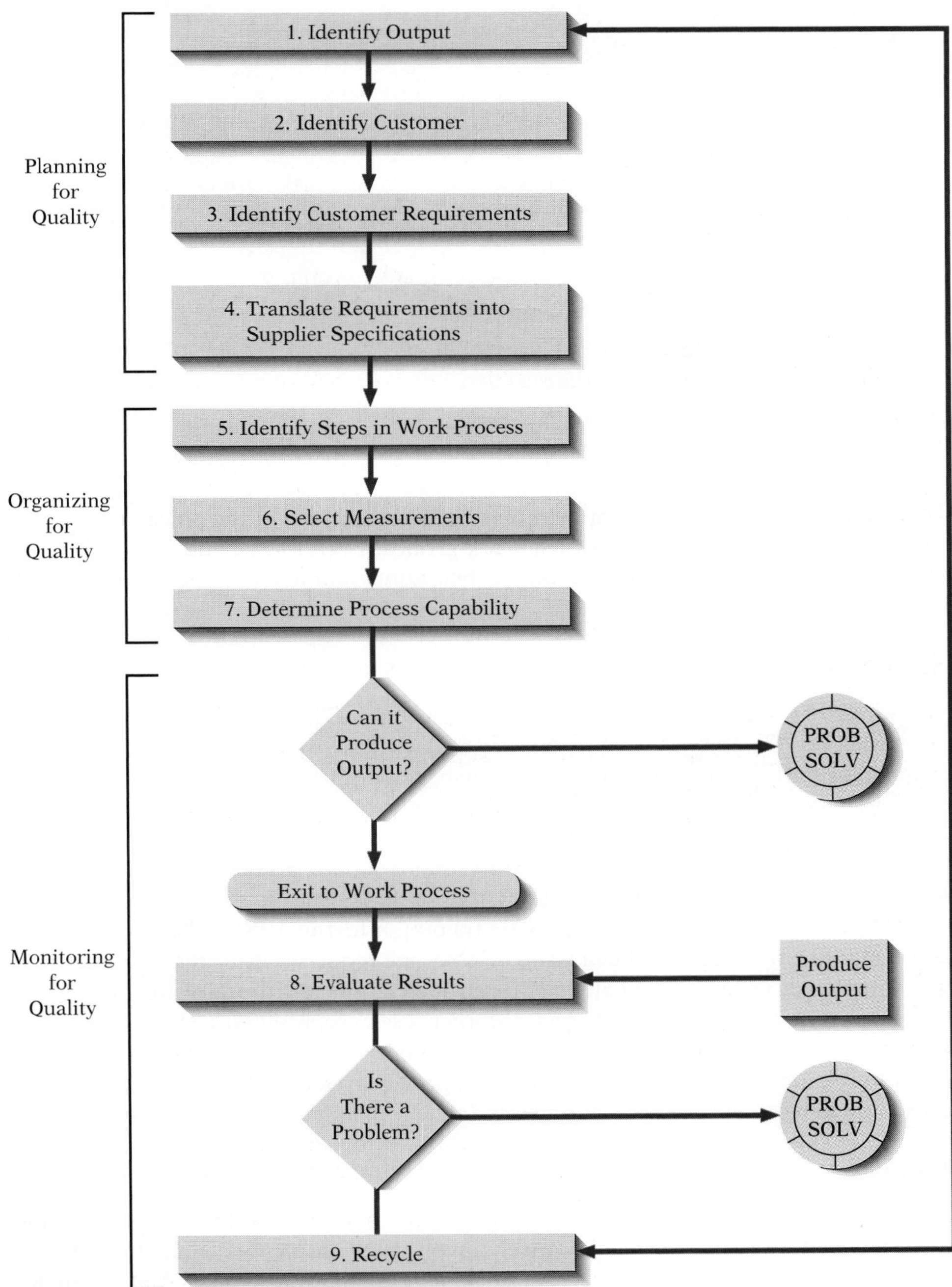

FIGURE A.2 Xerox Quality Improvement Process

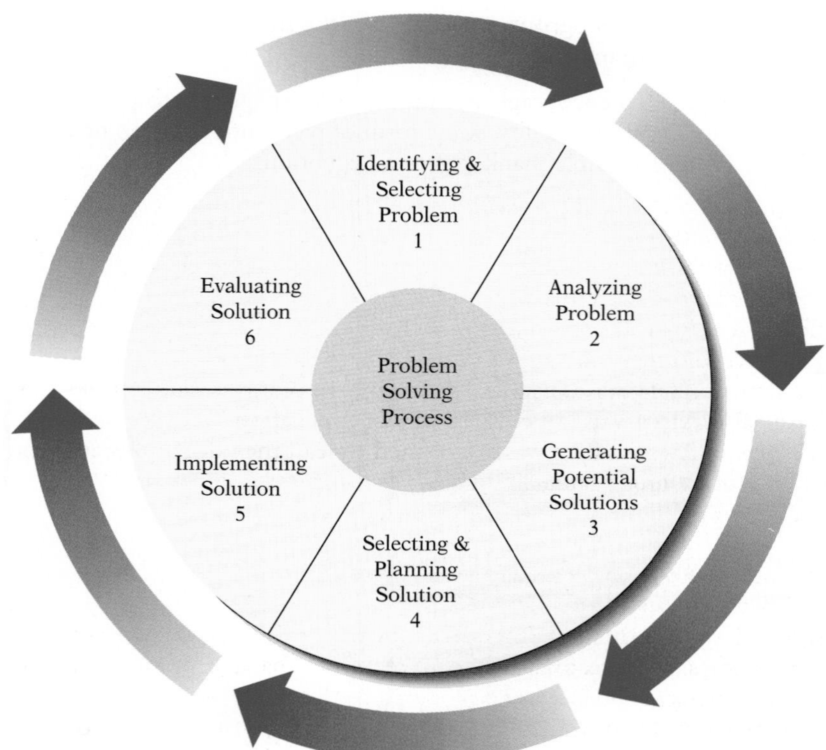

FIGURE A.3 Xerox Quality Improvement Process

Communication. All Xerox people were to be kept informed of the objectives and priorities of the corporation and of their work groups. Both formal and informal media were to be used, including films, company magazines and newsletters, and staff meetings.

Roll Out the Leadership Through Quality Process

"Early in 1984, we started the rollout of our Leadership Through Quality process," reports Malone. "Training started at the very top, with Mr. Kearns, the CEO, personally training his staff. From there, each level of management trained its staff and it cascaded down the line until every employee, worldwide, was trained. All employees were given a common set of tools to work with: a common language for quality, and a common approach through two models; the quality improvement process and the problem-solving process. (See Figures A.2 and A.3.)

"We completed our initial worldwide training effort in 1988, when every one of our 100,000 employees had been trained," Malone reports. "After the training effort was completed, we could pull any employee—an engineer from Holland, a designer from France, a service engineer from California, a sales representative from Texas, and a production worker from New York—into a conference room, and they would all be able to walk into that room and use the same process to tackle the business issues that caused them to come together," he asserts.

Continue To Increase the Number of Worldwide Problem-Solving Teams

Both the QWL and EI Teams were pulled into the mainstream. By the end of 1984, there were more than 300 teams actively involved in problem-solving. In 1985, all teams became known as Quality Improvement Teams. By 1986, 2,500 Quality Improvement Teams were solving problems worldwide.

INCREASED EFFECTIVENESS LEADS TO BALDRIGE APPLICATION—AND XEROX WINS

In 1987, an Act of Congress established the Malcolm Baldrige National Quality Award (see Module 1). Of course, Xerox had started its internal quality revolution in 1983—long before the establishment of the Baldrige Award. However, Xerox did not apply during the first year of the Award's existence. In late 1988, Xerox's senior management team made the decision to prepare an application for possible submission in 1989.

"It was not a foregone conclusion that we would actually submit the application," says Malone. "We positioned our efforts as a 'learning experience.' We said that 10 percent of our effort was to win the Baldrige and 90 percent was to learn and to educate ourselves. Further, we said that the application effort would cover our Xerox Business Products and Systems organization, which had 50,200 employees. Our second business, Xerox Financial Services, was not covered by our application."

A National Quality Award office was established to lead the effort. "Because the application covered such a broad range of functions, we formed a core team of 20 people whose job it was to do the research and then to write the application," Malone explains.

"The team consisted of a multifunctional cross section of the corporation. It included finance people, a union member, and people from personnel, sales, service, manufacturing and development, and others. Members varied as the team entered various stages of the process. Most team members were middle managers with an average of 20 years with the corporation.

"The team first had to learn what the Baldrige was about, and then draft our application. (It went through four drafts.) It was understood that if Xerox decided to submit the application, this team would also plan for a potential site visit. Following that, the team members were to deliver an assessment report to management based on their findings when writing the application and preparing for the site visit. This report would be the items that management would focus on for continuing the improvement of our internal quality process," Malone explains.

The decision was made in early April 1989 to submit the Xerox application. It was submitted on May 1, 1989. (Xerox was one of 40 companies submitting an application in 1989.)

On May 28, Xerox received notification that its application had been judged complete and was one of 23 in the manufacturing category to undergo a preliminary screening. This screening, conducted by a team of examiners, was based on an evaluation of 16 of the 44 questions responded to in the application.

On July 10, Xerox was notified that its application would move into the second stage of the review process, which meant that its entire application would now be evaluated.

Xerox was notified that it would receive a site visit. On August 17, 1989, the company was told that it had been selected to receive a site visit the week of September 17. A team of five members of the board of examiners conducted the site visit on Monday, Tuesday, and Wednesday of that week. They were accompanied by two observers representing the National Institute of Standards and Technology (NIST).

In those three days, the examiners visited a total of five different sites located in New York, Colorado, and California. Their task was to verify the contents of the application and to check the extent to which the company's quality efforts were deployed overall in the Business Products and Systems Organization. To accomplish this, the examiners talked with three different groups of employees. These groups were the following:

Category Teams

Groups of five to eight employees met with the examiners to answer specific questions on each of the seven categories covered in the Baldrige application.

Employee Involvement and Quality Improvement Teams

Examiners met with these teams to discuss their projects, processes, and results.

Individual Employees

"The examiners requested that they have lunch in the cafeteria unescorted during their visit," says Malone. "Examiners went through the cafeteria line and chose whom they would sit with. They would talk to the employees individually about the quality process, what they were doing to support it, and how they controlled their processes, among other significant factors.

"Many times, the examiners stopped people in the hall and talked to them or they got on an elevator and pushed the button for the floor they wanted," Malone notes. "They would get off the elevator, introduce themselves, and proceed to ask questions. They were free to wander anyplace they wanted to. All in all, they talked to over 425 Xerox employees during their three-day site visit."

Following their visit to Xerox, the examiners submitted their site-visit report to the panel of nine judges. The first week in October, the judges met to review all the site-visit reports and to select the recipients of the 1989 awards.

Of course, the rest was history: Xerox *did* win the 1989 Malcolm Baldrige National Quality Award. On November 2, 1989, at the Department of Commerce, President Bush presented the Award to Xerox's Business Products and Systems Unit and Milliken & Company. (The judges did not feel that any of the 1989 applicants in the service and small business categories met their stringent criteria, so no Awards were bestowed in these areas.)

THE "RACE FOR QUALITY" HAS NO FINISH LINE

According to Xerox President and CEO David Kearns, "The race for quality has no finish line." He reinforced that belief in his acceptance remarks at the Department of Commerce.

Kearns said, "Based on our findings during the application process, we have already made changes, and more will come in our ongoing quest for continuous quality improvement and customer satisfaction. This moment is but a milestone in the Xerox continuing quality drive."

After Xerox accepted its Award, the team that originally wrote the application and coordinated the site visit drafted its assessment report. It noted more than 500 areas for further improvement. The team also developed a set of 51 action considerations for management's review that would enable Xerox to advance its "race" for improved quality and increased customer satisfaction.

"The senior management team accepted this report and took ownership of it," says Malone. "Mr. Kearns is on record as saying that this report is worth millions of dollars to Xerox because it really sets down what we need to do over the long haul to substantially improve the corporation."

THE SUCCESS IS SHARED FAR AND WIDE

"The Baldrige Award was really created to do three things," explains Malone. These are:

1. To focus America's attention on the need for improved quality
2. To recognize organizations that had achieved outstanding results using quality improvement processes
3. To share their successful strategies with others

"We have been very open in our sharing process," Malone notes. "We have shared our ideas with more than 110,000 businesspeople across the United States since winning the Baldrige Award in 1989.

"In 1990, we averaged 35 calls a day. And in 1991, we averaged 25 calls a day. These calls range from requests for our CEO to talk at functions to questions on how we went about winning the Baldrige Award."

QUALITY HAS MANY REWARDS—HAPPY CUSTOMERS IS NUMBER ONE

"Since 1985, we've had a 41 percent improvement in the ratings our customers give us in regard to their satisfaction with our products and services," Malone reports. "We mail about 40,000 surveys a month to our customers and ask them to tell us how we are doing.

"In September 1990, we implemented the Xerox Total Satisfaction Guarantee, which basically says that if you buy a Xerox product and you are unhappy with it, for any reason, within the first three years of ownership, let us know and we will replace it free of charge. Obviously, if we didn't have a comfort level about the quality of our products and services, we could not enter into that kind of agreement," explains Malone.

Other benefits Xerox has enjoyed from its Leadership Through Quality process include:

Increased revenues: In 1990, revenues grew to $17.6 billion; earnings increased 11 percent.

Product kudos: Buyers Laboratory, Inc., named Xerox as having the "most outstanding product line of 1990."

Additional awards: In 1983, the Rank Xerox Venray manufacturing facility was given the CIMEI Quality Award by the Dutch government. The following year, the Rank Xerox Limited Micheldean manufacturing facility received the British Quality Award. Many more quality awards were given to affiliates abroad in the following years. Xerox won additional national quality awards in Mexico and Australia in 1990, bringing to *nine* the total number of national quality awards won since 1980 by Xerox operating companies worldwide.

THE "RACE WITHOUT A FINISH LINE" KEEPS ON GOING

"The number-one corporate objective is customer satisfaction," stresses Malone. "Xerox is preoccupied with the customer. The Baldrige process is valuable because it forces you to look at your company the way the *customer* sees it—not the way *you* think it is.

"The quality race is a very frustrating race," he concedes. "The further you go, the more you realize how far you still have to go. That is why our president and CEO Mr. Kearns said at the Baldrige Awards ceremony, 'we're in a race without a finish line.' You have to continue to tighten up your processes and to *continuously improve* if you are to remain competitive in today's global marketplace."

Motorola, Inc.: A 1988 Winner

Six Sigma Performance and Quality Systems Review teams helped this winning company to set zero-defects performance goals, train employees in how to meet those goals, and then keep its quality process on track so that it could move ever onward toward success.

Although Motorola, Inc. (Schaumburg, Ill.), had always had quality initiatives in place, the Baldrige-winning company realized that it needed to become even *more* aggressive in the area of world-class quality. Recognizing that "quality is in the eye of the customer," one area that Motorola chose to place special emphasis on was customer satisfaction.

"Previously, most of our quality efforts had dealt exclusively with product quality," reports Carlton Braun, vice president and director of the Motorola Management Institute. "However, other areas besides poor product quality can have a negative impact on customer satisfaction. For example, if we have a problem with our billing process that takes two or three months to straighten out, the customer is not going to be satisfied, even if the product works perfectly."

With this type of situation in mind, Motorola set a goal to instill its Total Customer Satisfaction (TCS) philosophy throughout the organization. To do that requires breaking down "silos."

According to Braun, silos are conceptual representations of what might be termed "departmental isolation." Most companies tend to operate under this silo concept, in which employees in each department are interested only in "polishing silo walls" (that is, making sure they work for the good of their own departments rather than for the good of the whole company).

Motorola's goal was to break down these silos and get employees to realize the importance of seeing the larger picture—and ultimately performing their jobs with the *whole process* in mind. "We wanted our people to cooperate with one another for support of total customer satisfaction," Braun explains.

IDENTIFYING SYSTEM WEAKNESSES BREAKS DOWN BARRIERS

Part of breaking down barriers involves addressing the "system" weaknesses that lead to so many problems. In most organizations, as has been demonstrated time and again, 20 percent of errors are caused by employees themselves (factors within their own control), while the other 80 percent are caused by the problems within the systems in which the employees work (issues for which management has responsibility).

In production, for example, problems beyond an operator's control might include such factors as the following:

- poorly designed assemblies
- incorrect parts being ordered or shipped by suppliers
- defective or damaged parts from suppliers
- machinery incapable of operating within control limits
- insufficient training

"In almost all cases, employees *want* to do a good job, so it is important to give them the tools to perform their jobs properly," Braun asserts.

THE SIX SIGMA SOLUTION SETS TIGHT PERFORMANCE PARAMETERS

One step Motorola has taken to address the issue of customer satisfaction is "Six Sigma Performance." Six Sigma Performance is a level of variation in a process measured in standard deviations from the mean and is defined as 99.9997 percent defect-free, or 3.4 defects per million parts produced.

While many companies limit their process improvement efforts to monitoring production control charts, Six Sigma Performance, again, extends beyond production quality. "It addresses variation in performance of *all* kinds," emphasizes Braun. Not only that, but it also addresses performance in all areas of the company, including Order Entry, Sales, Purchasing, Manufacturing, Engineering/Design, Quality Control, and so on.

IT STARTS WITH COMPREHENSIVE EMPLOYEE TRAINING

To kick off the process, the company's training department developed a step-by-step process designed to promote understanding and implementation of Six Sigma Performance throughout the entire organization. All employees going through the training learn the concepts and tools that help them reduce variation in the work they perform.

The first module of training takes one to three days to complete, depending on the level of the employees in the organization who are taking the training. After training, employees work in teams in their departments and across functions to utilize what they have learned, which should include the following:

To understand the system in which they are working by mapping the system step-by-step.

To look for places where variations/errors occur. In many cases, simply mapping the work process itself helps employees to spot these variations.

To determine the cause of the problems. This may include lack of proper tools, improper training, or an incorrect system, to name a few.

To reduce the cycle time of a process as much as possible. "If you have a lengthy cycle time, you have more chance for errors than if you have a short cycle time," Braun notes. A reduction in cycle time, then, leads to an improvement in quality.

Training employees in the use of this procedure is one thing; making sure they use it on a regular basis—instead of reverting to "Band-Aid" solutions—is quite another. Motorola addresses this issue in two ways:

Providing Additional Training Opportunities for Employees

Employees have the opportunity to attend additional training programs covering statistical process control (SPC), design for manufacturing, design for assembly, short-cycle-time manufacturing, JIT, and other areas. "These programs help support Six Sigma Performance initiatives," explains Braun.

Manager Training in Coaching Skills

Managers receive training in the importance of coaching their employees. "It's easy for managers to get caught up in the day-to-day activities of their work and forget the importance of coaching employees in reducing variations," he says. "But when you find a manager who is committed to coaching employees in these procedures, you find employees who are ready, willing, and able to use the procedures," Braun notes.

REVIEWS KEEP THE SYSTEM GOING STRONG

A company can have the best quality system in the world. But if it fails to keep the process on course, its quality effort is doomed to failure. To keep *its* process on track, Motorola established a highly effective review system.

"One of the provisions of the award was that, in winning, a company share its non-proprietary systems with other companies," says Scott Shumway, vice president and director of Quality for Motorola's Semiconductor Sector (Phoenix, Ariz.). "We've done that with a series of presentations to customers and suppliers; we're always happy to tell what works for us."

"Motorola's quality progress started when we saw a need for much more intensive training in quality at all levels," Shumway explains. "This led to formation of our Motorola Corporate Quality Council, or MCQC, which directs quality efforts throughout the company." The Quality Systems Review is one significant tool that helped Motorola advance its zero-defect, Total Customer Satisfaction philosophy and receive one of the first Baldrige Awards in 1988.

QUALITY TEAMS CONDUCT THE SYSTEMS REVIEWS

Motorola's Quality Systems Review is an internal audit program in which teams of five people from the MCQC visit divisions and spend a week talking with people there and measuring operations against stated criteria.

The teams look at 10 sections or factors that Shumway says are remarkably similar to the points looked at by the administrators who bestow the Malcolm Baldrige Award.

Motorola's basic 10 factors (with assigned weights) are the following:

1. Quality System Management (15 Percent)

"Here, we look at the leadership, style, and effectiveness of the management team in the area of quality," Shumway explains.

2. Product Development Control (10 Percent)

This area is based on the Six Sigma process. As explained earlier, Sigma is a statistical unit of measurement that describes the distribution about the mean of a process or procedure. "A process or procedure that can achieve plus or minus Six Sigma capability can be expected to have a defect rate of no more than a few parts per million," Shumway says.

"In statistical terms, this approaches zero defects—and it's our goal to achieve this level of quality in *everything* we do."

3. Purchasing Material Control (10 Percent)

This looks at the level of quality being supplied by vendors and the systems in place to measure vendor quality.

4. Process Development and Operational Controls (10 Percent)

"This is aimed at the entire manufacturing flow process," says Shumway. "The critical question is, 'Is it working?' "

5. Quality Data Programs (5 Percent)

Are all necessary data available? Is this real information and not just databases? How is the information used — as a tool to improve quality?

6. Special Studies (10 Percent)

How sophisticated are the process methods? Are they state-of-the-art?

7. Quality Measurement and Control Equipment (5 Percent)

"This governs all our standards and calibrations," says Shumway. "Is the system in place and is it properly maintained?"

8. Human Resources Involvement (5 Percent)

"The team tries to determine whether the people are capable and properly trained," says Shumway. "We want to know if the work force can do the job assigned."

This area is particularly important to Motorola, Shumway explains, because it's a recognized national leader in the participative management process, with people down the ranks involved in decision-making — and sharing in the rewards of correct decisions.

9. Customer Satisfaction Assessment (20 Percent)

All organizations must have methods and systems in place to assess customers' satisfaction with their shipments.

10. Software Quality Assurance (10 Percent)

"This was a later addition to our list," notes Shumway. "We're getting more and more sophisticated in software related to quality. We spent several years getting people prepared in this area before we tailored it into a score. We've developed the system to the point that we can see at a glance trends against goals, cost of nonconformance, quality of delivery, service to customers, and so on, complete with a summary."

Putting it all together, the division being examined knows how it is doing. "If its score is below the satisfactory mark, the division knows that it needs corrective action," he says.

REVIEW TEAM MEMBERS SELECTED ON A ROTATING BASIS

Motorola's divisions can expect a Quality Service Review every two years. The corporate council puts together a special team for each review, and the five members are selected from various parts of the company. There's no one committee that does all the checking, Shumway notes.

"We thought about having one fixed team do all the reviews, but decided against it," he explains. "It's better to have people rotated so that every quality director gets an opportunity to work on a team. We also are careful about selecting leaders of each team. No one can be the leader without having participated in Quality Service Reviews in the past.

"At the end of the week of review, the general manager and his or her staff have a session with the team. They go over the review. The strengths and weaknesses are discussed, and recommendations are given to local management as to what improvements have to be made," he says.

Results of the survey are reported to the steering committee, the MCQC, at the next meeting. Results aren't negotiable; what the team sees is what is reported. At the MCQC meeting, the division manager of the review division reports on what corrective action his or her organization will be taking.

CORPORATE CHAMPIONSHIP CREATES QUALITY CHAMPS

"The Quality Service Review is championed by the corporation," Shumway reports. "That's a key point that we've made to other corporations as we've shared our experiences under the provisions of the Malcolm Baldrige Award.

"Of course, there are some considerations that are proprietary," he concedes. "But for the most part, we're open as to what we do and how it works.

"Our system has worked well for us," Shumway continues. "Over the years, it gives us uniformity and consistency. Corporate goals are driven down through the organization, and that's a powerful quality tool," he concludes.

QUALITY MODULE 3

Selected Baldrige Winners from the Services Companies Award Category

AT&T Universal Card Services: A 1992 Winner

Many companies have used the Baldrige Award process as a turnaround tool or as a validation vehicle. But can it be used to *design a business* from the beginning? Can a start-up service company achieve success simply by following the Baldrige criteria? This 1992 winner did just that—and in under three years, catapulted itself to second place in its industry in total number of credit card accounts and customer dollars spent.

Following the Baldrige path has been very rewarding for AT&T's Universal Card Services (UCS). In just two and one-half years, the financial "youngster" grew from a start-up team of 35 people to a profitable multibillion-dollar concern with 2,500 associates.

The AT&T UCS business unit is headed by President and CEO Paul G. Kahn. Ninety percent of its work is done at UCS's Jacksonville, Florida, headquarters. The remaining associates are located at the collections operation in Houston and the payment processing center in Columbus, Ga. Two thirds of the associates are in customer-contact positions.

"Our quality approach has three major components," explains Rob Davis, vice president and chief quality officer at the Jacksonville headquarters. "First, we have always had a very strong focus on *customer delight;* we really have an obsession with delighting our customers," Davis stresses. "We insist on 'delighting' customers as opposed to 'satisfying' them.

"The second component we focus on is *delighting the associates (employees) who work here,*" he continues. "And the third component is *continuous improvement in both of these areas.*"

DELIGHTING EXTERNAL CUSTOMERS

How does UCS go beyond merely satisfying its external customers? On a daily basis, the group uses more than a hundred process measures to evaluate customer delight. These process measures include factors such as the following:

Did the associate answer the phone in a timely fashion?
Was the call handled accurately with the correct information given?
What was the cycle time on the credit cards issued?

Excerpted from *Quality Assurance Bulletin,* Number 1608, April 25, 1993, and from Allyn and Bacon's *Profiles of Malcolm Baldrige Award Winners,* originally published by the Bureau of Business Practice as *Award Winning Quality: Strategies from the Winners of the Malcolm Baldrige National Quality Award* (BBP © 1992). Used with permission of the Bureau of Business Practice (BBP), a division of the Business and Professional Group of Paramount Publishing, a Paramount Communications Company.

Are the outgoing letters to customers accurate?
Are the billing statements accurate?

"We have a group that meets every morning at 8:30 to look at the measurements and to determine how we performed on each of them the day before," says Davis. "Then they look at the diagnostic measurements and use these to make course corrections. They work on the issues immediately." The results are reported to the entire business operation every day so that everyone always knows how the entire operation is performing.

Everyone in the business—from the CEO to the last associate hired—uses the same set of quality measures and, as a team, is paid a bonus based on the results: When they meet the daily measurements, everyone earns a bonus; when they don't meet them, everybody loses. The results are reflected in the associates' compensation each quarter. (The average bonus earned per associate last year was $2,200.)

UCS has also established some quality measures for its suppliers. UCS uses many of the same measures with its suppliers that it uses in its own shop. For instance, two of UCS's suppliers are telemarketing companies, so the same measures that are important to UCS's telephone people are also important to the supplier's telemarketing people.

Every morning, UCS examines the status of its supplier measures at meetings that are routinely attended by two of its largest suppliers. If there is a problem, the person responsible for the particular area reports it, suggests a probable cause or causes, and discusses any solutions that have been proposed or are being implemented.

GAUGING EXTERNAL CUSTOMER SATISFACTION

To gauge the satisfaction level of its external customers, UCS calls over 4,000 customers every month and asks them for input on the interactions they've had with the company. "We do this to get specific feedback about particular activities," explains Davis. "For example, we call customers who phoned our 800 number. We ask them whether we met their expectations and their needs. Then we give this feedback to the people who do the job."

UCS asks customers several different questions. "We ask them whether we *met*, *failed*, or *exceeded* their expectations," Davis points out. "We also ask them to rate the call as *good*, *excellent*, *fair*, or *poor*. Since almost everyone who has a credit card has more than one card, we have a good point of reference. We can ask people whether the service we provide is worse than, equal to, or better than [that of the other card services]. Whenever people tell us that it is worse than or equal to [others], we ask followup questions that start, 'What would it take to be better than. . . ?' By doing this, we get specific information about what we could do that would delight this customer."

In addition to taking daily process measurements and calling customers every month, UCS uses what it calls its Customer Satisfier Model. "Most people would refer to this as a 'customer attribute study' in that we believe we have determined 98 percent of what it takes to make a customer delighted in the credit card business," says Davis. "From that, we have developed eight key attributes, or satisfiers, as well as secondary and tertiary satisfiers. The satisfiers include factors such as *price* and *customer service*. Each is weighted so that we know which is most important." UCS has also worked with customers to determine the importance they place on each satisfier. "This helps us focus on measuring the things that really *are* important to customers, as opposed to measuring the things we only *think* are important to them," Davis points out.

DELIGHTING INTERNAL CUSTOMERS

How does UCS delight its *internal* customers? One surefire way to do it at any organization is to give staffers the knowledge, resources, responsibility, and recognition they need to put more into and get more out of their jobs. With this in mind, UCS takes the following steps:

Encourage Teamwork

"We have a very loose definition of teams," Davis points out. "Many companies have quality improvement teams or continuous improvement teams. We have some teams that gather together to solve a particular issue which they may solve in one or two meetings and then disband.

"We have other teams that are process teams. These teams work with a particular set of tools to improve—in a long-term way—a process that is important to our business." These teams are usually cross-functional.

Teams' accomplishments are always recognized at UCS. "We focus on acknowledging the outcomes of teams and what they are able to accomplish, and we celebrate outcomes with the teams," Davis notes.

Train Teams According to Individual Needs

"Some of the teams are going to be together only a few days or a week, so they may not need help with process work," says Davis. "Other teams are ready for that type of training. We found that it works better to provide training when they are ready for it and can go out and use it immediately."

Solicit Associate Suggestions

"We have a very active suggestion program that is focused on the fact that the associates making the suggestions are the real customers here," Davis reports. "In 1992, we received over 7,500 suggestions from our employees.

"We believe that what makes the suggestion program work is the same thing that makes the rest of the business work: We have a strict set of measurements for it," he adds. Within 24 hours of submitting a suggestion, an associate is to be told the suggestion has been received. Then within 48 hours, the suggestion is to be placed in the hands of a review manager. Within two weeks, the review manager is to get an answer on it and get back to the associate. If at the end of two weeks, it appears that it will take longer to get an answer, a longer than two-week commitment must be negotiated with the associate. "We follow that up," Davis stresses. "Nothing gets lost. We keep the person who made the suggestion informed along the way as to what is happening with the suggestion. In some cases, the associate contributes more information or possible solutions to the review manager. This is a good way for people to participate in the business."

Have a "Meeting of the Minds"

Another way UCS associates can get involved in the business is through a program called Meeting of the Minds. "This is a session where our senior executives sit down with up to 10 associates for an open dialogue," says Davis. "We do at least one or two of these a week over breakfast, lunch, or dinner. It is a chance to keep senior people close to the business and it opens up a great dialogue."

Empower Employees to Take Responsibility for Customer Satisfaction

UCS phone associates are empowered to take whatever actions they feel are necessary when card members need help. As a result, associates have had an opportunity to troubleshoot some unique problems.

In one case, a stranded tourist in Paris called collect to say that her card had been "eaten by the ATM" on a Saturday afternoon. The card member was broke, scheduled to leave the next day, and desperate. While the customer stayed on the phone, the UCS associate called the U.S. embassy, arranged for a limo to carry the traveler to the one bank still open in Paris, and authorized an emergency cash advance.

Another call was from a desperate husband whose wife, suffering from Alzheimer's disease, had vanished. The police had not been able to find her and the husband hoped they could use her Universal Card to trace her. The UCS associate placed a hold on the account and arranged to be called personally if there was any attempted activity. One week later the card was used and the associate conferenced the woman's husband, doctor, and the police. The missing woman was found and helped home.

Provide Excellent Benefits

Benefits such as fully paid tuition for undergraduate or graduate work (whether or not the course is job related), quality childcare alternatives for associates' children, and a free 24-hour, on-site health club open to associates and their spouses help UCS employees maintain a high level of delight. "Associate delight is a commitment by our organization that any place we operate will be the best place to work," Davis emphasizes. "Therefore, it is one of those things we have to attend to constantly."

Conduct Telephone Surveys to Gauge Associate Satisfaction

It is critical to talk to employees about what makes them happy—or *un*happy. "Originally, we did an extensive survey once a year to get feedback on how well we were doing in particular areas," Davis recalls. "But we determined that once a year was not often enough—so now we call a sampling of employees at their homes every month to see how they are doing." As a result of these surveys, UCS found that

96 percent of associates say that the work they do is important and worthwhile. That is 21 points above the benchmark of 75 UCS found in other companies.

88 percent of associates feel that the UCS reward and recognition programs are effective.

87 percent of associates feel that the managers at UCS will try to resolve problems identified through the employee opinion survey. That's double the U.S. business norm.

THE BALDRIGE CONNECTION

A focus on external and internal customer delight coupled with an emphasis on the Baldrige process has helped UCS create its highly successful business. The company has used the Baldrige process since its inception in 1990. Several months after its start-up, UCS had some qualified Baldrige examiners do 100 interviews around the organization. Then UCS used that information to develop its strategic business plan.

At AT&T there is a Chairman's Quality Award process that mirrors the Baldrige process. It uses the same criteria, site visits, and scoring as the Baldrige Award. (AT&T uses the Baldrige criteria to evaluate its businesses each year. Those business units that meet the standards get the Chairman's Quality Award. The Chairman's Award process is used to select the AT&T business unit that will apply for the Baldrige Award.) "Within our first year, we decided to take the information we had gathered and write an application for the Chairman's Award," says Davis. This gave UCS valuable feedback from people outside the organization. This feedback was used to develop a gap list, which determined what things UCS needed to work on as a business.

In 1991 (its second year in business), UCS completed another Baldrige application and involved a few more people. In 1992, UCS decided to involve many *more* people in gathering information. "We had at least one person from each functional area on what we called the Business Improvement Team," explains Davis. "We assigned each person on the team different sectional responsibilities for the application. Their job was to collect information from the rest of the business and then write their piece of the application. Vice presidents, middle managers, and [first-line] managers all participated on the team, and some associates were involved in reviewing the application and giving feedback on it."

At first, the information was gathered with no attempt to constrain the number of pages, although only 75 pages are allowed by the Baldrige application. "Once we had pulled all that together, two of us were sequestered away for a couple of weeks and worked to ensure that the wording and sentence structure sounded as though they were written by one person," says Davis. "So in 1992, we submitted our first application for the Baldrige Award—and won."

UCS is deriving many positive results from the Baldrige process. "One benefit is that it helped us define our attributes," says Davis. "As I said earlier, we had identified the eight things it takes to satisfy our customers. We now lead the credit card business in all eight of those attributes. We have moved to this position over time; we started out strong, but because we used the Baldrige process, we also identified and improved areas where we were weaker. When we did our Chairman's Quality Award process, for example, we studied our feedback in great detail and determined that there were 119 gaps in our business. We assigned people to be responsible for those gaps. We gave a priority level to the 119 gaps and then they started to work on closing them. The good news is that in one year, we closed over 90 of them. The other good news is that we keep adding things to the list because we keep finding things to work on."

THE TEN MOST WANTED

In order to prioritize the improvements that need to take place, UCS people developed a "10 most wanted" list. "This is a list of the 10 quality improvements we want to make next," Davis explains. There are 10 slats on each of the "most wanted" boards scattered about the building. Each slat lists a needed improvement area and has an "owner" who is responsible for correcting it. "As the improvements are made, we ceremoniously retire them," he notes.

"Not only do we have a list for the business now but we also have one for each of our functional areas and some of the subfunctional areas," Davis continues. "We also have an 'apprehended' list of the things we have improved. At UCS's quarterly business meetings, we celebrate successes, retiring those most wanted items. The retired slat is the trophy that is given to the person or team who retires it. The slats are now hanging in their offices or sitting on their desks."

SOME ADVICE FROM A BALDRIGE WINNER

Here are some tips that Davis says helped UCS to become both a Baldrige winner and highly successful in its industry: "Work hard at keeping your business focused on improvement, and use the Baldrige template as an *improvement* mechanism rather than an award mechanism," he stresses. "Many people lose sight of that. You should use it to identify gaps—places where your business is weak—and then you should strengthen those spots. The Baldrige application asks you all the right questions. It causes you to look at your business with a keen eye.

"The other thing I would say is that you really have to *keep at it.* I think this is true of most things in the quality arena. It's not a situation where you can plant a seed, leave, and come back a year later and harvest. Rather, you need to attend to it pretty constantly. We found this to be true in the areas of both associate and customer delight.

"The Baldrige template is a good tool to improve productivity and customer focus, and I believe it works: It is good for American business," Davis concludes.

The Ritz-Carlton® Hotel Company: A 1992 Winner

Although two service companies may receive a Baldrige Award each year, only one such organization—Federal Express—actually won during the first four years the Award was bestowed. However, in 1992, two service companies captured the coveted MBNQA. In this article, we'll provide one of these service category winners—the first hotel to win the Award.

How did a hotel firm merit one of the 1992 Baldrige Awards given in the service category? From the start, the Ritz-Carlton has focused on providing excellent service to its customers. In fact, it trains employees to anticipate guests' wishes *before they are even spoken*.

In 1983, W.B. Johnson Properties (Atlanta) acquired the U.S. rights to the Ritz-Carlton trademark, a name that has been associated with luxury hotels for nearly 100 years. The Ritz-Carlton Hotel Company now manages 23 business and resort hotels in the United States and 2 in Australia; 20 of these hotels have been opened since the acquisition.

The quality efforts of the Ritz-Carlton are led by President and Chief Operating Officer Horst Schulze, along with 13 senior executives who make up its steering committee. Corporate Director of Quality Patrick Mene is a member of this committee, which doubles as the senior quality management team. It meets weekly to review the quality of the company's products and services.

Since the Ritz-Carlton's focus has always been the prestigious travel consumer, it turned to industry watchers such as AAA and Mobil to learn what customers expect in a luxury hotel. Senior management condensed these requirements into some key basics that have become known as the Gold Standards. "There are four components to the Gold Standards," explains Devan Banks, assistant director of Quality for the Ritz-Carlton Hotel Company. These components are:

1. The Mission Statement

The Ritz-Carlton Hotel is a place where the genuine care and comfort of our guests is our highest mission. We pledge to provide the finest personal service and facilities for our guests, who will always enjoy a warm, relaxed, yet refined ambience. The Ritz-Carlton experience enlivens the senses, instills well-being, and fulfills even the unexpressed wishes and needs of our guests.

2. The Ritz-Carlton Motto

We are ladies and gentlemen serving ladies and gentlemen.

"That motto tries to instill an extra level of pride in the company and in the work we are doing," says Banks. "With the country moving more into service industries, that's important for all of us. We are using the lessons we learned in striving for the Baldrige Award not only to help us improve the quality of our services but also to try to change the mind-set of the hotel business as a whole."

3. The Three Steps of Service

Which are composed of

1. **A warm and sincere greeting.** Hotel employees are instructed to address their guests by name as they are greeting them (if and when possible).

Quality Assurance Bulletin, Number 1608, April 25, 1993. BBP

2. **Anticipation of and compliance with guests' needs.**
3. **A fond farewell.** Hotel employees are instructed to give their guests a warm good-bye and, when doing so, to use the guests' names (if and when possible).

4. The Ritz-Carlton Basics

"These are the 20 key issues that drive the company," Banks explains. (Please see items listed at the end of the article.) "They cover everything from the fact that any employee that receives a guest complaint 'owns' that complaint to customers' expectations that employees will always use proper vocabulary and [be] well groomed. Even safety issues and environmental issues are included.

These 'Gold Standards' are printed on a trifold laminated card that is carried by all employees to help them understand and use these steps in their interactions with customers. Company studies prove that practicing these standards is paying dividends to our customers and, ultimately, to the Ritz-Carlton."

EMPLOYEE TRAINING IS EXTENSIVE

The Ritz-Carlton selects its employees very carefully, and then orients and trains them to follow the Gold Standards. "We recognized from the beginning that our strength was in the [positive] attitudes of our people, which could be fostered by careful employee selection and proper training. This helped us win the Baldrige Award," Banks says.

"Our employees are not just here to check people in or to make the beds. They are here primarily to *serve our guests,*" he stresses. With that in mind, all employees—from general managers to dishwashers—attend a two-day orientation program that emphasizes caring service. Part of the training focuses on the importance of serving both the external *and* the internal customer.

After this initial training program, employees are placed in their specific work areas, where they are trained by departmental trainers in the various technical aspects of their jobs. Each employee is then certified in his or her particular position as part of the Company's training/certification program.

On a daily basis, each department has a "lineup," a short 10- to 15-minute segment used to "reenergize" employees and reinforce their training. "We get the employees together just before they come on their shift," says Banks. "Most of our training is done in these lineup sessions. We give our employees standardized capsules of information on a regular basis."

Each hotel has its own full-time training manager whose primary responsibility is conducting the initial two-day orientations, held weekly, as well as providing a follow-up orientation three weeks after the initial orientation. Each hotel also has a quality leader who is in charge of driving the quality effort and facilitating team activities at the hotel level, including departmental strategic-planning and problem-solving teams. These people are trained in quality management skills and in the Ritz-Carlton's TQM strategy. They work closely with their hotel's senior managers to drive the fundamentals of quality throughout the organization.

THREE KEYS TO BALDRIGE SUCCESS

1992 was the second year in which the Ritz-Carlton applied for the Baldrige Award. The Company already had a strong head start toward qualifying: It had always empowered employees and trained them to *understand its quality mission* and *make it their personal mission* in all their interactions with hotel guests. Here are some steps that further assisted the Ritz-Carlton in its Baldrige bid:

Preparation

The Ritz-Carlton's leaders selected a seasoned hotel general manager, Pat Mene, to head their quality effort. Over the next two years, Mene went to school to learn quality terminology and to understand the Baldrige criteria. He then became the driving force in the quality effort and was one of the principal writers of (the Baldrige application) document. The Company also brought in an outside consultant to understand how everything it did fit into the Baldrige criteria. "These two factors—along with the senior management group at the corporate level and the quality leaders in the hotels—really drove us along," Banks says.

Documentation

Documenting your operation is a critical part of the Baldrige application process. "To help in the documenting process, we assigned topics to data collectors who worked out of our central office," says Banks. "The data collectors were from different hotels. Each data collector wrote up his or her own individual documentation. As a final step, they all came together to rewrite the document so that it flowed as though one person had written it.

"A lot of the things the Baldrige auditors asked for we had already measured very well, so it was easy to access the information. We explained to the examiners during their site visit that it is the Gold Standards that really drive the Company."

Process Orientation

The Ritz-Carlton at first found it difficult to correlate its service functions with the Baldrige criteria, which seemed more applicable to manufacturing. "The criteria can make it difficult for a service company to apply," Banks says. "On the other hand, things worked out well, because [the application process] gave us a chance to get a different perspective on how quality comes about. When you think about it, there *is* a lot

Measuring Customer Satisfaction

"Customer satisfaction is a really big issue with us," says Devan Banks, assistant director of Quality for the Ritz-Carlton. "Up until the last two years, we measured satisfaction by having guests fill out comment cards. Usually, we got two ends of the spectrum: Either customers wanted to tell us how happy they were with their stay or to tell us about problems they encountered.

"However, these extremes did not provide a good cross section of what guests were experiencing. So we've implemented quarterly guest surveys. These written surveys are handed out during a specified three-day interval each quarter to all arriving guests in each of our hotels," Banks explains. "The idea is to get a companywide picture of what our guests are experiencing. We also analyze the surveys by individual hotels to see what the guests at [each] hotel are experiencing." The four-page survey forms are given to guests with a self-addressed envelope so that the forms may be sent directly to the Ritz-Carton's president. Guests are given the option of identifying themselves.

If a guest has had a problem, the hotel is notified so that the general manager can respond to and resolve it immediately. The 25 hotels have up to 100,000 customer interactions a day. Every one of these interactions must be carried out correctly, otherwise customer dissatisfaction may result. "Our goal is to eliminate problems as fast as we can," Banks stresses.

The Ritz-Carton tracks defects daily to determine which problems may be occurring in patterns. This information is reported in Daily Quality Production Reports. All departments receive these reports and use them as an early warning of potential problems. The data are then analyzed quarterly to pinpoint areas of greatest concern. "The chief benefit of the surveys and the defect reports is that they give our senior management team specific targets to use when they go out to examine a hotel or to work on companywide problems," says Banks. "Wherever we spot a problem, we use teams to determine the root cause, develop a solution, and implement [remedies] as appropriate."

of manufacturing going on in a hotel, whether its 'manufacturing' a dinner, cleaning a guest room, or checking in a guest. We realized how process oriented service is and *should be*."

BIG BENEFITS OF THE BALDRIGE PROCESS

The Baldrige examiners visited nine hotels in all, plus two international sales offices. One benefit the Ritz-Carlton enjoyed from the Baldrige process came when the Company let employees know that they were going to have site visits at some of their hotels.

"With the announcement of the site visits, it was like a grand opening for every one of our hotels all over again. You can't imagine all the excitement," Banks says. "We had anticipated that employees would shy away from talking to the examiners during the site visits, but we had employees *begging* to be asked questions. They wanted to meet the examiners and tell them what we are doing as a company."

The Ritz-Carton Basics*

1. The Credo will be known, owned, and energized by all employees.
2. Our motto is: "We are Ladies and Gentlemen serving Ladies and Gentlemen". Practice teamwork and "lateral service" to create a positive work environment.
3. The three steps of service shall be practiced by all employees.
4. All employees will successfully complete Training Certification to ensure they understand how to perform to The Ritz-Carlton standards in their position.
5. Each employee will understand their work area and Hotel goals as established in each strategic plan.
6. All employees will know the needs of their internal and external customers (guests and employees) so that we may deliver the products and services they expect. Use guest preference pads to record specific needs.
7. Each employee will continuously identify defects (Mr. BIV) throughout the Hotel.
8. Any employee who receives a customer complaint "owns" the complaint.
9. Instant guest pacification will be ensured by all. React quickly to correct the problem immediately. Follow-up with a telephone call within twenty minutes to verify the problem has been resolved to the customer's satisfaction. Do everything you possibly can to never lose a guest.
10. Guest incident action forms are used to record and communicate every incident of guest dissatisfaction. Every employee is empowered to resolve the problem and to prevent a repeat occurance.
11. Uncompromising levels of cleanliness are the responsibility of every employee.
12. "Smile—We are on stage." Always maintain positive eye contact. Use the proper vocabulary with our guests. (Use words like - "Good Morning," "Certainly," "I'll be happy to" and "My pleasure").
13. Be an ambassador of your Hotel in and outside of the work place. Always talk positively. No negative comments.
14. Escort guests rather than pointing out directions to another area of the Hotel.
15. Be knowledgeable of Hotel information (hours of operation, etc.) to answer guest inquiries. Always recommend the hotel's retail and food and beverage outlets prior to outside facilities.
16. Use proper telephone etiquette. Answer within three rings and with a "smile." When necessary, ask the caller, "May I place you on hold." Do not screen calls. Eliminate call transfers when possible.
17. Uniforms are to be immaculate; Wear proper and safe footwear (clean and polished), and your correct name tag. Take pride and care in your personal appearance (adhering to all grooming standards).
18. Ensure all employees know their roles during emergency situations and are aware of fire and life safety response processes.
19. Notify your supervisor immediately of hazards, injuries, equipment or assistance that you need. Practice energy conservation and proper maintenance and repair of Hotel property and equipment.
20. Protecting the assets of a Ritz-Carlton Hotel is the responsibility of every employee.

*© The Ritz-Carlton Hotel Company

ADVICE TO OTHER COMPANIES

What advice would Banks pass along to other companies that are interested in applying for the Baldrige Award? "I think that [the Baldrige application process] is one of the best self-tests you can take," he stresses. "This is the advice that Mr. Schulze has given us. He said that 'even if you don't apply for the Baldrige, just going through the application and answering those questions will give you great insight into how your company actually works and what you can do to improve it.' "

A lot of companies would like to find a book that would tell them how to put a successful quality process into place, but it's not that easy, Banks suggests.

"You cannot simply buy a recipe and put it into place. You must create quality processes of your own," he stresses. "The Baldrige [process] played a prime role in steering us in that direction. It is a rigorous process, but it is a useful challenge. And it's an exhilarating feeling when you win the Award!"

Federal Express Corporation: A 1990 Winner

A 10-step Baldrige self-analysis and self-improvement process and 12 Quality Indicators are the catalysts that helped this top-notch organization deliver superior quality—and become the first Baldrige Award winner in the service category.

The first Malcolm Baldrige National Quality Awards were given in 1988. However, it wasn't until 1990 that a large service company captured one of the prized awards. It's not too surprising that the winner was Federal Express, an organization that's been setting standards for service quality since its inception.

Starting in 1973 with eight aircraft, the company rapidly expanded its overnight airborne delivery service to a fleet of 200 aircraft (in 1991), while maintaining customer satisfaction levels of better than 95 percent. However, its sustained success has never allowed Federal Express to sit back and take it easy; the organization is always looking for ways to improve even *more*—which is where the Baldrige Award came in.

"Our approach to the Baldrige Award was one of self-analysis and self-improvement," explains John R. West, manager of Corporate Quality Improvement for Federal Express Corporation (Memphis, Tenn.). "We recognized that the Award process was a great blueprint for quality."

A TEN-STEP PROCESS FOR IMPROVEMENT

With self-assessment and self-betterment foremost in mind, Federal Express took the following 10 steps, using the Baldrige application as a quality tool:

1. Have Each Division Apply for the Baldrige Individually

"Each of our divisions applied as a separate entity," West explains. "As their first step in the process, Corporate assigned the division heads the responsibility of appointing a managing director to lead their individual application processes.

"The idea was to take the completed division applications and compile them into one corporate application. While doing this, each division was going through a valuable self-analysis and self-improvement process."

2. Have Each Division Submit an Action Plan for Improvement

"By August 1, 1989, the divisions were ready for the second step," relates West. "They were asked to submit an action plan telling the chief executive and chief operating officers what they were going to do to close any gaps between Baldrige Award requirements and their actual performance."

3. Bring in Expert Help

In the middle of writing the applications, some people had trouble understanding the exact meaning of some questions and how the scoring worked. "To get answers to these questions we brought in a consultant who was an authorized Baldrige examiner," says West. "Our purpose in hiring him was to make sure we were on the right track; we did *not* employ him to write our exam for us or to do our work for us."

4. Hold an Application Workshop

The consultant held a workshop for key players in each of the divisions participating in the completion of the application guidelines. Approximately 30 people spent a day and a half getting answers to their questions and ensuring that they were on the right track.

5. Make Some Needed Changes

"As a result of the workshop, we realized that we had to change our course a little bit," says West. "We now understood the scoring, and we found that we had not always understood exactly what answers the questions were looking for.

"For example, if the application asks for charts, graphs, or trends, that's what it means. Notice the three significant things they focus on in the application guidelines: *approach, deployment,* and *results.* Include these factors in your answers whenever it's appropriate.

"Because of this new understanding, we extended the deadline for the divisions' completion of their work by two months. That was a turning point."

6. Have the Divisions Polish Their Applications

Most divisions finished writing up their applications by the end of January, with the rest finishing up in February.

7. Write the Corporate Application

West and six vice presidents led teams that compiled the division applications into the corporate application, working category by category. "Divisions sent their experts to the seven category meetings to share their information and help write the corporate application," he notes.

8. Have an Objective Outside Observer Critique the Corporate Application

"Once we had the rough draft for each of the seven Baldrige categories completed, we submitted the written manuscript to a consultant and asked him to give it a hard critique," West reports. "We wanted to know everything that was not good in the application."

9. Have Professional Writers Help with the Final Application

"After we got the consultant's feedback, we had professional, in-house writers write the final application," West explains. "That way, we had someone who was both knowledgeable about the company *and* had expertise in writing.

"The Baldrige application questions are very thorough," he points out. "One of the biggest points I can make is that people should be sure to answer the questions *directly.* That was the biggest advantage of having professional writers help write the final draft for us."

10. Send in the Application

"It wasn't until a consultant told us that we had a good chance of having a site visit [by Baldrige examiners] that we made the decision to send in our application," says West. "Our main intent all along was self-analysis that would lead to self-improvement. We wanted to be good enough to warrant a site visit before we threw our hat into the ring in 1990."

Of course, Federal Express *did* eventually receive a site visit. This is an intensive examination by a team of four to six people, a process that can last up to four days. The examiners rate the applications based on their observations, and then give their site visit report to a panel of judges, which selects the winners.

A DOZEN SERVICE QUALITY INDICATORS HELP KEEP EFFORTS ON TRACK

On December 13, 1990, company representatives accepted the Baldrige Award from President George Bush during a ceremony at the Department of Commerce Building. Since receiving the Award, Federal Express has shared nonproprietary information about its quality improvement process with other companies, government agencies, and education divisions. Federal Express also enlightens visitors at weekly quality forums.

One thing visitors learn when they attend these quality forums is that the company has always taken quality seriously, as evidenced by its quality measuring system.

"We have what we call a Service Quality Indicator," explains West. "This is analogous to Motorola's Six Sigma program, which helped it win the Baldrige Award previously."

Sigma is a statistical symbol: The higher the sigma number, the fewer the failures or variations, and the better the quality. "We did not use the Six Sigma program as a model when we developed this," West says. "Our Service Quality Indicator was based on our own complaint-handling system. Our purpose was to reduce the actual number of mistakes and failures made in a year, despite volume growth."

The Service Quality Indicator is based on these 12 service components:

Wrong day, late delivery
Right day, late delivery
Invoice adjustments (When people call to ask that their invoices be adjusted, it is treated and measured as a failure.)
Trace requests (When a customer calls in to track a package and the information is not on the computer, it is treated as a failure.)
Lost packages
Damaged packages
Overgoods (This concerns lost-and-found items: When the identification comes off a package, it is sent to the Overgoods Department, where an attempt is made to find out who the package belongs to.)
Missed pickups (This occurs when a customer calls to have a package picked up today, and the package is still sitting there tomorrow.)
Complaints reopened (When a customer calls back about a complaint that was considered "closed"— or resolved—the complaint is "reopened.")
Abandoned calls (This term is used when a customer hangs up because his or her call isn't answered within ten seconds or two rings.)
Missing proof of delivery (Federal Express promises that on each and every invoice it will have proof of delivery. This includes the name of the person receiving the package, the date, and the time received. If this information is not on the invoice, it is treated as a failure.)
International (This refers to any operations that are offshore of the United States.)

"The components for International are much the same as for Domestic, but they measure their own Service Quality Indicator," explains West. "We just compile the entire International Service Quality Indicator into this one category and include it as one of *our* 12 components.

"Our five-year goal on the Service Quality Indicator is to have only one tenth of the actual number of failures at the end of the fifth year that we had at the beginning of the first year—despite an annual growth of usually about 20 percent."

But just how does Federal Express determine how well it is doing in each area? It has very extensive automatic tracking systems. For instance, consider the two methods used for monitoring late deliveries:

The courier time cards require couriers to code and note any late deliveries. This information goes into a database each day, so by the next morning, the company knows the service level from the previous day.

Because the delivery information goes onto each invoice, it is therefore on the billing database, which provides a second report on service-quality levels.

EMPLOYEE SATISFACTION RANKS UP THERE WITH CUSTOMER SATISFACTION

As customer satisfaction is of vital importance to Federal Express, so is *employee* satisfaction. After all, there's a strong connection between the two: If the people who are expected to provide quality service to customers are unhappy, they aren't really going to be able to provide the level of service the company expects— and the customers demand.

West explains that Federal Express took special steps to keep employees content during the Baldrige qualification process. "During the 15 months we worked on this, we spread the work out so that it was a team effort. This meant that there would be no pressure put on any one group or individual at the company. Some divisions put in a lot of hours, but they found that it was a rewarding team experience," he notes.

To make sure the company is generally on track regarding worker satisfaction, "we hold an anonymous employee survey each year," says West. "This is a mandatory survey, so the percentage of returns is high—and the anonymity lets employees tell us what they actually feel. The goal is to have our employees feel as satisfied as they were last year (provided, of course, that we did *well* last year). If we did *not* do well, our goal is to make them *more* satisfied than they were last year.

"The penalty if we don't meet that goal is that no one in management— and in the higher professional ranks across the board—gets any bonus money at the end of the year," West explains. "The same applies to the service goal on the Service Quality Indictor: If we don't meet our goal, based on a six-month target, no one in management or the higher professional ranks gets any bonus money."

NOT AWARDS, BUT <u>IMPROVEMENT</u> IS THE PRIME OBJECTIVE

However, neither money nor awards are the primary incentives for the company's stringent quality standards: It's actually the quest for excellence that drives Federal Express to get as close as it can to 100 percent employee and customer satisfaction.

"I think it's important for people to go after the Award with self-improvement in mind," West asserts. "Many companies that call me for advice sound as if they feel that they aren't good enough to go for the Award. I think some of them are too self-critical and should give the Baldrige process a chance.

"People need to realize that they should always make *self-analysis* and *self-improvement* their goals, not winning the Award," West stresses. "They should work on meeting the criteria for the application and *then* decide whether they want to enter the application."

Solectron Corporation: A 1991 Winner

This fast-growing customized products manufacturer used the Baldrige application to fortify its already strong quality foundation—and then it actually became an Award recipient.

Solectron Corporation is a leading independent provider of customized integrated manufacturing services to original equipment manufacturers (OEMs) in the electronics industry. The company specializes in the assembly of complex printed circuit boards and subsystems for makers of computers and other electronic products. It also provides system-level assembly services of personal computers and mainframe mass storage subsystems, and it does turnkey materials management, board design, and manufacturability consultation and testing.

By most standards, Solectron is a young company; it was founded in 1977 as an assembly job shop with initial revenues of several hundred thousand dollars. By 1991, Solectron had become a $265-million-a-year business occupying approximately 750,000 square feet of building space in five locations in San Jose and Milpitas, California. (As of this writing, the company has plans to consolidate its locations onto a campus in the Milpitas area; in 1991, Solectron opened its first off-shore plant in Panang, Malaysia.)

How did this relatively new company achieve such rapid growth *and* join the ranks of Baldrige Award recipients? Part of Solectron's success lies in the fact that it used the Baldrige criteria to polish every facet of its already quality-conscious operation. Director of Quality Richard Allen shares with you some of the philosophies and actions that have caused the organization to achieve its enviable level of excellence.

CULTURE BASED ON CONTINUOUS IMPROVEMENT AND CUSTOMER SATISFACTION

"The Chief Executive Officer of Solectron, Dr. Winston Chen, has always been dedicated to quality, continuous improvement, and customer satisfaction," Allen reports. "So Dr. Chen has been the driving force of this philosophy in our organization. His focus has always been on customer satisfaction and reviving American competitiveness in manufacturing.

"As our company grew, Dr. Chen helped drive these philosophies down to every employee in the company," Allen continues. "From the very early days of the company's existence, he worked on the floor with the production people, and continued upward from there. He put together a lot of the initial training programs and was instrumental in implementing statistical process control throughout the whole company."

Allen notes that although larger companies often give sophisticated titles to their quality processes, Solectron has always kept it simple: "We simply call it our 'Quality Process' or 'Continuous Improvement Process' when we talk to our employees."

FLUCTUATING DEFECT RATES LED TO BALDRIGE CRITERIA

Although Solectron's level of defects was not high, it still wanted to see them decrease—preferably to the point where they were eliminated altogether. "As time went by, our defect rates dropped, but then they would level off," recalls Allen. "We had to figure out a method that would keep them continuously dropping. In addition, we were looking for a good improvement system that would affect *all* aspects of the company.

"We looked at Deming, Juran, and Crosby. Then we looked at the Baldrige criteria. It seemed as if the actual process of going through the Baldrige application and using the questions as a basis for improvement was a very good process. So we incorporated the whole process into our improvement strategy."

It should be stressed that Solectron's goal in applying the Baldrige criteria to its operation wasn't to win the Award, but to achieve continuous improvement throughout the organization. "We felt initially that the Award would be nice to win, but it was secondary to improving Solectron's quality. We had no plans to win when we first started to apply," Allen asserts. "We looked at the application completion and feedback as *an evolutionary process of improvement.* If we won the Award, it would be icing on the cake."

Initially, Solectron brought in consultants to provide a basic understanding of what to do to meet the Baldrige criteria. "Three years ago, when we wrote our first application, we initially brought in three consultants to help us understand the application process. Dr. Thomas Kennedy, vice president of Quality and Engineering Technology, and I worked with the consultants for approximately two weeks to learn the Baldrige application processes and what we had to do to apply. They explained how to answer the questions and the format that past applicants had used.

"During this time, the consultants also toured our facilities and reviewed many of our processes," Allen continues. "Before they left, they told us we had a pretty good story."

"Then we wrote our first application. The first year, Tom and I were the primary writers of the application. We utilized an outside professional technical writer to help with technical writing and act as a wordsmith. We also used internal secretarial help for proofreading. As I generated the charts, Tom took on the role of editor for the entire application."

Allen explains that the Baldrige criteria examined seven critical areas: Leadership; Information and Analysis; Strategic Quality Planning; Human Resource Utilization; Quality Assurance of Products and Services; Quality Results; and Customer Satisfaction. Applicants must answer specific questions within each category. Strong emphasis is placed on quality achievement and improvements based on quantitative data furnished by the applicants.

Many companies have sought the Baldrige Award, but few have won one because they cannot meet the stringent requirements of this self-examination. However, Solectron's philosophy had been quality and customer oriented from the start, and it had collected data in these areas through the years.

Each year, there were some changes in the application, notes Allen. "The application itself was noticeably different in the early stages from what it is now. It was more 'quality cited by example' in the first couple of years. Now they are looking for you to show them your process and to show how you are working the process. So there's a big difference in the question structure." However, Allen says, these changes were to Solectron's advantage. "Because Solectron has always collected a lot of data, it wasn't too hard to go back to the early stages of the application process. We had a lot of the information. All we had to do was write about what we already had."

THE CUSTOMER DRIVES SOLECTRON'S QUALITY EFFORTS

Focusing on the customer is one factor that has helped Solectron gain its quality edge. "Everything is driven from the customer backward," Allen stresses. "As a contract manufacturing company, Solectron manufactures products designed by its customers. We compete on the basis of service, quality, and cost. Therefore, we go to great lengths to determine how existing and prospective customers define superior performance."

How does Solectron gauge its customers' level of satisfaction with its products—and then assure their ongoing satisfaction? Here are some of the techniques it uses:

Carry Out Weekly Customer Satisfaction Polls

"We have a very unique approach to understanding whether we are satisfying our customers," says Allen. "This approach has been ongoing since the early years of the company's existence. What we do every week is to poll *every single* customer. We ask them to rate us in four different categories":

Quality—How good was the quality of the product that we sent you?
Delivery—Was our delivery on time? Did the product arrive in good shape?
Communication—Are we returning your phone calls? Are we paying attention to your needs?
Service—How good are we at meeting your needs? Are you happy with our service?

"Our customers are asked to provide a letter grade: A, B, C, or D for each of these categories each week. The first two categories, quality and delivery, are objective. The second two categories, communication and service, are subjective. We might be meeting their quality needs and we might be delivering their goods on time, but we are also concerned about how our customers *feel* about us and our products," Allen asserts.

"We use a very strict grading curve," he continues. "It works this way: Nothing is acceptable except an A. It gets negative from there. An A-minus is 90, B is 80, C is 0, and a D is a minus 100. We pay a huge penalty for any customer that rates us at C (average) or lower in any category, because we do a straight average of all those numbers. So every week, we get all this information back and we average it out by customer.

"We also ask them for any comments they have on things we've done that they liked or didn't like. We record those comments *verbatim*. We have found that customers who don't 'feel' like they are getting good service often react to that emotionally, and we get the brunt of [their displeasure], so we believe it is important to react to their feelings.

"This information is gathered from the customers on Monday. On Tuesday, it all gets compiled, and that information goes back to the respective divisions that service those customers. They have to come up with answers to any negative comments or questions or grades. We essentially have to come up with an action plan every week as to what we did or didn't do for that customer the previous week.

"On Thursday morning at 7:30, we have a senior management staff meeting, which includes the CEO, the COO, all the vice presidents, directors, division managers, and a number of the managers and supervisors. In this large forum, we review the entire package every week. That way, the whole company gets to see what is going on with every single customer."

Give Customers Feedback Every Week

We used to give our customers feedback by phone," Allen recalls. "Sometimes, we would send back a formal response in the form of an incident report.

"This year, however, we have formalized the process even more. Now we send back an actual customer complaint and resolution plan that lists the problem and what we're doing about it, gives the customer the time frame in which the problem will be corrected, and explains how it will be corrected. This package is then kept on record for future reference."

Provide Customer Support

At Solectron, customers are supported by two teams:

Customer Focus Teams. "The purpose of these teams is to evaluate production for each customer," explains Allen. "Their goals are to prevent potential problems and to identify ways to improve process yields. "These teams meet with their customers weekly—at a minimum—and in a lot of cases, they meet more frequently than that.

"They put together and send a formal weekly report to the customers, which provides a snapshot status of what happened during the week with respect to schedules, quality, test yields, product deliveries, and any other open action items that need to be discussed. The teams and their customers mutually review and use the reports and any feedback to make sure that customers are continuously satisfied with the products being delivered. That report can be up to a half inch thick, to give you an idea of the amount of paperwork involved," Allen adds.

Project-Planning Teams. These teams work with customers in planning, scheduling, and defining material requirements," says Allen. "These teams' key concern is ensuring customer on-time delivery.

"The project-planning teams are really geared toward our turnkey-type customers, for whom we will actually buy all the parts, assemble them, and give them a finished product because there is a lot more to do for these customers," Allen continues.

"If there are special requirements for a customer, this team gets the right people together up-front so that the job can proceed quickly. As a normal course of events, when products are running, we have a customer focus team, which has people from Quality, Manufacturing, Engineering, and Scheduling—these key people are the ones who can assure that the product will continue to get to the customer on time, on an ongoing basis."

Set up Customized Centers for Specific Customers

"The assembly operations at Solectron are designed for specific customer' products, so the same people work on the same products over time," says Allen. "We don't have many high volume, standardized products. We have just the opposite; very short runs and a very high mix of products.

"If a customer has a large amount of work, we will create a division, essentially a P&L (profit and loss) center, for the customer. Otherwise, we'll create P&L centers for a group of customers. We tend to staff divisions to be no larger than 200 or 300 people."

INSTITUTE A FORMAL QUALITY TRAINING PROGRAM

Many companies train their employees on a need-to-know basis. In other words, they teach them what they need to know to complete a certain job that comes in, but they don't have a comprehensive, quality-oriented training plan to ensure broader skills, knowledge, and comprehension. However, a formalized training plan is necessary to assure total quality and to meet the stringent Baldrige criteria.

"We used to have a training program based on needs," Allen says. "For instance, when someone needed to be trained on an assembly process, we'd work on developing the needed skills. We did not have a formal training program, which was something we were criticized for on our first application.

"To formalize our training program and give it direction, we created a position called vice president of training. This job was to assess the total training needs of the company from the lowest to the highest level and put in place a training program that would meet not only our current needs but our future needs as well." Here's a look at each element of Solectron's formalized training program:

Quality-Awareness Training

"We trained heavily in quality awareness," says Allen. "In these sessions, we included the Baldrige application and criteria training. We tried to make Baldrige-awareness training a part of everyone's daily job."

Management-Leadership Training

"All senior management was next put through a management leadership training program. To do this, several of our instructors attended a 'train the trainer' program and taught the management leadership course to all our executives," Allen explains. "We are now teaching a more basic form of this course to our supervisors."

Technical Training

"It was also determined that we needed technical training in certain areas. At Solectron, we are fortunate to have a number of good technical experts. We have nine Ph.D.s in different disciplines, and these people helped develop courses to support our technical needs such as reliability, waste-solder processes, and board cleanliness. Seminar training is conducted for our technical staff to elevate its knowledge of our business."

Statistical Process Control, (SPC) Training

"We offered SPC training at three levels: first, the operator level; second, the supervisory and engineering level, and third, advanced SPC techniques and design of experiments. This third level was strictly for the engineering groups. Practically everyone in the company, including the secretaries and administrative people, received the first-level statistical process control training," Allen explains.

To help eliminate defects—and also to encourage individual responsibility for quality—Solectron asks all its operators to do statistical analyses of their own work, generate control charts for their internal processes, and then correct any problems they uncover.

"Our operators are working in an area where there are a lot of small parts being assembled," Allen points out. "The statistical process controls that we put into place go right down to the operator level. They actually do self-corrections to the processes when they fluctuate beyond what is normal."

All departments at Solectron are now required to use SPC regularly. SPC charts track performance of each machine with measurements recorded in an SPC database. Division quality managers and the corporate quality director track and review results daily. Since 1987, average product quality has improved. Here are two examples of SPC at work in two critical areas:

Solder Monitoring

"One of the very critical areas that we have to continually monitor is the actual solder applied to the circuit boards," Allen explains. "This is because the devices currently being used on circuit boards have very small leads and are soldered directly to the surface of the circuit board—they don't go through holes any more.

"The solder used is in the form of a solder paste. It's very critical how much of this paste is put on every pad. So every hour, the operators will actually take physical-height readings of that solder paste and then record those readings on control charts.

"If the height goes above a certain limit, we know the machine has gone out of control, the paste is wrong, or something else is going amiss. By looking at the control charts, the operators can see early warning signs of possible problems. Corrections are then made to bring the process back under control."

Board Cleanliness

"Another critical area is the *cleanliness* of the boards," Allen reports. "We have found that the most critical components in our process are the raw PC boards— or printed circuit boards—without any components on them. If they are not clean, they will not hold solder, and the components won't become—or remain—soldered to the boards.

"Because of the complexity of the devices today, the spacing between components is very small, which makes it almost impossible to visually inspect for defects in the solder. All material has to be able to accept solder before we actually begin the solder process, so all bare-board lots are sampled for cleanliness and solderability," Allen explains. "As the solder process begins, we measure and monitor conveyor speed, temperature, and 10 to 15 other checkpoints in that process alone. These measurements are then recorded on statistical process control charts by operators.

"The operators are empowered to stop the line if they see any problems. If it is something that they don't understand, then they'll get an engineer or somebody else involved. In most cases, it is a minor adjustment that they can correct themselves."

CREATE AN ENVIRONMENT THAT ENCOURAGES A QUALITY ATTITUDE

Solectron takes several steps to create an environment in which all employees are encouraged to put quality first every day. Here's how it accomplishes this:

Give Workers Responsibility for Meeting Quality Goals

Solectron requires the support of its employees to meet its quality goals, notes Allen. So division managers go to their people and ask, "How are you going to meet these goals, and how will you do it as an operating division?"

"Many teams are created to help this process," Allen says. "Examples may include a production control team, a materials team, an operations team for soldering, or a team for auto-inserting parts. They all pull together to decide what we need to do."

Encourage a Strong "Family Atmosphere"

Solectron started out with a primarily Asian workforce, but now has 2,200 employees representing over 20 different cultures, reports Allen. "Solectron's high-energy, customer-focused work force has developed a strong family orientation," he points out. "That initial corporate culture was set up when the company started, and it has grown and led each employee to have a positive attitude toward the person working next to him or her. We've had virtually no problems interculturally throughout the whole company."

Promote Clear and Effective Communications

Because of the many languages and dialects spoken at Solectron, the company finds communicating with its employees to be one of its key challenges. The company had to ensure a way to communicate effectively with its diverse work force.

"Almost everyone in the company speaks *some* English," says Allen. "To help everyone improve their English, the company offers ESL (English as a Second Language) courses on site through a local community college. To get information to our employees, training materials and other printed materials such as publications or announcements are published in four languages: English, Spanish, Chinese, and Vietnamese."

Implement a Recognition and Reward Program

"In most cases, we give rewards and recognition to groups, rather than individuals," says Allen. "We have only two or three individualized awards, given for exceptional performance for a specific task.

"On a quarterly basis, we may give out two or three awards to specific groups. This is usually done by our CEO, Dr. Winston Chen, or our president, Dr. Ko Nishim.

Recognition may be given because a customer has called up to praise the customer focus team working with it and that has done an exceptional job. These types of actions trigger our executive management to publicly reward that group of people.

Other ways management rewards groups include:

Buying a whole division lunch
Bringing in ice cream for the entire corporation or the entire operation
Providing monetary rewards to a complete operating division
Giving monetary rewards to an improvement team

THE QUALITY JOURNEY KNOWS NO END

Although Solectron has joined the winner's circle of Baldrige winners, it is hardly resting on its laurels. The company aims to improve its products and processes *continuously,* aiming toward ever-tougher quality goals. "We've defined our goals through 1995. These include goals for on-time delivery, customer satisfaction, number of hours of training, how we want to look at our suppliers, and how we want to measure them," says Allen. "This way, we know what must be achieved at all times.

"After our goals are set, we meet with the division general managers and the quality managers to determine how best to meet these goals and what support from upper-level management is required. A plan is then put together that defines what is needed in terms of equipment, work force, training, and so forth. Then we work together to meet those goals.

"One of our goals is to achieve Six Sigma quality in all critical processes," Allen continues. "In some cases, we're at Three Sigma, and other cases we are up to Five Sigma. We're currently on track to where we think we should be, and we are continuing to use the Malcolm Baldrige guidelines and our other continuous-improvement methods to reach our Six Sigma target.

"Some of the challenges we are facing include the fact that the boards are getting more complex and customer requirements are getting tougher," Allen continues. "To remain a leader in quality, we need to further reduce our rejects and internal errors to less than ten parts per million (ppm). We don't believe we are anywhere near where we need to be.

"We'll continue to follow the Baldrige criteria because we feel that they are an excellent road map to world-class quality and customer satisfaction. They can be applied to all areas of the company—not only in manufacturing, but in areas such as finance, human resources, and material procurement as well. Our goal is to have *every single area and every single process* at the Six Sigma level, with zero defects."

Solectron has won over 37 awards for superior customer satisfaction over the last 10 years, many since 1990. After a recent quality audit, a customer rated Solectron as the "Best contract manufacturer of electronic assemblies in the United States."

"We've seen tremendous results in customer satisfaction and quality over the past three years by following the Malcolm Baldrige Award guidelines," Allen reports. "Defect rates have dropped substantially, and currently fall within the Five Sigma range, or 233 parts per million. On-time delivery to customers is at 97.7 percent."

He notes that 90 percent of new business comes from established customers, and many have closed their internal assembly operations after determining that Solectron can assemble better quality products at a lower price than they can. "The goal we're driving for is to be a billion-dollar corporation at the world-class level within three years," Allen points out.

But it isn't just *external* customers and their business that Solectron is concerned about. The company is committed to quality for its *internal* customers—its employees—too. "We are very dedicated to quality and making things better for everyone—our customers *and employees* alike," Allen stresses. "Solectron is very much aware that the whole winning of the Award was accomplished through the combination of the work and efforts of *everyone* at the company."

Selected Winners from the Baldrige Small Businesses Award Category

Granite Rock: A 1992 Winner

Can a small, family-owned company charge a *higher* rate for its products than its high-powered competitors do and still capture a hefty market share? You bet! Consistently high-quality products and speedy service have enabled this Lilliputian firm to beat out its Brobdingnagian competitors *and* win the 1992 Baldrige Award in the small business category.

Winning a Malcolm Baldrige National Quality Award in 1992 was just another quality milestone, albeit an important one, for Granite Rock (Watsonville, CA). Founded in 1900, this small but highly progressive organization has focused on making and delivering top-quality products and services for almost 100 years.

Granite Rock produces rock, sand, and gravel aggregates, concrete, asphalt, road treatments, and recycled road-base materials. It also operates a highway paving operation and retails other manufacturers' materials. The firm employs 400 people at its branch offices, quarries, batch plants, and other facilities.

Since 1987, Granite Rock has been operated by Bruce and Steve Woolpert, two grandsons of the company's founder. Both brought a plenitude of business moxie to the $90 million organization, and they needed it. The competition was tough, and getting tougher all the time. In fact, although Granite Rock only does business in a six-county area that extends from San Francisco south to Monterey, it really competes in a *global* market.

"Every other major player in our market has been purchased by an international corporation; we're the only family-owned player left," notes Val Verutti, director of Quality Support. "Instead of vying against small competitors like we used to, we have two or three major competitors owned by foreign conglomerates with world capital."

How has Granite Rock managed to thrive in the face of such formidable adversaries? The key is a strong *customer focus.*

NINE OBJECTIVES FOR TOTAL QUALITY

Although Granite Rock had always emphasized quality, the company realized it needed to go even further to win customer loyalty in such a challenging market. So in 1985, Granite Rock initiated a formal Total Quality Management program. This has brought

Excerpted from Allyn and Bacon's *Profiles of Malcolm Baldrige Award Winners,* originally published by the Bureau of Business Practice as *Award Winning Quality: Strategies from the Winners of the Malcolm Baldrige National Quality Award* (BBP © 1992). Used with permission of the Bureau of Business Practice (BBP), a division of the Business and Professional Group of Paramount Publishing, a Paramount Communications Company.

Make Suppliers Your Quality Partners

Forming partnerships with suppliers is one "secret to success" that has helped Granite Rock achieve customer-pleasing, award-winning quality. And it's no wonder—it only makes sense that *you* cannot become a top-notch supplier if *your own* suppliers are sorely lacking in quality themselves.

However, if you join forces with a select group of suppliers—letting them know what your needs are, sharing information on how they can better meet those needs, and asking them to make their own commitment to excellence—you've found one of the keys to Total Quality. And you're well on your way to unlocking the door behind which customer loyalty lies.

"We seek partnering arrangements with our suppliers," says Director of Quality Support Val Verutti. "We have reduced the number of our suppliers, and we don't play one against the other for low price. For example, we do most of our business with one cement company now. We let it know that we expect real data on its variability averages. We get day-to-day variability figures, so we know more about what the company is doing."

Granite Rock's commitment to supplier partnerships is evidenced by its refusal to settle for second best—even when it would be more expedient to do so. "We don't want cement from Mexico in the summer when supplies get low—we want cement from [our established] supplier's plant," stresses Verutti. "It's common in the industry to buy cement from various competing plants or to import it—especially if the other sources are on the coast where their materials can come in by boat. However, we want *consistency*. The cement we get today should be just like it was yesterday."

Your quality team is not complete unless you have given your suppliers an integral part to play on it. So get your suppliers involved in your efforts from day one, foster two-way communication and mutual commitment to quality, and reap the many rewards.

about an increase in market share as well as an increase in employee productivity. Revenue earned per employee has steadily risen to the point where it is now about 30 percent above the national average for the industry.

Under its Total Quality strategy, Granite Rock began to take a proactive approach to assessing the needs and expectations of its customers, with the goal of consistently providing each and every one with faultless products and impeccable service. "Nine corporate objectives serve as the cornerstone of our Total Quality program and service [strategy]," explains Verutti. "They were derived from our analyses of customers' requirements." Each component is considered equally important, he notes. They are:

1. Customer satisfaction and service
2. Safety
3. Production efficiency
4. Financial performance and growth
5. Community commitment
6. Management
7. Profit
8. Product quality assurance
9. People

Annually, the senior executives evaluate company data and develop measurable baseline goals to help Granite Rock advance toward meeting each of its quality objectives. These goals are communicated to each branch and division, which are expected to develop and implement plans to meet them.

FOUR STEPS TO SUCCESS

To help ensure that its facilities are able to meet their quality goals, Granite Rock takes a number of steps, including the following:

Put Quality Teams to Work

Ten Corporate Quality Teams coordinate and help carry out the improvement efforts across the entire organization. These teams, which carry out the day-to-day quality activities, are chaired by senior executives, but members include managers, salaried professional and technical workers, and hourly union employees.

Invest in New Technology

One of Granite Rock's largest investments was in a loading system called "Granite Xpress," which allows truckers to drive up to the system at the quarry any time, day or night. The Granite Xpress operates like an ATM system. The driver sticks a magnetic card into a slot and punches in an order on the computer, and the truck is automatically loaded from an overhead bin. Average loading time has been cut in half, from about 20 minutes to under 10 minutes.

Implement Statistical Problem-Solving Techniques

Granite Rock began to use statistical process control (SPC) to help assure customers that materials will exceed specs and will always arrive on time. Employees generate SPC charts for all products, tracking variables such as *size variability* of aggregate products and *mix variability* of the concrete recipes. They also track key measures of external customer service (such as on-time delivery, which is close to 95 percent), and performance and satisfaction levels of internal customers. Statistics are posted so that everyone can see them. (As far as Verutti knows, Granite Rock is the only firm in its industry that is using SPC.)

Gather and Communicate Quality Information throughout the Organization

Verutti and Dave Franceschi, who make up the quality support department, are mainly responsible for gathering and dispersing quality information throughout Granite Rock. For example, Franceschi gathers SPC data and other key information and puts the graphs together, while Verutti writes the first draft of the Baldrige application, which management uses (along with the resulting feedback) to help evaluate the company's Total Quality process.

One of Verutti's and Franceschi's other responsibilities is to give managers the data they need to "manage by fact." "We present management with information on batching accuracy, on-time delivery, complaints, invoice errors—everything we consider to be key data from our product lines and support services. Our executives manage from the data that we get from all the departments," says Verutti.

CONNECTING WITH CUSTOMERS

No matter how effective your quality strategy may be, you can't just *assume* you're pleasing your outside customers. You've got to keep in close contact with them to *make sure* you're on target, to find out where you're falling short, and to assess their changing needs and expectations so that you can better respond to them. Granite Rock "connects" with its customers in the following ways:

Make Management More Accessible to Customers

"We have a matrix management system that reduces the layers of management and puts top management much closer to our customers," Verutti explains. "We also have an absolute open-door policy right up to the president, and this is known by our customers as well as by our people."

Gather Customer Satisfaction Data

Granite Rock uses several methods to get feedback on how well it is doing in the area of customer satisfaction. The information gathered is analyzed and shared with *all* employees. The methods used to gather customer satisfaction data include

Annual "report cards." Once each year, customers are asked to grade their top three suppliers, which would include Granite Rock and two of its competitors.

Long, comprehensive surveys, conducted every two to three years. These give the company detailed information as to how well it is meeting customer needs.

"Quick response" cards. These ask for feedback on services rendered that day.

Customer complaint reports. Complaints are handled through Product/Service Discrepancy Reports. These are analyzed and the root cause of each problem is identified.

Short-pay system. Granite Rock customers don't have to pay for services or products they're not happy with. The company follows up on all negative

Employee Training and Involvement at Granite Rock

Like all quality leaders, Granite Rock knows that without well-trained, involved employees, it's impossible to achieve excellence. And the company doesn't just pay lip service to this idea—it puts its money where its mouth is. Granite Rock's training budget far exceeds the industry average: In 1991, for example, its people averaged 37 hours of training at an approximate cost of $1,697 per employee—three times more than the construction industry norm. On-the-job safety is paramount to Granite Rock, so much of this money goes into safety training programs. The effectiveness of these programs is reflected in the company's safety record, which is two times better than the state of California's average for the industry.

"Training our people is important because the quality teams are running the company. The teams make all the local decisions," Val Verutti points out. It's critical that the people running the teams that run the organization have the skills and resources they need to do a quality job.

With this in mind, Granite Rock encourages all of its employees to learn continuously. It sponsors a series of in-house classes and speakers on technical topics. Here, as part of the effort to reduce process variability and increase product reliability, employees are trained in statistical process control, root-cause analysis, and various other problem-solving methods. Granite Rock also pays for tuition at local colleges and sends its employees to industry-sponsored seminars. "For instance, we've sent young technicians to the Portland Cement Association in Skokie, Illinois," Verutti notes. "In fact, in 1991 we sent 21 people and took over a whole class—a first in the Portland Cement Association's history. We sent truck drivers, employees from the credit and batch departments, and dispatchers, as well as technical people—all to learn about the concrete industry. We've done the same thing with the National Association for Paving Asphalt (NAPA) and the National Ready-Mix Association."

To further facilitate its employees' ongoing development, Granite Rock introduced the Individual Professional Development Plan (IPDP) in 1987. Seventy-four percent of its people participate in this voluntary program. At least once each year, these employees sit down and evaluate their accomplishments, assess their skills, and set skill- and career-development goals. "Our Individual Professional Development Plan has brought us more attention than anything else we have done," says Verutti. "Instead of using the typical performance evaluation system where you just grade your employee's performance, we develop an IPDP for employees based on where they want to go and what they want to do. If an employee is a truck driver and wants to become a salesperson, learn how to operate a computer, or simply improve work skills—the person sits down with his or her supervisor and develops a plan to help reach those goals.

"We track goal accomplishment, how many classes employees take, and how well they do. We also promote from within, so the people who do well [in the IPDP] go the furthest, the fastest," he notes.

feedback to find out why customers are unhappy and to come up with ways to avoid future problems. "When customers short-pay us, they get *instant* action," says Verutti. "They don't have to fill out a form or wade through [red tape]. Whatever the problem is—a billing error or a product quality problem—we iron it out. Surprisingly, customers don't take advantage of this system, but they do use it. It really works."

Partner with Contractors

"What makes our industry unique is that our primary customer is the building contractor who makes the purchasing decision," says Verutti. "Beyond the primary contractor is *another* customer who is building the patio or the bridge or the sewer system. That is the end-point customer whose perception of quality often differs from the contractor's perception of quality.

"The primary contractor is mainly concerned about cost and service. The person on the end, who is paying the bill, really wants concrete that is going to last a long time."

In order to make sure that the end-point customer receives quality product, installed in a way that will help it perform well over time, Granite Rock forges partnering arrangements with contractors.

"We try to educate the contractors because they get the concrete in a plastic state and can influence its performance in many ways—how it is placed, whether they add water to it, whether the ground underneath it is prepared properly, etc.," Verutti explains. "For the end-point user to receive quality, we're not the only ones who have to do a good job—the contractor does, too.

"There are some contractors who do not qualify as our customers," he adds. "If we learn that [some contractors] ethics aren't as they should be or their history of performance is such that we could get in trouble as a result of it, we won't sell to them."

BELIEVERS IN THE BALDRIGE

Several companies that have won the Baldrige Award used the application process as a learning and improvement tool for years before actually winning. As mentioned above, Granite Rock is one of them. In fact, Verutti points out, the Baldrige process was one factor that helped Granite Rock beat the odds when the competition was getting fierce and the recession was hitting much of the United States—including California—hard. "During the early part of the recession, our business slowed. At that time, many people in the company felt that perhaps we were putting too much time into the Baldrige," he recalls.

"Then they noticed the turnaround in our business while other companies in the United States were losing business and laying off people. The market for our products had dropped way off, but every year we got a bigger and bigger share of it [and] we maintained our price, which is something our competitors didn't do. Our employees saw this happening and began to feel that pursuing the Baldrige was a good thing after all. It was apparent to the examiners that our employees really believed in the Baldrige process."

After being part of the Baldrige process for four years, Verutti speaks with authority when he offers this advice: "It takes time; you have to be patient. You may need to keep applying for a few years until you have it all in place." (Keep in mind that the Baldrige examiners now look for quality trends over a period of years.) "We've gone for the Award four times. I think the key to our winning this time is that we tied our quality programs in with our market share increases so that the examiners could see that our quality processes were working and were really paying off. Once we demonstrated that clearly, we won the Baldrige."

Bringing Quality Service to the Community and the Environment

Granite Rock extends its quality attitude well *beyond* its facilities' doors, by encouraging its employees to serve their *communities* as well as their customers, and recognizing them for their efforts. The company is involved in a long list of charitable activities, sponsorships and contributions. For example, it produces a Fourth of July concert to benefit community organizations. It is also involved in an "Adopt-a-School" program.

Perhaps the most important way in which Granite Rock takes quality beyond company limits is in its quality treatment of the environment. The company is involved in quarry reclamation, water conservation, and plant beautification projects, and it has received local and national recognition for its responsible use of natural resources.

Globe Metallurgical Inc.: A 1988 Winner

By talking with customers, finding out exactly what they expect in terms of products and services, and incorporating their suggestions and teachings into its quality process, this company achieved excellence—and easily earned the first Baldrige Award for a small business.

Globe Metallurgical Inc. (Beverly, Ohio)—a 210-employee producer of metal and ferrosilicon products—can be noted for three significant factors regarding its winning the Malcolm Baldrige National Quality Award in 1988:

1. It won the first year the Award was offered.
2. It was the first small business to win the Award.
3. One vice president sat down and wrote Globe's Award winning application in one weekend.

In addition to these items, another point that makes Globe's winning the Baldrige Award noteworthy is that the facility is really not what might come to mind when one envisions the ultimate high-quality workplace. When most people think of quality, they tend to picture clean, neat, sparkling, high-tech workplaces. But Globe far from fits that ideal.

"We are probably one of the 'heaviest' industries to ever be involved in the Baldrige process," concedes Curtis W. Goins, director of Quality and Research and Development. "By that, I mean we don't have a nice, wonderful, clean place to work in: We have an open, unheated, smoky, hot place because we handle molten metals, which generate a lot of smoke and sparks. Globe is not a pristine electronic corporation, or a Xerox, or a company like that. It's very much a 'smokestack' business."

Yet another interesting fact about Globe's winning the Baldrige Award is that the company became aware of the Award only about *two weeks* before they applied for it, Goins recalls. "That was the first year the Award was offered. Baldrige representatives were at a booth passing out applications at a Quality Conference we attended. We reviewed the application very quickly and decided to apply."

SIMPLY "TELLING IT LIKE IT IS" BRINGS BALDRIGE SURPRISE

The information for Globe's application was initially gathered by four people at the Beverly, Ohio plant: the vice president of Human Resources, the plant manager, the quality manager, and Goins. They divided up the seven sections of the application according to what they thought each person could best handle. (Each of the four actually contributed to several sections.) All the information they gathered was then given to the vice president of Quality and Administration, who sat down at his computer and wrote the complete application over one weekend.

"We won the first time we submitted an application, so naturally, we were very pleased with our results," Goins reports. "However, we did not *expect* to win—we simply wanted to use the Baldrige application as another means of improving ourselves."

Although it came easily, there was no trick to Globe's win: The company simply stated the quality facts as they were. "We just told about the systems we had established over the last two to three years," Goins explains. "We were able to give examples of what we had done to address various questions because the Baldrige criteria were very similar to the criteria that our customers had in their quality systems.

"We had also made great strides in productivity improvement," he continues. "Many of the sections in the Baldrige application recognized improvements in productivity as part of the total management system. Our systems were already in place—the Baldrige people simply recognized that they were superior, and recognized us with the Award.

"For Globe, it was not a matter of *get the Baldrige and then develop a system*. It was a matter of *develop a system, and then apply for the Baldrige*," Goins stresses.

Indeed, Globe had managed to easily skate through a process that often befuddles other organizations. Many companies that seek to apply for the Baldrige Award are completely confused by the complexity of the questions and the requests for data to support their statements. How did Globe seem to so easily cut through this process with one sweep of the blade?

First, the firm already had a well-established quality process in place that met the Baldrige criteria.

Second, this process was very well documented, so Globe was able to readily provide the statistical data and other information necessary to win the Award.

What steps did Globe follow to arrive at such an effective quality process? A detailed look at its strategy is provided below.

THE DEVELOPMENT OF A FIRST-RATE QUALITY PROCESS

Globe had long been well established in the domestic ferroalloy marketplace, but in the mid-1980s, quality became even more important to the way the company provided and marketed its products. This occurred for two reasons:

- Customers started emphasizing quality.
- International competition was on the rise.

To survive in an industry where companies were being forced out of business, Globe had to go the extra mile to prove its capabilities. The company shifted its focus from commodity markets, such as steel manufacturing, to higher value-added markets, such as foundries. It also started a quality program that involved customers, employees, and suppliers in its effort

"We concentrated on improving the quality of products and processes, and lowering the cost of producing the alloys that we do best," Goins explains. "It would be meaningless to have the best quality in the world if it was so expensive that no one could afford it. By the same turn, if we had the lowest price in the world but no one wanted the product because of poor quality, we'd be missing the mark."

Here are the steps Globe took to develop the process that helped it to assure both cost- and quality-effectiveness:

Learn from Customers

Some of Globe's larger customers, primarily auto makers, had started focusing on consolidating their supplier bases by doing business only with suppliers that were able to meet their stringent specifications and deliver top-quality materials. To make sure they chose the best of the best, some customers had begun providing suppliers such as Globe with stringent specifications, and auditing these suppliers' quality systems.

To become a recognized quality supplier, Globe turned to its customers for help, studying their requirements for awards and/or certifications. "We worked with our customers to develop an improved quality system, and we took advantage of all the insight that they could give us," Goins says. "These customers were such companies as

Ford Motor Company, General Motors Corporation, and several iron, steel, and chemical companies. They helped us by auditing our quality system and providing information about how to develop a 'world class' quality process."

For example, to make its quality expectations abundantly clear to its suppliers, Ford issued a document called Q-101, which is a manual of quality specs. Ford also established the American Supplier Institute to train suppliers in specific methods to improve quality. In addition, Ford offered exceptional suppliers a Q-1 Award, while General Motors offered its suppliers a SPEAR certification.

"We also took some courses ourselves to find out how to create and manage a quality system," Goins adds. "We went through the Q-1 process with Ford, and we learned a great deal about quality systems and statistical quality control."

Provide Quality Training

Quality training at Globe includes these two components:

Employee Training. When Globe realized that its entire work force had to be trained in at least the fundamentals of SPC, they had Ford's American Supplier Institute send a trainer to Beverly to train in-house. Following this, a Globe quality team trained the Selma, Alabama, division employees themselves. After that, their quality manager developed their programs.

Supplier Training. "Suppliers that want to improve quality and lower costs are the only ones we want to talk to," Goins asserts. Globe wants its suppliers to respond to its needs as effectively as Globe responds to its own customers' needs. So the company shows its suppliers the improvements it has made in response to customer suggestions, and teaches them how to implement SPC so that they can better control *their own* products.

This supplier involvement effort started after Globe trained all its own employees in quality methods. The company invited five major suppliers in and trained them in the fundamentals of quality and SPC. Then they visited other major suppliers and trained *their* employees in SPC. The Globe trainers left training materials, blank charts, and even calculators at each supplier's site so that the suppliers could continue training *their own* employees.

Suppliers are asked to furnish the same types of control charts that Globe uses internally to check its own processes. These charts must be provided on all critical parameters, and they must indicate whether the product is consistent, what variations occurred during processing, and other pertinent information.

(To add another link to the supplier quality chain, Globe also asks its suppliers to audit *their* suppliers, which further improves consistency and lowers costs, Goins notes.)

"As a result of these efforts, our suppliers' quality systems mirror Globe's quite closely, and the charts they provide match the parameters the QEC Committee expects," Goins reports. "The same processes that improve product quality and consistency also lower costs, so it's a win-win situation," he adds.

When suppliers deliver more consistent materials, Globe saves money in two ways:

There are fewer process upsets due to fluctuations in materials, so more product can be manufactured using the same amount of raw materials.

When suppliers save money, those savings are passed on to customers. "Suppliers get a larger share of our business as their product improves and their costs go down," says Goins. "Eventually, we may target one to be a certified supplier and maybe even a single-source supplier."

Implement Statistical Process Control (SPC)

Goins explains that SPC is a means for plotting data to determine whether processes are operating within specified quality parameters. For example, suppose employees need to check the length of some metal bars that must be four feet long. Plotting the lengths of the bars as they are being manufactured enables employees to

Determine the average length of the bars being produced and how much the length varies during the process. This then allows workers to spot and correct defect trends *before* the bars actually fall out of spec.

Monitor the range between the longest and shortest bars so that employees can narrow this range and keep it under control.

"You can use SPC procedures with any type of measurement, whether it's a percentage, rate of return, or other measurement," asserts Goins. "The real challenge is to identify the right variables to manage, and then learn what to do when a process starts to show a trend toward going out of spec. You need to determine what to correct and what not to correct. And that's all covered by statistical process control training."

Supervisors at Globe were given SPC training, and later, hourly workers were trained as well. Also, the American Supplier Institute customized a general SPC program specifically for Globe. "We wanted to talk about pouring temperatures, percent silicon, and other matters that were important to Globe," explains Goins. "We asked trainers to help our people to prepare real charts with real data so that after they completed their training, they could take those charts and continue to use them on the floor."

With SPC charting, management can track process quality. "Part of statistical process control is being able to calculate process capability," says Goins. "In other words, you can determine how well the process meets the needs of the customer. If you track the process capability from month to month, you can see improvements in the ability of that particular process to meet either internal or external customer needs." Current output, including statistical goals for product parameters and control variables (see below), are posted daily for all employees to see.

Conduct Quality Systems Audits

Globe had always been regarded as a producer of the highest quality alloys in the industry. Chemical laboratories at both of Globe's plants had state-of-the-art analytical equipment, and all products were carefully scrutinized before shipment. This 100-percent inspection proved costly but effective.

When the auto giants started offering quality audits, Globe asked Ford to audit its quality systems. Globe scored 139 points out of a possible 200, only one point short of the 140 needed to pass. With the need to install even more sophisticated quality systems, Globe formed an in-house team to assess customer audits.

The team was initially composed of the quality manager, staff metallurgist, and the vice president of Human Resources. It was called the Quality, Efficiency, and Cost (QEC) committee. Later, it became known as the QEC Steering Committee, and all top company officials became members. Soon afterward, QEC Committees composed of the plant managers and department heads were formed at each plant. These Committees examine their plants' SPC results daily, and meet with individuals or teams in problem areas to discuss what resources they need to do a quality job.

Utilize Audit Information to Develop Effective, Company-Specific Quality Tools

After conducting its initial in-house audits, the original QEC team identified five key "tools" that would become essential parts of Globe's quality system. These elements were

1. **Procedures.** These include exactly what steps are involved in making a particular product, and how employees in different functions interact to make that product.
2. **Job Work Instructions (JWIs).** These are similar to procedures but are much narrower in scope. They include specific instructions on how each indi-

vidual controls the process to generate a consistent product, and what parameters to measure for a consistent product.

3. **Critical Process Variables (CPVs).** These are the variables that must be controlled within the system to assure that the final product is within parameters.
4. **Product Parameters (PPs).** These are the parameters the customer is particularly interested in controlling. They involve SPC charting and process capability assessment.
5. **Failure Mode Effects Analysis (FMEAs).** These involve assessing such matters as what causes a parameter to go out of control? What is the probability that the company will detect the problem before the customer does? FMEAs can be used in the following ways:

First, they enable management to prioritize activities according to what products have the highest probability of reaching a customer with defects.

Second, they can be a source of information when posted with SPC charts. "What might go out of control and how it might be corrected can be gleaned from FMEAs and posted as a list of factors to check when a process is out of control," Goins explains.

Enlist Top Management Leadership

"To get total employee involvement, you must first have *leadership* in your company—the very top corporate management must be committed to the quality process," Goins stresses.

"You must also have top corporate management explain to workers that if they expect to keep their jobs and to keep the company open and running, they are going to have to make some rather dramatic changes in the way they do things. Employees needed to understand that we *had* to improve the quality of our products and our systems to ensure top quality, as well as to improve the way the company is run.

"As we found out, if management is *persistent* and *consistent,* particularly persistent—and exhibits real dedication to the process in a way that makes employees *see, feel,* and *know* their commitment is true—then employees begin to come on board almost in a landslide," Goins continues. "When this starts, the leaders in the hourly work force are the ones to say that the workers have to do this or that to improve. Pretty soon, *everyone* becomes part of the process and makes suggestions on ways to improve."

Involve and Recognize Employees

One way Globe keeps its employees involved and motivated is with *empowerment.* "We let employees know that the success or failure of the business or of the product group they are involved with depends upon the quality of the product they produce and the decisions they make," says Goins.

"We train employees to handle the responsibility of decision-making, and we give them the tools and support they need. Every success they have in problem-solving or in product improvement generates pride and ownership."

Employees at Globe serve on problem-solving teams that started out as quality circles, and have since become more product oriented, instead of process oriented. A team may be composed of employees who would otherwise not be exposed to an entire process—from purchasing raw materials to shipping finished products.

The teams examine the technology behind products, the products' characteristics, and other key factors. They may also investigate causes of product failure by learning how products are used and by tracing the manufacture of products from suppliers in the plant, to their internal customers, and then out to external customers.

Recognition plays a large role in Globe's employee participation effort, and takes several forms:

A Master Calendar Helps Keep a Master Quality Plan on Track

To keep an award winning quality plan on track, you need an effective, yet nonthreatening way to remind all company managers about deadlines, milestones, appointments, and other significant dates and events. To that end, Globe Metallurgical Inc. uses a "master calendar" as a critical planning tool in conjunction with its five-year strategy for improving quality and cutting costs.

According to Curtis W. Goins, director of Quality and Research and Development, this calendar keeps the company's 30 managers informed and helps them organize their time. "Everyone in the company has different functions to perform," he says. "There are audits, evaluations, benchmarks, and agendas, and they have to be done by certain dates.

"The calendar is a resource-planning tool. We use it as a reminder so they everyone knows what everyone else is working on, what the deadlines are, and to whom to go for help, etc. This draws us all a little closer together."

Making Their Marks

"People always mark appointments and things they have to do on a calendar," Goins explains. "So we just extended this idea for our managers and mark things for them." Keeping everyone on track is important at Globe, where the company's five-year plan consists of a 20-page list containing more than 100 items. With so many projects, the master calendar lets managers know what they must accomplish in the coming year.

The calendar is produced by computer software and consists of a page for each month. A Quality, Efficiency, and Cost Committee develops a proposed calendar that managers review and amend as needed. Once managers approve the calendar, entries are filled in, and each manager is given a completed calendar. Entries may be added later as additional appointments or other activities are scheduled.

The blocks for each day contain shorthand references to items on the five-year plan. One day's entry might read: *#56—Curt Goins, visit Union Carbide Corp., perform supplier quality audit.* Managers can then refer to the numbered plan for more details and deadlines.

"We try to plan activities in advance and prevent conflicts on the calendar," Goins says. "We don't want to send too many of our salaried people away from the plant at any given time. We also don't want to overload them with too many things to do.

"At the same time, the calendar is also a management tool for assigning responsibility and completion dates." However, its purpose is not simply to make managers accountable, but to constantly remind them of what steps to take to meet deadlines. "The calendar prods them," Goins notes. "They look at their calendars every day. They know what they have to do and to whom they have to talk. They can flip the page and see what's coming up the next month and organize their time so that they can get activities scheduled in advance and not wait until the last minute."

Get Full Agreement from Everyone Involved

Goins advises companies interested in using a calendar to *be sure that managers agree to what is scheduled* before it is finalized and distributed. He also notes that you don't need any tools to devise your own calendar. "You can use any tool you want; you don't need software," he says. "You can take a piece of paper and a pencil and draw up a calendar. What's more important is *to have an effective plan that is dedicated to continuous quality improvement.*" That's what Globe has, and it's got an Award to prove it.

Visits to Customer Sites. Individual workers and teams who contribute particularly noteworthy ideas are recognized by being invited to travel to customers' facilities. There, the employees get a real quality learning experience under their belts: They have the opportunity to talk to the customers' employees and find out how Globe's products are used, what the customers' employees consider important about the products, and what, if anything, they might like to see changed about the products.

"Our employees may think that the products themselves are what's important, but it may actually be the *packaging* that's a problem to the customers," notes Goins. "The customers' employees who do the handling may never complain to anyone else, but they'll tell our hourly employees about the problem."

During these visits, Globe employees also learn how their products contribute to society and how product failure can result in tragedy. "For instance, workers learn that the failure of a part made with poor product may lead to a car crash," says Goins. "And they don't want to be responsible for that type of failure."

Letters of Recognition. Workers who contribute suggestions for improvement are also given personal recognition in the form of letters from the company president, which are mailed to their homes so that the employees' families can participate in the reward, too.

Gifts. Other forms of recognition are jackets, hats, and other gifts, which are awarded for team as well as for individual efforts.

PRIZES ACCRUE AS QUALITY IMPROVEMENTS CONTINUE

Since implementing its comprehensive quality program, Globe has made extensive headway in penetrating international markets. It has also made significant internal improvements concerning efficiency, products returned for replacement, customer complaints, employee accidents, and absenteeism.

Goins attributes the success of Globe's quality efforts to two key factors: employee enthusiasm and customer satisfaction. "Had it not been for our customers' urging, instruction, patience, and guidance, I don't think we could have done it," he says, "It would have been much more difficult."

The efforts to improve continue onward. "We certainly didn't stop our quality improvement efforts with the Malcolm Baldrige [application process]," Goins adds. "We have continued to improve our system. We now call it the 'Total Management System,' rather than just the 'Quality System.' This new system has been recognized with the first-ever Shingo Prize for manufacturing excellence, administered out of the University of Utah. We won the Shingo the year after we won the Baldrige."

"We are also one of fewer than 20 suppliers worldwide to receive Ford's Total Quality Excellence Award,' which requires that you have a Total Quality Management system in place," he continues. "In addition, we've received General Motors' 'Targets for Excellence,' which is another total quality management system review.

"More recently, in 1991 our European division received ISO (International Standards Organization) 9000 certification. We have become the only certified supplier to Saturn Motors Corporation in the world.

"So we have continued to advance our quality systems," Goins stresses. "We continue to seek internal and external advice on how to correct deficiencies. We *listen,* we *learn,* and we *act* constantly so that the quality of our products and services will keep improving."

GLOSSARY

This glossary contains important management terms and their definitions as used in this text. Since it is sometimes difficult to understand a term fully simply by reading its definition, page numbers after each definition indicate where a more complete discussion of the term can be found.

Accountability: Management philosophy that individuals are held liable, or accountable, for how well they use their authority and live up to their responsibility of performing predetermined activities. (page 247)

Activities: In the PERT network, specified sets of behavior within a project. (page 199)

Affirmative action programs: In the area of equal employment opportunity, programs whose basic purpose is to eliminate barriers against and increase opportunities for underutilized or disadvantaged individuals. (page 270)

Alderfer's ERG Theory: An explanation of human needs that divides them into three basic types: existence needs, relatedness needs, and growth needs. (page 382)

Appropriate human resources: The individuals in the organization who make a valuable contribution to management system goal attainment. (page 264)

Argyris's maturity-immaturity continuum: A concept that furnishes insights on human needs by focusing on an individual's natural growth process from immaturity to maturity. (page 382)

Assessment center: A program in which participants engage in and are evaluated on a number of individual and group exercises constructed to simulate important activities at the organizational levels to which these participants aspire. (page 274)

Authority: The right to perform or command. (page 242)

Behavioral approach to management: Management approach that emphasizes increasing organizational success by focusing on human variables within the organization. (page 35)

Behavior modification: Program that focuses on managing human activity by controlling the consequences of performing that activity. (page 391)

Bicultural stress: The stress of coping with membership in two cultures simultaneously. (page 578)

Breakeven analysis: Control tool based on the process of generating information that summarizes various levels of profit or loss associated with various levels of production. (page 479)

Breakeven point: The situation wherein the total revenue of an organization equals its total costs. (page 479)

Budget: Control tool that outlines how funds in a given period will be spent, as well as how they will be obtained. (pages 189, 474)

Bureaucracy: Management system with detailed procedures and rules, a clearly outlined organizational hierarchy, and, mainly, impersonal relationships among organization members. (page 217)

Business ethics: Involve the capacity to reflect on values in the corporate decision-making process, to determine how these values and decisions affect the various stakeholder groups, and to establish how managers can use these observations in day-to-day company management. (page 73)

Business portfolio analysis: The development of business related strategy that is based primarily on the market share of businesses and the growth of markets in which businesses exist. (page 166)

Capacity strategy: An operational plan of action aimed at providing the organization with the right facilities to produce the needed output at the right time. (page 466)

Career: An individual's perceived sequence of attitudes and behaviors associated with the performance of work related experiences and activities over the span of the person's working life. (page 13)

Career plateauing: A period of little or no apparent progress in the growth of a career. (page 14)

Centralization: The situation in which a minimal number of job activities and a minimal amount of authority are delegated to subordinates. (page 251)

Change agent: Anyone inside or outside the organization who tries to modify an existing organizational situation. (page 295)

Changing: The second of Kurt Lewin's three related conditions, or states, that result in behavioral change—the state in which individuals begin to experiment with performing new behaviors. (page 304)

Changing an organization: The process of modifying an existing organization to increase organizational effectiveness. (page 292)

Classical approach to management: Management approach that emphasizes organizational efficiency to increase organizational success. (page 28)

Classical organizing theory: The cumulative insights of early management writers on how organizational resources can best be used to enhance goal attainment. (page 217)

Closed system: System that is not influenced by and does not interact with its environment (page 40)

Code of Ethics: A formal statement that acts as a guide for making decisions and acting within an organization. (page 74)

Command groups: Formal groups that are outlined in the chain of command on an organization chart. (page 404)

Commitment principle: Management guideline that advises managers to commit funds for planning only if they can anticipate, in the foreseeable future, a return on planning expenses as a result of the long-range planning analysis. (page 156)

Committee: Task group that is charged with performing some type of specific activity. (page 404)

Communication: The process of sharing information with other individuals. (page 325)

Communication effectiveness index: Intended message reactions divided by the total number of transmitted messages. (page 330)

Communication macrobarriers: The factors that hinder successful communication and that relate primarily to the communication environment and the larger world in which communication takes place. (page 327)

Communication microbarriers: The factors that hinder successful communication and that relate primarily to such variables as the communication message, the source, and the destination. (page 327)

Comparative management: The study of the management process in different countries to examine the potential of management action under different environmental conditions. (page 536)

Complete certainty condition: The decision-making situation in which the decision maker knows exactly what the results of an implemented alternative will be. (page 143)

Complete uncertainty condition: The decision-making situation in which the decision maker has absolutely no idea what the results of an implemented alternative will be. (page 144)

Comprehensive analysis of management: Studying the management function as a whole. (page 33)

Computer: Electronic tool capable of accepting data, interpreting data, performing ordered operations on data, and reporting on the outcome of these operations. (page 496)

Computer-aided design (CAD): A computerized technique for designing new products or modifying existing ones. (page 482)

Computer-aided manufacturing (CAM): Technique using computers to plan and program production equipment in the production of manufactured items. (page 482)

Conceptual skills: Skills that involve the ability to see the organization as a whole. (page 11)

Concurrent control: Control that takes place as some unit of work is being performed. (page 441)

Consensus: Agreement on a decision by all individuals involved in making the decision. (page 137)

Consideration behavior: Leadership behavior that reflects friendship, mutual trust, respect, and warmth in the relationship between the leader and the followers. (page 358)

Content theories of motivation: Explanations of motivation that emphasize internal characteristics of people. (page 376)

Contingency approach to management: Management approach that emphasizes that what managers do in practice depends on a given set of circumstances—a situation. (page 39)

Contingency theory of leadership: Leadership concept that hypothesizes that, in any given leadership situation, success is determined primarily by (1) the degree to which the task being performed by the followers is structured, (2) the degree of position power possessed by the leader, and (3) the type of relationship that exists between the leader and the followers. (page 363)

Control: Making something happen the way it was planned to happen. (page 434)

Control function: Computer activities that dictate the order in which other computer functions are performed. (page 498)

Control tool: A specific procedure or technique that presents pertinent organizational information in such a way that a manager is aided in developing and implementing an appropriate control strategy. (page 477)

Controller: Staff individual whose basic responsibility is assisting line managers with the controlling function by gathering appropriate information and generating necessary reports that reflect this information. (page 443)

Controlling: The process the manager goes through to control. (page 434)

Coordination: The orderly arrangement of group effort to provide unity of action in the pursuit of a common purpose. (page 224)

Corporate culture: A set of shared values and beliefs that organization members have regarding the functioning and existence of their organization. (page 418)

Corporate database: *See* Database.

Corporate social responsibility: The managerial obligation to take action that protects and improves the welfare of society as a whole and organizational interests as well. (page 52)

Corrective action: Managerial activity aimed at bringing organizational performance up to the level of performance standards. (page 439)

Cost-benefit analysis: The process of comparing the cost of some activity to the benefit or revenue that results from the activity to determine the total worth of the activity to the organization. (page 444)

Cost leadership: A strategy that focuses on making an organization more competitive by producing its products more cheaply than competitors can. (page 171)

Critical path: The sequence of events and activities within a program evaluation and review technique (PERT) network that requires the longest period of time to complete. (page 200)

Critical question analysis: Strategy development tool composed mainly of four questions: What are the purposes and objectives of the organization? Where is the organization presently going? In what kind of environment does the organization presently exist? What can be done to better achieve organizational objectives in the future? (page 165)

Culture: The total characteristics of a given group of people and their environment. (page 533)

Data: Facts or statistics. (page 492)

Database: A reservoir of corporate facts consistently organized to fit the information needs of a variety of organization members. Also termed corporate database. (page 509)

Decentralization: The situation in which a significant number of job activities and a maximum amount of authority are delegated to subordinates. (page 251)

Decision: Choice made between two or more available alternatives. (page 134)

Decision-making process: The steps a decision maker takes to make a decision. (page 140)

Decision tree: Graphic decision-making tool typically used to evaluate decisions containing a series of steps. (page 146)

Decision tree analysis: A statistical and graphical multi-phased decision-making technique that shows the sequence and interdependence of decisions. (page 481)

Decline stage: The fourth and last stage in career evolution, which occurs near retirement and during which individuals about sixty-five years of age or older show declining productivity. (page 14)

Decoder/destination: The person or people in the interpersonal communication situation with whom the source/encoder attempts to share information. (page 326)

Delegation: The process of assigning job activities and related authority to specific individuals in the organization. (page 249)

Demographics: The statistical characteristics of a population. (page 159)

Department: Unique group of resources established by management to perform some organizational task. (page 219)

Departmentalization: The process of establishing departments in the management system. (page 219)

Dialogue capability: The ability of a management decision support system (MDSS) user to interact with a management decision support system. (page 511)

Differentiation: A strategy that focuses on making an organization more competitive by developing a product(s) that customers perceive as being different from products offered by competitors. (page 170)

Direct investing: Using the assets of one company to purchase the operating assets of another company. (page 531)

Discrimination: The act of treating an issue, person, or behavior unjustly or inequitably. (page 576)

Diversity: The degree of basic human differences among a given population. Areas of diversity include gender, race, ethnicity, religion, social class, physical ability, sexual orientation, and age. (page 570)

Diversity training: A learning process designed to raise managers' awareness and develop competencies of the issues and needs involved in managing a diverse workforce. (page 586)

Divestiture: Strategy generally adopted to eliminate a strategic business unit that is not generating a satisfactory amount of business and has little hope of doing so in the future. (page 171)

Division of labor: The assignment of various portions of a particular task among a number of organization members. (page 224)

Downward organizational communication: Communication that flows from any point on an organization chart downward to another point on the organization chart. (page 334)

Economics: Science that focuses on understanding how people of a particular community or nation produce, distribute, and use various goods and services. (page 159)

Effectiveness: The degree to which managers attain organizational objectives; it is doing the right things. (page 466)

Efficiency: The degree to which organizational resources contribute to production; it is doing things right. (page 466)

Employee-centered behavior: Leader behavior through which the leader focuses primary attention on subordinates as people. (page 358)

Environmental analysis: Study of the organizational environment to pinpoint environmental factors that can significantly influence organizational operations. (page 158)

Equal Employment Opportunity Commission (EEOC): Agency established to enforce the laws that regulate recruiting and other managerial practices. (page 270)

Equity theory of motivation: An explanation of motivation that emphasizes an individual's perceived fairness of an employment situation and how perceived inequities can cause certain behaviors. (page 378)

Establishment stage: The second stage in career evolution, during which individuals of about twenty-five to forty-five years of age typically start to become more productive or higher performers. (page 13)

Esteem needs: Maslow's fourth set of human needs—including the desires for self-respect and respect from others. (page 380)

Ethics: Our concern for good behavior; our obligation to consider not only our own personal well-being but also that of other human beings. (page 73)

Ethnocentric attitude: Attitude that reflects a belief that multinational corporations should regard home country management practices as superior to foreign country management practices. (page 533)

Ethnocentrism: The belief that one's own group, culture, country, or customs are superior to others'. (page 576)

Events: In the PERT network, the completions of major product tasks. (page 199)

Expected value: Measurement of the anticipated value of some event; determined by multiplying the income an event would produce by its probability of making that income. (page 145)

Exploration stage: The first stage in career evolution, which occurs at the beginning of a career and is characterized by self-analysis and the exploration of different types of available jobs by individuals of about fifteen to twenty-five years of age. (page 13)

Exporting: Selling goods or services to another country. (page 632)

Extrinsic rewards: Rewards that are extraneous to the task accomplished. (page 378)

Feedback: In the interpersonal communication situation, the decoder/destination's reaction to a message. (page 330)

Feedback control: Control that takes place after some unit of work has been performed. (page 441)

Financial objectives: Organizational targets relating to monetary issues. (page 97)

Fixed costs: Expenses incurred by an organization regardless of the number of products produced. (page 479)

Fixed position layout: A layout plan appropriate for organizations involved in a large number of different tasks that require low volumes, multipurpose equipment, and broad employee skills. (page 470)

Flat organization chart: Organization chart that is characterized by few levels and relatively large spans of management. (page 227)

Flextime: Program that allows workers to complete their jobs within a workweek of a normal number of hours that they schedule themselves. (page 390)

Focus: A strategy that emphasizes making an organization more competitive by targeting a particular customer. (page 171)

Forecasting: Planning tool used to predict future environmental happenings that will influence the operation of the organization. (page 192)

Formal group: Group that exists in an organization by virtue of management decree to perform tasks that enhance the attainment of organizational objectives. (page 402)

Formal organizational communication: Organizational communication that follows the lines of the organization chart. (page 333)

Formal structure: Relationships among organizational resources as outlined by management. (page 219)

Friendship groups: Informal groups that form in organizations because of the personal affiliation members have with one another. (page 411)

Functional authority: The right to give orders within a segment of the management system in which the right is normally nonexistent. (page 246)

Functional objectives: Targets relating to key organizational functions. (page 98)

Functional similarity method: Method for dividing job activities in the organization. (page 239)

Gangplank: Communication channel extending from one organizational division to another but not shown in the lines of communication outlined on an organization chart. (page 229)

Gantt chart: Scheduling tool composed essentially of a bar chart with time on the horizontal axis and the resource to be scheduled on the vertical axis. (page 198)

Gender-role stereotypes: Perceptions about the sexes based on what society believes are appropriate behaviors for men and women. (page 577)

General environment: The level of an organization's external environment that contains components normally having broad long-term implications for managing the organization. (page 158)

Geocentric attitude: Attitude that reflects a belief that the overall quality of management recommendations, rather than the location of managers, should determine the acceptability of management practices used to guide multinational corporations. (page 533)

The glass ceiling: An invisible ceiling or limit that prevents women and minorities from advancing beyond a certain organizational level. (page 577)

Goal integration: Compatibility between individual and organizational objectives. (page 94)

Graicunas's formula: Formula that makes the span of management point that as the number of a manager's subordinates increases arithmetically, the number of possible relationships between the manager and the subordinates increases geometrically. (page 227)

Grapevine: Network for informal organizational communication. (page 336)

Grid organization development (grid OD): Commonly used organization development technique based on a theoretical model called the managerial grid. (page 300)

Group: Any number of people who (1) interact with one another, (2) are psychologically aware of one another, and (3) perceive themselves to be a group. (page 402)

Group cohesiveness: The attraction group members feel for one another in terms of the desire to remain a member of the group and to resist leaving it. (page 416)

Group norms: Appropriate or standard behavior that is required of informal group members. (page 417)

Groupthink: The mode of thinking that people engage in when seeking agreement becomes so dominant in a group that it tends to override the realistic appraisal of alternate problem solutions. (page 407)

Growth: Strategy adopted by management to increase the amount of business that a strategic business unit is currently generating. (page 171)

Hierarchy of objectives: The overall organizational objective(s) and the subobjectives assigned to the various people or units of the organization. (page 99)

Host country: The country in which an investment is made by a foreign company. (page 529)

Human resource inventory: Accumulation of information concerning the characteristics of organization members; this information focuses on the past performance of organization members as well as on how they might be trained and best used in the future. (page 267)

Human resource planning: Input planning that involves obtaining the human resources necessary for the organization to achieve its objectives. (page 192)

Human resource strategy: An operational plan to use the organization's human resources effectively and efficiently. (page 471)

Human resources: *See* Appropriate human resources.

Human skills: Skills involving the ability to build cooperation within the team being led. (page 11)

Hygiene, or maintenance, factors: Items that influence the degree of job dissatisfaction. (page 387)

Importing: Buying goods or services from another country. (page 530)

Individual objectives: Personal goals that each organization member would like to reach as a result of personal activity in the organization. (page 93)

Influencing: The process of guiding the activities of organization members in appropriate directions, involving the performance of four primary management activities: (1) leading, (2) motivating, (3) considering groups, and (4) communicating. (page 322)

Informal group: A collection of individuals whose common work experiences result in the development of a system of interpersonal relations that extends beyond those established by management. (page 410)

Informal organizational communication: Organizational communication that does not follow the lines of the organization chart. (page 336)

Informal structure: Patterns of relationships that develop because of the informal activities of organization members. (page 219)

Information: Conclusions derived from data analysis. (page 492)

Information appropriateness: The degree to which information is relevant to the decision-making situation that faces the manager. (page 493)

Information quality: The degree to which information represents reality. (page 493)

Information quantity: The amount of decision related information a manager possesses. (page 494)

Information timeliness: The extent to which the receipt of information allows decisions to be made and action to be taken so the organization can gain some benefit from possessing the information. (page 493)

Input function: Computer activities through which the computer enters the data to be analyzed and the instructions to be followed to analyze the data appropriately. (page 496)

Input planning: Development of proposed action that will furnish sufficient and appropriate organizational resources for reaching established organizational objectives. (page 189)

Interest groups: Informal groups that gain and maintain membership primarily because of special concern each member possesses about a specific issue. (page 410)

Intermediate-term objectives: Targets to be achieved within one to five years. (page 95)

Internal environment: The level of an organization's environment that exists inside the organization and normally has immediate and specific implications for managing the organization. (page 162)

International joint venture: A partnership formed by a company in one country with a company in another country for the purpose of pursuing some mutually desirable business undertaking. (page 531)

International management: Performing management activities across national borders. (page 524)

Intrinsic rewards: Rewards that come directly from performing a task. (page 378)

Job analysis: Technique commonly used to gain an understanding of what a task entails and the type of individual who should be hired to perform the task. (page 265)

Job description: A list of specific activities that must be performed to accomplish some task or job. (pages 238, 265)

Job design: An operational plan that determines who will do a specific job and how and where the job will be done. (page 471)

Job enlargement: The process of increasing the number of operations an individual performs in a job. (page 387)

Job enrichment: The process of incorporating motivators into a job situation. (page 388)

Job rotation: The process of moving individuals from one job to another and not requiring individuals to perform only one job over the long term. (page 385)

Job specification: Characteristics of the individual who should be hired to perform a specific task or job. (page 265)

Job-centered behavior: Leader behavior through which the leader focuses primary attention on the work a subordinate is doing. (page 358)

Jury of executive opinion method: Method of predicting future sales levels primarily by asking appropriate managers to give their opinions on what will happen to sales in the future. (page 194)

Just-in-time (JIT) inventory control: An inventory control technique that reduces inventories to a minimum by arranging for them to be delivered to the production facility just in time to be used. (page 472)

Lateral organizational communication: Communication that flows from any point on an organization chart horizontally to another point on the organization chart. (page 334)

Law of the situation: A law that indicates that managers continually analyze circumstances within their organizations and apply management concepts to fit them. (page 18)

Layout: The overall arrangement of equipment, work areas, service areas, and storage areas within a facility that produces goods or provides services. (page 470)

Layout strategy: An operational plan that determines the location and flow of organizational resources around, into, and within production and service facilities. (page 469)

Leader flexibility: The ability of leaders to change their leadership styles. (page 362)

Leadership: The process of directing the behavior of others toward the accomplishment of objectives. (page 348)

Leadership style: Behavioral pattern a leader establishes while guiding organization members in appropriate directions. (page 358)

Lecture: Primarily one-way communication situation in which an instructor trains by orally presenting information to an individual or group. (page 276)

Level dimension (of plans): The level of the organization at which plans are aimed. (page 185)

License agreement: Right granted by one company to another to use its brand name, technology, product specifications, and so on in the manufacture or sale of goods and services. (page 530)

Life cycle theory of leadership: Leadership concept that hypothesizes that leadership styles should reflect primarily the maturity level of the followers. (page 359)

Line authority: The right to make decisions and to give orders concerning the production-, sales-, or finance-related behavior of subordinates. (page 243)

Location strategy: An operational plan of action that provides the organization with a competitive location for its headquarters, manufacturing, services, and distribution activities. (page 467)

Long-term objectives: Targets to be achieved within five to seven years. (page 95)

Loss: The amount of the total costs of producing a product that exceeds the total revenue gained from selling the product. (page 479)

Maintenance stage: The third stage in career evolution, during which individuals of about forty-five to sixty-five years of age become more productive, stabilize, or become less productive. (page 14)

Majority group: The group of people holding the majority of the positions of decision-making power, control of resources and information, and access to system rewards. (page 570)

Malcolm Baldrige National Quality Awards: National awards given in the U.S. to companies doing exemplary work in the area of quality. (page 547)

Management: The process of reaching organizational goals by working with and through people and other organizational resources. (page 6)

Management by exception: Control tool that allows only significant deviations between planned and actual performance to be brought to the manager's attention. (page 478)

Management by objectives (MBO): Management approach that uses organizational objectives as the primary means by which to manage organizations (page 103)

Management decision support system (MDSS): An interdependent set of computer-oriented decision aids that help managers make nonprogrammed decisions. (page 509)

Management functions: Activities that make up the management process, including planning, organizing, influencing, and controlling. (page 7)

Management information system (MIS): Network established in an organization to provide managers with information that will assist them in decision making. (page 500)

Management inventory card: Form used in compiling a human resource inventory—containing an organizational history of an individual and an explanation of how the individual might be used in the future. (page 267)

Management manpower replacement chart: Form used in compiling a human resource inventory—people-oriented and presenting a total composite view of the individuals whom management considers significant to human resource planning. (page 267)

Management responsibility guide: Tool that can be used to clarify the responsibilities of various managers in the organization. (page 240)

Management science approach: Management approach that emphasizes the use of the scientific method and quantitative techniques to increase organizational success. (page 37)

Management system: Open system whose major parts are organizational input, organizational process, and organizational output. (page 41)

Managerial effectiveness: The degree to which management attains organizational objectives. (page 10)

Managerial efficiency: The degree to which organizational resources contribute to productivity. (page 10)

Managerial grid: Theoretical model based on the premise that concern for people and concern for production are the two primary attitudes that influence management style. (page 301)

Manpower planning: An operational plan that focuses on hiring the right employees for a job and training them to be productive. (page 471)

Materials control: An operational activity that determines the flow of materials from vendors through an operations system to customers. (page 476)

Matrix organization: Traditional organizational structure that is modified primarily for the purpose of completing some type of special project. (page 298)

Maturity: As used in the life cycle theory of leadership, an individual's ability to independently perform the job, to assume additional responsibility, and to desire success. (page 359)

McClelland's Acquired-Needs Theory: An explanation of human needs that focuses on desires for achievement, power, and affiliation as needs that people develop as a result of their life experiences. (page 382)

Means-ends analysis: The process of outlining the means by which various objectives, or ends, in the organization can be achieved. (page 102)

Message: Encoded information that the source/encoder intends to share with others. (page 325)

Message interference: Stimuli that compete with the communication message for the attention of the decoder/destination. (page 328)

Minority group: The smaller in number or lesser in granted rights and status of two groups together representing a whole. The larger group is called the majority group. (page 570)

Mission statement: A written document developed by management, normally based upon input by managers as well as nonmanagers, that describes and explains what the mission of an organization actually is. (page 164)

Model base: A collection of quantitative computer programs that can assist management decision support system (MDSS) users in analyzing data within databases. (page 510)

Motion study: Finding the one best way to accomplish a task by analyzing the movements necessary to perform the task. (page 30)

Motion study techniques: Operational tools that are used to improve productivity. (page 471)

Motivating factors: Items that influence the degree of job satisfaction. (page 387)

Motivation: The inner state that causes an individual to behave in a way that ensures the accomplishment of some goal. (page 376)

Motivation strength: Individual's degree of desire to perform a behavior. (page 377)

Multinational corporation (MNC): Company that has significant operations in more than one country. (page 526)

Murphy's Law: A lighthearted observation about organizations indicating that anything that can go wrong will go wrong. (page 434)

Needs-goal model: Motivation model that hypothesizes that felt needs cause human behavior. (page 376)

Negative norms: Informal group standards that limit organizational productivity. (page 417)

Negative reinforcement: Reward that is the elimination of an undesirable consequence of behavior. (page 391)

Nonprogrammed decisions: Decisions that typically are one-shot occurrences and usually are less structured than programmed decisions. (page 135)

Nonverbal communication: The sharing of ideas without the use of words. (page 332)

On-the-job training: Training technique that blends job related knowledge with experience in using that knowledge in the job. (page 279)

Open system: System that is influenced by and is constantly interacting with its environment. (page 40)

Operating environment: Level of the organization's external environment that contains components normally having relatively specific and immediate implications for managing the organization. (page 161)

Operational objectives: Objectives that are stated in observable or measurable terms. (page 100)

Operations control: An operational plan that specifies the operational activities of an organization. (page 472)

Operations management: The systematic direction (strategy) and control of operations processes that transform resources into finished goods and services; it is getting things done by working with or through other people. (page 465)

Organization chart: Graphic representation of organizational structure. (page 218)

Organization development: Process that emphasizes changing an organization by changing organization members and that bases these changes on an overview of structure, technology, and all other organizational ingredients. (page 300)

Organizational communication: Interpersonal communication in organizations. (page 333)

Organizational mission: The purpose for which or the reason why an organization exists. (page 163)

Organizational objectives: Targets toward which the open management system is directed. (page 90)

Organizational purpose: What the organization exists to do, given a particular group of customers and customer needs. (page 90)

Organizational resources: Assets available for activation during normal operations, among which are human resources, monetary resources, raw materials resources, and capital resources. (page 8)

Organizing: The process of establishing orderly uses for all resources in the organization. (page 214)

Output function: Computer activities that take the results of input, storage, processing, and control functions and transmit them outside the computer. (page 498)

Overlapping responsibility: Situation in which more than one individual is responsible for the same activity. (page 239)

Parent company: The company investing in international operations. (page 529)

Path-goal theory of leadership: A theory of leadership that suggests the primary activity of a leader should be to make desirable and achievable rewards available to organization members as a result of attaining organizational goals and to clarify the kinds of behavior that must be performed to earn those rewards. (page 364)

People change: Changing certain aspects of organization members to increase organizational effectiveness. (page 300)

People factors: Attitudes, leadership skills, communication skills, and all other characteristics of the organization's employees. (page 296)

Perception: Interpretation of a message as observed by an individual. (page 328)

Performance appraisal: The process of reviewing past productive activity to evaluate the contribution individuals have made toward attaining management system objectives. (page 280)

Personal power: Power derived from the relationship that one person has with another. (page 446)

PERT: *See* Program evaluation and review technique (PERT). (page 199)

Physiological needs: Maslow's first set of human needs—for the normal functioning of the body—including the desire for water, food, rest, sex, and air. (page 380)

Plan: Specific action proposed to help the organization achieve its objectives. (page 184)

Plan for planning: Listing of all steps that must be taken to plan for an organization. (page 121)

Planning: The process of determining how the management system will achieve its objectives. (page 114)

Planning tools: Techniques managers can use to help develop plans. (page 192)

Plant facilities planning: Input planning that involves developing the type of work facility an organization will need to reach its objectives. (page 189)

Pluralism: An environment in which cultural, group, and individual differences are acknowledged, accepted, and viewed as a significant contribution to the whole. (page 583)

Policy: Standing plan that furnishes broad guidelines for channeling management thinking in specified directions. (page 186)

Polycentric attitude: Attitude that reflects a belief that since foreign managers are closer to foreign organizational units, they probably understand them better—and therefore that foreign management practices generally should be viewed as more insightful than home country management practices. (page 533)

Porter-Lawler model: Motivation model that hypothesizes that felt needs cause human behavior and that motivation strength is determined primarily by the perceived value of the result of performing the behavior and the perceived probability that the behavior performed will cause the result to materialize. (page 378)

Position power: Power derived from the organizational position that one holds. (page 446)

Position replacement form: Form used in compiling a human resource inventory—summarizing information about organization members who could fill a position should it open. (page 267)

Positive norms: Informal group standards that contribute to organizational productivity. (page 417)

Positive reinforcement: Reward that is a desirable consequence of behavior. (page 391)

Power: The extent to which an individual is able to influence others so they respond to orders. (page 446)

Precontrol: Control that takes place before some unit of work is actually performed. (page 440)

Prejudices: Preconceived judgments, opinions, or assumptions about issues, behaviors, individuals, or groups of people. (page 576)

Premises: Assumptions on which alternative ways of accomplishing objectives are based. (page 116)

Principle of supportive relationships: Management guideline that indicates that all human interaction with an organization should build and maintain the sense of personal worth and the importance of those involved in the interaction. (page 393)

Principle of the objective: Management guideline that recommends that before managers initiate any action, organizational objectives should be clearly determined, understood, and stated. (page 96)

Probability theory: Decision-making tool used in risk situations—

situations in which the decision maker is not completely sure of the outcome of an implemented alternative. (page 145)

Problems: Factors within organizations that are barriers to organizational goal attainment. (page 439)

Procedure: Standing plan that outlines a series of related actions that must be taken to accomplish a particular task. (page 186)

Process control: A technique that assists in monitoring production processes. (page 481)

Process (functional) layout: A layout pattern based primarily on grouping together similar types of equipment. (page 470)

Process strategy: An operational plan of action that determines which means and methods the organization will use to transform resources into goods and services. (page 468)

Process theories of motivation: Explanations of motivation that emphasize how individuals are motivated. (page 376)

Processing function: Computer activities involved with performing the logic and calculation steps necessary to analyze data appropriately. (page 498)

Product layout: A layout designed to accommodate a limited number of different products that require high volumes, highly specialized equipment, and narrow employee skills. (page 470)

Product life cycle: Five stages through which most new products and services pass—introduction, growth, maturity, saturation, and decline. (page 196)

Product strategy: An operational plan of action that determines which goods and services an organization will produce and market. (page 468)

Product-market mix objectives: Objectives that outline which products and the relative number or mix of these products the organization will attempt to sell. (page 98)

Production: The transformation of organizational resources into products. (page 458)

Production control: Ensuring that an organization produces goods and services as planned. (page 458)

Productivity: The relationship between the total amount of goods or services being produced (output) and the organizational resources needed (input) to produce the goods or services. (page 458)

Profits: The amount of total revenue that exceeds total costs. (page 479)

Program: Single-use plan designed to carry out a special project in an organization. (page 187)

Program evaluation and review technique (PERT): Scheduling tool that is essentially a network of project activities showing estimates of time necessary to complete each activity and the sequential relationship of activities that must be followed to complete the project. (page 199)

Programmed decisions: Decisions that are routine and repetitive and that typically require specific handling methods. (page 134)

Programmed learning: Technique for instructing without the presence of a human instructor—small pieces of information requiring responses are presented to individual trainees. (page 277)

Punishment: The presentation of an undesirable behavioral consequence or the removal of a desirable one that decreases the likelihood of the behavior continuing. (page 391)

Pure-breakdown (repair) policy: A policy whereby machine adjustments, lubrication, cleaning, parts replacement, painting, and needed repairs and overhaul are performed after malfunction of facilities or machines occurs. (page 473)

Pure-preventive maintenance policy: A policy that assures that machine adjustments, lubrication, cleaning, parts replacement, painting, and needed repairs and overhauls are performed before malfunction of facilities or machines occurs. (page 473)

Quality: The extent to which a product does what it is supposed to do—how closely and reliably it satisfies the specifications to which it is built. (pages 459, 544)

Quality assurance: An operational activity aimed at achieving the organization's quality objectives. (page 460)

Quality circles: Small groups of workers that meet regularly with management to discuss quality related problems. (page 461)

Quality control: The process of making the quality of finished goods and services what it was planned to be. (page 565)

Quality-oriented policy: A standing plan that furnishes broad, general guidelines for channeling management thinking toward taking action consistent with reaching quality objectives. (page 555)

Ratio analysis: Control tool based on the process of generating information that summarizes the financial position of an organization by calculating ratio based on various financial measures appearing on balance sheets and income statements. (page 475)

Recruitment: The initial screening of the total supply of prospective human resources available to fill a position. (page 264)

Refreezing: The third of Kurt Lewin's three related conditions, or states, that result in behavioral change—the state in which an individual's experimentally performed behaviors become part of the person. (page 305)

Relevant alternatives: Alternatives that are considered feasible for implementation and for solving an existing problem. (page 139)

Repetitiveness dimension (of plans): The extent to which plans are used again and again. (page 184)

Responsibility: The obligation to perform assigned activities. (page 238)

Responsibility gap: Situation in which certain organizational tasks are not included in the responsibility area of any individual organization member. (page 239)

Retrenchment: Strategy adopted by management to strengthen or protect the amount of business a strategic business unit is currently generating. (page 171)

Reverse discrimination: An inequity affecting members of the majority group as an outcome of programs designed to help underrepresented groups and women. (page 590)

Risk condition: The decision-making situation in which the decision maker has only enough information to estimate how probable the outcome of implemented alternatives will be. (page 144)

Robot: Mechanical device built to perform repetitive tasks efficiently. (page 463)

Robotics: The study of the development and use of robots. (page 463)

Role conflict: The conflict resulting when a person fills competing roles from two cultures. (page 578)

Role overload: The result of a person having too many expectations to comfortably fulfill. (page 578)

Rule: Standing plan that designates specific required action. (page 186)

Sales force estimation method: Method of predicting future sales levels primarily by asking appropriate salespeople for their opinions of what will happen to sales in the future. (page 195)

Scalar relationships: The chain of command positioning of individuals on an organization chart. (page 228)

Scheduling: The process of formulating detailed listings of activities that must be performed to accomplish a task, allocating resources necessary to complete the task, and setting up and following timetables for completing the task. (page 198)

Scientific management: Management approach that emphasizes the one best way to perform a task. (page 28)

Scientific method: Problem-solving method that entails the following sequential steps: (1) observing a system, (2) constructing a framework that is consistent with the observations and from which the consequences of changing the systems can be predicted, (3) predicting how various changes would influence the system, and (4) testing to see if these changes influence the system as intended. (page 37)

Scope dimension (of plans): The portion of the total management system at which the plans are aimed. (page 185)

Scope of the decision: The proportion of the total management system that a particular decision will affect. (page 136)

Security, or safety, needs: Maslow's second set of human needs—reflecting the human desire to keep free from physical harm. (page 380)

Selection: Choosing an individual to hire from all of those who have been recruited. (page 272)

Self-actualization needs: Maslow's fifth set of human needs—reflecting the human desire to maximize potential. (page 380)

Serial transmission: The passing of information from one individual through a series of individuals. (page 334)

Short-term objectives: Targets to be achieved in one year or less. (page 95)

Signal: A message that has been transmitted from one person to another. (page 325)

Single-use plans: Plans that are used only once or several times because they focus on organizational situations that do not occur repeatedly. (page 186)

Site selection: Determining where a plant facility should be located. (page 189)

Situational approach to leadership: Relatively modern view of leadership that suggests that successful leadership requires a unique combination of leaders, followers, and leadership situations. (page 350)

Social audit: The process of measuring the social responsibility activities of an organization. (page 71)

Social needs: Maslow's third set of human needs—reflecting the human desire to belong, including the desire for friendship, companionship, and love. (page 380)

Social obligation approach: Approach to meeting social obligations that reflects an attitude that considers business to have primarily economic purposes and confines social responsibility activity mainly to conformance to existing legislation. (page 64)

Social responsibility approach: Approach to meeting social obligations that is characterized by an attitude that considers business as having both societal and economic goals. (page 64)

Social responsiveness: The degree of effectiveness and efficiency an organization displays in pursuing its social responsibilities. (page 61)

Social responsiveness approach: Approach to meeting social obligations that reflects an attitude that considers business to have societal and economic goals as well as the obligation to anticipate upcoming social problems and to work actively toward preventing their appearance. (page 64)

Social values: The relative degrees of worth society places on the manner in which it exists and functions. (page 159)

Sociogram: Sociometric diagram that summarizes the personal feelings of organization members about the people in the organization with whom they would like to spend free time. (page 412)

Sociometry: Analytical tool that can be used to determine what informal groups exist in an organization and who the members of those groups are. (page 412)

Source/encoder: The person in the interpersonal communication situation who originates and encodes information that the person wants to share with others. (page 325)

Span of management: The number of individuals a manager supervises. (page 226)

Stabilty: Strategy adopted by management to maintain or slightly improve the amount of business a strategic business unit is generating (page 171)

Staff authority: The right to advise or assist those who possess line authority. (page 243)

Standard: The level of activity established to serve as a model for evaluating organizational performance. (page 437)

Standing plans: Plans that are used over and over because they focus on organizational situations that occur repeatedly. (page 186)

Statistical quality control: Process used to determine how many products from a larger number should be inspected to calculate a probability that the total number of products meets organizational quality standards. (page 460)

Status: The positioning of importance of a group member in relation to other group members. (page 418)

Stereotypes: Positive or negative assessments or perceived attributes toward members of a group. (page 576)

Storage function: Computer activities involved with retaining the material entered into the computer during the performance of the input function. (page 496)

Strategic business unit (SBU): In business portfolio analysis, a significant organizational segment that is analyzed to develop organizational strategy aimed at generating future business or revenue. (page 166)

Strategic control: The last step of the strategy management process, monitoring and evaluating the strategy management process as a whole in order to make sure that it is operating properly. (page 173)

Strategic planning: Long-term planning that focuses on the organization as a whole. (page 156)

Strategy: Broad and general plan developed to reach long-term organizational objectives. (page 156)

Strategy formulation: The process of determining appropriate courses of action for achieving organizational objectives and thereby accomplishing organizational purpose. (page 165)

Strategy implementation: The fourth step of the strategy management process, putting formulated strategy into action. (page 172)

Strategy management: The process of ensuring that an organization possesses and benefits from the use of an appropriate organization strategy. (page 156)

Stress: The bodily strain that an individual experiences as a result of coping with some environmental factor. (page 306)

Stressor: Environmental demand that causes people to feel stress. (page 308)

Structural change: Type of organizational change that emphasizes modifying an existing organizational structure. (page 297)

Structural factors: Organizational controls, such as policies and procedures. (page 296)

Structure: Designated relationships among resources of the management system. (page 218)

Structure behavior: Leadership activity that (1) delineates the relationship between the leader and the leader's followers or (2) establishes well-defined procedures that the followers should adhere to in performing their jobs. (page 357)

Suboptimization: Condition wherein organizational subobjectives are conflicting or not directly aimed at accomplishing overall organizational objectives. (page 99)

Subsystem: System created as part of the process of the overall management system. (page 118)

Successful communication: Interpersonal communication situation in which the information the source/encoder intends to share with the decoder/destination and the meaning the decoder destination derives from the transmitted message are the same. (page 326)

Suppliers: Individuals or agencies that provide organizations with resources needed to produce organizational goods or services. (page 161)

SWOT analysis: Strategy development tool that matches internal organizational strengths and weaknesses with external opportunities and threats. (page 166)

Symptom: Sign that a problem exists. (page 439)

System: Number of interdependent parts functioning as a whole for some purpose. (page 40)

System approach to management: Management approach based on general system theory—the theory that to understand fully the operation of an entity, the entity must be viewed as a system. (page 40)

Tactical planning: Short-range planning that emphasizes current operations of various parts of the organization. (page 174)

Tall organization chart: Organization chart that is characterized by many levels and relatively small spans of management. (page 272)

Task groups: Formal groups of organization members who interact with one another to accomplish mostly nonroutine organizational tasks (members of any one task group can and often do come from various levels and segments of an organization). (page 404)

Technical skills: The ability to apply specialized knowledge and expertise to work related techniques and procedures. (page 11)

Technological change: Type of organizational change that emphasizes modifying the level of technology in the management system. (page 297)

Technological factors: Any types of equipment or processes that assist organization members in the performance of their jobs. (page 296)

Theory X: Set of essentially negative assumptions about the nature of people. (page 385)

Theory Y: Set of essentially positive assumptions about the nature of people. (page 385)

Theory Z: Effectiveness dimension that implies that managers who use either Theory X or Theory Y assumptions when dealing with people can be successful, depending on their situation. (pages 385, 537)

Time dimension (of plans): The length of time plans cover. (page 185)

Time series analysis method: Method of predicting future sales levels by analyzing the historical relationship in an organization between sales and time. (page 195)

Tokenism: Refers to being one of very few members of a group in an organization. (page 577)

Total costs: The sum of fixed costs and variable costs associated with production. (page 479)

Total power: The entire amount of power an individual in an organization possesses, mainly the amount of position power and the amount of personal power possessed by the individual. (page 446)

Total quality management (TQM): The continuous process of involving all organization members in ensuring that every activity related to the production of goods and services has an appropriate role in establishing product quality. (page 544)

Total revenue: All sales dollars accumulated from selling goods or services that are produced. (page 479)

Training: The process of developing qualities in human resources that ultimately will enable them to be more productive and thus to contribute more to organizational goal attainment. (page 274)

Training need: Information or skill area of an individual or group that requires further development to increase the organizational productivity of the individual or group. (page 275)

Trait approach to leadership: Outdated view of leadership that sees the personal characteristics of an individual as the main determinants of how successful the individual could be as a leader. (page 349)

Transformational leadership: Leadership that inspires organizational success by profoundly affecting followers' beliefs in what an organization should be, as well as followers' values like justice and integrity. (page 366)

Triangular management: Management approach that emphasizes using information from the classical, behavioral, and management science schools of thought to manage the open management system. (page 42)

Unfreezing: The first of Kurt Lewin's three related conditions, or states, that result in behavioral change—the state in which individuals experience a need to learn new behaviors. (page 304)

Unity of command: Management principle that recommends that an individual have only one boss. (page 229)

Universality of management principles: The idea that the principles of management are universal, or applicable to all types of organizations and organizational levels. (page 12)

Unsuccessful communication: Interpersonal communication situation in which the information the source/encoder intends to share with the decoder/destination and the meaning the decoder/destination derives from the transmitted message are different. (page 326)

Upward organizational communication: Communication that flows from any point on an organization chart upward to another point on the organization chart. (page 334)

User database: Database developed by an individual manager or other user. (page 510)

Value analysis: A cost control and cost reduction technique that examines all the parts, materials, and functions of an operation. (page 482)

Variable budgets: Budgets that outline various levels of resources to be allocated for each organizational activity, depending on the level of production within the organization. Also called flexible budgets. (page 475)

Variable costs: Organizational expenses that fluctuate with the number of products produced. (page 479)

Verbal communication: The sharing of ideas through words. (page 332)

Vroom expectancy model: Motivation model that hypothesizes that felt needs cause human behavior and that motivation strength depends on an individual's degree of desire to perform a behavior. (page 377)

"What if" analysis: The simulation of a business situation over and over again using somewhat different data for selected decision areas. (page 510)

Work measurement methods: Operational tools that are used to establish labor standards. (page 471)

Work methods analysis: An operational tool used to improve productivity and ensure the safety of workers. (page 471)

Work team: Task group used in organizations to achieve greater organizational flexibility or to cope with rapid growth. (page 407)

Zero-base budgeting: The planning and budgeting process that requires managers to justify their entire budget request in detail rather than simply to refer to budget amounts established in previous years. (page 474)

ENDNOTES

CHAPTER 1

1. For an interesting discussion of differences between managers and leaders, see Abraham Zaleznik, "Managers and Leaders: Are They Different?" *Harvard Business Review* (March/April 1992), 126–135.
2. Peter F. Drucker, "Management's New Role," *Harvard Business Review* (November/December 1969), 54.
3. U.S. Bureau of the Census, *Statistical Abstract of the United States,* 108th ed. (Washington, D.C.: Government Printing Office, 1987), 230.
4. Geoffrey Colvin, "How to Pay the CEO Right," *Fortune.* April 6, 1992, 60–69.
5. Dana Wechsler, "Just Deserts," *Forbes.* May 28, 1990, 208.
6. Robert Albanese, *Management* (Cincinnati: Southwestern, 1988), 8.
7. For a more detailed description of each of these definitions of management, see Dalton E. McFarland, *Management: Principles and Practice,* 4th ed. (New York: Macmillan, 1974), 6–10.
8. William Wiggenhorn, "Motorola U: When Training Becomes an Education," *Harvard Business Review* (July/August 1990) 71–83.
9. Robert L. Katz, "Skills of an Effective Administrator," *Harvard Business Review* (January/February 1955), 33–41.
10. Ruth Davidhizar, "The Two-Minute Manager," *Health Supervisor* 7(April 1989), 25–29.
11. For an article that demonstrates how important human skills are for middle managers, see also Philip A. Rudolph and Brian H. Kleiner, "The Art of Motivating Employees," *Journal of Managerial Psychology* 4 (1989), *i–iv.*
12. Henri Fayol, *General and Industrial Management* (London: Sir Isaac Pitman & Sons, 1949).
13. B.C. Forbes, *Forbes.* March 15, 1976, 128.
14. Douglas T. Hall, *Careers in Organizations* (Santa Monica, Calif.: Goodyear Publishing, 1976), 4.
15. John Ivancevich and Michael T. Matteson, *Organizational Behavior and Management* (Homewood, Ill.: BPI/Irwin, 1990), 593–95.
16. John W. Slocum, Jr., William L. Cron, and Linda C. Yows, "Whose Career Is Likely to Plateau?" *Business Horizons* (March/April 1987), 31–38.
17. Lynn Slavenski, "Career Development: A Systems Approach," *Training and Development Journal* (February 1987), 56–59.
18. Joseph E. McKendrick, Jr., "What Are You Doing the Rest of Your Life?" *Management World* (September/October 1987), 2.
19. Carl Anderson, *Management: Skills, Functions, and Organization Performance,* 2d ed. (Boston: Allyn and Bacon, 1988).
20. Kenneth Labich, "Take Control of Your Career," *Fortune.* November 18, 1991, 87–90.
21. Paul H. Thompson, Robin Zenger Baker, and Norman Smallwood, "Improving Personal Development by Applying the Four-Stage Career Model," *Organizational Dynamics* (Autumn 1986), 49–62.
22. Buck Blessing, "Career Planning: Five Fatal Assumptions," *Training and Development Journal* (September 1986), 49–51.
23. Thomas J. Peters, Jr., "The Best New Managers Will Listen, Motivate, Support," *Working Woman* (September 1990), 142–143, 216–217.
24. For related information, see Colin Leinster, "The Young Exec as Superdad," *Fortune.* April 25, 1988, 237–42; Uma Sekaran, *Dual-Career Families* (San Francisco: Jossey-Bass, 1986); F.S. Hall and T.D. Hall, "Dual Careers—How Do Couples and Companies Cope with the Problems?" *Organizational Dynamics* 6 (1978), 57–77.
25. Carol Milano, "Reevaluating Recruitment to Better Target Top Minority Talent," *Management Review* (August 1989), 29–32.
26. Colin Leinster, "Black Executives: How They're Doing," *Fortune.* January 18, 1988, 109–20.
27. James F. Wolf, "The Legacy of Mary Parker Follett," *Bureaucrat* 17 (Winter 1988–89), 53–57.
28. For a useful discussion of special training issues related to such employees see Adrienne S. Harris, "And the Prepared Will Inherit the Future," *Black Enterprise* (February 1990), 121–128.
29. Neil J. DeCarlo and W. Kent Sterett, "History of the Malcolm Baldrige National Quality Award," *Quality Progress* 23 (March 1990), 21–27.

CHAPTER 2

1. James H. Donnelly, Jr., James L. Gibson, and John M. Ivancevich, *Fundamentals of Management* (Plano, Tex.: Business Publications, 1987), 6–8.
2. Harold Koontz, Cyril O'Donnell, and Heinz Weihrich, *Management,* 8th ed. (New York: McGraw-Hill, 1984), 52–69.
3. W. Warren Haynes and Joseph L. Massie, *Management,* 2d ed. (Englewood Cliffs, N.J.: Prentice-Hall, 1969), 4–13.
4. Frederick W. Taylor, *The Principles of Scientific Management* (New York: Harper & Bros., 1947), 66–71.
5. For a discussion of how Taylor stressed employee relationships see Hindy Schachter, "Taylor's Scientific Management," *Public Administration Review* (July/August 1990), 471–72.
6. Edward A. Michaels, "Work Measurement," *Small Business Reports* 14 (March 1989), 55–63.
7. Henry L. Gantt, *Industrial Leadership* (New Haven, Conn.: Yale University Press, 1916), 57.
8. Ralph V. Rogers, "An Interactive Graphical Aided Scheduling System," *Computers and Industrial Engineering* 17 (1989), 113–18. For more information on the Gantt chart see G. William Page, "Using Project Management Software in Planning," *Journal of the American Planning Association* 55 (Autumn 1989), 494–99.
9. Gantt, *Industrial Leadership,* 85.
10. Chester I. Barnard, *Organization and Management* (Cambridge, Mass.: Harvard University Press, 1952). For more current discussion of Barnard's work see Christopher Vasillopulos, "Heroism, Self-Abnegation and the Liberal Organization," *Journal of Business Ethics* 7 (August 1988), 585–91.
11. Alvin Brown, *Organization of Industry* (Englewood Cliffs, N.J.: Prentice-Hall, 1947).
12. Henry S. Dennison, *Organization Engineering* (New York: McGraw-Hill, 1931).
13. Luther Gulick and Lyndall Urwick, eds., *Papers on the Science of Administration* (New York: Institute of Public Administration, 1937).
14. J.D. Mooney and A.C. Reiley, *Onward Industry!* (New York: Harper & Bros., 1931). With some modifications, this book appeared as *The Principles of Organization* (New York: Harper & Bros., 1939).
15. Oliver Sheldon, *The Philosophy of Management* (London: Sir Isaac Pitman and Sons, 1923).
16. Henri Fayol, *General and Industrial Management* (London: Sir Isaac Pitman and Sons, 1949).
17. Charles A. Mowll, "Successful Management Based on Key Principles," *Healthcare Financial Management* 43 (June 1989), 122, 124.
18. Fayol, *General and Industrial Management,* 19–42. For an excellent discussion of the role of accountability and organization structure see Elliott Jaques, "In Praise of Hierarchy," *Harvard Business Review* 68 (January/February 1990), 127–133.
19. For an interesting discussion of how modern training programs are teaching managers to establish productive authority relationships in organizations see A. Glenn Kiser, Terry Humphries, and Chip Bell, "Breaking Through Rational Leadership," *Training and Development Journal* 44 (January 1990), 42–45.
20. For a discussion of the impact of remuneration on an organization see Jeffrey Bradt, "Pay for Impact," *Personnel Journal* (January 1992), 76–79.
21. Paul T. Mill and Josephine Bonan, "Site-Based Management: Decentralization and Accountability," *Education Digest* (September 1991), 23–25.
22. For detailed summaries of these studies, see: *Industrial Worker,* 2 vols. (Cambridge, Mass.: Harvard University Press, 1938); and F.J. Roethlisberger and W.J. Dickson, *Management and the Worker* (Cambridge, Mass.: Harvard University Press, 1939). For more recent discussion of the Hawthorne studies see Bev Geber, "The Hawthorne Effect: Orwell or Buscaglia?" *Training* 23 (November 1986), 113–14.
23. For additional information, see: George C. Homans, *Fatigue of Workers: Its Relation to Industrial Production* (New York: Committee on Work in Industry, National Research Council, Reinhold Publishing, 1941).
24. Homans, *Fatigue of Workers.*
25. Stephen Jones, "Worker Interdependence and Output: The Hawthorne Studies Reevaluated," *American Sociological Review,* (April 1990), 176–90.
26. Jennifer Laabs, "Corporate Anthropologists," *Personnel Journal* (January 1992), 81–91.
27. C. West Churchman, Russell L. Ackoff, and E. Leonard Arnoff, *Introduction to Operations Research* (New York: Wiley, 1957), 18.
28. Hamdy A. Taha, *Operations Research: An Introduction* (New York: Macmillan, 1988), 1–2.
29. James R. Emshoff, *Analysis of Behavioral Systems* (New York: Macmillan, 1971), 10. For an interesting account of how the scientific method can be applied to studying management problems like information system problems, see Allen S. Lee, "A Scientific Methodology for the MIS Case Studies," *MIS Quarterly* 13 (March 1989), 33–50.
30. C.C. Shumacher and B.E. Smith, "A Sample Survey of Industrial Operations Research Activities II," *Operations Research* 13 (1965): 1023–27.
31. Catherine L. Morgan, "A Survey of MS/OR Surveys," *Interfaces* 19 (November/December 1989), 95–103.
32. Discussion concerning these factors is adapted from: Donnelly, Gibson, and Ivancevich, *Fundamentals of Management,* 302–03; Efraim Turban and Jack R. Meredith, *Fundamentals of Management Science* (Plano, Tex.: Business Publications, 1981), 15–23.
33. Harold Koontz, "The Management Theory Jungle Revisited," *Academy of Management Review* 5 (1980), 175–87. For an excellent illustration of how the contingency approach might apply to developing strategies for handling competing firms see Moonkyu Lee, "Contingency Approach to Strategies for Service Firms," *Journal of Business Research* 19 (December 1989), 293–301.
34. Don Hellriegel, John W. Slocum, and Richard W. Woodman, *Organizational Behavior* (St. Paul, Minn.: West Publishing, 1986), 22.
35. J.W. Lorsch, "Organization Design: A Situational Perspective," *Organizational Dynamics* 6 (1977), 2–4.
36. Louis W. Fry and Deborah A. Smith, "Congruence, Contingency, and Theory Building," *Academy of Management Review* (January 1987), 117–32.
37. For a more detailed development of von Bertalanffy's ideas, see "General System Theory: A New Approach to Unity of Science," *Human Biology* (December 1951), 302–61.
38. L. Thomas Hopkins, *Integration: Its Meaning and Application* (New York: Appleton-Century-Crofts, 1937), 36–49.
39. Joe Schwartz, "Why They Buy," *American Demographics* 11 (March 1989), 40–41.

40. For a discussion of the value of teaching management through these management functions, see Stephen J. Carroll and Dennis A. Gillen, "Are the Classic Management Functions Useful in Describing Managerial Work?" *Academy of Management Review* (January 1987), 38–51.

CHAPTER 3

1. For a good discussion of many factors involved in the modern meanings of social responsibility, see Frederick D. Sturdivant, and Heidi Vernon-Wortzel, *Business and Society: A Managerial Approach*, 4th ed. (Homewood, Ill.: Irwin, 1990), 3–24.
2. Keith Davis and Robert L. Blomstrom, *Business and Society: Environment and Responsibility,* 3d. ed. (New York: McGraw-Hill, 1975), 6. Also see Richard A. Rodewald, "The Corporate Social Responsibility Debate: Unanswered Questions About the Consequences of Moral Reform," *American Business Law Journal* (Fall 1987), 443–66.
3. For an illustration of how social responsibility makes good economic sense see David Woodruff, "Herman Miller: How Green Is My Factory," *Business Week*. September 16, 1992, 54–56.
4. Peter L. Berger, "New Attack on the Legitimacy of Business," *Harvard Business Review* (September/October 1981), 82–89.
5. Keith Davis, "Five Propositions for Social Responsibility," *Business Horizons* (June 1975), 19–24.
6. Stahrl W. Edmunds, "Unifying Concepts in Social Responsibility," *Academy of Management Review* (January 1977), 38–45.
7. For a discussion of how pre-employment tests might discriminate against blacks, see Iris Randall, "The Great Debate," *Black Enterprise* (February 1992), 141–46.
8. For extended discussion of arguments for and against social responsibility, see William C. Frederick, Keith Davis, and James E. Post, *Business and Society: Corporate Strategy, Public Policy, Ethics,* 6th ed. (New York: McGraw-Hill, 1988), 36–43.
9. T.G.P. Rogers, "Partnership with Society: The Social Responsibility of Business," *Management Decision* (1987), 76–80.
10. K.E. Aupperle, A.B. Carroll, and J.D. Hatfield, "An Empirical Examination of the Relationship Between Corporate Social Responsibility and Profitability," *Academy of Management Journal* (June 1985), 446–63; J.B. McGuire, A. Sundgren, and T. Schneeweis, "Corporate Social Responsibility and Firm Financial Performance," *Academy of Management Journal* (December 1988), 854–72; Vogel, "Ethics and Profits Don't Always Go Hand in Hand," *Los Angeles Times* (December 28, 1988), 7.
11. For Friedman's current views see "Freedom and Philanthropy: An Interview with Milton Friedman," *Business and Society Review* (Fall 1989), 11–18.
12. Neil M. Brown and Paul F. Haas, "Social Responsibility: The Uncertain Hypothesis," *MSU Business Topics* (Summer 1974), 48.
13. Milton Friedman, "Does Business Have Social Responsibility?" *Bank Administration* (April 1971), 13–14.
14. Eric J. Savitz, "The Vision Thing: Control Data Abandons It for the Bottom Line," *Barron's* (May 7, 1990), 10–11, 22; and Jagannath Dubashi, "The Do-Gooder," *Financial World* (June 27, 1989), 70–74.
15. Joan E. Rigdon, "The Wrist Watch: How a Plant Handles Occupational Hazard with Common Sense," *Wall Street Journal,* September 28, 1992, 1.
16. Sandra L. Holmes, "Executive Perceptions of Corporate Social Responsibility," *Business Horizons* (June 1976), 34–40.
17. Sturdivant and Vernon-Wortzel, *Business and Society,* 9–11.
18. Harry A. Lipson, "Do Corporate Executives Plan for Social Responsibility?" *Business and Society Review* (Winter 1974–75), 80–81.
19. S. Prakash Sethi, "Dimensions of Corporate Social Performance: An Analytical Framework," *California Management Review* (Spring 1975), 58–64.
20. George Pilo, "Director Readiness for the Big Cleanup," *Directors & Boards* (Spring 1989), 22–27.
21. For information on a growing trend of businesses making contributions to support education, see Joel Keehn, "How Business Helps the Schools," *Fortune*. October 21, 1991, 161–71.
22. Frank H. Cassell, "The Social Cost of Doing Business," *MSU Business Topics* (Autumn 1974), 19–26.
23. Donald W. Garner, "The Cigarette Industry's Escape from Liability," *Business and Society Review,* 33 (Spring 1980), 22.
24. Meinolf Dierkes and Ariane Berthoin Antal, "Whither Corporate Social Reporting: Is It Time to Legislate?" *California Management Review* (Spring 1986), 106–21.
25. Raymond A. Bauer and Dan H. Fenn, Jr., "What Is a Corporate Social Audit?" *Harvard Business Review* (January/February 1973), 37–48.
26. Condensed from: Jerry McAfee, "How Society Can Help Business," *Newsweek*. July 3, 1978, 15. Copyright 1978 by Newsweek, Inc. All rights reserved. Reprinted by permission.
27. Leonard J. Brooks, Jr., "Corporate Codes of Ethics," *Journal of Business Ethics* (February/March 1989), 117–29; James Srodes, "Mr. Diogenes, Call Your Office," *Financial World* (June 27, 1989).
28. Archie B. Carroll, "In Search of the Moral Manager," *Business Horizons* (March/April 1987), 7–15.
29. John F. Akers, "Ethics and Competitiveness—Putting First Things First," *Sloan Management Review* (Winter 1989), 69–71.
30. Thaddeus Tuleja, "Can the Good Guys Finish First?" *Modern Office Technology* (November 1986), 16–20.
31. "Helping Workers Helps Bottom Line," *Employee Benefit Plan Review* (July 1990).
32. Patrick E. Murphy, "Creating Ethical Corporate Structures," *Sloan Management Review* (Winter 1989), 81–87.
33. Richard A. Spinell, "Lessons from the Salomon Scandal," *America*. December 28, 1991, 476–77.
34. Touche Ross, *Ethics in American Business* (New York: Touche Ross & Co., January, 1988).
35. Abby Brown, "Is Ethics Good Business?" *Personnel Administrator* (February 1987), 67–74.
36. For additional insights on how to create an ethical workplace, see Larry L. Axline, "The Bottom Line on Ethics," *Journal of Accountancy* (December 1990), 87–91.
37. Alan L. Otten, "Ethics on the Job: Companies Alert Employees to Potential Dilemmas," *Wall Street Journal,* July 14, 1986, 25.
38. Gene R. Laczniak, "Framework for Analyzing Marketing Ethics," *Journal of Macromarketing* (Spring 1983), 7–18.
39. Karen L. Fernicola, "Take the Highroad . . . To Ethical Management: An Interview with Kenneth Blanchard," *Association Management* (May 1988), 60–66.
40. Patricia Haddock and Marilyn Manning, "Ethically Speaking," *Sky* (March 1990), 128–31.
41. Saul W. Gellerman, "Managing Ethics from the Top Down," *Sloan Management Review* (Winter 1989), 73–79.
42. For an interesting discussion of what management should do when charged with unethical actions, see John A. Byrne, "Here's What to Do Next, Dow Corning," *Business Week*. February 24, 1992, 33.

CHAPTER 4

1. James F. Lincoln, "Intelligent Selfishness and Manufacturing," Bulletin 434 (New York: Lincoln Electric Company).
2. John F. Mee, "Management Philosophy for Professional Executives," *Business Horizons* (December 1956), 7.
3. Paul Psarouthakis, "Getting There by Goal Setting," *Supervisory Management* (June 1989), 14–15.
4. Hans Hinterhuber and Wolfgang Popp, "Are You a Strategist or Just a Manager?" *Harvard Business Review* (January/February 1992), 105–13. For more on objectives as the central driving force of organizations, see F.G. Harmon and G. Jacobs, "Company Personality: The Heart of the Matter," *Management Review* (October 1985), 36–40.
5. For insights on how the Compaq Computer Corporation uses objectives to evaluate performance, see Alan M. Webber, "Consensus, Continuity, and Common Sense," *Harvard Business Review* (July/August 1990), 120.
6. Y.K. Shetty, "New Look at Corporate Goals," *California Management Review* 22 (Winter 1979), 71–79. For more recent evidence that profitability, growth, and market share continue to be the most commonly set organizational objectives see Luiz Moutinho, "Goal Setting Process and Typologies: The Case of Professional Services," *Journal of Professional Services Marketing* (1989), 83–100.
7. Thomas J. Murray, "The Unseen Corporate 'War,'" *Dun's Review* (June 1980), 110–14.
8. Peter F. Drucker, *The Practice of Management* (New York: Harper & Bros., 1954), 62–65, 126–29. For a worthwhile discussion about the constituencies that organizational objectives must serve, see Hal B. Pickle and Royce L. Abrahamson, *Small Business Management* (New York: Wiley, 1986), 211–12.
9. Theodore Levitt, "Marketing Myopia," *Harvard Business Review* (July/August 1960), 45.
10. Mee, "Management Philosophy for Professional Executives," 7.
11. Jay T. Knippen and Thad B. Green, "Directing Employee Efforts Through Goal-Setting," *Supervisory Management* (April 1989), 32–36.
12. Tom Brown, "What You "Know" Could Be What Hurts You in Business," *Industry Week*. February 3, 1992, 13–19.
13. For a successful history of a company setting and meeting financial objectives over the long run, see Charles F. Knight, "Emerson Electric: Consistent Profits, Consistently," *Harvard Business Review* (January/February 1992), 57–70.
14. For an interesting account of how a mutual insurance company sets financial objectives see Patrick D. Burns, "Objective Setting," *Business Quarterly* (Autumn 1989), 75–79.
15. Joseph G. Louderback and George E. Manners, Jr., "Integrating ROI and CVP," *Management Accounting* (April 1981), 33–39. For a related discussion of financial objectives, see Gordon Donaldson, "Financial Goals and Strategic Consequences," *Harvard Business Review* (May/June 1985), 56–66.
16. Adapted, by permission of the publisher, from "How to Set Company Objectives," by Charles H. Granger, *Management Review* (July 1970). © 1970 by American Management Association, Inc. All rights reserved. See also Max D. Richards, *Setting Goals and Objectives* (St. Paul, Minn.: West Publishing, 1986).
17. Granger, "How to Set Company Objectives," 7. For an interesting example of overall company objectives set for a Japanese bank, see "Dai-Ichi Kangyo Aims for Balanced Expansion," *Business Japan* (October 1989), 33–34.
18. Charles H. Granger, "The Hierarchy of Objectives," *Harvard Business Review* (May/June 1964), 64–74. See also Heinz Weihrich, *Management Excellence: Productivity through MBO* (New York: McGraw-Hill, 1985), 65–84.
19. Edwin A. Locke, Dong-Ok Chah, Scott Harrison, and Nancy Lustgarten, "Separating the Effects of Goal Specificity from Goal Level," *Organizational Behavior and Human Decision Processes* (April 1989), 270–87.

20. Alan Roberts, "Setting Export Training Objectives," *International Trade Forum* (January/February 1989), 24–27.
21. James G. March and Herbert A. Simon, *Organizations* (New York: Wiley, 1958), 191.
22. Drucker, *The Practice of Management;* also Peter Drucker, Harold Smiddy, and Ronald G. Greenwood, "Management by Objectives," *Academy of Management Review* 6 (April 1981), 225.
23. Robert Rodgers and John E. Hunter, "A Foundation of Good Management Practices in Government: Management by Objectives," *Public Administration Review* (January/February 1992), 27–39.
24. Robert L. Mathis and John H. Jackson, *Personnel: Human Resource Management* (St. Paul, Minn.: West Publishing, 1985), 353–55.
25. Robert Rodgers and John E. Hunter, "Impact of Management by Objectives on Organizational Productivity," *Journal of Applied Psychology* (1991), 322–35.
26. Jerry L. Roslund, "Evaluating Management Objectives with the Quality Loss Function," *Quality Progress* (August 1989), 45–49.
27. William H. Franklin, Jr., "Create an Atmosphere of Positive Expectations," *Administrative Management* (April 1980), 32–34.
28. William J. Kretlow and Winford E. Holland, "Implementing Management by Objectives in Research Administration," *Journal of the Society of Research Administrators* (Summer 1988), 135–41.
29. Charles H. Ford, "Manage by Decisions, Not by Objectives," *Business Horizons* (February 1980), 7–18.
30. Kretlow and Holland, "Implementing Management by Objectives in Research Administration," 135–41.
31. E.J. Seyna, "MBO: The Fad That Changed Management," *Long-Range Planning* (December 1986), 116–23.

CHAPTER 5

1. Harry Jones, *Preparing Company Plans: A Workbook for Effective Corporate Planning* (New York: Wiley, 1974), 3.
2. Robert G. Reed, "Five Challenges Multiple-Line Companies Face," *MarketFacts* (January/February 1990), 5–6.
3. Brian Burrows and Ken G.B. Blakewell, "Management Functions and Librarians," *Library Management* (1989), 2–61.
4. C.W. Roney, "The Two Purposes of Business Planning," *Managerial Planning* (November/December 1976), 1–6.
5. Wendy Zellner, "Moving Tofu into the Mainstream," *Business Week.* May 25, 1992, 94.
6. Harold Koontz and Cyril O'Donnell, *Management: A Systems and Contingency Analysis of Management Functions* (New York: McGraw-Hill, 1976), 130.
7. For an interesting discussion on how the importance of planning relates to even day-to-day operations, see Teri Lammers, "The Custom-Made Day Planner," *Inc.* (February 1992), 61–62.
8. "How to Create a New Venture Business Plan," *Agency Sales Magazine* (July 1988), 39–41.
9. For a discussion of U.S. shortsightedness in planning, see Michael T. Jacobs, "A Cure for America's Corporate Short-termism," *Planning Review* (January/February 1992), 4–9.
10. For an article emphasizing the importance of pinpointing planning areas, see Hans Klauss and Thomas Wolter, "Total Quality at Siemens' Wurzburg Electric Motor Factory," *International Journal of Technology Management* (1990), 114–21.
11. For more detailed information on how strategic planning takes place, see Richard F. Vancil and Peter Lorange, "Strategic Planning in Diversified Companies," *Harvard Business Review* (January/February 1975), 81–90; William R. King and David I. Cleland, "A New Method for Strategic Systems Planning," *Business Horizons* (August 1975), 55–64.
12. Excerpted, by permission of the publisher, from *1974–75 Exploratory Planning Briefs: Planning for the Future by Corporations and Agencies, Domestic and International,* by William A. Simmons, © 1975 by AMACOM, a division of American Management Associations, 10–11. All rights reserved.
13. Robert Ackelsberg and William C. Harris, "How Danish Companies Plan," *Long-Range Planning* (December 1989), 111–16.
14. Henry Mintzberg, "A New Look at the Chief Executive's Job," *Organizational Dynamics* (Winter 1973), 20–40.
15. For similar questions focusing on strategic planning, see Hans Hinterhuber and Wolfgang Popp, "Are You a Strategist or Just a Manager?" *Harvard Business Review* (January/February 1992), 105–13.
16. James M. Hardy, *Corporate Planning for Nonprofit Organizations* (New York: Association Press, 1972), 37.
17. Peter Beck, "Creating a Path to the Future," *Director* (February 1989), 64–66.
18. Milton Leontiades, "The Dimensions of Planning in Large Industrialized Organizations," *California Management Review* 22 (Summer 1980), 82–86.
19. For an interesting discussion of individuals such as consultants who are outside a company and develop plans for business clients, see Donald F. Kuratko and Arnold Cirtin, "Developing a Business Plan for Your Clients," *National Public Accountant* (January 1990), 24–27.
20. The section "Qualifications of Planners" is adapted from John Argenti, *Systematic Corporate Planning* (New York: Wiley, 1974), 126.
21. These three duties are adapted from Walter B. Schaffir, "What Have We Learned about Corporate Planning?" *Management Review* (August 1973), 19–26.
22. For a discussion of how modern planners must focus more on gathering information related to the international environment, see William H. Davidson, "The Role of Global Scanning in Business Planning," *Organizational Dynamics* (Winter 1991), 4–16.
23. Frank Corcell, "How to Identify a Sick Company in Time to Help It," *Practical Accountant* (October 1989), 90–99.
24. Michael Muckian and Mary Auestad Arnold, "Manager, Appraise Thyself," *Credit Union Management* (December 1989), 26, 28.
25. Edward J. Green, *Workbook for Corporate Planning* (New York: American Management Association, 1970).
26. Z.A. Malik, "Formal Long-Range Planning and Organizational Performance" (Ph.D. diss., Rensselaer Polytechnic Institute, 1974).
27. James Brian Quinn, "Managing Strategic Change," *Sloan Management Review* 21 (Summer 1980), 3–20.
28. Kamal E. Said and Robert E. Seiler, "An Empirical Study of Long-Range Planning Systems: Strengths—Weaknesses—Outlook," *Managerial Planning* 28 (July/August 1979), 24–28.
29. George A. Steiner, "The Critical Role of Management in Long-Range Planning," *Arizona Review* (April 1966).
30. Myles L. Mace, "The President and Corporate Planning," *Harvard Business Review* (January/February 1965), 49–62.
31. Paul J. Stonich, "Formal Planning Pitfalls and How to Avoid Them," *Management Review* (June 1975), 5–6.
32. Nigel Piercy, "Diagnosing and Solving Implementation Problems in Strategic Planning," *Journal of General Management* (Autumn 1989), 19–38.
33. Peter F. Drucker, *Management: Tasks, Responsibilities, Practices* (New York: Harper & Row, 1973).
34. Bernard W. Taylor III and K. Roscoe David, "Implementing an Action Program via Organizational Change," *Journal of Economics and Business* (Spring/Summer 1976), 203–08.
35. William H. Reynolds, "The Edsel: Faulty Execution of a Sound Marketing Plan," *Business Horizons* (Fall 1967), 39–46.
36. Luis Ma.R. Calingo, "Achieving Excellence in Strategic Planning Systems," *Advanced Management Journal* (Spring 1989), 21– 23. For more discussion on including the right people in the planning process, see Gary Hines, "Strategic Planning Made Easy," *Training & Development Journal* (April 1991), 39–43.
37. Stonich, "Formal Planning Pitfalls and How to Avoid Them," 5.

CHAPTER 6

1. For an excellent discussion of various decisions that managers make, see Michael Verespej, "Gutsy Decisions of 1991," *Industry Week.* February 17, 1992, 21–31.
2. Abraham Zaleznik, "What Makes a Leader?" *Success* (June 1989), 42–45.
3. Mervin Kohn, *Dynamic Managing: Principles, Process, Practice* (Menlo Park, Calif.: Cummings, 1977), 58–62. For an interesting discussion of slowing down the decision-making process to train managers to be better decision makers, see Jack Falvey, "Making Great Managers," *Small Business Reports* (February 1990), 15–18.
4. Herbert A. Simon, *The New Science of Management Decision* (New York: Harper & Bros., 1960), 5–8.
5. Anthony C. LaRusso, "Shutting It Down: A Test for Management," *Business Horizons* (July/August 1989), 59–62.
6. *The D of Research and Development* (Wilmington, Del.: DuPont, 1966), 28–29.
7. Marcia V. Wilkof, "Organizational Culture and Decision Making: A Case of Consensus Management," *R&D Management* (April 1989), 185–99.
8. For tips on how to build a consensus, see Joseph D. O'Brian, "Negotiating with Peers: Consensus, Not Power," *Supervisory Management* (January 1992), 4
9. Charles Wilson and Marcus Alexis, "Basic Frameworks for Decision," *Academy of Management Journal* 5 (August 1962), 151–64.
10. Robert B. Duncan, "Characteristics of Organizational Environments and Perceived Environmental Uncertainty," *Administrative Science Quarterly* 17 (September 1972), 313–27.
11. For a discussion on the importance of understanding decision makers in other organizations, see Walter D. Barndt, Jr., "Profiling Rival Decision Makers," *Journal of Business Strategy* (January/February 1991), 8–11.
12. See Ernest Dale, *Management: Theory and Practice* (New York: McGraw-Hill, 1973), 548–49.
13. "New OCC Guidelines for Appraising Management," *Issues in Bank Regulation* (Fall 1989), 20–22.
14. For an extended discussion of this model, see William B. Werther, Jr., "Productivity Through People: The Decision-Making Process," *Management Decisions* (1988), 37–41.
15. These assumptions are adapted from James G. March and Herbert A. Simon, *Organizations* (New York: Wiley, 1958), 137–38.
16. William C. Symonds, "There's More than Beer in Molson's Mug," *Business Week.* February 10, 1992, 108.
17. Chester I. Barnard, *The Function of the Executive* (Cambridge, Mass.: Harvard University Press, 1938).
18. For further elaboration on these factors, see Robert Tannenbaum, Irving R. Weschler, and Fred Massarik, *Leadership and Organization: A Behavioral Science Approach* (New York: McGraw-Hill, 1961), 277–78.
19. For more discussion of these factors, see F.A. Shull, Jr., A.L. Delbecq, and L.L. Cummings, *Organizational Decision Making* (New York: McGraw-Hill, 1970).

20. For worthwhile discussion of forecasting and evaluating the outcomes of alternatives, see J.R.C. Wensley, "Effective Decision Aids in Marketing," *European Journal of Marketing* (1989), 70–79.
21. Timothy A. Park and Frances Antonovitz, "Econometric Tests of Firm Decision Making under Uncertainty: Optimal Output and Hedging Decisions," *Southern Economic Journal* (January 1992), 593–609.
22. For a recent discussion of risk and decisions, see Sim B. Sitkin and Amy L. Pablo, "Reconceptualizing the Determinants of Risk Behavior," *Academy of Management Review* (January 1992), 11.
23. Steven C. Harper, "What Separates Executives from Managers," *Business Horizons* (September/October 1988), 13–19; Russ Holloman, "The Light and Dark Sides of Decision Making," *Supervisory Management* (December 1989), 33–34.
24. The scope of this text does not permit elaboration on these three decision-making tools. However, for an excellent discussion on how they are used in decision making, see Richard M. Hodgetts, *Management: Theory, Process and Practice* (Philadelphia: Saunders, 1975), 254–66.
25. Richard C. Mosier, "Expected Value: Applying Research to Uncertainty," *Appraisal Journal* (July 1989), 293–96.
26. Peter Boys, "Answers Grow on Decision Trees," *Accountancy* (January 1990), 86–89; Olen L. Greer, "A Decision-Tree Approach to the Design and Implementation of Accounting and Information Systems for Small Businesses," *Journal of Small Business Management* (January 1989), 8–16.
27. John F. Magee, "Decision Trees for Decision Making," *Harvard Business Review* (July/August 1964).

CHAPTER 7

1. Tony Grundy and Dave King, "Using Strategic Planning to Drive Strategic Change," *Long-Range Planning* (February 1992), 100–108.
2. Andrall E. Pearson, "Six Basics for General Managers," *Harvard Business Review* (July/August 1989), 94–101.
3. Charles R. Greer, "Counter-Cyclical Hiring as a Staffing Strategy for Managerial and Professional Personnel: Some Considerations and Issues," *Academy of Management Review* 9 (April 1984), 324–30.
4. Yedzi M. Godiwalla, Wayne A. Meinhart, and William D. Warde, "How CEOs Form Corporate Strategy," *Management World* (May 1981), 28–29, 44.
5. Richard B. Robinson, Jr., and John A. Pearce II, "Research Thrusts in Small Firm Strategic Planning," *Academy of Management Review* 9 (January 1984), 128–37.
6. George Sawyer, "Elements of Strategy," *Managerial Planning* (May/June 1981), 3–59.
7. This section is based on Samuel C. Certo and J. Paul Peter, *Strategic Management: Concepts and Applications* (New York: McGraw-Hill, 1991), 3–27.
8. Samuel C. Certo and J. Paul Peter, *Strategic Management: Concepts and Applications* (New York: Random House, 1988).
9. Philip S. Thomas, "Environment Analysis for Corporate Planning," *Business Horizons* (October 1974), 27–38.
10. For more information about several of these examples, see Abraham Katz, "Evaluating the Environment: Economic and Technological Factors," in *Handbook of Business Strategy,* ed. William D. Guth (Boston: Warren, Gorham & Lamont, 1985), 2–9.
11. This section is based on William F. Glueck and Lawrence R. Jauch, *Business Policy and Strategic Management* (New York: McGraw-Hill, 1984), 99–110.
12. D. Stanley Eitzen, *Social Structure and Social Problems in America* (Boston: Allyn & Bacon, 1974), 12–14.
13. Bruce Henderson, "The Origin of Strategy," *Harvard Business Review* (November/December 1989), 139–43.
14. R.S. Wilson, "Managing in the Competitive Environment," *Long-Range Planning* 17 (1984), 50–63.
15. Peter Wright, "MNC—Third World Business Unit Performance: Application of Strategic Elements," *Strategic Management Journal* 5 (1984), 231–240.
16. M. Klemm, S. Sanderson, and G. Luffman, "Mission Statements: Selling Corporate Values to Employees," *Long-Range Planning* (June 1991), 73–78.
17. Colin Coulson-Thomas, "Strategic Vision or Strategic Con?: Rhetoric or Reality," *Long-Range Planning* (February 1992), 81–89.
18. Discussion in this section is based primarily on Thomas H. Naylor and Kristin Neva, "Design of a Strategic Planning Process," *Managerial Planning* (January/February 1980), 2–7; Donald W. Mitchell, "Pursuing Strategic Potential," *Managerial Planning* (May/June 1980), 6–10; Benton E. Gup, "Begin Strategic Planning by Asking Three Questions," *Managerial Planning* (November/December 1979); 28–31, 35; L.V. Gerstner, Jr., "Can Strategic Planning Pay Off?" *Business Horizons* 15 (1972), 5–16.
19. This section is based on Arthur A. Thompson and A.J. Strickland III, *Strategy Formulation and Implementation* (Plano, Tex.: Business Publications, 1983), 277–91.
20. For more extended discussion of business portfolio analysis, see Certo and Peter, *Strategic Management,* 102–11.
21. Bruce D. Henderson, *Henderson on Corporate Strategy* (Cambridge, Mass.: ABT Books, 1979).
22. Philip Kotler, *Marketing Management: Analysis, Planning and Control,* 4th ed. (Englewood Cliffs, N.J.: Prentice-Hall, 1980), 76.
23. Harold W. Fox, "The Frontiers of Strategic Planning: Intuition or Formal Models?" *Management Review* (April 1981), 8–14.
24. This discussion of Porter's model is based on chapters 1 and 2 of Porter's *Competitive Strategy* (New York: The Free Press, 1980), and chapter 1 of Porter's *Competitive Advantage: Creating and Sustaining Superior Performance* (New York: The Free Press, 1985).
25. Ian C. MacMillan, Donald C. Hambrick, and Diana L. Day, "The Product Portfolio and Profitability—A PIMS-Based Analysis of Industrial-Product Businesses," *Academy of Management Journal* (December 1982), 733–55.
26. Bill Saporito, "Black & Decker's Gamble on Globalization," *Fortune.* May 14, 1984, 40–48.
27. Walecia Konrad and Bruce Einhorn, "Famous Amos Gets a Chinese Accent," *Business Week.* September 28, 1992, 76.
28. Doron P. Levin, "Westinghouse's New Chief Aims to Push New Lines, Revitalize Traditional Ones," *Wall Street Journal,* November 28, 1983, 10.
29. William Sandy, "Avoid the Breakdowns between Planning and Implementation," *Journal of Business Strategy* (September/October 1991), 30–33.
30. Thomas V. Bonoma, "Making Your Marketing Strategy Work," *Harvard Business Review* (March/April 1984), 69–76.
31. For a good discussion of the importance of monitoring the progress of the strategic planning process, see William B. Carper and Terry A. Bresnick, "Strategic Planning Conferences," *Business Horizons* (September/October 1989), 34–40.
32. Stephen Bungay and Michael Goold, "Creating a Strategic Control System," *Long-Range Planning* (June 1991), 32–39.
33. For a detailed discussion of the characteristics of strategic and tactical planning, see George A. Steiner, *Top Management Planning* (Toronto, Canada: Collier-Macmillan, 1969), 37–39.
34. Russell L. Ackoff, *A Concept of Corporate Planning* (New York: Wiley, 1970), 4.
35. "The New Breed of Strategic Planner," *Business Week.* September 17, 1984, 62–67.

CHAPTER 8

1. Charles B. Ames, "Straight Talk from the New CEO" *Harvard Business Review* (November/December 1989), 132–38.
2. Fremont E. Kast and James E. Rosenzweig, *Organization and Management: A Systems Approach* (New York: McGraw-Hill, 1970), 443–49.
3. For discussion on expanding this list of four characteristics to thirteen, see P. LeBreton and D.A. Henning, *Planning Theory* (Englewood Cliffs, N.J.: Prentice-Hall, 1961), 320–44. These authors list the dimensions of a plan as (1) complexity, (2) significance, (3) comprehensiveness, (4) time, (5) specificity, (6) completeness, (7) flexibility, (8) frequency, (9) formality, (10) confidential nature, (11) authorization, (12) ease of implementation, and (13) ease of control.
4. For a discussion of this rule and its difficult enforcement, see Sherry C. Hammond, David A. DeCenzo, and Mollie H. Bowers, "How One Company Went Smokeless," *Harvard Business Review* (November/December 1987), 44–45.
5. From "Seize the Future—Make Top Trends Pay Off Now," *Success* (March 1990), 39–45.
6. For an interesting article outlining how currency exchange rates complicate budgets that relate to operations in more than one country, see Paul V. Mannino and Ken Milani, "Budgeting for an International Business," *Management Accounting* (February 1992), 36–41.
7. J. Fred Weston and Eugene F. Brigham, *Essentials of Managerial Finance* (New York: Holt, Rinehart & Winston, 1971), 107; Mark M. Klein, "Questions to Ask Before You Sharpen Your Budget Knife," *Bottomline* (March 1990), 32–37; Pierre Filiatrault and Jean-Charles Chebat, "How Service Firms Set Their Marketing Budgets," *Industrial Marketing Management* (February 1990), 63–67.
8. Kjell A. Ringbakk, "Why Planning Fails," *European Business* (July 1970).
9. For a good discussion on involving people in the planning process, see Margaret M. Lucas, "Business Plan Is the Key to Agency Success," *National Underwriter* 94 (March 5, 1990), 15, 17.
10. For information that ranks U.S. cities on the possible site selection criterion of growth, see John Case, "Where the Growth Is," *Inc.* (June 1991), 66–79.
11. Walt Yesberg, "Get a Grip on Building Costs," *ABA Banking Journal* 82 (March 1990), 90, 92; Robert Bowman, "Key Logistics Issues in Site Selection," *Distribution* 88 (December 1989), 56–57.
12. Douglas P. Woodward, "Locational Determinants of Japanese Manufacturing Start-Ups in the United States," *Southern Economic Journal* (January 1992), 690–708.
13. Greg Nakanishi, "Building Business through Partnerships," *HRMagazine* (June 1991), 108–112.
14. Dale S. Beach, *Personnel: The Management of People at Work* (New York: Macmillan, 1975), 220.
15. Henri Fayol, *General and Industrial Management* (New York: Pitman, 1949).
16. Charles F. Kettering, "A Glimpse at the Future," *Industry Week.* July 1, 1991, 34.
17. William C. House, "Environmental Analysis: Key to More Effective Dynamic Planning," *Managerial Planning* (January/February 1977), 25–29.
18. Olfa Hemler, "The Uses of Delphi Techniques in Problems of Educational Innovations," no. 3499, RAND Corporation, December 1966.

19. For an interesting illustration of how the delphi method works, see Yeong Wee Yong, Kau Ah Keng, and Tan Leng Leng, "A Delphi Forecast for the Singapore Tourism Industry," *International Marketing Review* 6 (1989), 35–46.
20. James E. Cox, Jr., "Approaches for Improving Salespersons' Forecasts," *Industrial Marketing Management* 18 (November 1989), 307–11.
21. N. Carroll Mohn, "Forecasting Sales with Trend Models—Coca-Cola's Experience," *Journal of Business Forecasting* 8 (Fall 1989), 6–8.
22. For elaboration on these methods, see George A. Steiner, *Top Management Planning* (London: Collier-Macmillan, 1969), 223–27.
23. Willard Fazar, "The Origin of PERT," *The Controller* (December 1962).
24. Harold L. Wattel, *Network Scheduling and Control Systems CAP/PERT* (Hempstead, N.Y.: Hofstra University, 1964); see also Khaled A. Bushait, "The Application of Project Management Techniques to Construction and Research and Development Projects," *Project Management Journal* 20 (June 1989), 17–22.
25. R.J. Schonberger, "Custom-Tailored PERT/CPM Systems," *Business Horizons* 15 (1972): 64–66.
26. Avraham Shtub, "The Integration of CPM and Material Management in Project Management," *Construction Management and Economics* 6 (Winter 1988), 261–72.
27. For extended discussion of these steps see Edward K. Shelmerdine, "Planning for Project Management," *Journal of Systems Management* 40 (January 1989), 16–20.

CHAPTER 9

1. Douglas S. Sherwin, "Management of Objectives," *Harvard Business Review* (May/June 1976), 149–60.
2. Lloyd Sandelands and Robert Drazin, "On the Language of Organization Theory," *Organizational Studies* 10 (1989), 457–77.
3. Henri Fayol, *General and Industrial Management* (London: Sir Isaac Pitman and Sons, 1949), 53–54.
4. For a discussion emphasizing the importance of continually adapting organization structure, see Michael A. Verespej, "When Change Becomes the Norm," *Industry Week*. March 16, 1992, 35–36.
5. Burt K. Scanlan, "Managerial Leadership in Perspective: Getting Back to Basics," *Personnel Journal* (March 1979), 168–70.
6. Saul W. Gellerman, "In Organizations, as in Architecture, Form Follows Function," *Organizational Dynamics* 18 (Winter 1990), 57–68.
7. For a discussion of how this evaluation can contribute to increased worker productivity, see Eugene F. Finkin, "Techniques for Making People More Productive," *Journal of Business Strategy* (March/April 1991), 53–56.
8. Max Weber, *Theory of Social and Economic Organization,* trans. and ed. A.M. Henderson and Talcott Parsons (London: Oxford University Press, 1947); Stanley Vanagunas, "Max Weber's Authority Models and the Theory of X-Inefficiency: The Economic Sociologist's Analysis Adds More Structure to Leibenstein's Critique of Rationality," *American Journal of Economics and Sociology* 48 (October 1989), 393–400; Foad Derakhshan and Kamal Fatehi, "Bureaucracy as a Leadership Substitute: A Review of History," *Leadership and Organization Development Journal* 6 (1985), 13–16.
9. Richard Bendix, *Max Weber: An Intellectual Portrait* (New York: Doubleday, 1960).
10. Lyndall Urwich, *Notes on the Theory of Organization* (New York: American Management Association, 1952).
11. For an interesting discussion of a nontraditional organization structure, see John E. Tropman, "The Organizational Circle: A New Approach to Drawing an Organizational Chart," *Administration in Social Work* 13 (1989), 35–44.
12. Sally Helgesen, *The Female Advantage: Women's Ways of Leadership* (New York: Doubleday/Currency, 1990).
13. Tom Peters, "The Best New Managers Will Listen, Motivate, Support," *Working Woman* (September 1990), 142–43, 216–17.
14. Raef T. Hussein, "Informal Groups, Leadership, and Productivity," *Leadership and Organization Development Journal* 10 (1989), 9–16.
15. Geary A. Rummler and Alan P. Brache, "Managing the White Space on the Organization Chart," *Supervision* (May 1991), 6–12. For an article arguing in favor of having organizations designed by function, see Jack Cohen, "Managing the Managers," *Supermarket Business* 44 (September 1989), 16, 244.
16. Roderick E. White and Thomas A. Poynter, "Organizing for Worldwide Advantage," *Business Quarterly* 54 (Summer 1989), 84–89.
17. Y.K. Shetty and Howard M. Carlisle, "A Contingency Model of Organization Design," *California Management Review* 15 (1972), 38–45.
18. For insights on how Ralph Larsen, CEO of Johnson & Johnson, views problems and how this view might influence the formal structure of his organization, see Brian Dumaine, "Is Big Still Good?" *Fortune*. April 30, 1992, 50–60.
19. C.R. Walker and R.H. Guest, *The Man on the Assembly Line* (Cambridge, Mass.: Harvard University Press, 1952). For an excellent example of how technology can affect division of labor, see John P. Walsh, "Technological Change and the Division of Labor: The Case of Retail Meatcutters," *Work and Occupations* 16 (May 1989), 165–83.
20. J. Mooney, "The Principles of Organization," in *Ideas and Issues in Public Administration,* ed. D. Waldo (New York: McGraw-Hill, 1953), 86. For discussion of the importance of cooperation and coordination in division of labor, see Jason Magidson and Andrew E. Polcha, "Creating Market Economies within Organizations," *The Planning Forum* (January/February 1992), 37–40.
21. Bruce D. Sanders, "Making Work Groups Work," *Computerwrold* 24 (March 5, 1990), 85–89.
22. George D. Greenberg, "The Coordinating Roles of Management," *Midwest Review of Public Administration* 10 (1976), 66–76.
23. Henry C. Metcalf and Lyndall F. Urwich, eds., *Dynamic Administration: The Collected Papers of Mary Parker Follett* (New York: Harper & Bros., 1942), 297–99; James F. Wolf, "The Legacy of Mary Parker Follett," Bureaucrat (Winter 1988–89), 53–57.
24. Leon McKenzie, "Supervision: Learning from Experience," *Health Care Supervisor* 8 (January 1990), 1–11.
25. Harold Koontz, "Making Theory Operational: The Span of Management," *Journal of Management Studies* (October 1966), 229–43; see also John S. McClenahen, "Managing More People in the '90s," *Industry Week* 238 (March 1989), 30–38.
26. V.A. Graicunas, "Relationships in Organization," *Bulletin of International Management Institute* (March 1933), 183–87. For more on the life of Graicunas, see Arthur C. Bedeian, "Vytautas Andrius Graicunas: A Biographical Note," *Academy of Management Journal* 17 (June 1974), 347–49.
27. L.F. Urwick, "V.A. Graicunas and the Span of Control," *Academy of Management Journal* 17 (June 1974), 349–54.
28. Philip R. Nienstedt, "Effectively Downsizing Management Structures," *Human Resource Planning* 12 (1989), 155–65.
29. Robin Bellis-Jones and Max Hand, "Improving Managerial Spans of Control," *Management Accounting* 67 (October 1989), 20–21.
30. Cass Bettinger, "The Nine Principles of War," *Bank Marketing* 21 (December 1989), 32–34; Charles A. Mowll, "Successful Management Based on Key Principles," *Healthcare Financial Management* 43 (June 1989), 122, 124.
31. Henri Fayol, *General and Industrial Administration* (Belmont, Calif.: Pitman, 1949).

CHAPTER 10

1. Andre Nelson, "Have I the Right Stuff to Be a Supervisor?" *Supervision* 51 (January 1990), 10–12.
2. J.E. Osborne, "Job Descriptions Do More Than Describe Duties," *Supervisory Management* (February 1992), 8.
3. Stephen X. Doyle and Benson P. Shapiro, "What Counts Most in Motivating Your Sales Force?" *Harvard Business Review* (May/June 1980), 133–40. See also G.F. Scollard, "Dynamic Descriptions: Job Descriptions Should Work for You," *Management World* (May 1985), 34–35.
4. Bruce Shawkey, "Job Descriptions," *Credit Union Executive* 29 (Winter 1989/1990), 20–23.
5. Robert J. Theirauf, Robert C. Klekamp, and Daniel W. Geeding, *Management Principles and Practices: A Contingency and Questionnaire Approach* (New York: Wiley, 1977), 334.
6. Deborah S. Kezsbom, "Managing the Chaos: Conflict Among Project Teams," *AACE Transactions* (1989), A.4.1–A.4.8.
7. Robert D. Melcher, "Roles and Relationships: Clarifying the Manager's Job," *Personnel* 44 (May/June 1967), 34–41.
8. This section is based primarily on John H. Zenger, "Responsible Behavior: Stamp of the Effective Manager," *Supervisory Management* (July 1976), 18–24.
9. Stephen Bushardt, David Duhon, and Aubrey Fowler, "Management Delegation Myths and the Paradox of Task Assignment," *Business Horizons* (March/April 1991), 37–43.
10. Jack J. Phillips, "Authority: It Just Doesn't Come with Your Job," *Management Solutions* 31 (August 1986), 35–37.
11. Max Weber, "The Three Types of Legitimate Rule," trans. Hans Gerth, *Berkeley Journal of Sociology* 4 (1953), 1–11; for a current illustration of this concept, see Gail DeGeorge, "Yo, Ho, Ho, and a Battle for Bacardi," *Business Week*. April 16, 1990, 47–48.
12. John Gardner, "The Anti-Leadership Vaccine," *Carnegie Foundation Annual Report,* 1965.
13. Chester I. Barnard, *The Functions of the Executive* (Cambridge, Mass.: Harvard University Press, 1938).
14. Patti Wolf, Gerald Grimes, and John Dayani, "Getting the Most out of Staff Functions," *Small Business Reports* 14 (October 1989), 68–70.
15. Harold Stieglitz, "On Concepts of Corporate Structure," *Conference Board Record* 11 (February 1974), 7–13.
16. Wendell L. French, *The Personnel Management Process: Human Resource Administration and Development* (Boston: Houghton Mifflin, 1987), 66–68.
17. Derek Sheane, "When and How to Intervene in Conflict," *Personnel Management* (November 1979), 32–36; John M. Ivancevich and Michael T. Matteson, "Intergroup Behavior and Conflict," in their *Organizational Behavior and Management* (Plano, Tex.: Business Publications, 1987), 305–45.
18. Robert Albanese, *Management* (Cincinnati: South-Western Publishing, 1988), 313. For an excellent discussion of the role of accountability and organization structure see Elliott Jacques, "In Praise of Hierarchy," *Harvard Business Review* 68 (January/February 1990), 127–133.
19. "How Ylvisaker Makes 'Produce or Else' Work," *Business Week*. October 27, 1973, 112.
20. William H. Newman and E. Kirby Warren, *The Process of Management: Concepts, Behavior, and Practice,* 4th ed. (Englewood Cliffs, N.J.: Prentice-Hall, 1977), 39–40; these steps are also discussed in Jay T. Knippen and Thad B. Green, "Delegation," *Supervision* 51 (March 1990), 7–9, 17.

21. Robert Rohrer, "Does the Buck Ever Really Stop?" *Supervision* (July 1991), 7–8.
22. R. S. Dreyer, "The Ultimate Frustration," *Supervision* May 1991), 22–23.
23. Robert B. Nelson, "Mastering Delegation," *Executive Excellence* 7 (January 1990), 13–14.
24. Jimmy Calano and Jeff Salzman, "How Delegation Can Lead Your Team to Victory," *Working Woman* (August 1989), 86–87, 95.
25. Roz Ayres-Williams, "Mastering the Fine Art of Delegation," *Black Enterprise* (April 1992), 91–93.
26. Harold Koontz, Cyril O'Donnell, and Heinz Weihrich, *Essentials of Management,* 8th ed. (New York: McGraw-Hill, 1986), 231–33.
27. H. Gilman, "J.C. Penney Decentralizes Its Purchasing," *Wall Street Journal.* May 8, 1986, 6.
28. Donald O. Harper, "Project Management as a Control and Planning Tool in the Decentralized Company," *Management Accounting* (November 1968), 29–33.
29. For further discussion on positive and negative centralization and decentralization, see Terence R. Mitchell and James R. Larson, Jr., *People in Organizations* (New York: McGraw-Hill, 1987), 49–50.
30. Information for this section is mainly from John G. Staiger, "What Cannot Be Decentralized," *Management Record* 25 (January 1963), 19–21. At the time the article was written, Staiger was vice president of administration, North American Operations, Massey-Ferguson, Limited.
31. Staiger, "What Cannot Be Decentralized," 19.
32. Staiger, "What Cannot Be Decentralized," 21.
33. Staiger, "What Cannot Be Decentralized," 21.

CHAPTER 11

1. Bruce Shawkey, "Job Descriptions," *Credit Union Executive* 29 (Winter 1989/1990), 20–23; Howard D. Feldman, "Why Are Similar Managerial Jobs So Different?" *Review of Business* 11 (Winter 1989), 15–22.
2. "Job Analysis," *Bureau of Intergovernmental Personnel Programs* (December 1973), 135–52.
3. Gundars E. Kaupins, "Lies, Damn Lies, and Job Evaluations," *Personnel* 66 (November 1989), 62–65.
4. Thomas J. Murray, "The Coming Glut in Executives," *Dun's Review* (May 1977), 64. An even more recent article pointing out this trend is "Slackening in Executive Demand," *Personnel Management* 17 (September 1985), 74.
5. Fred K. Foulkes, "How Top Nonunion Companies Manage Employees," *Harvard Business Review* (September/October 1981), 90.
6. John Perham, "Management Succession: A Hard Game to Play," *Dun's Review* (April 1981), 54–55, 58.
7. Walter S. Wikstrom, "Developing Managerial Competence: Concepts, Emerging Practices," *Studies in Personnel Policy,* no. 189, National Industrial Conference Board (1964), 95–105.
8. Patricia Panchak, "Resourceful Software Boosts HR Efficiency," *Modern Office Technology* 35 (April 1990), 76–80.
9. Ray H. Hodges, "Developing an Effective Affirmative Action Program," *Journal of Intergroup Relations* 5 (November 1976), 13. For a more philosophical argument supporting affirmative action see Leo Goarke, "Affirmative Action as a Form of Restitution," *Journal of Business Ethics* 9 (March 1990), 207–13.
10. R. Roosevelt Thomas, Jr., "From Affirmative Action to Affirming Diversity," *Harvard Business Review* 68 (March/April, 1990), 107–17. For an argument on how quotas as part of affirmative action may harm business, see George Weimer, "Quotas and Other Dumb Ideas," *Industry Week.* April 6, 1992, 86.
11. For insights on how to select high performers see: "Can you Spot A Peak Performer?," *Personnel Journal,* Michael Rozek, June 1991, pages 77–78.
12. For more discussion on the stages of the selection process, see David J. Cherrington, *Personnel Management: The Management of Human Resources* (Dubuque, Iowa: Wm. C. Brown Publishers, 1987), 186–231.
13. This section is based on Andrew F. Sikula, *Personnel Administration and Human Resource Management* (New York: Wiley, 1976), 188–90.
14. For information on various tests available, see O.K. Buros, ed., *The 8th Mental Measurements Yearbook* (Highland Park, N.J.: Gryphon Press, 1978).
15. John W. Jones, Philip Ash, Catalina Soto, and William Terris, "Preemployment Testing: An Occasion for Invasion?" *Security Management* 34 (April 1990), 68–72.
16. Robin Inwald, "Preemployment Testing: Those Seven Deadly Sins," *Security Management* 34 (April 1990), 73–76.
17. D.W. Bray and D.L. Grant, "The Assessment Center in the Measurement of Potential for Business Management," *Psychological Monographs* 80, no. 17 (1966), 1–27.
18. Susan O. Hendricks and Susan E. Ogborn, "Supervisory and Managerial Assessment Centers in Health Care," *Health Care Supervisor* 8 (April 1990), 65–75.
19. Barry M. Cohen, "Assessment Centers," *Supervisory Management* (June 1975), 30. See also T.J. Hanson and J.C. Balestreri-Sepro, "An Alternative to Interviews: Pre-employment Assessment Process," *Personnel Journal* (June 1985), 114.
20. Ann Howard, "An Assessment of Assessment Centers," *Academy of Management Journal* 17 (March 1974), 117.
21. William Umiker and Thomas Conlin, "Assessing the Need for Supervisory Training: Use of Performance Appraisals," *Health Care Supervisor* 8 (January 1990), 40–45.
22. Bass and Vaughn, *Training in Industry.*
23. David Sutton, "Further Thoughts on Action Learning," *Journal of European Industrial Training* 13 (1989), 32–35.
24. For more information on training techniques, see Cherrington, *Personnel Management,* 304–36.
25. Samuel C. Certo, "The Experiential Exercise Situation: A Comment on Instructional Role and Pedagogy Evaluation," *Academy of Management Review* (July 1976), 113–16.
26. For more information on instructional roles in various situations, see Bernard Keys, "The Management of Learning Grid for Management Development," *Academy of Management Review* (April 1977), 289–97.
27. "Training Program's Results Measured in Unique Way," *Supervision* Editors-Supervision, (February 1992), 18–19.
28. William Keenan, Jr., "Are You Overspending on Training?" *Sales and Marketing Management* 142 (January 1990), 56–60.
29. For a review of the literature linking performance appraisal and training needs, see Glenn Herbert and Dennis Doverspike, "Performance Appraisal in the Training Needs Analysis Process: A Review and Critique," *Public Personnel Management* (Fall, 1990), 253–270.
30. Mike Deblieux, "Performance Reviews Support the Quest for Quality," *HR Focus* (November 1991), 3–4.
31. For more information on the performance appraisal process, see Robert L. Mathis and John H. Jackson, "Appraisal of Human Resources," in their *Personnel: Human Resource Management* (St. Paul, Minn.: West Publishing, 1985), 337–66.
32. Douglas McGregor, "An Uneasy Look at Performance Appraisal," *Harvard Business Review* (September/October 1972), 133–34. For insights on how performance appraisal can motivate employees see Kenneth M. Dawson and Sheryl N. Dawson, "How to Motivate Your Employees," *HRMagazine* 35 (April 1990), 78–80.
33. Harold Koontz, "Making Managerial Appraisal Effective," *California Management Review* 15 (Winter 1972), 46–55.
34. Linda J. Segall, "KISS Appraisal Woes Goodbye," *Supervisory Management* 34 (December 1989), 23–28.
35. George A. Rider, "Performance Review: A Mixed Bag," *Harvard Business Review* (July/August 1973), 61–67; Robert Loo, "Quality Performance Appraisals," *Canadian Manager* 14 (December 1989), 24–26.

CHAPTER 12

1. Rosabeth Moss Kanter, "The New Managerial Work," *Harvard Business Review* (November/December 1989), 85–92.
2. John S. Morgan, *Managing Change: The Strategies of Making Change Work for You* (New York: McGraw-Hill, 1972), 99.
3. Bart Nooteboom, "Paradox, Identity, and Change in Management," *Human Systems Management* 8 (1989), 291–300.
4. For an interesting discussion of how to handle employee stress, see Alan Farnham, "Who Beats Stress Best—And How," *Fortune.* October 7, 1991, 71–86.
5. For a discussion of the value of outside change agents, see John H. Sheridan, "Careers on the Line," *Fortune.* September 16, 1991, 29–30.
6. Myron Tribus, "Changing the Corporate Culture—A Roadmap for the Change Agent," *Human Systems Management* 8 (1989), 11–22.
7. W.F. Glueck, "Organization Change in Business and Government," *Academy of Management Journal* 12 (1969), 440–41.
8. Saul W. Gellerman, "In Organizations, as in Architecture, Form Follows Function," *Organizational Dynamics* 18 (Winter 1990), 57–68.
9. C.J. Middleton, "How to Set Up a Project Organization," *Harvard Business Review* (March/April 1967), 73.
10. George J. Chambers, "The Individual in a Matrix Organization," *Project Management Journal* 20 (December 1989), 37–42, 50.
11. John F. Mee, "Matrix Organization," *Business Horizons* (Summer 1964).
12. Middleton, "How to Set Up a Project Organization," 74; Deborah S. Kezsbom, "Managing the Chaos: Conflict Among Project Teams," *AACE Transactions* (1989), A.4.1–A.4.8.
13. Harvey F. Kolodny, "Managing in a Matrix," *Business Horizons* (March/April 1981), 17–24.
14. This section is based primarily on R. Blake, J. Mouton, and L. Greiner, "Breakthrough in Organization Development," *Harvard Business Review* (November/December 1964), 133–55. For a discussion of other methods for implementing OD change, see William F. Glueck, *Organization Planning and Development* (New York: American Management Association, 1971).
15. Blake, Mouton, and Greiner, "Breakthrough in Organization Development."
16. W.J. Heisler, "Patterns of OD in Practice," *Business Horizons* (February 1975), 77–84.
17. Martin G. Evans, "Failures in OD Programs—What Went Wrong," *Business Horizons* (April 1974), 18–22.
18. David Coghlan, "OD Interventions in Catholic Religious Orders," *Journal of Managerial Psychology* 4 (1989), 4–6.
19. Paul A. Iles and Thomas Johnston, "Searching for Excellence in Second-Hand Clothes?: A Note," *Personnel Review* 18 (1989), 32–35; Ewa Maslyk-Musial, "Organization Development in Poland: Stages of Growth," *Public Administration Quarterly* 13 (Summer 1989), 196–214.
20. For an interesting discussion of resistance to change from inherited staff, see: Margaret Russell, "Records Management Program-Directing: Inherited Staff," *ARMA Records Management Quarterly* 24 (January 1990), 18–22.

21. This strategy for minimizing the resistance to change is based on "How Companies Overcome Resistance to Change," *Management Review* (November 1972), 17–25; see also: Hank Williams, "Learning to Manage Change," *Industrial and Commercial Training* 21 (May/June 1989), 17–20.
22. John P. Kotter and Leonard A. Schlesinger, "Choosing Strategies for Change," *Harvard Business Review* (March/April 1979), 106–13.
23. "How Companies Overcome Resistance," 25.
24. Arnold S. Judson, *A Manager's Guide to Making Changes* (New York: Wiley, 1966), 118.
25. Kurt Lewin, "Frontiers in Group Dynamics: Concept, Method, and Reality of Social Sciences—Social Equilibria and Social Change," *Human Relations* 1 (June 1947), 5–14; Ivan Louis Bare, "The Three Phases of Change," *Quality Progress* 19 (November 1986), 47–49.
26. Edgar H. Schein, "Management Development as a Process of Influence," *Industrial Management Review* (May 1961), 59–76. For a more current discussion of the phases of change, see Dottie Perlman and George J. Takacs, "The 10 Stages of Change," *Nursing Management* 21 (April 1990), 33–38.
27. Newton Margulies and John Wallace, *Organizational Change: Techniques and Applications* (Chicago: Scott, Foresman, 1973), 14.
28. Larry E. Greiner, "Patterns of Organizational Change," *Harvard Business Review* (May/June 1967), 119–30.
29. Edgar C. Williams, "Changing Systems and Behavior: People's Perspectives on Prospective Changes," *Business Horizons* (August 1969), 53.
30. Hans Selye, *The Stress of Life* (New York: McGraw-Hill, 1956).
31. James C. Quick and Jonathan D. Quick, *Organizational Stress and Preventive Management* (New York: McGraw-Hill, 1984).
32. James D. Bodzinski, Robert F. Scherer, and Karen A. Goyer, "Workplace Stress," *Personnel Administrator* 34 (July 1989), 76–80; Richard M. Steers, *Introduction to Organizational Behavior* (Glenview, Ill.: Scott, Foresman, 1981), 340–41.
33. Corinne M. Smereka, "Outwitting, Controlling Stress for a Healthier Lifestyle," *Healthcare Financial Management* 44 (March 1990), 70–75.
34. For more discussion of this area, see Keith Davis and John W. Newstrom, *Human Behavior at Work: Organizational Behavior* (New York: McGraw-Hill, 1985), 469–70.
35. J. Clifton Williams, *Human Behavior in Organizations* (Cincinnati: South-Western, 1982), 212–13; Thomas L. Brown, "Are You Living in 'Quiet Desperation'?" *Industry Week*. March 16, 1992, 17.
36. John M. Ivancevich and Michael T. Matteson, "Organizations and Coronary Heart Disease: The Stress Connection," *Management Review* 67 (October 1978), 14–19.
37. For a discussion of other stressors, see "Workplace Stress," *HRMagazine*, Society of Human Resource Management (August 1991), 75–76.
38. For an interesting article addressing how managers can handle their stress, see Thomas Brown, "Are You Stressed Out?" *Industry Week*. September 16, 1991, 21.
39. Fred Luthans, *Organizational Behavior* (New York: McGraw-Hill, 1985), 146–48.
40. Donald B. Miller, "Career Planning and Management in Organizations," *S.A.M. Advanced Management Journal* 43 (Spring 1978), 33–43.

CHAPTER 13

1. Derek Torrington and Jane Weightman, "Middle Management Work," *Journal of General Management* 13 (Winter 1987), 74–89.
2. For insights into and examples of how communication is related to the performance of management activities, see Larry Penley and Brian Hawkins, "Studying Interpersonal Communication in Organizations: A Leadership Application," *Academy of Management Journal* (June 1985), 309–26; H.M. Shatshat and Bong-Gon P. Shin, "Organizational Communication—A Key to Successful Strategic Planning," *Managerial Planning* 30 (September/October 1981), 37–40.
3. Bernard Reilly and Joseph DiAngelo, Jr., "Communication: A Cultural System of Meaning and Value," *Human Relations* 43 (February 1990), 129–40.
4. Paul Sandwith, "Effective Communication," *Training and Development* (January 1992), 29–32.
5. This section is based on the following classic article on interpersonal communication: Wilbur Schramm, "How Communication Works," *The Process and Effects of Mass Communication,* ed. Wilbur Schramm (Urbana: University of Illinois Press, 1954), 3–10.
6. David S. Brown, "Barriers to Successful Communication: Part I, Macrobarriers," *Management Review* (December 1975), 24–29.
7. James K. Weekly and Raj Aggarwal, *International Business: Operating in the Global Economy* (New York: Dryden Press, 1987).
8. Davis S. Brown, "Barriers to Successful Communication: Part II, Microbarriers," *Management Review* (January 1976), 15–21.
9. Sally Bulkley Pancrazio and James J. Pancrazio, "Better Communication for Managers," *Supervisory Management* (June 1981), 31–37.
10. Gene E. Burton, "Barriers to Effective Communication," *Management World* (March 1977), 4–8.
11. John S. Fielden, "Why Can't Managers Communicate? *Business* 39 (January/February/March 1989), 41–44.
12. Lydia Strong, "Do You Know How to Listen?" in *Effective Communications on the Job,* ed. M. Joseph Dooher and Vivienne Marquis (New York: American Management Association, 1956), 28.
13. John R. White, "Some Thoughts on Lexicon and Syntax," *Appraisal Journal* 57 (July 1989), 417–21.
14. Robert E. Callahan, C. Patrick Fleenor, and Harry R. Knudson, *Understanding Organizational Behavior: A Managerial Viewpoint* (Columbus, Ohio: Charles E. Merrill, 1986).
15. For a discussion on the process of generating feedback, see Elizabeth Wolfe Morrison and Robert J. Bies, "Impression Management in the Feedback-Seeking Process: Literature Review and Research Agenda," *Academy of Management Review* (July 1991), 522–541.
16. For more on nonverbal issues, see I.T. Sheppard, "Silent Signals," *Supervisory Management* (March 1986), 31–33.
17. Robert S. Goyer, "Interpersonal Communication and Human Interaction: A Behavioral View," paper presented at the 138th annual meeting of the American Association for the Advancement of Science, 1971. For an article that complements this orientation toward feedback, see R. Abrams, "Do You Get What You Ask For?" *Supervisory Management* (April 1986), 32–34.
18. Verne Burnett, "Management's Tower of Babel," *Management Review* (June 1961), 4–11.
19. Reprinted, by permission of the publisher, from "Ten Commandments of Good Communication," by American Management Association AMACOM, et al. from *Management Review* (October 1955). © 1955 American Management Association, Inc. All rights reserved.
20. Robb Ware, "Communication Problems," *Journal of Systems Management* September 1991, 20.
21. Albert Mehrabian, "Communication Without Words," *Psychology Today* (September 1968), 53–55.
22. For a practical article emphasizing the role of gestures in communication, see S.D. Gladis, "Notes Are Not Enough," *Training and Development Journal* (August 1985), 35–38.
23. Nicole Steckler and Robert Rosenthal, "Sex Differences in Nonverbal and Verbal Communication with Bosses, Peers, and Subordinates," *Journal of Applied Psychology* (February 1985), 157–63.
24. Andrew J. DuBrin, *Contemporary Applied Management* (Plano, Tex.: Business Publications, 1982), 127–34.
25. W. Alan Randolph, *Understanding and Managing Organizational Behavior* (Homewood, Ill.: Richard D. Irwin, 1985), 349–50.
26. Gerald M. Goldhaber, *Organizational Communication* (Dubuque, Iowa: Wm. C. Brown, 1983).
27. Kenneth R. Van Voorhis, "Organizational Communication: Advances Made during the Period from World War II Through the 1950s," *Journal of Business Communication* 11 (1974), 11–18.
28. Phillip J. Lewis, "The Status of 'Organizational Communication,' in Colleges of Business," *Journal of Business Communication* 12 (1975), 25–28.
29. Paul Preston, "The Critical 'Mix' in Managerial Communications," *Industrial Management* (March/April 1976), 5–9.
30. Arnold E. Schneider, William C. Donaghy, and Pamela J. Newman, "Communication Climate within an Organization," *Management Controls* (October/November 1976), 159–62.
31. For discussion on how to communicate failures upward in an organization, see Jay T. Knippen, Thad B. Green and Kurt Sutton, "How to Communicate Failures to Your Boss," *Supervisory Management* (September 1991), 10.
32. "Upward/Downward Communication—Critical Information Channels," *Small Business Report* 10 (October 1985), 85–88. Anne B. Fisher, "CEOs Think That Morale is Dandy," *Fortune*. November 18, 1991, 70–71.
33. William V. Haney, "Serial Communication of Information in Organizations," in *Concepts and Issues in Administrative Behavior,* ed. Sidney Mailick and Edward H. Van Ness (Englewood Cliffs, N.J.: Prentice-Hall, 1962), 150.
34. Haney, "Serial Communication," 150.
35. Alex Bavelas and Dermot Barrett, "An Experimental Approach to Organizational Communication," *Personnel* 27 (1951), 366–71.
36. George de Mare, "Communicating: The Key to Establishing Good Working Relationships," *Price Waterhouse Review* 33 (1989), 30–37.
37. Alan Zaremba, "Working with the Organizational Grapevine," *Personnel Journal* 67 (July 1988), 38–42.
38. Stanley J. Modic, "Grapevine Rated Most Believable," *Industry Week*. May 15, 1989, 11, 14.
39. Keith Davis, "Management Communication and the Grapevine," *Harvard Business Review* (January/February 1953), 43–49.
40. Linda McCallister, "The Interpersonal Side of Internal Communications," *Public Relations Journal* (February 1981), 20–23.
41. Joseph M. Putti, Samuel Aryee, and Joseph Phua, "Communication Relationship Satisfaction and Organizational Commitment," *Group and Organizational Studies* 15 (March 1990), 44–52.
42. For an article defending the value of grapevines, see W. Kiechel, "In Praise of Office Gossip," *Fortune*. August 19, 1985, 253–54.

CHAPTER 14

1. David Nadler and Michael L. Tushman, "Beyond the Charismatic Leader: Leadership and Organizational Change," *California Management Review* 32 (Winter 1990), 77–97.
2. Abraham Zaleznik, "Executives and Organizations: Real Work," *Harvard Business Review* (January/February 1989), 57–64.
3. Abraham Zaleznik, "Managers and Leaders: Are They Different?" *Harvard Business Review* (May/June 1977), 67–78.
4. Theodore Levitt, "Management and the Post-Industrial Society," *Public Interest* (Summer 1976), 73.

5. Patrick L. Townsend and Joan E. Gebhardt, "We Have Lots of Managers . . . We Need Leaders," *Journal for Quality and Participation* (September 1989), 18–20.
6. Craig Hickman, "The Winning Mix: Mind of a Manager, Soul of a Leader," *Canadian Business* 63 (February 1990), 69–72.
7. As an example, see R.D. Mann, "A Review of the Relationship Between Personality and Performance in Small Groups," *Psychological Bulletin* 56 (1959), 241–70.
8. Ralph M. Stogdill, "Personal Factors Associated with Leadership: A Survey of the Literature," *Journal of Psychology* 25 (January 1948), 35–64.
9. Cecil A. Gibb, "Leadership," in *Handbook of Social Psychology*, ed. Gardner Lindzey (Reading, Mass.: Addison-Wesley, 1954).
10. Eugene E. Jennings, "The Anatomy of Leadership," *Management of Personnel Quarterly* 1 (Autumn 1961).
11. J. Oliver Crom, "What's New in Leadership?" *Executive Excellence* 7 (January 1990), 15–16.
12. For an interesting discussion of followers in a leadership situation, see Robert E. Kelly, "In Praise of Followers," *Harvard Business Review* (November/December 1988), 142–48.
13. Robert Tannenbaum and Warren H. Schmidt, "How to Choose a Leadership Pattern," *Harvard Business Review* (March/April 1957), 95–101.
14. William E. Zierden, "Leading through the Follower's Point of View," *Organizational Dynamics* (Spring 1980), 27–46.
15. Tannenbaum and Schmidt, "How to Choose a Leadership Pattern."
16. This point is elaborated in "The Art of Handling Technical Workers," *Electrical World* 204 (February 1990), 29–30.
17. Robert Tannenbaum and Warren H. Schmidt, "How to Choose a Leadership Pattern," *Harvard Business Review* (May/June 1973), 162–80.
18. Victor H. Vroom and Philip H. Yetton, *Leadership and Decision-Making* (Pittsburgh: University of Pittsburgh Press, 1973).
19. Victor H. Vroom and Arthur G. Jago, *The New Leadership* (Englewood Cliffs, N.J.: Prentice-Hall, 1988).
20. Vroom and Yetton, *Leadership and Decision-Making.*
21. Vroom and Jago, *New Leadership.*
22. Gary A. Yukl, *Leadership in Organizations*, 2d ed. (Englewood Cliffs, N.J.: Prentice-Hall, 1989).
23. "How Basic Management Principles Pay Off: Lessons in Leadership," *Nation's Business* (March 1977), 46–53.
24. Vishwanath V. Baba and Merle E. Ace, "Serendipity in Leadership: Initiating Structure and Consideration in the Classroom," *Human Relations* 42 (June 1989), 509–25; Desmond Nolan, "Leadership Appraisals: Your Management Style Can Affect Productivity," *Credit Union Executive* 28 (Winter 1988), 36–37.
25. Rensis Likert, *New Patterns of Management* (New York: McGraw-Hill, 1961).
26. Andrew W. Halpin, *The Leadership Behavior of School Superintendents* (Chicago: University of Chicago Midwest Administration Center, 1959).
27. Harvey A. Hornstein, Madeline E. Heilman, Edward Mone, and Ross Tartell, "Responding to Contingent Leadership Behavior," *Organizational Dynamics* 15 (Spring 1987), 56–65.
28. Rick Roskin, "Management Style and Achievement: A Model Synthesis," *Management Decision* 27 (1989), 17–22.
29. A.K. Korman, "'Consideration,' 'Initiating Structure,' and Organizational Criteria—A Review," *Personnel Psychology* 19 (Winter 1966), 349–61.
30. P. Hersey and K.H. Blanchard, "Life Cycle Theory of Leadership," *Training and Development Journal* (May 1969), 26–34.
31. Mary J. Keenan, Joseph B. Hurst, Robert S. Dennis, and Glenna Frey, "Situational Leadership for Collaboration in Health Care Settings," *Health Care Supervisor* 8 (April 1990), 19–25.
32. Claude L. Graeff, "The Situational Leadership Theory: A Critical View," *Academy of Management Review* 8, (1983), 285–91; Robert P. Vecchio, "Situational Leadership Theory: An Examination of a Prescriptive Theory," *Journal of Applied Psychology* 72 (August 1987), 444–51; Jane R. Goodson, Gail W. McGee, and James F. Cashman, "Situational Leadership Theory: A Test of Leadership Prescriptions," *Group and Organizational Studies* 14 (December 1989), 446–61.
33. Fred E. Fiedler, "Engineer the Job to Fit the Manager," *Harvard Business Review* (September/October 1965), 115–22. See also Fred E. Fiedler, *A Theory of Leadership Effectiveness* (New York: McGraw-Hill, 1967).
34. Rensis Likert, *New Patterns of Management.*
35. From *A Theory of Leadership Effectiveness*, 255–56 by F.E. Fiedler. Copyright © 1967 by McGraw-Hill, Inc. Used with permission of McGraw-Hill Book Company.
36. Fred E. Fiedler, "How Do You Make Leaders More Effective? New Answers to an Old Puzzle," *Organizational Dynamics* (Autumn 1972), 3–18.
37. L.H. Peters, D.D. Harike, and J.T. Pohlmann, "Fiedler's Contingency Theory of Leadership: An Application of the Meta-analysis Procedures of Schmidt and Hunter," *Psychological Bulletin* 97 (1985), 224–285.
38. Robert J. House and Terence R. Mitchell, "Path-Goal Theory of Leadership," *Journal of Contemporary Business* (Autumn 1974), 81–98; Gary A. Yukl, *Leadership in Organizations.*
39. Alan C. Filley, Robert House, and Steven Kerr, *Managerial Process and Organizational Behavior* (Glenview, Ill.: Scott, Foresman, 1976), 256–60.
40. For a worthwhile review of the path-goal theory of leadership see: Gary A. Yukl, *Leadership in Organizations.*
41. F.E. Fiedler and M.M. Chemers, *Leadership and Effective Management* (Glenview, Ill.: Scott Foresman, 1974).
42. Karl W. Kuhnert and Philip Lewis, "Transactional and Transformational Leadership: A Constructive/Developmental Analysis," *Academy of Management Review* (October 1987), 648–57.
43. Bernard M. Bass, *Leadership and Performance Beyond Expectations* (New York: Free Press, 1985).
44. Noel M. Tichy and David M. Ulrich, "The Leadership Challenge: A Call for Transformational Leadership," *Sloan Management Review* (Fall 1984), 59–68.
45. S. Kerr and J.M. Jermier, "Substitutes for Leadership: Their Meaning and Measurement," *Organizational Behavior and Human Performance* 22 (1978): 375–403.
46. J. Pfeffer, "The Ambiguity of Leadership," *Academy of Management Review* 2 (1977), 104–12.
47. C.C. Manz and H.P. Sims, Jr., "Leading Workers to Lead Themselves: The External Leadership on Self-Managing Work Teams," *Administrative Science Quarterly* (March 1987), 106–29.
48. J.R. Meindl and S.B. Ehrlich, "The Romance of Leadership and the Evaluation of Organizational Performance," *Academy of Man-agement Journal* 30, 91–109.
49. Ralph M. Stogdill, *Handbook of Leadership*, (New York: Free Press, 1974).
50. U.S. Department of Labor, Bureau of Labor Statistics, 1989. *Employment and Earnings* (Washington, D.C.: Table 1–22), 29.
51. "Workforce 2000 is Welcome Today at Digital," *Business Ethics* (July/August 1990), 5–16.
52. Any Salzman, "Trouble at the Top," *U.S. News and World Report.* June 17, 1991.
53. Susan B. Garland, "Throwing Stones at the Glass Ceiling," *Business Week.* August 19, 1991, 29.
54. J.B. Rosener, "Ways Women Lead," *Harvard Business Review* (May/June 1990), 103–11.
55. B.M. Bass Leadership. "Good, Better, Best," *Organizational Dynamics* (Winter 1985), 26–40.
56. Rosener, "Ways Women Lead."
57. Ibid.

CHAPTER 15

1. Philip A. Rudolph and Brian H. Kleiner, "The Art of Motivating Employees," *Journal of Managerial Psychology* 4 (1989), *i–iv.*
2. Craig Miller, "How to Construct Programs for Teams," *Reward & Recognition* (August/September 1991), 4–6.
3. Walter F. Charsley, "Management, Morale, and Motivation," *Management World* 17 (July/August 1988), 27–28.
4. Victor H. Vroom, *Work and Motivation* (New York: Wiley, 1964); Thomas L. Quick, "How to Motivate People," *Working Woman* 12 (September 1987), 15, 17.
4. J. Stacy Adams, "Towards an Understanding of Inequity," *Journal of Abnormal and Social Psychology* 67, no. 5 (1963), 422–36.
5. For a rationale linking expectancy and equity theories, see Joseph W. Harder, "Equity Theory versus Expectancy Theory: The Case of Major League Baseball Free Agents," *Journal of Applied Psychology* (June 1991), 458–464.
6. L.W. Porter and E.E. Lawler, *Managerial Attitudes and Performance* (Homewood, Ill.: Richard D. Irwin, 1968).
7. For more information on intrinsic and extrinsic rewards, see Pat Buhler, "Rewards in the Organization," *Supervision* 50 (January 1989), 5–7.
8. Eric G. Flamholtz and Yvonne Randle, "The Inner Game of Management," *Management Review* 77 (April 1988), 24–30.
9. Abraham Maslow, *Motivation and Personality*, 2d ed. (New York: Harper & Row, 1970). For a current discussion of the value of Maslow's ideas see Edward Hoffman, "Abraham Maslow: Father of Enlightened Management," *Training* 25 (September 1988), 79–82.
10. Robert J. Kelly and Jack Barnathan, "Out on a Limb: Executives Abroad," *Security Management* 32 (November 1988), 117–27.
11. Abraham Maslow, *Eupsychian Management* (Homewood, Ill.: Richard D. Irwin, 1965).
12. Jack W. Duncan, *Essentials of Management* (Hinsdale, Ill.: Dryden Press, 1975), 105.
13. C.P. Alderfer, "An Empirical Test of a New Theory of Human Needs," *Organizational Behavior and Human Performance* 4, no. 2 (1969), 142–75.
14. D.T. Hall and K. Nougaim, "An Examination of Maslow's Need Hierarchy in an Organizational Setting," *Organizational Behavior and Human Performance* 3, no. 1 (1968), 12–35.
15. Hoffman, "Abraham Maslow: Father of Enlightened Management;" Dale L. Mort, "Lead Your Team to the Top," *Security Management* 32 (January 1988), 43–45.
16. Clayton Alderfer, *Existence, Relatedness, and Growth* (New York: Free Press, 1972). For a reconstruction of Maslow's hierarchy, see Francis Heylighen, "A Cognitive-Systemic Reconstruction of Maslow's Theory of Self-Actualization," *Behavioral Science* (January 1992), 39–58.
17. Chris Argyris, *Personality and Organization* (New York: Harper & Bros., 1957).
18. Charles R. Davis, "The Primacy of Self-Development in Chris Argyris's Writings," *International Journal of Public Administration* 10 (September 1987), 177–207.

19. David C. McClelland and David G. Winter, *Motivating Economic Achievement* (New York: Free Press, 1969); David C. McClelland, "Power Is the Great Motivator," *Harvard Business Review* (March/April 1976), 100–10.
20. Burt K. Scanlan, "Creating a Climate for Achievement," *Business Horizons* 24 (March/April 1981), 5–9; Lawrence Holp, "Achievement Motivation and Kaizen," *Training and Development Journal* 43 (October 1989), 53–63.
21. David C. McClelland, *The Achieving Society* (New York: Van Nostrand, 1961).
22. Douglas McGregor, *The Human Side of Enterprise* (New York: McGraw-Hill, 1960). For a current illustration of how Theory X-Theory Y relates to modern business see Kenneth B. Slutsky "Viewpoint: Why Not Theory Z?" *Security Management* 33 (April 1989), 110, 112.
23. W.J. Reddin, "The Tri-Dimensional Grid," *Training and Development Journal* (July 1964).
24. For more discussion on the implications of job rotation in organizations, see Alan W. Farrant, "Job Rotation Is Important," *Supervision* (August 1987), 14–16.
25. L.E. Davis and E.S. Valfer, "Intervening Responses to Changes in Supervisor Job Designs," *Occupational Psychology* (July 1965), 171–90.
26. M.D. Kilbridge, "Do Workers Prefer Larger Jobs?" *Personnel* (September/October 1960), 45–48.
27. This section is based on Frederick Herzberg, "One More Time: How Do You Motivate Employees?" *Harvard Business Review* (January/February 1968), 53–62.
28. Scott M. Meyers, "Who Are Your Motivated Workers?" *Harvard Business Review* (January/February 1964), 73–88.
29. John M. Roach, "Why Volvo Abolished the Assembly Line," *Management Review* (September 1977), 50.
30. Matt Oechsli, "Million Dollar Success Habits," *Managers Magazine* 65 (February 1990), 6–14; J. Barton Cunningham and Ted Eberle, "A Guide to Job Enrichment and Redesign," *Personnel* 67 (February 1990), 56–61.
31. Richard J. Hackman, "Is Job Enrichment Just a Fad?" *Harvard Business Review* (September/October 1975), 129–38.
32. Bob Smith and Karen Matthes, "Flexibility Now for the Future," *HR Focus* (January 1992), 5.
33. D.A. Bratton, "Moving Away from Nine to Five," *Canadian Business Review* 13 (Spring 1986), 15–17.
34. Douglas L. Fleuter, "Flextime—A Social Phenomenon," *Personnel Journal* (June 1975), 318–19.
35. Lee A. Graf, "An Analysis of the Effect of Flexible Working Hours on the Management Functions of the First-Line Supervisor" (Ph.D. diss., Mississippi State University, 1976).
36. Jill Kanin-Lovers, "Meeting the Challenge of Workforce 2000," *Journal of Compensation and Benefits* 5 (January/February 1990), 233–36.
37. William Wong, "Rather Come in Late or Go Home Earlier? More Bosses Say OK," *Wall Street Journal,* July 12, 1973, 1.
38. B.F. Skinner, *Contingencies of Reinforcement* (New York: Appleton-Century-Crofts, 1969).
39. E.L. Thorndike, "The Original Nature of Man," *Educational Psychology* 1 (1903).
40. Fred Luthans and Robert Kreitner, *Organizational Behavior Modification and Beyond* (Glenview, Ill.: Scott, Foresman, 1985).
41. P.M. Padsokaff, "Relationships between Leader Reward and Punishment Behavior and Group Process and Productivity," *Journal of Management* 11 (Spring 1985), 55–73.
42. For another practical discussion on punishment, see Bruce R. McAfee and William Poffenberger, *Productivity Strategies: Enhancing Employee Job Performance* (Englewood Cliffs, N.J.: Prentice-Hall, Spectrum, 1982).
43. Ricky W. Griffin and Gregory Moorhead, *Organizational Behavior* (Boston: Houghton Mifflin, 1986), 183–89.
44. "New Tool: Reinforcement for Good Work," *Psychology Today* (April 1972), 68–69.
45. W. Clay Hamner and Ellen P. Hamner, "Behavior Modification on the Bottom Line," *Organizational Dynamics* 4 (Spring 1976), 6–8.
46. Rensis Likert, *New Patterns of Management* (New York: McGraw-Hill, 1961). For an interesting discussion of the worth of Likert's ideas see Marvin R. Weisbord, "For More Productive Workplaces," *Journal of Management Consulting* 4 (1988), 7–14.
47. These descriptions are based on the table of organizational and performance characteristics of different management systems in Rensis Likert, *The Human Organization* (New York: McGraw-Hill, 1967), 4–10.
48. Likert, *New Patterns of Management,* 103.
49. For discussion of a novel monetary incentive program, see Charles A. Cerami, "Special Incentives May Appeal to Valued Employees," *HR Focus* (November 1991), 17
50. "Incentive Pay Plan Replaces Wage Hikes: Lump Sum Bonuses, Profit-Sharing Attract and Maintain Good Workers," *Chain Store Age Executive* (February 1989), 78, 79.
51. Jeffrey P. Davidson, "A Great Place to Work: Seven Strategies for Keeping Employees Committed to Your Company," *Management World* (June/August 1987), 24–25.

CHAPTER 16

1. For an article illustrating the importance of managing groups in organizations see Gregory E. Kaebnick, "Notes from Underground: Walter Corbitt Talks About Monitoring Paperwork for 35,000 Underground Storage Tanks," *Inform* 3 (July/August 1989), 21–22, 48.
2. Edgar H. Schein, *Organizational Psychology* (Englewood Cliffs, N.J.: Prentice-Hall, 1965), 67.
3. George C. Homans, *The Human Group* (New York: Harcourt, Brace & World, 1950), 1.
4. Dorwin Cartwright and Ronald Lippitt, "Group Dynamics and the Individual," *International Journal of Group Psychotherapy* 7 (January 1957), 86–102.
5. Edgar H. Schein, *Organizational Psychology,* 2d ed. (Englewood Cliffs, N.J.: Prentice-Hall, 1970), 82.
6. For useful guidelines on how to make committees work, see Arthur R. Pell, "Making Committees Work," *Managers Magazine* 64 (September 1989), 28.
7. For insights on what causes groups to fail as organizational problem-solvers, see Harvey J. Brightman and Penny Verhoeven, "Why Managerial Problem-Solving Groups Fail," *Business* 36 (January/February/March 1986), 24–29.
8. Raymond McLeod, Jr., and Jack W. Jones, "Making Executive Information Systems More Effective," *Business Horizons* (September/October 1986), 29–37.
9. Cyril O'Donnell, "Ground Rules for Using Committees," *Management Review* 50 (October 1961), 63–67. See also "Making Committees Work," *Infosystems* (October 1985), 38–39.
10. These and other guidelines are discussed in "Applying Small-Group Behavior Dynamics to Improve Action-Team Performance," *Employment Relations Today* (Autumn 1991), 343–353. For additional guidelines, see Peggy S. Williams, "Physical Fitness for Committees: Getting on Track," *Association Management* 41 (June 1989), 104–11.
11. Irving L. Janis, *Groupthink* (Boston: Houghton Mifflin, 1982).
12. For insights on how to avoid groupthink, see Michael J. Woodruff, "Understanding-and Combatting-Groupthink," *Supervisory Management* (October 1991), 8.
13. To see how teams can increase productivity, see Jana Schilder, "Work Teams Boost Productivity," *Personnel Journal* 67–71.
14. For suggestions on how to build a team, see Edward Glassman, "Silence Is Not Consent," *Supervisory Management* (March 1992), 6–7.
15. Robert B. Reich, "Entrepreneurship Reconsidered: The Team as a Hero," *Harvard Business Review* (May/June 1987), 77–83.
16. Craig Cina, "Company Study: Five Steps to Service Excellence," *Journal of Services Marketing* 4 (Spring 1990), 39–47.
17. Bernard Bass, *Organizational Psychology* (Boston: Allyn and Bacon, 1965), 197–98.
18. Bass, *Organizational Psychology,* 199. For more insights on characteristics of productive groups, see Edward Glassman, "Self-Directed Team Building without a Consultant," *Supervisory Management* (March 1992), 6.
19. Raef T. Hussein, "Informal Groups, Leadership, and Productivity," *Leadership and Organization Development Journal* 10 (1989), 9–16.
20. Keith Davis and John W. Newstrom, *Human Behavior at Work: Organizational Behavior* (New York: McGraw-Hill, 1985), 310–12.
21. Muhammad Jamal, "Shift Work Related to Job Attitudes, Social Participation, and Withdrawal Behavior: A Study of Nurses and Industrial Workers," *Personnel Psychology* 34 (Autumn 1981), 535–47.
22. For the importance of determining such information see Dave Day, "New Supervisors and the Informal Group," *Supervisory Management* 34 (May 1989), 31–33.
23. For a classic study illustrating sociometry and sociometric procedures see Muzafer Sherif, "A Preliminary Experimental Study of Intergroup Relations," in *Social Psychology at the Crossroads,* ed. John H. Rohrer and Muzafer Sherif (New York: Harper & Bros., 1951).
24. Edgar H. Schein, "SMR Forum: Improving Face-to-Face Relationships," *Sloan Management Review* 22 (Winter 1981), 43–52.
25. Homans, *The Human Group.*
26. W. Alan Randolph, *Understanding and Managing Organizational Behavior* (Homewood, Ill.: Richard D. Irwin, 1985), 398–99.
27. Davis and Newstrom, *Human Behavior at Work,* 218.
28. Don Hellriegel and John W. Slocum, Jr., *Management* (Reading, Mass.: Addison-Wesley, 1986), 539–42.
29. Stanley E. Seashore, *Group Cohesiveness in the Industrial Work Group* (Ann Arbor: University of Michigan Press, 1954).
30. For an excellent critical comment on the quality of research in this area see Peter E. Mudrack, "Group Cohesiveness and Productivity: A Closer Look," *Human Relations* 42 (September 1989), 771–85.
31. O. Jeff Harris, *Managing People at Work* (New York: Wiley, 1976), 122. For an interesting discussion of how employee ownership affects group cohesiveness, see Jon L. Pierce and Candace A. Furo, "Employee Ownership: Implications for Management," *Organizational Dynamics* 18 (Winter 1990), 32–43.
32. J.R. Hackman, "Group Influence on Individuals," in *Handbook for Industrial and Organizational Psychology,* ed. M.P. Dunnette (Chicago: Rand McNally, 1976).
33. This section is based primarily on P.C. André De la Porte, "Group Norms: Key to Building a Winning Team," *Personnel* (September/October 1974): 60–67.
34. Peter F. Drucker, "Is Executive Pay Excessive?" *Wall Street Journal,* May 23, 1977, 22.
35. T.N. Whitehead, "The Inevitability of the Informal Organization and Its Possible Value," in *Readings in Management,* ed. Ernest Dale (New York: McGraw-Hill, 1970).

36. This section draws from Samuel C. Certo and J. Paul Peter, *Strategic Management: Concepts and Applications* (New York: McGraw-Hill, 1991), 141–46.
37. Cass Bettinger, "Use Corporate Culture to Trigger High Performance," *The Journal of Business Strategy* (March/April 1989), 38–42.
38. John Hassard and Sudi Sharifi, "Corporate Culture and Strategic Change," *Journal of General Management* 15 (Winter 1989), 4–19.
39. Discussion of these mechanisms is based on Edgar H. Schein, *Organizational Culture and Leadership* (San Francisco: Jossey-Bass Publishers, 1985), 223–43.

CHAPTER 17

1. For an illustration of the complexity of control in an international context, see Jean-Francois Hennart, "Control in Multinational Firms: The Role of Price and Hierarchy," *Management International Review* (Special Issue 1991), 71–96.
2. L.R. Bittle and J.E. Ramsey (eds.), *Handbook for Professional Managers* (New York: McGraw-Hill, 1985).
3. K.A. Merchant, "The Control Function of Management," *Sloan Management Review* 23 (Summer 1982), 43–55.
4. For an example of how a control system can be used with a formal planning model, see A.M. Jaeger and B.R. Baliga, "Control Systems and Strategic Adaptations: Lessons from the Japanese Experience," *Strategic Management Journal* 6 (April/June 1985), 115–34.
5. Robert L. Dewelt, "Control: Key to Making Financial Strategy Work," *Management Review* (March 1977), 18.
6. For more discussion on Murphy's Law, see George Box, "When Murphy Speaks—Listen," *Quality Progress* 22 (October 1989), 79–84.
7. Robert J. Mockler, ed., *Readings in Management Control* (New York: Appleton-Century-Crofts, 1970), 14.
8. Francis V. McCrory and Peter Gerstberger, "The New Math of Performance Measurement," *Journal of Business Strategy,* (March/April 1991) 33–38.
9. For a discussion of how standards are set, see James B. Dilworth, *Production and Operations Management: Manufacturing and Nonmanufacturing* (New York: Random House, 1986), 637–50.
10. Len Eglo, "Save Dollars on Maintenance Management," *Chemical Engineering* 97 (June 1990), 157–62.
11. Alden M. Hayashi, "GE Says Solid State Is Here to Stay," *Electronic Business* 14 (April 1, 1988), 52–56.
12. Frank Rose, "A New Age for Business?" *Fortune.* October 8, 1990, 156–64.
13. Edward Basset, "Diamond Is Forever," *New England Business* 12 (October 1990), 40–44.
14. David Sheridan, "Getting the Big Picture," *Training* (September 1990), 12–15.
15. Thomas A. Foster and Joseph V. Barks, "The Right Chemistry for Single Sourcing," *Distribution* 89 (September 1990), 44–52.
16. Joseph Conlin, "The House That G.E. Built," *Successful Meetings* 38 (August 1989), 50–58.
17. Robert W. Mann, "A Building-Blocks Approach to Strategic Change," *Training and Development Journal* 44 (August 1990), 23–25.
18. For an example of a company surpassing performance standards, see Peter Nulty, "How to Live by Your Wits," *Fortune.* April 20, 1992, 119–120.
19. For an illustration of the problem/symptom relationship see Elizabeth Dougherty, "Waste Minimization: Reduce Wastes and Reap the Benefits," *R & D* 32 (April 1990), 62–68.
20. Y.K. Shetty, "Product Quality and Competitive Strategy," *Business Horizons* (May/June 1987), 46–52.
21. Harold Koontz, Cyril O'Donnell, and Heinz Weihrich, *Essentials of Management* (New York: McGraw-Hill, 1986), 454–59.
22. For an example of concurrent control in the health-care industry, see Teri Lammers, "The Troubleshooter's Guide," *Inc.,* (January 1992), 65–67.
23. Vijay Sathe, *Controller Involvement in Management* (Englewood Cliffs, N.J.: Prentice-Hall, 1982).
24. James D. Wilson, *Controllership: The Work of the Managerial Accountant* (New York: Wiley, 1981).
25. For other ways in which cost-benefit analysis can be used by managers, see G.S. Smith and M.S. Tseng, "Benefit-Cost Analysis as a Performance Indicator," *Management Accounting* (June 1986), 44–49; "The IS (Information System) Payoff," *Infosystems* (April 1987), 18–20.
26. Amitai Etzioni, *A Comparative Analysis of Complex Organizations* (New York: Free Press, 1961), 4–6.
27. For a study discussing the utility of various types of power to managers, see Gary Yukl and Cecilia Falbe, "Importance of Different Power Sources in Downward and Lateral Relations," *Journal of Applied Psychology* (June 1991), 416–423.
28. John P. Kotter, "Power, Dependence, and Effective Management," *Harvard Business Review* (July/August 1977), 128.
29. Kotter, "Power, Dependence, and Effective Management," 135–36.
30. Kotter, "Power, Dependence, and Effective Management," 131.
31. For further discussion of overcoming the potential negative effects of control, see Ramon J. Aldag and Timothy M. Stearns, *Management* (Cincinnati, Ohio: South-Western Publishing, 1987), 653–54.
32. Arnold F. Emch, "Control Means Action," *Harvard Business Review* (July/August 1954), 92–98. See also K. Hall and L.K. Savery, "Tight Rein, More Stress," *Harvard Business Review* (January/February 1986), 160–64.
33. James T. McKenna, "Eastern, Maintenance Heads Indicted by U.S. Grand Jury," *Aviation Week & Space Technology* 133 (July 1990), 84–86.
34. W. Jerome III, *Executive Control: The Catalyst* (New York: Wiley, 1961), 31–34.
35. William Bruns, Jr. and E. Warren McFarlan, "Information Technology Puts Power in Control Systems," *Harvard Business Review* (September/October 1987), 89–94.
36. C. Jackson Grayson, Jr., "Management Science and Business Practice," *Harvard Business Review* (July/August 1973), 41–48.
37. For an article emphasizing the importance of management understanding and being supportive of organizational control efforts, see Richard M. Morris III, "Management Support: An Underlying Premise," *Industrial Management* 31 (March/April 1989), 2–3.

CHAPTER 18

1. James B. Dilworth, *Production and Operations Management: Manufacturing and Non-Manufacturing* (New York: Random House, 1986), 3.
2. John W. Kendrick, *Understanding Productivity: An Introduction to the Dynamics of Productivity Change* (Baltimore: Johns Hopkins University Press, 1977), 14.
3. Lester C. Thurow, "Other Countries Are as Smart as We Are," *New York Times,* April 5, 1981.
4. W. Edwards Deming, *Out of the Crisis* (Boston: MIT Center for Advanced Engineering Study, 1986).
5. Rafael Aguayo, *Dr. Deming: The American Who Taught the Japanese about Quality* (New York: Carol Publishing Group, 1990), 160–164.
6. John B. Miner, *Organizational Behavior: Performance and Productivity* (New York: Random House, 1988), 308–16.
7. Robert E. Kemper and Joseph Yehudai, *Experiencing Operations Management: A Walk-Through* (Boston: PWS-Kent Publishing Company, 1991), 48.
8. Richard B. Chase and Nicholas J. Aquilano, *Production and Operations Management: A Life Cycle Approach* (Homewood, Ill.: Richard D. Irwin, 1981), 4.
9. Lee J. Krajewski and Larry P. Ritzman, *Operations Management: Strategy and Analysis* (Reading, Mass,: Addison-Wesley, 1987), 573.
10. Krajewski and Ritzman, *Operations Management,* 572–84.
11. A. Ansari and Modarress Batoul, "Just-in-Time Purchasing: Problems and Solutions," *Journal of Purchasing and Materials Management* (August 1986), 11–15.
12. Albert F. Celley, William H. Clegg, Arthur W. Smith, and Mark A. Vonderembse, "Implementation of JIT in the United States," *Journal of Purchasing and Materials Management* (Winter 1987), 9–15.
13. John D. Baxter, "Kanban Works Wonders, but Will It Work in U.S. Industry?" *Iron Age,* June 7, 1982, 44–48.
14. Robert L. Dewelt, "Control: Key to Making Financial Strategy Work," *Management Review* (March 1977), 20.
15. George S. Minmier, "Zero-Base Budgeting: A New Budgeting Technique for Discretionary Costs," *Mid-South Quarterly Business Review* 14 (October 1976), 2–8.
16. Peter A. Phyrr, "Zero-Base Budgeting," *Harvard Business Review* (November/December 1970), 111–21. See also E.A. Kurbis, "The Case for Zero-Base Budgeting," *CA Magazine* (April 1986), 104–05.
17. Linda J. Shinn and M. Sue Sturgeon, "Budgeting from Ground Zero," *Association Management* 42 (September 1990), 45–48.
18. Gregory E. Becwar and Jack L. Armitage, "Zero-Base Budgeting: Is It Really Dead?" *Ohio CPA Journal* 48 (Winter 1989), 52–54.
19. Aaron Wildausky and Arthur Hammann, "Comprehensive Versus Incremental Budgeting in the Department of Agriculture," in *Planning Programming Budgeting: A Systems Approach to Management,* ed. Fremont J. Lyden and Ernest G. Miller (Chicago: Markham Publishing, 1968), 143–44.
20. Chris Argyris, "Human Problems with Budgets," *Harvard Business Review* (January/February 1953), 108.
21. Argyris, "Human Problems with Budgets," 109.
22. This section is based primarily on J. Fred Weston and Eugene F. Brigham, *Essentials of Managerial Finance,* 7th ed. (Hinsdale, Ill.: Dryden Press, 1985).
23. F.L. Patrone and Donald duBois, "Financial Ratio Analysis for the Small Business," *Journal of Small Business Management* (January 1981), 35.
24. For an excellent discussion of ratio analysis in a small business, see Patrone and duBois, "Financial Ratio Analysis," 35–40.
25. Aguayo, *Dr. Deming,* 139–148.
26. Lester R. Bittle, *Management by Exception* (New York: McGraw-Hill, 1964).
27. Frederick W. Taylor, *Shop Management* (New York: Harper & Bros., 1911), 126–27.
28. These two rules are adapted from *Boardroom Reports* 5 (May 1976), 4.
29. Robert J. Lambrix and Surendra S. Singhvi, "How to Set Volume-Sensitive ROI Targets," *Harvard Business Review* (March/April 1981), 174.
30. For a listing and discussion of quantitative tools and their appropriate uses, see Kemper and Yehudai, *Experiencing Operations Management,* 341–355.
31. For a clear discussion, illustrations, and examples of linear programming, break-even analysis, work measurement, acceptance sampling, payoff tables, value analysis, computer-aided design (CAD), computer-aided engineering (CAE), computer-aided manufacturing (CAM), manufacturing

resource planning, program evaluation and review technique (PERT), capacity requirements planning (CRP), and input/output control, see Jay Heizer and Barry Render, *Production and Operations Management: Strategies and Tactics* (Needham Heights, MA: Allyn and Bacon, 1993).

32. For additional information on these software packages, see *Lotus 1-2-3 Reference Manual* (Cambridge, Mass.: Lotus Development Corporation, 1985); Timothy J. O'Leary, *The Student Edition of Lotus 1-2-3* (Reading, Mass.: Addison-Wesley, 1989); *IFPS User's Manual* (Austin, Tex.: Execucom Systems Corporation, 1984).

CHAPTER 19

1. Garland R. Hadley and Mike C. Patterson, "Are Middle-Paying Jobs Really Declining?" *Oklahoma Business Bulletin* 56 (June 1988), 12–14.
2. A. Essam Radwan and Jerome Fields, "Keeping Tabs on Toxic Spills," *Civil Engineering* 60 (April 1990), 70–72.
3. Dean C. Minderman, "Marketing: Desktop Demographics," *Credit Union Management* 13 (February 1990), 26.
4. Henry Mintzberg, "The Myths of MIS," *California Management Review* (Fall 1972), 92–97.
5. Jay W. Forrester, "Managerial Decision Making," in *Management and the Computer of the Future*, ed. Martin Greenberger (Cambridge, Mass., and New York: MIT Press and Wiley, 1962), 37.
6. The following discussion is based largely on Robert H. Gregory and Richard L. Van Horn, "Value and Cost of Information," in *Systems Analysis Techniques*, ed. J. Daniel Conger and Robert W. Knapp (New York: Wiley, 1974), 473–89.
7. John T. Small and William B. Lee, "In Search of MIS," *MSU Business Topics* (Autumn 1975), 47–55.
8. G. Anthony Gorry and Michael S. Scott Morton, "A Framework for Management Information Systems," *Sloan Management Review* 13 (Fall 1971), 55–70.
9. Stephen L. Cohen, "Managing Human-Resource Data: Keeping Your Data Clean," *Training & Development Journal* 43 (August 1989), 50–54.
10. David Harvey, "Making Sense of the Data Deluge," *Director* 42 (April 1989), 139–40.
11. Robert Chaiken, "Pitfalls of Computers in a CPA's Office," *Ohio CPA Journal* 46 (Spring 1987), 45–46.
12. John E. Framel, "Managing Information Costs and Technologies as Assets," *Journal of Systems Management* 41 (February 1990), 12–18.
13. Martin D.J. Buss, "Penny-wise Approach to Data Processing," *Harvard Business Review* (July/August 1981), 111.
14. James A. Yardley and Parez R. Sopariwala, "Break-Even Utilization Analysis," *Journal of Commercial Bank Lending* 72 (March 1990), 49–56.
15. T. Mukhopadhyay and R. B. Cooper, "Impact of Management Information Systems on Decisions," *Omega* 20 (1992), 37–49.
16. Robert W. Holmes, "Twelve Areas to Investigate for Better MIS," *Financial Executive* (July 1970), 24. A similar definition is presented and illustrated in Jeffrey A. Coopersmith, "Modern Times: Computerized Systems Are Changing the Way Today's Modern Catalog Company Is Structured," *Catalog Age* 7 (June 1990), 77–78. For an interesting example of how a company can decentralize an MIS, see John E. Framel and Leo F. Haas III, "Managing the Dispersed Computing Environment at Mapco, Inc.," *Journal of Systems Management* 43, 6–12.
17. For an article discussing how a well-managed MIS promotes the usefulness of information, see Albert Lederer and Veronica Gardner, "Meeting Tomorrow's Business Demands through Strategic Information Systems Planning," *Information Strategy: The Executive's Journal* (Summer 1992), 20–27.
18. This section is based on Richard A. Johnson, R. Joseph Monsen, Henry P. Knowles, and Borge O. Saxberg, *Management, Systems, and Society: An Introduction* (Santa Monica, Calif.: Goodyear, 1976), 113–20.
19. James Emery, "Information Technology in the 21st Century Enterprise," *MIS Quarterly* (December 1991), xxi–xxiii.
20. Robert G. Murdick, "MIS for MBO," *Journal of Systems Management* (March 1977), 34–40.
21. F. Warren McFarlan, "Problems in Planning the Information System," *Harvard Business Review* (March/April 1971), 75.
22. David S. Stoller and Richard L. Van Horn, *Design of a Management Information System* (Santa Monica, Calif.: RAND Corporation, 1958).
23. Craig Barrow, "Implementing an Executive Information System: Seven Steps for Success," *Journal of Information Systems Management* 7 (Spring 1990), 41–46.
24. Bertram A. Colbert, "The Management Information System," *Management Services* 4 (September/October 1967), 15–24.
25. Adapted from Henry Mintzberg, "The Manager's Job: Folklore and Fact," *Harvard Business Review* (July/August 1975), 58.
26. William R. King and David I. Cleland, "Manager-Analysts Teamwork in MIS," *Business Horizons* 14 (April 1971), 59–68.
27. Regina Herzlinger, "Why Data Systems in Nonprofit Organizations Fail," *Harvard Business Review* (January/February 1977), 81–86.
28. John Sculley, "The Human Use of Information," *Journal for Quality and Participation* (January/February 1990), 10–13; Richard Discenza and Donald G. Gardner, "Improving Productivity by Managing for Retention," *Information Strategy: The Executive's Journal* (Spring 1992), 34–38.
29. G.W. Dickson and John K. Simmons, "The Behavioral Side of MIS," *Business Horizons* (August 1970), 59, 71.
30. Steven L. Mandell, *Computers and Data Processing: Concepts and Applications with BASIC* (St. Paul, Minn.: West Publishing, 1982), 370–91.
31. Mark G. Simkin, *Computer Information Systems for Business* (Dubuque, Iowa: Wm. C. Brown, 1987), 299–301.

CHAPTER 20

1. Alyssa A. Lappen, "Worldwide Connections," *Forbes*. June 27, 1988, 78–82.
2. Lee Smith, "Japan Hustles for Foreign Investment," *Fortune*. May 28, 1984, 163.
3. "Trying to Copy Past Success," *Economist*. February 6, 1982, 70.
4. Ben J. Wattenberg, "Their Deepest Concerns," *Business Month* (January 1988), 27–33.
5. American Assembly of Collegiate Schools of Business, *Accreditation Council Policies, Procedures, and Standards, 1990–92*. St. Louis, Mo.; Sylvia Nasar, "America's Competitive Revival," *Fortune*. January 4, 1988, 44–52.
6. U.S. Department of Commerce, *The Multinational Corporation: Studies on U.S. Foreign Investment*, vol. 1 (Washington, D.C.: Government Printing Office).
7. Grover Starling, *The Changing Environment of Business* (Boston: Kent, 1980), 140.
8. This section is based primarily on Richard D. Robinson, *International Management* (New York: Holt, Rinehart & Winston, 1967), 3–5.
9. 1971 Survey of National Foreign Trade Council, cited in Frederick D. Sturdivant, *Business and Society: A Managerial Approach* (Homewood, Ill.: Richard D. Irwin, 1977), 425. For an interesting discussion of diversification as an advantage to internationalizing see Jeff Madura and Ann Marie Whyte, "Diversification Benefits of Direct Foreign Investment," *Management International Review* 30 (First quarter 1990), 73–85.
10. Barrie James, "Reducing the Risks of Globalization," *Long Range Planning* 23 (February 1990), 80–88.
11. Robert O. Knorr, "Managing for World-Class Performance," *Journal of Business Strategy* 11 (January/February 1990), 48–50.
12. "The Bug Comes Back," *Newsweek*. April 4, 1983, 60.
13. Karen Paul, "Fading Images at Eastman Kodak," *Business and Society Review* 48 (Winter 1984), 56.
14. "The Mattress Maker That Woke Up Wall Street," *Fortune*. August 20, 1984, 37. For an interesting discussion of issues to consider when licensing software in Japan, see Fred M. Greguras, "Software Licensing in Japan: Checklist for U.S. Licensors," *East Asian Executive Reports*. February 15, 1989, 17–20.
15. Joan Servaas Marie, "Robinson Nugent, Inc.: Working Smarter, Not Harder," *Indiana Business* (June 1983), 4–7.
16. Peter J. Mullins, "Survival through Joint Ventures," *Automotive Industries* (May 1983), 17–18.
17. Howard V. Perlmutter, "The Tortuous Evolution of the Multinational Corporation," *Columbia Journal of World Business* (January/February 1969), 9–18.
18. Rose Knotts, "Cross-Cultural Management: Transformations and Adaptations," *Business Horizons* (January/February 1989), 29–33.
19. Geert Hofstede, "Motivation, Leadership, and Organization: Do American Theories Apply Abroad?" *Organizational Dynamics* 9 (Summer 1980), 42–63.
20. Walter Sweet, "International Firms Strive for Uniform Nets Abroad," *Network World*. May 28, 1990, 35–36.
21. R.N. Farmer, "International Management," in *Contemporary Management Issues and Viewpoints*, ed. J.W. McGuire (Englewood Cliffs, N.J.: Prentice-Hall, 1974), 302.
22. Frank Ching, "China's Managers Get U.S. Lessons," *Wall Street Journal*, January 23, 1981, 27.
23. Malcolm Baldrige National Quality Award, correspondence to stockholders, November 1992.
24. Otis Port and Geoffrey Smith, "Beg, Borrow—and Benchmark," *Business Week*. November 30, 1992, 74–75.
25. Philip R. Catoera, *International Marketing*, 8th ed. (Homewood, Ill.: Richard D. Irwin, 1993).
26. Charles McMillan, "Is Japanese Management Really So Different?" *Business Quarterly* (Autumn 1980), 26–31.
27. Masaru Ibuka, "Management Opinion," *Administrative Management*. May 5, 1980, 86.
28. "How Japan Does It," *Time*. March 30, 1981, 55.
29. Lane Kelly and Reginald Worthley, "The Role of Culture in Comparative Management," *Academy of Management Journal* 24, no. 1 (1981), 164–73.
30. Linda S. Dillon, "Adopting Japanese Management: Some Cultural Stumbling Blocks," *Personnel* (July/August 1983), 73–77.
31. Isaac Shapiro, "Second Thoughts About Japan," *Wall Street Journal*, June 5, 1981.
32. William Ouchi, *Theory Z* (Reading, Mass.: Addison-Wesley, 1981).
33. Gene Koretz, "Yankees Go East—On a Scale That's Startling," *Business Week*. January 18, 1993, 26.
34. Rose Brady and Peter Galuszka, "The Soviet Lurch toward Capitalism," *Business Week*. October 21, 1991, 50.
35. John A. Byrne "Management's New Gurus: Business Is Hungry for Fresh Approaches to the Global Marketplace," *Business Week*. August 31, 1992, 44–52.

CHAPTER 21

1. "The Push for Quality," Business Week. June 8, 1987, 131.
2. A.V. Feigenbaum, *Total Quality Control* (New York: McGraw-Hill, 1983).
3. From Michael Schroeder, "Heart Trouble at Pfizer," *Business Week* February 26, 1990, 47–48.
4. For more information on these three contributors, see Charles H. Fine and David H. Bridge, "Managing Quality Improvement," in *Quest for Quality: Managing the Total System*, ed. by M. Sepehri (Norcross, Ga.: Institute of Industrial Engineers, 1987), 66–74.
5. For some of Crosby's more notable books in this area, see Philip B. Crosby, *Quality Is Free* (New York: McGraw-Hill, 1979); *Quality Without Tears* (New York: McGraw-Hill, 1984); *Let's Talk Quality: 96 Questions You Always Wanted to Ask Phil Crosby* (New York: McGraw-Hill, 1989); and *Leading* (New York: McGraw-Hill, 1990).
6. Deming's 14 Points (January 1990 revision) reprinted by permission from *Out of Crisis* by W. Edwards Deming by permission of MIT and W. Edwards Deming. Published by MIT, Center for Advanced Engineering Study, Cambridge, MA 02139. Copyright 1986 by W. Edwards Deming.
7. Alan Robinson, *Modern Approaches to Manufacturing Improvement: The Shingo System* (Productivity Press, 1990), 267–268.
8. Ross Johnson and William O. Winchell, *Strategy and Quality* (Milwaukee, Wisc.: American Society for Quality Control, 1989), 1–2.
9. Company Mission Statement, All America Inc., 1991, used by permission.
10. For a discussion supporting how important training can be in a company-wide quality effort, see "Dr. W. Edwards Deming," *EBS Journal* (Spring 1989), 3.
11. Tom Peters, *Thriving on Chaos: Handbook for a Management Revolution* (Harper & Row, 1987), 88, 98.
12. Peters, *Thriving on Chaos,* 326.
13. Joseph Juran, *Juran on Quality Leadership: How to Go from Here to There* (Juran Institute, Inc., 1987), 6.
14. *Manpower Argus,* published by Manpower Temporary Services, February 1993, 10. Used by permission.
15. Michael Hammer, "Reeingineering Work: Don't Automate, Obliterate," *Harvard Business Review* (July/August 1990), 104–112.

CHAPTER 22

1. Ann M. Morrison, "Leadership Diversity as Strategy," in *The New Leaders: Guidelines on Leadership Diversity in America* (San Francisco: Jossey-Bass Publishers), 11–28.
2. William B. Johnston and Arnold E. Packer, "Executive Summary," *Workforce 2000: Work and Workers for the Twenty-First Century.* (Indianapolis: Hudson Institute, June 1987), xiii–xiv.
3. Roosevelt Thomas, "Affirmative Action or Affirming Diversity," *Harvard Business Review,* (1990), 110.
4. Rosabeth Moss Kanter, *Men and Women of the Corporation* (New York: Basic Books, 1977).
5. Rosabeth Moss Kanter, "Numbers: Minorities and Majorities," in *Men and Women of the Corporation* (New York: Basic Books, 1977), 206–244.
6. Ann M. Morrison, *Breaking the Glass Ceiling: Can Women Reach the Top of America's Largest Corporations?* (Reading, Massachusetts: Addison Wesley Publishing Company, 1992).
7. Susan Webb, *Step Forward: Sexual Harassment in the Workplace* (New York: MasterMedia, 1991).
8. Ella Bell, "The Bicultural Life Experience of Career Oriented Black Women," *Journal of Organizational Behavior* 11 (November 1990), 459–478.
9. Jeffrey Sonnenfeld, "Dealing With the Aging Workforce," *Harvard Business Review* 56, 6 (1978), 81–92.
10. Ibid.
11. Joan Shinault, *"Change Agent in Action: Organizational Change and Development Through Employee Initiatives"* (Master's thesis, Binghamton University, 1992).
12. William B. Johnston and Arnold E. Packer, "Executive Summary," *Workforce 2000: Work and Workers for the Twenty-First Century.* (Indianapolis: Hudson Institute, June 1987), xii–xiv.
13. Jean Kim, "Issues in Workforce Diversity," Panel Presentation at the First Annual National Diversity Conference. (San Francisco, May 1991).
14. *The Holy Bible.* Authorized King James Version. (Holman Bible Publishers: Nashville, 1984).
15. J. Stewart Black and Hal B. Gregersen, "Serving Two Masters: Managing the Dual Allegiance of Expatriate Employees," *Sloan Management Review* (Summer 1992), 61–71.
16. Morrison, *The New Leaders,* 5–7.
17. Les Donaldson and Edward E. Scannell, *Human Resource Development: The New Trainer's Guide,* 2nd ed. (Reading, Massachusetts: Addison-Wesley Publishing Company, 1986), 8–9.

CREDITS

CHAPTER 1

Figure 1.2: Shawn Tully, "What CEOs Really Make," *Fortune,* (June 15, 1992): 95. © 1992 Time, Inc. All rights reserved. **Table 1.2:** "The Eight Attributes" from *In Search of Excellence* by Thomas J. Peters and Robert H. Waterman Jr., pp. 13–16. Copyright © 1982 by Thomas J. Peters and Robert H. Waterman, Jr. Reprinted by permission of HarperCollins Publishers. **Figure 1.6:** Paul Hersey and Kenneth Blanchard, *Management of Organizational Behavior: Utilizing Human Resources,* 5th ed., © 1988, p. 8. Reprinted by permission of Prentice-Hall, Inc., Englewood Cliffs, NJ. **Figure 1.7:** Douglas T. Hall, *Careers in Organizations,* © 1976 Scott, Foresman and Company. Reprinted by permission. **Table 1.3:** Lynn Slavenski, "Career Development: A Systems Approach," *Training and Development Journal* (February 1987): 58. Copyright 1987, *Training and Development Journal,* American Society for Training and Development. Reprinted with permission. All rights reserved. **Table 1.4:** Reprinted, by permission of the publisher, from "Improving Professional Development by Applying the Four-Stage Career Model," by Paul H. Thompson, Robin Zenger Baker, and Norman Smallwood, *Organizational Dynamics* (Autumn/1986): 59, © 1986. American Management Association, New York. All rights reserved. **Table 1.5:** Copyright 1976 by the Regents of the University of California. Reprinted from Ross A. Webber, "Career Problems of Young Managers," *California Management Review,* Vol. 18, No. 4 (Summer 1976): 29. By permission of the Regents.

CHAPTER 2

Global Highlight: Anne M. Hayer, "Packaging Solutions at Delta," *Manufacturing Engineering* 103 (August 1989): 69–70. **Table 2.1:** From Anne M. Hayner, "Packaging Solutions at Delta," *Manufacturing Engineering* 103 (August 1989): 69–70. **Table 2.2:** William R. Spriegel and Clark E. Myers, *The Writings of the Gilbreths,* Easton, PA: Richard D. Irwin (1953): 56. By permission of Hive Publishing Company. **Diversity Highlight:** Cathy Wallace, "Creating a Family-Friendly Workplace," *Credit Union Management* 15 (February 1992): 18–21. **Quality Highlight:** Jeremy Main, "How to Win the Baldridge Award," *Fortune Magazine* (April 23, 1990): 101–116; Christopher W. I. Hart, Christopher Bogan, and Dan O'Brien, "When Winning Isn't Everything," *Harvard Business Review* (January/February 1990): 209. **Ethics Highlight:** Annette Kondo, "Disaster Plans Prove Sound after San Francisco Shake-Up," *Wall Street Computer Review* 17 (December 1989): 6–10. **Case Study:** Peter B. Peterson, "The Pioneering Efforts of Major General William Crozier (1855–1942) in the Field of Management," *Journal of Management* 15 (1989): 3.

CHAPTER 3

Quality Highlight: Alan Halcrow, "Social Service at Xerox," *Personnel Journal* (March 1987): 10–15. **Table 3.1:** Adapted from Terry W. McAdams, "How to Put Corporate Responsibility into Practice." Reprinted by permission from *Business and Society Review* (Summer 1973): 12–13. Copyright 1973, Warren, Gorham and Lamont Inc., 210 South St., Boston, MA. All rights reserved. **Ethics Highlight:** Barbara Clark O'Hare, *American Demographics* 13 (September 1991): 38–42. **Global Highlight:** Edgar S. Wollard, Jr. "The 'Soul' Factor in Corporate Growth and Prosperity," *Directors and Boards* (Winter 1989): 4–8. **Table 3.4:** Sandra L. Holmes, "Executive Perceptions of Social Responsibility," *Business Horizons* (June 1976). Copyright, 1976, by the Foundation for the School of Business at Indiana University. Reprinted by permission. **Figure 3.1:** Ramon J. Aldag and Donald W. Jackson, Jr., "A Managerial Framework for Social Decision Making," *MSU Business Topics* (Winter 1975): 34. Reprinted by permission of the publisher, Division of Research, Graduate School of Business Administration, Michigan State University. **Table 3.5:** © 1975 by the Regents of the University of California. Reprinted from S. Prakash Sethi, "Dimensions of Corporate Social Performance: An Analytical Framework," *California Management Review* 17 (Spring 1975): 63. By permission of the Regents. **Figure 3.2:** Kenneth E. Newgren, "Social Forecasting: An Overview of Current Business Practices," in Archie B. Carroll, ed., *Managing Corporate Social Responsibility.* Copyright © 1977 by Little, Brown and Company (Inc.). Reprinted by permission of the author. **Figure 3.3:** Reprinted by permission of the *Harvard Business Review,* from "How Companies Respond to Social Demands" by Robert W. Ackerman (July/August 1973): 96. Copyright © 1973 by the President and Fellows of Harvard College; all rights reserved. **Figure 3.4:** John L. Paulszek, "How Three Companies Organize for Social Responsibility." Reprinted by permission from *Business and Society Review* (Summer 1973): 18, Warren, Gorham and Lamont, Inc., 210 South St., Boston, MA. All rights reserved. **Diversity Highlight:** Glenn Hasek, "Breaking Barriers: Education Erases False Perceptions of Minority Opportunities," *Hotel & Motel Management* 207 (February 24, 1992): 21–22. **Table 3.6:** Bernard Butcher, "Anatomy of a Social Performance Report." Reprinted by permission from *Business and Society Review* (Autumn 1973): 29, Warren, Gorham and Lamont, Inc., 210 South St., Boston, MA. All rights reserved. **Table 3.7:** Reprinted by permission of Johnson & Johnson. **Table 3.8:** Reprinted by permission from "Code of Ethics and Standards of Conduct" (Orlando, FL: Martin Marietta, n.d.): 3. **Case Study:** Archie B. Carroll and Frank Hoy, "Integrating Corporate Social Policy into Strategic Management," *Journal of Business Strategy* (Winter 1984): 48–57; Cindy Milto, "Companies with a Conscience," *Working Woman* (January 1990): 10; Proctor & Gamble advertisement, *American Baby* (December 1992): 27; additional information obtained from P&G's toll-free number (1–800–866–0971) and from P&G pamphlets.

CHAPTER 4

Figure 4.2: Jon H. Barrett, *Individual Goals and Organizational Objectives: A Study of Integration Mechanisms,* p. 5. Copyright © 1970 by the Institute for Social Research, The University of Michigan. Reprinted with permission. **Global Highlight:** Ted Agres, "Asea Brown Boveri—A Model for Global Management," *R & D* 33 (December 1991): 30–34; Paul R. Sullivan, "Executive Excellence," *R & D* 8 (September 1991): 9–10. **Ethics Highlight:** Stacy Shapiro, "Employer Fights AIDS with Education," *Business Insurance* (October 30, 1989): 31. **Quality Highlight:** Barry Z. Posner and William H. Schmidt, "Values of American Managers: Then and Now," *HR Focus* 69 (March 1992): 13. **Diversity Highlight:** Samuel K. Skinner, "Workforce Diversity," *Bureaucrat* 20 (Summer 1991): 29–31. **Figure 4.4:** Joseph L. Massie and John Douglas, *Managing,* © 1985, p. 244. Reprinted by permission of Prentice-Hall, Inc., Englewood Cliffs, NJ. **Table 4.2:** Howard M. Carlisle, *Management Concepts and Situations,* p. 598, © 1976. Published by Science Research Associates. Reprinted by permission of the author. **Table 4.3:** Reprinted by permission from A. N. Geller, *Executive Information Needs in Hotel Companies* (New York: Peat Marwick Main, 1984): 17. © Peat Marwick Main & Co., 1984. **Figure 4.5:** From Samuel C. Certo, Stewart T. Husted, and Max E. Douglas, *Business,* 3rd ed., p. 205. Copyright © 1990 by Allyn and Bacon. Reprinted by permission. **Case Study:** Ronald Henkoff, "Companies That Train Best," *Fortune Magazine* (March 22, 1993): 62; "The Trade-Off No One Wants," *Los Angeles Times* (March 21, 1993): M4; Joel Kotkin and David Friedman, "Clinton's Troubling Welfare Plan for the State—Defense Conversion," *Los Angeles Times* (March 21, 1993): M6; Myron Magnet, "Why Job Growth Has Stalled," *Fortune Magazine* (March 8, 1993): 51.

CHAPTER 5

Global Highlight: Robert P. Bauman, "Creating a Global Health Care Company," *Journal of Business Strategy* 13 (March/April 1992): 4–7. **Diversity Highlight:** Karen Matthes, "Companies Can Make It Their Business to Care," *HR Focus* 69 (February 1992): 4–5. **Figure 5.5:** William R. King and David I. Cleland, "A New Method for Strategic Systems Planning," *Business Horizons* (August 1975): 56. Copyright, 1975, by the Foundation for the School of Business Administration at Indiana University. Reprinted by permission. **Ethics Highlight:** Jean Marie Hubert van Engelshoven, "Corporate Environmental Policy in Shell," *Long-Range Planning* 24 (December 1991): 17–24. **Quality Highlight:** Bryan Siegel, "Organizing for a Successful CE Process," *Industrial Engineering* 23 (December 1991): 15–19. **Case Study:** D'Anastasio, "PepsiCo's Pizza Hut Signs Agreement for Soviet Venture; McDonald's Next?" *Wall Street Journal* (September 18, 1987): 12; Paul Farhi, "Pizza Rising Fast in Fast Good Market," *Washington Post* (September 20, 1988): E1, E6; "Pizza Hut Outlets to Open in Moscow Under New Pact," *Wall Street Journal* (February 23, 1989); "Pizza Hut Plans Brazil Expansion," *New York Times* (October 19, 1990); "Pizza Huts for Moscow, Beijing," *Wall Street Journal* (September 11, 1990); Charles P. Wallace, "Exotic Dining in Bangkok Means the Pizza Hut," *Los Angeles Times* (August 21, 1990): H4.

CHAPTER 6

Diversity Highlight: Wendell H. Joice, "Home Based Employment—A Consideration for Public Personnel Management," *Public Personnel Management* 20 (Spring 1991): 49–60. **Table 6.1:** Herbert A. Simon, *The Shape of Automation* (New York: Harper & Row, 1965): 62. Used with permission of the author. **Figure 6.3:** Republished with permission of E. I. du Pont de Nemours & Company. **Table 6.2:** Reprinted from "Characteristics of Organizational Environment and Perceived Environmental Uncertainty" by Robert B. Duncan. Published by *Administrative Science Quarterly* 17 (September 1972): 315, Table 1. By permission of *Administrative Science Quarterly.* **Global Highlight:** "United Technologies: Like Japan, but Different," *Economist* (UK) 317 (November 3, 1990): 76–77. **Ethics Highlight:** Cynthia Starr, "To Sell or Not to Sell Cigarette Products?" *Drug Topics* (May 1988): 28–34. **Quality Highlight:** Brian Dumaine, "Those High-Flying PepsiCo Managers," *Fortune Magazine* (April 10, 1989): 78–86. **Figure 6.8:** Reprinted by permission of *Harvard Business Review.* An exhibit from "Decision Trees for Decision Making" by John F. Magee (July/August 1964): 130. Copyright © 1964 by the President and Fellows of Harvard College; all rights reserved. **Case Study:** Thomas A. Stewart, "The King is Dead," *Fortune Magazine* (January 11, 1993): 34; Alex Taylor III, "U.S. Cars Come Back," *Fortune Magazine* (November 16, 1992): 52; Alex Taylor III, "Can GM Remodel Itself," *Fortune Magazine* (January 13, 1993): 26.

CHAPTER 7

Table 7.1: (a) and (b) based on E. Meadows, "How Three Companies Increased Their Productivity," *Fortune Magazine* (March 10, 1980): 92–101. (c) based on William B. Johnson, "The Transformation of a Railroad," *Long-Range Planning* 9 (December 1976): 18–23. **Figure 7.1:** Adapted from Samuel C. Certo and J. Paul Peter, *Strategic Management: Concepts and Applications* (New York: McGraw-Hill, Inc., 1991). Reprinted by permission of the authors. **Table 7.2:** William F. Glueck and Lawrence R. Jauch, *Business Policy and Strategic Management,* p. 102. © 1984 McGraw-Hill Book Company, New York. Reprinted by permission. **Ethics Highlight:** Joshua Levine, "Locking Up the Weekend Warriors," *Forbes* (October 2, 1989): 234–235. **Global Highlight:** Steven B. Weiner, "The Unlimited?" *Forbes* (April 6, 1987): 76–80; "The World Without Boundaries," Mast Industries, Inc. Recruitment Brochure. **Table 7.3:** Adapted from Arvind V. Phatak, *International Dimensions of Management,* 2nd ed., 1989, p. 6. Copyright © 1989 by Wadsworth, Inc. Reprinted by permission of the publisher. **Table 7.5:** [1]From the Roy E. Crummer Graduate School of Business Handbook, 1989; [2]Reprinted by permission from IBM 1990 Annual Report 1 © 1990 International Business Machines Corporation; [3]From the Federal Express Manager's Guide, 1990. **Quality Highlight:** Julie Johnson, "New Mission Statement Creates Unity for Health Care System," *Trustee* 45

(February 1992): 10, 23. **Table 7.6:** Arthur A. Thompson, Jr. and A. J. Strickland III, *Strategy Formulation and Implementation,* 4th ed., p. 109. Copyright © 1989 Business Publications, Inc. Reprinted by permission of Richard D. Irwin, Inc. **Figure 7.3:** © 1970 The Boston Consulting Group, Inc. All rights reserved. Published by permission. **Figure 7.4:** Reprinted by permission from p. 32 (adaptation of Figure 2.2) of *Strategy Formulation: Analytical Concepts* by Charles W. Hofer and Dan Schendel. Copyright © 1978 by West Publishing Company. All rights reserved. **Figure 7.5:** Reprinted with the permission of The Free Press, a Division of Macmillan, Inc. from *Competitive Advantage: Creating and Sustaining Superior Performance* by Michael E. Porter, p. 6. Copyright © 1985 by Michael E. Porter. **Diversity Highlight:** Paula Eubanks, "Workforce Diversity in Health Care: Managing the Melting Pot," *Hospitals* 64 (June 20, 1990): 48–52. **Figure 7.7:** Reprinted with the special permission of *Dun's Review* from R. M. Besse, "Company Planning Must Be Planned," (April 1957): 48. Copyright 1957, Dun & Bradstreet Publications Corporation.

CHAPTER 8

Ethics Highlight: Yoshihiko Shimizu, "Toyota Buckles Down to Overtake GM," *Tokyo Business Today* (Japan) 59 (February 1991): 32–34. **Table 8.1:** Reprinted by permission from *Indiana State University Handbook* 1969. Revised in 1970 and 1972, Terre Haute, Indiana. **Diversity Highlight:** Sue Shea and Ruby K. Okada, "Benefiting from Workforce Diversity," *Healthcare Forum* 35 (January/February 1992): 23–26. **Tables 8.2, 8.3:** Adapted from E. S. Groo, "Choosing Foreign Locations: One Company's Experience," *Columbia Journal of World Business* (September/October 1977): 77. Used with permission. **Global Highlight:** Mary B. Teagarden, Mark C. Sutler, and Mary Ann Von Glinow, "Mexico's Maquiladora Industry: Where Strategic Resource Management Makes a Difference," *Organizational Dynamics* 20 (Winter 1992): 34–47. **Quality Highlight:** Bill Stack, "Toyota in Bluegrass Country," *Industry Week* (June 5, 1989): 30–33; William J. Holstein, Peter Engardio, and Dan Cook., "Will Sake and Sour Mash Go Together?" *Business Week* (July 14, 1986): 53–55. **Figure 8.4:** Bruce Colman, "An Integrated System for Manpower Planning," *Business Horizons* (October 1970): 89–95. Copyright 1970, by the Foundation for the School of Business at Indiana University. Reprinted by permission. **Table 8.4:** Adapted, with permission, from W. C. House, "Environmental Analysis: Key to More Effective Dynamic Planning," *Managerial Planning* (January/February 1977): 27. Published by the Planning Executive Institute, Oxford, Ohio 45046. **Figure 8.6:** Philip Kotler, *Marketing Management Analysis, Planning and Control,* © 1967, p. 291. Adapted by permission of Prentice-Hall, Inc. Englewood Cliffs, NJ. **Table 8.5:** Adapted from *Sales Forecasting* (New York: The Conference Board, Inc., 1978): pp. 11–12, 31–44, 47–80. Used with permission.

CHAPTER 9

Diversity Highlight: "How to Manage a Diverse Workforce," *ABA Banking Journal* 83 (October 1991): 122, 124. **Global Highlight:** Tim Davis, "Crowning Achievement," *Beverage World* 111 (February 1992): 66, 78. **Ethics Highlight:** Carolyn Garrett Cline and Michael D. Cline, "The Gerber Baby Cries Foul!" *Business & Society Review* (Winter 1987): 14–19. **Figure 9.11:** © 1972 by the Regents of the University of California. Reprinted from Y. K. Shetty and H. M. Carlisle, "A Contingency Model of Organizational Behavior," *California Management Review*, Vol. 15, No. 1, p. 44. By permission of the Regents. **Quality Highlight:** Robert F. Huber, "Mercedes Manufacturing Strategy Is to Keep the Company's Market Niche Full," *Production* 103 (October 1991): 60–63. **Table 9.2:** Harold Koontz and Cyril O'Donnell, *Principles of Management*, p. 253. Copyright © 1972 by McGraw-Hill, Inc. Used by permission of McGraw-Hill Book Co. **Figure 9.14**: H. Fayol, *General and Industrial Management*, trans. Constance Storrs (London: Sir Issac Pitman & Son, Ltd., 1963): 34. Used with permission. **Case Study:** Sedona Fire Department, "Modernizing Current Job Descriptions, Performance Evaluations and Grievance Procedures," *Solicitation for Bid: Sedona Fire Department, Personnel Division*, 1991.

CHAPTER 10

Quality Highlight: Phil Niestedt and Richard Wintermantel, "Motorola Restructures to Improve Productivity," *Management Review* 76 (January 1987): 47–49. **Table 10.1:** Reprinted, by permission of the publisher, from "Roles and Relationships Clarifying the Manager's Job," by Robert D. Melcher, *Management Review* (May/June/1967): 35, 38–39, © 1967. American Management Association, New York. All rights reserved. **Table 10.3:** Adapted from ASPA-BNA Survey No. 47, "Personnel Activities, Budgets, and Staffs: 1983–1984," *Bulletin to Management* No. 1785—Part II, June 21, 1984. Copyright 1984 by the Bureau of National Affairs, Inc. Reprinted by permission. **Ethics Highlight:** Joseph Conlin, "The House That GE Built," *Successful Meetings* 38 (August 1989): 50–58. **Table 10.4:** Reprinted with the permission of Macmillan Publishing Company from *The New Management* by Robert M. Fulmer. Copyright © 1974 by Macmillan Publishing Company. **Diversity Highlight:** Zachary Schiller, "No More Mr. Nice Guy at P&G—Not by a Long Shot," *Business Week* (February 3, 1992): 54–56. **Figure 10.3:** David B. Starkweather, "The Rationale for Decentralization in Large Hospitals," *Hospital Administration* 15 (Spring 1970): 139. Courtesy of Dr. P. N. Ghei, Secretary General, Indian Hospital Association, New Delhi, India. **Global Highlight:** Maria Shao, "For Levi's, a Flattering Fit Overseas," *Business Week* (November 5, 1990): 76–77; Marcy Magiera and Pat Sloan, "Basic Jeans Shine for Levi's, Lee" *Advertising Age* 63 (February 17, 1992): 22. **Case Study:** George Anders, "Weak Trend: Value Line is Hurt by Low Morale, Slide in Interest in Stocks," *Wall Street Journal* (August 2, 1989): 1, A2; Value Line Inc., *Compact Disclosure*, 1991.

CHAPTER 11

Figure 11.2: Reprinted with the permission of Macmillan Publishing Company from *The Management of People at Work: Readings in Personnel,* 2nd ed. by Dale S. Beach. Copyright © 1970 by Macmillan Publishing Company. **Table 11.1:** U. S. Civil Service Commission. **Figures 11.3, 11.4, 11.5:** Walter S. Wikstrom, "Developing Managerial Competence: Concepts, Emerging Practices," *Studies in Personnel Policy* No. 189, pp. 9, 14. Used with permission. **Table 11.2:** Gene E. Burton, Dev S. Pathak, and David B. Burton, "Equal Employment Opportunity: Law and Labyrinth," *Management World* (September 1976): 29–30. Published by Administrative Management Society. **Figure 11.6:** Reprinted by permission from L. C. Megginson, *Providing Management Talent for Small Business* (Baton Rouge, LA, Division of Research, College of Business Administration, Louisiana State University, 1961): 108. **Global Highlight:** Anne Ferguson, "Compaq's Personnel Solution," *Management Today* (May 1989): 127–128; Prabhu Guptara, "Searching the Organization for the Cross-Cultural Operators," *International Management* 41 (August 1986): 40–42. **Table 11.3:** Dale Feuer, "Where the Dollars Go." Reprinted from the October 1985 issue of *Training*, The Magazine of Human Resources Development, p. 53. Copyright 1985, Lakewood Publications, Inc., Minneapolis, MN, 612-333-0471. All rights reserved. **Quality Highlight:** Kathryn W. Porter, "Tuning in to TV Training," *Training and Development Journal* 44 (April 1990): 73–77. **Figure 11.8:** George R. Terry and Leslie W. Rue, *Personal Learning Aid for Principles of Management*, p. 138. Copyright © 1982 Dow Jones-Irwin. Reprinted by permission. **Diversity Highlight:** Shari Caudron, "US WEST Finds Strength in Diversity," *Personnel Journal* 71 (March 1992): 40–44. **Table 11.4:** Compiled from Andrew F. Sikula, *Personnel Administration and Human Resource Management* (New York: John Wiley & Sons, 1976): 208–211. **Ethics Highlight:** Ken Sternberg, "Mobil Fights a Cover-up Charge," *Chemical Week* 146 (January 3, 1990/January 10, 1990): 10. **Case Study:** Marilyn Loden and Judy B. Rosener, *Workforce America! Managing Employee Diversity as a Vital Resource* (Homewood, IL: Business One Irwin, 1991).

CHAPTER 12

Figure 12.1: Don Hellriegel and John W. Slocum, Jr., "Integrating Systems Concepts and Organizational Strategy," *Business Horizons* 15 (April 1972): 73. Copyright, 1972, by the Foundation for the School of Business at Indiana University. Reprinted by permission. **Global Highlight:** Garry Evans, "Conde Fights Back," *Euromoney* (UK) (June 1991): 33–37. **Quality Highlight:** John Butman, "Quality Comes Full Circle," *Management Review* 81 (February 1992): 49–51. **Ethics Highlight:** Jonathan Lee, *Pulp & Paper* 66 (March 1992): 198–200. **Figures 12.4, 12.5:** John F. Mee, "Matrix Organization," *Business Horizons* (Summer 1964): 71. Copyright, 1964, by the Foundation for the School of Business at Indiana University. Reprinted by permission. **Diversity Highlight:** Beverly Geber, "The Disabled: Ready, Willing and Able," *Training* 27 (December 1990): 29–36. **Figure 12.6:** Richard J. Selfridge and Stanley I. Sokolik, "A Comprehensive View of Organization Development," *MSU Business Topics* (Winter 1975): 47. Reprinted by permission of the publishers, Division of Research, Graduate School of Business Administration, Michigan State University. **Figure 12.7:** Reprinted by permission of *Harvard Business Review*. From "Breakthrough in Organization Development" by Robert R. Blake, Jane S. Mouton, Louis Barnes, and Larry Greiner (November/December 1964): 136. Copyright © 1964 by the President and Fellows of Harvard College; all rights reserved. **Figure 12.9:** Reprinted by permission of the authors from Arthur P. Brief, Randall S. Schuller, and Mary Van Sell, *Managing Job Stress* (Boston: Little, Brown, 1981): 66. **Case Study:** Chris Sauula, "Prime Users Still on Hold," *Datamation* (September 1, 1990); Gary Slutsker, "The Company They Couldn't Sell," *Forbes* (October 2, 1989); Neil Margolis, "Big Overhaul Set at Prime," *Computer World* (December 19, 1988); Interview with Kathleen A. Cote, President and General Manager of Prime Service, by Sylvia Keyes, Bridgewater State College. **Integrative Case:** Interview with James Fogarty, Senior Director of Quality Assurance and Flight Training, USAir Corporation by Cheryl Macon, Butler Community College; *Beaver Country Times*, (December 1992): 8–11, 22–23; *Beaver Country Times*, (January 1993): 7; *USAir Corporate Policy Manual* (July 20, 1992): 1–14, 18–20.

CHAPTER 13

Table 13.1: Reprinted by permission from Stephen C. Harper, "Business Education: A View from the Top," *Business Forum* (Summer 1987): 25. **Global Highlight:** Patricia Crane and James W. Johnson, "A Bright Future for International Teleconferencing," *Satellite Communications* 13 (November 1989): 16a, 18a. **Figures 13.4, 13.5:** Wilber Schramm, *The Process and Effects of Mass Communication*, © 1954 University of Illinois Press, Champaign, IL. Reprinted by permission. **Diversity Highlight:** Brian M. Cook, "Joel Beck 'Grows Up' at Bull," *Industry Week* 240 (September 16, 1991): 22–26. **Ethics Highlight:** John A. Byrne, "The Best-Laid Ethics Programs," *Business Week* (March 9, 1992): 67–69. **Figure 13.7:** Reprinted, by permission of the publisher, from "An Experimental Approach to Organizational Communication," by Alex Bavelas and Dermont Barrett, *Personnel* (March/1951): 370, © 1951. American Management Association, New York. All rights reserved. **Quality Highlight:** Alan Salomon, "Bass Gains Base of Confidence," *Hotel & Motel Management* 206 (November 25, 1991): 2, 42. **Figure 13.8:** Reprinted by permission of *Harvard Business Review*. An exhibit from "Management Communication and the Grapevine" by Keith Davis (September/October 1953): 45. Copyright © 1953 by the President and Fellows of Harvard College; all rights reserved. **Table 13.2:** Keith Davis, *Human Behavior at Work*, p. 396. Copyright © 1972 by

McGraw-Hill, Inc. Used with permission of McGraw-Hill Book Company. **Case Study:** Vance H. Trimble, *Sam Walton, Founder of Wal-Mart: The Inside Story of America's Richest Man.* (New York: Dutton, 1990); Wal-Mart Stores Incorporated, *Compact Disclosure*, 1991. **Part 4 Integrative Case:** Navajo Arts and Crafts Enterprise, "Personnel Policies and Procedures" (July 1987); Navajo Arts and Crafts Enterprise, "Strategic and Operational Management Guide" (July 1987).

CHAPTER 14

Global Highlight: Esther Lee Yao, "Cultivating Guan-Xi (Personal Relationships) with Chinese Partners," *Business Marketing* 72 (January 1987): 62–66. **Figure 14.2:** Reprinted by permission of *Harvard Business Review.* From "How to Choose a Leadership Pattern" by Robert Tannenbaum and Warren H. Schmidt (May/June 1973). Copyright © 1973 by the President and Fellows of Harvard College; all rights reserved. **Figure 14.4:** Reprinted from *Leadership and Decision-Making* by Victor H. Vroom and Philip W. Yetton (Table 2.1, p. 13), by permission of the University of Pittsburgh Press. © 1973 by University of Pittsburgh Press. **Figure 14.5:** Reprinted from *The New Leadership: Managing Participation in Organizations by* Victor H. Vroom and Arthur G. Jago, 1988, Englewood Cliffs, NJ: Prentice-Hall. Copyright 1987 by V.H. Vroom and A. G . Jago. Used with permission of the authors. **Ethics Highlight:** Elizabeth Jensen, "NBC News President, Burned by Staged Fire and GM, Will Resign," *Wall Street Journal* (March 2, 1993): A1, A8; Douglas Lavin, "GM Accuses NBC of Rigging Test Crash of Pickup Truck on 'Dateline' Program," *Wall Street Journal* (February 9, 1993): A3, A6; Bill Loftus, "NBC Admits Forest Report Erred," *Lewiston Morning Tribune* (February 25, 1993) A1, A15; Elizabeth Jensen and Douglas Lavin, "How GM One-Upped an Embarrassed NBC on Staged News Event," *Wall Street Journal* (February 11, 1993): A1, A7; Howard Kirtz, "NBC News Credibility Crashes with GM Story," *Washington Post* (February 10, 1993): A1, A5; "A Safety Expert under Fire," *Business Week* (March 1, 1993): 42. **Figure 14.7:** Paul Hersey and Kenneth H. Blanchard, *Management of Organizational Behavior: Utilizing Human Resources*, 3rd ed., p. 103, © 1977. Reprinted by permission of Prentice-Hall, Inc., Englewood, Cliffs, NJ. **Table 14.1:** Paul Hersey and Kenneth H. Blanchard, *Management of Organizational Behavior: Utilizing Human Resources*, 3rd ed., © 1977 by Prentice-Hall, Inc., Englewood, Cliffs, NJ. Used with permission of Dr. W. J. Reddin, University of New Brunswick. **Table 14.2:** F. E. Fiedler, *A Theory of Leadership Effectiveness*, p. 34. Copyright © 1967 by McGraw-Hill, Inc. Used with permission of McGraw-Hill Book Company. **Figure 14.8:** Reprinted by permission of the *Harvard Business Review.* From "Engineer the Job to Fit the Manager" by Fred Fiedler (September/October 1965). Copyright © 1965 by the President and Fellows of Harvard College; all rights reserved. **Diversity Highlight:** Kevin D. Thompson, "Blazing New Trails," *Black Enterprise* 21 (January 1991): 54–57. **Case Study:** Interview with Al Scott by Stephen M. Beckstead, Utah State University.

CHAPTER 15

Figure 15.3: Lyman Porter and Edward Lawler III, *Managerial Attitudes and Performance*, p. 165. Copyright © 1968 Richard D. Irwin Inc. Reprinted by permission. **Global Highlight:** Ikushi Yamaguchii, "A Mechanism of Motivational Processes in a Chinese, Japanese, and U.S. Multicultural Corporation: Presentation of 'A Contingent Motivational Model'" *Management Japan* 24 (Autumn 1991): 27–32. **Figure 15.5:** Adapted from B. Kolasa, *Introduction to Behavioral Science in Business* (New York: Wiley, 1969): 256. Used with permission. **Table 15.1:** Douglas McGregor, *The Human Side of Enterprise.* Copyright © 1960 by McGraw-Hill, Inc. Used with permission of McGraw-Hill Book Company. **Figure 15.6:** W.J. Reddin, "The Tri-Dimensional Grid." Reproduced by special permission from the July 1964 *Training and Development Journal.* Copyright 1964 by the American Society for Training and Development Inc. **Diversity Highlight:** Gregory B. Northcraft, Terri L. Griffith, and Christina E. Shalley, "Building Top Management Muscle in a Slow Growth Environment: How Different Is Better at Greyhound Financial Corporation," *Academy of Management Executive* 6 (February 1992): 32–41. **Tables 15.2, 15.3:** Reprinted by permission of *Harvard Business Review*. From "One More Time: How Do You Motivate Employees?" by Frederick Herzberg (January/February 1968). Copyright © 1968 by the President and Fellows of Harvard College; all rights reserved. **Quality Highlight:** Jim Brahan, "A Rewarding Place to Work," *Industry Week* 238 (September 18, 1989): 15–19. **Table 15.4:** Reprinted by permission from Edward G. Thomas, "Workers Who Set Their Own Time Clocks," *Business and Society Review* (Spring 1987): 50. **Ethics Highlight:** Gail T. Young, "Is the Reward System the Problem?" *Bureaucrat* 18 (Spring 1989): 11–13. **Case Study:** Don Dedera, "Building an Airline with its Hub in the Desert," *Financial Enterprise: The Magazine of GE Capital* (Spring 1990); James O'Toole, "The Spirit of Phoenix," *Business Month* (October 1989); Michael Conway, "Doing the Right Thing," *Executive Financial Woman* (Spring 1990).

CHAPTER 16

Figure 16.2: Rensis Likert, *New Patterns of Management*, p. 104. Copyright © 1961 by McGraw-Hill, Inc. Used with permission of McGraw-Hill Book Company. **Diversity Highlight:** Sherri K. Lindenberg, "Managing a Multi-Ethnic Field Force," *National Underwriter* 95 (January 7, 1991): 16–18, 24. **Figure 16.3:** Reprinted by permission of *Harvard Business Review.* From "Committees on Trial" (Problems in Review) by Rollie Tillman, Jr. (May/June 1960): 163. Copyright © 1960 by the President and Fellows of Harvard College; all rights reserved. **Ethics Highlight:** Colleen Scanlon and Cornelia Fleming, "Confronting Ethical Issues: A Nursing Survey," *Nursing Management* 21 (May 1990): 63–65. **Figure 16.4:** Adapted from Raymond McLeod, Jr. and Jack W. Jones, "Making Executive Information Systems More Effective," *Business Horizons* (September/October 1986): 32. Copyright, 1986, by the Foundation for the School of Business at Indiana University. Reprinted by permission. **Quality Highlight:** George W. Hess, "Setting the New Standard in Quality," *Iron Age* 7 (September 1991): 33–36. **Figure 16.6:** Figure 11.5 from *Social Psychology* by Muzafer Sherif and Carolyn W. Sherif. Copyright © 1969 by Muzafer Sherif and Carolyn W. Sherif. Reprinted by permission of HarperCollins Publishers, Inc. **Table 16.1:** Reprinted with permission from Don Hellriegel and John W. Slocum, Jr., "Organizational Behavior Contingency Views," p. 166. Copyright © 1976 by West Publishing Co. **Global Highlight:** Gregg LaBar, "Ergonomics: the Mazda Way," *Occupational Hazards* 52 (April 1990): 43–46. **Figure 16.9:** Reprinted, by permission of the publisher, from "Group Norms Key to Building a Winning Team," by P.C. Andre de la Porte, *Personnel* (September/October/1974): 64, © 1974. American Management Association, New York. All rights reserved. **Table 16.2:** Reprinted, by permission of the publisher, from "What Raises a Man's Morale," by Morris S. Viteles, *Personnel,* (January/1954): 305, © 1954. American Management Association, New York. All rights reserved. **Case Study:** Barbara Buell, Jonathan B. Levine, and Nell Gross, "Apple: New Team, New Strategy," *Business Week* (October 15, 1990); James Kaplan, "Rethinking the Feel-Good Manager," *Business Month* (March 1990); Evelyn Richards, "Changes Eating Away at Apple's Core," *Washington Post* (February 23, 1990); G. Pascal Zachary, "Bruised Apple," *Wall Street Journal* (1990).

CHAPTER 17

Global Highlight: Sarah Grey, "Not a Mickey Mouse Organization," *Accountancy* 104 (November 1989): 16–17. **Quality Highlight:** Brian S. Moskal, "Quality Cow Gives Free Milk," *Industry Week* 239 (March 19, 1990): 27, 30. **Table 17.1:** Adapted from Y. K. Shetty, "Product Quality and Competitive Strategy," *Business Horizons* (May/June 1987): 47. Copyright, 1987, by the Foundation for the School of Business at Indiana University. Reprinted by permission. **Ethics Highlight:** Glen Schriever, "Reducing Fire Risk in Propane Appliances," *Appliance Manufacturer* 40 (February 1992): 28, 34. **Diversity Highlight:** Lisa Lebowitz, "A Rainbow Coalition, *Working Woman* 16 (December 1991): 72–74. **Figure 17.3:** Reprinted by permission of *Harvard Business Review*. An exhibit from "Better Reports for Better Control" by John G. McLean (May/June 1957): 98. Copyright © 1957 by the President and Fellows of Harvard College; all rights reserved. **Table 17.2:** Reprinted by permission from p. 13 of *Cost Accounting: A Managerial Approach,* 2/e, by Cherrington, Hubbard, and Luthy; Copyright © 1988 by West Publishing Company. All rights reserved. **Case Study:** Texaco, Inc., "Is It Really System 3? Samples Can Tell," *Texaco Marketer* (March 1990): 18–19; Robert C. Samuels, "System 3: How Good It Is," *Texaco Today* (1990): 6–9; "Pursuing and Benefiting from a Quality Initiative," *Texaco Inc. Annual Report 1989.*

CHAPTER 18

Figure 18.1: Joseph W. Wilkinson, *Accounting and Information Systems.* Copyright © 1982 John Wiley & Sons, Inc. Reprinted by permission of John Wiley & Sons, Inc. **Figure 18.2**: Reprinted from *Out of Crisis* by W. Edwards Deming by permission of MIT and W. Edwards Deming. Published by MIT, Center for Advanced Engineering, Cambridge, MA 02139. Copyright 1986 by W. Edwards Deming. **Quality Highlight:** Stephen Barr, "Adidas on the Rebound," *CFO: The Magazine for Senior Financial Executives* (September 1991): 48–56; Richard A. Melcher, "Now This Should Get Adidas on Its Feet," *Business Week* (July 20, 1992): 42. **Table 18.1:** Robert Kemper and Joseph Yehudai, *Experiencing Operations Management: A Walk-Through,* 1991, pp. 7–8. Copyright © 1991 by Wadsworth, Inc. Reprinted by permission of the publisher. **Global Highlight:** From Andrew Tanzer and Ruth Simon, "Why Japan Loves Robots and We Don't," *Forbes* (April 1990): 148–153. **Figure 18.4:** Richard B. Chase and Nicholas J. Aquilano, *Production and Operations Management: A Life Cycle Approach,* 4th ed., p. 5. © 1985 Richard D. Irwin, Inc. Reprinted by permission. **Ethics Highlight:** Mary Walton, *Deming Management at Work: Six Successful Companies that Use the Quality Principles of the World-Famous W. Edwards Deming* (New York: G.P. Putnam's Sons, 1991): 185–205; Kathleen Morris, "A Bridge Far Enough: Four Years after Buying Firestone Bridgestone Finally Gets Tough," *Financial World* (June 9, 1992): 52–54. **Diversity Highlight:** Reprinted, by permission of the publisher, from "Will the ADA Disable Your Company?" by Don Nichols, from *Small Business Report* 17 (January/1992): 28–38, © 1992. American Management Association, New York. All rights reserved. **Case Study:** Annual Report, Caterpillar, 1988; "Caterpillar's Fundamental English," *Training and Development Journal* (February 1973); "Caterpillar's Triple Whammy," *Fortune Magazine* (October 27, 1986); Shirley Carver, "Off-highway Industry Takes a New Path to Profits," *Purchasing* (August 17, 1989); Jeremy Main, "Manufacturing the Right Way," *Fortune Magazine* (May 21, 1990)

CHAPTER 19

Figure 19.1: Reprinted by permission from G. Anthony Gorry and Michael S. Scott Morton, "A Framework for Management Information Systems," *Sloan Management Review* 13 (Fall 1971): 59. **Figure 19.2, Table 19.1:** Roman R. Andrus, "Approaches to Information Evaluation," *MSU Business Topics* (Summer 1971): 44. Reprinted by permission of the publisher, Division of Research, Graduate School of Business Administration, Michigan State University. **Table 19.2:** Reprinted by permission from Alice M. Greene, "Computers Big Pay-off for Small Companies," *Iron Age* (March 30, 1972): 63–64. **Ethics Highlight:** Neil A. Burger, "Let's Talk Benefits—Electronically," *Personnel* 66 (September 1989): 58–59. **Global Highlight:** Oles

Gadacz, "Steel Giant Pioneers Korean IS," *Datamation* 35 (June 1, 1989): 64g–64h. **Table 19.3:** Reprinted by permission of *Harvard Business Review.* An exhibit from "Manufacturing—Missing Link in Corporate Strategy" by Wickham Skinner (May/June 1969): 141. Copyright © 1969 by the President and Fellows of Harvard College; all rights reserved. **Figure 19.5:** Adapted from Robert G. Murdick, "MIS for MBO," *Journal of Systems Management* (March 1977): 34–40. Used with permission of *Journal of Systems Management*, 24587 Bagley Road, Cleveland, OH 44138. **Diversity Highlight:** Jay L. Johnson, "Target's New Dynamics," *Discount Merchandiser* 31 (August 1991): 30–46; Terry E. Hedrick, "New Challenges for Government Managers," *Bureaucrat* 19 (Spring 1990): 17–20. **Quality Highlight:** Catherine Marenghi, "Nashua Keeps Quality Flame Burning in Customer Service," *Computerworld* 26 (January 6, 1992): 61. **Figure 19.6:** Reprinted by permission from R. E. Breen et al., *Management Information Systems: A Subcommittee Report on Definitions* (Schenectady, NY: General Electric Co., 1969): 21. **Table 19.4:** Reprinted by permission of the Institute of Management Services from Bertram A. Colbert, "The Management Information System," *Management Services* 4 (September/October 1967): 18. **Table 19.5:** Dickson/Simmons, "The Behavioral Side of MIS," *Business Horizons* (August 1970): 68. Copyright, 1970, by the Foundation for the School of Business at Indiana University. Reprinted by permission. **Figure 19.7:** "Parts of the Personal Computer and What They Do," *Time* (January 3, 1983): 39. Copyright 1982 Time Inc. Magazine Company. Reprinted by permission. **Figure 19.8:** From Mark G. Simkin, *Introduction to Computer Information Systems for Business*, p. 299. Copyright © 1987 by Wm. C. Brown Publishers, Dubuque, Iowa. All Rights Reserved. Reprinted by permission. **Case Study:** "The Changing Role of the Mainframe," *IS Analyzer* 31 (January 1993): 1–4. Reprinted by permission. **Part 5 Integrative Case:** Paul B. Brown, "Mag Instruments." Reprinted with permission, *Inc.* Magazine (August 1989). Copyright 1989 by Goldhirsh Group, Inc., 38 Commercial Wharf, Boston, MA 02110.

CHAPTER 20

Figure 20.1: "U.S. Direct Investment Abroad: Detail for Position and Balance of Payment Flows," *Survey of Current Business* 70 (August 1990): 56–98, *Survey of Current Business* 71 (August 1991): 81–107; "Historical-Cost Position and Balance of Payment Flows, 1991," *Survey of Current Business* 72 (August 1992): 116–144. **Figure 20.2:** "Foreign Direct Investment in the U.S.: Detail for Position and Balance of Payment Flows," *Survey of Current Business* 70 (August 1990): 41–55, *Survey of Current Business* 71 (August 1991): 47–79; "Foreign Direct Investment in the U.S.: Detail for Historical Cost Position and Balance of Payment Flows, 1991" *Survey of Current Business* 72 (August 1992): 87–115. **Table 20.1:** "U.S. Corporations with the Biggest Foreign Revenues," *Forbes* (July 20, 1992): 298. Reprinted by permission of *Forbes* magazine. © Forbes, Inc., 1992. **Table 20.2:** "Fewer Deals, Less Investment," *Forbes* (July 20, 1992): 290. Reprinted by permission of *Forbes* magazine. © Forbes, Inc., 1992. **Table 20.3:** Neil H. Jacoby, "The Multinational Corporation," reprinted by permission from *Center Magazine* 3 (May 1970): 37–55. **Ethics Highlight:** "Japanese New Earth 21 Plan," Peter Jennings on *World News Tonight*, ABC network (December 14, 1992). **Global Highlight:** "Trade with China: More of a One-Way Than Two-Way Street," *Business Week* (November 30, 1992): 28. **Table 20.4:** Stefan H. Robock and Kenneth Simmonds, *International Business and Multinational Enterprise*, 4th ed., p. 383. Copyright © 1989 Richard D. Irwin, Inc. Reprinted by permission. **Figure 20.3:** Reprinted by permission of the author from Richard D. Robinson, *International Management* (Hinsdale, IL: Dryden Press, 1967). **Diversity Highlight:** Barry Louis Rubin, "Europeans Value Diversity," *HRMagazine* 36 (January 1991): 38–41, 78. **Table 20.5:** Reprinted with permission from Howard V. Perlmutter, "The Tortuous Evolution of the Multinational Corporation," *Columbia Journal of World Business* 4 (January/February 1989): 12. **Quality Highlight:** Carol Hiderbrand, *Computer World*, 100. **Figure 20.4:** William Ouchi, *Theory Z*, p. 58, © 1981 Addison-Wesley Publishing Company, Inc. Reprinted with permission of the publisher. **Figure 20.5:** "The Evolution of Worker Participation in the U. S.," p. 57. Reprinted from July 10, 1989 issue of *Business Week*, by special permission, copyright © 1989 by McGraw-Hill, Inc. **Case Study:** Matt Moffett, "Culture Shock," *Wall Street Journal* (September 24, 1992): R13–R14; Jim Carlston, "The Lure of Cheap Labor," *Wall Street Journal* (September 24, 1992): R16; Walter E. Greene, "The Maquiladora—Japan's New Competitive Weapon," *Business* (October/December 1989): 52–56; "Is Free Trade with Mexico Good or Bad for the U.S.?" *Business Week* (November 12, 1990): 112–113; Jane LeMaster, "A Survey of the Maquiladora Industry in Mexico" (term paper, University of North Texas, Spring 1990).

CHAPTER 21

Quality Highlight: Tom Peters, *Thriving on Chaos: Handbook for a Management Revolution*, Harper & Row, 1987, p. 87. **Table 21.1:** Adapted with the permission of The Free Press, a Division of Macmillan, Inc. from *Japanese Manufacturing Techniques*, p. 47–82 and *World Class Manufacturing* p. 122–143, by Richard J. Schonberger. (JMT) Copyright © 1982 by Richard J. Schonberger. (WCM) Copyright © 1986 by Schonberger & Associates, Inc. **Figure 21.1:** David A. Gavin, "What Does Product Quality Really Mean?" *Sloan Management Review* 26 (Fall 1984): 37. Reprinted by permission of the publisher. Copyright 1984 by the Sloan Management Review Association. All rights reserved. **Table 21.2:** Philip B. Crosby, *Quality Without Tears*, (New York: McGraw-Hill, 1979): 8–9. Copyright 1979. Reprinted with permission of McGraw-Hill, Inc. **Ethics Highlight:** Rajendra S. Sisodia, "We Need Zero-Tolerance Ethics Violations," *Marketing News* 24 (March 5, 1990): 4, 14. **Figure 21.2:** Shigeo Shingo, *Zero Quality Control: Source Inspection and the Poka-Yoke System*. Copyright © 1986 by Productivity Press, Inc., Portland, OR, 1-800-394-6868. Reprinted by permission. **Global Highlight:** Excerpt from Ronald E. Yates "US Lags on Rigorous New Quality Standard," *Chicago Tribune*, November 16, 1992. Reprinted by permission: Tribune Media Services. **Figure 21.3:** Philip B. Crosby, *Quality Without Tears* (New York: McGraw-Hill, 1979): 38–39. Copyright 1979. Reprinted with permission of McGraw-Hill, Inc. **Case Study:** Ellis Booker, "Quality in IS: Managing with Facts, Not Intuition," *Computerworld* (December 11, 1989): 97; Florida Power and Light Company, *Compact Disclosure* (1991); Carol Hilderbrand, "The Deming Prize: No Longer a Stranger at Home," *Computerworld* (December 11, 1989): 100; Carol Hilderbrand, "Take It From the Top," *Computerworld* (December 11, 1989): 96; "Information Systems Anchor the Entire Organization," *Computerworld* (December 11, 1989): 96; Alan J. Ryan, "For Programmers, a Night's Sleep," *Computerworld* (December 11, 1989): 97; Alan J. Ryan, "Where Quality Takes Command," *Computerworld* (December 11, 1989): 1, 95–100.

CHAPTER 22

Quality Highlight: Parker R. Goodwin, Laying the Groundwork for Diversity Training at CAE-LINK: Demographics and Process Issues, Binghamton University (1993): 31–33. Reprinted by permission. **Table 22.1:** Ann M. Morrison, *The New Leaders: Guidelines on Leadership Diversity in America* (San Francisco: Josey-Bass, Inc., 1992): 5–7, 18–27. Copyright © 1992 by Ann M. Morrison and Josey-Bass, Inc., Publishers. Reprinted by permission. **Diversity Highlight:** Parker R. Goodwin, *Laying the Groundwork for Diversity Training at CAE-LINK: Demographic and Process Issues*, (Reprinted by permission) Binghamton University (1993): 31–33. **Table 22.2:** William B. Johnston and Arnold E. Packer, *Workforce 2000: Work and Workers for the 21st Century.* (Indianapolis: Hudson Institute, June 1987): pp. xix–xx, pp. 105–106. Reprinted by permission. **Figure 22.1:** William B. Johnston and Arnold E. Packer, "Executive Summary," *Workforce 2000: Work and Workers for the 21st Century.* (Indianapolis: Hudson Institute, June 1987): 95. Reprinted by permission. **Global Highlight:** "Connecting the World," *Focus: For and About the People of AT&T* (September 1992). **Ethics Highlight:** Parker R. Goodwin, *Laying the Groundwork for Diversity Training at CAE-LINK: Demographic and Process Issues*, Binghamton University (1993): 20. Reprinted by permission. **Case Study:** Patrick Lee, "Diverse Opinions on Where to Focus," *Los Angeles Times* (November 29, 1992): D1; John Naisbitt and Patricia Aburdene, *Megatrends 2000* (New York: Avon Books, 1991); Robert Scheer, "Peter Ueberroth," *Los Angeles Times* (May 17, 1992): M3; "Touched by Fire: Understanding the Riots—Six Months Later," *Los Angeles Times* (November 19, 1992): JJ2; Jonathan Weber, "Rebuild California," *Los Angeles Times* (November 29, 1992): D1.

PHOTO CREDITS

Allyn & Bacon acknowledges the following photo copyright holders.

Part I: Page 1, D. Fabricius/Stock Boston.

Chapter 1: **Introductory Case,** Michael Abramson/Woodfin Camp; page 16, D. Fabricius/Stock Boston; page 19, Joel Feingersh/Stock Boston.

Chapter 2: **Introductory Case,** Andy Levin/Photo Researchers; **Global Highlight,** Delta Faucet; **Diversity Highlight,** North Island Federal Credit Union; **Quality Highlight,** Ritz Carlton Hotel Company; **Ethics Highlight,** Ron Haviv/SABA.

Chapter 3: **Introductory Case,** Rich Maiman/Sygma; **Quality Highlight,** Jeff Reinking/The Picture Group; **Ethics Highlight,** Stephen R. Brown/Gamma-Liaison; **Diversity Highlight,** Opryland Hotel; **Global Highlight,** Jesse Hemerofsky/Picture Group.

Part 2: Page 87, SmithKline Beecham Corporation.

Chapter 4: **Introductory Case,** Stuart Cohen/Comstock; **Global Highlight,** Asea Brown Boveri Company; **Ethics Highlight,** Canadian Public Health Association; **Quality Highlight,** Tony Freeman/Photo Edit; **Diversity Highlight,** Department of Transportation.

Chapter 5: **Introductory Case,** Margaret Miller/Photo Researchers; **Diversity Highlight,** Johnson & Johnson; **Global Highlight,** SmithKline Beecham Corporation; **Ethics Highlight,** N. Tully/Sygma; **Quality Highlight,** Sun Microsystems.

Chapter 6: **Introductory Case,** R. Maiman/Sygma; **Diversity Highlight,** Paul Conklin/PhotoEdit; **Global Highlight,** George Hall/Leo DeWys; **Ethics Highlight,** Bob Daemmrich/Stock Boston; **Quality Highlight,** PepsiCo, Inc.

Chapter 7: **Introductory Case,** Jay Clarke/Miami Herald; **Ethics Highlight,** Bob Daemmrich/Stock Boston; **Global Highlight,** Bill Freeman/PhotoEdit; **Quality Highlight,** Lutheran General Health Care System; **Diversity Highlight,** Miro Vintoniu/Stock Boston.

Chapter 8: **Introductory Case,** Fiat; **Ethics Highlight,** Carlo Carino/SABA; **Diversity Highlight,** Burroughs/PhotoEdit; **Quality Highlight,** Jack McKigney/Picture Group; **Global Highlight,** R. Perry/Sygma.

Part 3: Page 211, Hutchinson Technology, Inc.

Chapter 9: **Introductory Case,** MCI; **Diversity Highlight,** Robert Rathe/Stock Boston; **Global Highlight,** Will & Deni McIntyre/Allstock; **Ethics Highlight,** David Dempster; **Quality Highlight,** Douglas Mesney/Leo de Wys, Inc.

Chapter 10: **Introductory Case,** Susanna Pashko/Envision; **Quality Highlight,** Jacques Chenet/Woodfin Camp; **Ethics Highlight,** Dennis Young-Wolff/Photo Edit; **Diversity Highlight,** Frank Fournier/Contact Press Images/Woodfin Camp; **Global Highlight,** Maggie Murray/Impact Visuals.

Chapter 11: **Introductory Case,** Universal Studios; **Global Highlight,** Compaq Computer Corporation; **Quality Highlight,** Aetna Life and Casualty Company; **Diversity Highlight,** US West; **Ethics Highlight,** Russ Kinne/Comstock.

Chapter 12: **Introductory Case,** PepsiCo, Inc.; **Global Highlight,** Ralph-Sinn Hestoff/Picture Group; **Quality Highlight,** Hutchinson Technology; **Ethics Highlight,** Sonoco Products Company; **Diversity Highlight,** Lawrence Migdale/Tony Stone Worldwide.

Part 4: Page 319, Greyhound Financial Corporation.

Chapter 13: **Introductory Case,** Eaton Corporation; **Global Highlight,** Arnie Katz/Stock South; **Diversity Highlight,** Michael Newman/PhotoEdit; **Ethics Highlight,** Najlah Feanny/SABA; **Quality Highlight,** Holiday Inn.

Chapter 14: **Introductory Case,** William Taufic; **Global Highlight,** Will & Deni McIntyre/Allstock; **Ethics Highlight,** Yvonne Hemsey/Gamma-Liaison; **Quality Highlight,** Paul Chesley/Tony Stone Worldwide; **Diversity Highlight,** Katherine Lambert.

Chapter 15: **Introductory Case,** David R. Frazier/Tony Stone Worldwide; **Global Highlight,** Hiroshi Harada/Dung/Photo Researchers Inc.; **Diversity Highlight,** Greyhound Financial Corporation; **Quality Highlight,** Apple Computer; **Ethics Highlights,** Bruce Hoertel/Woodfin Camp.

Chapter 16: **Introductory Case,** Tom Stoddart/Katz/SABA; **Diversity Highlight,** Tim Brown/Tony Stone Worldwide; **Quality Highlight,** George Hunter/Tony Stone Worldwide; **Ethics Highlight,** Calvary Hospital; **Global Highlight,** Peter Yates.

Part 5: Page 431, Dick Luria/Photo Researchers.

Chapter 17: **Introductory Case,** James Wilson/Woodfin Camp; **Global Highlight,** Sipa; **Quality Highlight,** Walter Hodges/Allstock; **Ethics Highlight,** Al Clayton/Stock South; **Diversity Highlight,** Peter Menzel/Stock Boston.

Chapter 18: **Introductory Case,** Bridgestone Inc.; **Quality Highlight,** R. Bossu/Sygma; **Global Highlight,** W. Estap/The Stock Market; **Ethics Highlight,** Bridgestone Inc.; **Diversity Highlight,** J. Pickerell/The Image Works.

Chapter 19: **Introductory Case,** Greg L. Ryan/Allstock; **Ethics Highlight,** Will & Deni McIntyre; **Global Highlight,** David Pollack/The Stock Market; **Diversity Highlight,** Target Store; **Quality Highlight,** Dick Luria/Photo Researchers.

Part 6: Page 521, ISO 9000.

Chapter 20: **Introductory Case,** Epaymoy/Sygma; **Ethics Highlight,** David Flock/Gamma-Liaison; **Global Highlight,** Kevin Morris/Allstock; **Diversity Highlight,** Hewlett Packard, Inc.; **Quality Highlight,** Deming Prize/Florida Power and Light Company.

Chapter 21: **Introductory Case,** Iomega Corporation; **Quality Highlight,** Ford Motor Company; **Ethics Highlight,** Bob Daemmrich/Image Works; **Global Highlight,** ISO 9000; **Diversity Highlight,** Bob Daemmrich/Image Works.

Chapter 22: **Introductory Case,** Ferguson & Katzman/ Allstock; **Quality Highlight,** Lawrence Migdale/Photo Researchers; **Diversity Highlight,** Frank Herholdt/Tony Stone Worldwide; **Global Highlight,** AT&T; **Ethics Highlight,** Mark Richards/PhotoEdit.

INDEXES

COMPANIES

Adidas USA, 462–463
Aetna Life and Casualty Company, 277
Alixandre Furs, 234–235
All America Inc., 553
American Can Company, 75, 260
American Greetings, 375–376, 379, 383, 385–386, 390–391, 394
American Heart Association, 14
American Home Products, 97
American Stock Exchange (Amex), 130–131
America West Airlines, 397
AMP, Inc., 524
Anheuser-Busch, 155–156, 524
A&P, 526
Apple Computer, 41, 389–390
Arkansas Freightways, 89–90, 92–93, 98–99, 101–102, 104
Arthur Young, 437
Asea Brown Boveri, 91
AT&T, 18, 172, 213, 274, 574
AT&T Universal Card Services, 38
Avon, 18, 160

Banco Espanol de Credito, 293–294
Baskin-Robbins, 205
B.A.T. Industries Plc/Imasco Ltd., 527
Beecham, 114–115
Ben & Jerry's, 592
Bethlehem Steel Comapny, 29
Black & Decker, 171
Blanes Industrial Incorporated, 84–85
Body Shop, 82–83
Boeing Co., 189, 425
Boston Consulting Group, 166–168
Brant Manufacturing, 109
Bridgestone Corporation, 457–458, 465, 467–468, 469, 476–477, 482–483
Bristol-Meyers Squibb, 84–85, 208–209
British Petroleum Plc, 526, 527
Brooklyn Union Gas, 14
Bull Worldwide Information Services, 329
Burger King, 13, 49, 526
Burns & McCallister, 581
Burroughs Wellcome, 497–498
Butterick Company, 260–261

Cajun Joe's, 48
Calvary Hospital, 405
Carts of Colorado, Inc., 129
Carvel, 205
Caterpillar, 487
Charles Schwab, 40
Chemical Bank, 75
Chevron, 526
Chrysler Corporation, 133–134, 138, 140, 143, 144, 147, 151, 221, 366, 539, 580
Citicorp, 92, 526
Coca-Cola Company, 15, 196, 229, 309
Colgate-Palmolive, 531
3Com Corporation, 515
Compaq Computer Company, 273
Compression, 325–326
ComputerVision, 313
Control Data Corporation, 55, 73
Corning, 38, 39, 368, 506, 572
Crown Cork & Seal Company, 221
Cypress Semiconductor Corporation, 499

Dell Computer, 221
Delta Faucet Company, 30
Denny's, 584
Development Dimensions, 353
Digital Equipment Corporation, 9, 23, 381, 561
Dominos, 129
Dow Chemical, 531
Dow Corning Corporation, 333–334
Drexel Burnham Lambert, 119
Dun & Bradstreet, 476

Eastern Airlines, 448
Eastman Kodak, 539
Eastman Kodak Co., 136
Eaton Corporation, 321–322, 324–325, 329–330, 333, 336, 338–339
E.I. duPont de Nemours and Company, 60–61, 136–137, 526
Elsie Y. Cross Associates, 569
Emery Air Freight Company, 391
Emery Worldwide, 391
EPI Products, 179
Equitable Life Assurance Company, 18, 403–404
Esprit de Corps, 314–315
Essence Communications, 110–111
Estee Lauder, 523–524, 526, 529–530
Euro Disneyland, 437
Exxon, 267, 526

Famous Amos, 171, 237–238, 240, 241, 243, 246, 249, 251, 253, 254–255
Fanuc, 463
Federal Express, 38, 165, 398–399, 594–595
Federal-Mogul Corporation, 463
Federated Department Stores, 13
Fiat, 183–184, 185–186, 192, 197–198, 200, 531
Firestone, 467–468
Firestone Tire and Rubber Company, 457
Ford Motor Co., 3, 125, 133, 151, 157, 239, 409, 421, 526, 539, 544
Friendly's, 205
Frigidaire Company, 288, 289
Frito-Lay, 9, 571
Frusen Gladje, 205
Fuller Brush, 160

Gannett, 433
General Dynamics, 75
General Electric, 168–169, 171, 246, 267, 364, 437–438, 446, 461, 473, 491, 527, 539, 573
General Motors, 3–4, 11, 12–13, 20, 114, 133, 151, 221, 292, 418, 463, 526, 539, 552–553, 566–567
Gerber Products Company, 160, 222–223
Geuman Corporation, 548
Gillian Group, 426–427
Globe Metallurgical, 38
GMFanuc, 463–464
Goodyear, 457
Grand Metropolitan, 526
Grand Metropolitan Plc, 527
Granite Rock Company, 38
Great American Cookie Company, 444
Greene Furniture Company, 220, 221
Green Giant, 539
Greyhound Financial Corporation, 387
Ground Round, 526
Gulf Oil, 71–72

Haagen Dazs, 205
Hammond, Inc., 516–517
Hanson, 526, 527
Hardee's, 526
Heinz, 472, 528
Hertz, 454–455
Hewlett-Packard, 9, 18, 259, 532, 561
Hoare Govett, 183
Holiday Inn, 92, 335–336
Honda, 170, 174
House of Natori, 24
Hughes, 151
Hutchinson Technology, 295

IBM, 9, 14, 18, 54–55, 73, 141, 165, 192, 196, 221, 252, 274, 310, 526, 540
IBM France, 95
IBM Rochester, 38
Imasco, 526
Infinity, 225

Insect Control Services Company, 193–194
Intel, 539
International Paper, 152–153
International Telephone and Telegraph, 539
Intuit, 545
IOMEGA Corporation, 259, 543–544, 548, 552, 558, 562

JAS Manufacturing, 565
J.C. Penney, 252, 274
J.D. Powers and Associates, 3
Johnson & Johnson, 9, 73–74, 117–118

Kentucky Fried Chicken, 291
KFC, 129
Kingsbury Machine Tool Company, 30
Kokotu Rubber Industry, 439
Komatsu, 467, 487

Labconco, 390
Larami Corporation, 51–52, 55, 58, 61, 65, 66–68, 71, 76
Laura Ashley, 386
Levi Strauss, 253, 287
Lexus, 225
Little Caesar's, 129
Liz Claiborne, 347–348, 349–350, 352–353, 357, 362, 367
Lockheed, 527
Lutheran General Health System, 164

3M, 9
Manila Philharmonic, 24
March of Dimes, 14
Marshfield Inc., 440
Mars Inc., 532
Martin Marietta, 75
Massey-Ferguson, 253–254
Mattel, 160
Maytag, 9
Mazda, 157, 239, 415–416
MCA, Inc., 263
McCormick and Company, 180–181
McDonalds Corporation, 578
McDonald's Corporation, 9, 14, 41, 43, 300, 394
McDonnell Douglas, 75
MCI Communications Corporation, 213–214, 216–217, 223, 225, 230
McKinsey and Company, 168–169, 218
Mercedes-Benz, 225
Merrill Lynch, 24
Methodist Hospital, 172
Michelin, 457
Mickey's Kitchen, 27–28, 33, 37, 43
Miller, Cooper, and Co. Ltd., 473
Mobil, 526
Mobil Chemical, 282
Molson, 141
Monsanto, 14
Motorola Inc., 38, 195, 240, 288, 381, 421, 551
Mrs. Fields' Cookies, 246

Nashua Corporation, 502–504
National Steel, 524
Nationwide Insurance, 13
Natori Company, 24
NBC News, 356–357
NCR, 193
Nike, 170, 221
Nippon Kokan, 524
Nissan, 121, 467
North Isalnd Federal Credit Union, 32
Northwestern National Life Insurance, 309
N.V. Phillips, 528
Nynex, 524, 531

Ohio Mattress Company, 530
Olive Garden, 129
Opryland Hotel, 64–65
Ortho Pharmaceutical, 569–570, 572, 581, 583, 588

Pacific Gas & Electric, 344–345
Pentland Group, 463
People's Car Company, 530
PepsiCo, 129, 142, 291–292, 294, 296, 299–300, 306, 310, 332
Perkin-Elmer Corporation, 141
Petroleos de Venezuela, 527
Peugeot, 531
Philip Morris, 18, 526
Pillsbury, 526
Pizza Hut, 129, 291, 294, 296, 300, 303, 306, 310, 349
Plain Jane, 314
Pohang Iron & Steel Company, 500–501
Potlatch Corporation, 361–362
PPG, 94
President Enterprises, 171
Price Waterhouse & Company, 507
Prime Computer, 313
Procter & Gamble, 9, 81, 160, 248, 528, 583
Publix supermarkets, 14

Quad/Graphics, 392
Quaker Oats, 159–161
Quaker Oats Company, 119
QVC, 117

Ralston Purina, 524
Rath & Strong, 295
Rebuild LA, 591
Remington Products Inc., 179
Renault, 531
Rich Products, 488–489
Ritz-Carlton Hotel Company, 38
Robert Morris Associates, 476
Robinson Nugent Inc., 531
Rolls-Royce Motor Cars Ltd., 410, 411, 414, 421
Rolls-Royce Motors Cars Ltd., 401–402, 404, 408–409
Royal Dutch/Shell Group, 527
Ryder, 441

Saks Fifth Avenue, 523
Samsonite, 390
Samsung, 385
Sara Lee Bakery, 59
SCC, Inc., 494
Scott Paper, 390
Seagram Co., Ltd., 526, 527
Sealy, 530
Sea World, 155–156, 157, 163, 173, 175–176
Security Pacific Bank, 188–189
Sedona Fire Department, 233
Sensomatic Electronics, 498
Service Corps of Retired Executives (SCORE), 14
Sharp, 467, 539
Shearson Lehman Brothers, 24
Shell Oil Company, 124, 168, 526
Shiseido Company, 500
Siemens, 540
Silicon Graphics, 499
Simmons Associates, 493
Skytrain, 372
Smith Corona, 526
SmithKline Beckman, 114–115
SmithKline Beecham, 114–115
Sonoco Products Company, 296–297
Sony Corporation, 411, 526, 527, 544
St. Gillian, 426
Standard Oil of Ohio, 68–69, 274
Standard Steel Company, 408
Steelcase, 592, 593
Subway Sandwiches, 48
SunExpress, 23
Sun Microsystems Inc., 23, 126
Sun Oil Company, 93, 119, 390

Taco Bell, 129, 291, 294, 296, 300, 303, 306, 310
Target, 502
Tengelmann, 526
Tengelmann Group, 527
Texaco, 206–207, 303, 453, 526
Texas Instruments, 9, 38, 388, 474
The Crummer School, 165
The Disney Store, 27–28, 33, 37, 43
The Limited, 161–162
The Rank Organisation PLC, 263, 265
The Virgin Group, 372
Thorn EMI, 372
Time Warner, 572
Toshiba, 467, 539
Toyota Motor Company, 184, 191, 472, 555
Tupperware, 9
TW Services, 584
Tyco Toys Inc., 51

Unilever, 528
Unilever NV/ Unilever Plc, 527
United Technologies, 139
Universal Studios Florida, 155, 173, 263–264, 271–272, 274, 276, 280, 282–283
U.S. Army Corps of Engineers, 355

USADirect Service, 574
USA Today, 433–434, 435, 438, 440, 443, 445, 447, 449–450
US West, 280

Virgin Atlantic Airways, 372, 373
Virgin Megastores, 372
Virgin Music, 372
Volkswagon, 531
Volvo, 388, 531

Wallace Company, 38
WalMart Stores Incorporated, 129
Wal-Mart Stores Incorporated, 343, 491–492, 495, 500, 505, 508–509, 511, 571
Walt Disney World, 155, 437
Wang Laboratories, 313
Watertown Arsenal, 47
Wegmans Food Markets, 113
Western Electric Company, 35–36, 99
Westinghouse, 168, 171
Weyerhauser Co., 113–114, 116, 119–120, 123–124, 126
Whirlpool Corporation, 461
Whole Foods Market, 114
Wilson Sporting Goods, 371

Xerox Corporation, 18, 53, 421, 524, 592

YDAC, Inc., 494

NAMES

Abraham, Bobby, 113
Ackoff, Russell L., 37, 174
Adams, J. Stacy, 378
Adler, Nancy J., 571, 576
Akers, John F., 73
Alderefer, Clayton, 381
Alford, Leon P., 28
Amos, Wally "Famous," 237
Argyris, Chris, 475
Arnoff, 37
Artzt, Edwin L., 248

Baer, Jeffrey, 237
Baer, Ronald, 237
Baldrige, Malcolm, 536
Barnard, Chester, 33, 242–243
Barnard, Kurt, 491
Baron, Tosh, 172, 592
Barrett, Dermot, 325
Barrett, Jon, 93–94
Barrier, Michael, 536
Barth, Carl, 47
Bartlett, Christopher A., 528
Baskin, Burton, 205
Bass, Bernard, 409
Bavelas, Alex, 335
Beauvais, Edward, 397
Beck, Joel, 329
Beckstead, Stephen M., 259
Bell, Ella, 577–578
Bergeron, Stephanie, 580
Black, Stewart, 584
Blackburn, Joseph, 548
Blanes, Juan, 84–85
Bogle, Bob, 491
Bonsall, Brian, 205
Borgschulte, Donald F., 536
Bowman, Valcar Jr., 282
Brandon, David A., 1
Branson, Richard, 372
Brokaw, Tom, 356
Brooks, Andy, 539
Brown, Alvin, 33
Buck, Peter, 48
Burke, James E., 73
Burns, Tom, 37
Burris, Mary Ellen, 113
Bush, George, 300
Butler, Graham, 291
Byman, William C., 353
Byrom, Fletcher, 9

Caldwell, Philip, 409
Calloway, Wayne, 144, 291
Carey, Emastine Gilbreth, 28
Carlzon, Jan, 365
Case, John, 544
Cassell, Dean, 548
Certo, Samuel C., 205, 397, 453
Chazen, Jerome, 347
Chiampa, Dan, 295
Chupa, Dennis, 375
Claiborne, Elisabeth "Liz," 347
Clarke, Richard, 344
Colbert, Bertram A., 507–508
Conde, Mario, 293
Condit, Phil, 189
Conway, Michael, 397
Cote, Kathleen A., 313
Crosby, Philip B., 521, 548, 549, 556
Cross, Elsie, 569
Crozier, Will, 47
Curley, Thomas, 433

Danforth, Douglas D., 171
Davis, Al, 51
Davis, Bill, 155
Davis, Keith, 52–53, 336–337
Dean, Carol, 527
DeLuca, Fred, 48
Deming, W. Edwards, 460, 461, 478, 521, 536–537, 547, 548–550
Dennison, Henry, 33
Dettloff, George, 321
Deutch, Claudia, 586
Dewelt, Robert L., 434
DiNello, Gilbert, 51
DiTomaso, Nancy, 572
Dowd, Ann Reilly, 36
Downs, Hugh, 155
Doz, Yves, 528
Drucker, Peter, 4, 94–95, 103, 124, 125
Duncan, Robert B., 138
Dyer, Robert, 321

Easton, Sue, 403

Fayol, Henri, 12, 28, 29, 33–35, 214
Feigenbaum, Armand V., 552
Feldberg, Warren, 502
Felsenthal, Edward, 578
Fiedler, Fred, 362
Fleuter, Douglas, 390
Flynn, Raymond, 51
Follet, Mary Parker, 16, 224–225
Forbes, B.C., 12
Ford, Henry, 12
Fried, Lisa I., 523
Friedman, Milton, 55, 77
Fuchburg, Gilbert, 581

Gallagher, Tim, 503
Galusha, Joe, 415–416
Gantt, Henry L., 28, 32–33, 198
Garrison, Sheridan, 89, 90, 92–93, 98–99, 101, 104
Gartner, Michael, 356
Gaye, Marvin, 237
Georges, John, 152
Gercik, Patricia, 537
Gergerson, Hal, 584
Gerner, John, 155
Gerringer, Juanita, 113–114
Gerstner, Louis V. Jr., 143
Gilbreth, Frank, 28, 29, 30–31
Gilbreth, Lillian, 28, 29, 30–31
Gill, Mark Stuart, 551
Glass, David, 343
Gorbachev, Mikhail, 523
Graicunas, V.A., 227
Green, Judson, 437
Greenfield, Jerry, 592
Griffin, Sarah, 415
Guisewithe, Cathy, 36
Gulick, Luther, 33
Gumbel, Peter, 523

Haas, Robert, 287
Hammer, Michael, 558–561
Hammond, Caleb Dean III, 516

Harness, Edward G., 9
Herrigan, Kathryn, 540
Hastings, K. Neil, 546
Hayner, Anne M., 30
Hedlund, Gunner, 528
Heldman, Lou, 433
Helegesen, Sally, 218
Herzberg, Frederick, 387–388
Hess, Bob, 246
Hines, Andrew P., 463
Hirch, James S., 535
Hite, George, 502
Holden, Benjamin J., 584
Holden, Ted, 581
Holland, William, 36
Holmes, Sandra, 59
Homans, George, 412–413
Honda, Soichiro, 174
Hopkins, L. Thomas, 40
Houghton, Tom, 38
House, William C., 193
Hudiburg, John J., 536
Hunter, John, 229

Iacocca, Lee, 133–134
Icahn, Carl, 206
Ivestor, M. Douglas, 229

Jacoby, Neil H., 526–527
Johnson, Robert M., 433
Johnson, Robert W., 9
Jones, Dennis, 401
Jones, Jim, 130–131
Juran, Joseph M., 521, 536, 550–551, 555–556

Kaiser, James G., 368
Kanter, Rosabeth Moss, 546, 577
Katz, Robert L., 11
Kavner, Bob, 172
Kearns, Tom, 39
Kelley, Robert, 375
Kelly, Phil, 321, 551
Kemper, Robert E., 84–85, 233, 343, 428, 515, 518–519, 594–595
Kennedy, Marilyn Moats, 375
Keough, Donald R., 229
Keyes, Sylvia, 313
Kim, Jean, 579–580, 583–584
King, Rodney, 591
Kinnear, James, 206–207
Kirby, Carol, 205
Koontz, Harold, 226
Korman, A.K., 359
Kotter, John P., 348
Krok, Arlene, 179
Krok, Loren, 179
Krok, Sharon, 179
Krok, Solomon, 179
Kume, Tadashi, 174
Kunde, Diane, 574

Lacy, Chuck, 592
Landlo, Linda, 537
Lawlor, Edward, 239
Lear, Norman, 72, 73
Lee, Dalton, 585
Lehmann, John, 260–261
Leven, Mike, 336
Levitt, Theodore, 95–96, 348
Levy, John, 426
Lewin, Kurt, 304
Lewis, Edward, 110
Likert, Rensis, 358, 392–393
Lorenzo, Frank, 59
Lowe, Barbara, 65
Lublin, Joann S., 531, 534
Luther, David, 39

Macon, Cheryl, 81
Magee, John F., 146
Maglica, Claire, 518–519
Maglica, Tony, 518–519
Malandrakis, Joseph E., 141
Marsh, Barbara, 586
Marszewski, Carl, 325
Martin, John, 291
Maslow, Abraham, 380
Maxim, James, 386
McAfee, Jerry, 71, 77
McClelland, Davis C., 382–383
McConnell, John, 390
McCormick, Charles "Buzz," 180–181
McCormick, Willoughby, 180
McCraken, Ed, 499
McGregor, Douglas, 281, 385
McNeally, Scott, 23
Mee, John F., 90–91, 298
Mehrabian, Albert, 332
Miller, R.S. Jr., 160
Mintzberg, Henry, 120
Mitchell, Bedford, 453
Mockler, Robert, 434
Mooney, J.D., 33
Morales, Emilio, 109
Morita, Akio, 544
Mork, William J., 440
Morrison, Ann, 571–573
Murdick, Robert G., 504
Myers, Jerry, 592, 593

Natori, Jose Cruz, 24–25
Natori, Ken, 24
Nixon, Richard, 136
Norris, William, 55

Ohno, Taiichi, 551
Oliver, Susanne, 183
Olson, Frank, 454
Ortega, Tony, 109, 151, 591
Ortenberg, Arthur, 347
Osei-Amoako, Yaw, 574
Ouchi, William, 537–538

Paddock, Susan C., 585
Parkel, James, 54
Parlin, Gary, 569, 581, 583
Parnes, Francine, 523
Patterson, W.A. "Pat," 59
Pattillo, Jim, 361–362
Paul, Ron, 291
Peale, Norman V., 417
Peters, Tom, 8, 16, 218, 555
Petersen, Peter B., 47
Phillips, Richard L., 164
Plane, Martin, 20
Prichard, Peter, 433
Pryor, Mildred Golden, 565

Reddy, Helen, 237
Reese, Wendy, 198
Reidy, John, 433
Reiley, A.C., 33
Reinemund, Steve, 291
Resnick, Judy, *1
Rich, Robert, 488
Rigg, Ricky, 321
Ringbakk, K.A., 189
Rittenhouse, John, 573
Robbins, Irene, 205
Roberts, Bert C. Jr., 213
Roddick, Anita, 82
Rodgers, Francis G., 9
Rolander, Dag, 528
Roney, C.W., 114

Sarni, Vincent A., 94
Sawyett, Olukem, 533
Schein, Edgar, 304
Schramm, Wilbur, 326
Schwartz, Alan, 314
Schwartz, Felice, 282
Schweitzer, Albert, 73
Scott, Al, 371
Segal, Joseph, 117
Selye, Hans, 306
Sethi, S. Prakash, 62–64
Shad, John, 72
Sharna, Abraham, 530
Sheldon, Oliver, 33
Shellenger, Rita J., 156
Shepherd, Mark, 9
Shetty, Y.K., 93, 439–440
Shewhart, Walter A., 562
Shilit, Warren Keith, 15
Shulman, Edward, 234
Shulman, Samuel, 234
Shulman, Stanley, 234
Singo, Shigeo, 551
Skagen, Anne, 550
Skinner, B.F., 391
Sloan, Alfred P., 114, 151
Smale, John, 151
Smith, Clarence, 110
Smith, Jack, 151
Smith, Raymond, 428
Smith, Roger, 151

Sonnenfeld, Jeffrey, 578
Stalker, G.M., 37
Steele, Murray, 446
Steffen, Christopher J., 136
Steinmetz, Charles, 553
Stempel, Robert, 3, 4, 151
Stickler, Michael J., 548
Stieglitz, Harold, 244–245
Strong, Lydia, 329
Stronich, Paul J., 125
Suquet, Jose S., 403

Taylor, Alex, 3
Taylor, Frederick W., 28–29, 47
Terrell, Dorothy, 23
Thibodeaux, Mary S., 287, 425, 487, 539–540
Thomas, Bailey, 180
Thomas, Paulette, 577
Thomas, Peter, 198
Thomas, R. Roosevelt Jr., 585
Thompson, Donna, 572
Tice, Jane, 314
Tompkins, Doug, 314
Tompkins, Susie, 314
Toombs, Leslie A., 129, 179
Toyoda, Shoichiro, 184
Trost, Cathy, 577
Trust, Martin, 162

Ueberroth, Peter, 591
Ummel, Stephen, 164
Unger, Kay, 426
Urwick, Lyndall, 33

Valtierra, Susan, 539
Vaughn, Vicki, 27
Vernot, Pierre, 95
Vohringer, Klaus-Dieter, 225
von Vertalanffy, Ludwig, 40

Wachner, Linda, *1
Wald, Jeff, 237
Walsh, Michael H., 303
Walton, Sam, 343, 491, 500
Ward, Peter, 401–402
Waterman, Robert H. Jr., 8
Watner, Jeanette, 523
Watson, Thomas J. Jr., 9
Weber, Max, 217
Welch, John F. Jr., 364, 437, 446, 491
Wellins, Richard, 403
Wenninger, Fred, 259, 552
Wexner, Leslie, 161
Whipple, Marian, 53
White, J.P., 569
Wiener, Jennifer, 581
Wikstrom, Walter S., 267
Wilson, Kammon, 92
Wynter, Leon W., 572

Zamaryonov, Kira, 523

SUBJECT

Acceptance stage, of formal group development, 409
Accountability, 247
Achievement, need for, 382
Achievement behavior, leadership and, 365
Achievement tests, 273
Acquired-need theory, McClelland's, 382–383
Activities, in program evaluation and review technique, 199
Activity ratio, 475
Advisory role, of staff personnel, 245
Affiliation, need for, 382
Affirmative action, 270–271, 580
Aging, of work force, 578
Alderfer's ERG theory, 381–382
Algebraic breakeven analysis, 479–480
Allocating skill, 172
American Society of Quality and Control, 547
Americans with Disabilities Act, 300, 471–472
Appropriate human resources, 264. *See also* Human resource management
Appropriateness, of information, 493
Aptitude tests, 273
Argyris's maturity-immaturity continuum, 382
Assessment centers, 274
Assimilation, 584
Association for Manufacturing Excellence, 547
Attitudes
  employee standards and, 438
  influencing people in multinational corporations and, 533–534
  of managers in multinational corporations, 533
Audit, social, 70–71
Authority, 34, 242–248
  accountability and, 247
  defined, 242
  functional, 246–247, 248
  line and staff, 243–244
  power and, 446
Automation, 463–464

Bank wiring observation room experiments, 36
Behavioral approach to management, 35–36
Behavioral side of change, 304–305
Behavior modification, motivating and, 391
Bicultural stress, 578
Bonus system, 33
Boston Consulting Group (BCG), growth-share matrix of, 166–168
Breakeven analysis, 479–481
  algebraic, 479–480
  basic ingredients of, 479
  control and, 480–481
  graphic, 480
Breakeven point, 479
Budgets, 188, 474–475
  people considerations in using, 475
  pitfalls of, 474–475
  variable, 475
  zero-based, 474
Bureaucracy, 217
Business ethics. *See* Ethics.
Business portfolio analysis, 166–170
  BCG growth-share matrix and, 166–168
  GE multifactor portfolio matrix, 168–170

CAD. *See* Computer-aided design
CAM. *See* Computer-aided manufacturing
Capacity strategy, 466–467
Career counseling, 304
Career(s)
  decline stage of, 14
  defined, 12
  establishment stage of, 13
  exploration stage of, 13
  maintenance stage of, 14
  management, 12–13
  plateauing, 14
  self-promotion of, 14–16
Cash cows, 167
Categorical imperative, ethics and, 76
Centralization, 34
  delegation and, 251, 252
Change. *See* Organizational change
Change agents, 294–295
Changing, 304
Civil Rights Act of 1964, 270
Civil Service Commission, U.S., 265
Classical approach to management, 28–29, 35
Classical organizing theory, 217–225
  division of labor and, 224–225
  scalar relationships and, 228–229
  span of management and, 226–228
  structure and, 218–223
Clean Air Act of 1963, 160
Clean Air Act Amendments of 1990, 59

Closed Systems, 38, 40
Cluster grapevine, 337
Code of ethics, 74–75
Cohesiveness, of groups, 416–417
Command
  authority and, 242–248
  unity of, 34, 229
Command groups, 404
Commitment principle, 156
Committees
  reasons for using, 404–406
  successful, 407
Communication, 325–341
  barriers to, 326–330
  of degree of social responsibility involvement, 61
  formal. *See* Formal organizational communication
  informal. *See* Informal organizational communication
  interpersonal. *See* Interpersonal communication
  managerial, motivating and, 384
  recommendations for, 331
  successful and unsuccessful, 326
  verbal and nonverbal, 332–333
Communication and decision-making stage, of formal group development, 409
Communication effectiveness index, 330
Communication macrobarriers, 327
Communication microbarriers, 327
Community relations, in site selection, 190, 191
Company image, quality and, 546
Company-wide quality, 521, 544, 548–552
Comparative management, 536–539
  defined, 536
  Japanese motivation strategies and, 537
  Theory Z and, 537–538
Compensation
  Gantt's contributions to, 34
  of managers, 4, 6
Competition, as component of operating environment, 161
Competitors, as source of human resources, 270
Complete certainty condition, decision making, 143
Complete uncertainty condition, decision making, 144
Comprehensive analysis of management, 33–35
Comprehensive Environmental Response, Compensation, and Liability Act of 1980, 160
Comptroller. *See* Controller
Computer-aided design (CAD), 482
Computer-aided manufacturing (CAM), 482
Computer(s), 496. *See also* Management information systems
  main functions of, 496–498
  pitfalls in using, 499
Conceptual skills, 11
Concurrent control, 441
Conflict, in line-staff relationships, 246
Conflict of interest, 55
Consensus, 137
Consideration behavior, leadership and, 358
Consistency, organizational, 92
Consumer Product Safety Commission, 59
Consumer Products Safety Act of 1972, 160
Content theories of motivation, 376, 379–381
Contingency approach to management, 37, 39–40
  decentralization and, 252–253
  departmentalization and formal structure and, 219
  span of management and, 226–227
Contingency theory of leadership, 362–364
Control
  amount of, 444–445
  breakeven analysis and, 479–481
  concurrent, 441
  controller and, 443–445
  defined, 434
  inventory, just-in-time, 472–473
  materials requirements, 476
  power and, 446–447
  strategic, 172–173
  types of, 440–443
Control function, of computers, 498
Controller
  amount of control and, 444–445
  job of, 443–444
Controlling, 431–455
  barriers to, 448–449
  comparing measured performance to standards, 437–438
  corrective action and, 438–440
  defined, 434–435
  as management function, 8
  minority recruitment and, 586
  multinational corporations, 535
  performance measurement and, 435–437
  process, 435
  of social responsibility activities, 69–71
  strategic, 556
  subsystem of, 435, 436
  successful, 447, 449
Control role, of staff personnel, 245
Control tool
  defined, 477
  for operations, 477–482
Coordination
  division of labor and, 224–225
  span of management and, 226
Corporate culture, 418–421
Corporate database, 510
Corporate social responsibility. *See* Social responsibility
Corporation, international. *See* Multinational corporation
Corrective action, 439–440
Cost-benefit analysis, control and, 444–445
Cost control, 473–474
Cost leadership, 171
  Porter's model for industry analysis and, 169–170
Costs
  breakeven analysis and, 479–481
  fixed, 479
  product liability and, 546
  quality and, 546
  total, 479
  variable, 479
Cost savings, diversity and, 572
Counseling role, of staff personnel, 245
Critical path, in program evaluation and review technique, 200
Critical question analysis, 165–166
Crosby's vaccination for quality, 548–549
Cultural environment, 162
Culture
  corporate, 418–421
  diversity in. *See* Diversity
  influencing people in multinational corporations and, 533–534
Culture-specific approach, 584
Customer
  as component of operating environment, 161
  departmentalization on basis of, 221
Customer service, as organizational objective, 91
CWQ. *See* Company-wide quality

Data, 492
Database, 509–510
Decentralization
  contingency viewpoint of, 252–253
  delegation and, 251–255
  examples of, 254–255
Decision
  defined, 134
  nonprogrammed, 134–135, 136
  programmed, 134, 135
  scope of, 136
Decision areas, for human resource director, 245
Decision makers, orientation of, 139
Decision making, 132–153
  alternatives and, 140
  communication and decision making stage of formal group development, 409
  conditions for, 143–144
  consensus, 137
  decision makers and, 139
  decisions and, 134–135
  goals and, 139
  management decision support system and, 509–511
  ordering of alternatives, 140
  organizational objectives and, 92
  relevant alternatives and, 139–140
  responsibility for, 136–137
  social responsiveness and, 61–63
  state of nature and, 138
  Tannenbaum and Schmidt leadership continuum and, 350–362
  techniques, 135
Decision-making conditions
  complete certainty, 143
  complete uncertainty, 144
  risk, 144
Decision-making process, 140–143
  defined, 140
  feedback and, 142–143
  implementation and, 142

listing alternative solutions and, 141
problem identification and, 141
selecting most beneficial alternative and, 142
Decision-making tools, 145–147
decision trees, 146–147
probability theory, 145–146
Decision-tree analysis, 481
Decision trees, 146–147
Decline stage, of careers, 14
Decoder/destination, 326
Deducing, in scientific method, 37
Degrees of risk, 144
Delegation, 249–255
centralization and decentralization and, 251–255
obstacles to, 249–251
steps in, 249, 250
Deming Prize, 536–537, 547
Deming's quality advice, 548, 550
Demographics
changing, 574, 575
general environment and, 159
Department, 219
Departmentalization, formal structure and, 219
Dialogue capability, 511
Differentiation, 170
Differentiation, Porter's model for industry analysis and, 170
Direct investing, multinational corporations and, 531
Directive behavior, leadership and, 365
Disabilities, workers with, 578–579
Discipline, 34
Discretionary area, in decision making, 141
Discrimination, 576–577
Discrimination, reverse, 580
Diversity
advantages of, 571–573
challenges for managers, 574–579
defined, 570
management development and training, 586–588
managing, 143, 156, 568–595
role of managers, 584–586
strategies for promoting, 579–584
training, 586–587
Divestiture, 171–172
Division of labor, 224–225
advantages and disadvantages of, 224
coordination and, 224–225
Division of work, 34
Dogs, 167
Downshifting, 297
Downward organizational communication, 334
Dual-career couples, 16–17
Dun & Bradstreet's *Ratios for Selected Industries,* 97

EAPs. *See* Employee Advisory Programs
Economic component, of general environment, 158–159
Economic environment, 162
Economic function area, measuring social responsibility in, 69
Educational institutions, as source of human resources, 270
EEOC. *See* Equal Employment Opportunity Commission
Effectiveness
of communication, 326
of delegation, 250
of leadership styles, 359–362
managerial, 10
of operations management, 466
of planning process, 124–126
of work groups, 414–416
Efficiency
managerial, 10–11
of operations management, 466
organizational, 92
scientific approach to, 29–31
Employee Advisory Programs (EAPs), 73
Employee attitudes standards, 438
Employee-centered behavior, leadership and, 358–359
Employee education, training, and support, social responsibility in, 56
Employee morale, reducing, 448
Employee relations, 57
Employee safety and health, 57
Employee stock ownership plans (ESOP), 393–394
Employment agencies, as source of human resources, 270
Empowerment, and quality, 554
Entrophy, 38
Environment, decision making and, 138
Environmental analysis
general environment, 158–161
internal environment, 162–163
operating environment, 161–162
quality and, 552–553
Environmental control, social responsibility in, 56
Environmental Protection Agency (EPA), 59
Equal Employment Opportunity Commission (EEOC), 270–271, 580
Equal Opportunity Act of 1972, 59, 64–65
Equal Pay Act of 1963, 59
Equity, 34
Equity theory of motivation, 378
ERG theory, 381–382
ESOP. *See* Employee stock ownership plans
Esprit de corps, 35
Establishment stage, of careers, 13
Esteem needs, 380
job enrichment and, 387–389
Ethics, 72–76
code of, 74–75
creating ethical workplace and, 75–76
defined, 73
importance of, 73–74
Ethnocentric attitude, multinational corporations and, 533, 534
Ethnocentrism, 576
EV. *See* Expected value
Evaluation. *See also* Program Evaluation and Review Technique
of change, 305–306
of information, 494–495
of planners, 122–123
of sales forecasting methods, 196–197
of training programs, 279
Events, in program evaluation and review technique, 199
Expected value (EV), decision making and, 145–146
Exploration stage, of careers, 13
Exporting, 530
External relations, social responsibility in, 56
Extrinsic rewards, 378–379

Feedback
decision making and, 142–143
interpersonal communication and, 330–332
Feedback control, 441–442
Feigenbaum's advice on quality, 552
Fiedler's contingency theory of leadership, 362–364
Financial objectives, 97
Financial resources, organizational objectives for, 95
Fixed costs, 479
Fixed position layout, 470
Flat organizational chart, 227
Flextime, 389–390
Focus, 171
Porter's model of industry analysis and, 169–170
Forecasting, 192–197
sales, 193–197
Formal group(s), 402–410. *See also* Work groups
command groups, 404
committees, 404–407
development of, 409–410
task groups, 404
work teams, 407–409
Formal organizational communication, 333–336, 338
downward, 334
lateral, 334
upward, 334
Formal structure, 219
factors influencing, 223
Four-way test, ethics and, 76
Friendship groups, 411
Functional authority, 246–247, 248
Functional layout, 470
Functional objectives, 98
Functional similarity method, 239
Future, in decision making, 143

Gangplank, 229
Gantt chart, 32, 198–199
Gender-role stereotypes, 577
General Electric multifactor portfolio matrix, 166–168
General environment, 158–161
economic component of, 158–159
political component of, 160

social component of, 159–160
technology component of, 160–161
Geocentric attitude, multinational corporations and, 533, 534
Glass ceiling, 577
Goal(s)
attainment of, management functions and, 8–11
consistency of, 92
decision making and, 139
integration of, 93–94
setting, 93
standard reflecting relative balance between and long- and short-term goals, 438
stressing, 449
"Golden Rule" approach, 583
"Golden Rule," ethics and, 75
Gossip grapevine, 337
Government agencies, social responsibility and, 59
Graicunas' formula, 227
Grapevine, 336–337
cluster, 337
gossip, 337
probability, 337
single-strand, 336–337
Graphic breakeven analysis, 480
Grid OD, 300–302
Group cohesiveness, 416–417
Group members, group size and, 415
Group norms, 417–418
positive and negative, 417
Group processes, group size and, 415
Groups
defined, 402
formal. *See* Formal groups
majority, 578
minority, 570
operations research, 37–38
Group solidarity stage, of formal group development, 409
Group technology layout, 470
Groupthink, 407
Growth strategy, 171

Hawthorne experiments, 36
Hersey-Blanchard life cycle theory of leadership, 359–361
Hierarchy of needs, 380–381
job enrichment and, 387–389
Hierarchy of organizational objectives, 99–100
Highway Safety Act of 1978, 59
Hoarding orientation, decision making and, 139
Host country, 529
Human resource director, decision areas for, 245
Human resource inventory, 267
Human resource management, 262–289
assessment centers and, 274
defining appropriate, 264
job analysis and, 265–267
law and, 270–272
performance appraisal and, 280–283
recruitment and, 264–265
selection and, 272–274
sources of human resources and, 267–270
testing and, 273–274
training and, 274–280
Human resource planning, 192, 193
Human resources, 8
job design, 471
manpower planning, 471
motion study, 471
sources of, 267–270
strategy for, 471
work measurement methods, 471
work method analysis, 471
Human skills, 11
Hygiene factors, job enrichment and, 387–389

Identification, 304
Image, quality and, 546
Implementation-focused planning orientation, 125
Importing, 530
Improvement, and quality, 555
Inappropriate human resources, 264
Incentives, monetary and nonmonetary, 393–394
Incremental improvement process, 558–560
Industry analysis, Porter's model for, 169–170
Influencing, 319–325
defined, 322
individuals performing social responsibility, 69
as management function, 7
minority recruitment and, 585–586
in multinational corporations, 533–534
subsystem for, 322–325
Influencing subsystem, 322–325
Informal group(s), 410–411
benefits of membership in, 411
evolution of, 412–414
friendship groups, 411
interest groups, 410–411
Informal organizational communication, 336–339
discouraging, 337–339
grapevine and, 336–337
Informal structure, 219. *See also* Informal group(s)
Information, 490–519
appropriateness of, 493
computer assistance in using, 496–499
evaluating, 494–495
management. *See* Management information system (MIS)
for management system analysis, 42–43
quality and, 554–555
quality of, 493
and quality of management, 249
quantity of, 494
timeliness of, 493–494
value of, 492–494
Information overload, 327
Initiative, 35
Innovation
diversity and, 572
organizational objectives for, 95
and quality, 555
Input function, of computers, 496
Input planning, 189–191
Inspection, 478
Interacting skill, 172
Interest groups, 410–411
Intermediate-term objectives, 95
Internal environment, 162–163
Internalization, 304–305
International component, of operating environment, 162
International joint venture, 531
International management, 522–541. *See also* Multinational corporation
Interpersonal communication, 325–335
barriers to, 326–330
decoder/destination and, 326
feedback and, 330–332
in organizations, 333–339
signal and, 325
source/encoder and, 325
successful and unsuccessful, 326
verbal and nonverbal, 332–333
Intrinsic rewards, 378–379
Inventory control, just-in-time, 472–473
Investment, 525, 527
return on, 97–98
Investment costs, in site selection, 190, 191

Japanese, quality and, 544–545
Japanese management, 537–540
Deming Prize and, 536–537
kanban, 472–473
motivational strategies of, 537
robotics and, 463
Theory Z and, 537–538
JIT. *See* Just-in-time (JIT) inventory control
Job activities
clarifying managers', 240–241
dividing, 238–240
Job analysis, 265–267
Job-centered behavior, leadership and, 358
Job description, 238, 265
Job design, 471
flextime and, 389–390
job enlargement and, 387
job enrichment and, 387–389
job rotation and, 386–387
motivating and, 386–390
Job enlargement, 387
Job enrichment, 387–389
Job rotation, 386–387
Job specification, 265
Joint ventures, international, 531
Juran's advice on quality, 500–551
Jury of executive opinion method, 194–195
Just-in-time (JIT) inventory control, 472–473

Kanban, 472–473
Keiretsus, 214, 537

Labor
as component of operating environment, 161
considerations in site selection, 190, 191
division of. *See* Division of labor
Language, influencing people in multinational corporations and, 534
Lateral organizational communication, 334
Law, human resources management and, 270–272
Law of the situation, 16
Laws, in site selection, 190, 191
Layout, 470
Layout strategy, 469–470
Leader flexibility, 362
Leader-member relations, 363
Leaders, women as, 367–368
Leadership, 346–373
defined, 348
Fiedler's contingency theory of, 362–364
group size and, 415
Hersey-Blanchard life cycle theory of, 359–361
manager versus, 348–349
Michigan studies of, 358–359
OSU studies of, 357–358
path-goal theory of, 364
quality and, 554
recent emphasis on, 365–367
situational approach to, 350–365
style of. *See* Leadership style
substitutes for, 366–367
Tannenbaum and Schmidt leadership continuum for, 350–354
trait approach to, 349
transformational, 366
Vroom-Yetton-Jago model of, 354–356
women in, 367–368
Leadership style, 357–365
consideration behavior and, 358
contingency theory of leadership and, 362–364
defined, 358
effectiveness of, 359, 360
employee-centered behavior and, 358–359
job-centered behavior and, 358
leader flexibility and, 362
life-cycle theory of leadership and, 359–361
path-goal theory of leadership and, 364
structure behavior and, 357
Lectures, training programs and, 276–277
Legal component, of general environment, 160
Legal environment, 162
Level dimension, of plans, 185
License agreements, multinational corporations and, 530
Life cycle theory of leadership, 359–361
Likert's management systems, 392–393
Line authority, 243–244, 247, 248
conflict in line-staff relationships, 246
organizational chart and, 244
Liquidity ratio, 475
Listening, active, 338
Living conditions, in site selection, 190, 191
Location strategy, 467
Long-term goals, 438
Long-term objectives, 95

Maintenance control, 473
Maintenance stage of careers, 14
Majority group, 570
Malcolm Baldrige National Quality Awards, 19, 38–39, 547
Malcolm Baldrige National Quality Improvement Act of 1987, 19
Management
behavioral approach to, 35–36
careers in, 5, 13–18
classical approach to, 28–29, 35
closed system approach, 38
commitment to just-in-time inventory control, 472
comparative. *See* Comparative management
under condition of risk, 145
contingency approach to, 37, 39–40
defined, 6–7
diversity and, 568–595
dual-career couples, 16–17
goal attainment and, 8–11
importance of, 4–5
international. *See* International management; Multinational corporation
leadership versus, 348–349
levels of, in decision making, 136
multicultural work force and, 17–18
organizational resources and, 8–10
in planning process, 124
quality improved through diversity, 572
responsible behavior of, 241–242
role of, 6
scientific, 27–28, 37–39
span of, 226–228
system approach to, 40–43
women in, 16, 367–368
of work groups, 412–418
Management analysis
comprehensive, 33–35
lower-level, 27–28
Management by exception, 478
Management by objectives (MBO), 103–104, 478
Management career, enhancing, 17
Management decision support system (MDSS), 509–511
Management functions, 7, 8
interrelationship of, 8
multinational corporations and, 528, 530–535
social responsibility and, 62–64, 65–66
Management information system (MIS), 500–509
defined, 500
different needs for information and, 604
establishing, 505–507
improving, 507–508
inadequate, symptoms of, 507
operating, 501–504
Management inventory card, 267, 268
Management levels
information needs and, 504
and planning, 175–176
Management manpower replacement card, 267, 269
Management responsibility guide, 239–242
Management science approach, 37–39
Management skills, 11
Management system, 41–42
information for analysis, 42–43
Likert's, 392–393
organizational objectives and, 90
Managerial effectiveness, 10
Managerial efficiency, 10–11
Managerial grid, 300–301
Managerial performance, organizational objectives for, 95
Manager(s)
communication by, motivation and, 384
compensation of, 4, 6
decision making and, 136–137, 350–362
development of goal statements and, 99–100
job activities of, 240–241
minority recruitment and, 584–585
for multinational corporation, selection of, 533
Manpower planning, 471
Manufacturing process, departmentalization on basis of, 221
Maquiladoras, 189–190
Marketing, social responsibility in, 56
Market position standards, 437
Market share
diversity and, 571
quality and, 546
Market standing, organizational objectives for, 94
Maslow's hierarchy of needs, 380–381
Materials control, 476
Matrix organization, 297–298
Maturity, in life cycle theory of leadership, 359
Maturity-immaturity continuum, Argyris's, 382
MBO. *See* Management by objectives
McClelland's acquired-need theory, 382–383
Means-end analysis, 102
Message, 325
Message interference, 328
Mining Enforcement and Safety Commission, 59
Minorities, 577–578
Minority employees, 57
Minority groups, 570. *See also* Affirmative action programs
Minority groups, in management, 17–18
MIS. *See* Management information system
Mission. *See* Organizational mission
Mission statement, 164
Model
construction of in scientific method, 37
testing of in scientific method, 37
Model database, 510
Modular corporation, 221
Monetary incentives, 393–394

Monitoring skill, 172
Motion analysis, at Bethlehem Steel, 31
Motion study, 30–31, 471
Motivation, 374–398
  Alderfer's ERG theory, 381–382
  Argyris' maturity-immaturity continuum, 382
  behavior modification and, 391–392
  content theories of, 376, 379–383
  contingency theory of, 379–383
  defined, 376
  equity theory of, 378
  Japanese strategies for, 537
  job design and, 386–391
  Likert's management systems and, 392–393
  managerial communication and, 384
  Maslow's hierarchy of needs, 380–381
  McClelland's acquired-needs theory, 382–383
  monetary incentives and, 393–394
  needs-goals theory of, 376–377
  nonmonetary incentives and, 394
  Porter-Lawlor theory of, 378–379
  process theories of, 376–379
  strategies for, 383–394
  Theory X, 385–386
  Theory Y, 385–386
  Theory Z, 385
  Vroom expectancy theory of, 377–378
Motivation strength, 377
Multicultural approach, 584
Multiculturalism, 582
Multicultural work force, 17–18
  and management, 17–18
Multinational corporation, 526–539
  controlling, 535
  defined, 526–527
  influencing people in, 533–534
  managing, 528, 530–535
  organizing, 531–533
  planning for, 530–533
  risk and, 528–529
Murphy's Law, 434

National Association of Manufacturers, 547
National Highway Traffic Safety Administration, 59
Need(s)
  for achievement, 382
  for affiliation, 382
  Alderfer's ERG theory and, 381–382
  Argyris's maturity-immaturity continuum, 382
  esteem, 380
  influencing people in multinational corporations and, 534
  Maslow's hierarchy of, 380–381
  McClelland's acquired-needs theory, 382–383
  physiological, 380
  for power, 382
  security, 380
  self-actualization, 380
  social, 380
Needs-goal theory of motivation, 376–377
Negative norms, 416
Negative reinforcement, 391
Net expected gain, in decision trees, 147
Nonmonetary incentives, 394
Nonprogrammed decisions, 134–135, 136
Non-traditional organization, 218
Nonverbal communication, 332–333
Norms, group, 417–418

Objective, principle of the, 96
Objective(s). *See also* Organizational objectives
  individual, 93–94
Occupational Health and Safety Act, 41, 57, 59, 160
Office of Federal Contract Compliance Programs, 59
"One best way." *See* Scientific management
On-the-job training, 279
Open system, 40, 41
Operating costs, in site selection, 190, 191
Operating environment, 161–162
  competition component of, 161
  customer component of, 161
  international component of, 162
  labor component of, 161
  supplier component of, 161–162
Operational objectives, 100–101
Operations control, 472–483
  breakeven analysis and, 479–481
  budgets for, 474–475
  computer-aided design and, 482
  computer-aided manufacturing and, 482
  cost control, 473–474
  decision-tree analysis and, 481
  defined, 472
  inspection and, 478
  just-in-time inventory control, 472–473
  maintenance control, 473
  management by exception and, 478
  management by objectives and, 478
  materials control and, 476
  process control and, 481–482
  ratio analysis, 475–476
  value analysis and, 482
Operations management, 465–472
  capacity strategy of, 466–467
  defined, 465
  effectiveness of, 466
  efficiency of, 466
  human resources strategy for, 470
  layout strategy for, 469–470
  location strategy for, 467
  process strategy for, 468–469
  product strategy for, 468
Operations research (OR) groups, 37–38
Order, 34
Organization, 214
Organizational change, 292–310
  behavioral side of, 304–305
  change agent, 294–295
  defined, 292–293
  determining what should be changed, 296
  evaluation of, 305–306
  individuals and, 303–304
  kind of change and, 297
  people, 300–303
  resistance to, 303–304
  stability versus, 293
  stress and, 306–310
  structural, 297–299
  technological, 297
Organizational communication
  formal, 333–336, 338
  informal, 336–339
Organizational consistency, organizational objectives and, 92
Organizational direction
  establishing, 163–165
  quality and, 553
Organizational efficiency, organizational objectives and, 92
Organizational mission, 163–165
  determining, 163
  importance of, 164
  mission statement and, 164
  objectives and, 164–165
Organizational objectives, 88–93
  areas for, 94–95
  attainment of, 102
  defined, 90
  establishing, 96
  financial, 97
  functional, 98
  goal integration and, 93–94
  hierarchy of, 99–100
  importance of, 92
  management by objectives (MBO), 103–104
  mission and, 164–165
  operational, 100–101
  planning and, 116
  principle of the objective and, 96
  product-market mix and, 98
  quality and, 100, 555
  types of, 93–94
  use of, 102–103
Organizational purpose, 90–91
Organizational resources, 8–11
Organization chart, 218
  authority and, 242
  height of, span of management and, 227–228
  line-staff relationships on, 244
  for multinational corporation, 532
Organization development (OD), 300–302
  grid, 300–302
  status of, 302
Organization structure. *See* Structure
Organizing, 211–235
  classical organizing theory and. *See* Classical organizing theory
  defined, 214
  importance of, 214–215
  as management function, 7
  minority recruitment and, 585
  multinational corporations and, 531–533
  process of, 215–216
  social responsibility activities, 68–69
  subsystems of, 216
Organizing skill, 172

OSHA. *See* Occupational Health and Safety Act
OSU studies, of leadership, 357–358
Output function, of computers, 498
Overlapping responsibility, 239

Parent company, 529
Participative behavior, leadership and, 365
Partnering, and quality, 554
Path-goal theory of leadership, 364–365
People change, 300–302
  describing, 300
  grid organization development and, 300–302
  status of organization development and, 302
People factors, organizational change and, 296
Perception, communication and, 328
Performance appraisal, 280–283
  handling, 281
  reasons for using, 281
  weaknesses of, 282
Performance evaluation, organizational objectives as guide for, 92
Performance measurement, 436–437
  comparing measured performance to standards, 437–438
Personality tests, 273
Personal power, 446
  increasing, 446–447
Personnel, tenure of, 34–35
Personnel development standards, 438
Perspective, narrow, 448–449
PERT. *See* Program evaluation and review technique
Philanthropy, 56
Physical resources, organizational objectives for, 95
Physiological needs, 380
Piece-rate system, 32
Planners, 120–123
  duties of, 121–122, 123
  evaluation of, 122–123
  qualifications of, 121
Planning, 87, 112–126
  advantages and disadvantages of, 115
  chief executive and, 120
  defined, 114
  efficient and effective organization of, 125
  human resource, 192
  implementation-focused orientation to, 125
  including right people in, 125–126
  input, 189–191
  levels of management and, 175–176
  as management function, 7
  materials requirements, 472–474
  maximizing effectiveness of, 124–126
  minority recruitment and, 585
  for multinational corporations, 530–533
  plant facilities, 189–191
  primacy of, 115
  purposes of, 114–115
  social responsibility activities, 65–66
  steps in process of, 116–117
  subsystem, 118–119
  tactical, 174
  top management support for, 124
Planning subsystem, 118–119
Planning tools, 192–200
  forecasting, 192–197
  scheduling, 198–200
Plans, 184–192
  defined, 184
  dimensions of, 184–186
  failure of, 189
  single-use, 187–189
  standing, 186–187
  types of, 186–189
Plant facilities planning, 189–191
Pluralism, 583
Policy, 186
  social responsibility, converting into action, 66
Political component, of general environment, 160
Political risk, 529
Political system, 162
Polycentric attitude, multinational corporations and, 533, 534
Porter-Lawlor theory of motivation, 378–379
Porter's model for industry analysis, 169–170
Position power, 446
  leadership and, 363
Position replacement form, 267, 268
Positive norms, 416
Positive reinforcement, 391
Power
  authority and, 446
  control and, 446–447
  defined, 446
  increasing, 446–447
  need for, 382
  personal, 446
  position and, 446
  total, of manager, 446–447
Precontrol, 440–441
Prejudices, 576
Premises, 116
Principle of supportive relationships, 393
Principle of the objective, 96
Probability grapevine, 337
Probability theory, in decision making, 145–146
Problem identification, decision making and, 141
Problem-solving area, measuring social responsibility in, 69
Problem-solving teams, 539
Procedure, 186
Process, production, 465
Process control, 481–482
Processing function, of computers, 498
Process layout, 470
Process strategy, 468–469
Process theories of motivation, 376–379
Production, 458–465
  automation and, 463–464
  defined, 458
  productivity and, 458–459
  quality and, 459–463
  strategies, systems, and processes, 464–465
Production facility, layout patterns and, 470
Production management, 456–489
Productivity
  defined, 458
  diversity and, 572
  organizational objectives for, 95
  standards for, 437
Product layout, 470
Product leadership standards, 437–438
Product liability costs, 546
Product line, social responsibility in, 56
Product-market mix objectives, 98
Product(s)
  departmentalization on basis of, 220
  quality of. *See* Quality; Quality control
Product strategy, 468
Professional ethic, 76
Profit
  as organizational objective, 91
  in site selection, 190, 191
Profitability, organizational objectives for, 95
Profitability standards, 437
Profits, 479
Program, 187–188
Program evaluation and review technique (PERT), 199–200
  activities and events and, 199
  critical path, 200
  defined, 199–200
  steps in designing network for, 200
  training for, 278
Programmed decisions, 134, 135
Programmed learning, training programs and, 277–279
Promotion, from within, 267–269
Publications, as source of human resources, 270
Public responsibility, organizational objectives for, 95
Punishment, 391
Pure-breakdown policy, 473
Pure-preventative maintenance policy, 473

Quality, 542–567
  achieving, 548–552
  assurance, 460–461
  awards, 547–548
  importance of, 544–546
  improvement process, 558–562
  of information, 493
  just-in-time inventory control and, 472–473
  organizational objectives for, 100
  productivity and, 459–460
  strategic planning and, 552–556
  total quality management and, 543–544
  traditional approach to, 545
Quality circles, 461–462
Quality control
  inspection and, 478
  quality circles, 461–462

Quality council, 555
Quality Management Maturity Grid, 557
Quality-of-life area, measuring social responsibility in, 69
Quality-oriented policy, 555
Quantity, of information, 494
Question marks, 167

Ratio analysis, 475–476
  activity, 475
  leverage, 475
  liquidity, 475
  profitability, 475
Ratios for Selected Industries, 97
Raw materials, 8
Recruitment, 264–265
Refreezing, 305
Reinforcement, positive and negative, 391
Relay assembly test room experiments, 35–36
Relevant alternatives
  choice of, 140
  decision making and, 139–140
Reliability, of tests, 273
Repetitiveness dimension, 184
Report falsification, 448
Resistance to change, 303–304
Resources, organizational objectives for, 95
Responsibility, 238–241
  clarifying job activities of managers, 240–241
  decision making and, 136–137
  dividing job activities and, 238–240
  overlapping, 239
  responsible management behavior and, 241–242
  social. *See* Social responsibility
Responsibility gap, 239
Retrenchment strategy, 171
Return on investment (ROI), 97–98
Revenue, total, 479
Reverse discrimination, 580
Rewards
  extrinsic, 378–379
  Gantt's contribution to, 32
  intrinsic, 378–379
Righting the wrongs, 584
Risk, multinational corporations and, 528–529
Risk condition, decision making, 144
Robotics, 463
Robots, 463
Role conflict, 578
Role overload, 578
Rule, 186

Safety needs, 380
Sales force estimation method, 195
Sales forecasting, 193–197
  evaluating method for, 196–197
  jury of executive opinion method for, 194–195
  sales force estimation method for, 195
  time series analysis method for, 195–196
Sample organizational strategy, 171
SBUs. *See* Strategic Business Units
Scalar chain, 34
Scalar relationships, 228–230
Scheduling, 198–200
  Gantt charts and, 32, 198–199
  program evaluation and review technique and, 199–200
Scientific management, 28–35
  Fayol's contribution to, 34–25
  Gantt's contribution to, 32
  Gilbreth and Gilbreth's contribution to, 30–32
  Taylor's contribution to, 28–29
Scientific method, 37–38
Scope dimension, of plans, 185
Scope of the decision, 136
Security needs, 380
  international differences in, 534
Selection
  by human resources managers, 272–274
  of managers for multinational corporations, 533
Self-actualization needs, 380
  international differences in, 534
Self-managing work teams, 539
Self-promotion, of careers, 14–16
Serial transmission, 334–335
Service role, of staff personnel, 245
Sexual harassment, 271, 577
Shingo Prize for Excellence in American Manufacturing, 547
Shingo's advice on quality, 551
Short- and long-term goals, relative balance between, 438
Short range, 174
Short-term objectives, 95
Short-term production, steering away from, 448
Signal, interpersonal communication and, 325
Single-strand grapevine, 336–337
Single-use plans, 187–189
Site selection, 190–191
Situation, law of the, 16
Situational approach, to management, 350–365
Skill development techniques, 279
Social audit, 70–71
Social component, of general environment, 159–160
Social investment area, measuring social responsibility in, 69
Social needs, 380
  international differences in, 534
Social obligation approach, 64
Social responsibility, 51–72
  areas of, 54
  arguments against, 55, 58
  arguments for, 54, 58
  communicating degree of involvement, 61
  controlling activities, 69–71
  converting policies into action, 66–68
  Davis model of, 52–53
  defined, 52
  influencing individuals performing, 69
  management functions and, 62–64, 65–66
  as organizational objective, 91
  organizing activities, 68–69
  planning, 65–66
  required activities and, 59
  social audit and, 62
  society's responsibilities and, 81–82
  standards for, 438
Social responsibility approach, 64
Social responsiveness, 55
  decision making and, 61–62
  defined, 61
Social responsiveness approach, 64
Social values, general environment and, 159–160
Society, responsibilities to business, 71–72
Sociograms, 412, 413
Sociometry, 412
Source/encoder, 325
Span of management, 226–228
  contingency viewpoint on, 226–227
  Graicunas' formula and, 227
  height of organizational chart and, 227–228
Special-purpose teams, 407–408, 539
Stability, change versus, 293
Stability of tenure of personnel, 34–35
Stability strategy, 171
Staff authority, 243–244, 247, 248
  conflict in line-staff relationships, 246
  organizational chart and, 244
  roles of staff personnel and, 244–245
Standards, comparing measured performance to, 437–438
Standing plans, 186–187
Stars, 167
State of nature, decision making and, 138
Statistical quality control, 460
Status, of work group members, 417–418
Stereotypes, 576
Storage function, of computers, 496
Strategic business units (SBUs), 166–172
  BCG growth-share matrix and, 166–168
  divestiture and, 171–172
  GE multifactor portfolio analysis and, 168–169
  growth strategy and, 171
  Porter's model for industry analysis and, 169–170
  retrenchment and, 171
  stability and, 171
Strategic control, 172, 173
  quality and, 556
Strategic planning, 154–181
  defined, 156
  for multinational corporations, 530–533
  tactical planning and, 174
Strategy
  capacity, 466–467
  cost leadership, 171
  defined, 156
  differentiation, 170
  divestiture, 171–172
  focus, 171
  growth, 171
  human resources, 471
  implementation of, 172–173
  layout, 469–470
  location, 467

for motivation, 383–394
process, 468–469
product, 468
production, 464–467
retrenchment, 171
sample organizational, 171
stability, 171
Strategy formulation, 165–172
business portfolio analysis and, 166
critical question analysis and, 165–166
Porter's model for industry analysis and, 169–170
quality and, 554–555
SWOT analysis and, 166
Strategy implementation, 172–173
Strategy management, 156–173
environmental analysis and, 158
establishing organizational direction, 163–165
strategic control and, 173
strategy formulation and, 165–172
strategy implementation and, 172–173
Stress
defined, 306
helping employees handle, 308–310
importance of studying, 307
managing in organizations, 307
organizational change and, 306–310
unhealthy, identifying, 308
worker performance and, 307
Stressor, 308–309
Structural change, 297–299
advantages and disadvantages of, 298–299
describing, 297–298
matrix organizations and, 298–299
organizational development, 300–302
people, 300
Structure, 218–223
formal and informal, 219
of multinational corporations, 531–532
Structured behavior, leadership and, 357
Suboptimization, 99–100
Subordinates
confidence in, decision-making and, 351
leadership behavior in decision-making and, 353–354
Subordination of individual interests, 34
Subsystem
controlling, 436–437
influencing, 322–323
planning, 118–119
Successful communication, 326
Suppliers, as component of operating environment, 161–162
Supportive behavior, leadership and, 365
Supportive relationships, principle of, 393
SWOT analysis, 166, 167
Symptoms, 439
System approach to management, 40–43
System(s), 40
closed, 38, 40
management, 40–43
open, 40, 41

Tactical planning, 174
Tall organizational chart, 227
Tannenbaum and Schmidt leadership continuum, 350–362
Task groups, 404
Task structure, leadership and, 363
Technical skills, 11
Technological change, 297
Technological factors
in general environment, 160–161
organizational change and, 296
Territory, departmentalization on basis of, 220
Testing, 273–274
Theory X, 385–386
Theory Y, 385–386
Theory Z, 385, 537–538
Time dimension, of plans, 185
Timeliness, of information, 493–494
Times series analysis method, 195–196
Tokenism, 577
Total costs, 479
Total power, 446–447
Total quality management (TQM), 544–545
Total revenue, 479
Training, 274–280
administering program for, 276–279
designing program for, 276
evaluating program of, 279
needs for, 275–276
on-the-job, 279
Trait approach, to leadership, 349–350
Transformational leadership, 366
Transportation, site selection and, 190, 191
Trends, establishing organizational objectives and, 96
Triangular management, 42
TV test, ethics and, 76

Uncertainty, decision making and, 144
Unfreezing, 304
Unionization, site selection and, 190, 191
Unity of command, 34, 229
Unity of direction, 34
Universality, of management principles, 12–13
Unsuccessful communication, 326
Upward organizational communication, 334
User database, 509–510
Utilitarian principle, ethics and, 75

Validity, of tests, 273
Value, of information, 492–494
Value adding, quality and, 554
Value analysis, 482
Variable budgets, 475
Variable costs, 479
Verbal communication, 332
Vocational interest tests, 273
Vroom expectancy theory of motivation, 377–378
Vroom-Yetton-Jago model of leadership, 354–356

"What if" analysis, 510–511
Wholeness, of systems, 40–41
Women
as employees, 57
in management, 16, 367–368, 577
Work, division of, 34
Worker participation, evolution of in U.S., 539
Work force
aging of, 581
multicultural, 17–18
Workforce 2000, 579–580
Work functions, 219
departmentalization on basis of, 219–220
Work groups, 412–418
cohesiveness of, 416–417
determining existence of, 412
evolution of informal groups and, 412–414
maximizing effectiveness of, 414
norms of, 417–418
size of, 414–415
status of members, 418
Work measurement methods, 471
Work methods analysis, 471
Work teams, 403, 407–408

Zaibatsus, 537
Zero-base budgeting, 474
Zero inventory, 472–473